AF207891

Flanders

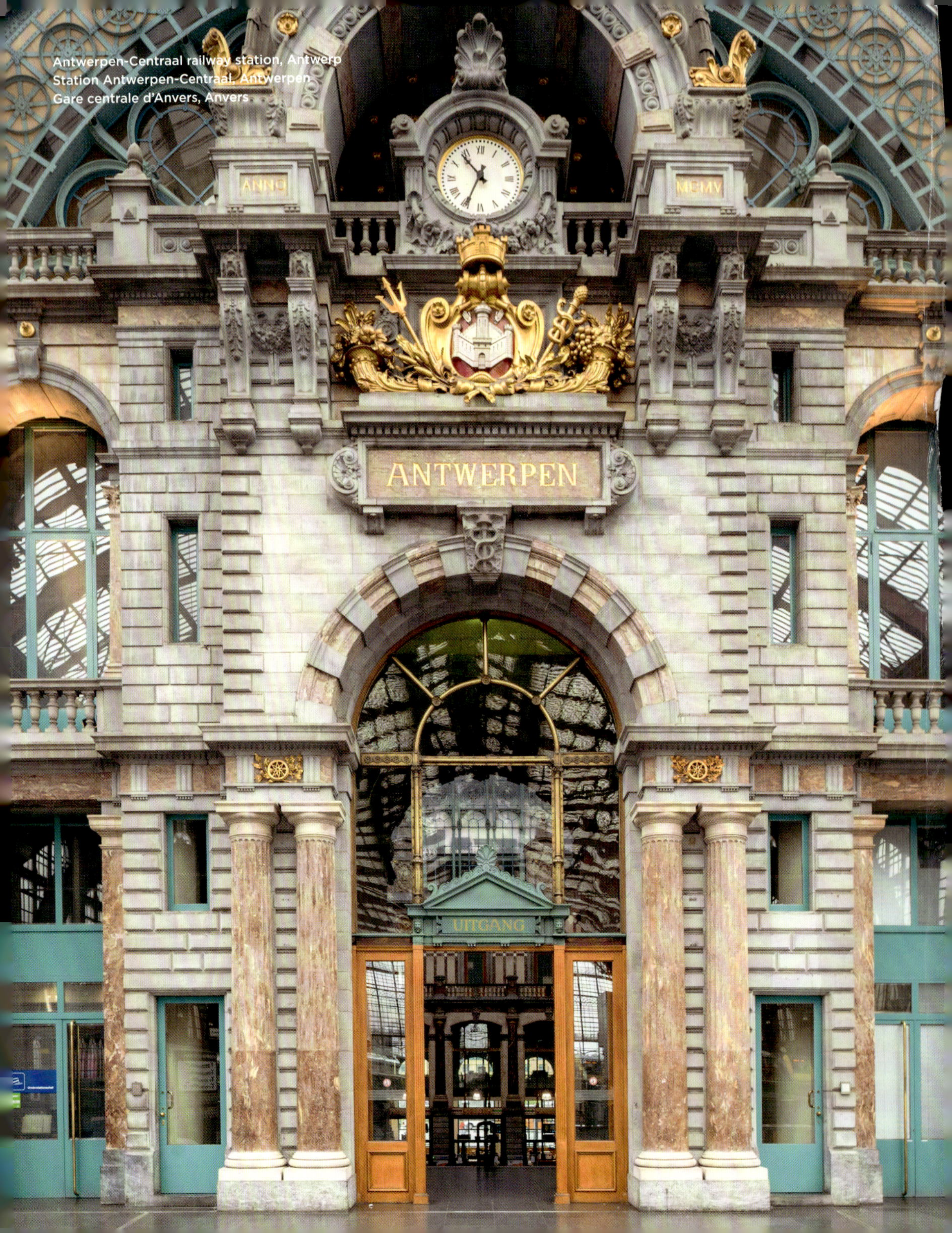

Antwerpen-Centraal railway station, Antwerp
Station Antwerpen-Centraal, Antwerpen
Gare centrale d'Anvers, Anvers

Flanders & Brussels

Flandres

Flandern & Brüssel

Flandes & Bruselas

Flandres & Bruxelas

Vlaanderen & Brussel

Joel Etzold
Katja Sassmannshausen

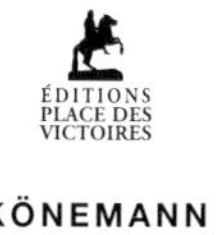

ÉDITIONS
PLACE DES
VICTOIRES

KÖNEMANN

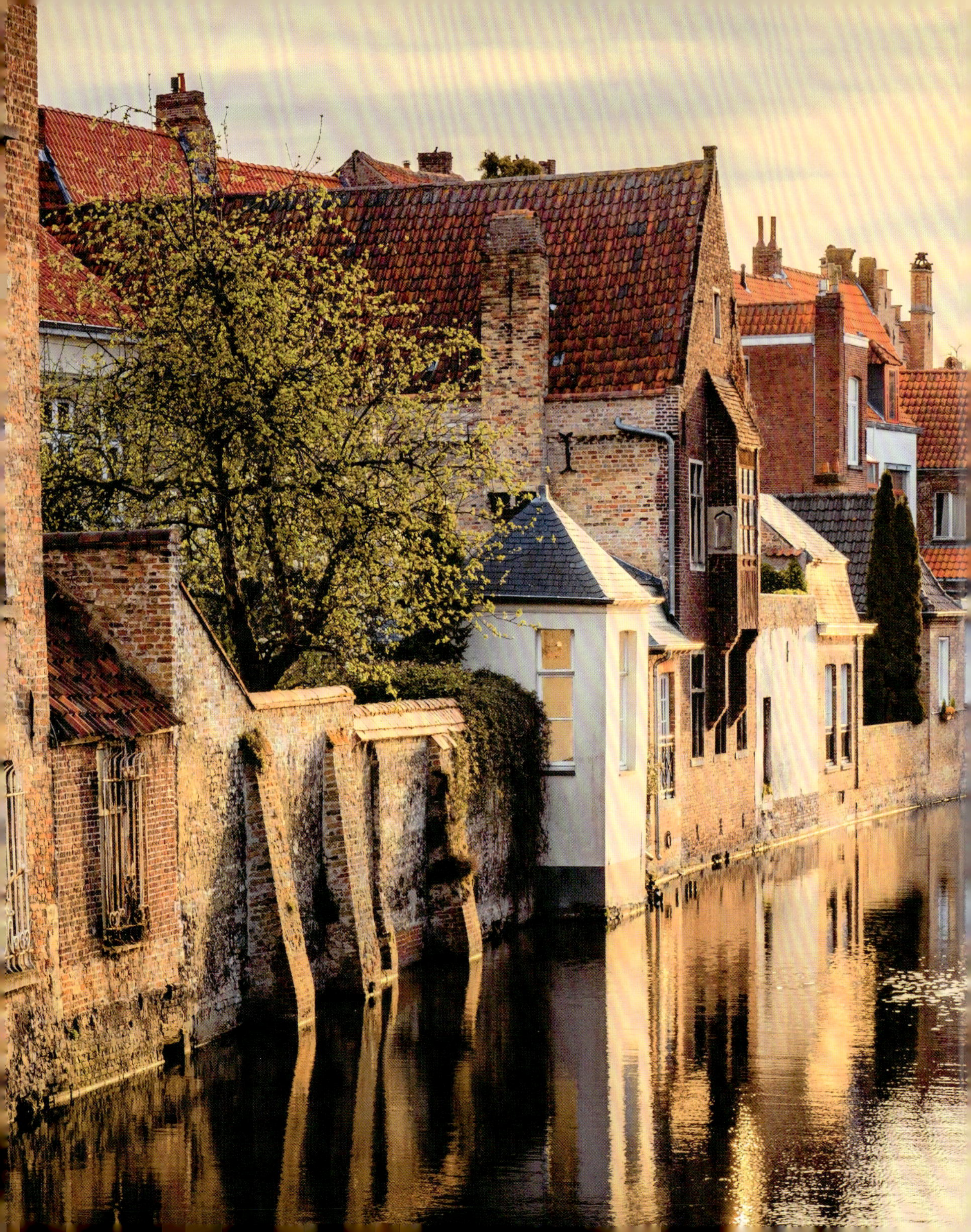

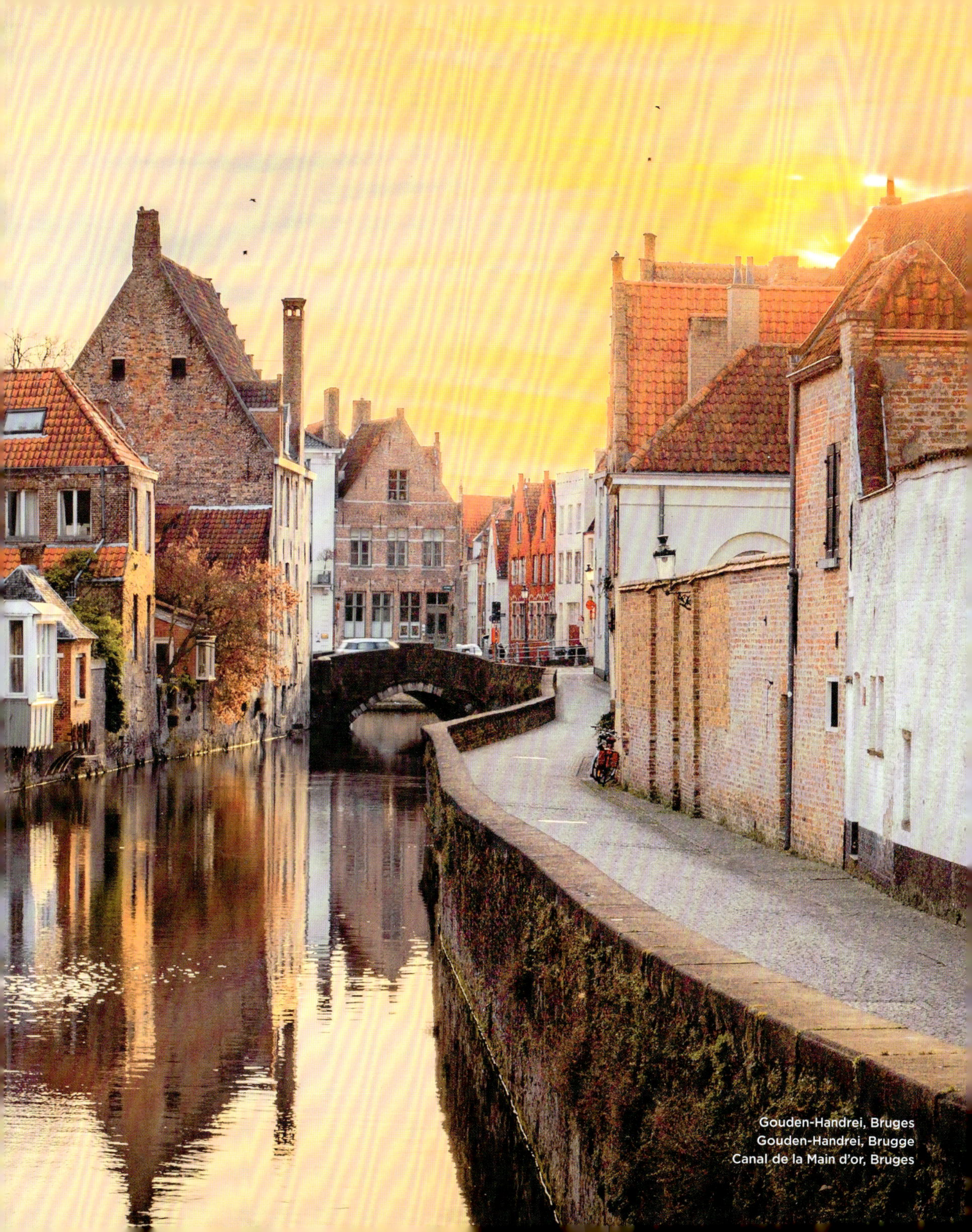

Gouden-Handrei, Bruges
Gouden-Handrei, Brugge
Canal de la Main d'or, Bruges

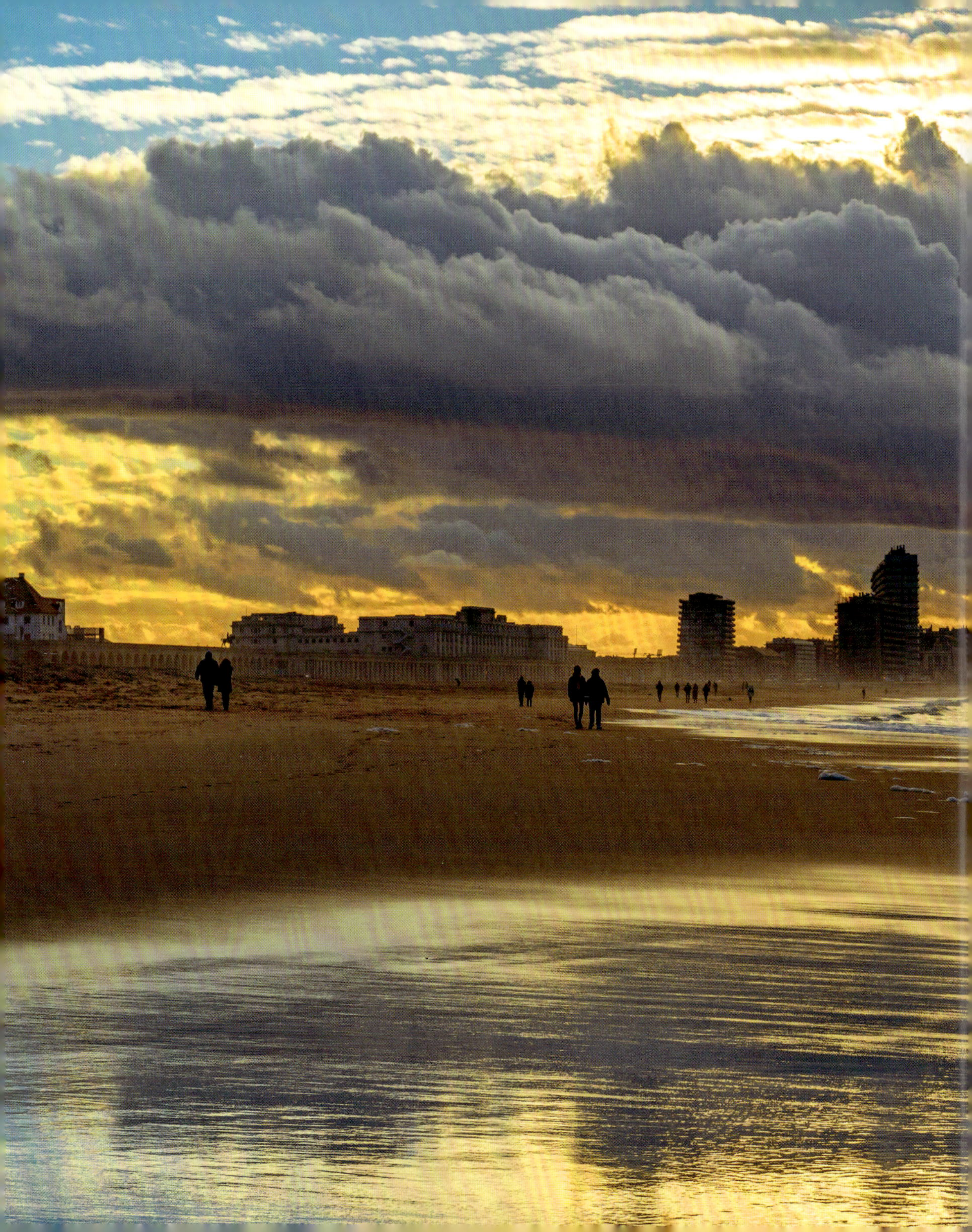

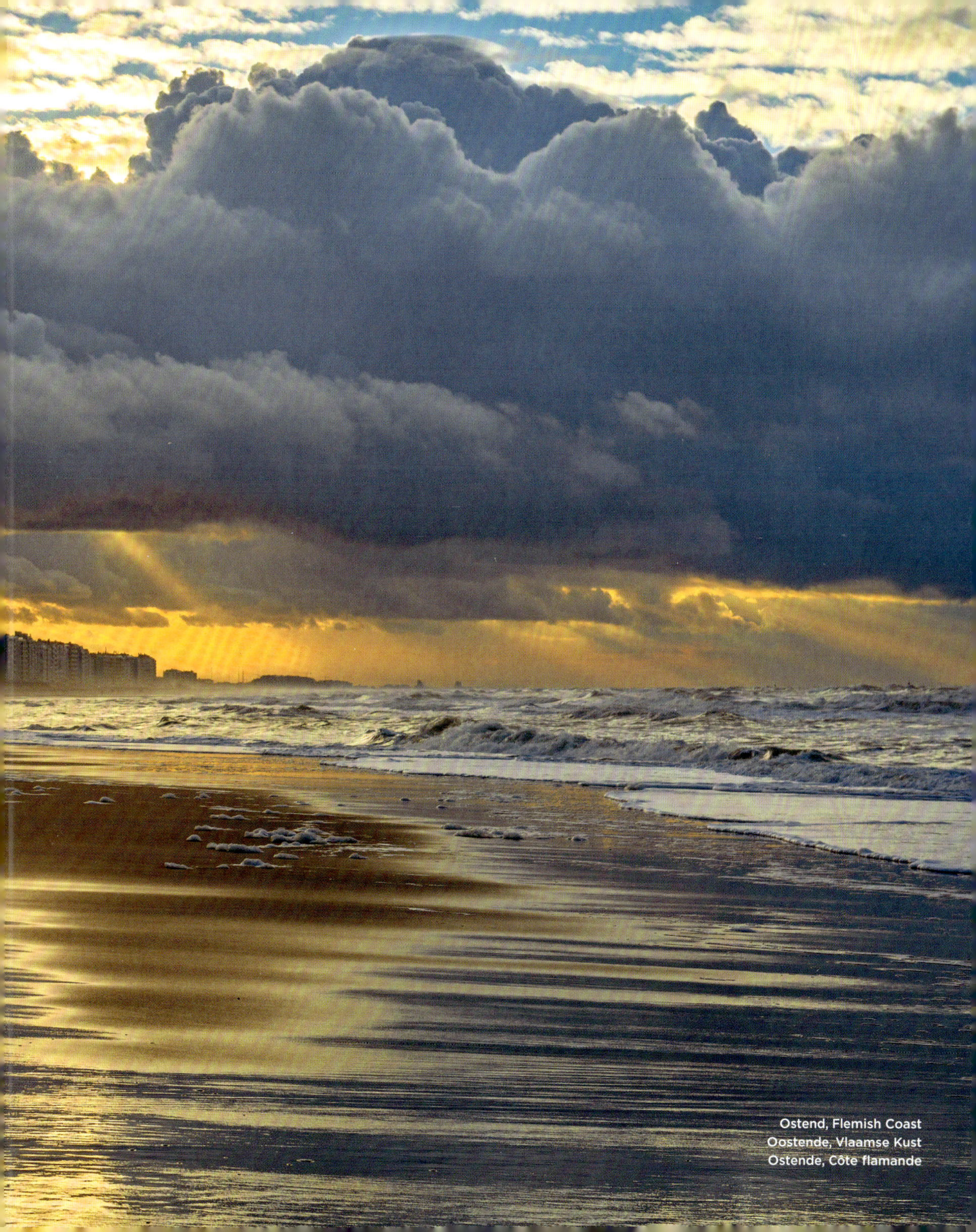

Ostend, Flemish Coast
Oostende, Vlaamse Kust
Ostende, Côte flamande

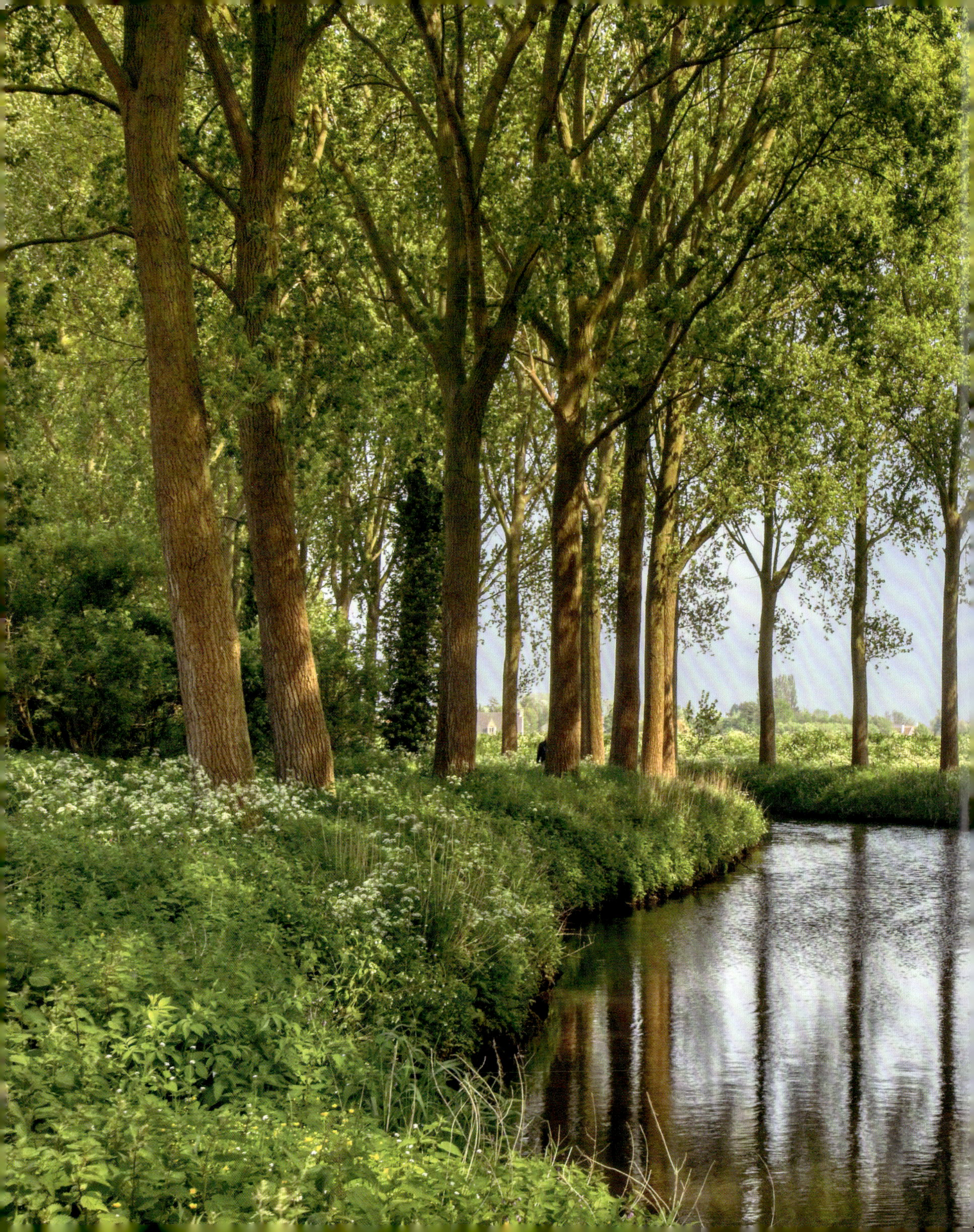

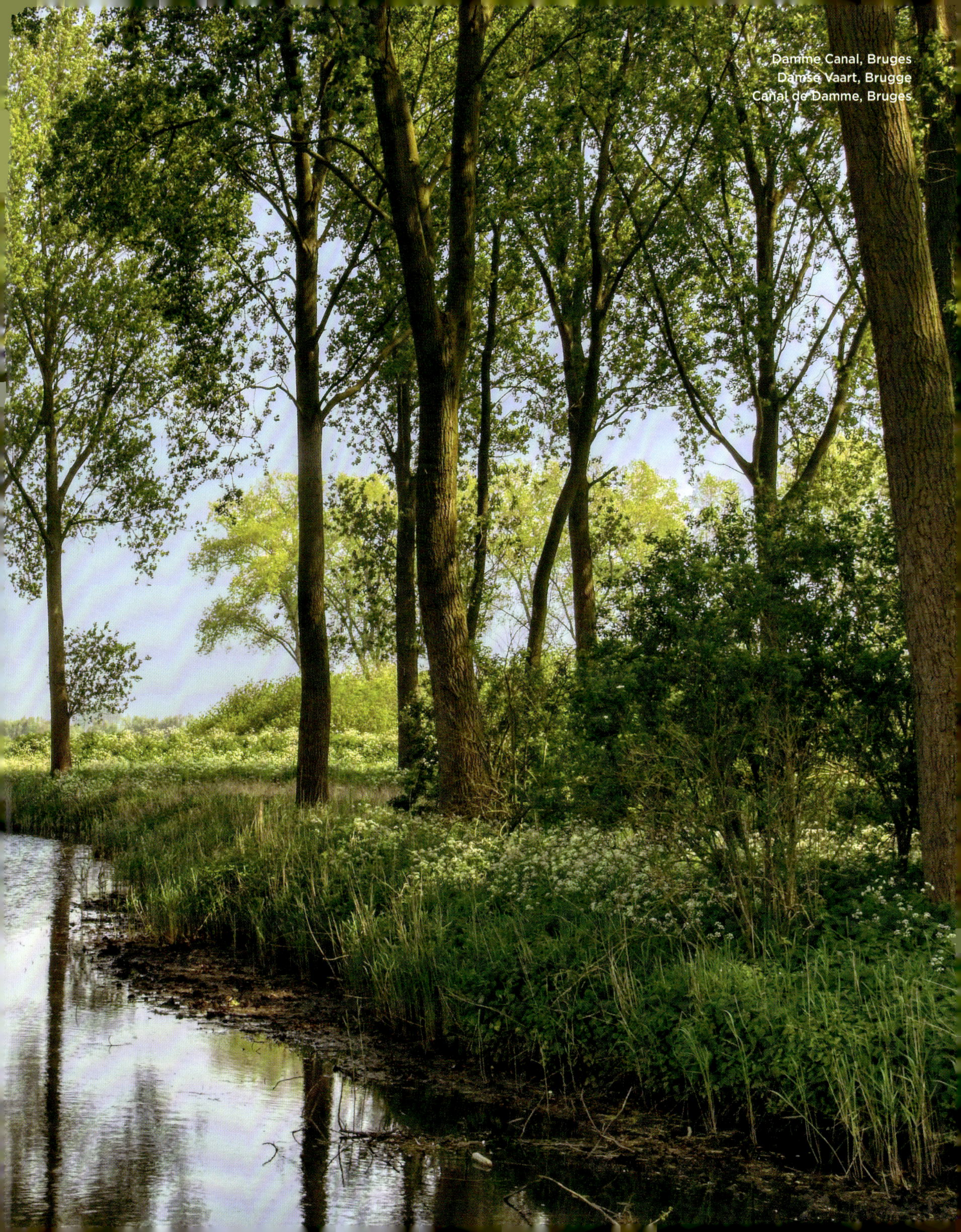

Damme Canal, Bruges
Damse Vaart, Brugge
Canal de Damme, Bruges

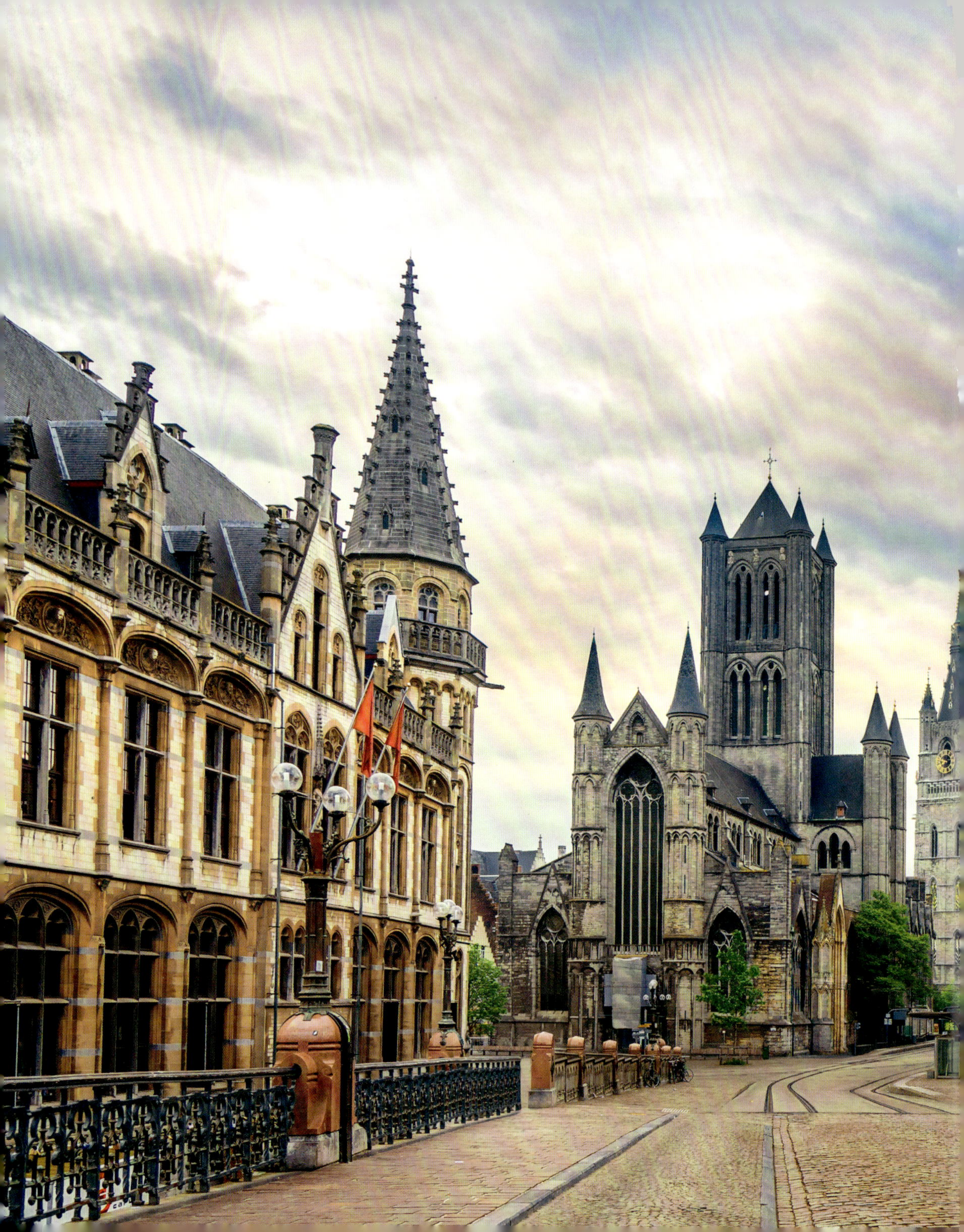

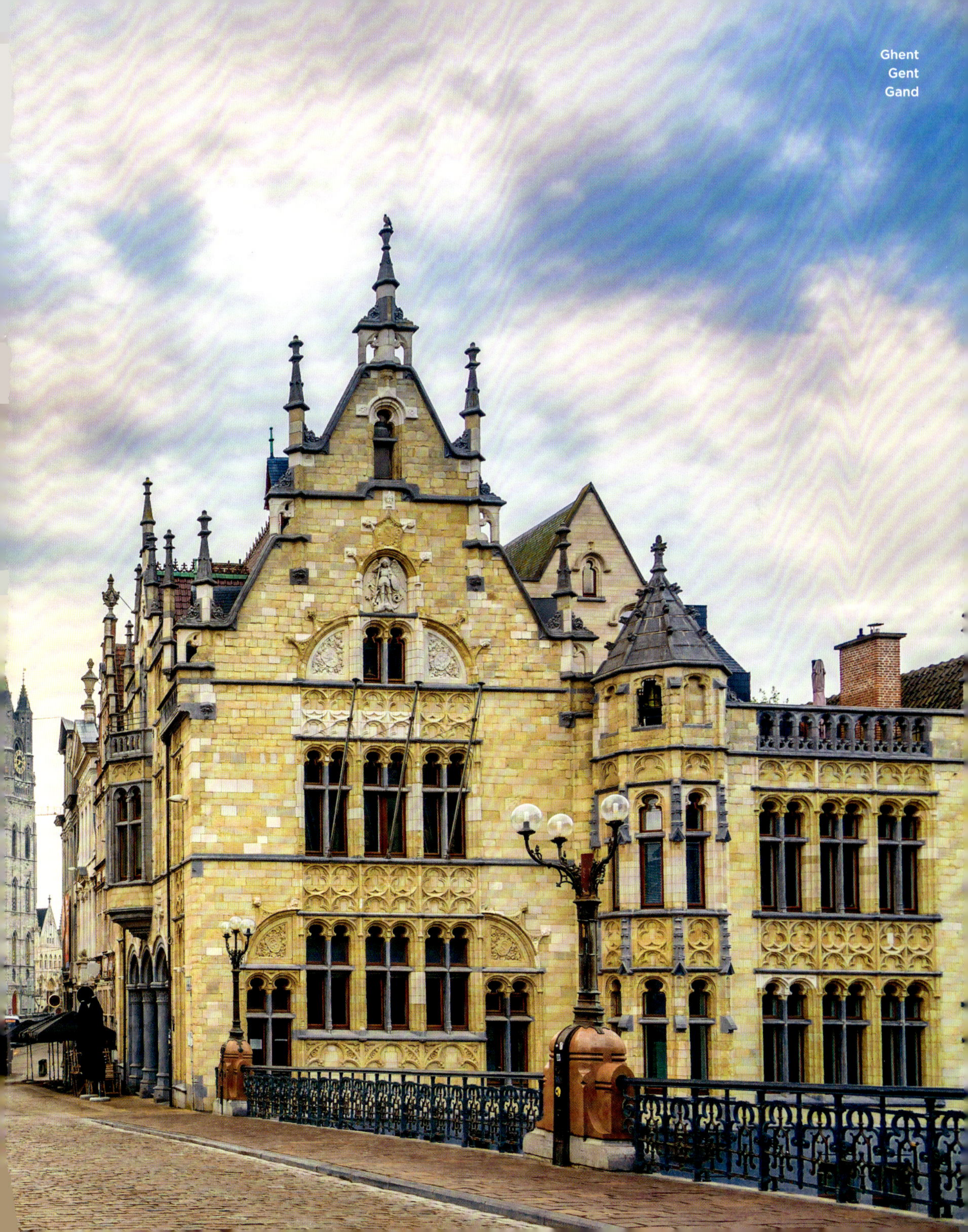

Ghent
Gent
Gand

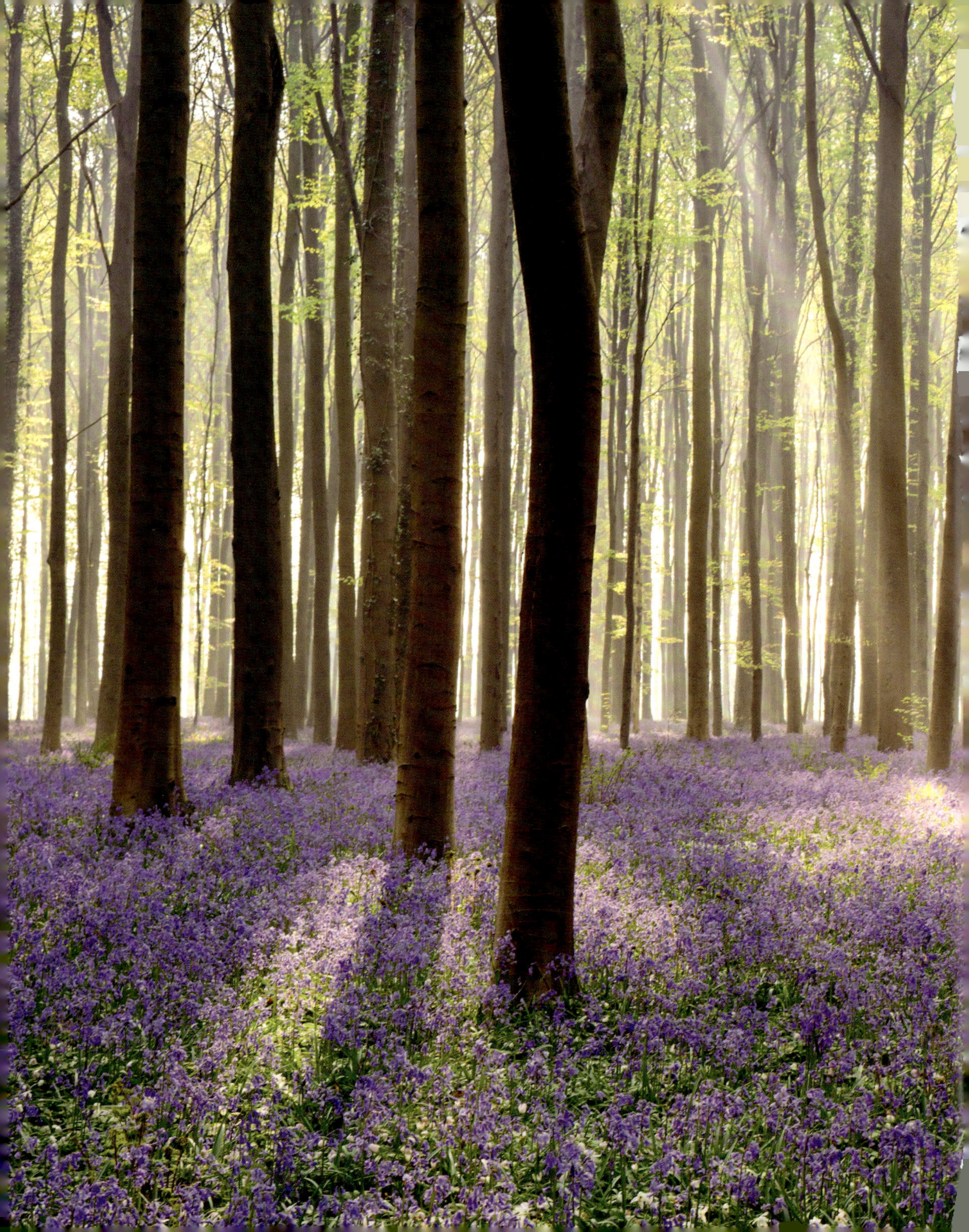

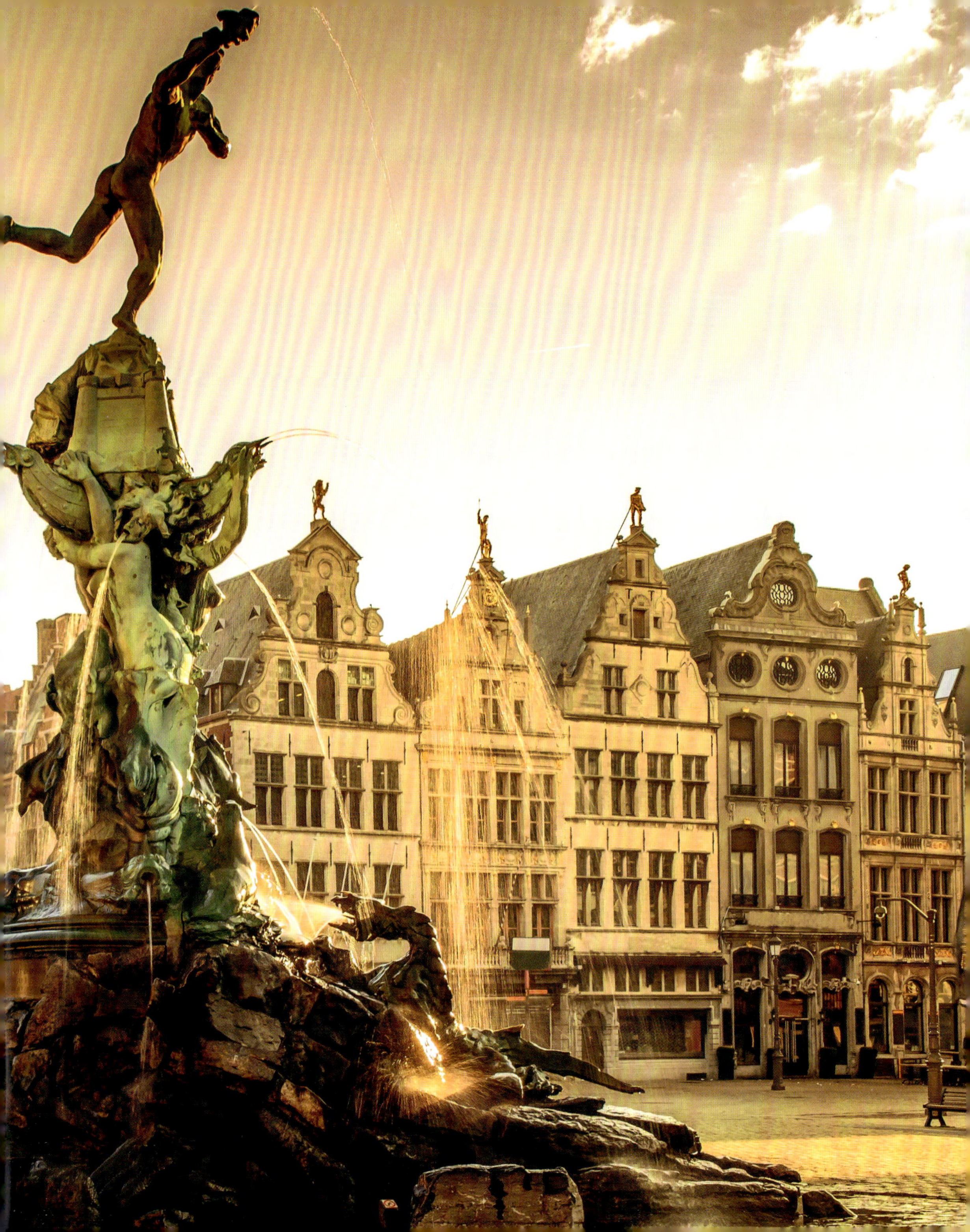

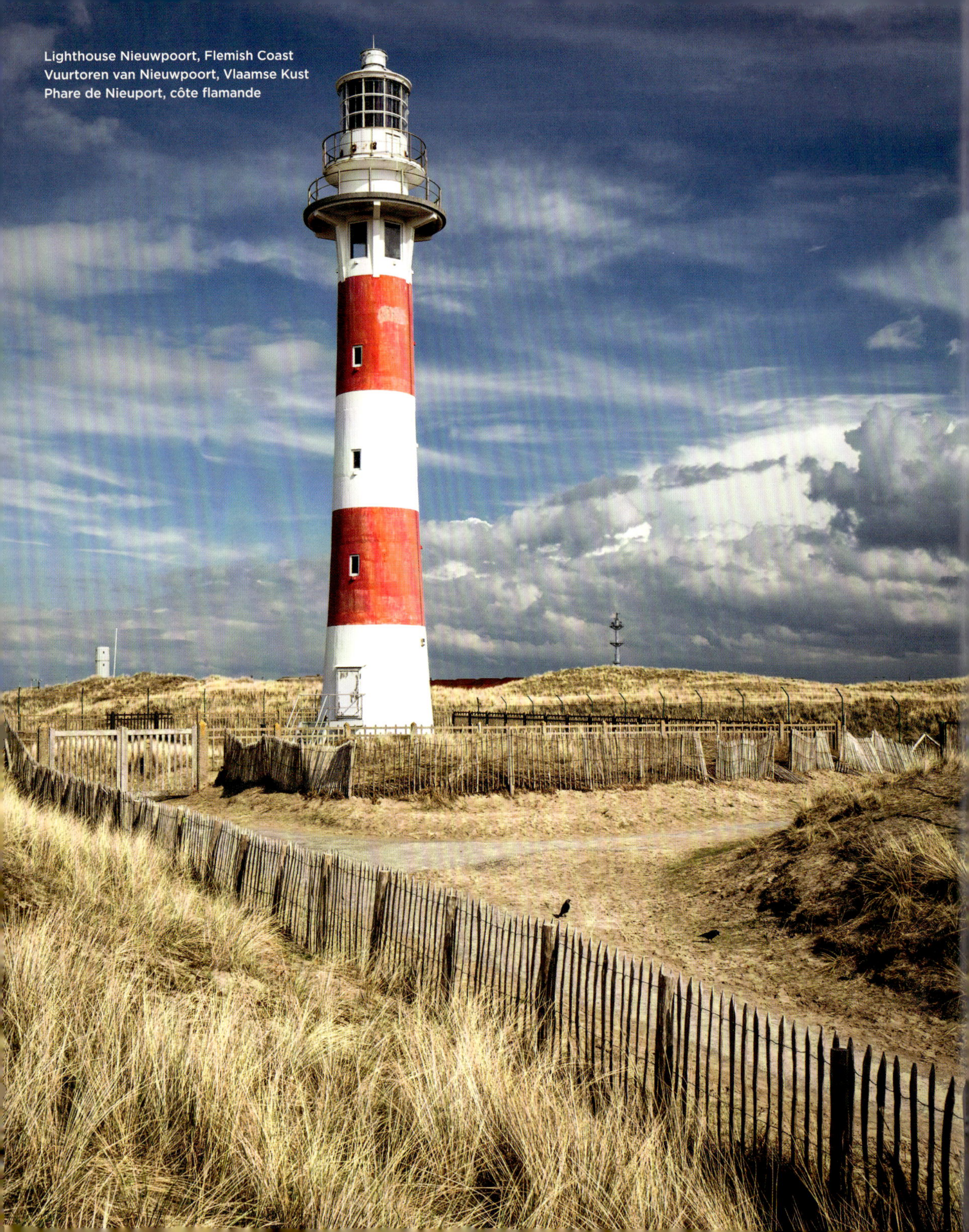
Lighthouse Nieuwpoort, Flemish Coast
Vuurtoren van Nieuwpoort, Vlaamse Kust
Phare de Nieuport, côte flamande

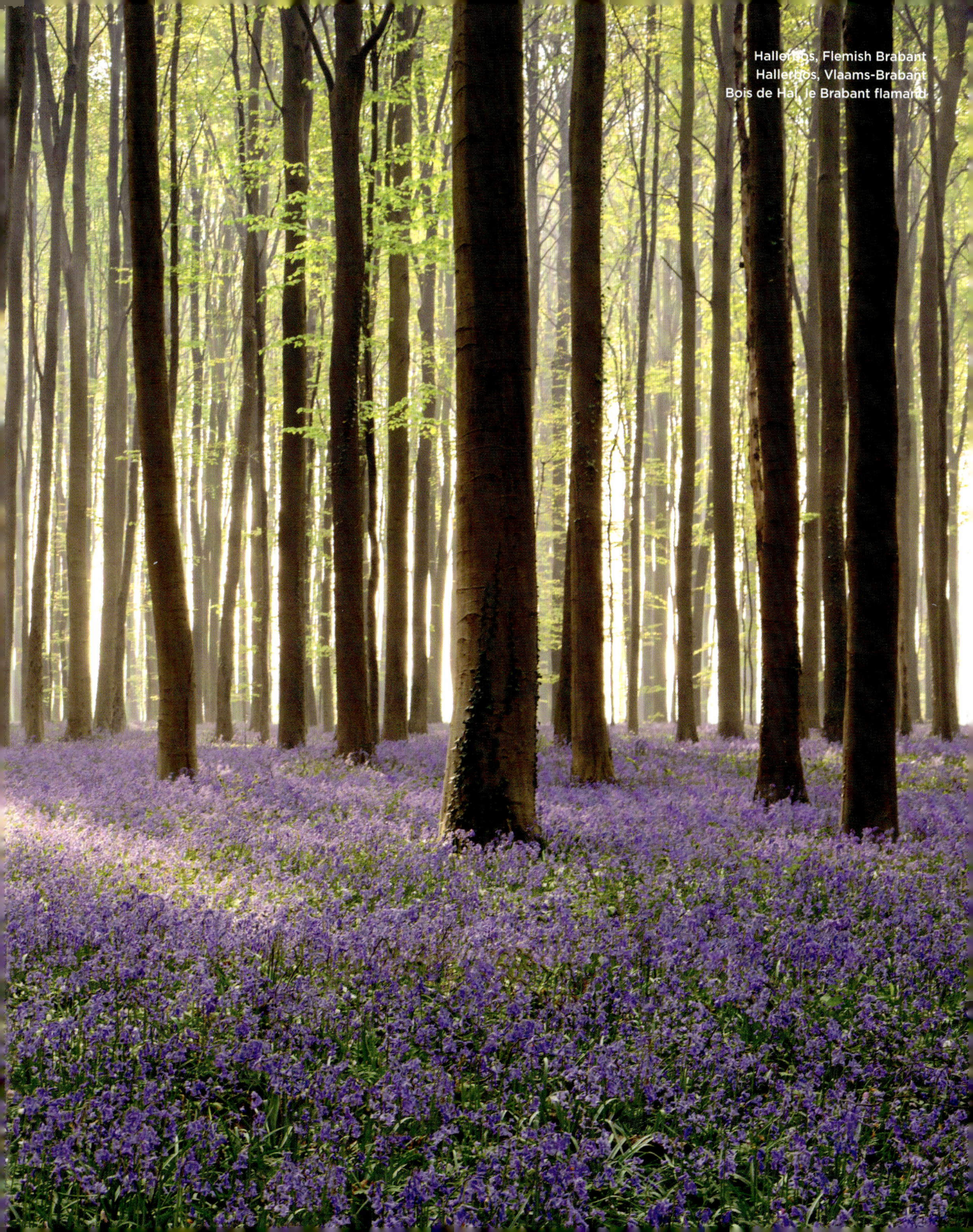
Hallerbos, Flemish Brabant
Hallerbos, Vlaams-Brabant
Bois de Hal, le Brabant flamand

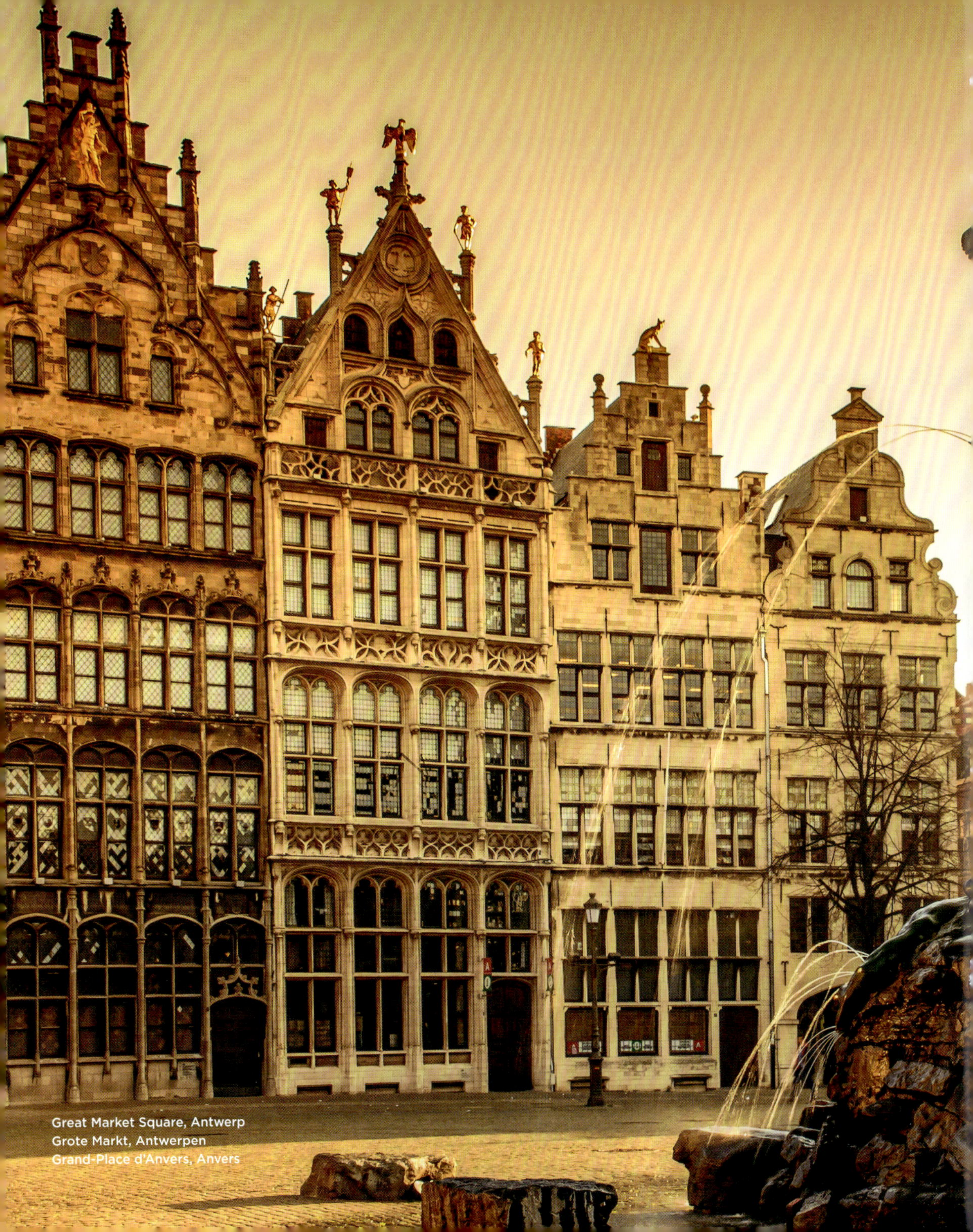

Great Market Square, Antwerp
Grote Markt, Antwerpen
Grand-Place d'Anvers, Anvers

Contents · Sommaire · Inhalt · Índice · Inhoud

Flanders

Proud towers, picturesque market squares with magnificent town halls, canals and bridges: Flanders owes everything to the sea and trade. With its cities of art, Flanders has been one of the most important centers of Western art and culture since the Middle Ages. The name of this diverse region means "waterlogged land". It is a land wrested from the sea by monks, utilizing dikes and windmills. Today it forms the typical Flemish landscape: from the horse-riding fishermen on the beaches of the North Sea to the gentle hills of the Flemish Ardennes. In the Middle Ages, the ports made Flanders the most important trading center north of the Alps and a center of linen processing. Precious fabrics were stored in huge cloth halls guarded by mighty belfries. The port cities of Bruges, Antwerp, Ghent and Brussels were among the wealthiest in Europe. Whether lively market squares with their numerous cafés and terraces, dreamy beguinage courts or pompous city palaces from the *belle époque,* the rich heritage of the golden age is omnipresent. The traces of the famous Flemish masters such as Rubens, Bruegel or Van Eyck are as much a part of Flanders as the desire for pleasure and good food. It is no wonder then, that the creative Flemings also draw comics, brew 1000 different beers, invent chocolates, cook masterfully and of course make the best French fries.

Les Flandres

Tours majestueuses, grand-places pittoresques ourlées de somptueux hôtels de ville, ponts et canaux : les Flandres doivent tout à la mer et au commerce. Avec leurs villes d'art, elles font partie, depuis l'époque médiévale, des principaux centres artistiques et culturels en Occident. Le nom de cette région riche et diverse signifie « terres inondées ». Des terres que les moines ont arrachées à la mer, à l'aide de digues et de moulins à vent. C'est le paysage flamand typique d'aujourd'hui, des pêcheurs à cheval sur les plages de la mer du Nord jusqu'aux douces collines des Ardennes flamandes. Au Moyen Âge, les ports flamands firent des Flandres la principale place commerciale au nord des Alpes et le centre du travail du lin. De précieuses étoffes étaient stockées dans d'immenses halles aux draps, sur lesquelles veillaient d'imposants beffrois. Les villes portuaires de Bruges, d'Anvers, de Gand et de Bruxelles faisaient partie des cités les plus fortunées d'Europe. À travers des places vivantes agrémentées d'innombrables cafés et terrasses, d'idylliques béguinages ou de pompeux hôtels particuliers de la Belle Époque, le riche héritage de l'âge d'or est omniprésent. Les traces des célèbres maîtres flamands comme Rubens, Brueghel ou Van Eyck font tout autant partie des Flandres que le plaisir et la bonne chère. Que les Flamands créatifs fassent des bandes dessinées, brassent mille bières différentes, inventent des chocolats fourrés, cuisinent comme des chefs et bien sûr, soient les rois des frites n'a donc rien d'étonnant.

Flandern

Stolze Türme, malerische Marktplätze mit prächtigen Rathäusern, Grachten und Brücken: Flandern verdankt alles dem Meer und dem Handel. Mit seinen Kunststädten gehört Flandern seit dem Mittelalter zu den bedeutendsten Zentren abendländischer Kunst und Kultur. Der Name der vielfältigen Region bedeutet „überschwemmtes Gebiet". Ein Land, das von Mönchen mit Deichen und Windmühlen dem Meer abgerungen wurde. Es bildet heute die typisch flämische Landschaft: von den Pferdefischern an den Stränden der Nordsee bis zu den sanften Hügeln der flämischen Ardennen. Die Häfen machten Flandern im Mittelalter zum wichtigsten Handelsplatz nördlich der Alpen und zum Zentrum der Leinenverarbeitung. Kostbare Stoffe lagerten in riesigen Tuchhallen bewacht von mächtigen Belfrieden. Die Hafenstädte Brügge, Antwerpen, Gent und Brüssel gehörten zu den wohlhabendsten in Europa. Ob lebhafte Marktplätze mit zahlreichen Cafés und Terrassen, verträumte Beginenhöfe oder pompöse Stadtpaläste aus der Belle Époque, das reiche Erbe der goldenen Zeit ist allgegenwärtig. Die Spuren der berühmten Flämischen Meister wie Rubens, Bruegel oder Van Eyck gehören dabei ebenso zu Flandern, wie die Lust auf Genuss und gutes Essen. So ist es kein Wunder, dass die kreativen Flamen, Comics zeichnen, 1000 verschiedene Biere brauen, Pralinen erfinden, meisterhaft Kochen und natürlich die besten Pommes frittieren.

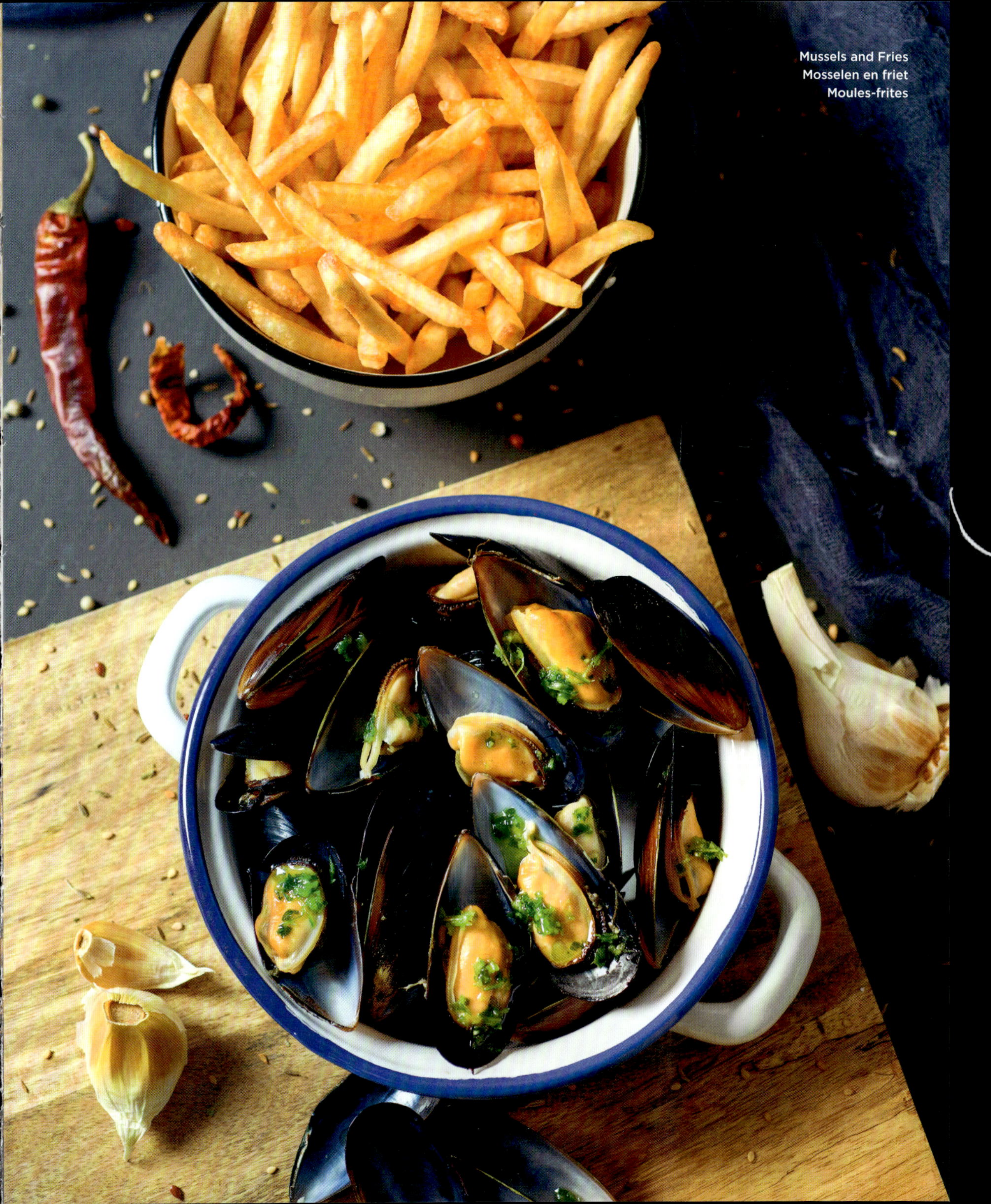
Mussels and Fries
Mosselen en friet
Moules-frites

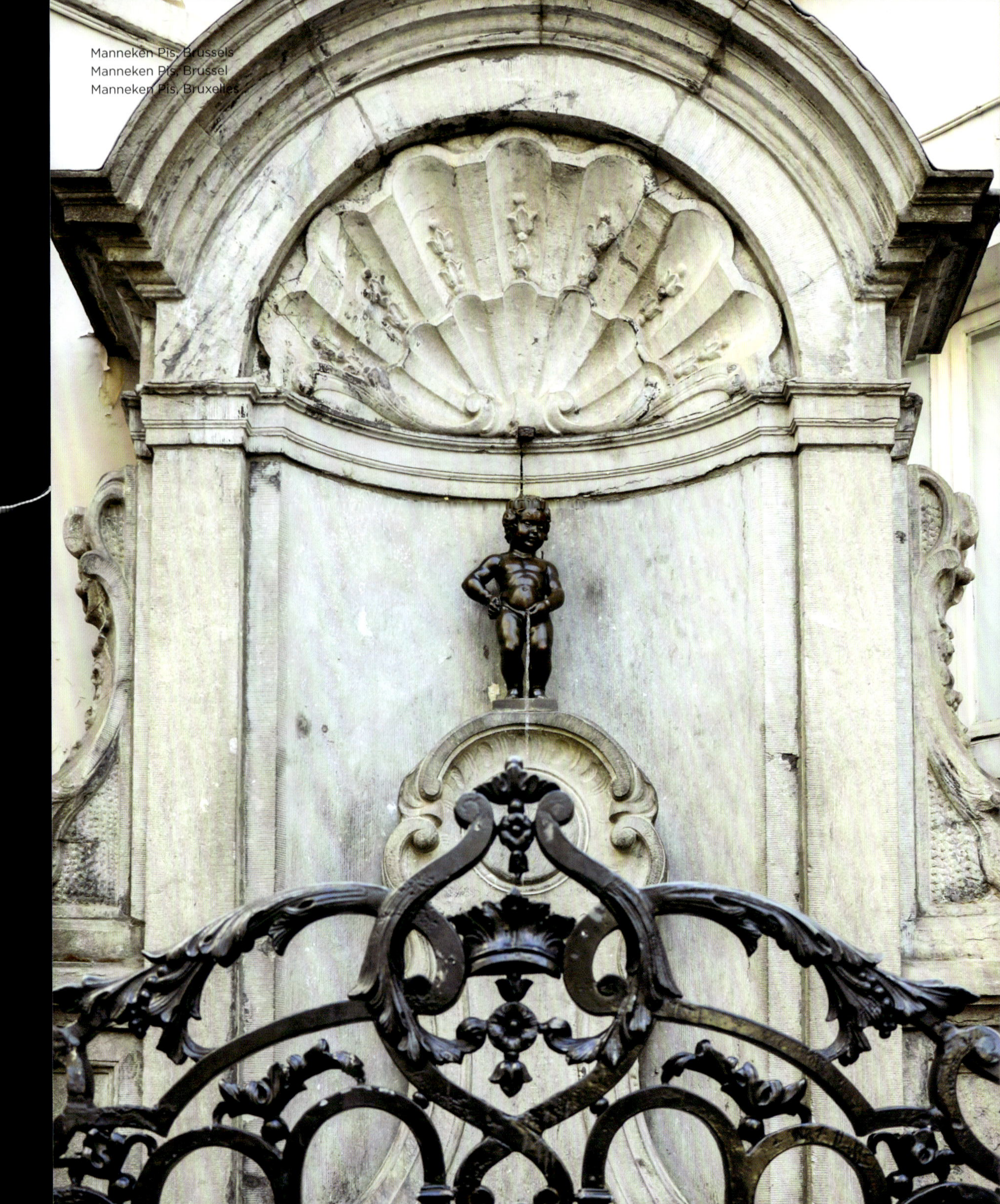

Manneken Pis, Brussels
Manneken Pis, Brussel
Manneken Pis, Bruxelles

Flandes

Orgullosas torres, pintorescas plazas de mercado con magníficos ayuntamientos, canales y puentes: Flandes debe todo al mar y al comercio. Con sus ciudades de arte, Flandes ha sido uno de los centros más importantes del arte y la cultura occidentales desde la Edad Media. El nombre de esta región tan diversa significa "zona inundada". Una tierra arrancada del mar por monjes con diques y molinos de viento. Hoy en día forma el típico paisaje flamenco: desde los pescadores a caballo en las playas del Mar del Norte hasta las suaves colinas de las Ardenas flamencas. En la Edad Media, los puertos convirtieron a Flandes en el centro comercial más importante al norte de los Alpes y en el centro del procesamiento de la ropa. Las valiosas telas se almacenaban en enormes salas de telas custodiadas por poderosos beligerantes. Las ciudades portuarias de Brujas, Amberes, Gante y Bruselas se encuentran entre las más ricas de Europa. Ya se trate de animadas plazas de mercado con numerosas cafeterías y terrazas, patios de ensueño o pomposos palacios de la Belle Époque, el rico patrimonio de la época dorada es omnipresente. Las huellas de los famosos maestros flamencos como Rubens, Bruegel o Van Eyck forman parte de Flandes tanto como el deseo de placer y buena comida. Así que no es de extrañar que los creativos flamencos dibujen cómics, elaboren 1000 cervezas diferentes, inventen chocolates, cocinen con maestría y, por supuesto, hagan las mejores patatas fritas.

Flandres

Torres maravilhosas, praças de mercado pitorescas com magníficas câmaras municipais, canais e pontes: A Flanders deve tudo ao mar e ao comércio. Com as suas cidades artísticas, a Flandres tem sido um dos mais importantes centros de arte e cultura ocidentais desde a Idade Média. O nome desta diversa região significa "área inundada". Uma terra com diques e moinhos de vento que foi arrancada do mar por monges. Hoje forma a típica paisagem flamenga: desde os pescadores a cavalo nas praias do Mar do Norte até às suaves colinas das Ardenas flamengas. Na Idade Média, os portos fizeram da Flandres tanto o centro comercial mais importante ao norte dos Alpes como também o centro de processamento de linho. Tecidos preciosos eram armazenados em enormes salões de pano vigiados por poderosos campanários. As cidades portuárias de Bruges, Antuérpia, Gante e Bruxelas estavam entre as mais ricas da Europa. Sejam praças de mercado animadas com inúmeros cafés e terraços, os pátios de sonho das beguinas ou palácios urbanos pomposos da Belle Époque, a rica herança da época dourada é onipresente. Os vestígios dos famosos mestres flamengos como Rubens, Bruegel ou Van Eyck fazem tanto parte da Flandres como o desejo de diversão e boa comida. Portanto, não é de admirar que os criativos flamengos desenhem histórias em quadrinhos, preparem 1000 cervejas diferentes, inventem chocolates, cozinhem magistralmente e, é claro, fritem as melhores batatas fritas.

Vlaanderen

Trotse torens, pittoreske marktpleintjes met prachtige stadhuizen, grachten en bruggen: Vlaanderen heeft alles te danken aan de zee en de handel. Met zijn kunststeden behoort Vlaanderen sinds de middeleeuwen tot één van de belangrijkste centra van westerse kunst en cultuur. De naam van deze gevarieerde regio betekent "overstroomd gebied". Een land dat door monniken met dijken en molens aan de zee werd onttrokken. Vandaag vormt dit het typisch Vlaamse landschap: van de paardenvissers op de stranden van de Noordzee tot de glooiende heuvels van de Vlaamse Ardennen. De havens maakten in de middeleeuwen van Vlaanderen het belangrijkste handelscentrum ten noorden van de Alpen en het centrum van de linnenverwerking. Kostbare stoffen werden opgeslagen in grote lakenhallen, bewaakt door machtige belforten. De havensteden Brugge, Antwerpen, Gent en Brussel behoorden tot de rijkste van Europa. Of het nu gaat om levendige marktpleinen met talrijke cafés en terrassen, dromerige begijnhofjes of pompeuze stadspaleizen uit de belle époque, het rijke erfgoed van de gouden eeuw is alomtegenwoordig. De sporen van de beroemde Vlaamse meesters zoals Rubens, Bruegel of Van Eyck maken evenzeer deel uit van Vlaanderen als het verlangen naar plezier en goed eten. Het is dus geen wonder dat de creatieve Vlamingen strips tekenen, 1000 verschillende bieren brouwen, pralines uitvinden, meesterlijk koken en natuurlijk de beste frieten bakken.

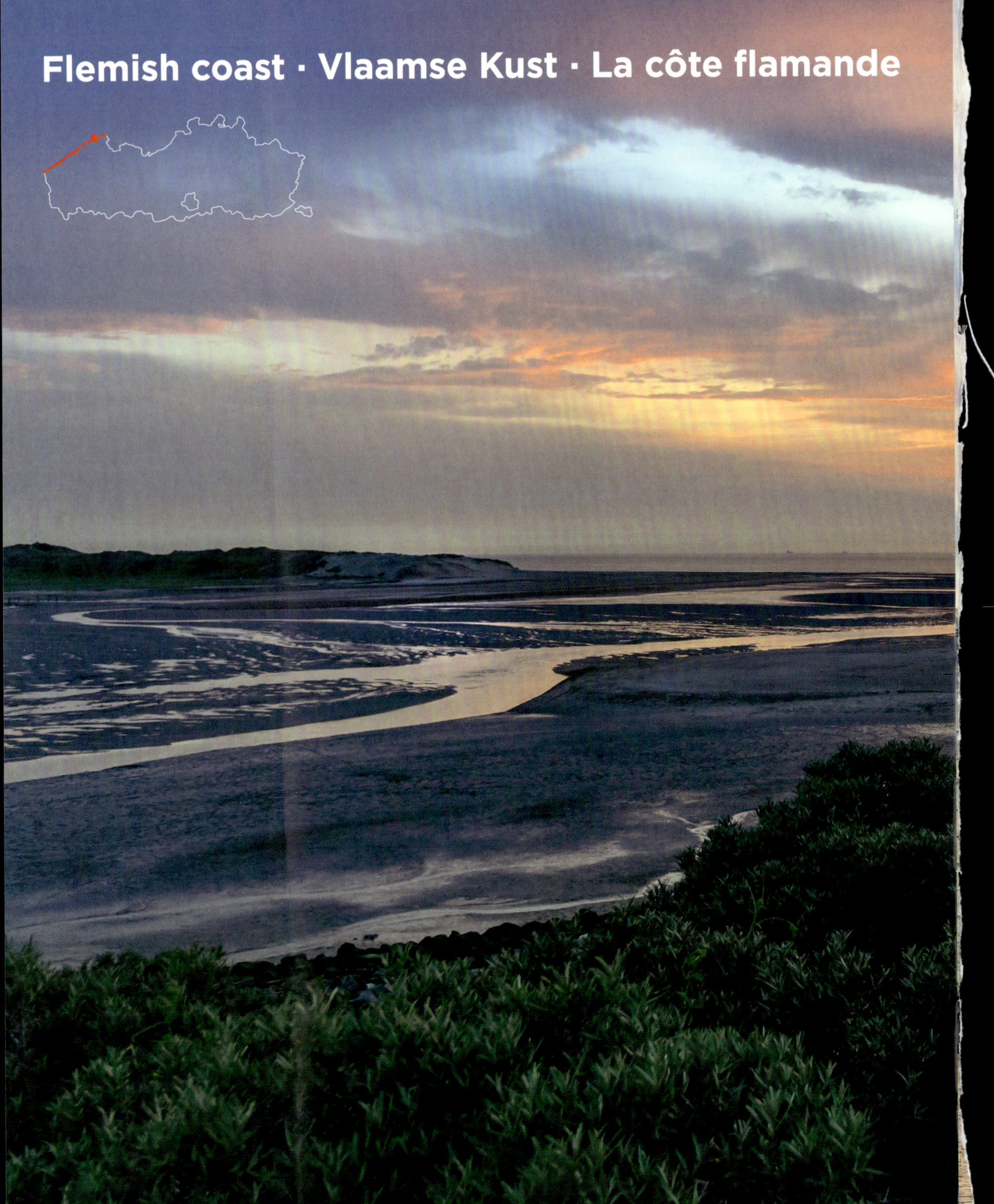

Flemish coast · Vlaamse Kust · La côte flamande

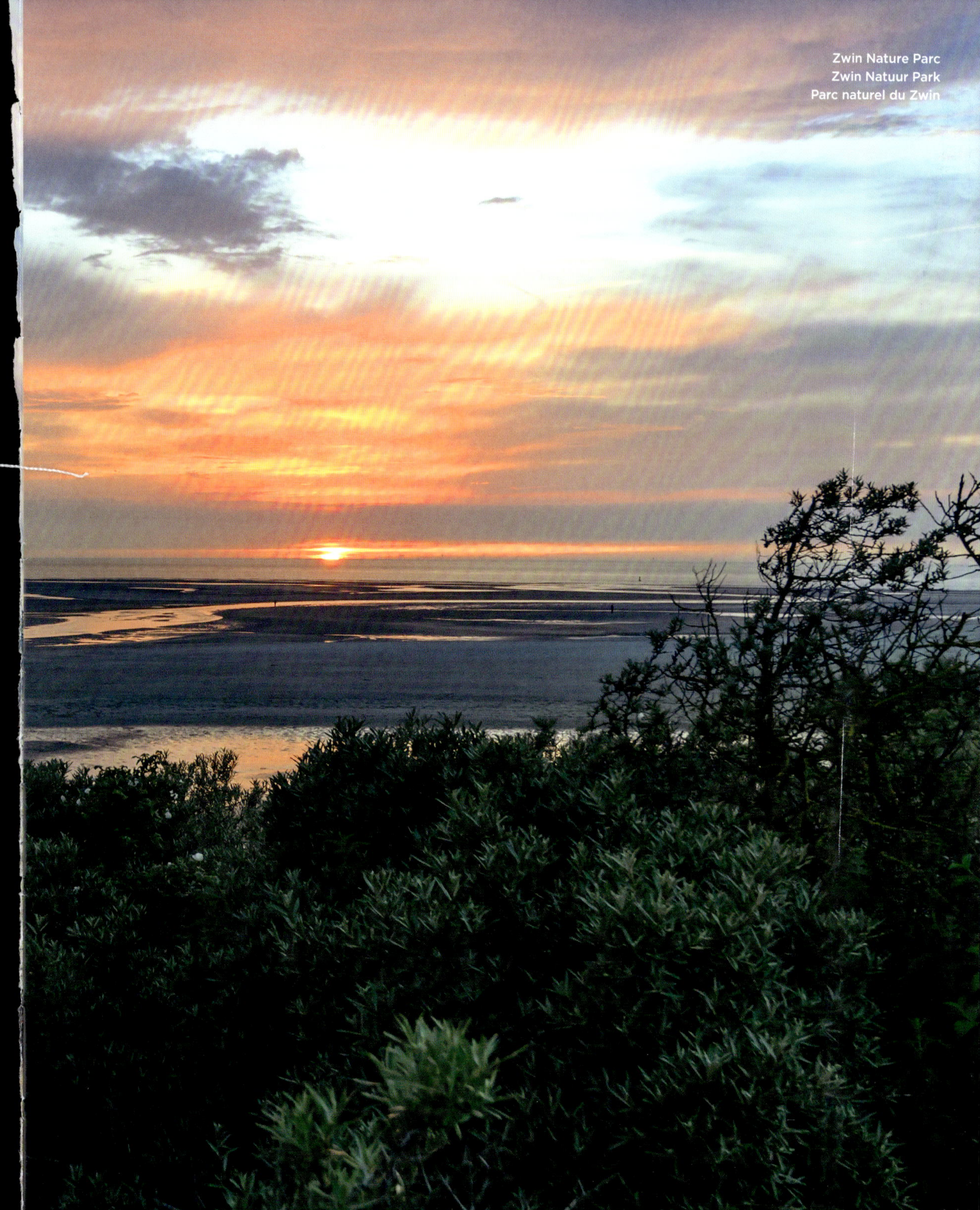
Zwin Nature Parc
Zwin Natuur Park
Parc naturel du Zwin

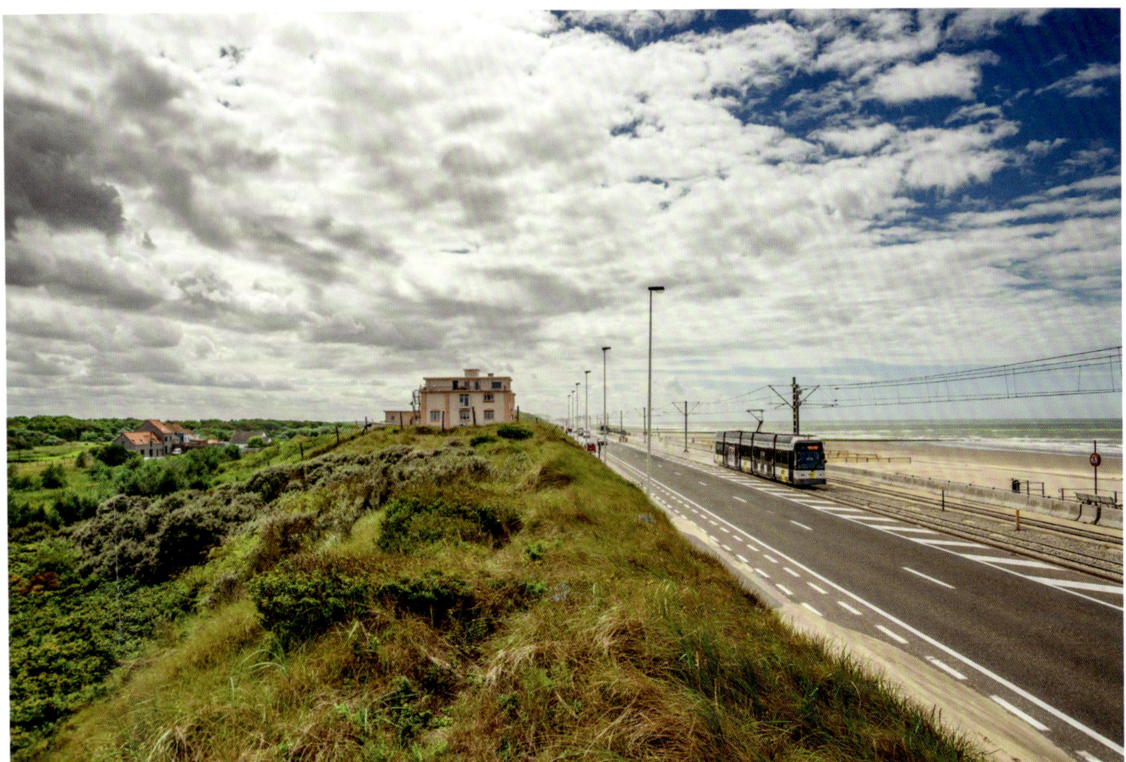

Coast Tram
Kusttram
Tramway de la côte flamande

Flemish Coast

Whether in the rain or in the sunshine, comfortably watching the sea by tram, from the Netherlands to France, from beach to beach, from seaside resort to seaside resort, this is the Flemish way to discover the coast. At the tram stops there are, wide, flat sandy beaches with colorful cabins and tempting cosy cafés on the promenades.

Costa de Flandes

Ya sea bajo la lluvia o bajo el sol, mirando cómodamente al mar desde el tranvía, de los Países Bajos a Francia, de playa en playa, de balneario en balneario, esta es la forma flamenca de descubrir la costa. En las estaciones de tranvía, las lisas playas de arena de un kilómetro de ancho, las coloridas casetas de playa y los paseos marítimos con acogedores cafeterías son tentadores.

La côte flamande

Observer la mer confortablement installé dans le tramway, des Pays-Bas à la France, au fil des plages, au fil des stations balnéaires, par pluie ou par beau temps : voilà l'art d'explorer la côte à la flamande. Les stations de tram sont situées près d'immenses plages de sable agrémentées de cabines colorées et de promenades de bord de mer ourlées d'agréables cafés, qui s'étendent sur des kilomètres.

Costa da Flandres

Faça sol ou faça chuva, confortavelmente observando o mar em um passeio de elétrico, da Holanda à França, de praia à praia, de balneário a balneário, esta é a forma flamenga de descobrir a costa. Nas estações de bonde, as praias de areia plana, com quilômetros de extensão, as cabines coloridas e os calçadões de praia com cafés acolhedores são atraentes.

Flanderns Küste

Ob bei Regen oder Sonnenschein, bequem in der Straßenbahn das Meer betrachten, von den Niederlanden bis nach Frankreich, von Strand zu Strand, von Seebad zu Seebad, das ist die flämische Art die Küste zu entdecken. An den Tramstationen locken kilometerweite, flache Sandstrände, bunte Strandkabinen und Strandpromenaden mit behaglichen Cafés.

Vlaamse Kust

In de regen of in de zon, comfortabel vanuit de tram de zee bekijken, van Nederland tot aan Frankrijk, van strand naar strand, van badplaats naar badplaats, dat is de Vlaamse manier om de kust te ontdekken. Bij de tramhaltes lokken kilometerslange, vlakke zandstranden, kleurrijke strandcabines en promenades met gezellige cafés.

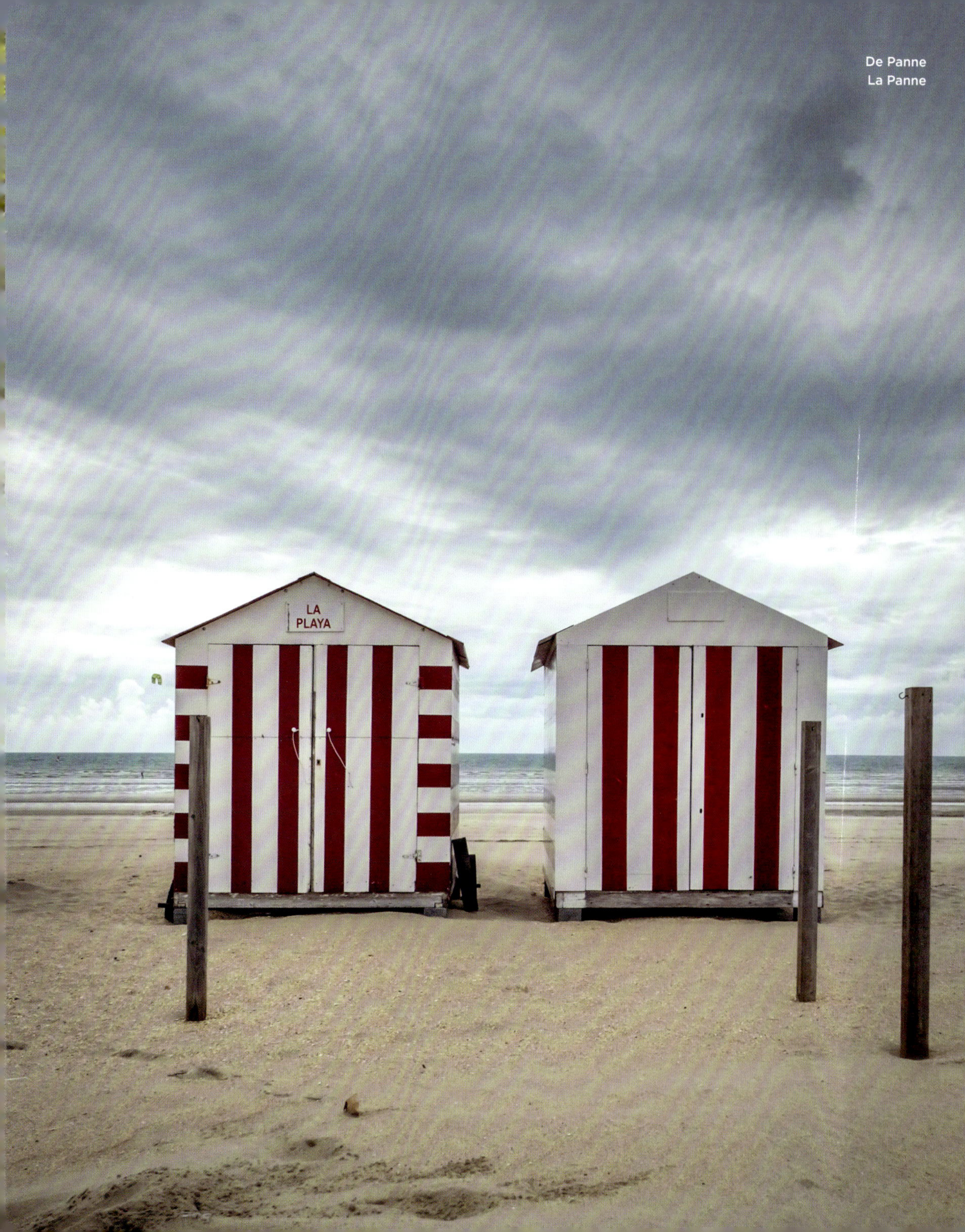
De Panne
La Panne
LA
PLAYA

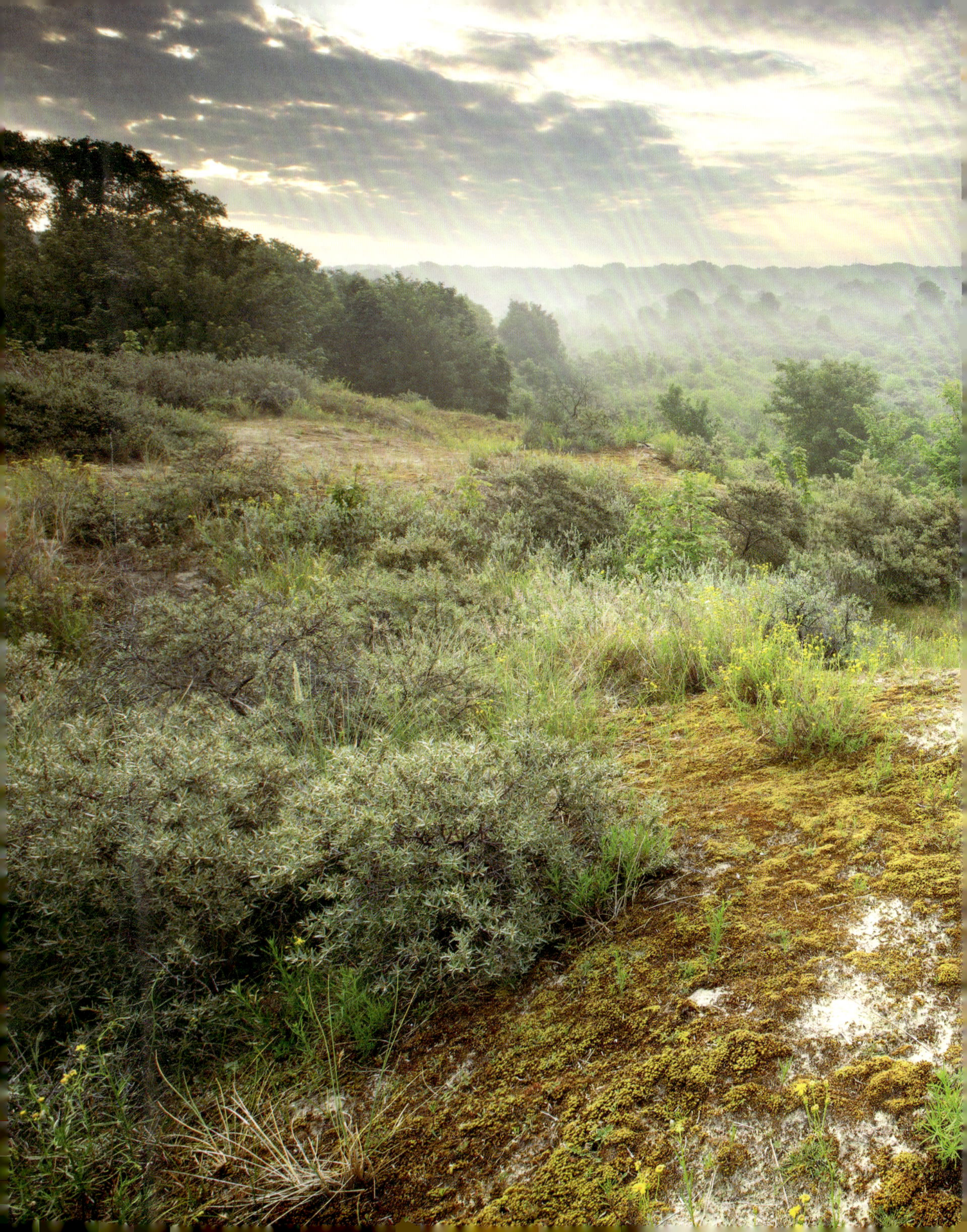

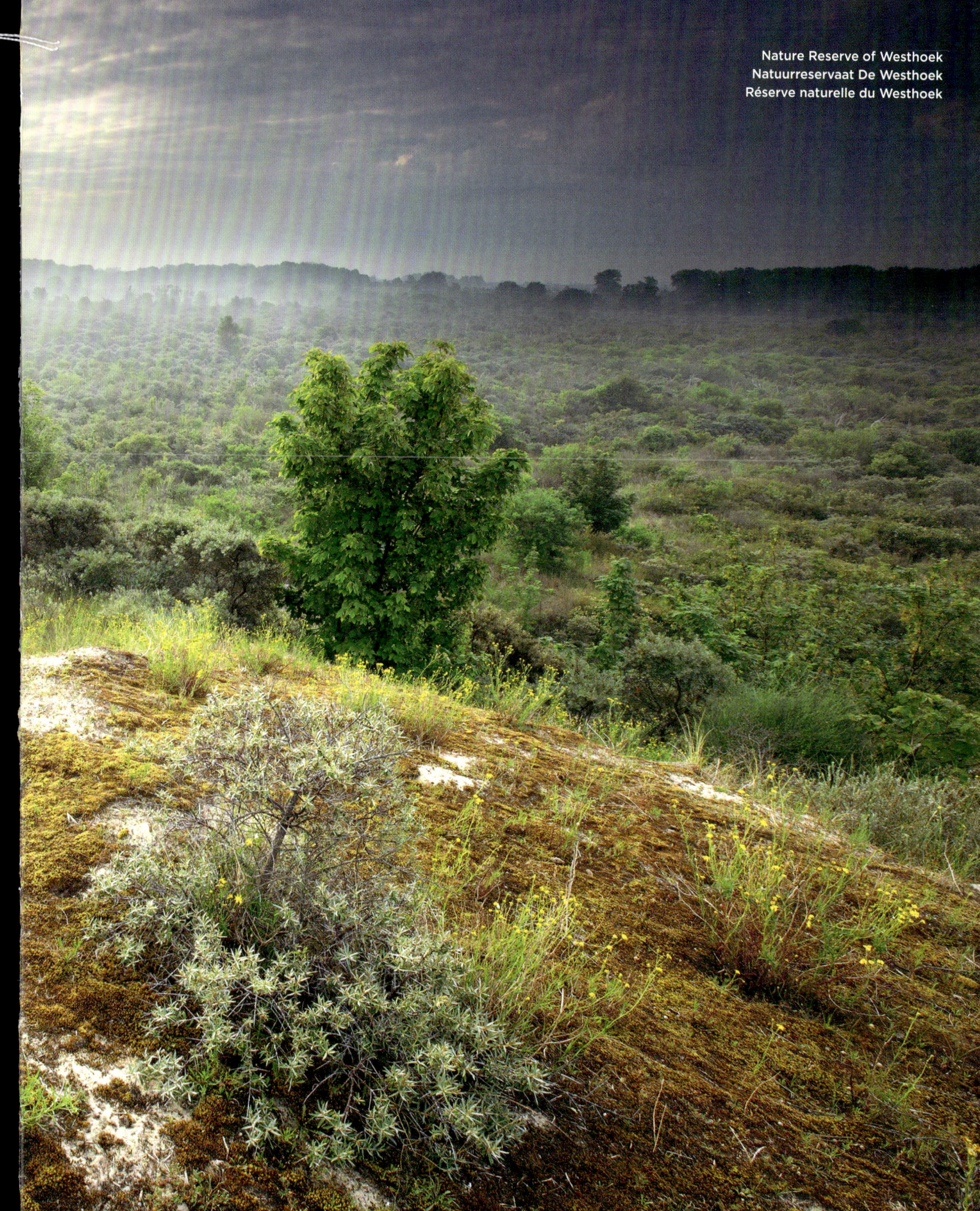
Nature Reserve of Westhoek
Natuurreservaat De Westhoek
Réserve naturelle du Westhoek

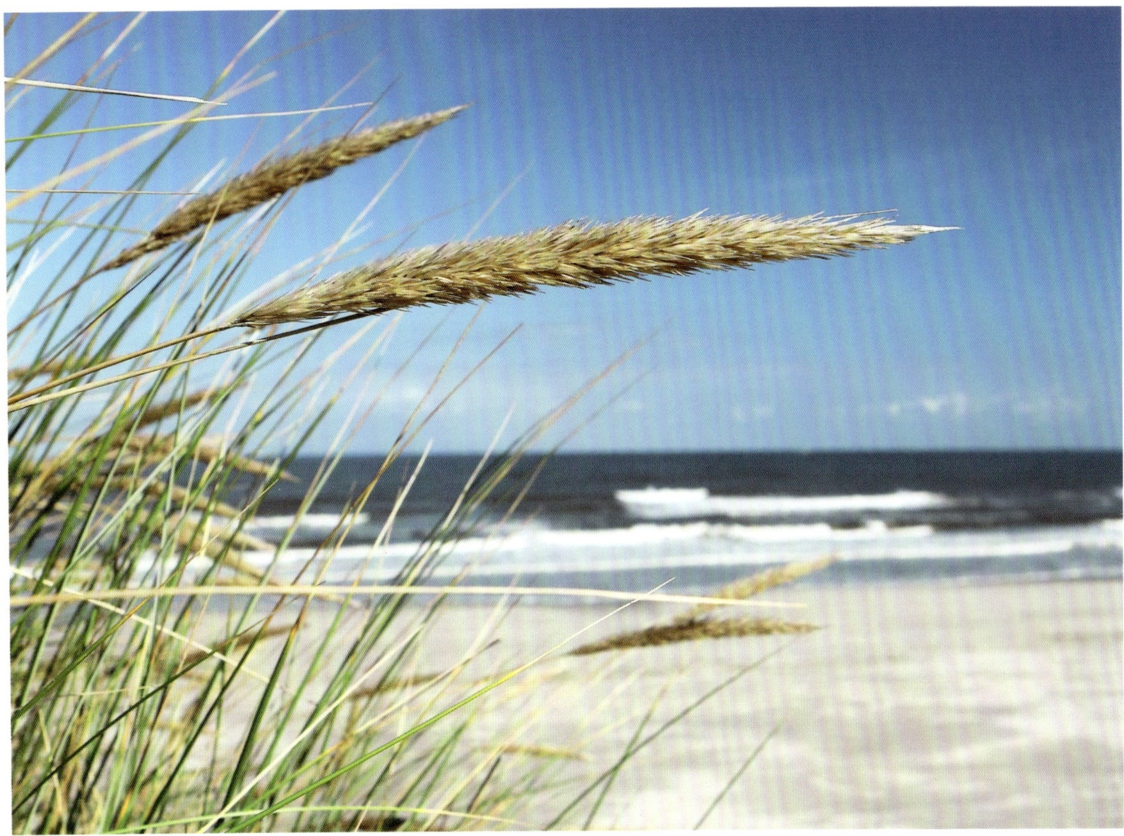

European marram grass, De Panne
Helmgras, De Panne
Oyat, La Panne

Flat beaches and dunes

At low tide the sea retreats for miles, leaving behind a wide sandy beach, with the coast at De Panne providing an ideal spot for land sailing. The omnipresent wind shapes the dune landscapes of Flanders into a "Flemish Sahara", giving the unique dune topography which makes up the border to France. The dunes constitute a natural barrier against storm tides. The dune grass, along with many other simple plant varieties, fortifies the dunes and forms a valuable biotope for rare breeding birds. The coastal hiking route leads through the dunes along the 68 km (42 mi) long Flemish coast.

Vastes plages et dunes ondoyantes

À marée basse, la mer se retire sur des kilomètres et fait apparaître une vaste plage de sable. Celle de la Panne, notamment, constitue le repère idéal des amateurs de char à voile. Le vent, qui y souffle en permanence, façonne les dunes flamandes, tout comme le « Sahara flamand », ce paysage unique à la frontière avec la France. Les dunes forment un rempart naturel contre les raz-de-marée. L'oyat et beaucoup d'autres plantes pionnières les maintiennent et offrent à de rares espèces d'oiseaux nicheurs un précieux biotope. Le chemin de randonnée côtier sillonne les 68 km de dunes de la côte flamande.

Flache Strände und Dünenlandschaften

Bei Ebbe zieht sich das Meer kilometerweit zurück und hinterlässt einen weiten Sandstrand. Insbesondere der Strand von De Panne bildet ein ideales Revier für Strandsegler. Der allgegenwärtige Wind formt die Dünenlandschaften Flanderns, so auch die „Flämische Sahara", die einzigartige Dünenlandschaft an der Grenze zu Frankreich. Die Dünen bilden einen natürlichen Schutzwall vor Sturmfluten. Das Dünengras und viele weitere Pionierpflanzen befestigen die Dünen und bilden ein wertvolles Biotop für seltene Brutvögel. Durch die Dünen führt die Küstenwanderroute längs der 68 km langen flämischen Küste.

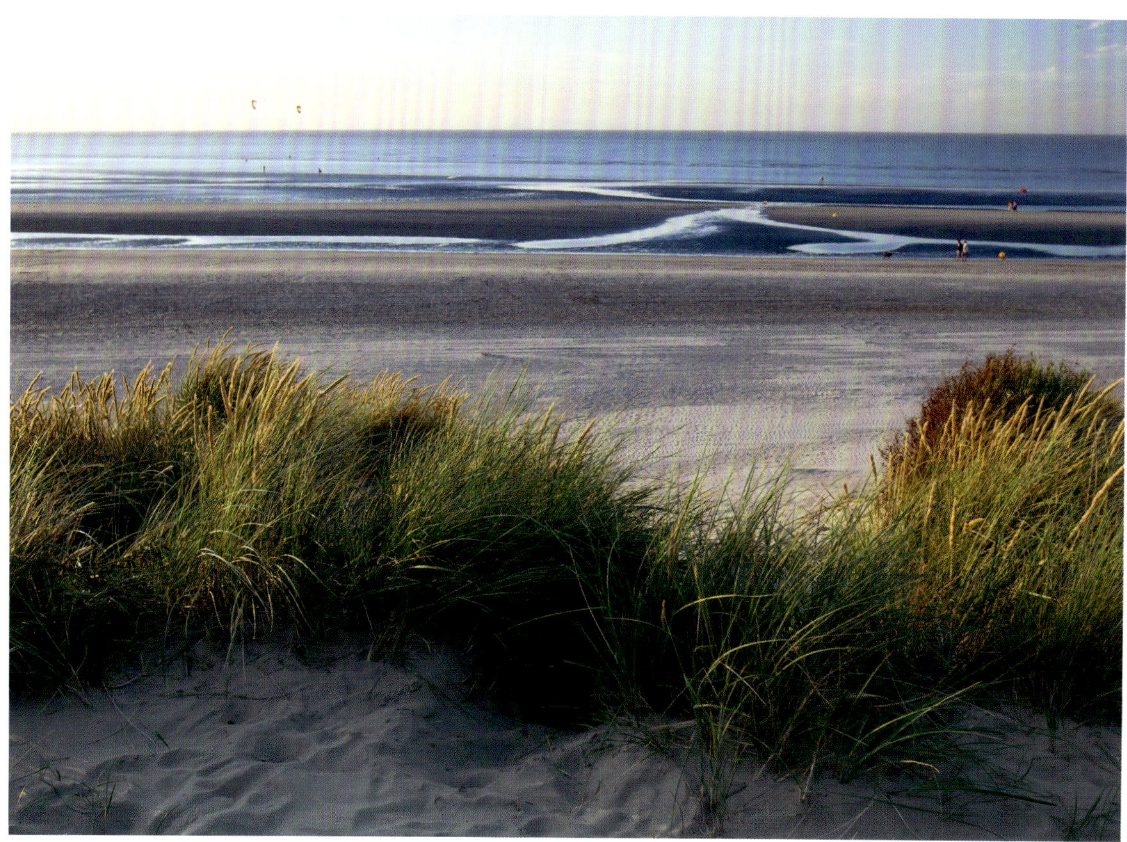

De Panne
La Panne

Playas lisas y parajes de dunas

Cuando baja la marea, el mar retrocede
varios kilómetros y deja atrás una
amplia playa de arena. Especialmente
la playa de De Panne es un lugar ideal
para los navegantes de playa. El viento
omnipresente forma los paisajes dunares
de Flandes, como el "Sahara Flamenco",
el paisaje dunar único en la frontera con
Francia. Las dunas forman una barrera
natural contra las mareas tormentosas. El
pasto de las dunas y muchas otras plantas
pioneras son un refuerzo para las dunas y
forman un valioso biotopo para las raras
aves reproductoras. La ruta de senderismo
costero conduce a través de las dunas a lo
largo de los 68 km de la costa flamenca.

Praias planas e paisagens de dunas

Na maré baixa, o mar se recua por
quilômetros e deixa para trás uma ampla
praia de areia. A praia de De Panne,
especialmente, é um local ideal para
velejadores de praia. O vento omnipresente
forma as paisagens dunares da Flandres,
como o "Saara Flamengo", a paisagem
única das dunas na fronteira com a
França. As dunas formam uma barreira
natural contra as tempestades do mar.
A grama das dunas e muitas outras
plantas pioneiras fortalecem as dunas e
formam um biótopo valioso para aves
raras reprodutoras. A rota de caminhada
costeira leva pelas dunas ao longo da costa
flamenga de 68 km deextensão.

Vlakke stranden en duinlandschappen

Bij eb trekt de zee zich mijlenver terug en
laat een breed zandstrand achter. Vooral
het strand van De Panne is een ideale plek
voor strandzeilers. De alomtegenwoordige
wind vormt de duinlandschappen van
Vlaanderen, zoals de "Vlaamse Sahara", het
unieke duinlandschap dichtbij de grens met
Frankrijk. De duinen vormen een natuurlijke
bescherming tegen stormvloeden. Het
duingras en vele andere pionierplanten
versterken de duinen en vormen een
waardevolle biotoop voor zeldzame
broedvogels. De kustwandelroute loopt
door de duinen langs de 68 km lange
Vlaamse kust.

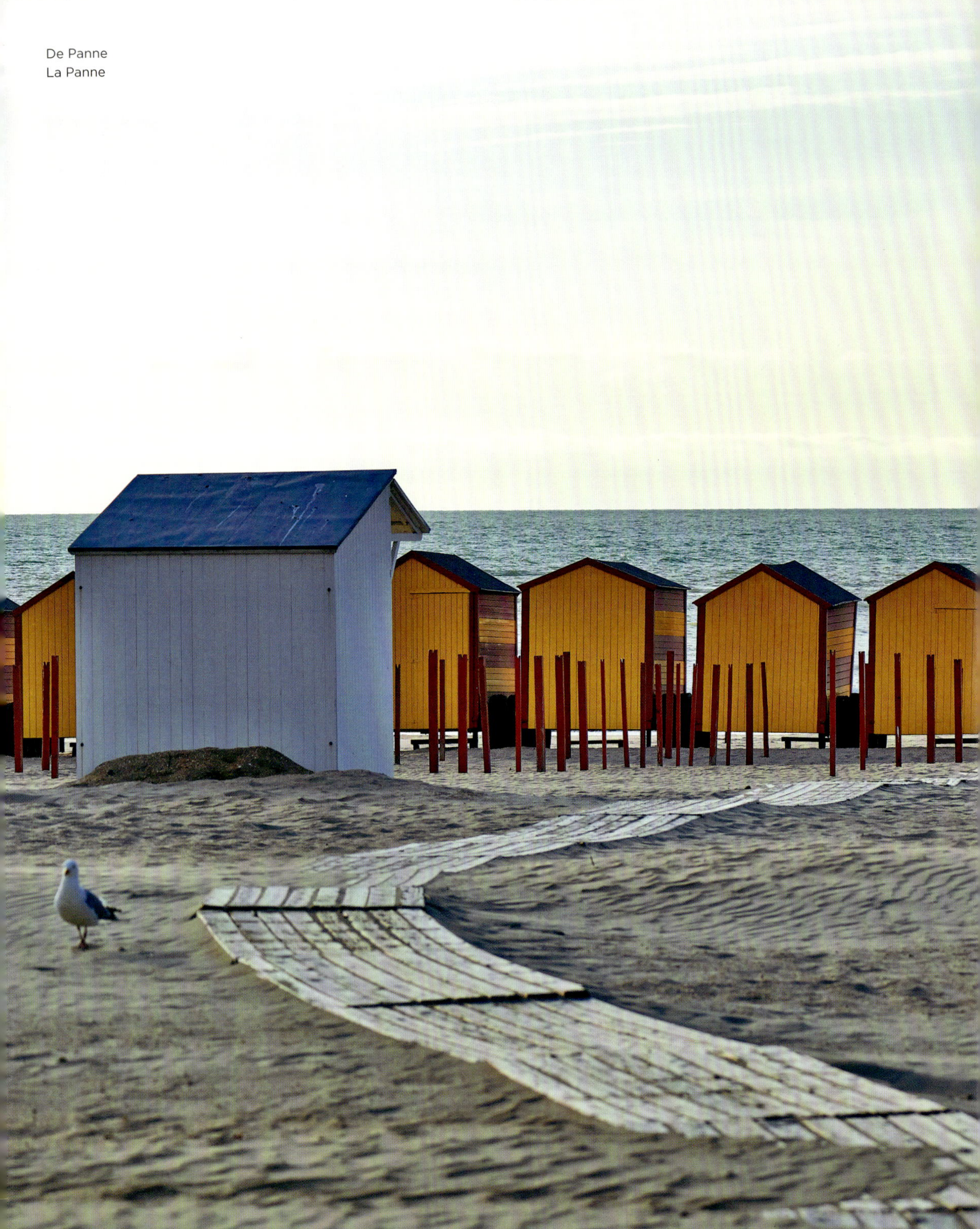
De Panne
La Panne

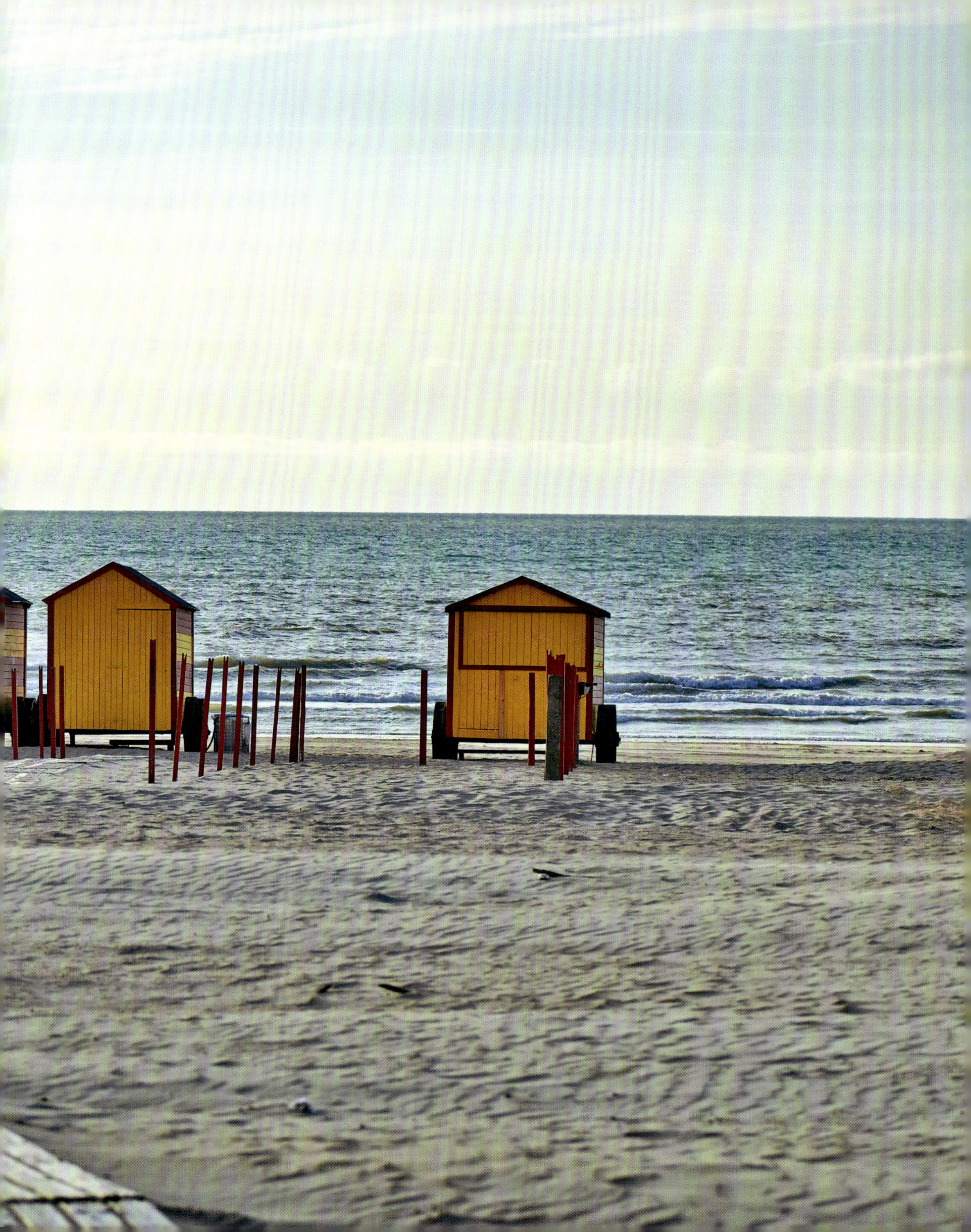

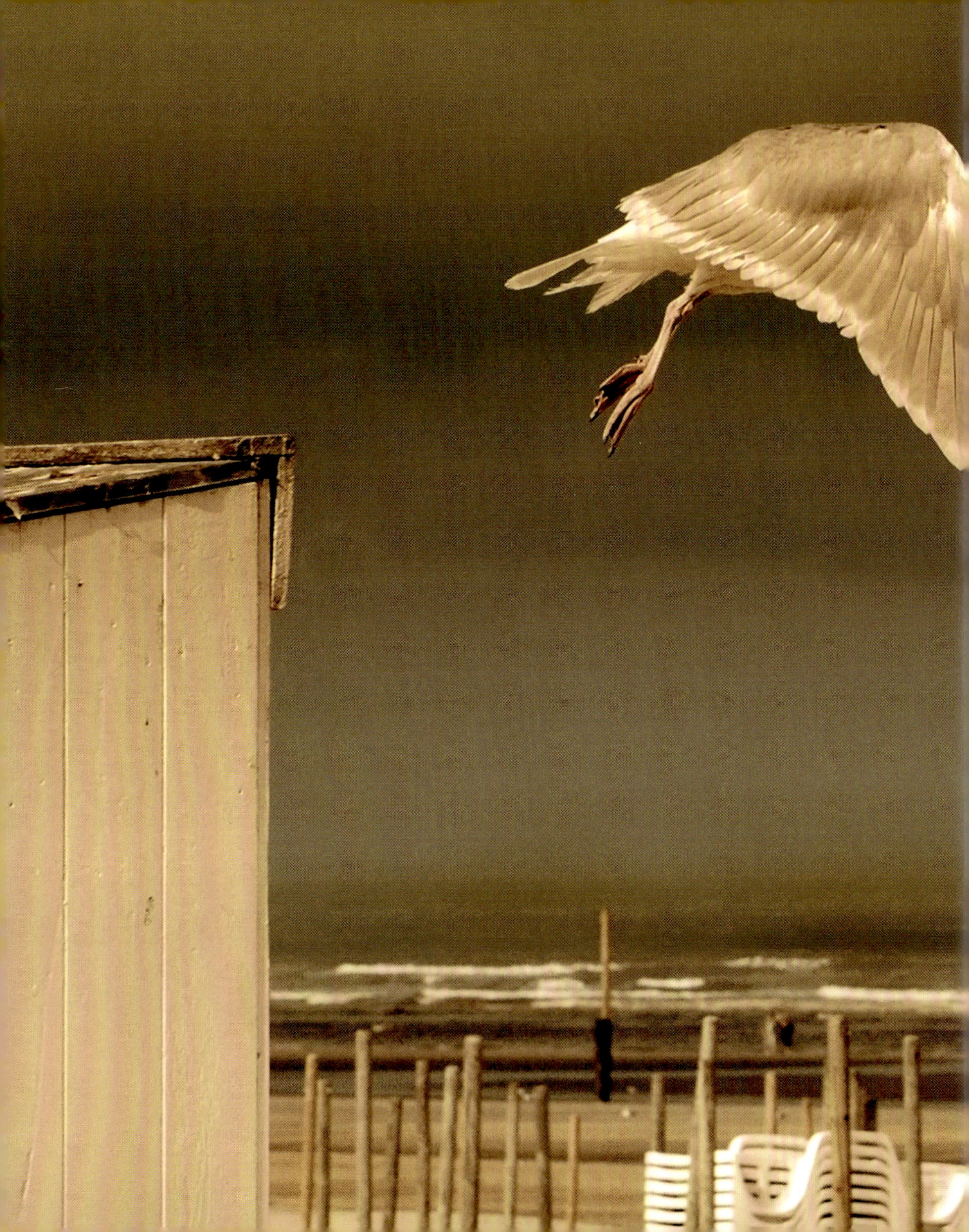

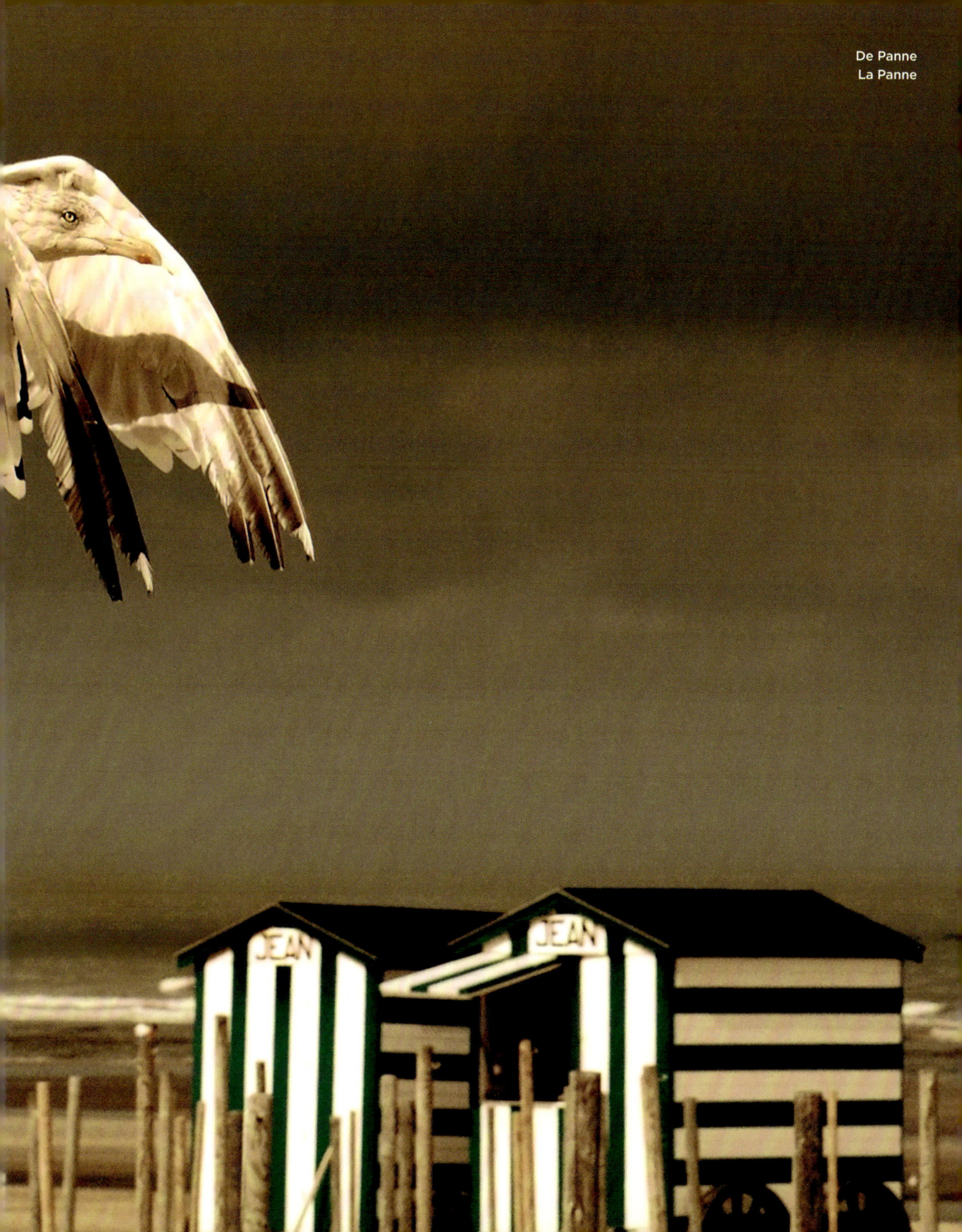
De Panne
La Panne

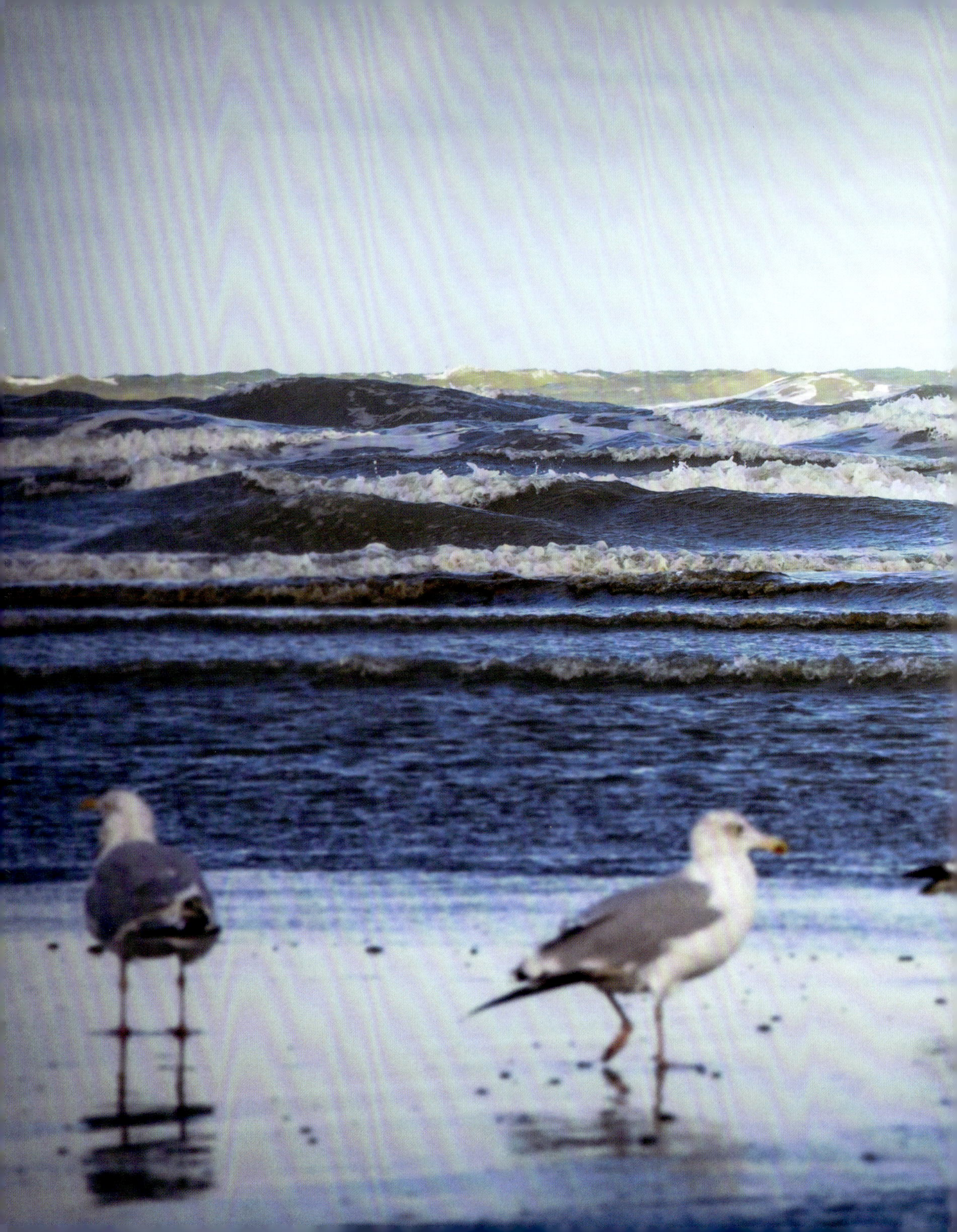

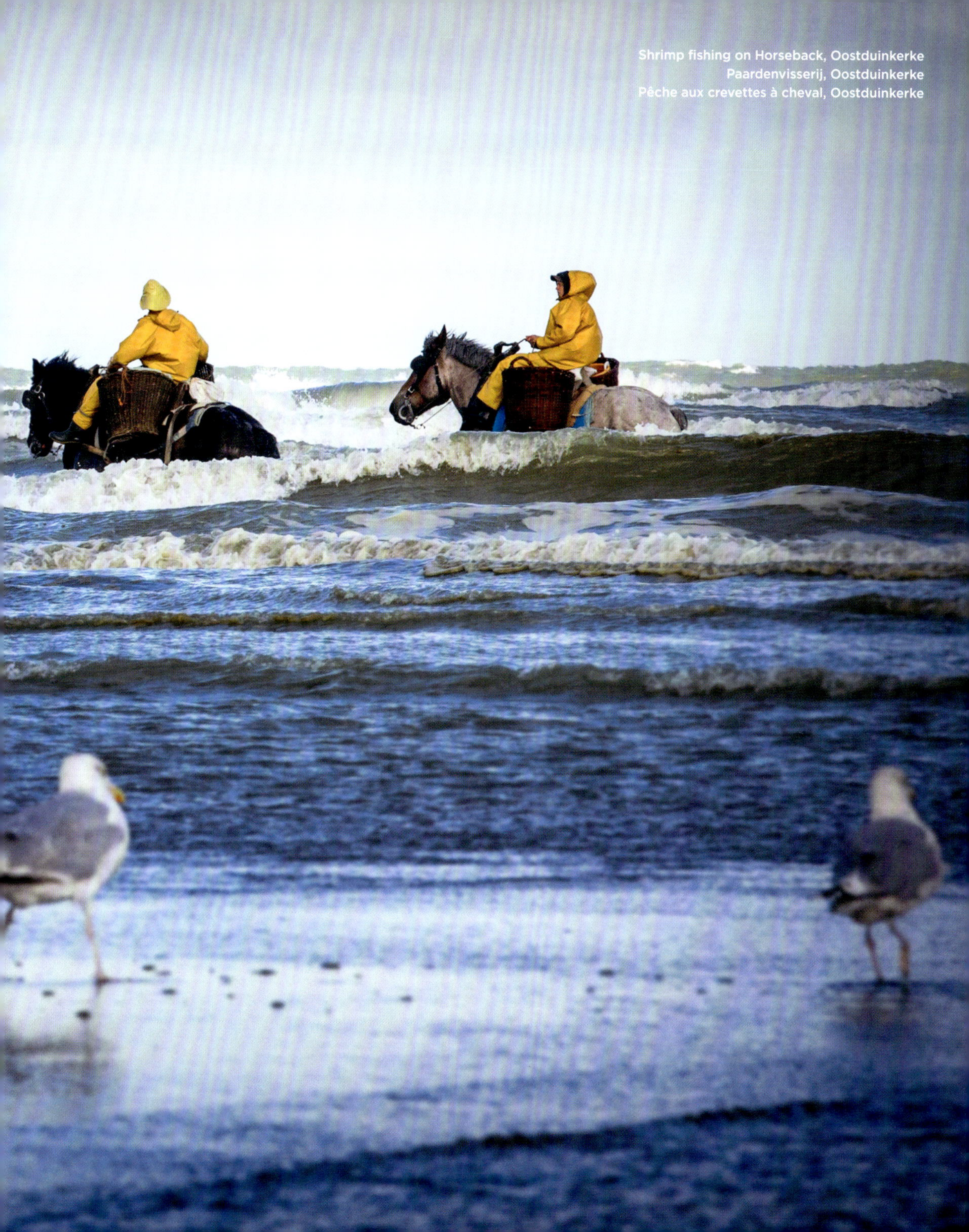

Shrimp fishing on Horseback, Oostduinkerke
Paardenvisserij, Oostduinkerke
Pêche aux crevettes à cheval, Oostduinkerke

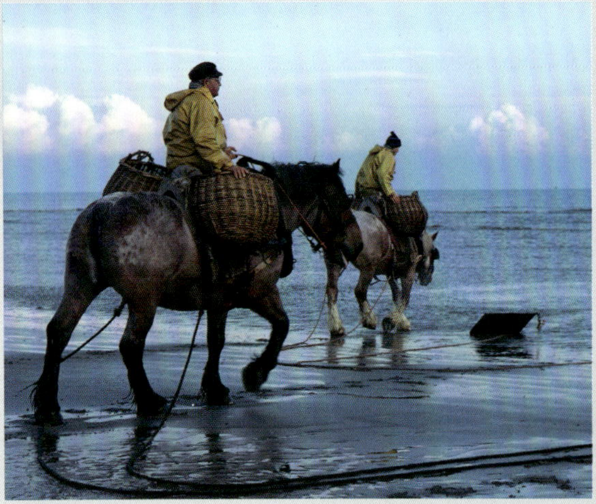

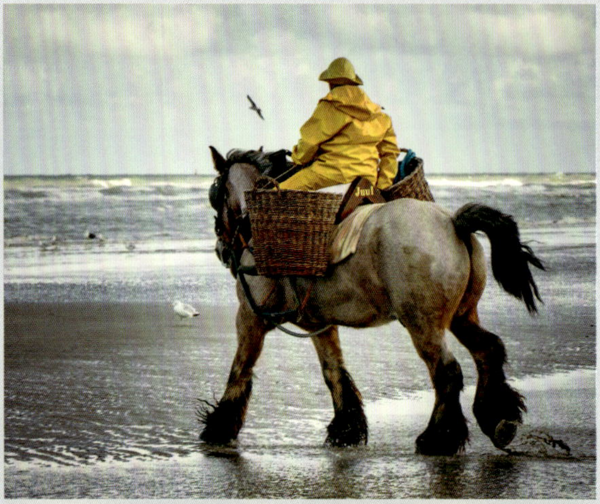

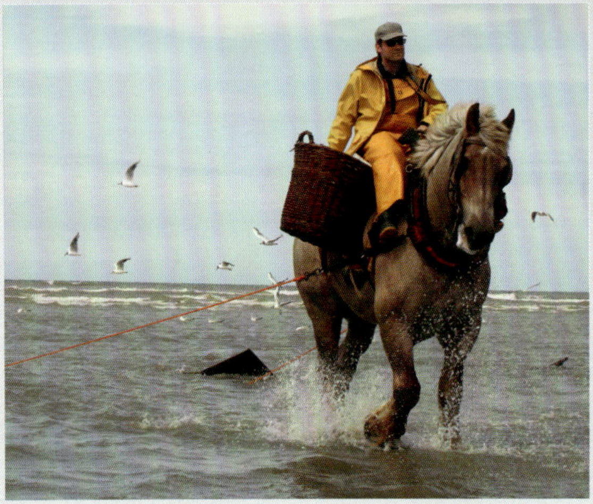

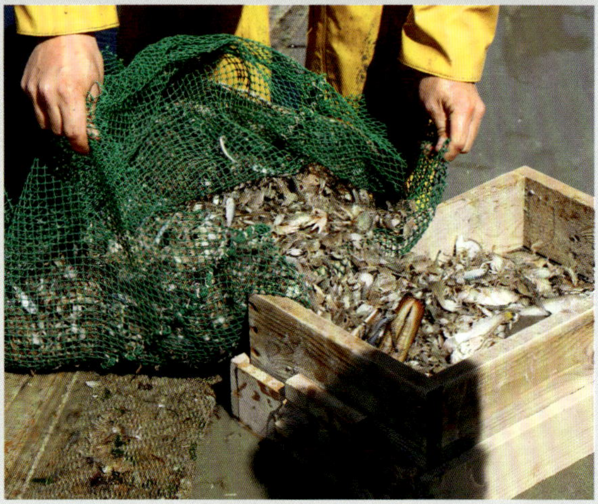

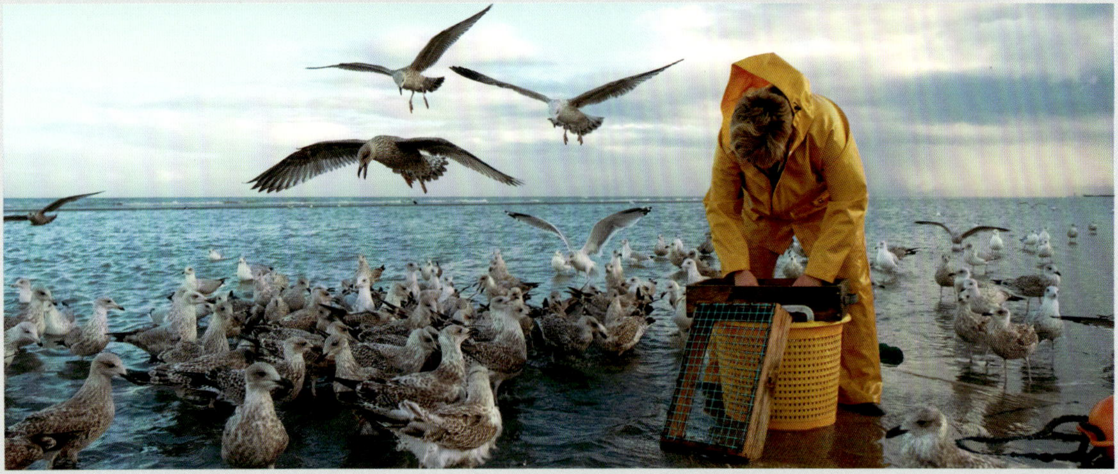

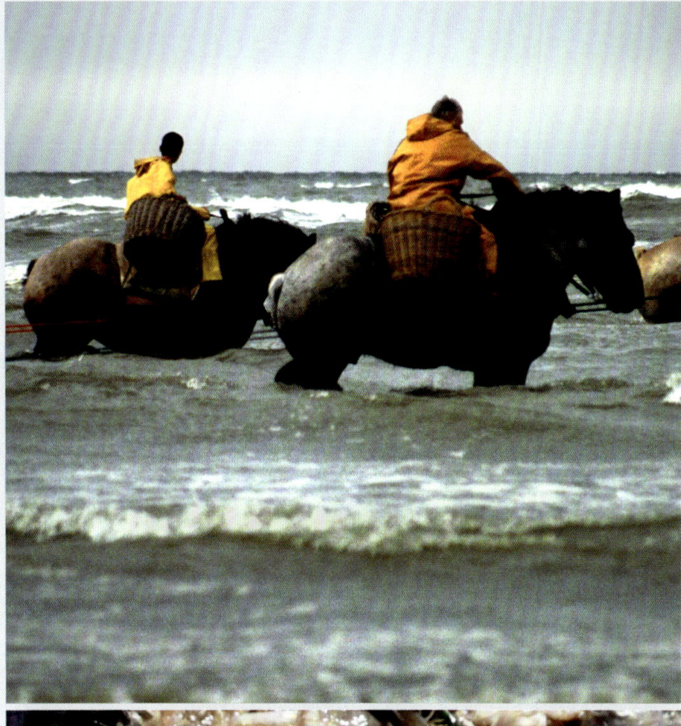

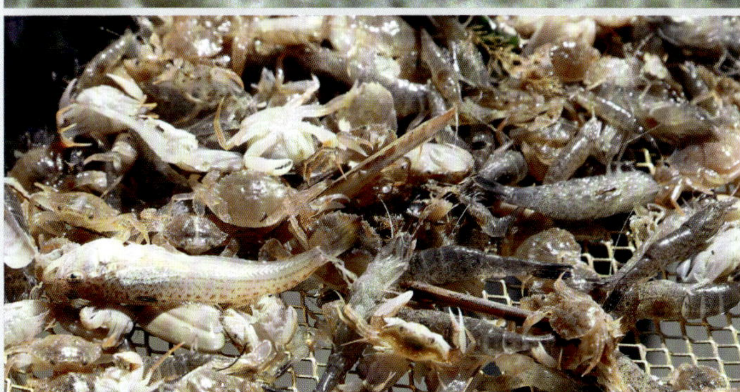

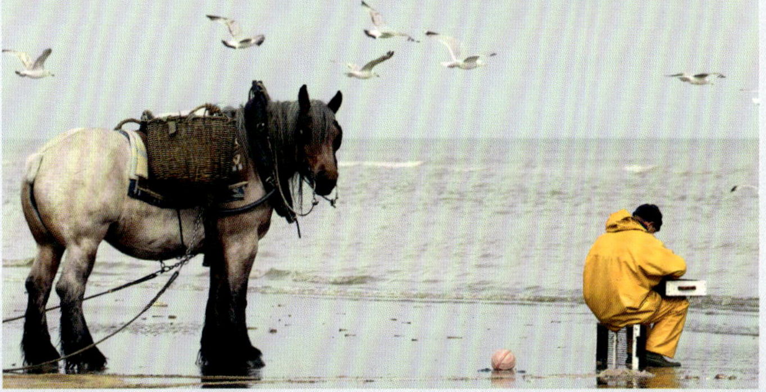

Fishermen on horseback

The Flemish coast is the only place in Europe where fishermen still ride on horseback trawling for shrimps. At low tide the horses ply the sea up to their bellies, pulling the heavy nets and from time to time, horses and fishermen come ashore to empty these nets. The grey North Sea shrimps caught in this way are then cooked, a real treat for gourmets.

Pêcheurs à cheval

La côte flamande est le seul lieu en Europe où la pêche aux crevettes se fait encore à cheval. À marée basse, les chevaux s'enfoncent dans la mer jusqu'au poitrail, tirant derrière eux les lourds filets de pêche. De temps en temps, cheval et pêcheur reviennent sur la terre ferme pour les vider. Pêchées ainsi et ensuite cuisinées, les crevettes grises de la mer du Nord sont un véritable plaisir de gourmet.

Fischer zu Pferde

Die flämische Küste ist der einzige Ort in Europa, an dem Fischer noch zu Pferd Krabben fangen. Bei Ebbe laufen die Pferde bis zur Brust durch das Meer und ziehen die schweren Netze. Ab und zu kommen Pferd und Fischer an Land, um die Netze zu entleeren. Die grauen Nordseekrabben, die auf diese Weise gefangen und gekocht werden, sind für Feinschmecker ein wahrer Leckerbissen.

Pescadores a caballo

La costa flamenca es el único lugar de Europa donde los pescadores todavía pescan cangrejos a caballo. Cuando la marea está baja, los caballos avanzan por el mar hasta que el agua les llega por el pecho y tiran de las pesadas redes. De vez en cuando, los caballos y los pescadores van a la orilla para vaciar las redes. Las gambas grises capturadas y cocinadas de esta manera son un verdadero placer para los gourmets.

Pescadores a cavalo

A costa flamenga é o único local da Europa onde os pescadores ainda pescam caranguejos a cavalo. Na maré baixa, os cavalos andam pelo mar com água até as suas barrigas e puxam as redes pesadas. De vez em quando, cavalos e pescadores retornam à praia para esvaziar as redes. Os caranguejos cinzentos do Mar do Norte, que são capturados desta forma e cozinhados, são um verdadeiro deleite para os gourmets.

Paardenvissers

De Vlaamse kust is de enige plaats in Europa waar vissers nog steeds te paard krabben vangen. Bij eb rennen de paarden tot aan de borst door de zee en trekken aan zware netten. Soms komen er paarden en vissers aan land om de netten te legen. De grijze Noordzeekrabben, die op deze manier gevangen en gekookt worden, zijn een echte traktatie voor fijnproevers.

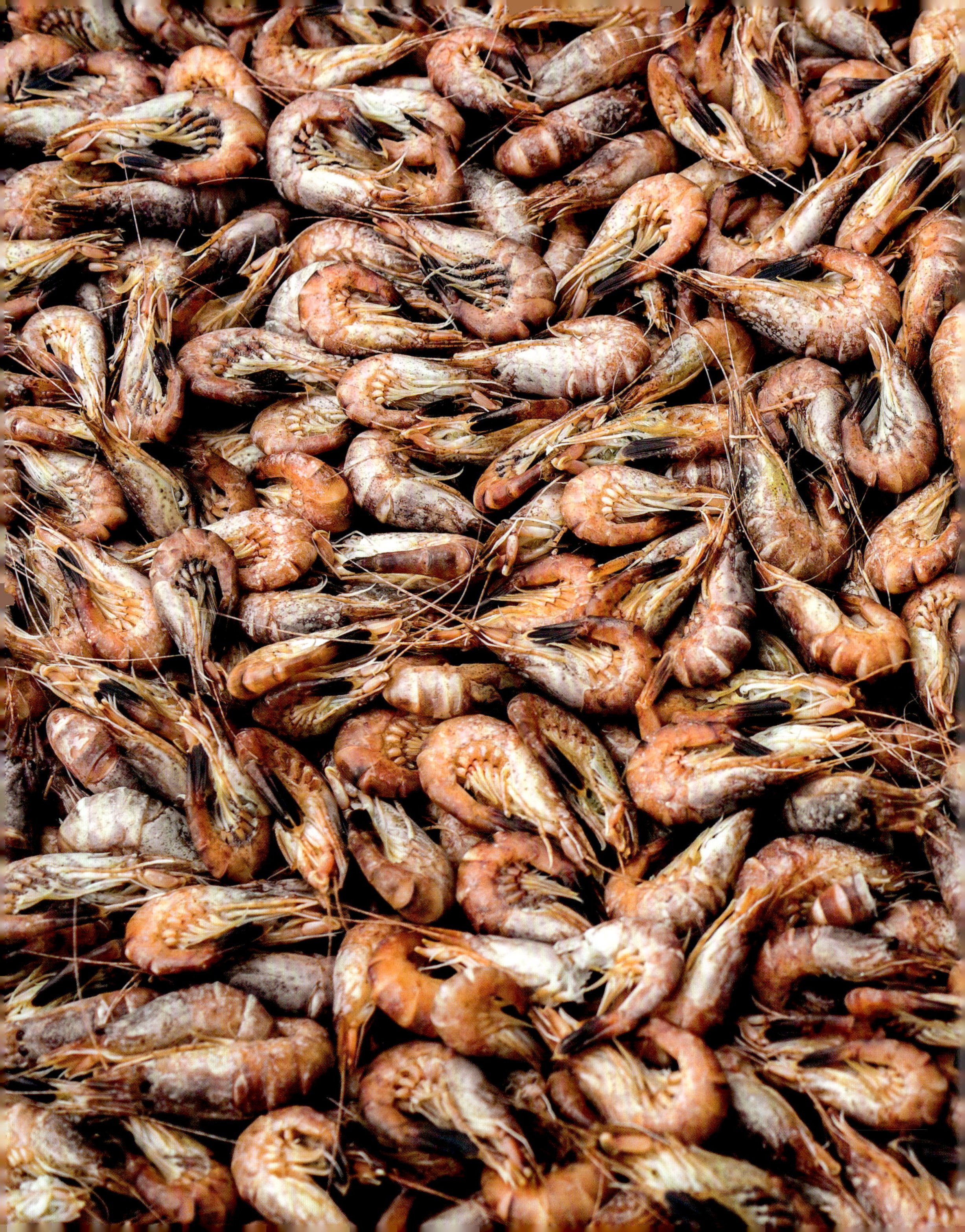

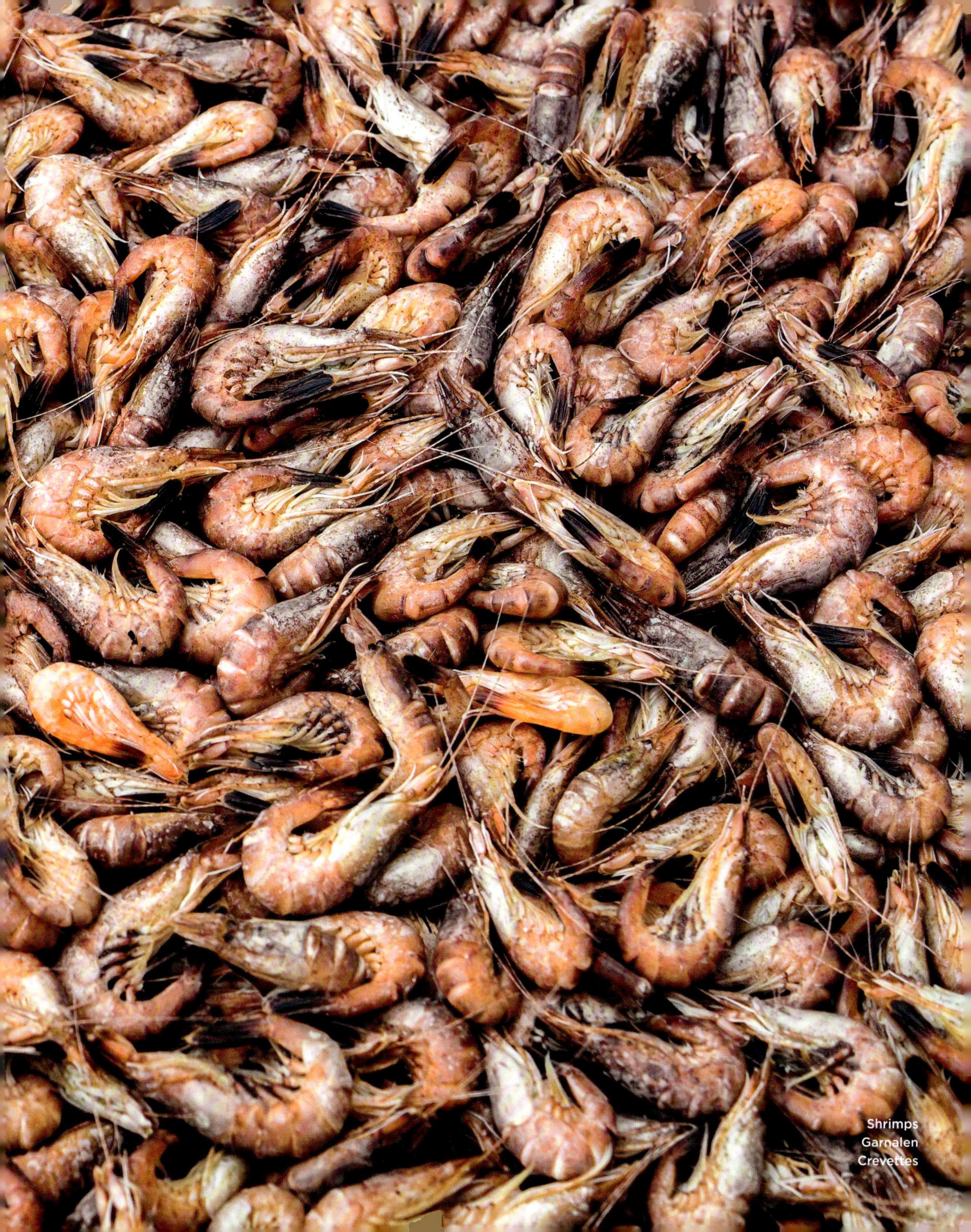
Shrimps
Garnalen
Crevettes

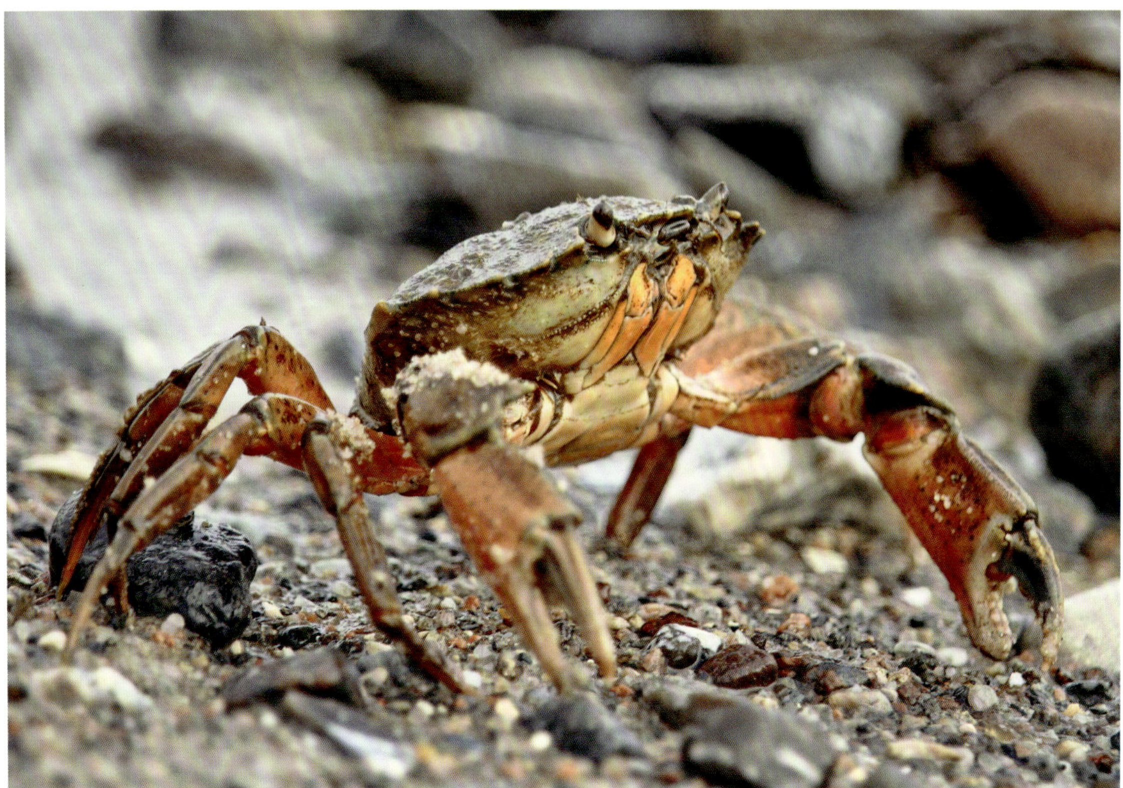

Shore crab
Strandkrab
Crabe enragé

Land sailing

As early as the 15th century, the Flemish mathematician Simon Stevin built a fleet of 27 land yachts for Prince Maurice of Orange and others, which were propelled by the wind and could easily overtake the conventional horse-drawn carriages. It was not until 1898, however, that the inventor André Dumont developed the first sporting land yacht, establishing the sport on the wide sandy beach of De Panne.

Navegación playera

Ya en el siglo XV, el matemático flamenco Simon Stevin construyó una flota de 27 coches de vela para Mauricio de Nassau, que eran más rápidos que el viento y superaban fácilmente a los habituales coches de caballos. No fue hasta 1898 que el inventor André Dumont desarrolló el primer velero deportivo y estableció el deporte en la amplia playa de De Panne.

Char à voile

Au XVe siècle déjà, le mathématicien flamand Simon Stevin construisit pour Maurice de Nassau une flotte de 27 chars à voile qui avançaient plus vite que le vent, doublant sans problème les calèches. Ce n'est qu'en 1898 que l'amateur de bricolage André Dumont mit au point le premier char à voile de sport et établit cette activité sportive sur la vaste plage de sable de Panne.

Vela na praia

Já no século XV, o matemático flamengo Simon Stevin construiu uma frota de 27 veículos movidos a velas para Maurício, Príncipe de Orange, que eram mais rápidos do que o vento e facilmente ultrapassavam as carruagens puxadas a cavalo habituais. Foi só em 1898 que o inventor, André Dumont, desenvolveu o primeiro carro à vela esportivo e estabeleceu o esporte na larga praia arenosa de De Panne.

Strandsegeln

Bereits im 15. Jahrhundert baute der flämische Mathematiker Simon Stevin für Moritz von Oranien eine Flotte von 27 Segelwagen, die schneller fuhren als der Wind und die üblichen Pferdekutschen locker überholten. Erst 1898 entwickelte der Tüftler, André Dumont den ersten sportlichen Segelwagen und etablierte den Sport am weiten Sandstrand von De Panne.

Strandzeilen

Al in de 15de eeuw bouwde de Vlaamse wiskundige Simon Stevin voor Maurits van Oranje een vloot van 27 zeilwagens die sneller waren dan de wind en met gemak de gebruikelijke paardenkoetsen inhaalden. Pas in 1898 ontwikkelde de knutselaar en hobbyist André Dumont de 1e sportieve zeilwagen en legde de grondslag voor de sport op het brede zandstrand van De Panne.

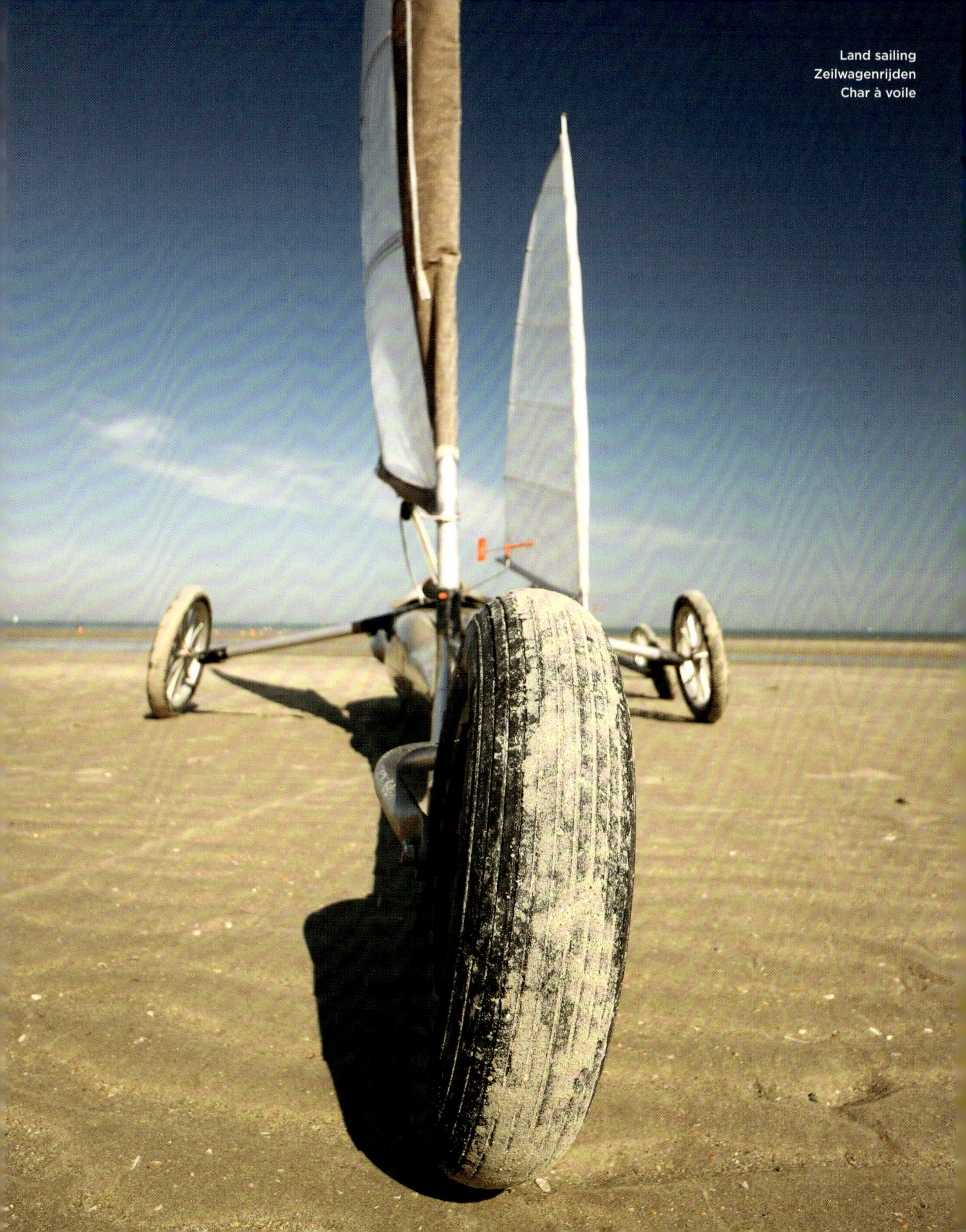
Land sailing
Zeilwagenrijden
Char à voile

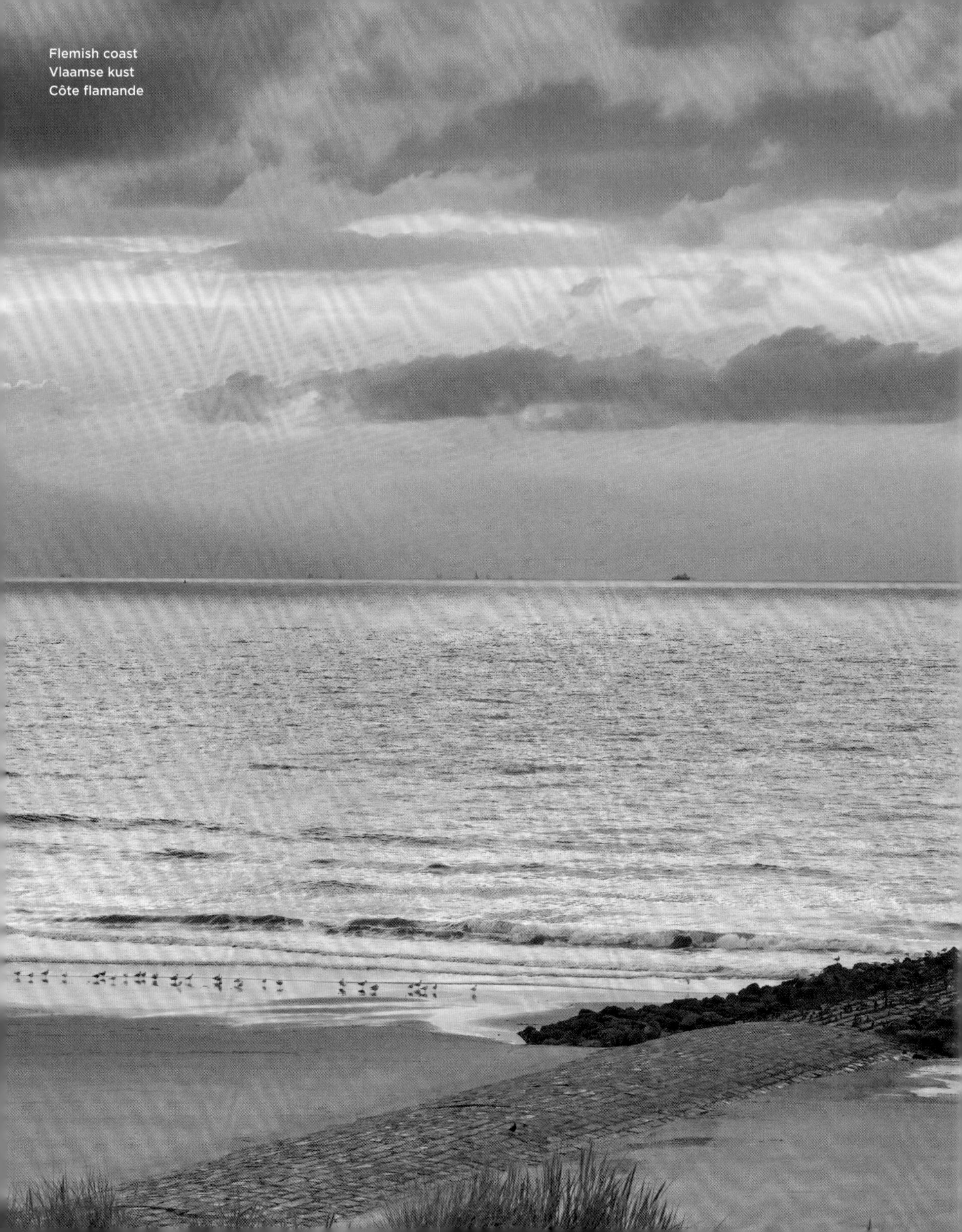
Flemish coast
Vlaamse kust
Côte flamande

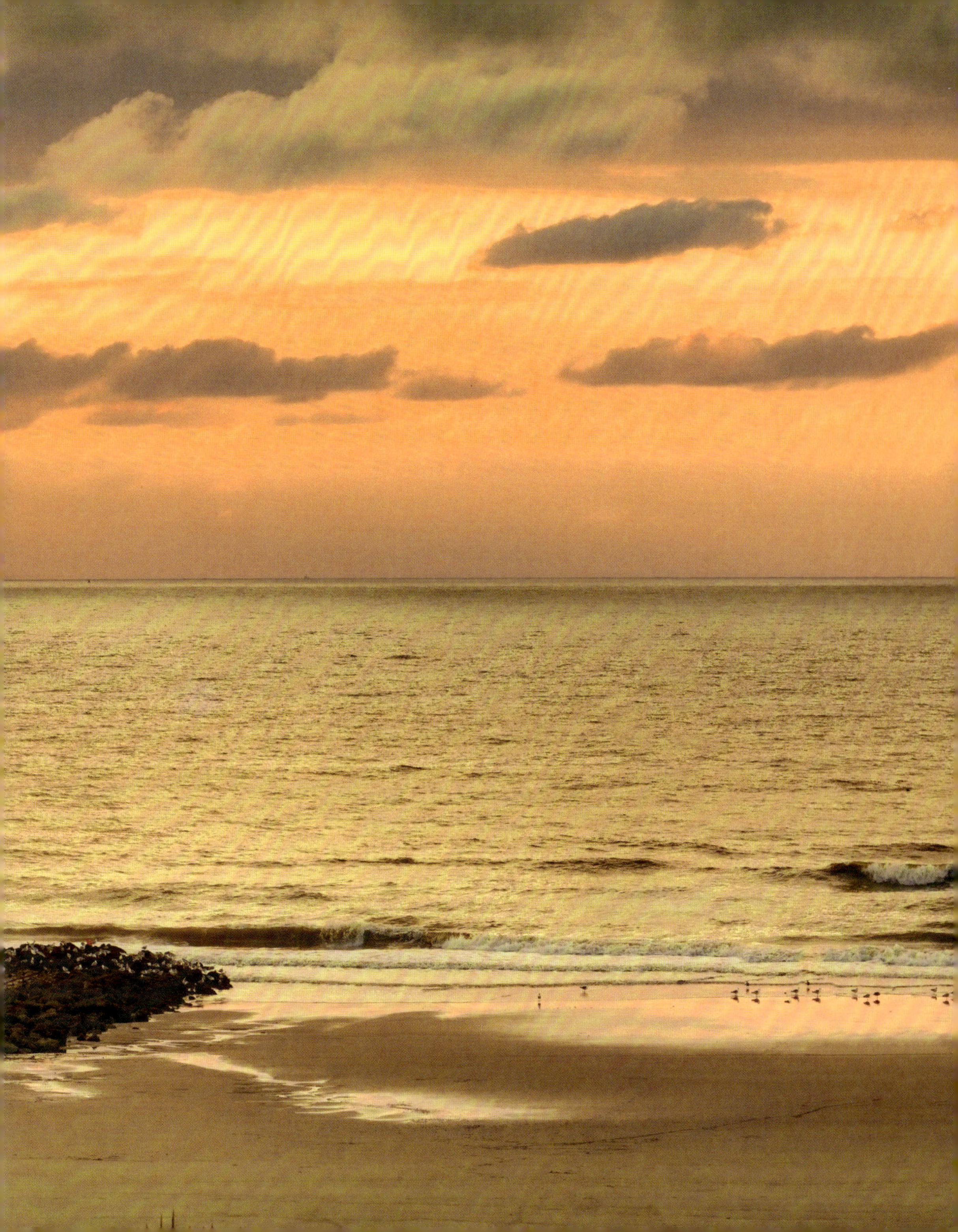

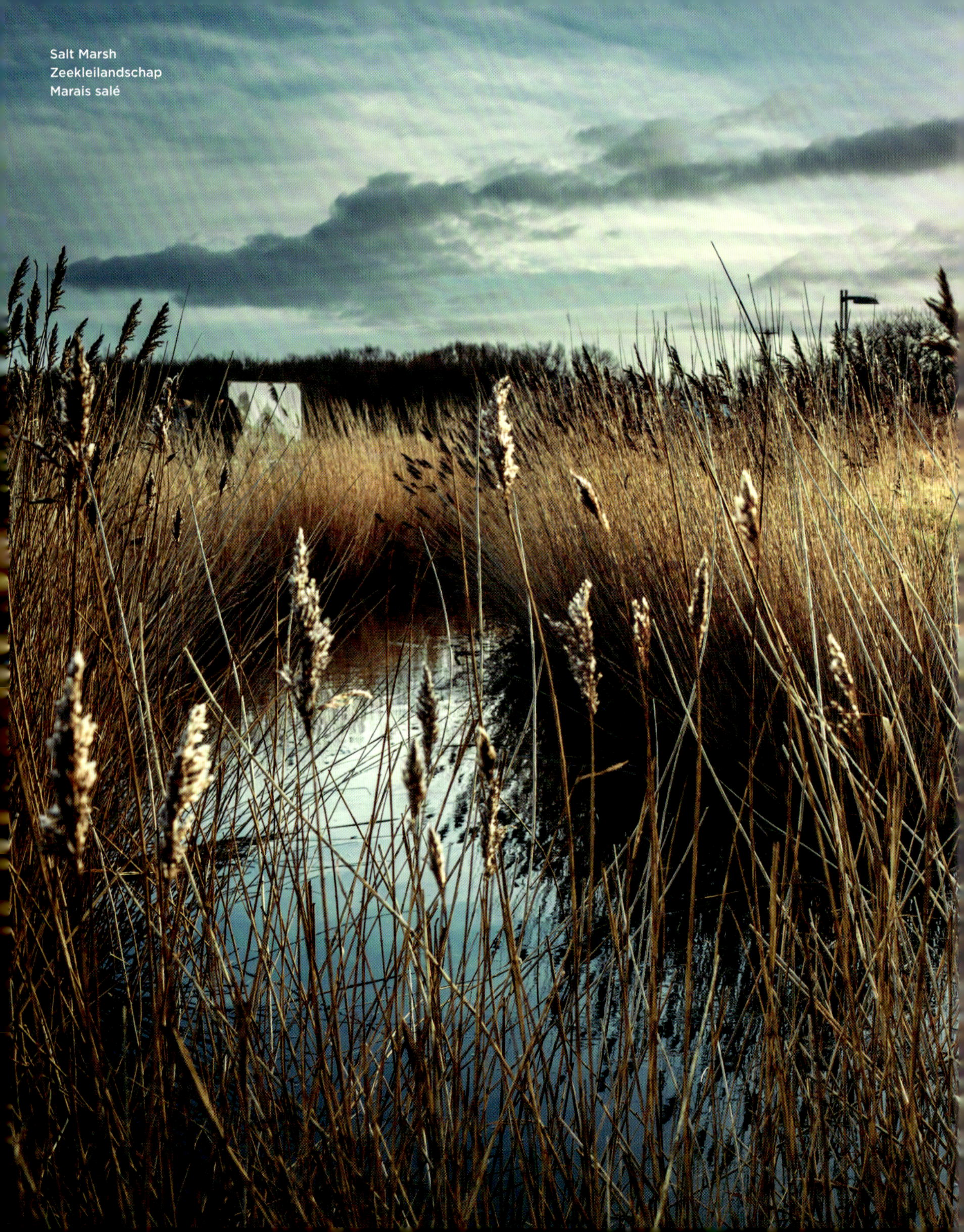
Salt Marsh
Zeekleilandschap
Marais salé

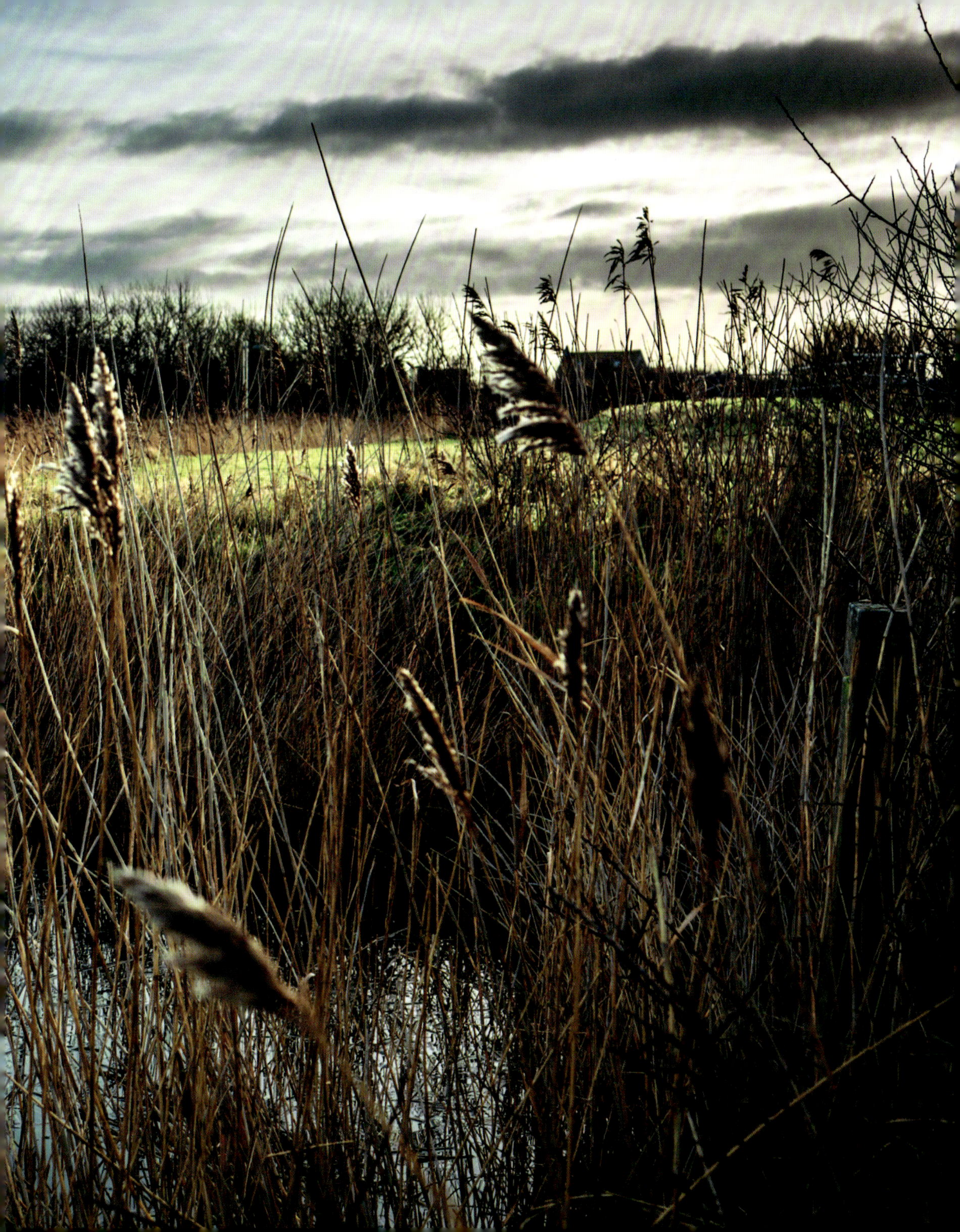

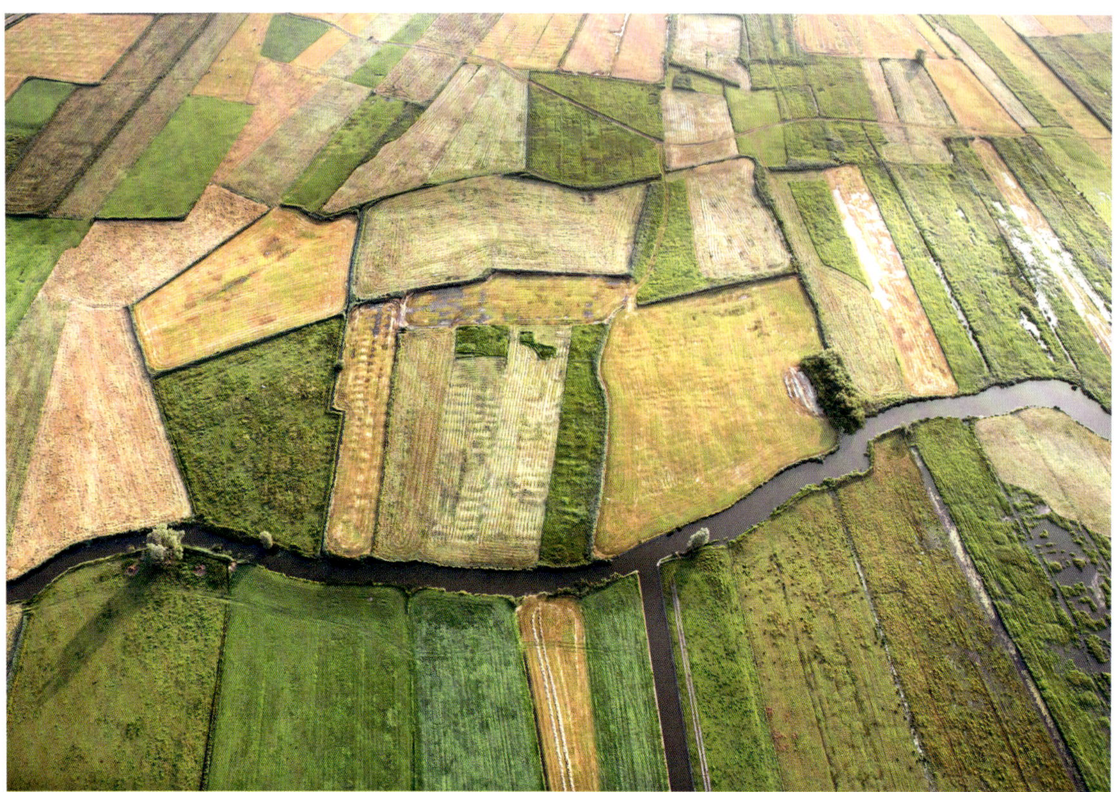

Yser
IJser

Polder and Windmills

Further to the west, the Flemish wrested fertile farmland from the sea. A large part of Flanders today consists of polders: a dike-enclosed landscape crossed by canals, which was drained by windmills. The Flemings also owe this to the polymath, Simon Stevin, who significantly improved windmill design in the 15th century.

Polders et moulins à vent

Côté ouest, les Flamands prirent de plus en plus de fertiles terres arables à la mer. Une grande partie des Flandres se compose aujourd'hui de polders : un paysage de digues, drainé par des moulins à vent et sillonné de canaux. Encore le fruit des travaux du polymathe Simon Stevin, qui améliora considérablement les moulins à vent au XVe siècle.

Polder und Windmühlen

Immer weiter nach Westen rangen die Flamen dem Meer das fruchtbare Ackerland ab. Ein Großteil Flanderns besteht heute aus Poldern: eine von Kanälen durchzogene Deichlandschaft, die mittels Windmühlen entwässert wurde. Auch das verdanken die Flamen dem Universalgelehrten, Simon Stevin, der die Windmühlen im 15. Jahrhundert maßgeblich verbesserte.

Pólder y molinos de viento

Más al oeste, los flamencos ganaros tierras fértiles de cultivo al mar. Una gran parte de Flandes consiste hoy en día en pólderes: un paisaje de diques atravesado por canales, que fue drenado por molinos de viento. Esto también se lo deben al erudito universal Simon Stevin, que mejoró considerablemente los molinos de viento en el siglo XV.

Polder e moinhos de vento

Cada vez mais a oeste, os flamengos arrancavam as terras férteis do mar. Uma grande parte da Flandres consiste hoje em polders: uma paisagem de diques atravessada por canais, que foi drenada por moinhos de vento. Os flamengos também devem isso ao estudioso universal, Simon Stevin, que melhorou significativamente os moinhos de vento no século XV.

Polder en Windmolens

Nog meer westwaarts ontrukten de Vlamingen de vruchtbare landbouwgronden aan de zee. Een groot deel van Vlaanderen bestaat nu uit polders: een door kanalen doorkruist dijkenlandschap dat door windmolens werd gedraineerd. De Vlamingen hebben dit ook dit te danken aan de universele geleerde Simon Stevin die de windmolens in de 15e eeuw flink verbeterde.

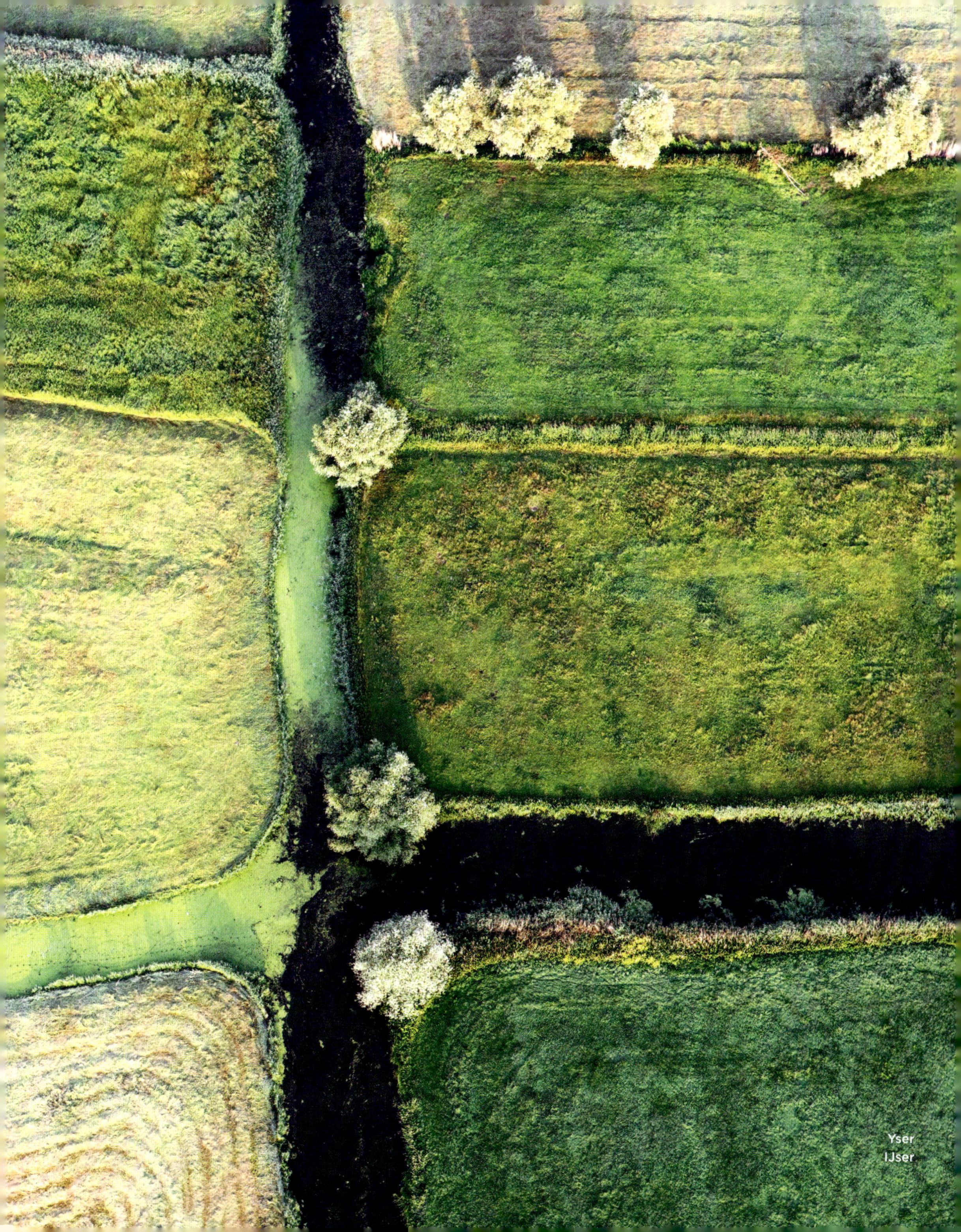

Yser
IJser

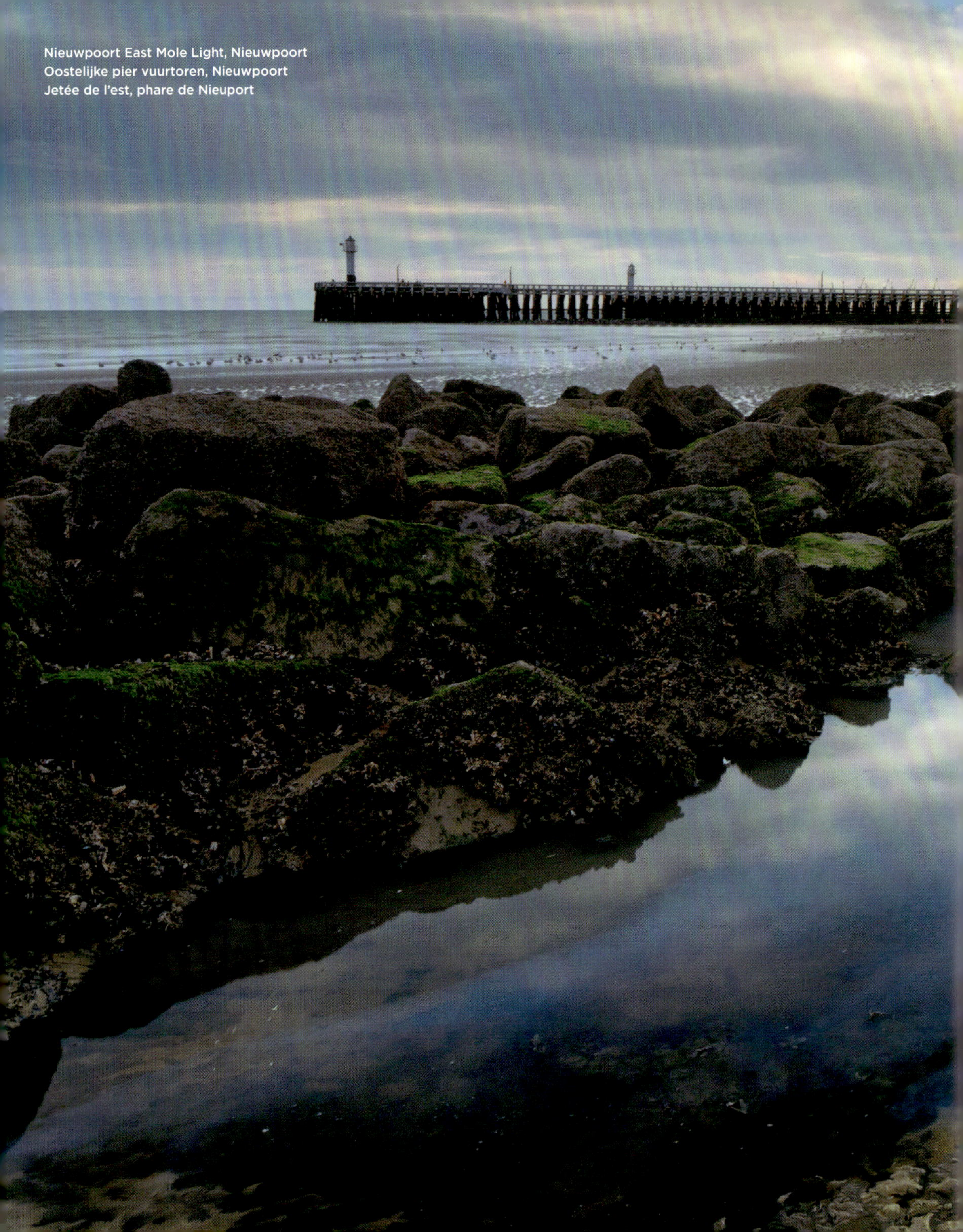

Nieuwpoort East Mole Light, Nieuwpoort
Oostelijke pier vuurtoren, Nieuwpoort
Jetée de l'est, phare de Nieuport

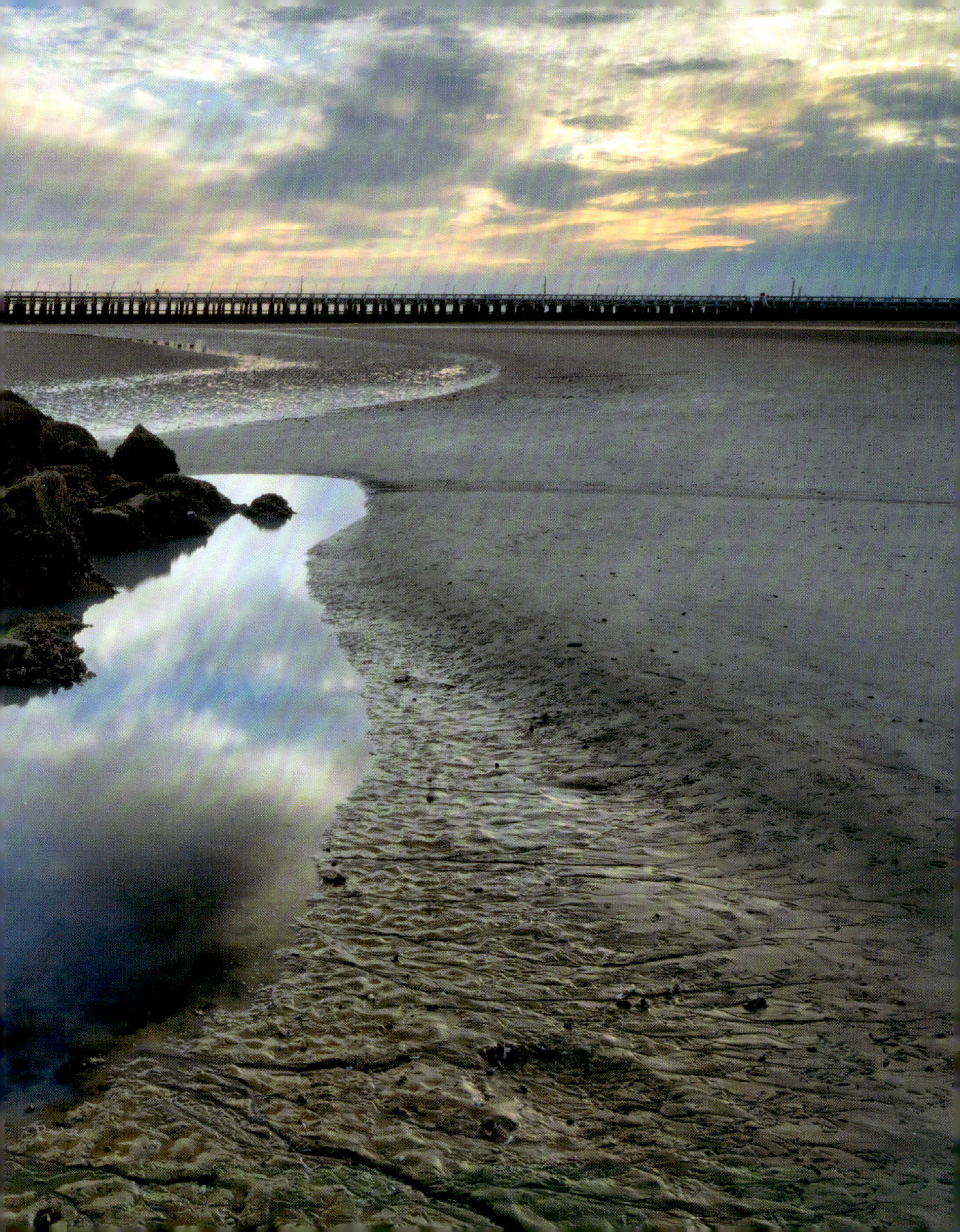

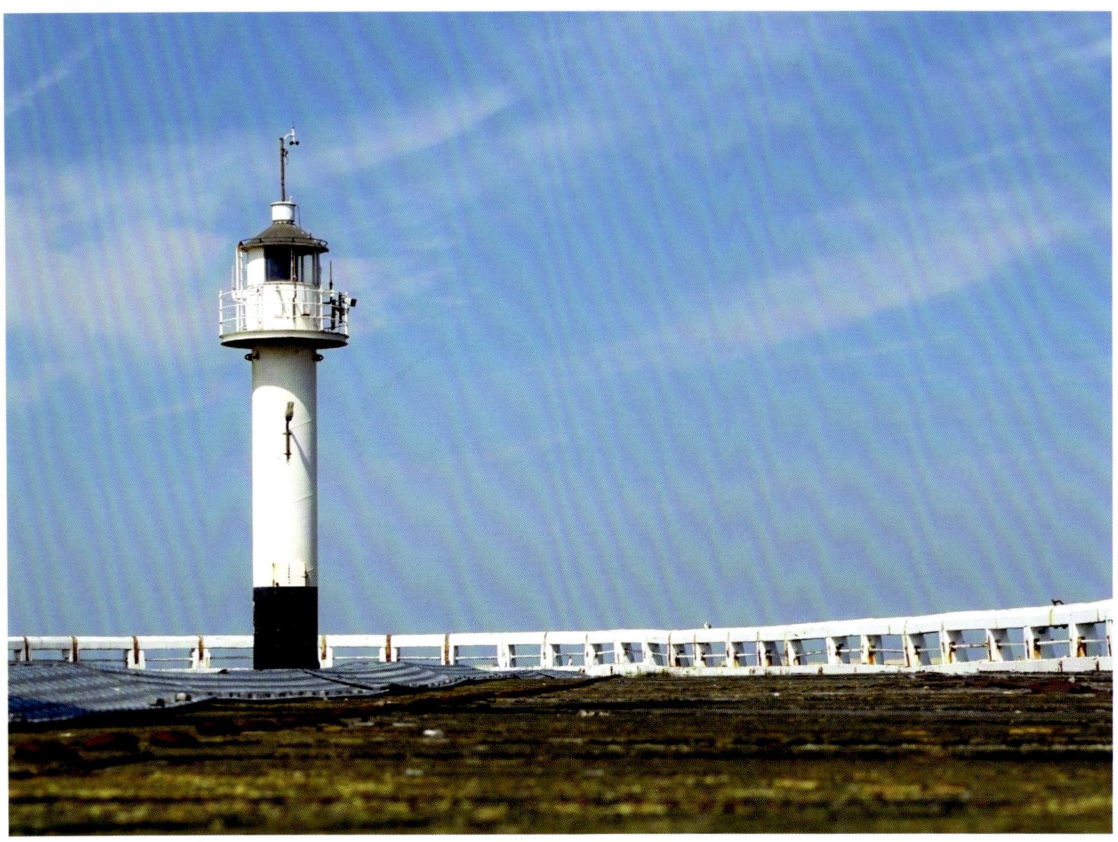

Lighthouse, Ostend
Vuurtoren, Oostende
Phare, Ostende

Piers

The up-and-coming Ostend owed its economic blooming in the 18th century to its port. With the coming of the first tourists, piers were built into the sea in the English style, as was appropriate for a sophisticated seaside resort of the *belle époque*. On the piers, to the right and left of the harbour exit, people could feel the wildness of the sea and watch the ships up close. The wooden, white-painted pier in Ostend measures a proud 650 m (184 ft) and supports a cast-iron lighthouse. In addition to two piers in Ostend, there are other piers in Nieuwpoort and Blankenberge.

Des ponts vers le large

Au XVIIIe siècle, la florissante ville d'Ostende devait sa prospérité économique à son port. Avec les premiers touristes, on bâtit des jetées, suivant le modèle anglais, comme il seyait aux baigneurs mondains de la Belle Époque. De part et d'autre de la sortie du port, les badauds pouvaient ainsi avancer vers le large, sentir l'embrun de la mer sauvage et observer les bateaux de près. Parée d'un phare en fonte, la jetée en bois peinte en blanc ne mesure pas moins de 650 m. Outre les deux jetées d'Ostende, deux autres estacades s'élancent dans la mer à Nieuport et à Blankenberge.

Brücken ins Meer

Das aufstrebende Ostende verdankte seine wirtschaftliche Blüte im 18. Jahrhundert seinem Hafen. Mit den ersten Touristen wurden, wie es sich für mondäne Seebäder in der Belle Époque gehörte, nach englischem Vorbild, Seebrücken ins Meer gebaut. Schaulustige konnten auf den Pieren rechts und links der Hafenausfahrt die Wildheit des Meeres spüren und die Schiffe aus nächster Nähe beobachten. Die hölzerne, weiß gestrichene Seebrücke in Ostende misst stolze 650 m und trägt einen gusseisernen Leuchtturm. Neben zwei Pieren in Ostende gibt es noch weitere Seebrücken in Nieuwpoort und Blankenberge.

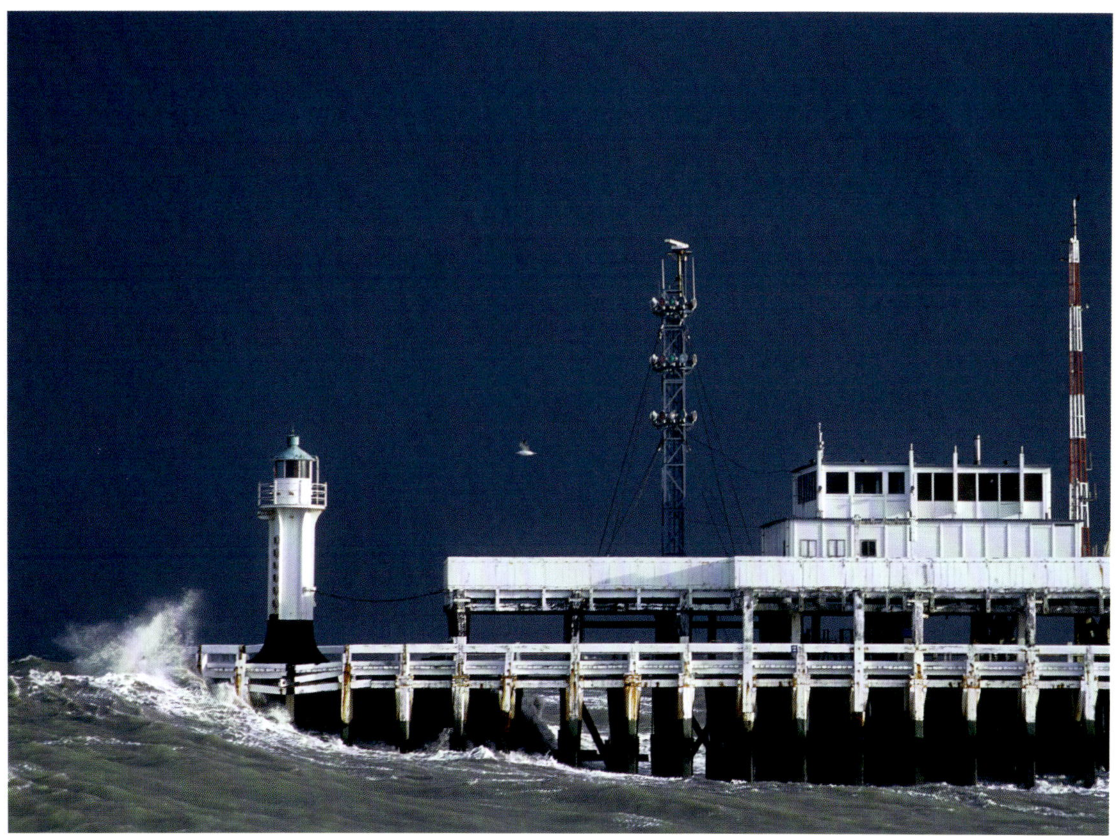

Lighthouse, Ostend
Vuurtoren, Oostende
Phare, Ostende

Puentes hacia el mar

El prometedor Ostende debió su apogeo
económico en el siglo XVIII a su puerto.
Con los primeros turistas, se construyeron
puentes marítimos en el mar según el
modelo inglés, como era apropiado para
los sofisticados balnearios de la Belle
Époque. En los muelles a la derecha y a
la izquierda de la salida del puerto, los
espectadores podían sentir la naturaleza
salvaje del mar y observar de cerca los
barcos. El puente marítimo de madera
pintado de blanco en Ostende mide ni
más ni menos que 650 m y lleva un faro de
hierro fundido. Además de dos muelles en
Ostende, hay otros muelles en Nieuwpoort
y Blankenberge.

Pontes para o mar

O Ostende emergente deve o seu apogeu
económico ao seu porto no século XVIII.
Com os primeiros turistas, as pontes
marítimas foram construídas no mar
baseadas no modelo inglês, como era
apropriado para as sofisticados estâncias
balneares da moda na Belle Époque. Nos
cais à direita e à esquerda da saída do
porto, os espectadores podiam sentir a
natureza selvagem do mar e observar
de perto os navios. A ponte marítima de
madeira pintada de branco em Ostend
mede uns orgulhosos 650 m e sobre ela
está situado um farol de ferro fundido.
Além de dois cais em Ostende, há outros
cais em Nieuwpoort e Blankenberge.

Pieren

Het opkomende Oostende dankt zijn
economische bloeitijd in de 18e eeuw
aan zijn haven. Met de eerste toeristen
werden ook, naar Engels model, pieren in
de zee gebouwd, zoals dat bij mondaine
badplaatsen in de belle époque paste.
Op de pieren rechts en links van de
havenuitgang konden de toeschouwers
de wildheid van de zee voelen en de
schepen van dichtbij bekijken. De houten,
wit geschilderde pier in Oostende meet
650 m en draagt een gietijzeren vuurtoren.
Naast twee pieren in Oostende zijn er
nog andere havenhoofden in Nieuwpoort
en Blankenberge.

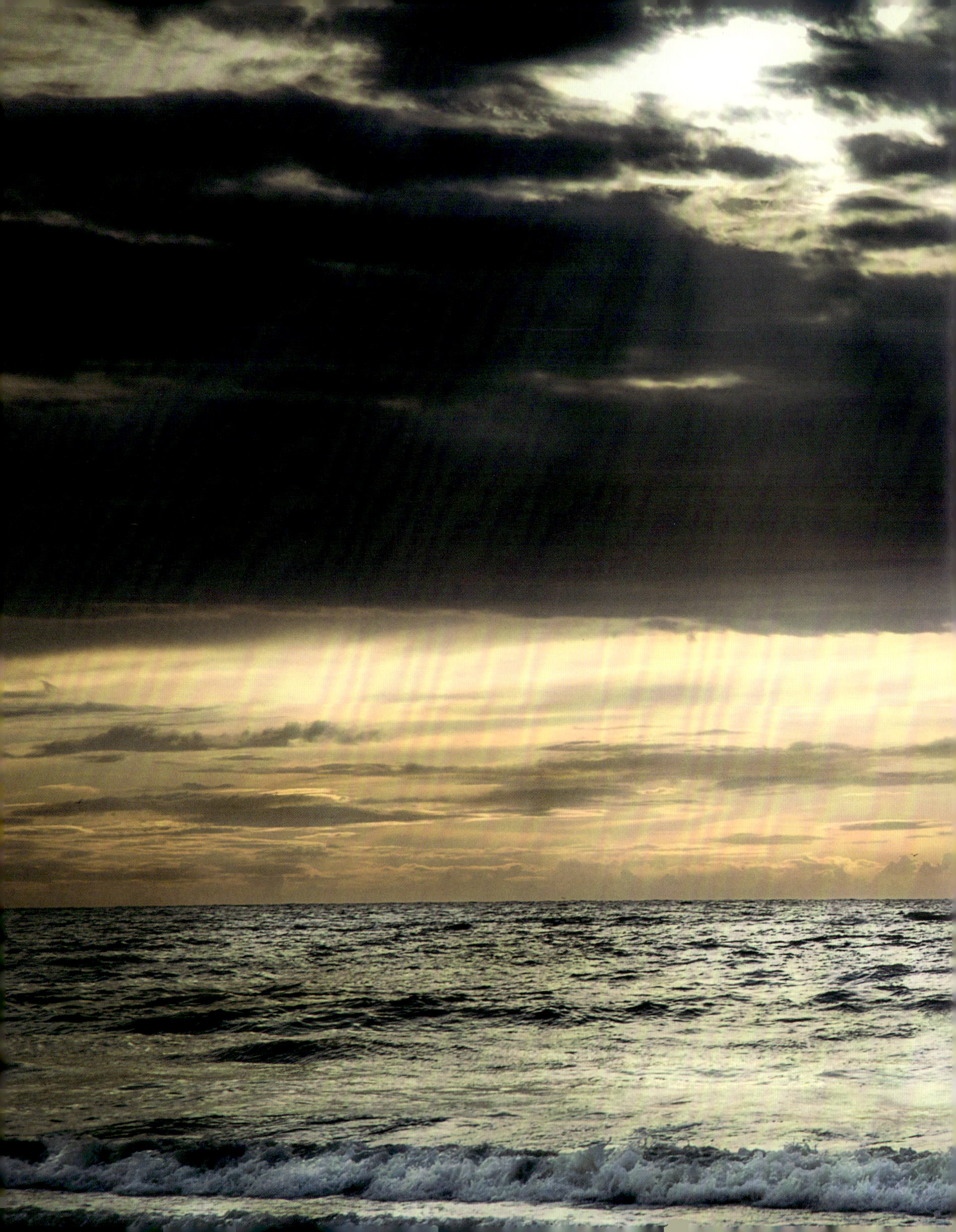

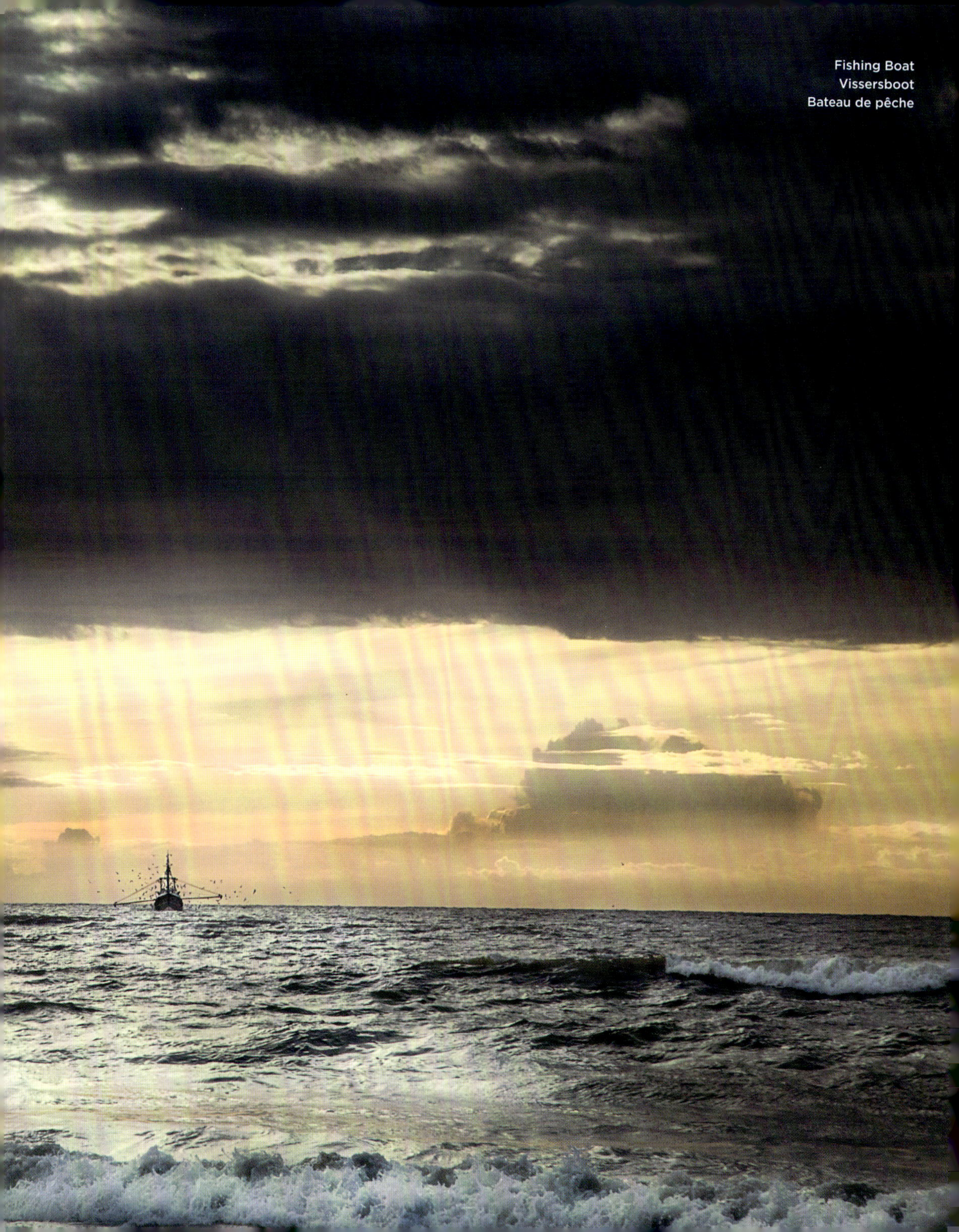

Fishing Boat
Vissersboot
Bateau de pêche

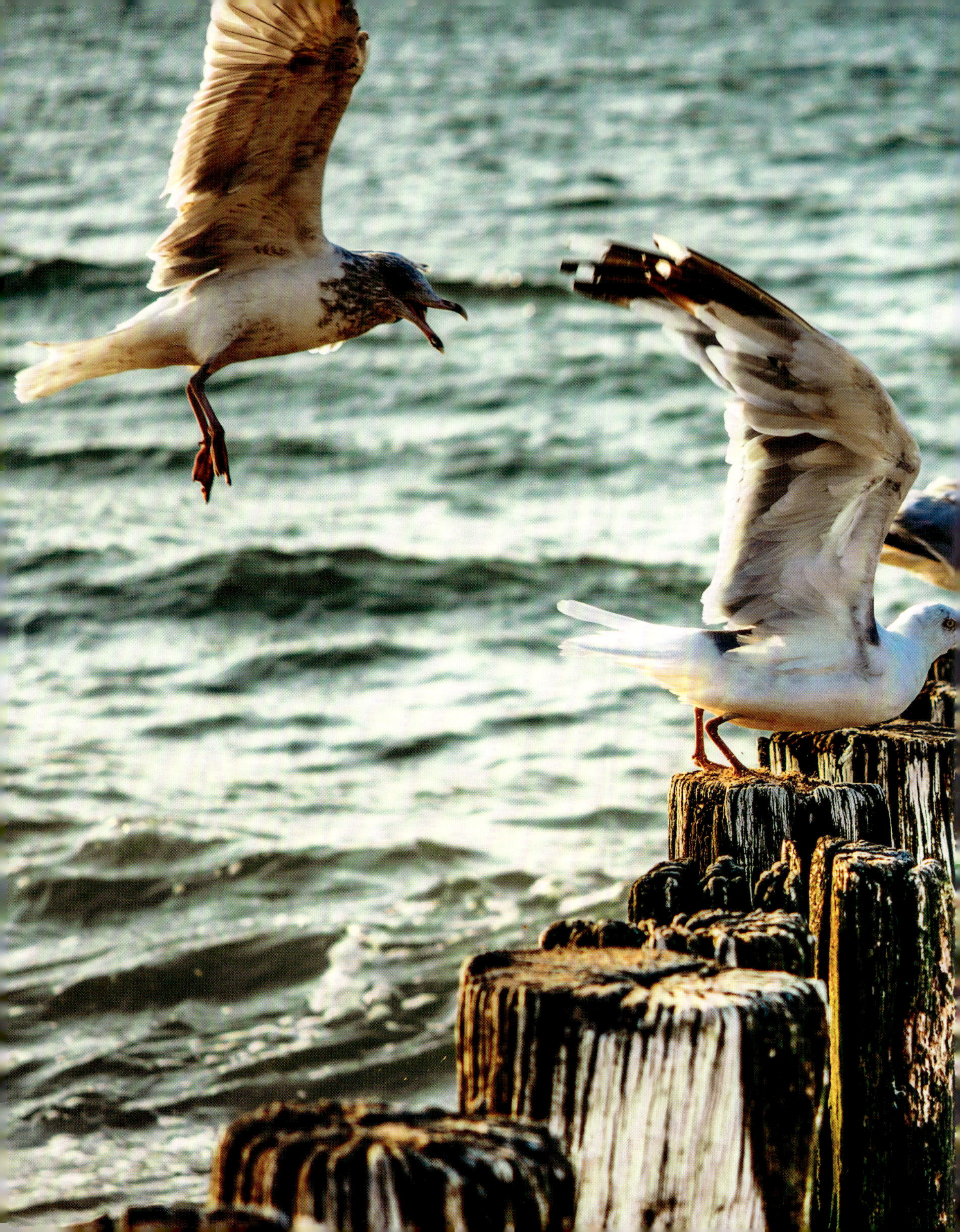

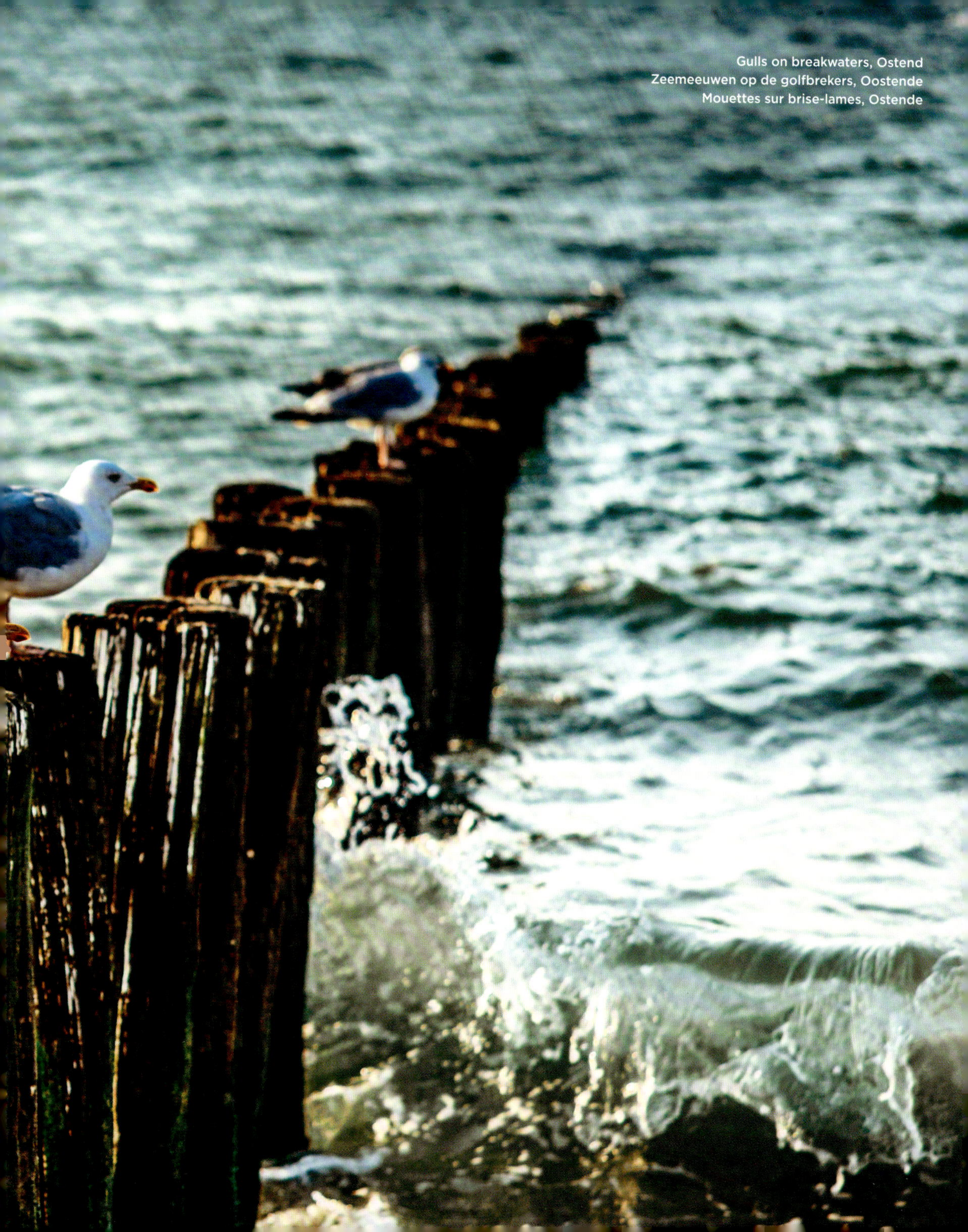

Gulls on breakwaters, Ostend
Zeemeeuwen op de golfbrekers, Oostende
Mouettes sur brise-lames, Ostende

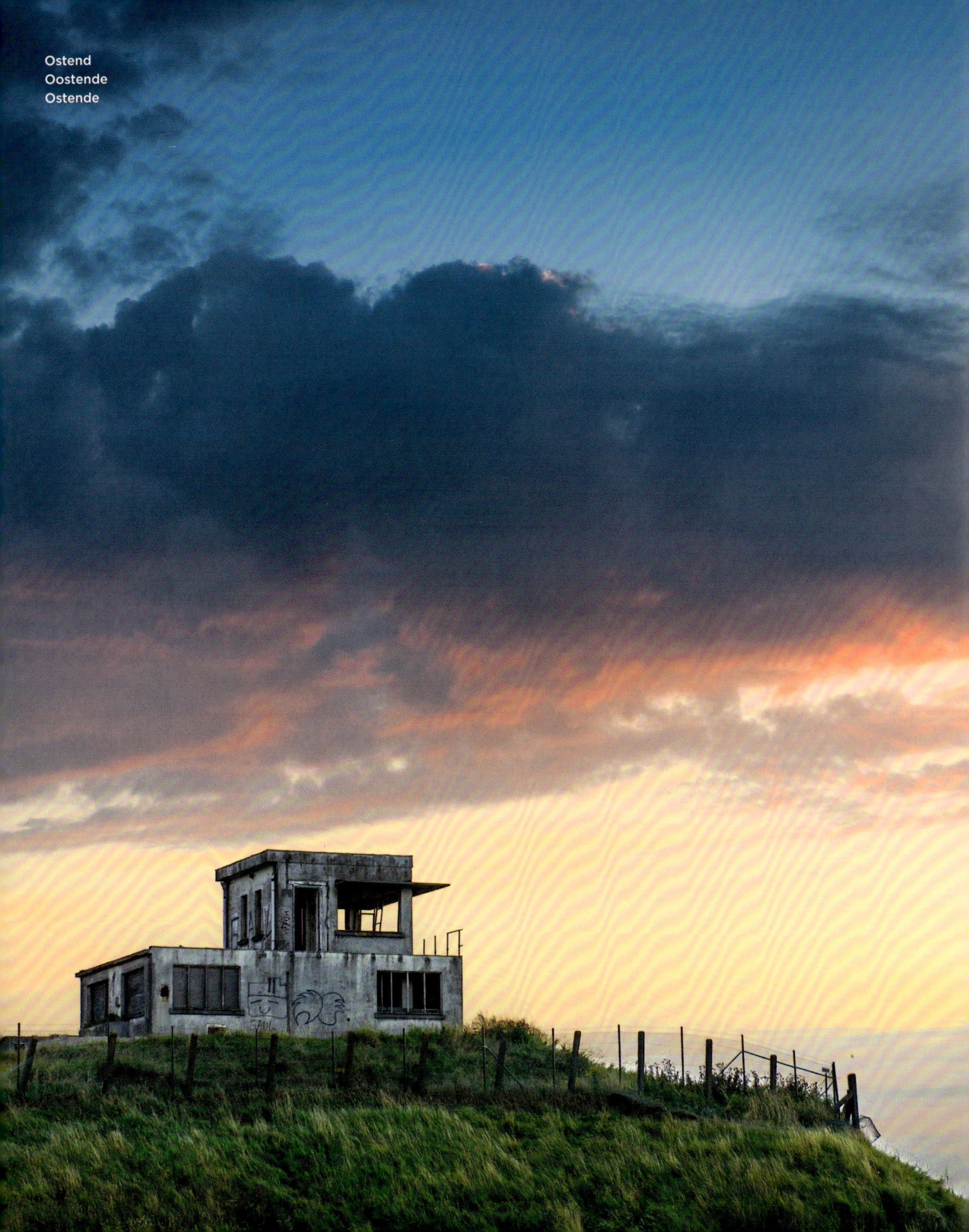

Ostend
Oostende
Ostende

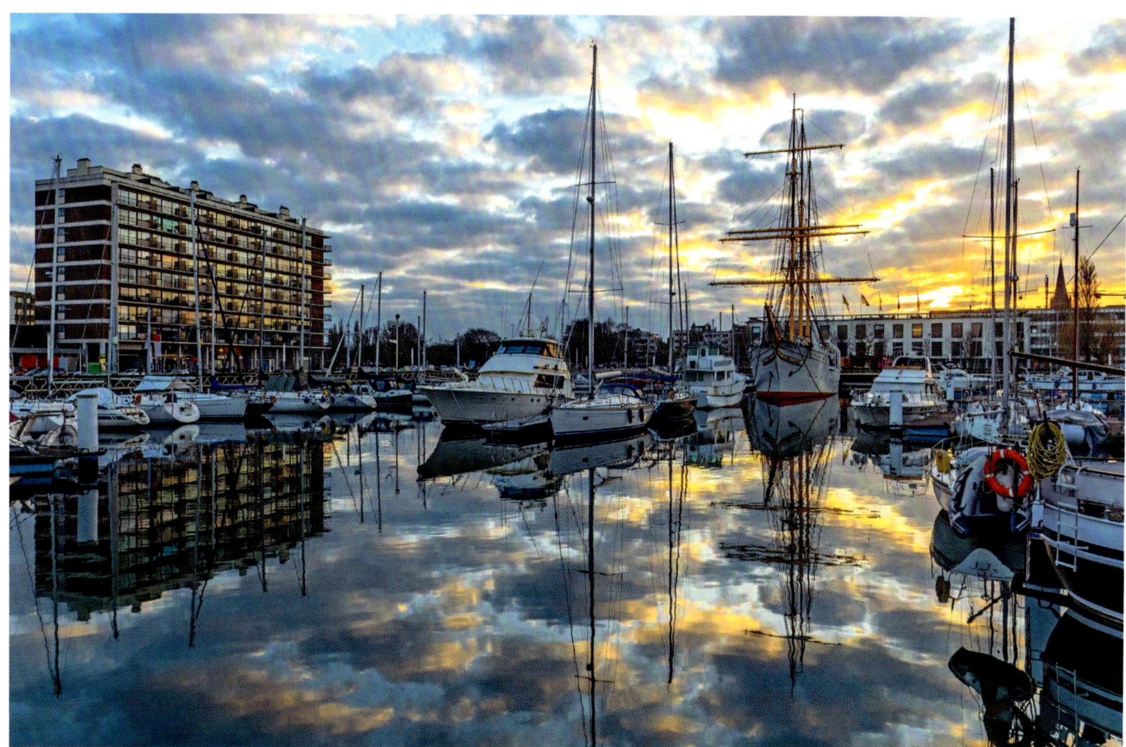

Mercator Marina, Ostend
Mercator Marina, Oostende
Port de plaisance, Ostende

Ostend—Dover

The most important ferry connection to England, the legendary "Oostende Lines", made the queen of seaside resorts famous. Directly next to the ferry port, and the now much too large railway station, is the marina with the schooner barque *Mercator*. Built in Scotland, the former sailing training ship of the Belgian Navy is now a museum ship and belongs to the maritime cultural heritage of Flanders.

Ostende – Dover

La conexión de transbordador más importante a Inglaterra, la legendaria línea Ostende - Dover, hizo famosa a la reina de los balnearios. Justo al lado del puerto de transbordadores y de la estación de ferrocarril, ahora de enormes dimensiones, se encuentra el puerto deportivo con el *Mercator*. El antiguo barco escuela de vela de la Armada belga es ahora un barco museo y pertenece al patrimonio cultural marítimo de Flandes.

Ostende – Douvres

La reine des stations balnéaires doit sa célébrité à la principale liaison maritime avec l'Angleterre, la ligne légendaire Ostende-Douvres. Juste à côté du port de ferry et de la gare, désormais surdimensionnée, s'étend le port de plaisance avec le *Mercator*. Transformé en musée, cet ancien voilier-école de la marine belge fait partie de l'héritage culturel maritime des Flandres.

Ostende – Dover

A mais importante conexão de balsa para a Inglaterra, a lendária linha Ostende - Dover tornou famosa a rainha dos resorts à beira-mar. Diretamente ao lado do terminal de balsas e da estação ferroviária, que agora é superdimensionada, está a marina com o *Mercator*. O antigo navio de treinamento de vela da Marinha Belga é agora um navio-museu e pertence ao patrimônio cultural marítimo da Flandres.

Ostende – Dover

Die wichtigste Fährverbindung nach England, die legendäre Linie Ostende – Dover machte die Königin der Seebäder bekannt. Direkt neben dem Fährhafen und dem inzwischen überdimensionierten Bahnhof befindet sich der Jachthafen mit der *Mercator*. Das ehemalige Segelschulschiff der belgischen Marine ist ein Museumsschiff und gehört zum maritimen Kulturerbe Flanderns.

Oostende – Dover

De belangrijkste ferryverbinding naar Engeland, de legendarische lijn Oostende - Dover, maakte de parel van de badplaatsen beroemd. Naast de veerhaven en het inmiddels enorme treinstation ligt de jachthaven met de *Mercator*. Het voormalige opleidingsschip van de Belgische marine is nu museumschip en behoort tot het maritieme, culturele erfgoed van Vlaanderen.

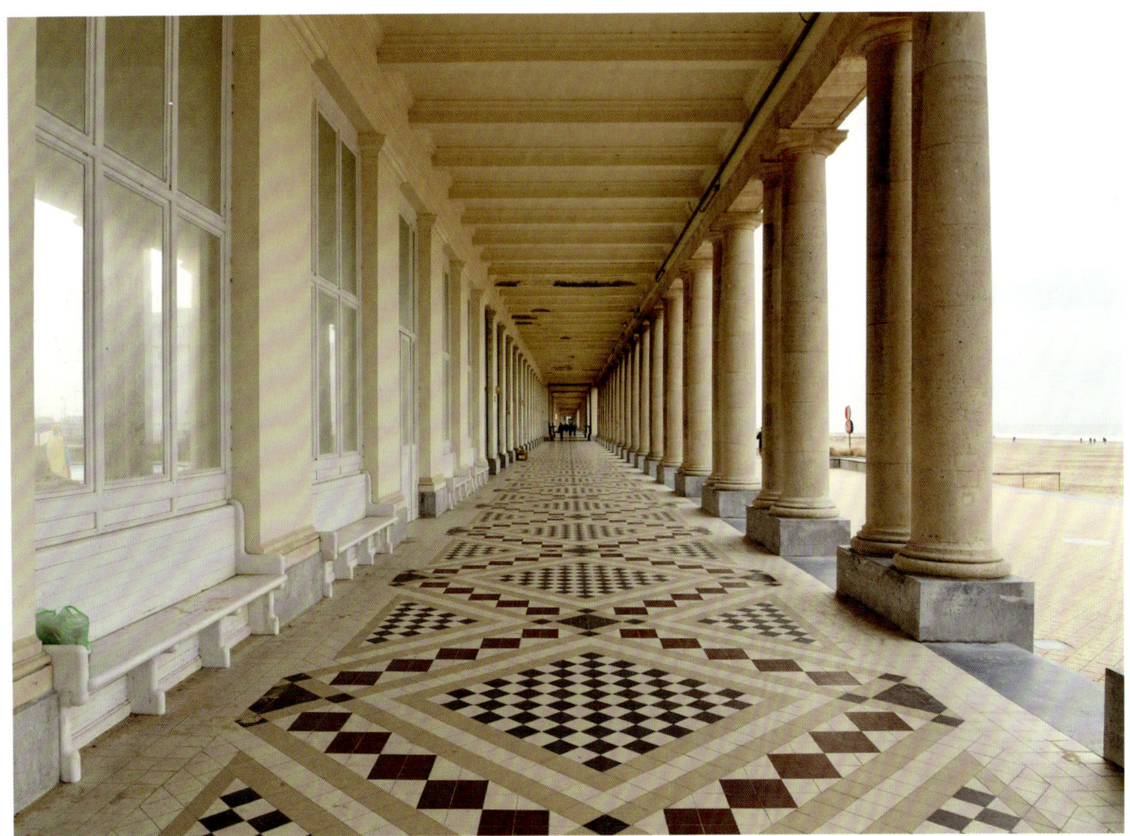

Royal Galleries of Ostend
Koninklijke Gaanderijen te Oostende
Galeries royales d'Ostende

Beach promenade for the nobility

Protected from sun and rain, the noble lords and ladies could stroll under the Royal Galleries of Ostend and admire the sea. The Galleries consists of two aisles, some of which is separated by a glass wall. In this way, the strollers could use one of the two sides, depending on the wind direction. The almost 400 m (1312 ft) long gallery connects the royal villa with the Hippodrome Wellington racecourse. When the Belgian royal family decided not to use their seaside residence, the building became an exhibition centre. The adjoining Thermae Palace is now a nostalgic luxury hotel.

Promenade de bord de mer pour les nobles

À l'abri du soleil et de la pluie, les nobles pouvaient flâner dans «les galeries royales» et admirer la mer. La galerie se compose de deux nefs partiellement séparées par un mur en verre. Ainsi, les flâneurs empruntaient l'une des deux allées en fonction de la direction du vent. Avec ses presque 400 m de longueur, la galerie relie le chalet royal à l'hippodrome Wellington. Lorsque la famille royale belge décida d'abandonner sa résidence balnéaire, le bâtiment fut transformé en un centre d'exposition. Le palais des Thermes attenant est désormais un hôtel de luxe à l'atmosphère nostalgique.

Strandpromenade für den Adel

Geschützt vor Sonne und Regen konnten die noblen Herrschaften unter der „Königlichen Galerie" flanieren und das Meer bewundern. Die Galerie besteht aus zwei Schiffen, die teilweise durch eine gläserne Wand getrennt werden. Auf diese Weise konnten die Flaneure abhängig von der Windrichtung einen der beiden Wandelgänge benutzen. Die fast 400 m lange Galerie verbindet die königliche Villa mit der Wellington-Rennbahn. Als die belgische Königsfamilie beschloss, ihre Residenz am Meer nicht mehr zu benutzen, wurden die Gebäude zu einem Ausstellungszentrum. Der angrenzende Thermenpalast ist heute ein nostalgisches Luxushotel.

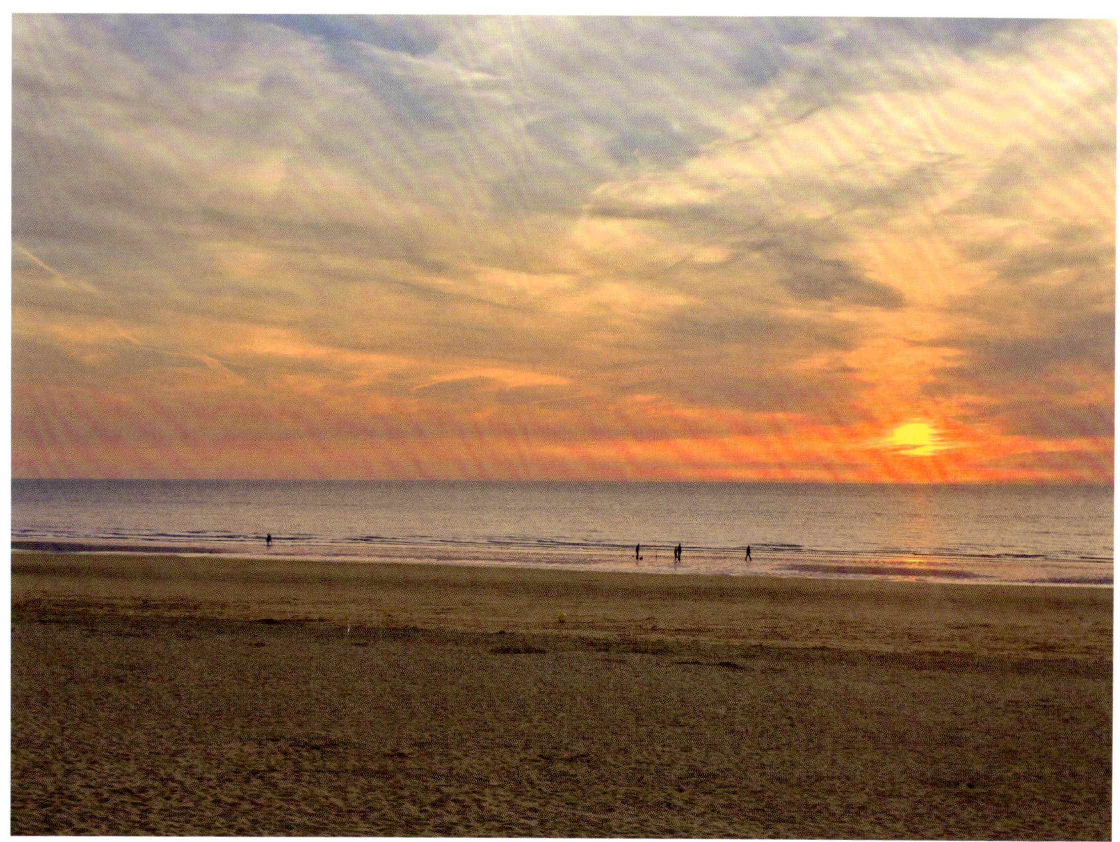

Beach, Ostend
Strand, Oostende
Plage d'Ostende

Paseo marítimo para la nobleza

Protegidos del sol y de la lluvia, los nobles señores podían pasear bajo la "Royal Gallery" y admirar el mar. La galería consta de dos naves, parte de las cuales está separada por un muro de cristal. De esta manera, los paseantes pueden utilizar uno de los dos pasillos, dependiendo de la dirección del viento. La galería de casi 400 m de largo conecta la villa real con el hipódromo de Wellington. Cuando la familia real belga decidió no utilizar su residencia junto al mar, los edificios se convirtieron en un centro de exposiciones. El palacio de aguas termales que había al lado es ahora un hotel de lujo nostálgico.

Passeio marítimo para a nobreza

Protegidos do sol e da chuva, os nobres senhores podiam passear sob a "Galeria Real" e admirar o mar. A galeria é constituída por duas navios, alguns dos quais separados por uma parede de vidro. Desta forma, os flâneurs poderiam utilizar uma das duas passagens, dependendo da direção do vento. A galeria de quase 400 m de comprimento liga a vila real com o hipódromo de Wellington. Quando a família real belga decidiu não utilizar mais a sua residência à beira-mar, os edifícios tornaram-se um centro de exposições. O "Thermenpalast" adjacente é agora um hotel de luxo nostálgico.

Strandpromenade voor de adel

Beschermd tegen zon en regen konden de edele heren onder de "Koninklijke Gaanderije" wandelen en de zee bewonderen. De galerij bestaat uit twee zuilengangen die deels door een glazen wand worden gescheiden. Op deze manier konden flaneurs afhankelijk van de windrichting van een van de beide wandelgangen gebruik maken. De bijna 400 m lange galerij verbindt de koninklijke villa met de Wellingtonrenbaan. Toen de Belgische koninklijke familie besloot hun residentie aan zee niet meer te gebruiken, veranderden de gebouwen in een tentoonstellingscentrum. Het aangrenzende Thermenpaleis is nu een nostalgisch luxe hotel.

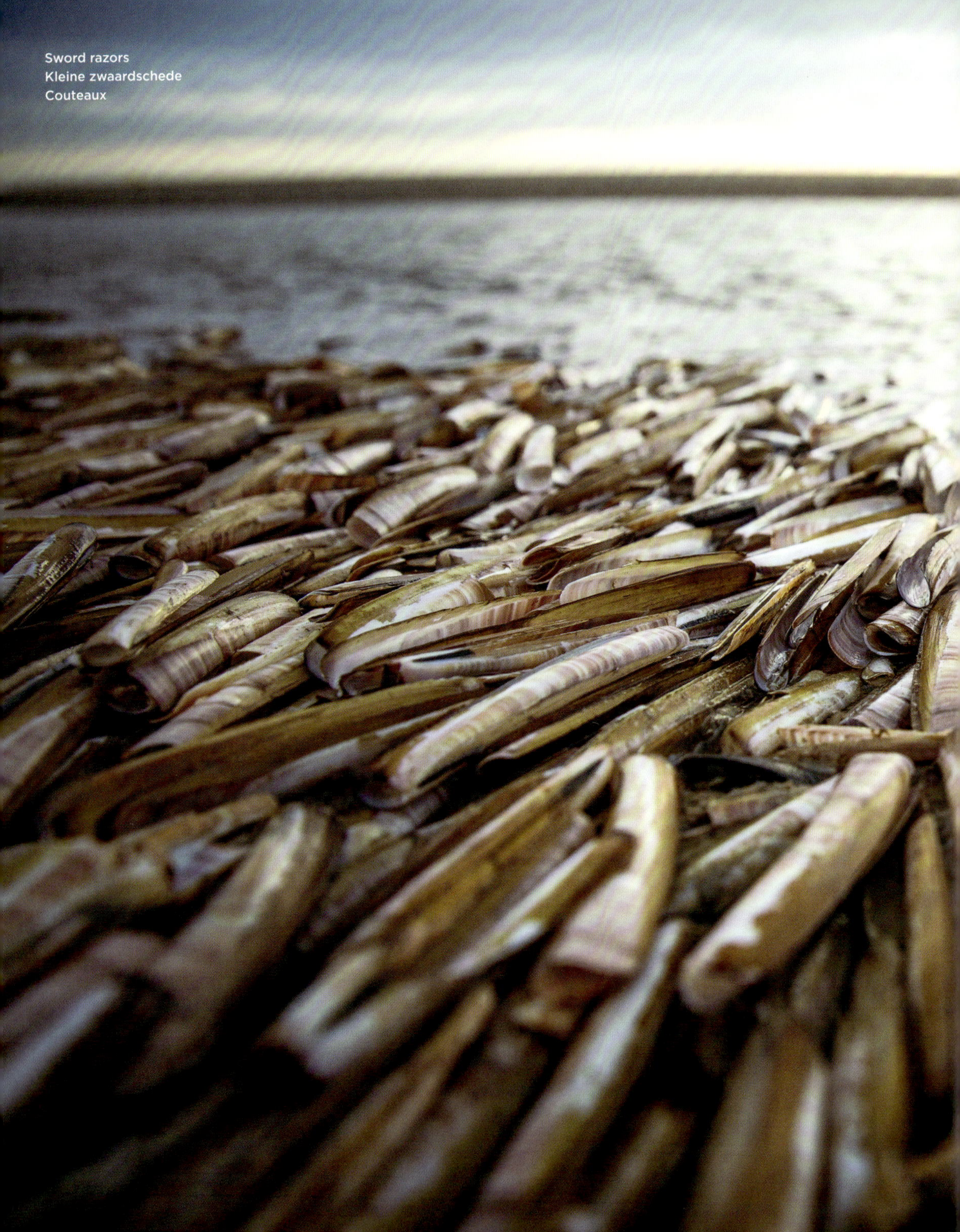

Sword razors
Kleine zwaardschede
Couteaux

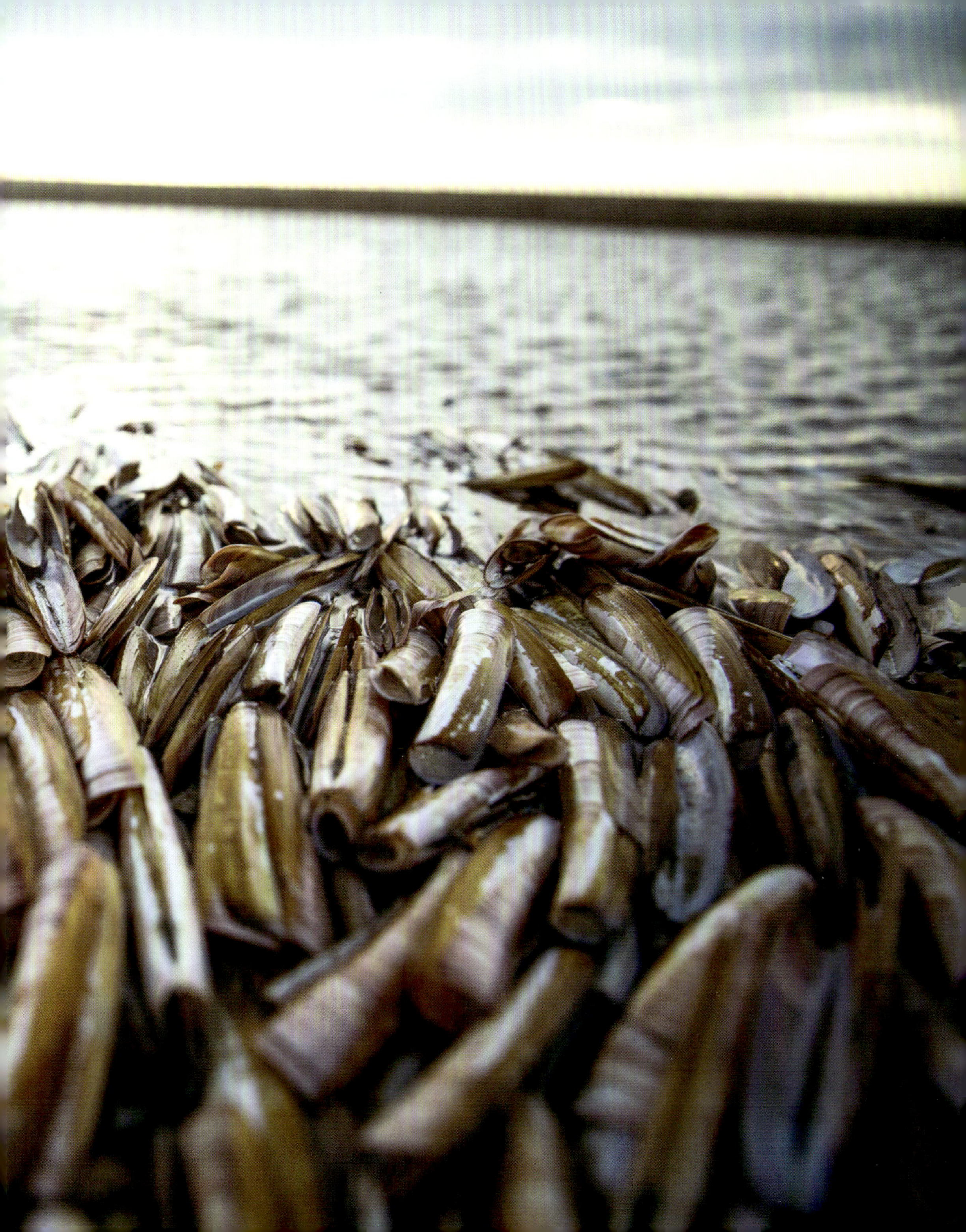

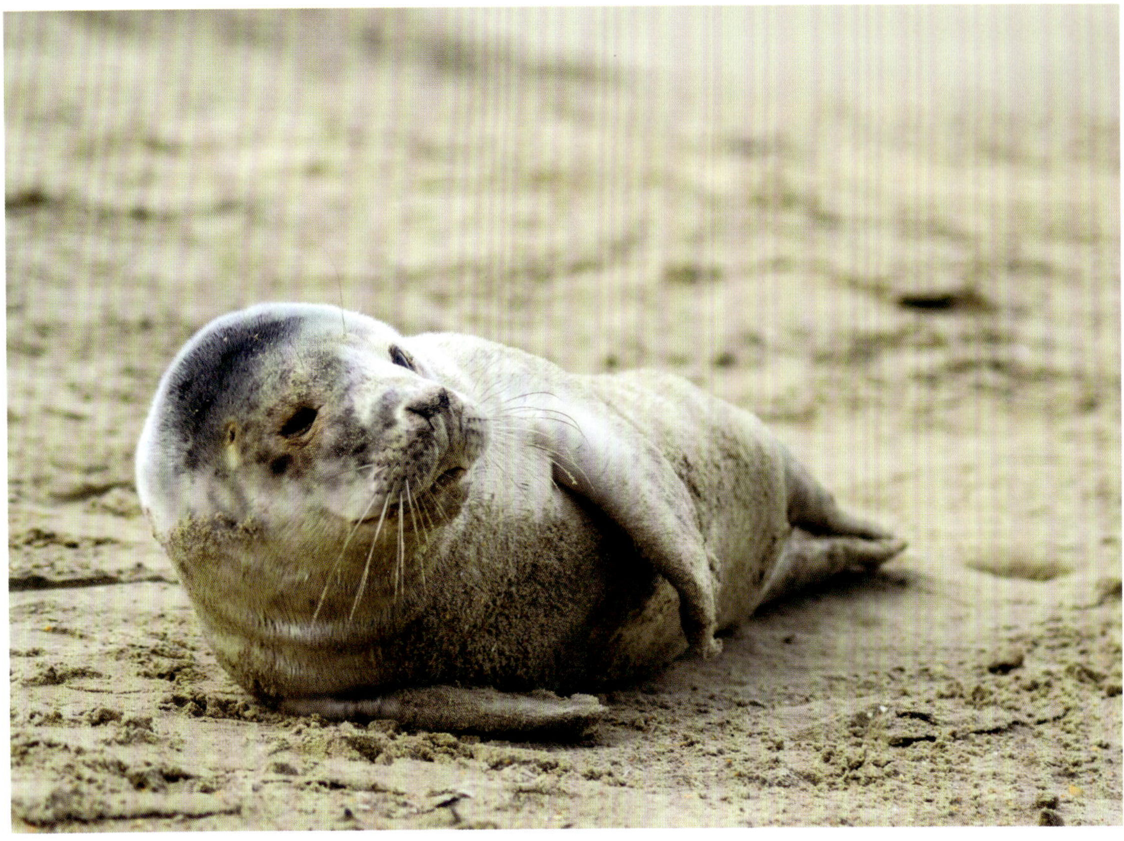

Harbor seal
Gewone zeehond
Phoque commun

Seals on the beach

Seals may now be seen more frequently again on Flanders' beaches and, if discovered, should be left alone and observed quietly from at least 20 m (66 ft) away. How one can recognize whether a seal could be unwell is detailed on signs put up by the beach of Nieuwpoort, where the animals frequently come ashore. In Blankenberge, a refuge for seals was established on a pontoon. Another beach dweller is the ruddy turnstone. This bird owes its name to its particular way of foraging for food, which is by flipping stones and shells on the beach.

Phoque sur la plage

Aujourd'hui, les phoques reviennent plus régulièrement sur les plages flamandes. Si vous en découvrez un, laissez-le en paix et gardez au moins 20 m de distance pour l'observer tranquillement. Sur la plage de Nieuport, fort prisée des phoques, des panneaux expliquent comment savoir si l'un d'eux est peut-être malade. À Blankenberge aussi, on leur a aménagé un espace de repos. Autre habitant des plages : le tournepierre à collier. Cet oiseau doit son nom à sa manière toute particulière de chercher sa nourriture : il retourne pierres et coquillages.

Seehund am Strand

Seehunde sind inzwischen wieder häufiger an Flanderns Stränden zu sehen. Wer also Robben entdeckt, der sollte sie in Ruhe lassen und aus mindestens 20 m Entfernung ruhig beobachten. Woran man erkennen kann, ob ein Seehund krank sein könnte, erklären Schilder, die am Strand von Nieuwpoort angebracht wurden, wo häufiger Seehunde an den Strand kommen. Aber auch in Blankenberge wurde auf einem Ponton ein Ruheplatz für Robben eingerichtet. Ein weiterer Strandbewohner ist der Steinwälzer. Dieser Vogel verdankt seinen Namen seiner speziellen Art der Nahrungssuche, bei der er am Strand Steine und Muscheln umdreht.

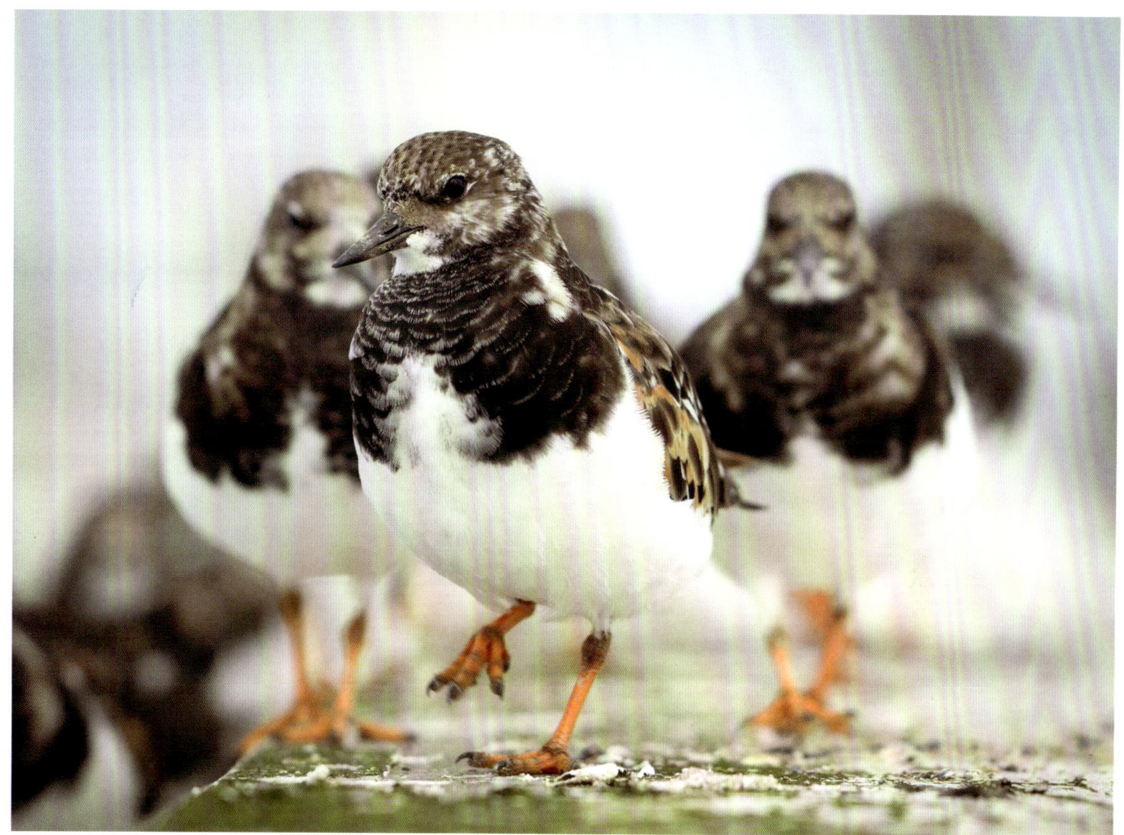

Ruddy turnstones
Steenloper
Tournepierre à collier

Foca en la playa

Las focas vuelven a verse con más frecuencia en las playas de Flandes. Por lo tanto, cuando se ven focas, deben dejarse en paz y observarse tranquilamente desde una distancia de al menos 20 m. En las señales que se colocaron en la playa de Nieuwpoort, donde las focas acuden con frecuencia a la playa, se explica cómo se puede saber si una foca puede estar enferma. Pero también en Blankenberge se estableció un lugar de descanso para las focas en un pontón. Otro habitante de la playa es el vuelvepiedras común. Este ave debe su nombre a su especial forma de buscar comida girando piedras y conchas en la playa.

Foca na praia

As focas podem agora ser vistas mais frequentemente nas praias da Flandres. Por isso, se você descobrir alguma foca, deve deixá-la em paz e observá-la calmamente a pelo menos a 20 m de distância. Como se pode saber se uma foca pode estar doente ou não é explicado por placas anexadas à praia de Nieuwpoort, onde as focas frequentemente chegam à praia. Mas também em Blankenberge, um local de descanso para as focas foi estabelecido num pontão. Outro morador da praia é a rola-do-mar ou vira-pedras. Este pássaro deve o seu nome à sua forma especial de procurar alimentos, virando pedras e conchas na praia.

Zeehonden op het strand

Op de Vlaamse stranden zijn weer meer zeehonden te zien. Wie zeehonden ontdekt, dient ze met rust te laten en ze vanaf minstens 20 m afstand rustig observeren. Hoe men kan herkennen of een zeehond ziek zou kunnen zijn, dat maken de infoborden duidelijk die op het strand van Nieuwpoort zijn geplaatst, de plek waar vaker zeehonden op het strand komen. Maar ook in Blankenberge werd op een ponton een rustplaats voor zeehonden ingericht. Een andere strandbewoner is de steenloper. Deze vogel dankt zijn naam aan zijn speciale manier van voedsel zoeken door stenen en schelpen op het strand om te draaien.

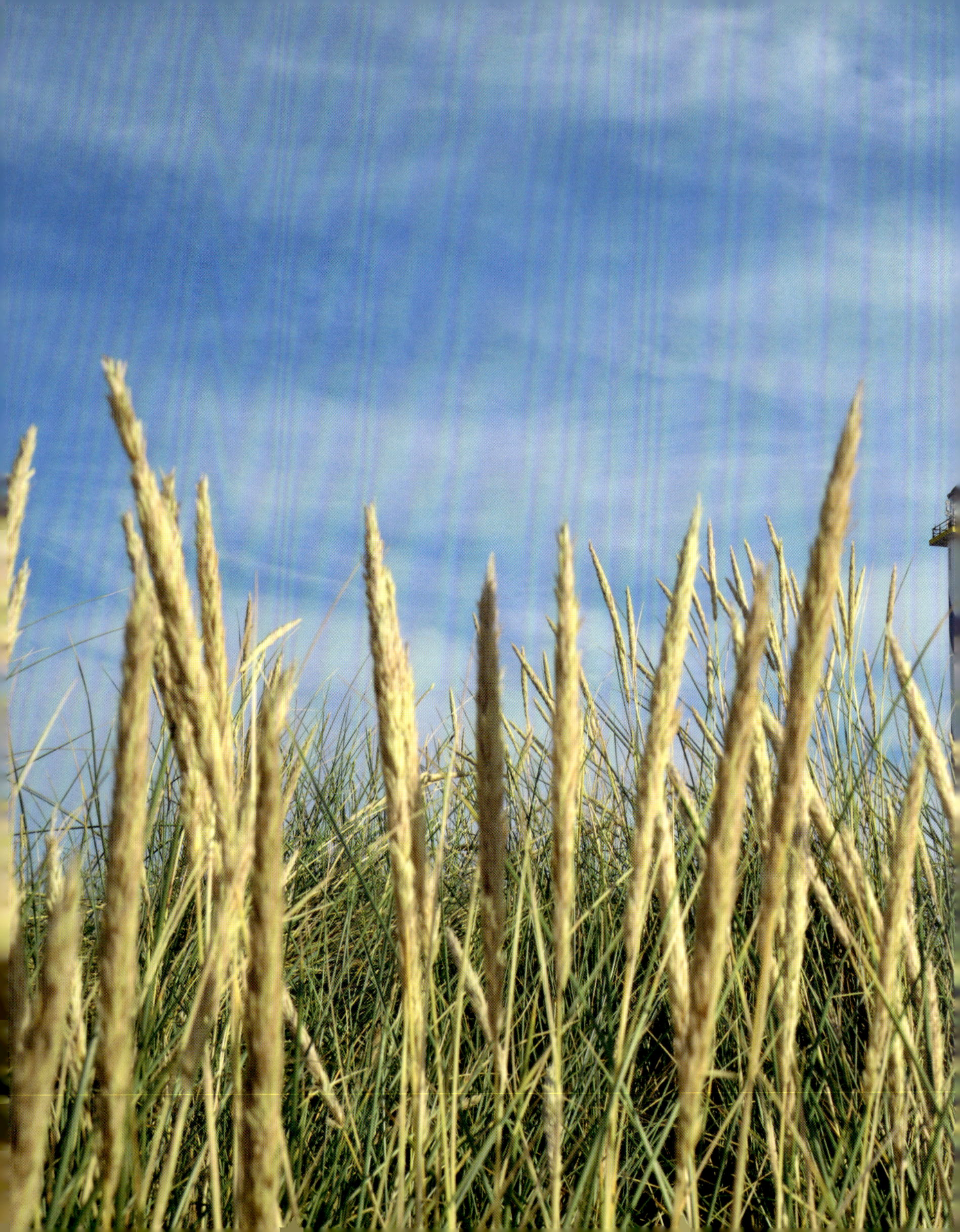

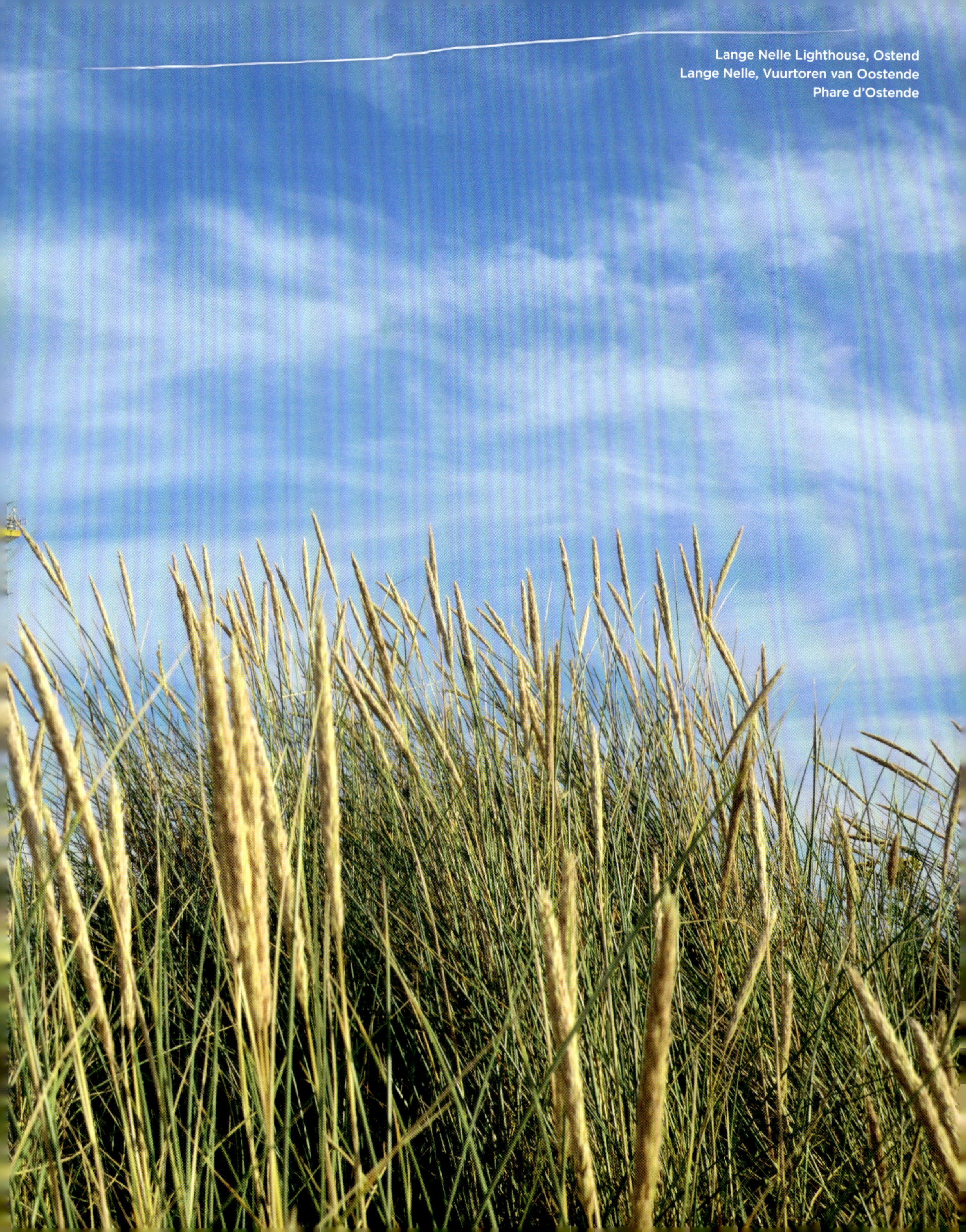

Lange Nelle Lighthouse, Ostend
Lange Nelle, Vuurtoren van Oostende
Phare d'Ostende

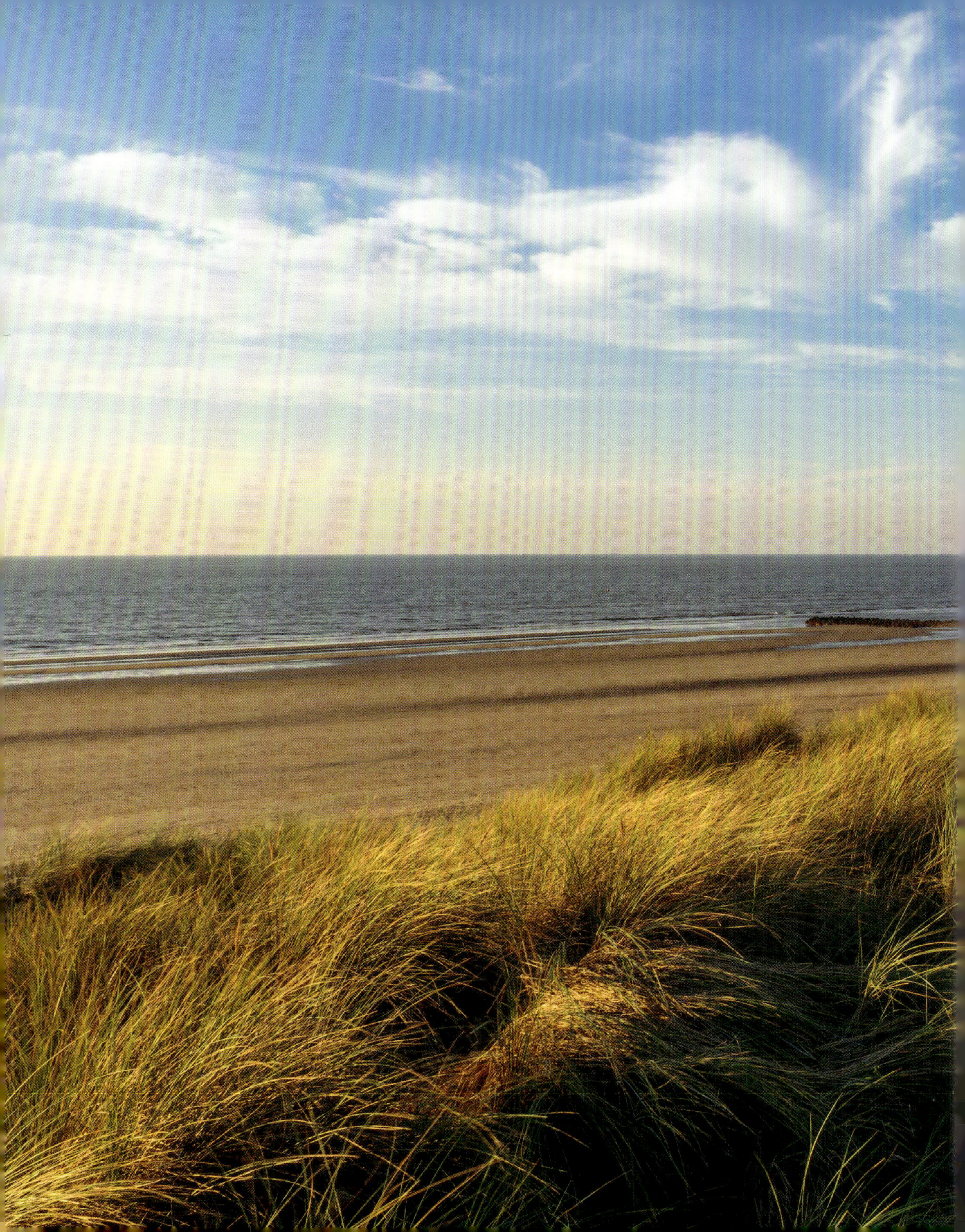

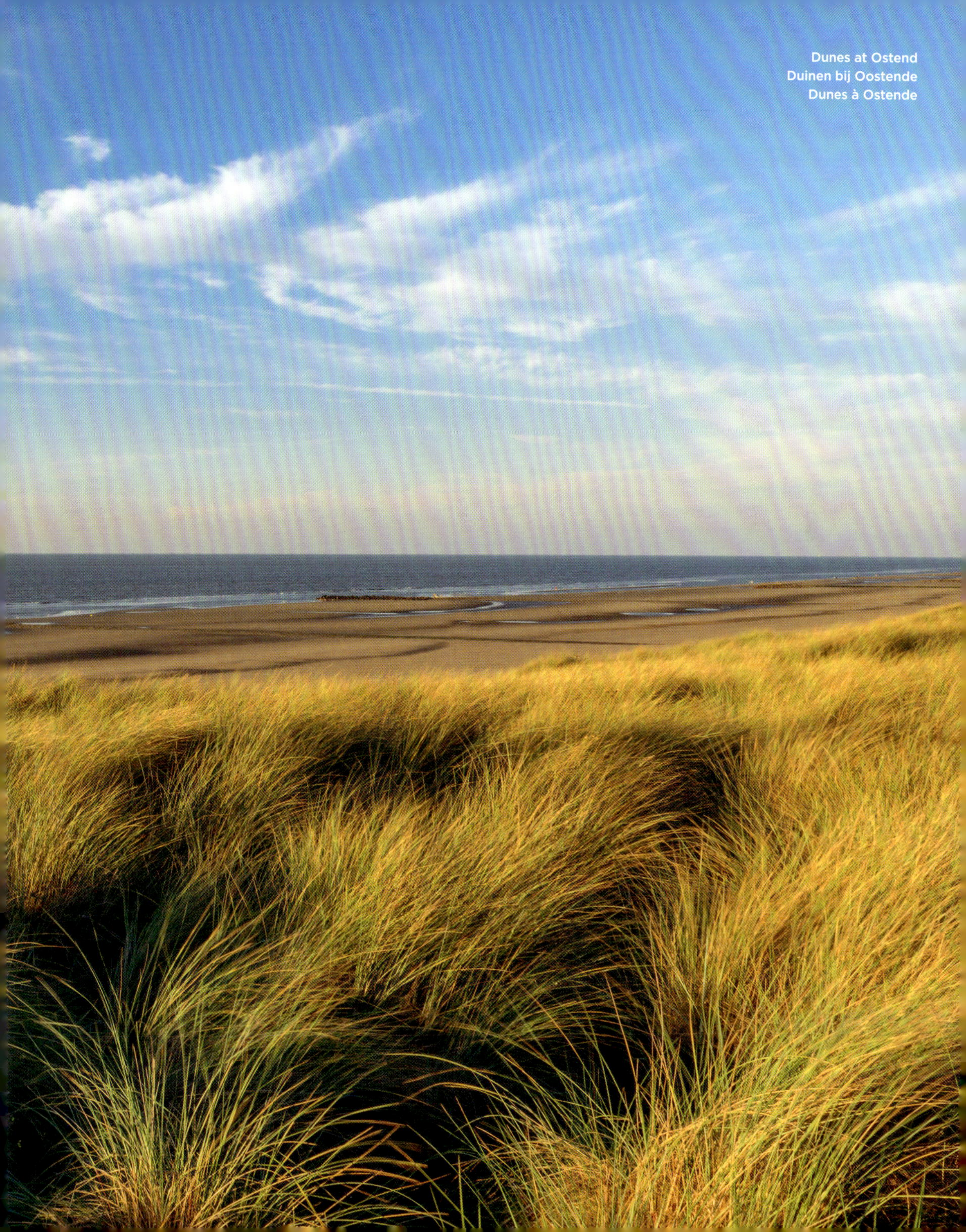
Dunes at Ostend
Duinen bij Oostende
Dunes à Ostende

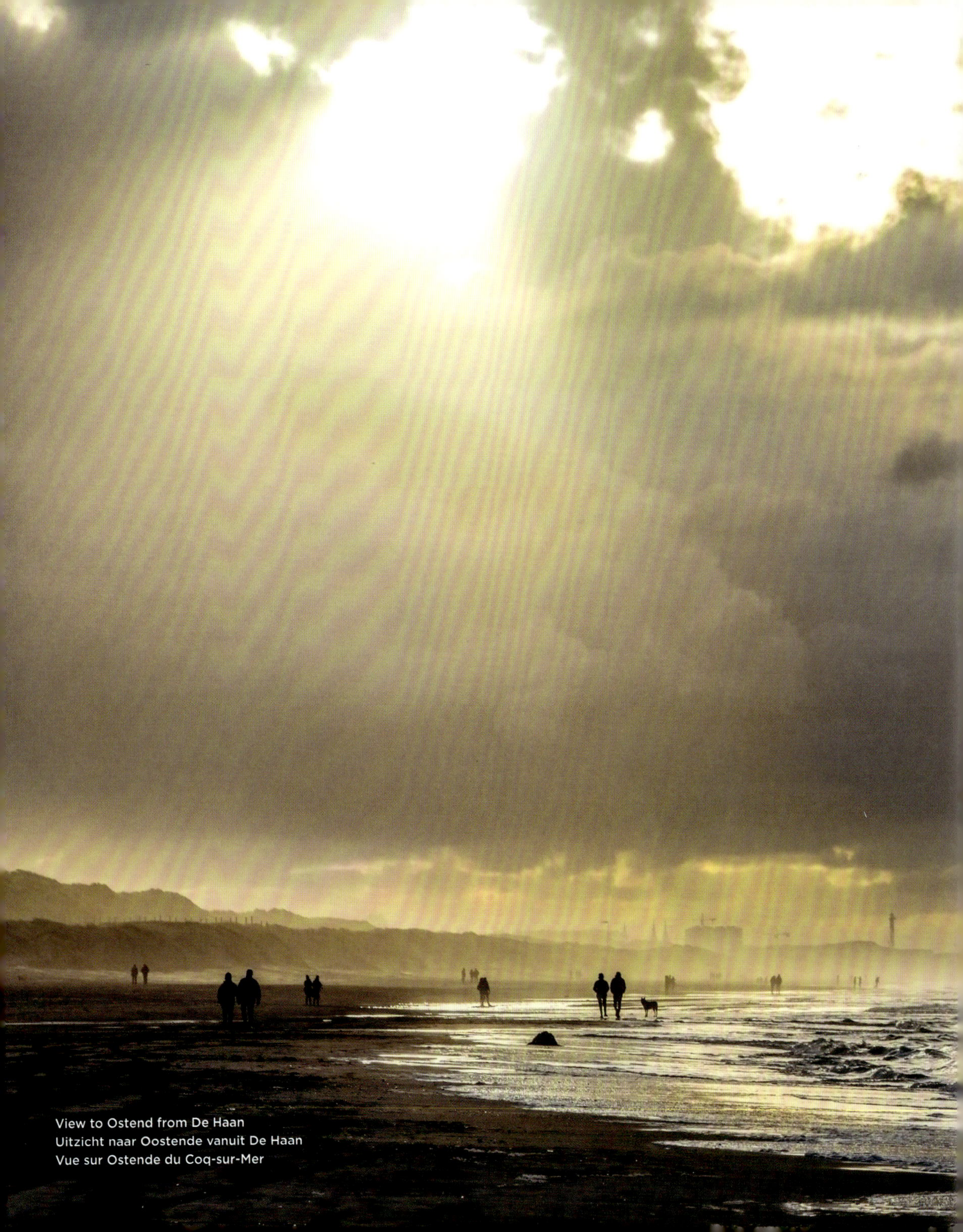

View to Ostend from De Haan
Uitzicht naar Oostende vanuit De Haan
Vue sur Ostende du Coq-sur-Mer

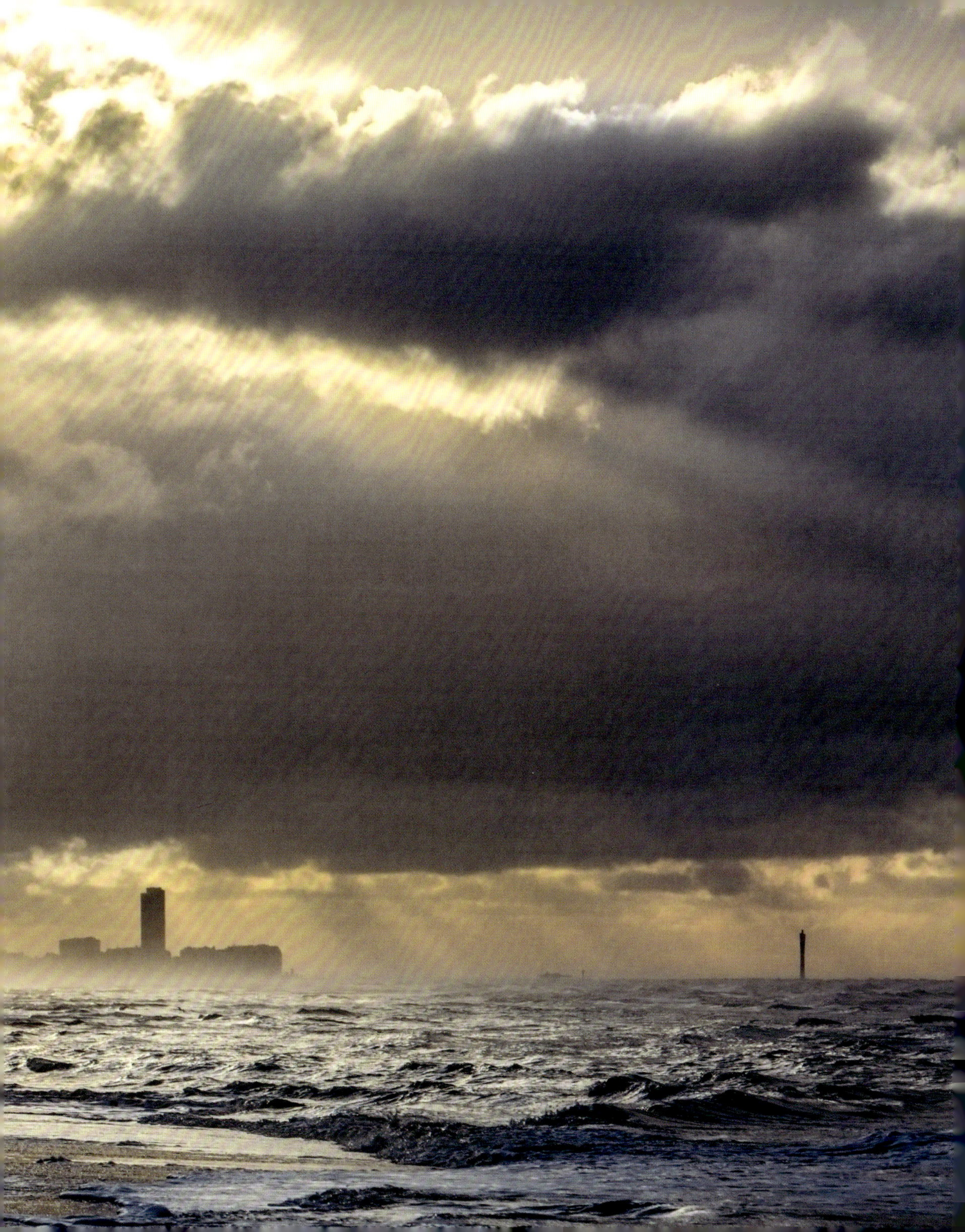

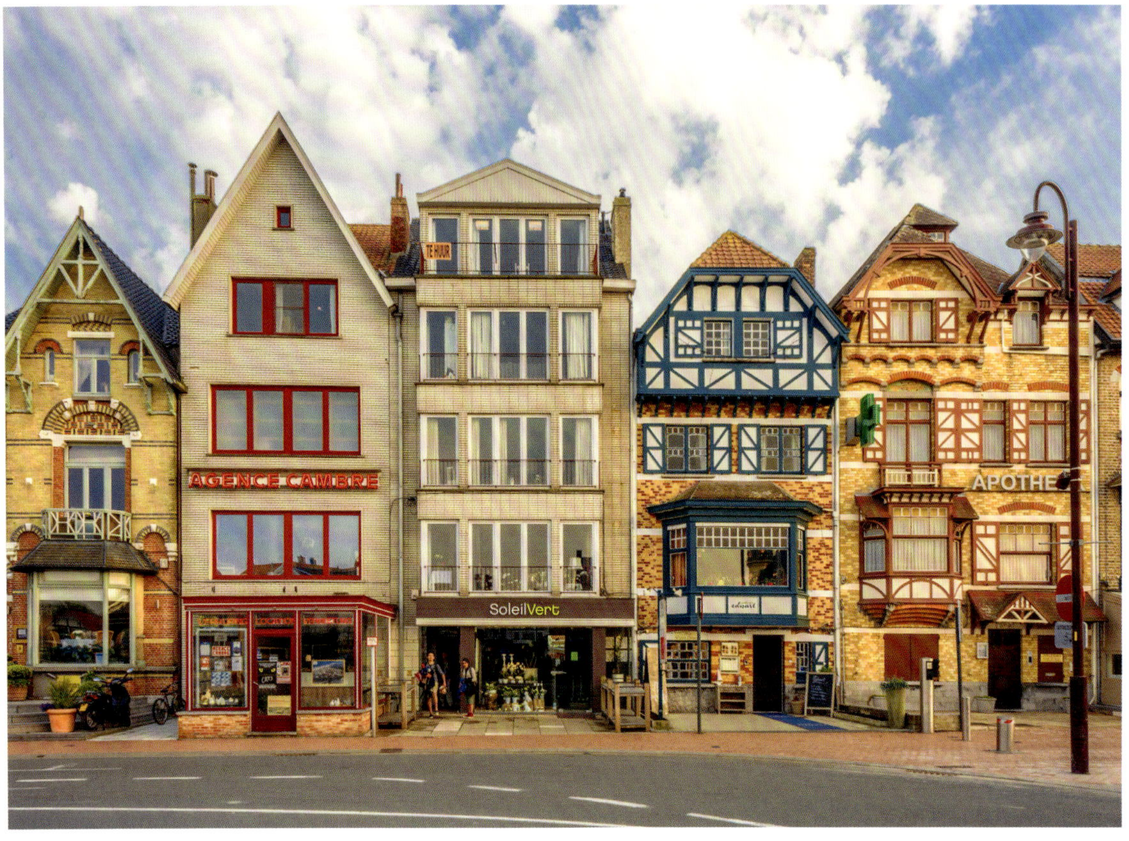

De Haan
Le Coq-sur-Mer

De Haan

The picturesque seaside resort, with many gardens and white villas in Norman cottage style, has hardly changed. The arrival of the Coast Tram at the historic wooden tram station gives the visitor a nostalgic feeling for the time when tourists first discovered the sea and longed for summer holidays. The nostalgic flair unfolds in the winding avenues between the dunes, where the gardens and villas from the belle époque merge into a quiet park landscape. De Haan is best discovered on foot, or like the Flemish do, in a typical North Sea coast pedal car.

Le Coq-sur-Mer

Avec ses nombreux jardins et villas blanches dans le style des cottages normands, la pittoresque station balnéaire n'a guère changé. Dès son arrivée par le tramway côtier à la station de tram historique en bois, le visiteur est pris de nostalgie, se projetant à une époque où les citoyens découvraient la mer et attendaient avec impatience les vacances estivales. Cette nostalgie ambiante se fait sentir dans les allées sinueuses entre les dunes, où jardins et villas de la Belle Époque se fondent pour offrir un paisible parc paysager. Découvrez Le Coq-sur-Mer à pied ou, comme les Flamands, en voiture à pédales, un engin typique de la côte de la mer du Nord.

De Haan

Das malerische Seebad mit vielen Gärten und weißen Villen im normannischen Cottage-Stil hat sich kaum verändert. Schon bei der Ankunft mit der Küstenstraßenbahn an der historischen Tramstation aus Holz ergreift den Besucher ein nostalgisches Gefühl an eine Zeit, als die Bürger das Meer entdeckten und die Sommerferien herbeisehnten. Das nostalgische Flair entfaltet sich in den gewundenen Alleen zwischen den Dünen, wo die Gärten und Villen aus der Belle Époque zu einer ruhigen Parklandschaft verschmelzen. De Haan entdeckt man am besten zu Fuß oder wie die Flamen mit dem für die Nordseeküste typischen Tretwagen.

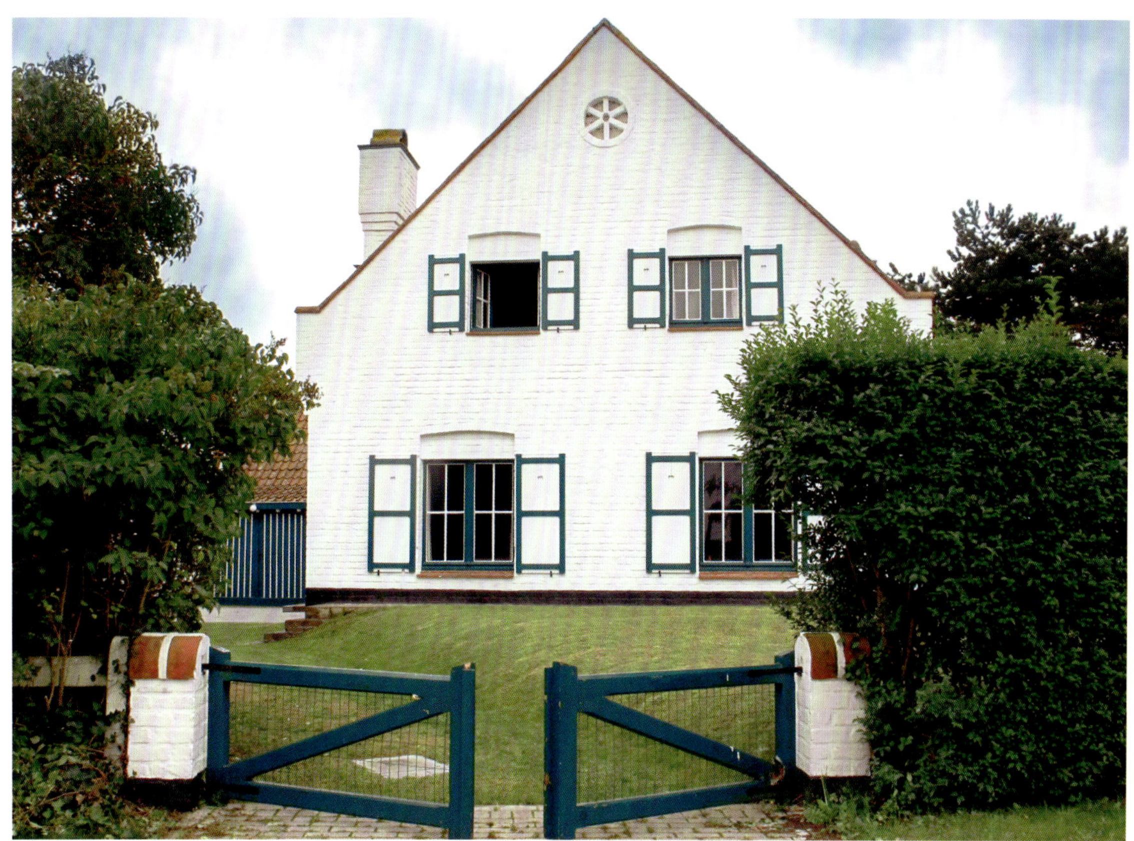

De Haan
Le Coq-sur-Mer

De Haan

El pintoresco balneario con muchos jardines y villas blancas de estilo rústico normando apenas ha cambiado. Ya al llegar con el tranvía costero a la histórica estación de tranvía de madera, el visitante tiene una sensación de nostalgia de una época en la que los ciudadanos descubrían el mar y anhelaban unas vacaciones de verano. El aire nostálgico se despliega en las sinuosas avenidas entre las dunas, donde los jardines y las villas de la Belle Époque se funden en un tranquilo paisaje de parques. De Haan se descubre mejor a pie o, como hacen los flamencos: en el típico coche de pedales de la costa del Mar del Norte.

De Haan

O pitoresco balneário com seus muitos jardins e moradias brancas em estilo de casa de campo normanda quase não mudou. A chegada do bonde costeiro à histórica estação de bonde de madeira dá ao visitante uma sensação nostálgica de uma época em que os cidadãos descobriram o mar e ansiaram pelas férias de verão. O toque nostálgico desdobra-se nos sinuosos becos entre as dunas, onde os jardins e moradias da Belle Époque se fundem numa tranquila paisagem de parque. De Haan é descoberto melhor a pé ou como os flamengos no típico carro a pedal da costa do Mar do Norte.

De Haan

De pittoreske badplaats met vele tuinen en witte villa's in Normandische cottagestijl is nauwelijks veranderd. Alleen al de aankomst met de Kusttram bij het historische houten tramstation bezorgt de bezoeker een nostalgisch gevoel van een tijd waarin de burgers de zee ontdekten en naar de zomervakantie snakten. De nostalgische flair ontvouwt zich in de kronkelende lanen tussen de duinen waar de tuinen en villa's uit de belle époque opgaan in een rustig parklandschap. De Haan is het best te voet te ontdekken of zoals de Vlamingen het doen met de voor de Noorzeekust typische skelter.

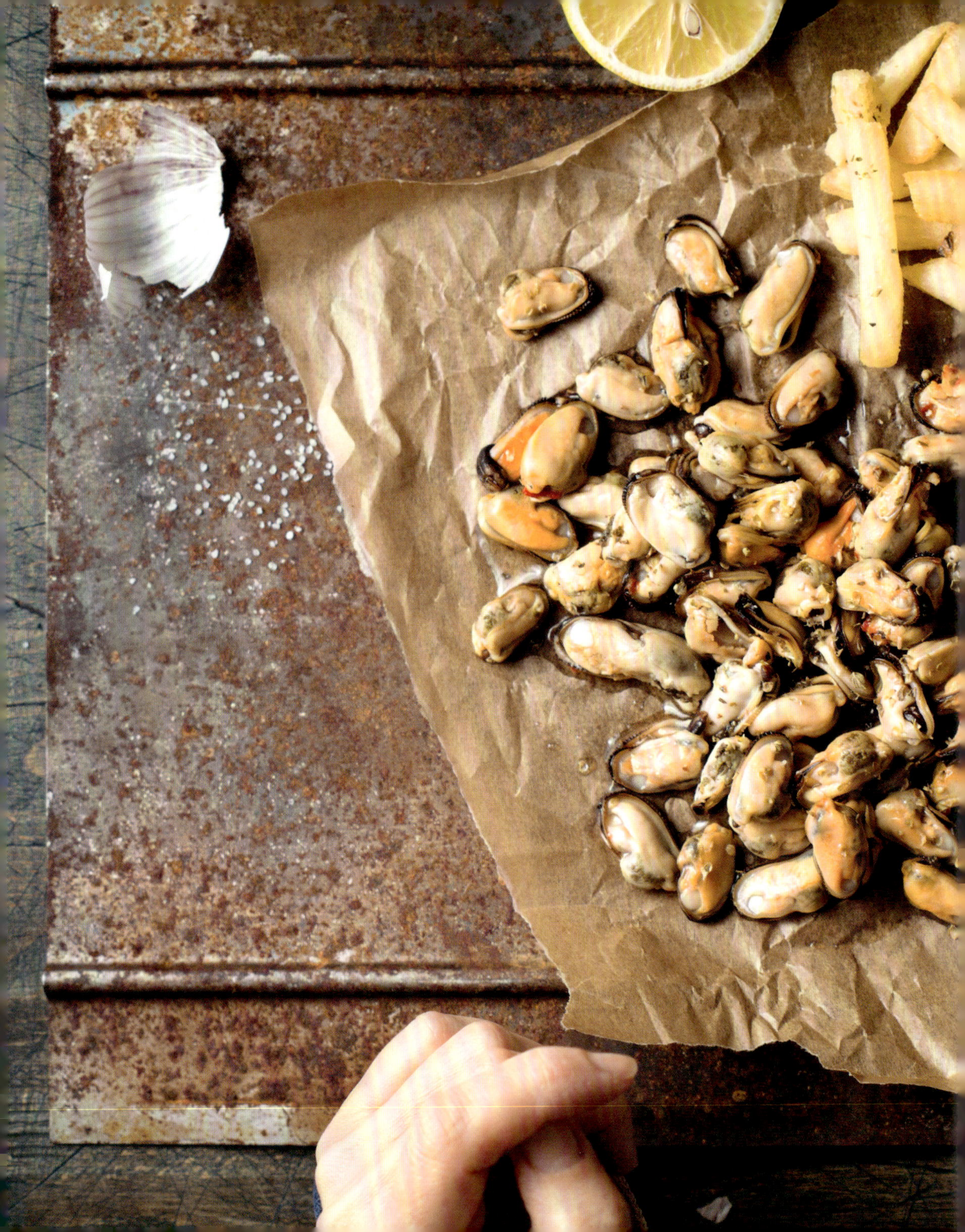

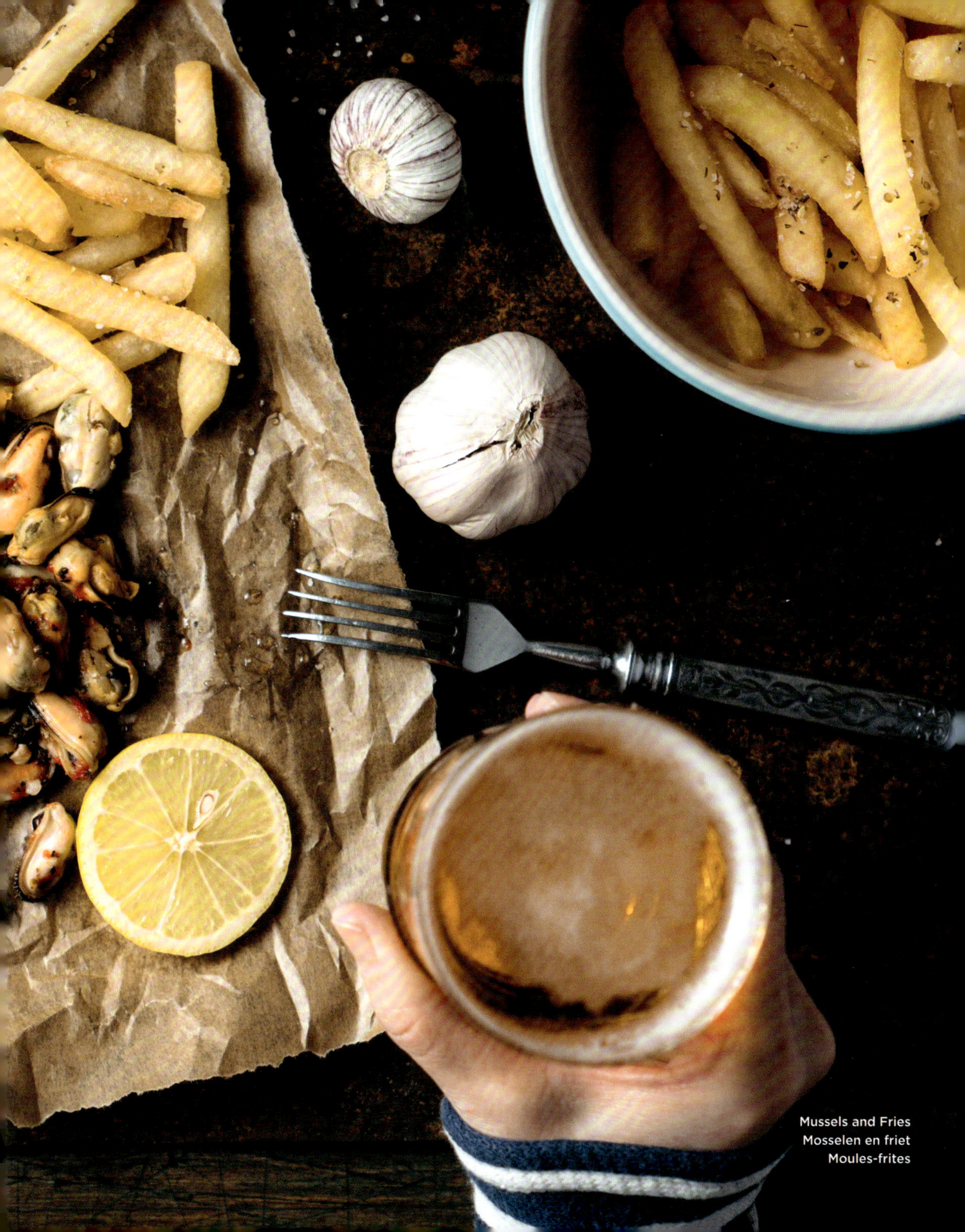

Mussels and Fries
Mosselen en friet
Moules-frites

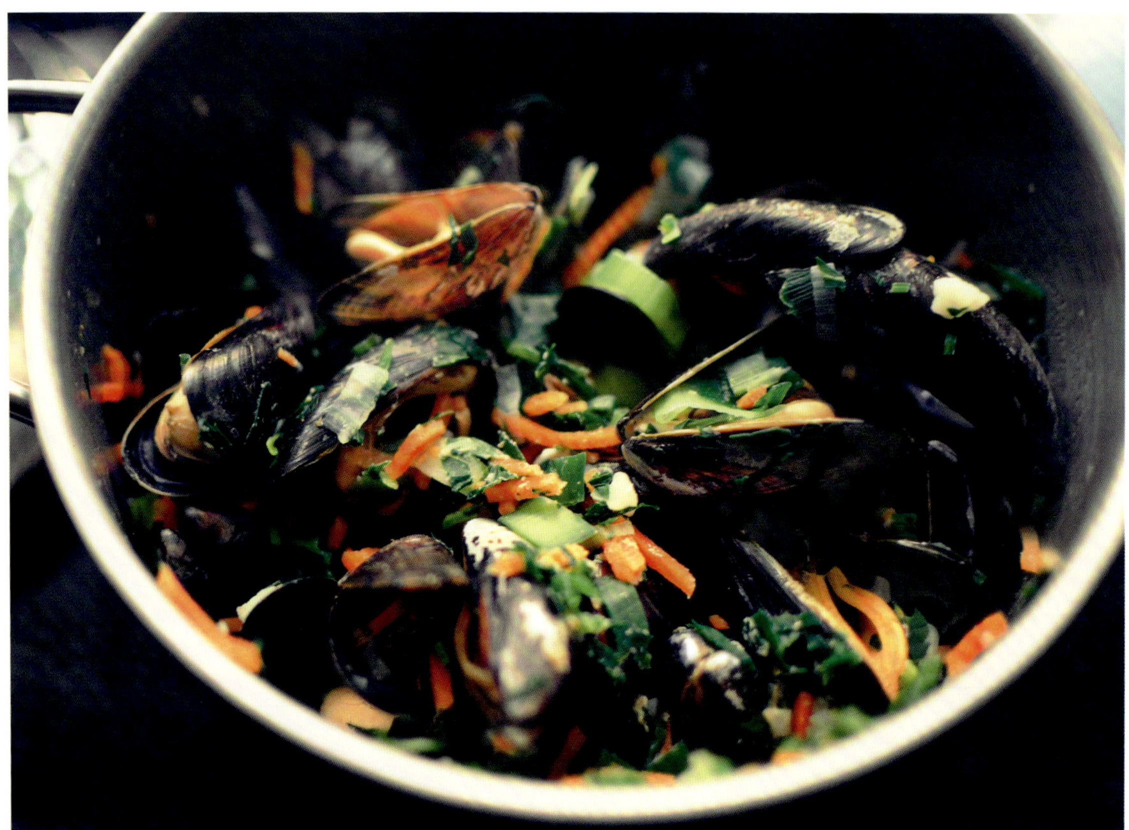

Mussels
Mosselen
Moules

Mussels and french fries

Fresh mussels with homemade french
fries are probably the most popular dish
in Flanders. The season for this North Sea
delicacy traditionally lasts from July to
February. For the Flemish, french fries are
anything but a side dish. From the right
cutting technique to the second cooking
process—the preparation of French fries
is an art. Although they are known all
over the world as "french fries", they have
less to do with France than with French-
speaking Belgians and American soldiers.
The Americans stationed in Flanders
during the First World War ate their first
French fries there.

Moules-frites

Moules fraîches et frites faites maison –
voilà sans doute le plat le plus apprécié
en Flandres. Traditionnellement, la saison
permettant de goûter ce délice de la mer
du Nord s'étend de juillet à février. Pour
les Flamands, les frites ne se réduisent
pas à un simple accompagnement. De la
bonne technique de coupe à la seconde
cuisson, leur préparation est un véritable
art. Même si on les appelle souvent, à
l'étranger, des « french fries », elles n'ont
guère de lien avec la France et davantage
avec des Flamands parlant français et des
soldats américains. En effet, les Américains
stationnés en Flandres pendant la Première
Guerre mondiale y goûtèrent leurs
premières frites.

Muscheln und Fritten

Frische Miesmuscheln mit selbst
gemachten Pommes sind das wohl
beliebteste Gericht Flanderns.
Traditionell dauert die Saison für diese
Nordseeköstlichkeit von Juli bis Februar.
Für die Flamen sind Pommes frites alles
andere als eine Beilage. Von der richtigen
Schneidetechnik bis zum zweiten Garen
– die Zubereitung von Pommes frites ist
eine Kunst. Obwohl sie auf der ganzen
Welt als „French fries" bekannt sind,
haben sie weniger mit Frankreich zu
tun, als mit Französisch sprechenden
Flamen und amerikanischen Soldaten. Die
während des Ersten Weltkriegs in Flandern
stationierten Amerikaner probierten dort
ihre ersten Fritten.

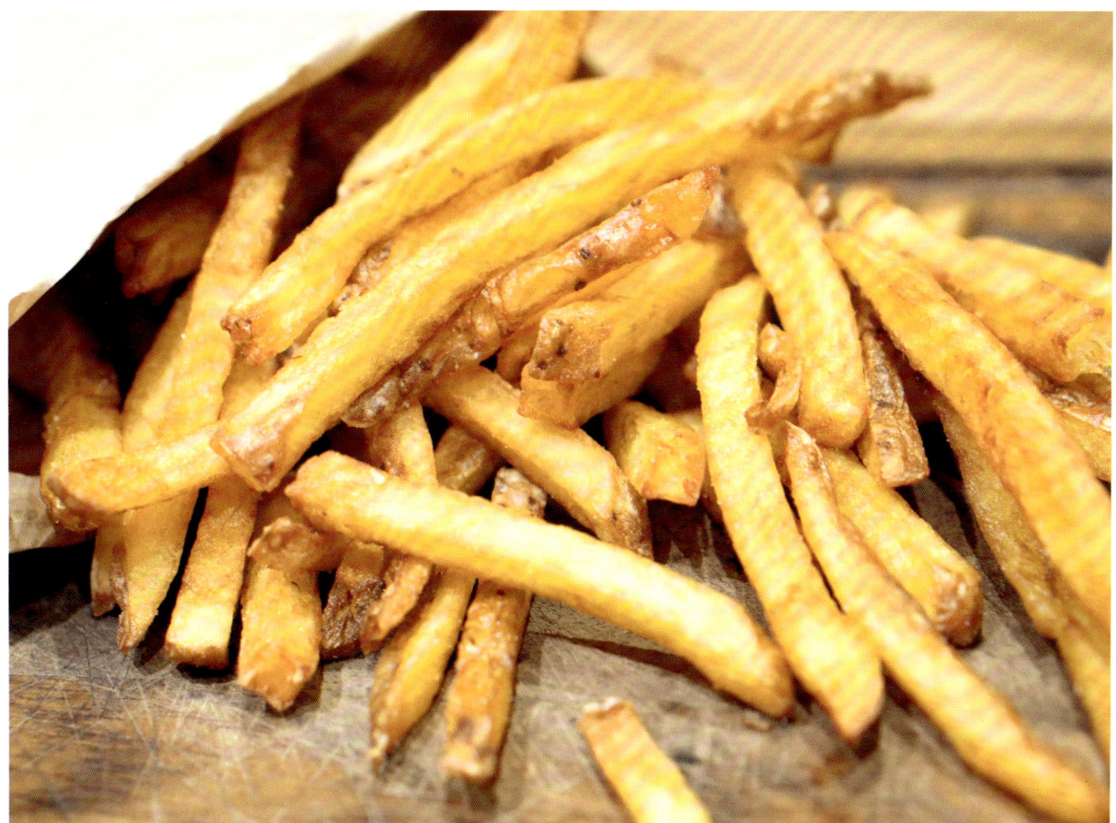

Fries
Friet
Frites

Mejillones y patatas fritas

Los mejillones frescos con patatas fritas
caseras son probablemente el plato
más popular en Flandes. La temporada
de este manjar del Mar del Norte dura
tradicionalmente de julio a febrero. Para
los flamencos, las patatas fritas no son
simplemente un acompañamiento. Desde
la técnica de corte adecuada hasta la
segunda cocción, la preparación de
patatas fritas es un arte. Aunque en todo
el mundo se las conoce como "French
fries", tienen menos que ver con Francia
que con los flamencos francófonos y los
soldados estadounidenses. Los americanos
estacionados en Flandes durante la
Primera Guerra Mundial probaron sus
primeras patatas fritas allí.

Mexilhões e batatas fritas

Os mexilhões frescos com batatas fritas
caseiras é provavelmente o prato mais
popular na Flandres. A temporada
para esta iguaria do Mar do Norte dura
tradicionalmente de julho a fevereiro. Para
os Flamengos, as batatas fritas são tudo
menos somente um acompanhamento.
Desde a técnica correta de corte até a
segunda cozedura – a preparação de
batatas fritas é uma arte. Embora sejam
conhecidas em todo o mundo como
"batatas fritas", têm menos a ver com
a França do que com os flamengos
francófonos e soldados americanos.
Foi em Flanderes, que os americanos
estacionados durante a Primeira Guerra
Mundial provaramtentaram suas primeiras
batatas fritas.

Mosselen en friet

Verse mosselen met zelfgemaakte frieten
zijn waarschijnlijk het populairste gerecht
in Vlaanderen. Het seizoen voor deze
Noordzee delicatesse duurt traditioneel
van juli tot februari. Voor de Vlamingen
zijn frieten allesbehalve een bijgerecht.
Van de juiste snijtechniek tot de tweede
keer bakken - het bereiden van friet is
een kunst. Hoewel ze over de hele wereld
bekend staan als "Frensh fries", hebben ze
minder met Frankrijk te maken dan met
Franstalige Vlamingen en Amerikaanse
soldaten. De Amerikanen die tijdens
de Eerste Wereldoorlog in Vlaanderen
gestationeerd waren, probeerden er hun
eerste frieten.

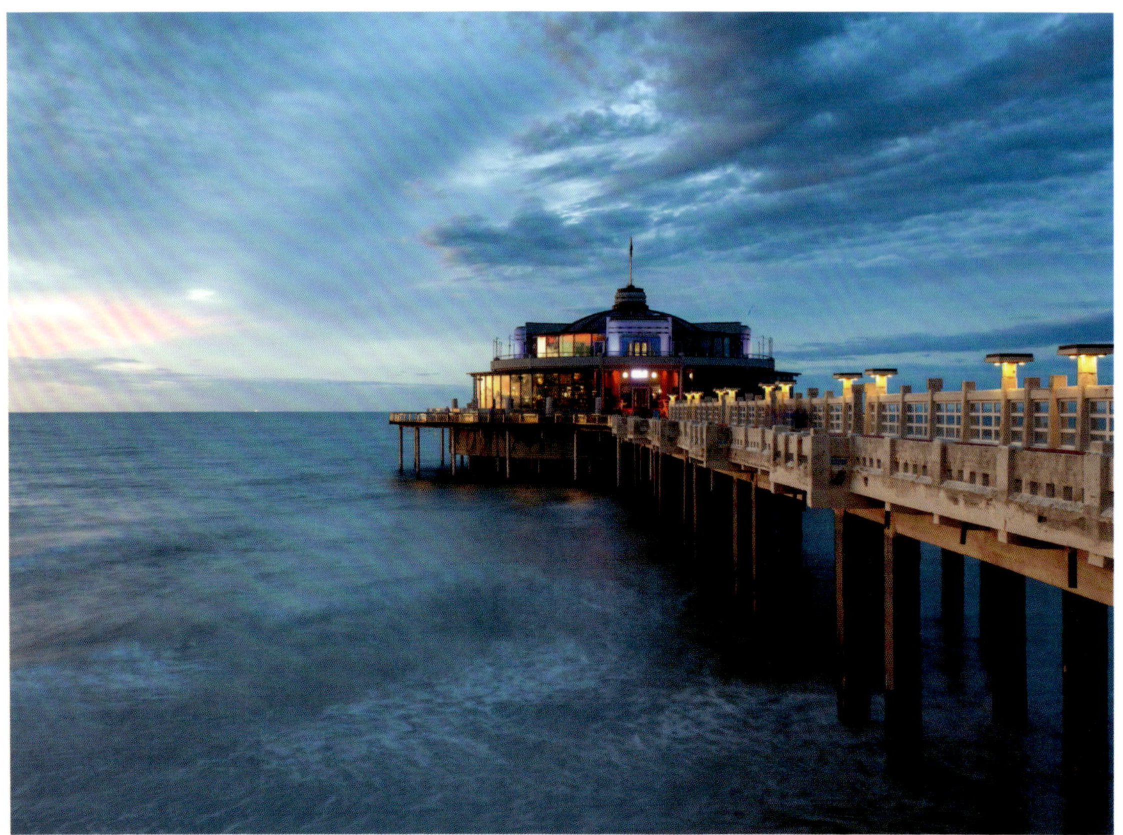

Belgium Pier, Blankenberge
Pier van Blankenberge
Jetée de Blankenberge

Drinking tea on the high seas

Following the arrival of the railway line, the fishing village of Blankenberge became a sophisticated seaside resort. In 1894, the first tourists strolled along the 350 m (1148 ft) long pier to the open sea. The heart of the monumental attraction, made of cast iron, was the tea salon in the pavilion. The old pier was destroyed during the First World War and later rebuilt in Art Deco style. A fishing boat, a sunset or even a storm—still today visitors can enjoy their tea or cocktail on the 360-degree sea terrace. Nearby is another small pier, the Oosterstaketsel, which features a brasserie.

Prendre le thé en haute mer

Dès lors qu'il fut accessible en train, le village de pêcheurs de Blankenberge se transforma en une station balnéaire moderne. En 1894, les premiers touristes flânaient sur la jetée de 350 m conduisant au large. Au cœur de cette attraction monumentale en fonte : le salon de thé dans le pavillon. L'ancienne jetée fut détruite pendant la Première Guerre mondiale et reconstruite dans le style Art Déco. Un bateau de pêcheur, un coucher de soleil, une tempête : aujourd'hui encore, les visiteurs peuvent siroter un thé ou un cocktail sur la terrasse avec vue à 360° sur la mer. À proximité immédiate, une autre petite jetée, l'Oosterstaketsel, est pourvue d'une brasserie.

Teetrinken auf hoher See

Mit dem Anschluss an die Eisenbahnlinie wurde aus dem Fischerdorf Blankenberge ein mondänes Seebad. 1894 flanierten die ersten Touristen über die rund 350 m lange Seebrücke aufs offene Meer. Das Herz der monumentalen Attraktion aus Gusseisen war der Tee-Salon im Pavillon. Der alte Pier wurde während des Ersten Weltkriegs zerstört und im Art-déco-Stil wiederaufgebaut. Ein Fischerboot, ein Sonnenuntergang oder gar ein Sturm – auch heute können die Besucher auf der 360-Grad-Seeterrasse ihren Tee oder Cocktail genießen. Ganz in der Nähe befindet sich noch ein weiterer kleiner Pier, der Oosterstaketsel, mit einer Brasserie.

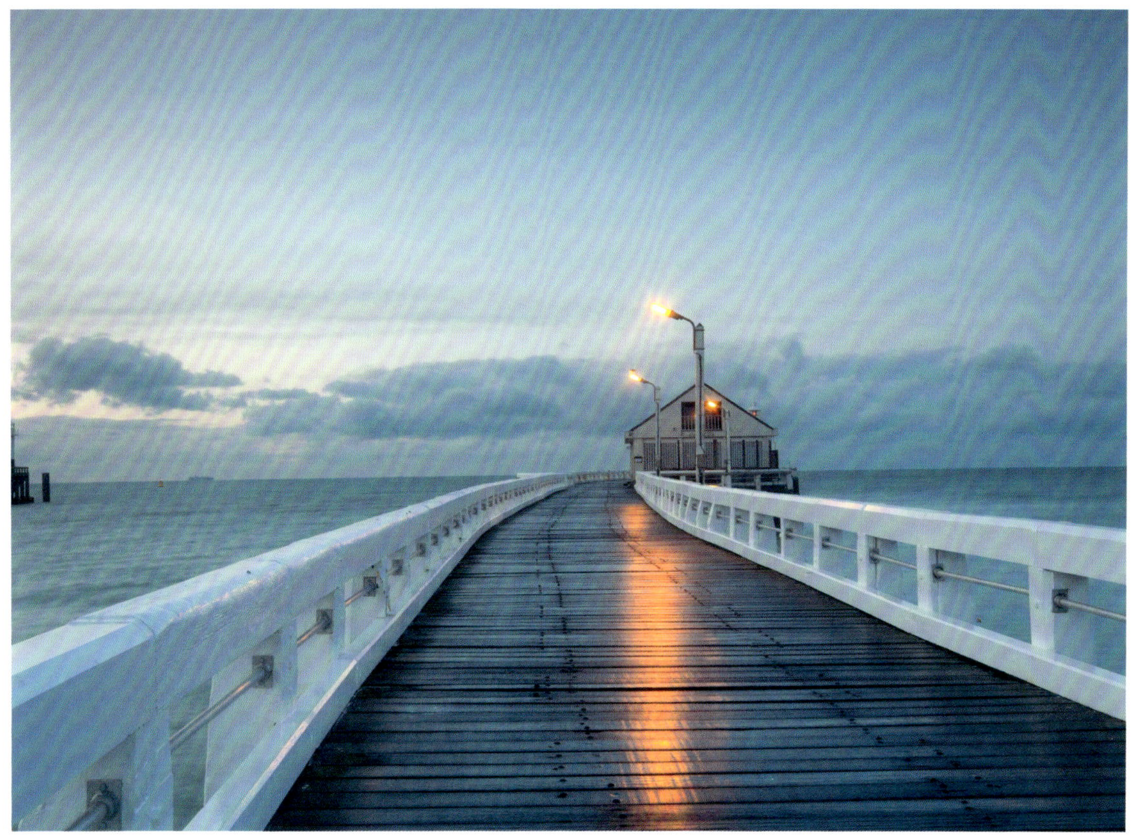

Oosterstaketsel—Eastern Pier, Blankenberge
Oosterstaketsel, Blankenberge
Jetée de l'est, Blankenberge

Beber té en alta mar

Con la conexión a la línea de ferrocarril, el pueblo pesquero de Blankenberge se convirtió en una sofisticada estación balnearia. En 1894 los primeros turistas pasearon por el muelle de 350 m de largo hasta el mar abierto. El corazón de la monumental atracción de hierro fundido era el salón de té en el pabellón. El antiguo muelle fue destruido durante la Primera Guerra Mundial y reconstruido en estilo Art Déco. Un barco de pesca, una puesta de sol o hasta una tormenta; incluso hoy en día los visitantes pueden disfrutar de su té o cóctel en la terraza marina de 360 grados. Cerca hay otro pequeño muelle, el Oosterstaketsel, con una brasserie.

Beber chá em alto mar

Com a conexão à linha férrea, a aldeia piscatória Blankenberge tornou-se um sofisticado resort à beira-mar. Em 1894, os primeiros turistas passearam pelo cais de aproximadamente 350 m de comprimento até o mar aberto. O coração da monumental atração feita de ferro fundido foi o salão de chá no pavilhão. O antigo cais foi destruído durante a Primeira Guerra Mundial e reconstruído no estilo Art Deco. Um barco de pesca, um pôr-do-sol ou mesmo uma tempestade – ainda hoje os visitantes podem desfrutar do seu chá ou de um cocktail no terraço de 360 graus com vista para o mar. Perto está outro pequeno cais, o Oosterstaketsel, com uma brasserie.

Theedrinken op volle zee

Door de aansluiting op de spoorlijn werd het vissersdorp Blankenberge een mondaine badplaats. In 1894 liepen de eerste toeristen over de 350 m lange pier naar de open zee. Het hart van de monumentale attractie van gietijzer was de theesalon in het paviljoen. De oude pier werd tijdens de Eerste Wereldoorlog verwoest en in art deco-stijl herbouwd. Een vissersboot, een zonsondergang of zelfs een storm – ook vandaag nog kunnen bezoekers op het 360-graden zee-terras genieten van hun thee of cocktail. Vlakbij is nog een kleine pier, het Oosterstaketsel, met een brasserie.

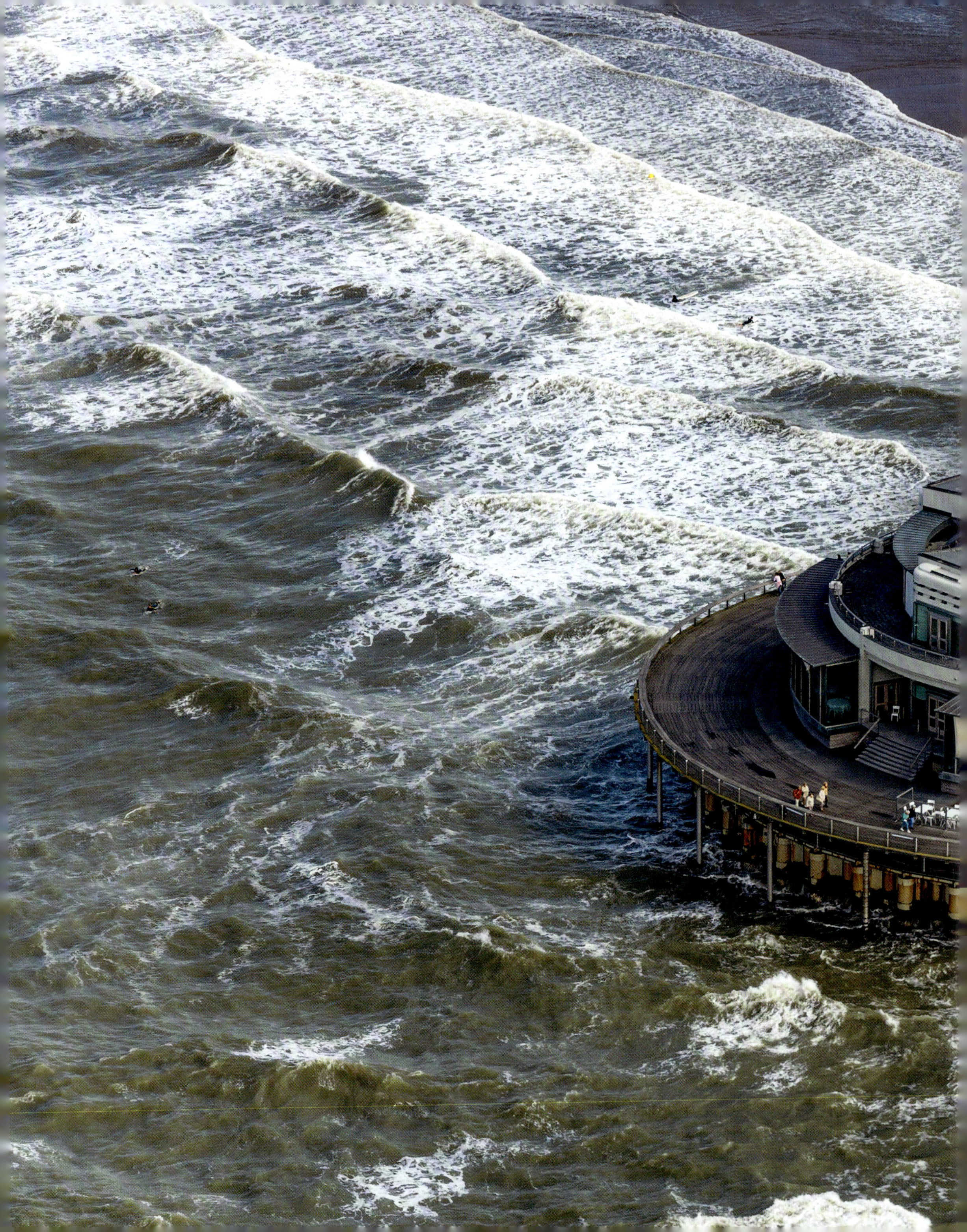

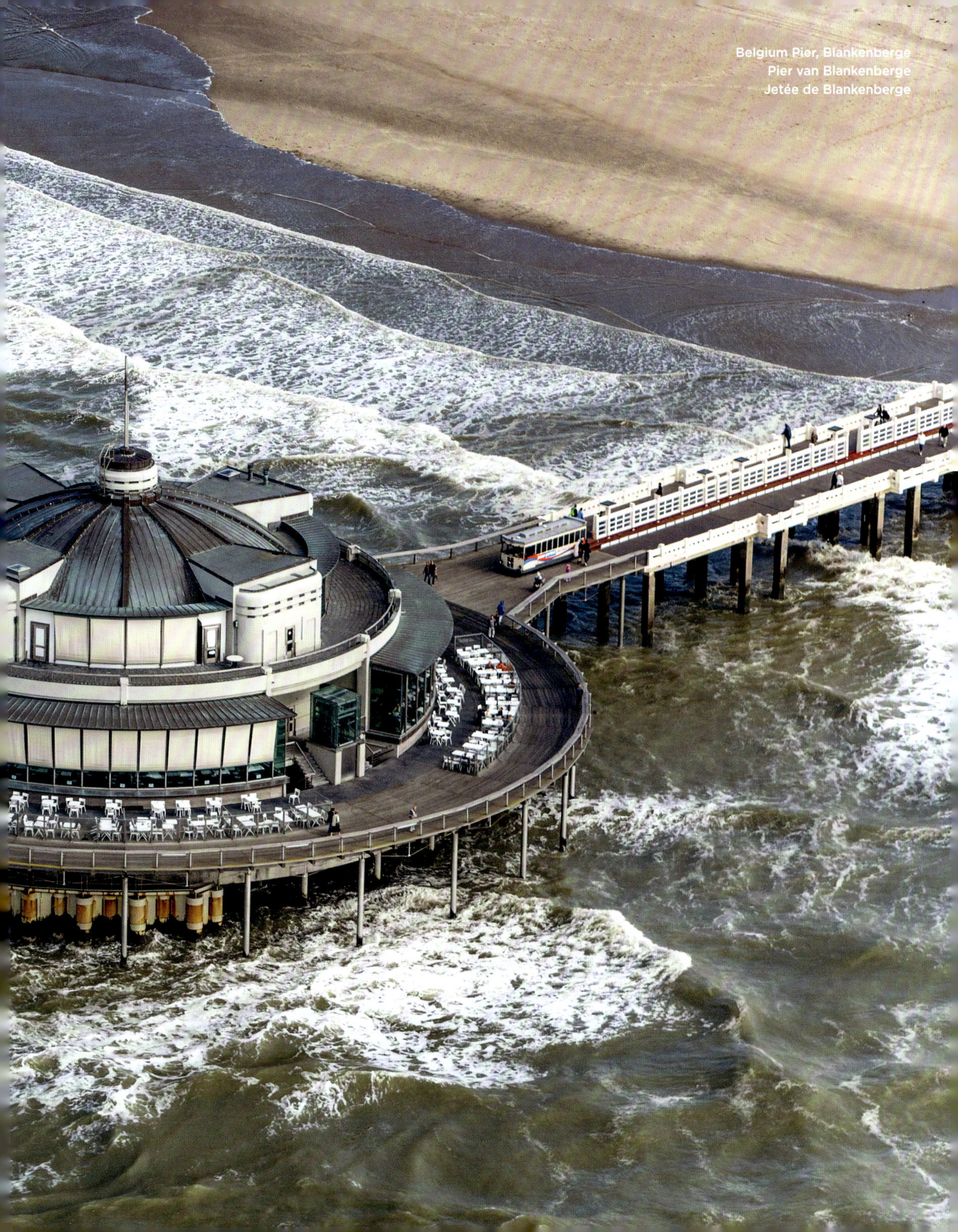
Belgium Pier, Blankenberge
Pier van Blankenberge
Jetée de Blankenberge

Seaside resort

The "beautiful age" (1870-1914) of the *belle époque* left
its mark on the 13 seaside resorts of Flanders with its
playful villas in the Art Nouveau style. In the seaside
resort of Blankenberge, three villas have been renovated
and converted into a museum. Faithful interiors, posters,
costumes and fashionable accessories illuminate the
world of the emerging tourism, fashion and music of the
belle époque.

Stations balnéaires

La Belle Époque (1870–1914) a laissé des traces dans les
treize stations balnéaires des Flandres : des villas fantaisie
aux allures de pièce montée ou de style Art nouveau.
À la station balnéaire de Blankenberge, trois villas ont
été restaurées et transformées en musée. Intérieurs
fidèlement conservés jusque dans les moindres détails,
affiches, costumes et accessoires de mode illustrent
un tourisme en plein essor, la mode et la musique à la
Belle Époque.

Seebäder

Die „schöne Zeit" (1870–1914) der Belle Époque hat ihre
Spuren in den 13 Seebädern Flanderns hinterlassen:
verspielte Villen im Zuckerbäcker- oder Art nouveau-Stil.
Im Seebad Blankenberge wurden drei Villen saniert und
in ein Museum umfunktioniert. Detailgetreue Interieurs,
Plakate, Kostüme und modische Accessoires beleuchten
die Welt des aufkommenden Tourismus, der Mode und
der Musik in der Belle Époque.

Estaciones balnearias

La "bella época" (1870–1914) de la Belle Époque dejó su
huella en las 13 estaciones balnearias de Flandes: villas
lúdicas de estilo ornamental o Art Nouveau. En la estación
balnearia de Blankenberge, tres villas han sido renovadas
y convertidas en un museo. Interiores con abundantes
detalles, carteles, trajes y accesorios de moda iluminan el
mundo del turismo emergente, la moda y la música de la
Belle Époque.

Estâncias balneares

O "bons momentos" (1870–1914) da Belle Époque deixou
a sua marca nas 13 estâncias balneares da Flandres: vilas
lúdicas no estilo bolo de casamento ou em Art Nouveau.
Na estância balnear de Blankenberge, três moradias
foram renovadas e transformadas em museu. Interiores
requintados, cartazes, figurinos e acessórios da moda
iluminam o mundo do turismo emergente, da moda e da
música da Belle Époque.

Badplaats

De "mooie tijd" (1870–1914) van de belle époque
heeft in de 13 badplaatsen van Vlaanderen zijn sporen
achtergelaten: vrolijke villa's in suikerbakkers- of art
nouveaustijl. In de badplaats Blankenberge werden drie
villa's gerenoveerd en omgebouwd tot een museum.
Detailgetrouwe interieurs, affiches, kostuums en modieuze
accessoires belichten de wereld van het opkomende
toerisme, de mode en de muziek van de belle époque.

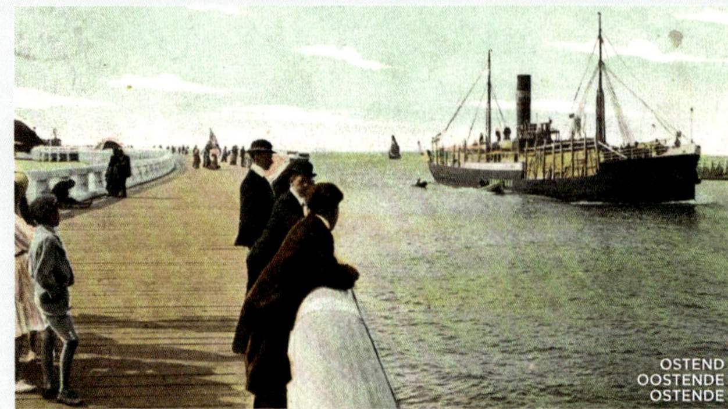

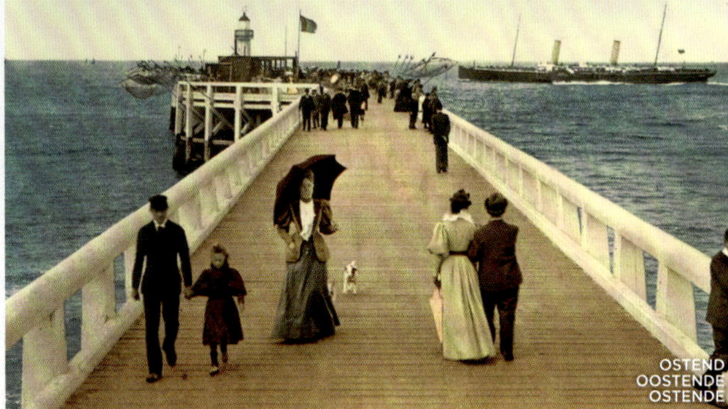

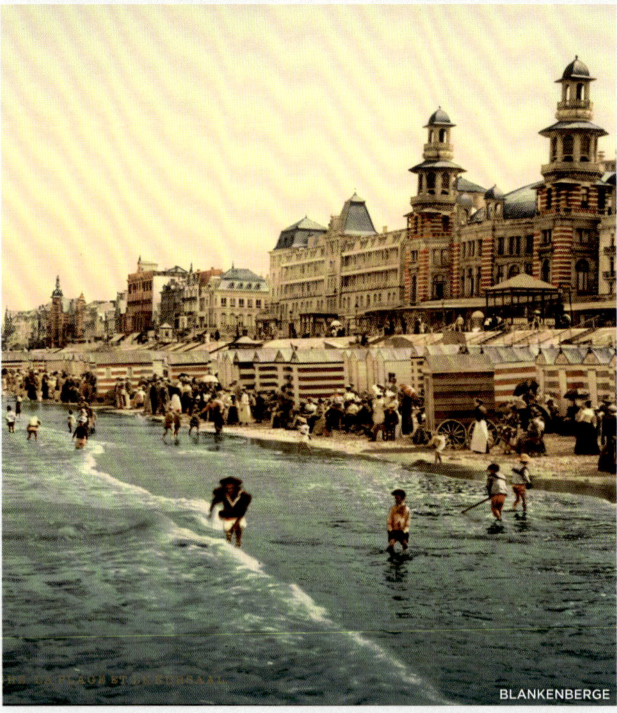

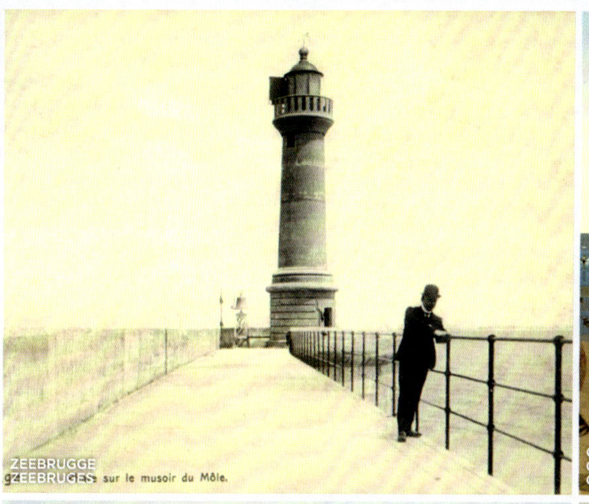

ZEEBRUGGE
ZEEBRUGES sur le musoir du Môle.

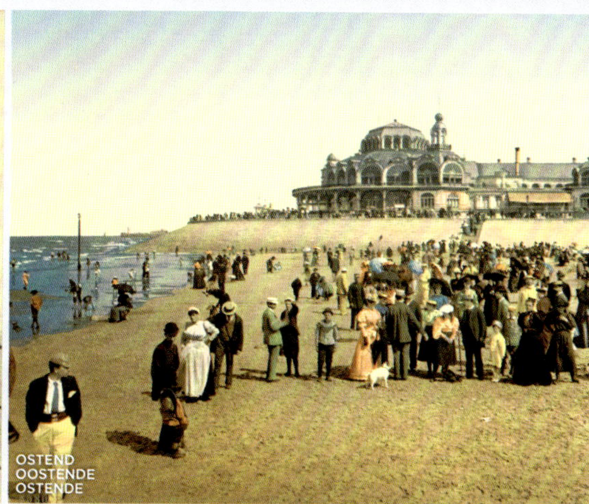

OSTEND
OOSTENDE
OSTENDE

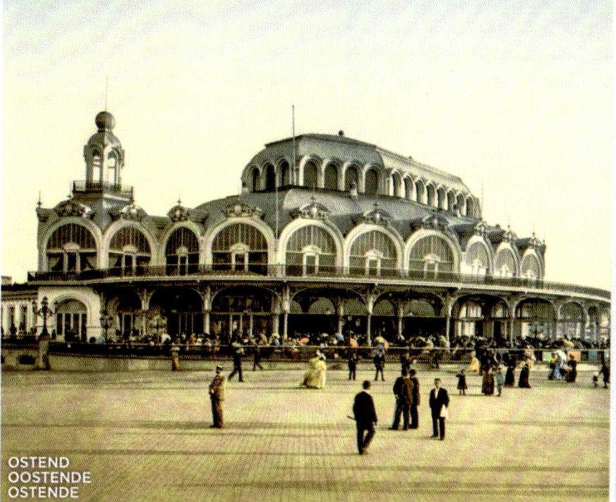

OSTEND
OOSTENDE
OSTENDE

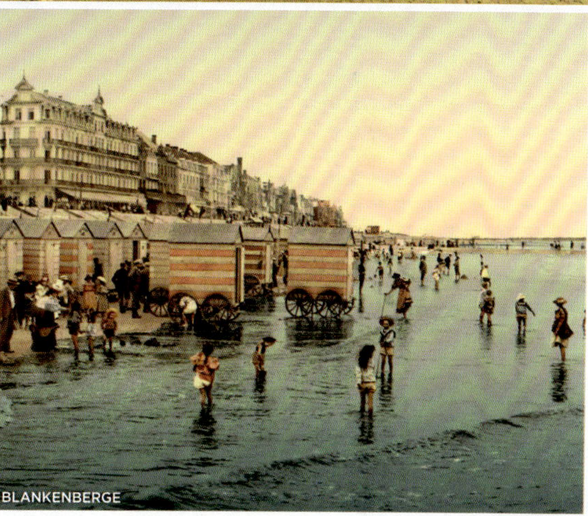

BLANKENBERGE

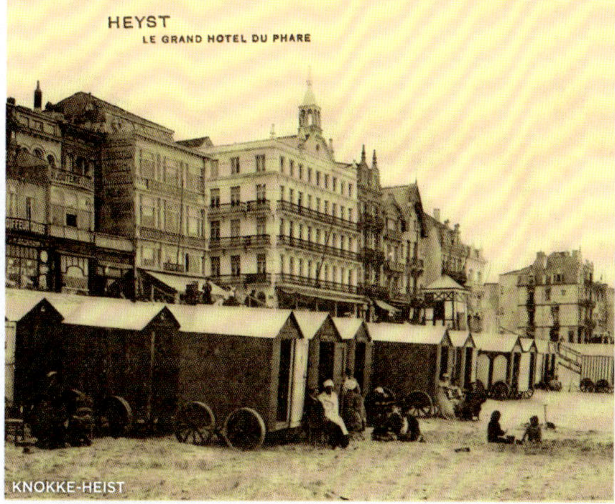

HEYST
LE GRAND HOTEL DU PHARE
KNOKKE-HEIST

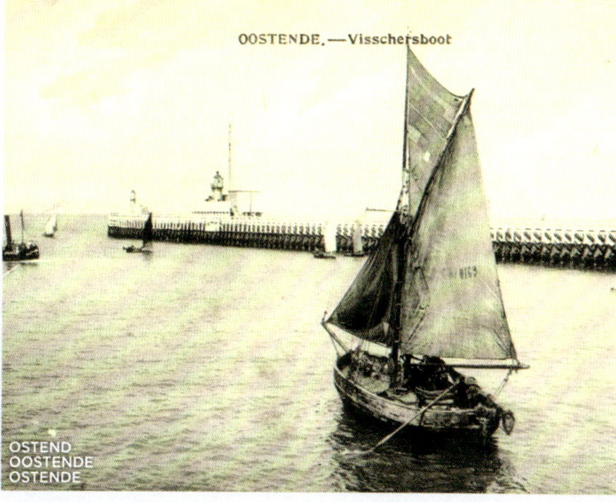

OOSTENDE. — Visschersboot
OSTEND
OOSTENDE
OSTENDE

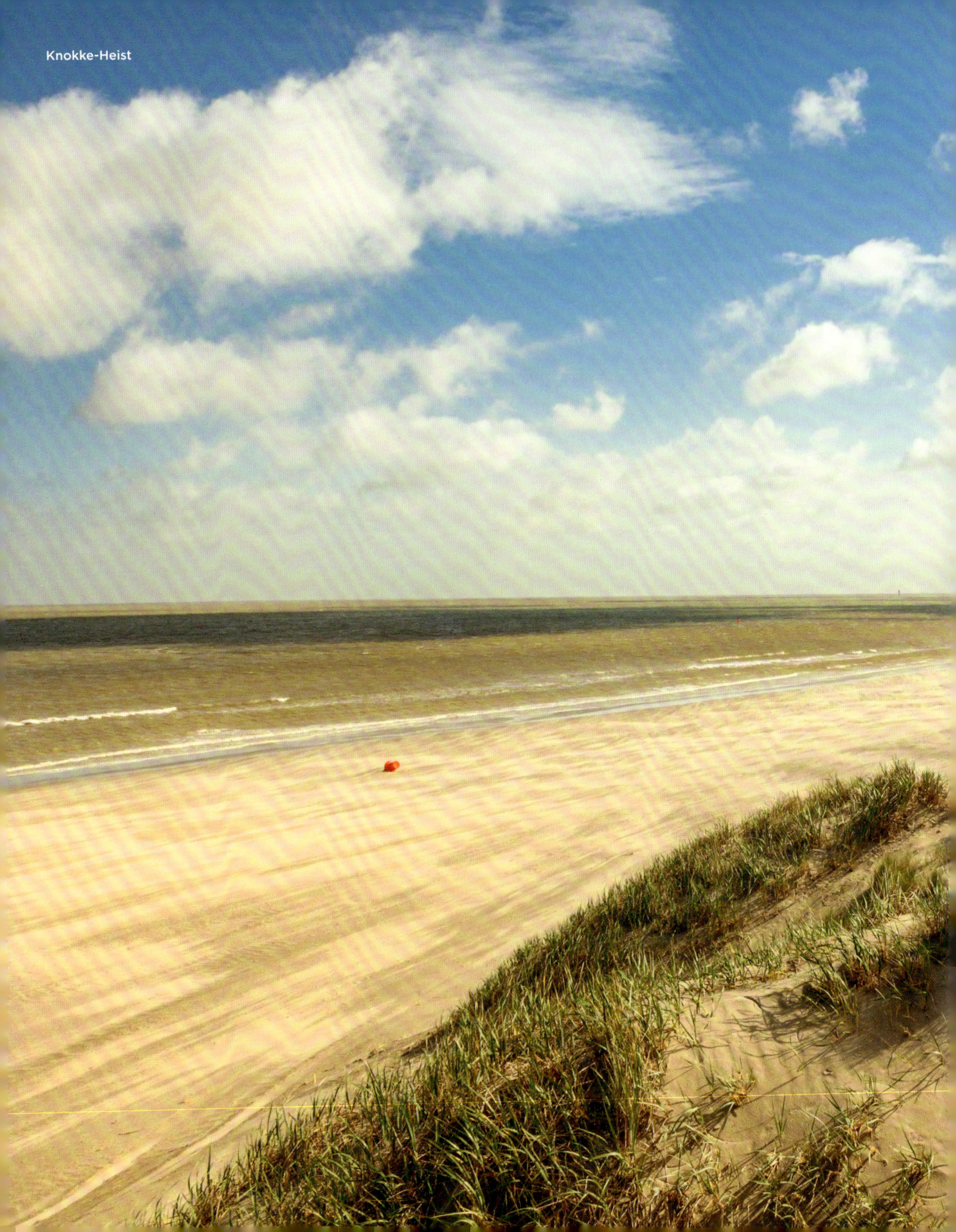
Knokke-Heist

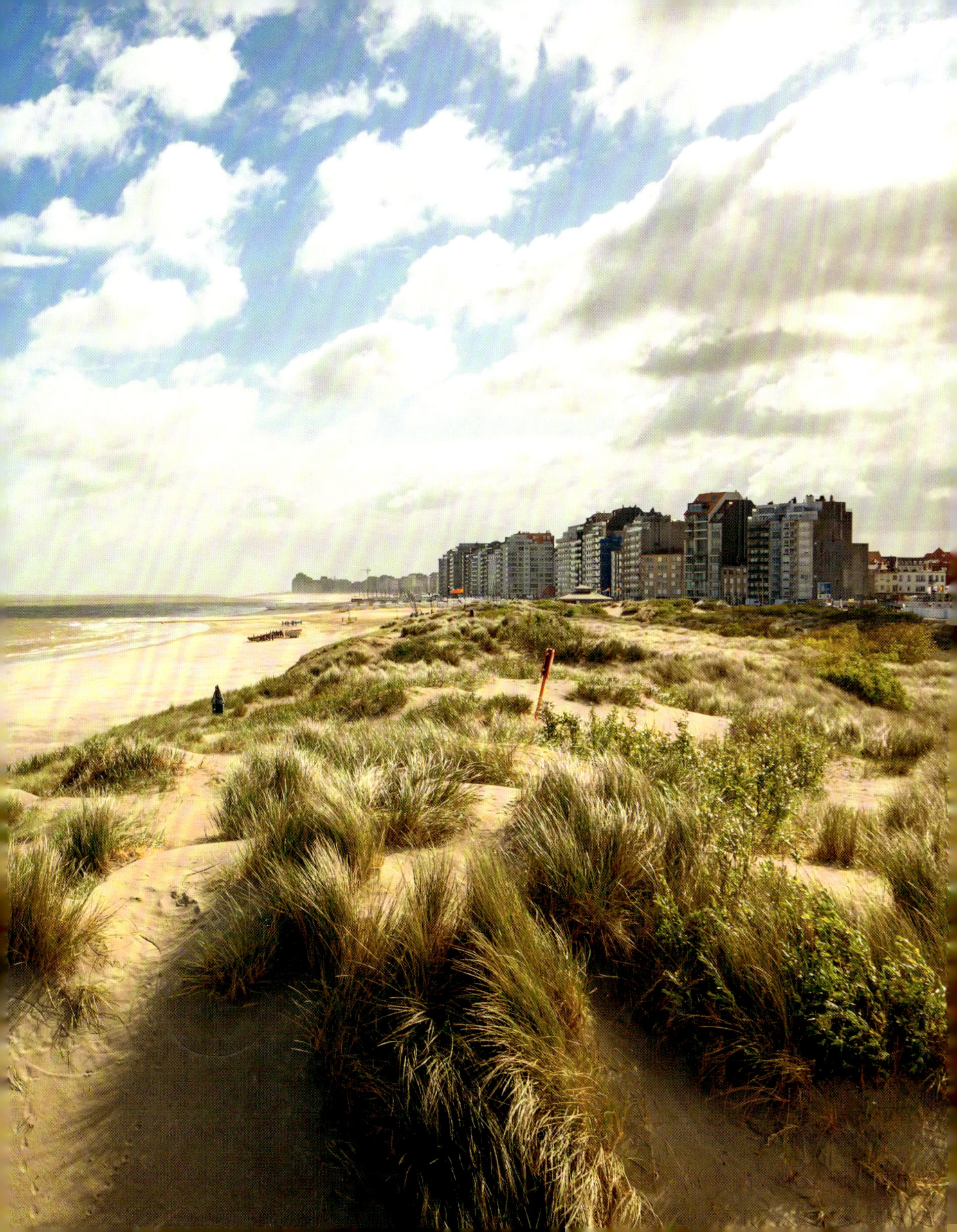

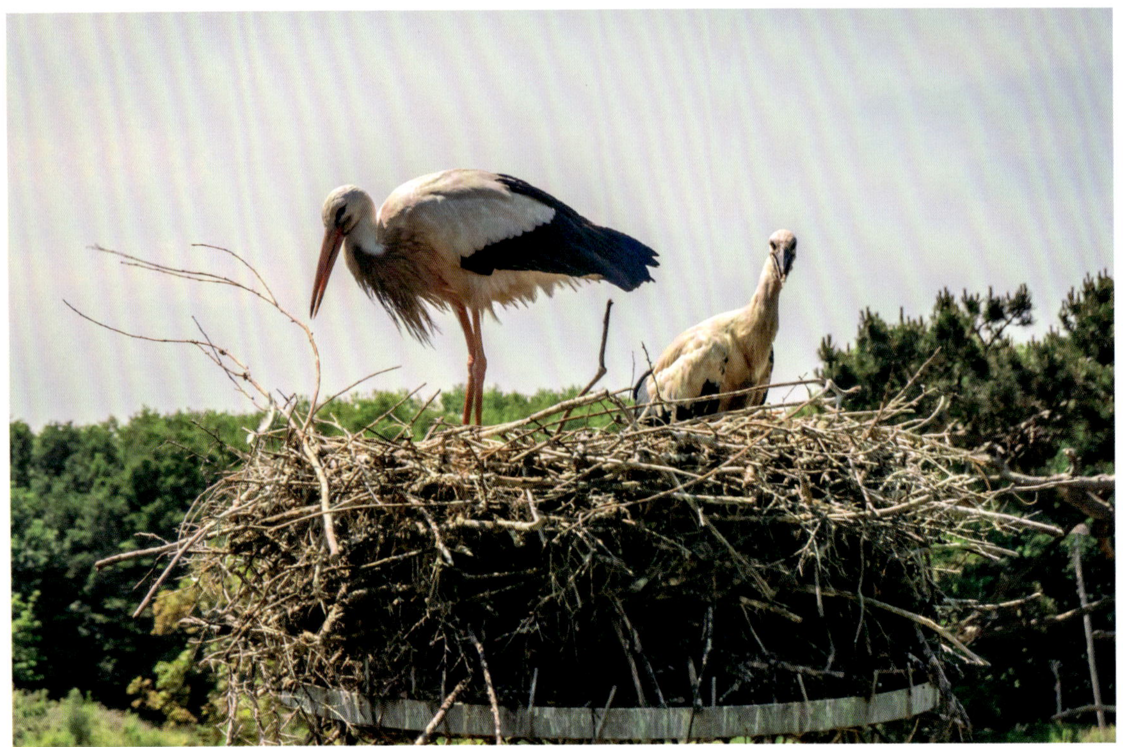

White Storks, Zwin Nature Reserve
Ooievaar, Zwin Natuur Park
Cigognes blanches, parc naturel du Zwin

Bird paradise Zwin

The Zwin nature reserve, encompassing about 350 ha (865 ac) and the largest nature reserve on the Belgian coast, is known for its great biodiversity of migratory birds. White storks can often be seen traversing the Zwin or the beach, wading through the meadows in search of food, sitting on lamp posts or chimneys, or breeding on their nests.

Zwin: un paraíso para las aves

Con aproximadamente 350 ha, el parque natural es la mayor reserva natural de la costa belga, y es conocido por su gran biodiversidad de aves migratorias. A menudo se pueden ver cigüeñas blancas sobrevolando el Zwin o la playa, vadeando los prados en busca de comida, sentadas en farolas o chimeneas o reproduciéndose en puestos de cría.

Le Zwin, paradis des oiseaux

Avec ses 350 hectares, cette réserve naturelle célèbre pour sa grande diversité d'oiseaux migrateurs est la plus grande de la côte belge. Souvent, on aperçoit des cigognes blanches survoler le Zwin ou la plage, sillonner les prés à la recherche de nourriture, couver sur des plateformes de couvaison installées à leur intention, ou encore postées sur des lampadaires ou des cheminées.

Paraíso das aves Zwin

O parque natural, com cerca de 350 ha, a maior reserva natural da costa belga, é conhecido pela sua grande biodiversidade de aves migratórias. As cegonhas-brancas podem muitas vezes ser vistas atravessando o Zwin ou a praia, percorrendo os prados em busca de alimento, sentadas em postes de iluminação ou chaminés ou reproduzindo-se em ninhos em postes de nidificação.

Vogelparadies Zwin

Der Naturpark, mit rund 350 ha das größte Naturschutzgebiet der belgischen Küste, ist für seine große Artenvielfalt von Zugvögeln bekannt. Häufig sieht man Weißstörche über dem Zwin oder dem Strand ihre Flugbahnen ziehen, auf Nahrungssuche durch die Wiesen waten, auf Laternenpfählen oder Schornsteinen sitzen oder auf Brutpfählen brüten.

Vogelparadijs Zwin

Het natuurpark, met ongeveer 350 ha het grootste natuurreservaat van de Belgische kust, staat bekend om zijn grote biodiversiteit trekvogels. Dikwijls zie je hier ooievaars over het Zwin of het strand hun banen trekken, door het weiland waden op zoek naar voedsel, op lantaarnpalen of schoorstenen zitten of op broedplaatsen broeden.

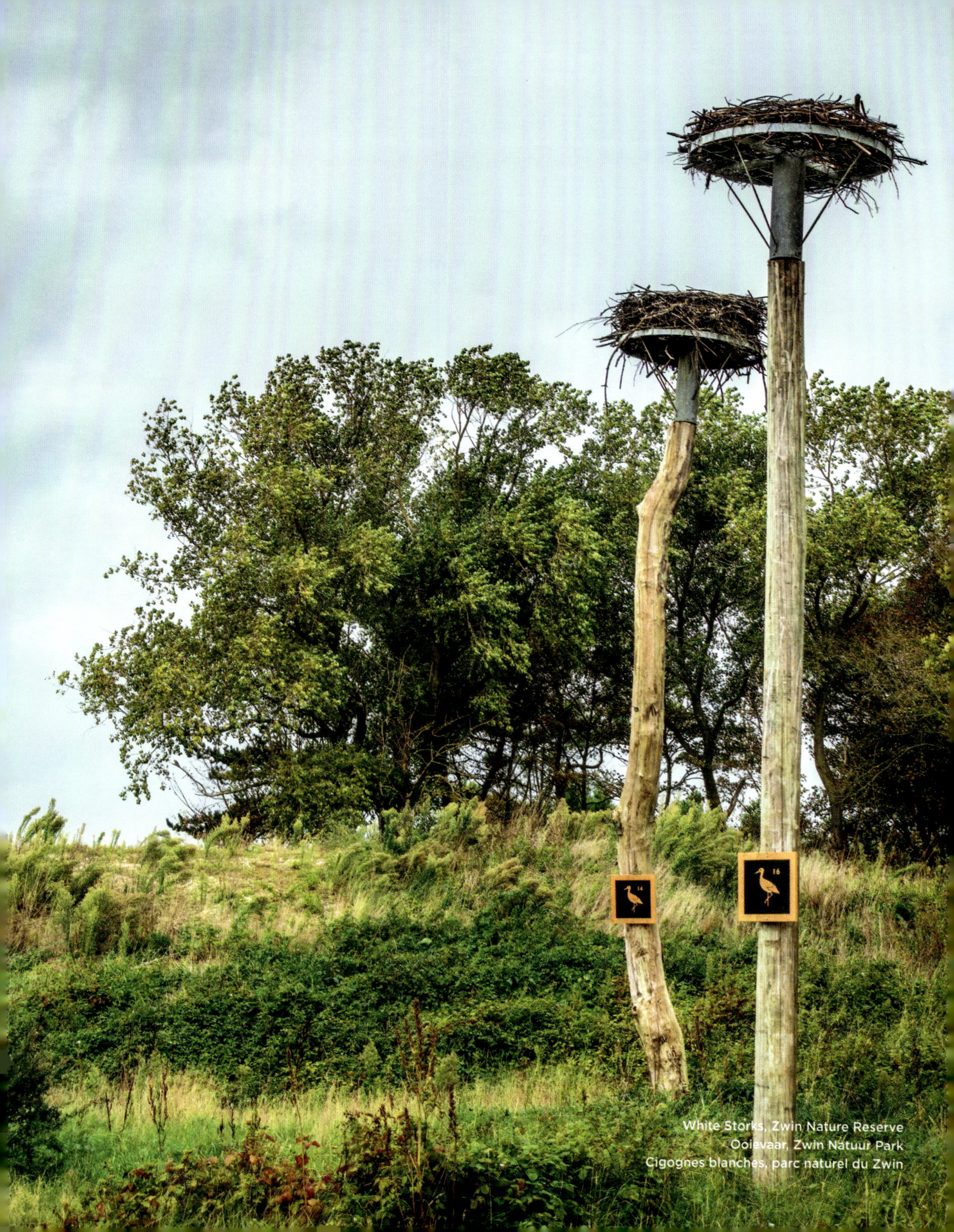

White Storks, Zwin Nature Reserve
Ooievaar, Zwin Natuur Park
Cigognes blanches, parc naturel du Zwin

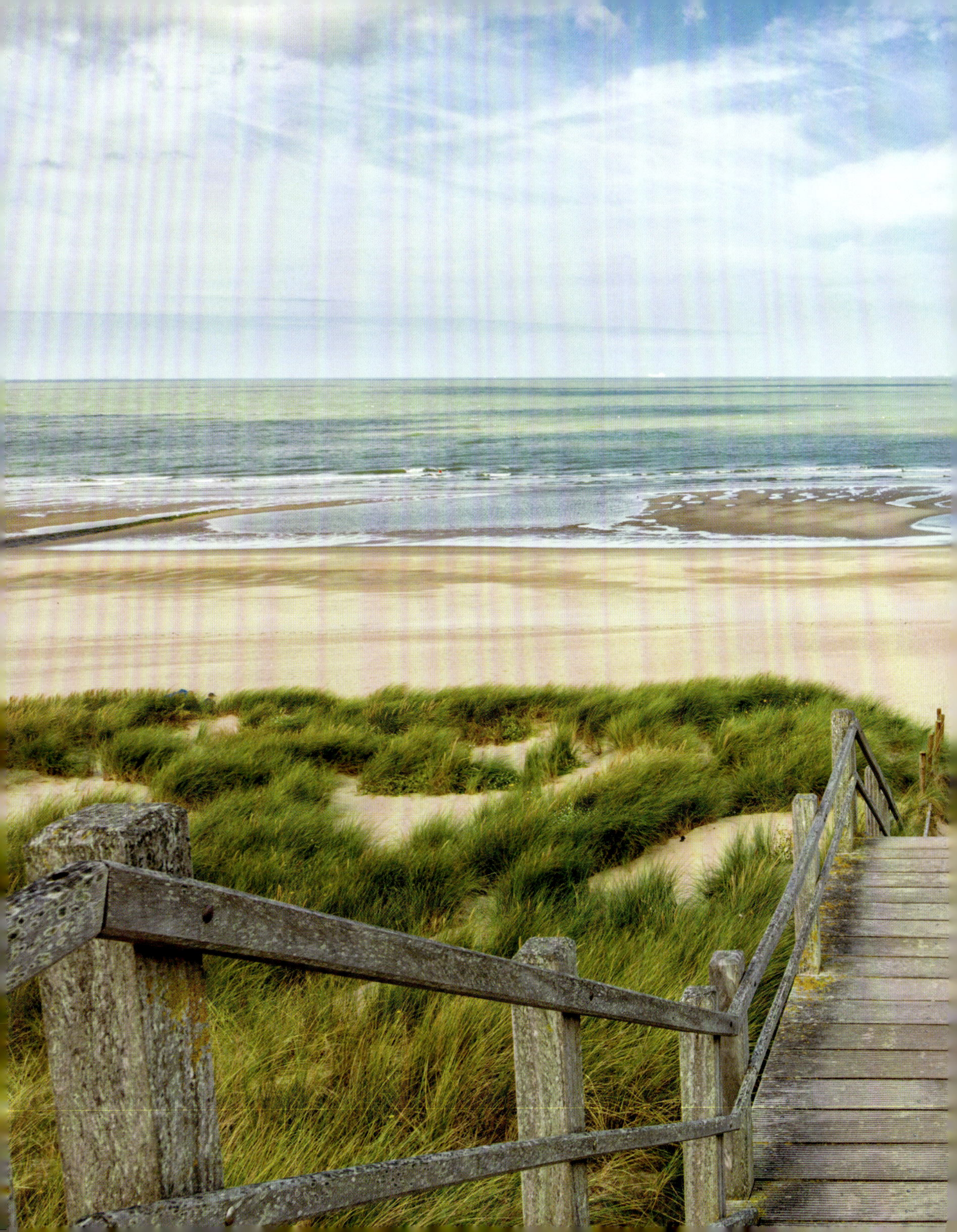

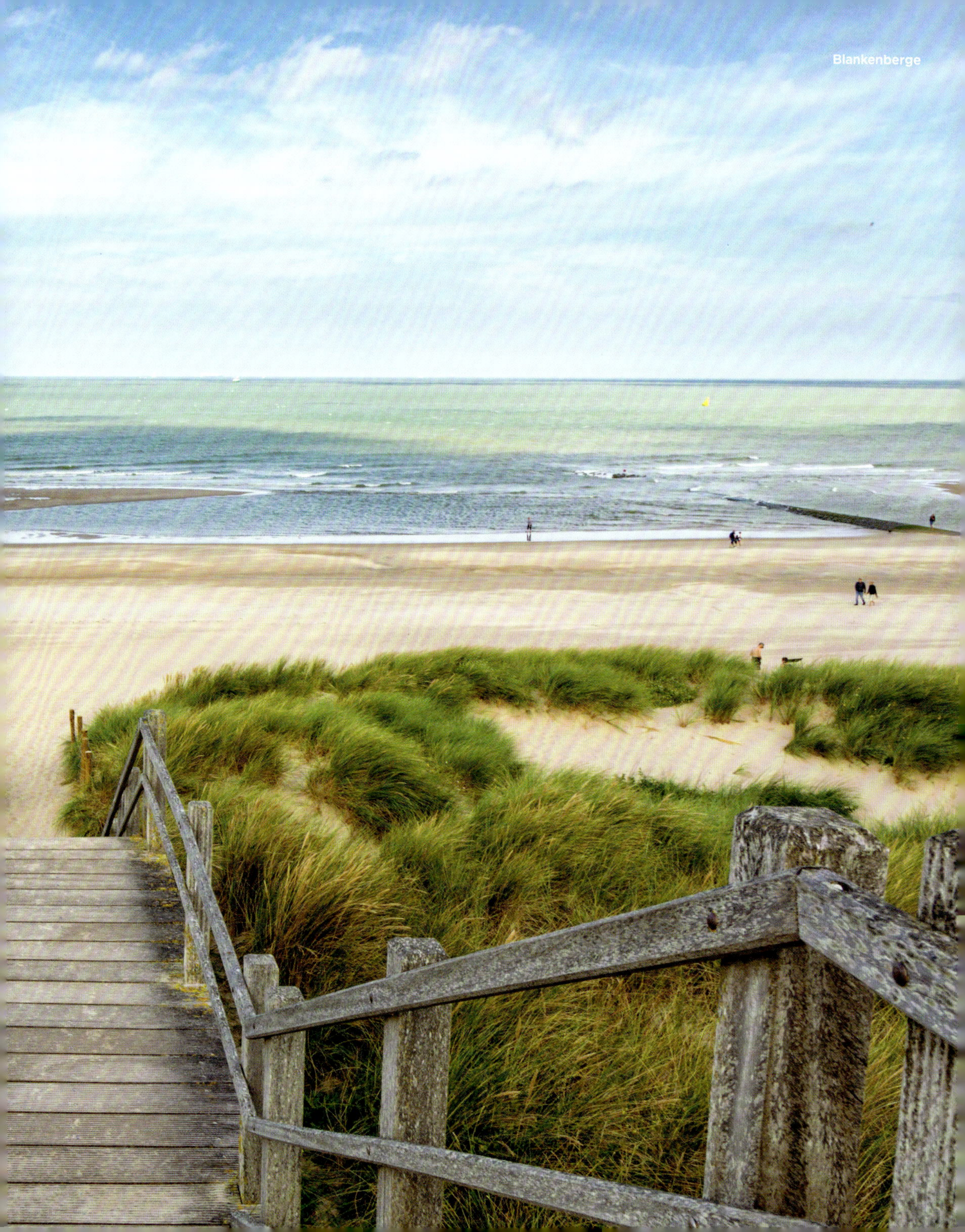
Blankenberge

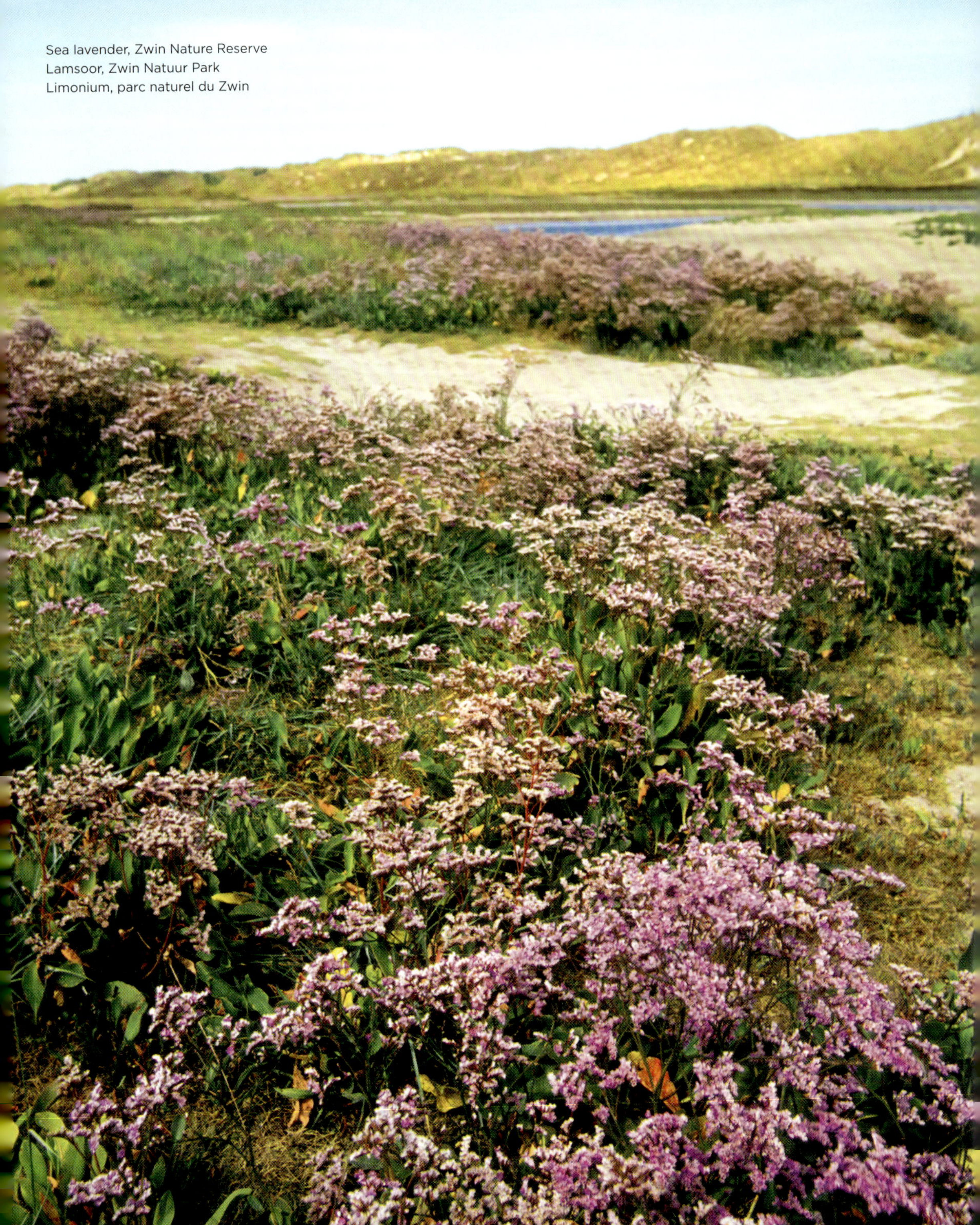
Sea lavender, Zwin Nature Reserve
Lamsoor, Zwin Natuur Park
Limonium, parc naturel du Zwin

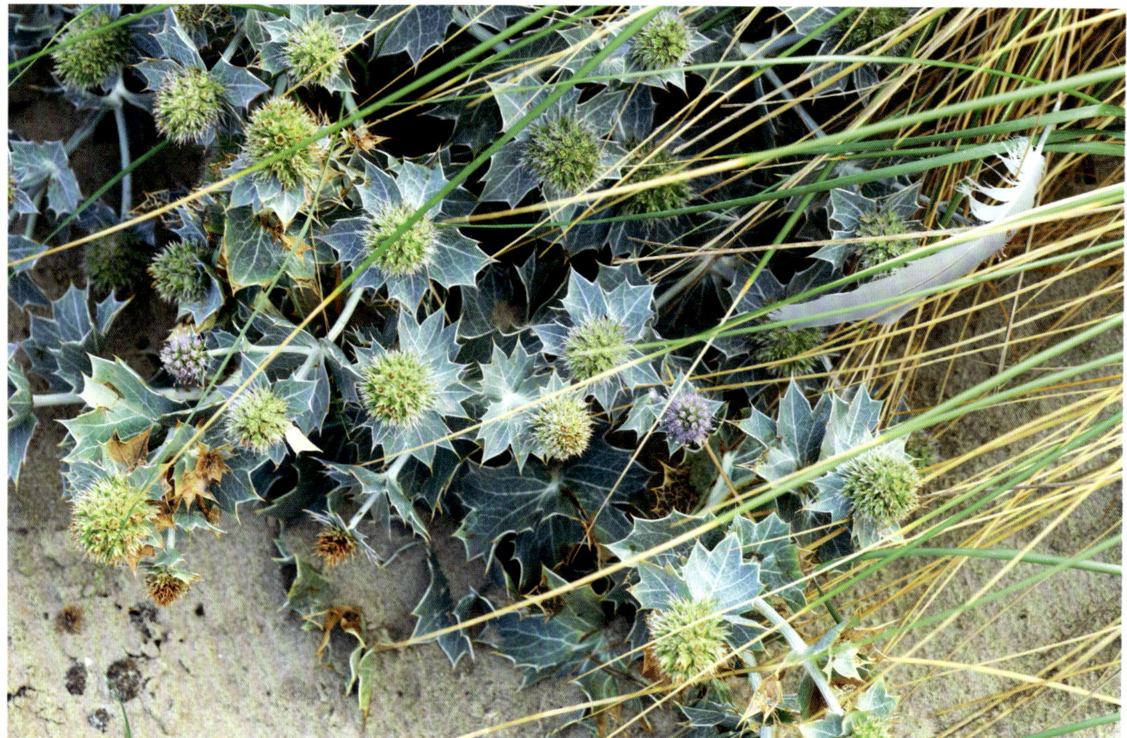

Sea Holly
Blauwe zeedistel
Panicaut maritime

Bruges estuary

In the Middle Ages, the inlet of Zwin stretched as far as the port of Bruges. However, in the 16th century this access to the sea silted up and the richest trading town of the Middle Ages became impoverished and depopulated. Today, the silted estuary is a natural paradise for highly endangered plants, such as the salt-loving sea lavender or the blue sea holly.

Estuario de Brujas

En la Edad Media, el Zwin, un estuario fluvial, se extendía hasta el puerto de Brujas. En el siglo XVI, el acceso al mar se encenagó y la ciudad comercial más rica de la Edad Media se empobreció y despobló. Hoy en día, el estuario encenagado es un paraíso natural para las plantas en peligro de extinción, como la siempreviva azul, que ama la sal, o el cardo marino azul.

Bras de mer de Bruges

Au Moyen Âge, le Zwin, une embouchure de fleuve, s'étendait jusqu'à la ville portuaire de Bruges. Au XVIᵉ siècle, l'accès à la mer s'ensabla et la ville commerciale la plus riche du Moyen Âge s'appauvrit et se dépeupla. Aujourd'hui, l'ancienne embouchure est un coin de nature paradisiaque agrémenté de plantes menacées d'extinction, comme le limonium, amateur de sel, ou le panicaut maritime et ses fleurs bleues.

Estuário de Bruges

Na Idade Média, o canal Zwin, um estuário fluvial, estendia-se até ao porto de Bruges. No século XVI, o acesso ao mar assoreou-se e a cidade comercial mais rica da Idade Média ficou empobrecida e despovoada. Hoje, o estuário assoreado é um paraíso natural para as plantas altamente ameaçadas de extinção, como o lavanda-do-mar amante do sal ou a salsa-da-praia azul.

Brügges Meeresarm

Im Mittelalter erstreckte sich der Zwin, eine Flussmündung, bis zur Hafenstadt Brügge. Im 16. Jahrhundert versandete der Zugang zum Meer und die reichste Handelsstadt des Mittelalters verarmte und entvölkerte sich. Heute ist die verlandete Mündung ein Naturparadies für stark gefährdete Pflanzen wie den salzliebenden Strandflieder oder die Blaue Stranddistel.

Brugge zeearm

In de Middeleeuwen strekte de riviermonding het Zwin zich uit tot aan de haven van Brugge. In de 16e eeuw verzandde de toegang tot de zee en verarmde en ontvolkte de rijkste handelsstad van de Middeleeuwen. Tegenwoordig is de verzandde zeearm een natuurparadijs voor sterk bedreigde planten zoals de zoutminnende zee-lavendel of de blauwe zeedistel.

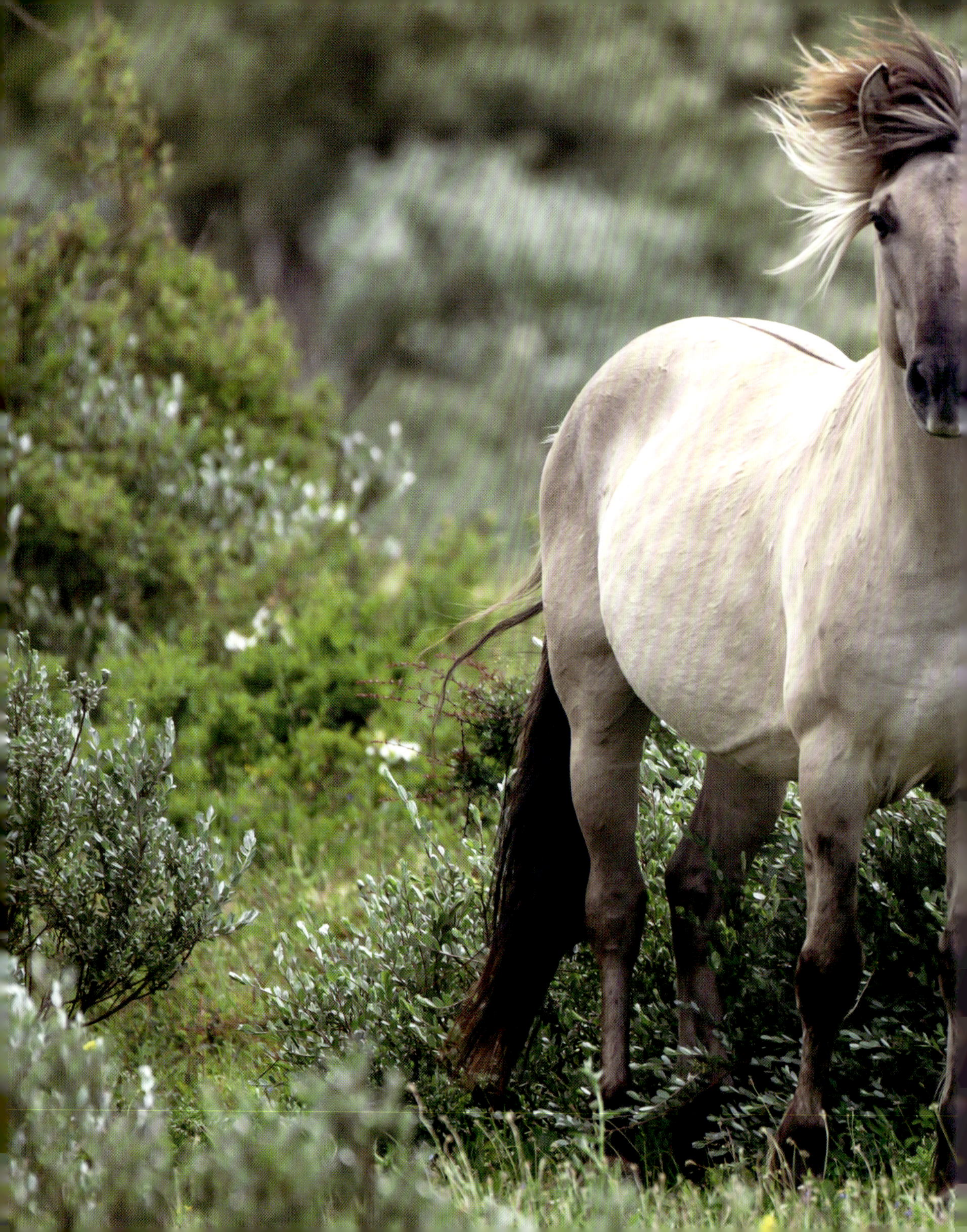

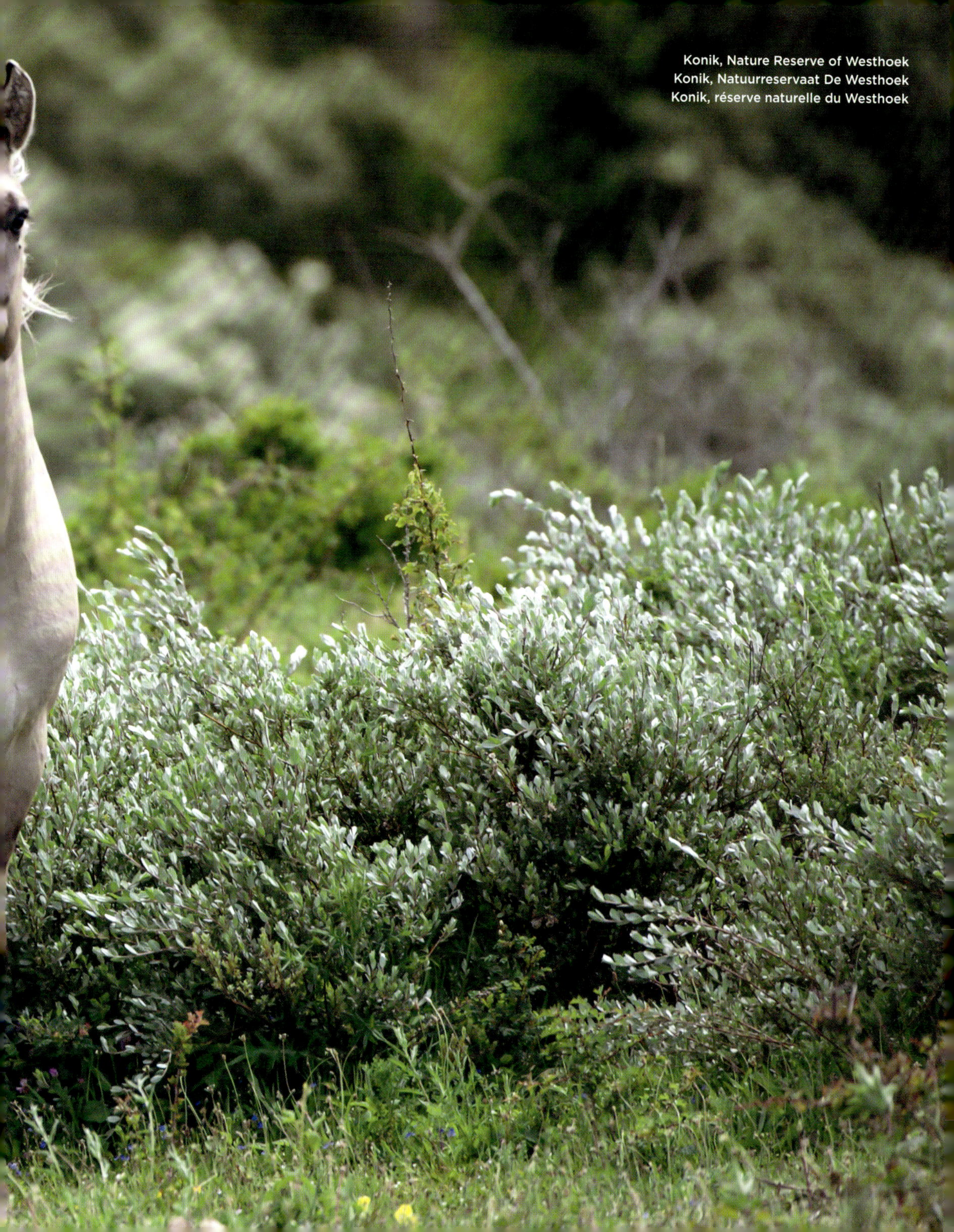

Konik, Nature Reserve of Westhoek
Konik, Natuurreservaat De Westhoek
Konik, réserve naturelle du Westhoek

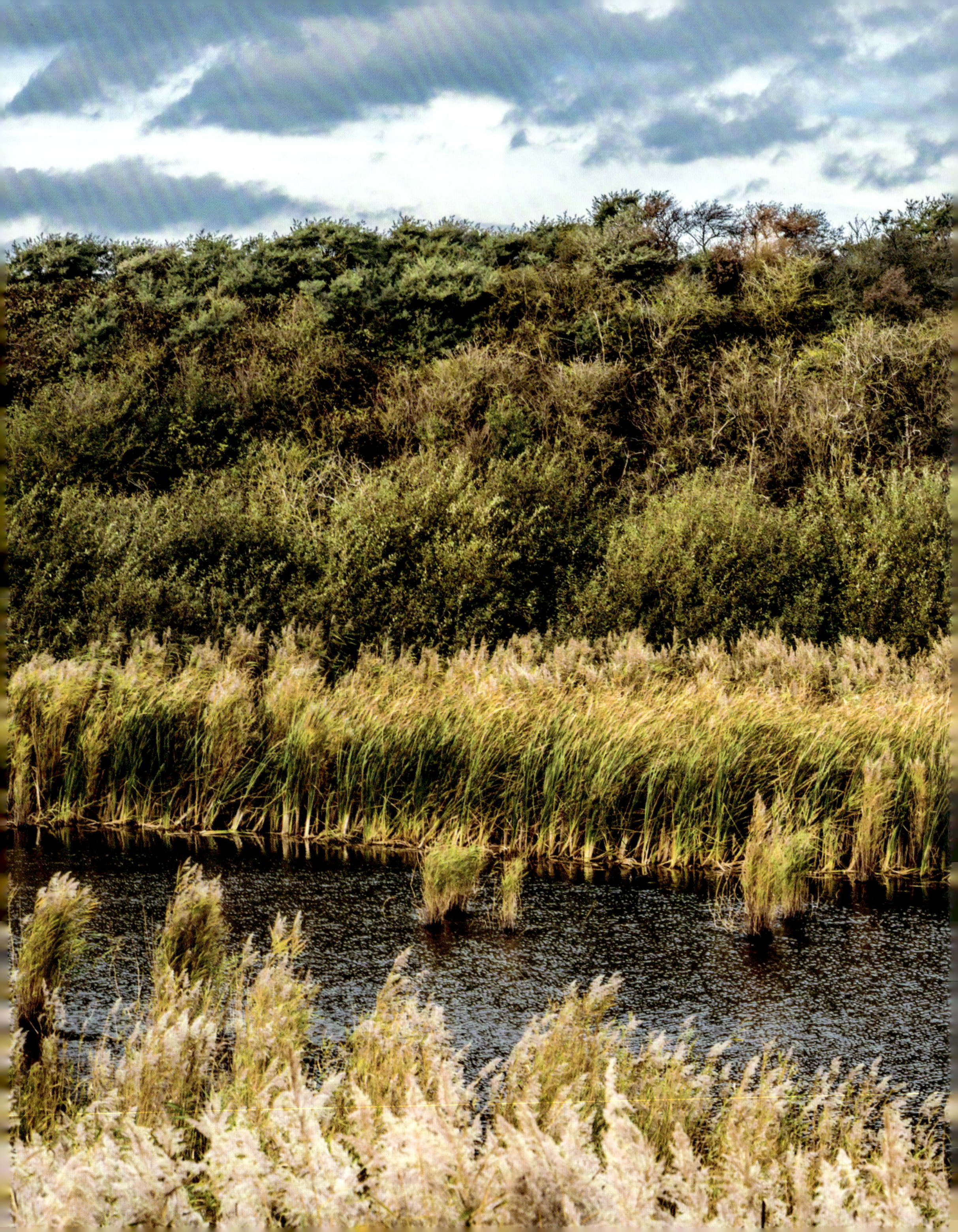

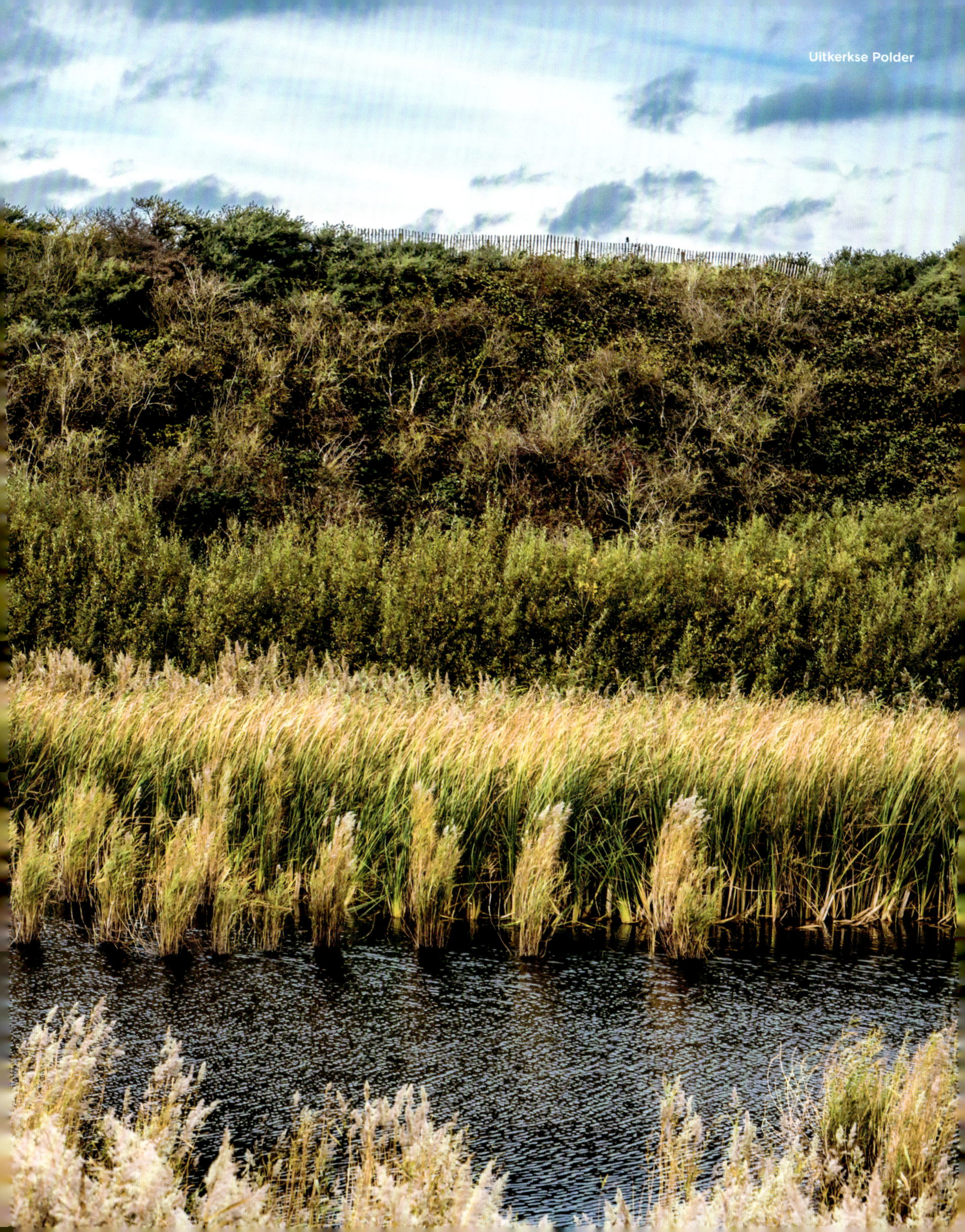
Uitkerkse Polder

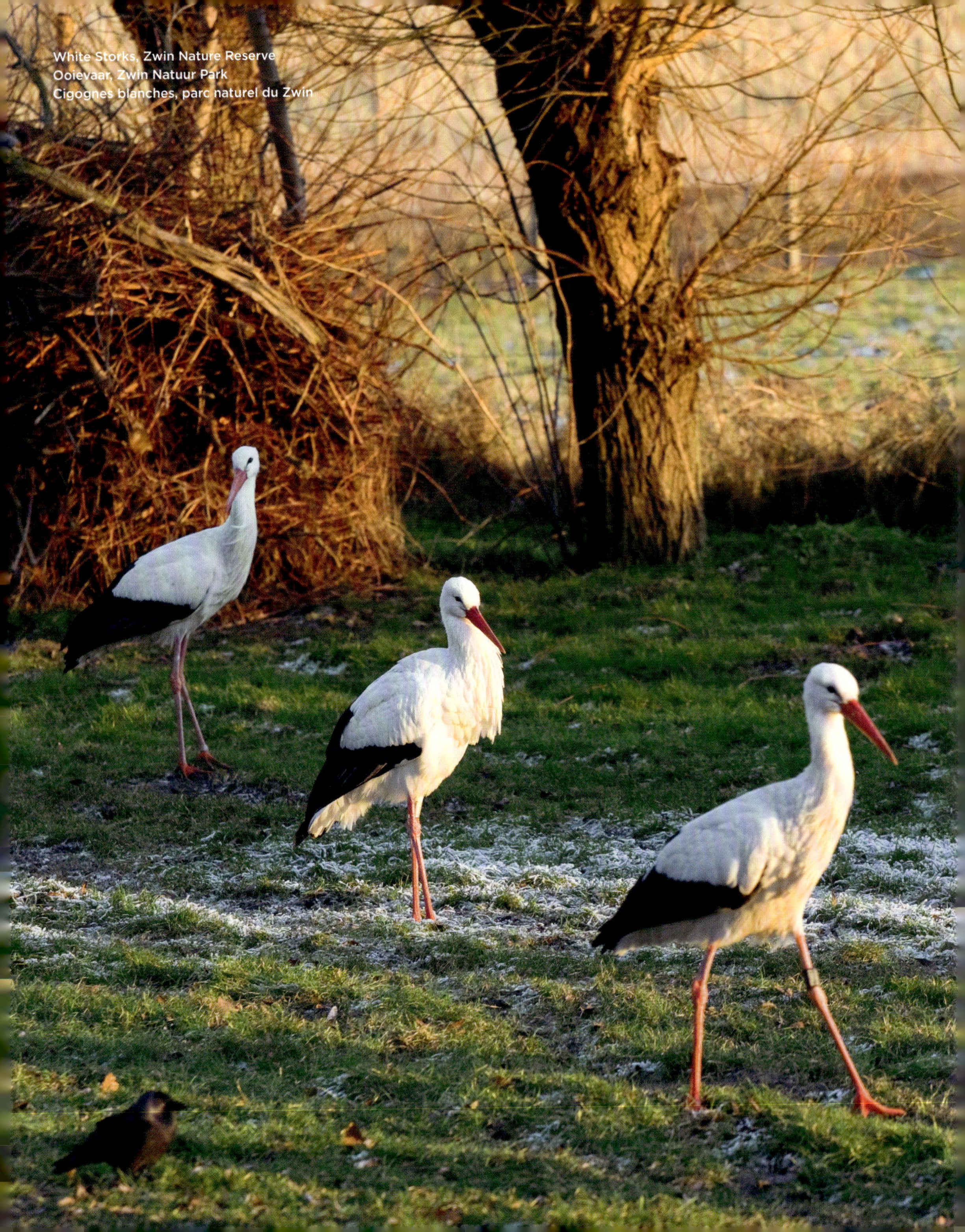

White Storks, Zwin Nature Reserve
Ooievaar, Zwin Natuur Park
Cigognes blanches, parc naturel du Zwin

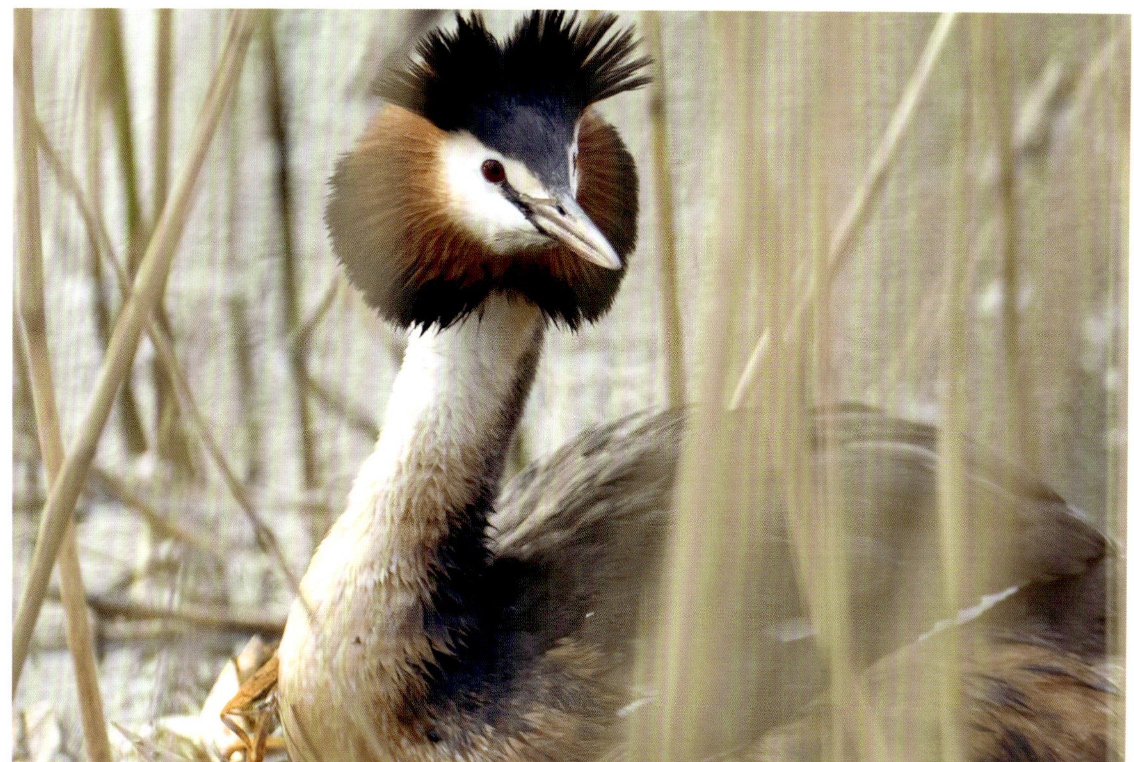

Great crested grebe
Fuut
Grèbe huppé

Unique biosphere reserve

Twice a day at high tide, large quantities of sea water flow into the Zwin. The salty North Sea water provides natural conditions unique in Europe and creates a biotope of silt and salt marshes. The Zwin is therefore the ideal habitat for worms, snails and mussels, which in turn provide food for a wide variety of birds.

Una reserva de biosfera única

Dos veces al día con marea alta, grandes cantidades de agua de mar fluyen hacia el Zwin. El agua salada del Mar del Norte proporciona unas condiciones naturales únicas en Europa y crea un biotopo de limo y marismas saladas. El Zwin es, por lo tanto, el hábitat ideal para gusanos, caracoles y mejillones, que a su vez proporcionan alimento a una gran variedad de aves.

Une réserve de biosphère unique

Deux fois par jour, à marée haute, de grandes quantités d'eau de mer affluent dans le Zwin. L'eau fort salée de la mer du Nord offre des conditions naturelles uniques en Europe et crée un paysage composé de vase et de marais salants. C'est pourquoi le Zwin est un biotope idéal pour les vers, escargots, coquillages, qui alimentent à leur tour les oiseaux les plus divers.

Reserva exclusiva da biosfera

Duas vezes por dia na maré alta, grandes quantidades de água do mar fluem para o Zwin. A água salgada do Mar do Norte proporciona condições naturais únicas na Europa e cria um biótopo de lodo e pântanos salgados. O Zwin é, portanto, o habitat ideal para minhocas, caracóis e mexilhões, que por sua vez fornecem alimento para uma grande variedade de aves.

Einmaliges Biosphären-Reservat

Zwei Mal am Tag strömen bei Flut große Mengen Meerwasser in das Zwin. Das salzhaltige Nordseewasser sorgt für, in Europa einmalige Naturbedingungen und schafft ein Biotop aus Schlick und Salzwiesen. Das Zwin ist deshalb der ideale Lebensraum für Würmer, Schnecken, Muscheln, die wiederum die Nahrung unterschiedlichster Vögel bilden.

Uniek biosfeerreservaat

Twee keer per dag stromen er bij vloed grote hoeveelheden zeewater in het Zwin. Het zouthoudende Noordzeewater zorgt voor unieke natuuromstandigheden in Europa en creëert een biotoop van slib en kwelders. Het Zwin is daarom de ideale leefomgeving voor wormen, slakken en mosselen die op hun beurt weer het voedsel voor diverse vogels verzorgen.

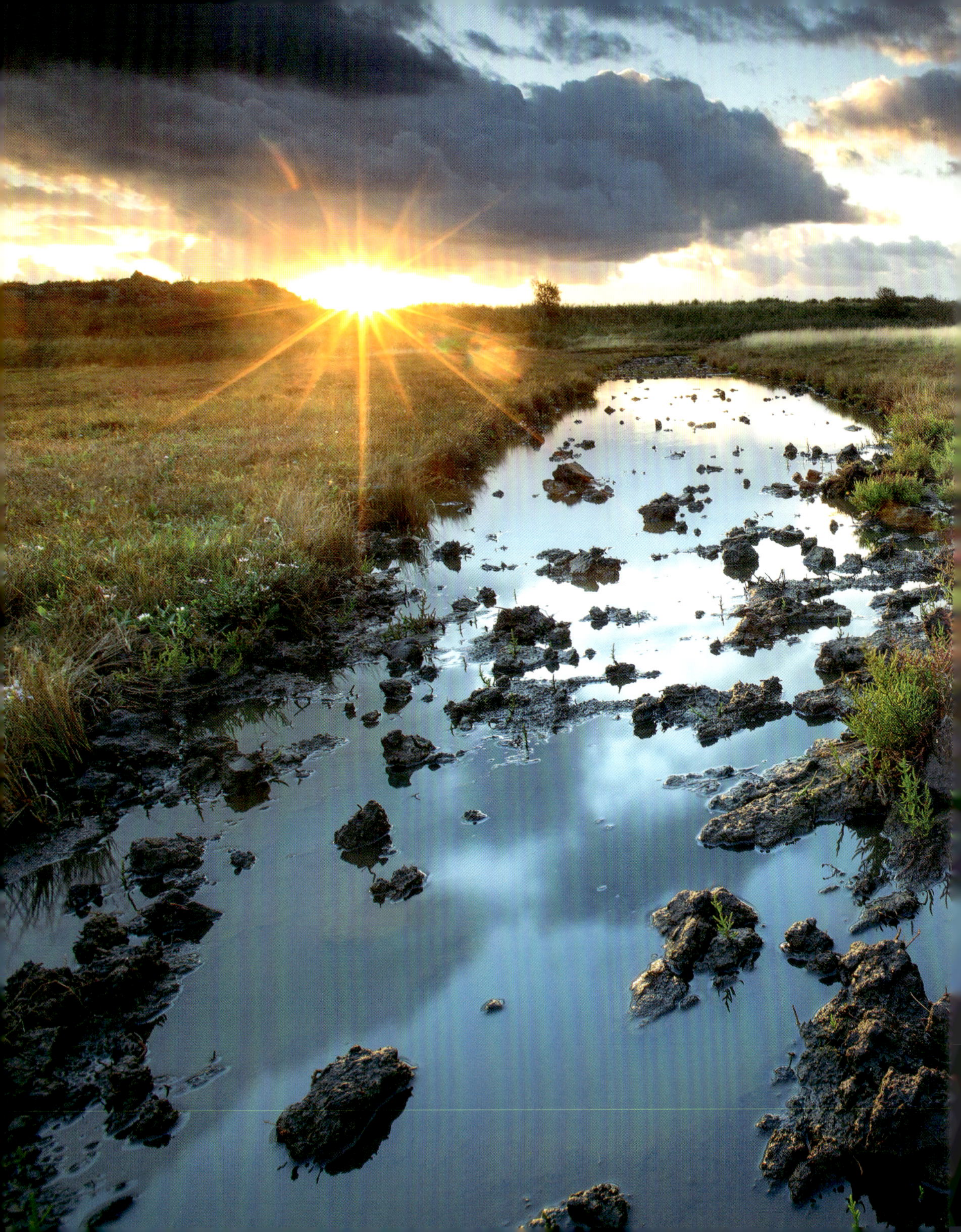

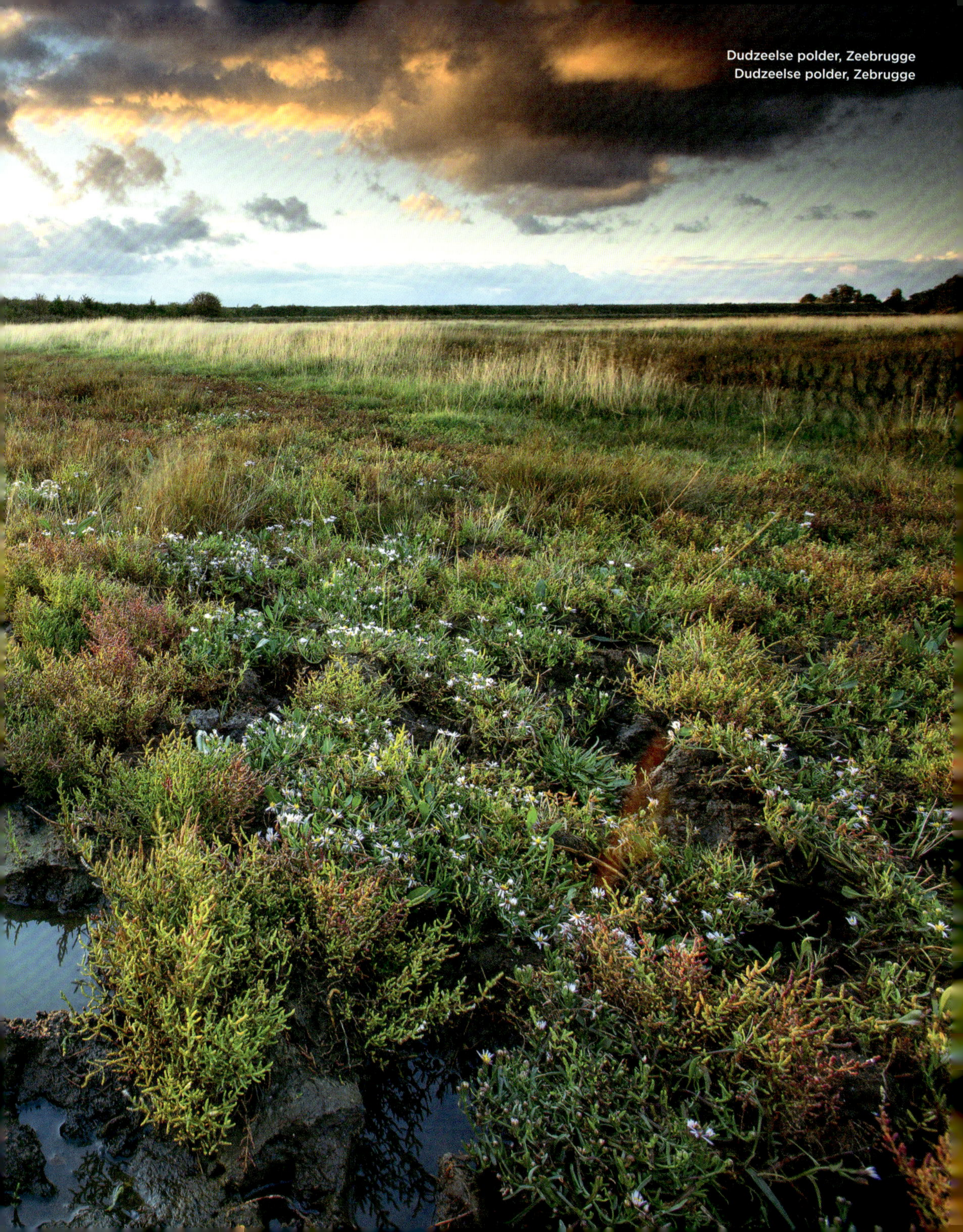

Dudzeelse polder, Zeebrugge
Dudzeelse polder, Zebrugge

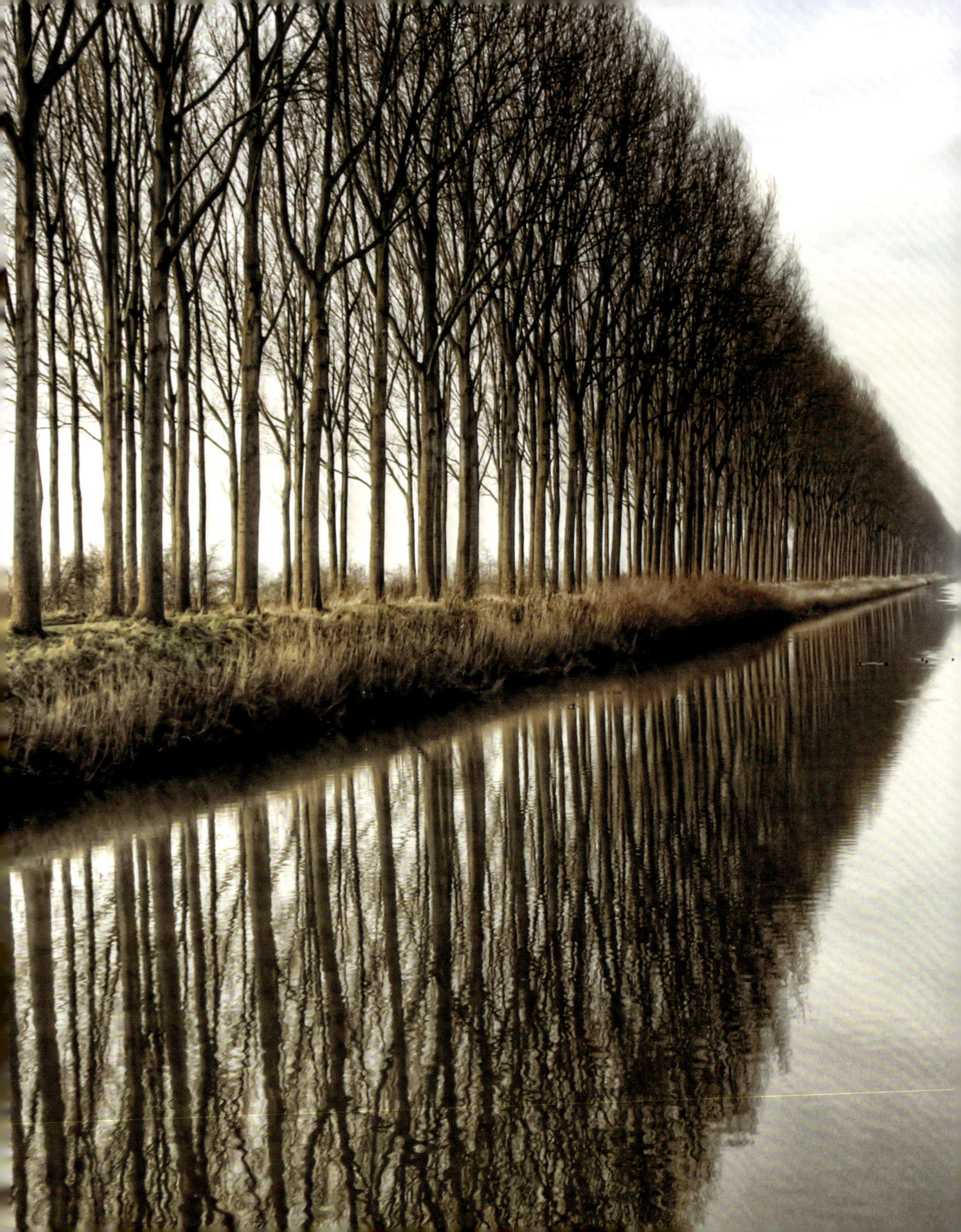

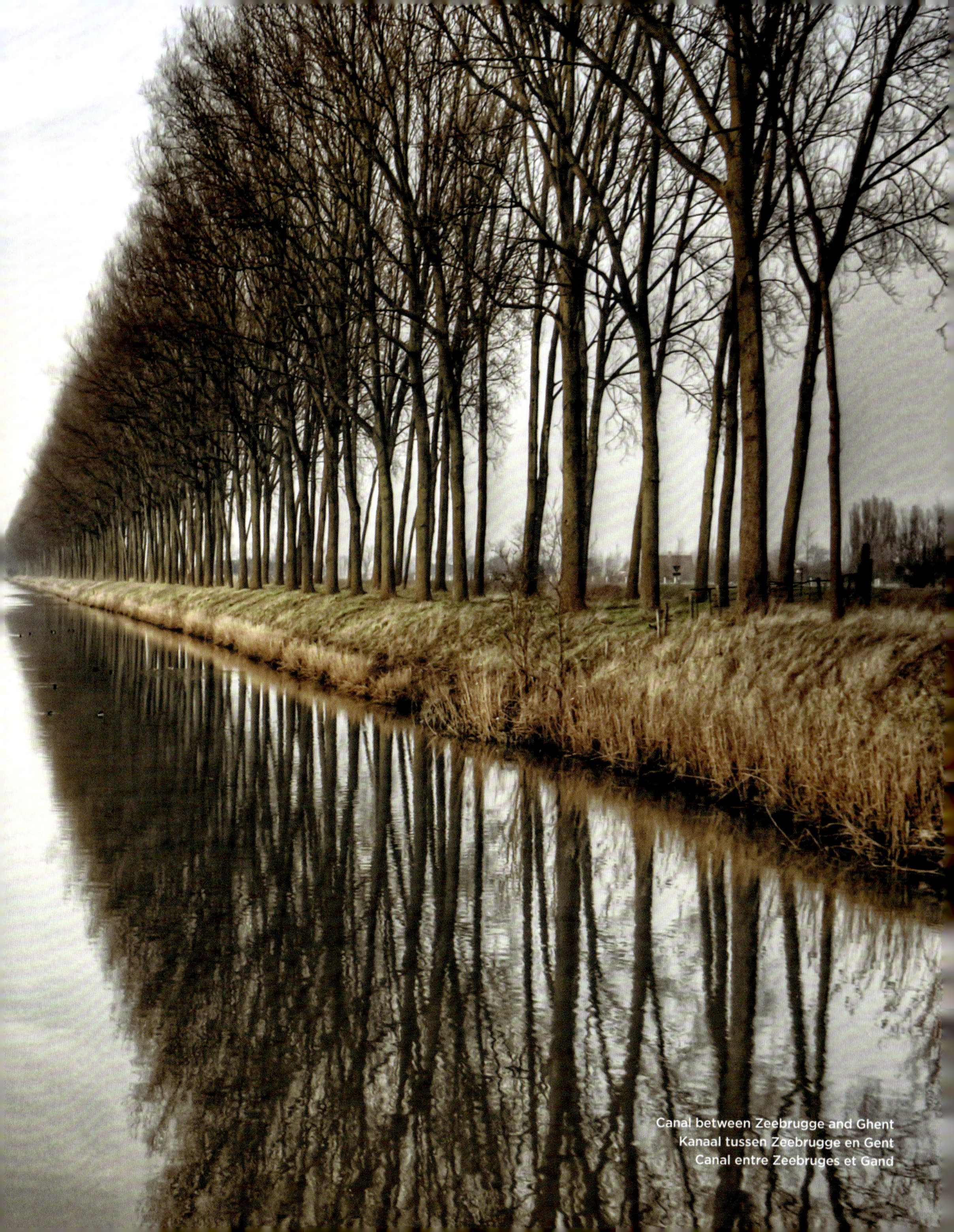

Canal between Zeebrugge and Ghent
Kanaal tussen Zeebrugge en Gent
Canal entre Zeebruges et Gand

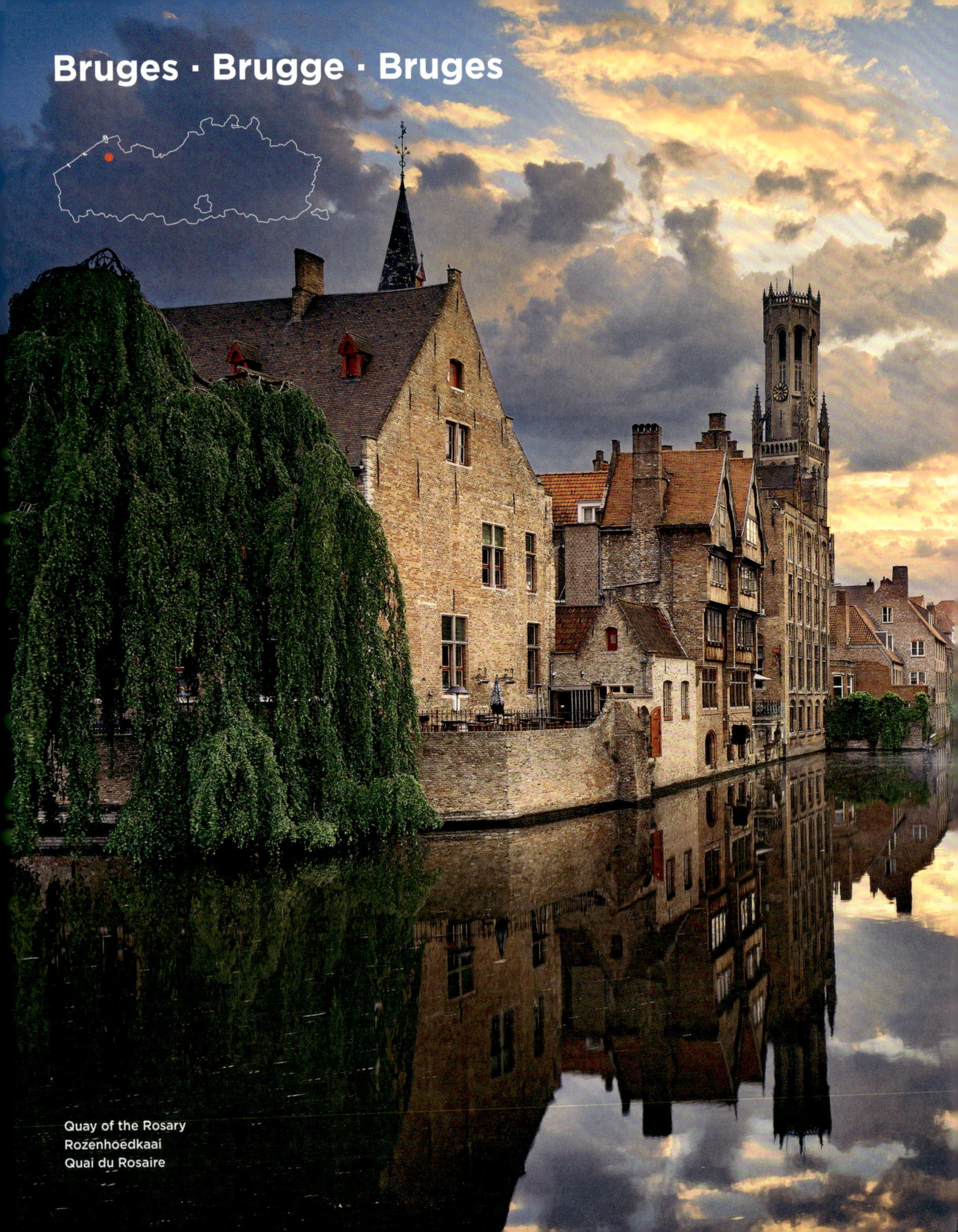

Quay of the Rosary
Rozenhoedkaai
Quai du Rosaire

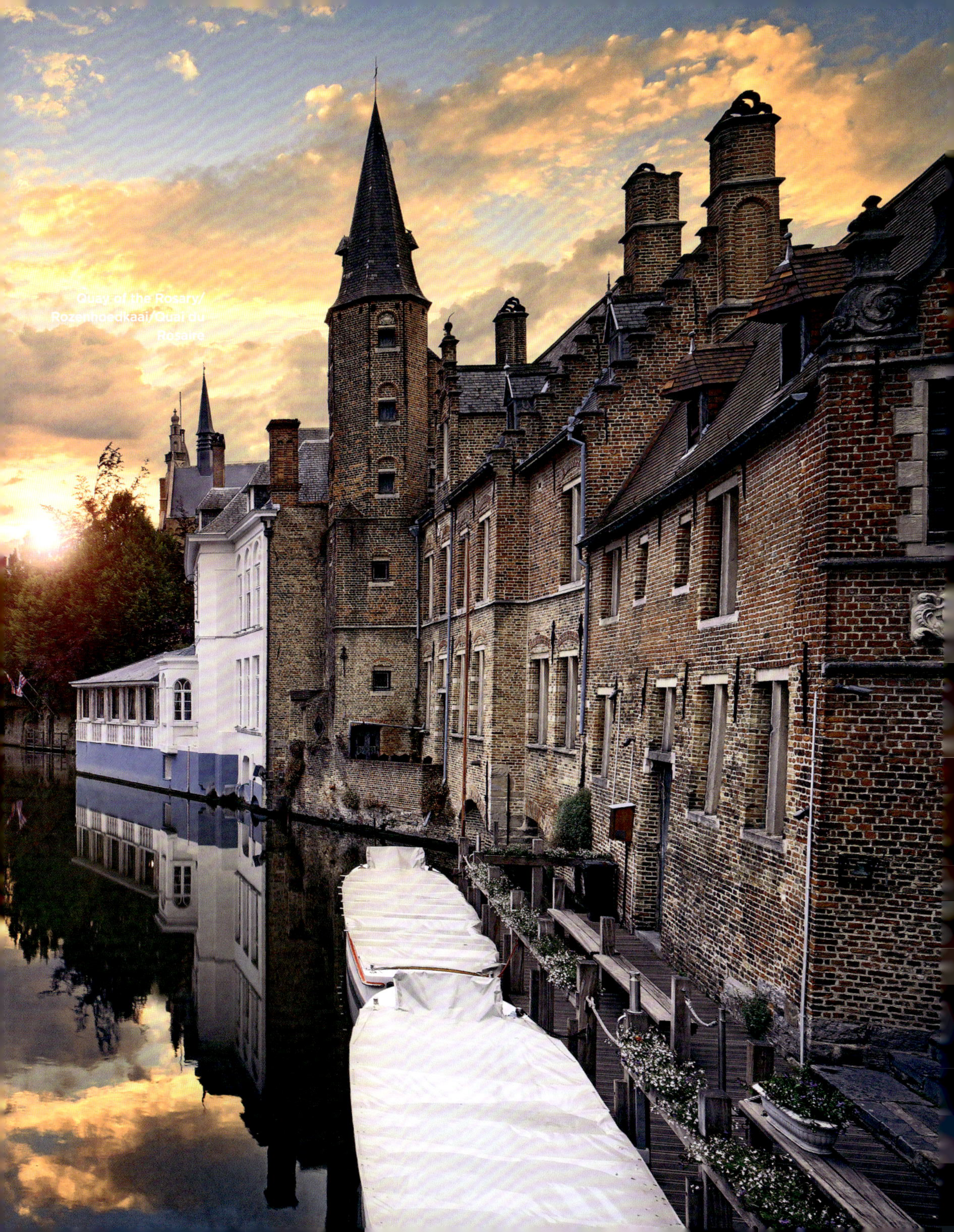
Quay of the Rosary/
Rozenhoedkaai/Quai du
Rosaire

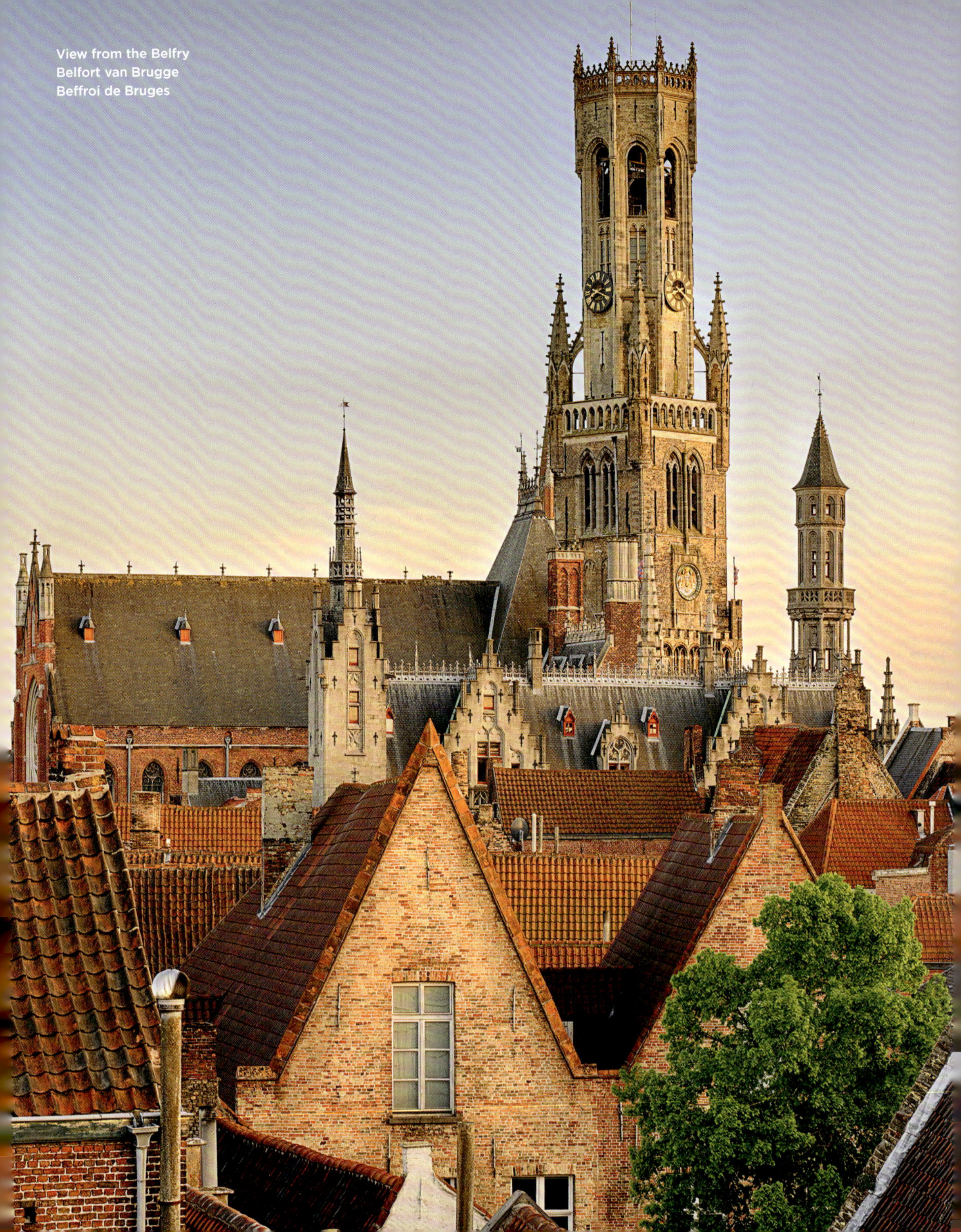

View from the Belfry
Belfort van Brugge
Beffroi de Bruges

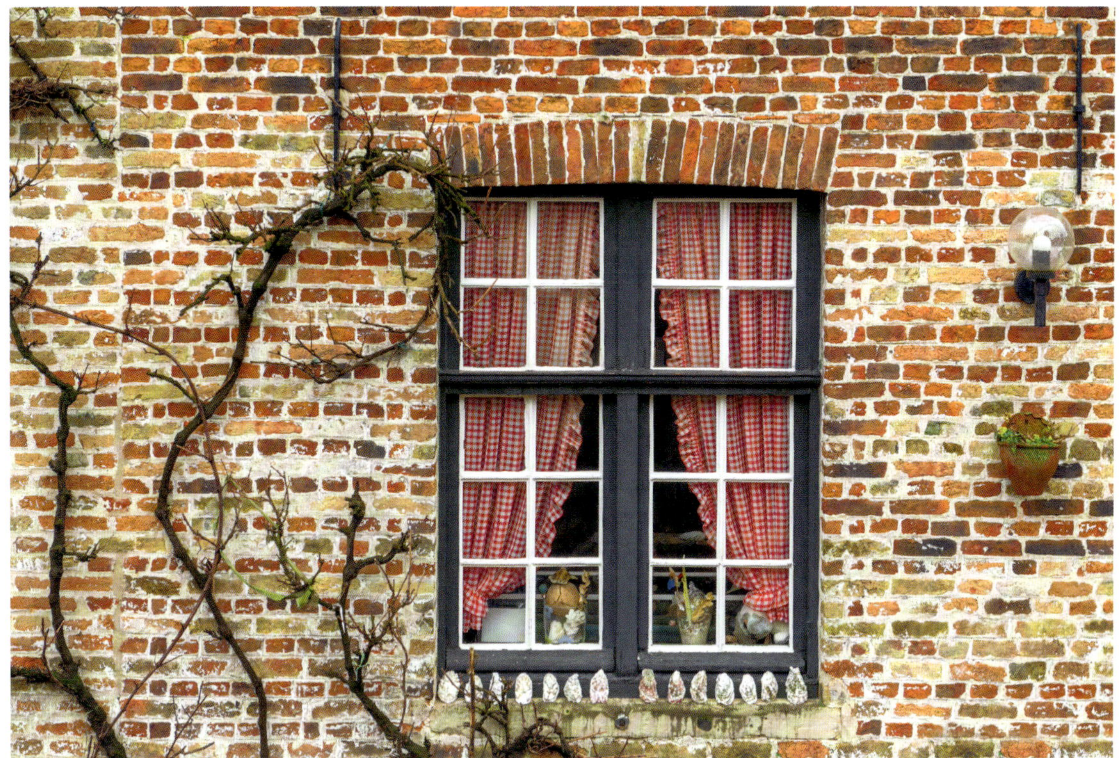

House in the historic city center
Huis in het historisch stadscentrum
Centre-ville historique

Bruges

The battlements of the Gothic Belfry, once a sign of the power of the Bruges merchants, still tower over the flat polder. Today, a visit to the old harbor town, with its canals, gabled houses and Gothic splendour, is like taking a journey back in time to the Middle Ages. Since 2000, the entire old town has been under UNESCO protection.

Brujas

Las almenas del campanario gótico, que en su día fueron una señal del poder de los mercaderes de Brujas, aún se elevan sobre el terreno llano del pólder. Hoy en día, una visita a la antigua ciudad portuaria con sus canales, sus casas a dos aguas y su esplendor gótico es como un viaje en el tiempo a la Edad Media. Desde el año 2000, todo el casco antiguo se encuentra bajo la protección de la UNESCO.

Bruges

De nos jours encore, les créneaux du beffroi gothique, jadis symbole du pouvoir des commerçants brugeois, s'élancent au-dessus du plat pays des polders. Une visite de l'ancienne ville portuaire, avec ses canaux, ses maisons à pignon et ses sompteux monuments gothiques, vous replonge au Moyen Âge. Depuis 2000, l'ensemble de la vieille ville fait partie du patrimoine culturel de l'Unesco.

Bruges

As ameias do campanário gótico, outrora um sinal do poder dos mercadores de Bruges, ainda se elevam sobre a terra plana de polder. Hoje, uma visita à antiga cidade portuária com seus canais, casas empedradas e esplendor gótico é como uma viagem de volta no tempo até a Idade Média. Desde 2000, toda a cidade velha está sob a proteção da UNESCO.

Brügge

Noch immer ragen die Zinnen des gotischen Belfrieds, einst ein Zeichen der Macht der Brügger Kaufleute, über das flache Polderland. Heute ist ein Besuch der alten Hafenstadt mit ihren Grachten, Giebelhäusern und gotischen Prachtbauten wie eine Zeitreise ins Mittelalter. Seit dem Jahr 2000 steht die gesamte Altstadt unter dem Schutz der UNESCO.

Brugge

Nog altijd torenen de kantelen van het gotische belfort, ooit een teken van de macht van de Brugse kooplieden, boven het vlakke polderland uit. Vandaag de dag is een bezoek aan de oude havenstad met zijn grachten, gevels en gotische pracht en praal als een tijdreis naar de Middeleeuwen. Sinds 2000 staat de complete oude stad onder UNESCO-bescherming.

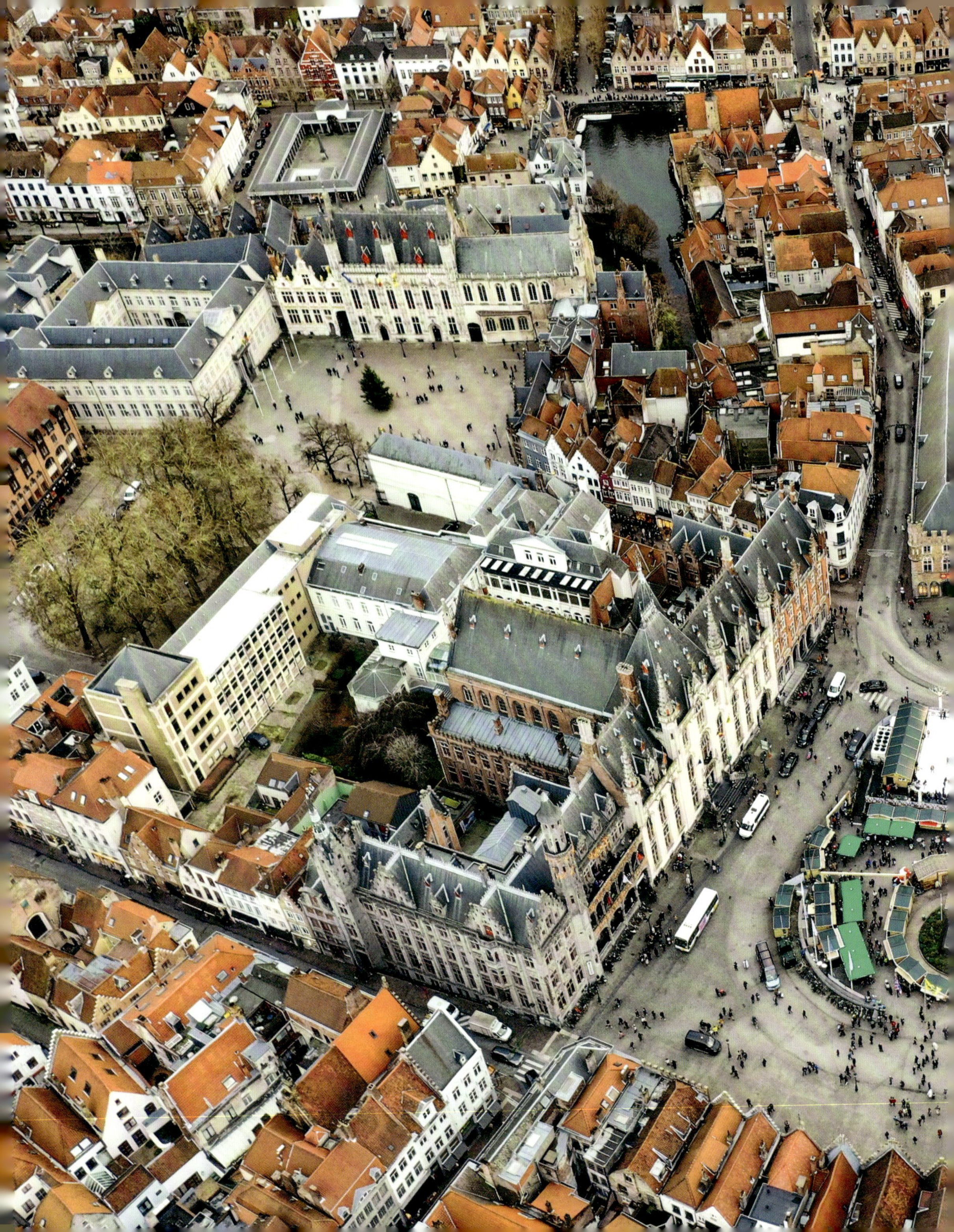

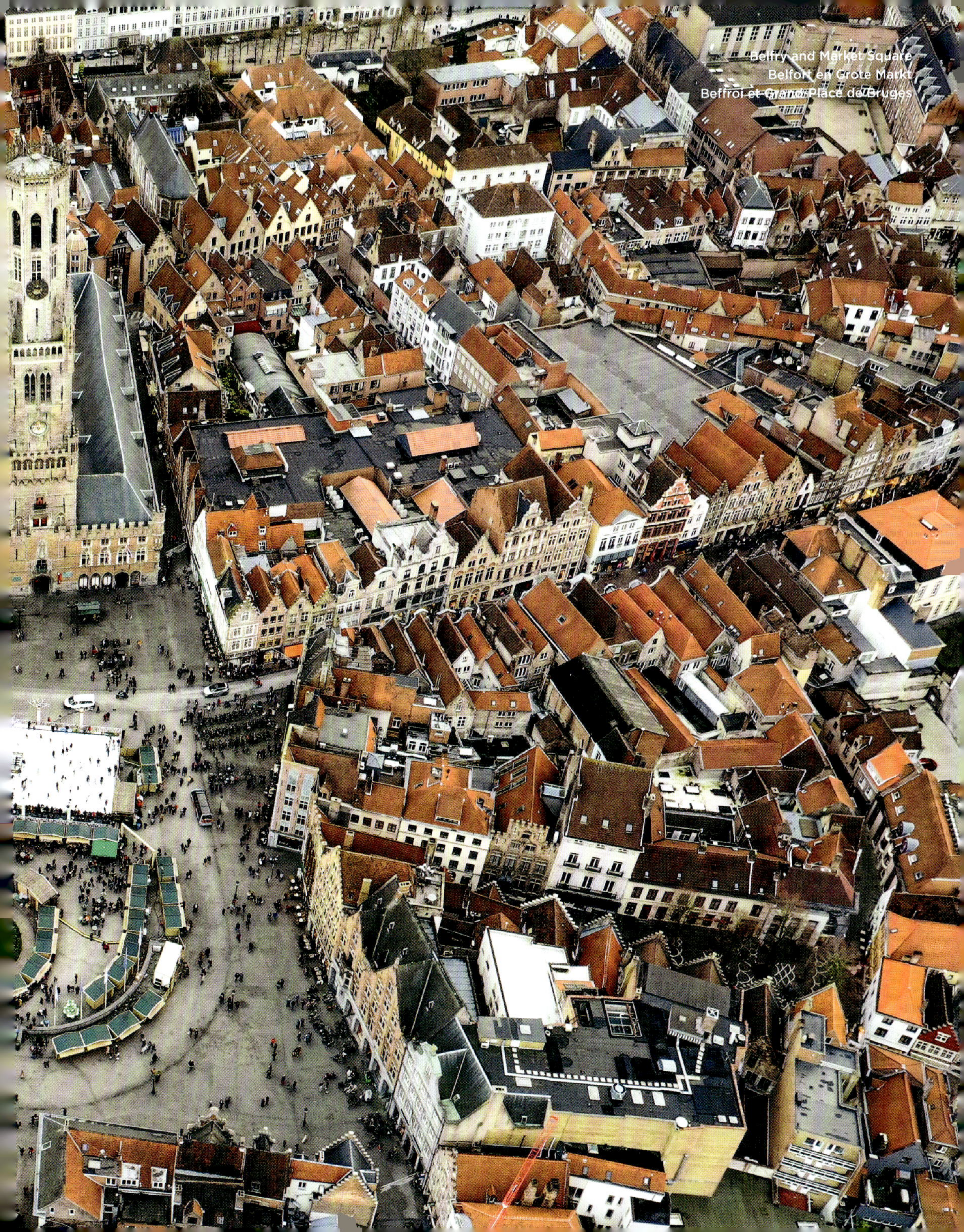

Belfry and Market Square
Belfort en Grote Markt
Beffroi et Grand Place de Bruges

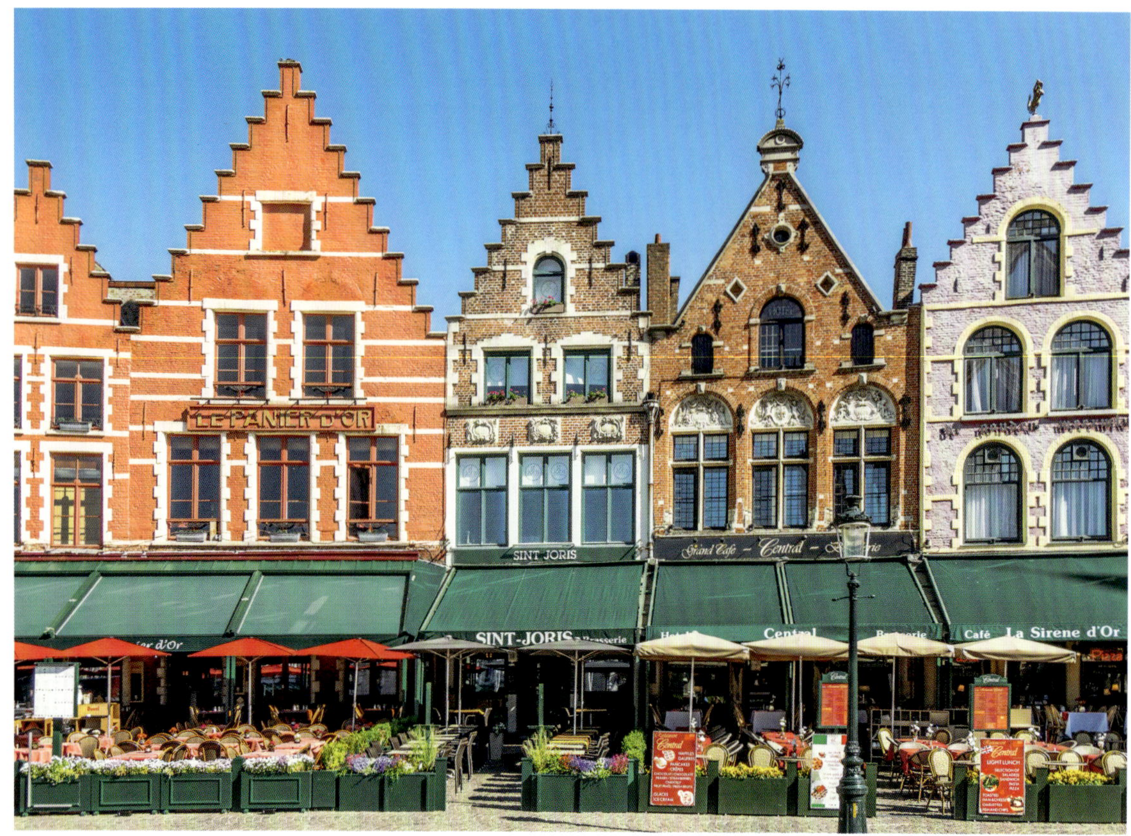

Market Square
Grote Markt
Grande-Place de Bruges

Market and Belfry

Directly on the central market square, the Grote Markt, the Belfry watches over the enormous cloth halls in which the most important export goods of Flanders, linen and wool fabrics, were stored. Visitors who climb the 366 steps of the octagonal Belfry can see as far as the North Sea on a clear day. The Grote Markt at the foot of the Belfry is lined by picturesque gabled houses and the magnificent Gothic Provinciaal Hof. Restaurants, cafés and bistros have moved into the former merchants' houses, but, as in centuries past, the market is still held there every Wednesday

Marché et Beffroi

Donnant directement sur la place centrale du marché, la Grand-Place, le beffroi veille sur l'imposante halle aux draps, qui abritait jadis des étoffes de lin et de laine, principal bien d'exportation des Flandres. Par temps dégagé, les visiteurs gravissant les 366 marches de la tour octogonale jouissent d'une vue s'étendant jusqu'à la mer du Nord. Au pied du beffroi, la Grand-Place est délimitée par de pittoresques maisons à pignons et un somptueux palais provincial gothique. Restaurants, cafés et bistrots ont investi les anciennes maisons de marchands. Mais le marché, lui, se tient tous les mercredis, depuis des siècles.

Markt und Belfried

Direkt am zentralen Marktplatz, dem Grote Markt, wacht der Belfried über die gewaltigen Tuchhallen, in denen das wichtigste Exportgut Flanderns, Leinen- und Wollstoffe, gelagert wurde. Besucher, die die 366 Stufen des oktogonalen Turms erklimmen, können an klaren Tagen bis an die Nordsee schauen. Der Grote Markt zu Füßen des Belfrieds wird von malerischen Giebelhäusern und dem prächtigen gotischen Provinzialhaus gesäumt. In die ehemaligen Kaufmannshäuser sind Restaurants, Cafés und Bistros eingezogen. Aber, wie schon vor Jahrhunderten, wird dort noch immer jeden Mittwoch Markt abgehalten.

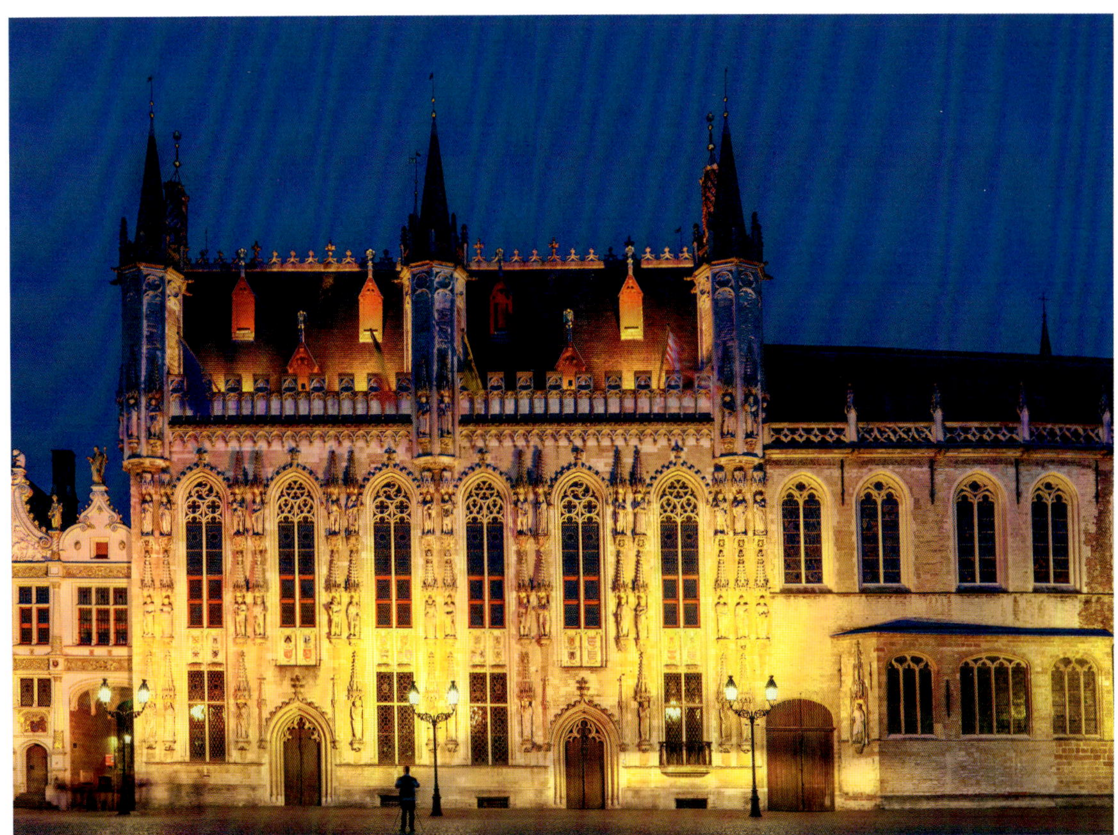

Bruges City Hall
Stadhuis van Brugge
Hôtel de ville de Bruges

Mercado y campanario

Directamente en la plaza central del mercado, el Grote Markt, Belfried vigila las enormes salas de telas en las que se almacenaba el bien de exportación más importante de Flandes, el lino y la lana. Los visitantes que suben los 366 escalones de la torre octogonal pueden ver hasta el Mar del Norte si el día está despejado. El Grote Markt, situado al pie del Belfried, está rodeado de pintorescas casas a dos aguas y del magnífico Juzgado Provincial gótico. En las casas de los antiguos comerciantes se han instalado restaurantes, cafeterías y bares. Pero, como hace siglos, el mercado sigue celebrándose allí todos los miércoles.

Mercado e campanário

Diretamente na praça central do mercado velho, o Grote Markt, o campanário, vigia os enormes salões de pano onde se armazenava o mais importante produto de exportação da Flandres, linho e tecidos de lã. Os visitantes que sobem os 366 degraus da torre octogonal podem ver todo o caminho até o Mar do Norte em um dia claro. O Grote Markt, ao pé do campanário, está cercado por casas pitorescas de duas águas e pela magnífica casa provincial gótica. Restaurantes, cafés e bistrôs mudaram-se para as antigas casas dos comerciantes. Mas, como acontecia há séculos atrás, o mercado continua acontecendo ainda lá todas as quartas feiras.

Markt en belfort

Direct op de centrale marktplaats, de Grote Markt, waakt het belfort over de enorme lakenhallen waarin het belangrijkste exportgoed van Vlaanderen, linnen en wol, werd opgeslagen. Bezoekers die de 366 treden van de achthoekige toren beklimmen, kunnen op heldere dagen tot aan de Noordzee kijken. De Grote Markt aan de voet van het belfort wordt omringd door pittoreske gevels en het prachtige gotische Provinciaal Hof. Restaurants, cafés en bistro's zijn de voormalige koopmanshuizen binnengetrokken. Maar, net zoals eeuwen geleden, wordt daar nog iedere woensdag markt gehouden.

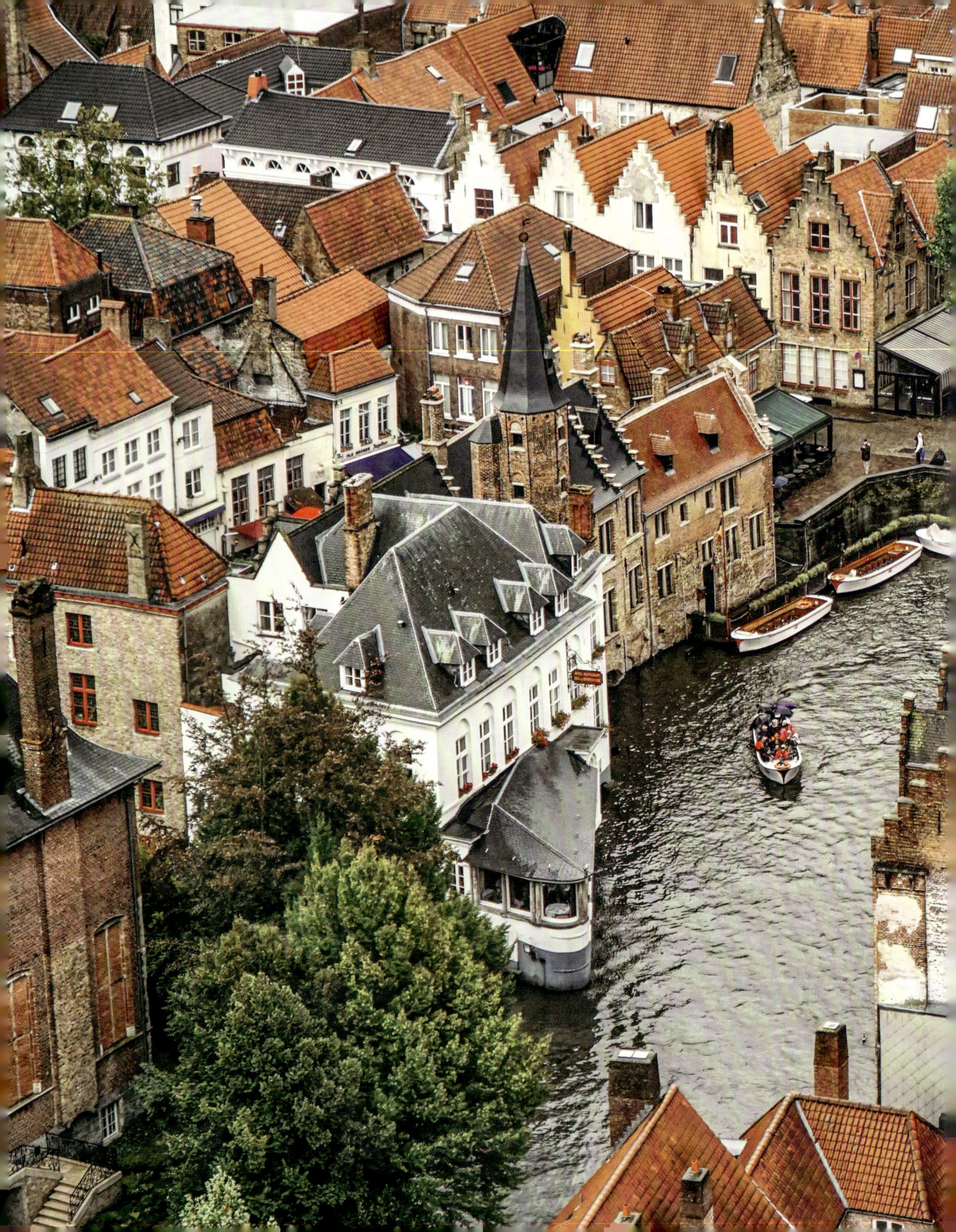

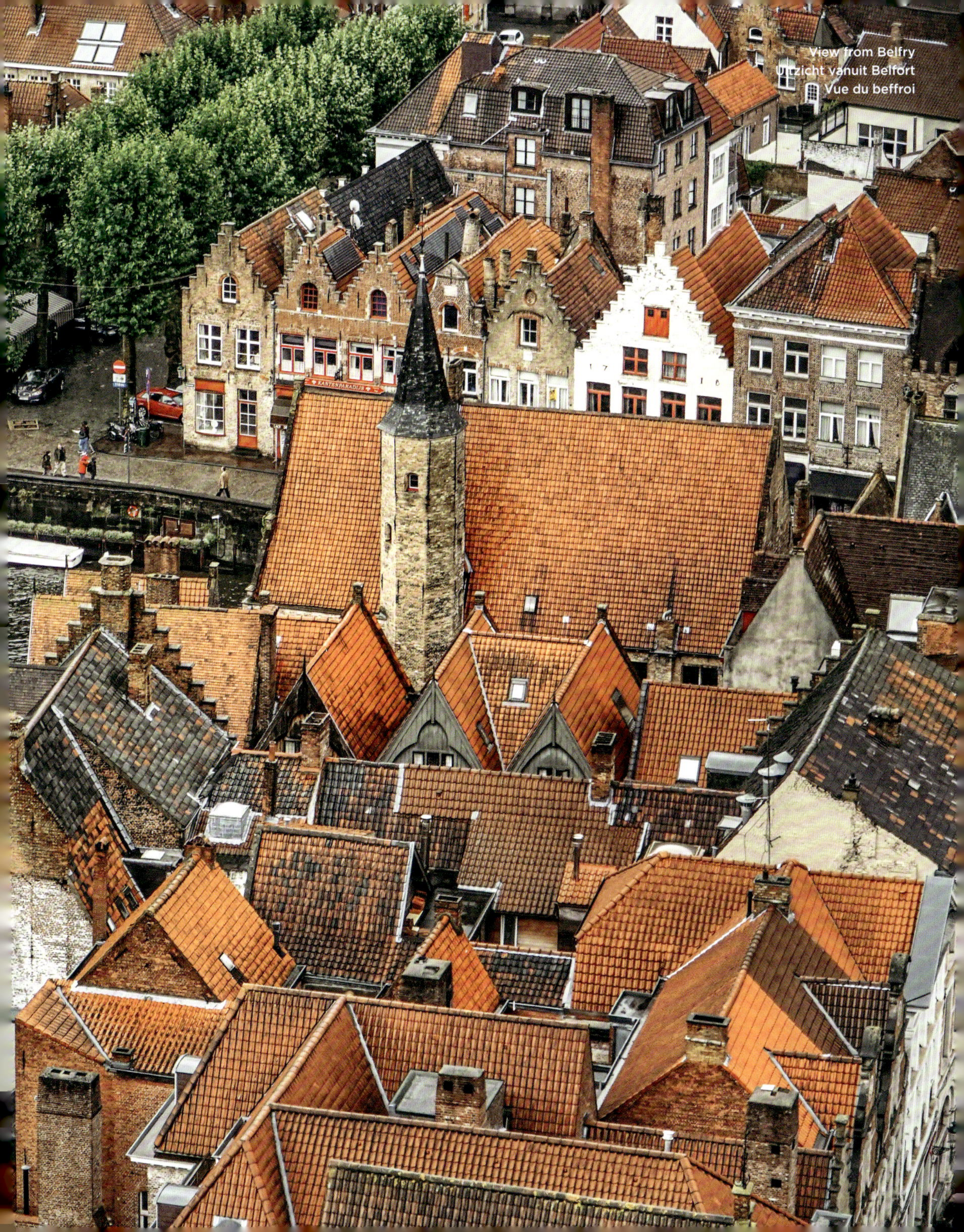

View from Belfry
Uitzicht vanuit Belfort
Vue du beffroi

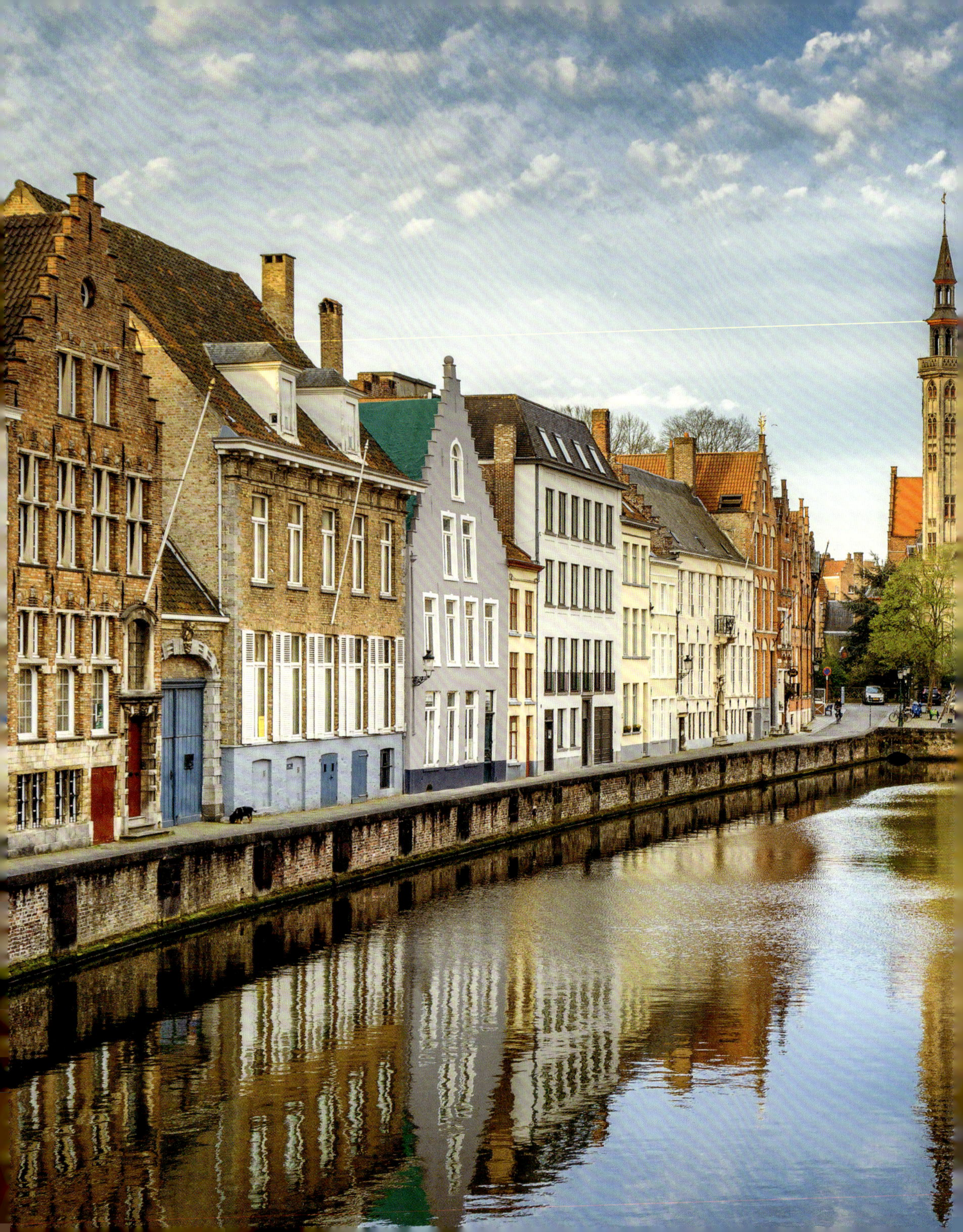

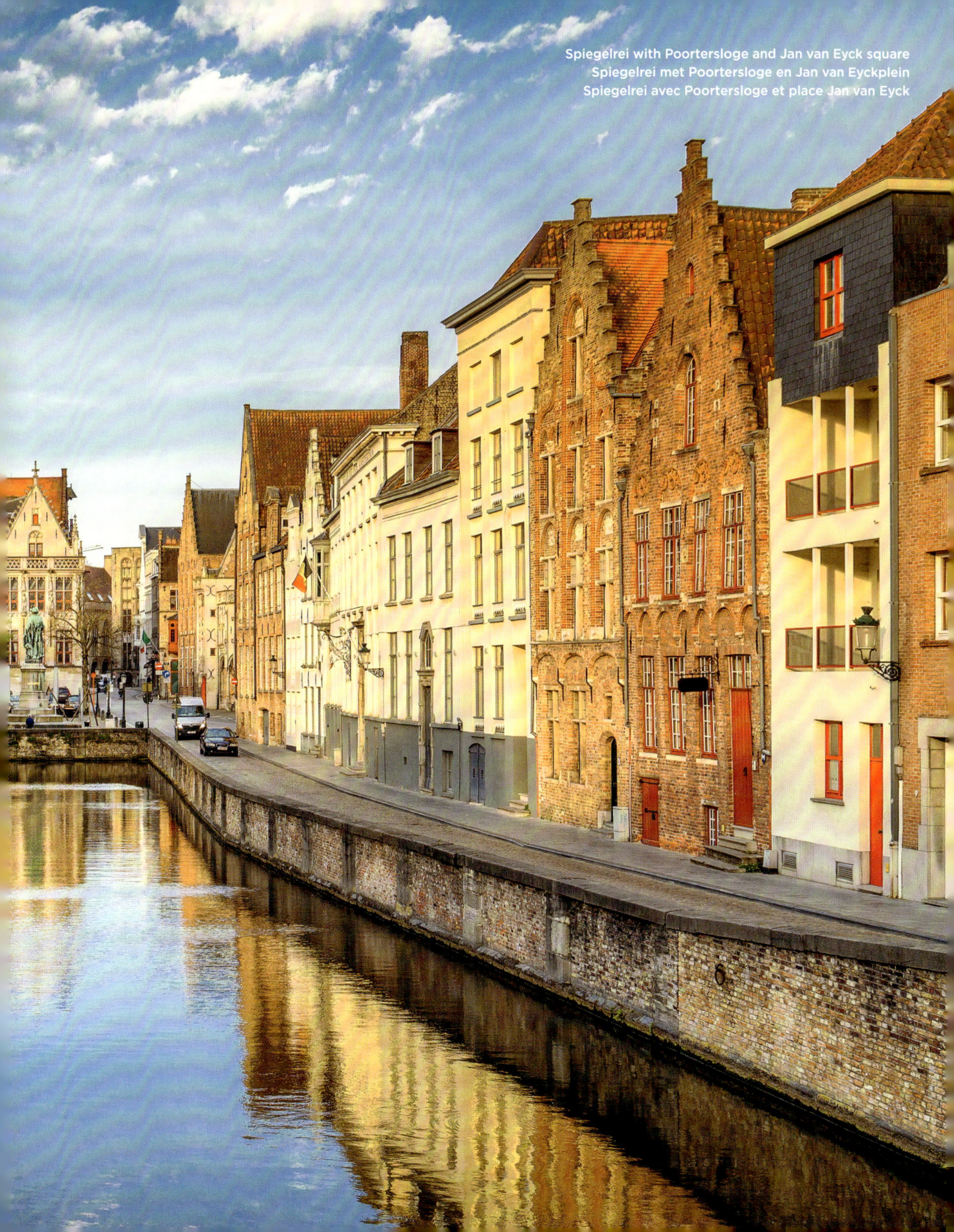
Spiegelrei with Poortersloge and Jan van Eyck square
Spiegelrei met Poortersloge en Jan van Eyckplein
Spiegelrei avec Poortersloge et place Jan van Eyck

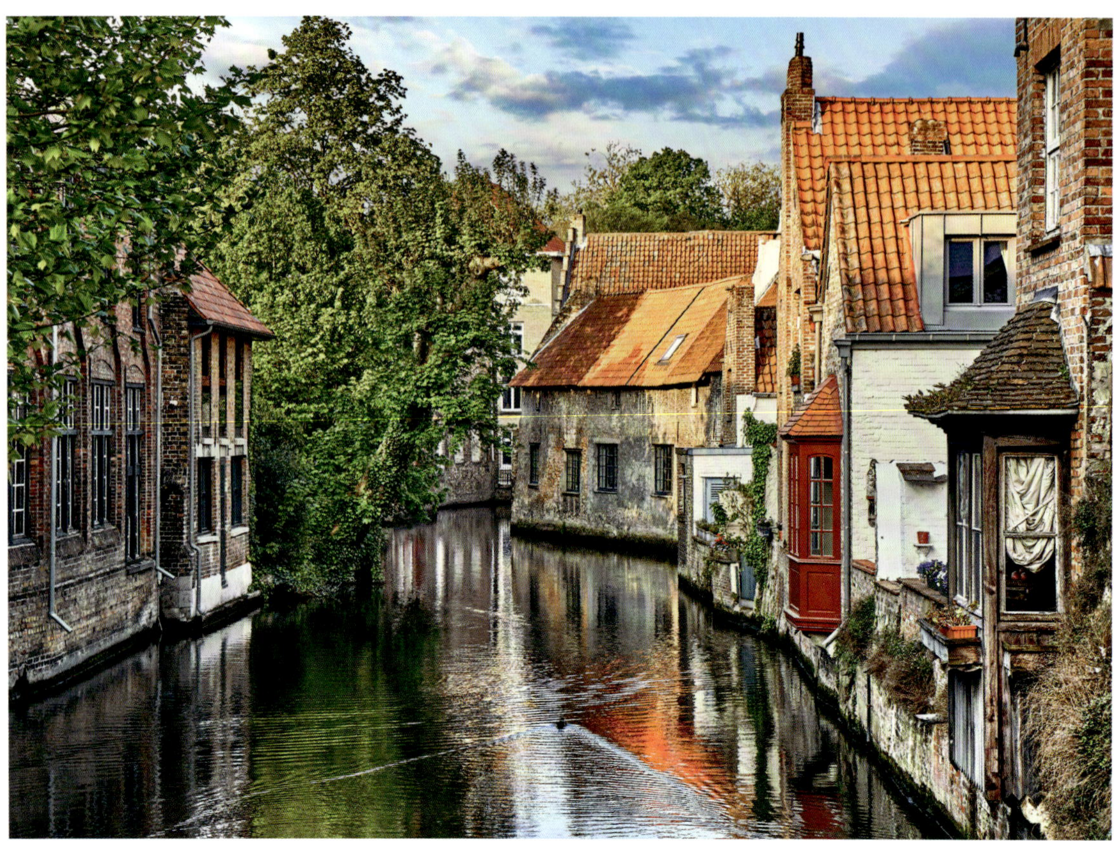

Quay of the Rosary
Rozenhoedkaai
Quai du Rosaire

Streets of the Middle Ages

Whether cloth, wool or grain, all traded goods were transported by ship during Bruges' heyday, and canals were more important than roads. Canals run through the former port city like veins, lined by ancient houses, bridges and gardens. The picturesque squares seem even more attractive if one admires them from the water. During a boat tour on the canals, one gets the feel of times long past, especially if ducking one's head under some bridges. There are altogether five moorings and the multilingual canal tours last approximately half an hour.

Rues médiévales

Qu'il s'agisse d'étoffes, de laine ou de céréales, toutes les marchandises étaient transportées en bateau à l'époque florissante de Bruges. Les canaux revêtaient plus d'importance que les rues. Bordés de maisonnettes, de ponts et de jardins d'une autre époque, ils sillonnent, telles des veines, l'ancienne ville portuaire. Les pittoresques places ont d'autant plus de charme lorsqu'on les contemple sur l'eau. Une promenade en bateau dans les canaux vous fait plonger dans des temps révolus, surtout lorsque certains ponts vous font baisser la tête. Il y a cinq embarcadères en tout et les visites plurilingues des canaux durent environ une demi-heure.

Straßen des Mittelalters

Ob Tuche, Wolle oder Korn, alle Handelsgüter wurden in der Blütezeit Brügges mit Schiffen transportiert. Kanäle waren wichtiger als Straßen. Grachten verlaufen durch die einstige Hafenstadt wie Adern, gesäumt von uralten Häuschen, Brücken und Gärten. Die malerischen Plätze gewinnen noch an Reiz, wenn man sie vom Wasser aus bewundert. Bei einer Bootstour auf den Grachten nimmt man die Perspektive längst vergangener Zeiten ein, besonders wenn man unter manchen Brücken den Kopf einziehen muss. Es gibt insgesamt fünf Anlegestellen und die mehrsprachigen Grachtentouren dauern rund eine halbe Stunde.

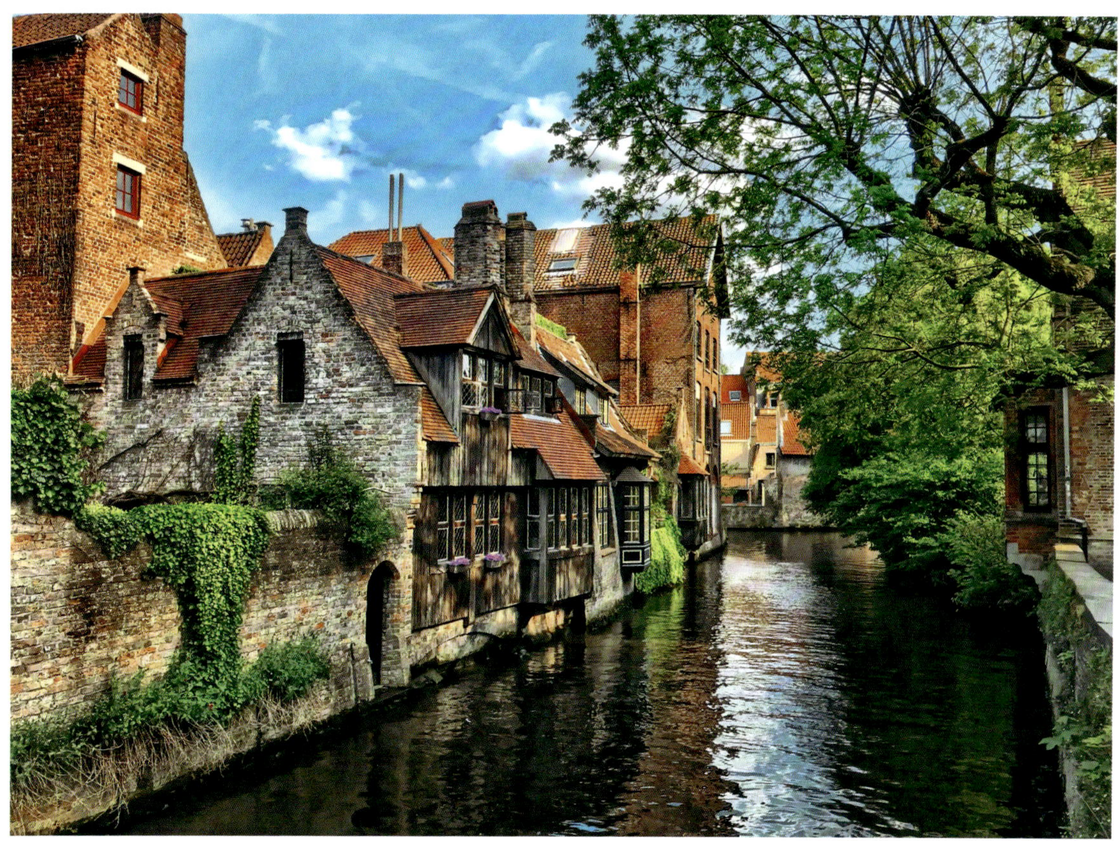

Dijver

Calles de la Edad Media

Ya sea tela, lana o grano, todos los productos comerciales se transportaban en barco durante el apogeo de Brujas. Los canales eran más importantes que las carreteras. Los canales atraviesan la antigua ciudad portuaria como venas, bordeados por antiguas casas, puentes y jardines. Las pintorescas plazas son aún más atractivas si se admiran desde el agua. Durante un paseo en barco por los canales, uno toma se remonta a tiempos pasados, especialmente cuando hay que bajar la cabeza para pasar por debajo de algunos puentes. Hay un total de cinco amarres y los recorridos multilingües por los canales duran aproximadamente media hora.

Ruas da Idade Média

Sejam tecidos, lã ou grãos, todos os produtos comercializados eram transportados por navio durante o apogeu de Bruges. Os canais eram mais importantes que as estradas. Os canais atravessam a antiga cidade portuária como veias, alinhadas com antigas casas, pontes e jardins. As praças pitorescas são ainda mais atraentes se as admirarmos da água. Durante um passeio de barco nos canais, a pessoa passa a ter a perspectiva de tempos muito passados, especialmente se tiver que retrair a cabeça debaixo de algumas pontes. No total, existem cinco ancoradouros e os passeios pelo canal multilingue duram aproximadamente meia hora.

Middeleeuwse straten

Lakens, wol of graan, alle handelsgoederen werden tijdens de hoogtijdagen van Brugge per schip vervoerd. De kanalen waren belangrijker dan de straten. Grachten lopen als aders door de voormalige havenstad, omringd door oeroude huisjes, bruggen en tuinen. De schilderachtige pleinen zijn nog aantrekkelijker als ze vanaf het water worden bewonderd. Tijdens een boottocht over de grachten heeft men het perspectief van lang vervlogen tijden, vooral als je onder enkele bruggen het hoofd moet intrekken. Er zijn in totaal vijf aanlegplaatsen en de meertalige grachtrondvaarten duren ongeveer een half uur.

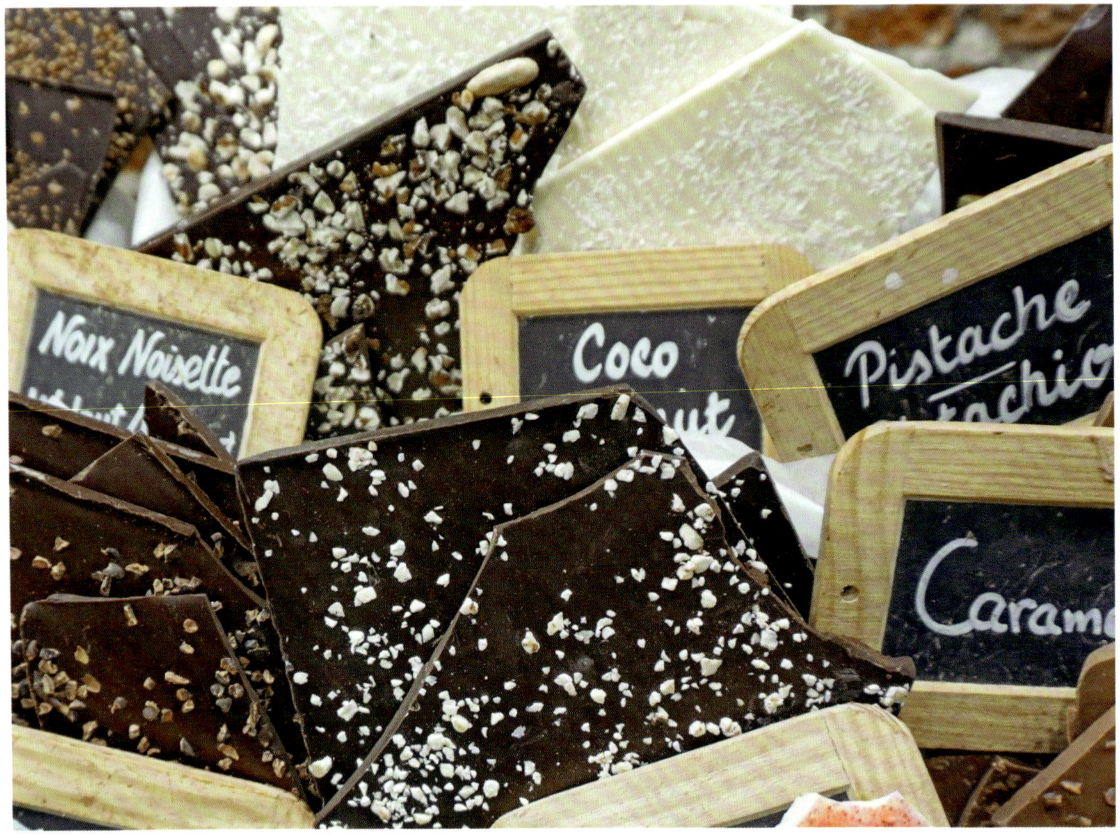

Belgian Chocolate
Belgische chocolade
Chocolat belge

Chocolate City Bruges

Almost everywhere in the old town, you can smell chocolate. In the Chocolate Museum, thick chocolate steams in the cups and 52 confectioneries tempt you with incredible chocolate creations. With cannabis or bacon, colourful poison frogs or skulls - hardly anyone who comes to Bruges goes home without a sweet souvenir. The star of the chocolatiers, Dominique Persoone, has a Michelin star and designed a "chocolate-snorter" for the Rolling Stones. The chocolate fever really began with Jean Neuhaus, who created the first praline in Brussels in 1912.

Bruges, ville du chocolat

Une douce odeur cacaotée plane dans presque tous les recoins de la vieille ville. Un épais chocolat fume dans les tasses au musée du Chocolat et 52 chocolateries vous attirent avec leurs délirantes créations pralinées. Qu'elles soient agrémentées de cannabis ou de lard, de phyllobates terribles ou de têtes de mort, difficile de repartir de Bruges sans l'un de ces charmants souvenirs en poche. La star des chocolatiers, Dominique Persoone, a décroché une étoile Michelin et inventé pour les Rolling Stones une machine à sniffer du chocolat. La fièvre chocolatée commença avec Jean Neuhaus, qui créa la première praline à Bruxelles en 1912.

Brügge Schokoladen-Stadt

Fast überall in der Altstadt kann man Schokolade schnuppern. Im Schokoladenmuseum dampft dickflüssige Schokolade in den Tassen und 52 Chocolaterien locken mit wahnwitzigen Pralinenkreationen. Mit Cannabis oder Speck, bunte Giftfrösche oder Totenköpfe - kaum einer, der nach Brügge kommt, fährt ohne ein süßes Andenken wieder nach Hause. Der Star der Chocolatiers, Dominique Persoone, hat einen Michelin-Stern ergattert und den Rolling Stones ein Schokoladen-Katapult für die Nase entworfen. Das Schokoladenfieber begann mit Jean Neuhaus, der in Brüssel im Jahr 1912 die erste Praline kreierte.

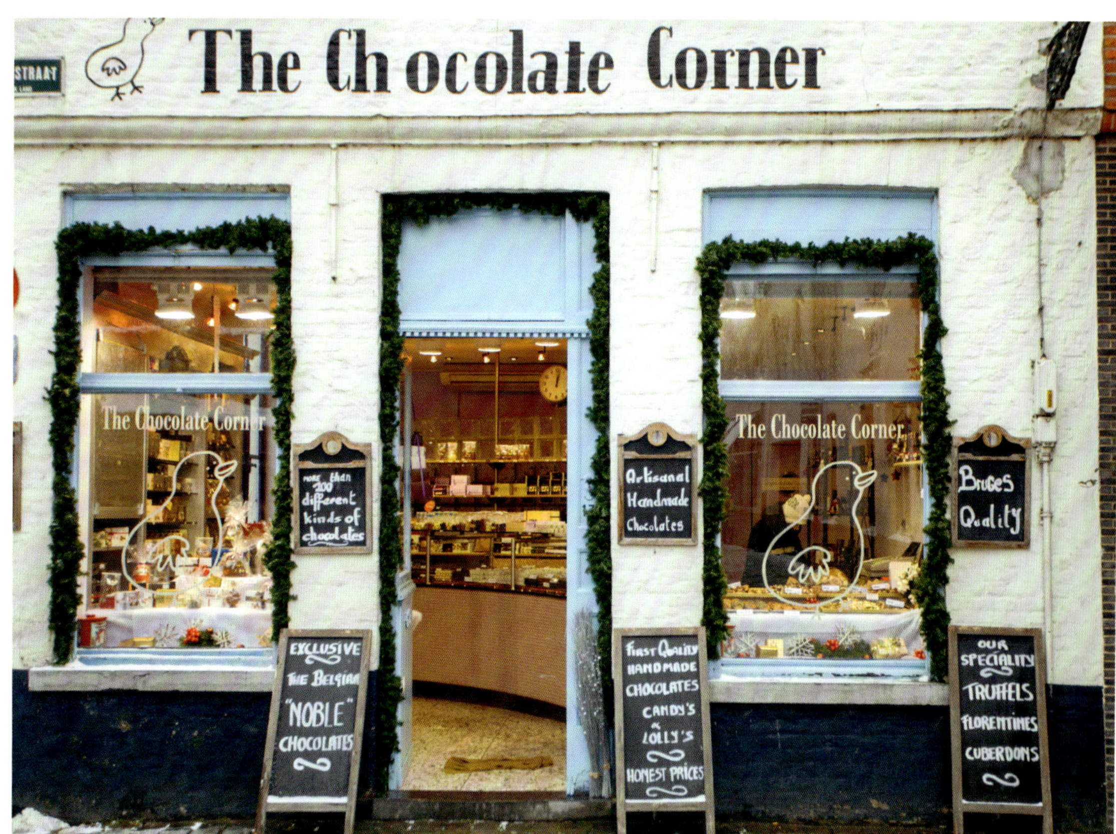

Chocolate Shop
Chocoladewinkel
Chocolaterie

Brujas: la ciudad del chocolate

En casi todas partes del casco antiguo se puede oler el chocolate. En el Museo del Chocolate, espesos vapores de chocolate en las tazas y 52 chocolaterías tientan a los visitantes con locas creaciones de chocolate. Con cannabis o panceta, coloridas ranas venenosas o cráneos... Casi nadie que viene a Brujas se va a casa sin un dulce souvenir. La estrella de los Chocolateros, Dominique Persoone, ha conseguido una estrella Michelin y ha diseñado una catapulta de chocolate para esnifar cacao para los Rolling Stones. La fiebre del chocolate comenzó con Jean Neuhaus, que creó el primer bombón en Bruselas en 1912.

Cidade de Chocolate de Bruges

Em quase todos os lugares da cidade velha, você pode cheirar o chocolate. No Museu do Chocolate, espessos vapores de chocolate nas xícaras e 52 chocolaterias o seduzem com criações loucas de bombons de chocolate. Com canábis ou bacon, em forma de rãs venenosas coloridas ou caveiras - quase ninguém que chega a Bruges vai para casa sem uma lembrança doce. A estrela dos chocolatiers, Dominique Persoone, tem uma estrela Michelin e projetou a catapulta de chocolate para o nariz dos Rolling Stones. A febre do chocolate começou com Jean Neuhaus, que criou o primeiro bombom em Bruxelas em 1912.

Chocoladestad Brugge

Bijna overal in de oude stad kun je de geur van chocolade opsnuiven. In het chocolademuseum dampt dikke, vloeibare chocolade in de kopjes en 52 chocoladewinkels lokken met waanzinnige pralinecreaties. Met cannabis of spek, kleurrijke gifkikkers of schedels - bijna niemand die naar Brugge keert zonder een zoet souvenir huiswaarts. Dominique Persoone, de ster onder chocolatiers, heeft een Michelin-ster in de wacht gesleept en voor de Rolling Stones de chocolate shooter voor de neus ontworpen. De chocoladekoorts begon met Jean Neuhaus, die in 1912 in Brussel de eerste praline maakte.

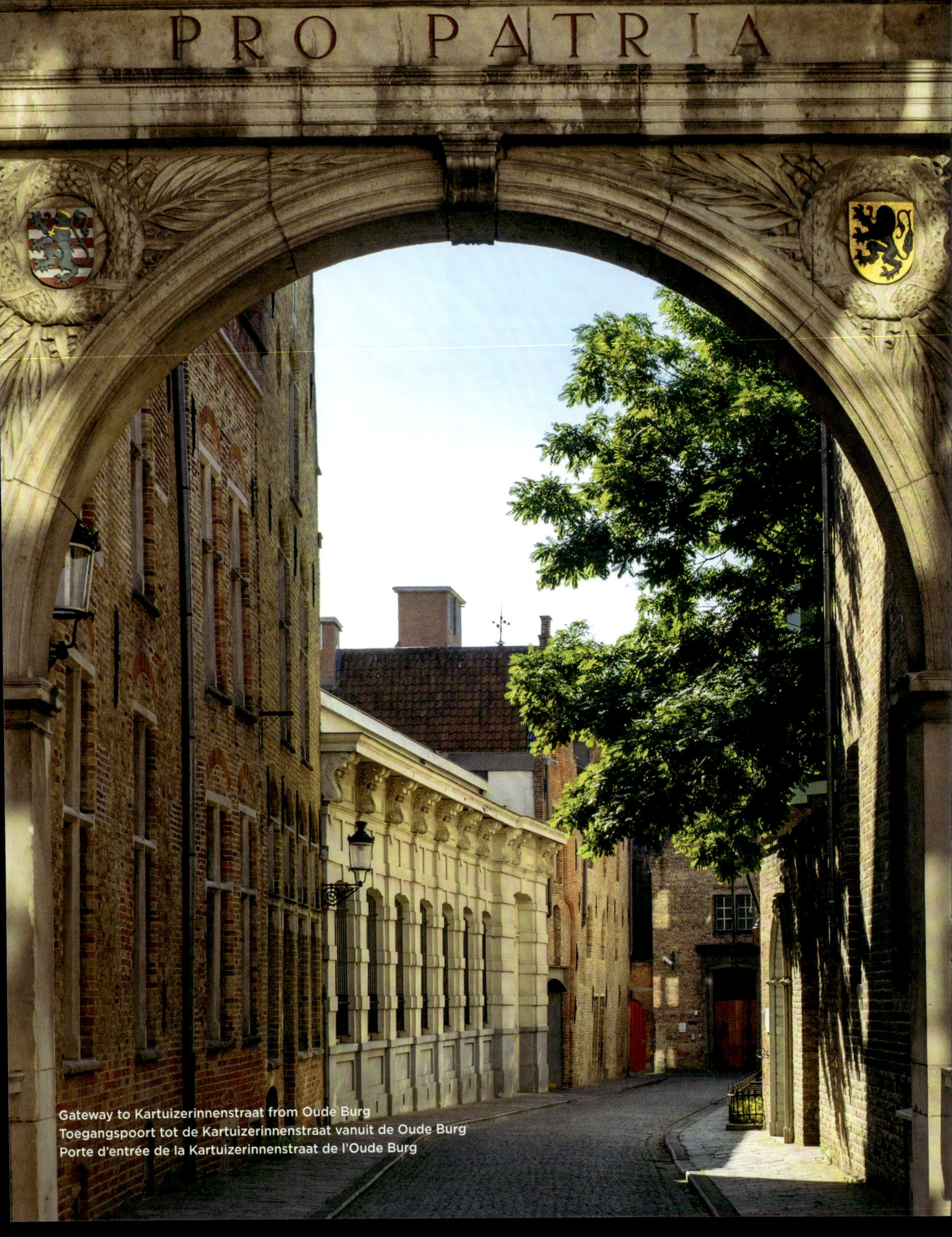

Gateway to Kartuizerinnenstraat from Oude Burg
Toegangspoort tot de Kartuizerinnenstraat vanuit de Oude Burg
Porte d'entrée de la Kartuizerinnenstraat de l'Oude Burg

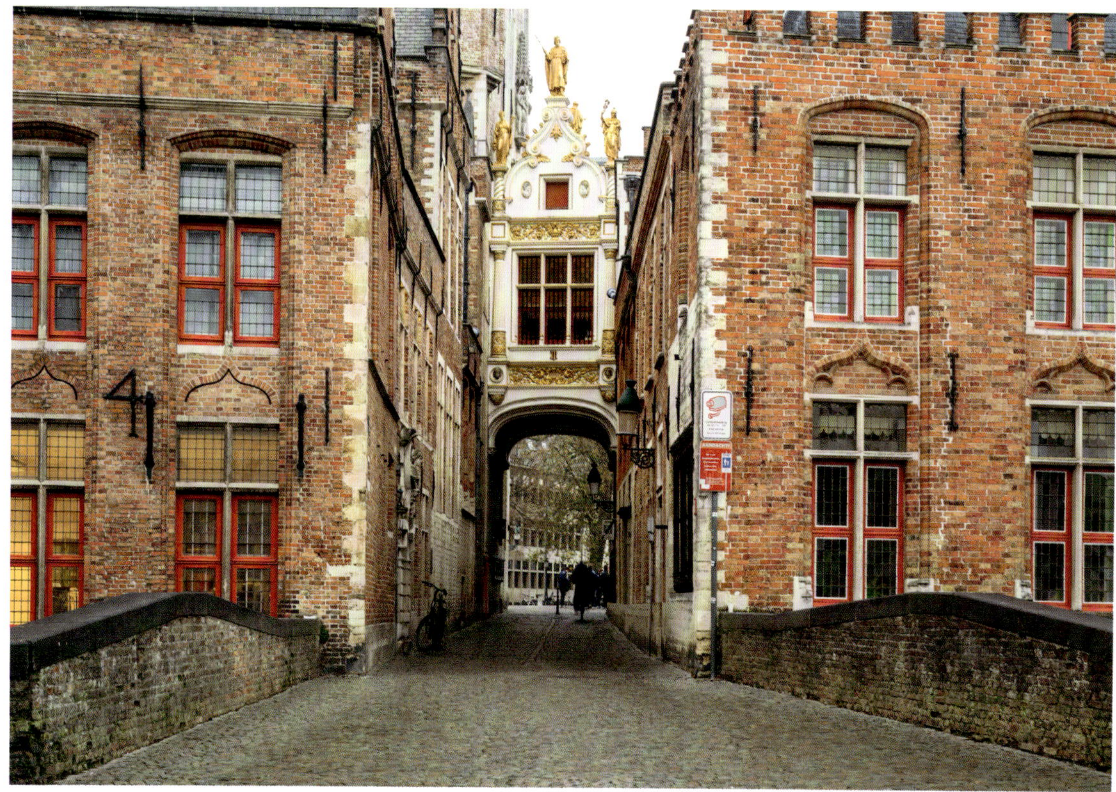

Pedestrian passageway "Blind Donkey Street"
Blinde-Ezelstraat
Passage piétonnier des « Ânes aveugles »

Old castle and blind donkeys

The "Burg" square belongs to the oldest core of the city and took its name from a fortress built there around the 9th century. Next to the town hall there is the "Blinde Ezelstraat" (Blind Donkey Street). The name refers to an old custom of the beer brewers, which was to blindfold the donkey on the treadmill so that it didn't get dizzy when circling.

Antiguo castillo y burros ciegos

La plaza "Burg" pertenece al núcleo más antiguo de la ciudad y fue un castillo en el siglo X. Al lado del ayuntamiento se encuentra la "Blinde Ezelstraat" (calle del burro ciego). El nombre hace referencia a una antigua costumbre de los cerveceros de vendar al burro en la calandria para que no se maree al dar vueltas.

Vieux château fort et ânes aveugles

La place « Burg » fait partie du plus ancien centre de la ville et un château fort s'y dressait au xᵉ siècle. À côté de la mairie : la « Blinde Ezelstraat » (rue des Ânes aveugles). Son nom renvoie à un ancien usage des brasseurs, qui bandaient les yeux des ânes dans le carrousel, pour qu'ils ne soient pas pris de tournis.

Velho castelo e burros cegos

A praça "Burg" pertence ao núcleo mais antigo da cidade e foi realmente um castelo no século X. Junto à Câmara Municipal encontra-se o "Blinde Ezelstraat" (rua dos burros cegos). O nome refere-se a um velho costume dos fabricantes de cerveja de vendar os olhos do burro na esteira para que ele não ficasse tonto ao circular.

Alte Burg und blinde Esel

Der Platz „Burg" gehört zum ältesten Kern der Stadt und war im 10. Jahrhundert tatsächlich eine Burg. Dort befindet sich neben dem Rathaus die „Blinde Ezelstraat" (Blinde-Esel-Straße). Die Bezeichnung bezieht sich auf einen alten Brauch der Bierbrauer, dem Esel in der Tretmühle die Augen zu verbinden, damit ihm beim Kreisen nicht schwindelig wird.

Oud kasteel en blinde ezels

De "Burg" behoort tot de oudste kern van de stad en was in de 10e eeuw daadwerkelijk eigenlijk een burcht. Naast het gemeentehuis ligt de Blinde-Ezelstraat. De naam verwijst naar een oude gewoonte van de bierbrouwers om de ezel in de tredmolen te blinddoeken, zodat hij bij het in de rondte lopen niet duizelig werd.

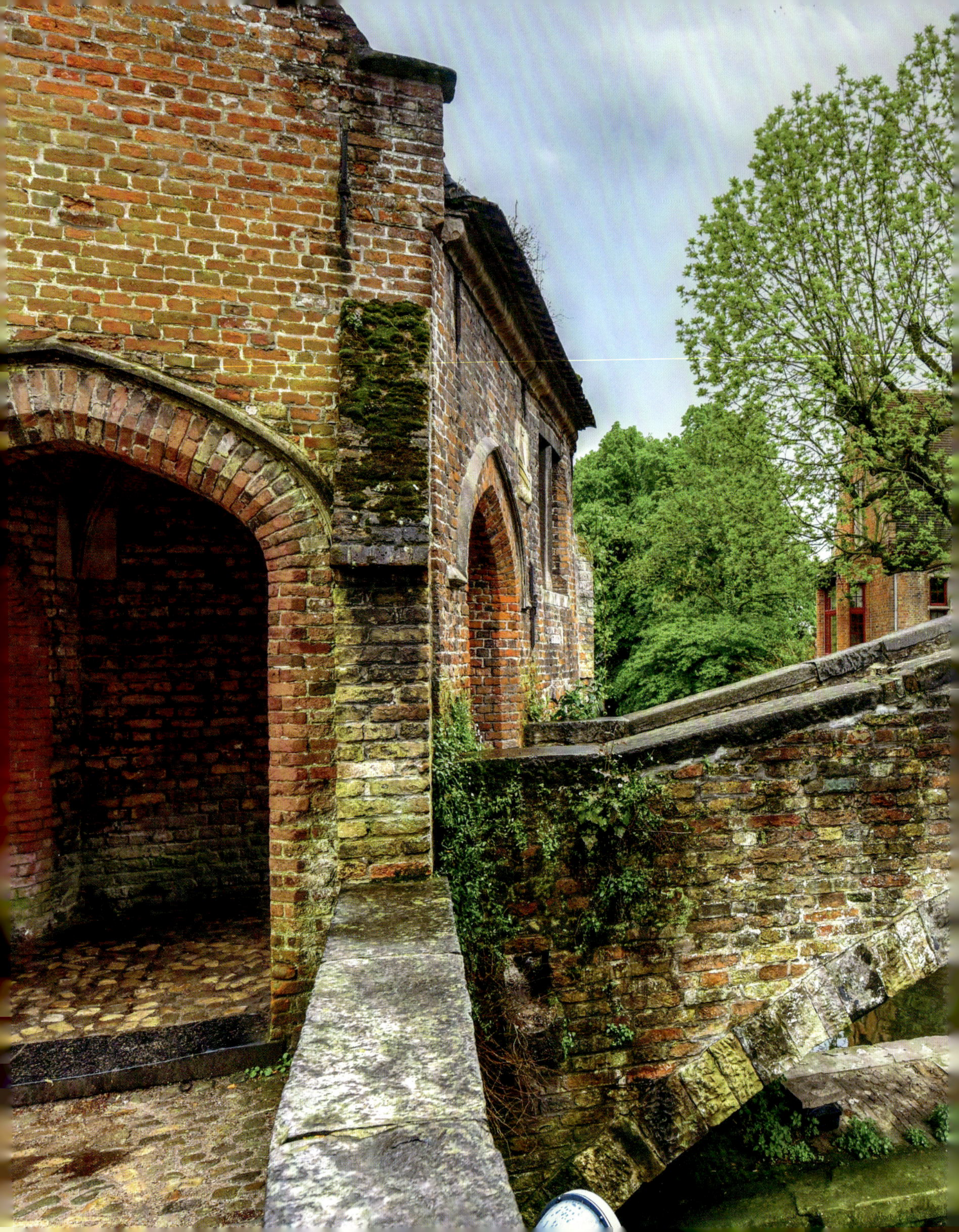

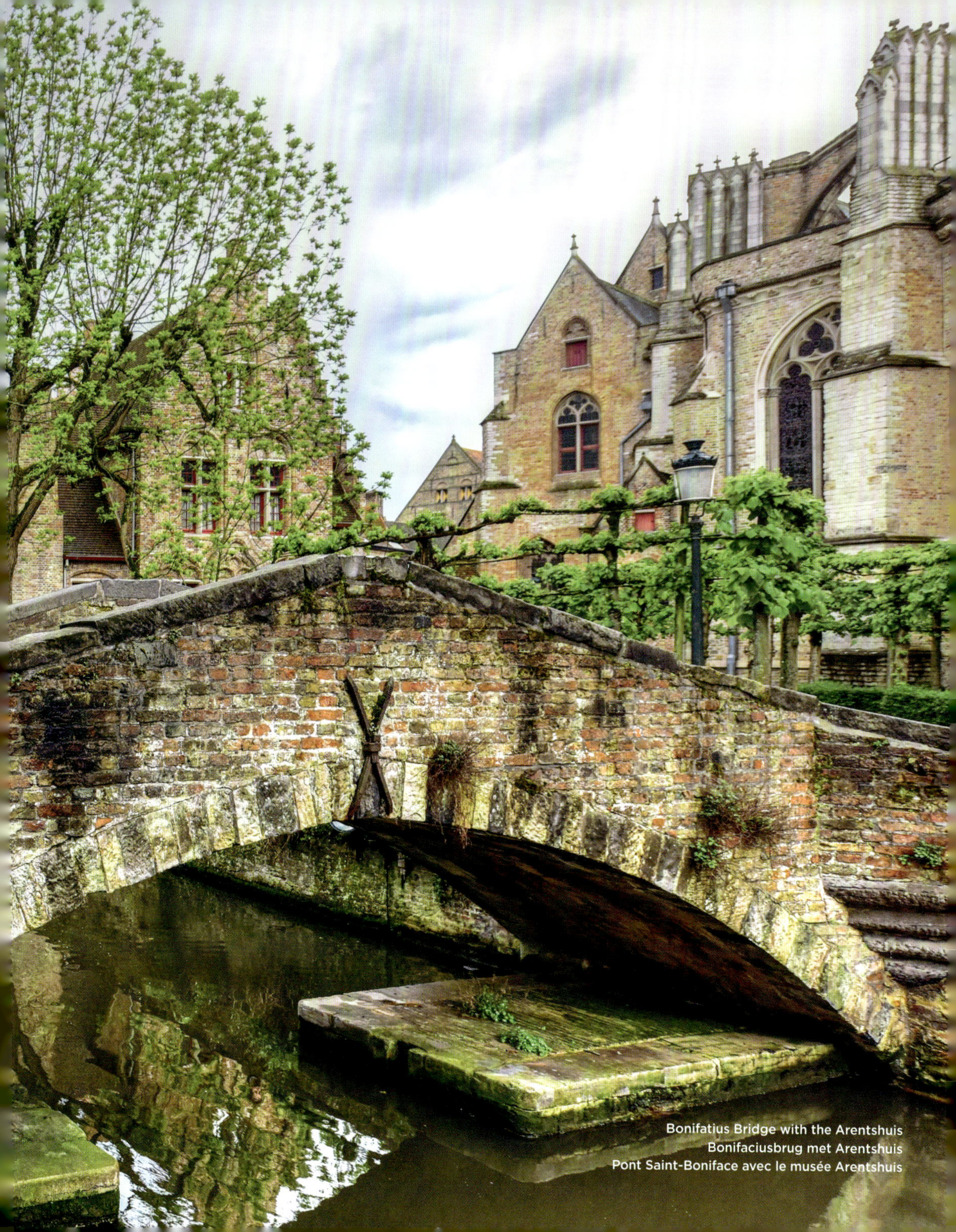

Bonifatius Bridge with the Arentshuis
Bonifaciusbrug met Arentshuis
Pont Saint-Boniface avec le musée Arentshuis

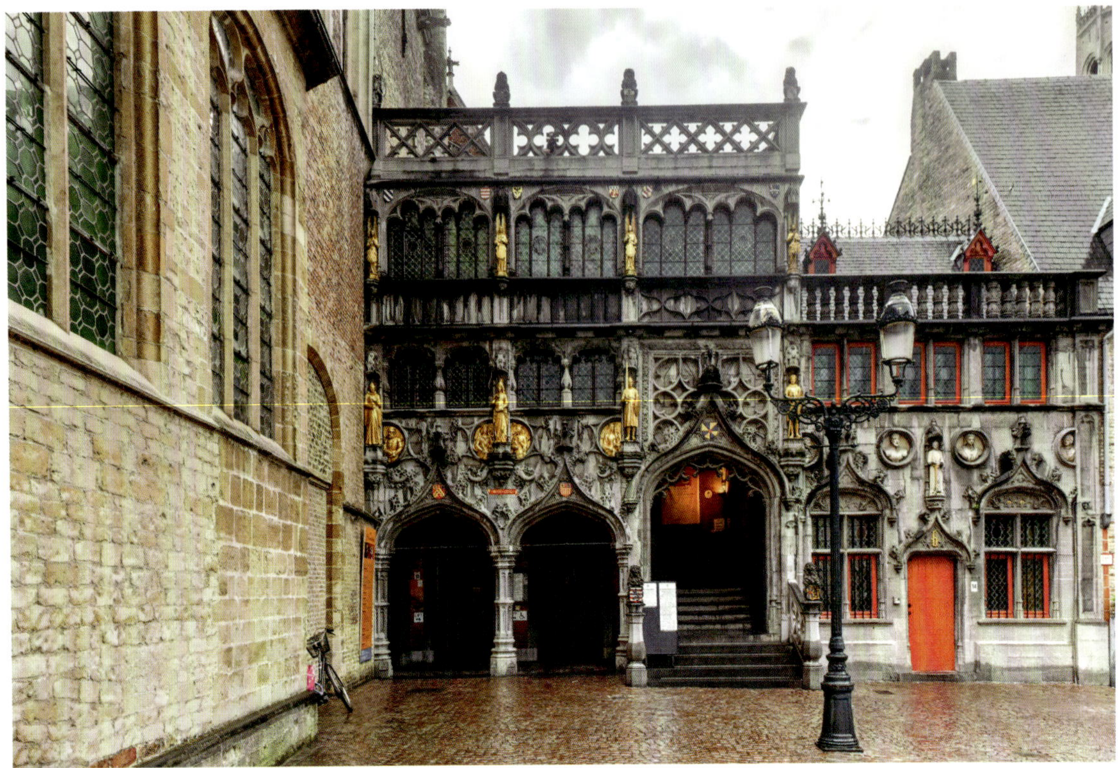

Basilica of the Holy Blood
Basiliek van het Heilig Bloed
Basilique du Saint-Sang de Bruges

The Basilica of the Holy Blood

The basilica houses one of the most important relics in Europe, an ampoule allegedly containing the blood of Christ. Since 1291, the relic has been carried through the city during the procession of the Holy Blood, always on Ascension Day. The Procession of the Holy Blood was added to Unesco's Representative List of the Intangible Cultural Heritage of Humanity in 2009.

Basílica de la Santa Sangre

La basílica alberga una de las reliquias más importantes de Europa, una ampolla que contiene la sangre de Cristo. Desde 1291, la reliquia ha sido llevada por la ciudad durante la procesión de la Santa Sangre, siempre en el Día de la Ascensión. La Procesión de la Santa Sangre fue añadida a la lista representativa del patrimonio cultural inmaterial de la humanidad en 2009.

La basilique du Saint-Sang

Cette basilique abrite l'une des reliques les plus importantes d'Europe, une ampoule contenant le sang du Christ. Depuis 1291, celle-ci est transportée à travers la ville lors de la procession du Saint-Sang, le jour de l'Ascension. Cette procession appartient au patrimoine culturel immatériel de l'humanité de l'Unesco depuis 2009.

A Basílica do Sangue Sagrado

A basílica abriga uma das relíquias mais importantes da Europa, uma ampola contendo o sangue de Cristo. Desde 1291, a relíquia percorre a cidade durante a procissão do Sangue Sagrado, sempre no Dia da Ascensão. A Procissão do Sangue Sagrado foi acrescentada à lista representativa do Património Cultural Imaterial da Humanidade em 2009.

Die Heilig-Blut-Basilika

In der Basilika wird eine der bedeutendsten Reliquien Europas, eine Ampulle mit dem Blut Christi aufbewahrt. Seit 1291 wird die Reliquie, immer zu Christi Himmelfahrt, während der Heilig-Blut-Prozession durch die Stadt getragen. Die Heilig-Blut-Prozession wurde 2009 in die repräsentative Liste des immateriellen Kulturerbes der Menschheit aufgenommen.

De Basiliek van het Heilig Bloed

De basiliek herbergt één van de belangrijkste relikwieën in Europa met het bloed van Christus. Sinds 1291 wordt het relikwie tijdens de Heilig Bloedprocessie door de stad gedragen, altijd op Hemelvaartsdag. De Heilig Bloedprocessie werd in 2009 toegevoegd aan de representatieve lijst van het immaterieel cultureel erfgoed van de mensheid.

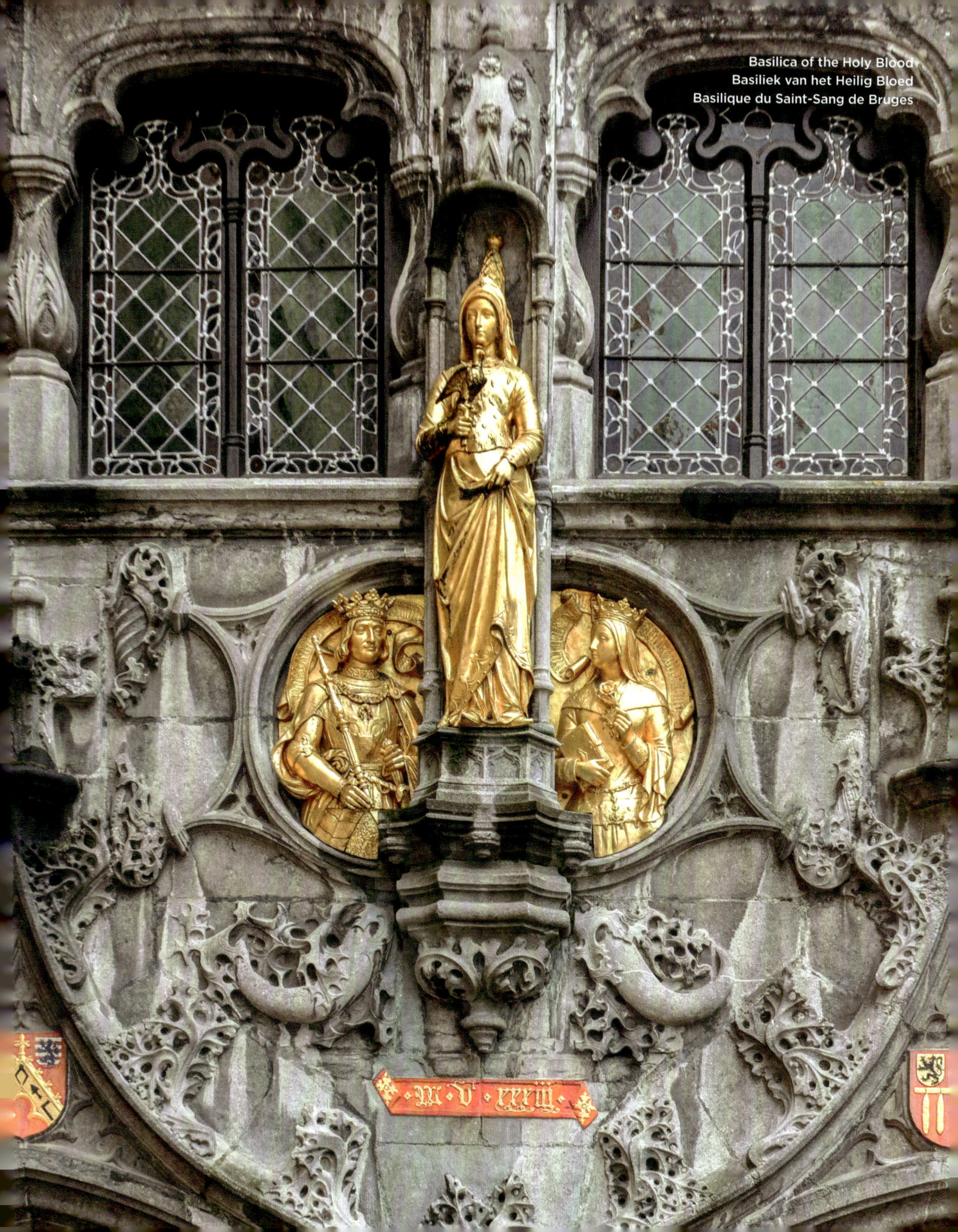

Basilica of the Holy Blood
Basiliek van het Heilig Bloed
Basilique du Saint-Sang de Bruges

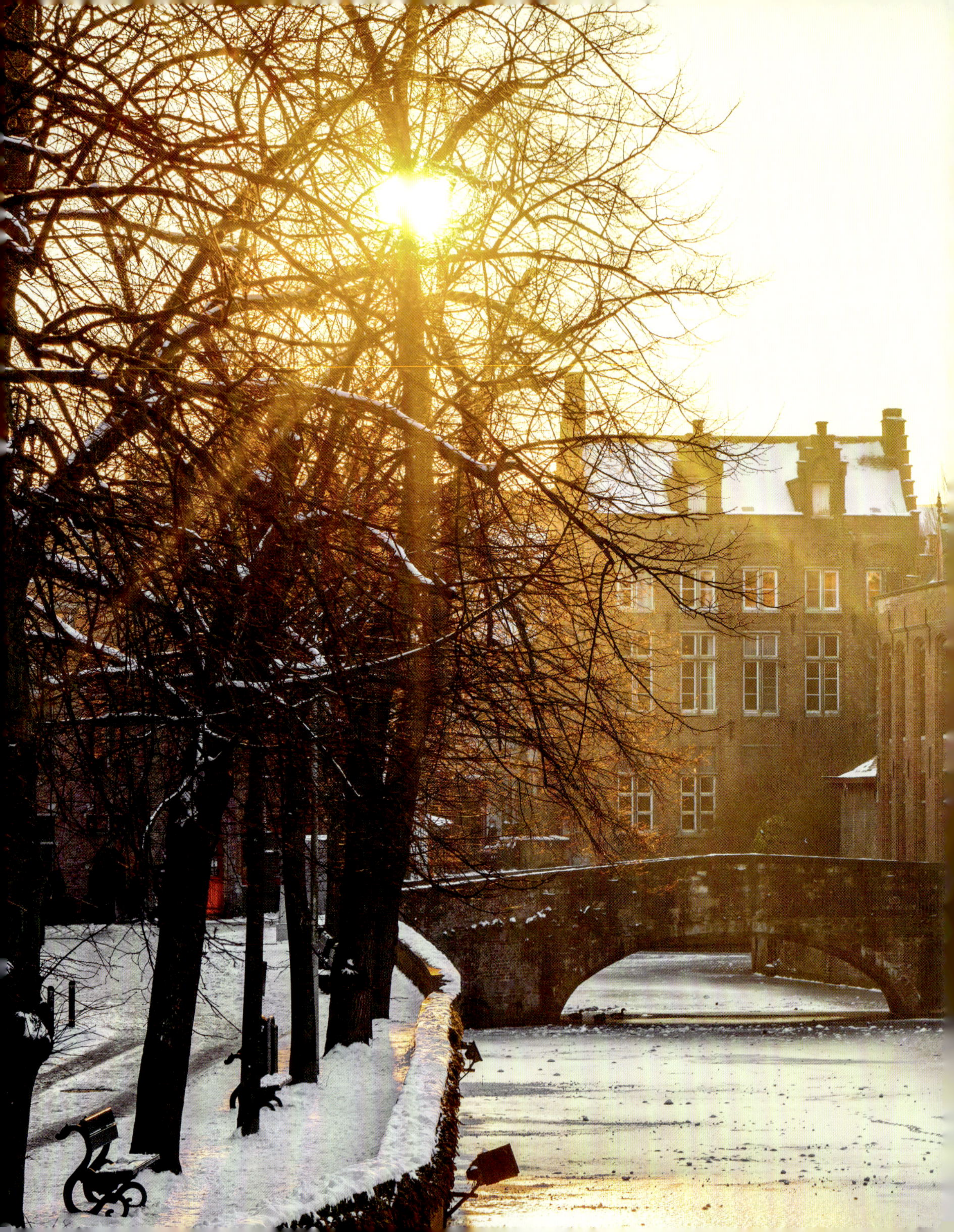

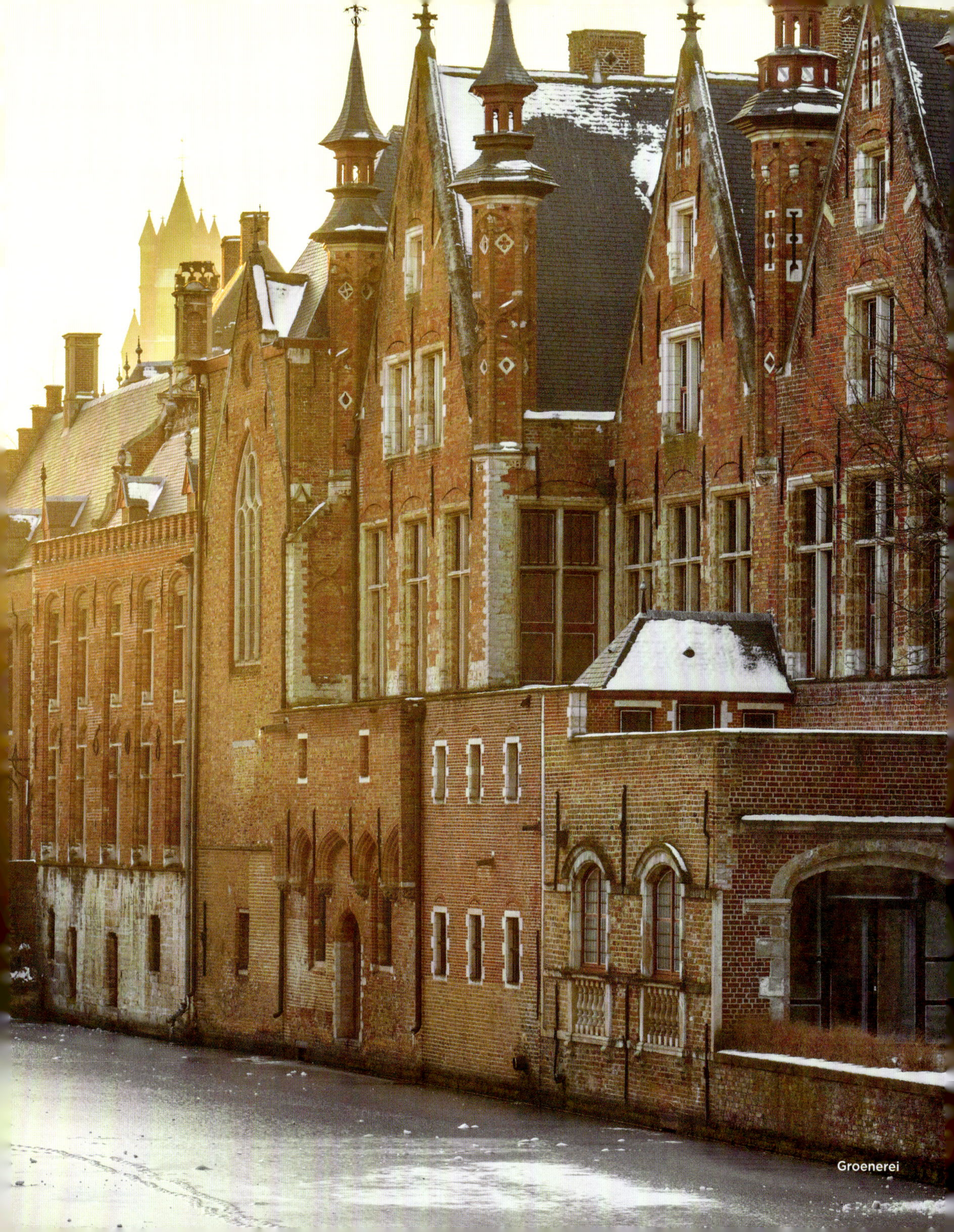
Groenerei

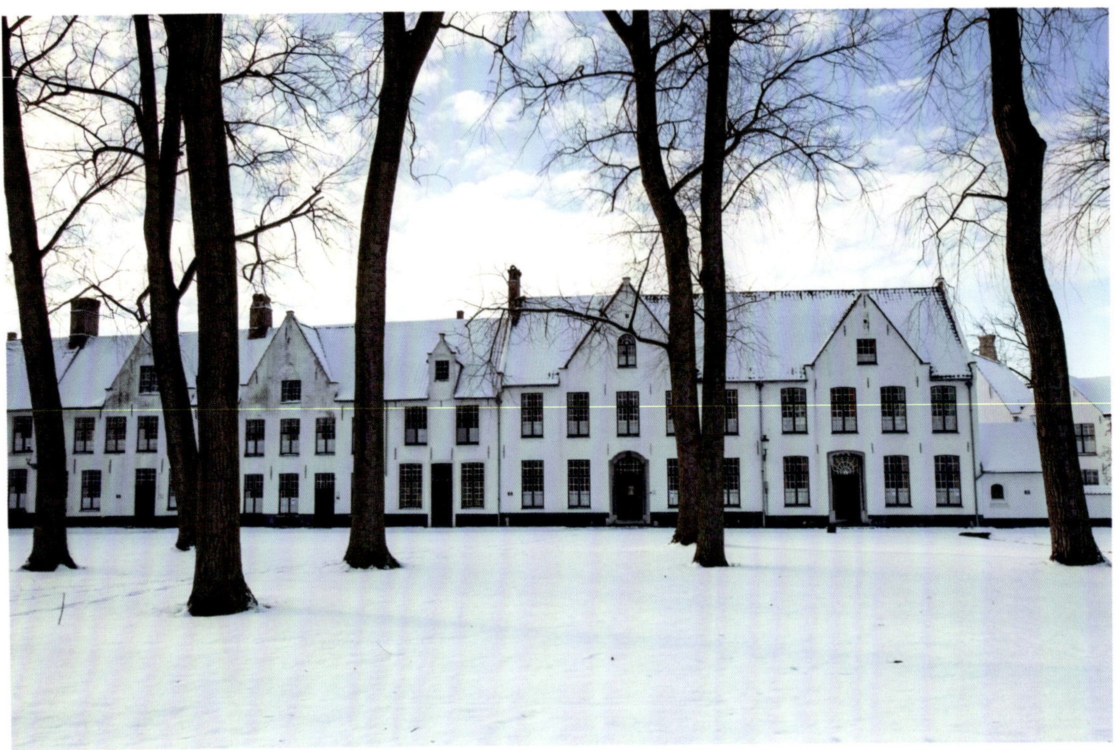

Princely Beguinage Ten Wijngaarde
Prinselijk Begijnhof Ten Wijngaarde
Béguinage princier Ten Wijngaarde

Beguines living independent lives

In the Beguinage "Ten Wijngaarde" lived Beguines, who were emancipated women leading a pious and celibate life. Today the Beguinage is a World Heritage Site and is inhabited by sisters of the Benedictine Order. The Beguinage Museum conveys a lively impression of the everyday life of the women in the 17th century.

La vie indépendante des béguines

Le béguinage « Ten Wijngaarde » abritait jadis des béguines : des femmes laïques, émancipées, qui menaient une vie pieuse et célibataire. Aujourd'hui, le béguinage fait partie du patrimoine culturel mondial de l'Unesco. Des bénédictines et des femmes seules y habitent. Le musée du Béguinage restitue de façon vivante le quotidien des femmes au XVIIᵉ siècle.

Beginen lebten selbstbestimmt

Im Beginenhof „Ten Wijngaarde" lebten früher Beginen: weltliche, emanzipierte Frauen, die ein frommes und eheloses Leben führten. Heute gehört der Beginenhof zum Weltkulturerbe und wird von Benediktinerinnen und alleinstehenden Frauen bewohnt. Das Beginenhaus-Museum vermittelt einen lebendigen Eindruck in das Alltagsleben der Frauen im 17. Jahrhundert.

Las beguinas vivían con autodeterminación

En el Beguinage "Ten Wijngaarde" vivían beguinas: mujeres mundanas y emancipadas que llevaban una vida piadosa y célibe. Hoy en día la Beguinage es Patrimonio de la Humanidad y está habitada por mujeres benedictinas y solteras. El Museo de Beguinage transmite una viva impresión de la vida cotidiana de las mujeres en el siglo XVII.

Os Beguines viveram a autodeterminação

Na beguinaria "Ten Wijngaarde" viviam as beguines: mulheres mundanas, emancipadas, que levavam uma vida piedosa e celibatária. Hoje a beguinaria é um Patrimônio Mundial e é habitada por mulheres beneditinas e mulheres solteiras. A Beguinaria de Bruges dá uma impressão viva da vida quotidiana das mulheres do século XVII.

Begijnen en zelfbeschikkingsrecht

In het begijnhof "Ten Wijngaarde" woonden begijnen: wereldlijke, geëmancipeerde vrouwen die een vroom en celibaat leven leidden. Vandaag de dag behoort het begijnhof tot het werelderfgoed en wordt door benedictijnse vrouwen en alleenstaande vrouwen bewoond. Het Begijnhofmuseum geeft een levendig beeld van het dagelijkse leven van vrouwen in de 17de eeuw.

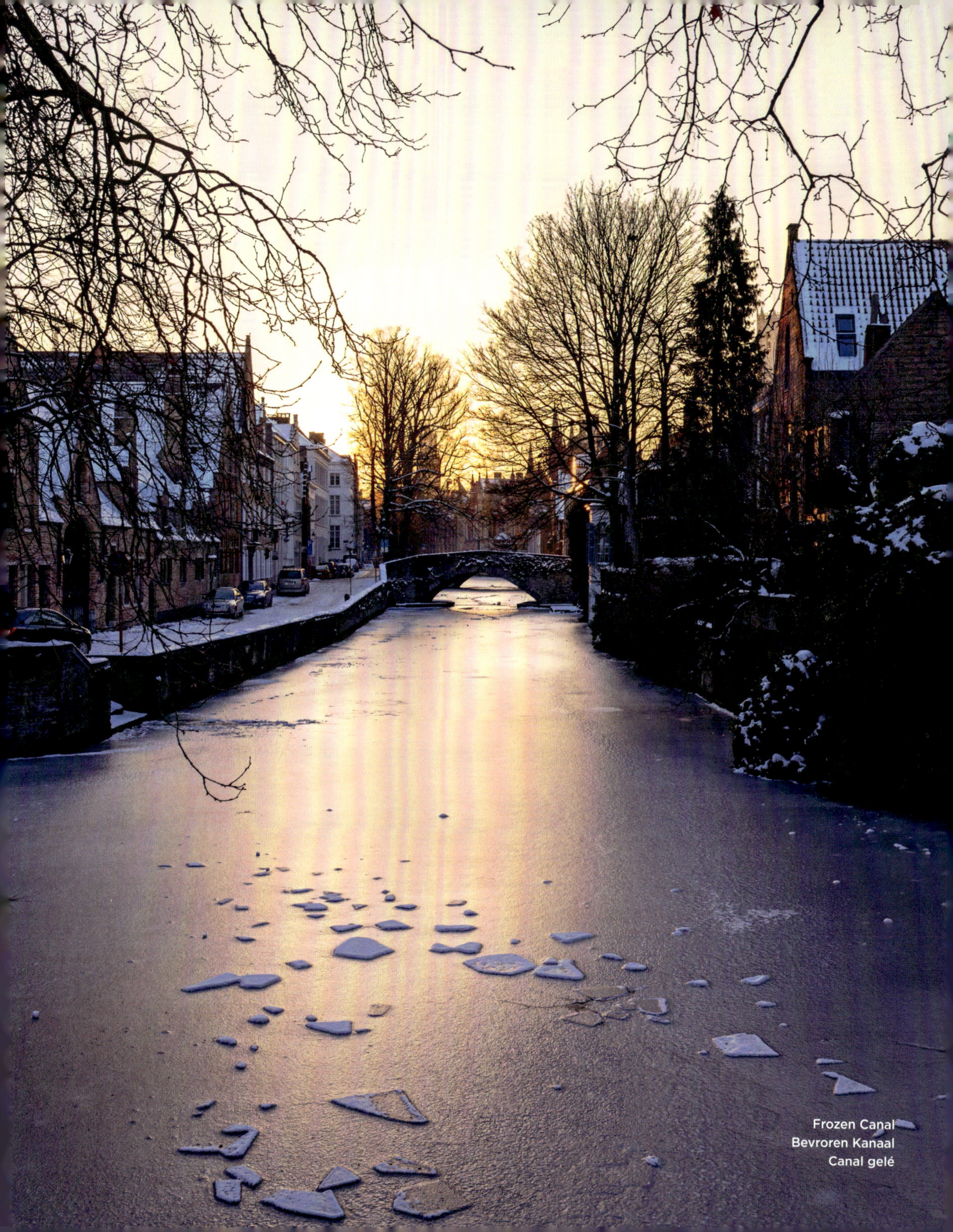

Frozen Canal
Bevroren Kanaal
Canal gelé

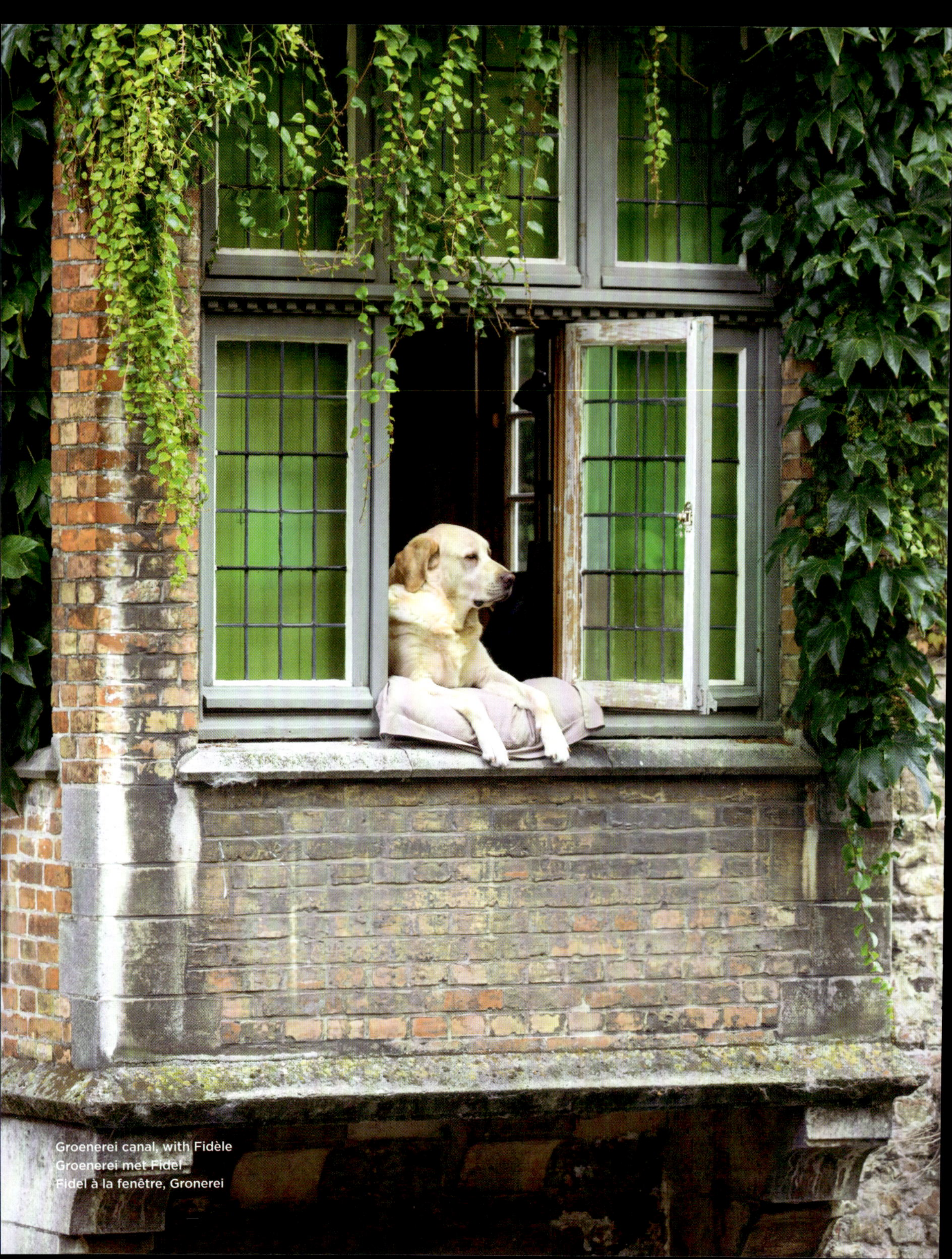

Groenerei canal, with Fidèle
Groenerei met Fidel
Fidel à la fenêtre, Gronerei

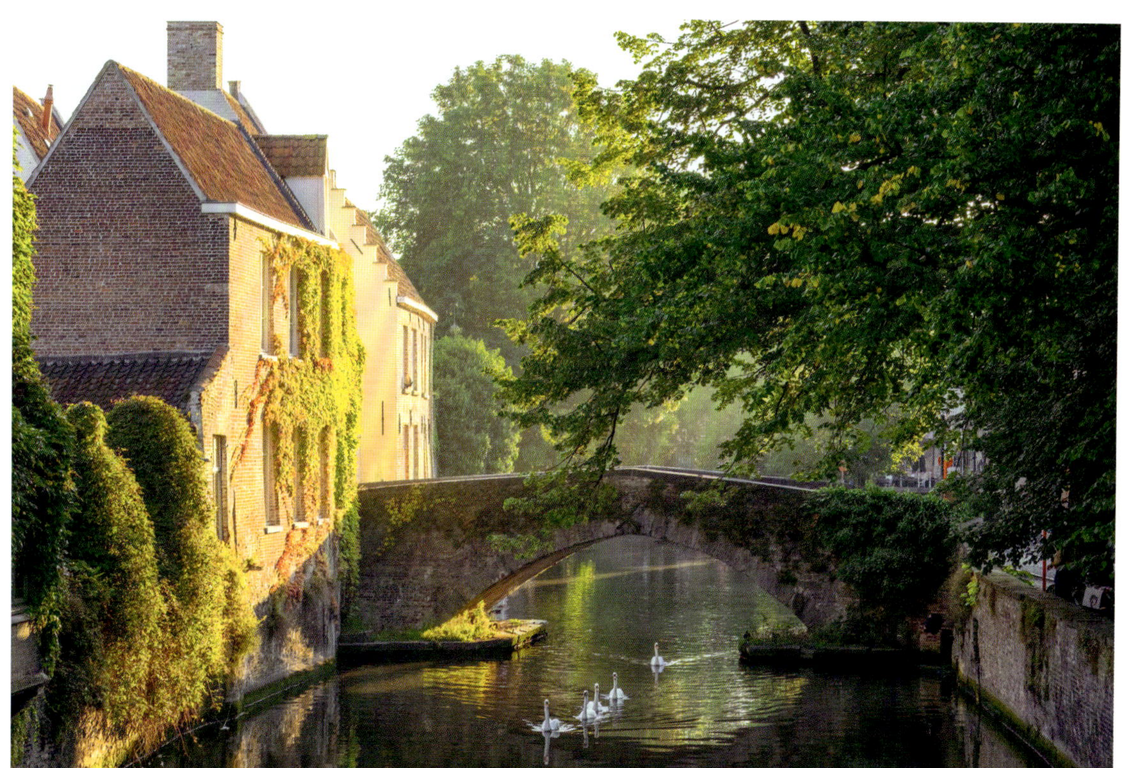

Meebrug bridge, Groenerei
Meebrug, Groenerei
Pont de Meestraat, Groenerei

Bridges, windows and a dog

The place name Bruges can probably be traced back to the existence of many bridges. Originally, all bridges were made of wood and did not survive long, with the oldest stone bridge being the Meebrug, dating from the 14th century. The picture on the left shows the most famous dog of the city, the labrador Fidèle, featured in the film "In Bruges", which would lie in the window from morning till evening.

Ponts, fenêtre et chien

Le nom de la ville de Bruges découle fort probablement de ses nombreux ponts, « brug » signifiant pont en néerlandais. À l'origine, tous les ponts étaient en bois et ils ne survécurent pas au temps ; le plus vieux pont de pierre est le Meerbrug, bâti au xive siècle. Sur la photo à gauche, vous apercevez le chien le plus célèbre de la ville, le labrador Fidel, qui se tient à la fenêtre du matin au soir.

Brücken, Fenster und Hund

Die Ortsname Brügge geht mit hoher Wahrscheinlichkeit auf die vielen Brücken zurück. Ursprünglich waren alle Brücken aus Holz und haben die Zeit nicht überstanden, die älteste Steinbrücke ist die Meebrug aus dem 14. Jahrhundert. Das Bild links zeigt den berühmtesten Hund der Stadt, den Labrador Fidel, der von morgens bis abends im Fenster liegt.

Puentes, ventanas y perros

El nombre de Brujas probablemente se remonta a los numerosos puentes. Originalmente todos los puentes eran de madera y no sobrevivieron al tiempo; el puente de piedra más antiguo es el puente Meebrug del siglo XIV. En la imagen de la izquierda aparece el perro más famoso de la ciudad, el Labrador Fidel, que se encuentra tubado en la ventana desde por la mañana hasta por la noche.

Pontes, janelas e cães

O nome do lugar, Bruges, provavelmente é proveniente das muitas pontes. Originalmente, todas as pontes eram feitas de madeira e não sobreviveram ao tempo, a ponte de pedra mais antiga é a ponte Meebrug do século XIV. A foto à esquerda mostra o cão mais famoso da cidade, o Labrador Fidel, que fica na janela de manhã à noite.

Bruggen, ramen en honden

De plaatsnaam Brugge heeft zijn oorsprong waarschijnlijk in de vele bruggen. Oorspronkelijk waren alle bruggen van hout en hebben de tijd niet overleefd, de oudste stenen brug is de Meebrug uit de 14e eeuw. De foto links toont de beroemdste hond van de stad, de labrador Fidel, die van 's morgens tot 's avonds in het raam ligt.

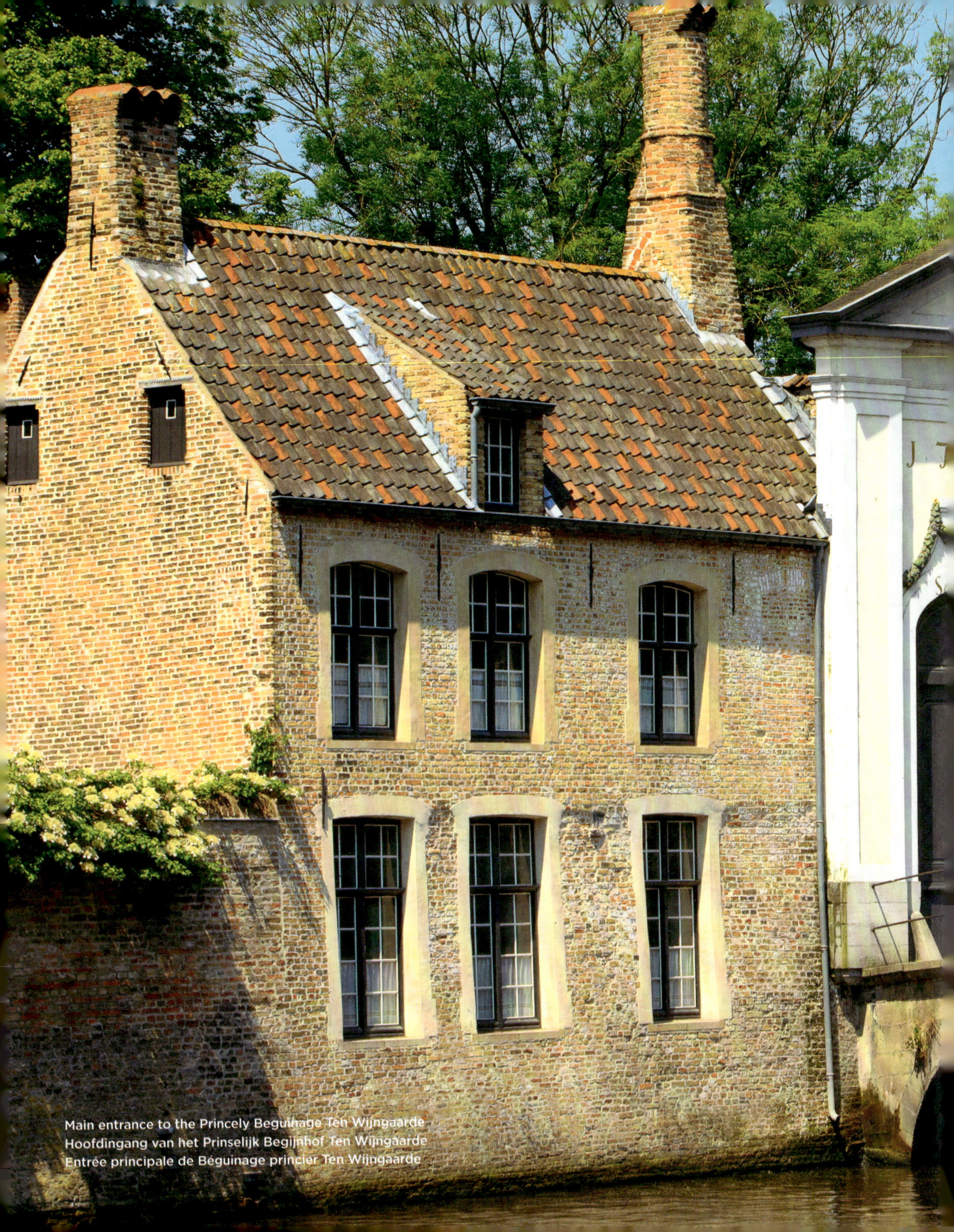

Main entrance to the Princely Beguinage Ten Wijngaarde
Hoofdingang van het Prinselijk Begijnhof Ten Wijngaarde
Entrée principale de Béguinage princier Ten Wijngaarde

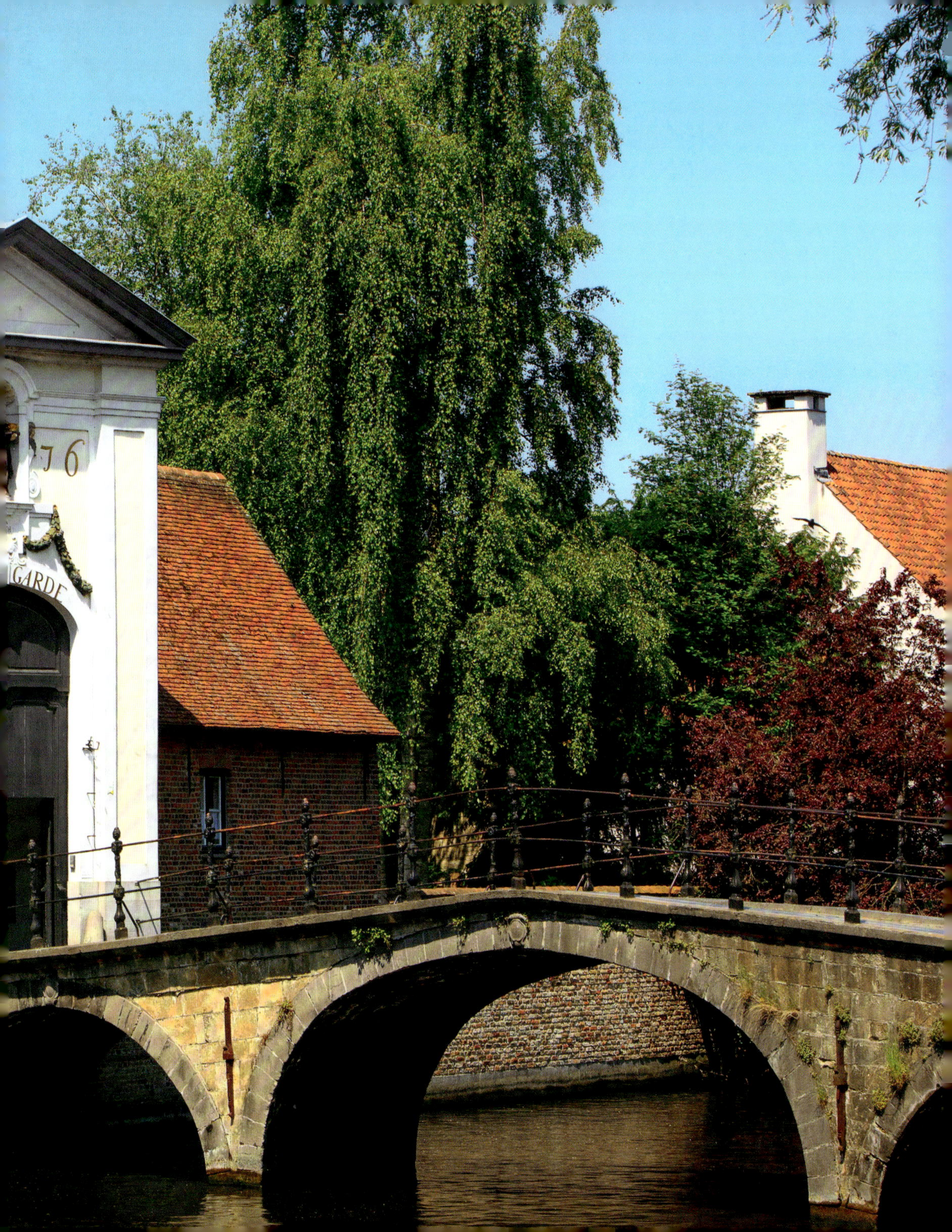

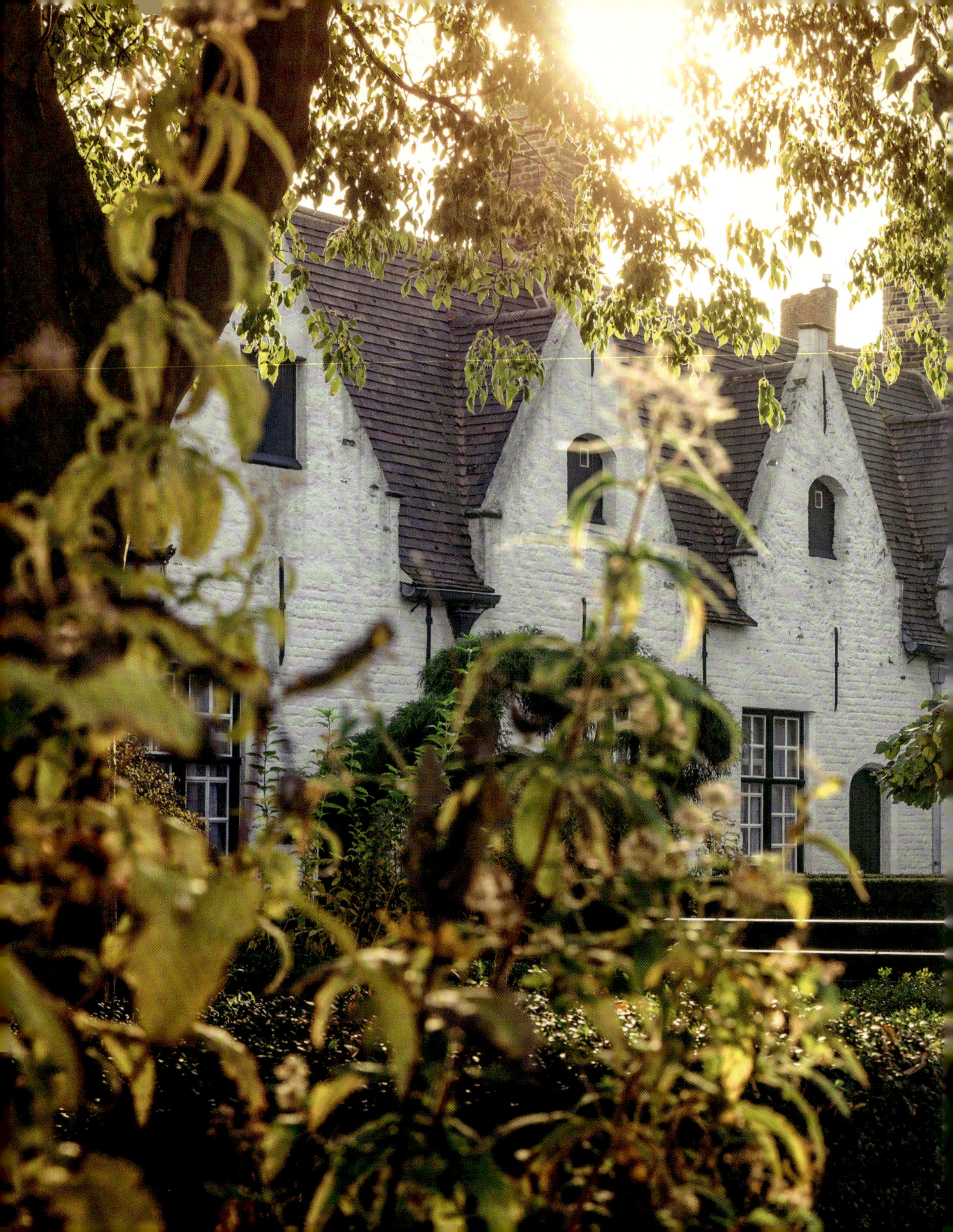

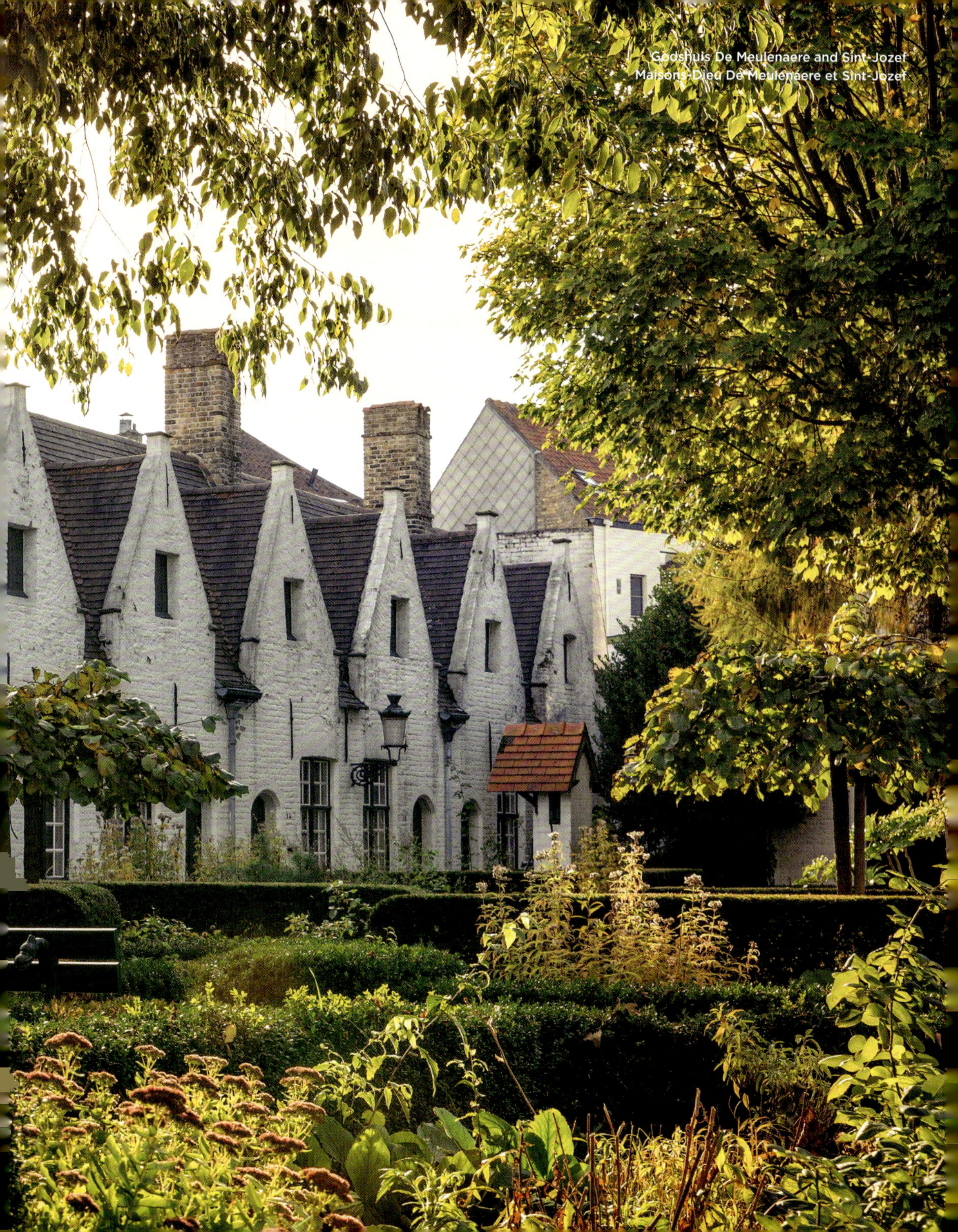

Godshuis De Meulenaere and Sint-Jozef
Maisons-Dieu De Meulenaere et Sint-Jozef

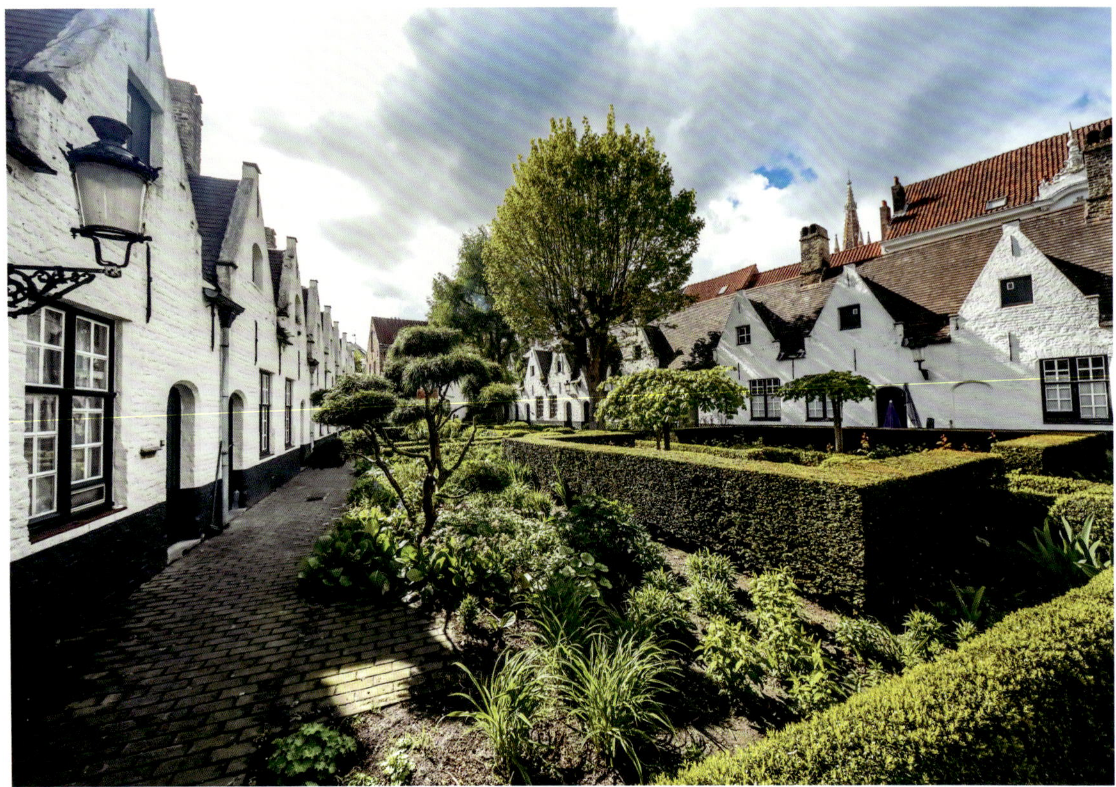

Almshouses
Godshuis De Vos
Maisons-Dieu

"Social housing" of the 14th century

In Bruges there are 46 almshouses consisting of whitewashed cottages, often around a courtyard, dating from the 14th century onwards. The cottages were built by rich citizens, or guilds, to give the poor and the elderly a roof over their heads. The inhabitants were obliged to pray daily for their generous donors and today 43 of these courtyards are still inhabited by the needy.

"Viviendas sociales" del siglo XIV

En Brujas hay 46 patios ocultos con casitas encaladas del siglo XIV. Las casitas fueron construidas por ciudadanos ricos o gremios para dar a los pobres y a los ancianos un techo bajo el que vivir. Los habitantes se vieron obligados a rezar diariamente por sus generosos donantes. 43 patios todavía están habitadas por los necesitados.

« Logements sociaux » du XIVᵉ siècle

Bruges abrite environ 46 cours ourlées de maisonnettes chaulées datant du XIVᵉ siècle. Ce sont les riches habitants de la ville ou les guildes qui les firent construire afin d'offrir un toit aux pauvres et aux personnes âgées. En contrepartie, ceux-ci devaient prier chaque jour pour leurs généreux bienfaiteurs. Aujourd'hui, 43 cours sont encore habitées par des personnes démunies.

"Habitação social" do século XIV

Em Bruges há 46 pátios um tanto escondidos, com casas caiadas de branco do século XIV. As casas foram construídas por cidadãos ricos ou corporações (guildas) para dar aos pobres e aos idosos um teto sobre suas cabeças. Os habitantes eram obrigados a rezar diariamente pelos seus generosos doadores. Hoje, 43 pátios ainda são habitados pelos necessitados.

„Sozialwohnungen" des 14. Jahrhunderts

In Brügge findet man etwas verborgen 46 Höfe mit weiß gekalkten Häuschen, aus dem 14. Jahrhundert. Die Häuschen wurden von reichen Bürgern oder Gilden errichtet, um Armen und Alten ein Dach über den Kopf zu geben. Die Bewohner waren verpflichtet täglich, für ihre großherzigen Stifter zu beten. 43 Höfe werden auch heute noch von Bedürftigen bewohnt.

"Sociale woningbouw" uit de 14e eeuw

In Brugge bevinden zich een beetje verstopt 46 hofjes met witgekalkte huisjes uit de 14e eeuw. De godshuizen werden gebouwd door rijke burgers of gilden om de armen en ouderen een dak boven hun hoofd te geven. De inwoners waren verplicht om dagelijks te bidden voor hun gulle donateurs. 43 hofjes worden nog steeds door de armen bewoond.

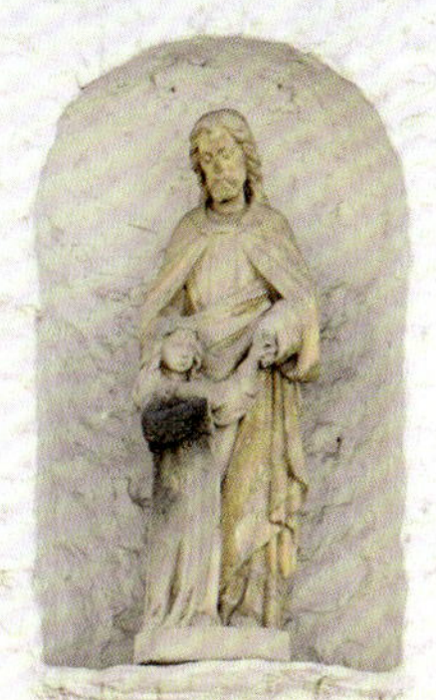

The Sint-Josef Almshouse
Godshuis Sint-Jozef
Maisons-Dieu

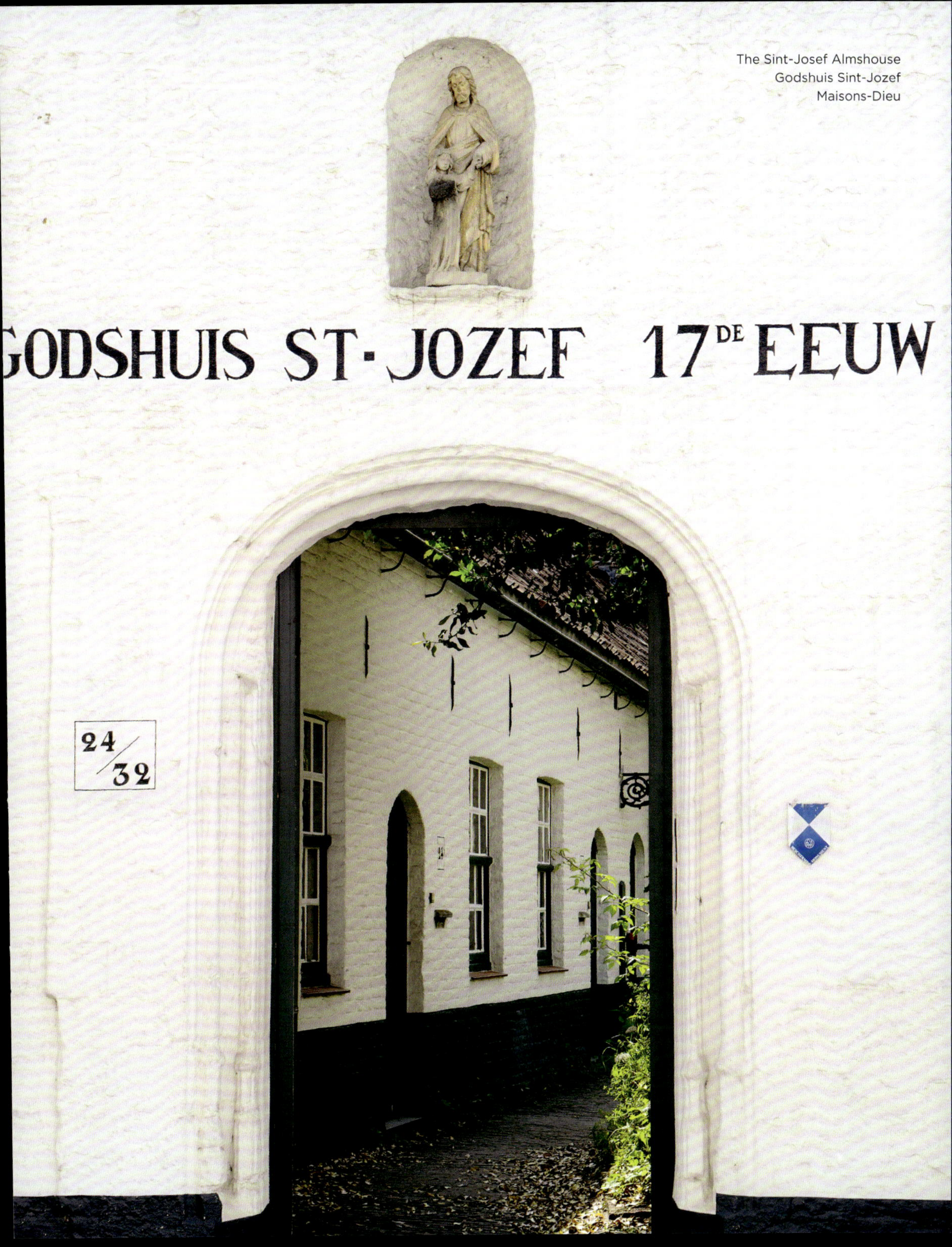

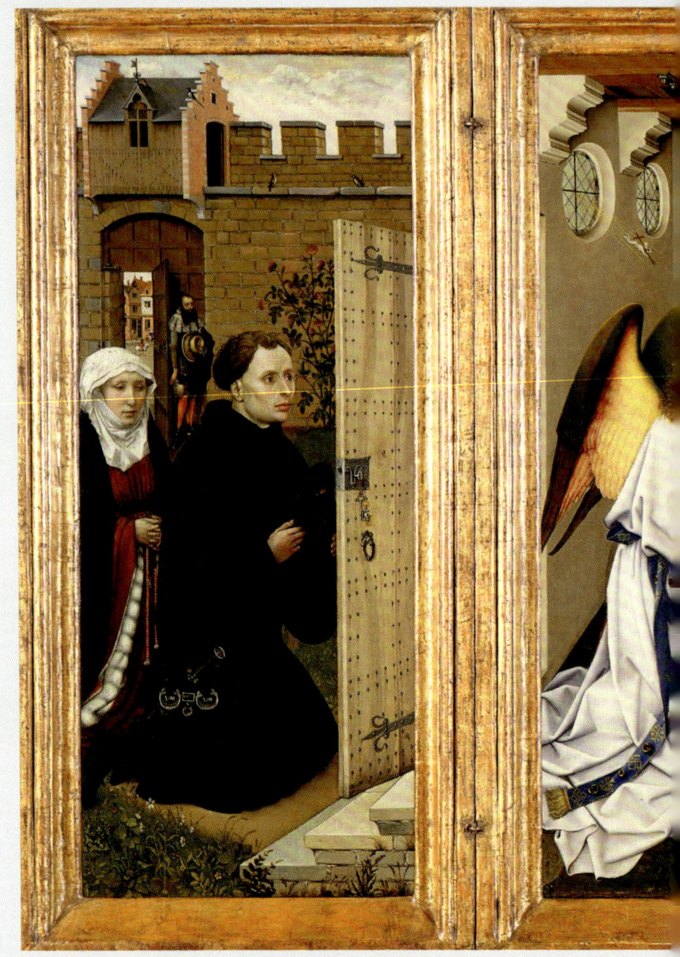

Annunciation Altar (Mérode Altar)

Triptyque de Mérode *ou*
Triptyque de l'Annonciation

Verkündigungsaltar (Mérode-Altar)

Altar de la Anunciación (Mérode Altar)

Altar da Anunciação (Altar de Mérode)

Aankondigingaltaar (Mérode-altaar)

ROBERT CAMPIN (WORKSHOP)
c. 1427–32, Oil on oak/Huile sur bois, c. 65 × c. 130 cm,
Metropolitan Museum of Art, New York

The Flemish Primitives

In the transition period between late Gothic and early Renaissance, a new style of painting developed in Flanders. Jan van Eyck and the Master of Flémalle (Robert Campin) are regarded as the protagonists of this new style, which is characterised by realistic depictions and detailed implementation. The use of magnifying glasses, fine brushes and, above all, the refined technique of oil painting made photorealistic depictions possible. The wealth acquired through trade in the metropolises of Bruges, Ghent and Brussels created the basis for numerous commissions of large altars, private devotional pictures and, increasingly, also portraits.

Les primitifs flamands

Lors du passage du gothique tardif à la Première Renaissance, un nouveau style de peinture émergea dans les Flandres. Jan van Eyck et le maître de Flémalle (Robert Campin) sont considérés comme les pionniers du nouveau style, caractérisé par des représentations fidèles de la réalité et riches en détails. Grâce à l'utilisation de la loupe, de pinceaux fins et surtout à la technique affinée de la peinture à l'huile, des tableaux dont le réalisme se rapproche de celui de la photographie virent le jour. La prospérité acquise par le commerce des métropoles de Bruges, de Gand et de Bruxelles offrit une base financière permettant de nombreuses commandes de grands autels, d'images de dévotion à usage privé et de plus en plus de portraits.

Die Flämischen Primitiven

In der Übergangszeit zwischen Spätgotik und Frührenaissance bildet sich in Flandern ein neuer Malstil heraus. Jan van Eyck und der Meister von Flémalle (Robert Campin) gelten als die Protagonisten des neuen Stils, der sich durch realitätsgetreue Darstellungen und detailreiche Ausführungen auszeichnet. Der Einsatz von Lupe, feinen Pinseln und vor allem die verfeinerte Technik der Ölmalerei ermöglichten gradezu fotorealistische Darstellungen. Der durch Handel erworbene Wohlstand in den Metropolen Brügge, Gent und Brüssel schuf die Grundlage für zahlreiche Aufträge von großen Altären, privaten Andachtsbilder und zunehmend auch Porträts.

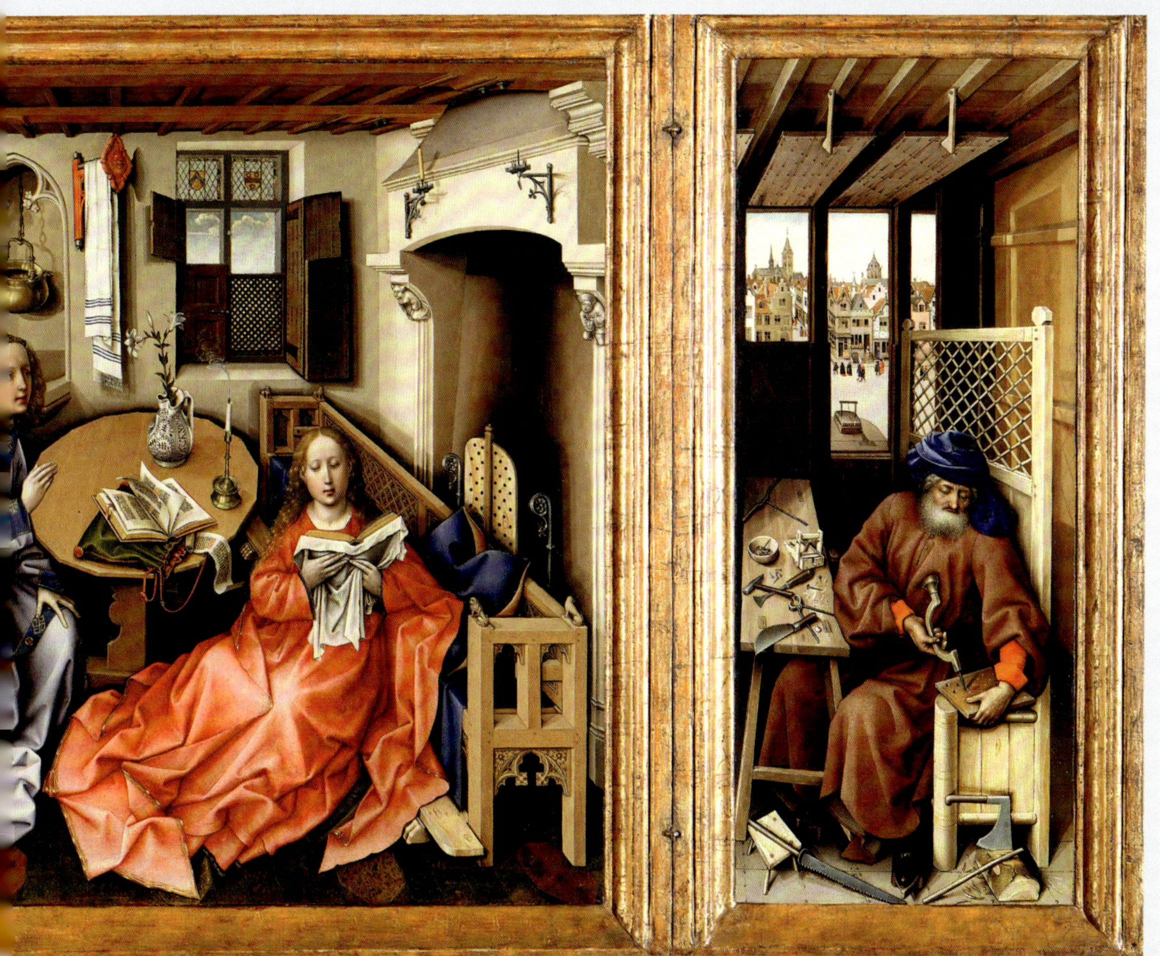

Los Primitivos Flamencos

En el período de transición entre
el Gótico tardío y el Renacimiento
temprano se desarrolló un nuevo estilo
de pintura en Flandes. Jan van Eyck y el
maestro de Flémalle (Robert Campin)
son considerados los protagonistas del
nuevo estilo, que se caracteriza por
representaciones realistas y explicaciones
detalladas. El uso de lupas, pinceles finos y,
sobre todo, la refinada técnica de la pintura
al óleo posibilitaron representaciones
fotorrealistas. La riqueza adquirida a través
del comercio en las metrópolis de Brujas,
Gante y Bruselas sirvió de base para
numerosos encargos de grandes altares,
cuadros devocionales privados y, cada vez
más, retratos.

Os Primitivos Flamengos

No período de transição entre o
Gótico Tardio e o Pré-Renascimento,
desenvolveu-se um novo estilo de
pintura na Flandres. Jan van Eyck e o
Mestre de Flémalle (Robert Campin) são
considerados os protagonistas do novo
estilo, caracterizado por representações
realistas e versões detalhadas. O uso
de lupas, pincéis finos e, acima de tudo,
a técnica refinada da pintura a óleo
tornaram possíveis as representações
quase fotorealistas. A riqueza adquirida
através do comércio nas metrópoles de
Bruges, Gante e Bruxelas criou a base para
numerosas encomendas de grandes altares,
imagens devocionais privadas e, cada vez
mais, também retratos.

De Vlaamse Primitieven

In de overgangsperiode tussen laatgotiek
en vroege Renaissance ontwikkelde zich
in Vlaanderen een nieuwe schilderstijl.
Jan van Eyck en Meester van Flémalle
(Robert Campin) worden beschouwd
als de protagonisten van de nieuwe stijl,
die gekenmerkt wordt door realistische
voorstellingen en gedetailleerde
uitvoeringen. Het gebruik van loepen, fijne
penselen en vooral de verfijnde techniek
van het schilderen met olieverf maakten
fotorealistische voorstellingen mogelijk.
De rijkdom die de handel in de Brugse,
Gentse en Brusselse metropolen opleverde,
vormde de basis voor tal van opdrachten
voor grote altaren, private devotiebeelden
en steeds vaker ook portretten.

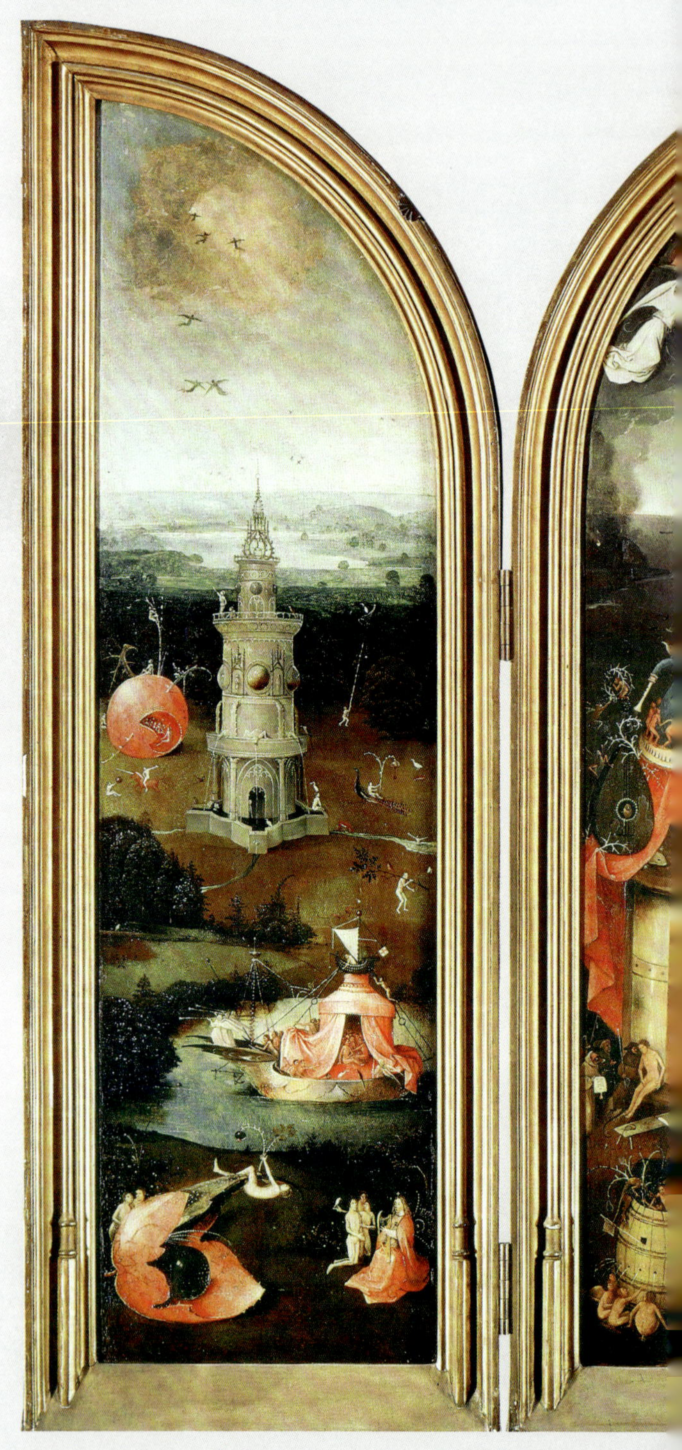

The Last Judgement

Le Jugement dernier

Das Jüngste Gericht

El Juicio Final

O Julgamento Final

Het laatste oordeel

HIERONYMUS BOSCH (C.1450–1516) AND WORKSHOP
c. 1500–05, Oil on wood/ Huile sur panneau de chêne,
98,7 x 110 cm, Groeningemuseum, Brugge

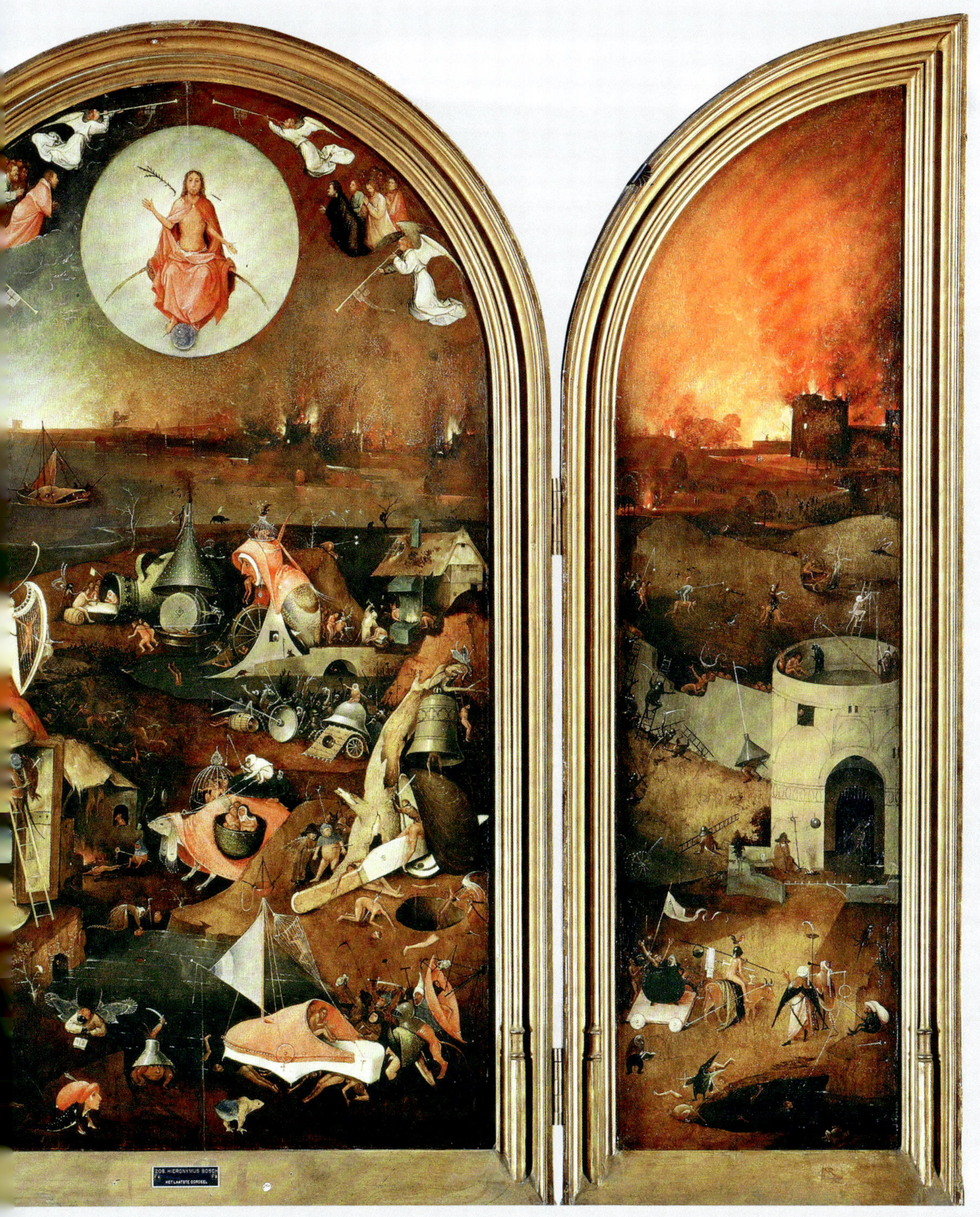

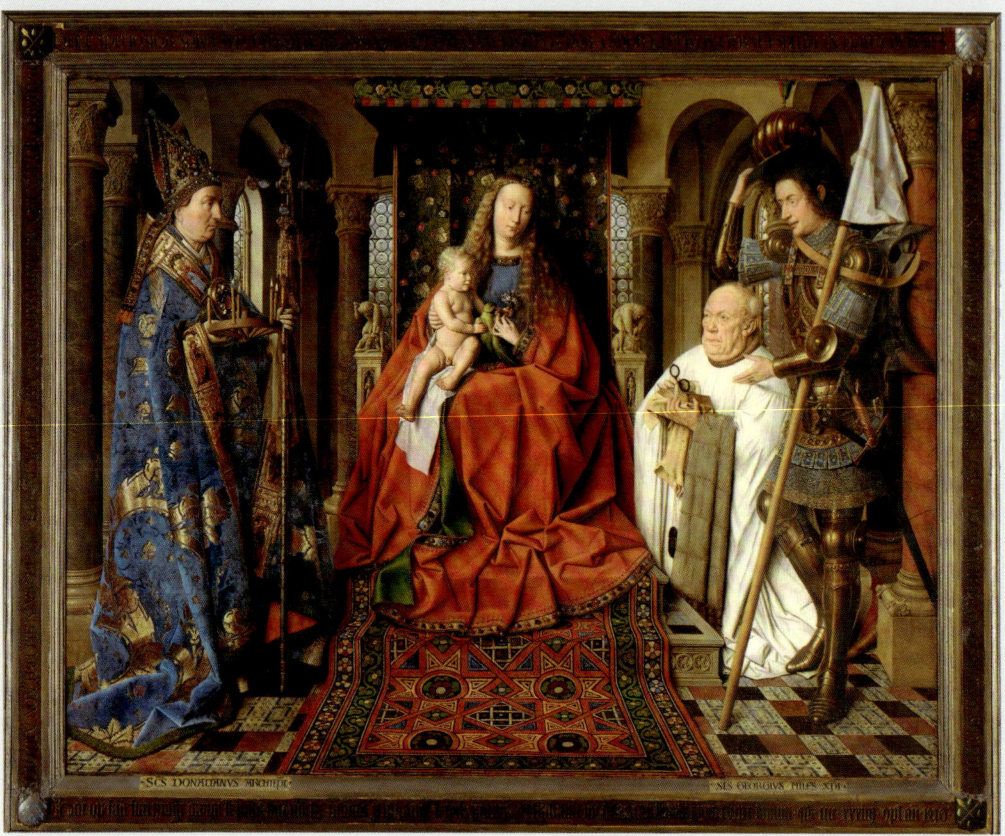

The Madonna with the Canon Joris van der Paele (Paele Madonna)

The new painting style can be clearly discerned here. The robe of Maria is tangible in its materiality, with the carpet and floor tiles, as well as the entire interior also being reproduced in great detail. Canon van der Paele, who commissioned the painting, is depicted unembellished, as an elderly man with a wrinkled face.

La Virgen con el canónigo Joris van der Paele (La Virgen de Paele)

El nuevo estilo de pintura se puede ver muy bien aquí: la túnica de María es tangible en su materialidad; la alfombra y las baldosas del suelo, así como todo el interior se reproducen con gran detalle. Y el donante de la pintura está representado sin adornos como un anciano con la cara arrugada.

La Madone au chanoine Joris van der Paele (Paele-Madone)

Voici un bel exemple du nouveau style pictural: l'étoffe dont Marie est vêtue semble quasiment palpable dans sa matérialité; le tapis et les dalles, tout comme l'intérieur, sont pourvus d'innombrables détails. Et le donateur du tableau est représenté sans complaisance sous les traits d'un vieil homme au visage ridé.

Virgem e o Menino com o Cónego van der Paele (Paele Madonna)

O novo estilo de pintura pode ser visto muito bem nesta obra: O manto de Maria é tangível na sua materialidade, o tapete e os azulejos, bem como todo o interior são reproduzidos com grande detalhe. E o doador da pintura é retratado sem embelezamento como um homem mais velho, com um rosto enrugado.

Die Madonna mit dem Kanoniker Joris van der Paele (Paele-Madonna)

Der neue Malstil lässt sich hier sehr gut erkennen: Das Gewand der Maria wirkt in seiner Stofflichkeit greifbar, Teppich und Bodenfliesen sowie das gesamte Interieur sind äußerst detailliert wiedergegeben. Und der Stifter des Bildes ist ungeschönt als älterer Mann mit faltigem Gesicht dargestellt.

De Madonna met de kanunnik Joris van der Paele (Paele Madonna)

De nieuwe schilderstijl is zeer goed herkenbaar: De mantel van Maria is voelbaar als stof, tapijt en vloertegels en het hele interieur zijn uiterst gedetailleerd weergegeven. En de opdrachtgever van het schilderij is onvervalst afgebeeld als een oudere man met een gerimpeld gezicht.

JAN VAN EYCK (C. 1390–1441)
1436, Oil on wood/Huile sur bois, 124,5 × 160 cm, Groeningemuseum, Brugge

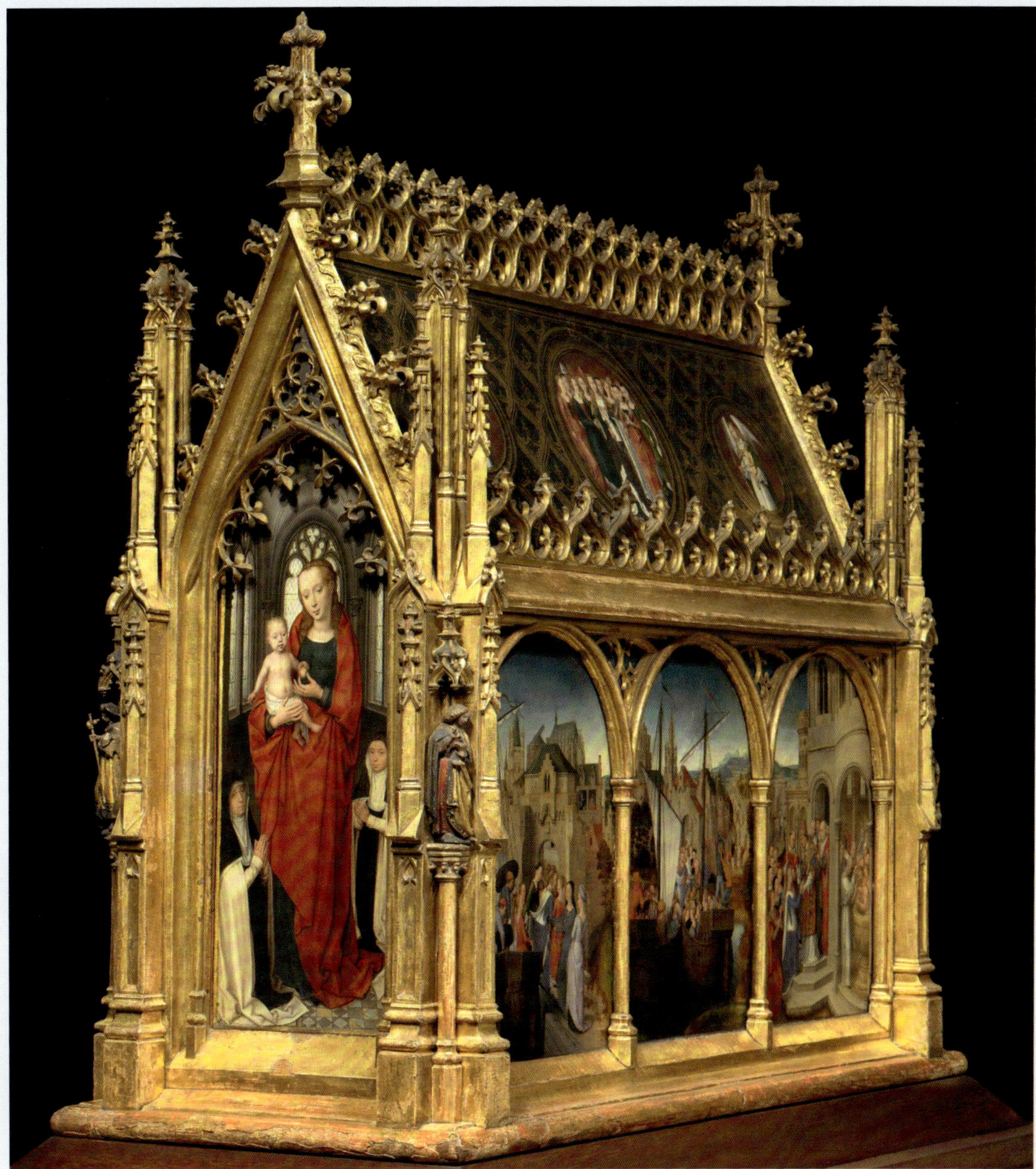

Ursula shrine   Châsse de sainte Ursule   Ursulaschrein

Santuario de Úrsula   Santuário de Ursula   Ursulaschrijn

HANS MEMLING (1433/40–94)
before/avant 1489, Carved and gilded oak, oil on oak/Chêne
sculpté et peint à l'huile, Sint-Janshospitaal, Brugge

The Baptism of Christ

Gerard David was a pupil of Hans Memling, and after his death (1494) took over the position of the official city painter of Bruges. On the centre panel of the triptych is the baptism of Christ, in an extremely detailed landscape. This landscape continues in the side wings, which depict the donors. In the background of the baptism portrayal may be seen further episodes from the life of John the Baptist.

Le baptême du Christ

Élève de Hans Memling, Gérard David lui succéda après sa mort (1494) comme peintre officiel de la ville de Bruges. Au centre, on aperçoit le baptême du Christ dans un paysage pourvu de nombreux détails. Ce paysage se prolonge sur les panneaux latéraux, représentant le couple de donateurs. À l'arrière-plan de la scène du baptême, on distingue d'autres étapes de la vie de Jean le Baptiste.

Die Taufe Christi

Gerard David war Schüler Hans Memlings und übernahm nach dessen Tod (1494) die Position des offiziellen Stadtmalers von Brügge. Im Zentrum steht die Taufe Christi, in einer äußerst detailliert geschilderten Landschaft. In den Seitenflügeln, die das Stifterpaar zeigen, setzt sich diese Landschaft fort. Im Hintergrund der Taufszene sind weitere Stationen aus dem Leben Johannes des Täufers zu erkennen

El Bautismo de Cristo

Gerard David fue alumno de Hans Memling y después de su muerte (1494) asumió el cargo de pintor oficial de la ciudad de Brujas. En el centro se representa el bautismo de Cristo, en un paisaje extremadamente detallado. Este paisaje continúa en las alas laterales que representan a los donantes. En el fondo de la escena del bautismo hay más estaciones de la vida de Juan el Bautista para ser vistas.

O Batismo de Cristo

Gerard David foi aluno de Hans Memling e após a sua morte (1494) assumiu a posição de pintor oficial da cidade de Bruges. No painel central está o batismo de Cristo, em uma paisagem extremamente detalhada. Nos painéis laterais, que mostram os doadores, a paisagem continua. No pano de fundo da cena do batismo são vistas outras cenas da vida de João Batista.

Het doopsel van Christus

Gerard David was een leerling van Hans Memling en werd na zijn dood (1494) officieel de Brugse stadsschilder. Centraal staat het doopsel van Christus in een zeer gedetailleerd geschilderd landschap. Op de zijpanelen met de opdrachtgever en zijn, loopt het landschap door. De achtergrond van de doopscène toont staties uit het leven van Johannes de Doper.

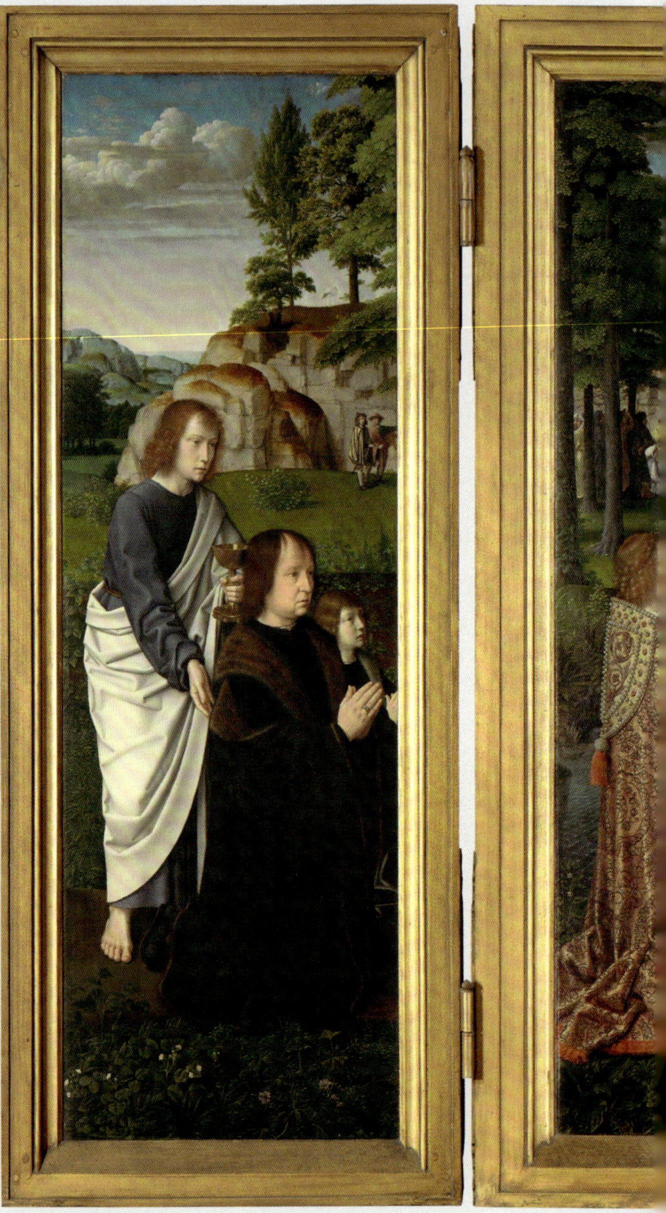

GERARD DAVID (C.1455–1523)
c. 1502–08, Oil on wood/Huile sur bois, 182 x 132,2 cm, Groeningemuseum, Brugge

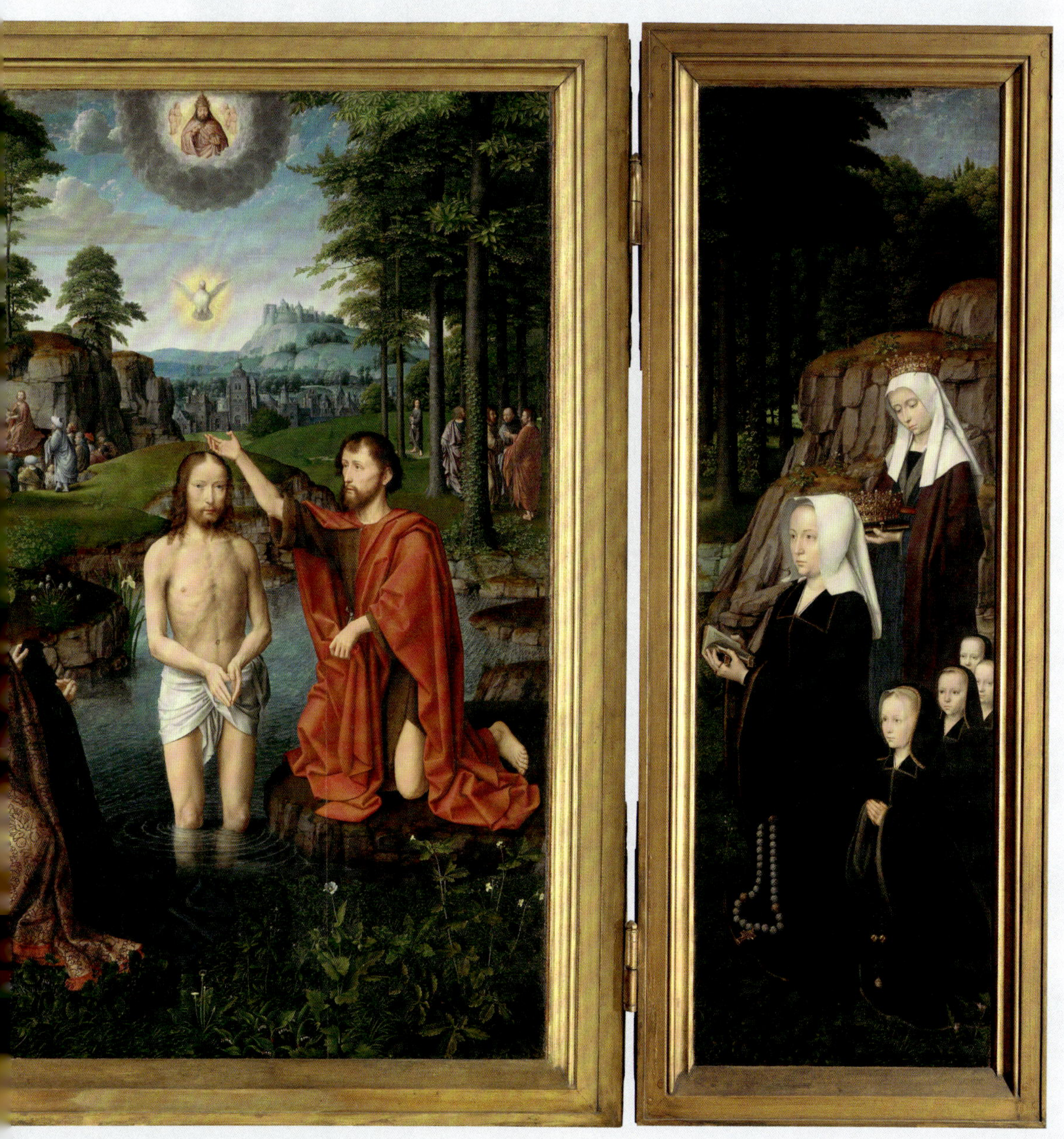

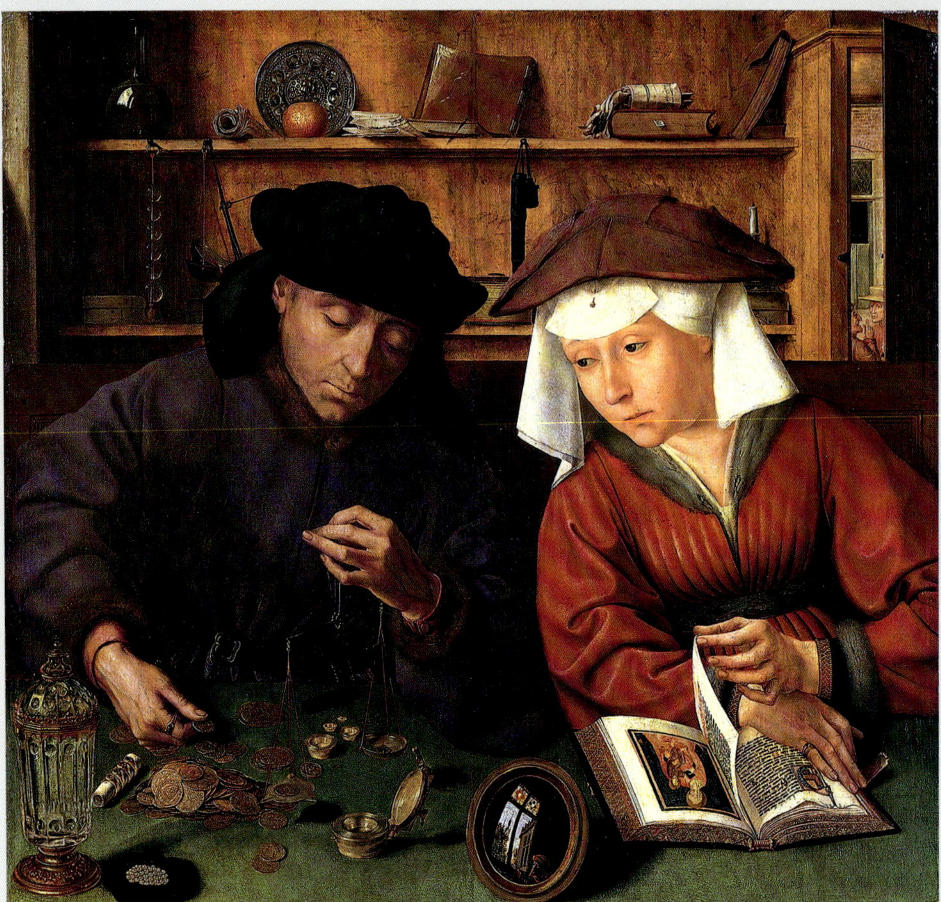

The money changer and his wife

Two worlds in one picture: whilst the man is checking the scales to determine the value of the gold, his wife is leafing through a book of hours. She thus forms the pious counterweight to her husband's work. The reflection in the round mirror reveals another person in the room.

El cambista y su mujer

Dos mundos en una sola imagen: mientras el hombre revisa la balanza para determinar el valor del oro, su esposa está hojeando un libro de horas. Ella forma así el contrapeso piadoso a las acciones de su marido. El reflejo del espejo redondo muestra a otra persona en la habitación.

Le prêteur et sa femme

Un tableau, deux univers : tandis que l'homme scrute sa balance pour définir la valeur de l'or, son épouse feuillette un livre d'Heures. Elle est ainsi le contrepoids pieux de l'activité de son mari. Le miroir rond révèle la présence d'une autre personne dans la pièce.

O cambista e sua esposa

Dois mundos em uma imagem: enquanto o homem segura a balança controlando-a para determinar o valor do ouro, sua esposa folheia um livro de horas. Ela forma assim o piedoso contrapeso às ações do marido. O reflexo do espelho redondo mostra outra pessoa na sala.

Der Geldwechsler und seine Frau

Zwei Welten auf einem Bild: Während der Mann prüfend die Waage hält, um den Wert des Goldes zu bestimmen, blättert seine Frau in einem Stundenbuch. Sie bildet so das fromme Gegengewicht zum Tun ihres Gatten. In der Spiegelung des Rundspiegels ist eine weitere im Raum befindliche Person zu erkennen.

De geldwisselaar en zijn vrouw

Twee werelden in één schilderij: Terwijl de man de weegschaal controleert om de waarde van het goud te bepalen, bladert zijn vrouw door een getijdenboek. Ze vormt dus het vrome tegenwicht van haar man. De reflectie van de ronde spiegel toont een andere persoon in de kamer.

QUENTIN METSYS (1466–1530)
1514, Oil on wood/Huile sur bois, 70,5 × 67 cm, Musée du Louvre, Paris

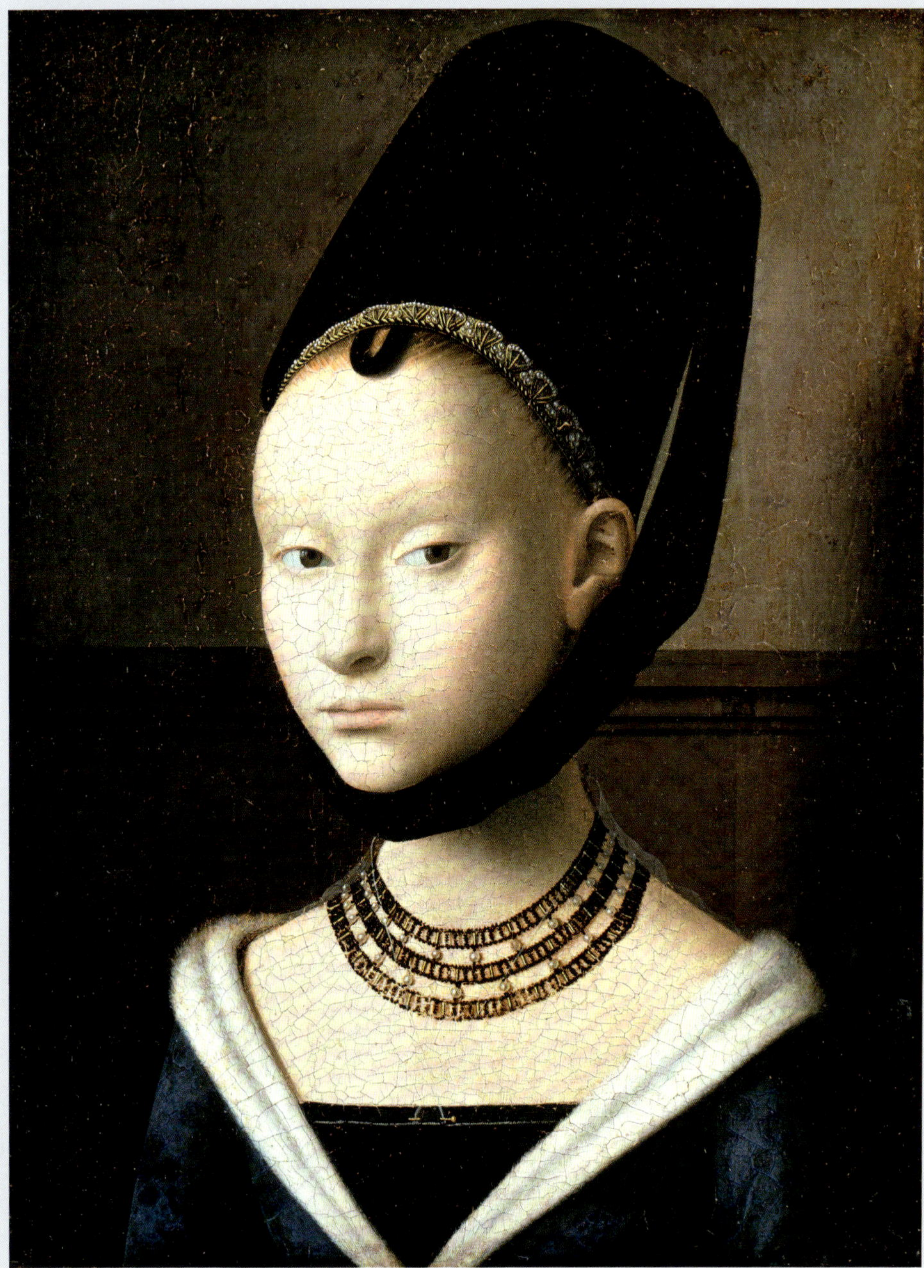

Portrait of a young lady   **Portrait d'une jeune fille**   **Bildnis einer jungen Dame**

Retrato de una joven   **Retrato de uma mocinha**   **Portret van een jongedame**

PETRUS CHRISTUS (C. 1410/20–75/76)
c. 1470, Tempera and oil on oak/Tempera et huile sur bois, 29 × 22,5 cm, Gemäldegalerie, Berlin

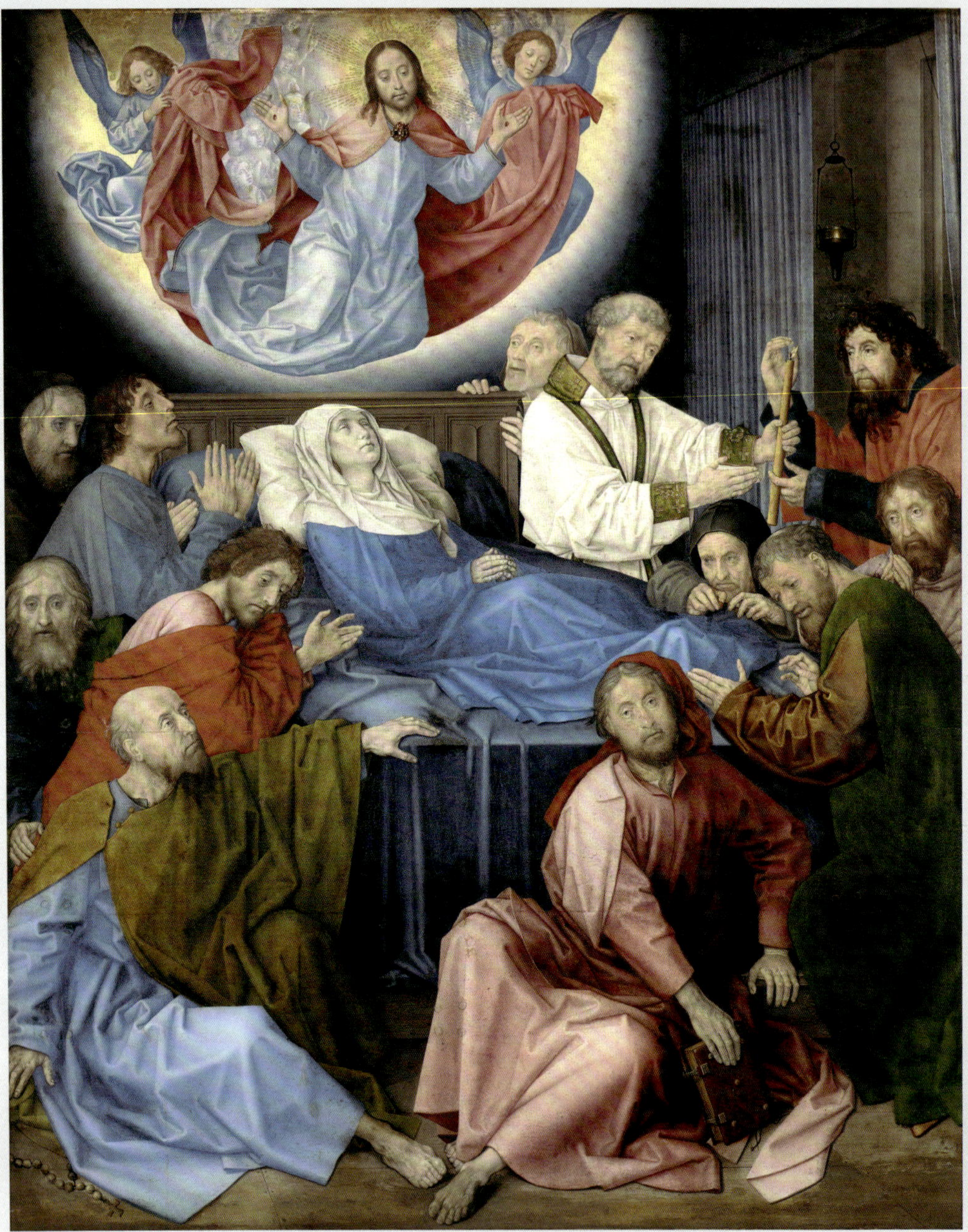

Death of the Virgin   **Tod Mariae**   **Morte de Maria**

La Mort de la Vierge   **Muerte de María**   **Dood van de Heilige Maagd**

HUGO VAN DER GOES (C. 1435/40–82)
c. 1480, Oil on wood/Huile sur bois, 147,8×122,5 cm, Groeningemuseum, Brugge

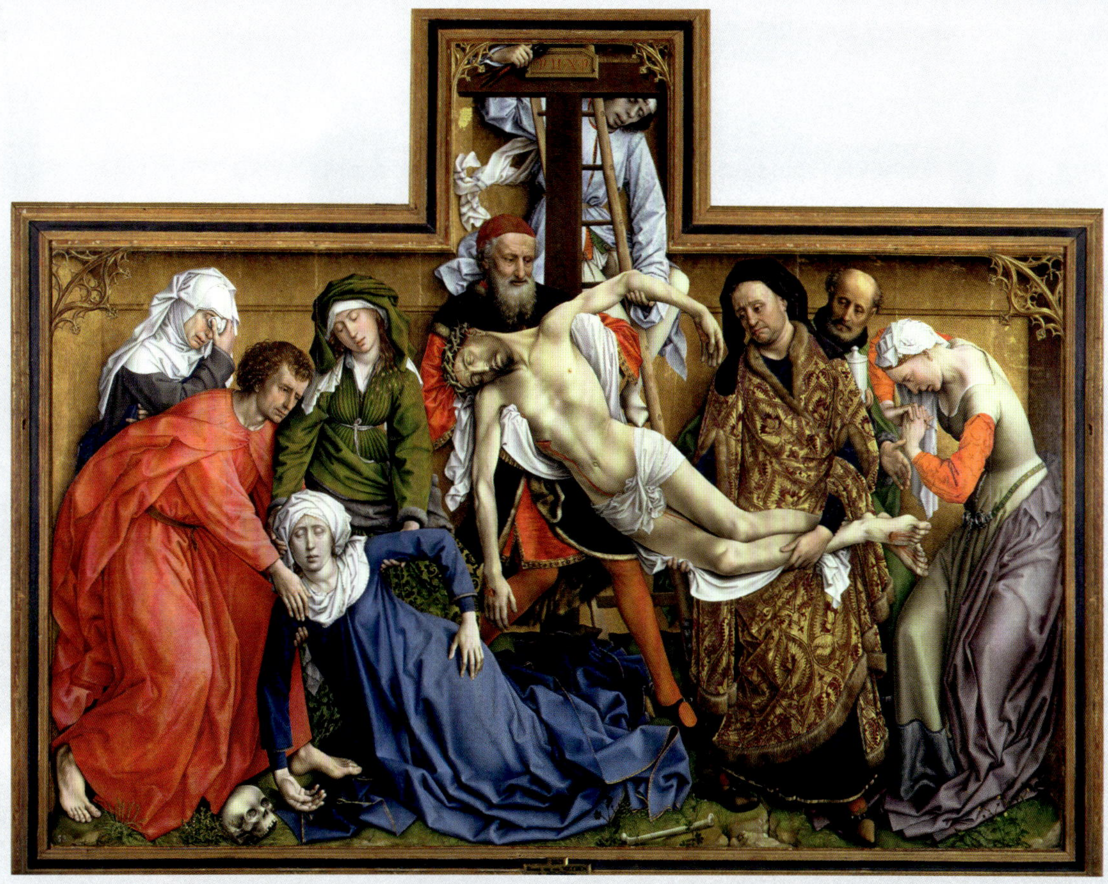

Descent from the Cross

The *Descent from the Cross* is one of the main works of the artist Rogier van der Weyden, who at times worked in Robert Campin's workshop. The panel was probably originally the central panel of a triptych. The painter impressively reproduces the different skin tones and garments.

Descendimiento de la cruz

El *Descendimiento de la cruz* es una de las principales obras del artista Rogier van der Weyden,, que a veces trabajó en el taller de Robert Campin. El panel fue probablemente originalmente el panel central de un tríptico. El pintor reproduce de forma impresionante los diferentes tonos de la piel y las prendas.

La Descente de croix

La Descente de croix fait partie des principales œuvres de l'artiste Rogier van der Weyden, qui travaillait par moments dans l'atelier de Robert Campin. Sans doute ce panneau fit-il jadis partie d'un triptyque. Le peintre rend de manière saisissante les différentes couleurs de peau et les diverses étoffes.

Deposição da Cruz

A *Deposição da Cruz* é uma das principais obras do artista Rogier van der Weyden,, que trabalhou temporariamente na oficina de Robert Campin. Provavelmente o painel teria sido originalmente o painel central de um tríptico. O pintor reproduz de forma impressionante os diferentes tons de pele e roupas.

Kreuzabnahme

Die *Kreuzabnahme* ist eines der Hauptwerke des Künstlers Rogier van der Weyden, der zeitweise in der Werkstatt Robert Campins arbeitete. Vermutlich war die Tafel ursprünglich die Mitteltafel eines Triptychons. In eindrucksvoller Weise gibt der Maler die unterschiedlichen Hauttöne und Gewandstoffe wieder.

Kruisafneming

De *Kruisafneming* is één van de belangrijkste werken van de kunstenaar Rogier van der Weyden, die soms in het atelier van Robert Campin werkte. Het paneel was waarschijnlijk oorspronkelijk het centrale paneel van een drieluik. De schilder reproduceert op indrukwekkende wijze de verschillende huidtinten en kledingstukken.

ROGIER VAN DER WEYDEN (1399–1464)

before/avant 1443, Oil on wood/Huile sur bois, 204,5 × 261,4 cm, Museo del Prado, Madrid

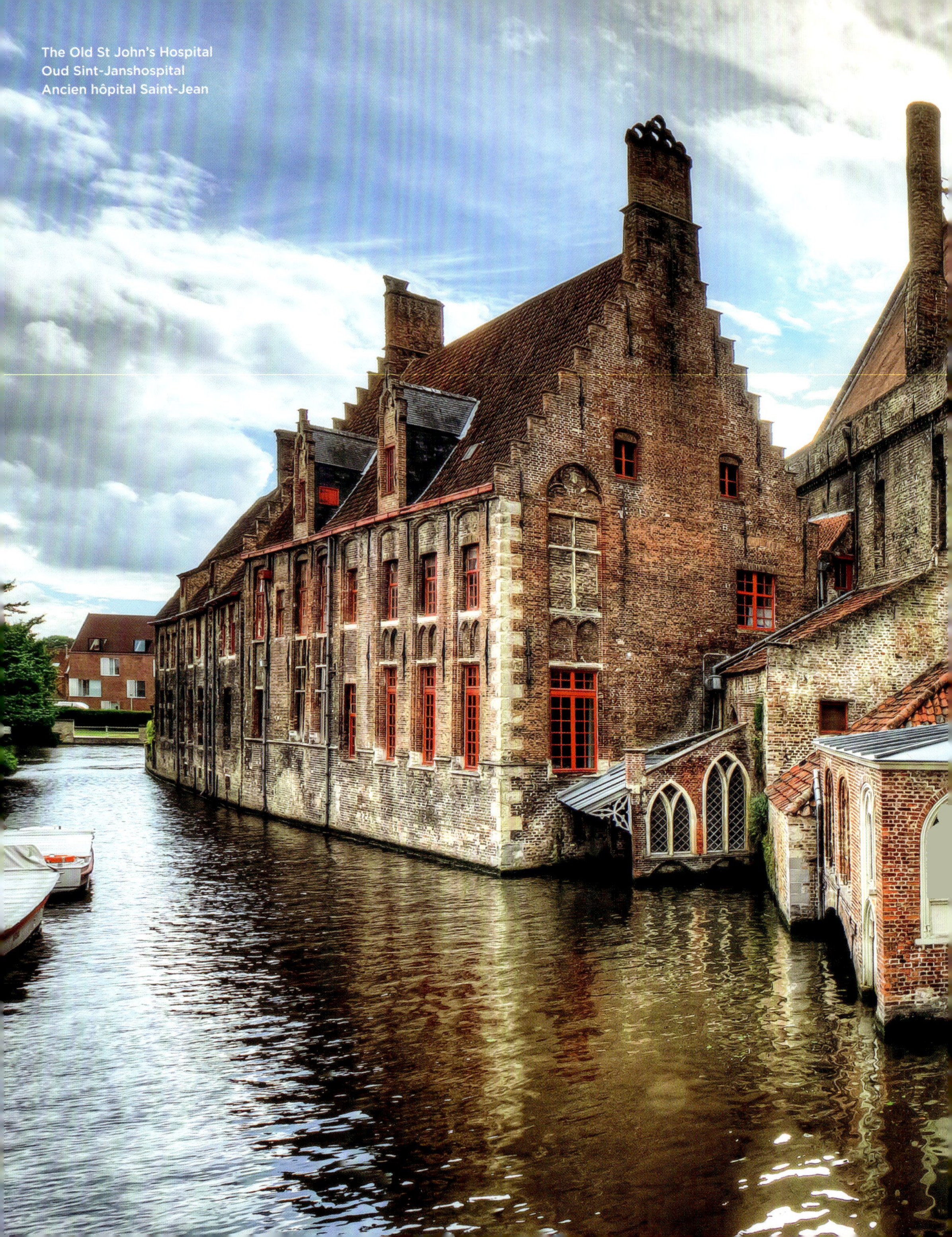

The Old St John's Hospital
Oud Sint-Janshospital
Ancien hôpital Saint-Jean

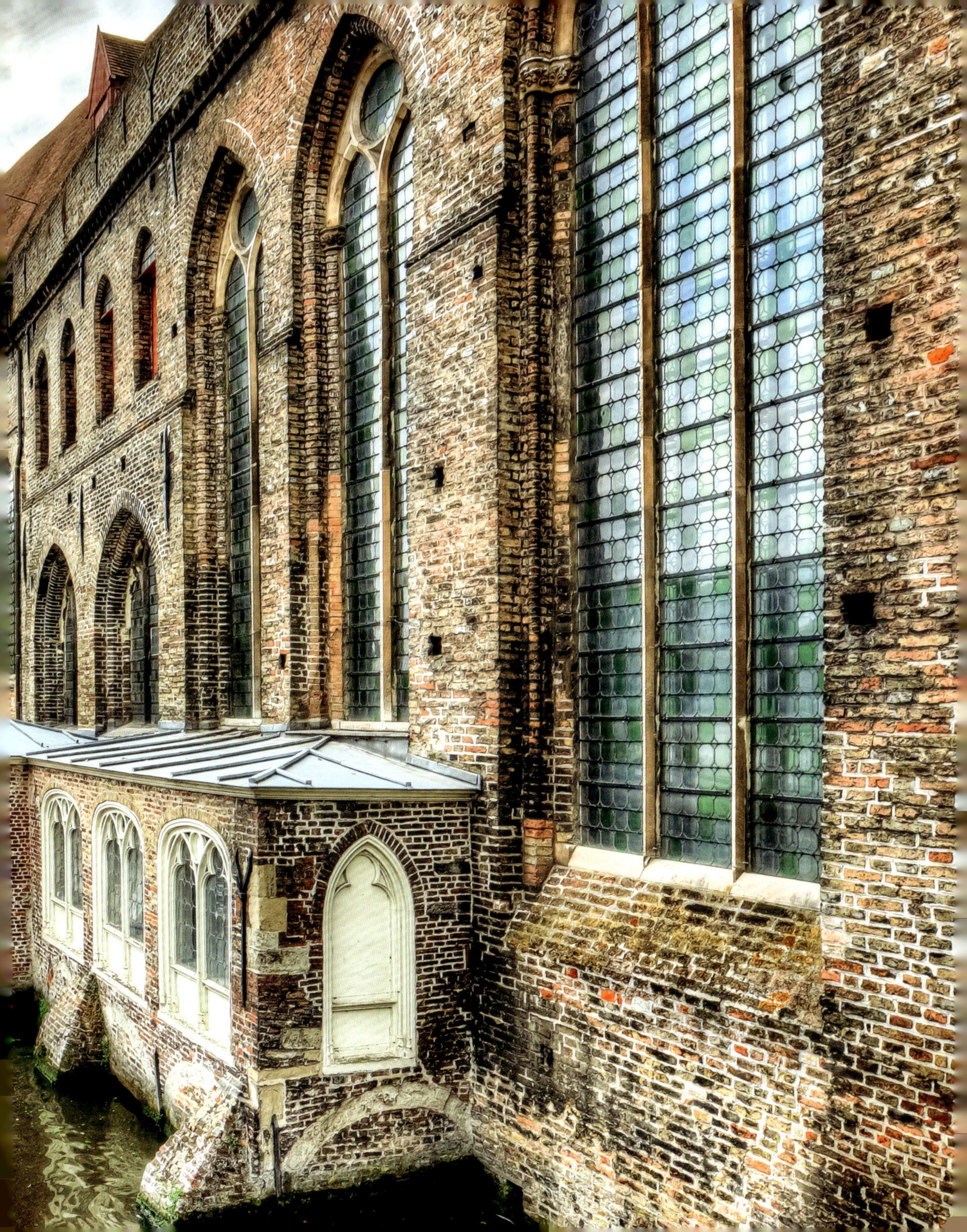

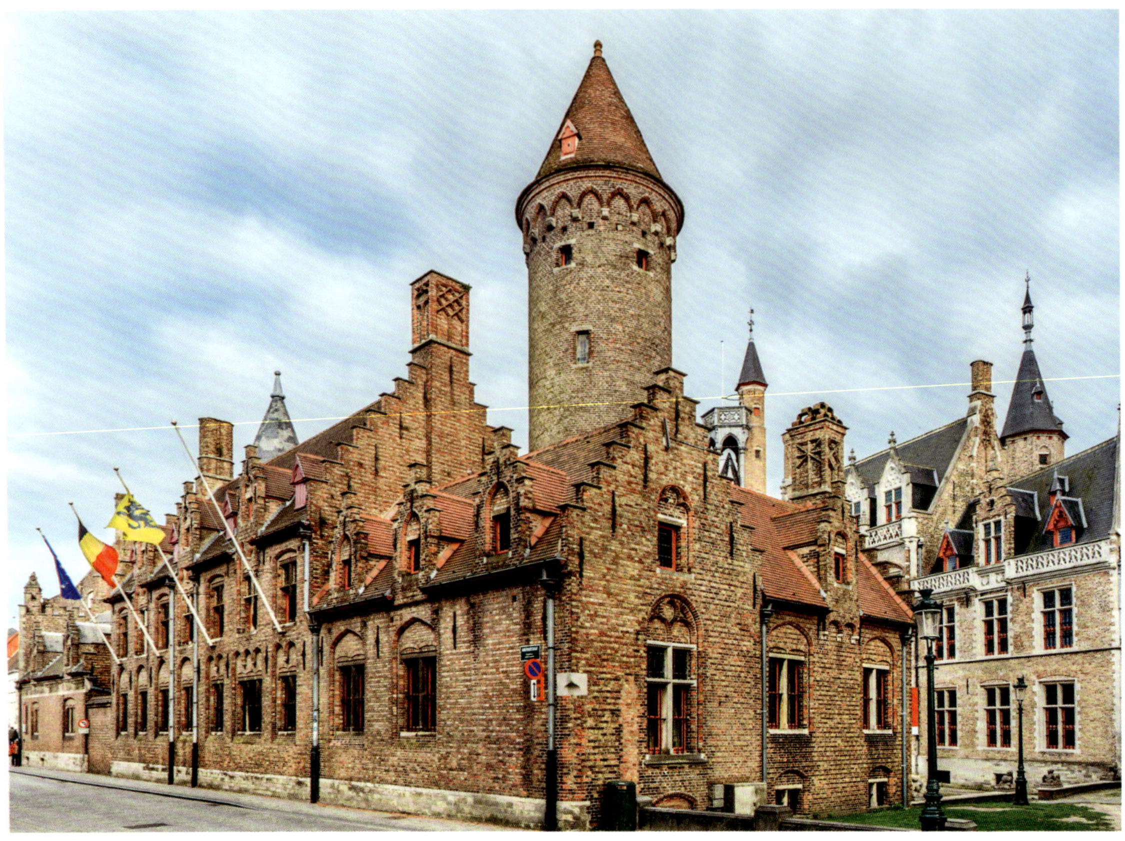

Gruuthusemuseum
Musée Gruuthuse

Gruuthuse Museum

The imposing city palace is a treasure trove of Bruges art history, filled with majestic tapestries, precious furniture and paintings. It is a museum of applied arts, with a collection of 20,000 objects. The theme of the museum is "Plus est en vous" (There is more in you), the motto of Louis de Gruuthuse, who made a fortune with "Gruut" (herbs added to beer instead of hops).

Musée Gruuthuse

Cet imposant palais de ville est un trésor de l'histoire de l'art brugeois, que l'on y découvre au fil de majestueuses tapisseries, de précieux meubles et tableaux. L'institut d'histoire culturelle renferme une collection de 20 000 objets. Le fil conducteur est « Plus est en vous », la devise de Louis de Gruuthuse, l'homme qui fit fortune grâce au « gruut » (mélange d'herbes ajoutées à la bière à la place du houblon).

Gruuthuse-Museum

Der imposante Stadtpalast ist eine Schatzkammer der Brügger Kunstgeschichte, gefüllt mit majestätischen Wandteppichen, kostbaren Möbeln und Gemälden. Es ist ein kulturgeschichtliches Institut mit einer Sammlung von 20 000 Objekten. Leitfaden ist hier „Plus est en vous" (Es steckt mehr in Dir), die Devise Ludwigs von Gruuthuse, dem Mann, der mit „Gruut" (Kräuter, die anstelle des Hopfens dem Bier zugefügt wurden) ein Vermögen machte.

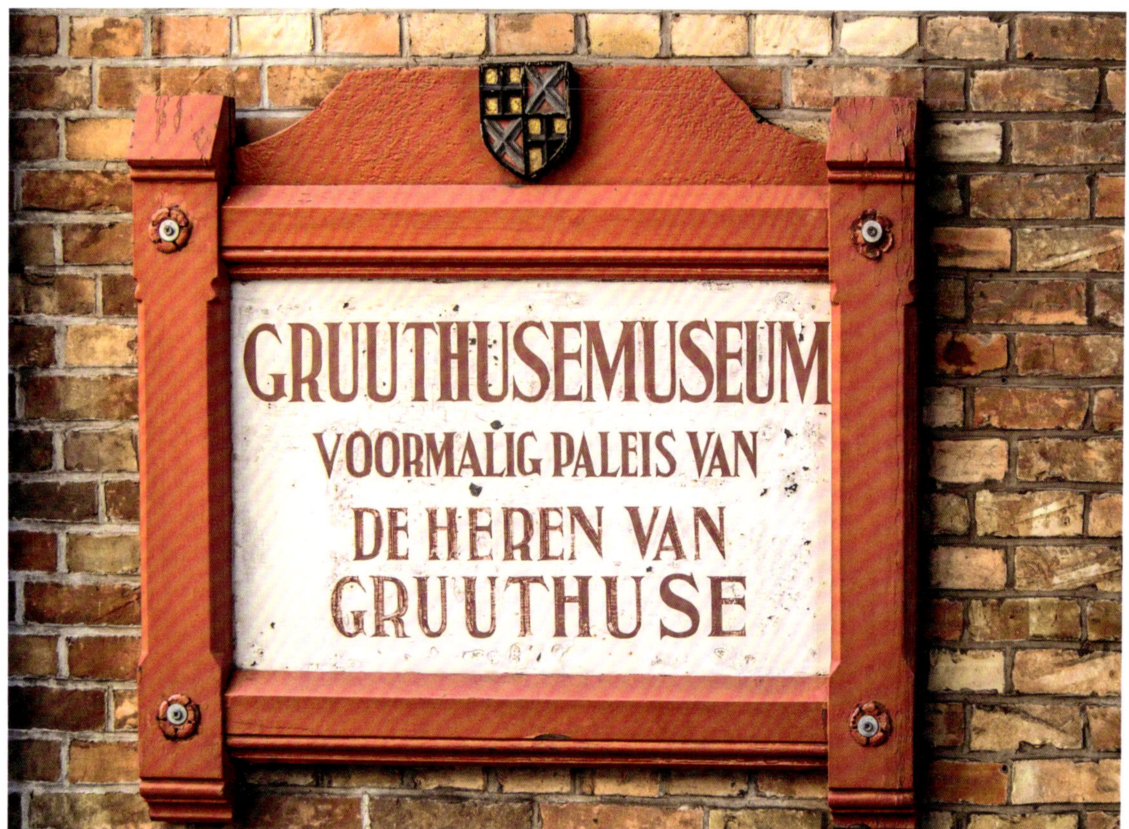

Gruuthusemuseum
Musée Gruuthuse

Museo Gruuthuse

El imponente palacio de la ciudad es un tesoro escondido de la historia del arte de Brujas, lleno de majestuosos tapices, muebles preciosos y pinturas. Es un instituto de historia cultural con una colección de 20 000 objetos. La guía es "Plus est en vous" (hay más en ti), el lema de Ludwig von Gruuthuse, el hombre que hizo una fortuna con "Gruut" (hierbas añadidas a la cerveza en lugar de lúpulo).

Museu Gruuthuse

O imponente palácio da cidade é um tesouro da história da arte de Bruges, repleto de tapeçarias majestosas, móveis preciosos e pinturas. É um instituto de história cultural com uma coleção de 20 000 objetos. O guia aqui é "Plus est en vous" (Há mais em você), o lema de Ludwig von Gruuthuse, o homem que fez uma fortuna com "Gruut" (ervas adicionadas à cerveja em vez de lúpulo).

Gruuthusemuseum

Het imposante stadspaleis is een schatkamer van de Brugse kunstgeschiedenis, gevuld met majestueuze wandtapijten, kostbare meubels en schilderijen: een cultuurhistorisch instituut met een 20 000 objecten. Hier geldt "Plus est en vous" (meer is in u), motto van Ludwig von Gruuthuse die een fortuin verdiende met "gruut" (kruiden toegevoegd aan bier i.p.v. hop).

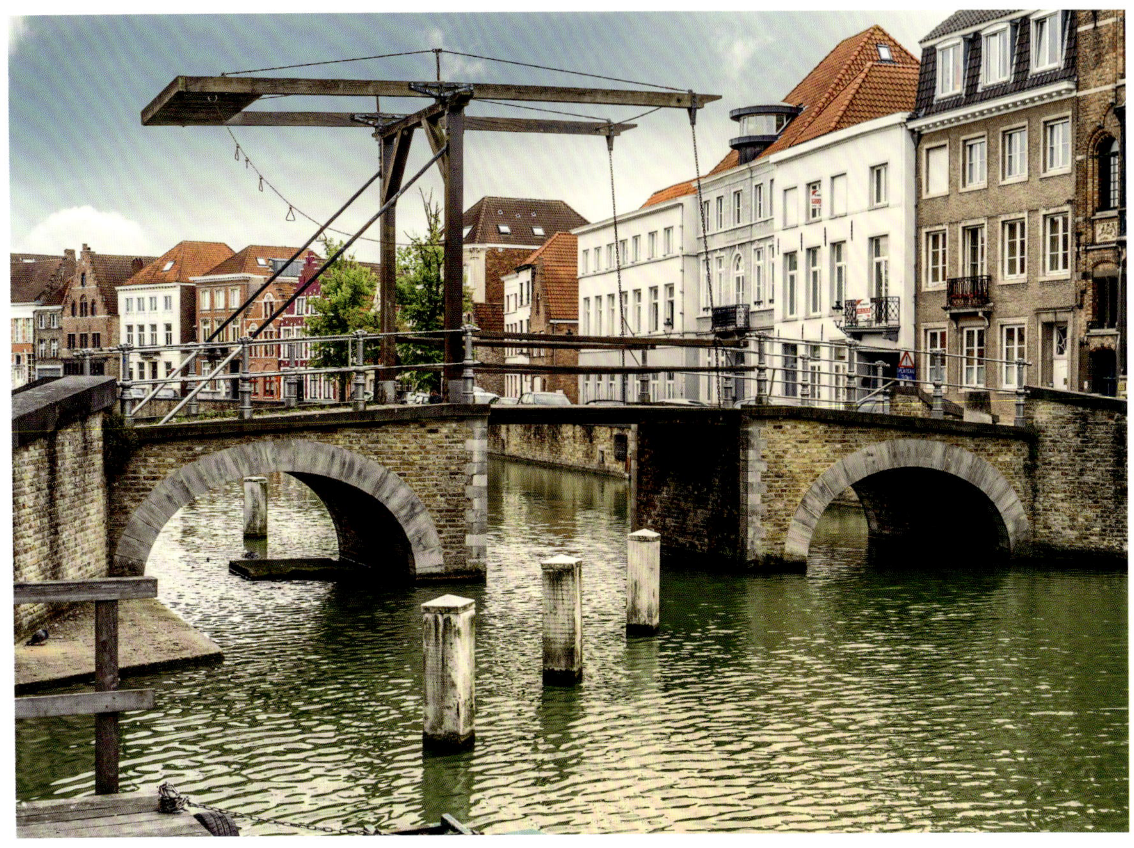

Small drawbridge connecting Langerei with Potterierei
Kleine ophaalbrug die Langerei met Potterierei verbindt
Petit pont-levis reliant Langerei à Potterierei

Splendour of the Middle Ages

With the canals, called Reien in Bruges, the river Reie formed the lifeline of the port city. With the loss of access to the sea, the once rich city lost its livelihood. The remaining inhabitants were so poor that the ghost town increasingly decayed. When the writer Georges Rodenbach published his melancholic novel *Bruges-la-Morte* (*Bruges, dead city,* 1892), he made the city famous. The weathered splendour of the Middle Ages aroused nostalgic feelings and Bruges became a tourist attraction drawing eight million visitors a year.

Splendeur du Moyen Âge

Avec ses canaux, appelés «reien» à Bruges, le fleuve Reie formait l'artère faisant battre le pouls de la ville portuaire. Mais son accès à la mer disparu, la ville jadis opulente perdit la base de son existence. Les habitants qui y restèrent étaient si pauvres que la ville fantôme se délabra de plus en plus. En publiant son roman mélancolique *Bruges-la-Morte* (1892), l'écrivain Georges Rodenbach rendit à la ville sa célébrité. La splendeur érodée du Moyen Âge éveilla des élans de nostalgie. Bruges se transforma en un bastion touristique, accueillant huit millions de visiteurs par an.

Glanz des Mittelalters

Mit den Kanälen, die in Brügge Reien genannt werden, bildete der Fluss Reie, die Lebensader der Hafenstadt. Mit dem Verlust des Zugangs zum Meer verlor die einst reiche Stadt ihre Lebensgrundlage. Die verbliebenen Einwohner waren so arm, dass die Geisterstadt zunehmend verfiel. Als der Schriftsteller Georges Rodenbach seinen melancholischen Roman *Bruges-la-Morte* (*Brügge, tote Stadt,* 1892) herausbrachte, machte er die Stadt berühmt. Der verwitternde Glanz des Mittelalters weckte nostalgische Gefühle. Brügge entwickelte sich, mit jährlich acht Millionen Besuchern, zu einer Touristenhochburg.

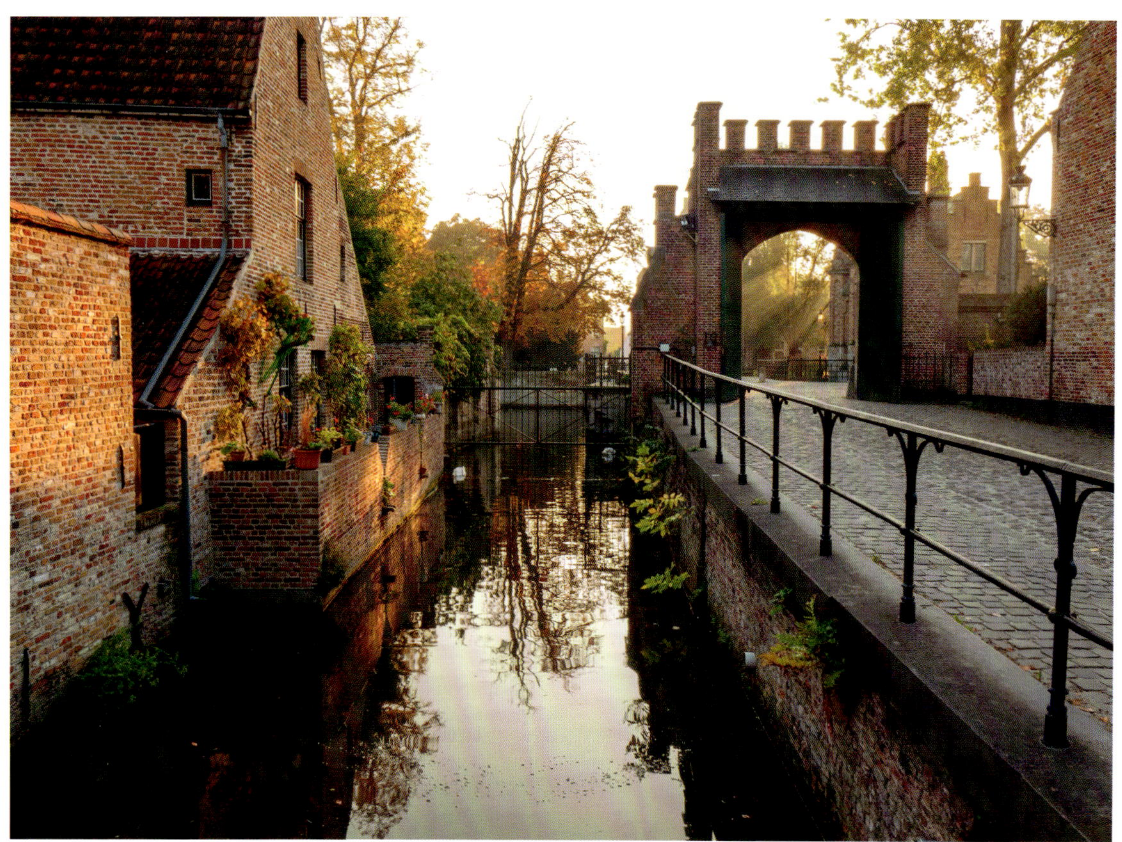

Canal at the end of Arsenaalstraat
Gracht aan het einde van de Arsenaalstraat
Canal au bout de l'Arsenaalstraat

Esplendor de la Edad Media

Con los canales llamados Reien en Brujas, el río Reie formó la línea de la vida de la ciudad portuaria. Con la pérdida del acceso al mar, la ciudad, que en su día había sido rica, perdió su sustento. Los habitantes restantes eran tan pobres que la ciudad fantasma se iba deteriorando cada vez más. Cuando el escritor Georges Rodenbach publicó su novela melancólica *Bruges-la-Morte* (*Brujas la muerta*, 1892), hizo famosa a la ciudad. El esplendor curtido de la Edad Media despertó sentimientos nostálgicos. Brujas se convirtió en un baluarte turístico con ocho millones de visitantes al año.

Esplendor da Idade Média

Com os canais chamados Reien em Bruges, o rio Reie formou a artéria vital da cidade portuária. Com a perda do acesso ao mar, a outrora rica cidade perdeu seu sustento. Os restantes habitantes eram tão pobres que a cidade fantasma se deteriorou cada vez mais. Quando o escritor Georges Rodenbach publicou seu romance melancólico *Bruges-la-Morte* (*Bruges, cidade morta*, 1892), ele tornou a cidade famosa. O esplendor desgastado da Idade Média despertou sentimentos nostálgicos. Bruges tornou-se um reduto turístico com oito milhões de visitantes por ano.

Schitterende Middeleeuwen

Met de grachten, die in Brugge reien worden genoemd, vormt de rivier de Reie de levensader van de havenstad. Met het verlies van de toegang tot de zee verloor de ooit rijke stad haar bestaansgrond. De overgebleven inwoners waren zo arm dat de spookstad steeds meer in verval raakte. Toen de schrijver Georges Rodenbach zijn melancholische roman *Bruges-la-Morte* (*Brugge-de-dode,* 1892) publiceerde, maakte hij de stad beroemd. De verweerde pracht en praal van de Middeleeuwen wekte nostalgische gevoelens op. Brugge ontwikkelde zich met jaarlijks acht miljoen bezoekers tot een toeristisch bolwerk.

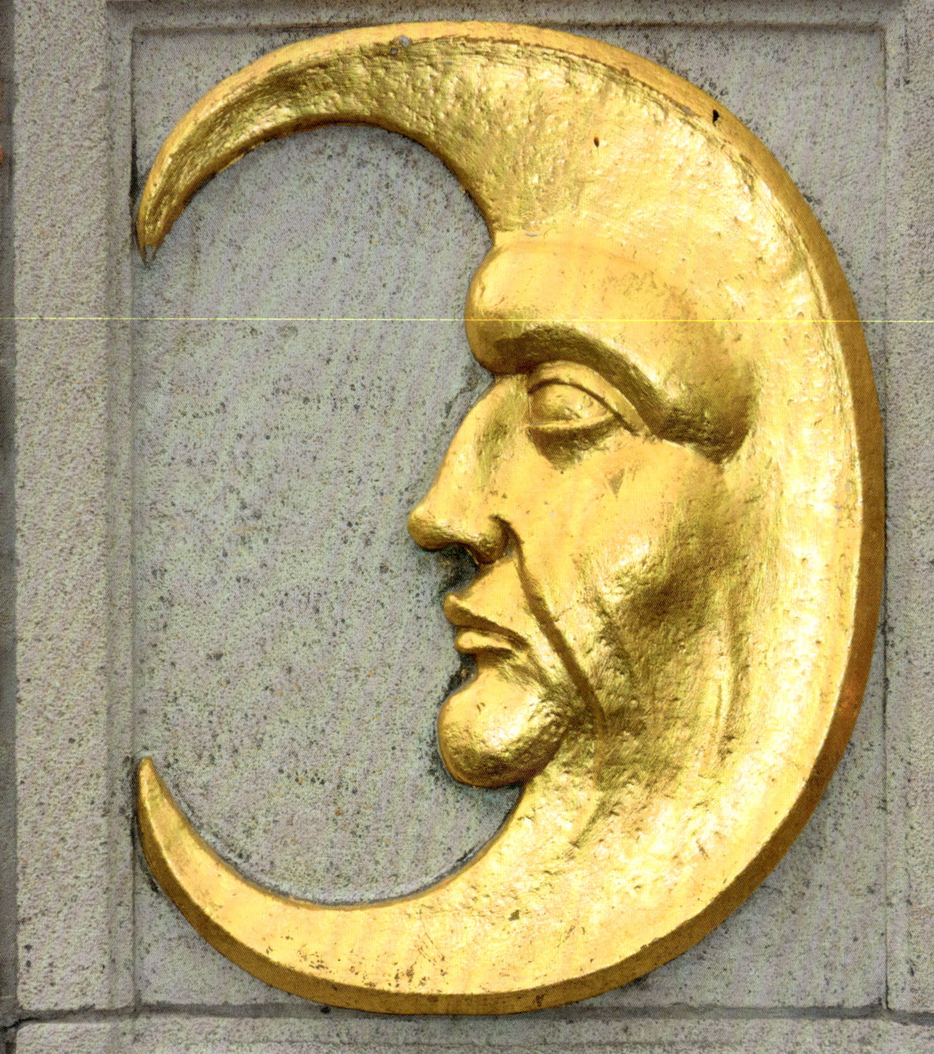

De Halve Maan Brewery
Brouwerij De Halve Maan
Brasserie De Halve Maan

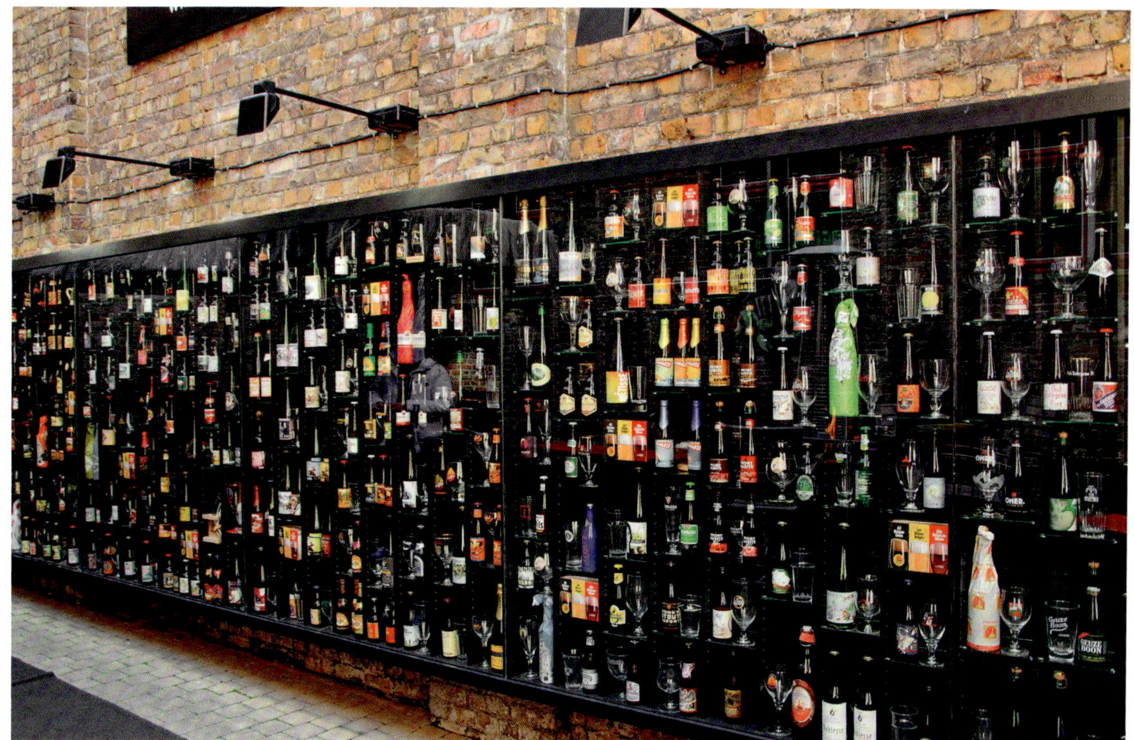

Beer varieties
Biersoorten
Variétés de bières

3 km beer pipeline

For over 500 years the traditional brewery "De Halve Maan" (The Half Moon) has been brewing its beers in Bruges' old town. The "Brugse Zot", a spicy top-fermented beer, flows between the brewery and the bottling plant at the edge of the city through a 3 km (1,68 mi) long underground beer pipeline. Guided tours with beer tasting take place daily.

Tubería de cerveza de 3 km

Desde hace más de 500 años, la cervecería tradicional "De Halve Maan" (media luna) elabora sus cervezas en el casco antiguo de Brujas. La "Brugse Zot", una cerveza picante de alta fermentación, fluye entre la cervecería y la planta de embotellado a las puertas de la ciudad a través de una tubería subterránea de cerveza de 3 km de longitud. Diariamente se realizan visitas guiadas con degustación de cerveza.

3 km de pipeline à bière

Depuis plus de 500 ans, la brasserie traditionnelle De Halve Maan (demi-lune) brasse sa bière dans la vieille ville de Bruges. Entre le lieu de brassage et celui de l'embouteillage, aux portes de la ville, la Brugse Zot, une bière épicée à haute fermentation, coule dans un pipeline à bière souterrain de 3 km. Chaque jour, les visiteurs peuvent participer à des visites guidées suivies d'une dégustation.

3 km de tubulação de cerveja

Há mais de 500 anos que a cervejaria tradicional "De Halve Maan" (meia-lua) fabrica as suas cervejas na cidade velha de Bruges. O "Brugse Zot", uma cerveja altamente fermentada, flui entre o tubo de fabricação de cerveja e a fábrica de engarrafamento nos arredores da cidade através de uma tubulação subterrânea de cerveja de 3 km de comprimento. Visitas guiadas com degustação de cerveja acontecem diariamente.

3 km Bier-Pipeline

Seit über 500 Jahren braut die Traditionsbrauerei „De Halve Maan" (Halber Mond) ihre Biere in Brügges Altstadt. Zwischen der Braustube und der Abfüllanlage vor den Toren der Stadt fließt das „Brugse Zot", ein würziges obergäriges Bier, durch eine 3 km lange unterirdische Bier-Pipeline. Täglich finden Führungen mit anschließender Bierverkostung statt.

3 km bierpijpleiding

Al meer dan 500 jaar brouwt de traditionele brouwerij "De Halve Maan" haar bieren in de oude Brugse binnenstad. Tussen het proeflokaal en de bottelarij voor de poorten van de stad vloeit de "Brugse Zot", een pittig bier van hoge gisting, door de 3 km lange onderaardse bierpijpleiding. Dagelijks vinden er rondleidingen met aansluitend een bierproeverij plaats.

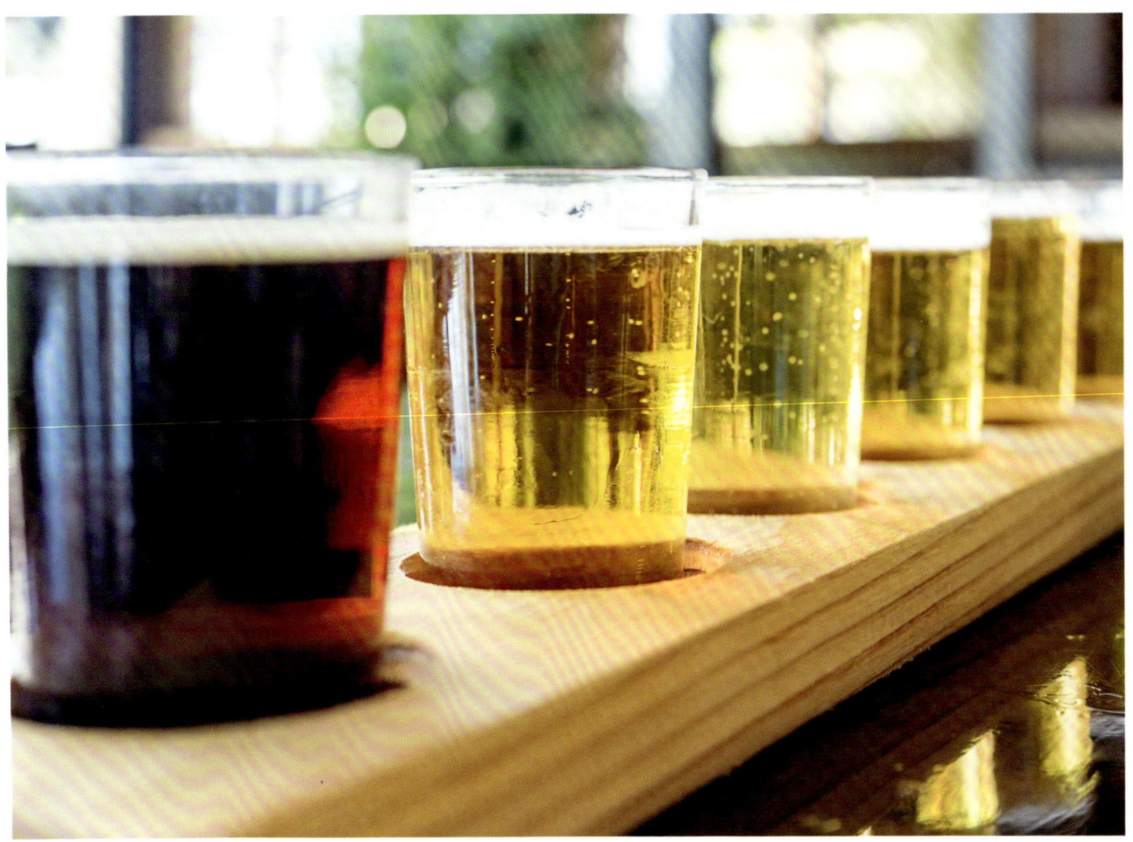

Beer varieties
Biersoorten
Variétés de bières

Flemish beer variety

Flanders is a beer province with a
centuries-old tradition. Nowhere else
in Europe are more, stronger and more
daring varieties brewed. From classic Pils
and legendary Trappist beers to Kriek
(cherry beer) and Geuze: the Flemish beer
varieties offers all colours, flavors and
alcohol contents. The tasty Trippel of the
pub "De Garre", which is somewhat hidden
down a long alley near the Burgplatz, has
much to offer in terms of alcohol: Only
two glasses are served per person! In 2016,
Belgian beer was added to UNESCO's List
of Intangible Cultural Heritage.

Diversité des bières flamandes

Les Flandres sont une région brassicole à
la tradition séculaire. Il n'est aucun autre
lieu en Europe où l'on brasse des variétés
plus nombreuses, plus fortes, plus osées.
De la Pils classique et des légendaires
bières trappistes à la bière de cerise et la
Gueuze: avec la bière flamande, vous avez
le choix en matière de couleurs, d'arômes,
de teneur en alcool. Au bar à bières De
Garre, dissimulé près de la place du Bourg,
la délicieuse Trippel, notamment, ne lésine
pas sur ce dernier point: c'est d'ailleurs la
raison pour laquelle on y sert au maximum
deux verres par personne ! La bière
belge fait partie du patrimoine culturel
immatériel de l'Unesco depuis 2016.

Flämische Biervielfalt

Flandern ist ein Bierland mit einer
Jahrhunderte alten Tradition. Nirgendwo
sonst in Europa werden mehr, stärkere
und gewagtere Sorten gebraut. Vom
klassischen Pils und legendären
Trappistenbieren bis hin zu Kirschbier und
Geuze: Die flämische Biervielfalt bietet
alle Farben, Aromen und Alkoholgehalte.
Insbesondere das leckere Trippel der
Bierkneipe de Garre, die etwas versteckt
nahe dem Burgplatz liegt, hat es in puncto
Alkohol in sich: Pro Person werden nur
zwei Gläser ausgeschenkt! 2016 wurde
das belgische Bier in die Liste der
UNESCO für immaterielles Kulturerbe der
Menschheit aufgenommen.

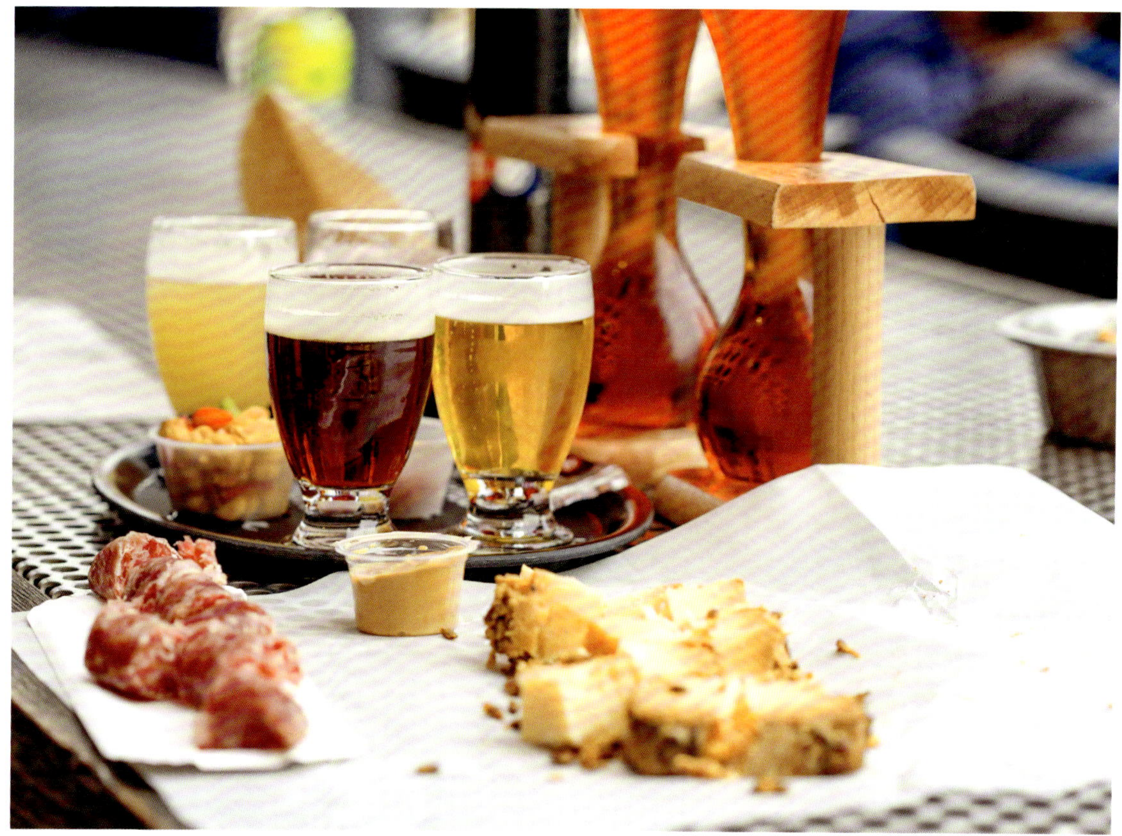

Different types of beer like cherry bear and coconut beer
Verschillende soorten bier zoals kerselaar en kokosnootbier
Différents types de bières comme la bière à la cerise et la bière à la noix de coco

Variedad de cerveza flamenca

Flandes es un país cervecero con una tradición de siglos. En ningún otro lugar de Europa se elaboran variedades más fuertes y atrevidas. Desde las clásicas Pils y las legendarias cervezas trapenses hasta la cerveza de cereza y gueuze: la cerveza flamenca ofrece todos los colores, sabores y grados alcohólicos. Especialmente el sabroso Trippel de la cervecería de Garre, que está un poco escondido cerca de la plaza Burgplatz, tiene mucho que ofrecer en términos de alcohol: ¡solo se sirven dos vasos por persona! En 2016, la cerveza belga fue añadida a la lista del patrimonio cultural inmaterial de la UNESCO.

Variedade de cerveja flamenga

A Flandres é uma terra da cerveja com uma tradição secular. Em nenhum outro lugar da Europa são fabricadas mais, mais fortes e mais ousadas variedades. Das clássicas Pilsen e lendárias cervejas Trappist até às Lambic Kriek e Gueuze: a variedade de cerveja flamenga oferece todas as cores, sabores e teor alcoólico. Especialmente a saborosa Tripel, no bar De Garre, que fica um pouco escondido perto da praça do castelo, tem muito a oferecer em termos de álcool: apenas dois copos são servidos por pessoa! Em 2016, a cerveja belga foi acrescentada à lista do Património Cultural Imaterial da UNESCO.

Vele Vlaamse biersoorten

Vlaanderen is een bierland met een eeuwenoude traditie. Nergens anders in Europa worden meer, sterkere en gedurfdere soorten gebrouwen. Van klassieke pils en legendarische trappistenbieren tot kersenbier en geuze: de vele Vlaamse biersoorten bieden alle kleuren, smaken en alcoholpercentages. Vooral de smakelijke trippel van biercafé De Garre, dat een beetje verscholen ligt in de buurt van de Burg, heeft veel te bieden op het gebied van alcohol: per persoon worden slechts twee glazen geserveerd! In 2016 werd het Belgische bier toegevoegd aan de UNESCO-Representatieve lijst van het immaterieel cultureel erfgoed van de mensheid.

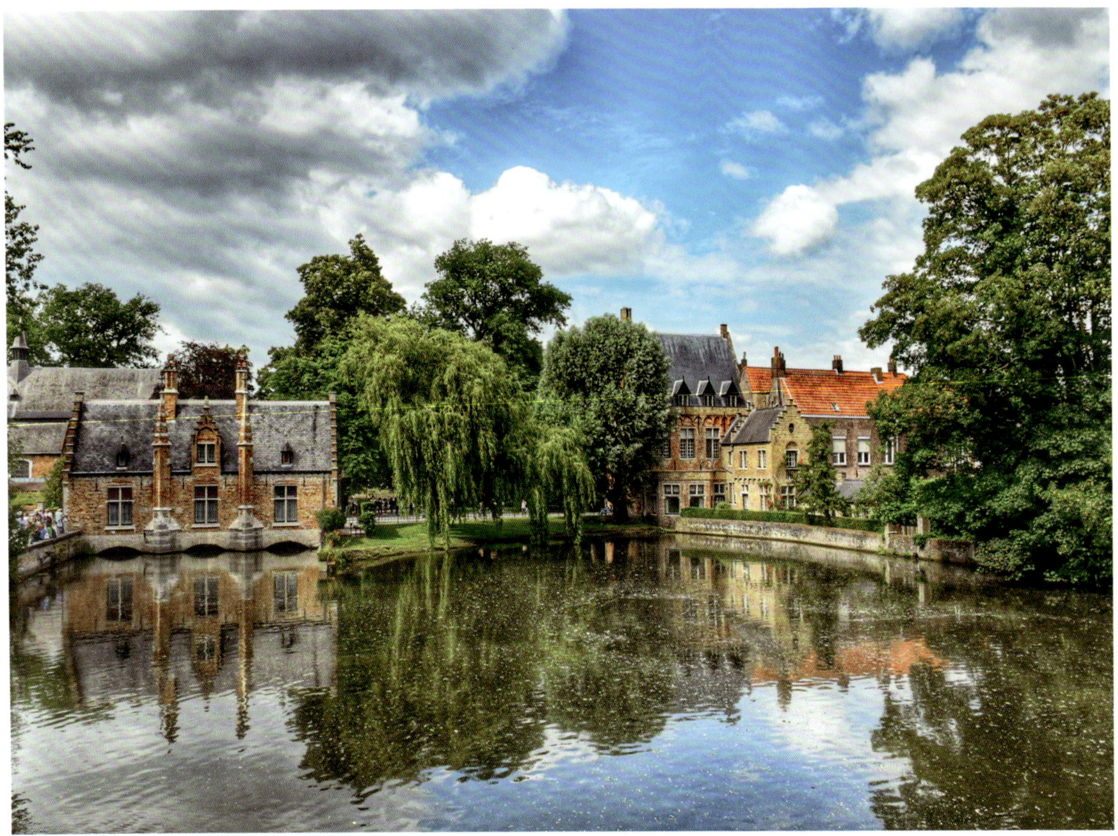

Minnewater, the Lake of Love
Minnewater, Minnewaterpark
Lac d'amour, parc du Minnewater

Minnewater—Lake of Love

In order to control the water level of the canals in Bruges, locks were built at the southern gates of the city in the 12th century and the water of the Reie river was dammed. The lake, today called Minnewater, served as a harbor basin. Here the ships were loaded, which ensured the regular exchange of goods with the city of Ghent. Today the lake with the magazine tower is a quiet and romantic place. The place name Minnewater or "Water of the Minns" is derived from the medieval popular belief in "Minns" or water spirits, who lived under bridges.

Minnewater – le lac d'Amour

Afin de contrôler le niveau des canaux à Bruges, on construisit au xiie siècle des écluses servant à retenir l'eau du fleuve Reie. Le lac qui en résulta, aujourd'hui appelé Minnewater, servait de bassin portuaire. On y chargeait les bateaux qui assuraient les échanges réguliers de marchandises avec la ville de Gand. Aujourd'hui, le lac, agrémenté de sa tour à poudre, est un lieu paisible et romantique. Il doit son nom à la croyance populaire médiévale relative aux esprits des eaux, ou «minnen», qui aimaient prendre leurs quartiers sous des ponts.

Minnewater – See der Liebe

Um den Wasserstand der Grachten in Brügge zu kontrollieren, wurden im 12. Jahrhundert an den südlichen Toren der Stadt Schleusen gebaut und das Wasser des Flusses Reie aufgestaut. Der entstandene See, heute Minnewater genannt, diente als Hafenbecken. Hier wurden die Schiffe beladen, die den regelmäßigen Warenaustausch mit der Stadt Gent sicherten. Heute ist der See mit dem Pulverturm ein ruhiger und romantischer Ort. Der Ortsname Minnewater oder „Wasser der Minnen" leitet sich aus dem mittelalterlichen Volksglauben an „Minnen" oder Wassergeister her, die vorzugsweise unter Brücken hausten.

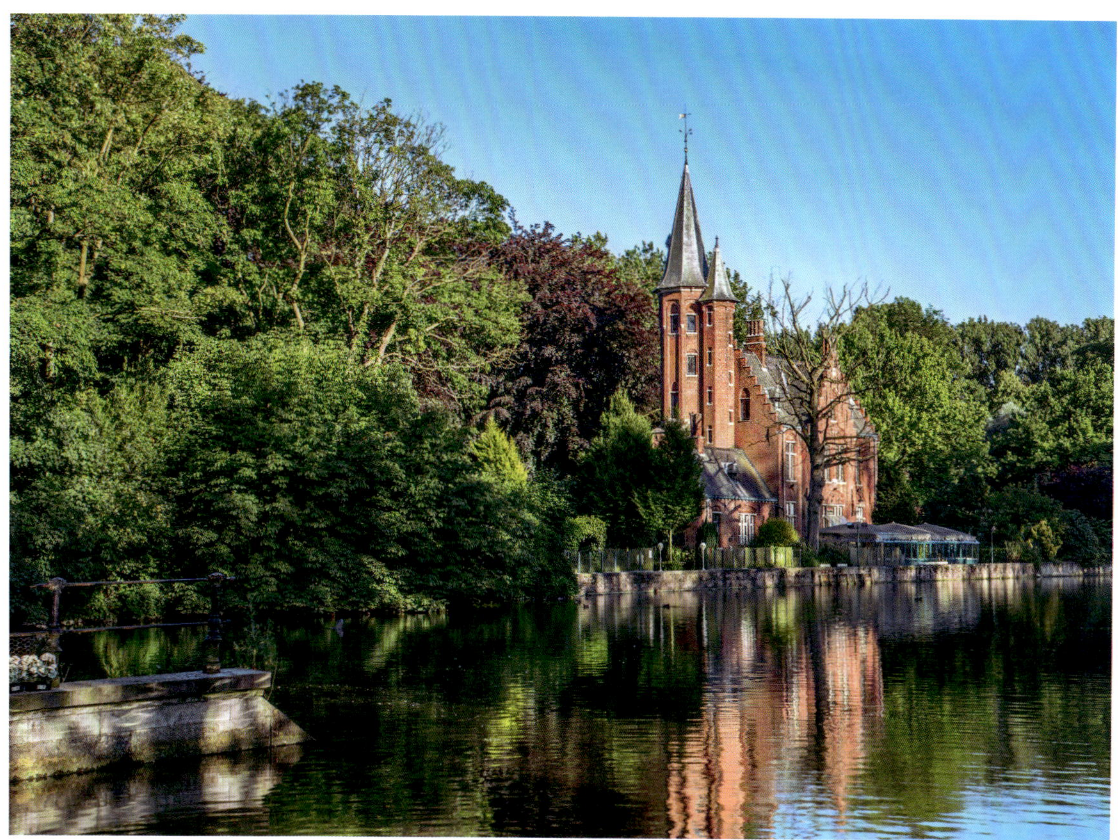

Minnewater Castle and the "Lake of Love", Minnewaterpark
Kasteel Minnewater en Minnewater
Château Minnewater et Lac d'amour, Parc du Minnewater

Minnewater– Lago del Amor

Para controlar el nivel del agua de los canales de Brujas, en el siglo XII se construyeron esclusas en las puertas del sur de la ciudad y se embalsamó el agua del río Reie. El lago que se formó y que ahora recibe el nombre de Minnewater, servía como cuenca portuaria. Aquí se cargaban los barcos, lo que aseguraba el intercambio regular de mercancías con la ciudad de Gante. Hoy en día el lago con la torre de polvo es un lugar tranquilo y romántico. El nombre del lugar Minnewater o "Agua de los Minnen" se deriva de la creencia popular medieval en los "Minnen" o espíritus del agua, a los que les encantaba vivir bajo los puentes.

Minnewater – Lago do Amor

Para controlar o nível da água dos canais de Bruges, foram construídas eclusas nas portas sul da cidade no século XII e as águas do rio Reie foram represadas. O lago resultante, hoje chamado Minnewater, serviu como uma bacia portuária. Aqui os navios eram carregados, o que assegurava a troca regular de mercadorias com a cidade de Gante. Hoje o lago com a Torre da Pólvora é um lugar tranquilo e romântico. O nome da localidade Minnewater ou "Água da Ondina", deve seu nome à crença popular medieval da deusa do amor Minne ou ondinas, espíritos da água, que de preferência viviam debaixo de pontes.

Minnewater – meer van de liefde

Om het waterpeil van de Brugse kanalen te controleren, werden in de 12de eeuw aan de zuidelijke poorten van de stad sluizen gebouwd en werd het water van de Reie opgestuwd. Het meer, tegenwoordig Minnewater genoemd, diende als havenbekken. Hier werden de schepen geladen die regelmatig goederen uitwisselden met de stad Gent. Vandaag de dag is het meer met de Poertoren een rustige en romantische plek. De naam Minnewater of "water van de minnen" is afgeleid van het middeleeuwse volksgeloof in "minnen" of watergeesten, die bij voorkeur onder bruggen leefden.

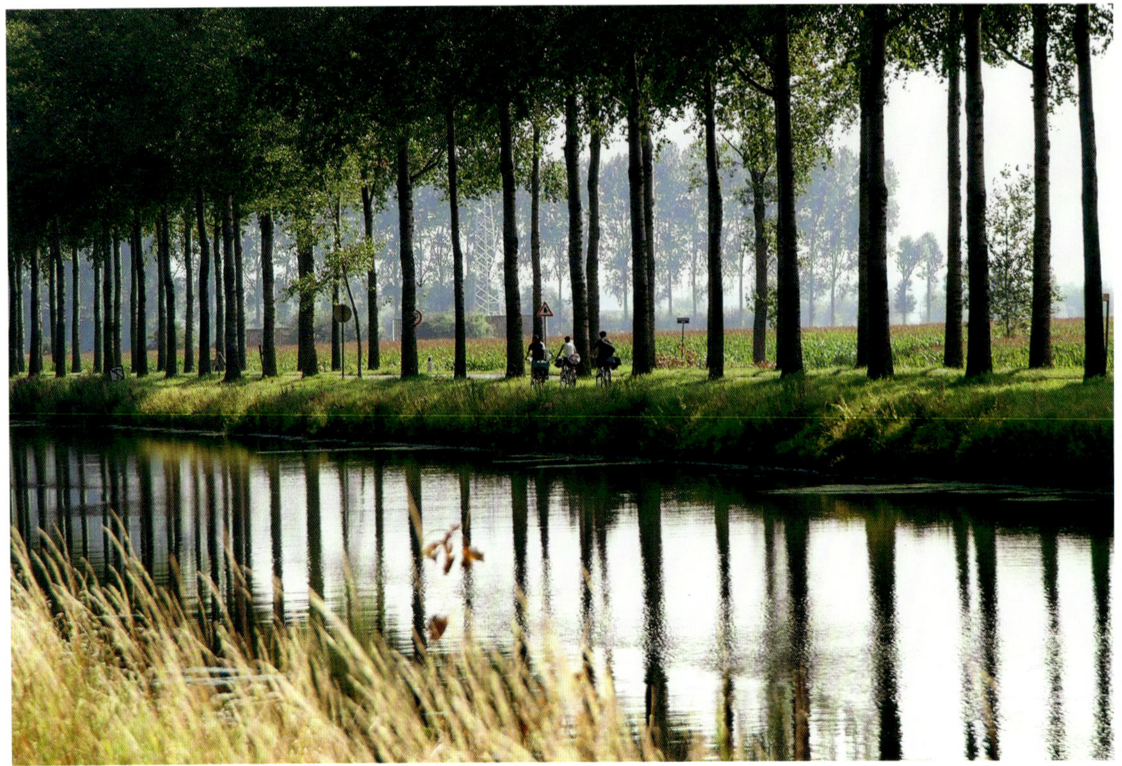

Damme Canal
Damse Vaart
Canal de Damme

Canal and dam

In the 11th century, to regain access to the sea, the city of Bruges built a canal and a levee to an estuary further north. There a new harbour and the settlement of Damme were founded. It developed into a lively transshipment centre, especially for wine from Bordeaux and herring from Sweden, for which it had medieval stacking rights.

Canal et digue

Pour récupérer son accès à la mer, la ville de Bruges construisit au XIᵉ siècle un canal et une digue rejoignant un bras de mer situé plus au nord. On y fonda un nouveau port et la cité de Damme. Celle-ci devint un lieu de transbordement vivant, surtout concernant le vin de Bordeaux et le hareng de Suède, pour lesquels elle possédait le droit d'étape.

Kanal und Damm

Um wieder Zugang zum Meer zu bekommen baute die Stadt Brügge im 11. Jahrhundert einen Kanal und einen Damm zu einem weiter nördlich liegenden Meeresarm. Dort wurde ein neuer Hafen und die Siedlung Damme gegründet. Sie entwickelte sich zu einem lebhaften Umschlagplatz, vor allem für Wein aus Bordeaux und Hering aus Schweden, für die es das Stapelrecht besaß.

Canal y presa

En el siglo XI, para recuperar el acceso al mar, la ciudad de Brujas construyó un canal y una presa en un estuario más al norte. Allí se fundó un nuevo puerto y el asentamiento Damme. Se convirtió en un animado centro de transbordo, especialmente para el vino de Burdeos y el arenque de Suecia, para los que tenía derechos de apilamiento.

Canal e barragem

No século XI, para recuperar o acesso ao mar, a cidade de Bruges construiu um canal e uma barragem para um estuário mais a norte. Lá, um novo porto e a colónia Damme foram fundados. Tornou-se um centro movimentado de transbordo, especialmente para o vinho de Bordeaux e o arenque da Suécia, para os quais tinha direitos de empilhamento.

Kanaal en dam

Om de toegang tot de zee te herwinnen, bouwde de stad Brugge in de 11e eeuw een kanaal en een dam naar een meer noordelijk gelegen zeearm. Daar werd een nieuwe haven en het stadje Damme gesticht. Het ontwikkelde zich tot een levendige overlaadplaats van vooral wijn uit de Bordeaux en haring uit Zweden waarvoor Damme de stapelrechten had.

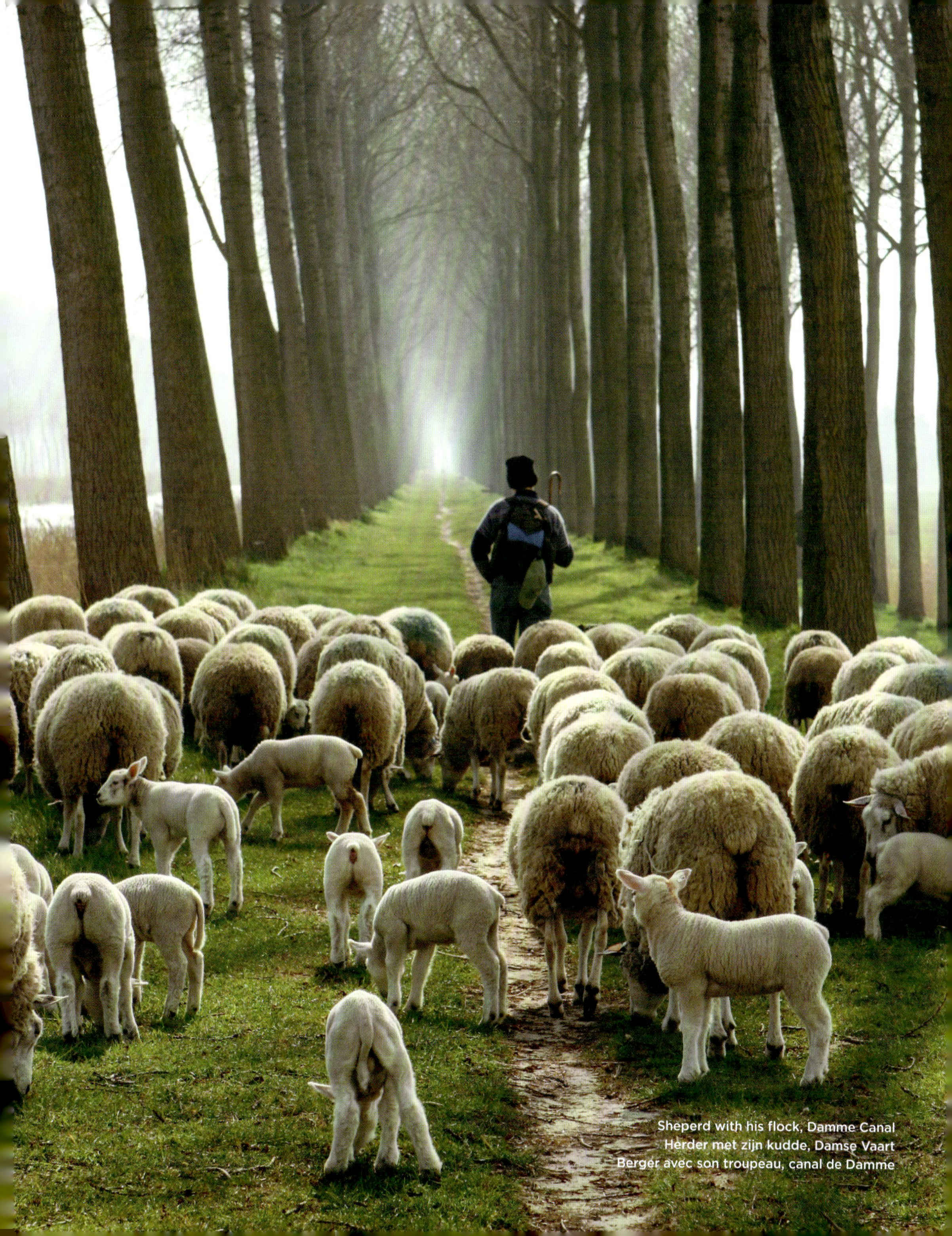

Sheperd with his flock, Damme Canal
Herder met zijn kudde, Damse Vaart
Berger avec son troupeau, canal de Damme

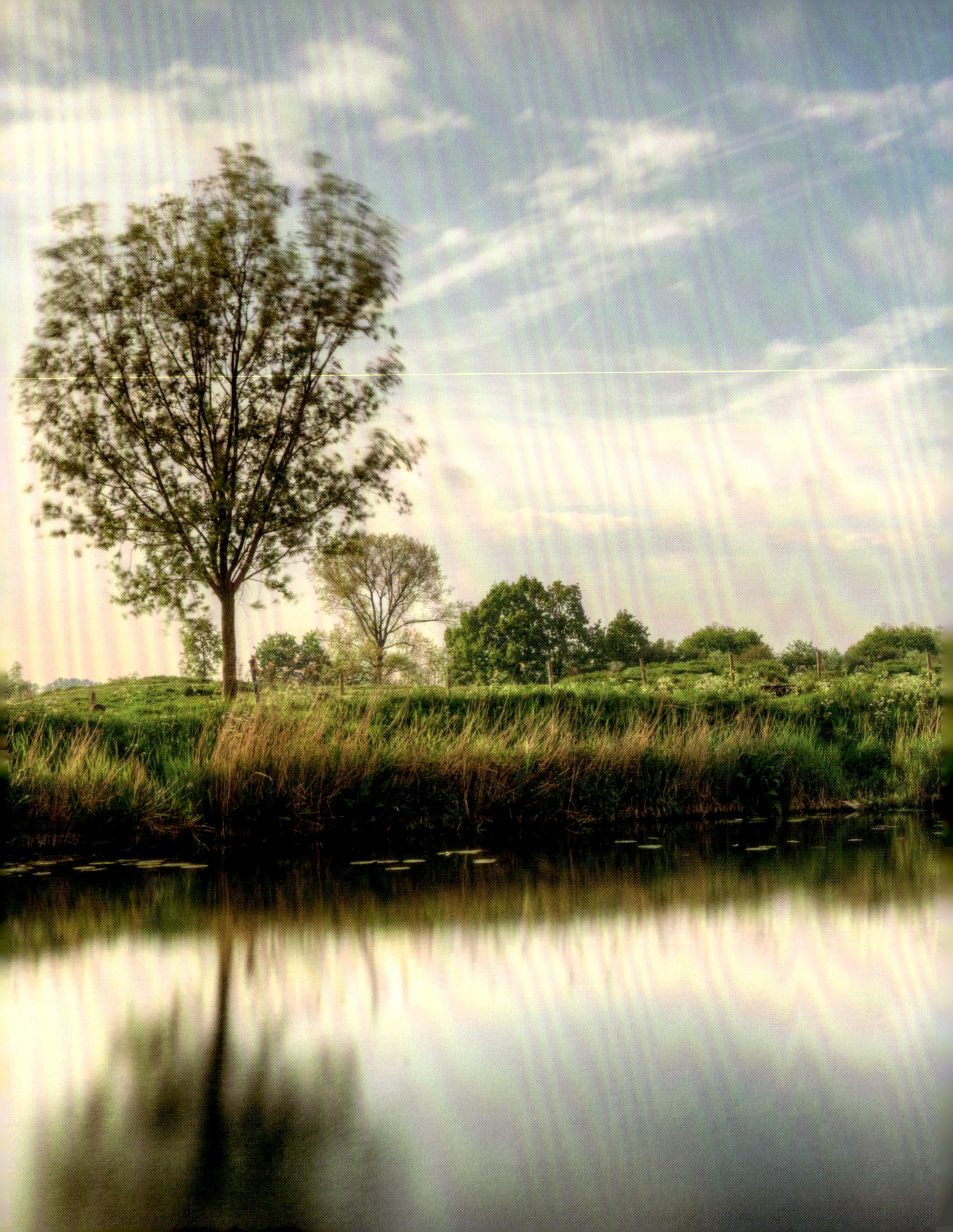

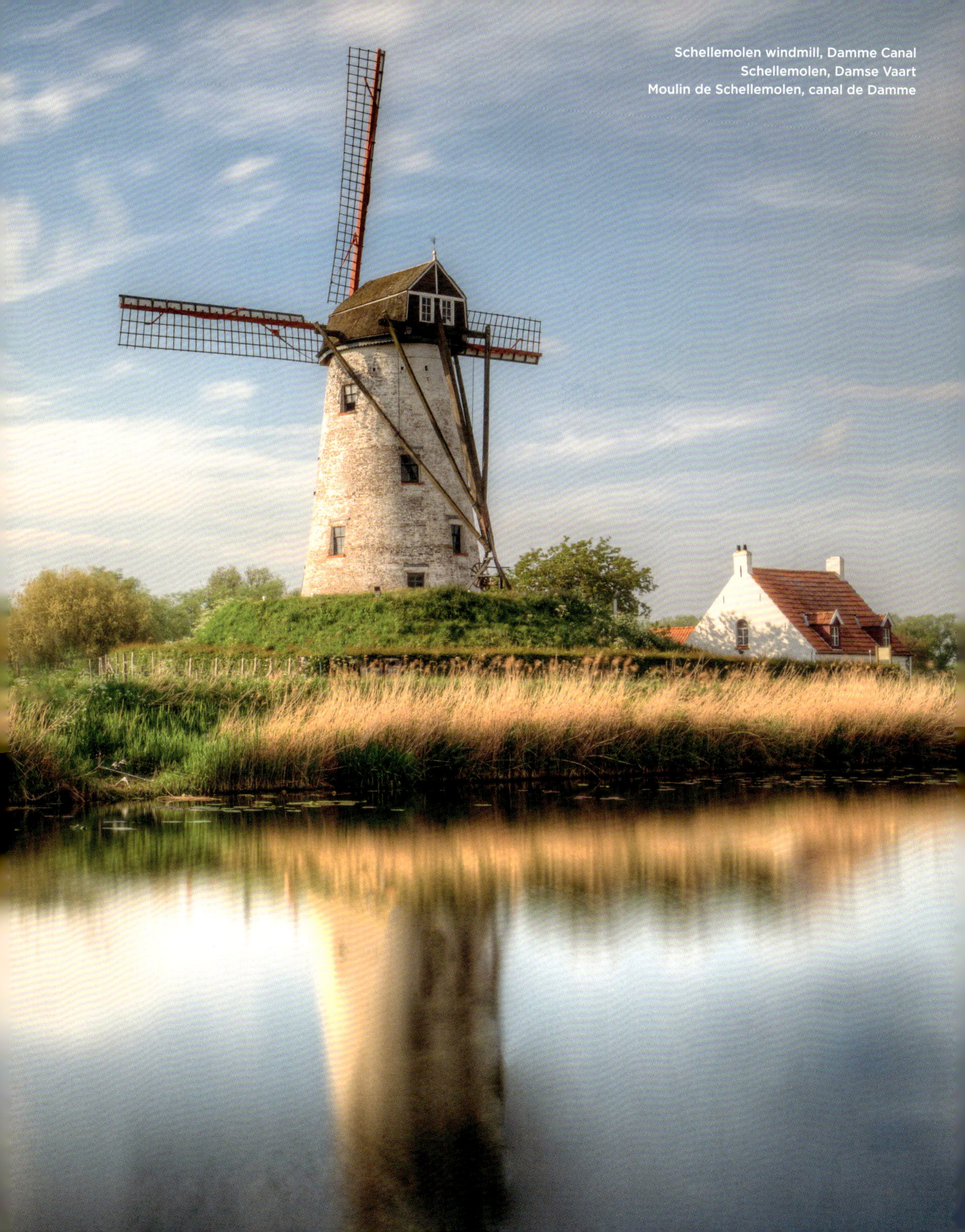

Schellemolen windmill, Damme Canal
Schellemolen, Damse Vaart
Moulin de Schellemolen, canal de Damme

West Flanders · West-Vlaanderen · Flandre occidentale

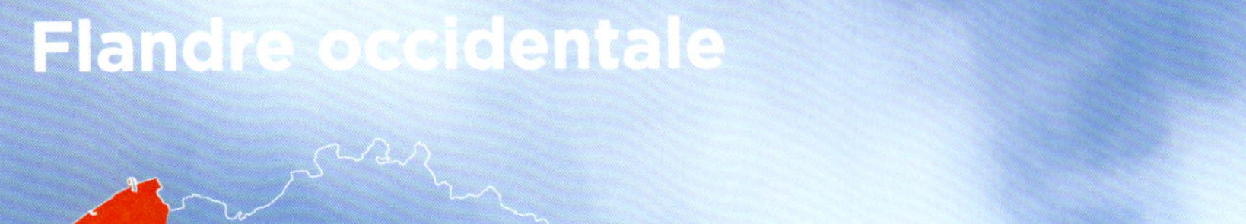

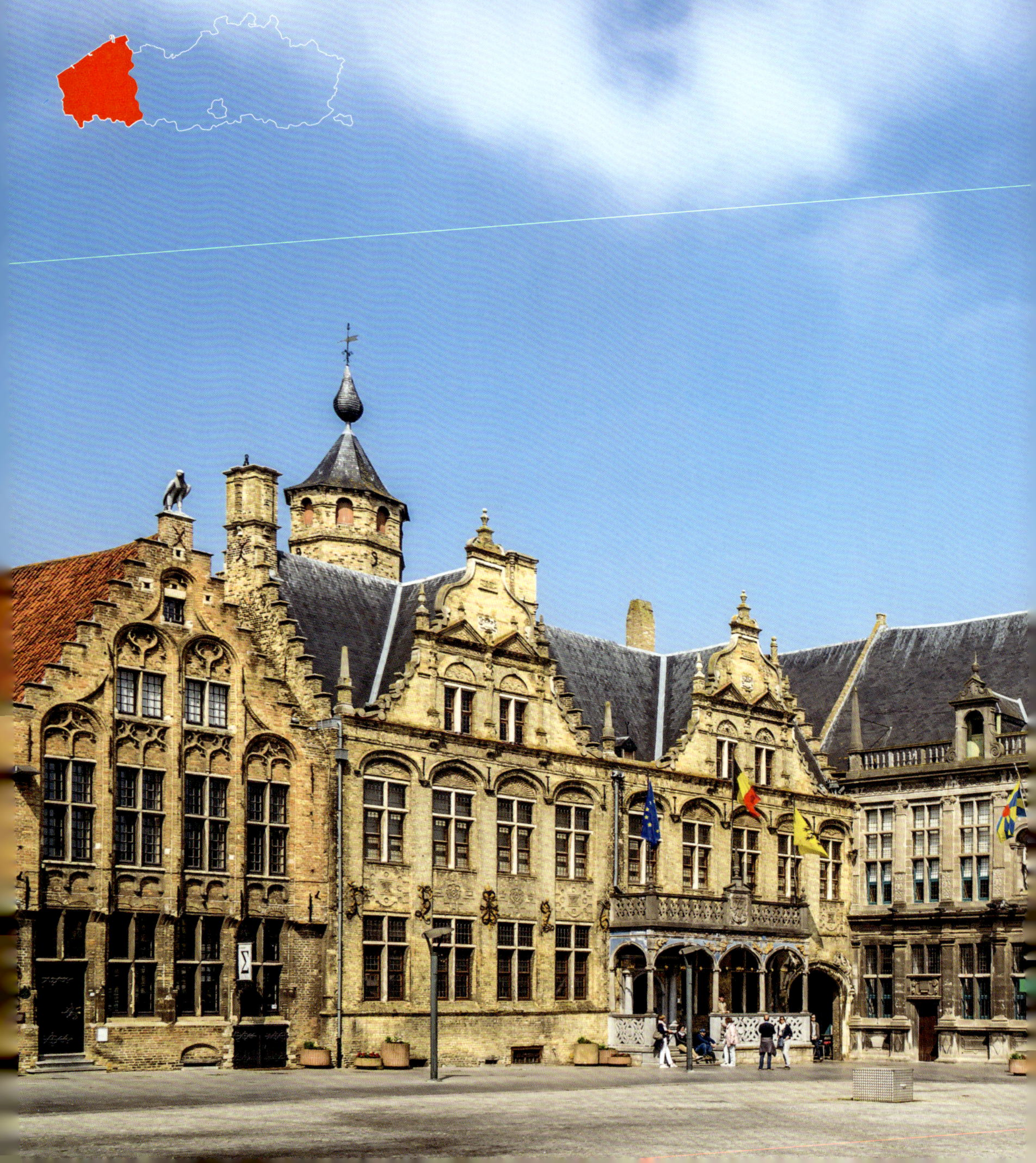

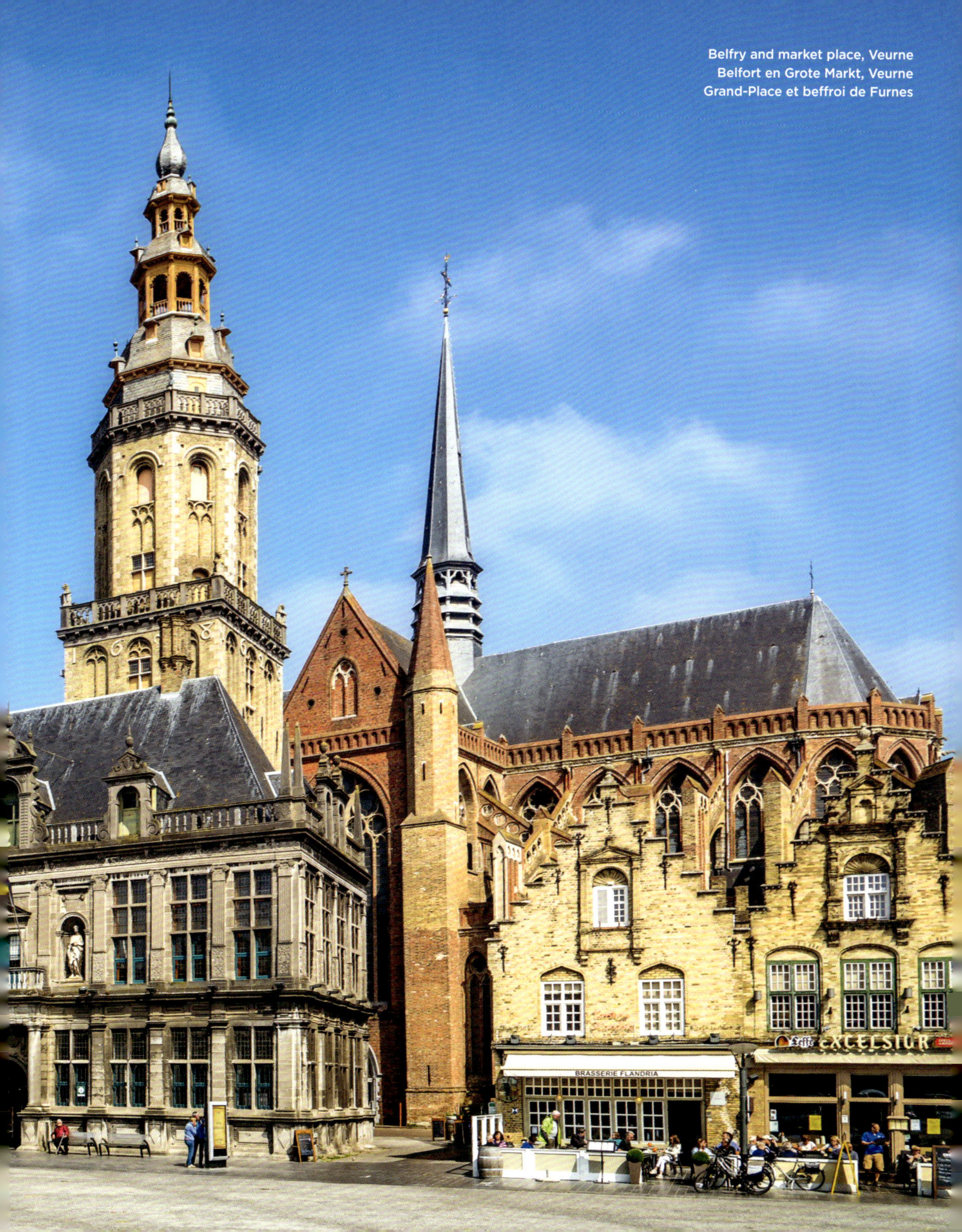

Belfry and market place, Veurne
Belfort en Grote Markt, Veurne
Grand-Place et beffroi de Furnes

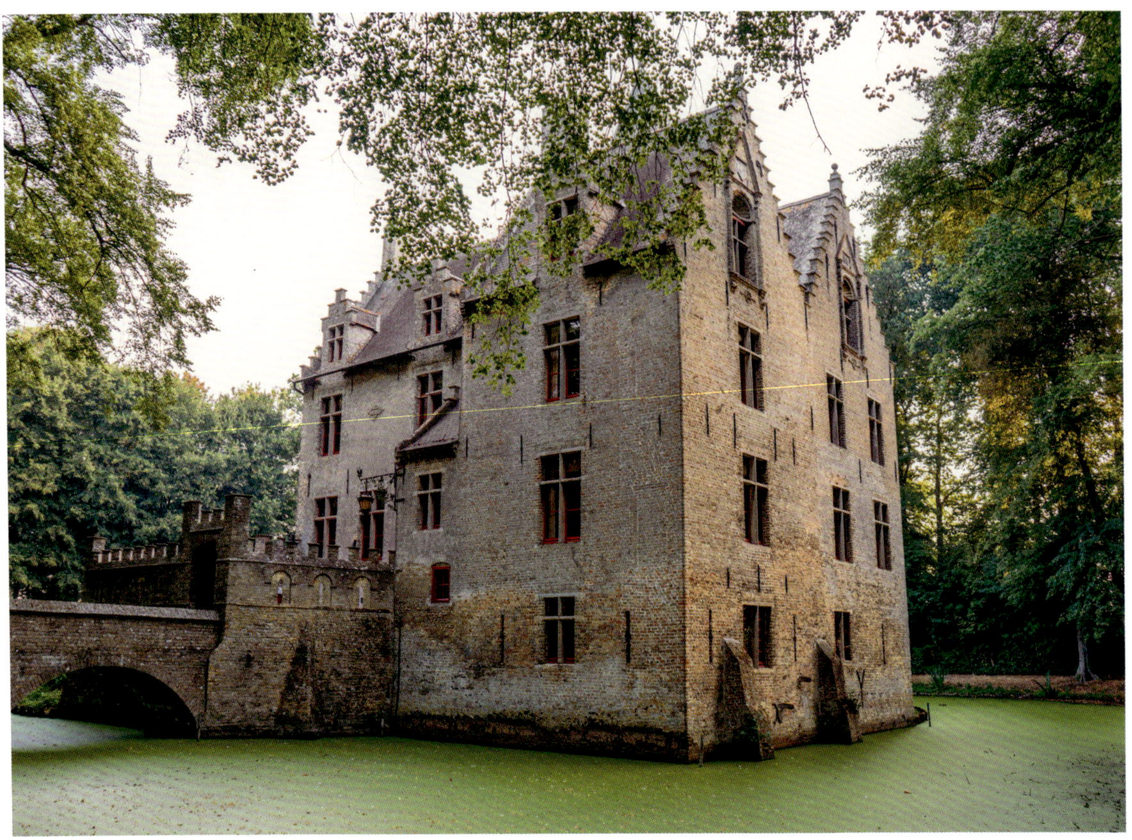

Beauvoorde Castle, near Veurne
Kasteel Beauvoorde, bij Veurne
Château Beauvoorde, près de Furnes

West Flanders

In the hinterland of the coast, far to the west, lies the tranquil city of Veurne, with its picturesque market square around which brick houses with stepped gables are grouped. The City Hall, the Palace of Justice and the old Meat Market all date from the early 17th century. The Belfry was added to the UNESCO World Heritage List in 1999. The nostalgic Beauvoorde Castle is also very close by. At the end of the 19th century, the eccentric aristocrat Arthur Merghelynck bought the dilapidated castle and had it rebuilt as he believed it had looked in the 17th century.

Flandre occidentale

À l'extrême ouest, dans l'arrière-pays, la paisible Furnes offre au visiteur sa pittoresque place du marché, autour de laquelle se groupent des maisons en briques agrémentées de pignons à échelons, la mairie, l'ancienne cour de justice avec sa tour et l'ancienne halle des bouchers – des bâtiments datant tous du début du XVIIe siècle. Depuis 1999, le beffroi fait partie du patrimoine mondial de l'Unesco. Non loin de là se dresse le château de Beauvoorde, d'où se dégage une atmosphère empreinte de nostalgie. À la fin du XIXe siècle, le noble excentrique Arthur Merghelynck acheta cette bâtisse délabrée et la fit reconstruire selon l'apparence qu'il supposa être la sienne au XVIIe siècle.

Westflandern

Im Hinterland der Küste, ganz im Westen, liegt das beschauliche Veurne mit seinem malerischen Marktplatz, um den sich Backsteinhäuser mit Treppengiebeln gruppieren: das Rathaus, der ehemalige Gerichtshof mit Turm und die alte Fleischhalle, alle aus dem frühen 17. Jahrhundert. Der Belfried wurde 1999 in die Liste des UNESCO-Welterbes aufgenommen. Ganz in der Nähe liegt auch das nostalgische Schloss Beauvoorde. Ende des 19. Jahrhunderts kaufte der exzentrische Adlige Arthur Merghelynck das verfallene Schloss und ließ es wiederaufbauen, so wie es seiner Ansicht nach im 17. Jahrhundert ausgesehen hatte.

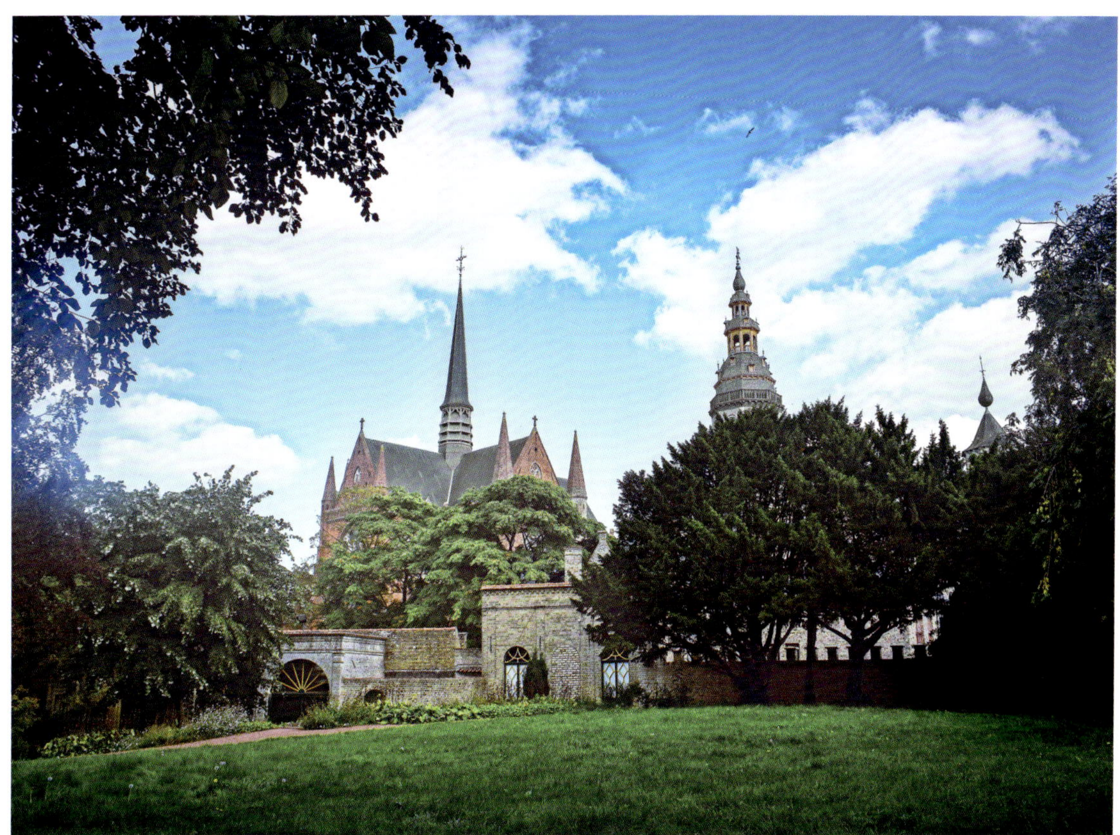

Veurne
Furnes

Flandes Occidental

En el interior de la costa, muy al oeste, se encuentra la tranquila Veurne con su pintoresca plaza de mercado, alrededor de la cual se agrupan las casas de ladrillo con frontones escalonados: el ayuntamiento, la antigua corte con torre y el antiguo almacén de carnes, todos ellos de principios del siglo XVII. El campanario fue inscrito en la Lista del Patrimonio Mundial de la UNESCO en 1999. El nostálgico castillo de Beauvoorde también está muy cerca. A finales del siglo XIX, el excéntrico aristócrata Arthur Merghelynck compró el castillo en ruinas y lo hizo reconstruir tal y como él creía que era en el siglo XVII.

Flandres Ocidental

No interior da costa, bem a oeste, encontra-se o tranquilo Veurne, com a sua pitoresca praça do mercado, em torno da qual se agrupam as casas de tijolo com empenas escalonadas: a câmara municipal, o antigo tribunal com torre e o antigo pavilhão da carne, todos datados do início do século XVII. O campanário foi acrescentado à Lista do Património Mundial da UNESCO em 1999. Nas proximidades fica o nostálgico Castelo de Beauvoorde. No final do século XIX, o excêntrico aristocrata Arthur Merghelynck comprou o castelo em ruínas e mandou reconstruí-lo como ele acreditava ter sido no século XVII.

West-Vlaanderen

In het achterland van de kust, ver naar het westen, ligt het rustige Veurne met zijn pittoreske marktplein waaromheen bakstenen huizen met trapgevels zijn gegroepeerd: het stadhuis, het voormalige gerechtsgebouw en de oude vleeshal, allemaal uit het begin van de 17e eeuw. Het belfort werd in 1999 toegevoegd aan de UNESCO Werelderfgoedlijst. Zeer dichtbij ligt ook het nostalgische Kasteel Beauvoorde. Aan het einde van de 19e eeuw kocht de excentrieke aristocraat Arthur Merghelynck het vervallen kasteel en liet het herbouwen zoals hij dacht dat het er in de 17e eeuw uitgezien moest hebben.

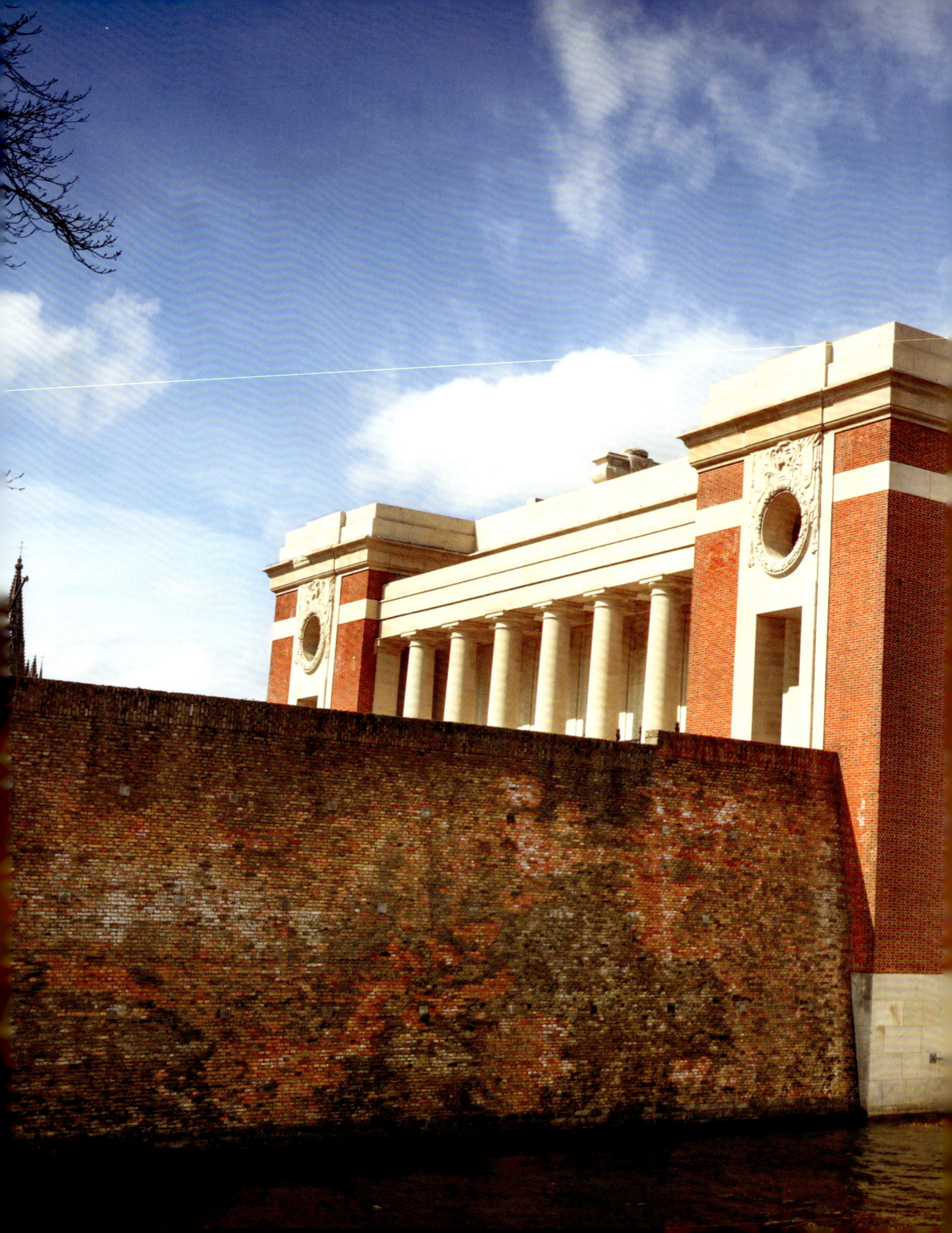

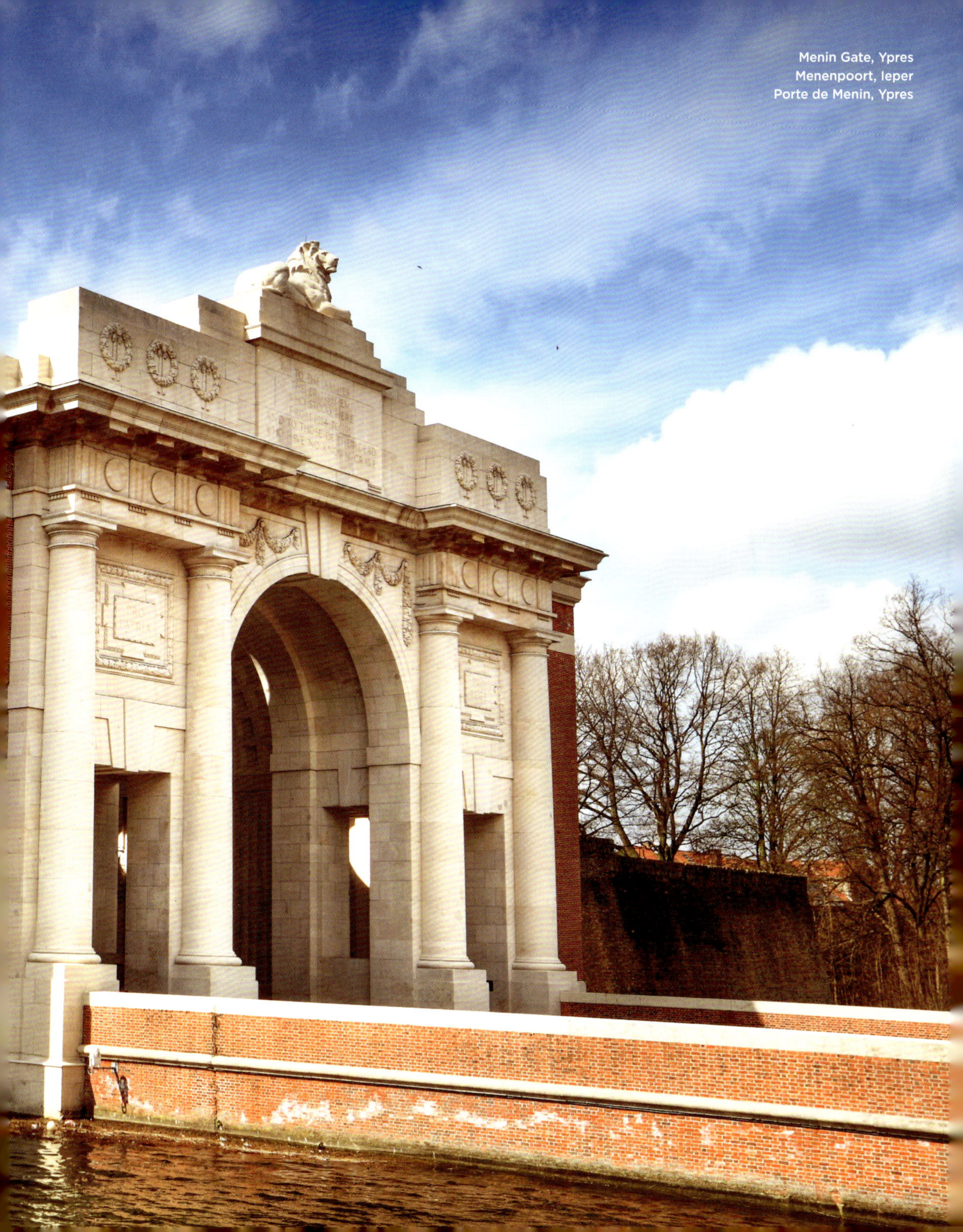
Menin Gate, Ypres
Menenpoort, Ieper
Porte de Menin, Ypres

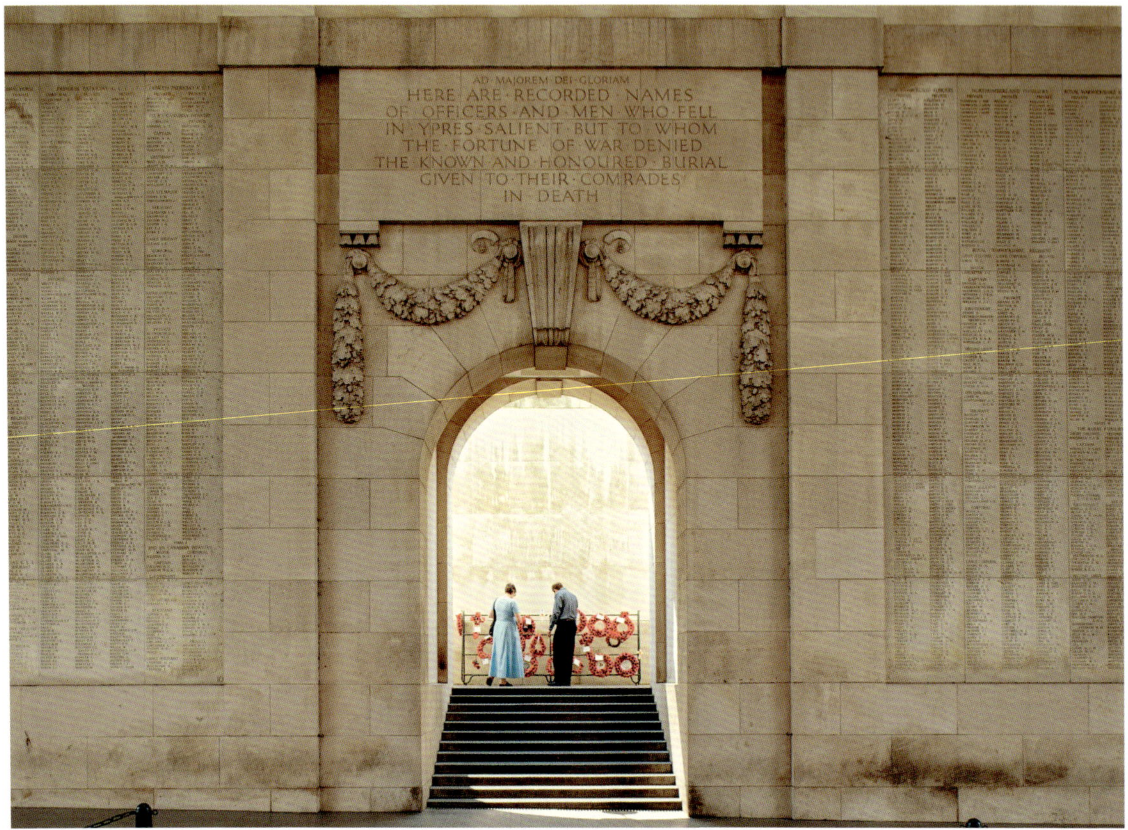

Interior of Menin Gate
Interieur van Menenpoort
Intérieure de la Porte de Menin

Menin Gate Memorial to the Missing and The Last Post

The memorial is dedicated to those missing and fallen soldiers of Great Britain and the Commonwealth who were not identified in the battles around Ypres, and remained without their own grave. The large memorial hall with its engraved names honours the 54,896 missing soldiers of the first three Flemish battles. Since 2 July 1928, car traffic has been interrupted every evening at 8 pm at the gate and the "Last Post" has been blown to commemorate the dead. The bugle call is usually made by five firemen from Ypres. This tradition was only interrupted during the Second World War.

Porte de Menin et Last Post

Ce monument aux morts fut édifié à la mémoire des soldats de Grande-Bretagne et du Commonwealth tombés lors des batailles autour d'Ypres, soldats restés non identifiés et dépourvus de sépulture. Dans la grande halle de mémoire sont gravés les noms des 54 896 soldats auxquels elle rend hommage, disparus lors des trois batailles des Flandres. Depuis le 2 juillet 1928, la route passant sous le mémorial est fermée chaque soir à 20 heures et le Last Post retentit à la mémoire des soldats morts. Ce sont généralement cinq pompiers d'Ypres qui sonnent le clairon. Cette tradition n'a été interrompue que durant la Seconde Guerre mondiale.

Menenpoort und Last Post

Das Ehrenmal ist den gefallenen Soldaten Großbritanniens und des Commonwealth gewidmet, die in den Schlachten um Ypern nicht identifiziert wurden und ohne eigenes Grab geblieben sind. Die große Gedenkhalle ehrt mit ihren eingemeißelten Namen die 54 896 vermissten Soldaten, der ersten drei Flandernschlachten. Seit dem 2. Juli 1928 wird jeden Abend um 20 Uhr der Autoverkehr durch das Tor unterbrochen und das „Last Post" zum Gedenken an die Gefallenen geblasen. Das Hornsignal blasen in der Regel fünf Feuerwehrleute aus Ypern. Nur während der Zeit des Zweiten Weltkriegs wurde diese Tradition unterbrochen.

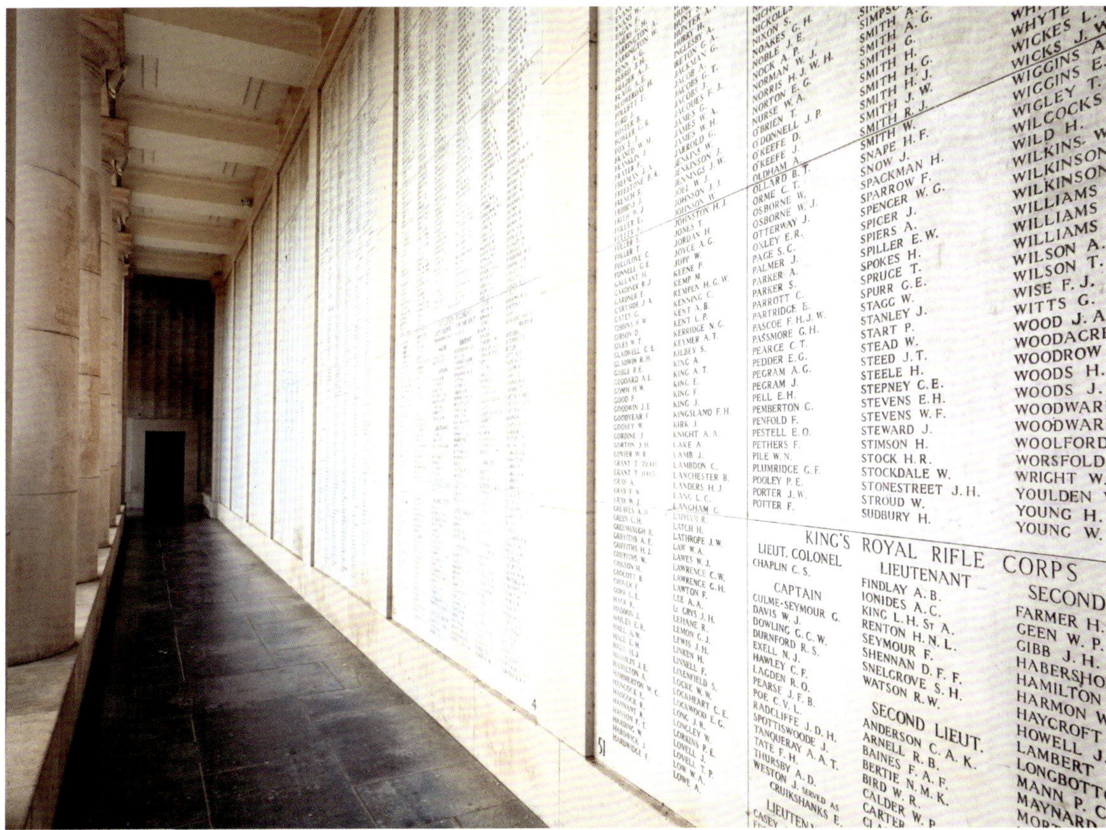

Stone panels bearing names of the missing dead
Panelen met namen van gestorven soldaten
Noms de soldats morts

Puerta de Menin y Last Post

El monumento está dedicado a los
soldados caídos de Gran Bretaña
y la Commonwealth que no fueron
identificados en las batallas alrededor de
Ypres y se quedaron sin tener su propia
tumba. La gran sala conmemorativa con
sus nombres grabados rinde homenaje a
los 54 896 soldados desaparecidos en las
tres primeras batallas flamencas. Desde el
2 de julio de 1928, el tráfico de coches se
interrumpe todas las noches a las 20 00
horas por la puerta y el "Last Post" se hace
sonar para conmemorar a los muertos. La
señal de la bocina normalmente la hacen
sonar cinco bomberos de Ypres. Esta
tradición solo se interrumpió durante la
Segunda Guerra Mundial.

Portão Menin e Cerimônia do "Último Post"

O memorial é dedicado aos soldados
caídos da Grã-Bretanha e da Comunidade
das Nações (Commonwealth), que não
foram identificados nas batalhas em
torno de Ypres e permaneceram sem seu
próprio túmulo. O grande salão memorial
com seus nomes gravados homenageia os
54 896 soldados desaparecidos das três
primeiras batalhas de Flandres. Desde 2
de Julho de 1928, todas as noites às 20
horas o tráfego de automóveis pelo portão
é interrompido e o "toque de silêncio" é
tocado para comemorar os mortos. O sinal
da trompeta é normalmente soprado por
cinco bombeiros da Ypres. Esta tradição
só foi interrompida durante a Segunda
Guerra Mundial.

De Menenpoort en Last Post

Het monument is gewijd aan de
gesneuvelde soldaten van Groot-Brittannië
en het Gemenebest die tijdens de
gevechten rond Iper niet geïdentificeerd
werden en zonder eigen graf zijn bleven.
De grote herdenkingszaal eert met zijn
ingebeitelde namen de 54 896 vermiste
soldaten van de eerste drie Vlaamse
veldslagen. Sinds 2 juli 1928 wordt elke
avond om 20.00 uur het autoverkeer
onderbroken en wordt de "Last Post"
gespeeld om de doden te herdenken.
Het zijn meestal vijf brandweermannen
uit Ieper die op een klaroen blazen. Deze
traditie werd enkel tijdens de Tweede
Wereldoorlog onderbroken.

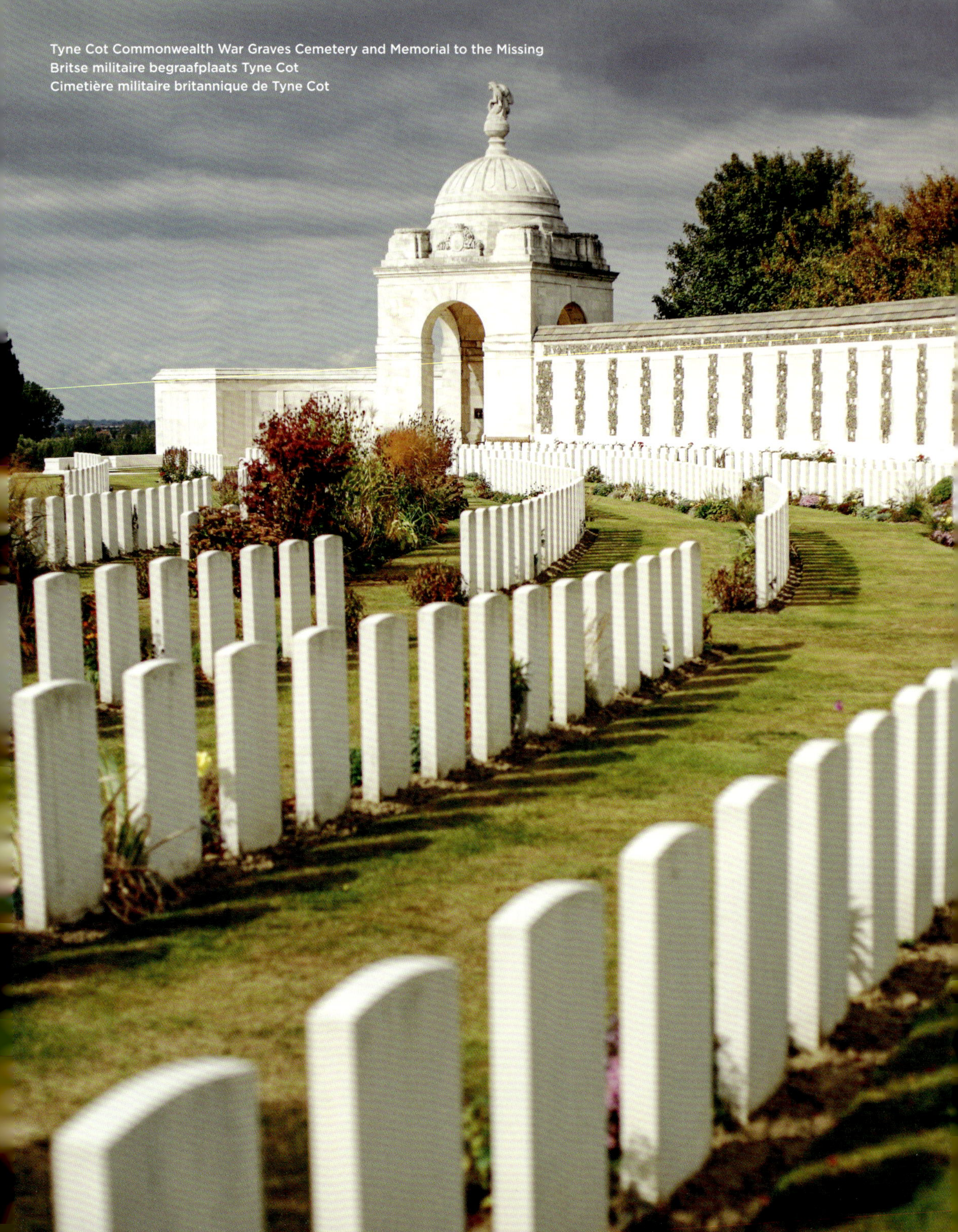

Tyne Cot Commonwealth War Graves Cemetery and Memorial to the Missing
Britse militaire begraafplaats Tyne Cot
Cimetière militaire britannique de Tyne Cot

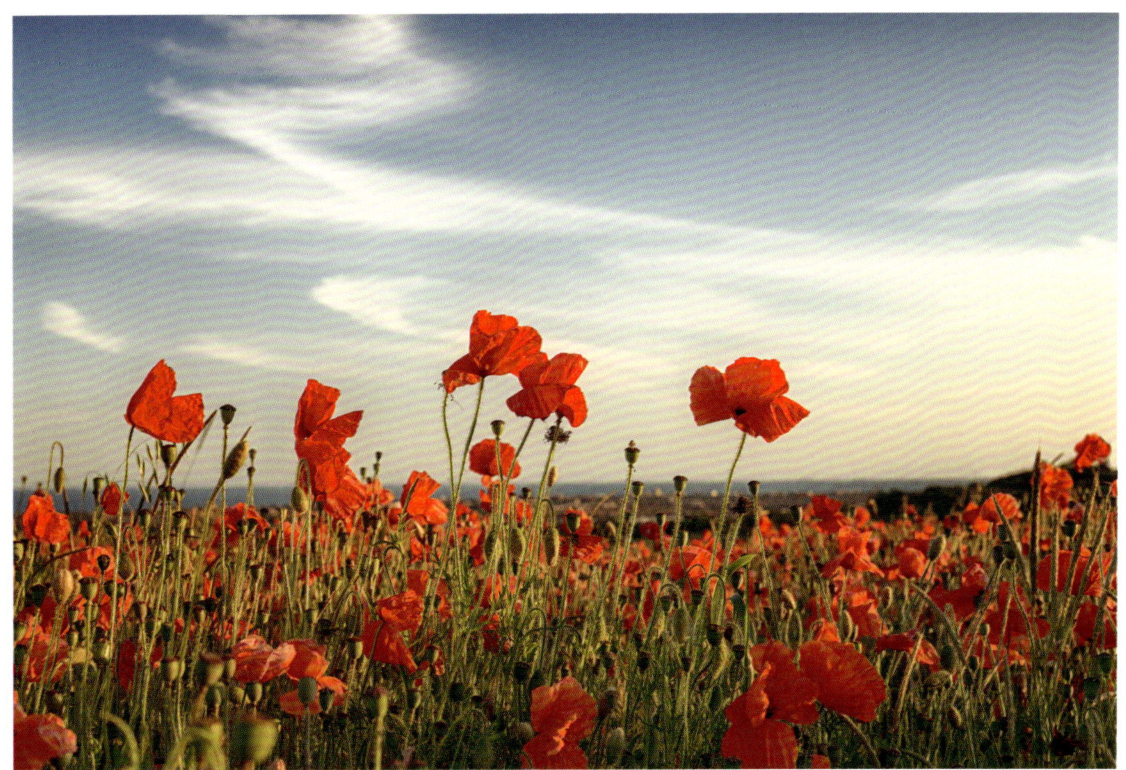

Field of Poppies
Veld met klaprozen
Champ de pavots

Tyne Cot military cemetery

With nearly 12,000 buried soldiers, this memorial is the largest Commonwealth cemetery in the world. White gravestones with colorful flowers line up on the field. The cemetery wall is a monument to the missing; it bears the names of nearly 35,000 men from the United Kingdom and Commonwealth who were never found and declared dead.

Cimetière militaire de Tyne Cot

Avec ses quasi 12 000 soldats enterrés, ce mémorial est le plus grand cimetière du Commonwealth au monde. Des pierres tombales blanches et des fleurs colorées s'y alignent. Le mur du cimetière rend hommage aux soldats disparus ; il porte les noms de près de 35 000 hommes britanniques, jamais retrouvés et déclarés morts.

Soldatenfriedhof Tyne Cot

Mit beinahe 12 000 beigesetzten Soldaten ist diese Gedenkstätte der größte Friedhof des Commonwealth weltweit. Weiße Grabsteine mit bunten Blumen reihen sich auf dem Feld aneinander. Die Friedhofsmauer ist ein Denkmal für die Vermissten; sie trägt die Namen von fast 35 000 Männer aus dem Vereinigten Königreich, die nie gefunden und für tot erklärt wurden.

Cementerio militar Tyne Cot

Con casi 12 000 soldados enterrados, este monumento es el mayor cementerio de la Commonwealth del mundo. Tumbas blancas con flores de colores se alinean en el campo. El muro del cementerio es un monumento a los desaparecidos; lleva los nombres de casi 35 000 hombres del Reino Unido que nunca fueron encontrados y que se declararon muertos.

Cemitério militar de Tyne Cot

Com quase 12 000 soldados enterrados, este memorial é o maior cemitério da Comunidade das Nações do mundo. As lápides brancas com flores coloridas alinham-se no campo. O muro do cemitério é um monumento aos desaparecidos; traz os nomes de quase 35 000 homens do Reino Unido que nunca foram encontrados e declarados como mortos.

Militaire begraafplaats Tyne Cot

Met bijna 12 000 bijgezette soldaten is deze gedenkplaats de grootste begraafplaats van de Commonwealth ter wereld. Op het veld staan rijnen witte grafstenen met bonte bloemen. De muur van de begraafplaats is een monument voor de vermisten en draagt de namen van bijna 35 000 mannen uit het Verenigd Koninkrijk die nooit zijn gevonden en dood werden verklaard.

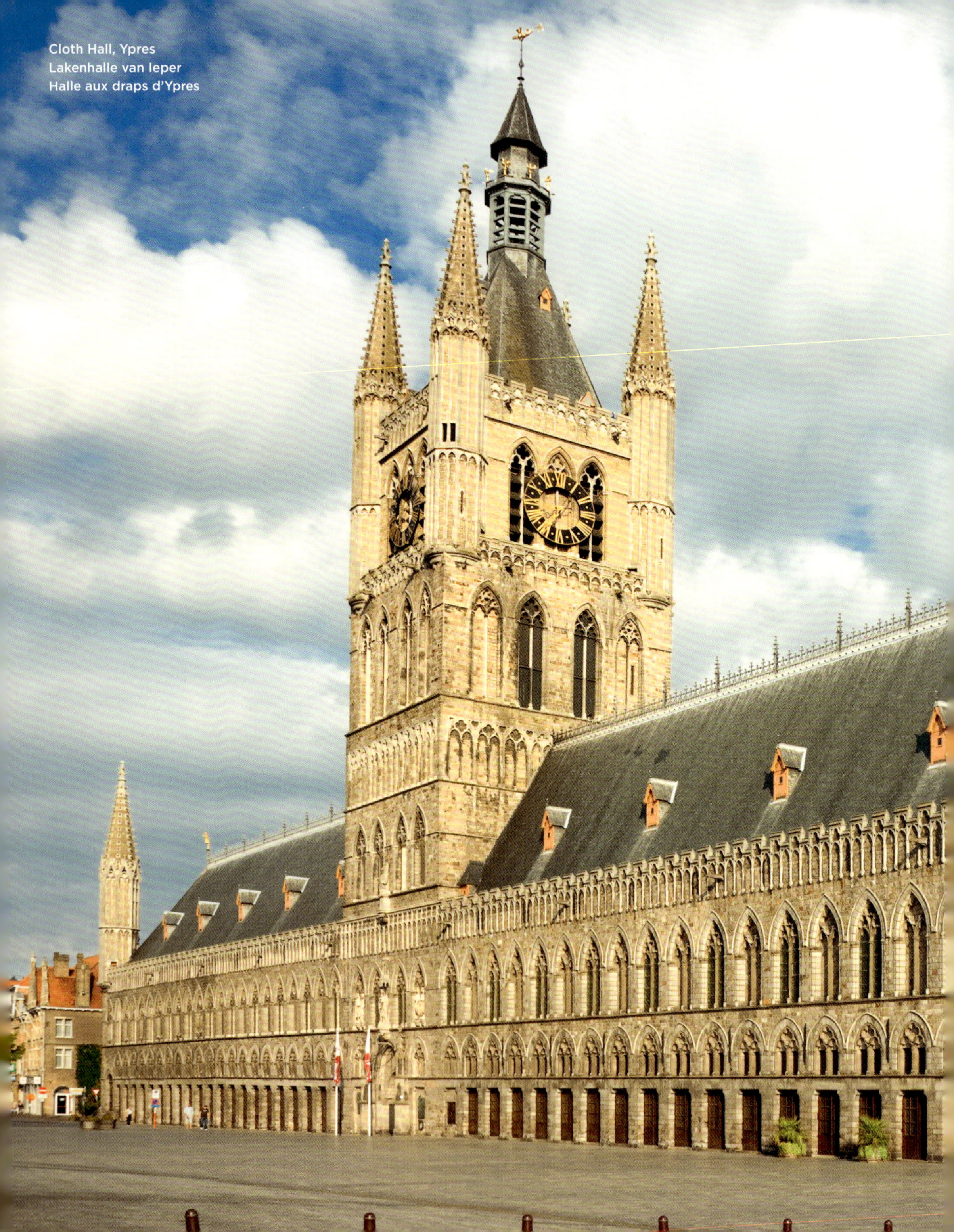
Cloth Hall, Ypres
Lakenhalle van Ieper
Halle aux draps d'Ypres

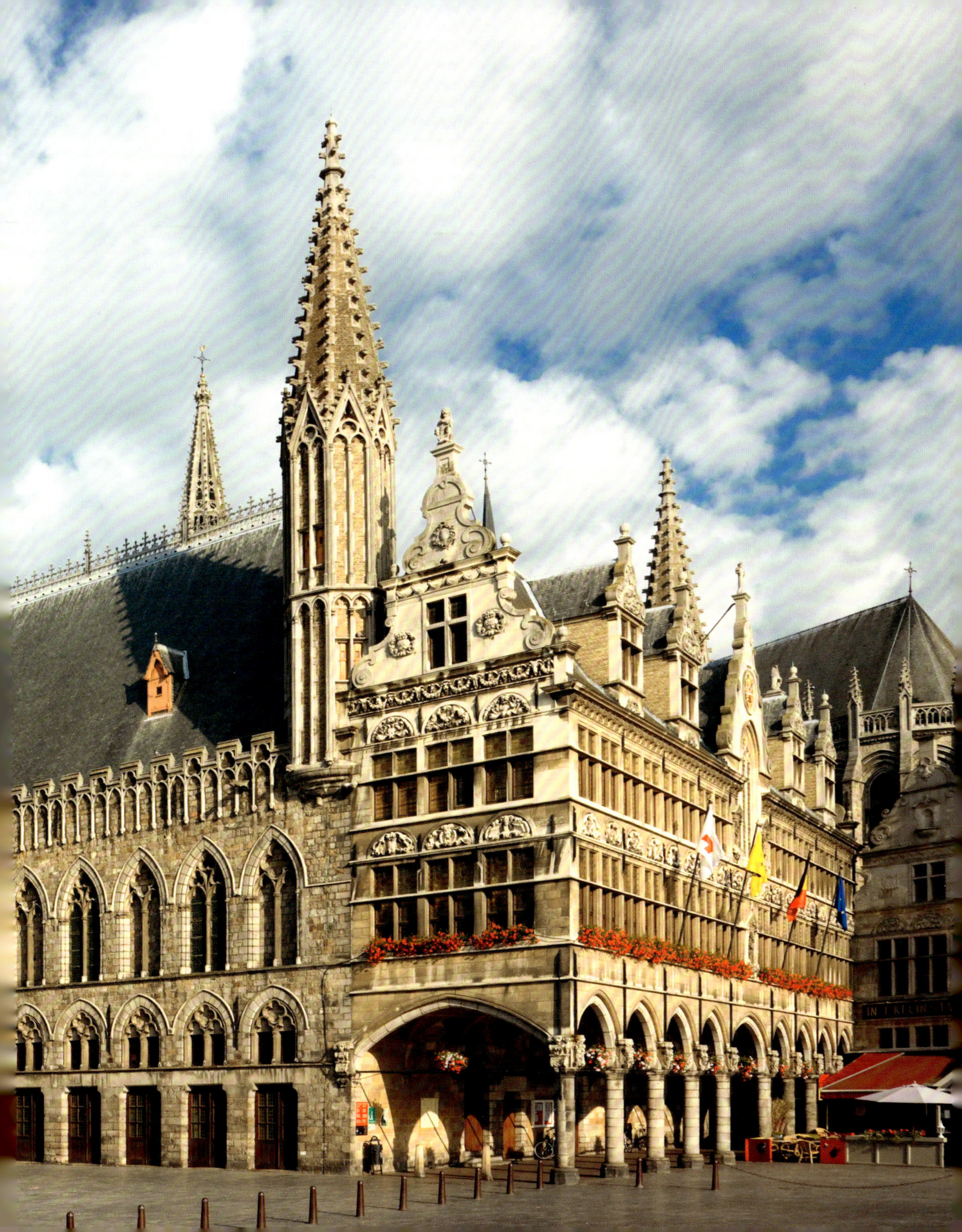

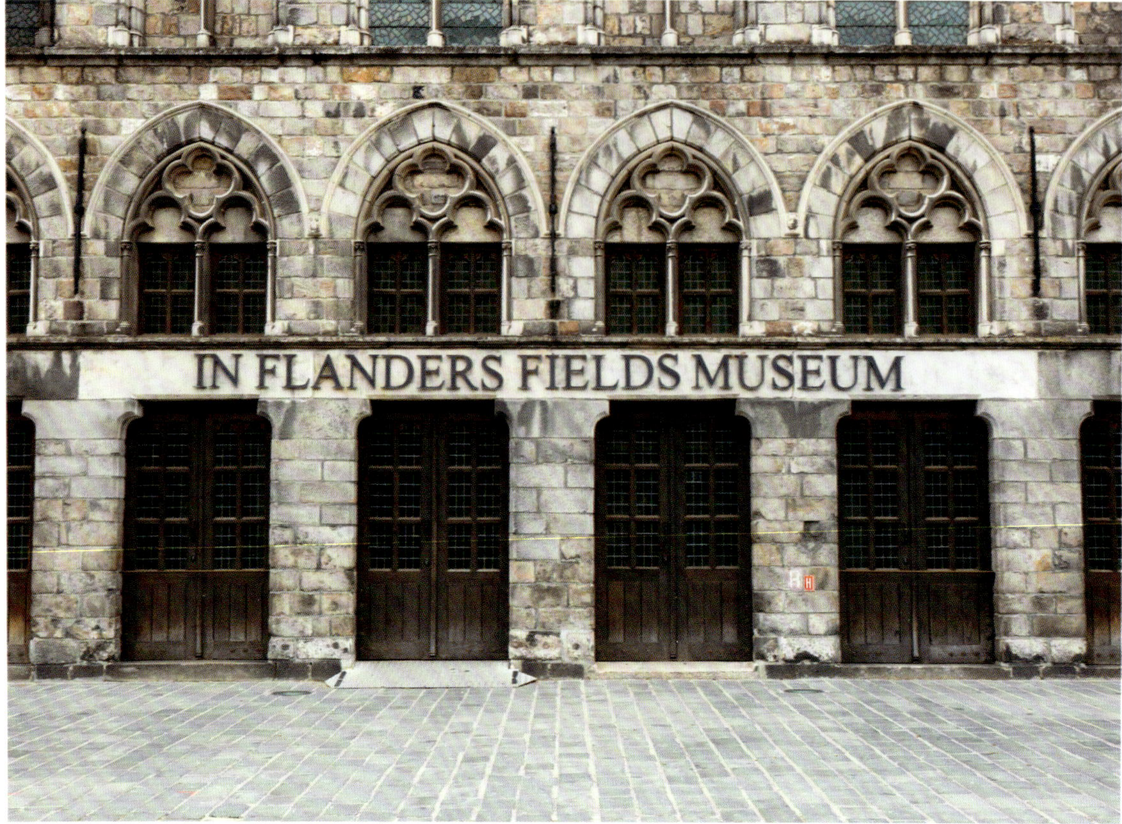

In Flanders Field Museum, Ypres
In Flanders Field Museum, Ieper

Ypres, memory of the Great War

Half a million soldiers died in the First World War in Flemish Ypres. British and French fought against German troops there. The once important textile city of Ypres is the starting point for exploring the memorials of the First World War. The Cloth Hall, the largest secular building of the medieval Gothic in Europe is, like the whole town, a symbol of the will to live on after 1918 and houses the "In Flanders Fields Museum", which is the central memorial of the region. Reconstructions and models illustrate how concrete bunkers and deep tunnels were used to protect people from the permanent bombardment.

Ypres, souvenir de la Grande Guerre

Lors de la Première Guerre mondiale, un demi-million de soldats est tombé dans l'Ypres flamande. Britanniques et Français y affrontèrent les troupes allemandes. L'ancienne grande cité drapière d'Ypres constitue le point de départ idéal pour découvrir les mémoriaux de la Première Guerre mondiale. La plus grande construction profane du gothique médiéval européen symbolise, tout comme l'ensemble de la ville, la volonté de continuer à vivre après 1918. Le musée In Flanders Fields est le principal lieu de mémoire de la région. Reconstructions et modèles montrent comment on se protégeait des bombardements permanents à l'aide de bunkers en béton et de profondes galeries.

Ypern, Erinnerung an den Großen Krieg

Eine halbe Million Soldaten sind im Ersten Weltkrieg im flämischen Ypern gefallen. Briten und Franzosen kämpften dort gegen deutsche Truppen. Die einst bedeutende Tuchstadt Ypern ist der Ausgangspunkt für die Erkundung der Gedenkstätten des 1. Weltkriegs. Der größte Profanbau der mittelalterlichen Gotik Europas ist, wie der gesamte Ort, ein Symbol für den Willen zum Weiterleben nach 1918. Das „In Flandern Fields Museum" bildet die zentrale Erinnerungsstätte der Region. Rekonstruktionen und Modelle verdeutlichen, wie man sich mit Betonbunkern und tief reichenden Stollen vor dem Dauerbombardement schützte.

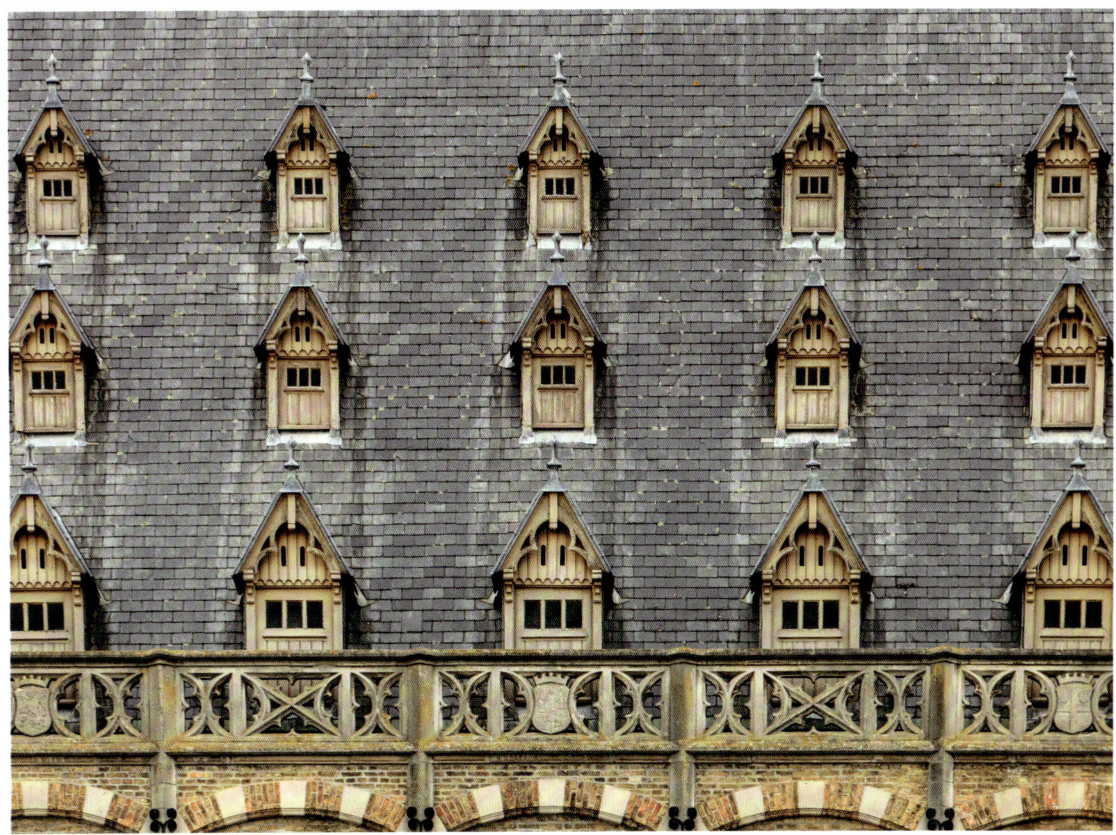

Kasselrijhof, Ypres
Kasselrijhof, Ieper

Ypres, recuerdo de la Gran Guerra

Medio millón de soldados murieron en la Primera Guerra Mundial en el Ypres flamenco. Los británicos y los franceses lucharon contra las tropas alemanas allí. La importante ciudad para la elaboración de tejidos, Ypres, es el punto de partida para explorar los monumentos conmemorativos de la Primera Guerra Mundial. El mayor edificio secular del gótico medieval de Europa es, como toda la ciudad, un símbolo de la voluntad de vivir después de 1918, y el "Museo de los Campos de Flandes" es el monumento central de la región. Las reconstrucciones y los modelos ilustran cómo se utilizaron los búnkeres de hormigón y los túneles profundos para proteger a las personas de los bombardeos permanentes.

Ypres, memória da Grande Guerra

Meio milhão de soldados morreram na Primeira Guerra Mundial em Ypres da Flandres. Britânicos e franceses lutaram lá contra as tropas alemãs. A outrora importante cidade medieval fabricante de tecidos, Ypres, é o ponto de partida para explorar os memoriais da Primeira Guerra Mundial. O maior edifício secular do gótico medieval na Europa é, como toda a cidade, um símbolo da vontade de viver depois de 1918. O "In Flanders Fields Museum" é o memorial central da região. Reconstruções e modelos ilustram como bunkers de concreto e túneis profundos foram usados para proteger as pessoas do bombardeio permanente.

Ieper, herinnering aan de Grote Oorlog

In het Vlaamse Ieper stierven tijdens de Eerste Wereldoorlog een half miljoen soldaten. Britten en Fransen vochten daar tegen Duitse troepen. De eens zo belangrijke lakenstad Ieper is het vertrekpunt voor het verkennen van de gedenkplaatsen m.b.t. de Eerste Wereldoorlog. Het grootste wereldlijke gebouw van de middeleeuwse gotiek in Europa is, net als de hele stad, een symbool van de wil om na 1918 verder te leven. Het "In Flanders Fields Museum" is de centrale gedenkplaats van de regio. Reconstructies en modellen verduidelijken hoe men zich met betonnen bunkers en diepe tunnels tegen de permanente bombardementen beschermde.

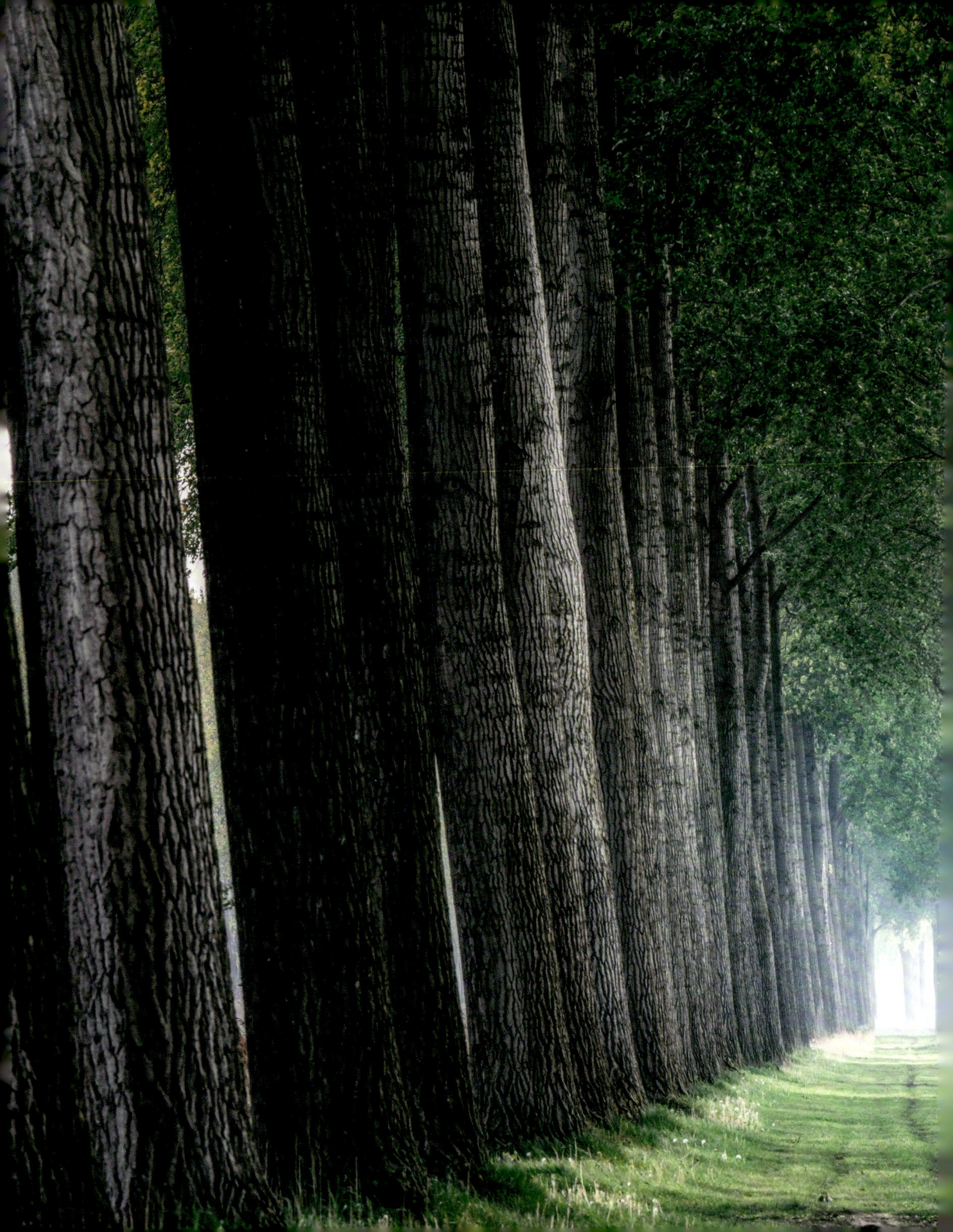

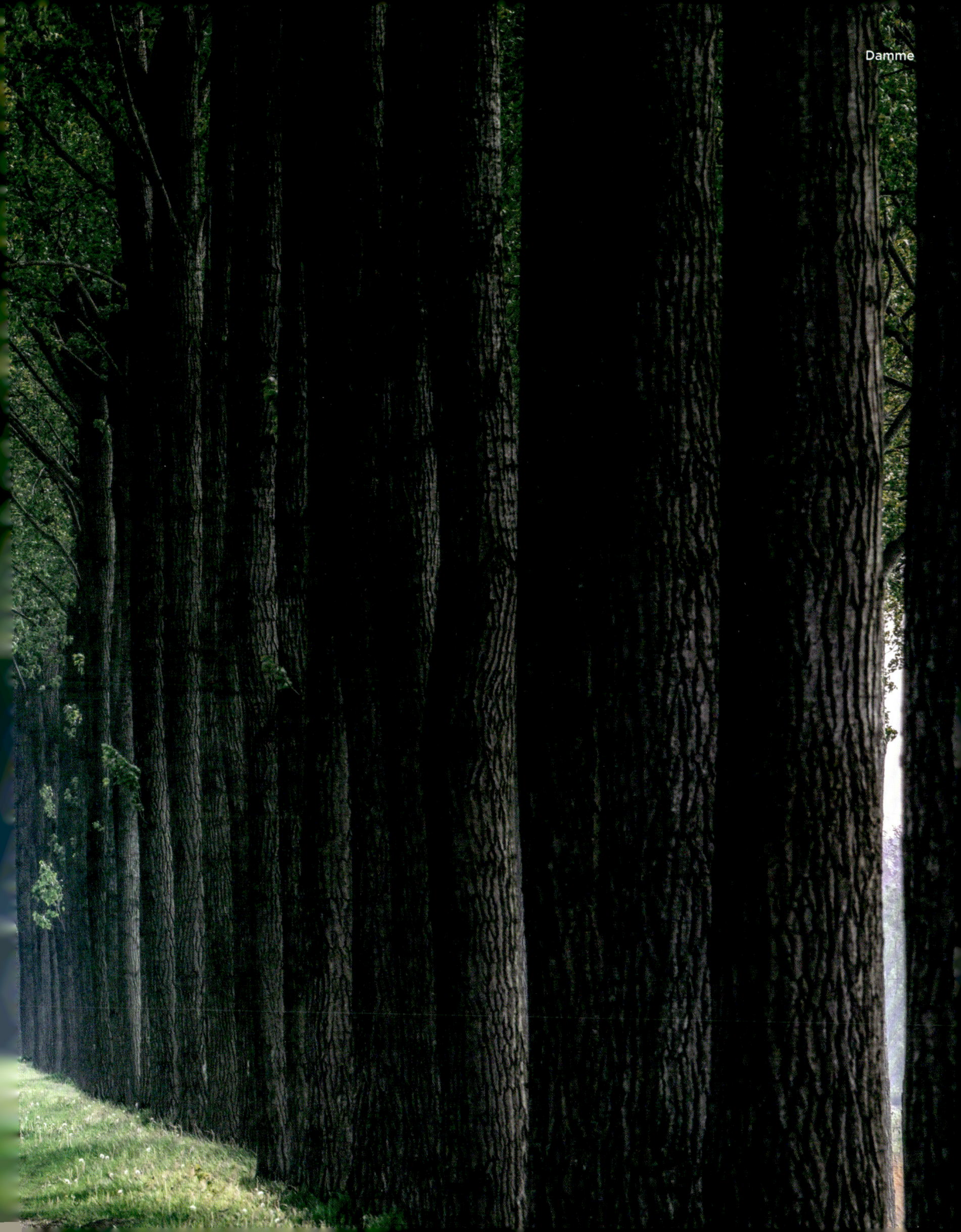
Damme

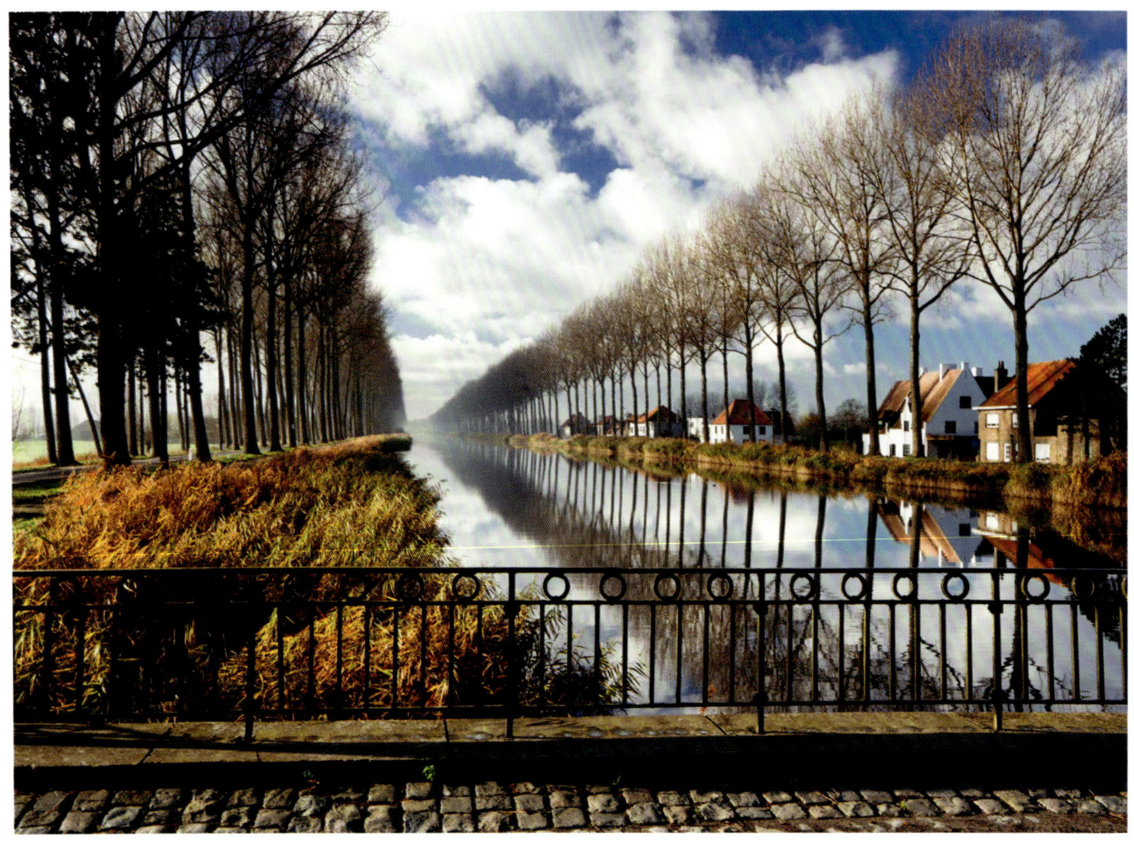

Damme Canal
Damse Vaart
Canal de Damme

By steamer from Bruges to Damme
A nostalgic excursion from Bruges to
Damme is offered by a boat trip with
the paddle steamer *Lamme Goedzak.*
Damme is the town where the Flemish Till
Eulenspiegel was born. Damme dedicated
a museum, sculptures and a gravestone to
the fool and freedom fighter. The paddle
steamer is named after his best friend,
Lamme Goedzak. The leisurely cruise
along the poplar-lined canal, passing small
Flemish cottages and windmills, takes
about 35 minutes. The towpath is also very
popular with cyclists. From April to the
end of September the boat runs five times
a day.

De Bruges à Damme en bateau à vapeur
C'est une excursion empreinte de nostalgie
qu'offre le trajet de Bruges à Damme à
bord du bateau à roues à aubes *Lamme
Goedzak.* Damme est le lieu de naissance
du personnage flamand Till l'Espiègle. La
ville a consacré à ce farceur et combattant
de la liberté un musée, des sculptures et
une pierre tombale. Le bateau porte le
nom de son meilleur ami. Le paisible trajet
sur le canal bordé de peupliers, laissant
apparaître de petites maisons flamandes
et des moulins à vent, dure environ 35
minutes. Le chemin de halage est fort prisé
des cyclistes. D'avril à fin septembre, le
bateau assure le trajet cinq fois par jour.

**Mit dem Dampfer von Brügge nach
Damme**
Einen nostalgischen Ausflug von Brügge
nach Damme bietet die Bootsfahrt mit
dem Schaufelraddampfer *Lamme Goedzak.*
Damme ist das Städtchen, in dem der
flämische Till Eulenspiegel geboren
wurde. Damme widmete dem Narren und
Freiheitskämpfer ein Museum, Skulpturen
und einen Grabstein. Der Raddampfer
ist nach seinem besten Freund benannt:
Lamme Goedzak. Die geruhsame Fahrt
auf dem von Pappeln gesäumten Kanal,
vorbei kleinen flämischen Häuschen und
Windmühlen, dauert rund 35 Minuten. Der
Treidelpfad ist auch bei Radfahrern sehr
beliebt. Von April bis zu Ende September
fährt das Boot fünfmal am Tag.

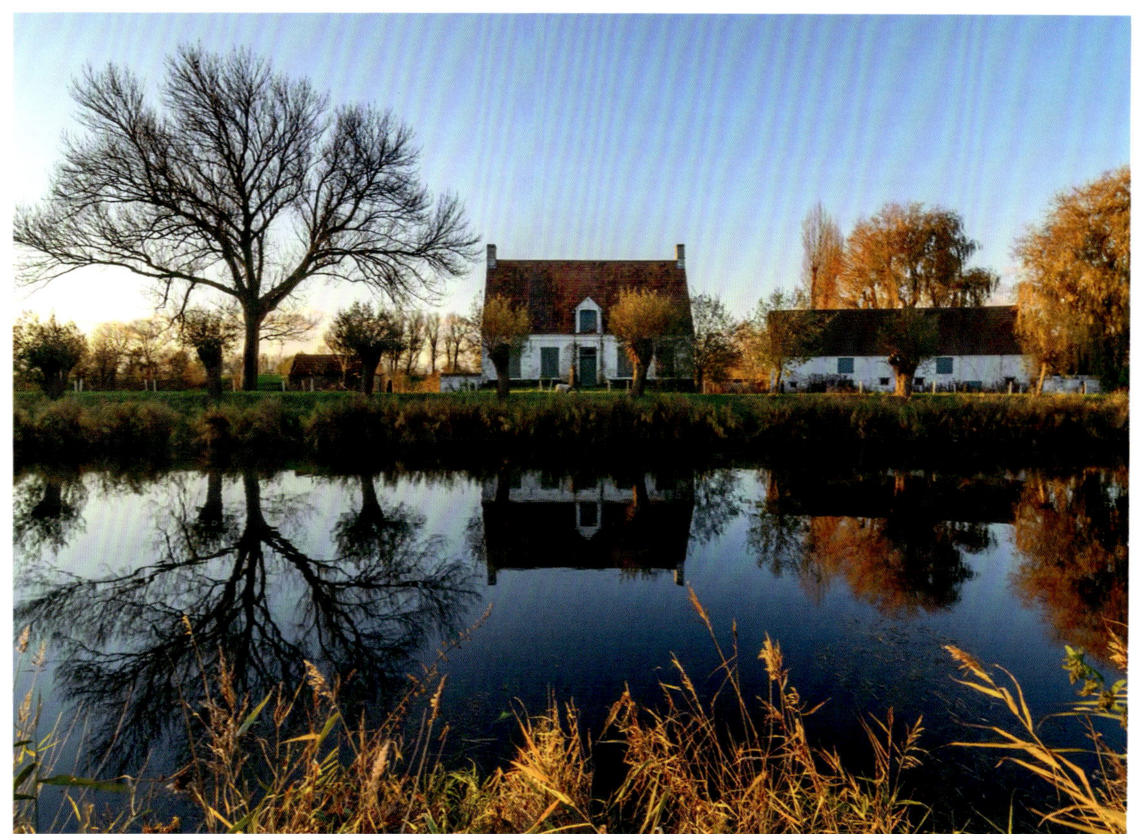

Damme Canal
Damse Vaart
Canal de Damme

En barco de Brujas a Damme

Se puede dar un paseo en el barco de
vapor *Lamme Goedzak* para hacer una
excursión nostálgica de Brujas a Damme.
Damme es una pequeña ciudad donde
nació el flamenco Till Eulenspiegel. Damme
dedicó un museo, esculturas y una lápida
al tonto y luchador por la libertad. El vapor
de vapor lleva el nombre de su mejor
amigo: Lamme Goedzak. El tranquilo
crucero a lo largo del canal bordeado de
álamos dura 35 minutos y se pasa por
pequeñas cabañas flamencas y molinos
de viento. El camino de sirga también es
muy popular entre los ciclistas. De abril a
finales de septiembre el barco ofrece esta
excursión cinco veces al día.

De navio a vapor de Bruges a Damme

Uma nostálgica excursão de Bruges
a Damme é oferecida por um passeio
em um barco a vapor de rodas *Lamme
Goedzak*. Damme é a cidade onde
nasceu o flamengo Till Eulenspiegel.
Damme dedicou um museu, esculturas
e uma lápide ao tolo e ao combatente
da liberdade. O barco a vapor recebeu
o nome do seu melhor amigo: Lamme
Goedzak. O cruzeiro de lazer ao longo
do canal cercado por choupos, passando
por pequenas casas e moinhos de vento
flamengos, leva cerca de 35 minutos. O
caminho ao longo das margens do canal
também é muito popular entre os ciclistas.
De abril até o final finais de setembro, o
barco faz o percurso cinco vezes por dia.

Met de stoomboot van Brugge naar Damme

Een nostalgische excursie van Brugge
naar Damme wordt aangeboden door
een boottocht met de raderstoomboot
Lamme Goedzak. Damme is de stad
waar de Vlaamse Tijl Uilenspiegel werd
geboren. Damme wijdde een museum,
beeldhouwwerken en een grafsteen aan de
nar en vrijheidsstrijder. De raderstoomboot
is vernoemd naar zijn beste vriend: Lamme
Goedzak. De ontspannen tocht langs het
met populieren omzoomde kanaal, langs
kleine Vlaamse huisjes en windmolens,
duurt ongeveer 35 minuten. Het jaagpad
is ook erg populair bij fietsers. Van april
tot eind september vaart de boot vijf keer
per dag.

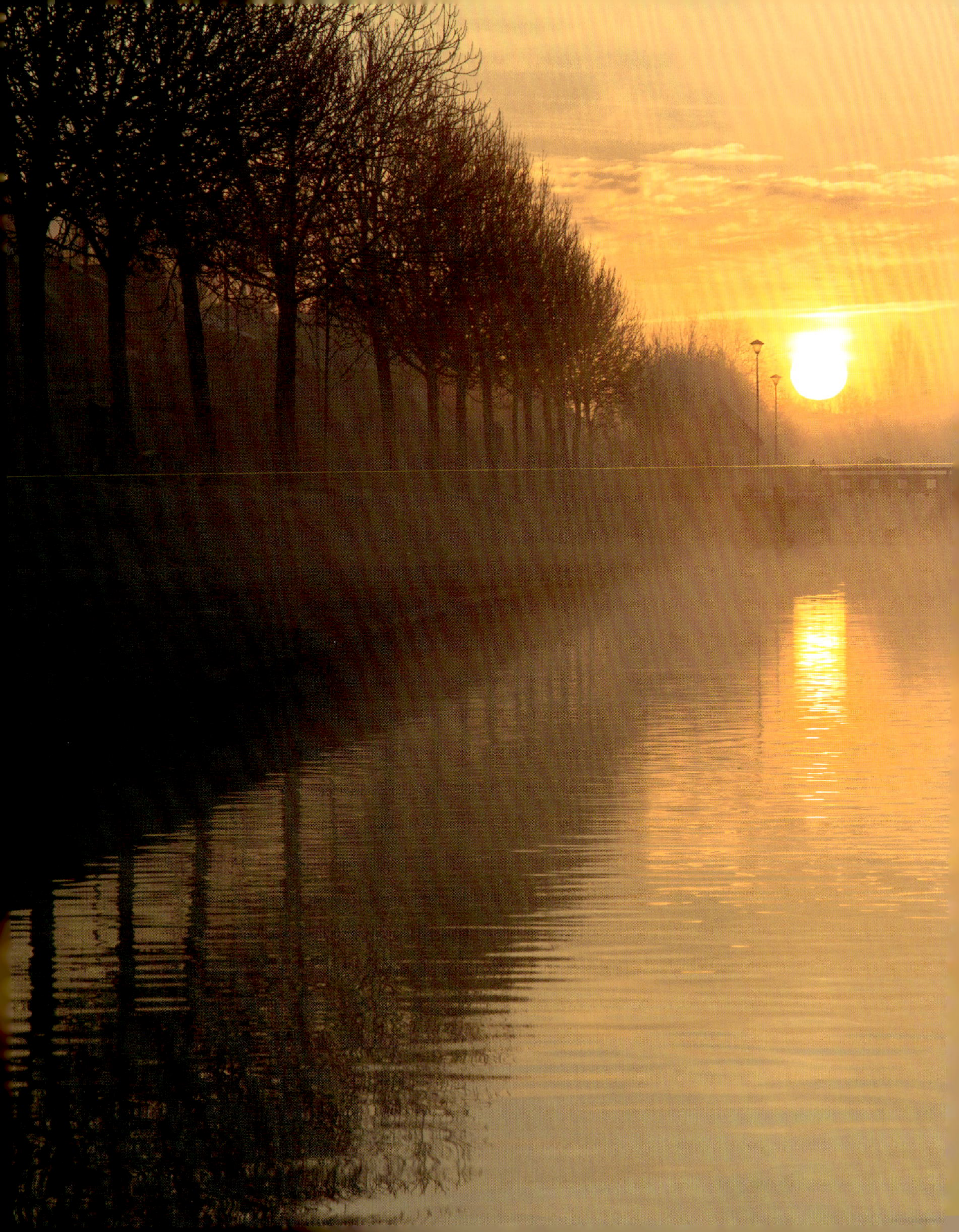

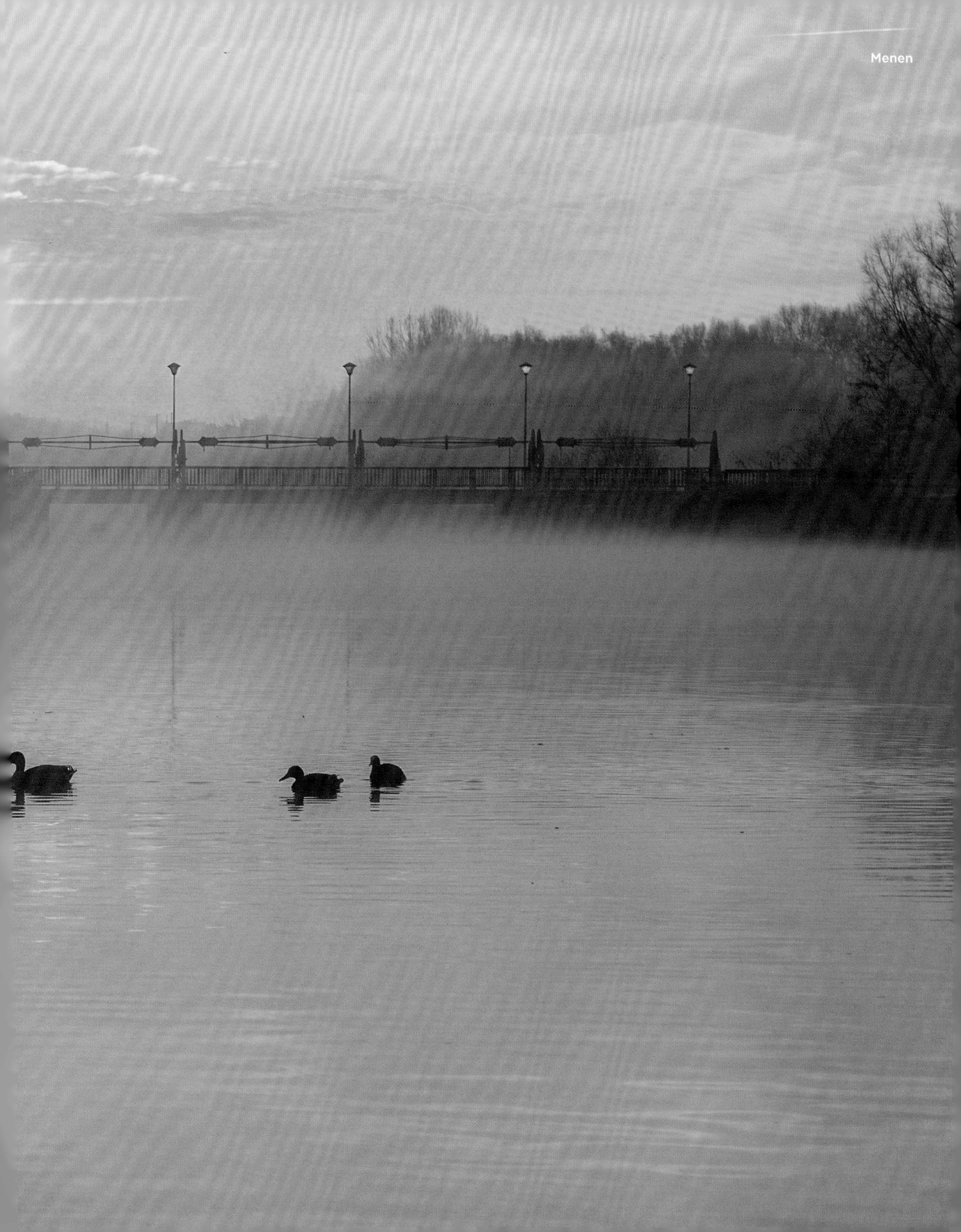
Menen

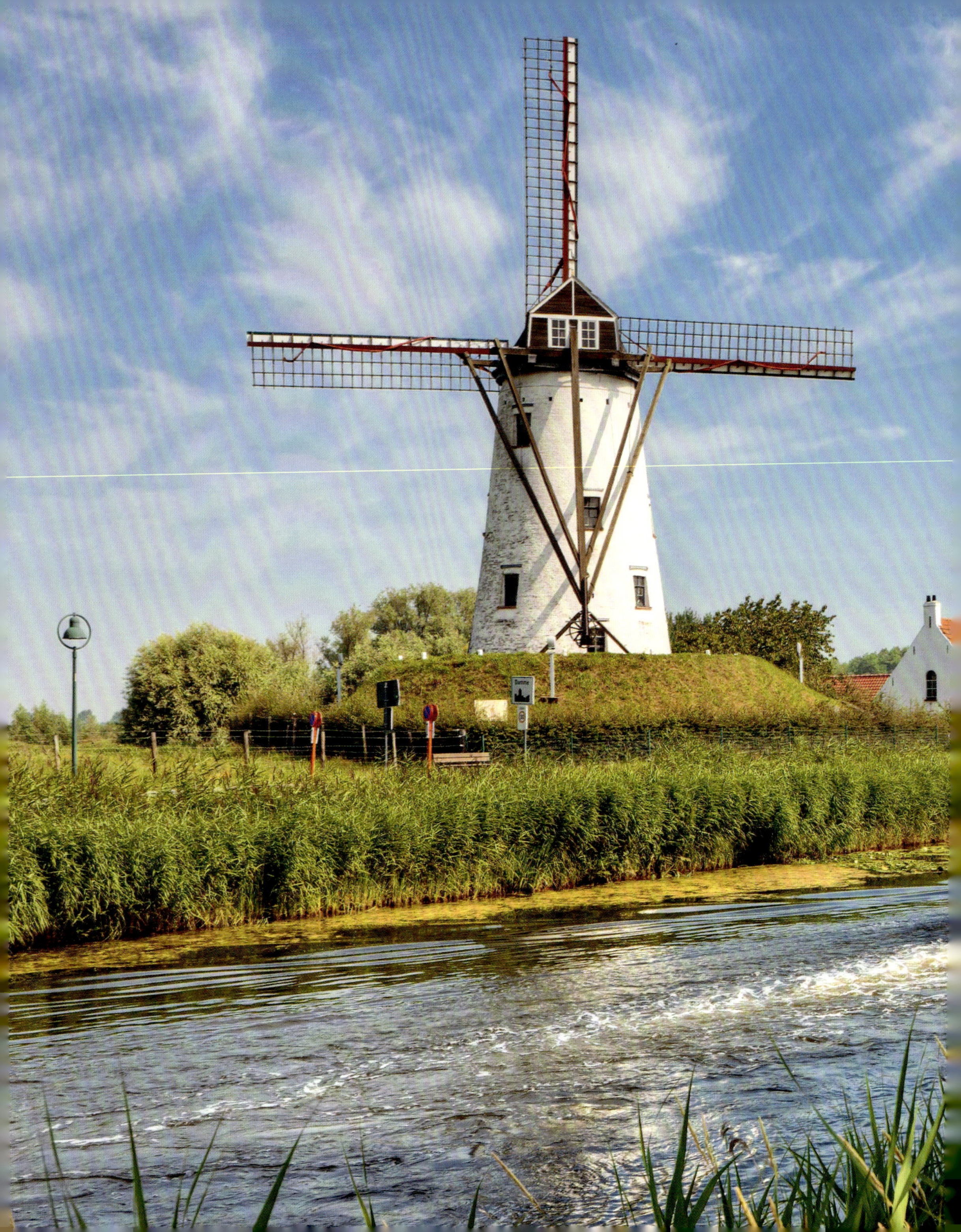

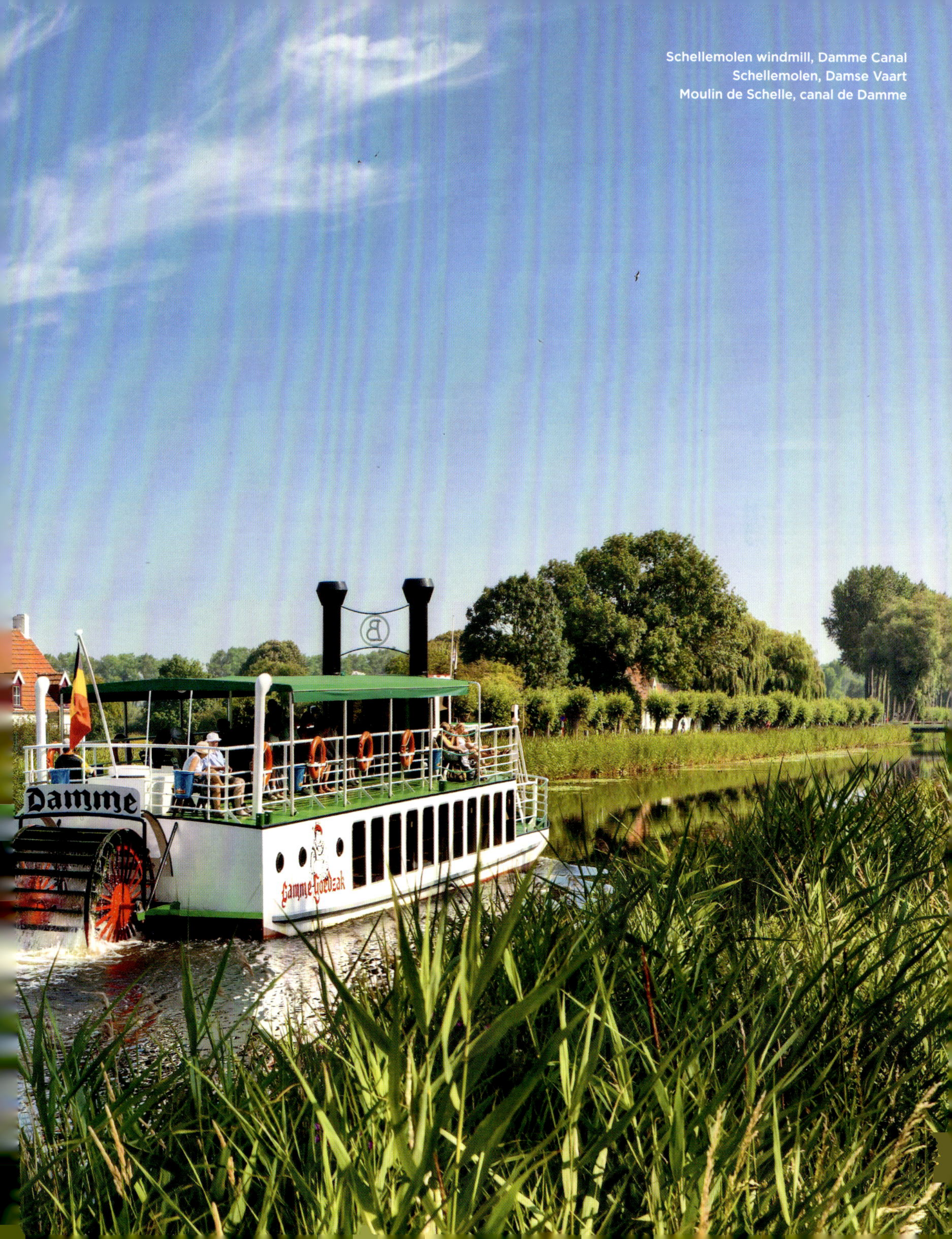

Schellemolen windmill, Damme Canal
Schellemolen, Damse Vaart
Moulin de Schelle, canal de Damme

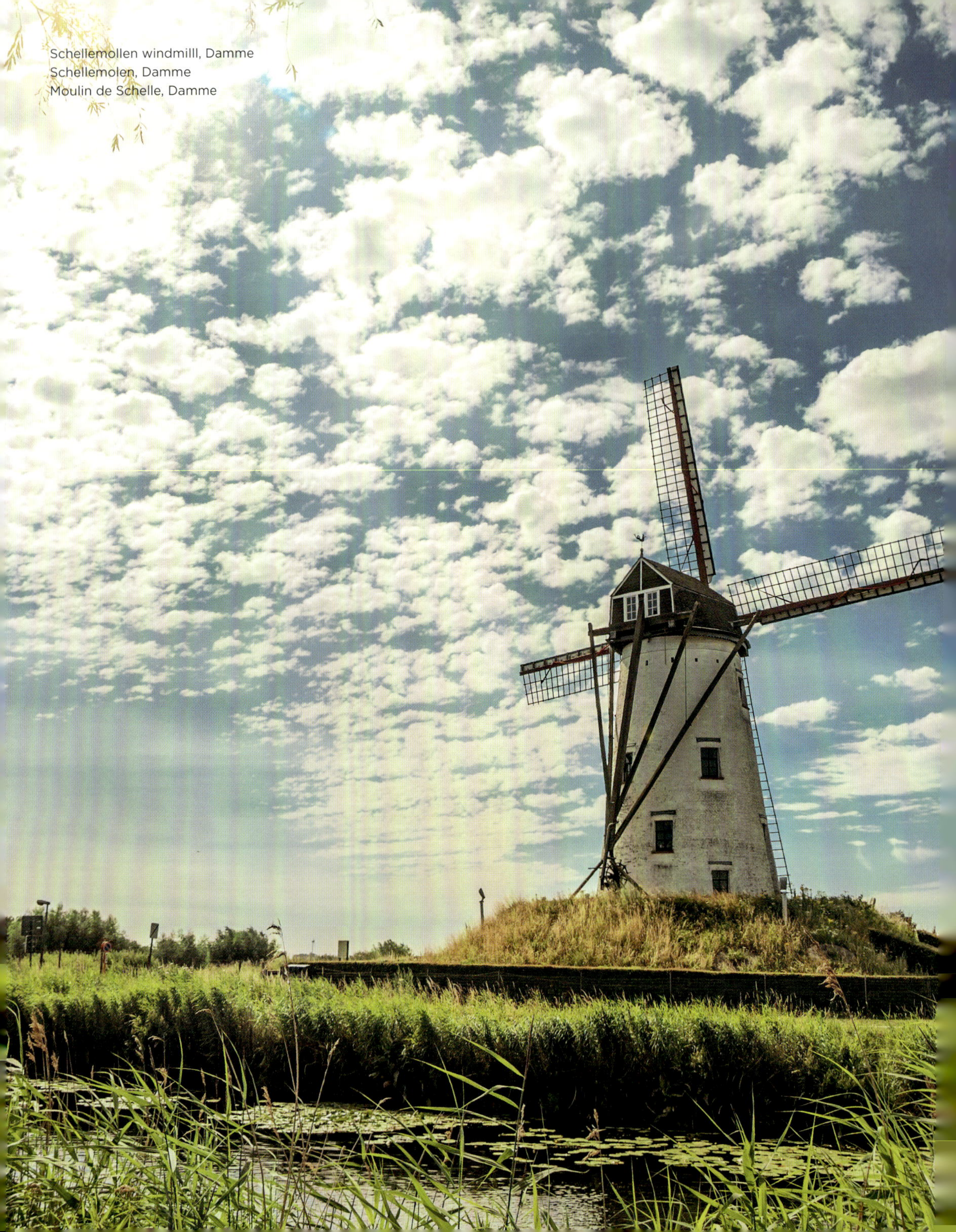
Schellemollen windmilll, Damme
Schellemolen, Damme
Moulin de Schelle, Damme

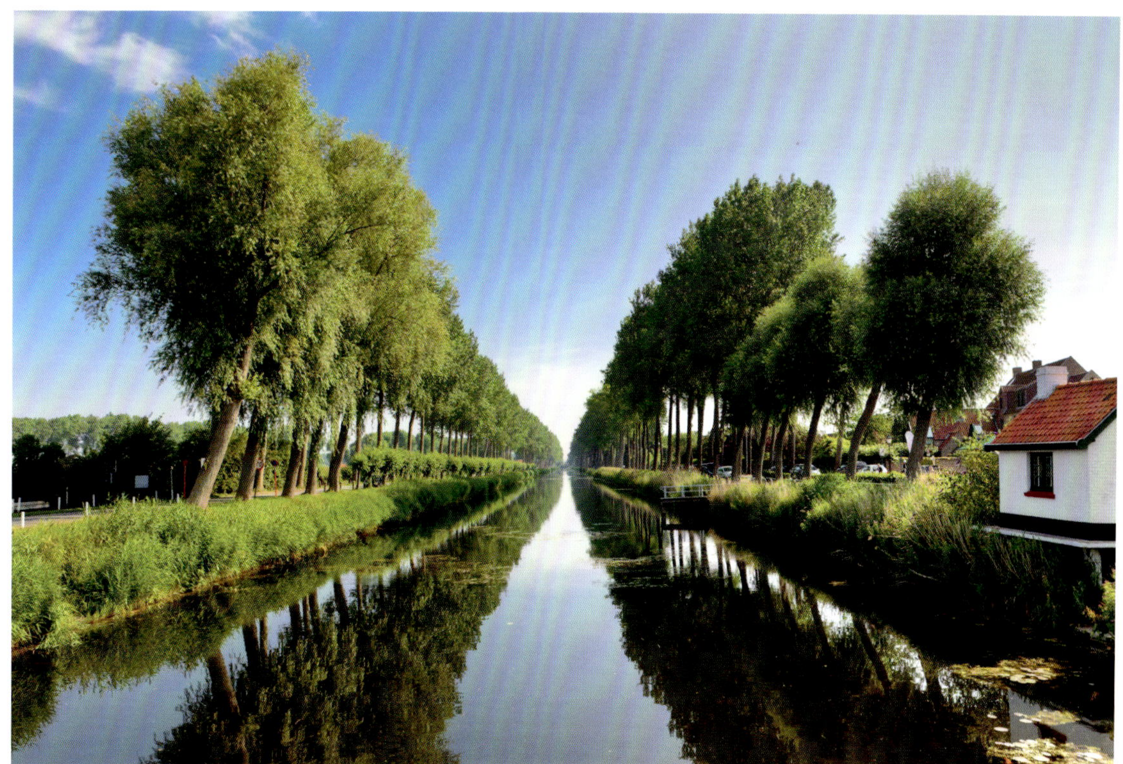

Damme Canal
Damse Vaart
Canal de Damme

Till Eulenspiegel, a rogue from Damme?

Charles de Coster wrote a famous literary work in the 19th century in which he transferred the legend of Till Eulenspiegel to the time of the 80-year war (from 1568 to 1648, the Netherlands fought against Spain). His main characters, Till and Lamme Goedzak, are freedom fighters from Damme and move out into the big world to play their well-known tricks.

¿Till Eulenspiegel, el pícaro de Damme?

Charles de Coster escribió una famosa obra literaria en el siglo XIX en la que trasladó la leyenda de Till Eulenspiegel a la época de la guerra de los 80 años (1568 a 1648, Holanda contra España). Sus protagonistas, Till y Lamme Goedzak, son luchadores por la libertad de Damme y se trasladan al gran mundo para realizar sus conocidos trucos.

Till l'Espiègle, le farceur de Damme ?

Au XIXe siècle, Charles de Coster écrivit une œuvre littéraire célèbre retraçant la légende de Till l'Espiègle à l'époque de la guerre de Quatre-Vingts ans (de 1568 à 1648, Pays-Bas contre Espagne). Ses personnages principaux sont Till et Lamme Goedzak, des combattants de la liberté originaires de Damme qui partent à la découverte du monde pour y jouer leurs tours bien connus.

Till Eulenspiegel, um malandro de Damme?

Charles de Coster escreveu uma famosa obra literária no século XIX, na qual transferiu a lenda de Till Eulenspiegel para a época da guerra de 80 anos (1568 a 1648, Holanda contra Espanha). Seus personagens principais, Till e Lamme Goedzak, são combatentes da liberdade de Damme e vão para o grande mundo para fazer as travessuras mais conhecidas.

Till Eulenspiegel, ein Schelm aus Damme?

Charles de Coster schrieb im 19. Jahrhundert ein berühmtes literarisches Werk, in dem er die Legende Till Eulenspiegels, in die Zeit des 80-jährigen Krieges (1568 bis 1648, Niederlande gegen Spanien) übertrug. Seine Hauptfiguren Till und Lamme Goedzak sind Freiheitskämpfer aus Damme und ziehen in die große Welt aus, um die bekannten Streiche zu spielen.

Tijl Uilenspiegel, een schelm uit Damme?

Charles de Coster schreef in de 19e eeuw een beroemd literair werk waarin hij de legende van Tijl Uilenspiegel overbrengt naar de tijd van de 80-jarige oorlog (1568-1648, Nederland tegen Spanje). Zijn hoofdpersonen, Tijl en Lamme Goedzak, zijn vrijheidsstrijders uit Damme en trekken de grote wereld in om de bekende streken uit te halen.

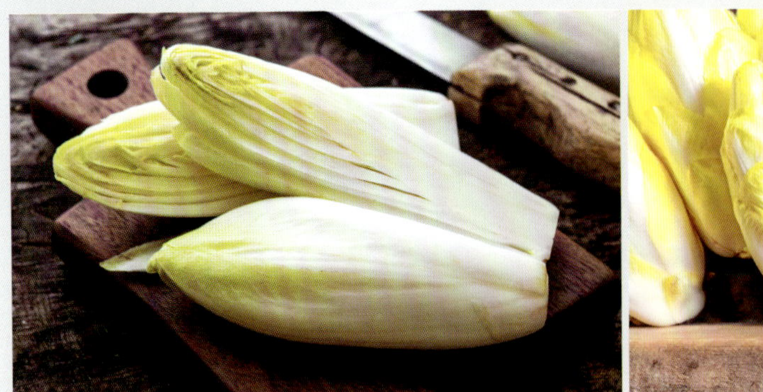
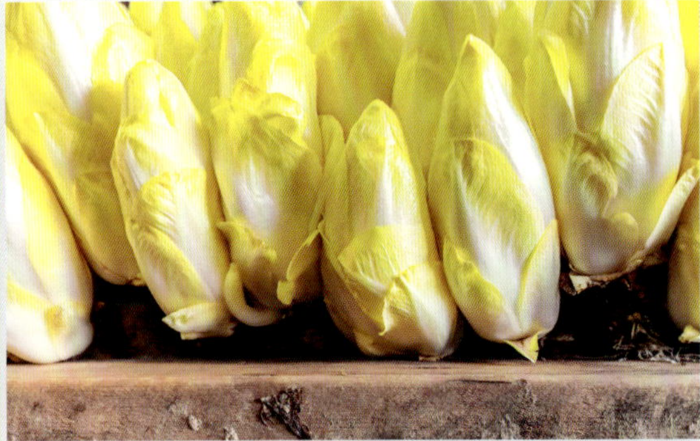

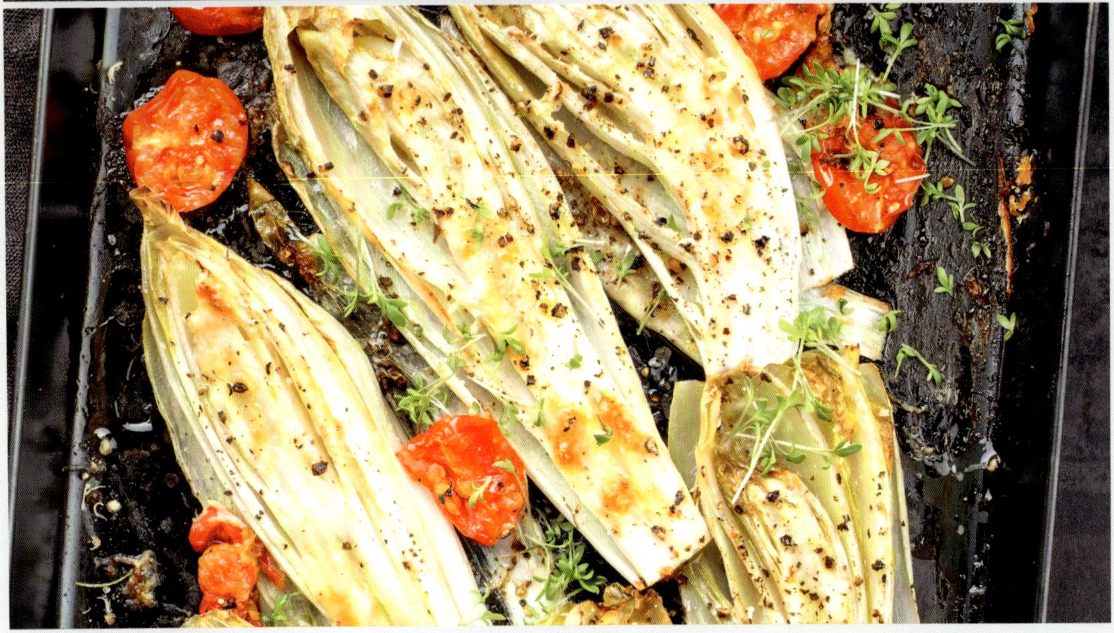

Chicory and Brussels sprouts

Chicory is the national vegetable of the Flemish. Nobody produces more and nobody consumes more. It was not until the 19th century that Flemish farmers discovered it by chance. When the chicory root grows in the dark, the plant develops only slightly bitter, crunchy leaves. After this discovery, the Flemish vegetable farmers cultivated their new vegetables and proudly presented them to the world in 1873. We also owe Brussels sprouts to the Flemish from Brussels. Due to the growing population within the city walls, the gardeners bred the space-saving new cabbage hybrids.

Endives et choux de Bruxelles

L'endive est le légume national des Flamands : nulle part ailleurs on n'en produit plus et personne n'en consomme plus qu'en Flandres. Ce n'est qu'au XIXe siècle que les agriculteurs la découvrirent par hasard. Si l'on cultive sa racine dans l'obscurité, ses feuilles craquantes et très légèrement amères se mettent à pousser. Suite à cette découverte, les agriculteurs flamands cultivèrent leur nouveau légume et le présentèrent fièrement au monde en 1873. Les choux de Bruxelles aussi, nous les devons aux Flamands : en raison de la population croissante à l'intérieur des murs de la ville, les maraîchers se mirent à faire pousser de nouveaux hybrides de chou ne nécessitant pas trop d'espace.

Chicorée und Rosenkohl

Chicorée ist das Nationalgemüse der Flamen: Keiner produziert mehr und auch niemand verzehrt mehr. Erst im 19. Jahrhundert entdeckten ihn flämische Bauern per Zufall. Wenn die Zichorienwurzel im Dunkeln treibt, entwickeln sich die nur leicht bitteren, knackigen Blätter. Nach dieser Entdeckung züchteten die flämischen Gemüsebauern ihr neues Gemüse und stellten es 1873 stolz der Weltöffentlichkeit vor. Auch den Rosenkohl haben wir den Flamen aus Brüssel zu verdanken. Aufgrund der wachsenden Bevölkerung innerhalb der Stadtmauern züchteten die Gärtner die platzsparenden neuen Kohlhybriden.

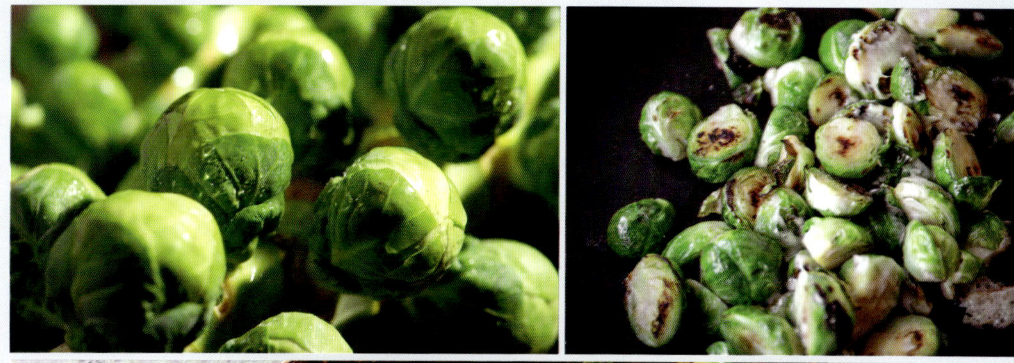

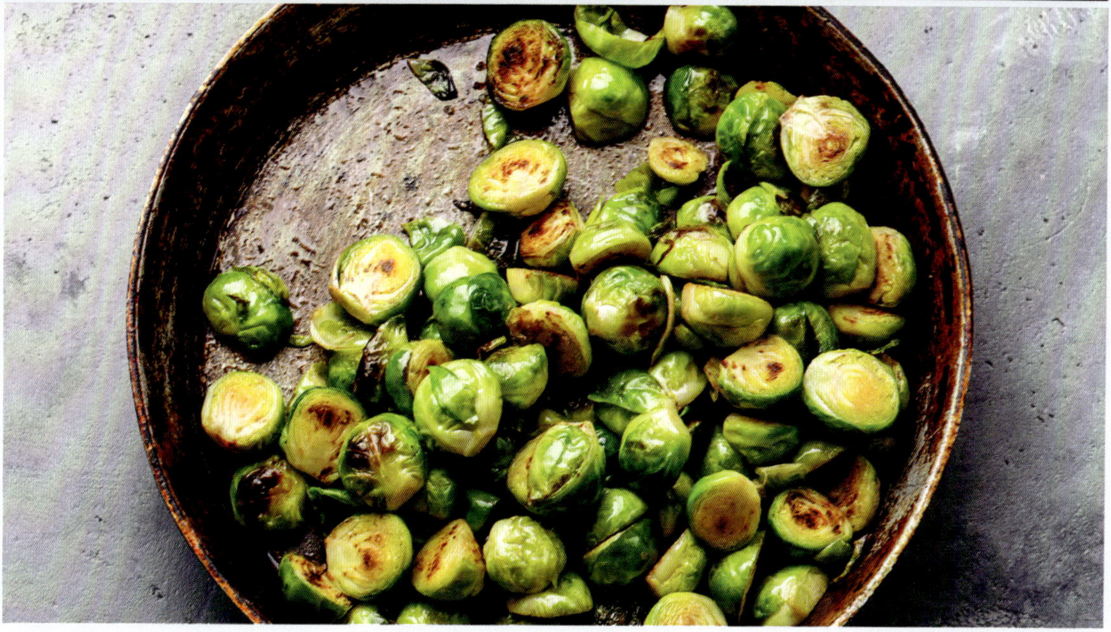

Achicoria y coles de Bruselas

La achicoria es el vegetal nacional de los flamencos: nadie la produce más y nadie la consume más. No fue hasta el siglo XIX que los agricultores flamencos lo descubrieron por casualidad. Cuando la achicoria echa raíces en la oscuridad, las hojas se vuelven ligeramente amargas y crujientes. Tras este descubrimiento, los horticultores flamencos cultivaron sus nuevas hortalizas y las presentaron con orgullo al público mundial en 1873. También debemos las coles de Bruselas a los flamencos de Bruselas. Debido a la creciente población dentro de las murallas de la ciudad, los jardineros criaron los nuevos híbridos de col que permiten ahorrar espacio.

Chicória e couve-de-bruxelas

A chicória é o vegetal nacional dos flamengos: ninguém produz mais e ninguém consome mais. Só no século XIX é que os agricultores flamengos o descobriram por acaso. Quando a raiz da chicória cresce no escuro, as folhas desenvolvem-se ligeiramente amargas e estaladiças. Após esta descoberta, os produtores de legumes flamengos cultivaram os seus novos legumes e apresentaram-nos orgulhosamente ao público mundial em 1873. Devemos também as couves-de-bruxelas aos flamengos de Bruxelas. Devido ao crescimento da população dentro das muralhas da cidade, os jardineiros criaram os novos híbridos de couve, que economizam espaço.

Witlof en spruitjes

Witlof is de nationale groente van de Vlamingen: niemand produceert meer en ook niemand consumeert meer. Pas in de 19e eeuw ontdekten de Vlaamse boeren het bij toeval. Wanneer de witlofwortel in het donker groeit, ontwikkelen de bladeren slechts licht bittere, knapperige bladeren. Na deze ontdekking kweekten de Vlaamse groentetelers hun nieuwe groenten en presenteerden ze in 1873 met trots aan de wereld. Ook de spruiten hebben we te danken aan de Vlamingen in Brussel. Door de groeiende bevolking binnen de stadsmuren kweekten de tuinders de ruimtebesparende, nieuwe koolhybriden.

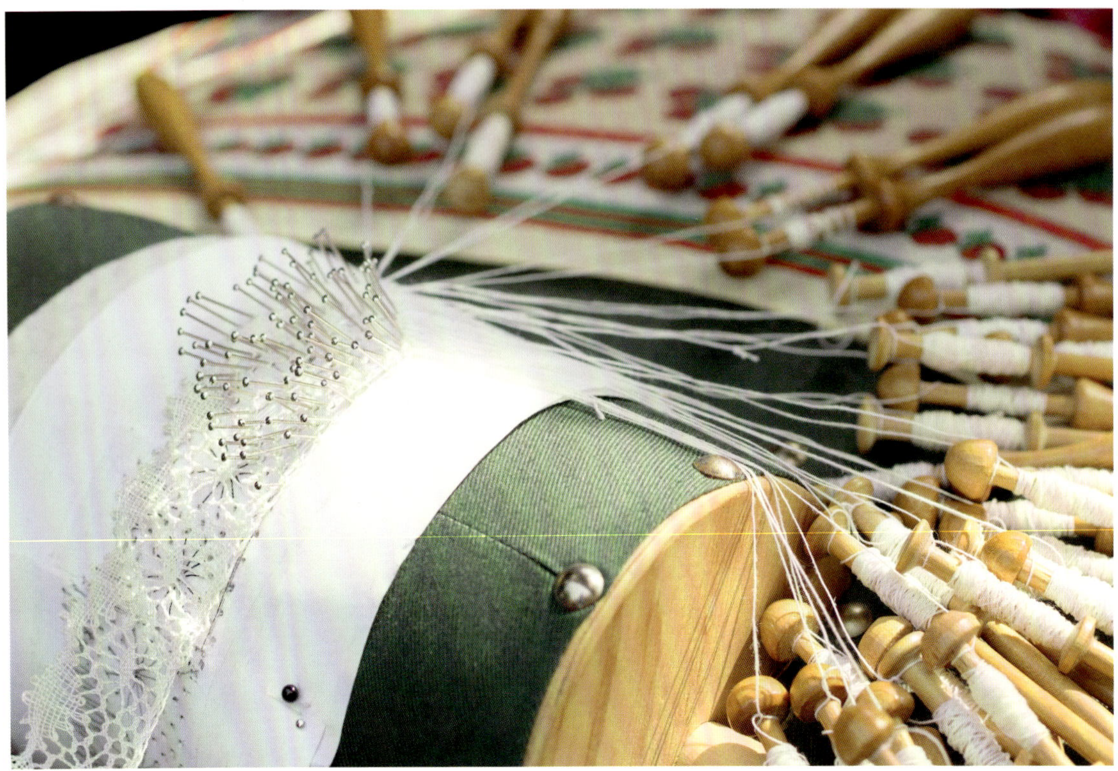

Handmade lace, bobbins and pins
Handgemaakte kant, houten spoelen en naalden spelden
Dentelle aux fuseaux, bobines et épingles

Flemish Lace

In Flanders, lace is part of the cultural heritage. In the early 20th century there were around 47,000 lace-makers. About 70 percent of them were in Bruges alone, which led to the founding of the Bruges lace-making school. The roots of the lace production go back to the 15th century. Even today, Flemish designers are developing new creations from lace.

Encaje flamenco

En Flandes, el encaje forma parte del patrimonio cultural. A principios del siglo XX había alrededor de 47 000 encajeras. Alrededor del 70 por ciento de ellas se encontraba solo en Brujas, lo que condujo a la fundación de la escuela de encaje de Brujas. Las raíces del encaje flamenco se remontan al siglo XV. Incluso hoy en día los diseñadores flamencos están desarrollando nuevas creaciones a partir del encaje.

Dentelle flamande

En Flandres, la dentelle fait partie de l'héritage culturel. Au début du XXᵉ siècle, on comptait environ 47 000 dentellières. Environ 70 % d'entre elles travaillaient à Bruges, ce qui conduisit à la fondation de l'école de fabrication de dentelle de Bruges. Les origines de la dentelle flamande remontent au XVᵉ siècle. Aujourd'hui encore, les stylistes flamands développent de nouvelles créations en dentelle.

Renda Flamenga

Na Flandres, a renda faz parte do património cultural. No início do século XX haviam cerca de 47 000 rendeiros. Cerca de 70 por cento deles só em Bruges, o que levou à fundação da escola de fabricação de rendas de Bruges. As raízes da renda flamenga remontam ao século XV. Ainda hoje, os designers flamengos desenvolvem novas criações feitas de renda.

Flämische Spitze

In Flandern sind Spitzen ein Teil des kulturellen Erbes. Im frühen 20. Jahrhundert gab es rund 47 000 Klöpplerinnen. Rund 70 Prozent davon allein in Brügge, was zur Gründung der Brügger Klöppelschule führte. Die Wurzeln der flämische Spitze reichen zurück bis ins 15. Jahrhundert. Auch heutzutage entwickeln flämische Designer neue Kreationen aus Spitze.

Vlaamse kant

In Vlaanderen maakt kant deel uit van het cultureel erfgoed. In het begin van de 20e eeuw waren er ongeveer 47 000 kantklossters. Ongeveer 70 procent daarvan alleen al in Brugge, wat leidde tot de oprichting van de Brugse kantschool. De wortels van het Vlaamse kant gaan terug tot de 15e eeuw. Ook vandaag nog ontwikkelen Vlaamse designers nieuwe creaties met kant.

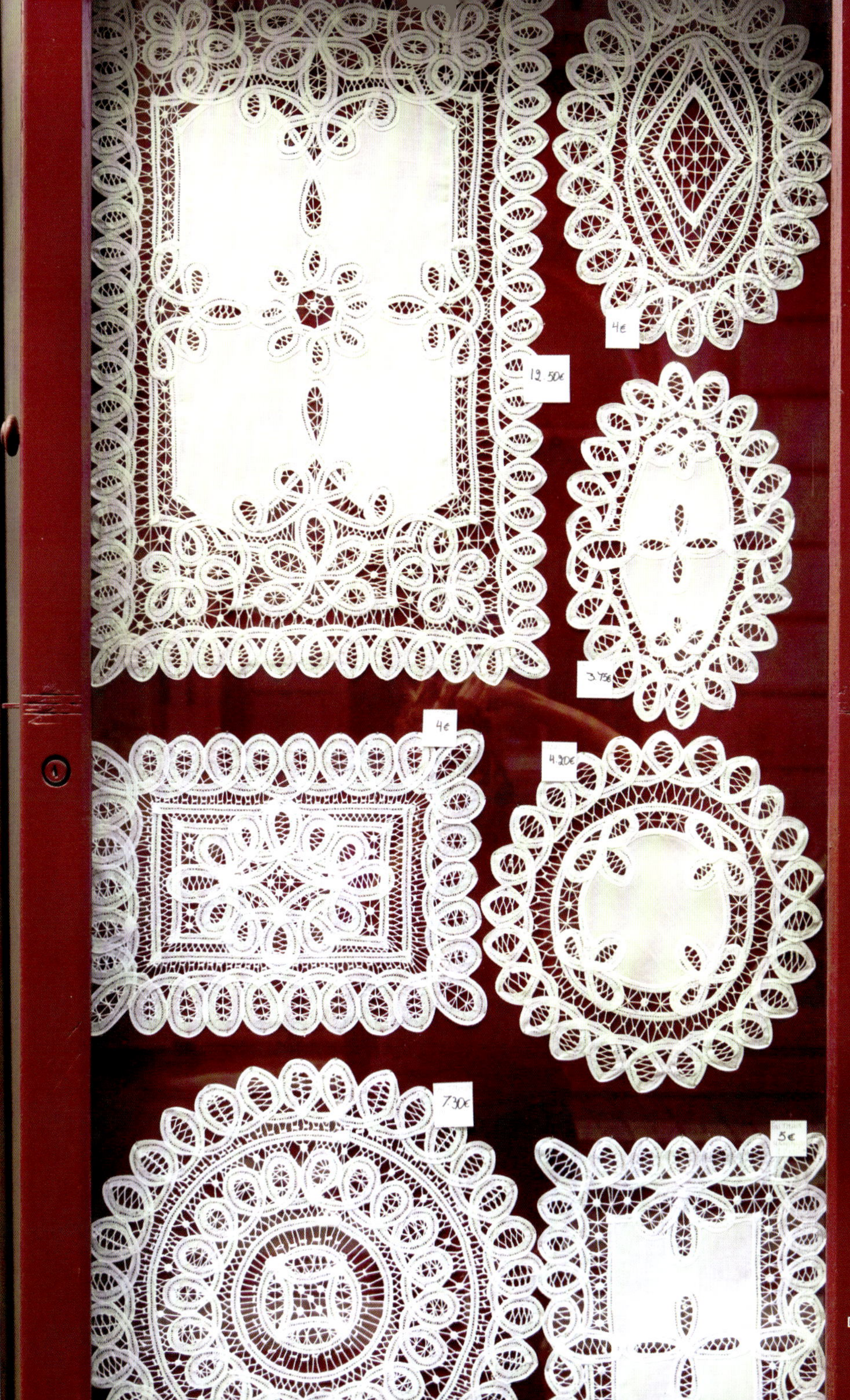

12.50€
4€
3.75€
4€
4.20€
7.30€
5€
Handmade lace
Handgemaakte kant
Dentelle aux fuseaux

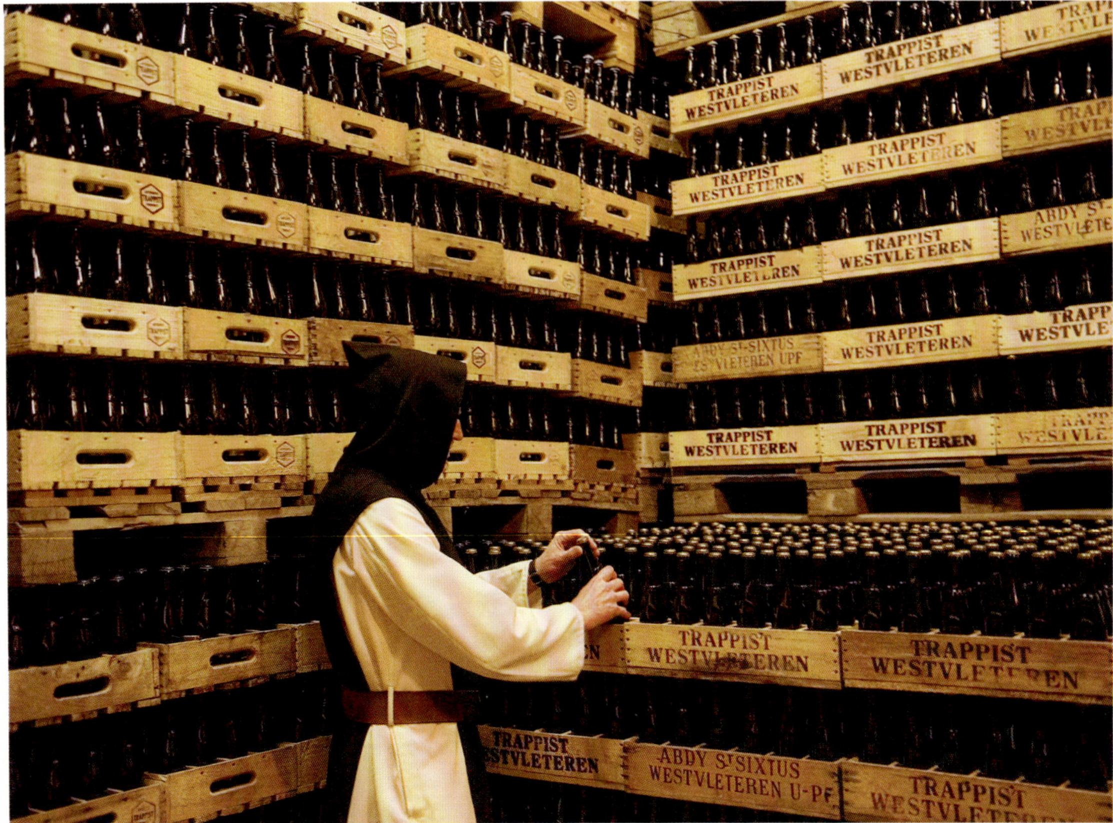

Saint-Sixtus Abbey of Westvleteren
Brouwerij de Sint-Sixtusabdij van Westvleteren
Abbaye Saint-Sixte de Westvleteren

Westvleteren, the best beer in the world?

Trappist monks have lived in seclusion at small monasteries in Flanders for centuries. They pray, read, work and produce their own food such as cheese, bread and beer. After "Westvleteren 12" was declared the best beer in the world in the USA in 2005, the tranquility was over. Week after week more and more thirsty tourists came, whole buses full, and now the monks have long since moved the restaurant to the other side of the street. Despite this success, the amount of beer produced has not been increased. The monastery remains a monastery—they brew to pray, they say.

Westvleteren, la meilleure bière du monde ?

Il était une fois une petite abbaye isolée dans les Flandres. Depuis des siècles, ses moines trappistes y prient, y lisent, y travaillent et y produisent leur propre nourriture comme le fromage, le pain et la bière. Mais en 2005, ce fut la fin de la tranquillité : aux États-Unis, on fit de leur Westvleteren 12 la meilleure bière du monde. Alors, au fil des semaines, les touristes assoiffés se succédèrent, toujours plus nombreux, par cars entiers, tant et si bien que les moines s'empressèrent de déplacer le restaurant de l'autre côté de la rue. Et malgré le succès, ils n'augmentent pas la quantité de bière produite. Après tout, cela reste une abbaye – s'ils brassent, c'est pour prier, affirment-ils.

Westvleteren, das beste Bier der Welt?

In einem kleinen Kloster in der Abgeschiedenheit Flanderns leben seit Jahrhunderten die Trappisten-Mönche. Sie beten, lesen, arbeiten und stellen ihre eigenen Nahrungsmittel wie Käse, Brot und Bier her. Nachdem 2005 in den USA „Westvleteren 12" zum besten Bier der Welt erklärt wurde, war es mit der Ruhe vorbei. Woche für Woche kamen mehr durstige Touristen, ganze Busse voll, da hatten die Mönche längst das Ausflugslokal auf die andere Straßenseite verlagert. Und trotz des Erfolges wird auch die Biermenge nicht erhöht. Das Kloster ist eben ein Kloster – sie brauen doch, um zu beten, sagen sie.

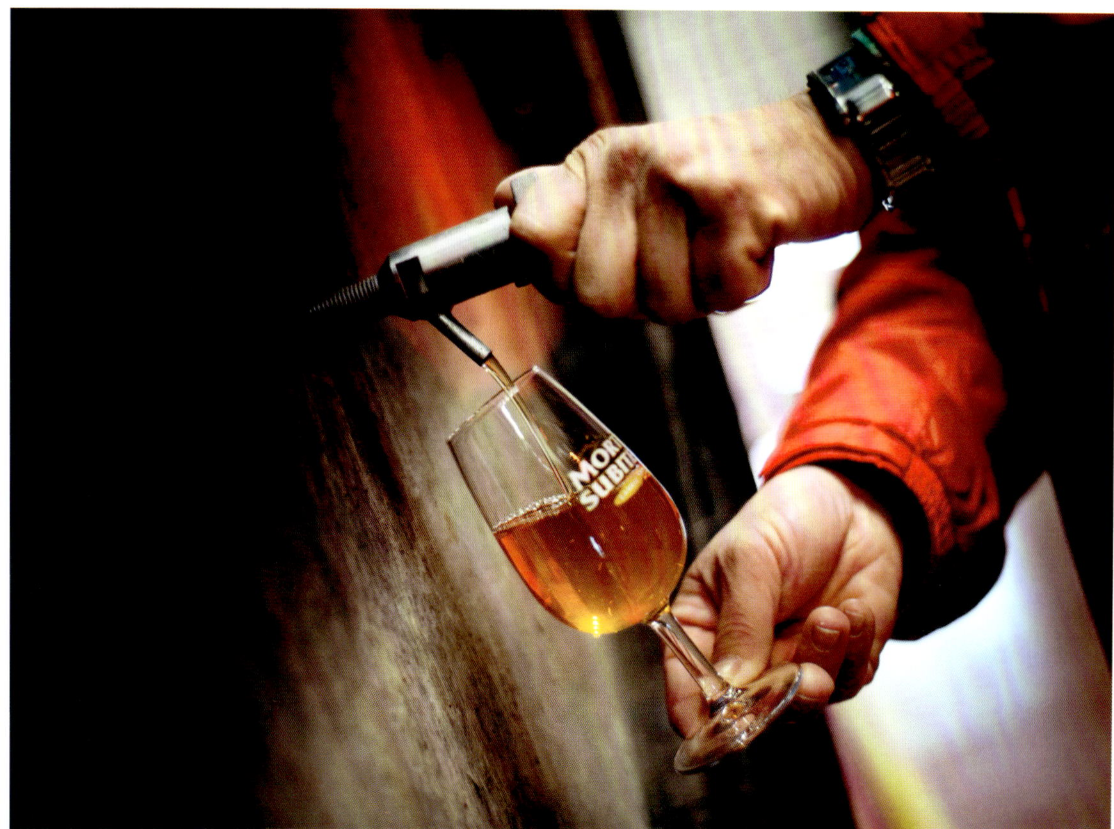

Mort Subite Brewery
Brouwerij Mort Subite
Brasserie Mort Subite

Westvleteren, ¿la mejor cerveza del mundo?

Los monjes trapenses han vivido aislados en un pequeño monasterio de Flandes durante siglos. Rezan, leen, trabajan y producen su propia comida como queso, pan y cerveza. Pero después de que "Westvleteren 12" fuera declarada la mejor cerveza del mundo en los EE. UU. en 2005, se les acabó la tranquilidad. Semana tras semana llegaron más y más turistas sedientos, autobuses enteros llenos. Los monjes habían trasladado hace mucho tiempo el restaurante al otro lado de la calle. Y a pesar del éxito, la cantidad de cerveza tampoco aumentó. El monasterio es un monasterio; dicen que preparan cerveza para rezar.

Westvleteren, a melhor cerveja do mundo?

Durantes séculos, os monges trapistas vivem num pequeno mosteiro em reclusão em Flandres.. Eles oram, lêem, trabalham e produzem seus próprios alimentos, como queijo, pão e cerveja. Depois que a "Westvleteren 12" foi declarada a melhor cerveja do mundo nos EUA em 2005, a paz e a tranquilidade acabaram. Semana após semana mais e mais turistas sedentos chegavam em ônibus inteiros lotados, e os monges tiveram há muito tempo que mudar o restaurante para o outro lado da rua. E apesar do sucesso, a quantidade de cerveja não foi aumentada. O mosteiro é apenas um mosteiro - eles fabricam a cerveja para rezar, dizem eles.

Westvleteren, het beste bier ter wereld?

In een klein klooster in een afgezonderd stuk Vlaanderen leven al eeuwenlang trappistenmonniken. Ze bidden, lezen, werken en produceren hun eigen voedsel zoals kaas, brood en bier. Nadat in 2015 in de Verenigde Staten "Westvleteren 12" tot het beste bier ter wereld werd uitgeroepen, was het gedaan met de rust. Wekelijks kwamen er meer en meer dorstige toeristen, hele bussen vol. Toen hadden de monniken het restaurant al lang naar de andere kant van de straat verplaatst. En ondanks het succes wordt de hoeveelheid bier ook niet verhoogd. Het klooster is nu eenmaal een klooster – ze brouwen toch om te bidden, zeggen ze.

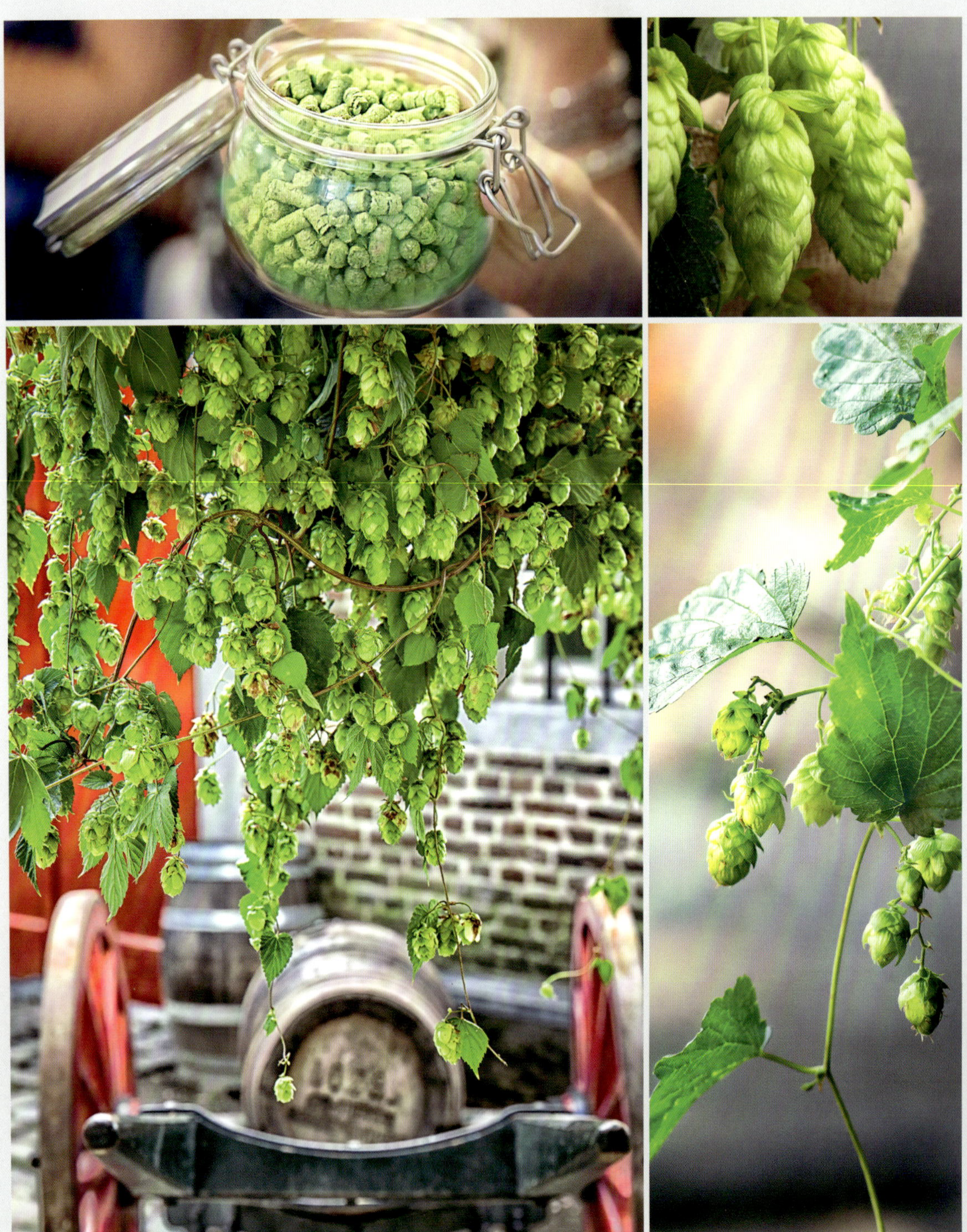

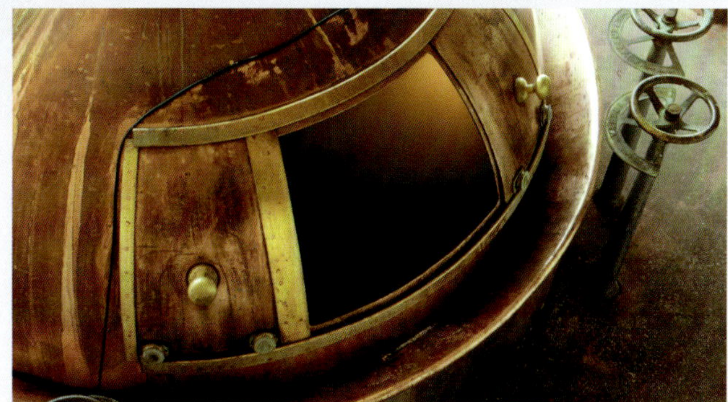

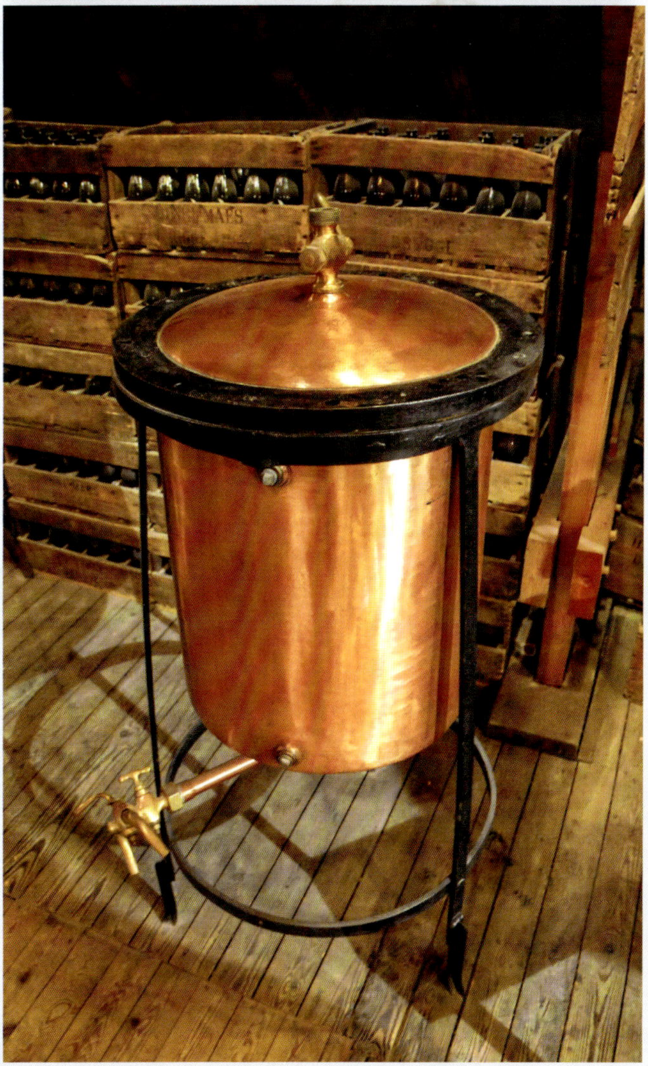

Hop Town Poperinge

Poperinge is the centre of Flemish hop-growing.
Worth seeing are the hop gardens, up to seven metres
high, and the Hop Museum in the city's former weigh-
house. Until the end of the 1960s, hops were tested,
weighed and pressed there. The museum shows the
history of hop growing and hop picking. The collection
of over 1900 Belgian beers is also impressive.

Poperinge, la ville du houblon

Poperinge est le centre de la culture flamande du
houblon. Les houblonnières, dont la hauteur peut
atteindre sept mètres, et le musée du Houblon,
installé dans les anciens bâtiments du «poids
public», valent le détour. Jusqu'à la fin des années
1960, on y contrôlait, pesait et pressait le houblon.
Le musée présente l'histoire de sa culture et de sa
cueillette. Sa collection de plus de 1900 bières belges
est saisissante.

Hopfenstadt Poperinge

Poperinge ist das Zentrum des flämischen
Hopfenanbaus. Sehenswert sind die bis zu sieben
m hohen Hopfengärten und das Hopfenmuseum im
Stadt-Waagen-Haus. Bis Ende der 1960er-Jahre wurde
dort der Hopfen geprüft, gewogen und gepresst. Das
Museum zeigt die Geschichte des Hopfenanbaus und
der Hopfenpflücker. Beeindruckend ist die Sammlung
mit über 1900 belgischen Bieren.

Poperinge, la ciudad del lúpulo

Poperinge es el centro de la producción flamenca de
lúpulo. Los jardines de lúpulo de hasta siete metros
de altura y el Museo del Lúpulo en el almacén de
pesaje de la ciudad son dignos de ver. Hasta finales
de los años 1960, el lúpulo se probaba, se pesaba y se
prensaba allí. El museo muestra la historia del cultivo y
la recolección del lúpulo. La colección de más de 1900
cervezas belgas es impresionante.

Poperinge Cidade do Lúpulo

Poperinge é o centro do cultivo do lúpudo flamengo.
Vale a pena ver os jardins de lúpulo de até sete
metros de altura e o Museu do Lúpulo na velha casa
de pesagem da cidade. Até o final dos anos 1960,
o lúpulo era lá testado, pesado e prensado. O
museu mostra a história do cultivo e da colheita do
lúpulo. A coleção de mais de 1900 cervejas belgas é
impressionante.

Hopstad Poperinge

Poperinge is het centrum van de Vlaamse
hopteelt. Bezienswaardig zijn de tot zeven
meter hoge hoptuinen en het hopmuseum in het
stadsschaalcomplex. Tot eind jaren 1960 werd daar de
hop getest, gewogen en geperst. Het museum toont
de geschiedenis van de hopteelt en het plukken van
de hop. De collectie van meer dan 1900 Belgische
bieren is indrukwekkend.

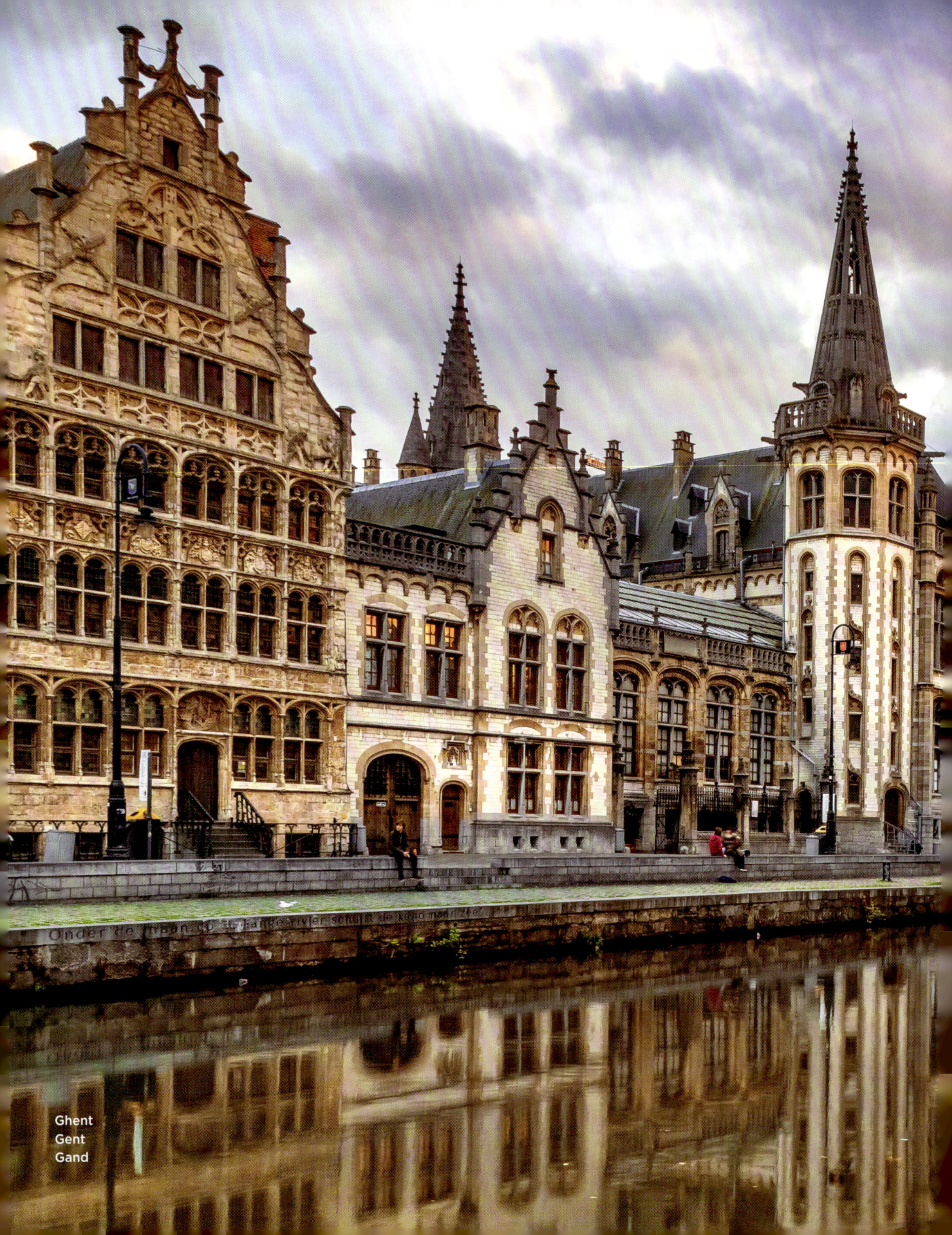

Ghent
Gent
Gand

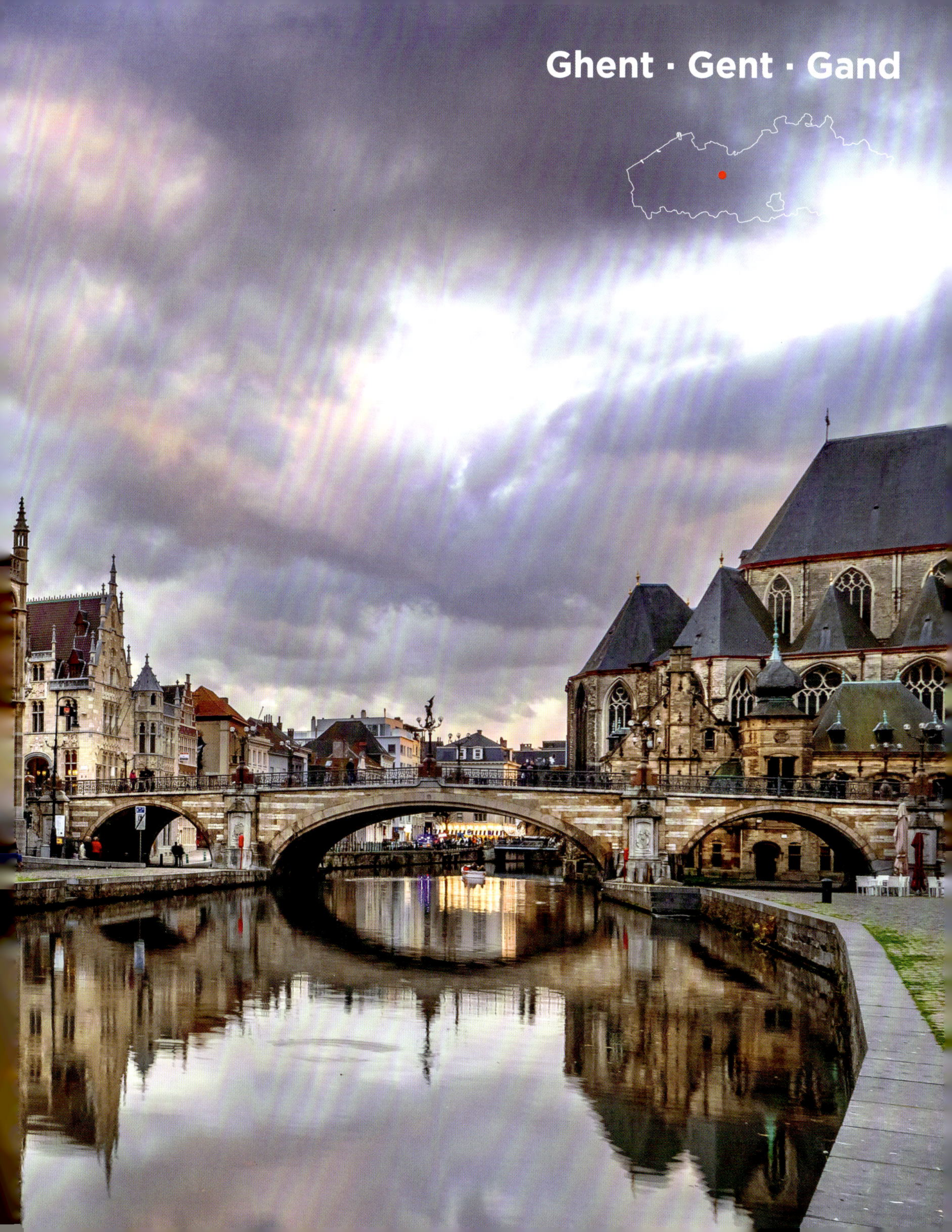
Ghent · Gent · Gand

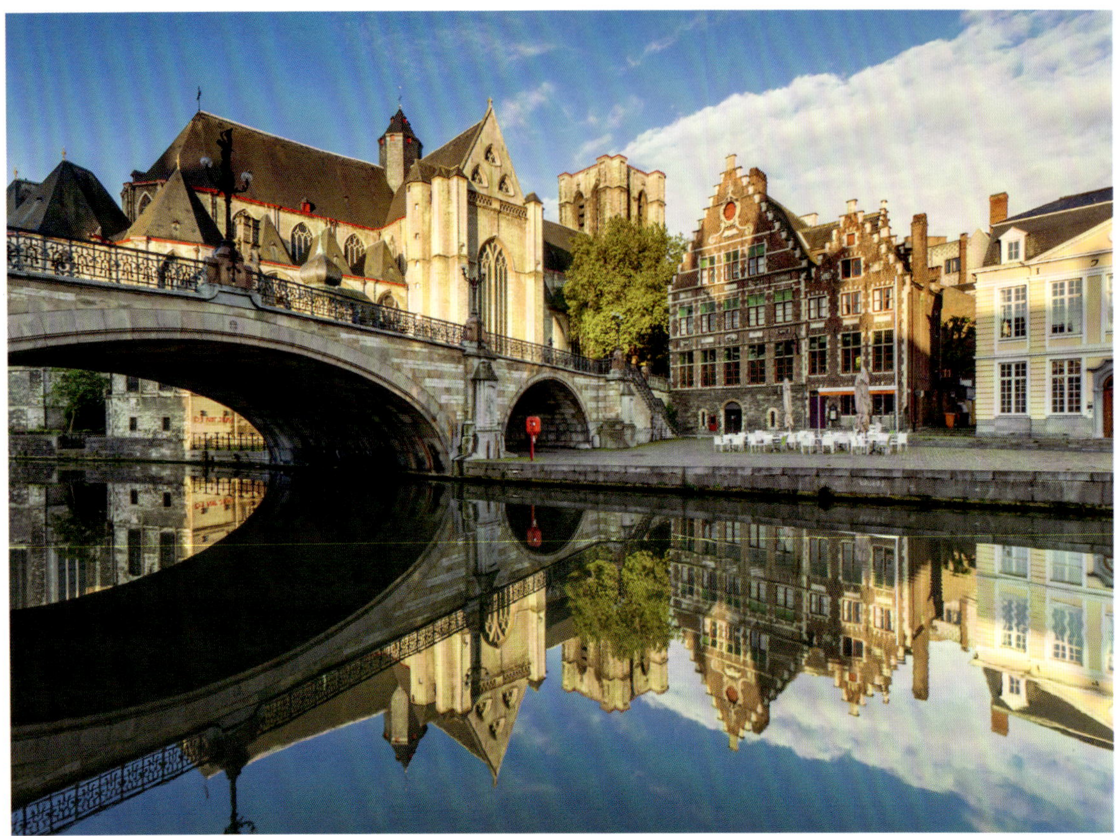

St Michael's Bridge
Sint-Michielsbrug
Pont Saint-Michel

Ghent

In the 14th century, Ghent was one of the largest cities north of the Alps, alongside Paris. Even today, the city has the most impressive historical buildings of all the art cities of Flanders. From the St Michael's Bridge you can see the Guild Houses on the Leie and one of the largest and oldest moated castles in the world, the imposing Gravensteen. To the east, you can see three towers; St Nicholas' Church, the Belfry and St. Bavo's Cathedral, forming the most important postcard motif in Ghent. The richly decorated palace, right next to the bridge, is a luxury hotel and shopping centre, but was originally the post office.

Gand

Au xive siècle, Gand faisait partie, avec Paris, des plus grandes villes au nord des Alpes. Aujourd'hui encore, la ville possède les bâtiments historiques les plus impressionnants parmi les villes d'art de Flandres. Le pont Saint-Michel offre une vue sur les maisons de corporations érigées sur les rives de la Lys et sur l'un des plus grands et plus anciens châteaux à douves au monde, l'imposant château des comtes. À l'est se dessinent trois tours : celles de l'église Saint-Nicolas, du beffroi et de la cathédrale Saint-Bavon, le principal motif de carte postale de Gand. Le palais richement décoré se dressant juste à côté du pont est l'ancien bureau de poste, désormais transformé en hôtel de luxe et en centre commercial.

Gent

Im 14. Jahrhundert gehörte Gent neben Paris zu den größten Städten nördlich der Alpen. Auch heute hat die Stadt von allen Kunststädten Flanderns die eindrucksvollsten historischen Bauten. Von der Michiels-Brücke schaut man auf die Gildehäuser an der Leie und auf eine der größten und ältesten Wasserburgen der Welt, die imposante Grafenburg. Im Osten fällt der Blick auf drei Türme: St.-Nikolaus-Kirche, Belfried und St.-Bavo-Kathedrale, das wichtigste Postkartenmotiv von Gent. Der reich verzierte Palast, gleich neben der Brücke, ist ein Luxushotel und Einkaufszentrum, war aber ursprünglich das Postamt.

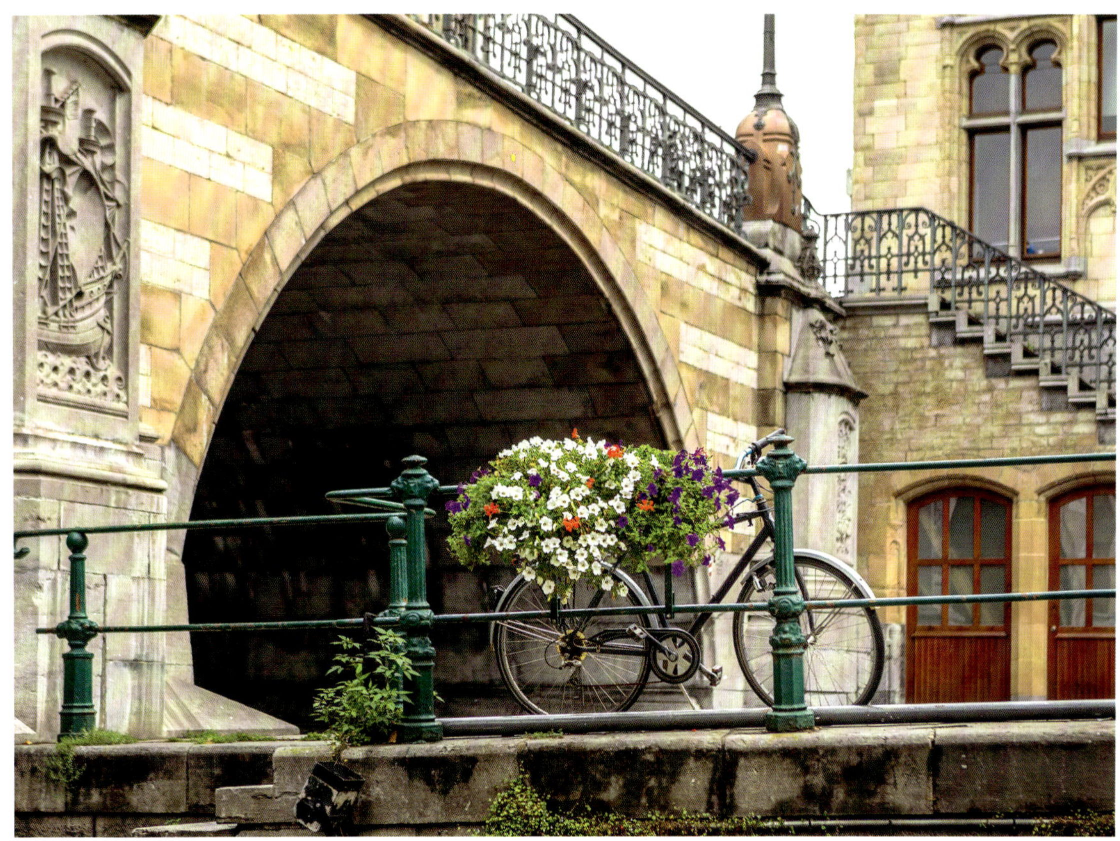

St Michael's Bridge
Sint-Michielsbrug
Pont Saint-Michel

Gante

En el siglo XIV, Gante era una de las ciudades más grandes al norte de los Alpes, junto con París. Aún hoy, la ciudad tiene los edificios históricos más impresionantes de todas las ciudades de arte de Flandes. Desde el puente de Michiels se pueden ver las casas gremiales en el Leie y uno de los castillos más grandes y antiguos del mundo: el imponente Castillo de los Condes. Al este se pueden ver tres torres: la iglesia de San Nicolás, el campanario y la catedral de San Bavo, el motivo de postal más importante de Gante. El palacio, que se encuentra ricamente decorado y se sitúa justo al lado del puente, es un lujoso hotel y centro comercial, pero fue originalmente la oficina de correos.

Gante

No século XIV, Gante era uma das maiores cidades ao norte dos Alpes, próximo a Paris. Ainda hoje, a cidade tem os edifícios históricos mais impressionantes de todas as cidades artísticas da Flandres. A partir da Ponte de São Miguel você pode ver casas das corporações no rio Leie e um dos maiores e mais antigos castelos do mundo, o imponente castelo de Gravensteen. A leste, você pode ver três torres: Igreja de São Nicolau, Campanário (Belfry) e Catedral de SãoBavo, o mais importante motivo de cartão postal de Gante. O palácio ricamente decorado, mesmo ao lado da ponte, é um hotel e centro comercial de luxo, mas era originalmente o correio.

Gent

In de 14e eeuw behoorde Gent naast Parijs tot de grootste steden ten noorden van de Alpen. Ook vandaag nog heeft de stad de meest indrukwekkende historische gebouwen van alle kunststeden van Vlaanderen. Vanaf de Sint-Michielsbrug kijkt u op de gildehuizen aan de Leie en op het Gravensteen, één van de grootste en oudste waterburchten ter wereld. In het oosten zie je drie torens: de Sint-Niklaaskerk, het belfort en de Sint-Baafskathedraal, het belangrijkste ansichtkaartmotief van Gent. Het rijk versierde paleis, direct naast de brug, is een luxe hotel en winkelcentrum, maar was oorspronkelijk het postkantoor.

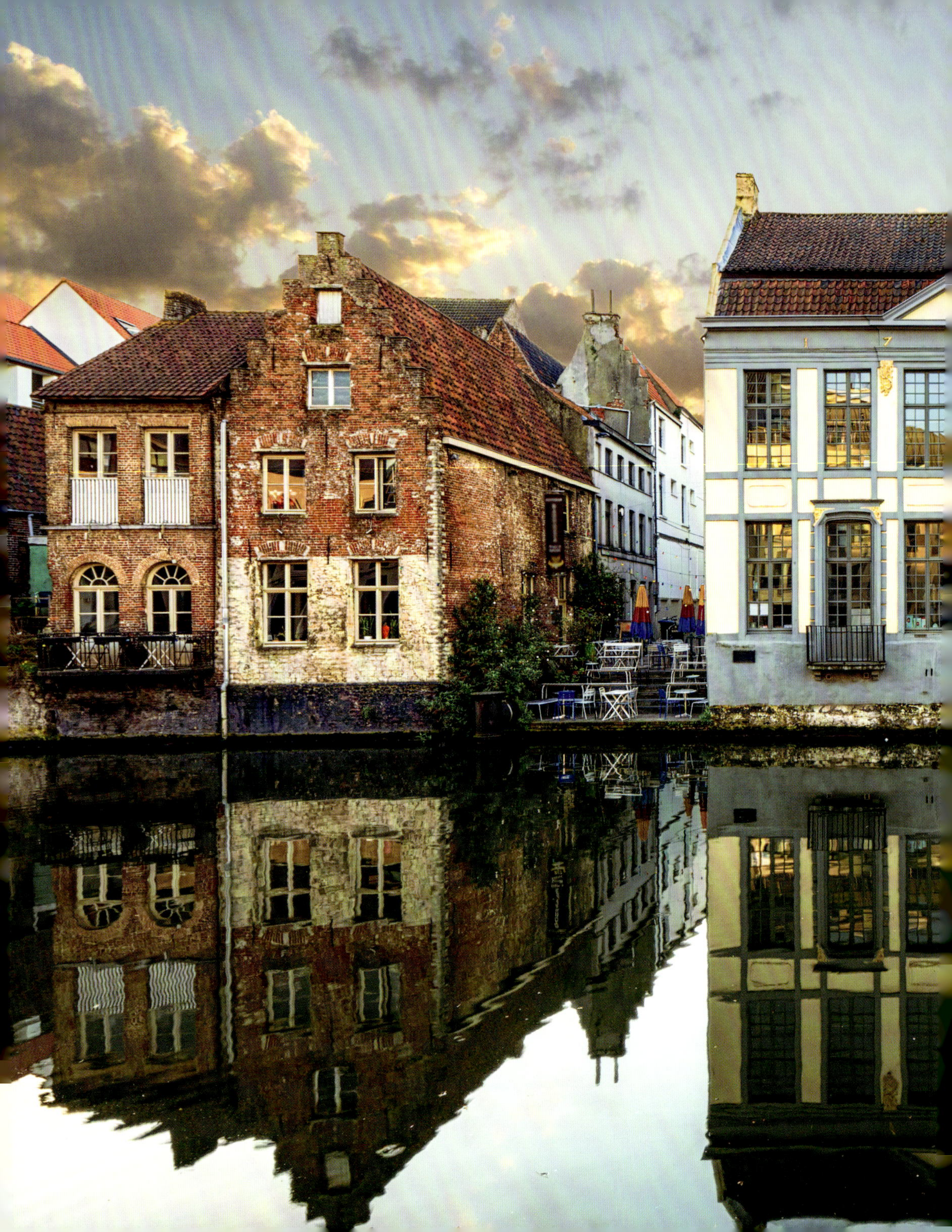

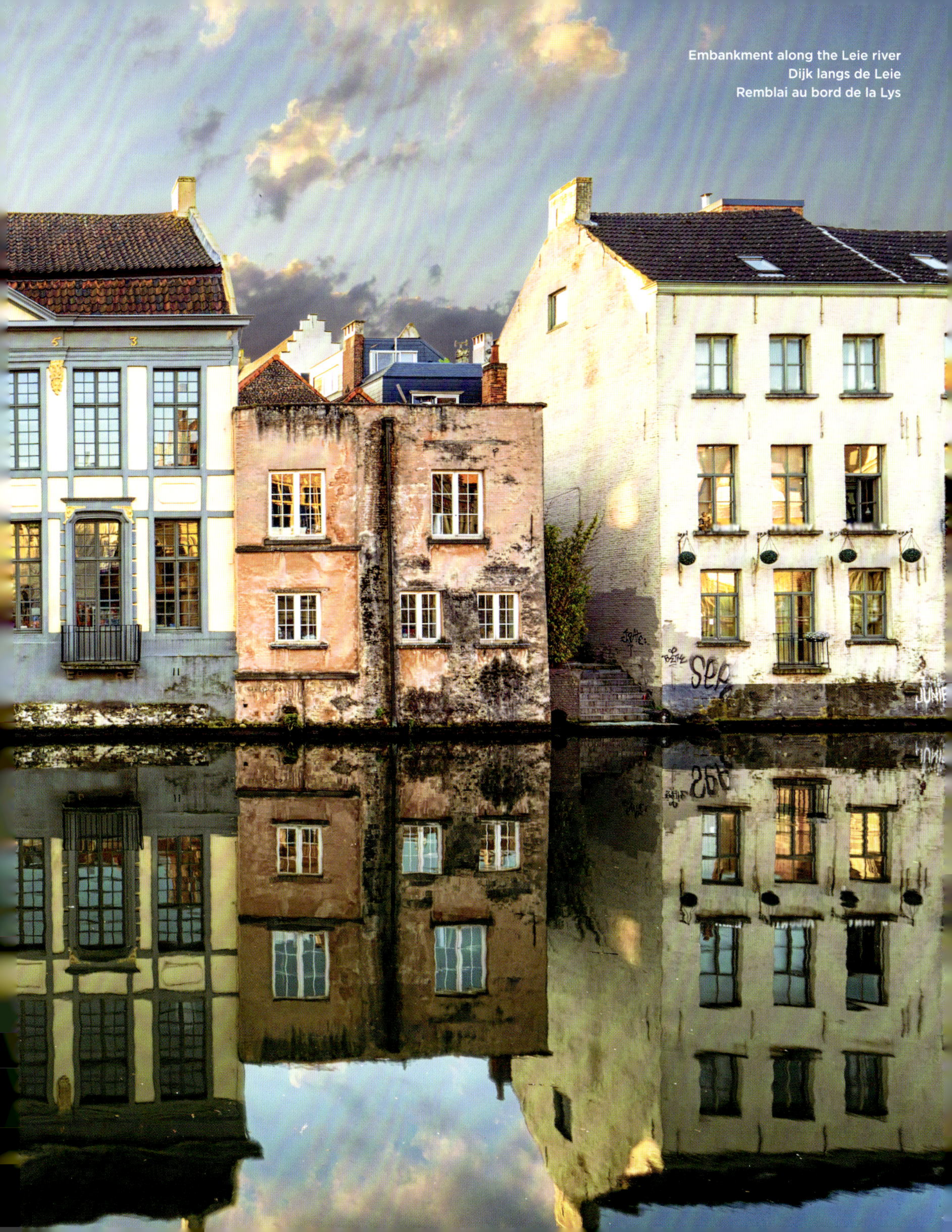

Embankment along the Leie river
Dijk langs de Leie
Remblai au bord de la Lys

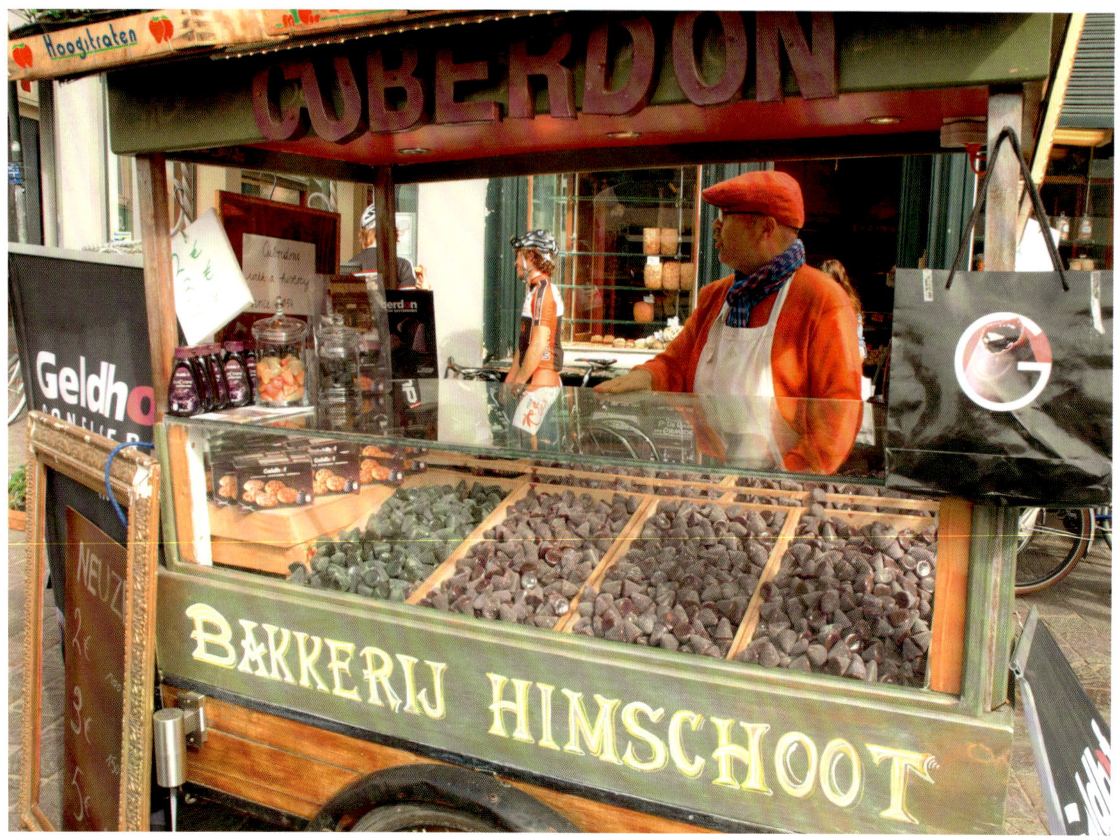

Cuberdon seller
Cuberdon verkoper
Vendeur de cuberdons

Ghent Noses

A "Gentse Neus" is a typical Ghent
speciality. The cone-shaped sweets,
also called cuberdons in French, taste
classically like raspberry syrup. The matt-
velvety surface of the Ghent Nose contains
a hard, jelly-like filling. Due to the limited
shelf life of three weeks, Ghent Noses
are not exported and are practically only
available in Belgium. They are sold in
delicatessen shops, but also by two dealers
at the Groentenmarkt, where they have
been standing for years with their historic
hand carts as they loudly claim to sell the
best Ghent Noses.

Nez gantois

Un «gentse neus» est une spécialité
gantoise typique. La version classique
de ce bonbon en forme de cône, aussi
appelé cuberdon en français, a un goût
de sirop de framboise. La surface mate et
veloutée du «nez gantois» est dure, son
intérieur renferme une texture ressemblant
à de la gelée. En raison de leur durée de
conservation, limitée à trois semaines, les
cuberdons ne peuvent être exportés et ne
sont vendus pratiquement qu'en Belgique.
On les trouve dans les épiceries fines,
mais aussi auprès de deux marchands du
Groentenmarkt. Avec leurs charrettes à
bras historiques, ils s'y tiennent depuis des
années et prétendent haut et fort vendre
les meilleurs «nez gantois» qui existent.

Genter Nasen

Eine „Gentse Neus" ist eine typisch Genter
Spezialität. Die kegelförmige Süßigkeit,
im Französischen auch Cuberdon
genannt, schmeckt klassischerweise
nach Himbeersirup. Die matt-samtige
Oberfläche der Genter Nase ist hart,
im Innern geleeartig. Aufgrund der
begrenzten Haltbarkeit von drei Wochen
werden Genter Nasen nicht exportiert
und sind praktisch nur in Belgien
erhältlich. Sie werden in Feinkostläden
angeboten, aber auch von zwei Händlern
am Groentenmarkt. Dort stehen sie seit
Jahren mit historischen Handkarren und
behaupten lautstark jeweils, die besten
Genter Nasen zu verkaufen.

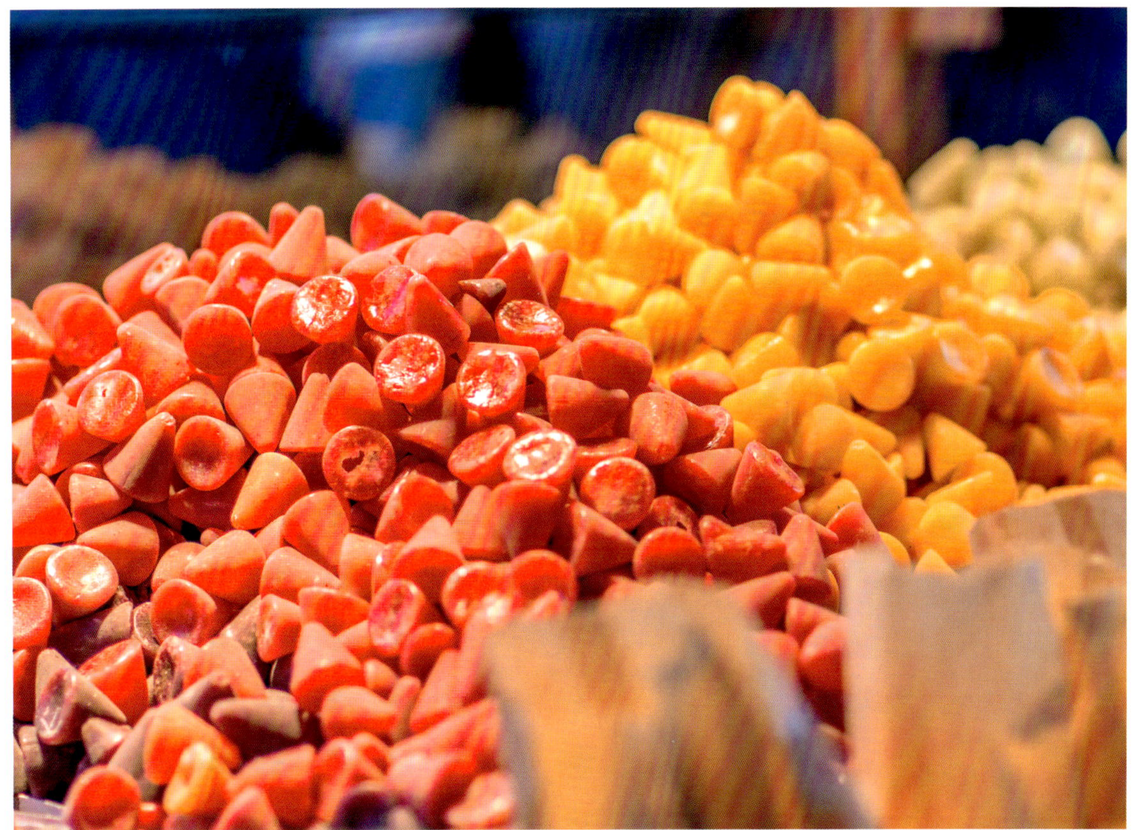

Cuberdon, also called "neuzekes" (little noses)
Cuberdon, ook "neuzekes" genoemd
Cuberdons, également appelés « nez gantois »

Narices de Gante

Un "Gentse neus" es una especialidad típica de Gante. El dulce en forma de cono, también llamado cuberdon en francés, tiene un sabor clásico a jarabe de frambuesa. La superficie mate y aterciopelada de la «nariz de Gante» es dura y gelatinosa por dentro. Dado que solo aguantan tres semanas, este dulce no se exporta y prácticamente solo está disponible en Bélgica. Se vende en tiendas de delicatessen, pero también a través de dos distribuidores en el mercado de Groente. Han estado allí durante años con carros de mano históricos y dicen en voz alta que venden las mejores narices de Gante.

Nariz de Gante

Um "Gentse Neus" é uma especialidade típica de Gante. O doce em forma de cone, também chamado "cuberdon" em francês, tem gosto clássico de xarope de framboesa. O "Nariz de Gante" possui uma superfície com uma casquinha fosca e avermelhadaGante, mas com uma consistência gelatinosa por dentro. Devido ao prazo de validade limitado de três semanas, os "narizes de Gante" não são exportados e praticamente só estão disponíveis na Bélgica. São vendidos em lojas de especialidades alimentares, mas também por dois comerciantes do Mercado Velho (Groentenmarkt). Eles têm estado lá há anos com carrinhos de mão históricos e reivindicam em voz alta cada um, para vender os melhores "narizes de Gante".

Gentse Neuzen

Een Gentse Neus is een typisch Gentse specialiteit. Dit kegelvormige zoete snoepje, in het Frans ook wel cuberdon genoemd, smaakt naar frambozensiroop. De matte buitenkant van de Gentse neus is hard, de binnenkant is gelatineus. Door de beperkte houdbaarheid van drie weken worden Gentse Neuzen niet geëxporteerd en zijn ze praktisch alleen in België verkrijgbaar. Ze worden verkocht in delicatessenwinkels, maar ook door twee handelaren op de Groentenmarkt. Ze staan er al jaren met historische handkarren en beweren luidkeels de beste Gentse neuzen te verkopen.

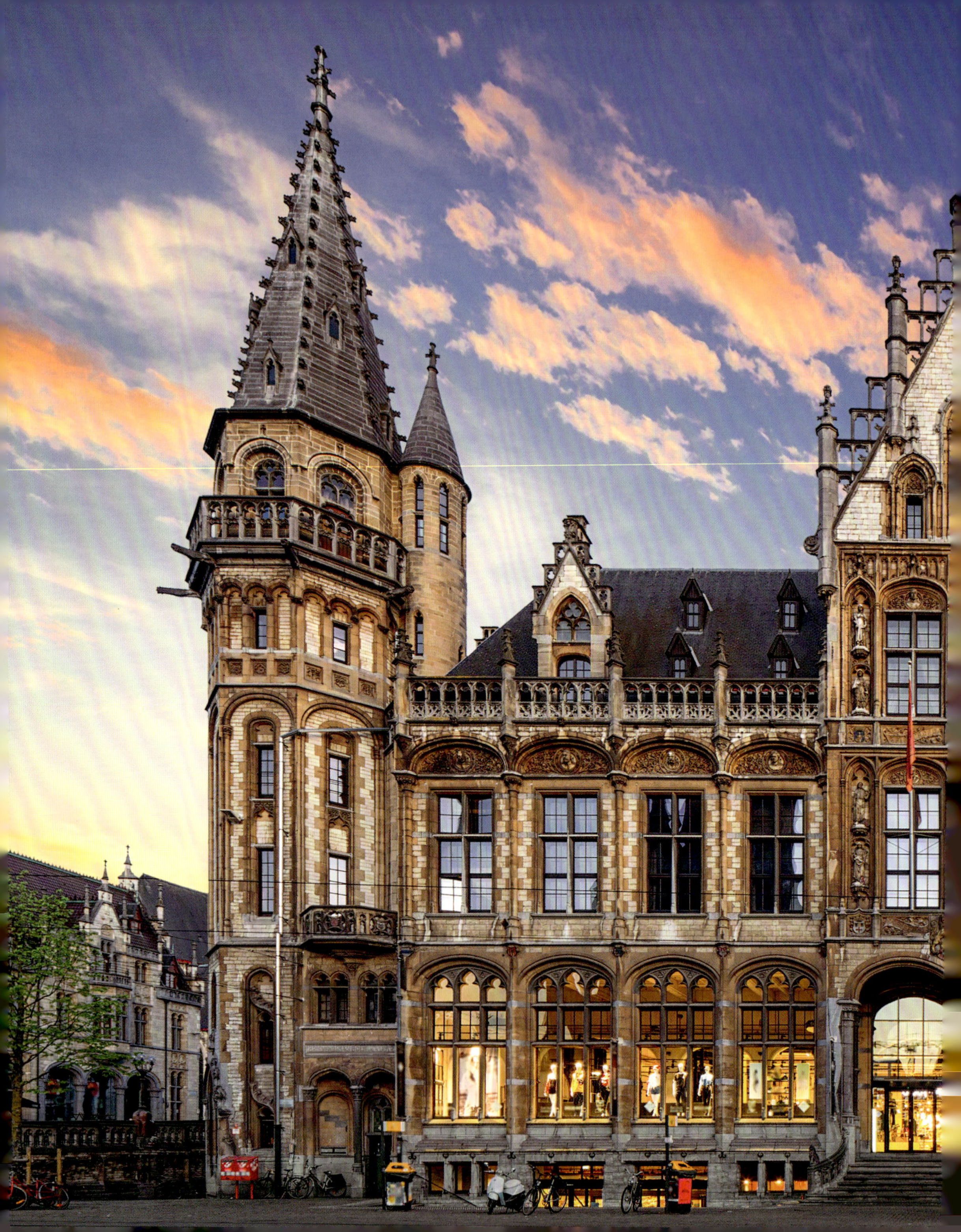

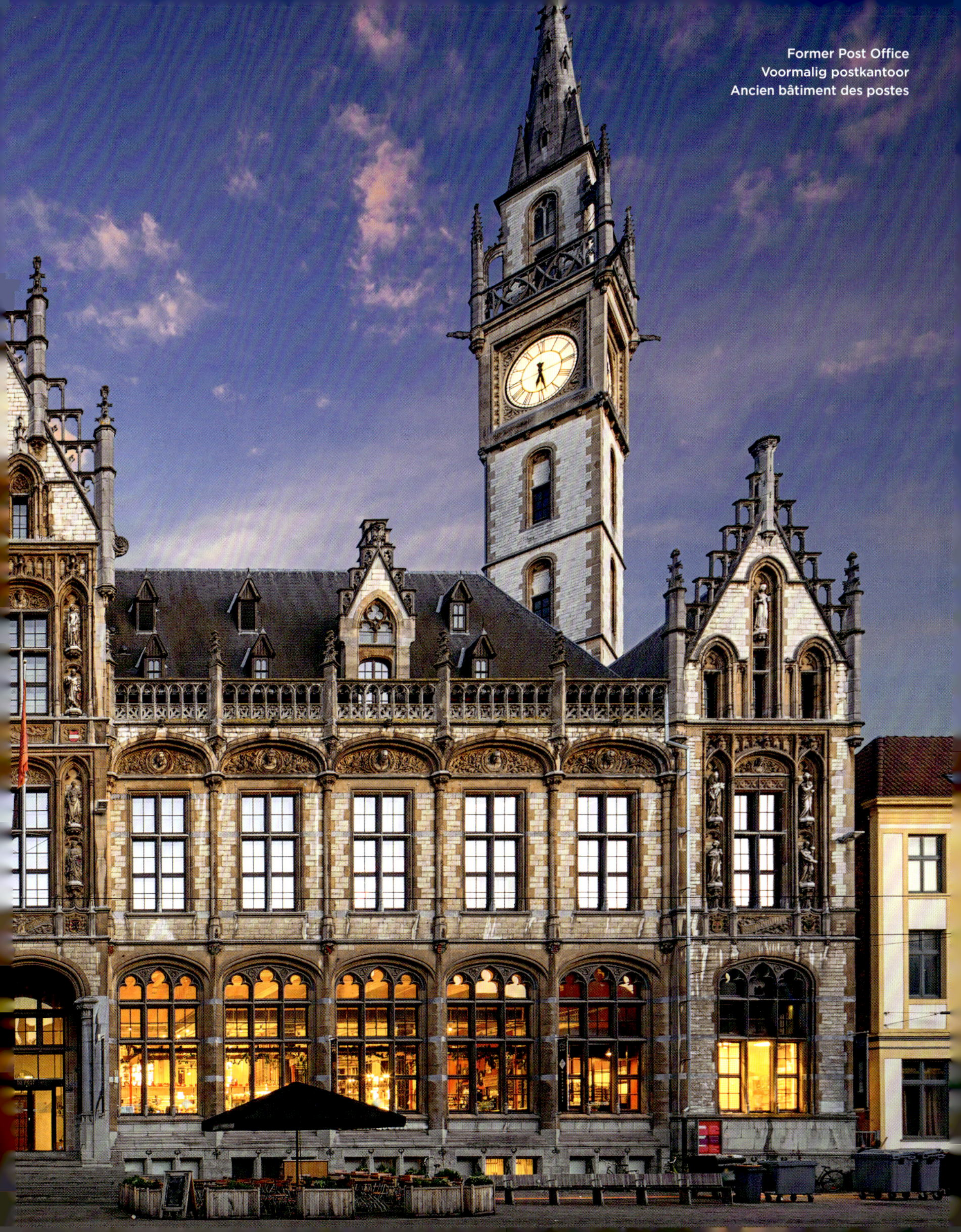

Former Post Office
Voormalig postkantoor
Ancien bâtiment des postes

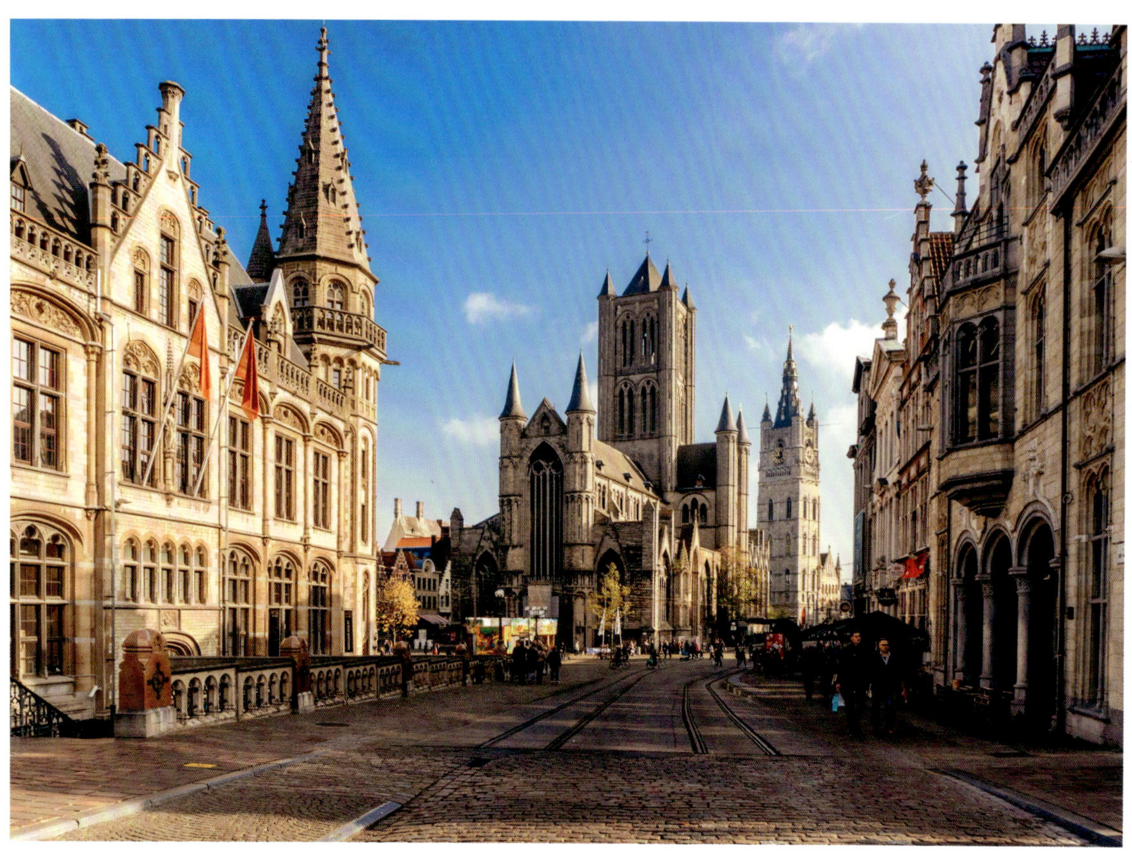

St Bavo's Cathedral
Sint-Baafskathedraal
Cathédrale Saint-Bavon de Gand

St Nicholas' Church and Belfry

The Nicholas' Church is one of the most important Gothic church buildings in western Europe. The Belfry in the background symbolizes the prosperity and independence of Ghent and is a UNESCO World Heritage Site. From the bell tower, one has a great view of the city and every Sunday morning the carillons can be heard chiming from above. The dragon, which has stood on the tower since 1377, not only watches over the town, but is also the symbolic treasure keeper of the belfry. The Cloth Hall in Brabant Gothic, attached to the belfry, celebrates the long tradition of the Ghent textile industry.

Église Saint-Nicolas et beffroi

L'église Saint-Nicolas compte parmi les plus importantes églises gothiques d'Europe centrale. Inscrit au patrimoine culturel mondial de l'Unesco, le beffroi à l'arrière-plan symbolise la prospérité et l'indépendance de Gand. Le clocher, dont le carillon retentit tous les dimanches matin, offre une vue imprenable sur la ville. Le dragon, qui se dresse sur la tour depuis 1377, veille sur Gand, mais il revêt aussi pour le beffroi la fonction symbolique de gardien du trésor. La halle aux draps jouxtant le beffroi, de style gothique brabançon, célèbre la longue tradition de l'industrie textile gantoise.

Nikolaus-Kirche und Belfried

Die Nikolaus-Kirche gehört zu den bedeutendsten gotischen Kirchenbauwerken Westeuropas. Der Belfried im Hintergrund symbolisiert den Wohlstand und die Unabhängigkeit von Gent und ist UNESCO-Weltkultur-Erbestätte. Vom Glockenturm hat man eine großartige Aussicht auf die Stadt und jeden Sonntagmorgen ertönt von oben das Stadtglockenspiel. Der Drache, der seit 1377 auf dem Turm steht, wacht nicht nur über die Stadt, sondern ist auch der symbolische Schatzhüter des Belfrieds. Die an den Belfried angebaute Tuchhalle in Brabanter Gotik zelebriert die lange Tradition der Genter Textilindustrie.

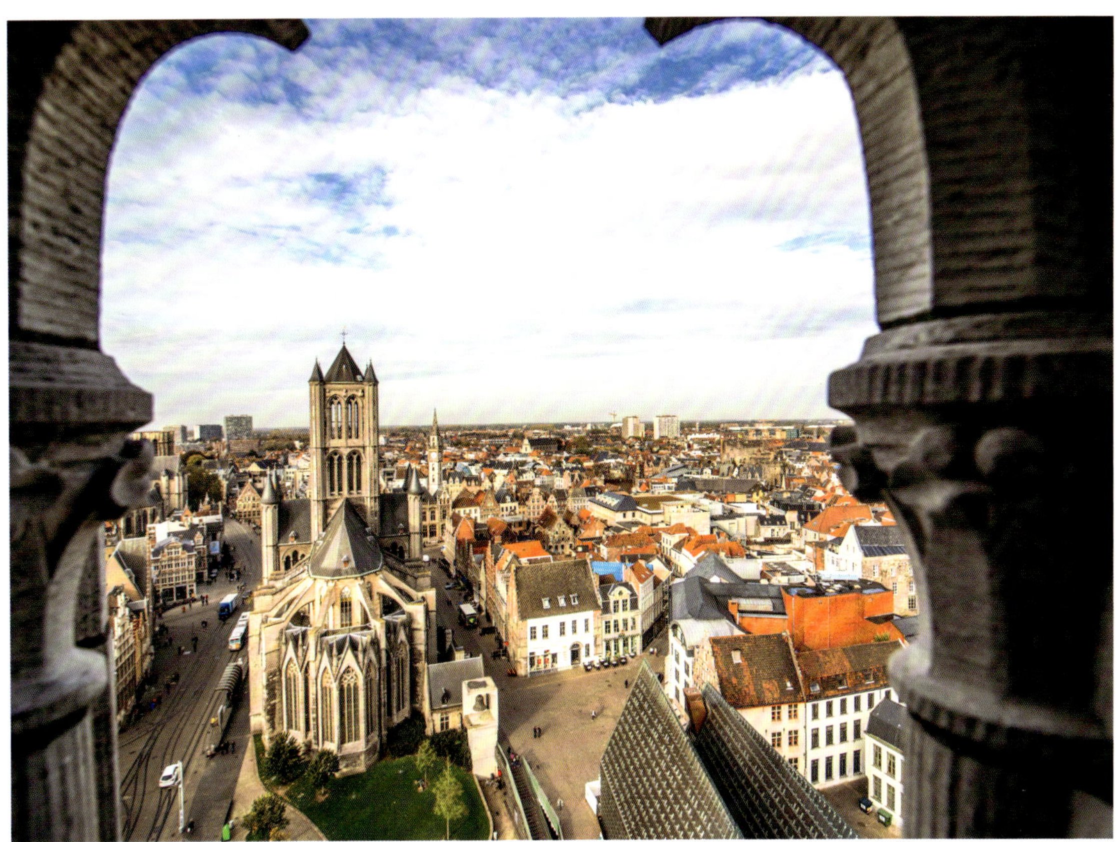

St Nicholas' Church
Sint-Niklaaskerk
Église Saint-Nicolas

Iglesia de San Nicolás y Beffroi

La iglesia de San Nicolás es uno de los edificios góticos más importantes de Europa del Oeste. El beffroi del fondo simboliza la prosperidad y la independencia de Gante y es Patrimonio de la Humanidad de la UNESCO. Desde el campanario se tiene una gran vista de la ciudad y todos los domingos por la mañana se pueden escuchar sonar las campanas de la ciudad desde arriba. El dragón, que se encuentra en la torre desde 1377, no solo vigila la ciudad, sino que también es el tesorero simbólico del beffroi. La sala de telas de estilo gótico brabanzón, adosada al beffroi, celebra la larga tradición de la industria textil de Gante.

Igreja de São Nicolau e Belfry

A Igreja de São Nicolau é uma das igrejas góticas mais importantes da Europa do Oeste. O campanário ao fundo simboliza a prosperidade e independência de Gante e é um Património Mundial da UNESCO. Da torre do sino você tem uma excelente vista da cidade e todos os domingos de manhã você pode ouvir do alto o som do carrilhão da cidade. O dragão, que está na torre desde 1377, não só vigia a cidade, mas é também o guardião simbólico do campanário. O Salão do Pano no estilo gótico brabantino, ligado ao campanário, celebra a longa tradição da indústria têxtil de Gante.

Sint-Niklaaskerk en belfort

De Sint-Niklaaskerk is één van de belangrijkste gotische kerkgebouwen in West-Europa. Het belfort op de achtergrond symboliseert de welvaart en onafhankelijkheid van Gent en staat op de UNESCO-werelderfgoedlijst. Vanaf de klokkentoren heeft u een prachtig uitzicht over de stad en elke zondagochtend kunt u het klokkenspel van de stad van bovenaf horen. De draak, die sinds 1377 op de toren staat, waakt niet alleen over de stad, maar is ook de symbolische schatbewaarder van het belfort. De aan het belfort aangebouwde lakenhal in Brabantse gotiek is opgedragen aan de lange traditie van de Gentse textielindustrie.

Van Eyck: Ghent Altarpiece

This polyptych altarpiece, commissioned by Ghent patricians, is considered van Eyck's main work. The history of salvation is told on a total of 24 panels. The main theme is the worship of the Lamb of God. The altar used to be open only on festive days, however visitors to St Bavo's Cathedral today can admire the altar in all its splendour.

Van Eyck: retable de l'Agneau mystique

Commandé par des patriciens gantois, ce polyptyque est considéré comme l'œuvre principale de Van Eyck. Sur un ensemble de 24 panneaux, l'artiste y retrace l'histoire du salut. Le thème principal est l'adoration de l'Agneau de Dieu. Jadis, le retable n'était ouvert que les jours de fête. Aujourd'hui, le visiteur peut l'admirer dans toute sa splendeur.

Van Eyck: Genter Altar

Dieser Flügelaltar, ein Auftrag Genter Patrizier, gilt als das Hauptwerk van Eycks. Auf insgesamt 24 Tafeln verteilt wird die Heilsgeschichte erzählt. Das Hauptthema ist die Anbetung des Lamm Gottes. Nur zu Festtagen wurde früher der Altar geöffnet. Der Besucher heute kann den Altar in seiner ganzen Pracht bestaunen.

Van Eyck: altar de Gante

Este altar alado, encargado por Genter Patrician, es considerado la obra principal de van Eyck. La historia de la salvación se cuenta en un total de 24 paneles. El tema principal es la adoración del cordero de Dios. El altar solía estar abierto solo los días festivos. Actualmente, los visitantes pueden admirar el altar en todo su esplendor.

Van Eyck: Retábulo de Gante

Este altar alado, encomendado pelos patrícios de Gante, é considerado a principal obra de van Eyck. A história da salvação é contada num total de 24 painéis. O tema principal é a adoração do Cordeiro de Deus. O altar costumava estar aberto apenas em dias festivos. Os visitantes de hoje podem admirar o altar em todo o seu esplendor.

Van Eyck: Het Lam Gods

Deze polyptiek, in opdracht van een Gentse patriciër, wordt beschouwd als het belangrijkste werk van Van Eyck. Op totaal 24 panelen wordt de heilsgeschiedenis verteld. Het hoofdthema is de aanbidding van het Lam Gods. Vroeger was het altaar alleen op zon- en feestdagen geopend. Vandaag de dag kunnen bezoekers het altaar in al zijn pracht en praal bewonderen.

JAN VAN EYCK (C. 1390–1441)
1430-32, Oil on wood, Huile sur bois, 375 × c. 520 cm, Sint-Baafskathedraal, Gent

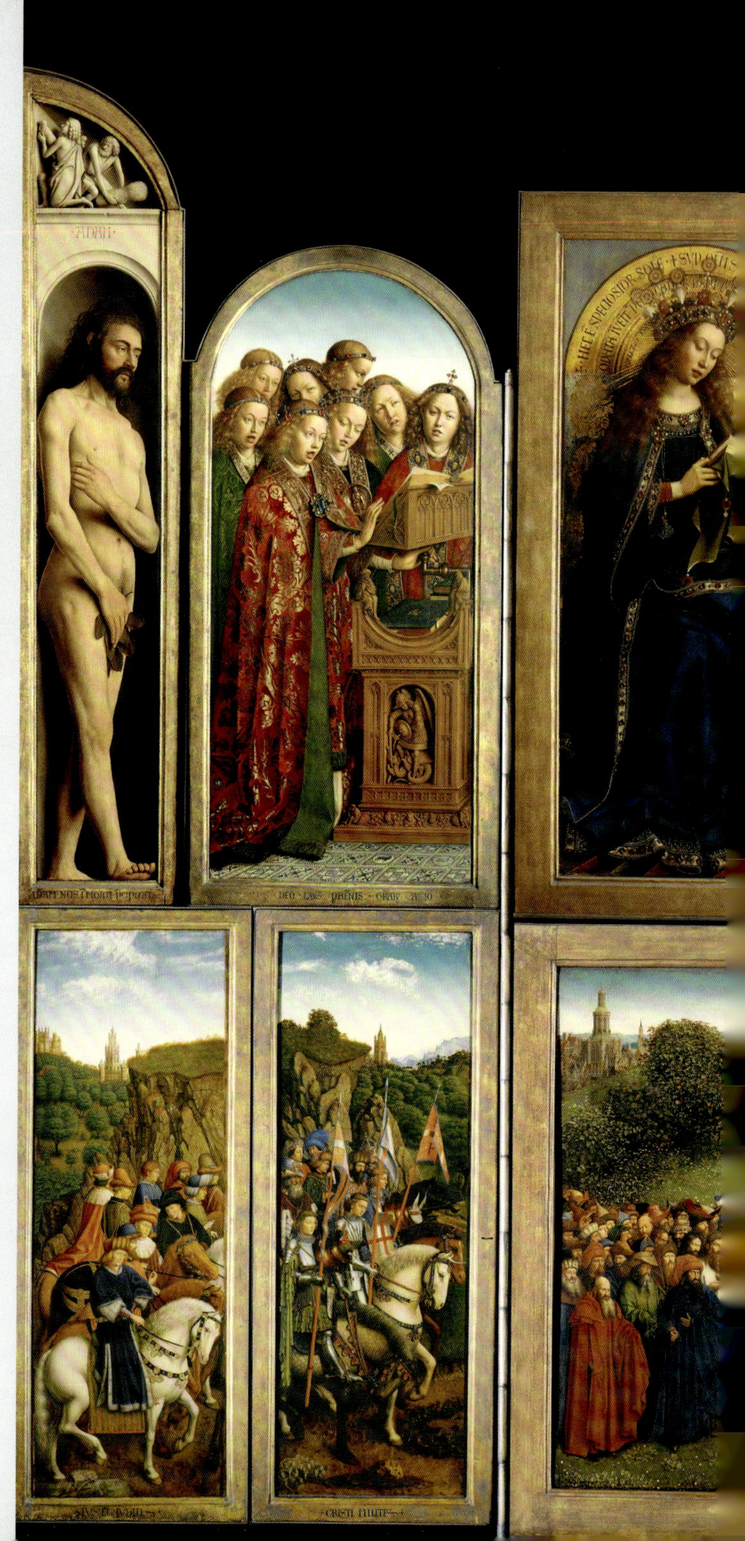

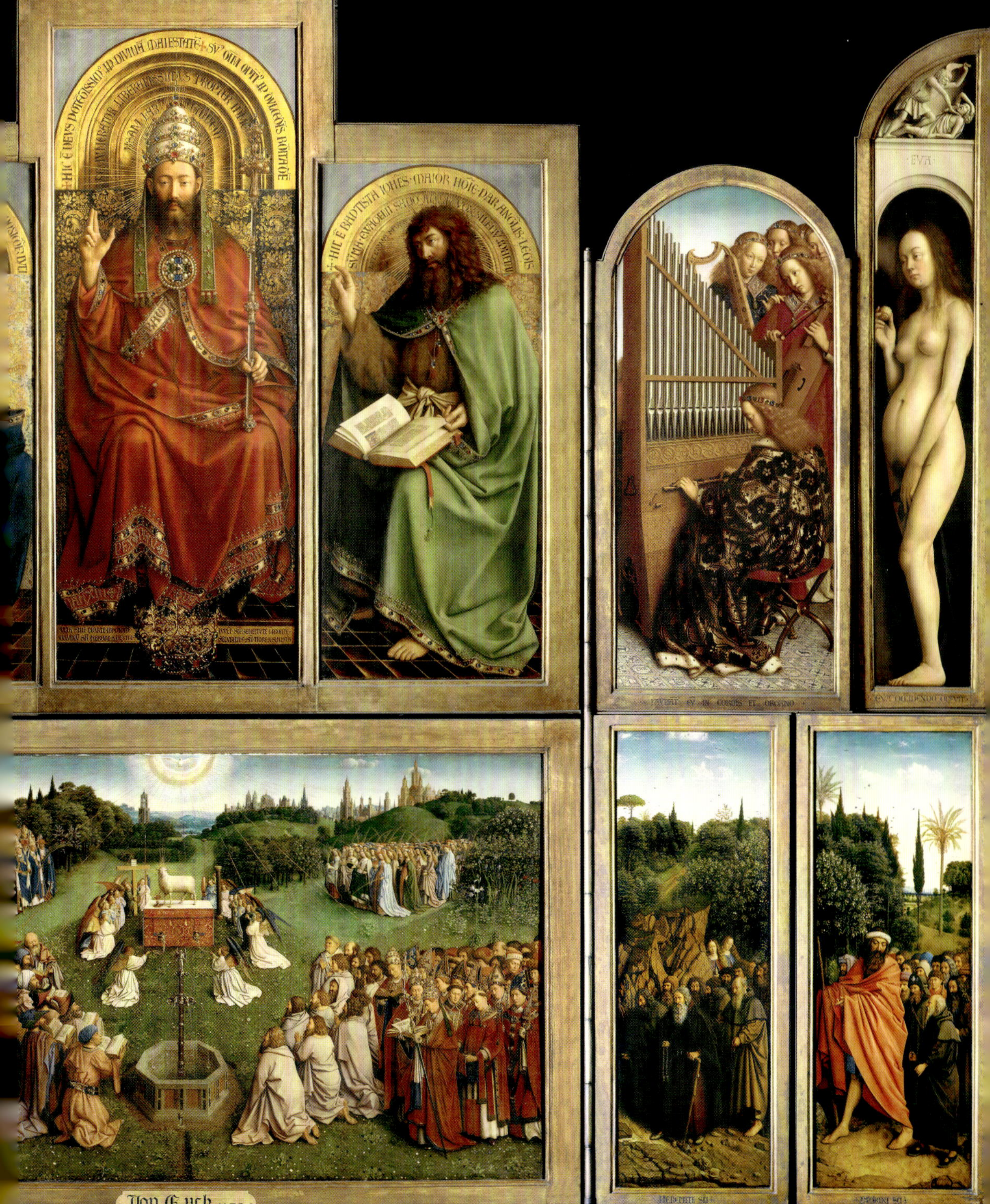

Van Eyck 1432

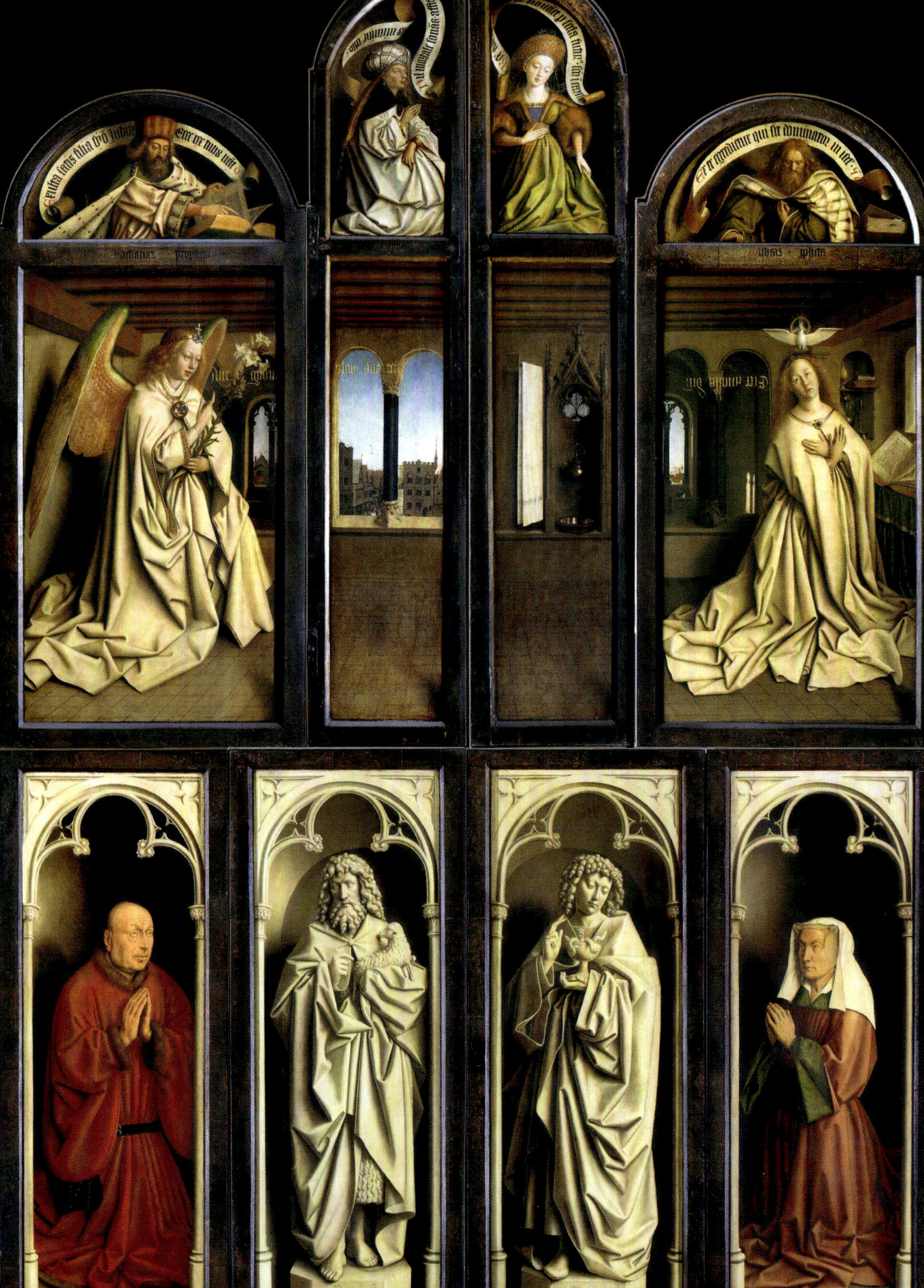

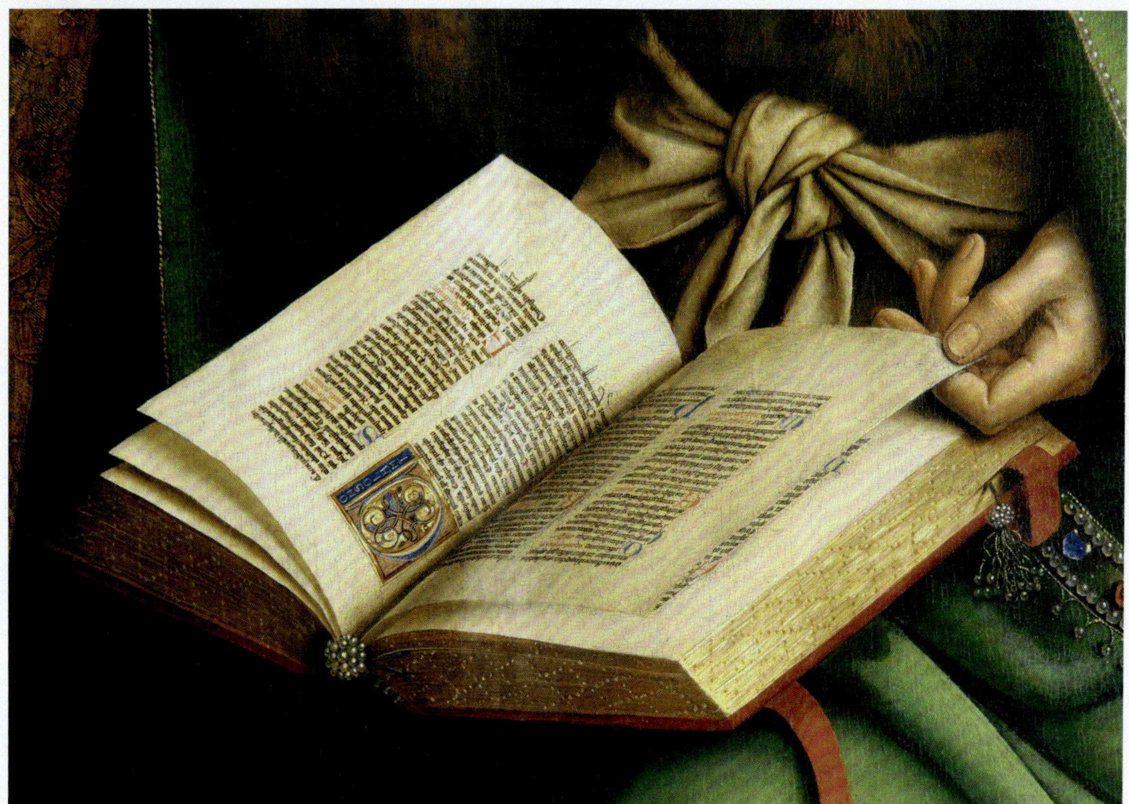

Three-zone construction

At the top there are round arches, in the middle is a scene of the Annunciation, distributed on four panels, and at the bottom are the two donors next to painted sculptures of John the Baptist and John the Evangelist. John the Baptist is the patron saint of Ghent.

Structure en trois espaces :

Dans la partie supérieure, des arcs en plein cintre achèvent le retable ; au centre, une scène de l'Annonciation est répartie sur quatre panneaux ; la partie inférieure présente le couple de donateurs aux côtés de sculptures de Jean le Baptiste et de Jean l'Évangéliste. Jean le Baptiste est le saint patron de Gand.

Dreizoniger Aufbau

Oben befinden sich Rundbögenabschlüsse, in der Mitte eine Verkündigunsszene auf vier Tafeln verteilt, und unten das Stifterpaar neben einer gemalten Skulptur von Johannes dem Täufer und Johannes dem Evangelisten. Johannes der Täufer ist der Stadtpatron von Gent.

Construcción de tres zonas

En la parte superior hay arcos de medio punto, en el centro una escena de la Anunciación distribuida en cuatro paneles, y en la parte inferior la pareja de donantes junto a una escultura pintada por Juan el Bautista y Juan el Evangelista. Juan el Bautista es el santo patrón de Gante.

Construção em três zonas

Na parte superior há arcos redondos, no meio uma cena da Anunciação distribuída em quatro painéis, e na parte inferior o casal de doadores ao lado de uma escultura pintada por João Batista e João Evangelista. João Batista é o santo padroeiro de Gante.

Bouwen in drie zones

Bovenaan bevinden zich ronde bogen, in het midden een scène van de Maria boodschap verdeeld over vier panelen en onderaan het schenkerspaar naast een geschilderde sculptuur van Johannes de Doper en Johannes de Evangelist. Johannes de Doper is de beschermheilige van Gent.

Detail, Ghent Altar (closed view)

Détail, retable de l'Agneau mystique (fermé)

Detail, Genter Altar (geschlossene Ansicht)

Detalle, altar de Gante (vista cerrada)

Detalhe, Retábulo de Gante (vista fechada)

Detail, altaar van Gent (gesloten zicht)

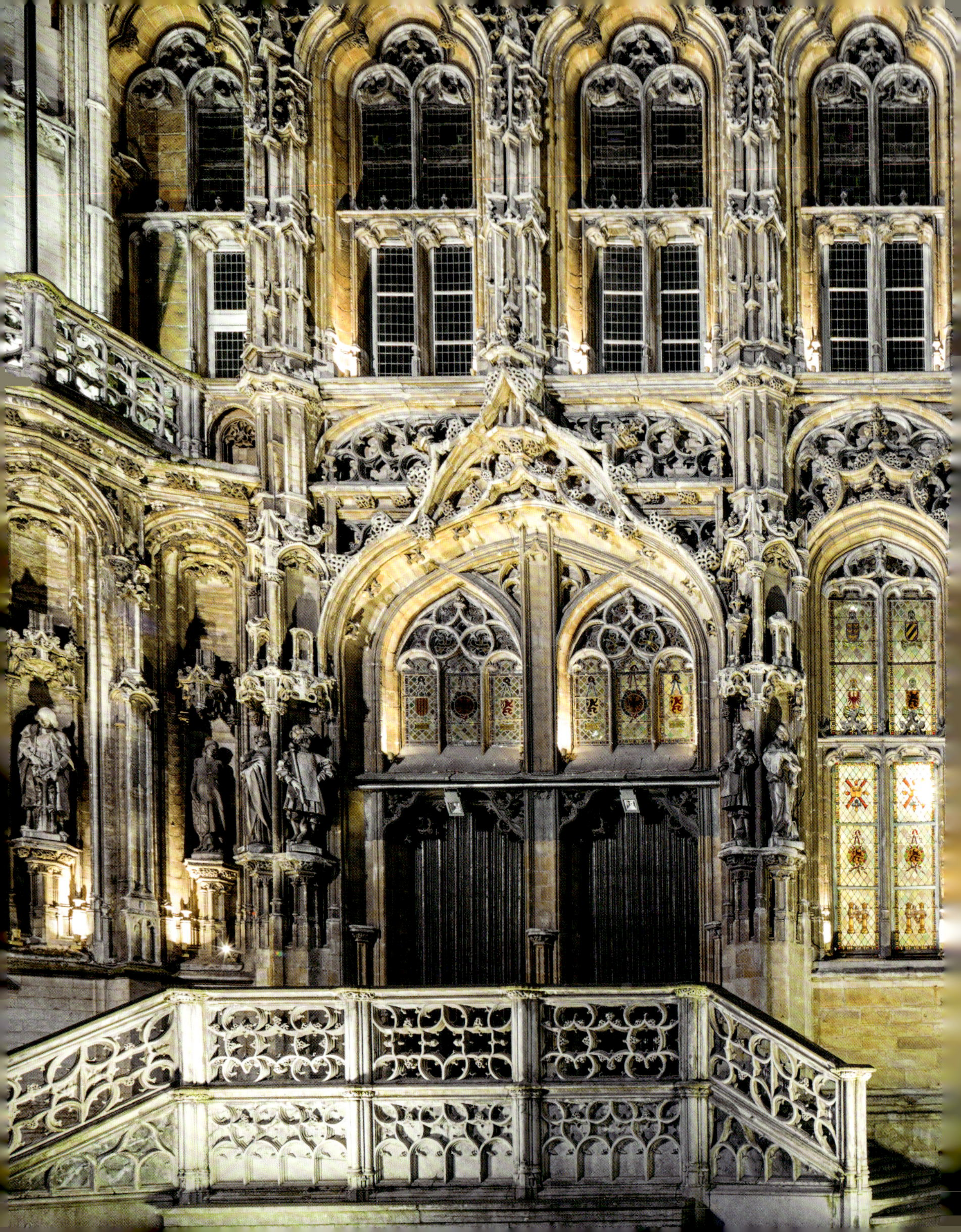

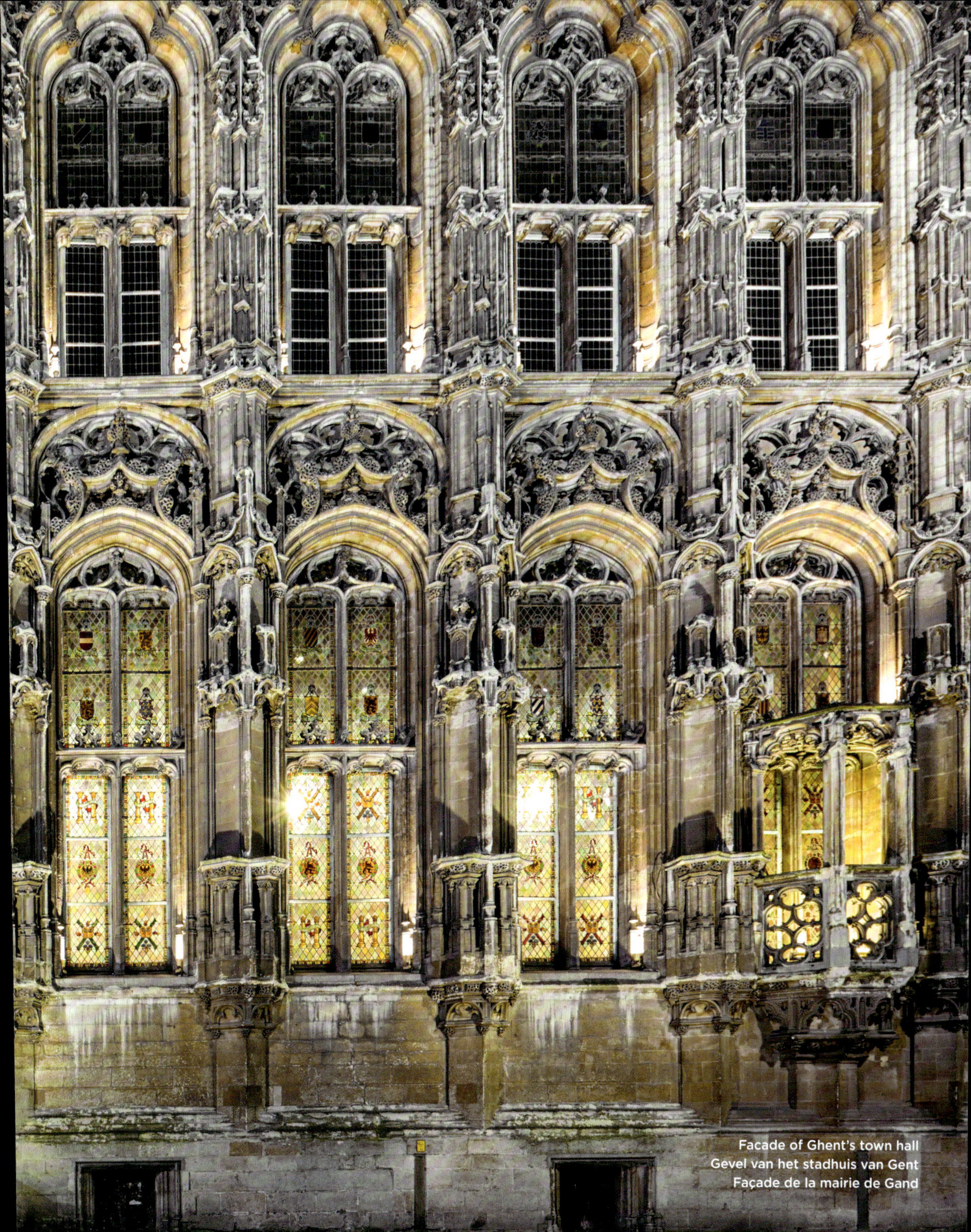

Facade of Ghent's town hall
Gevel van het stadhuis van Gent
Façade de la mairie de Gand

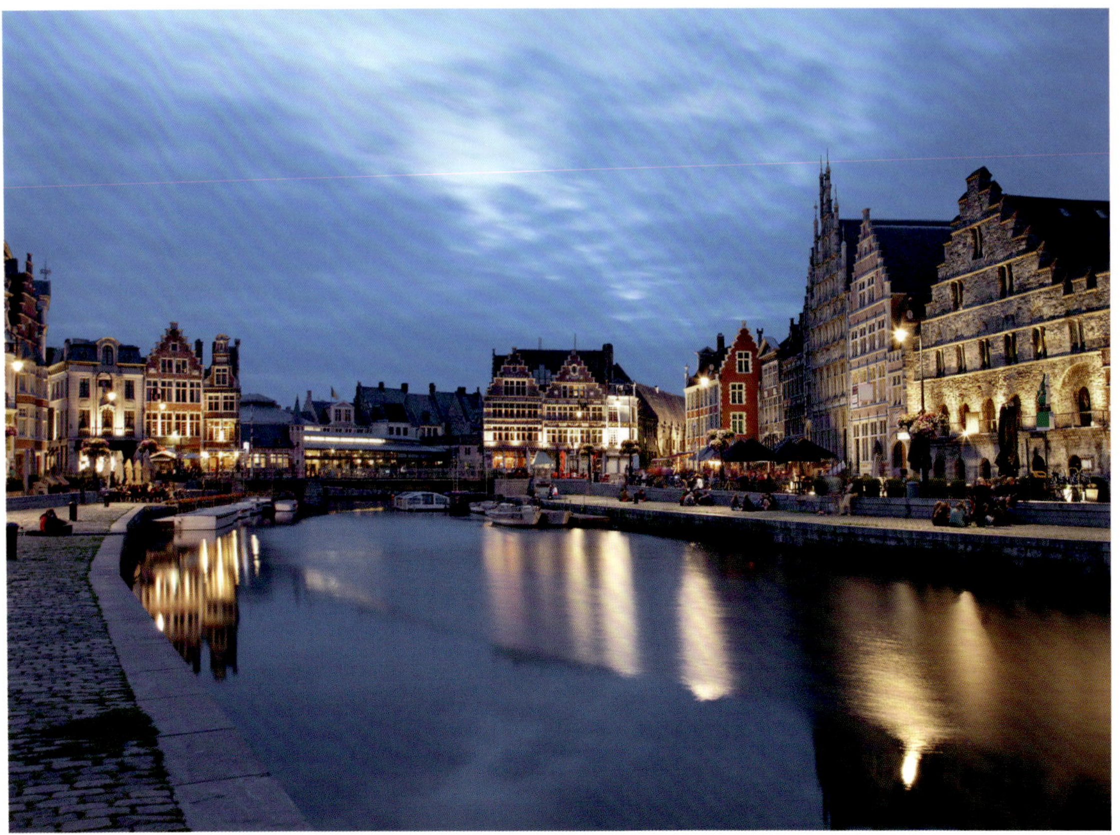

Graslei

Korenlei and Graslei

In the 13th century, Ghent was the most important port of Flanders. On one bank of the Leie, the Korenlei, was the landing stage for grain and on the opposite bank of the river, the Graslei, the landing stage for hay. The historic warehouses are reflected in the water of the Leie and form the heart of the town. The Romanesque building, the "Spijker" from the 12th century, where wheat was once stored, is the oldest house in Flanders. Other guild houses with magnificent facades and Gothic stepped gables, such as the House of the Free Boatmen or the Corn Measurer's House, bear witness to the importance of Ghent harbour.

Le Korenlei et le Graslei

Au XIIIe siècle, Gand était le principal port flamand. À droite de la rivière Lys, dans le Korenlei, on débarquait les céréales ; à gauche de la Lys, dans le Graslei, on débarquait le foin. Les anciens entrepôts qui se reflètent dans l'eau de la rivière forment le cœur de la ville. Datant du XIIe siècle, le bâtiment roman, ou « Spijker », où on entreposait jadis le blé, est la plus ancienne maison de Flandres. D'autres maisons de corporations aux somptueuses façades et aux pignons gothiques à gradins, telles la maison des Francs-Bateliers ou la maison des Mesureurs de grains, témoignent de l'importance du port de Gand.

Korenlei und Graslei

Im 13. Jahrhundert war Gent der wichtigste Hafen von Flandern. Rechts der Leie, die Korenlei, war die Anlegestelle für Korn und links der Leie, die Graslei, war die Landungsstelle für Heu. Im Wasser der Leie spiegeln sich die historischen Stapelhäuser und bilden das Herz der Stadt. Das romanische Gebäude, der „Spijker" aus dem 12. Jahrhunderts, wo man einst den Weizen lagerte, ist das älteste Haus Flanderns. Weitere Zunfthäuser, mit prächtigen Fassaden und gotischen Treppengiebeln, wie das Haus der freien Schiffer oder das Haus der Kornmesser, zeugen von der Bedeutung des Genter Hafens.

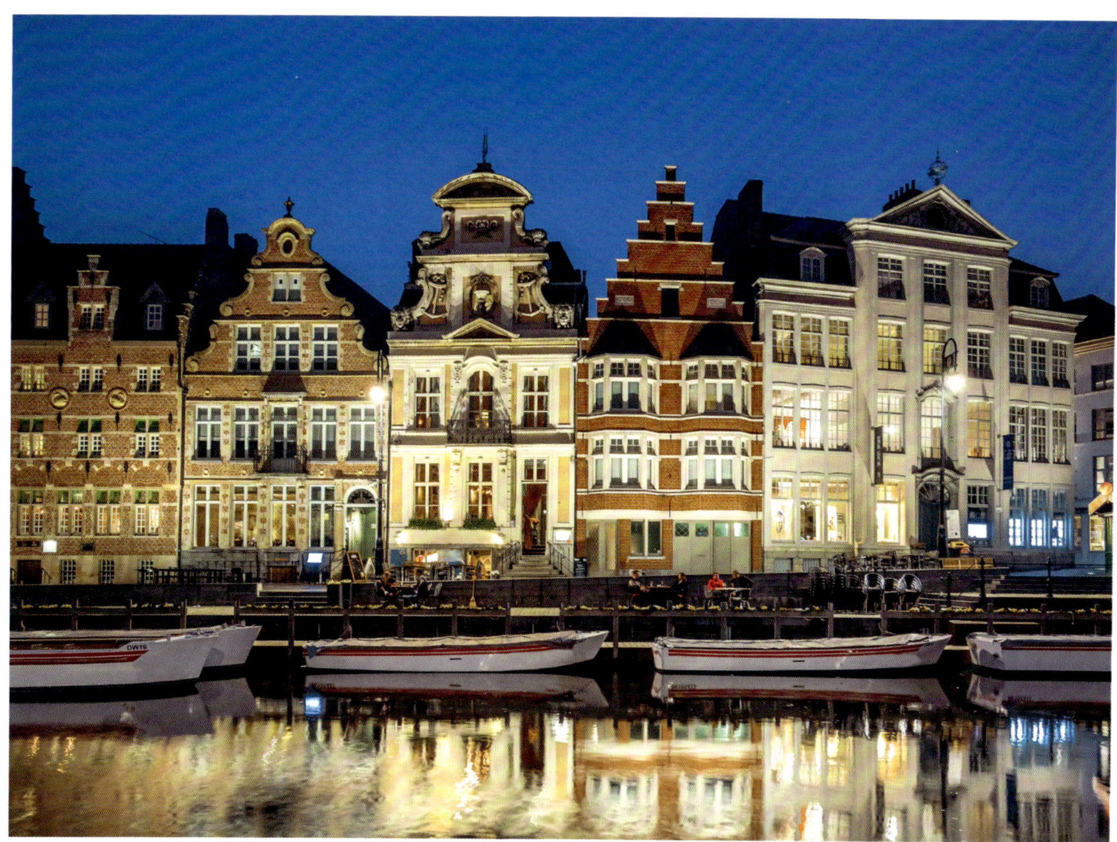

Korenlei

Korenlei y Graslei

En el siglo XIII Gante era el puerto más importante de Flandes. A la derecha del Leie, el Korenlei, era el muelle para el grano y a la izquierda del Leie, el Graslei, era el muelle para el heno. Las históricas casas de apilamiento se reflejan en el agua del Leie y forman el corazón de la ciudad. El edificio románico donde se almacenaba el trigo, el "Spijker" del siglo XII, es la casa más antigua de Flandes. Otras casas gremiales con magníficas fachadas y frontones góticos escalonados, como la Casa de los Marineros Libres o la Casa de los Medidores del Grano, dan fe de la importancia del puerto de Gante.

Korenlei e Graslei

No século XIII, Gante foi o porto mais importante da Flandres. À direita do rio Leie, o Korenlei, era o local de desembarque de grãos e à esquerda do rio Leie, o Graslei, estava o desembarque de feno. Nas águas do Leie refletem-se as casas de empilhamento históricas e formam o coração da cidade. O edifício românico, o "Spijker" do século XII, onde o trigo foi armazenado, é a casa mais antiga da Flandres. Outras casas das corporações com magníficas fachadas e empenas escalonadas góticos, como a Casa dos Barqueiros Livres ou a Casa dos Medidores de Grãos, testemunham a importância do porto de Gante.

Korenlei en Graslei

In de 13de eeuw was Gent de belangrijkste haven van Vlaanderen. Rechts van de Leie, de Korenlei, bevond zich de aanlegsteiger voor graan en links van de Leie, de Graslei, was de aanlegsteiger voor hooi. De historische stapelhuizen worden weerspiegeld in het water van de Leie en vormen het hart van de stad. Het romaanse gebouw de "Spijker" uit de 12e eeuw, waar ooit tarwe werd opgeslagen, is het oudste huis van Vlaanderen. Andere gildehuizen met prachtige gevels en gotische trapgevels, zoals het Gildehuis der Vrije Schippers of het Gildehuis van de korenmeters, getuigen van het belang van de Gentse haven.

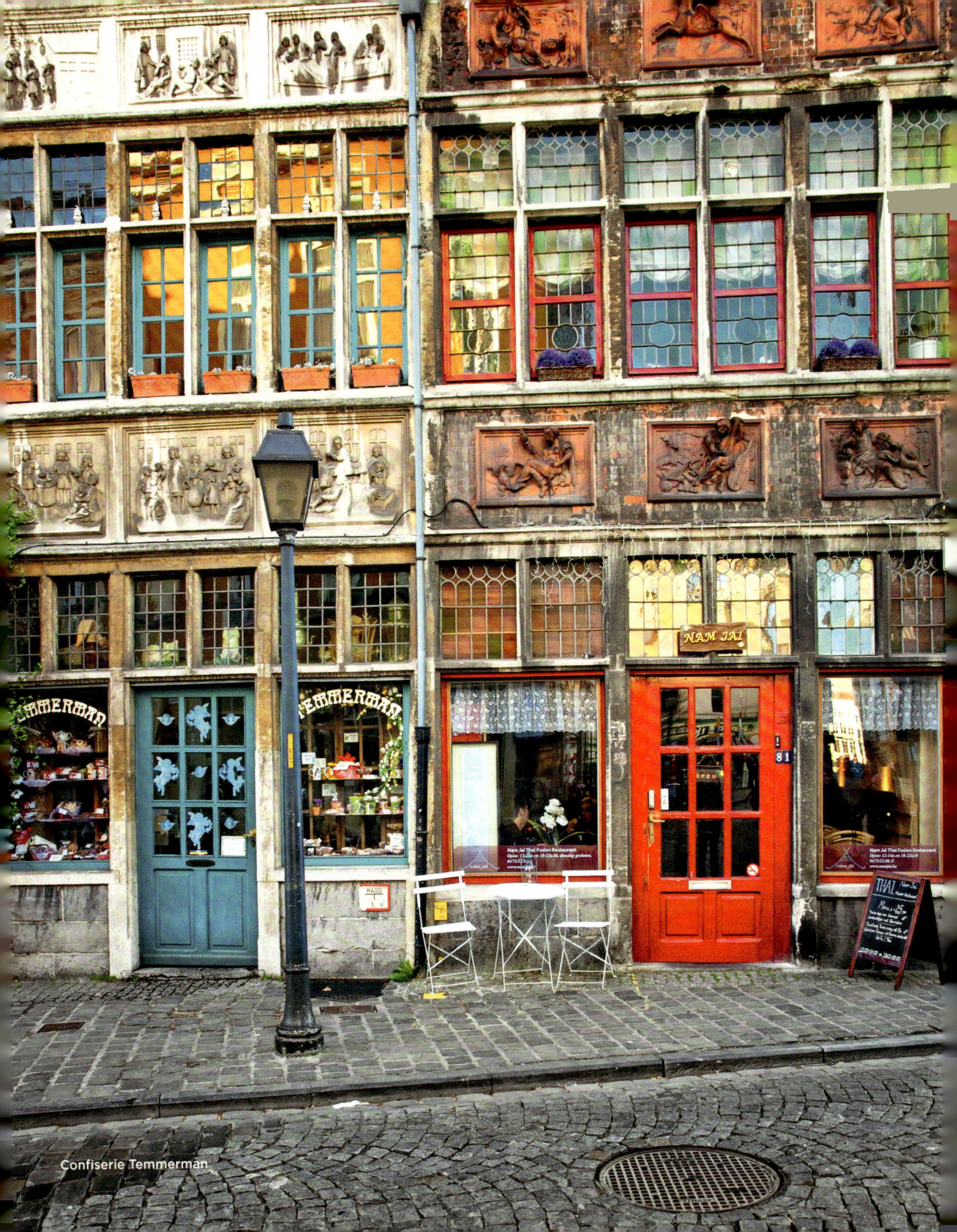

Confiserie Temmerman

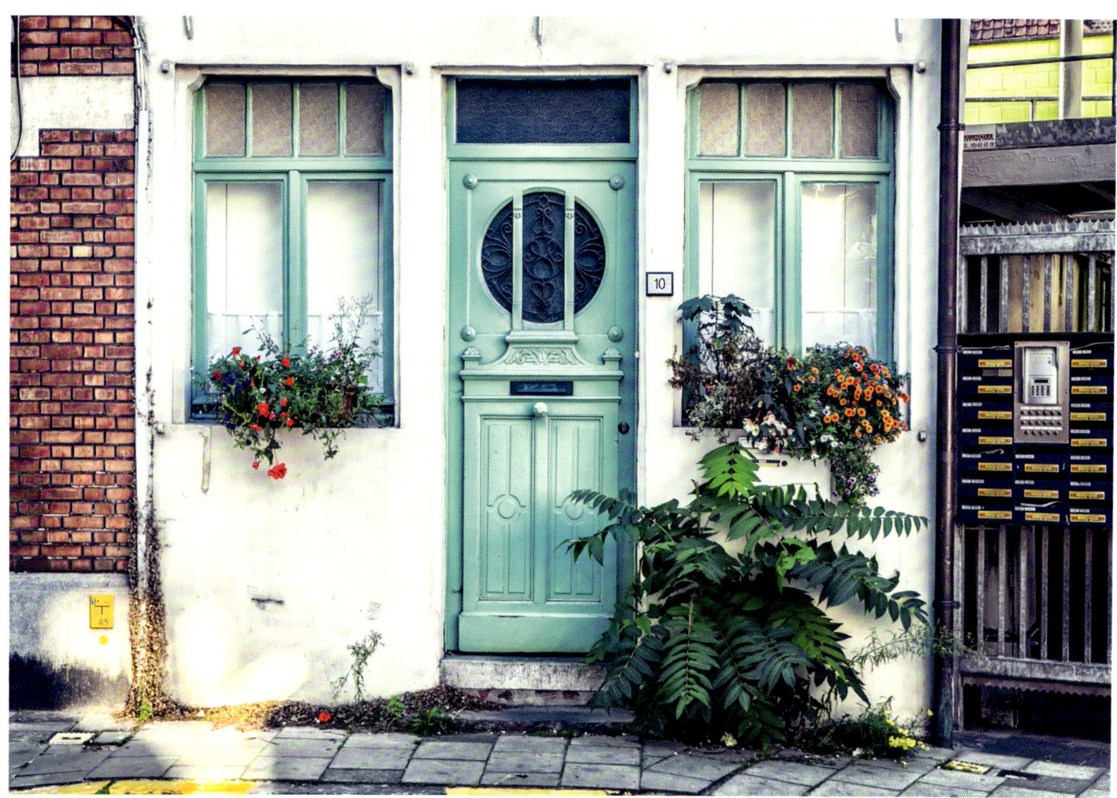

Typical house
Typisch huis
Maison typique

Mercy and Deadly Sins

At the edge of the quarter Patershol there are two remarkable houses in the "Confiserie Temmerman" and Bistro "De Hel" (Hell). The facade of the traditional confectioners illustrates six works of mercy in reliefs. The front of the bistro shows vividly, from pride to lust, the seven deadly sins.

Misericordia y pecados capitales

Al borde del barrio Patershol hay dos casas notables: Confiserie Temmerman y Bistro "De Hel" (el infierno). La fachada de la confitería tradicional muestra las obras de misericordia en seis relieves. El frente del bistro muestra vívidamente, desde el orgullo hasta la lujuria, los siete pecados capitales.

Miséricorde et péchés capitaux

À l'orée de ce quartier, Patershol, se dressent deux maisons remarquables : la confiserie Temmerman et le bistrot De Hel (l'Enfer). La façade de la confiserie traditionnelle est pourvue de six bas-reliefs représentant les œuvres de miséricorde. Celle du bistrot présente sans équivoque les sept péchés capitaux, de l'orgueil à la luxure.

Misericórdia e Pecados Capitais

Nos limites do bairro Patershol existem duas casas notáveis: a "Confiserie Temmerman" e o Bistro "De Hel" (Inferno). A fachada da confeitaria tradicional mostra as obras de misericórdia em seis relevos. A frente do bistrô mostra vividamente, do orgulho à luxúria, os sete pecados capitais.

Barmherzigkeit und Todsünden

Am Rande des Viertels Patershol stehen zwei bemerkenswerte Häuschen: die Confiserie Temmerman und das Bistro „De Hel" (Die Hölle). Die Fassade der traditionsreichen Confiserie, zeigt auf sechs Reliefs die Werke der Barmherzigkeit. Die Front des Bistros zeigt anschaulich, vom Hochmut bis zur Wollust, die sieben Todsünden.

Barmhartigheid en doodzonden

Aan de rand van de wijk Patershol staan twee opmerkelijke huizen: confiserie Temmerman en bistro "De Hel". De voorgevel van de traditionele banketbakkerij toont op zes reliëfs Bijbelse werken van barmhartigheid. De voorkant van de bistro toont op levendige wijze, van hoogmoed tot wellust, de zeven doodzonden.

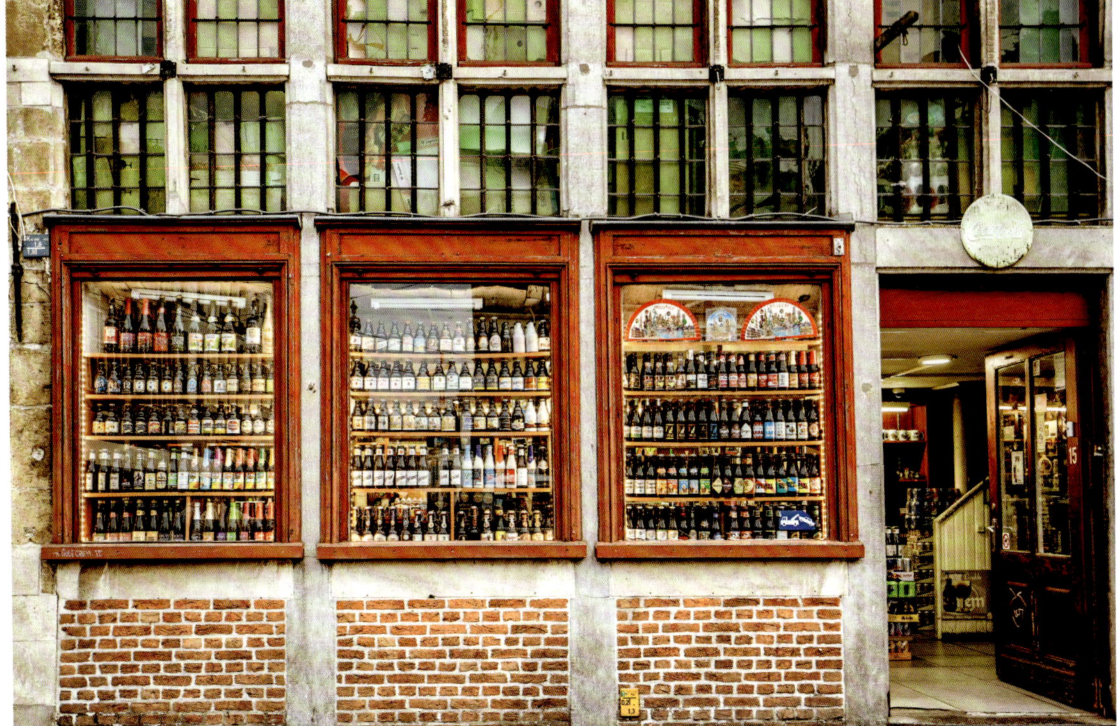

Beer shop
Bierwinkel
Magasin de bière

Beer and Herbs

In Ghent there are hundreds of pubs and beers, and also some breweries. The most famous brewery, "Gruut", does not brew with hops, but with Gruut (herbs). The tavern "Dulle Griet" has the largest range of beers, with around 500 on offer. Here, when ordering a "Max beer", you have to put a shoe in a basket as a deposit for the glass, which is then pulled up to the ceiling.

Bière et fines herbes

Gand renferme des centaines de pubs, proposant de nombreuses variétés de bières, ainsi que quelques brasseries. Parmi ces dernières, la plus célèbre, la Gruut, ne brasse pas sa bière avec du houblon, mais avec du «gruut» (des herbes). Avec ses 500 bières, le bar à bières Dulle Griet présente l'offre la plus large. Ici, en guise de consigne, il vous faudra placer une chaussure dans un panier tiré jusqu'au plafond.

Bier und Kräuter

In Gent gibt es Hunderte von Kneipen und Biersorten und einige Brauereien. Die bekannteste Brauerei, „Gruut", braut nicht mit Hopfen, sondern mit Gruut (Kräutern). Mit 500 Bieren das größte Angebot hat die Bierstube „Dulle Griet". Hier muss man für ein Max-Bier als Pfand einen Schuh in einen Korb legen, der dann bis unter die Decke hochgezogen wird.

Cerveza y hierbas

En Gante hay cientos de pubs y tipos de cerveza, así como algunas cervecerías. La cervecería más famosa, "Gruut", no produce con lúpulo, sino con Gruut (hierbas). La cervecería "Dulle Griet" tiene la oferta más grande de cerveza: ni más ni menos que 500 tipos de cerveza distintos. Aquí tienes que poner un zapato en una cesta como depósito para una cerveza Max, que luego se tira al techo.

Cerveja e Ervas

Em Gante, há centenas de bares e cervejas e algumas cervejarias. A cervejaria mais famosa, "Gruut", não fabrica cerveja com lúpulo, mas com Gruut (ervas). Com 500 cervejas a maior oferta, tem a cervejaria "Dulle Griet". Aqui para uma cerveja Max, você tem que colocar um sapato como um depósito em uma cesta, que é então puxado para cima até o teto.

Bier en kruiden

In Gent zijn er honderden cafés en bieren en enkele brouwerijen. De bekendste brouwerij "Gruut" brouwt niet met hop, maar met Gruut (kruiden). Café "Dulle Griet" heeft met 500 bieren het grootste aanbod. Hier moet je als borg voor hun huisbier Max een schoen in een mandje doen dat dan tot aan het plafond omhoog wordt getrokken.

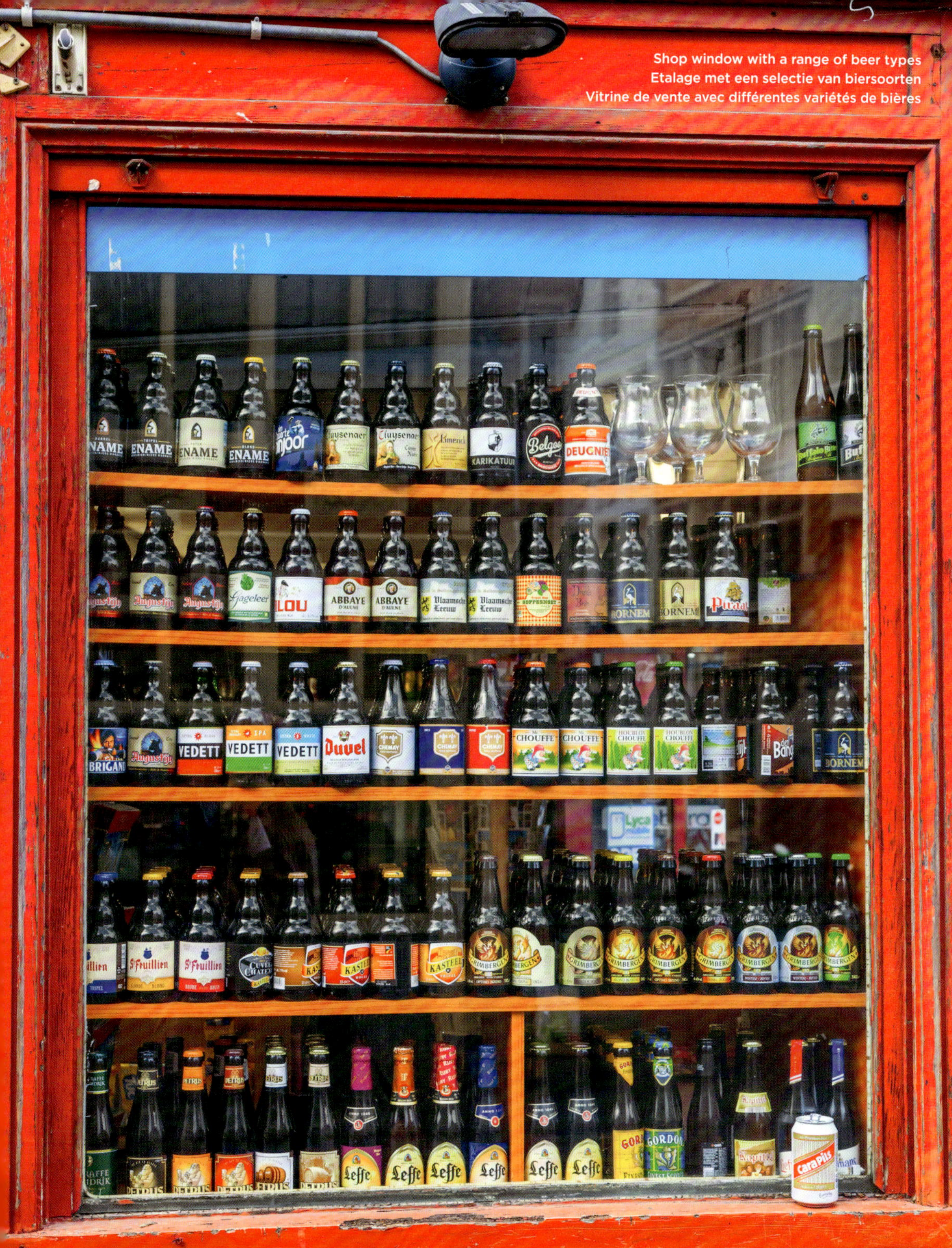

Shop window with a range of beer types
Etalage met een selectie van biersoorten
Vitrine de vente avec différentes variétés de bières

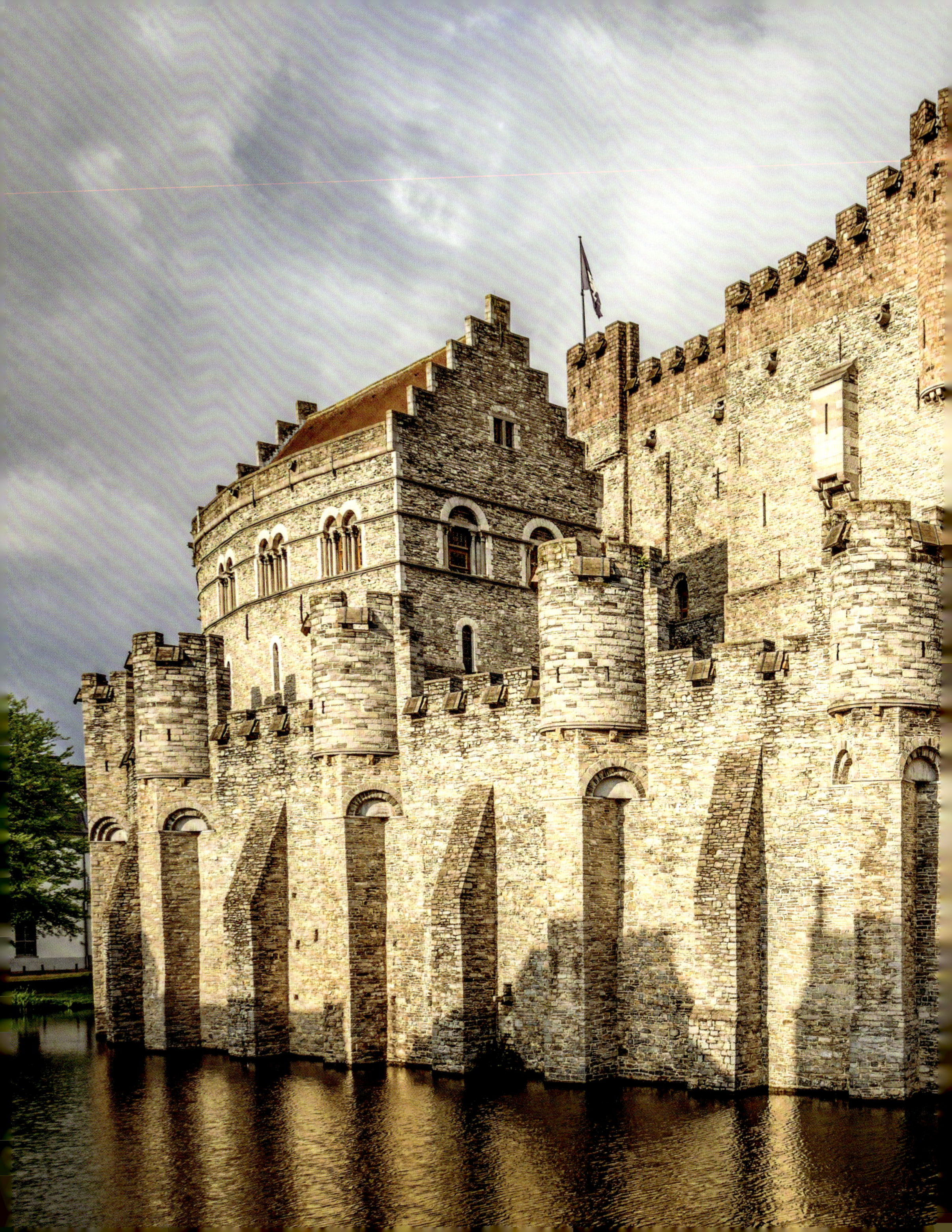

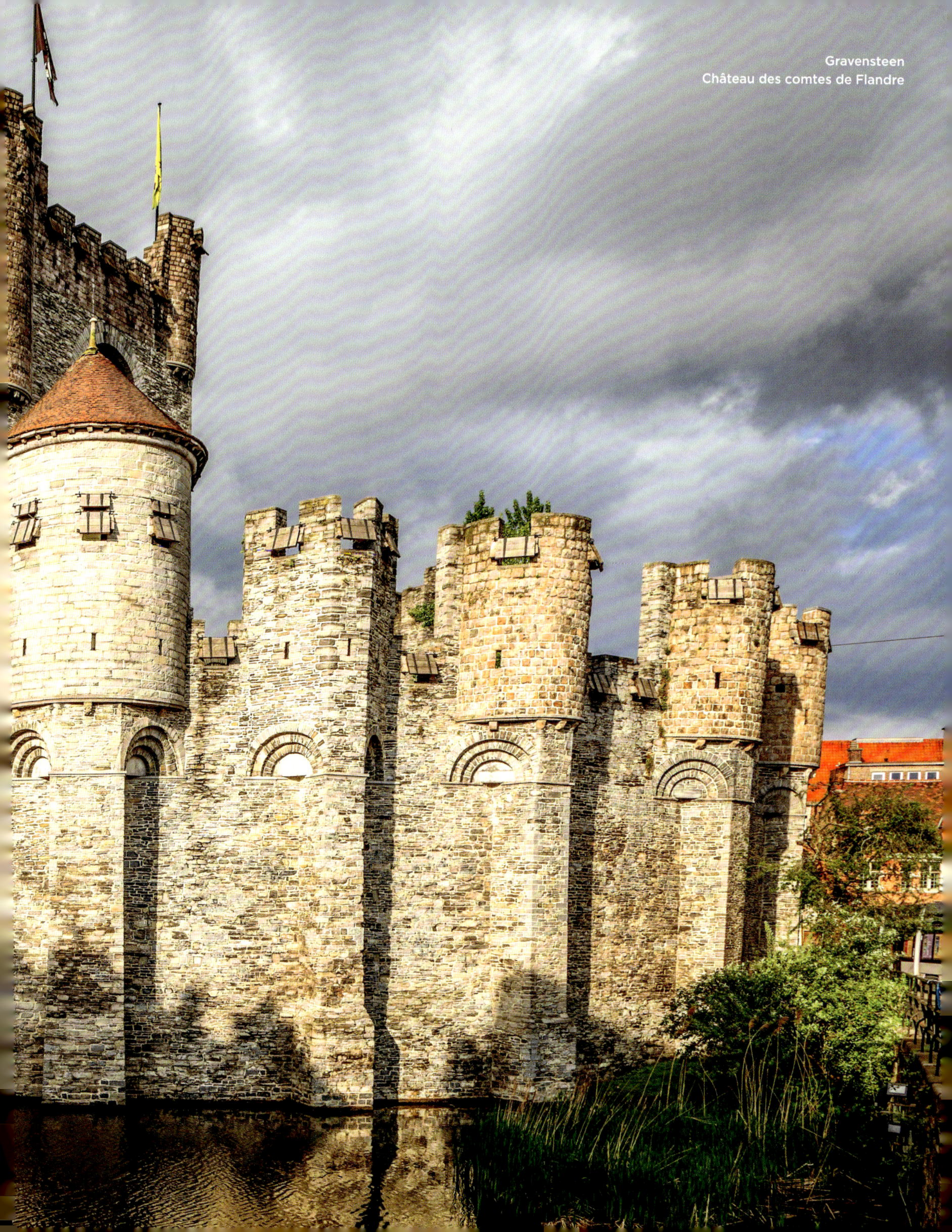
Gravensteen
Château des comtes de Flandre

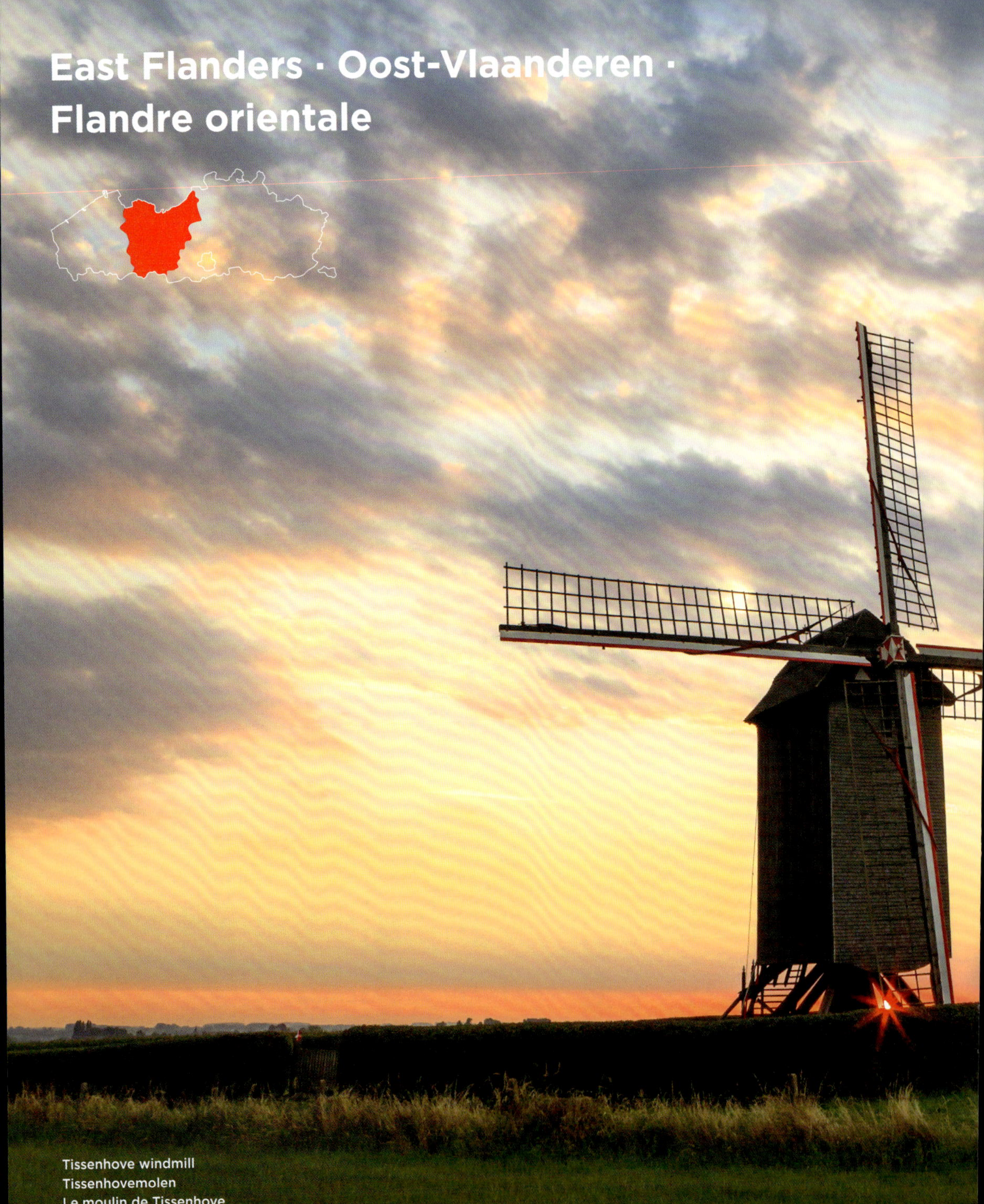

Tissenhove windmill
Tissenhovemolen
Le moulin de Tissenhove

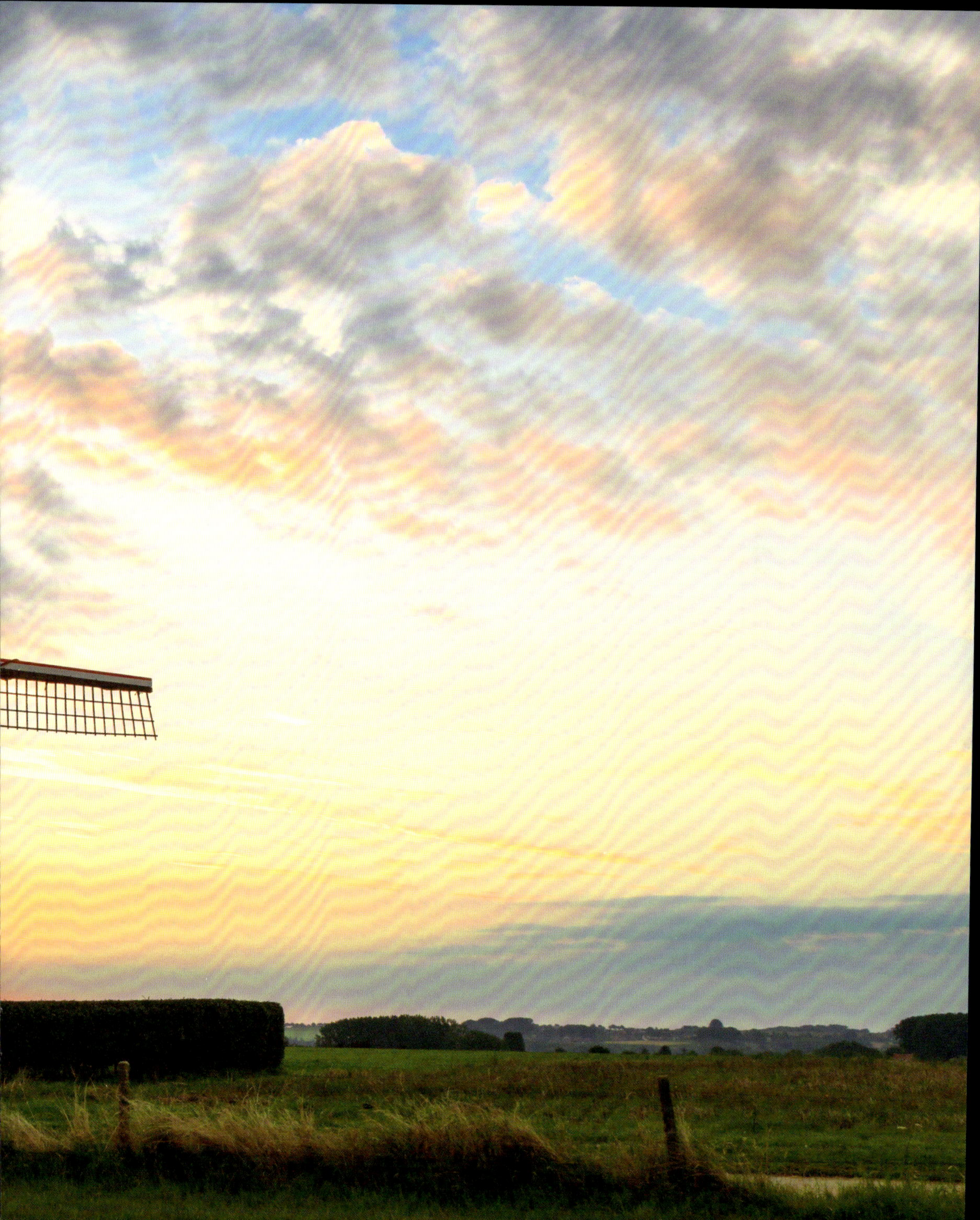

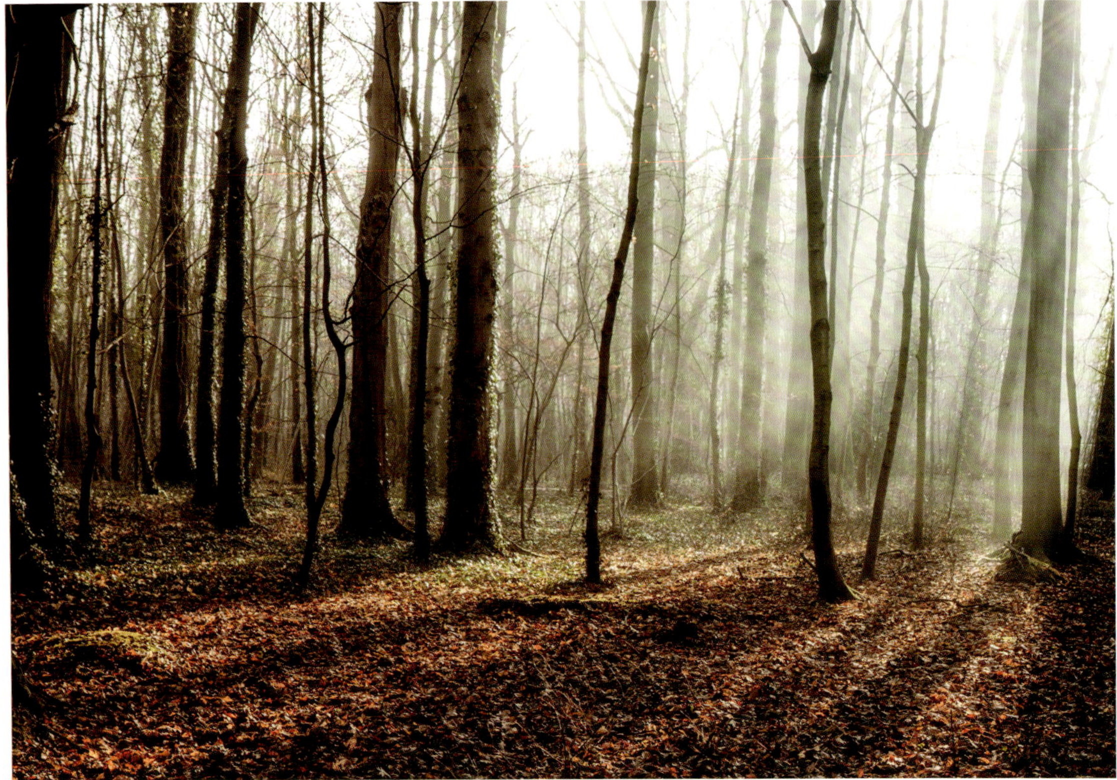

Kravaalbos, Aalst

East Flanders

The river landscapes of the Leie, with their villages, castles and gardens extend out before the gates of Gent. Inspired by their native idyll, Flemish painters and artists founded an artists' colony downstream in Sint-Martens-Latem. Further south, on the hills directly at the Flemish-French language divide, is the largest forest in East Flanders.

Flandes Oriental

Los paisajes fluviales del Leie con sus pueblos, castillos y jardines se extienden ante las puertas de Gante. Inspirados por su idilio nativo, pintores y artistas flamencos fundaron un pueblo de artistas río abajo en Sint-Martens-Latem. Más al sur, en las colinas directamente en la frontera de lengua flamenca y francesa, crece el bosque más grande de Flandes Oriental.

Flandre orientale

Émaillés de villages, châteaux et jardins, les paysages fluviaux de la Lys s'étendent devant les portes de Gand. Inspirés par leur région natale idyllique, des peintres et artistes flamands fondèrent un village d'artistes en aval, à Laethem-Saint-Martin. Plus au sud, la plus grande forêt de Flandre orientale s'étale sur les collines situées directement à la frontière franco-flamande.

Flandres Oriental

As paisagens fluviais do Leie com as suas aldeias, castelos e jardins estendem-se diante dos portões de Gante. Inspirados pelo seu idílio nativo, pintores e artistas flamengos fundaram uma vila de artistas às margens do rio Leie em Sint-Martens-Latem. Mais a sul, nas colinas diretamente na fronteira flamengo-francesa, cresce a maior floresta da Flandres Oriental.

Ostflandern

Vor den Toren Gents erstrecken sich die Flusslandschaften der Leie mit ihren Dörfern, Schlössern und Gärten. Von der heimatlichen Idylle inspiriert, gründeten flämische Maler und Künstler flussabwärts in Sint-Martens-Latem ein Künstlerdorf. Weiter südlich, auf den Hügeln direkt an der flämisch-französischen Sprachgrenze, wächst der größte Wald Ostflanderns.

Oost-Vlaanderen

Voor de poorten van Gent strekken zich de rivierlandschappen van de Leie met hun dorpen, kastelen en tuinen. Geïnspireerd door idylle van de plek, stichtten Vlaamse schilders en kunstenaars stroomafwaarts in Sint-Martens-Latem een kunstenaarsdorp. Verder zuidwaarts, op de heuvels direct aan de Vlaams-Franse taalgrens, groeit Oost-Vlaanderens grootste bos.

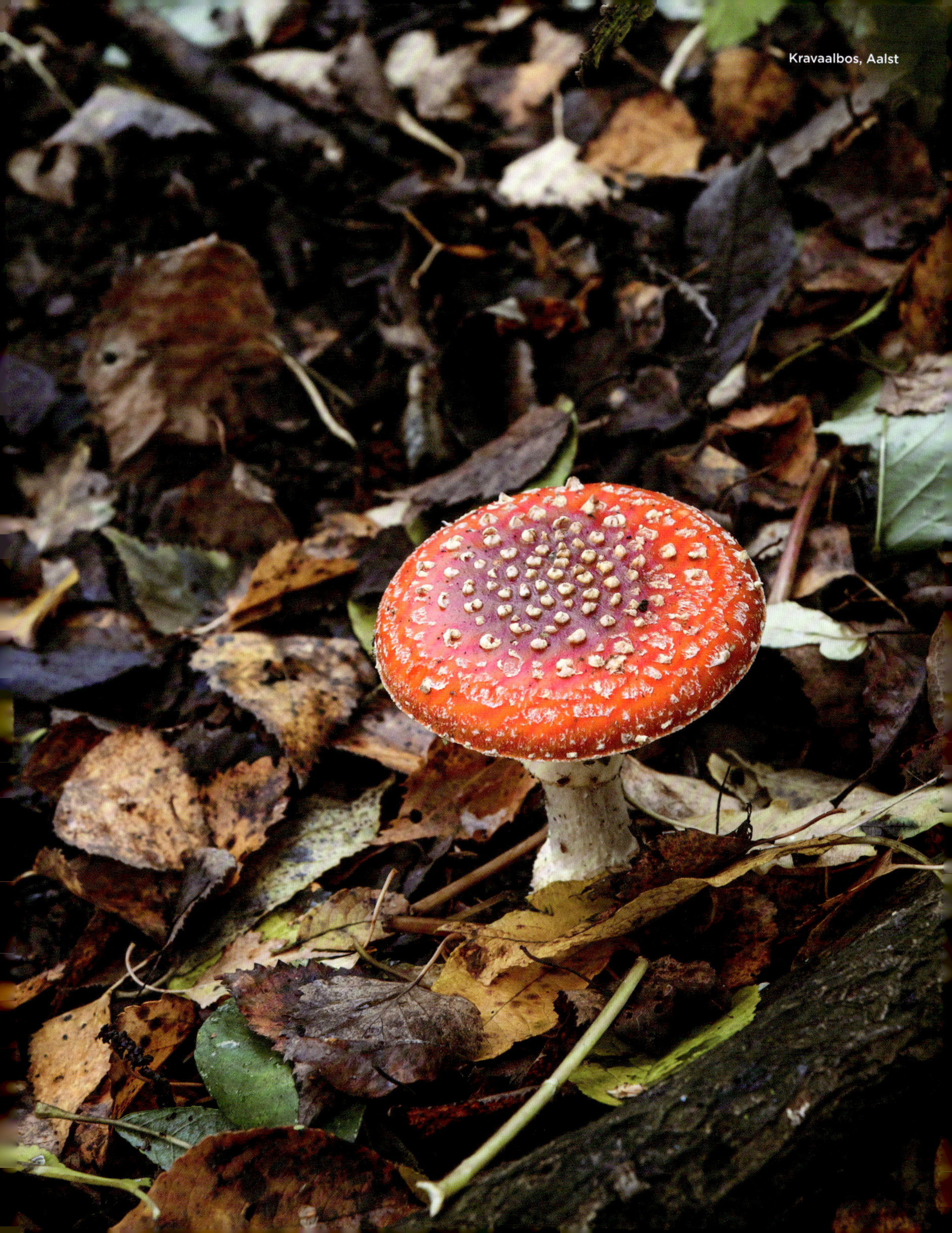

Kravaalbos, Aalst

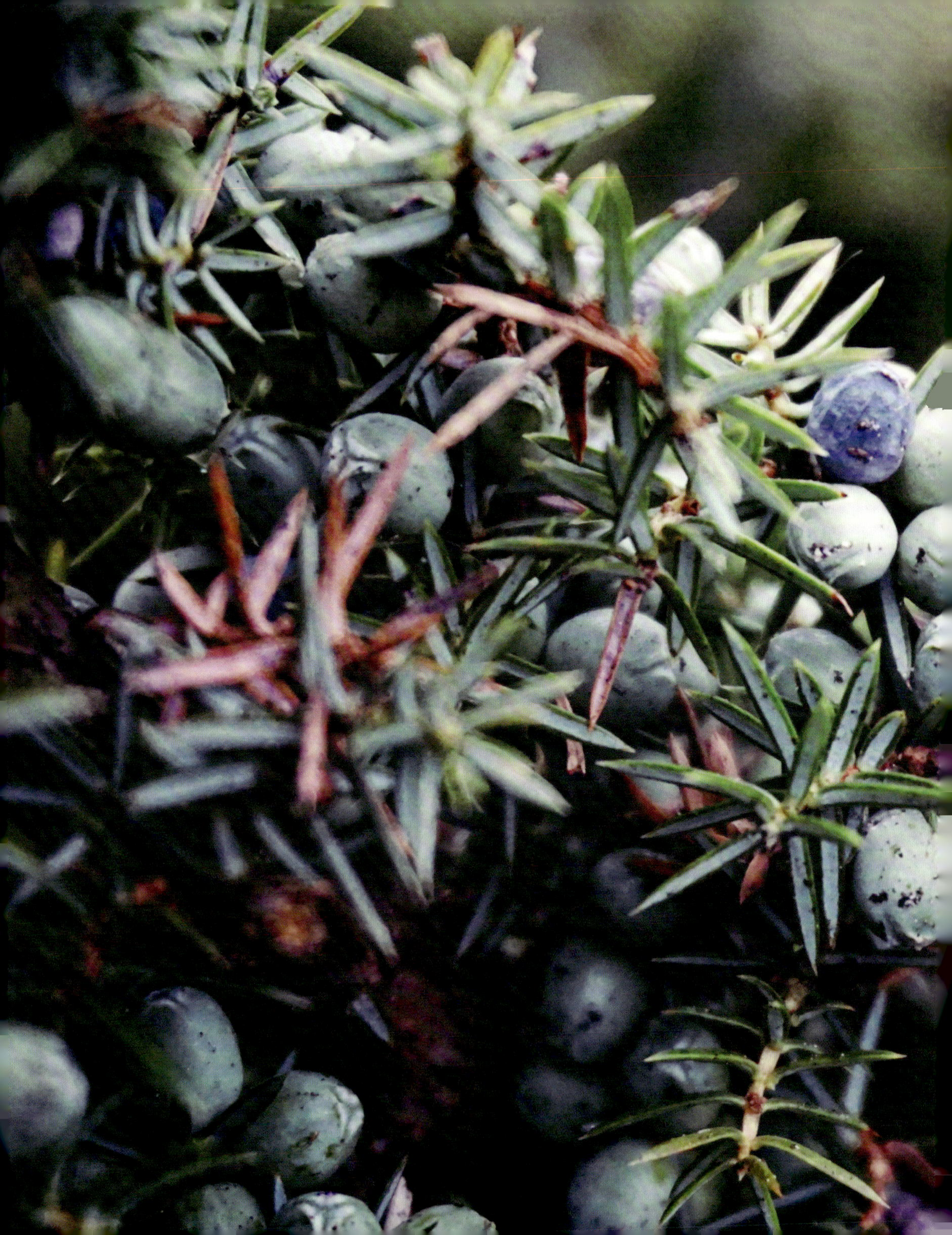

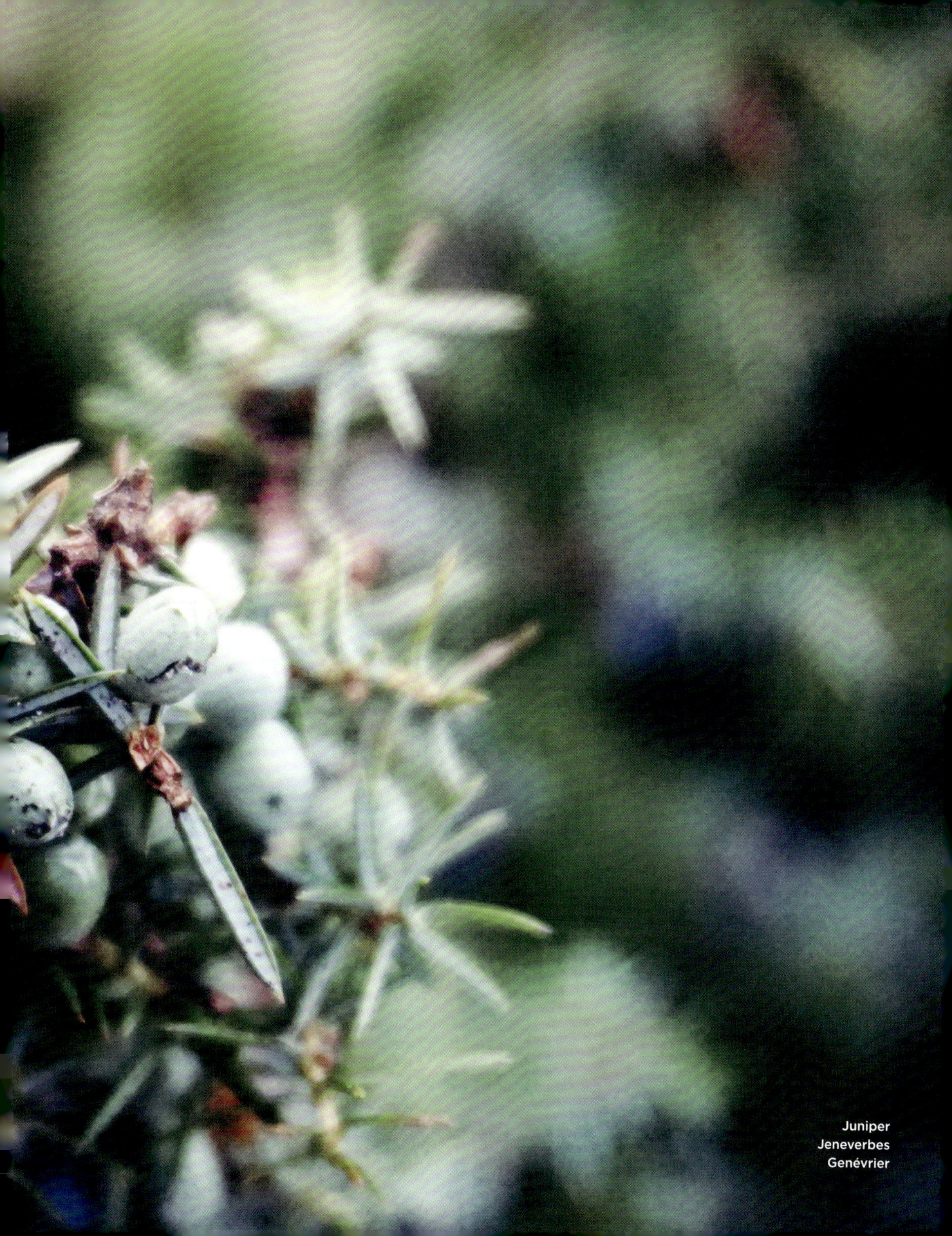
Juniper
Jeneverbes
Genévrier

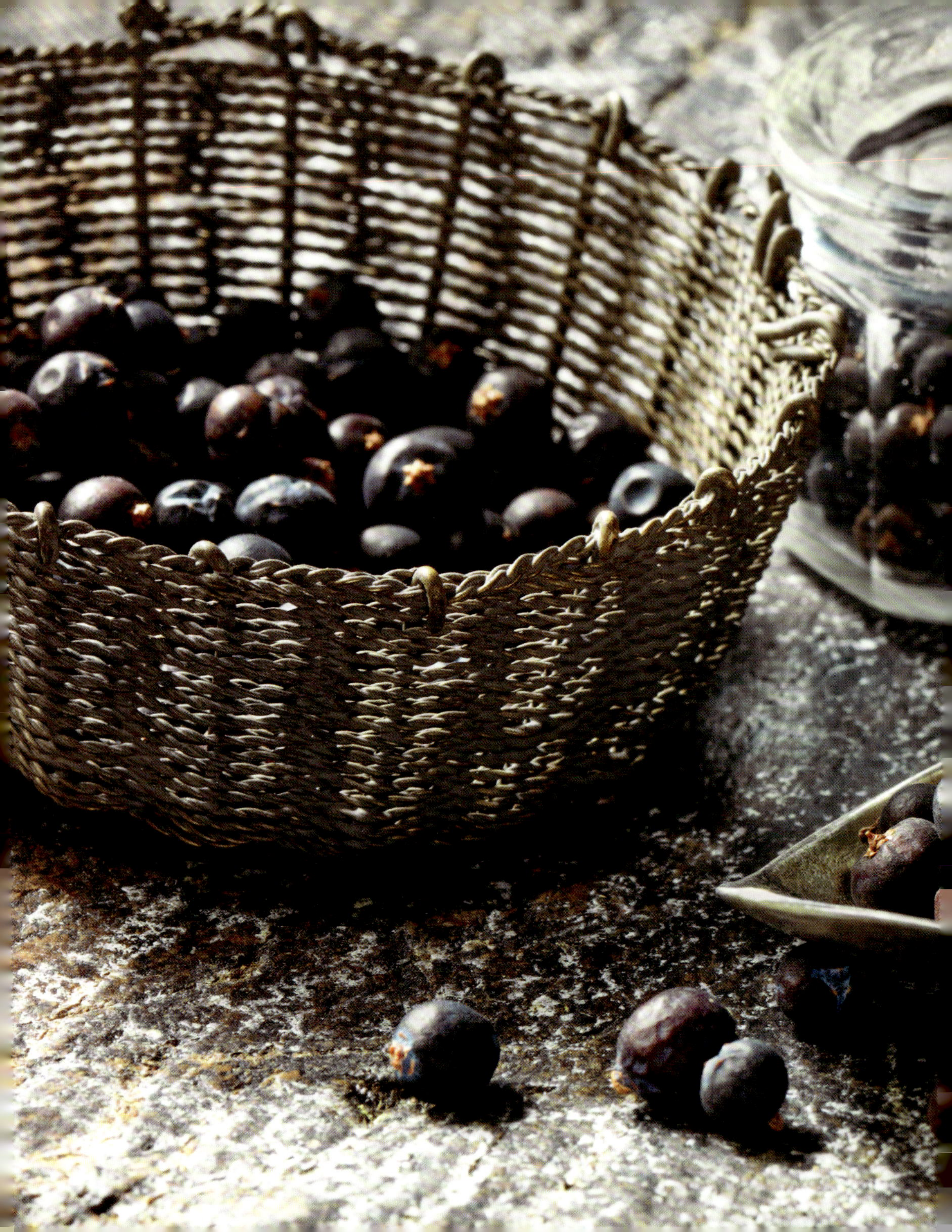

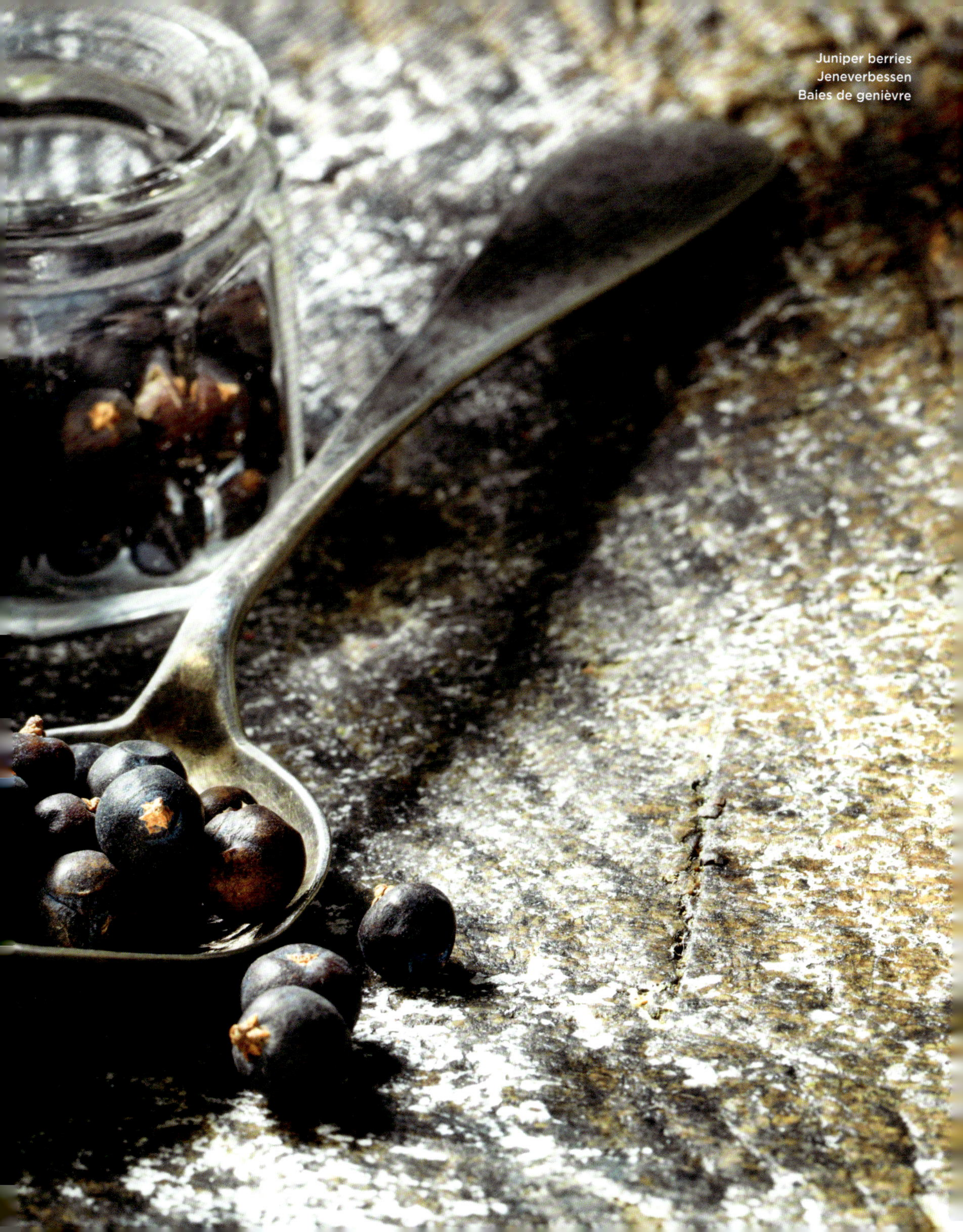
Juniper berries
Jeneverbessen
Baies de genièvre

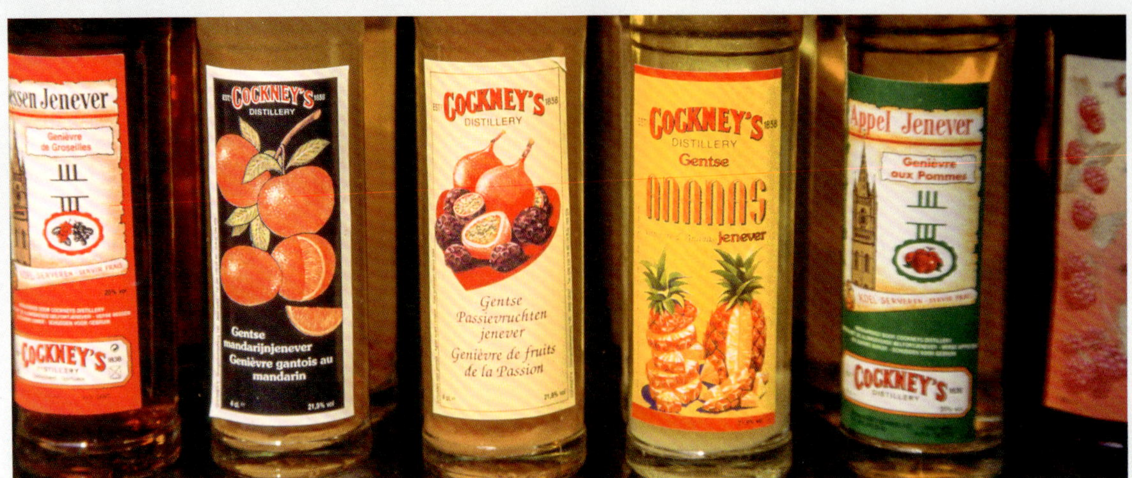
essen Jenever
Genièvre
de Groseilles
COCKNEY'S
DISTILLERY
COCKNEY'S
DISTILLERY
Gentse
mandarijnjenever
Genièvre gantois au
mandarin
COCKNEY'S
DISTILLERY
Gentse
Passievruchten
jenever
Genièvre de fruits
de la Passion
COCKNEY'S
DISTILLERY
Gentse
ANANAS
Jenever
Appel Jenever
Genièvre
aux Pommes
COCKNEY'S
DISTILLERY

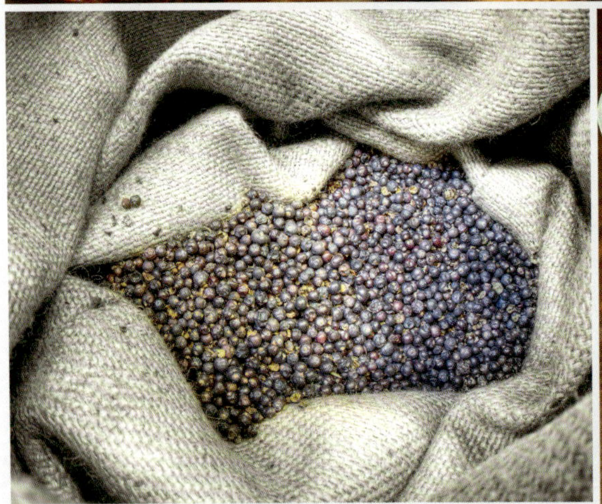

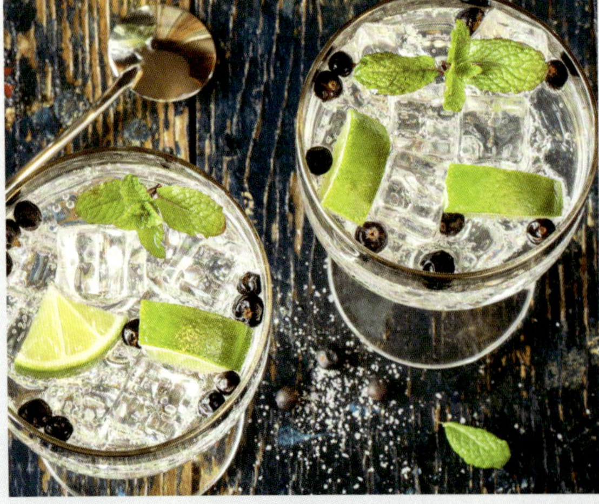

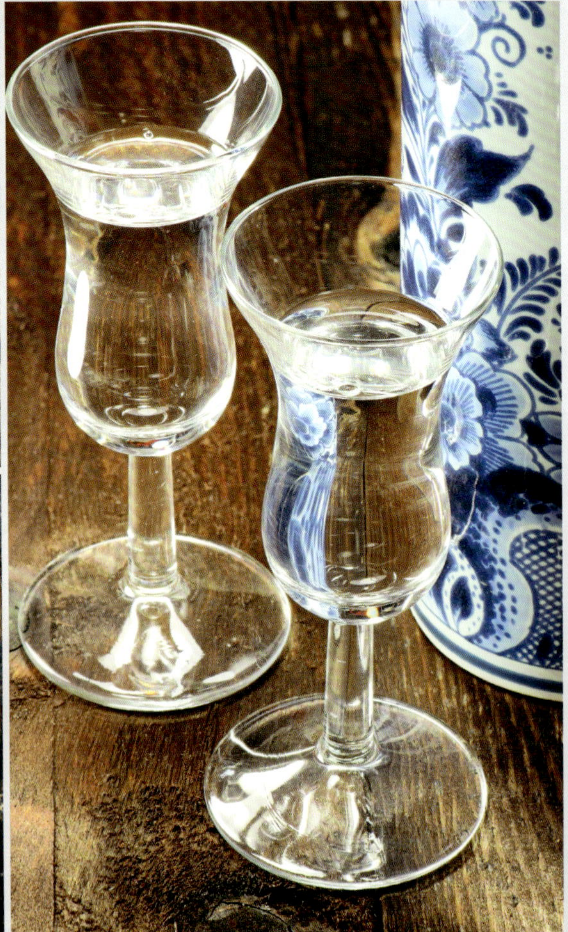

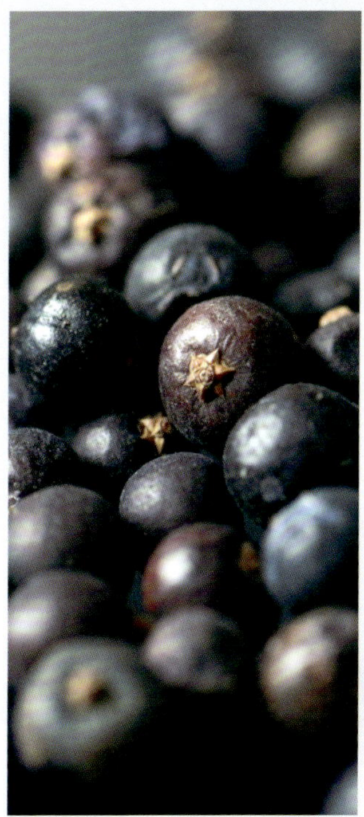

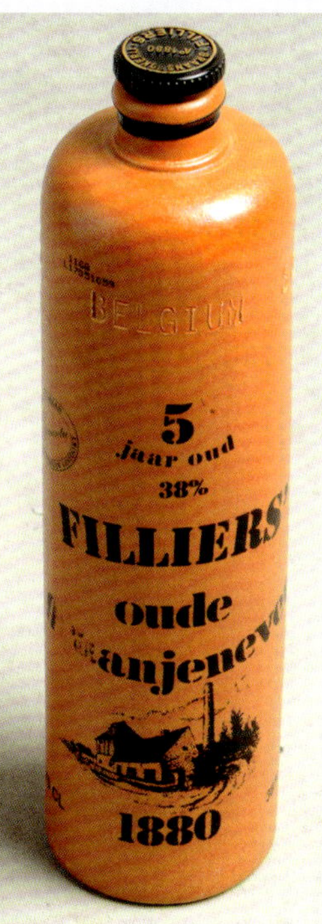

Genever

Almost every region of Flanders has its own genever. Not far from Ghent, on the river Leie, Filliers has been distilling genever for five generations in the family tradition. Malt wine from rye or barley forms the highly aromatic basis. The Classic Dry Gin, one of the best, is flavoured in small batches with juniper, coriander, lavender, hops and other herbs and then matured for eight years in oak barrels.

Genièvre

Presque toutes les régions des Flandres ont leur propre genièvre. Aux portes de Gand, en aval de la Lys, Filliers distille le genièvre depuis cinq générations dans la tradition familiale. Le vin de malt composé de seigle ou d'orge en constitue la base hautement aromatique. Le Classic Dry Gin fait partie des meilleurs genièvres. Mûri pendant huit ans en fût de chêne, il véhicule de subtils arômes de genièvre, de coriandre, de lavande, de houblon et d'autres herbes.

Genever

Fast jede Region Flandern hat ihren eigenen Genever. Vor den Toren Gents, flussabwärts an der Leie, wird bei Filliers, seit 5 Generationen in Familientradition Genever gebrannt. Malzwein aus Roggen oder Gerste bildet die hocharomatische Basis. Der Classic Dry Gin, einer der besten, wird in kleinen Chargen mit Wacholder, Koriander, Lavendel, Hopfen und weiteren Kräutern aromatisiert und acht Jahre in Eichenfässern gereift.

Genever

Casi todas las regiones de Flandes tienen su propio Genever. A las puertas de Gante, río abajo en el Leie, Filliers ha estado destilando Genever durante cinco generaciones en la tradición familiar. El vino de malta de centeno o de cebada constituye la base altamente aromática. El Classic Dry Gin, uno de los mejores, se aromatiza en pequeñas cantidades con enebro, cilantro, lavanda, lúpulo y otras hierbas y se deja envejecer durante ocho años en barriles de roble.

Genebra

Quase todas as regiões da Flandres têm a sua própria genebra. Nos portões de Gante, a jusante do Leie, a firma Filliers vem destilando genebra há 5 gerações na tradição familiar. O vinho maltado de centeio ou cevada constitui a base altamente aromática. O Gin Seco Clássico, um dos melhores, é aromatizado em pequenos lotes com zimbro, coentro, lavanda, lúpulo e outras ervas e amadurecido durante oito anos em barricas de carvalho.

Jenever

Bijna iedere Vlaamse regio heeft eigen jenever. Voor de stad Gent, stroomafwaarts van de Leie, distilleert Filliers 5 generaties traditionele jenever met de aromatische basis van moutwijn uit rogge of gerst. De klassieke Dry Gin wordt in kleine hoeveelheden op smaak gebracht met o.a. jeneverbes, koriander, lavendel en hop en acht jaar in eikenhouten vaten gerijpt.

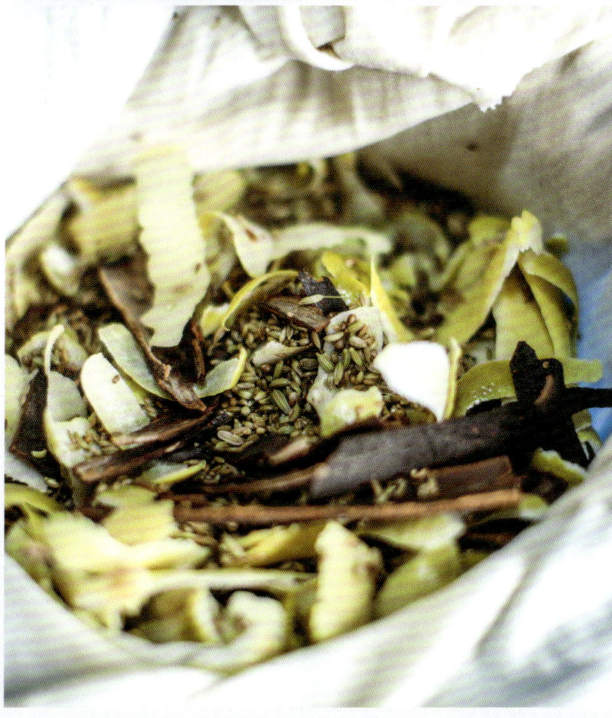

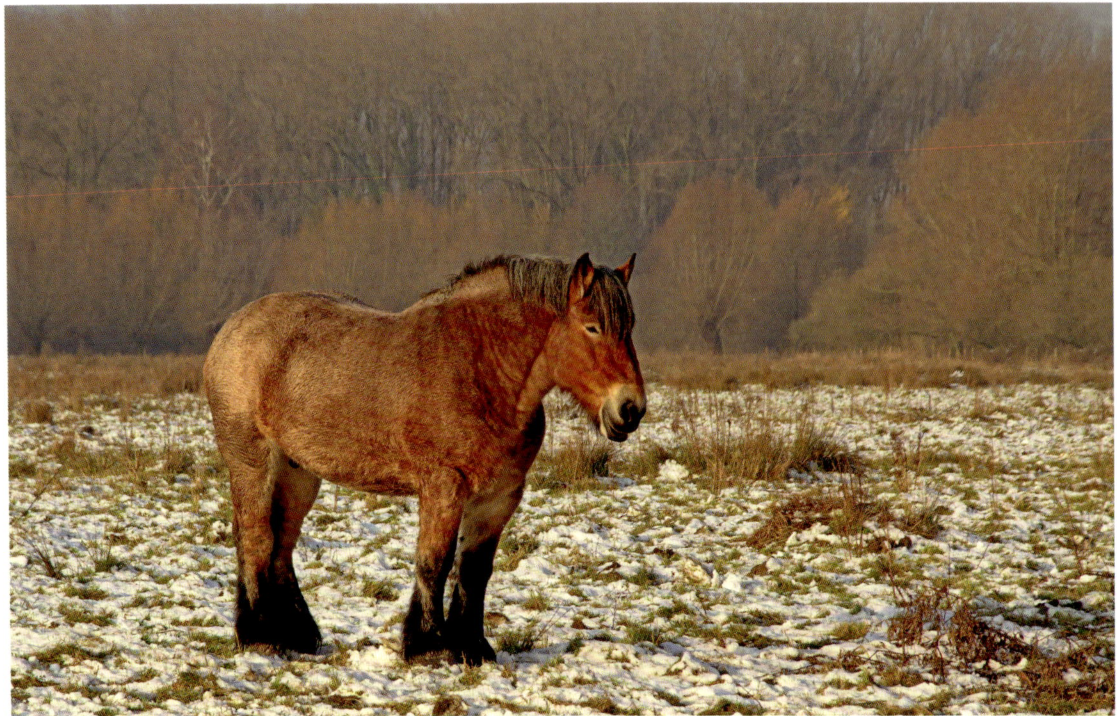

Begian Draft Horse
Belgisch trekpaard
Trait belge

Belgian Draft Horse

The Belgian Coldblood, one of the oldest coldblood breeds in Europe, was very popular as a workhorse because of its enormous traction and willingness to learn, leading to its export all over the world. With increased motorization, it was made redundant, and today the gentle Belgians find more and more devotees as robust and long-lived leisure horses.

Caballo de Flandes

El caballo belga de tiro, una de las razas de sangre fría más antiguas de Europa, era muy popular como caballo de batalla debido a su enorme fuerza de tracción y voluntad de aprender, y fue exportado a todo el mundo. Con el aumento de la motorización dejó de necesitarse. Hoy en día estos amables caballos belgas, que son caballos de ocio robustos y longevos, encuentran cada vez más entusiastas.

Le cheval flamand

Le trait belge est l'une des plus anciennes races de chevaux à sang froid d'Europe. Jadis, on aimait ce cheval de trait pour son énorme traction et sa volonté d'apprendre ; il était exporté dans le monde entier. Avec l'arrivée de la motorisation, on eut de moins en moins recours à lui. Aujourd'hui, ces doux chevaux belges ont toujours plus d'adeptes, qui voient en eux des animaux forts, adaptés aux loisirs et qui vivent longtemps.

Cavalo da Flandres

O cavalo belga de sangue frio, uma das raças de sangue frio mais antigas da Europa, era muito popular como cavalo de batalha devido à sua enorme tração e vontade de aprender e foi exportado para o mundo todo. Com a crescente motorização, já não era necessário. Hoje em dia, os gentis belgas, encontram cada vez mais amantes, como cavalos de lazer robustos e duradouros.

Flanderns Pferd

Das Belgische Kaltblut, eine der ältesten Kaltblutrassen Europas, war wegen seiner enormen Zugkraft und Lernwilligkeit als Arbeitspferd sehr begehrt und wurde in die ganze Welt exportiert. Mit der zunehmenden Motorisierung wurde es nicht mehr gebraucht. Heute finden die sanftmütigen Belgier als robuste und langlebige Freizeitpferde zunehmend Liebhaber.

Paard van Vlaanderen

Het Belgische koudbloed, één van de oudste koudbloedrassen in Europa, was als werkpaard erg populair vanwege de enorme trekkracht en leergierigheid en werd wereldwijd geëxporteerd. Met de toenemende motorisering werd het niet langer gebruikt. Vandaag de dag vinden deze zachtmoedige Belgen als robuuste en langlevende vrijetijdspaarden meer en meer liefhebbers.

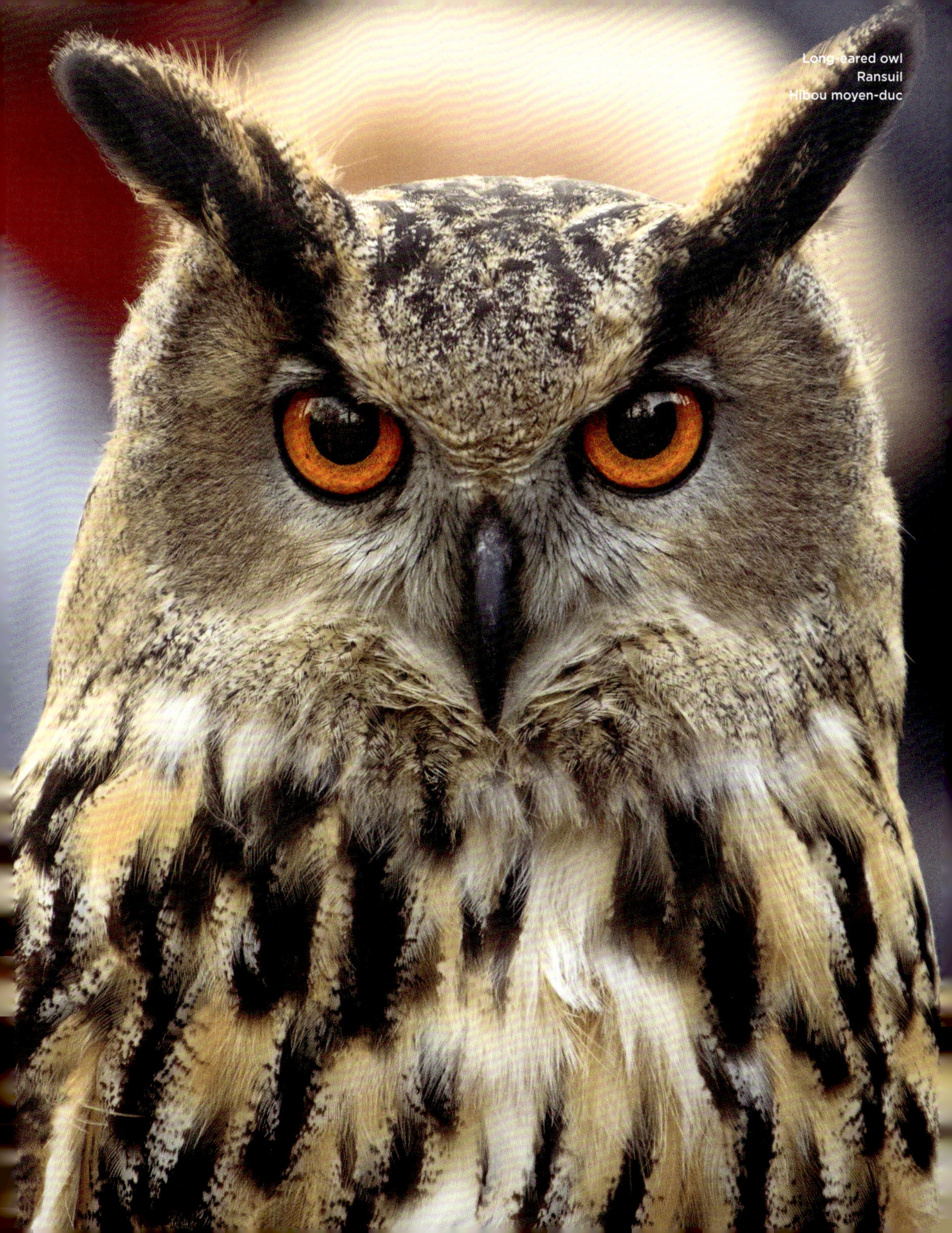

Long-eared owl
Ransuil
Hibou moyen-duc

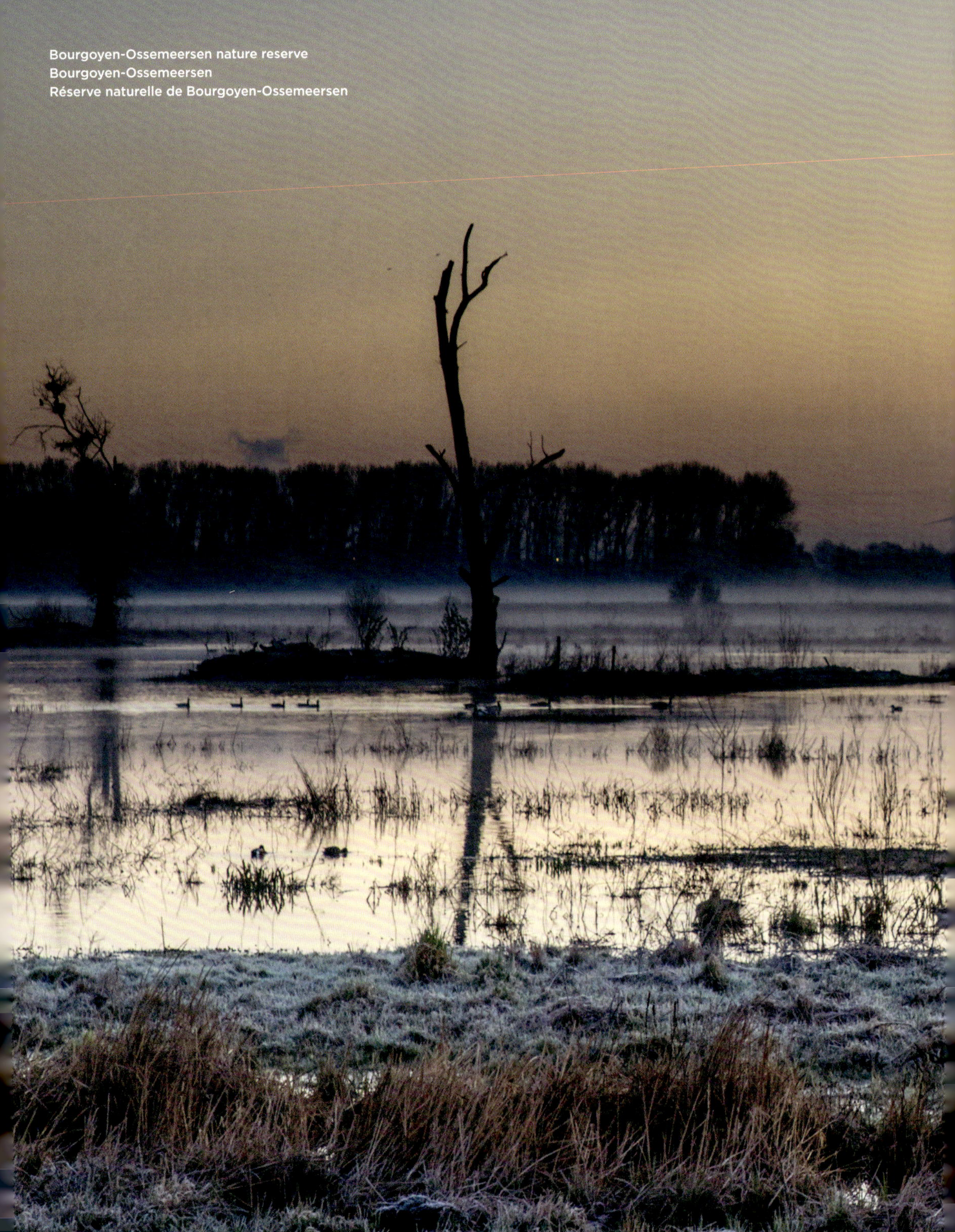

Bourgoyen-Ossemeersen nature reserve
Bourgoyen-Ossemeersen
Réserve naturelle de Bourgoyen-Ossemeersen

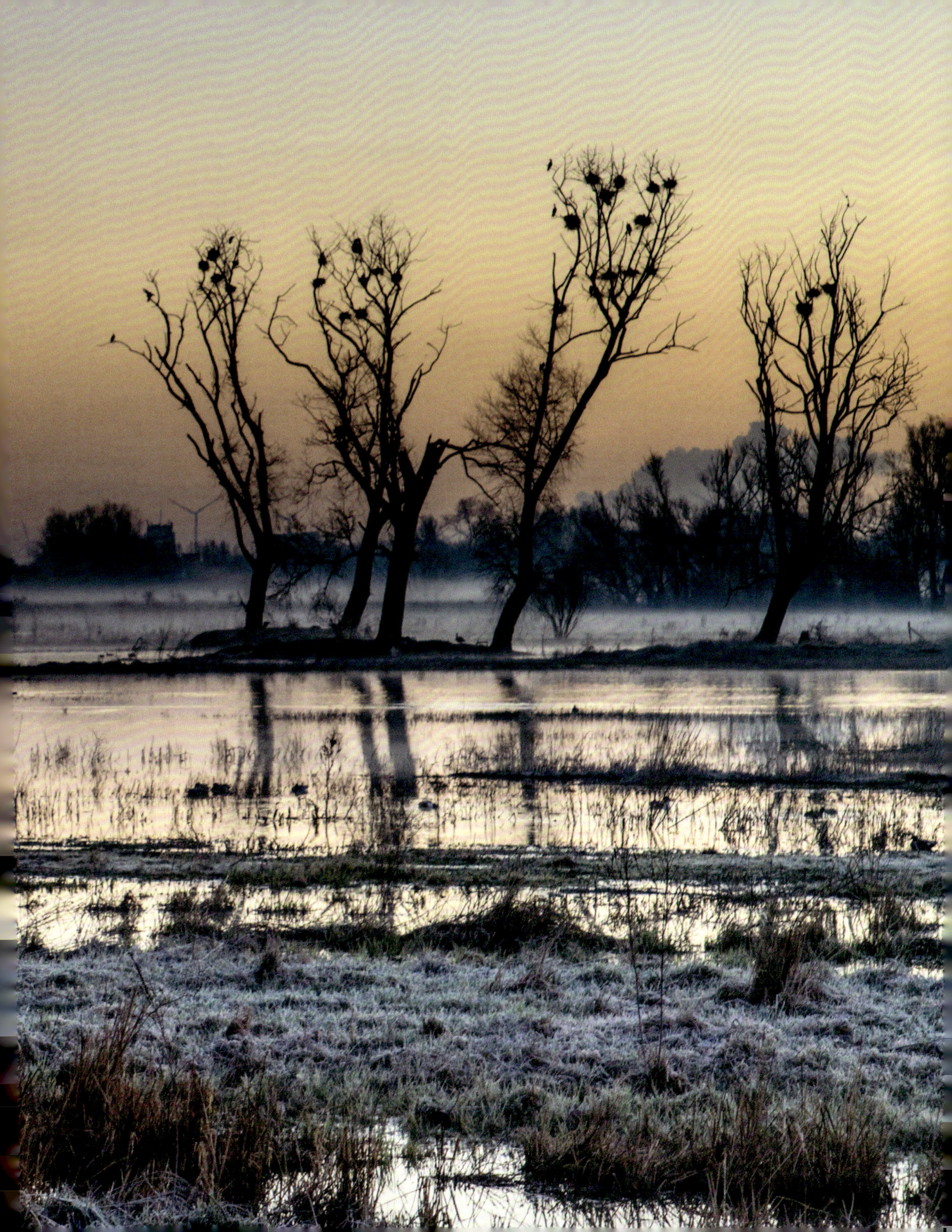

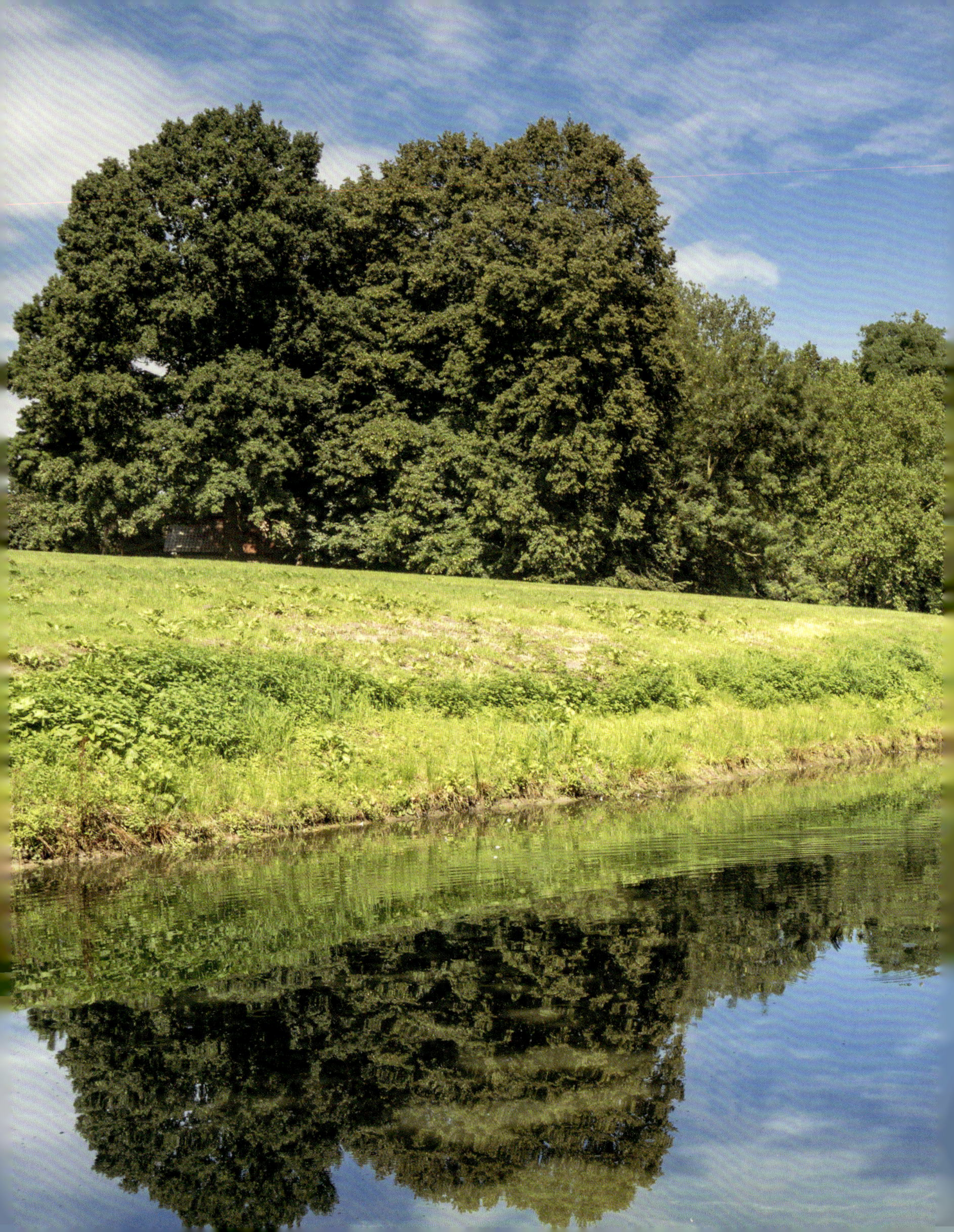

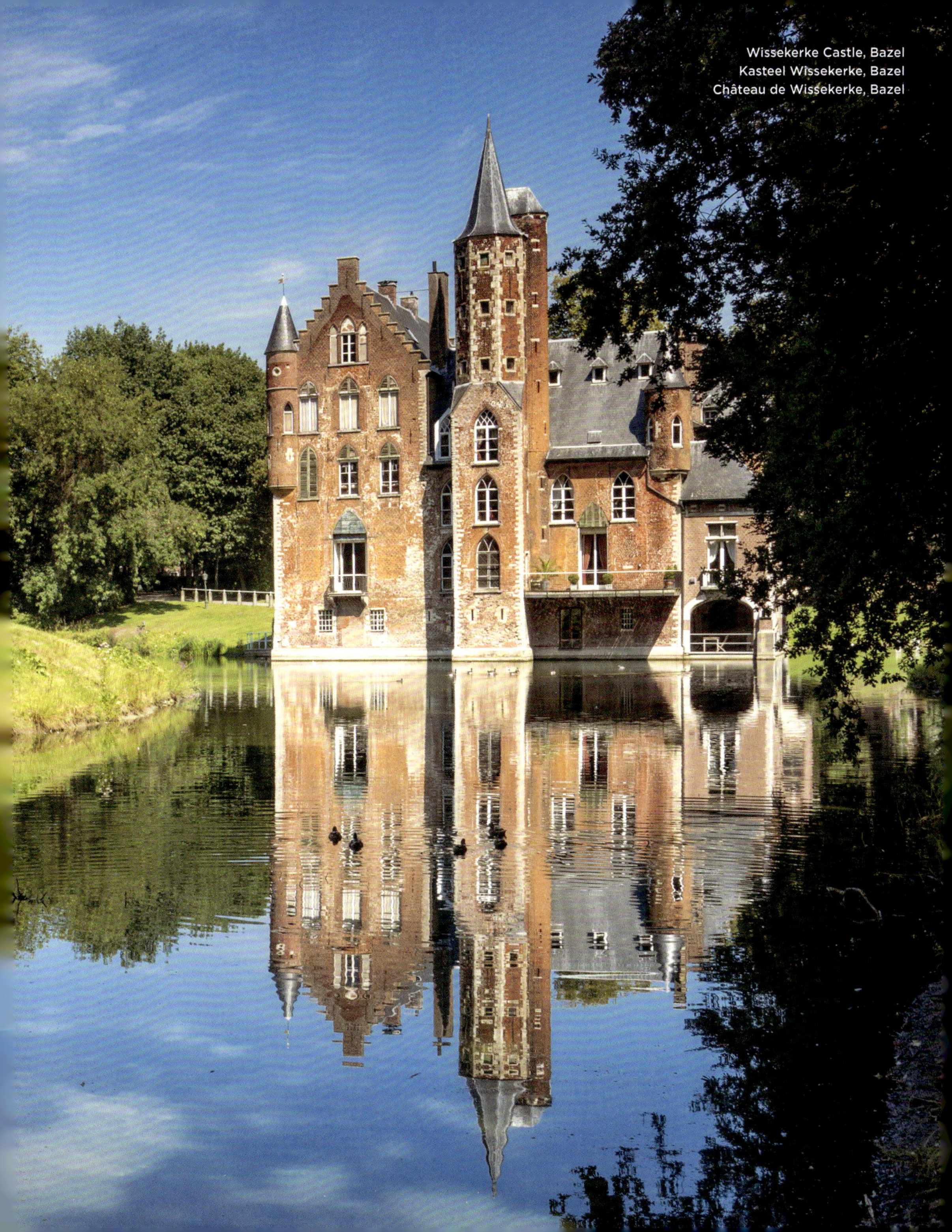
Wissekerke Castle, Bazel
Kasteel Wissekerke, Bazel
Château de Wissekerke, Bazel

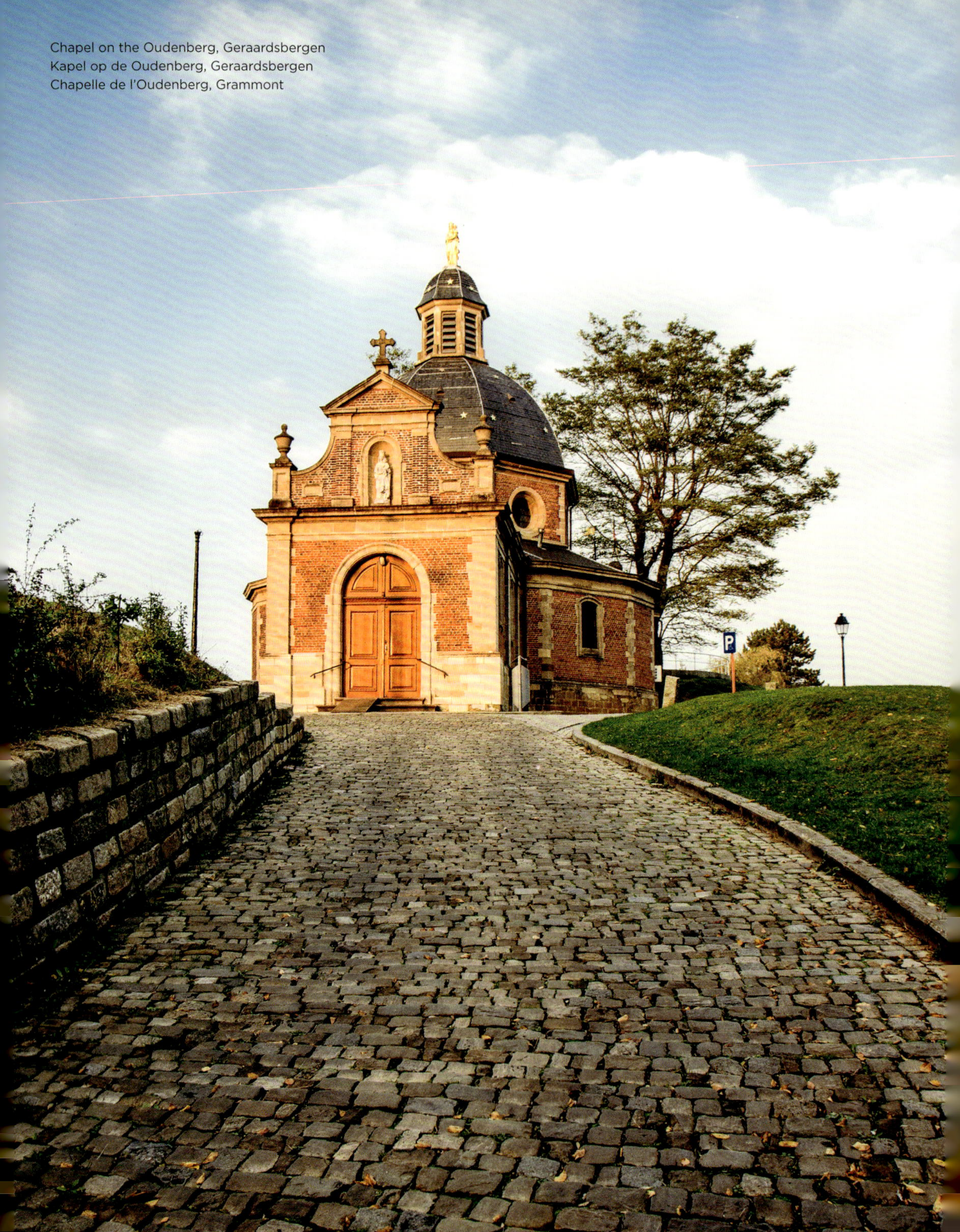

Chapel on the Oudenberg, Geraardsbergen
Kapel op de Oudenberg, Geraardsbergen
Chapelle de l'Oudenberg, Grammont

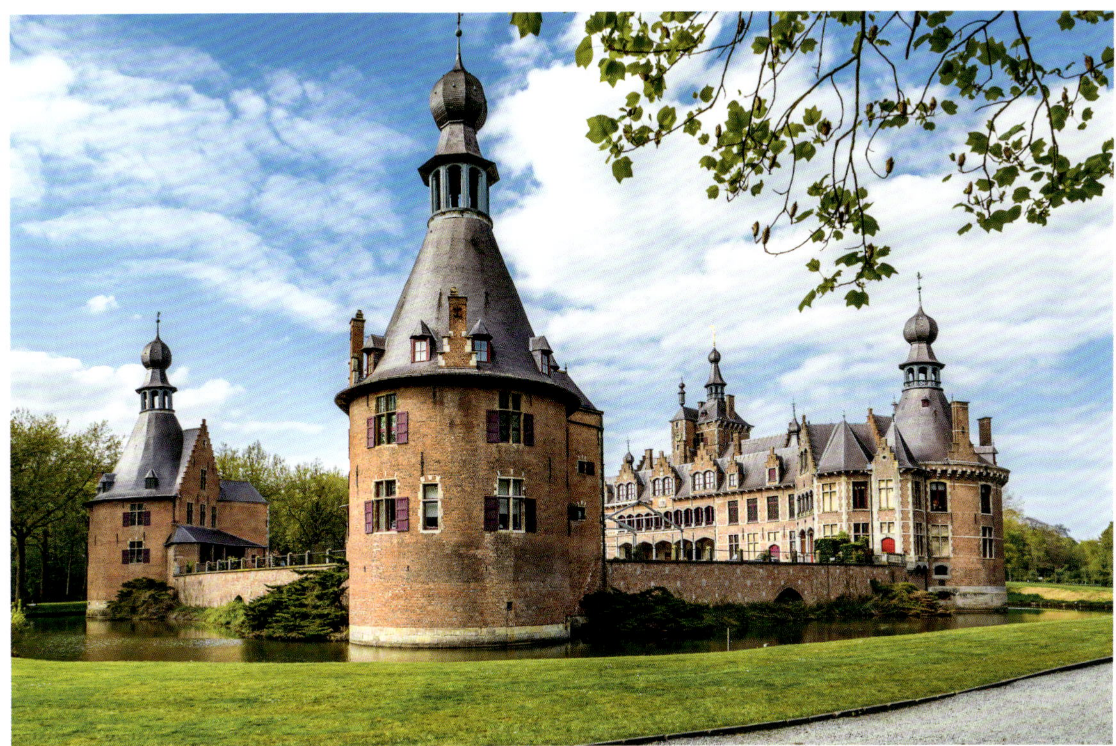

Ooidonk Castle, Deinze
Kasteel van Ooidonk, Deinze
Château d'Ooidonk, Deinze

Moated castle on the river Leie

Ooidonk, the Renaissance-style castle with its onion domes, graceful stone staircase and castle park is one of the most beautiful in Flanders. The massive towers hint at fortified and warlike times. The moated castle is still inhabited by a real count. The furniture and art objects inside are particularly worth seeing.

Château à douves au bord de la Lys

Avec ses tours à bulbe, son délicat escalier de pierre et son parc, le château d'Ooidonk, qui date de la Renaissance, est l'un des plus beaux des Flandres. Ses tours massives témoignent d'une époque guerrière où il était nécessaire de se défendre. Entouré de douves, le château est encore habité par un vrai comte. Les meubles et objets d'art à l'intérieur valent particulièrement le détour.

Wasserschloss an der Leie

Ooidonk, das Renaissance-Schloss mit den Zwiebeltürmchen, der zierlichen Steintreppe und dem Schlosspark zählt zu den schönsten Flanderns. Die wuchtigen Türme zeugen von Wehrhaftigkeit und kriegerischen Zeiten. Das Wasserschloss wird auch heute noch von einem echten Grafen bewohnt. Sehenswert sind insbesondere die Möbel und Kunstgegenstände in Innern.

Castillo rodeado de agua en el río Leie

Ooidonk, el castillo renacentista con sus cúpulas de cebolla, la elegante escalera de piedra y el parque del castillo es uno de los más bellos de Flandes. Las enormes torres son testigos de tiempos fortificados y de guerra. El castillo rodeado de agua todavía está habitado por un conde real. Los muebles y objetos de arte en su interior son especialmente dignos de ser vistos.

Castelo d'água no rio Leie

Ooidonk, o castelo renascentista com suas cúpulas em forma de cebola, a graciosa escadaria de pedra e com o parque do castelo é considerado um dos mais belos da Flandres. As enormes torres são testemunhas de tempos fortificados e bélicos. O castelo d'água ainda é habitado por uma contagem real. Os móveis e objetos de arte no interior são especialmente dignos de serem vistos.

Waterburcht aan de Leie

Ooidonk, het renaissancekasteel met zijn uivormige torens, de sierlijke stenen trap en het kasteelpark is één van de mooiste van Vlaanderen. De massieve torens getuigen van een strijdbaarheid en krijgszuchtige tijden. De waterburcht wordt nog steeds bewoond door een echte graaf. Vooral de meubels en kunstvoorwerpen binnenin zijn de moeite waard.

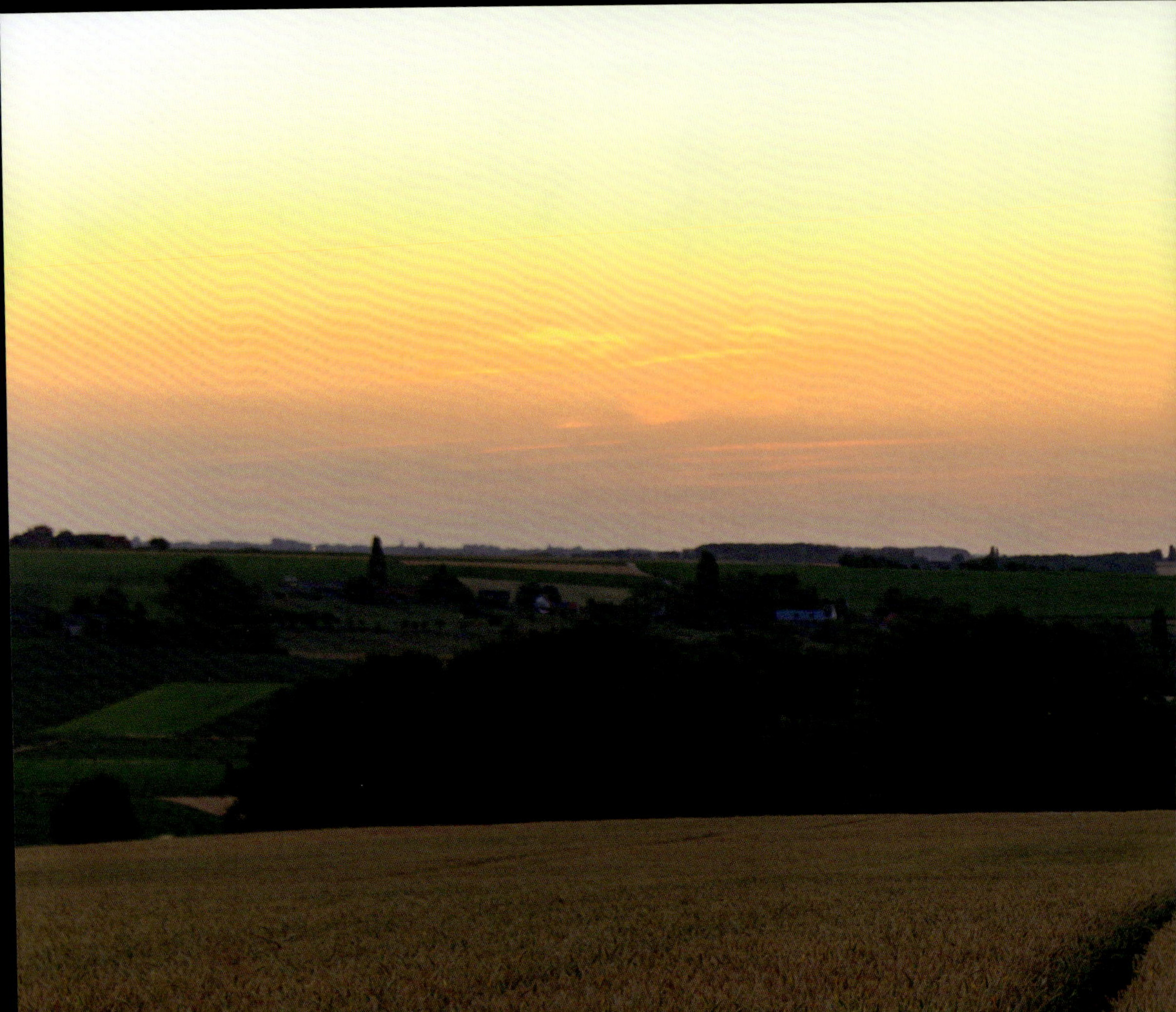

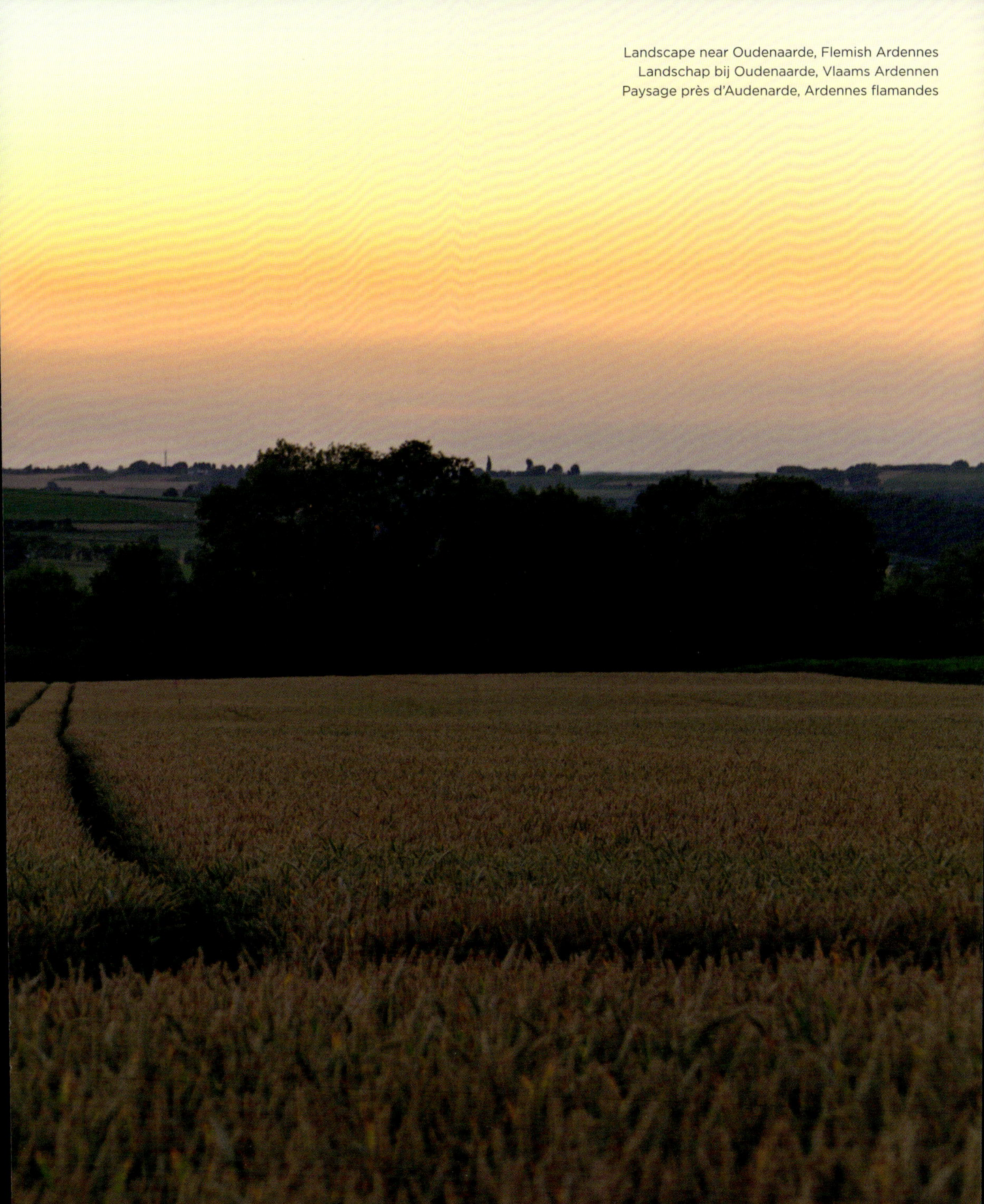
Landscape near Oudenaarde, Flemish Ardennes
Landschap bij Oudenaarde, Vlaams Ardennen
Paysage près d'Audenarde, Ardennes flamandes

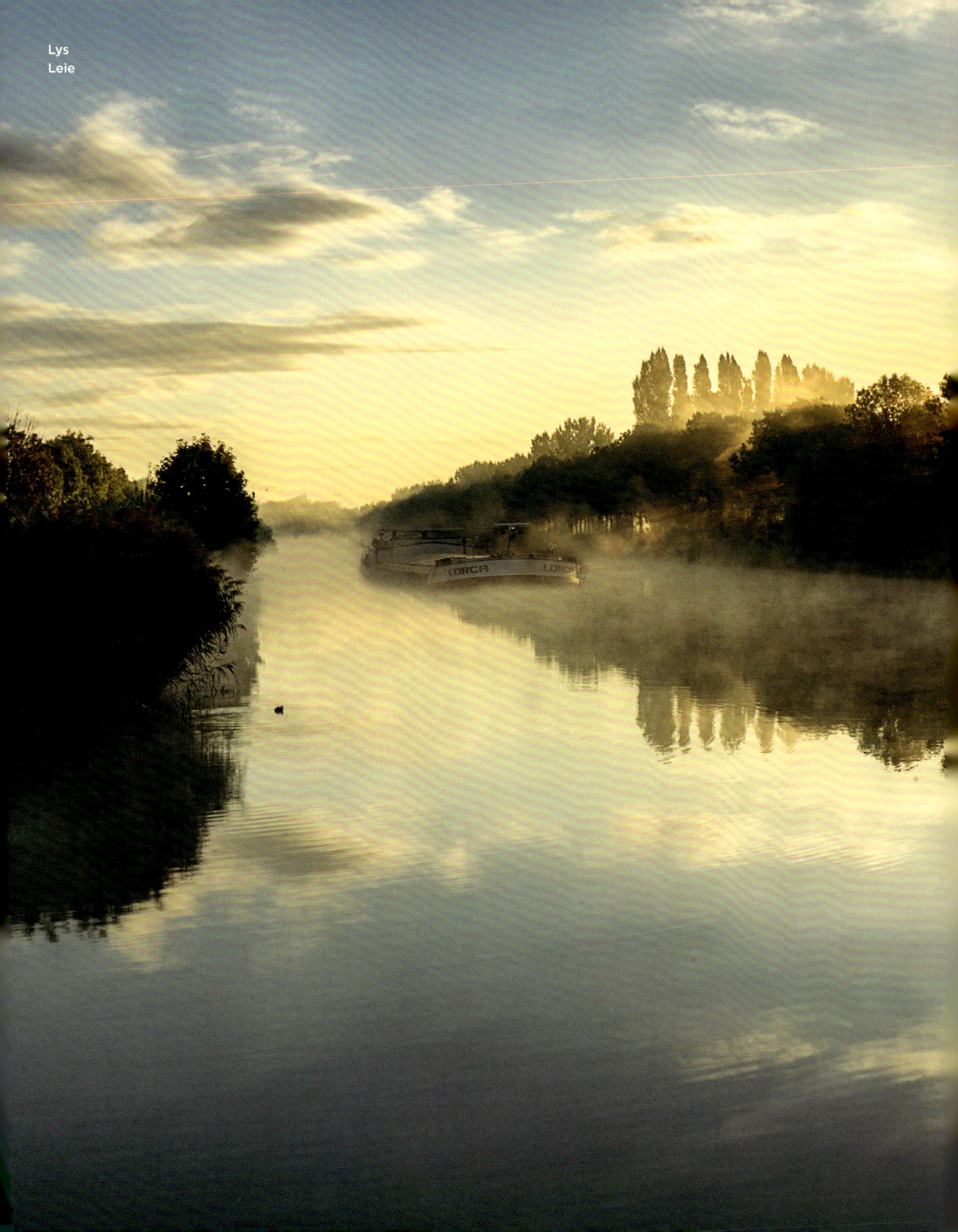
Lys
Leie

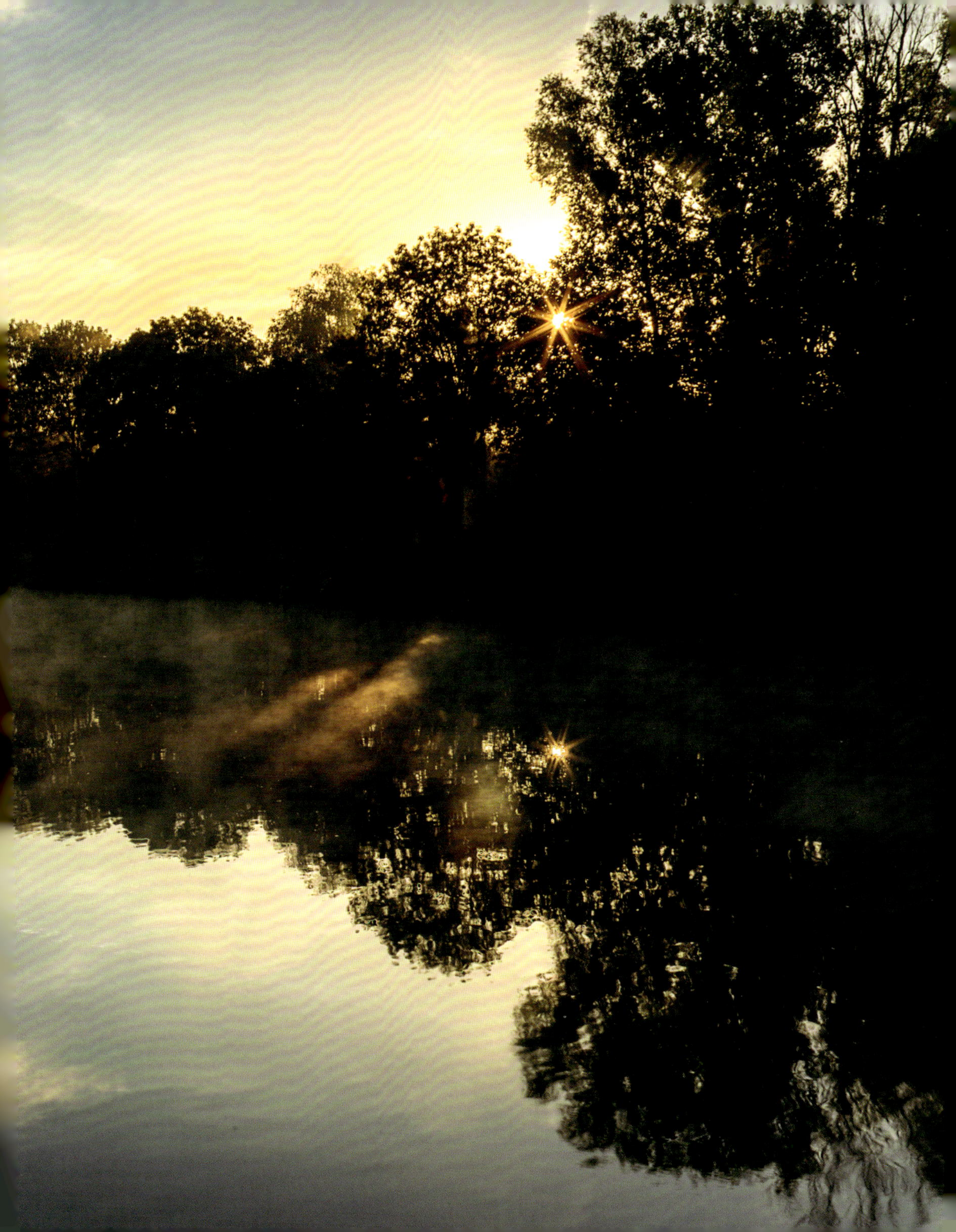

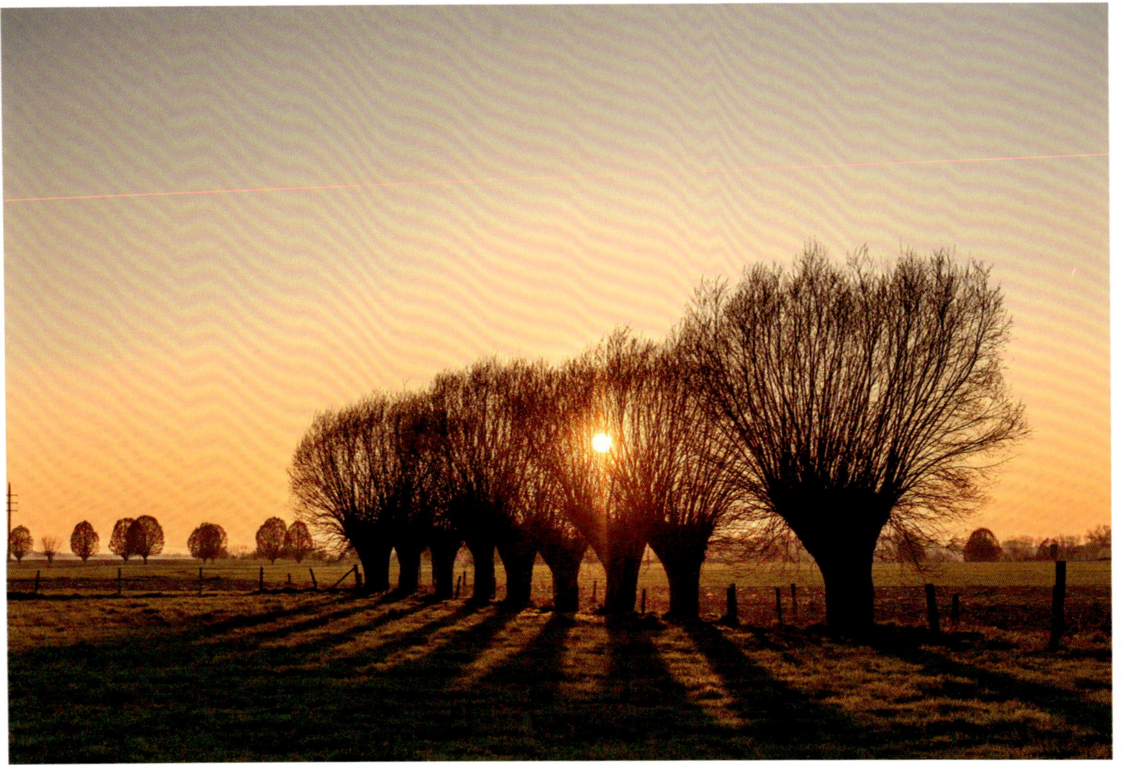

Rural landscape
Rustiek landschap
Paysage rural

Linen and the Golden River

The low-lime river water of the Leie was ideally suited for the so-called retting of the flax stems. After several weeks the linen takes on a golden shimmer. Thanks to the wealth which this work brought, the Leie also became known as the "Golden River". The Leie was also an inexhaustible source of inspiration for many painters and artists.

Lin et rivière dorée

Avec sa faible teneur en calcaire, l'eau de la Lys se prêtait à merveille au rouissage des tiges de lin. Au bout de plusieurs semaines, le lin prenait un reflet doré. La Lys doit son surnom de «rivière dorée» à la prospérité apportée par ce travail. Mais elle était aussi une source d'inspiration inépuisable pour les peintres et les artistes.

Leinen und goldener Fluss

Das kalkarme Flusswasser der Leie eignete sich ideal zum sogenannten Rösten der Flachsstängel. Nach mehreren Wochen bekam das Leinen einen goldenen Schimmer. Dank des Wohlstands, den diese Arbeit hervorbrachte, wurde der Beiname „Goldener Fluss" zu einem festen Begriff. Aber auch für Maler und Künstler war die Leie eine unerschöpfliche Inspirationsquelle.

Lino y río dorado

El agua del río Leie con bajo contenido de cal era ideal para el llamado tostado de los tallos de lino. Después de varias semanas, el lino adquiría un brillo dorado. Gracias a la prosperidad que produjo este trabajo, el apodo "río dorado " se convirtió en un nombre muy conocido. Pero el río fue también una fuente inagotable de inspiración para pintores y artistas.

Linho e rio dourado

A água de baixo cálcário do rio Leie era ideal para a chamada torrefação dos caules de linho. Depois de várias semanas, o linho ficava com um brilho dourado. Graças à prosperidade que este trabalho produziu, a alcunha "Rio Dourado" se tornou um nome familiar. Mas o rio era também uma fonte inesgotável de inspiração para pintores e artistas.

Linnen en gouden rivier

Het riverwater van de Leie heeft weinig kalk en was ideaal voor het zogenaamde roosteren van de vlasstengels. Na enkele weken kreeg het linnen een gouden glans. Dankzij de welvaart die dit werk opleverde, werd de bijnaam "Gouden Rivier" een begrip. Maar de rivier was ook een onuitputtelijke bron van inspiratie voor schilders en kunstenaars.

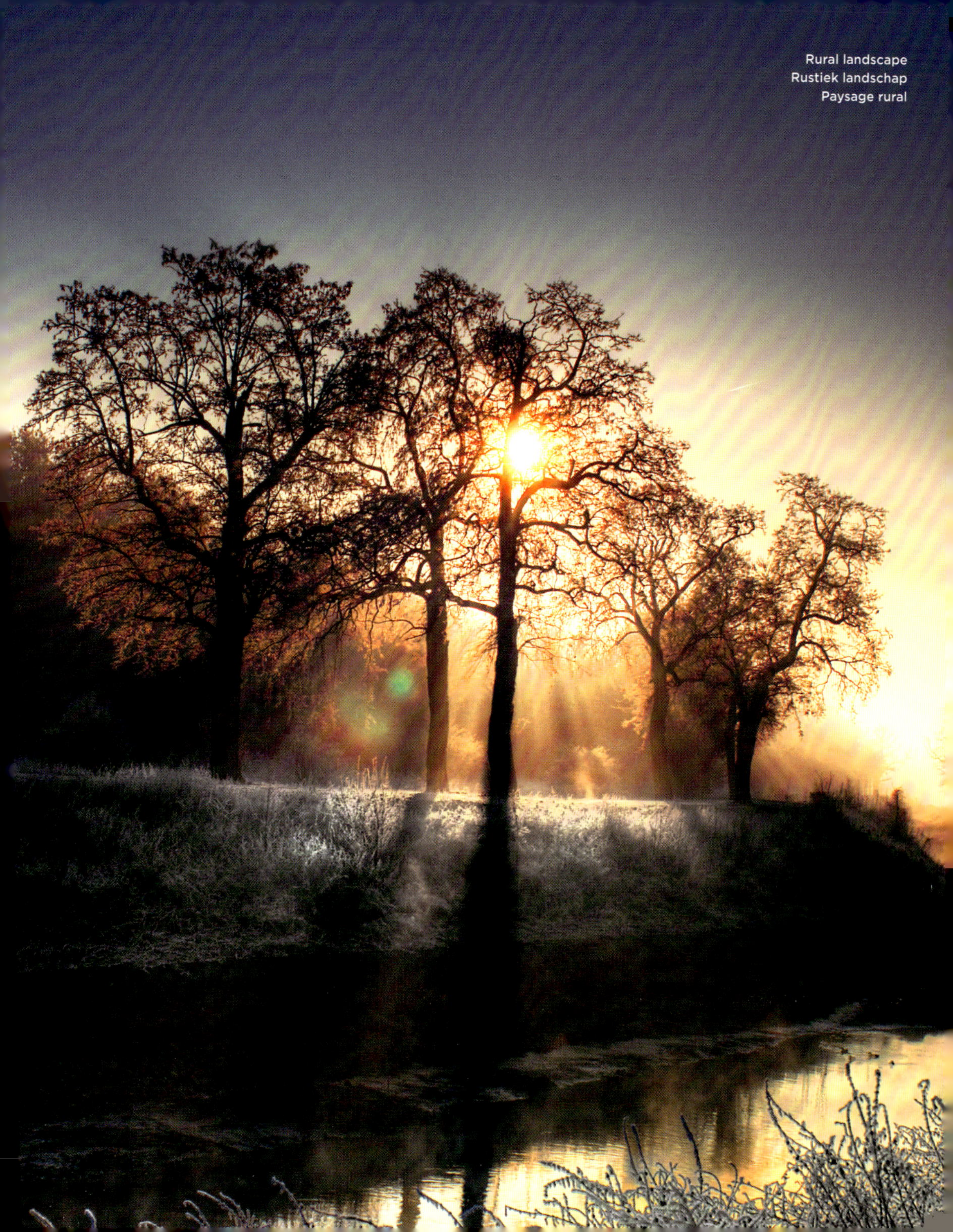
Rural landscape
Rustiek landschap
Paysage rural

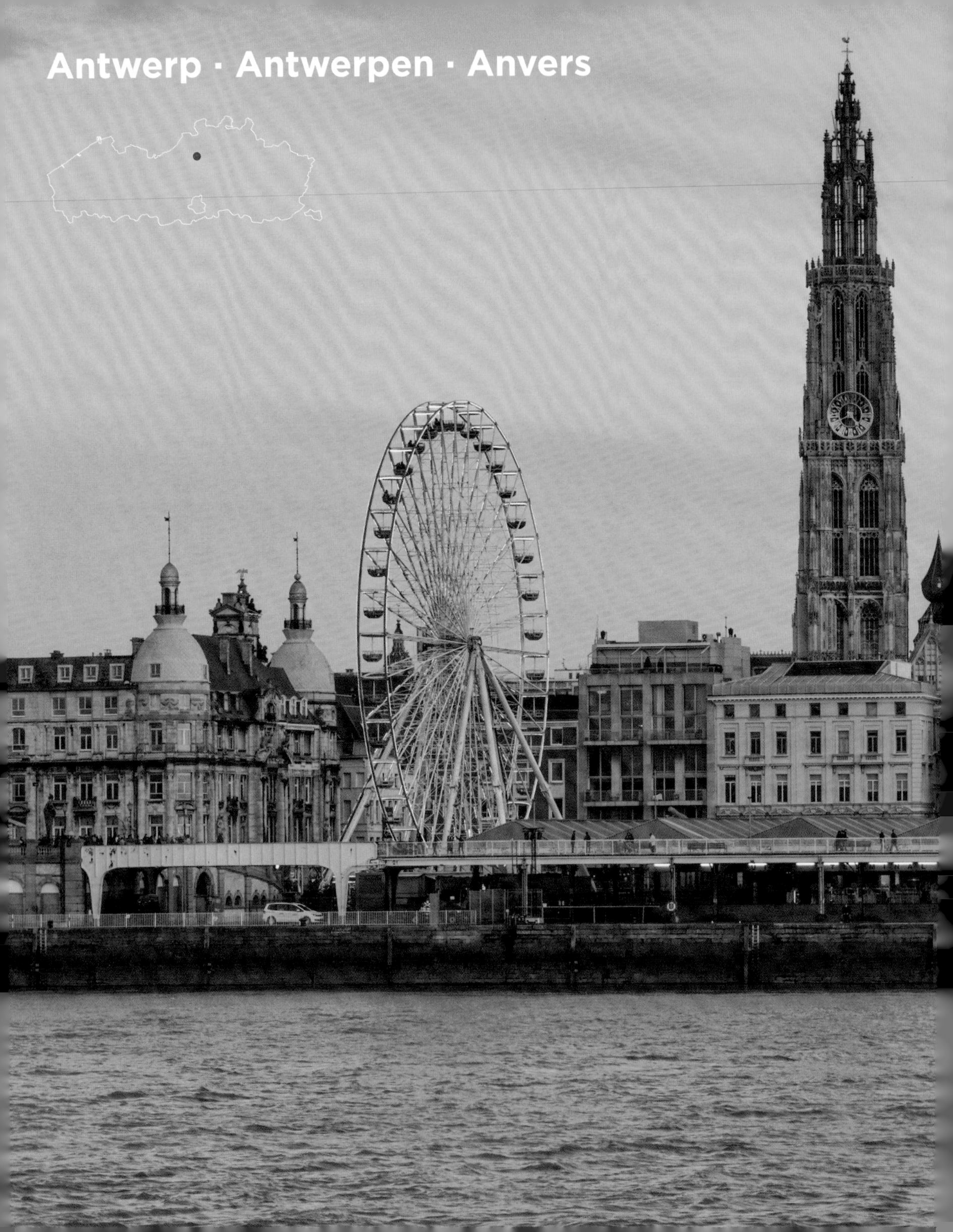
Antwerp · Antwerpen · Anvers

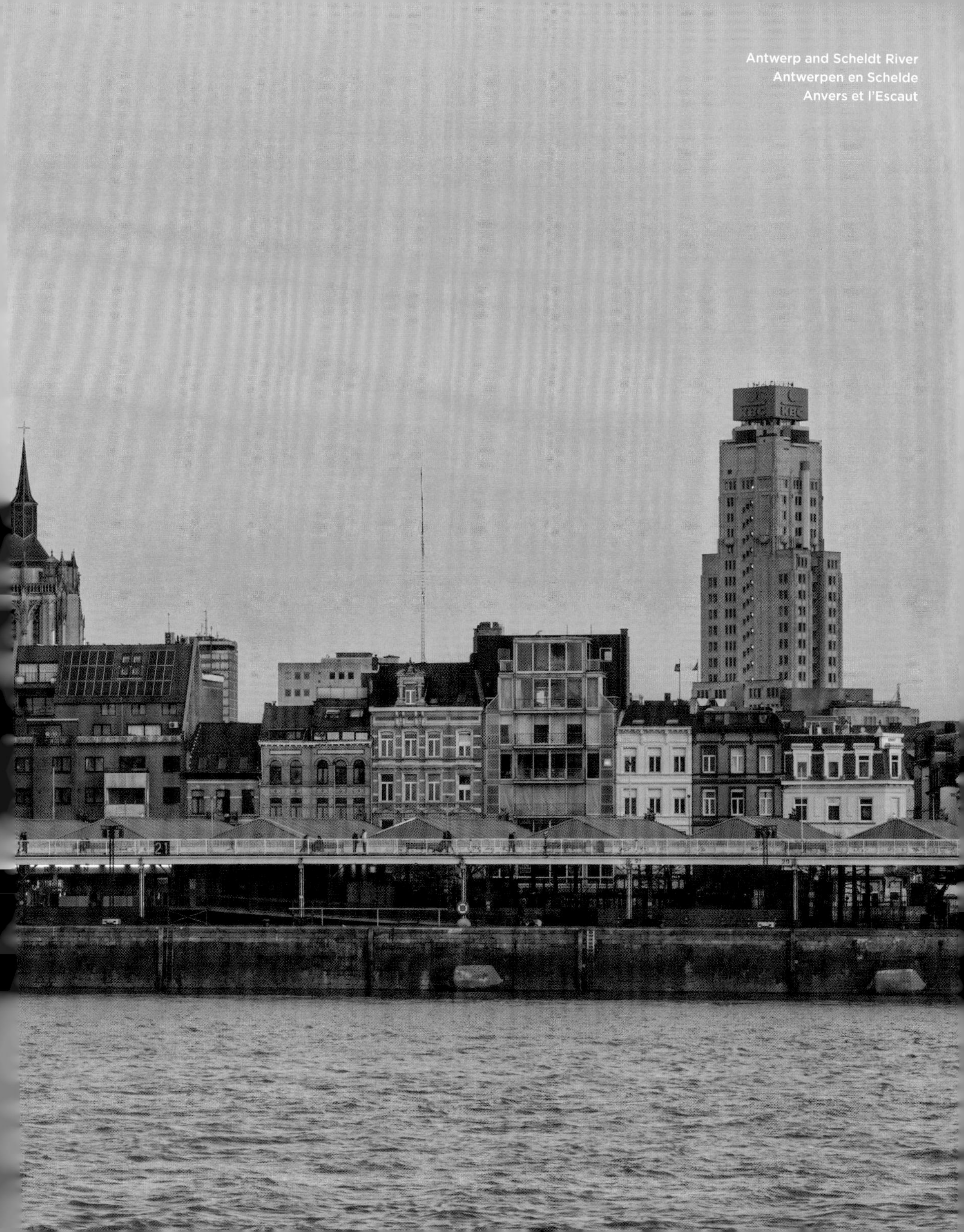
Antwerp and Scheldt River
Antwerpen en Schelde
Anvers et l'Escaut

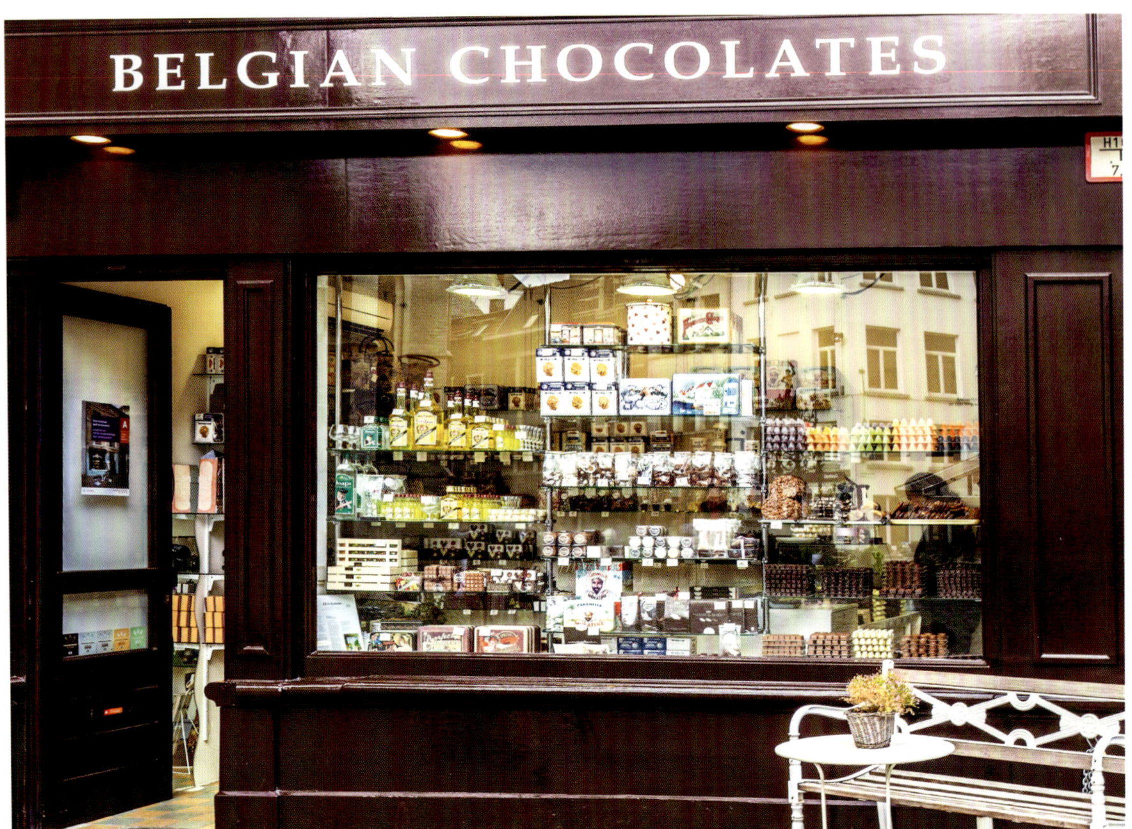

Chocolate Shop
Chocoladewinkel
Chocolaterie

Antwerp

Antwerp has been the world's largest diamond center for over five centuries. Even the products in the chocolate factories and in the experience museum "Chocolate Nation" have the shape of diamonds. Another curiosity is the hands made of chocolate or marzipan. The hand is the symbol of Antwerp, and "throwing hands" in Dutch translates to "handwerpen", which in turn sounds like Antwerp. Legend has it that the hero Silvius Brabo cut off the hand of an evil giant and threw it into the Scheldt river. A more diplomatic and well-known hero is the painter Peter Paul Rubens, who left many traces in his city.

Anvers

Cela fait plus de cinq siècles qu'Anvers est le plus grand centre de diamants au monde. Même les pralines des chocolateries et du musée expérimental Chocolate Nation en adoptent la forme. Autre curiosité : les mains en chocolat ou en pâte d'amande. La main est le symbole d'Anvers. Le nom néerlandais d'Anvers, « Antwerpen », provient du mot « handwerpen » ou jet de la main. La légende raconte que le héros Brabo aurait coupé la main d'un géant maléfique et l'aurait jetée dans l'Escaut. Autre héros plus diplomatique et plus connu, le génie de la peinture Pierre Paul Rubens a laissé de nombreuses traces dans sa ville.

Antwerpen

Seit über fünf Jahrhunderten ist Antwerpen das größte Diamantenzentrum der Welt. Sogar die Pralinen in den Chocolaterien und im Erlebnismuseum „Chocolate Nation" haben die Form von Brillanten. Eine weitere Kuriosität sind die Hände aus Schokolade oder Marzipan. Die Hand ist das Symbol Antwerpens. Handwerfen auf Niederländisch „handwerpen" hört sich wie Antwerpen an. Der Legende nach schnitt der Held Brabo einem bösen Riesen die Hand ab und warf sie über die Schelde. Ein diplomatischerer und bekannter Held ist der Malerfürst Peter Paul Rubens, der in seiner Stadt viele Spuren hinterlassen hat.

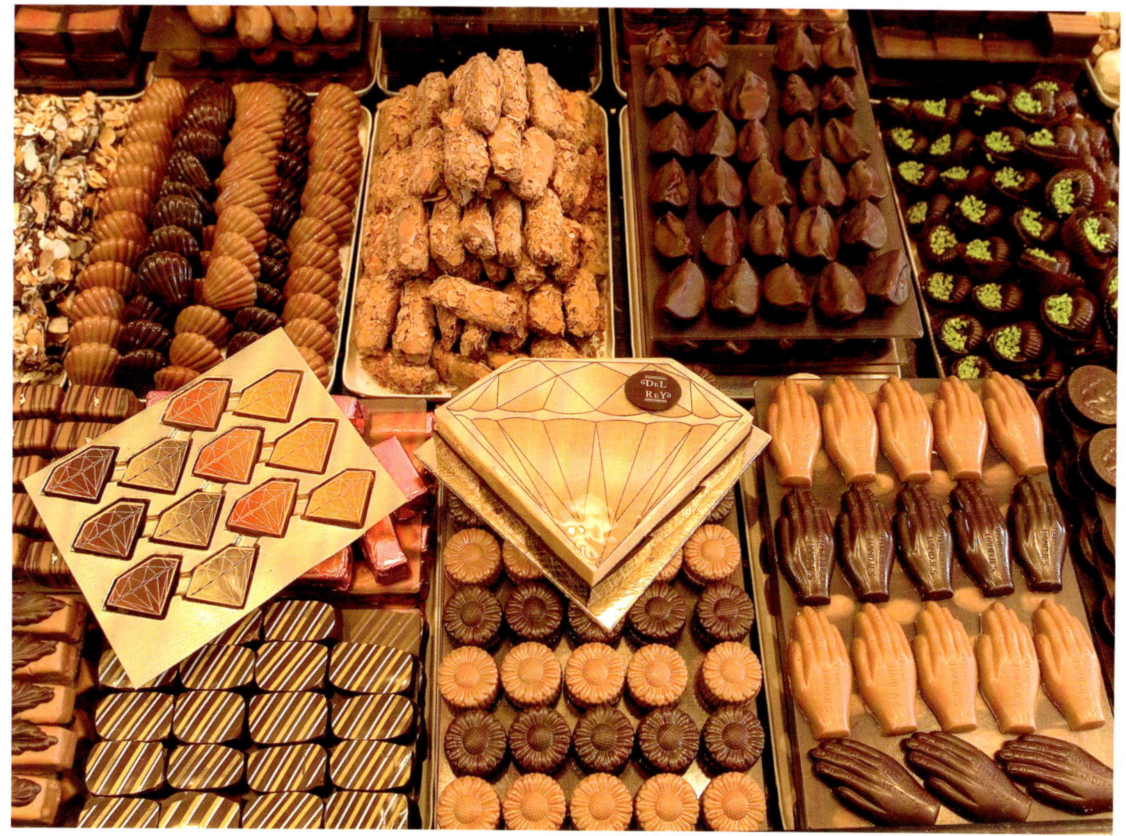

Belgian Chocolate
Belgische chocolade
Chocolat belge

Amberes

Amberes ha sido el mayor centro de diamantes del mundo desde hace más de cinco siglos. Incluso los chocolates en las chocolaterías y en el museo de la aventura "Chocolate Nation" tienen forma de diamantes. Otra curiosidad son las manos hechas de chocolate o mazapán. La mano es el símbolo de Amberes. Lanzar las manos en holandés se dice "Handerpen", que suena parecido a Amberes. Cuenta la leyenda que el héroe Brabo le cortó la mano a un gigante malvado y la arrojó sobre el río Escalda. Un héroe más diplomático y conocido es el príncipe pintor Peter Paul Rubens, que dejó numerosas huellas en su ciudad.

Antuérpia

Antuérpia tem sido o maior centro de diamantes do mundo há mais de cinco séculos. Até mesmo os chocolates nas lojas de chocolate e no museu de aventura "Chocolate Nation" têm a forma de diamantes. Outra curiosidade são as mãos feitas de chocolate ou maçapão. A mão é o símbolo de Antuérpia. Atirar as mãos em holandês "handwerpen" soa como Antuérpia. A lenda diz que o herói Brabo cortou a mão de um gigante malvado e atirou-a sobre o rio Esclada. Um herói mais diplomático e conhecido é o pintor príncipe Peter Paul Rubens, que deixou muitos vestígios em sua cidade.

Antwerpen

Antwerpen is al meer dan vijf eeuwen 's werelds grootste diamantencentrum. Zelfs de pralinen in de chocolaterieën en in het belevingsmuseum "Chocolate Nation" hebben de vorm van diamanten. Een andere curiositeit zijn de handen van chocolade of marsepein. De hand is het symbool van Antwerpen. "Handwerpen" klinkt als Antwerpen. Volgens de legende sneed de held Brabo de hand van een kwaadaardige reus af en wierp die over de Schelde. Een meer diplomatieke en bekende held is de schilder Peter Paul Rubens die veel sporen in zijn stad heeft achtergelaten.

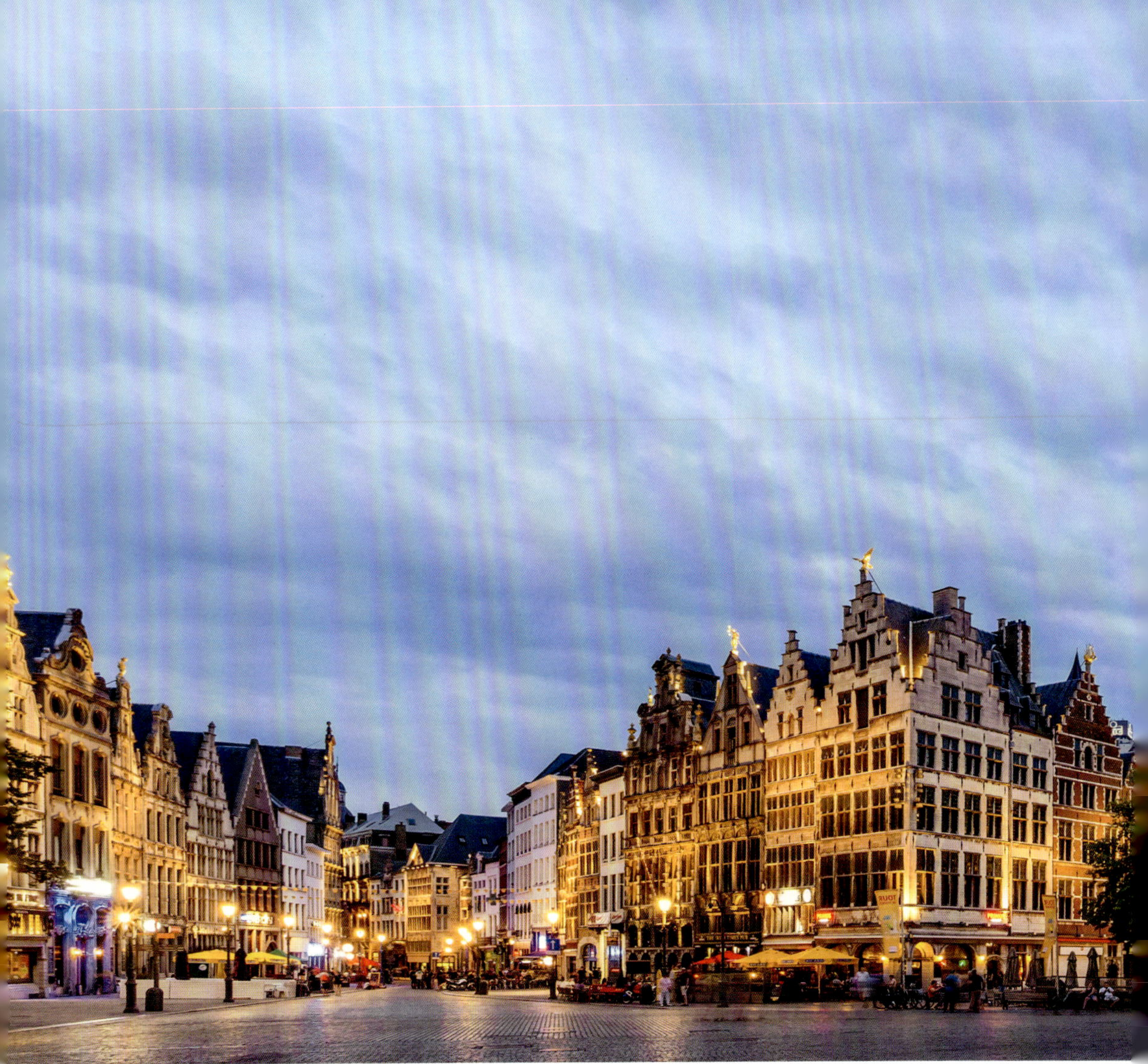

Cathedral of Our Lady

The filigreed cathedral is one of the highlights of Gothic architecture. Of the planned two-tower facade in the west, only the north tower was completed, but with its height of 123 m (403 ft) it rises above all other churches in Belgium and the Netherlands and houses several notable works of art, including four paintings by Peter Paul Rubens, who provided the most famous artworks within the church, *The Elevation of the Cross* and *The Descent from the Cross*.

Cathédrale Notre-Dame

La cathédrale finement ajourée fait partie des joyaux de l'architecture gothique. De la façade de deux tours prévue à l'ouest, seule la tour nord a été achevée, mais du haut de ses 123 m, elle surplombe toutes les églises de Belgique et des Pays-Bas. Aujourd'hui encore, la cathédrale possède diverses œuvres d'art, dont quatre tableaux de Pierre Paul Rubens. Le peintre fournit également à l'intérieur de l'église les œuvres retenant le plus l'attention : *L'Érection de la Croix* et *La Descente de la Croix*.

Liebfrauen-Kathedrale

Die filigrane Kathedrale zählt zu den Höhepunkten gotischer Baukunst. Von der geplanten Zweiturmfassade im Westen wurde nur der Nordturm vollendet, der allerdings mit seiner Höhe von 123 m alle Kirchen Belgiens und der Niederlande überragt. Noch heute ist sie im Besitz etlicher Kunstwerke, unter anderem vier Gemälde von Peter Paul Rubens. Der Maler sorgte auch für die größten Blickfänge innerhalb der Kirche: die *Kreuzaufrichtung* und die *Kreuzabnahme*.

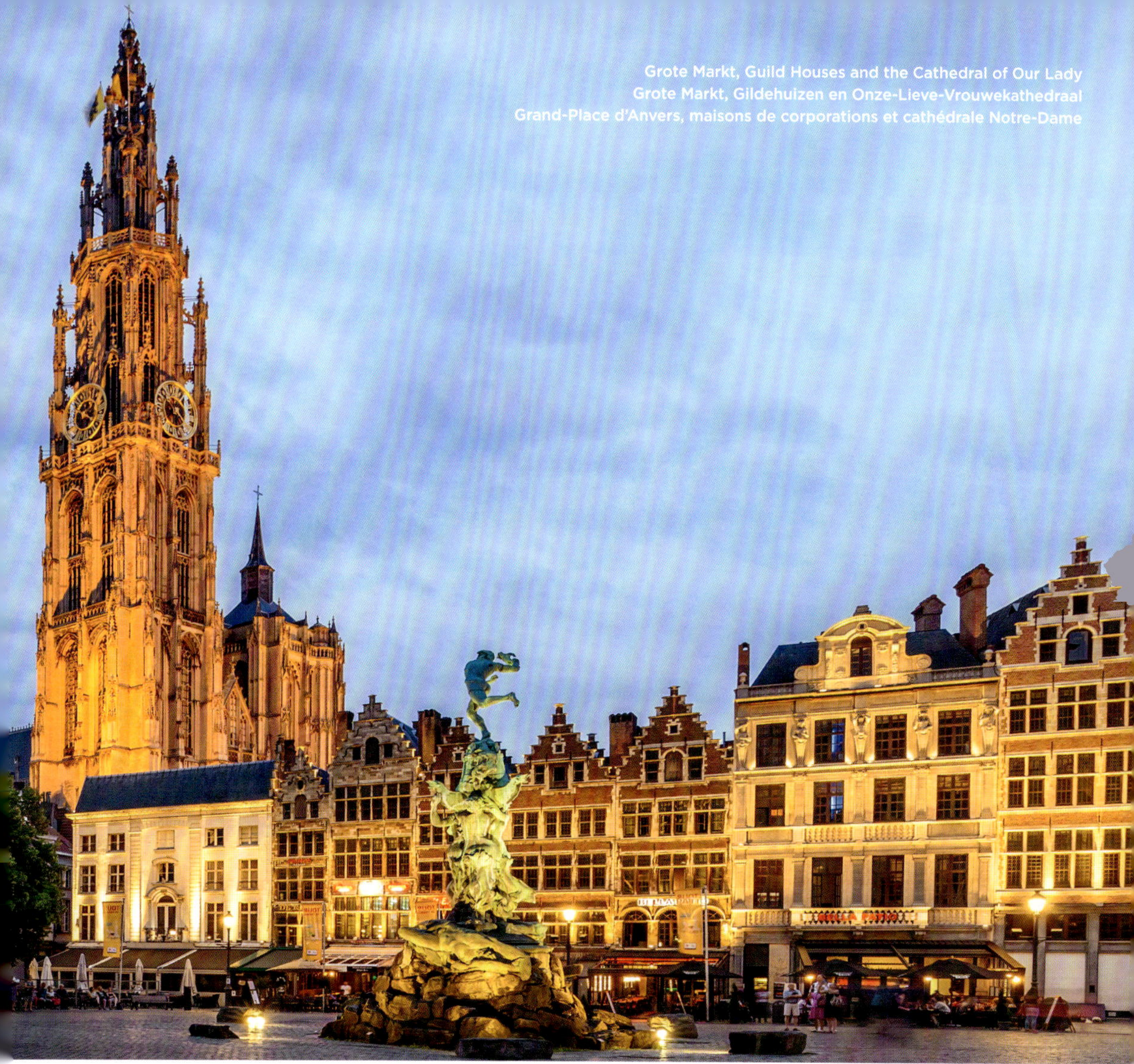

Catedral de Nuestra Señora

La filigrana catedral es uno de los puntos culminantes de la arquitectura gótica. De la fachada de dos torres proyectada en el oeste, solo se terminó la torre norte, pero con su altura de 123 m domina todas las iglesias de Bélgica y los Países Bajos. Aún hoy en día, sigue albergando varias obras de arte, incluyendo cuatro pinturas de Peter Paul Rubens. El pintor también fue el que más llamó la atención dentro de la iglesia: la *Elevación de la Cruz* y el *Descendimiento de la Cruz*.

Catedral de Nossa Senhora

A catedral de filigrana é um dos destaques da arquitetura gótica. Da fachada planejada de duas torres no oeste, apenas a torre norte foi concluída, mas com sua altura de 123 m impõe-se sobre todas as igrejas na Bélgica e na Holanda. Ainda hoje, ela possui várias obras de arte, incluindo quatro pinturas de Peter Paul Rubens. O pintor também foi responsável pelos maiores atrativos da igreja: a *Elevação da Cruz* e a *Deposição da Cruz*.

Onze-Lieve-Vrouwekathedraal

De sierlijke kathedraal is een van de hoogtepunten van de gotische architectuur. Van de geplande twee torens in het westen werd alleen de noordertoren voltooid, die met zijn hoogte van 123 m boven alle kerken in België en Nederland uitsteekt. Tot op de dag van vandaag is het nog steeds in het bezit van verschillende kunstwerken waaronder vier schilderijen van Peter Paul Rubens. De schilder zorgde ook voor de grootste blikvangers in de kerk: *De Kruisoprichting* en *De Kruisafneming*.

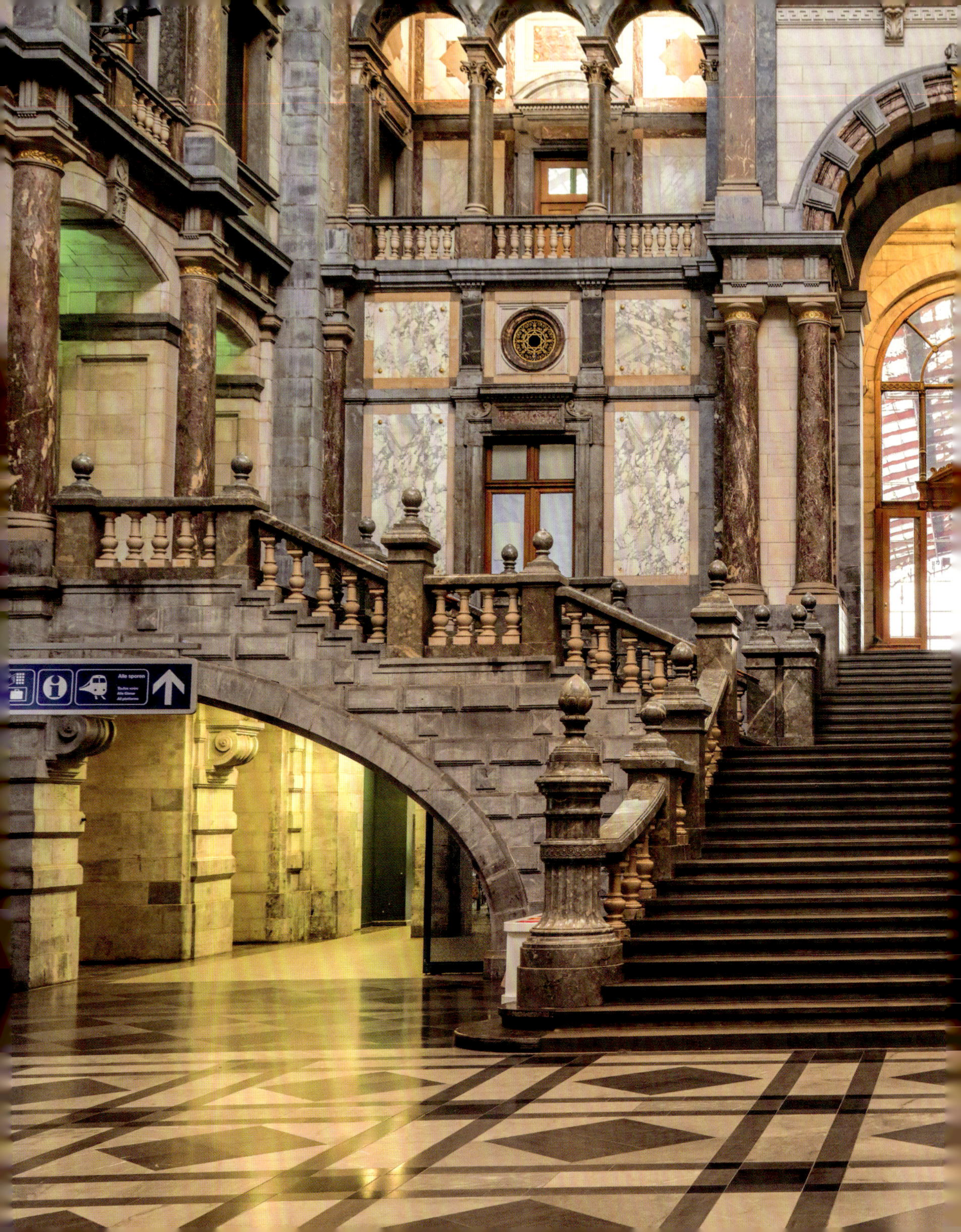
Alle sporen
Toutes voies
Alle Gleise
All platforms

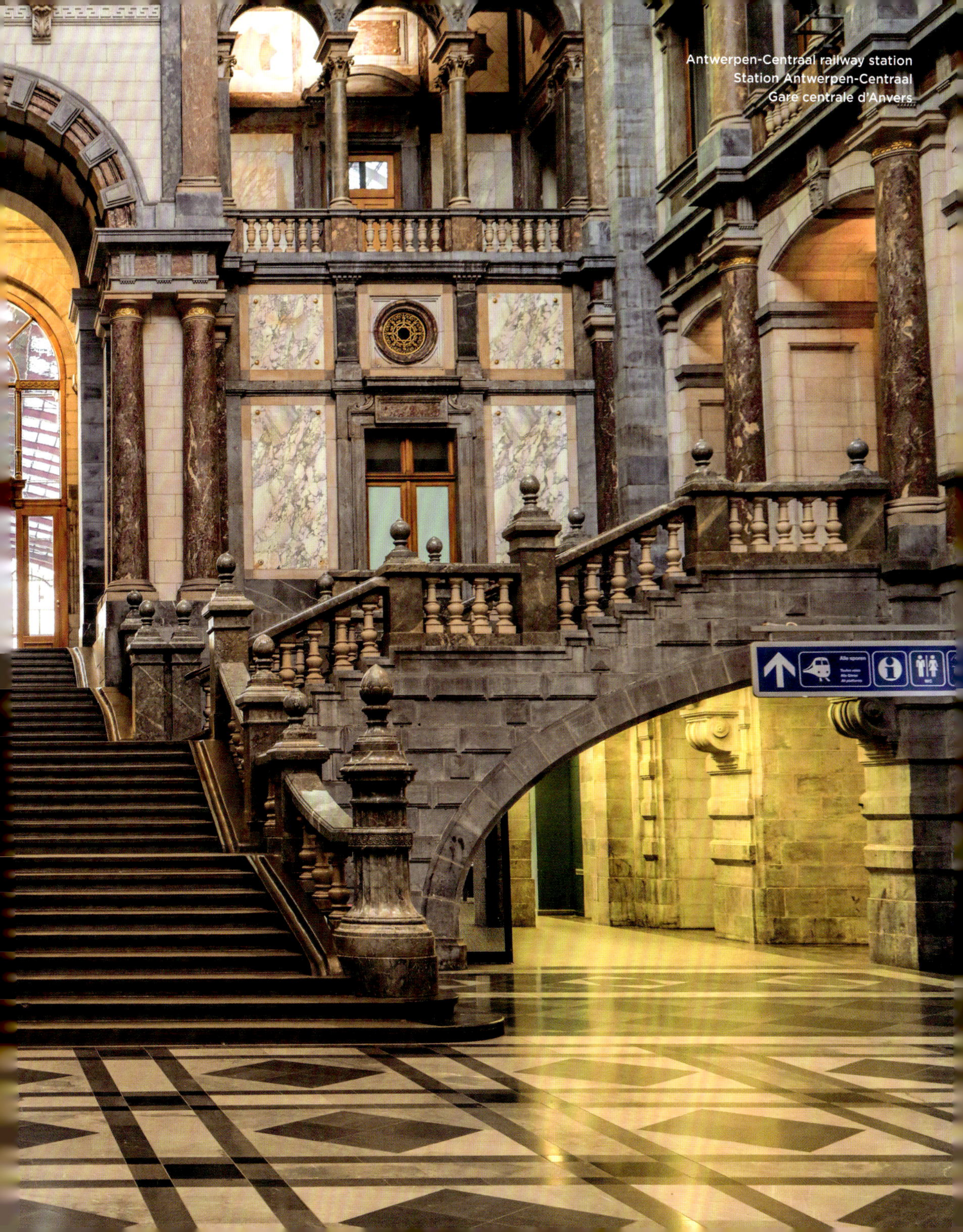

Antwerpen-Centraal railway station
Station Antwerpen-Centraal
Gare centrale d'Anvers

The railway station "cathedral"
The Neo-Renaissance Antwerp Central Station (built around 1899) is a magnificent monument to the Industrial Age. It is one of the most beautiful in the world and has become a popular backdrop for feature films. The opulent reception hall, made of marble, and the magnificent staircase are worthy of a castle. The eclectic secular building, with its dome, is also affectionately called the railway cathedral.

La cathédrale du rail
De style néo-Renaissance, la gare centrale d'Anvers (bâtie dès 1899) est un monument grandiose de l'ère industrielle. Décor fort prisé pour les longs métrages, elle compte parmi les plus belles gares du monde. L'opulent hall d'arrivée en marbre et le somptueux escalier sont dignes d'un château. Les Anversois ont affectueusement rebaptisé ce bâtiment séculier éclectique surmonté d'un dôme «la cathédrale du rail».

Bahnhofskathedrale
Antwerpens Zentralbahnhof im Stil der Neurenaissance (gebaut ab 1899) ist ein grandioses Denkmal des Industriezeitalters. Er zählt zu den schönsten der Welt und ist eine beliebte Kulisse für Spielfilme geworden. Die opulente Empfangshalle aus Marmor und die prunkvolle Treppe sind eines Schlosses würdig. Der eklektizistische Profanbau mit Domkuppel wird im Volksmund auch liebevoll Eisenbahnkathedrale genannt.

Catedral de trenes
La Estación Central Neorrenacentista de Amberes (construida a partir de 1899) es un magnífico monumento a la Edad Industrial. Es una de las más bellas del mundo y se ha convertido en un popular telón de fondo para largometrajes. El opulento salón de recepción de mármol y la magnífica escalera son dignos de un castillo. Este ecléctico edificio secular, con su cúpula, también recibe cariñosamente el nombre de "la catedral ferroviaria".

Catedral da estação
A Estação Central Neo-Renascentista de Antuérpia (construída em 1899) é um magnífico monumento da era industrial. É um dos mais belos do mundo e tornou-se um cenário popular para longas-metragens. A opulenta sala de recepção em mármore e a magnífica escadaria são dignas de um castelo. O eclético edifício secular com uma cúpula também é carinhosamente chamado de catedral ferroviária.

Spoorwegkathedraal
Het Centraal Station van Antwerpen in de stijl van de Neorenaissance (gebouwd in 1899) is een prachtig monument voor het industriële tijdperk. Het is één van de mooiste ter wereld en is een geliefd decor voor speelfilms geworden. De weelderige ontvangsthal van marmer en de prachtige trap zijn een kasteel waardig. Het eclectische, seculiere gebouw met zijn koepel wordt ook wel de spoorwegkathedraal genoemd.

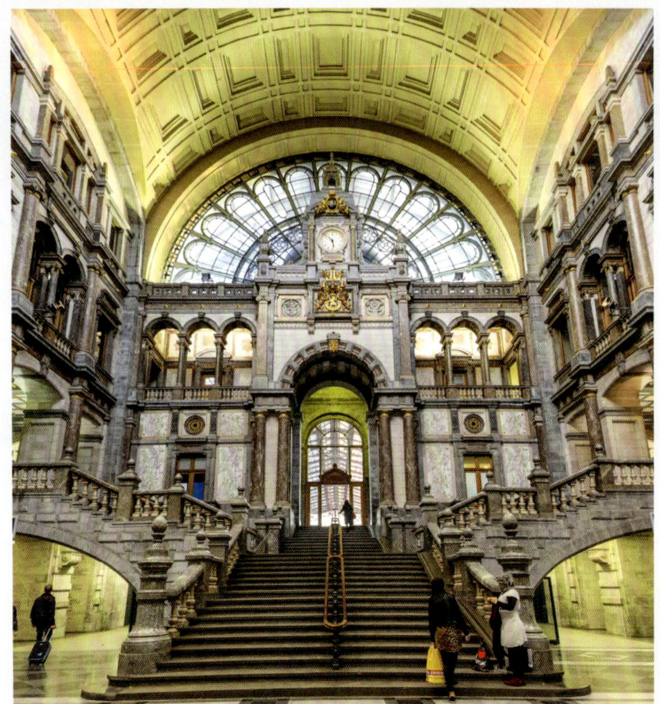

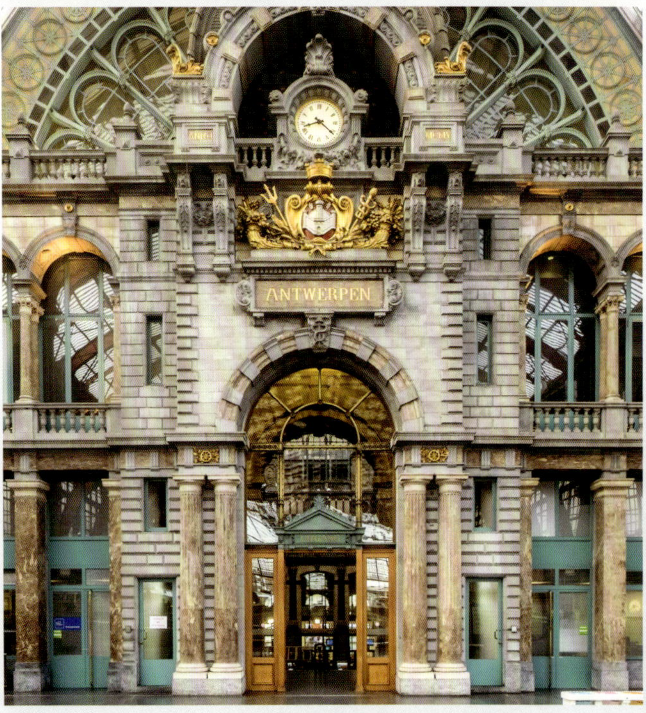

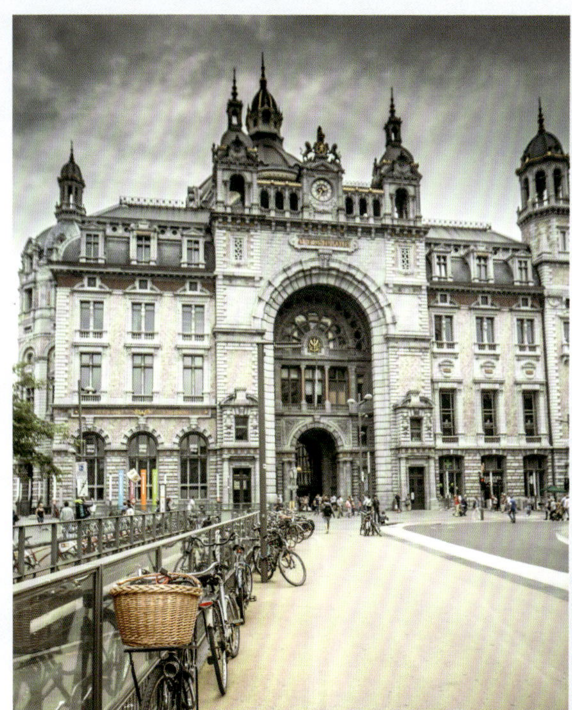
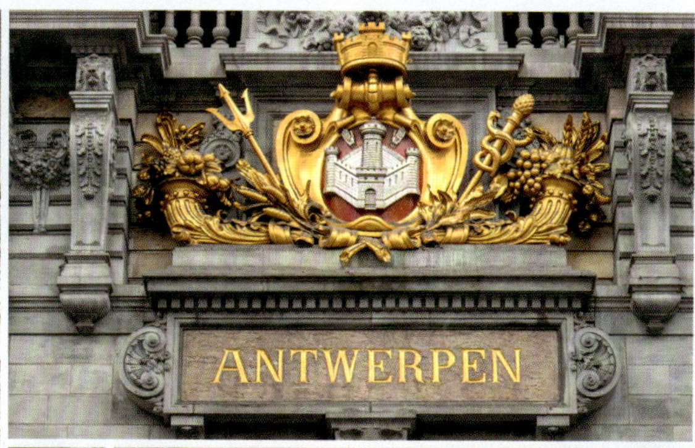

ANTWERPEN

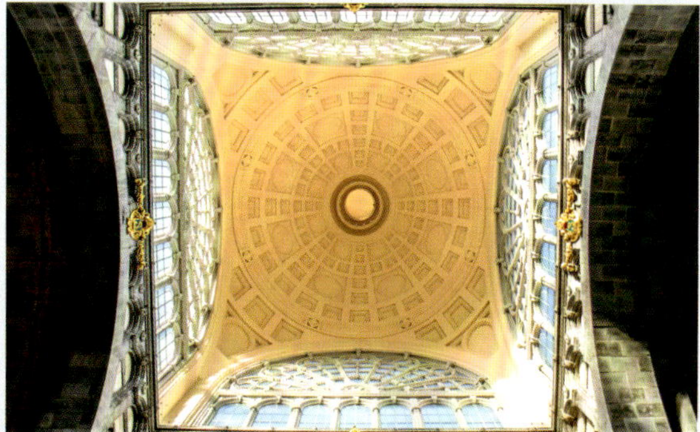
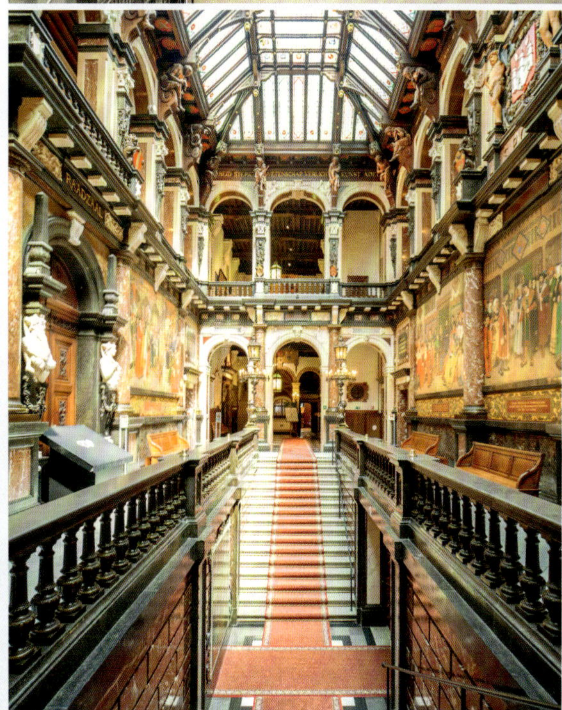
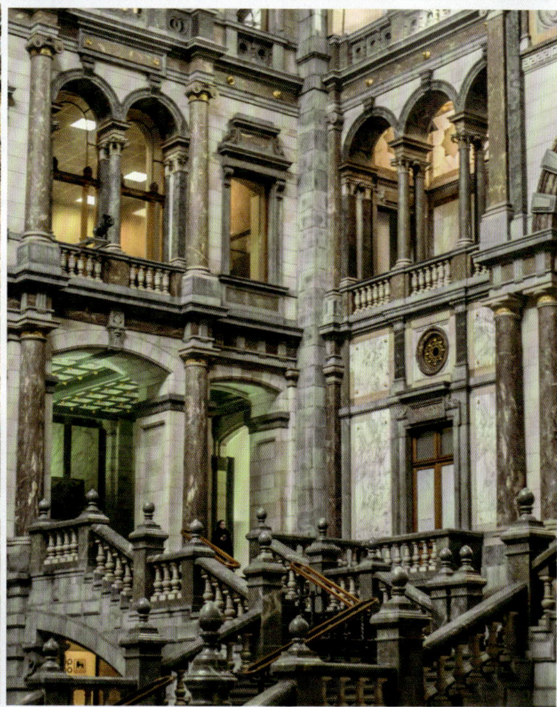

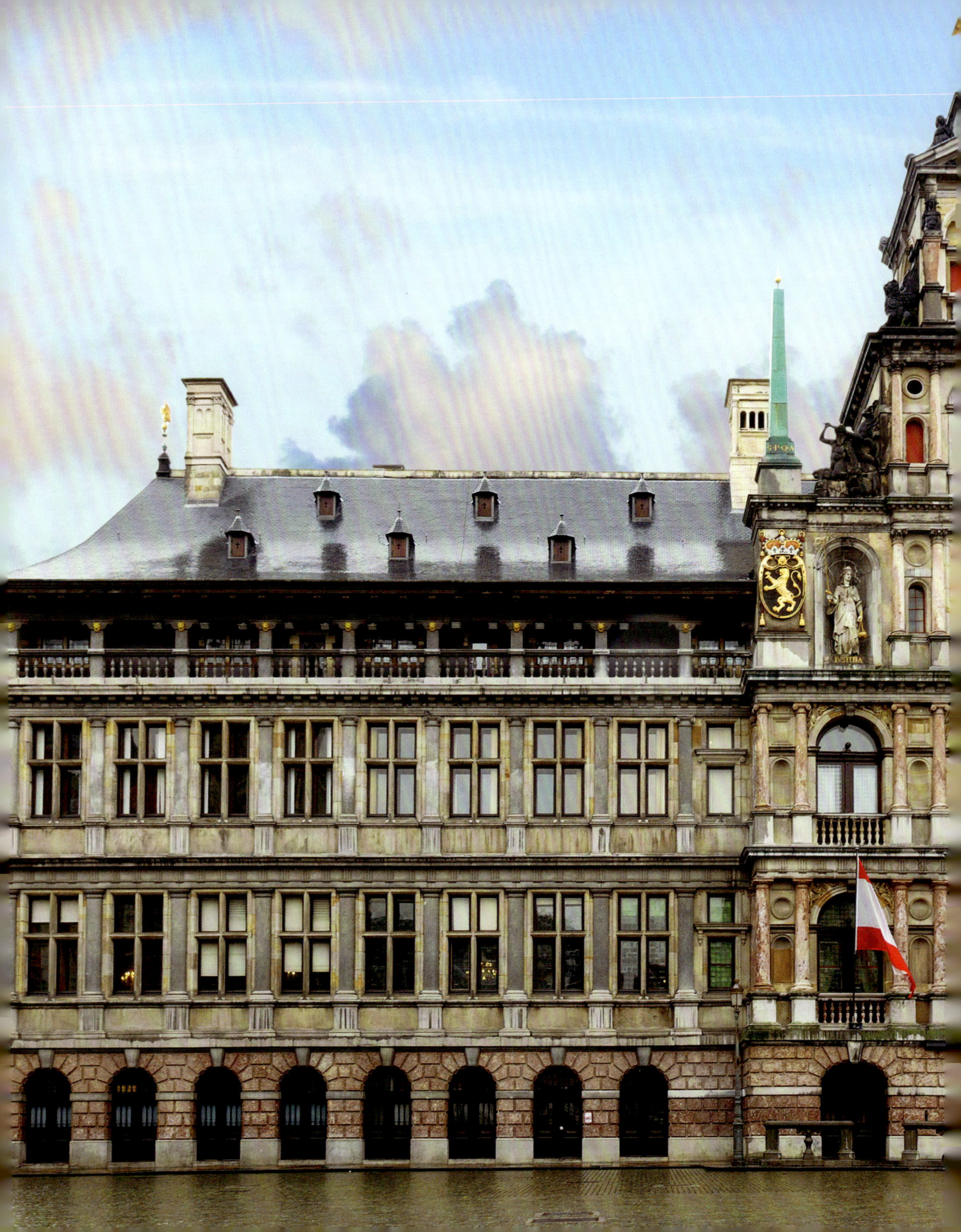

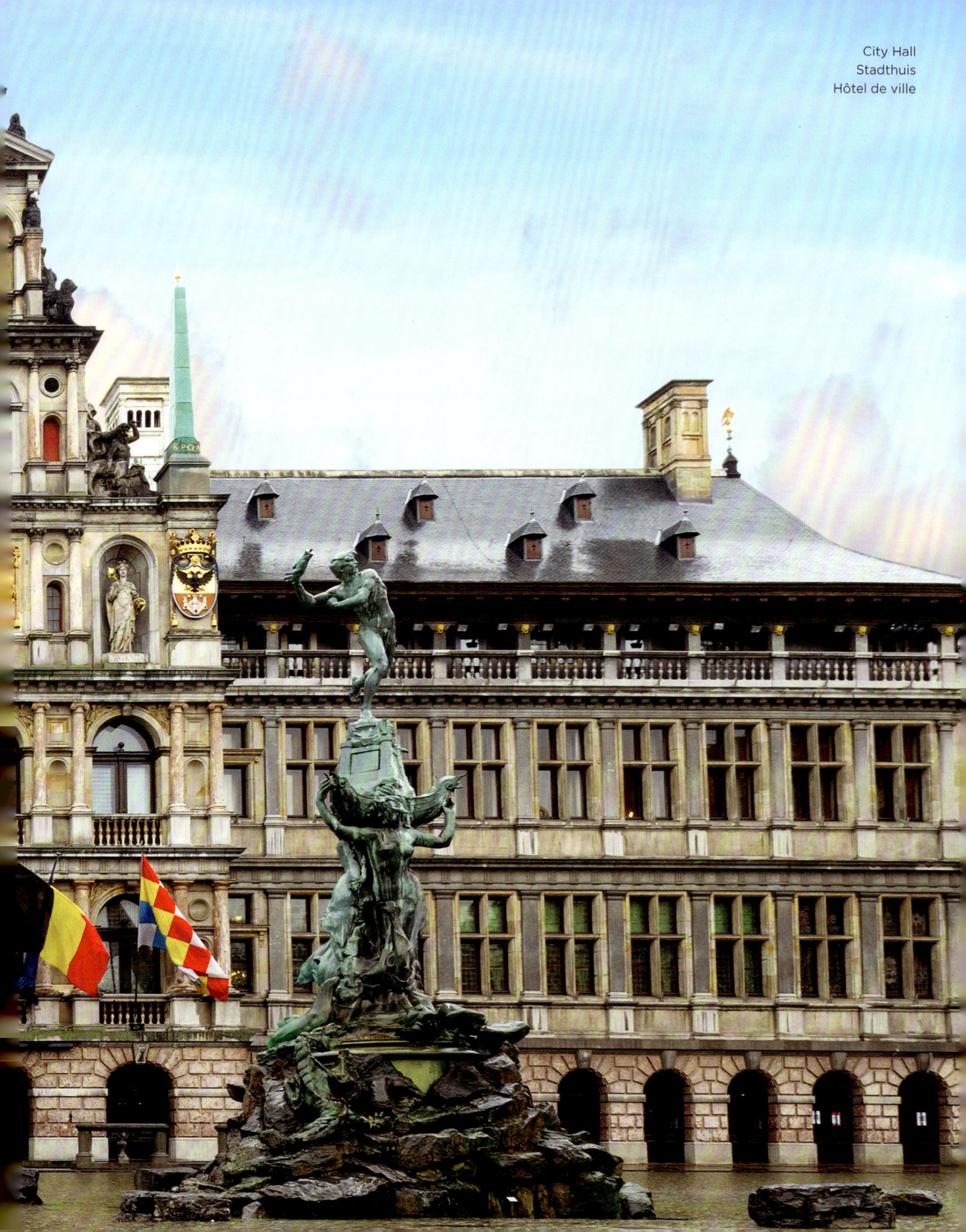

City Hall
Stadthuis
Hôtel de ville

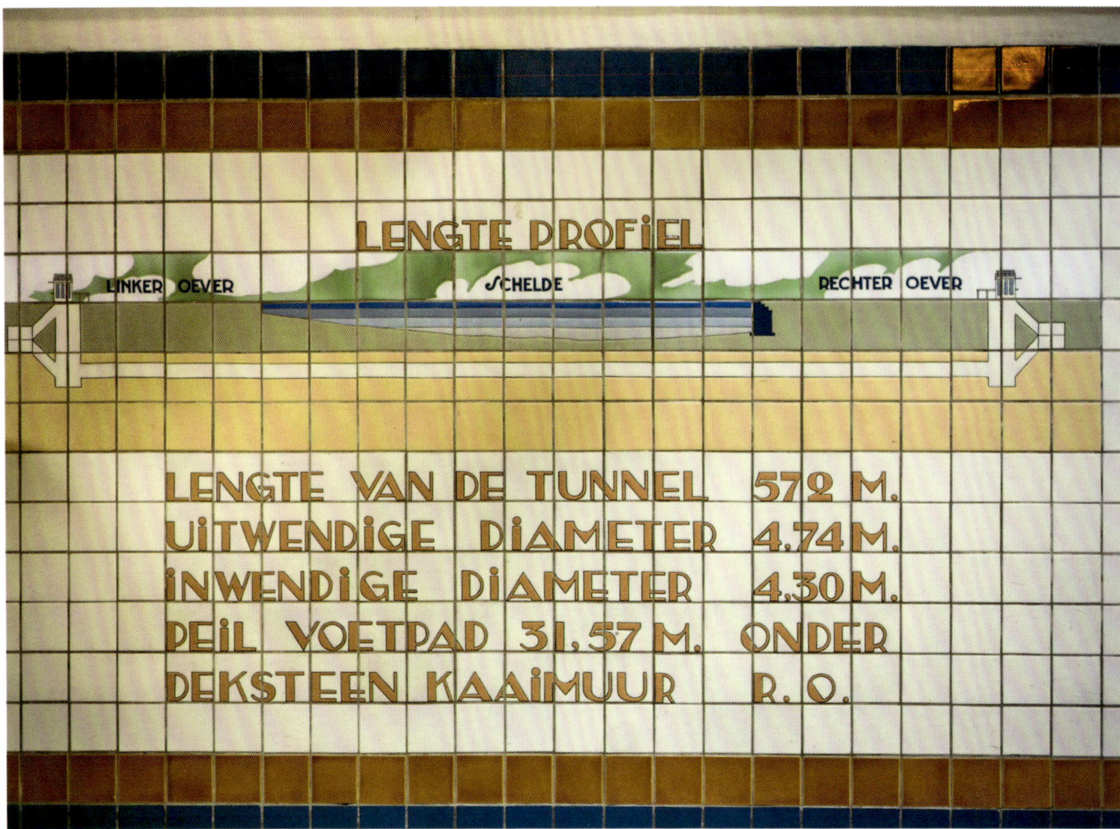

St Anna's Tunnel
Sint-Annatunnel
Tunnel Sainte-Anne

Saint Anna's Tunnel

The listed pedestrian tunnel below the Scheldt was opened in 1933. The entire facility is in original condition and still in operation, featuring not only the original wooden escalators, but also information signs and barriers. The 4.30 m (14 ft) wide tunnel, with a length of 572 m (1877 ft), leads from the old town to the other side of the Scheldt and into a park. The park on the left bank offers a beautiful view of Antwerp's old town. Also of interest is the photo exhibition in the yellow entrance house, showing pictures from the construction phase in the 1930s.

Tunnel piétonnier Sainte-Anne

Classé monument historique, le tunnel piétonnier passant sous l'Escaut a été inauguré en 1933. L'ensemble de l'installation est dans son état d'origine et toujours en service – tant les authentiques escaliers mécaniques en bois que les panneaux d'information et les barrières. Avec ses 4,30 m de diamètre intérieur et une longueur de 572 m, ce tunnel relie la vieille ville à un parc situé de l'autre côté de l'Escaut. Le parc, sur la rive gauche, offre une belle vue sur la vieille ville d'Anvers. Dans la maison jaune, à l'entrée, l'exposition de photos présentant la phase de construction dans les années 1930 vaut également le détour.

Fußgängertunnel Sint-Anna

Der denkmalgeschützte Fußgängertunnel unterhalb der Schelde wurde im Jahr 1933 eröffnet. Die gesamte Anlage ist im Originalzustand und immer noch in Funktion: die authentischen Rolltreppen aus Holz, aber auch Hinweisschilder und Absperrungen. Die im inneren Durchmesser 4,30 m breite Röhre, mit einer Länge von 572 m, führt von der Altstadt auf die andere Seite der Schelde in einen Park. Von dem Park am linken Ufer bietet sich ein schöner Blick auf die Antwerpener Altstadt. Interessant ist auch die Fotoausstellung, mit Bildern aus der Bauphase in den 1930er-Jahren, im gelben Eingangshaus.

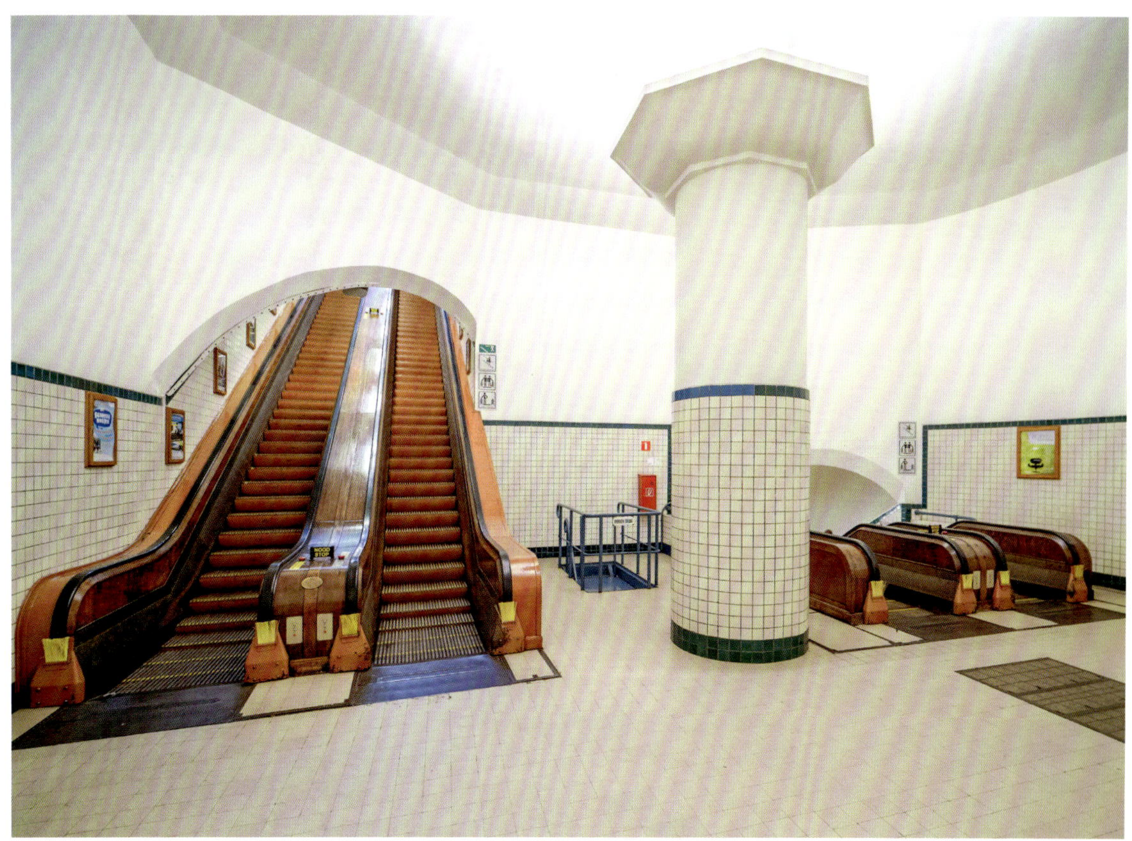

Wooden Escalator
Houten roltrap
Escalier roulant en bois

Túnel peatonal de Santa Ana

El túnel peatonal situado bajo el río Schelde fue inaugurado en 1933. Toda la instalación se encuentra en su estado original y sigue en funcionamiento: las auténticas escaleras mecánicas de madera, pero también las señales informativas y las barreras. El tubo de 4,30 m de ancho con un diámetro interior y una longitud de 572 m conduce desde el casco antiguo hasta el otro lado del río Schelde y hacia el interior de un parque. El parque de la orilla izquierda ofrece una hermosa vista del casco antiguo de Amberes. También es interesante la exposición fotográfica que hay en la casa de entrada amarilla y en la que se pueden observar imágenes de la fase de construcción de la década de 1930.

Túnel de pedestre de Santa Ana

O túnel de pedestres, tombado como monumento, situado abaixo do rio Escalda foi inaugurado em 1933. Toda a instalação está em condições originais e ainda em funcionamento: as autênticas escadas rolantes de madeira, mas também sinais de informação e barreiras. O tubo de 4,30 m de largura com um diâmetro interior e um comprimento de 572 m leva da cidade velha para o outro lado do Escalda em um parque. O parque na margem esquerda oferece uma bela vista da cidade velha de Antuérpia. Também interessante é a exposição fotográfica, com fotos da fase de construção na década de 1930, na entrada principal do pavilhão amarelo.

Voetgangerstunnel Sint-Anna

De als beschermd monument geldende voetgangerstunnel onder de Schelde werd in 1933 geopend. Het geheel is in originele staat en nog steeds in gebruik: de authentieke houten roltrappen, maar ook informatieborden en slagbomen. De brede buis met een diameter van 4,30 m en een lengte van 572 m leidt van de oude binnenstad naar een park aan de andere kant van de Schelde. Het park op de linkeroever biedt een prachtig uitzicht op de oude binnenstad van Antwerpen. Interessant is ook de fototentoonstelling in het gele entreegebouw met foto's uit de bouwfase in de jaren dertig van de vorige eeuw.

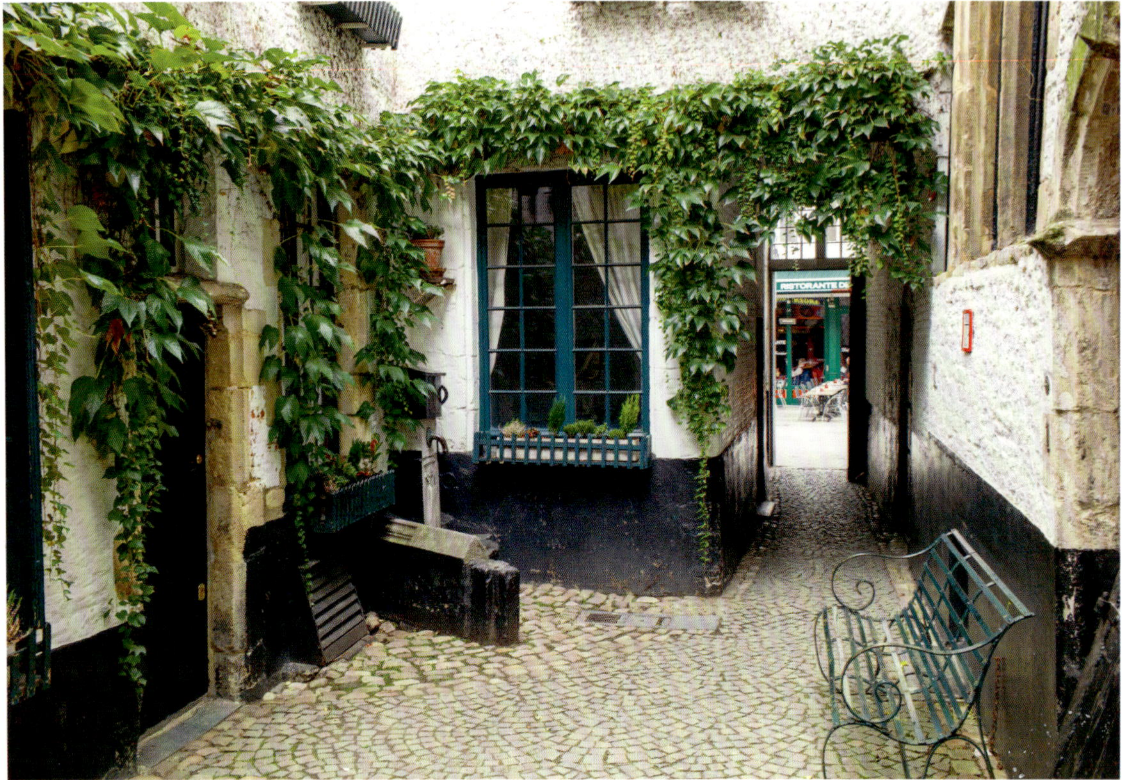

Vlaeykensgang

Vlaeykensgang alley

In the shadow of the cathedral lies a little hidden alley, the Vlaeykensgang. In the past, the crooked alley was home to shoemakers, who were also charged with ringing the cathedral's emergency bell. Today you will find there antique shops, art galleries and an exclusive restaurant. The alley is also a popular place to listen to the carillon concerts.

Callejón Vlaeykensgang

A la sombra de la catedral se encuentra, un poco escondido, el Vlaeykensgang. En el pasado, este callejón retorcido era el hogar de los zapateros que tenían que tocar la campana de emergencia de la catedral. Ahora aquí hay tiendas de antigüedades, galerías de arte y un restaurante exclusivo. El callejón es también un lugar popular para escuchar los conciertos de carillón.

Passage Vlaeykensgang

À l'ombre de la cathédrale, un peu caché, le Vlaeykensgang. Autrefois, c'était les cordonniers qui vivaient dans ce passage tortueux ; ils devaient sonner le tocsin de la cathédrale. Aujourd'hui, on y trouve des antiquaires, des galeries d'art et un restaurant de luxe. La ruelle est aussi un endroit fort prisé pour écouter les concerts de carillon.

Beco Vlaeykensgang

À sombra da catedral, um pouco escondido, o Vlaeykensgang. No passado, o beco torto era o lar de sapateiros que precissavam tocar o sino de emergência da catedral. Hoje você vai encontrar lojas de antiguidades, galerias de arte e um restaurante exclusivo. O beco também é um lugar popular para ouvir os concertos do carrilhão.

Gasse Vlaeykensgang

Im Schatten der Kathedrale liegt, ein wenig versteckt, der Vlaeykensgang. Früher wohnten in der verwinkelten Gasse die Schuhmacher, die die Notglocke der Kathedrale läuten mussten. Heute findet man hier Antiquitätengeschäfte, Kunstgalerien und ein exklusives Restaurant. Das Gässchen ist auch ein beliebter Ort, um den Glockenspielkonzerten zu lauschen.

Steegje Vlaeykensgang

In de schaduw van de kathedraal ligt, een beetje verborgen, de Vlaeykensgang. Vroeger was de kromme steeg de thuisbasis van schoenmakers die de noodklokken van de kathedraal moesten luiden. Vandaag de dag vindt u hier antiekwinkels, kunstgalerijen en een exclusief restaurant. De steeg is ook een populaire plek om naar de beiaardconcerten te luisteren.

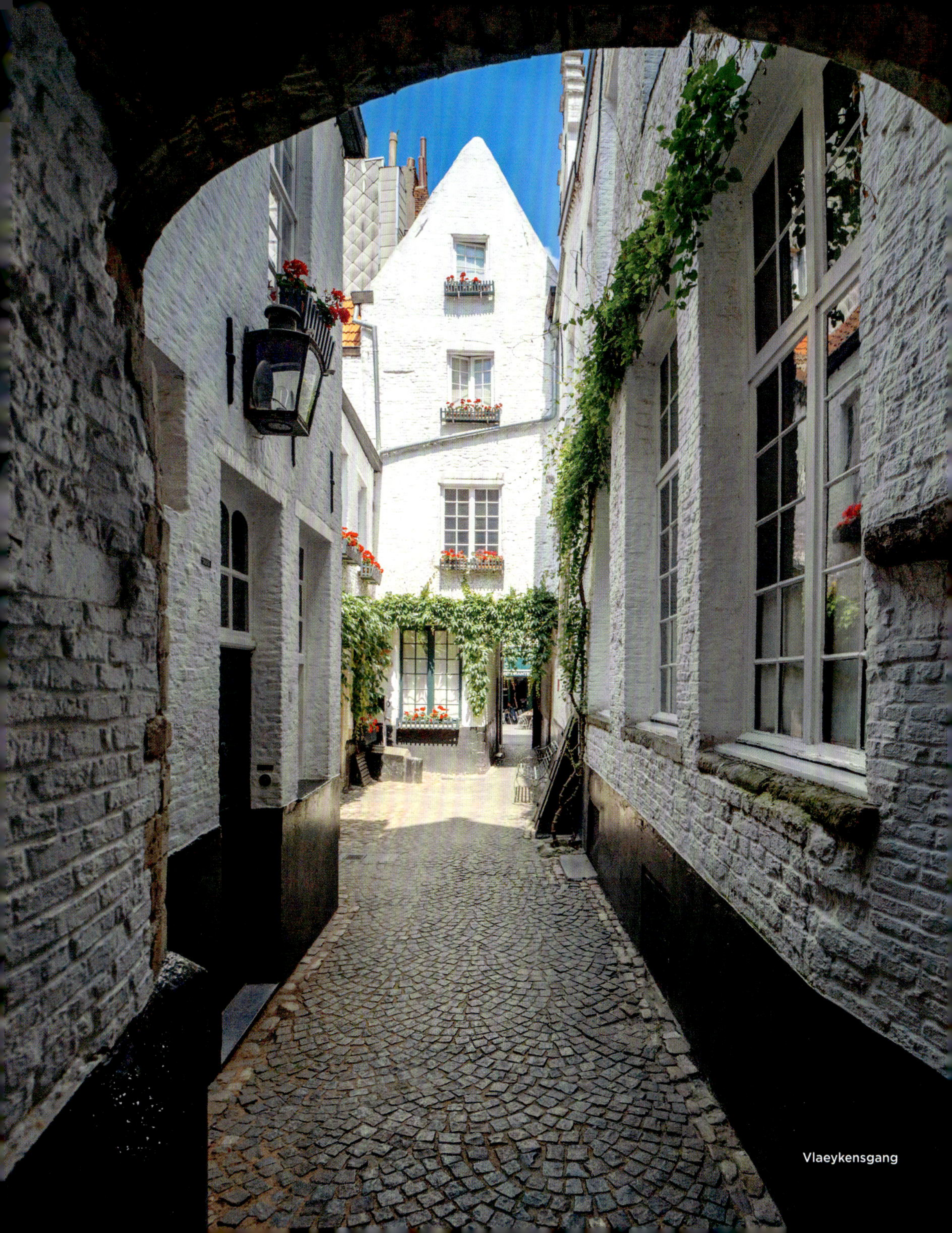
Vlaeykensgang

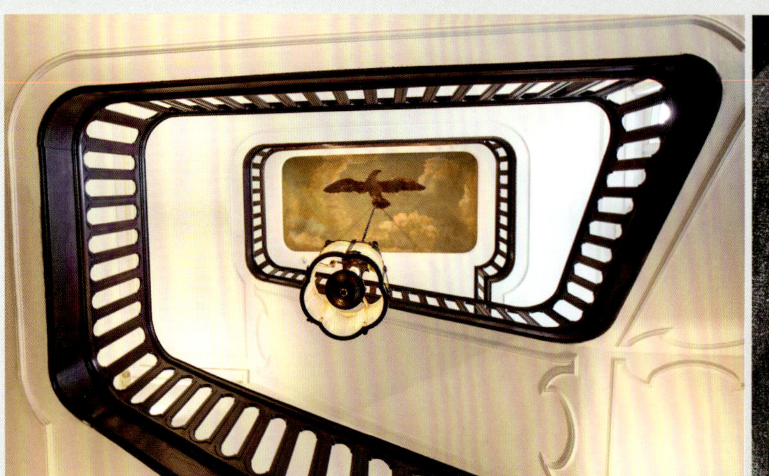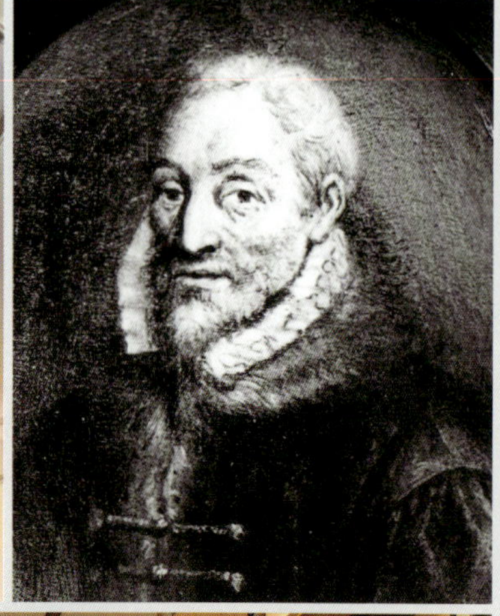

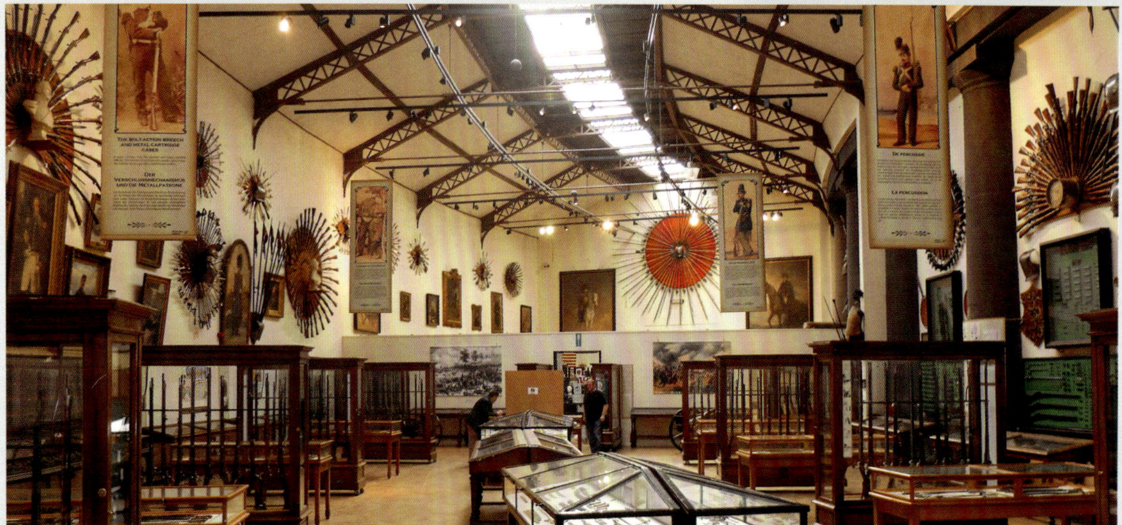

Plantin-Moretus Printing Museum

In the museum, there is the only still-functioning printing house dating from the Renaissance era, which is why UNESCO has included the house in the World Heritage List. Visitors may still admire the rooms, with their paintings, sculptures, tapestries and gold leather wallpaper, whilst also getting an overview of the development of the art of printing between the 15th and 18th centuries. Additionally worth visiting are the libraries and the verdant inner courtyard. The first "industrial" printing works, founded by Christophe Plantin in 1555, is located in the middle of the historic old town.

Imprimerie Plantin-Moretus

Ce musée abrite la seule imprimerie de la Renaissance encore en service, d'où son inscription au patrimoine culturel mondial de l'Unesco. Aujourd'hui encore, les visiteurs peuvent admirer ses salles avec leurs peintures, sculptures, tapisseries et papiers peints en cuir doré et avoir un aperçu de l'évolution de l'art de l'imprimerie du XVe au XVIIIe siècle. Les bibliothèques et la cour intérieure verdoyante valent également le détour. Fondée par Christophe Plantin en 1555, cette première imprimerie « industrielle » se trouve au cœur de la vieille ville historique.

Plantin-Moretus-Museum

In dem Museum befindet sich die einzige noch funktionsfähige Druckerei aus dem Zeitalter der Renaissance, aus diesem Grunde hat die UNESCO das Haus ins Weltkulturerbe aufgenommen. Noch heute können Besucher die Zimmer mitsamt Gemälden, Skulpturen, Wandteppichen und der Goldledertapete bewundern und erhalten einen Überblick über die Entwicklung der Buchdruckerkunst zwischen dem 15. und 18. Jahrhundert. Sehenswert sind auch die Bibliotheken und der grüne Innenhof. Die von Christoph Plantin im Jahr 1555 gegründete erste „industriellen" Druckerei, befindet sich mitten in der historischen Altstadt.

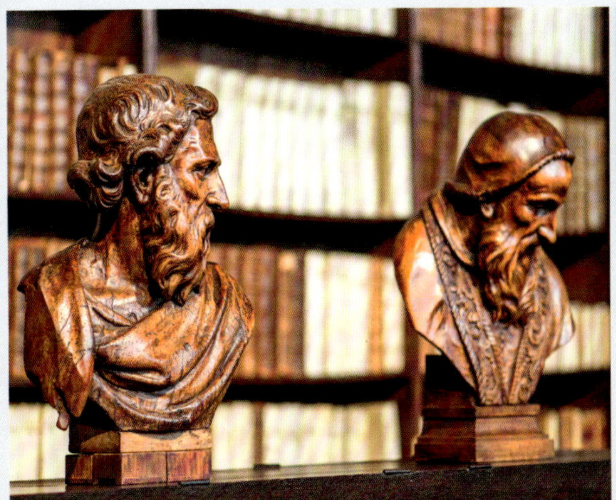

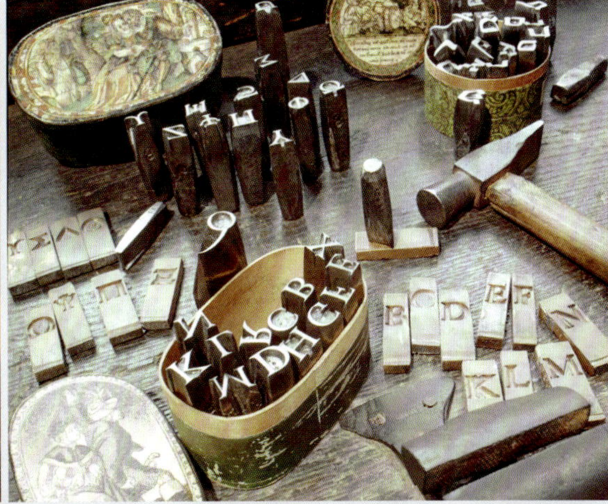

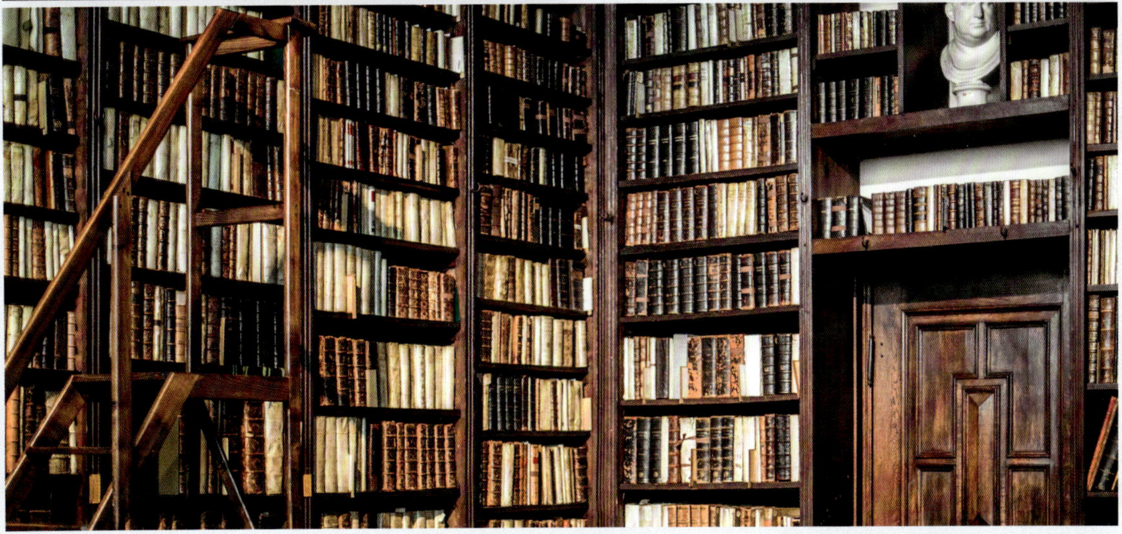

Museo Plantin-Moretus

En el museo se encuentra la única imprenta de la época del Renacimiento que aún funciona, por lo que la UNESCO la ha incluido en la Lista del Patrimonio Mundial. Los visitantes pueden admirar las salas con sus pinturas, esculturas, tapices y papeles pintados de cuero dorado y obtener una visión general de la evolución del arte de la impresión entre los siglos XV y XVIII. También vale la pena visitar las bibliotecas y el patio interior verde. La primera imprenta "industrial", que fue fundada por Christoph Plantin en 1555, se encuentra en el centro del casco histórico.

Museu tipográfico Plantin-Moretus

No museu abriga a única oficina tipográfica ainda em funcionamento da era renascentista, razão pela qual a UNESCO incluiu a casa na lista do Património Mundial. Os visitantes, ainda hoje, podem admirar as salas com suas pinturas, esculturas, tapeçarias e papel de parede de couro dourado e obter uma visão geral do desenvolvimento da arte da impressão entre os séculos XV e XVIII. Também vale a pena ver as bibliotecas e o pátio interior verde. A primeira gráfica "industrial", fundada por Christoph Plantin em 1555, está localizada no centro da cidade velha histórica.

Museum Plantin-Moretus

In het museum bevindt zich de enige nog functionerende drukkerij uit de renaissancetijd. Om die reden heeft de UNESCO het huis op de werelderfgoedlijst gezet. Nog steeds kunnen bezoekers de zalen met de schilderijen, sculpturen, wandtapijten en het goudleer aan de muur bewonderen en zo een overzicht krijgen van de ontwikkeling van de drukkunst tussen de 15e en 18e eeuw. Bezienswaardig zijn ook de bibliotheken en de groene binnenplaats. De in 1555 door Christoph Plantin opgerichte eerste "industriële" drukkerij bevindt zich midden in de historische, oude binnenstad.

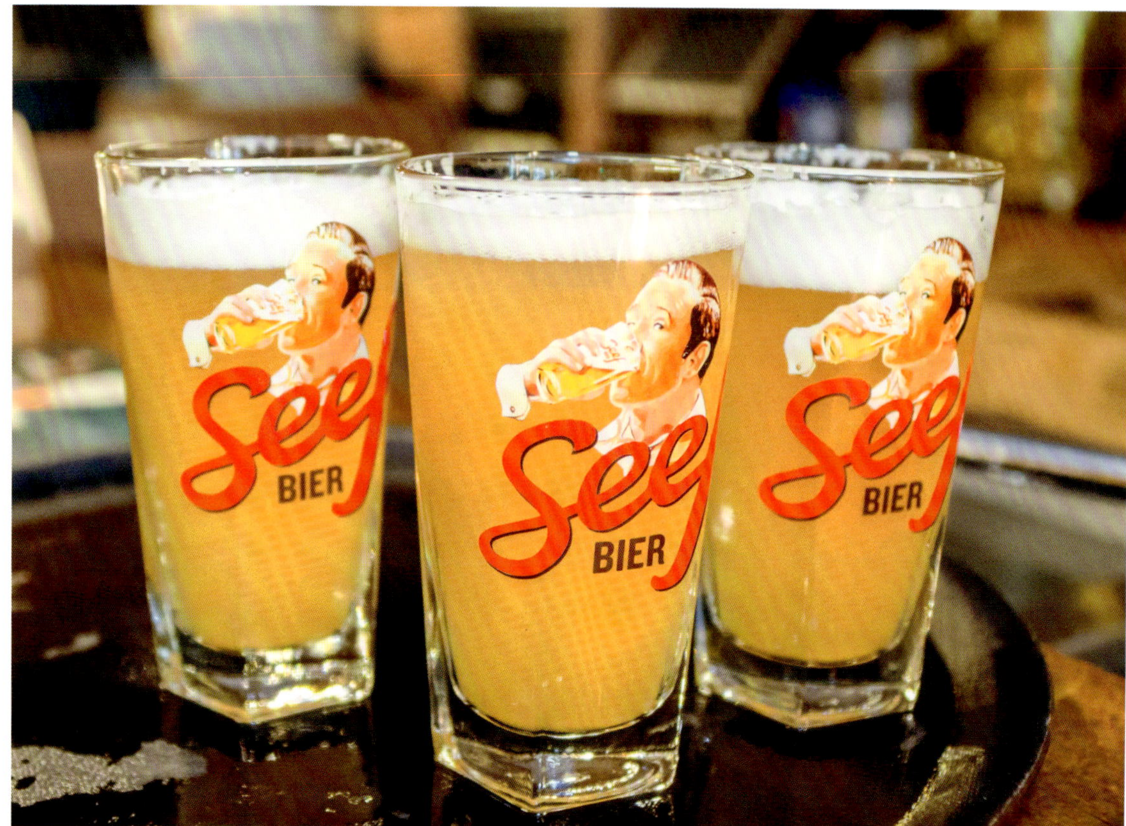

Seef beer
Seefbier
Bière de Seef

Seef—buckwheat beer

Just 100 years ago, Seef was brewed everywhere in the city, and a whole district was named after the beverage. With the advance of industrial beers, however, it fell out of fashion and was no longer produced. The brewer Johan Van Dyck found a recipe, and after three years of research and many trials was finally satisfied with his Seef. The jurors of the World Beer Cup were also satisfied, and Seefbier, although only recently introduced, received gold for the best Belgian beer without classification. Seef probably tastes best when drunk on a terrace by the Grote Markt, with a view of the guild houses and the Brabo Fountain.

Bière de sarrasin

Il y a 100 ans à peine, la Seef était brassée aux quatre coins de la ville et cette bière a donné son nom à un quartier entier. Mais avec l'essor des bières industrielles, elle tomba dans l'oubli. Après trois ans de recherche, le brasseur Johan Van Dyck en retrouva une recette et après de nombreux essais, il se montra satisfait de sa Seef – tout comme le jury de la World Beer Cup : malgré son entrée récente sur le marché, elle décrocha la médaille d'or de la meilleure bière belge non classée. Il n'y a rien de plus agréable que de siroter une Seef sur une terrasse de la Grand-Place, avec vue sur les maisons de corporations et la fontaine de Brabo.

Bier aus Buchweizen

Noch vor 100 Jahren wurde das Seef überall in der Stadt gebraut, ein ganzer Stadtteil wurde nach dem Bier benannt. Mit dem Vormarsch der industriellen Biere geriet es jedoch in Vergessenheit. Der Brauer Johan Van Dyck fand nach dreijähriger Recherche ein Rezept und war nach vielen Probe-Suden mit seinem Seef zufrieden. Zufrieden waren auch die Juroren des World Beer Cup: Seefbier, obwohl erst seit kurzem auf dem Markt, erhielt Gold für das beste belgische Bier ohne Klassifizierung. Seef schmeckt am besten auf einer Terrasse auf dem Grote Markt, mit Blick auf die Zunfthäuser und den Brabo-Brunnen.

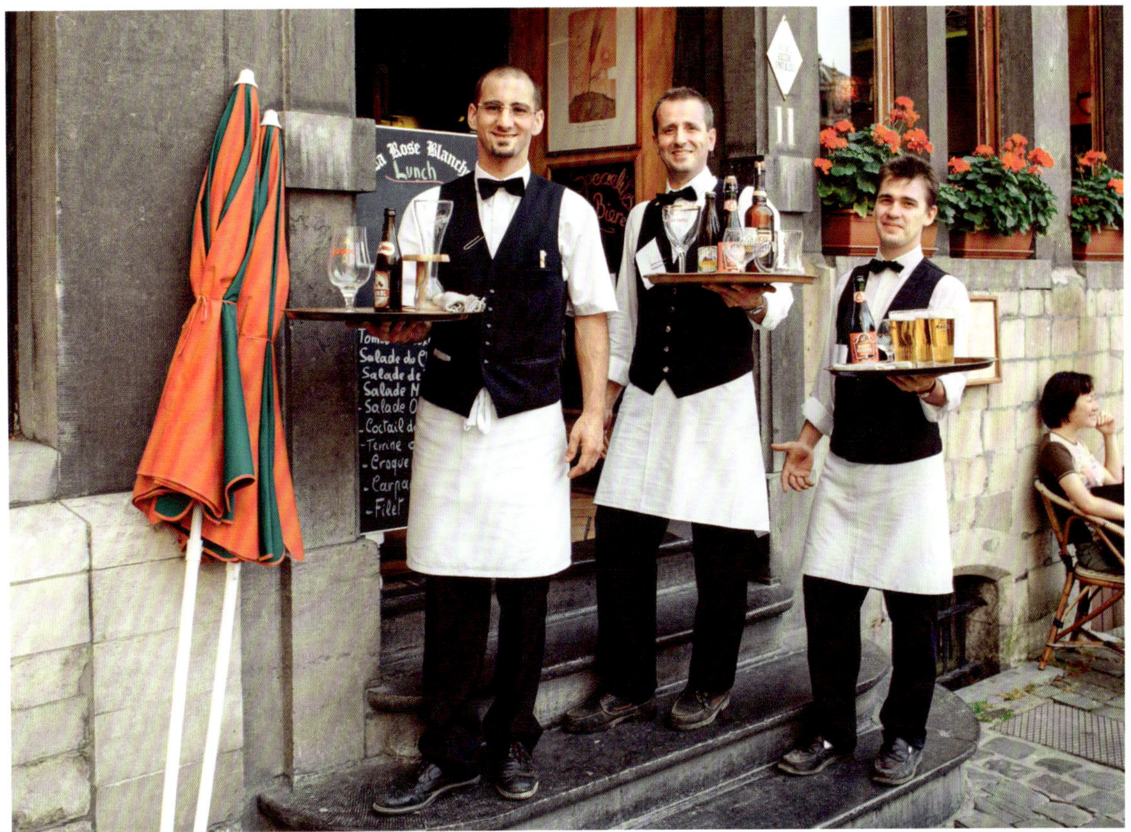

Waiters at Grote Markt
Kelners op de Grote Markt
Serveurs sur la Grande-Place d'Anvers

Cerveza de sarraceno

Hace solo 100 años, la Seef se fabricaba
en toda la ciudad y todo un distrito fue
bautizado con el nombre de la cerveza. Sin
embargo, con el avance de las cervezas
industriales cayó en el olvido. El cervecero
Johan Van Dyck encontró una receta
después de tres años de investigación y
quedó satisfecho con su Seef después
de muchas pruebas. Y los que también
quedaron satisfechos fueron los miembros
del jurado de la World Beer Cup: la cerveza
Seef, aunque no llevaba mucho tiempo
en el mercado, recibió el oro por la mejor
cerveza belga sin clasificación. Como
mejor sabe es si se bebe en una terraza de
la Grote Markt, con vistas a las casas del
gremio y a la fuente del Brabo.

Cerveza de sarraceno

Hace solo 100 años, la Seef se fabricaba
en toda la ciudad y todo un distrito fue
bautizado con el nombre de la cerveza. Sin
embargo, con el avance de las cervezas
industriales cayó en el olvido. El cervecero
Johan Van Dyck encontró una receta
después de tres años de investigación y
quedó satisfecho con su Seef después
de muchas pruebas. Y los que también
quedaron satisfechos fueron los miembros
del jurado de la World Beer Cup: la cerveza
Seef, aunque no llevaba mucho tiempo
en el mercado, recibió el oro por la mejor
cerveza belga sin clasificación. Como
mejor sabe es si se bebe en una terraza de
la Grote Markt, con vistas a las casas del
gremio y a la fuente del Brabo.

Boekweitbier

Nog maar 100 jaar geleden werd Seef
overal in de stad gebrouwen, een hele
wijk werd naar het bier genoemd. Met de
opmars van industriële bieren raakte het
echter in de vergetelheid. Brouwer Johan
Van Dyck vond na drie jaar onderzoek
een recept en was na vele testbrouwsels
tevreden met zijn Seefbier. Ook de
juryleden van de World Beer Cup waren
tevreden: Seefbier, hoewel nog niet zo lang
op de markt, kreeg goud voor het beste
Belgische bier zonder classificatie. Seef
smaakt het best op een terras op de Grote
Markt, met uitzicht op de gildehuizen en
de Brabofontein.

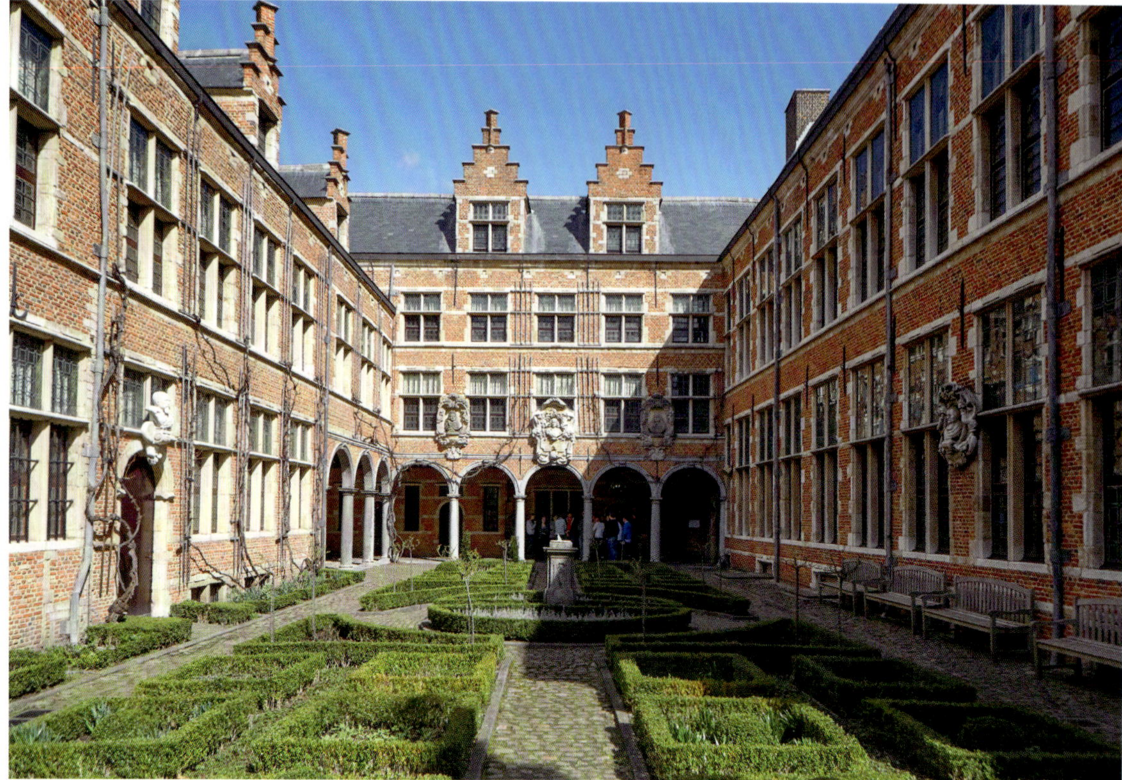

Rubens House
Rubenshuis
Maison de Rubens

Rubens House

The Rubens House is the former residence and workshop of the Flemish baroque painter Peter Paul Rubens (1577–1640). He himself designed his house in the Italian palazzo-style. A monumental portico leads to the baroque garden and his studio. The exhibition, including twelve works by the master, conveys a detailed picture of his impressive life.

Casa de Rubens

La Casa de Rubens es la antigua residencia y taller del pintor barroco flamenco Peter Paul Rubens (1577–1640). Él mismo diseñó su palacio al estilo italiano. Un portal barroco conduce al jardín y a su estudio. La exposición, que incluye doce obras del maestro, ofrece una imagen detallada de su impresionante vida.

Maison de Rubens

La maison de Rubens fut jadis la résidence et l'atelier du peintre baroque flamand Pierre Paul Rubens (1577–1640). Il conçut lui-même son palais à l'italienne. Un portail baroque conduit au jardin et à son atelier. L'exposition, qui comprend douze œuvres du maître, brosse un tableau détaillé de son impressionnante vie.

Casa de Rubens

A Casa de Rubens é a antiga residência e oficina do pintor barroco flamengo Peter Paul Rubens (1577–1640). Ele próprio projetou o seu palácio no estilo italiano. Um portal barroco leva ao jardim e ao seu estúdio. A exposição, incluindo doze obras do mestre, transmite uma imagem detalhada de sua impressionante vida.

Rubenshaus

Das Rubenshaus ist die ehemalige Wohn- und Werkstatt des flämischen Barockmalers Peter Paul Rubens (1577–1640). Seinen Palast im italienischen Stil entwarf er selbst. Durch ein Barockportal erreicht man den Garten und sein Atelier. Die Ausstellung, darunter zwölf Werke des Meisters, vermittelt ein detailliertes Bild seines beeindruckenden Lebens.

Rubenshuis

Het Rubenshuis is de voormalige residentie en werkplaats van de Vlaamse barokschilder Peter Paul Rubens (1577–1640). Zijn paleis in Italiaanse stijl ontwierp hij zelf. Een barok portaal biedt toegang tot de tuin en zijn atelier. De tentoonstelling, met twaalf werken van de meester, geeft een gedetailleerd beeld van zijn indrukwekkende leven.

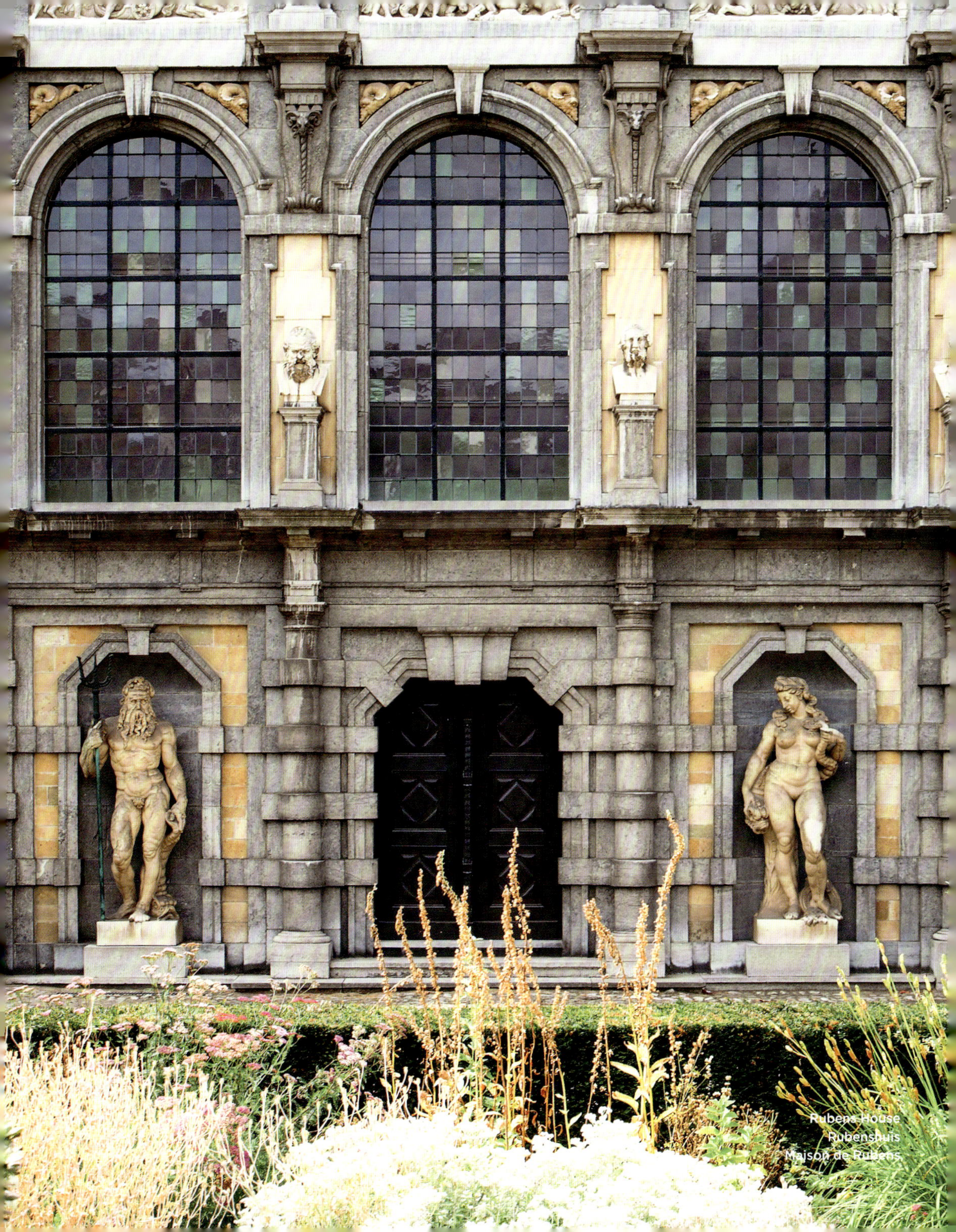

Rubens House
Rubenshuis
Maison de Rubens

Rubens—painter and diplomat

Already during his lifetime, Rubens enjoyed great
success as a painter. He worked not only in Flanders,
but also for clients in Italy, Spain and England and
was additionally entrusted with political missions.
The spacious house in Antwerp illustrates his status.
Depending on the commission, Rubens carried out
works with biblical or mythological scenes, made
portraits and also altarpieces.

Rubens, peintre et diplomate

De son vivant déjà, Rubens connut un grand succès
en tant que peintre. Il travaillait non seulement dans
les Flandres, mais honorait aussi des commandes
provenant d'Italie, d'Espagne et d'Angleterre – sans
compter qu'on lui confiait aussi des tâches politiques.
Sa maison spacieuse à Anvers symbolise son statut.
En fonction des commandes, Rubens réalisait
des œuvres représentant des scènes bibliques ou
mythologiques, des portraits ou des retables.

Rubens – Maler und Diplomat

Bereits zu Lebzeiten genoss Rubens einen großen
Erfolg als Maler. Er war nicht nur in Flandern sondern
auch für Auftraggeber in Italien, Spanien und England
tätig und wurde zudem mit politischen Aufgaben
betraut. Das großzügige Wohnhaus in Antwerpen
verdeutlicht seinen Status. Je nach Auftrag, führte
Rubens Werke mit biblischen oder mythologischen
Szenen aus, fertigte Porträts oder Altarstücke an.

Rubens: pintor y diplomático

Ya en vida, Rubens tuvo un gran éxito como pintor.
No solo trabajó en Flandes, sino también para
clientes en Italia, España e Inglaterra, y también se le
encomendaron tareas políticas. La espaciosa casa de
Amberes ilustra su estatus. Según el encargo, Rubens
realizaba trabajos con escenas bíblicas o mitológicas,
y realizaba retratos o retablos.

Rubens – pintor e diplomata

Já durante a sua vida, Rubens teve um grande
sucesso como pintor. Ele trabalhou não só na
Flandres, mas também para clientes na Itália,
Espanha e Inglaterra e também foi encarregado de
tarefas políticas. A espaçosa casa em Antuérpia
deixa mais claro o seu status. Conforme o tipo de
encomenda, Rubens realizou trabalhos com cenas
bíblicas ou mitológicas, fez retratos ou retábulos.

Rubens – kunstschilder en diplomaat

Tijdens zijn leven was Rubens zeer succesvol
als schilder. Hij werkte niet alleen in Vlaanderen,
maar ook voor opdrachtgevers in Italië, Spanje
en Engeland en nam politieke opdrachten aan.
Het ruime huis in Antwerpen illustreert zijn status.
Afhankelijk van de opdracht maakte hij werken met
Bijbelse of mythologische voorstellingen, portretten
of altaarstukken.

Self-Portrait

Autoportrait

Selbstbildnis

Autorretrato

Autoritratto

Zelfportret

PETER PAUL RUBENS (1577–1640)
c. 1638, Oil on canvas/Huile sur toile, 110 × 85,5 cm, Kunsthistorisches Museum, Wien

Rubens and Isabella Brant in the Honeysuckle Arbor

Rubens et Isabella Brant sous la tonnelle de chèvrefeuille

Rubens und Isabella Brant in der Geißblattlaube

Autorretrato con su esposa Isabel Brant

Autorretrato com sua esposa Isabella Brant

Rubens en Isabella Brant in het kamperfoelieprieel

PETER PAUL RUBENS (1577–1640)
1609/10, Oil on canvas, mounted on wood/Huile sur toile, montée
sur bois, 178 × 136,5 cm, Alte Pinakothek, München

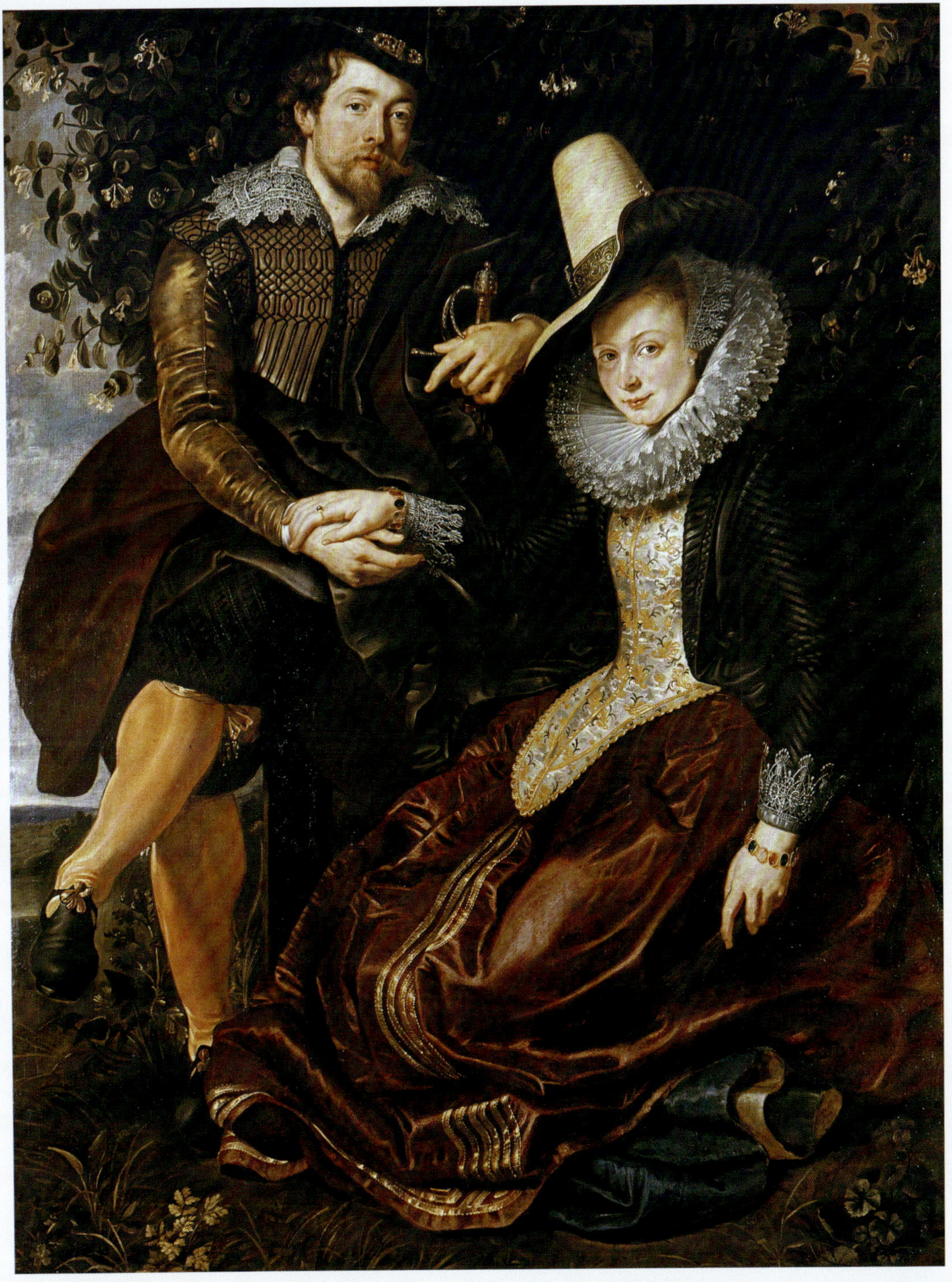

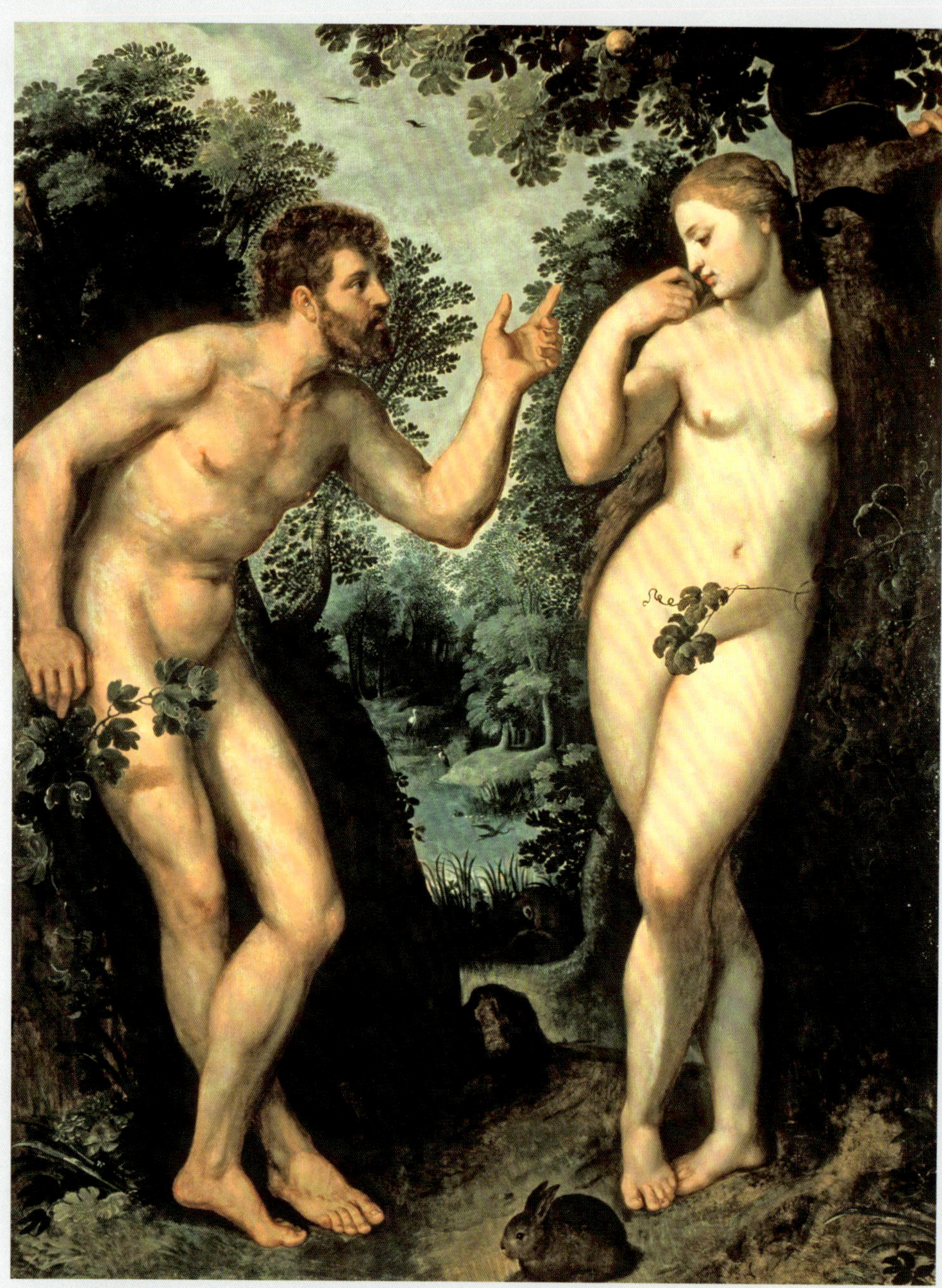

Adam and Eve

Adam et Ève

Adam und Eva

Adán y Eva

Adão e Eva

Adam en Eva

PETER PAUL RUBENS (1577–1640)
c. 1598–1600, Oil on wood/Huile sur bois, 180 × 158 cm, Rubenshuis, Antwerpen

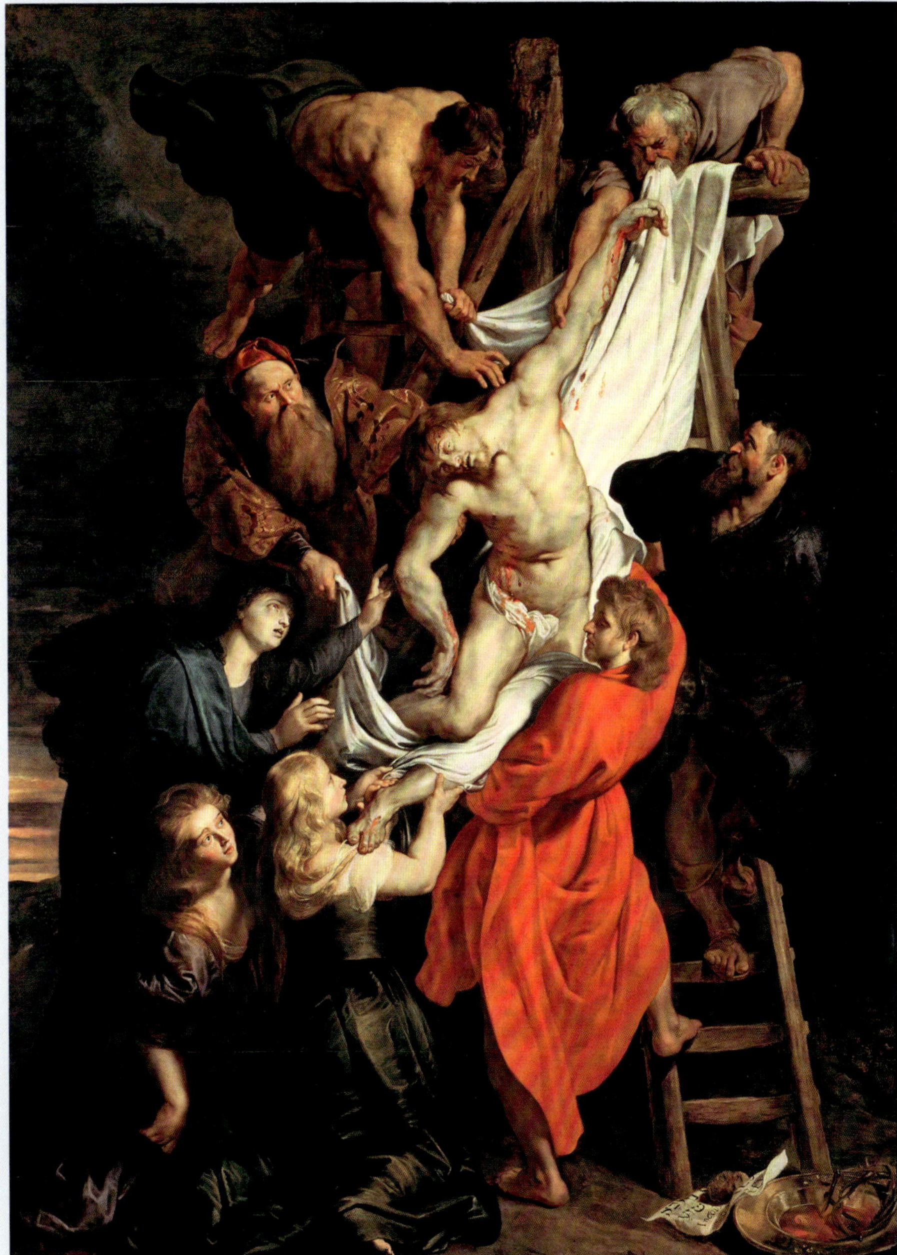

**The Deposition
from the Cross**

**Descente de croix,
panneau médian pour
le triptyque de la
cathédrale d'Anvers**

**Die Kreuzabnahme,
Mitteltafel des
Kreuzabnahme-
Triptychons**

**El Descendimiento
de Cristo, panel
central del Tríptico
del Descendimiento**

**Descida da Cruz, o
painel central do
tríptico Descida
da Cruz**

**De kruisafname,
middenpaneel van het
kruisafnemingstriptiek**

**PETER PAUL RUBENS
(1577–1640)**
1611–14, Oil on wood/
Huile sur bois,
421 × 311 cm, Onze-Lieve-
Vrouwekathedraal,
Antwerpen

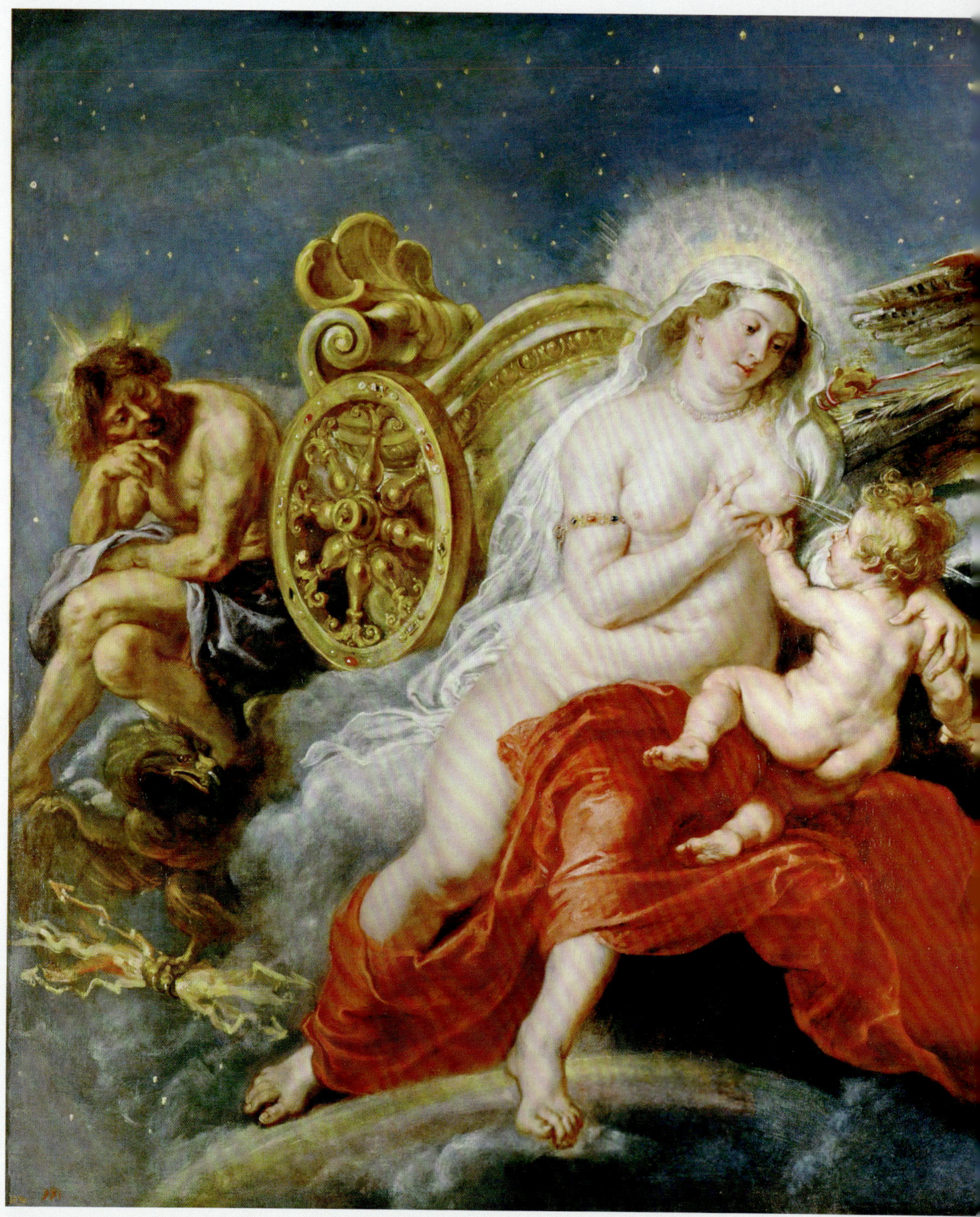

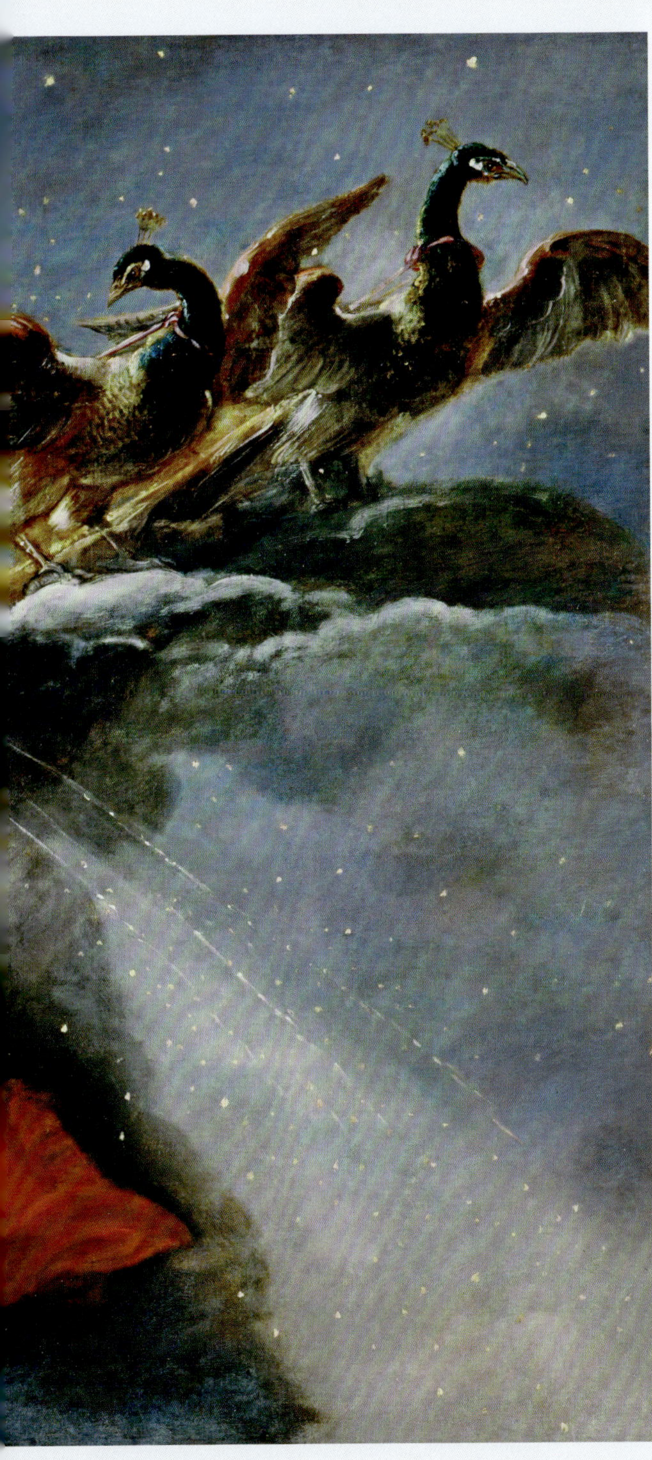

The Creation of the Milky Way

L'Origine de la Voie lactée

Die Entstehung der Milchstraße

La creación de la Vía Láctea

O Nascimento da Via Láctea

Het ontstaan van de melkweg

PETER PAUL RUBENS (1577–1640)
1636–38, Oil on canvas/Huile sur toile,
181 × 244 cm, Museo del Prado, Madrid

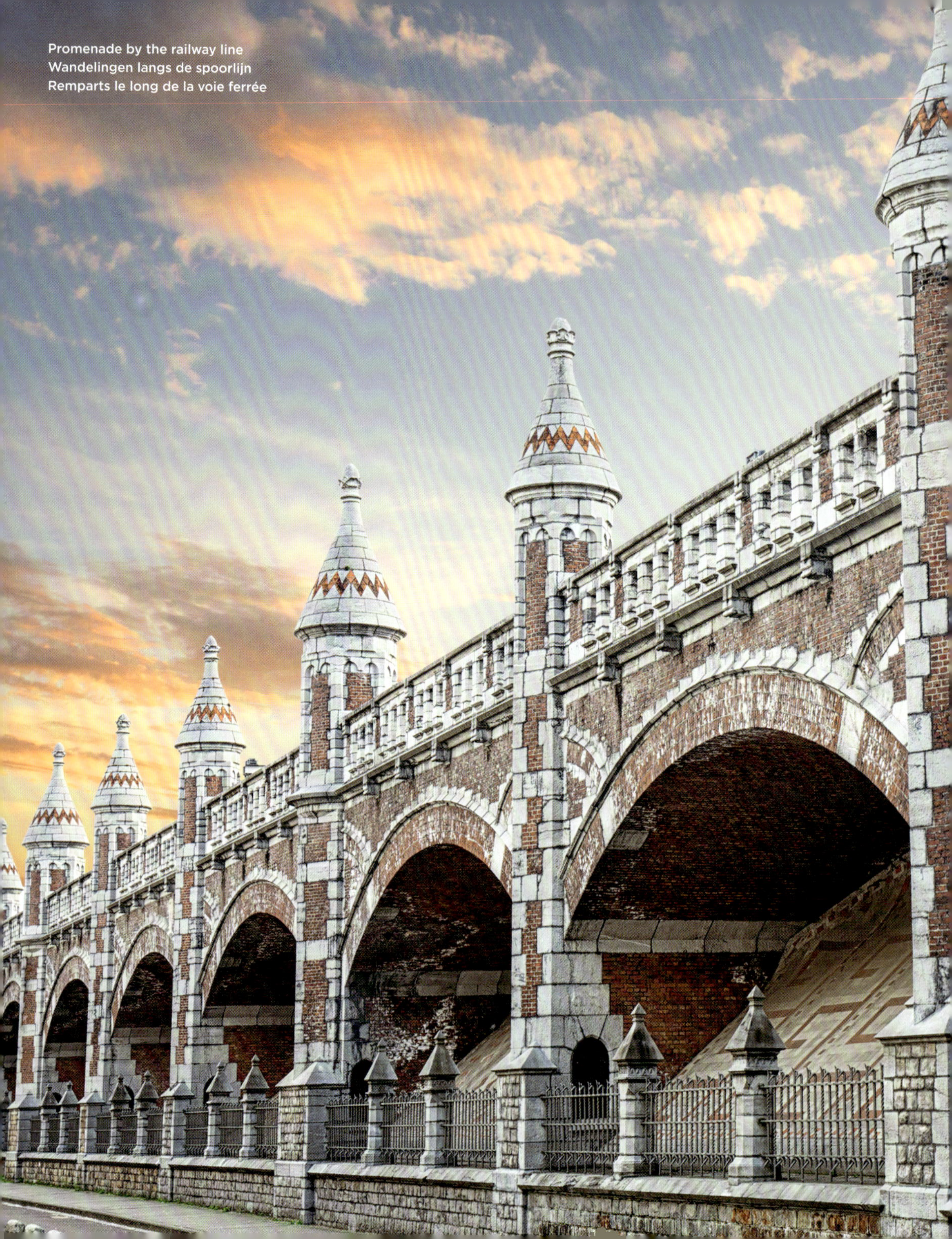

Promenade by the railway line
Wandelingen langs de spoorlijn
Remparts le long de la voie ferrée

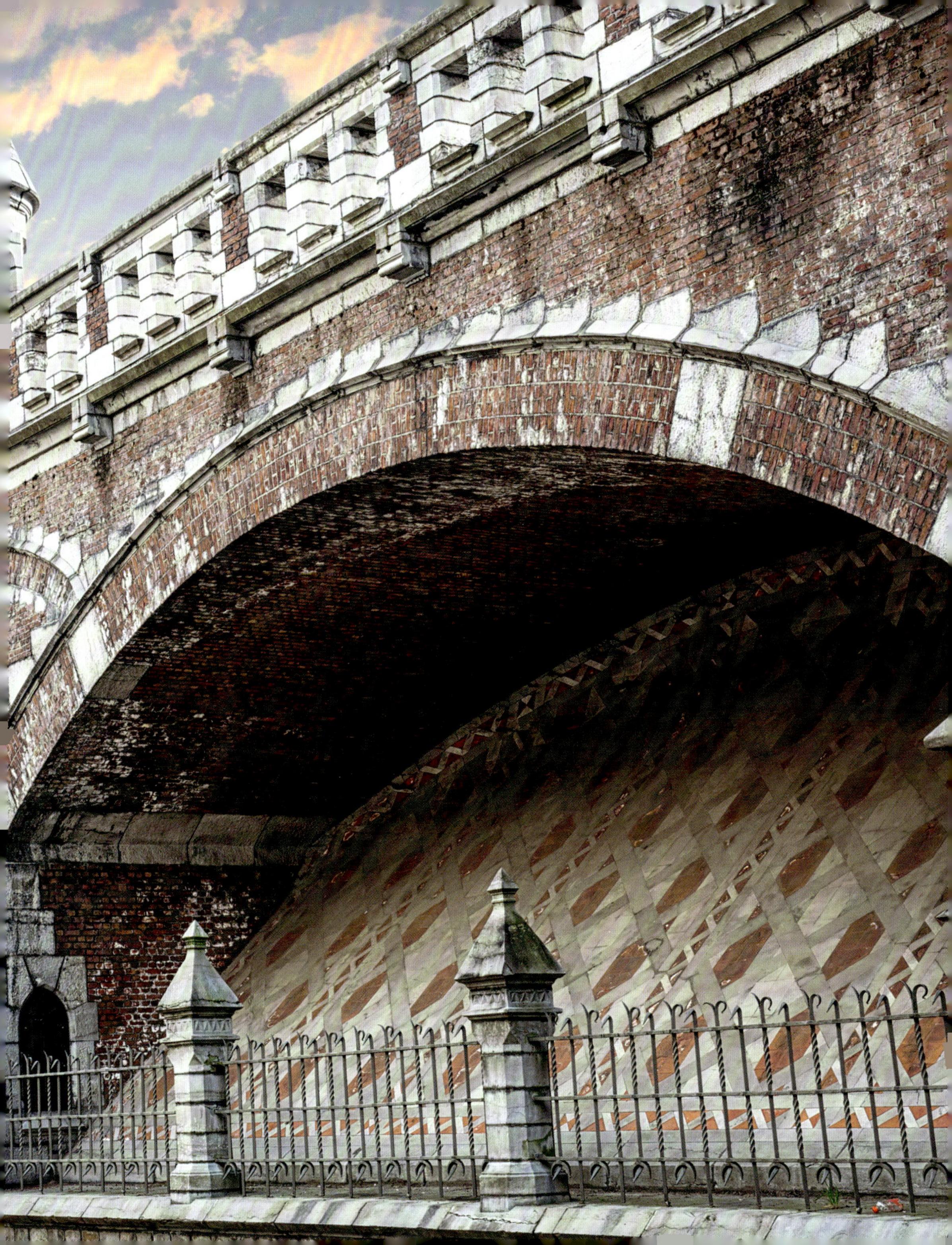

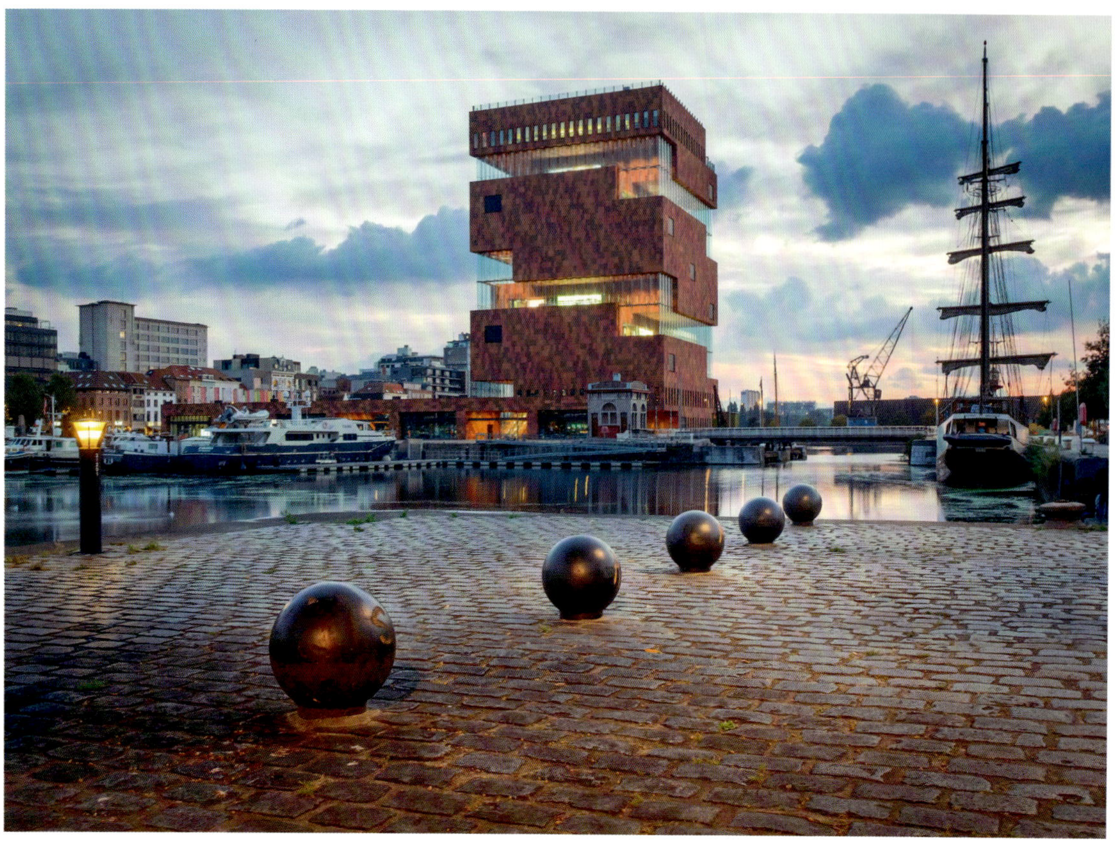

Museum aan de Stroom (MAS), Eilandje

Museum aan Stroom

A new landmark, visible from afar, has been standing in the harbour district since 2011—the Museum aan Stroom (Museum by the River). The exhibition rooms of the 62 m (203 ft) high museum tower are stacked like containers over ten floors. Each level is rotated through 90 degrees, so that the glass galleries in between allow changing views of the city and harbour. The facade of reddish Indian sandstone is decorated with 3000 hands of polished aluminium, an allusion to the city name of Antwerp. With a gigantic collection of nearly 500,000 art objects and utensils, the museum presents the history of the city.

Museum aan de Stroom

Depuis 2011, un nouvel emblème de la ville se dresse dans le quartier du port : le Museum aan de Stroom. Les salles d'exposition de cette tour muséale de 62 m de haut s'empilent sur dix étages, tels des containers. À chaque niveau, les galeries vitrées intermédiaires – formant des angles de 90° – offrent divers points de vue sur la ville et le port. La façade en grès indien rouge est ornée de 3 000 mains en aluminium poli, une allusion au nom de la ville d'Anvers. Le musée présente l'histoire de la ville au travers d'une gigantesque collection de 500 000 objets d'art et d'usage courant.

Museum am Strom

Im Hafenviertel steht seit 2011 ein neues weithin sichtbares Wahrzeichen: das Museum am Strom. Die Ausstellungsräume des 62 m hohen Museumsturms sind über zehn Etagen wie Container gestapelt. Dabei ist jede Ebene um 90 Grad gedreht, sodass die dazwischen liegenden Glasgalerien wechselnde Ausblicke auf Stadt und Hafen erlauben. Die Fassade aus rötlichem indischen Sandstein ist mit 3000 Händen aus poliertem Aluminium verziert, eine Anspielung auf den Stadtnamen Antwerpen. Mit einer gigantischen Sammlung von 500 000 Kunstobjekten und Gebrauchsgegenständen zeigt das Museum die Geschichte der Stadt.

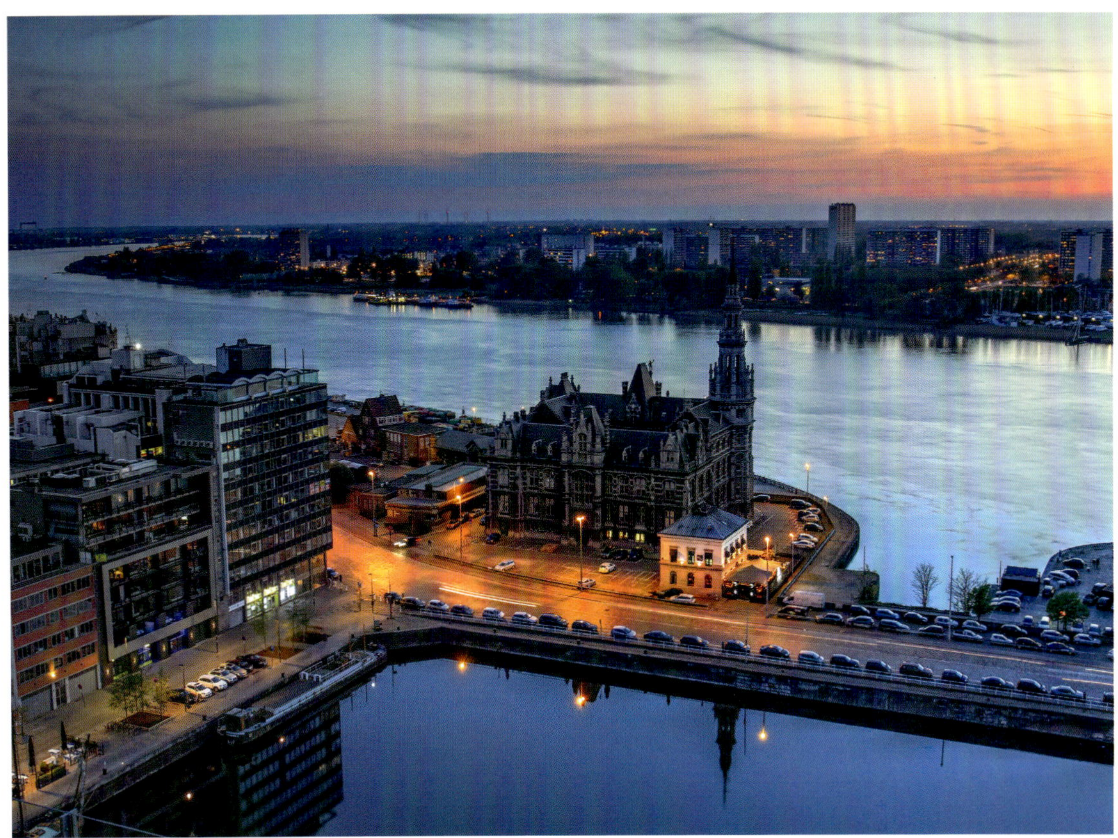

View from Museum aan de Stroom (MAS)
Uitzicht vanuit het Museum aan de Stroom (MAS)
Vue de Museum aan de Stroom (MAS)

Museo aan de Stroom

Un nuevo hito visible desde lejos se encuentra en el barrio portuario desde 2011: el Museo aan de Stroom (museo en la corriente). Las salas de exposición de la torre del museo, de 62 m de altura, están apiladas en diez pisos como contenedores. Cada piso está girado a 90 grados, de modo que las galerías de vidrio en el medio permiten cambiar las vistas de la ciudad y el puerto. La fachada de arenisca india rojiza está decorada con 3000 manos de aluminio pulido, una alusión al nombre de la ciudad de Amberes. Con una gigantesca colección de 500 000 objetos de arte y utensilios, el museo muestra la historia de la ciudad.

Museu à Beira-Rio

Um novo marco visível de longe está na zona portuária desde 2011: o Museu à Beira-rio (Museum am Strom – MAS). As salas de exposição da torre do museu de 62 m de altura estão empilhadas como contentores em dez andares. Cada nível é girado 90 graus, de modo que as galerias de vidro no meio permitem mudar as vistas da cidade e do porto. A fachada de arenito indiano avermelhado é decorada com 3000 mãos de alumínio polido, uma alusão ao nome da cidade de Antuérpia. Com uma gigantesca coleção de 500 000 objetos de arte e utensílios, o museu mostra a história da cidade.

Museum aan de Stroom

In het havengebied staat sinds 2011 een nieuw, al van ver zichtbaar, karakteristiek bouwwerk: het Museum aan de Stroom. De tentoonstellingsruimtes van de 62 m hoge museumtoren zijn als containers over tien verdiepingen gestapeld. Elk niveau is 90 graden gedraaid, zodat de tussenliggende glazen galerijen een wisselend uitzicht op de stad en de haven mogelijk maken. De gevel van roodachtig, Indisch zandsteen is versierd met 3000 handen van gepolijst aluminium, een verwijzing naar de Antwerpse stadsnaam. Met een gigantische collectie van 500 000 kunst- en gebruiksvoorwerpen toont het museum de geschiedenis van de stad.

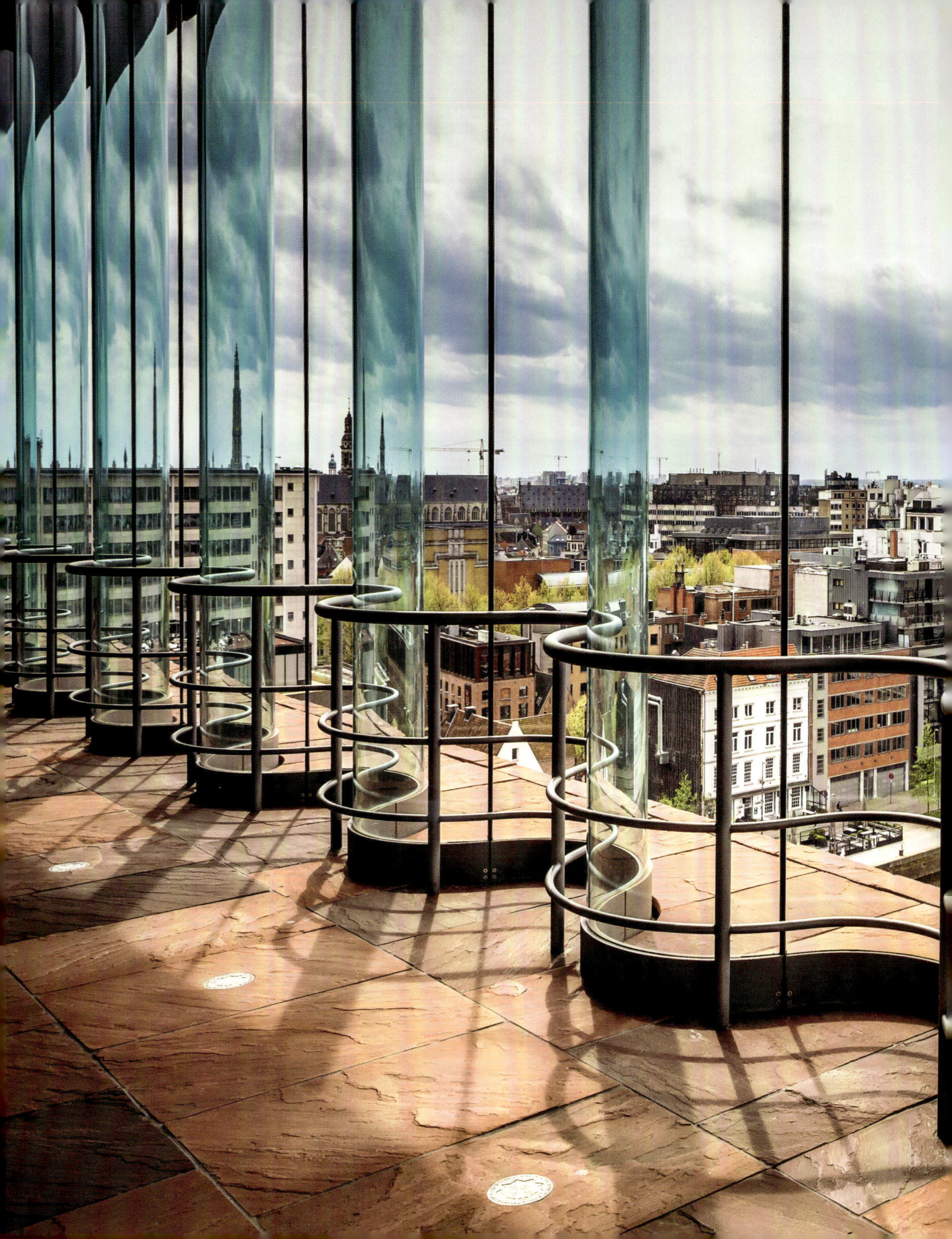

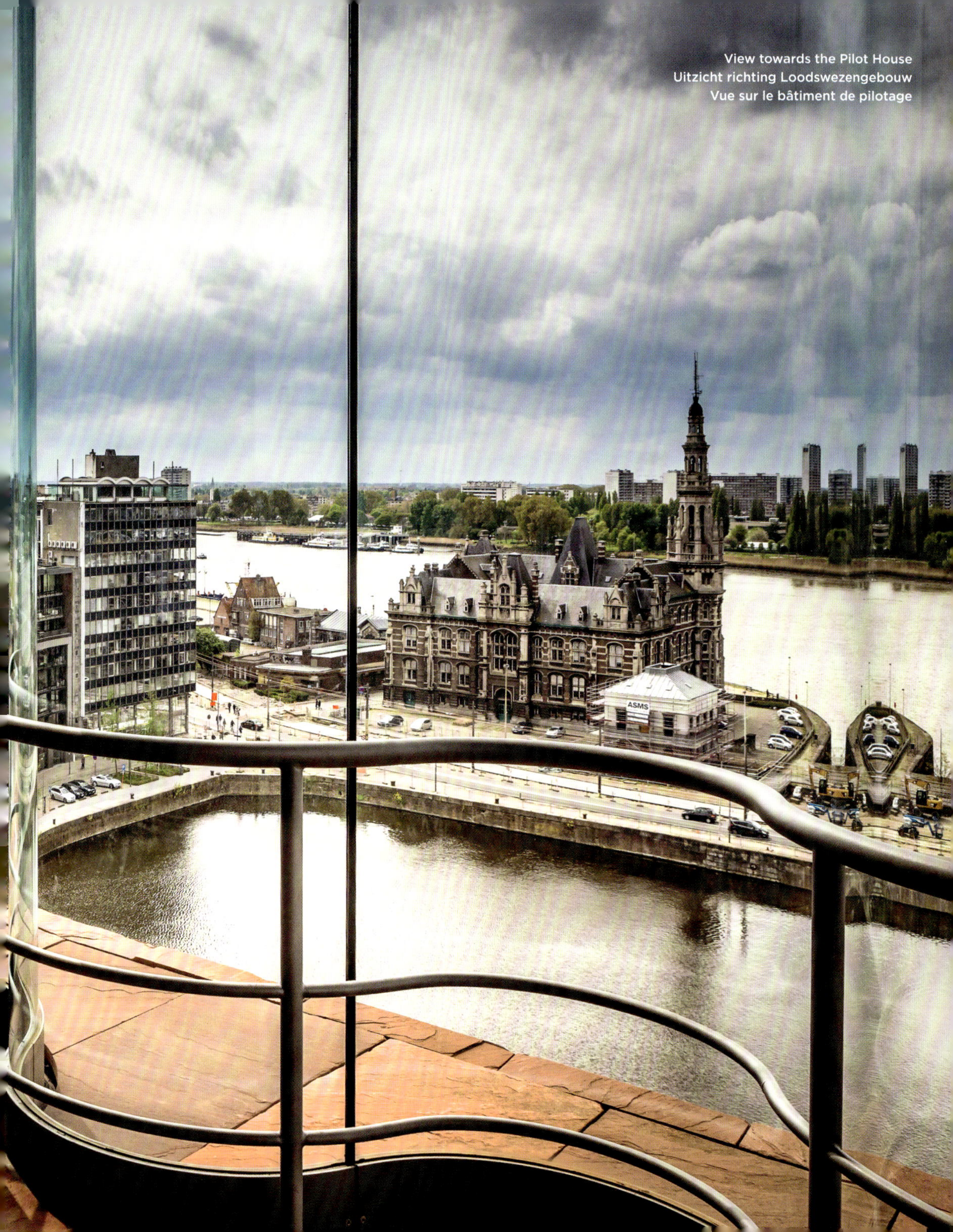

View towards the Pilot House
Uitzicht richting Loodswezengebouw
Vue sur le bâtiment de pilotage

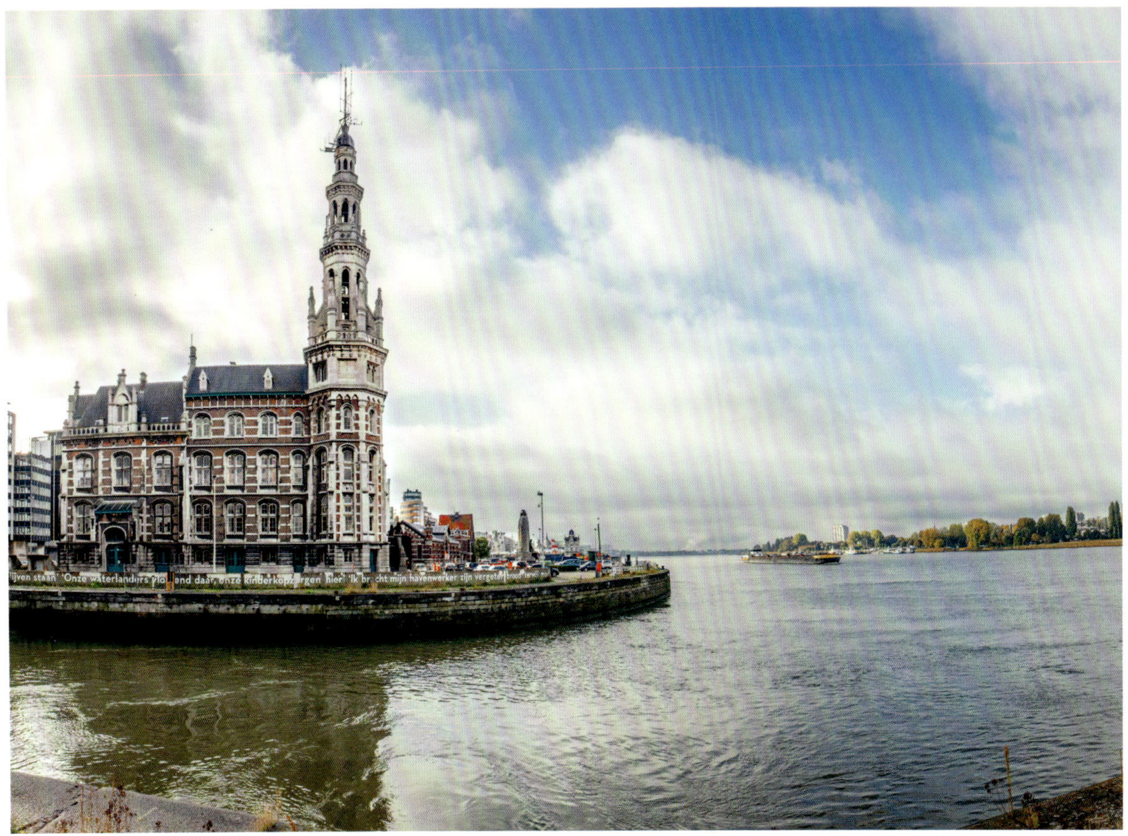

Pilot House
Loodswezengebouw
Bâtiment de pilotage

Islet and rowing boat harbor

The Eilandje (small island), the original port
of Antwerp, is surrounded by water. Today,
the harbor activity has migrated further
north, but with the new attractions of
the Museum am Strom, the Red Star Line
Museum and the many terrace cafés at the
docks, the quarter is flourishing and has
become a party mile. Opposite Bonaparte
Dock, from where Napoleon planned
his invasion of England, you will find the
eclectically styled Pilot House and also the
former rowing boat harbor, as those who
needed to board a ship at anchor in days
gone by had to rely on rowing boats.

Îlot et port des chaloupes

Entouré d'eau, l'Eilandje (qui signifie
îlot ou île) fut le premier port d'Anvers.
Aujourd'hui, l'activité portuaire s'est
déplacée vers le nord, mais les nouvelles
attractions, le Museum aan de Stroom, le
musée Red Star Line et les nombreuses
terrasses de café donnant sur les quais
rendent le quartier vivant et en ont fait
un lieu de fête. Face au quai Bonaparte,
d'où Napoléon planifia l'invasion de
l'Angleterre, se dressent le bâtiment de
pilotage, de style éclectique, et l'ancien
port des chaloupes. À l'époque, quiconque
souhaitait monter à bord d'un navire à
l'ancre en dépendait.

Inselchen und Ruderboot-Hafen

Das Eilandje (kleine Eiland, Insel), der
ursprüngliche Hafen von Antwerpen,
ist von Wasser umgeben. Heute ist
die Hafenaktivität weiter nach Norden
gewandert, aber mit den neuen
Attraktionen, dem Museum am Strom,
dem Red Star Line Museum und den
vielen Terrassencafés an den Docks blüht
das Viertel auf und wurde zur Party-
Meile. Gegenüber des Bonaparte Docks,
Napoleon plante von hier aus die Invasion
Englands, befinden sich das Lotsenhaus
im eklektizistischen Stil und der ehemalige
Ruderboot-Hafen. Wer damals an Bord
eines vor Anker liegenden Schiffes wollte,
war auf die Ruderboote angewiesen.

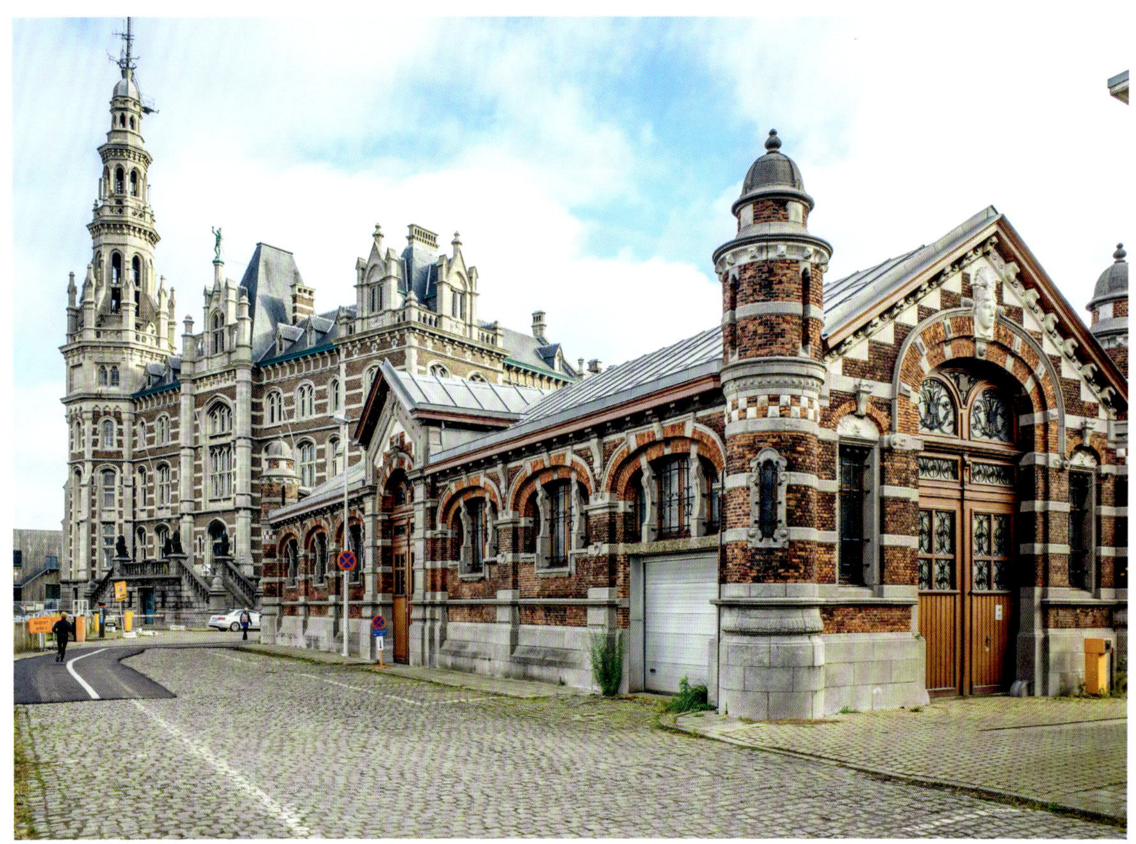

Marguerie Schuilhaven and Pilot House
Marguerie Schuilhaven en Loodswezengebouw
Marguerie Schuilhaven et bâtiment de pilotage

Islote y puerto de remos

El Eilandje (pequeña isla), el puerto original de Amberes, está rodeado de agua. Hoy en día la actividad portuaria ha migrado más al norte, pero con las nuevas atracciones, el Museo aan de Stroom, el Red Star Line Museum y las numerosas terrazas de los muelles, el barrio está floreciendo y se ha convertido en una milla de fiesta. Frente al muelle de Bonaparte, desde donde Napoleón planeó la invasión de Inglaterra, se encuentran la casa piloto de estilo ecléctico y el antiguo puerto de remos. Aquellos que querían embarcarse en un barco fondeado en ese momento tenían que confiar en los botes de remos.

Pequenas ilhas e porto de barcos a remos

O Eilandje (pequena ilha), o porto original de Antuérpia, é cercado por água. Hoje a atividade portuária migrou mais para o norte, mas com as novas atrações, o Museu am Strom, o Museu Red Star Line e os muitos cafés com terraço nas docas, o bairro está florescendo e se tornou uma milha de festa. Em frente à Doca de Bonaparte, de onde Napoleão planejou a invasão da Inglaterra, você encontrará a eclética casa de pilotos e o antigo porto de barcos a remos. Aqueles que queriam embarcar em um navio ancorado naquela época tinham que contar com barcos a remos.

Eiland- en roeiboothaven

Het Eilandje, de oorspronkelijke haven van Antwerpen, is omgeven door water. Vandaag de dag is de havenactiviteit verder naar het noorden getrokken, maar met de nieuwe attracties, het Museum aan de Stroom, het Red Star Line Museum en de vele terrasjes aan de haven komt de wijk tot bloei en is het een feestelijke locatie geworden. Tegenover het Bonapartedok, van waaruit Napoleon de invasie van Engeland heeft gepland, vindt u het Loodswezen, een gebouw in eclectische stijl, en de voormalige roeiboothaven. Wie destijds aan boord wilde gaan van een schip dat voor anker lag, was op roeiboten aangewezen.

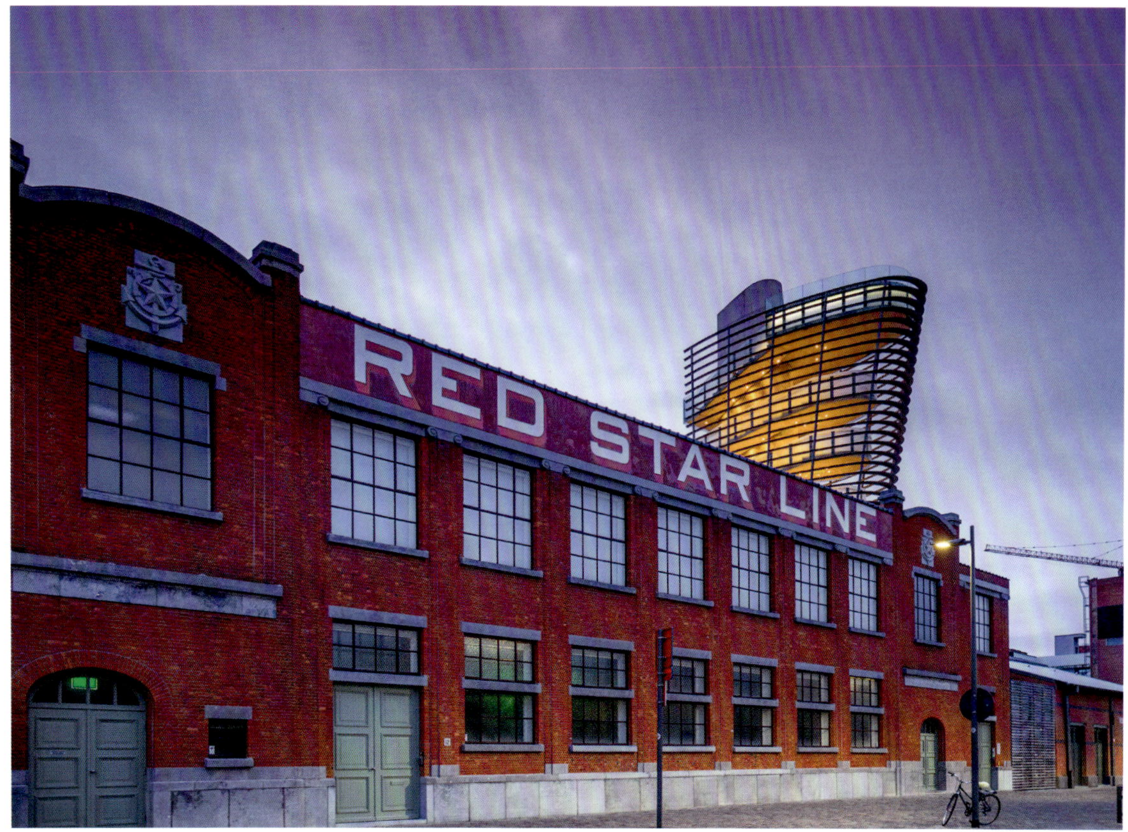

Red Star Line Museum
Musée Red Star Line

Red Star Line

With its interactive permanent exhibition, the "Red Star Line" maritime museum recalls the emigration wave at the beginning of the 20th century. Travelers who passed through the building of the shipping company were heading into an uncertain life in America. The ships of the Red Star Line, founded in 1872, mainly traveled the Philadelphia and New York passages, carrying almost three million people up until 1935. Among the passengers was, for example, the theoretical physicist Albert Einstein, who like many other German-Jewish intellectuals and artists fled the Nazi regime, from Europe into exile overseas.

Red Star Line

L'exposition permanente interactive du musée maritime Red Star Line fait revivre la vague d'émigration du début du xxᵉ siècle : jadis, quiconque passait le seuil du bâtiment de la compagnie maritime se lançait dans l'inconnu d'une vie en Amérique. Les navires de la Red Star Line, compagnie fondée en 1872, assuraient surtout le transport maritime vers Philadelphie et New York et transporta près de trois millions de personnes jusqu'en 1935. Parmi les passagers, la compagnie compta, ainsi l'astrophysicien Albert Einstein, qui, comme beaucoup d'autres intellectuels et artistes juifs allemands, s'enfuit d'Europe au moment de l'accession au pouvoir d'Hitler et s'exila à l'étranger.

Red Star Line

Das maritime Museum „Red Star Line" erinnert mit seiner interaktiven Dauerausstellung an die Auswanderungswelle zu Beginn des 20. Jahrhunderts: Wer einst das Gebäude der Reederei betrat, startete in ein ungewisses Leben in Amerika. Die Schiffe der 1872 gegründeten Red Star Line befuhren vor allem die Passagen Philadelphia und New York und beförderten bis 1935 fast drei Millionen Menschen. Unter den Passagieren war zum Beispiel auch der Physiker Albert Einstein, der wie viele andere deutsch-jüdische Intellektuelle und Künstler vor dem Naziregime aus Europa ins Exil nach Übersee flüchtete.

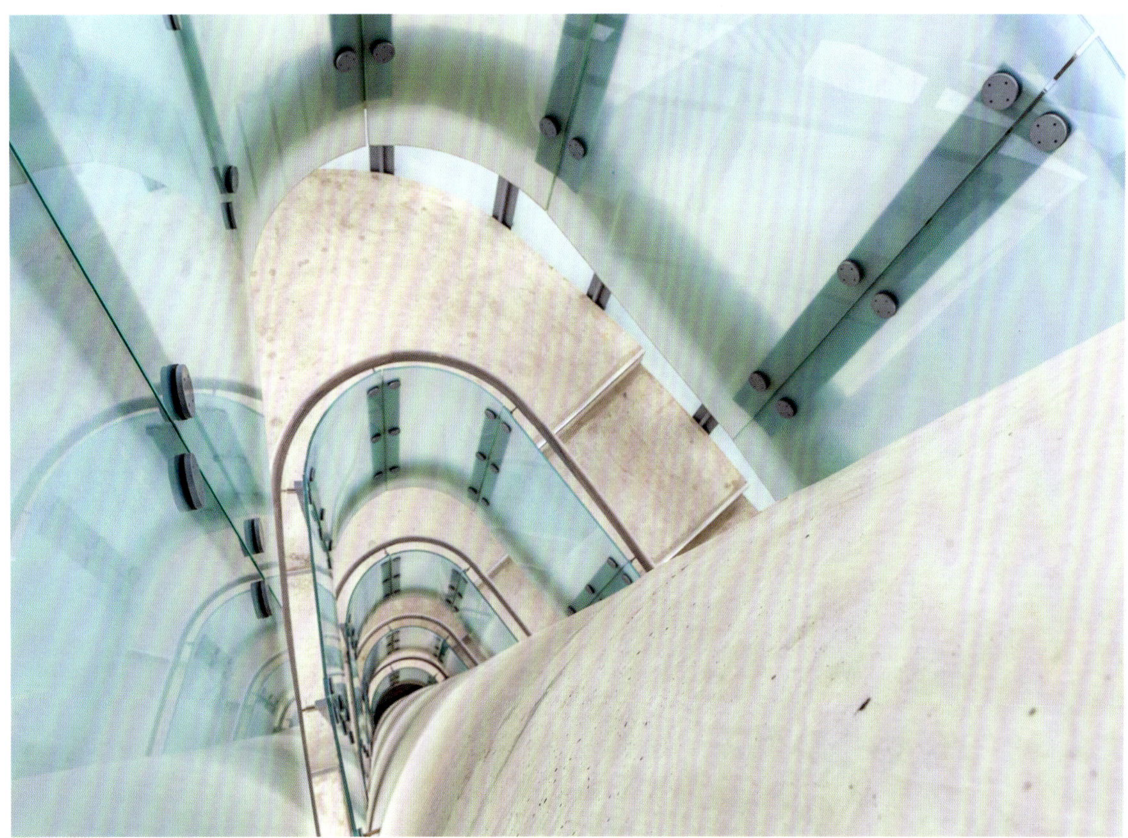

Staircase, Red Star Line Museum
Trap, Red Star Line Museum
L'escalier du Musée Red Star Line

Red Star Line

Con su exposición permanente interactiva, el museo marítimo "Red Star Line" recuerda la ola de emigración que tuvo lugar a principios del siglo XX: aquellos que entraron en el edificio de la compañía naviera comenzaron una vez una vida incierta en América. Los barcos de la Red Star Line, fundada en 1872, viajaron principalmente por los pasajes de Filadelfia y Nueva York y transportaron a casi tres millones de personas hasta 1935. Entre los pasajeros se encontraba, por ejemplo, el físico Albert Einstein que, como muchos otros intelectuales y artistas judíos alemanes, huyó del régimen nazi de Europa al exilio en ultramar.

Red Star Line

Com a sua exposição permanente interativa, o museu marítimo da linha estrela vermelha "Red Star Line" recorda a onda de emigração no início do século XX: aqueles que entraram no edifício da companhia de navegação tiveram um começo de vida incerta na América. Os navios da "Red Star Line", fundada em 1872, percorreram principalmente as passagens de Filadélfia e Nova Iorque e transportaram quase três milhões de pessoas até 1935. Entre os passageiros encontrava-se, por exemplo, o físico Albert Einstein, que, como muitos outros intelectuais e artistas judeus alemães, fugiu do regime nazista da Europa para o exílio no estrangeiro.

Red Star Line

Het maritiem "Red Star Line Museum" herinnert met zijn interactieve permanente tentoonstelling aan de emigratiegolf van begin 20e eeuw: wie destijds het gebouw van de rederij binnenkwam, begon aan een ongewis leven in Amerika. De schepen van de in 1872 opgerichte Red Star Line voeren voornamelijk naar Philadelphia en New York en vervoerden tot 1935 bijna drie miljoen mensen. Onder de passagiers was bijvoorbeeld ook de natuurkundige Albert Einstein die net als veel andere Duits-joodse intellectuelen en kunstenaars vanwege het naziregime uit Europa naar het buitenland vluchtte.

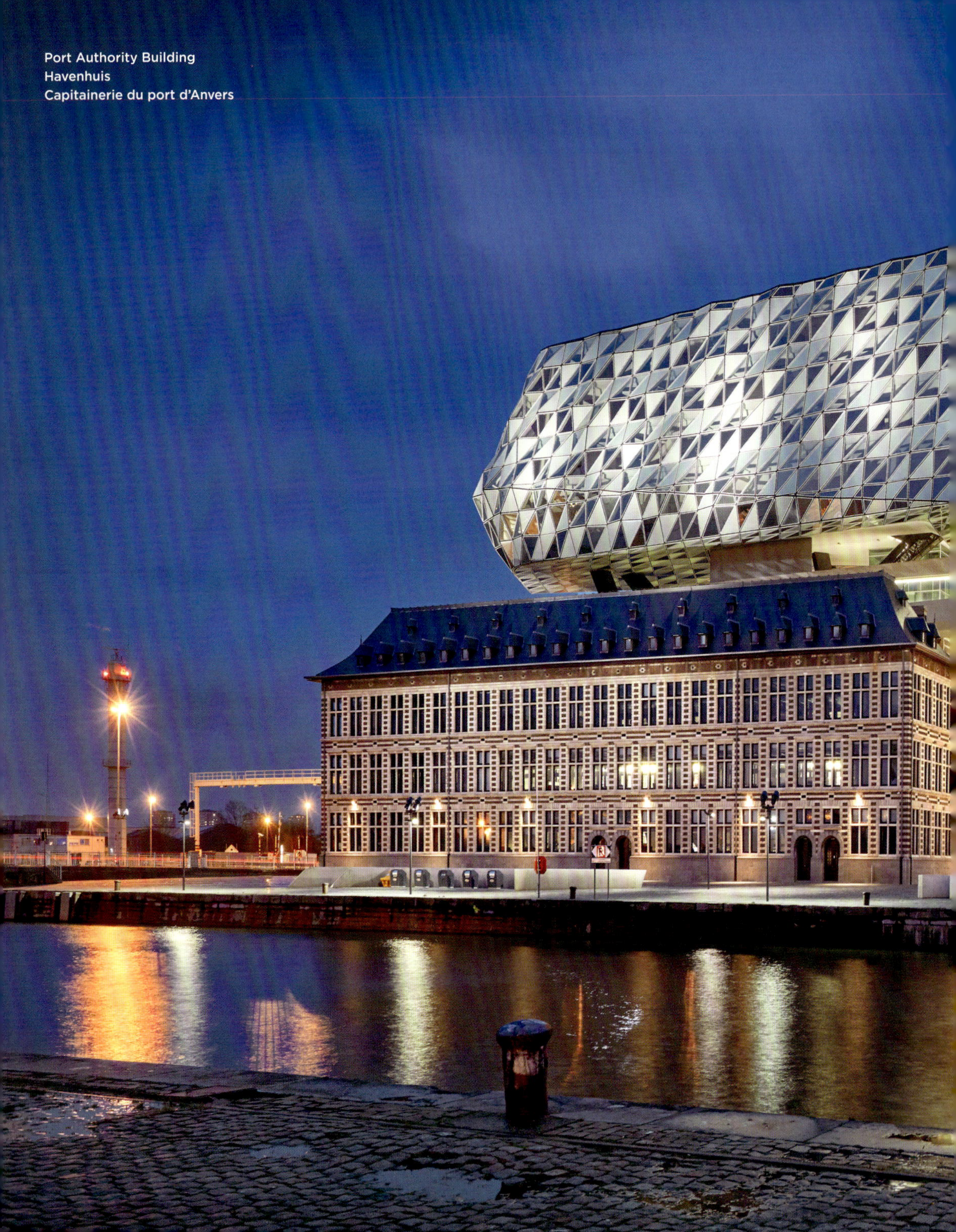
Port Authority Building
Havenhuis
Capitainerie du port d'Anvers

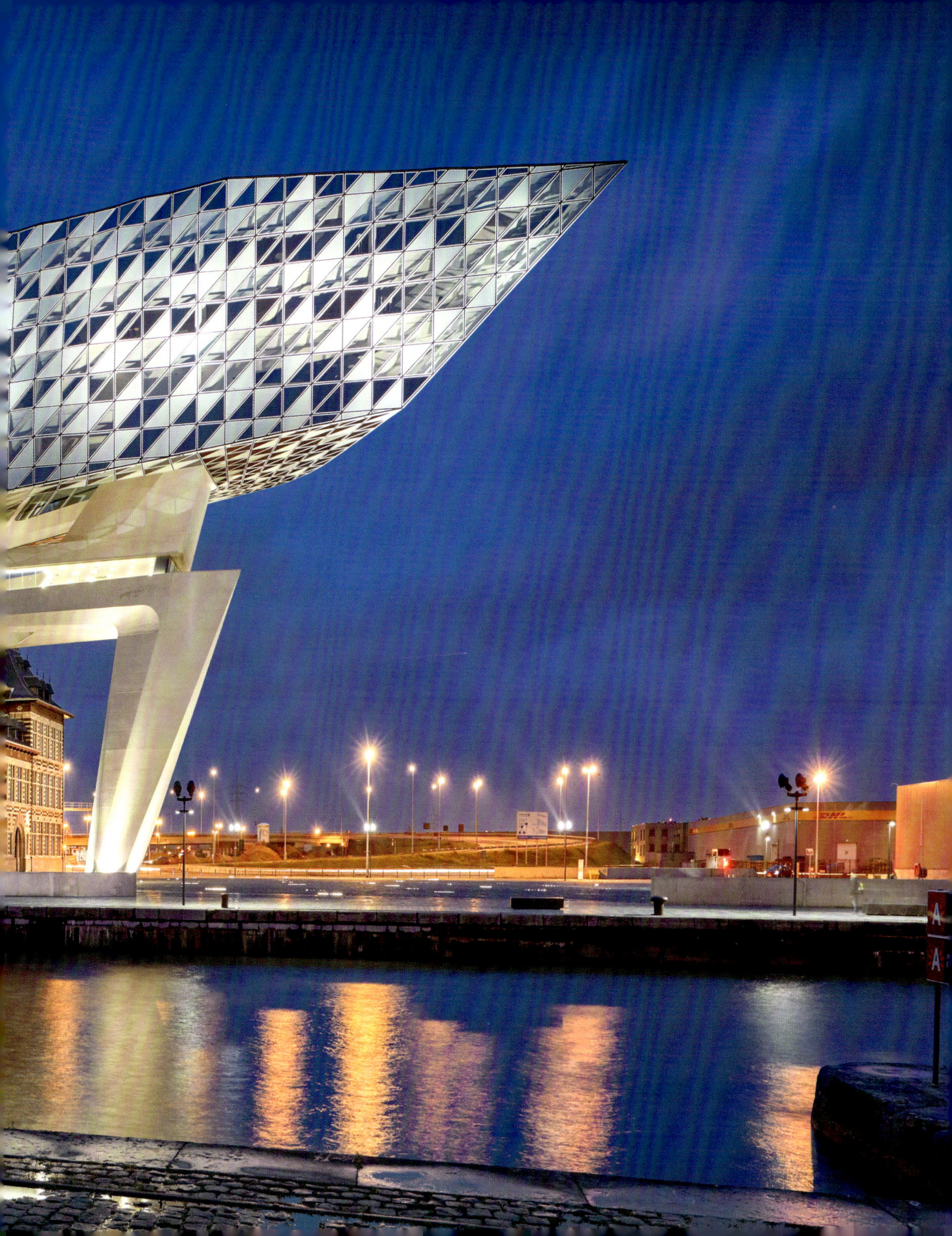

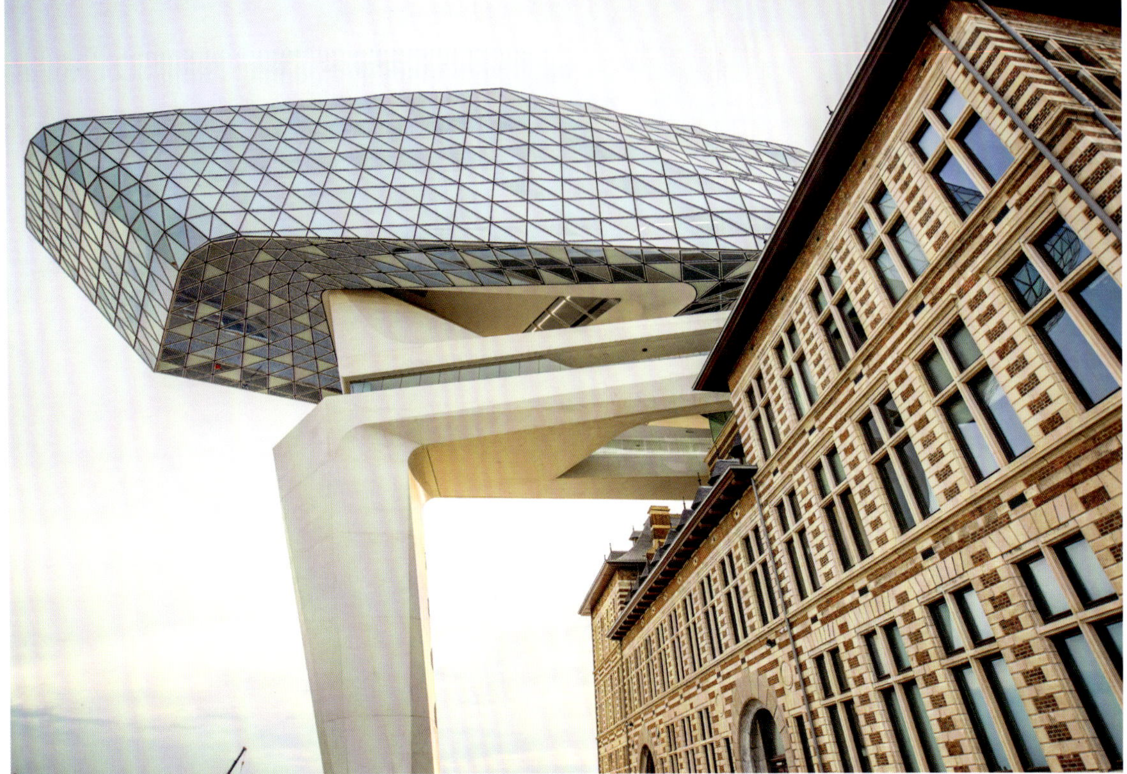

Port Authority Building
Havenhuis
Capitainerie du port d'Anvers

Port Authority Building

The star architect Zaha Hadid has had a spectacular glass construction, reminiscent of both a ship and a diamond, incorporated into and upon a former fire station. The new landmark was opened shortly before her death in 2016. One may also visit the futuristic building with a guide and enjoy the panoramic view.

Casa portuaria

La arquitecta estrella Zaha Hadid diseñó una espectacular construcción de vidrio que recuerda a un barco o a un diamante y está montada sobre un antiguo cuartel de bomberos. El nuevo hito se inauguró poco antes de su muerte en 2016. También puede visitar el edificio futurista con un guía y disfrutar de la vista panorámica.

Maison du Port

La célèbre architecte Zaha Hadid fit édifier sur une ancienne caserne de pompiers une spectaculaire construction en verre évoquant un navire ou un diamant. Le nouvel emblème de la ville fut inauguré peu avant sa mort en 2016. Ce bâtiment futuriste peut être exploré dans le cadre d'une visite guidée et offre une belle vue panoramique.

Casa do porto

A arquiteta estrela Zaha Hadid teve uma construção de vidro espetacular, que faz lembrar um navio ou um diamante, montada em um antigo quartel de bombeiros. O novo marco foi inaugurado pouco antes da sua morte em 2016. Você também pode visitar o edifício futurista com um guia e desfrutar da vista panorâmica.

Hafenhaus

Auf eine ehemalige Feuerwehrkaserne hat die Stararchitektin Zaha Hadid eine spektakuläre Glaskonstruktion setzen lassen, die an ein Schiff oder einen Diamanten erinnert. Kurz vor ihrem Tod im Jahr 2016 wurde das neue Wahrzeichen eröffnet. Darüber hinaus kann man das futuristische Gebäude im Rahmen einer Führung besichtigen und die Panoramaaussicht genießen.

Havenhuis

De sterarchitect Zaha Hadid liet op een voormalige brandweerkazerne een spectaculaire glazen constructie plaatsen die doet denken aan een schip of een diamant. Het nieuwe monument werd kort voor haar dood in 2016 geopend. U kunt het futuristische gebouw ook bezoeken met een gids en genieten van het panoramische uitzicht.

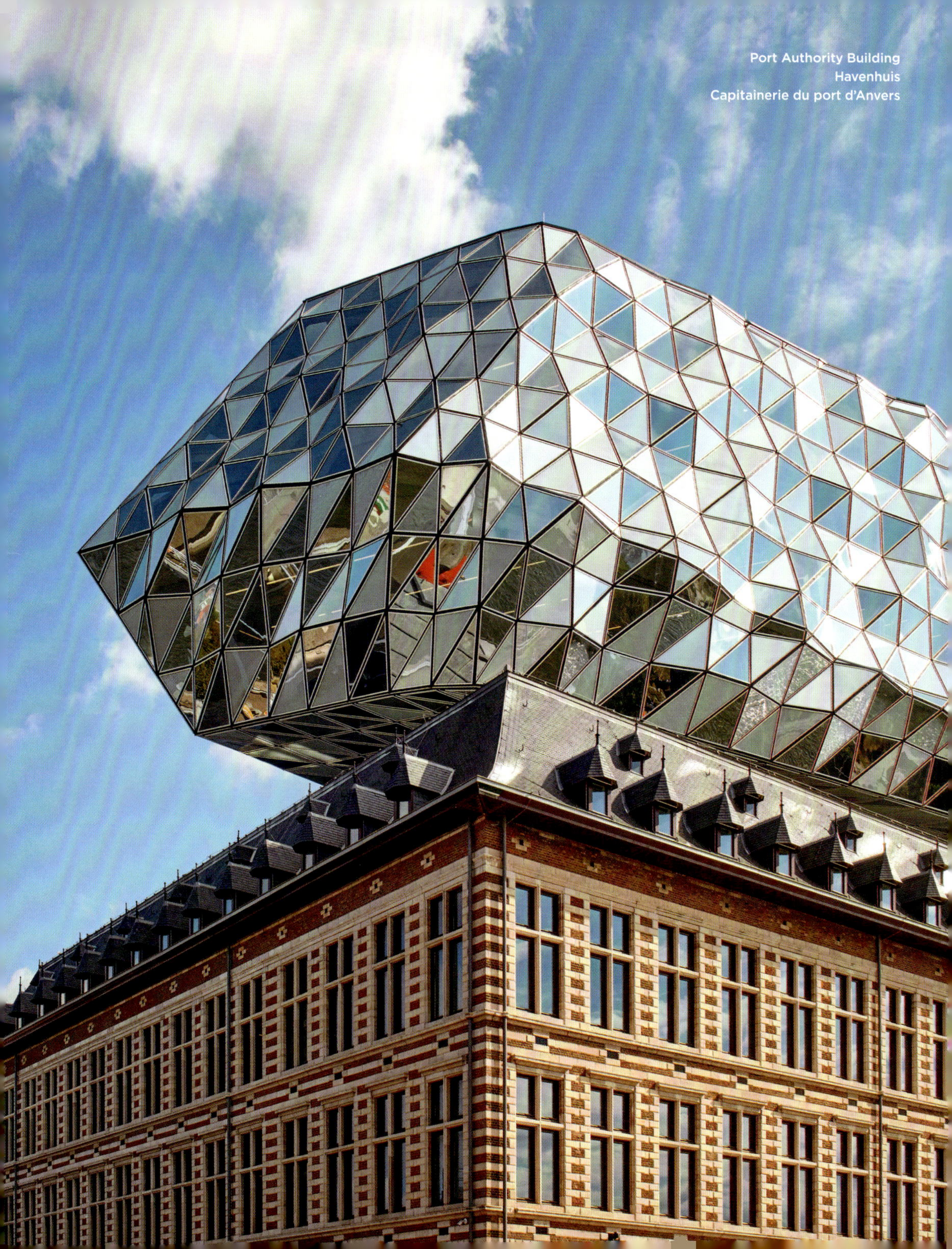

Port Authority Building
Havenhuis
Capitainerie du port d'Anvers

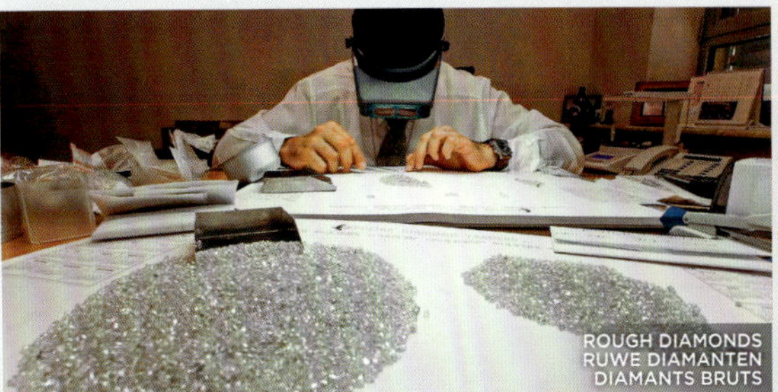

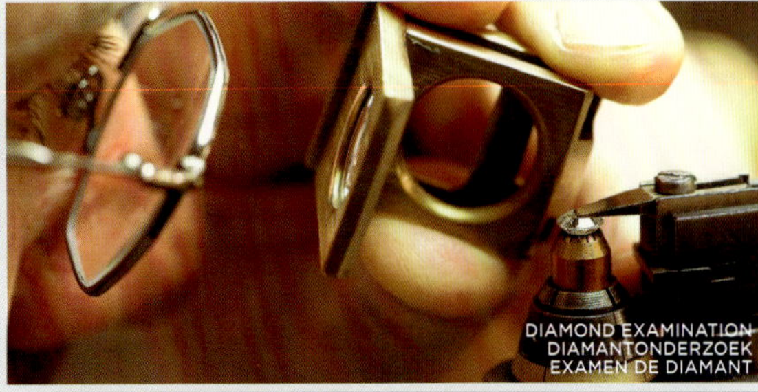

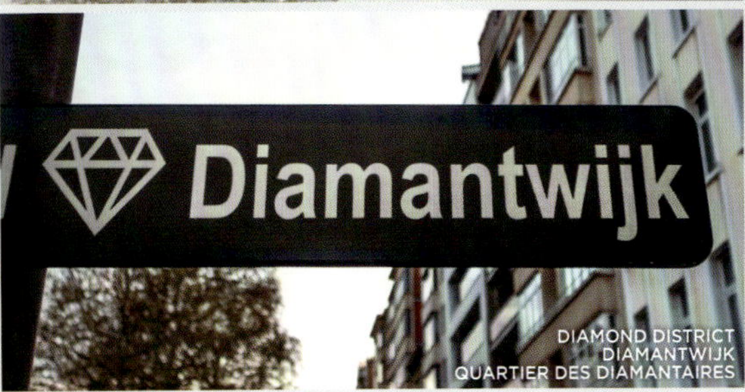

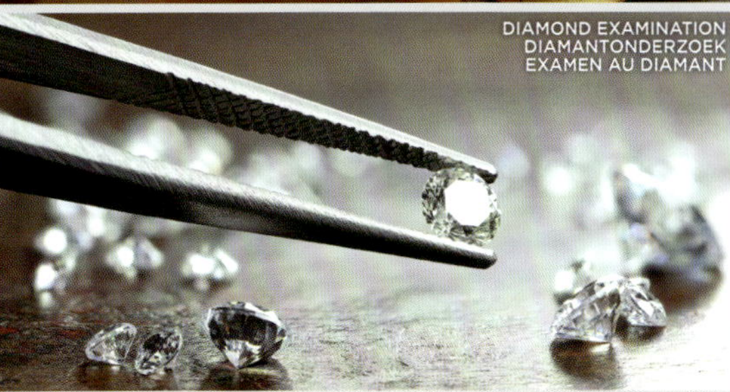

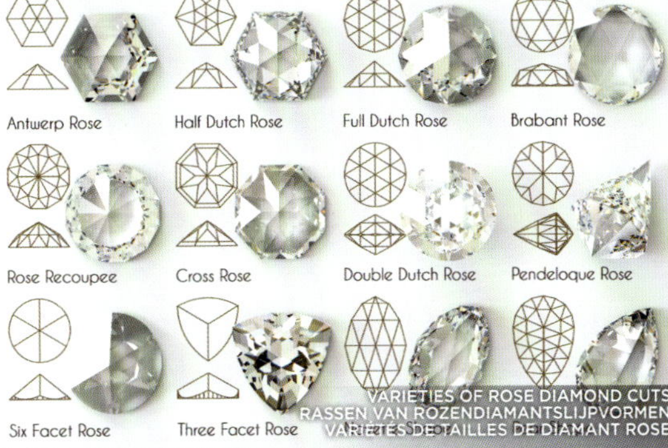

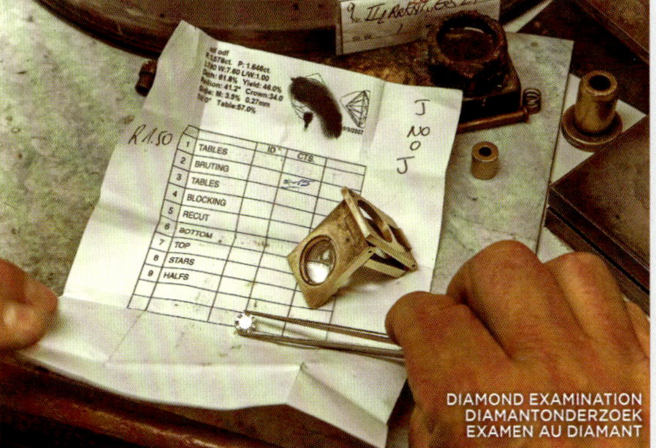

Diamond City

Four out of five rough diamonds mined worldwide are traded in Antwerp, with every second diamond being cut and returned to the city. In the diamond district near the main railway station, diamond cutters, jewellers and diamond traders work hand in hand and everyone knows everyone else. Even today a trade worth millions is sealed with a handshake and a "Mazal U'Bracha" (Hebrew for "luck and blessing"). In the quarter there are countless jewellers, four diamond exchanges, diamond showrooms and cutters. Despite strong competition, "Cut in Antwerp" remains the highest distinction for diamonds.

La ville du diamant

Parmi tous les diamants bruts extraits dans le monde, les quatre cinquièmes sont commercialisés à Anvers et la moitié y revient sous la forme de diamants taillés. Dans le quartier du diamant, près de la gare centrale, bijoutiers, tailleurs, diamantaires travaillent main dans la main et tout le monde se connaît. Aujourd'hui encore, une poignée de main et un « Mazal U'Bracha » (en hébreu, chance et bénédiction) scellent une transaction de plusieurs millions d'euros. Le quartier comprend d'innombrables bijoutiers, quatre bourses du diamant, des salles d'exposition et des tailleurs de diamants. Malgré une forte concurrence, « Cut in Antwerp » reste le meilleur label dans ce domaine.

Diamantenstadt

Vier von fünf weltweit geförderten Rohdiamanten werden in Antwerpen gehandelt; jeder zweite kommt als geschliffener Diamant in die Stadt zurück. Im Diamanten-Viertel nahe dem Hauptbahnhof arbeiten Diamantenschleifer, Juweliere und Diamantenhändler Hand in Hand und jeder kennt jeden. Noch heute wird ein millionenschwerer Handel per Handschlag und einem „Mazal U'Bracha" (hebräisch für „Glück und Segen") besiegelt. In dem Viertel gibt es unzählige Juweliere, vier Diamantbörsen, Diamanten-Showrooms und Schleifereien. Trotz starker Konkurrenz bleibt „Cut in Antwerp" das höchste Label für Diamanten.

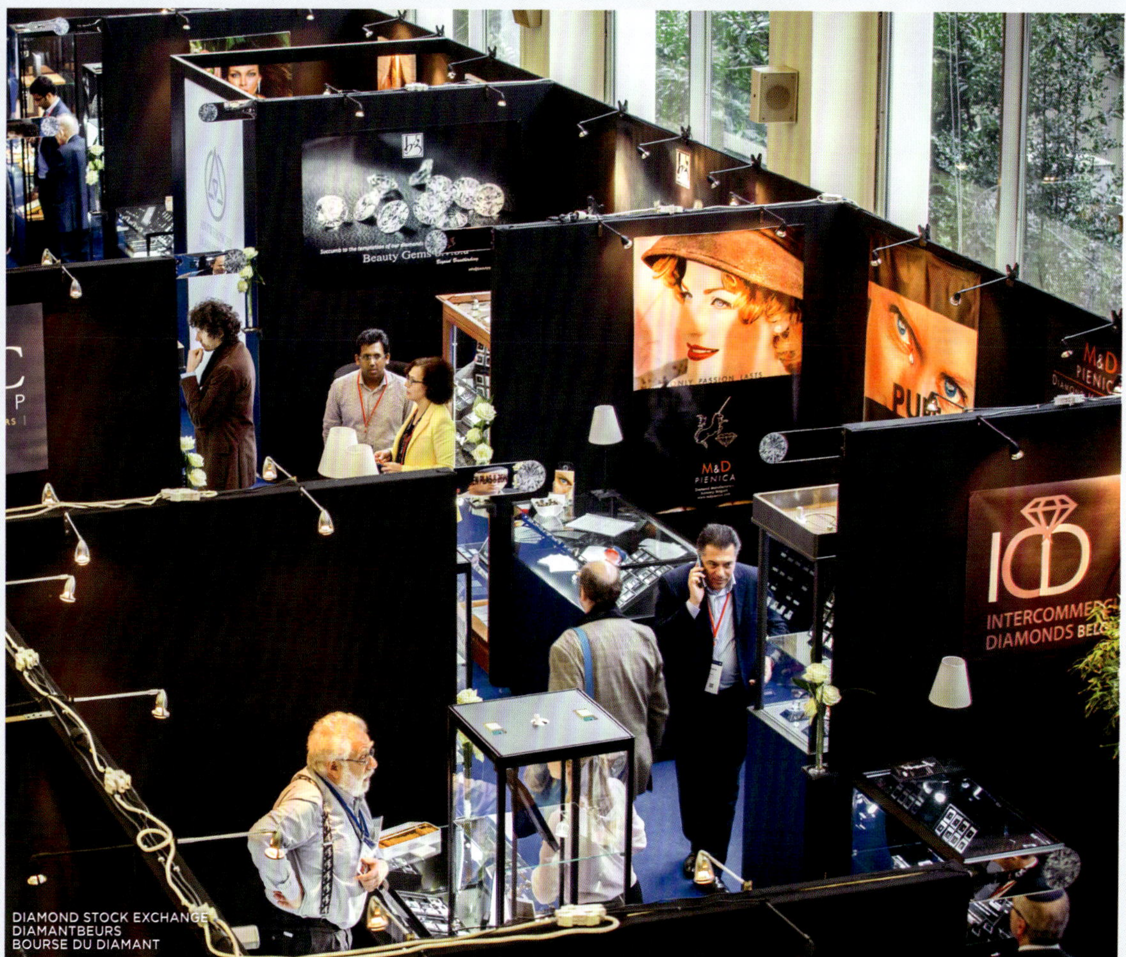

DIAMOND STOCK EXCHANGE
DIAMANTBEURS
BOURSE DU DIAMANT

Ciudad de diamantes

Cuatro de cada cinco diamantes en bruto extraídos en todo el mundo se comercializan en Amberes; uno de cada dos diamantes se talla y se devuelve a la ciudad. En el barrio de los diamantes, cerca de la estación principal de ferrocarril, los talladores de diamantes, los joyeros y los comerciantes de diamantes trabajan mano a mano y todo el mundo se conoce. Incluso hoy en día, un intercambio millonario se sella con un apretón de manos y un "Mazal U'Bracha" (que en hebreo significa "suerte y bendición"). En el barrio hay innumerables joyeros, cuatro bolsas de diamantes, salas de exposición de diamantes y cortadores. A pesar de la fuerte competencia, "Cut in Antwerp" sigue siendo la etiqueta más alta para diamantes.

Cidade dos diamantes

Quatro em cada cinco diamantes brutos extraídos em todo o mundo são comercializados em Antuérpia; cada segundo diamante volta à cidade como um diamante lapidado. No distrito diamantífero perto da estação ferroviária principal, os cortadores de diamantes, os joalheiros e os comerciantes de diamantes trabalham de mãos dadas e todo mundo conhece todo mundo. Ainda hoje um comércio que vale milhões de dólares é selado com um aperto de mão e um "Mazal U'Bracha" (hebraico para "boa sorte e bênção"). No bairro há inúmeros joalheiros, quatro bolsas de diamantes, showrooms de diamantes e lapidadores. Apesar da forte concorrência, a "Cut in Antuérpia" continua a ser a marca mais importante para os diamantes.

Diamantstad

Vier van de vijf wereldwijd gedolven ruwe diamanten worden in Antwerpen verhandeld; elke tweede diamant komt als geslepen diamant weer terug in de stad. In de diamantwijk nabij Station Antwerpen-Centraal werken diamantslijpers, juweliers en diamanthandelaren hand in hand en iedereen kent iedereen. Zelfs vandaag de dag wordt een miljoenen transactie bezegeld met een handdruk en een "Mazal U'Bracha" (Hebreeuws voor "geluk en zegen"). In de wijk zijn talloze juweliers, vier diamantenbeurzen, diamanten showrooms en slijperijen. Ondanks de sterke concurrentie blijft "Cut in Antwerp" het hoogste kwaliteitsmerk voor diamanten.

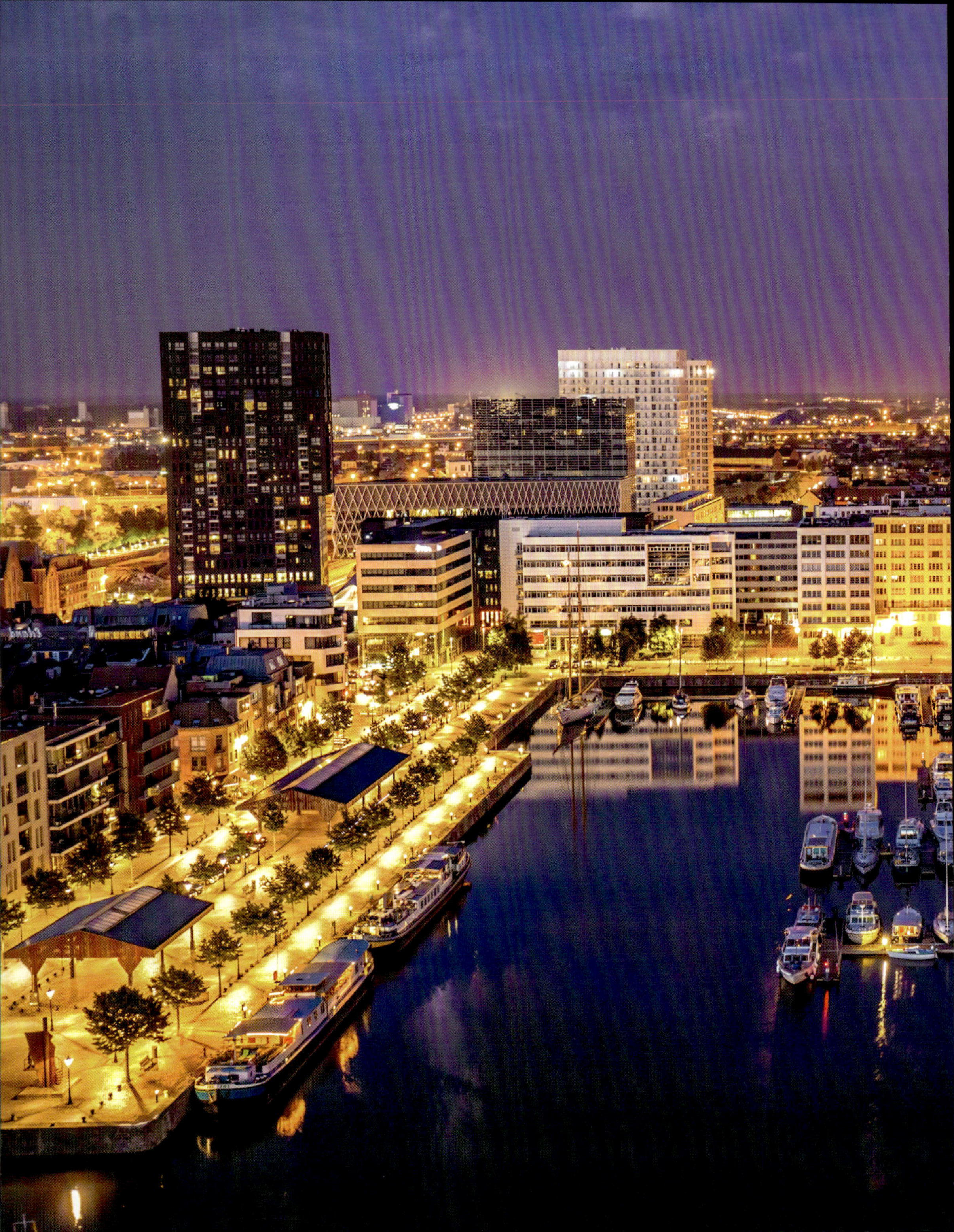

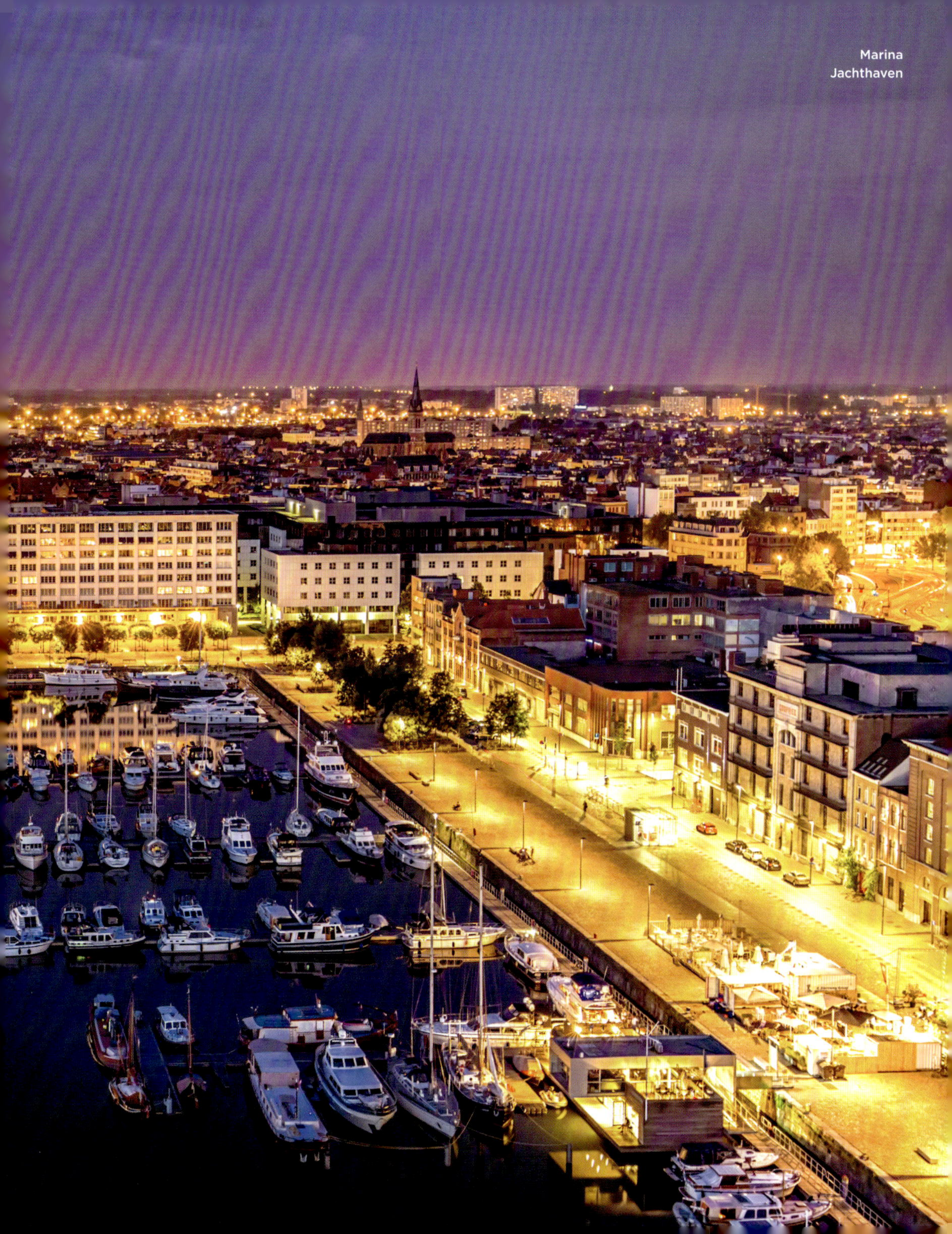
Marina
Jachthaven

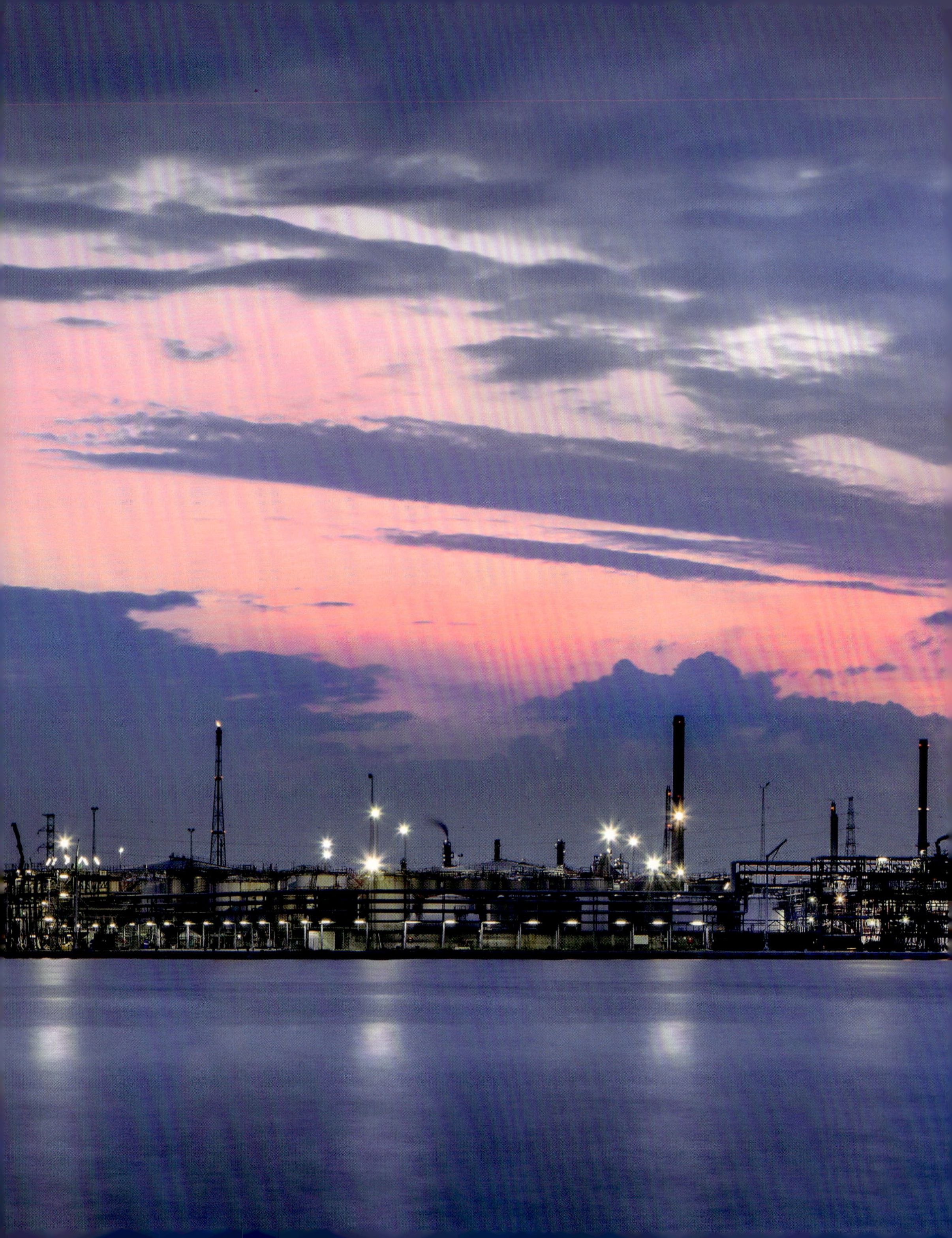

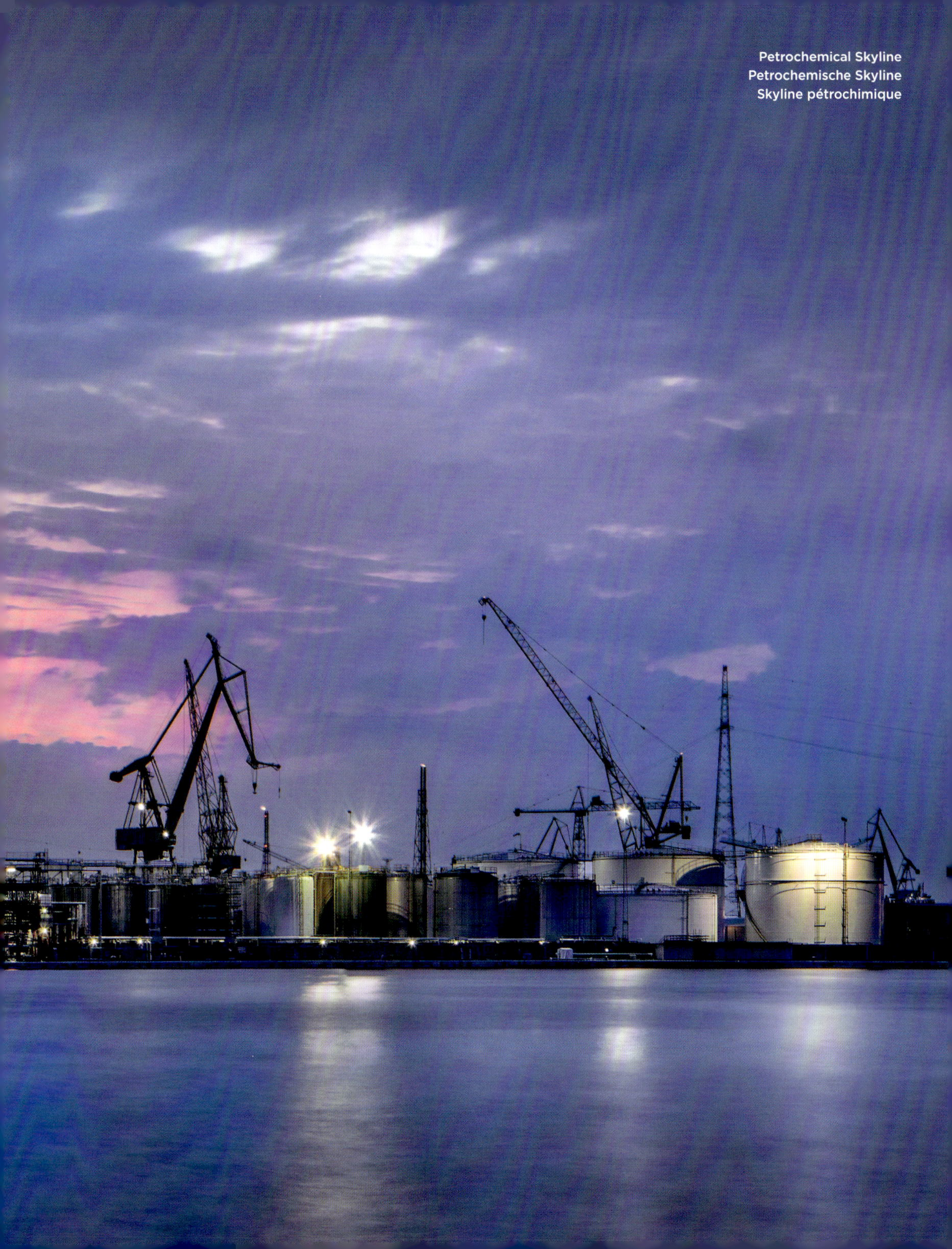

Petrochemical Skyline
Petrochemische Skyline
Skyline pétrochimique

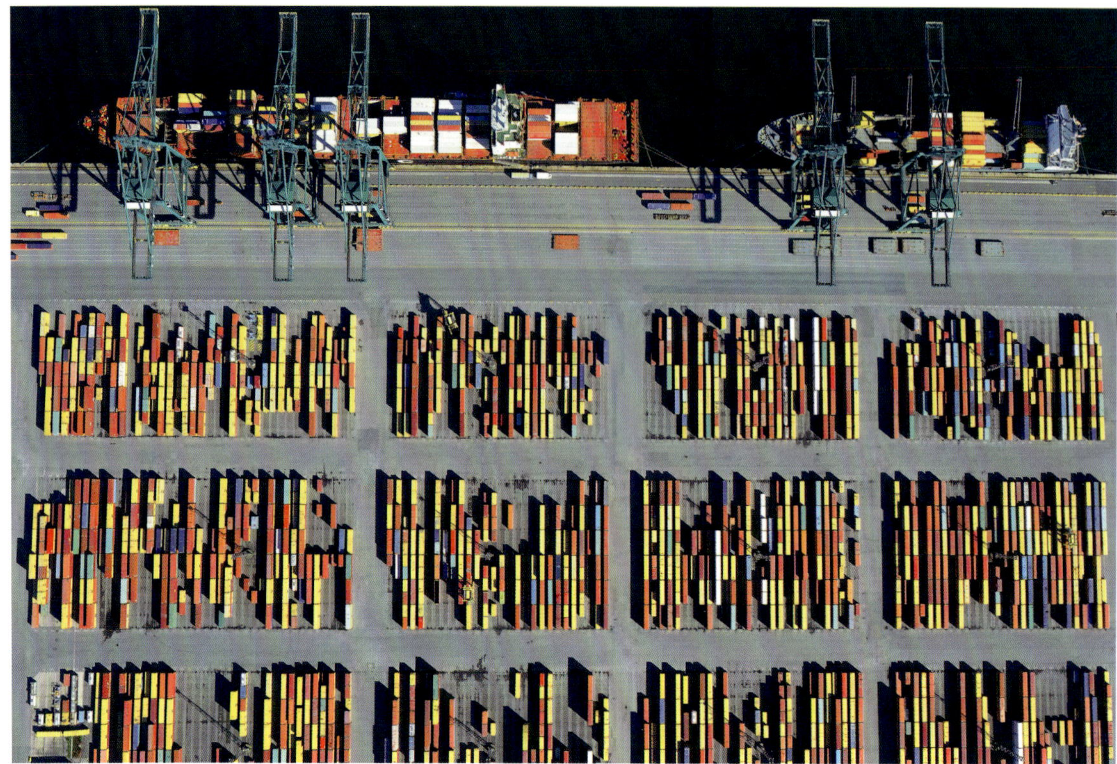

Container terminal, Delwaide Dock
Containerterminal, Delwaide Dok
Terminal à containers, quai de Delwaide

Port of Antwerp

The second largest port in Europe has the largest tidal lock in the world. Visitors can discover the fascinating cosmos full of gigantic buildings and machines on a harbor tour. A round trip is like a tour through a maze, past docks, locks, lifting bridges, hundreds of tankers and thousands of colourful containers.

Le port d'Anvers

C'est dans le deuxième port d'Europe que se trouve la plus grande écluse du monde. Un tour du port en bateau permet aux visiteurs d'explorer un univers fascinant, composé de gigantesques bâtiments et machines. Cette visite labyrinthique les fait passer le long de quais, devant des écluses, des ponts levants, des centaines de bateaux-citernes et des milliers de containers colorés.

Antwerpener Hafen

Der zweitgrößte Hafen Europas verfügt über die größte Schleuse der Welt. Besucher können den faszinierenden Kosmos voller gigantischer Bauwerke und Maschinen mit einer Hafenrundfahrt entdecken. Eine Rundfahrt ist wie eine Tour durch einen Irrgarten, vorbei an Docks, Schleusen, Hebebrücken, an Hunderten Tankern und an Tausenden bunten Containern.

Puerto de Amberes

El segundo puerto más grande de Europa tiene la esclusa más grande del mundo. Los visitantes pueden descubrir el fascinante cosmos lleno de gigantescos edificios y máquinas en un recorrido por el puerto. Dar una vuelta por aquí es como recorrer por un laberinto, pasando por muelles, esclusas, puentes elevadores, cientos de camiones cisterna y miles de coloridos contenedores.

Porto de Antuérpia

O segundo maior porto da Europa tem a maior eclusa do mundo. Os visitantes podem descobrir o fascinante cosmos cheio de edifícios gigantescos e máquinas em um passeio pelo porto. Uma viagem de ida e volta é como um passeio por um labirinto, docas, eclusas, pontes elevatórias, centenas de petroleiros e milhares de contentores coloridos.

Haven van Antwerpen

De op een na grootste haven van Europa heeft de grootste sluis ter wereld. Bezoekers kunnen met een havenrondvaart de fascinerende kosmos met zijn gigantische gebouwen en machines ontdekken. Een rondvaart is als een tocht door een doolhof, langs dokken, sluizen, hefbruggen, honderden tankers en duizenden kleurrijke containers.

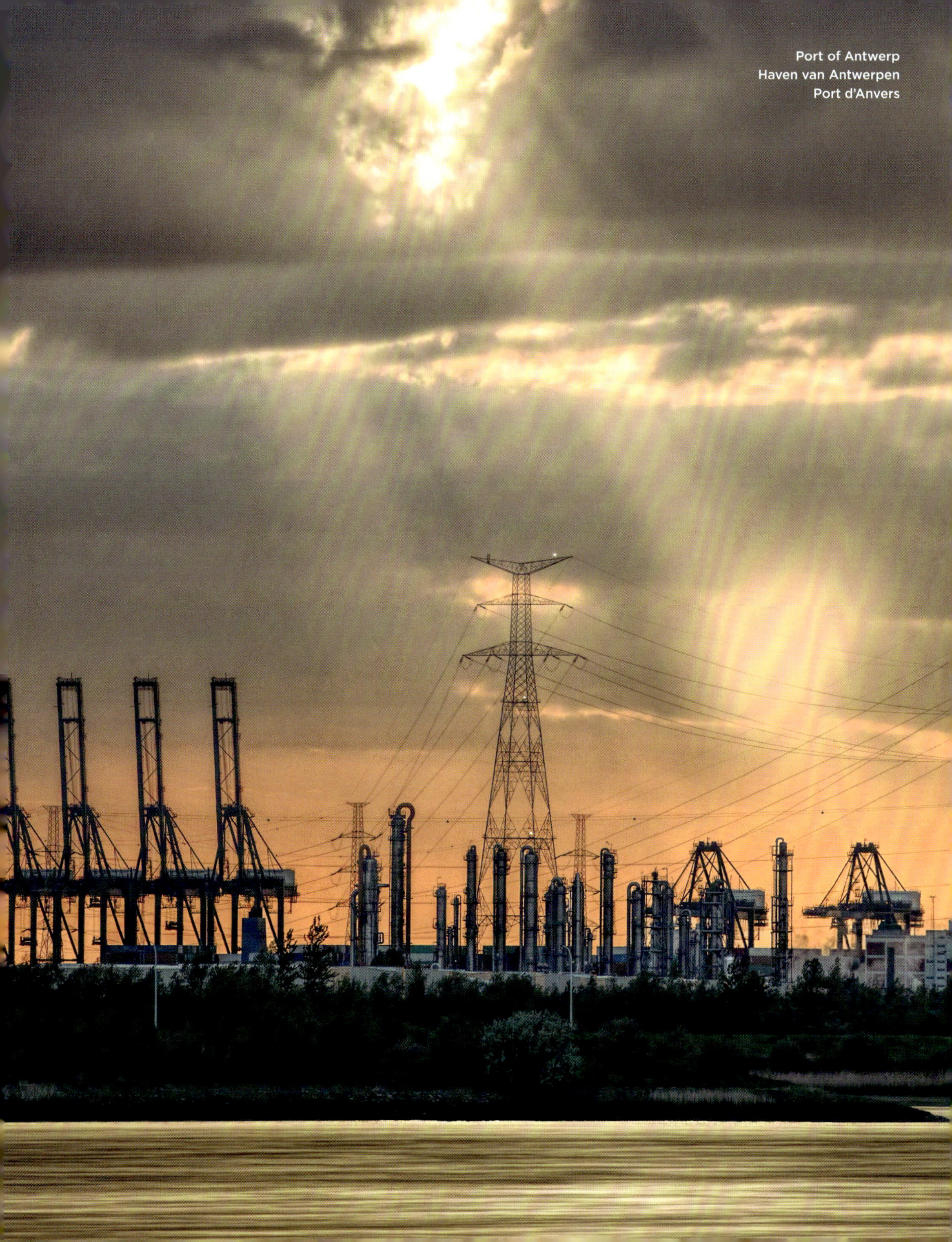

Port of Antwerp
Haven van Antwerpen
Port d'Anvers

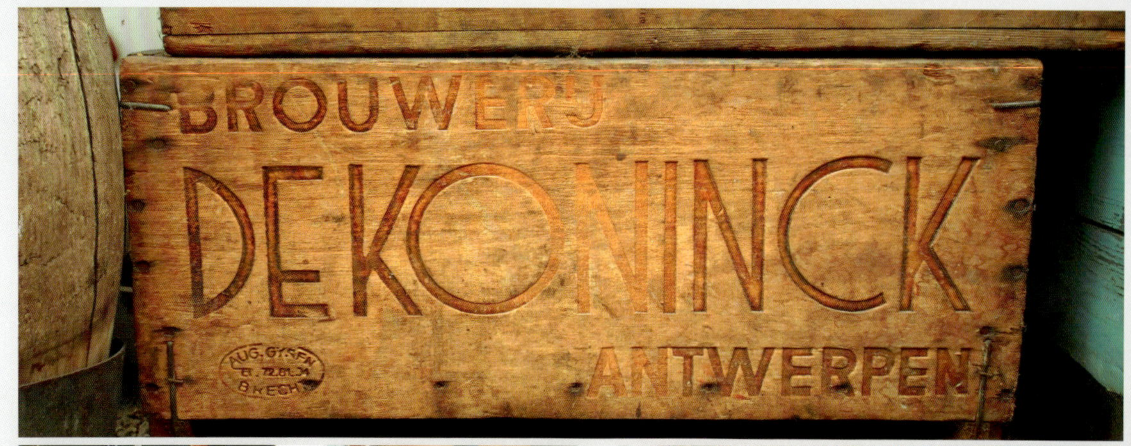

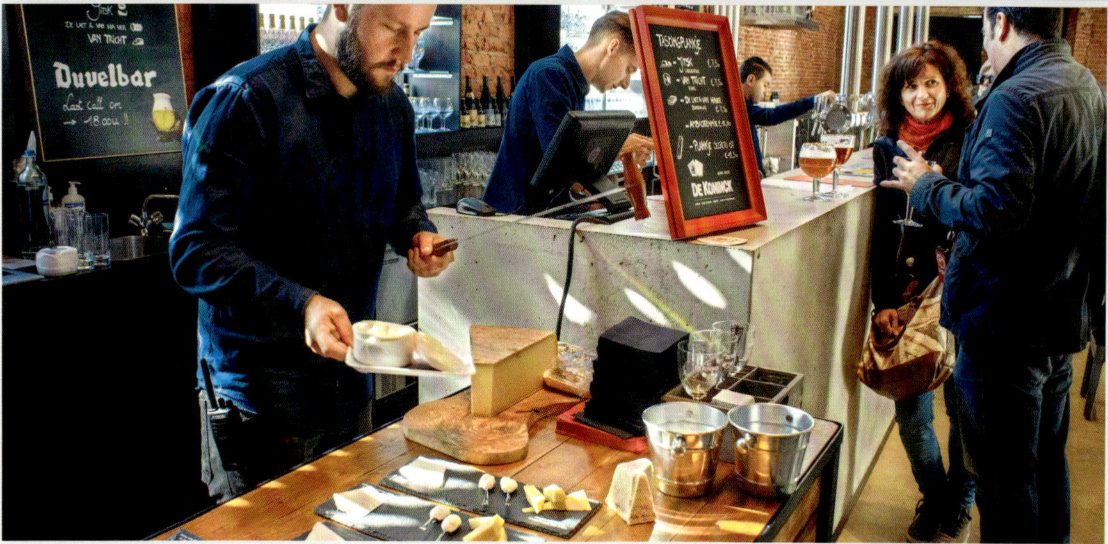

De Koninck Brewery

The brewery was originally a carriage station, but today it is the oldest brewery in Antwerp. Since 1833 beers such as the top-fermented, amber-coloured "De Koninck" have been brewed there. During a visit to the brewery, visitors discover the basics of brewing interactively, with multimedia presentations. For example, there is a picture gallery where generations of the operating families report from their respective epochs. Active guests can experience the ride on a beer cart or dragging of beer barrels. At the end of the tour, beer tasting takes place in a historic taproom

Brasserie De Koninck

À l'origine, la brasserie était une station de calèches ; aujourd'hui, c'est la plus ancienne brasserie de d'Anvers. Depuis 1833, on y brasse, par exemple, la De Koninck, une bière ambrée de fermentation haute. Dans le cadre de la visite, on y apprend de manière interactive et multimédia les bases du brassage. Grâce à une galerie de photos, plusieurs générations de familles de brasseurs donnent des informations sur leurs époques respectives. Les visiteurs audacieux peuvent expérimenter au plus près un trajet en chariot à bière ou le transport de barils. À la fin de la visite, la dégustation de bières se déroule dans une taverne historique.

Brauerei De Koninck

Die Brauerei war ursprünglich eine Kutschstation; heute ist sie die älteste Stadtbrauerei Antwerpens. Seit 1833 werden dort Biere wie das obergärige, bernsteinfarbene "De Koninck" gebraut. Bei einem Brauereibesuch entdecken die Besucher die Grundlagen des Brauens interaktiv und multimedial. So gibt es eine Bildergalerie, auf denen Generationen der Betreiberfamilien aus ihrer jeweiligen Epoche berichten. Unternehmungslustige Gäste können die Fahrt mit einem Bierfuhrwerk oder das Schleppen von Fässern hautnah erleben. Am Ende der Tour findet die Bierverkostung in einem historischen Schankraum statt.

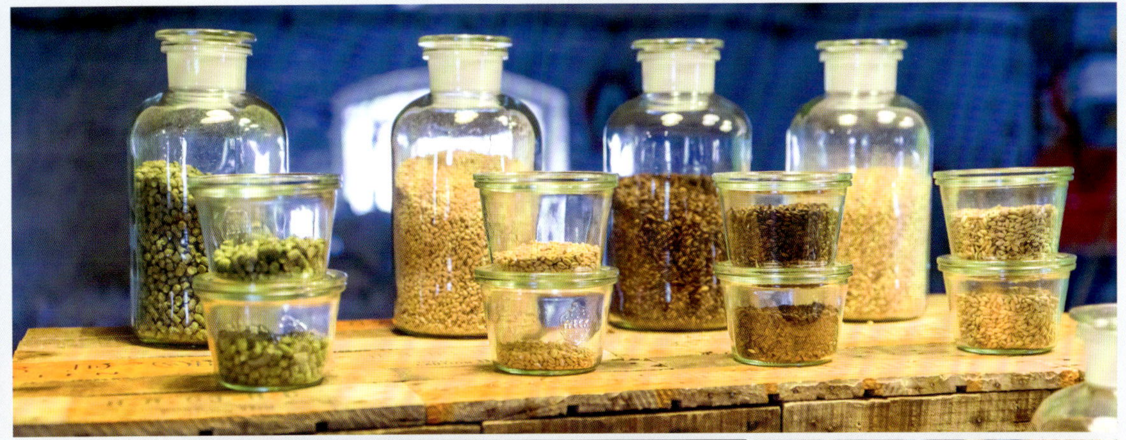

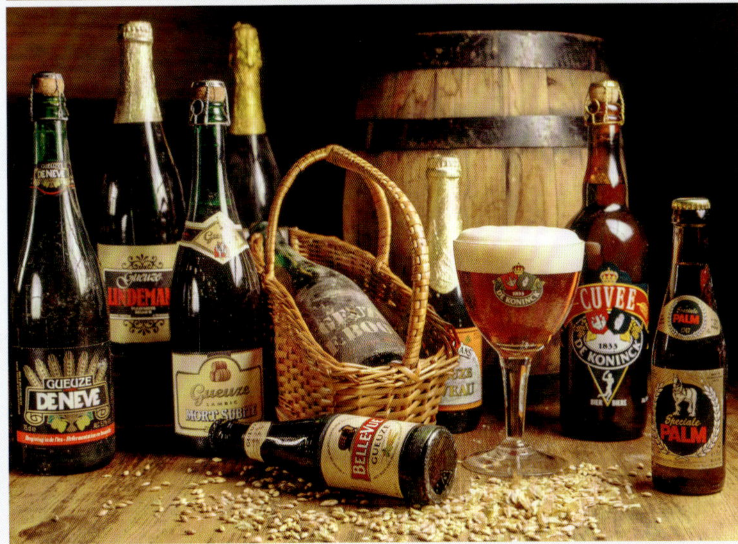

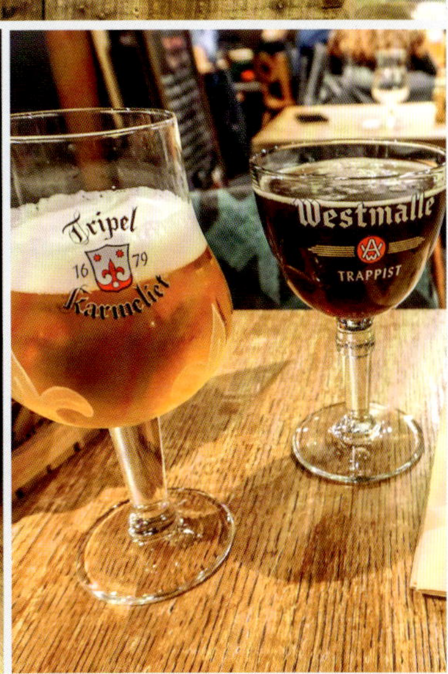

Cervecería De Koninck

La cervecería fue originalmente una estación de carruajes; hoy en día es la cervecería urbana más antigua de Amberes. Desde 1833 se elaboran allí cervezas como la "De Koninck" de fermentación alta y color ámbar. Durante una visita a la cervecería, los visitantes descubren los fundamentos de la elaboración interactiva y multimedia. Por ejemplo, hay una galería de imágenes donde las generaciones de las familias operadoras informan de sus respectivas épocas. Los huéspedes emprendedores pueden experimentar el paseo con un carrito de cerveza o el arrastre de barriles de cerca. Al final del recorrido, se puede degustar la cerveza en una histórica sala de bar.

Cervejaria De Koninck

A cervejaria era originalmente uma estação de carruagem; hoje é a mais antiga cervejaria da cidade de Antuérpia. Desde 1833, cervejas como a top-fermentada "De Koninck", de cor âmbar, são fabricadas lá. Durante uma visita à cervejaria, os visitantes descobrem os conceitos básicos da fabricação de cerveja de forma interativa e multimédia. Por exemplo, há uma galeria de fotos onde gerações de famílias operárias relatam suas respectivas épocas. Os hóspedes empreendedores podem experimentar de perto o passeio com um carroça de cerveja ou o transporte de barris. No final do passeio, a degustação de cerveja é realizada em uma taberna histórica.

Brouwerij De Koninck

Oorspronkelijk was de brouwerij een afspanning, vandaag is het de oudste stadsbrouwerij van Antwerpen. Sinds 1833 worden hier bieren zoals "De Koninck" gebrouwen, het amberkleurige bier van hoge gisting. Tijdens een bezoek aan de brouwerij ontdekken de bezoekers op een interactieve en multimediale manier de basisprincipes van het brouwen. Zo is er bijvoorbeeld fotogalerij waar generaties familiebedrijven van de brouwerij verslag doen van hun tijdperken. Ondernemende gasten kunnen de rit met een bierwagen of het slepen van vaten van dichtbij meemaken. Aan het einde van de tour vindt de bierdegustatie in een historisch proeflokaal plaats.

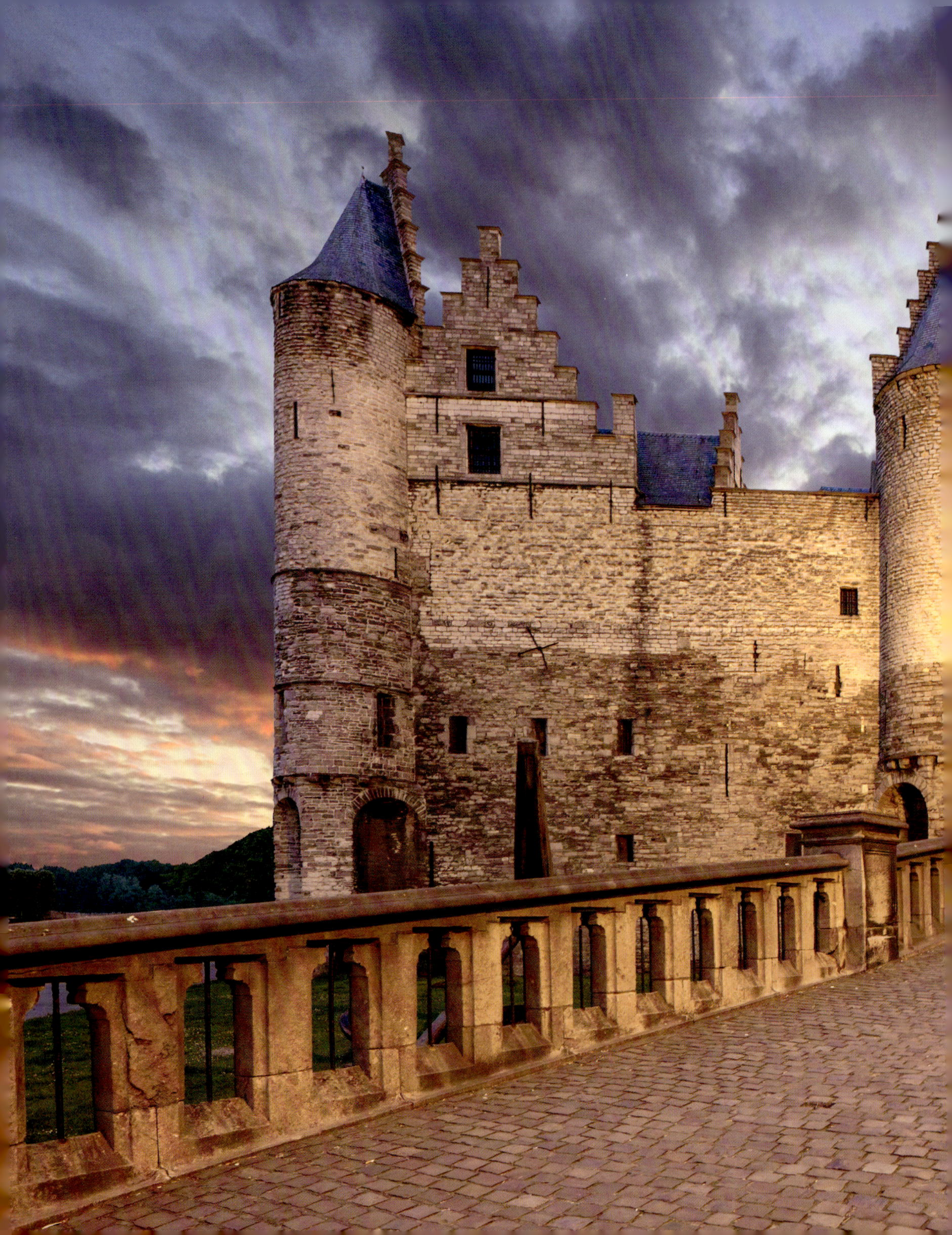

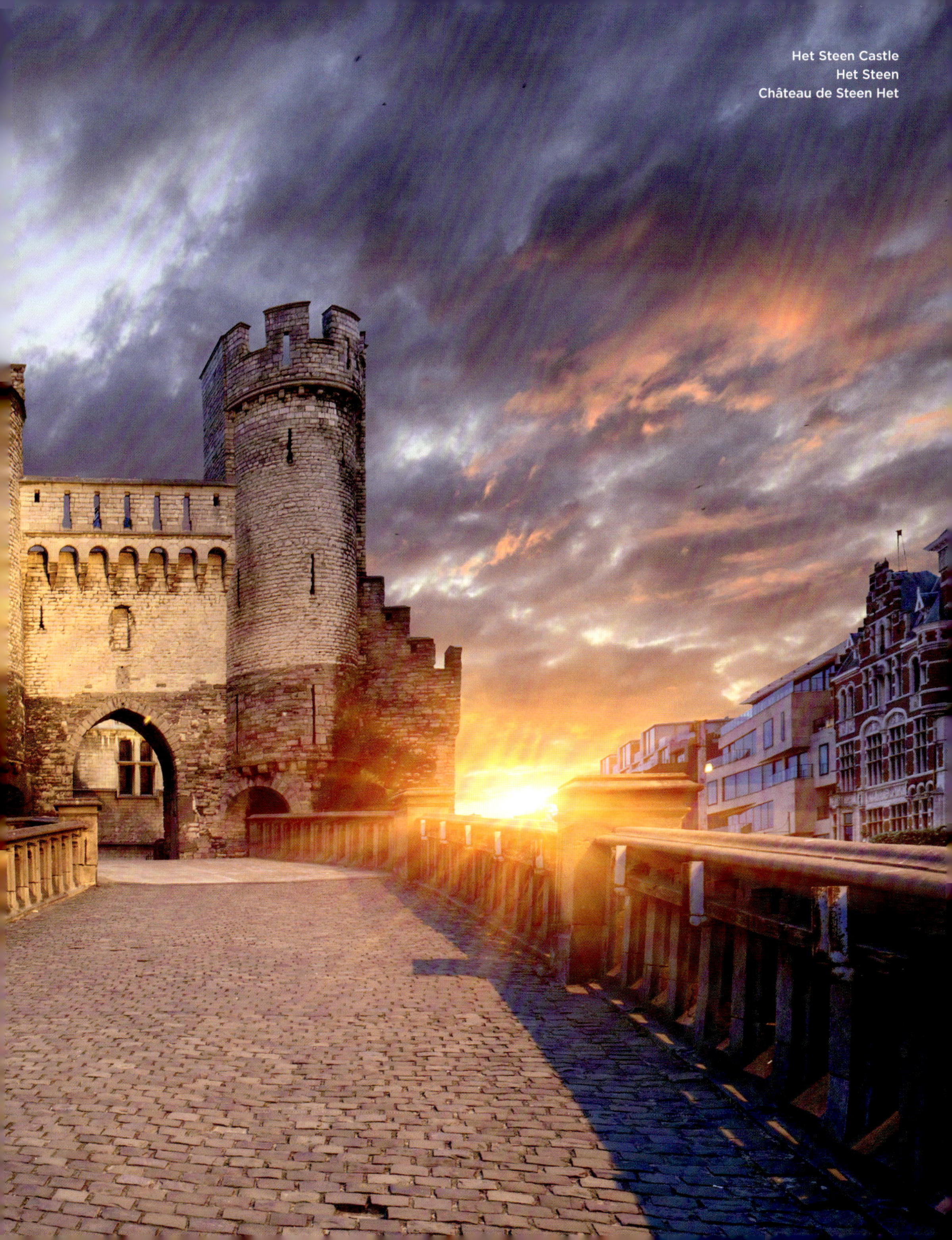
Het Steen Castle
Het Steen
Château de Steen Het

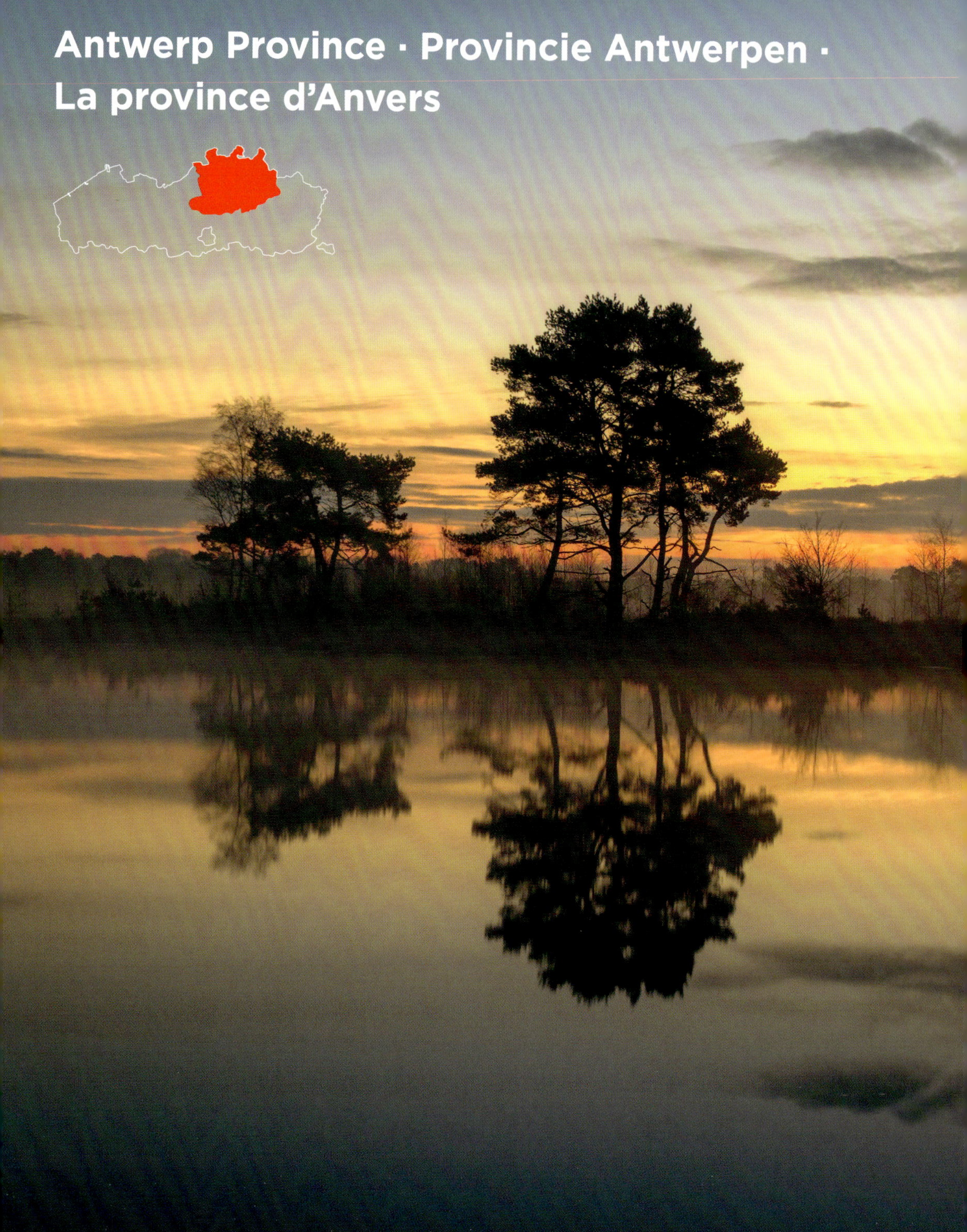

Antwerp Province · Provincie Antwerpen · La province d'Anvers

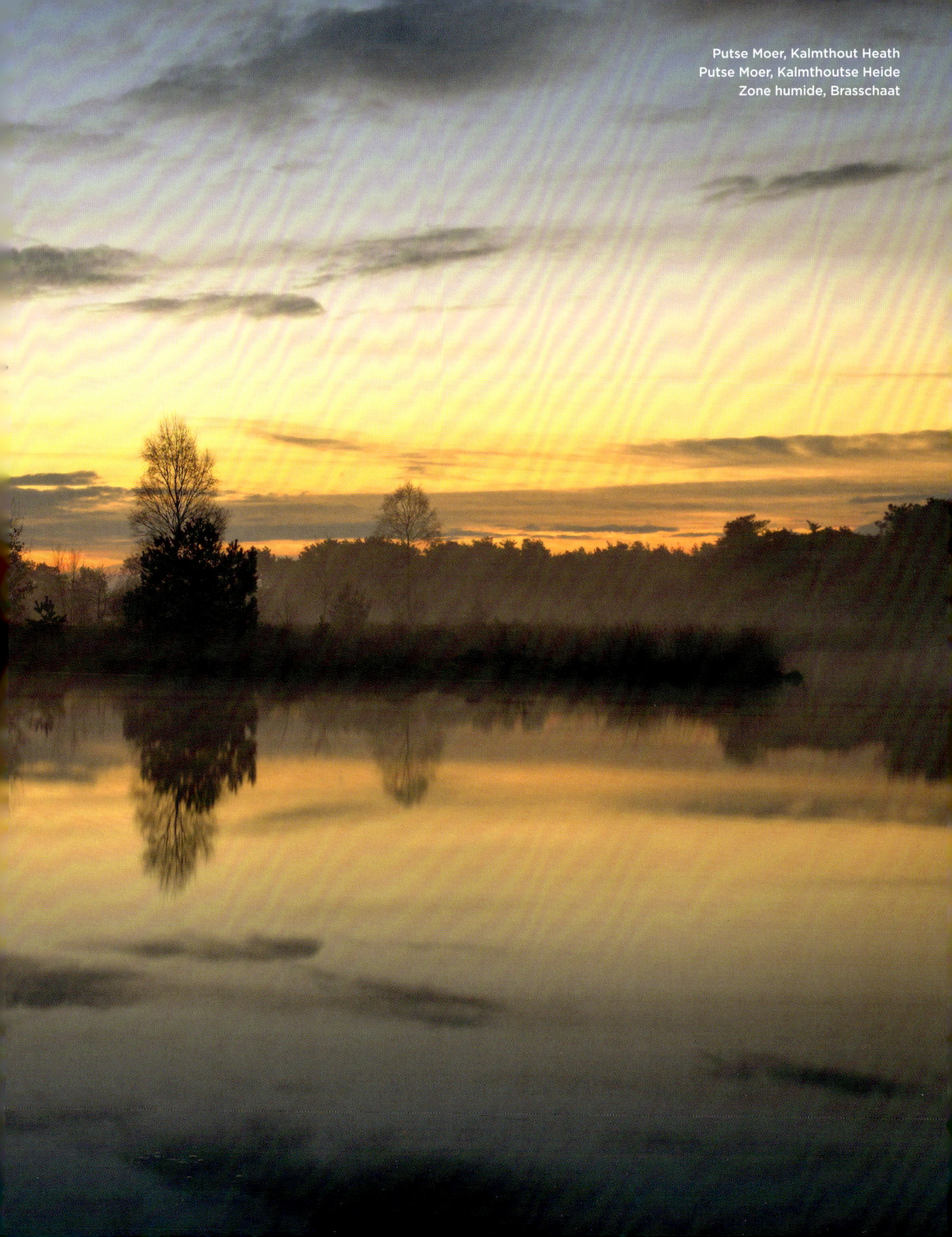
Putse Moer, Kalmthout Heath
Putse Moer, Kalmthoutse Heide
Zone humide, Brasschaat

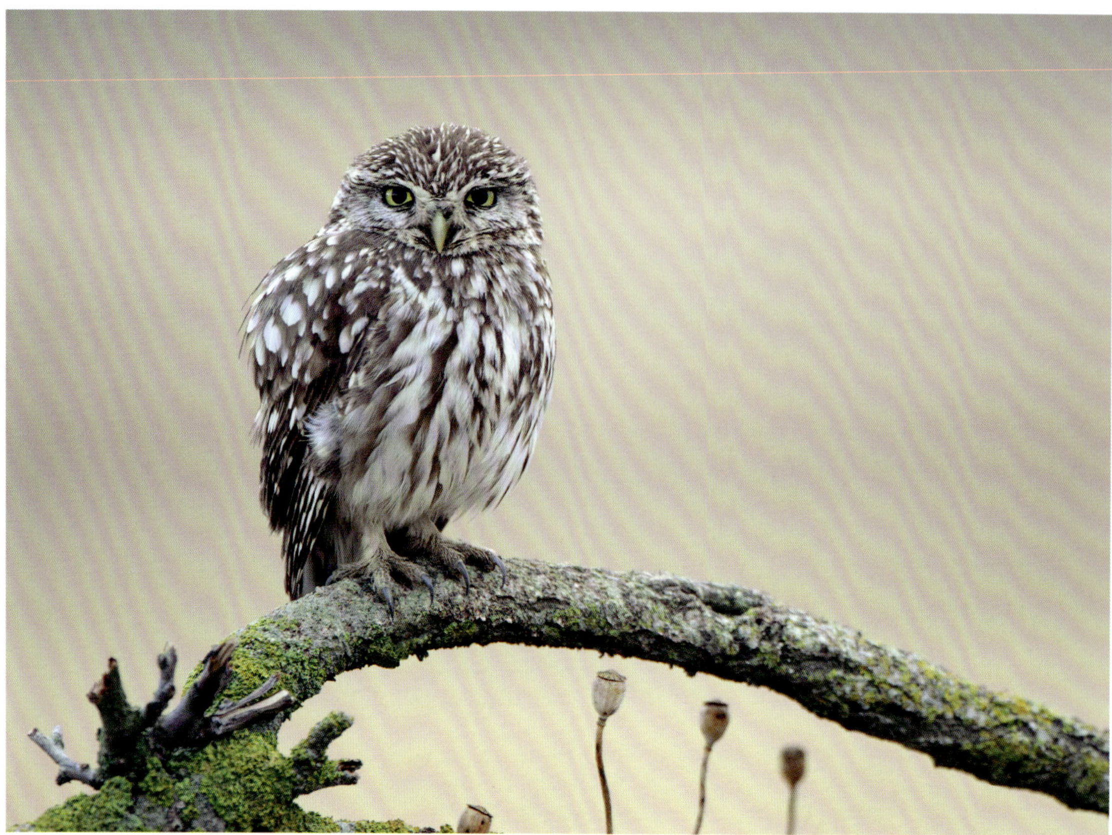

Little Owl
Steenuil
Chouette chevêche

Antwerp Province

The characteristic feature of North Flanders is its sandy soil, and until around 1860 the region was largely characterised by heath, pine forests, moors and peat extraction. Even today there are still a number of largely unchanged landscapes. The Schietveld Nature Reserve, a military training area, is known for the largest population of snakes in northwestern Europe. There are over 100 species of breeding birds, from the European honey buzzard to the nightjar and the short-toed snake eagle. The wetland biotope is also valuable as a habitat for bats, crested newts and its abundance of bog plants, from orchids to sundews.

La province d'Anvers

Du fait de son sol sablonneux, le nord des Flandres se caractérisait, jusqu'en 1860 environ, par sa lande, ses forêts de pins, ses marais et l'extraction de tourbe. Aujourd'hui encore, il se compose d'un certain nombre de paysages naturels. Terrain d'entraînement militaire, le parc naturel de Schietveld doit sa réputation à la plus grande population de serpents du nord-ouest de l'Europe. On y compte plus de 100 espèces d'oiseaux nicheurs, de la bondrée apivore à l'engoulevent en passant par le circaète Jean-le-Blanc. Ce biotope humide est également fort prisé par les chauves-souris, les tritons à crête et une abondance de plantes de marais, des orchidées aux droséras.

Provinz Antwerpen

Das charakteristische Merkmal Nordflanderns ist der sandige Boden, sodass die Region bis etwa 1860 weitgehend von Heide, Kiefernwäldern, Mooren und Torfabbau geprägt war. Auch heute gibt es noch eine Reihe von Naturlandschaften. Der Naturpark Schietveld, ein Truppenübungsgelände, ist bekannt für die größte Schlangenpopulation Nordwesteuropas. Man zählt über 100 Arten von Brutvögeln, vom Wespenbussard bis zum Ziegenmelker und Schlangenadler. Wertvoll ist das Feuchtbiotop auch als Lebensraum für Fledermäuse, Kammmolche und seinen Artenreichtum an Moorpflanzen, von Orchideen bis zu Sonnentau.

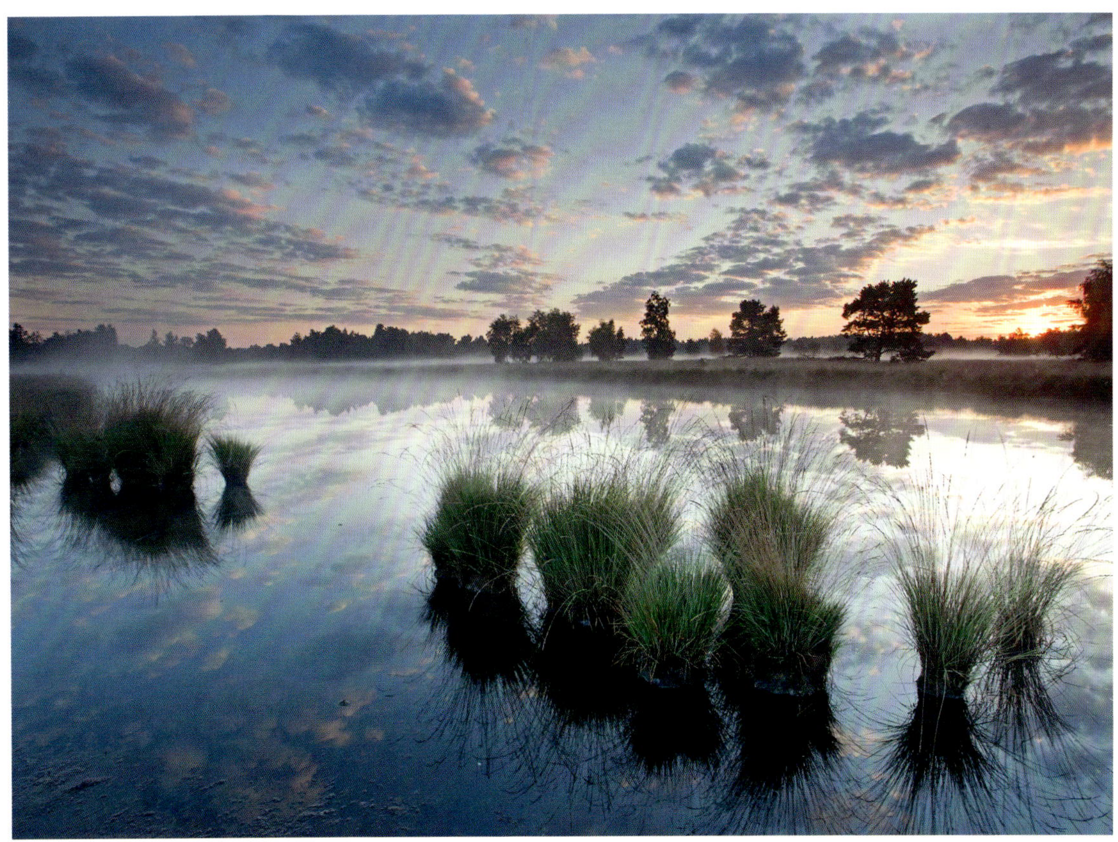

Klein Schietveld wetland, Brasschaat
Klein Schietveld, Brasschaat

Provincia de Amberes

El rasgo característico de Flandes
Septentrional es su suelo arenoso, de
modo que hasta alrededor de 1860 la
región se caracterizaba en gran medida
por los brezales, los bosques de pinos,
los páramos y la extracción de turba.
Incluso hoy en día todavía hay una serie
de paisajes naturales. El Parque Natural
de Schietveld, un área de entrenamiento
militar, es conocido por tener la mayor
población de serpientes del noroeste de
Europa. Hay más de 100 especies de aves
reproductoras, desde el abejero europeo
hasta el chotacabras europeo y la culebra
europea. El biotopo de humedal también
es valioso como hábitat de murciélagos,
tritones crestados y su abundancia de
plantas de pantano, desde orquídeas hasta
rocíos del sol.

Província de Antuérpia

A característica do norte da Flandres é o
solo arenoso, de modo que até cerca de
1860, a região se caracterizava em grande
parte por charnecas, pinhais, pântanos e
extração de turfa. Ainda hoje há uma série
de paisagens naturais. O Parque Natural
Schietveld, uma área de treinamento
militar, é conhecido pela maior população
de cobras do noroeste da Europa. Existem
mais de 100 espécies de aves reprodutoras,
desde o bútio-vespeiro até ao noitibó-da-
europa e à águia-cobreira. O biótopo das
zonas húmidas também é valioso como
habitat para morcego, tritões-de-crista e
a sua abundância de plantas de pântano,
desde orquídeas até as droseras.

Provincie Antwerpen

Karakteristiek voor Noord-Vlaanderen
is de zandige bodem, zodat de regio
tot ongeveer 1860 grotendeels werd
gekenmerkt door heide, dennenbossen,
heidevelden en veenwinning. Ook
vandaag de dag zijn er nog steeds een
aantal natuurlijke landschappen. Het
natuurpark Groot Schietveld, een militair
oefenterrein, staat bekend om de grootste
slangenpopulatie in Noordwest-Europa.
Hier telt men meer dan 100 soorten
broedvogels, van de wespendief tot de
nachtzwaluw en de slangenarend. Het
drasland is ook waardevol als thuisbasis
voor vleermuis, kamsalamanders en
zijn rijkdom aan moerasplanten, van
orchideeën tot zonnedauw.

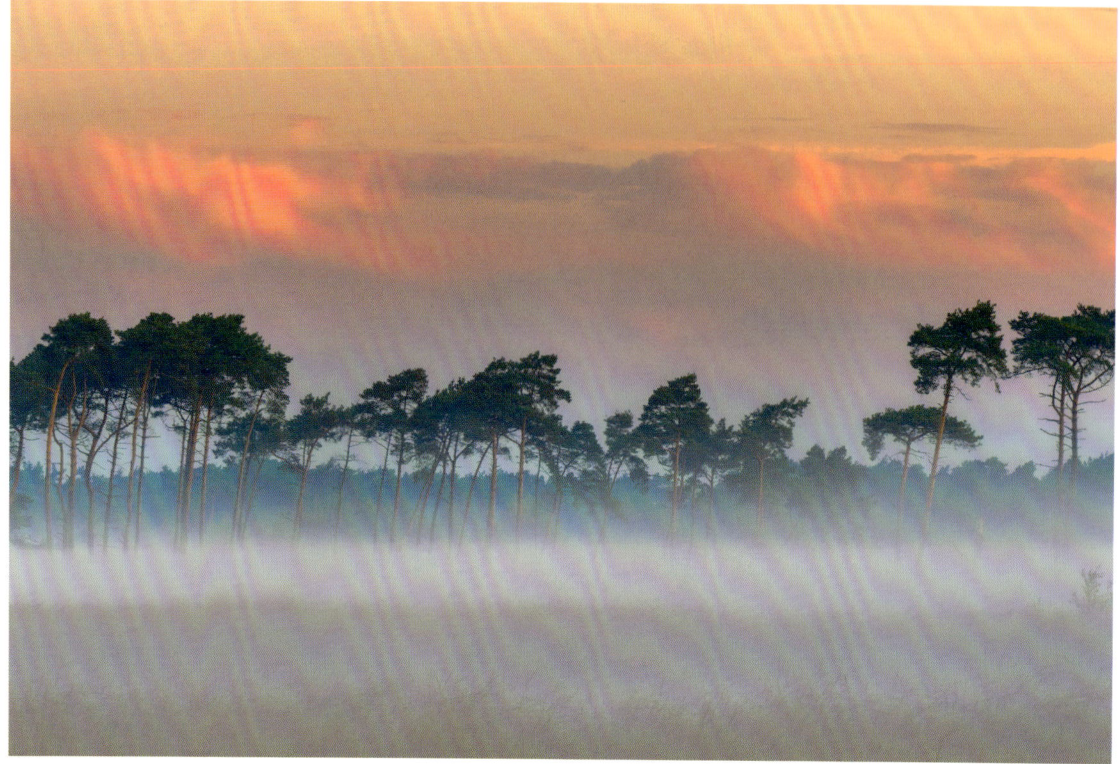

Kalmthout Heath
Kalmthoutse Heide

Kalmthoutse Heath

Heathland, dunes and numerous moors form a 6000 ha (14,826 ac) national park on both sides of the border separating Flanders from the Netherlands. Violet-flowering heather dominates the classic heath panorama from July to September. This landscape offers ideal conditions for countless insects, which feed a rich variety of birds.

Kalmthoutse Heide

Des landes, des dunes et de nombreux marais : voilà de quoi se compose le parc national de 6000 hectares qui s'étend de part et d'autre de la frontière séparant les Flandres des Pays-Bas. La bruyère à fleurs violettes domine le paysage classique des landes de juillet à septembre, un environnement qui offre des conditions de vie idéales à d'innombrables insectes, nourrissant à leur tour une riche population d'oiseaux.

Kalmthoutse Heide

Heideflächen, Dünen und zahlreiche Moore bilden einen 6000 ha großen Nationalpark beiderseits der Grenze zwischen Flandern und den Niederlanden. Die violett blühende Besenheide prägt von Juli bis September das klassische Heidepanorama. Die Heidelandschaft bietet ideale Bedingungen für unzählige Insekten, die einer reichen Vogelwelt als Nahrung dienen.

Kalmthoutse Heide

Zonas de brezales, dunas y numerosos páramos forman un parque nacional de 6000 ha a ambos lados de la frontera entre Flandes y los Países Bajos. El brezo de flores violetas domina el panorama clásico del brezal de julio a septiembre. El paisaje de brezales ofrece condiciones ideales para innumerables insectos, que alimentan un rico mundo de aves.

Kalmthoutse Heide

Áreas de urze, dunas e inúmeros pântanos formam um parque nacional de 6000 ha em ambos os lados da fronteira entre a Flandres e a Holanda. A urze-das-vassouras de flor violeta domina o panorama clássico da urze de julho a setembro. A paisagem de urze oferece condições ideais para inúmeros insetos, que servem de alimento para um mundo rico em aves.

Kalmthoutse Heide

Heidegebieden, duinen en talrijke veengronden vormen een 6000 ha groot nationaal park aan weerszijden van de grens tussen Vlaanderen en Nederland. De paars bloeiende struikhei domineert het klassieke heidepanorama van juli tot september. Het heidelandschap biedt ideale omstandigheden voor talloze insecten die een rijke vogelwereld tot voedsel dienen.

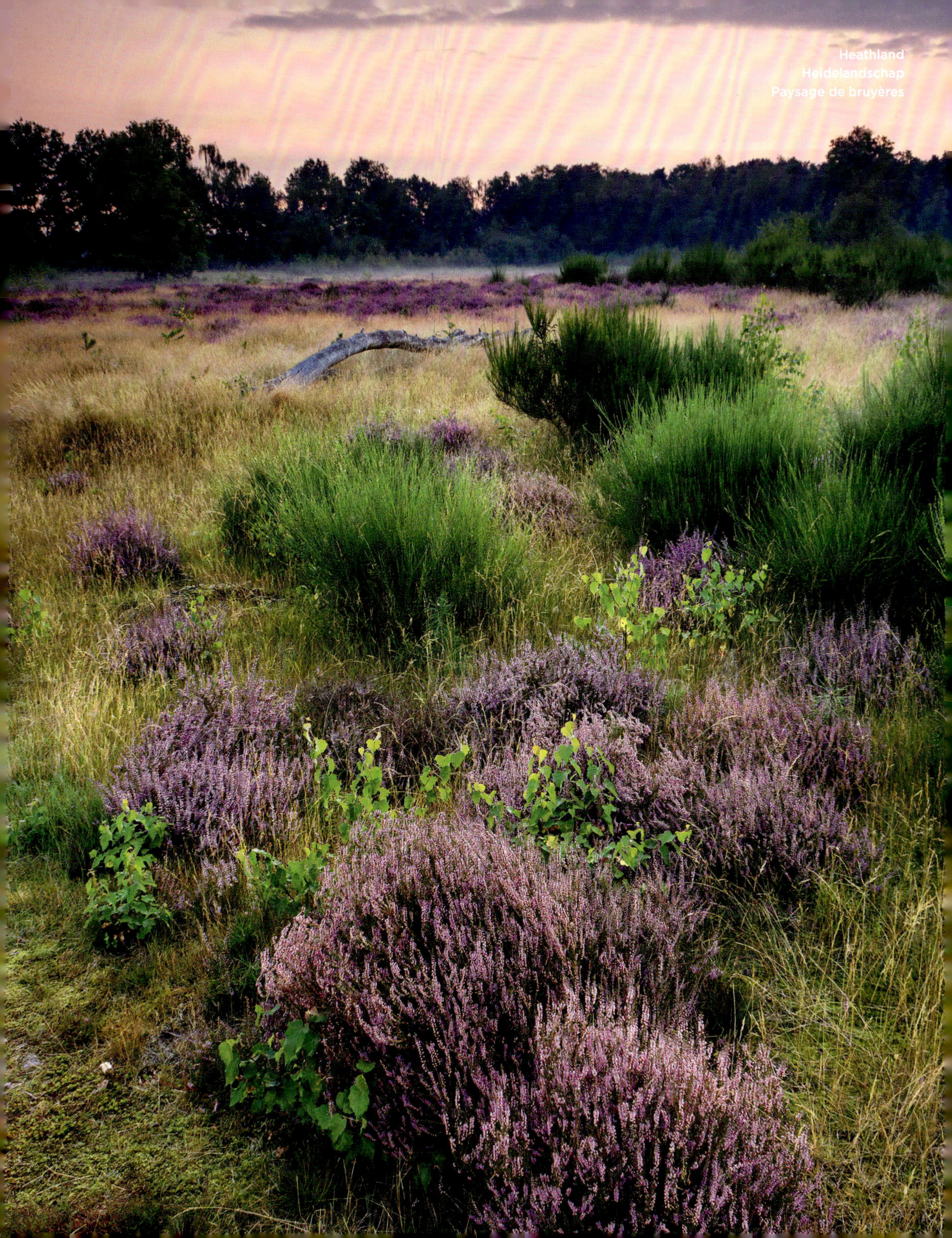
Heathland
Heidelandschap
Paysage de bruyères

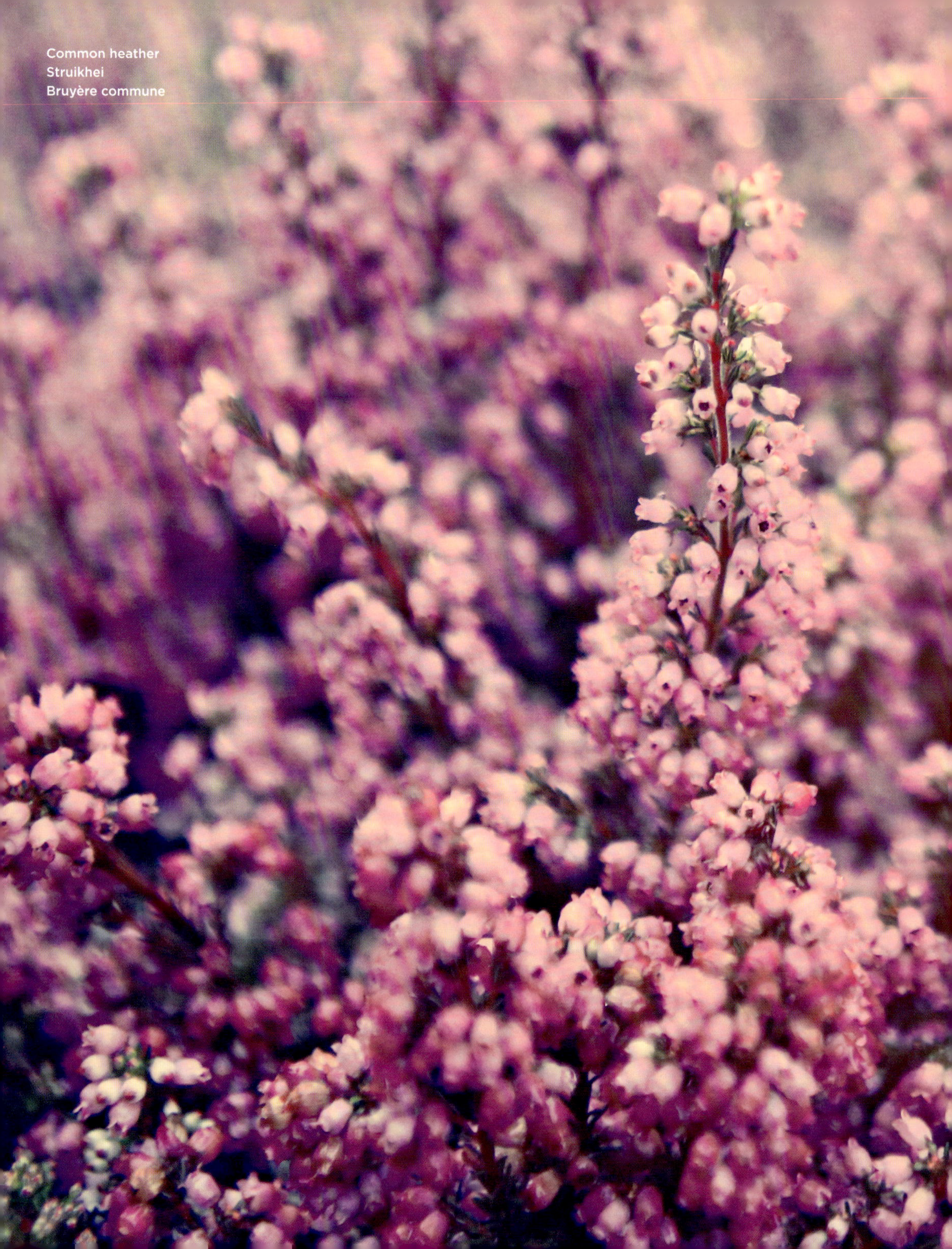
Common heather
Struikhei
Bruyère commune

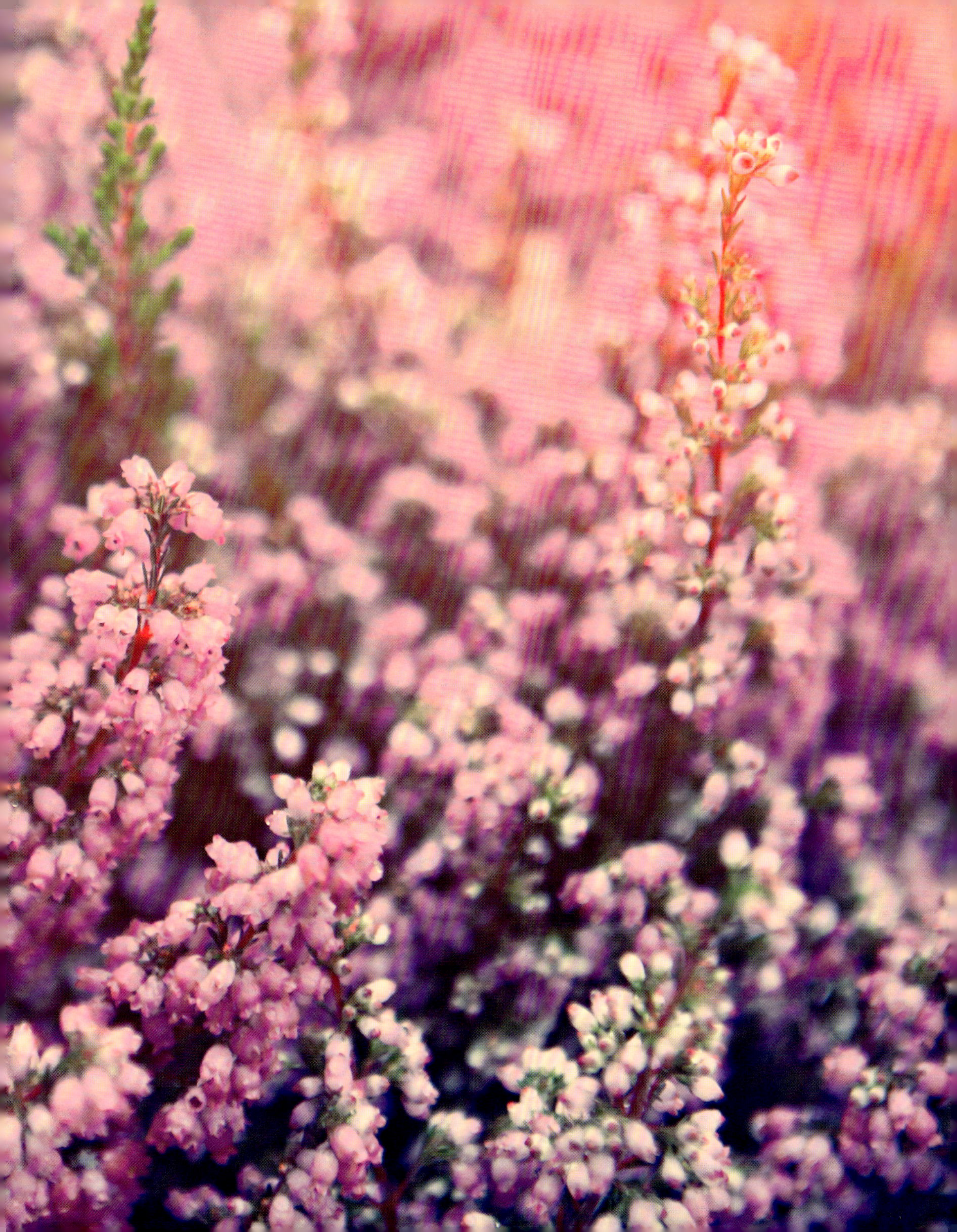

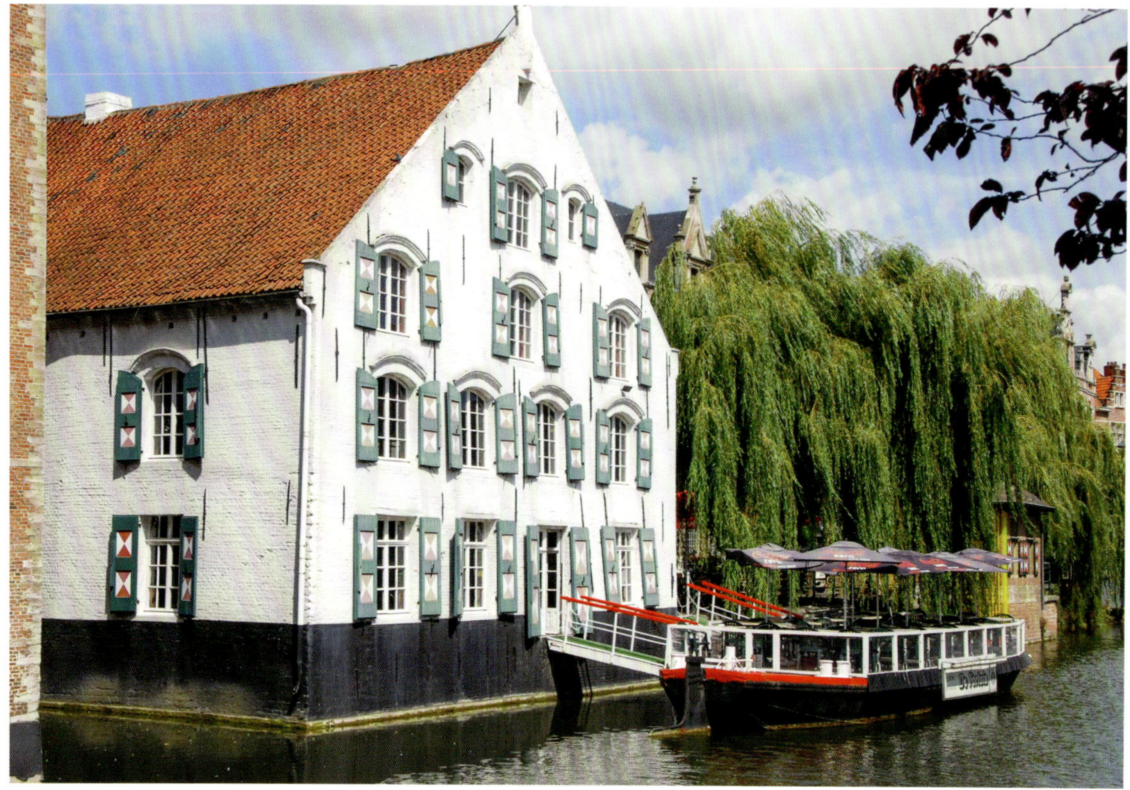

Nete River, Lier
Nete, Lier
La Nèthe, Lierre

The almond bean of Lier

With 150 cottages, the Lier Beguinage is one of the largest in Flanders. At the red brick houses with semicircular gates, there are names like "Paradise" or "Vineyard of the Lord" and in front of them are gardens with geraniums, dahlias and mallows. The Flemish poet Felix Timmermans described the nostalgic monastery of his hometown as the "almond bean of Lier".

Almendro de Lier

Con 150 casitas, el beguinaje es uno de los más grandes de Flandes. En las casas de ladrillo rojo con puertas semicirculares, hay nombres como "Paradieske" o "Viñedo del señor " y delante de ellas hay jardines con geranios, dalias y malvas. El poeta flamenco Felix Timmermans describió el nostálgico monasterio de su ciudad natal como la almendra de Lier.

L'amande de Lierre

Avec ses 150 maisonnettes, le béguinage de Lierre est l'un des plus grands des Flandres. Devant ses maisons de briques rouges aux portes semi-circulaires, qui portent des noms comme Paradieske ou Vignoble du Seigneur, s'étalent des jardinets avec géraniums, dahlias et mauves. Le poète flamand Félix Timmerman appela ce lieu nostalgique de sa ville natale l'amande de Lierre.

Amendoeira de Lier

Com 150 cabanas, a Béguinage é uma das maiores da Flandres. Nas casas de tijolo vermelho com portões semi circulares, encontram-se nomes como "Paraíso" ou "Vinhedo do Senhor" e em frente a eles há jardins com gerânios, dálias e malvas. O poeta flamengo Felix Timmermans descreveu o convento nostálgico de sua cidade natal como a amêndoa de Lier.

Mandelbaum von Lier

Mit 150 Häuschen zählt der Beginenhof zu den größten Flanderns. An den Häusern aus rotem Ziegelstein mit halbrunden Pforten, stehen Namen wie „Paradieske" oder „Weinberg des Herrn" und davor liegen Gärtchen mit Geranien, Dahlien und Malven. Der flämische Dichter Felix Timmermans beschrieb das nostalgische Stift seiner Heimatstadt als Mandel von Lier.

Amandelboom uit Lier

Het Begijnhof is met 150 huisjes één van de grootste van Vlaanderen. Op bakstenen huizen met halfronde poorten staan namen als "Stalleken van Bethlehem" of "Wijngaert des Heren". De tuinen bevatten geraniums, dahlia's of kruidachtige planten. Vlaams dichter Felix Timmermans omschreef het nostalgische klooster van zijn geboortestad als d'amandelboon van Lier.

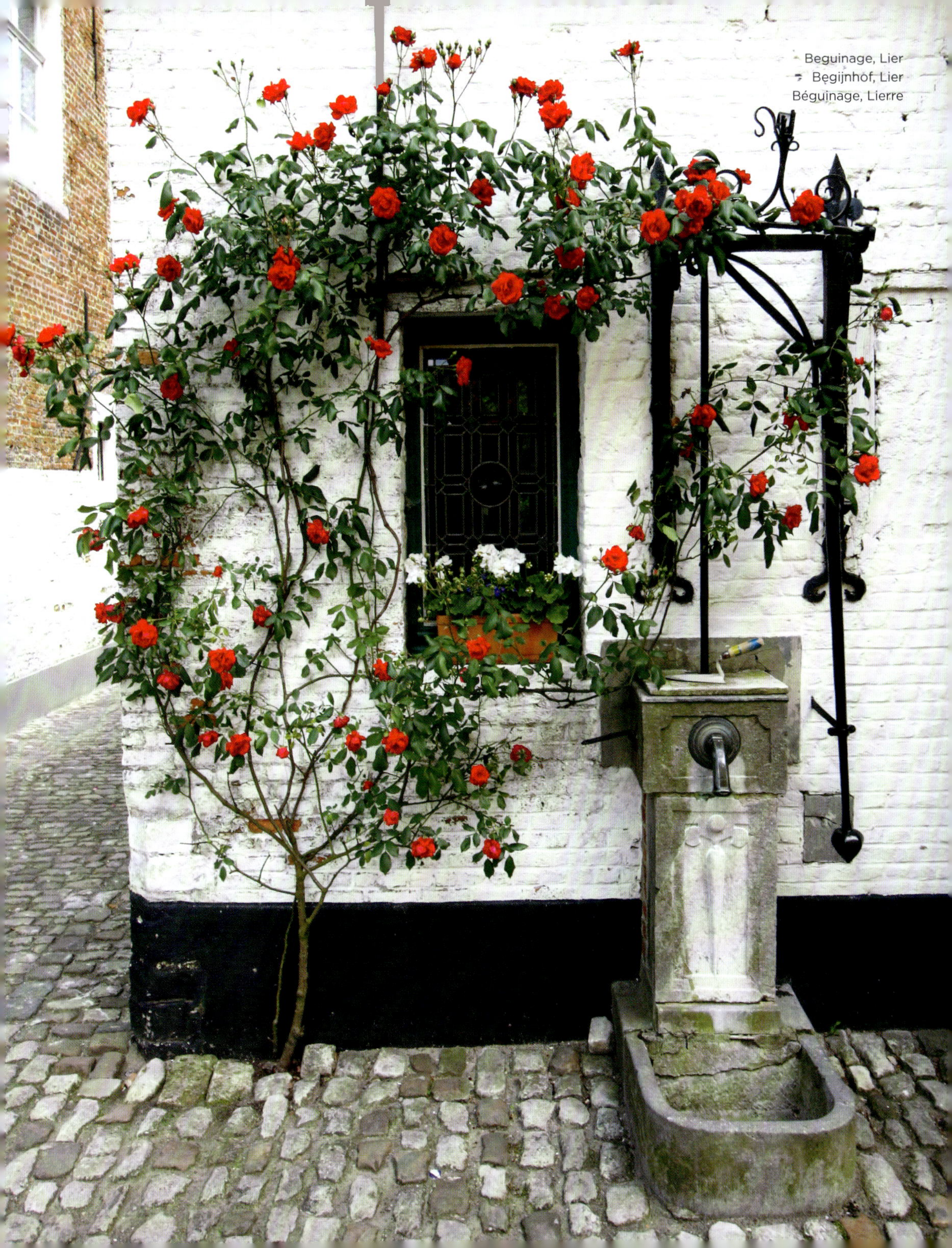

Beguinage, Lier
Begijnhof, Lier
Béguinage, Lierre

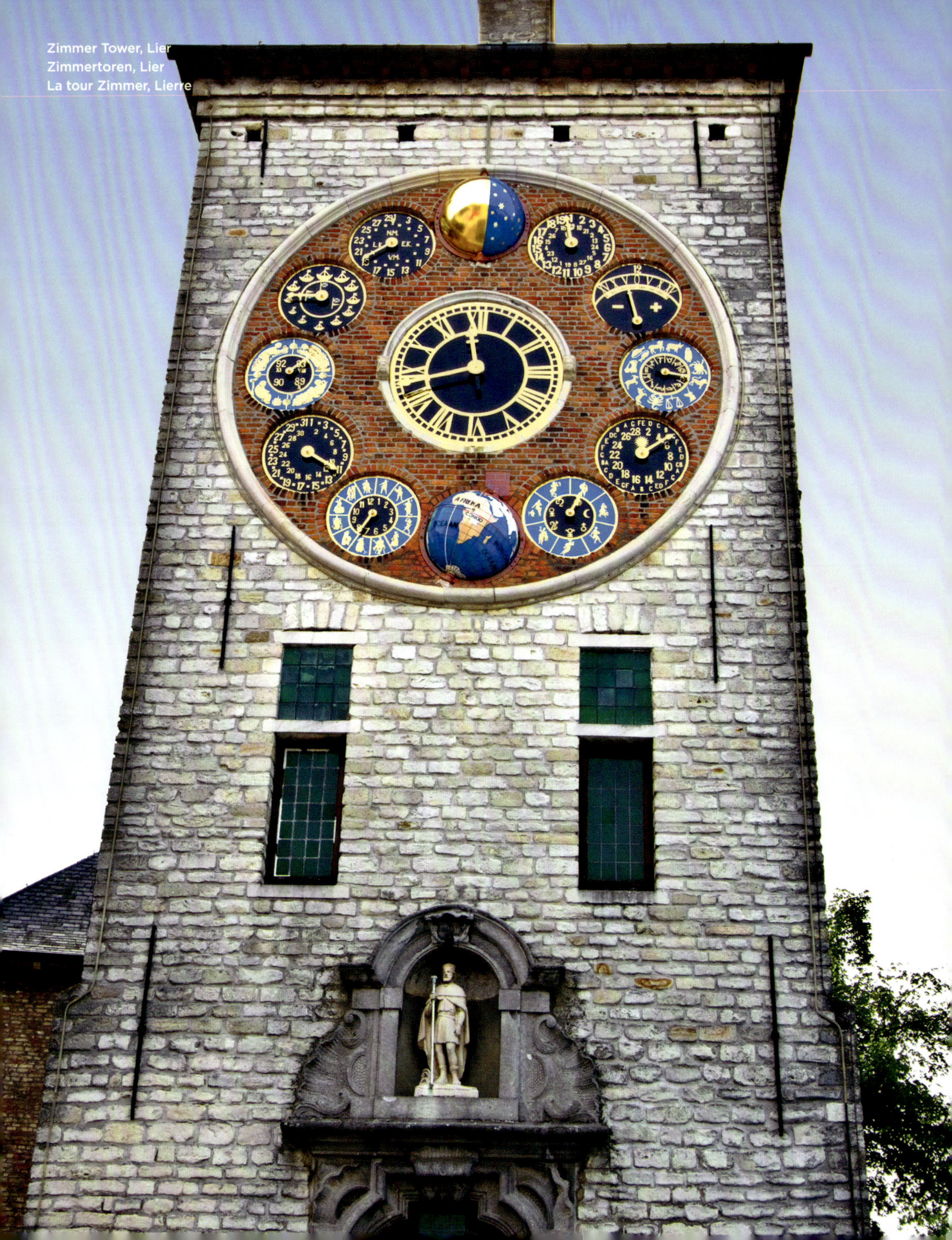

Zimmer Tower, Lier
Zimmertoren, Lier
La tour Zimmer, Lierre

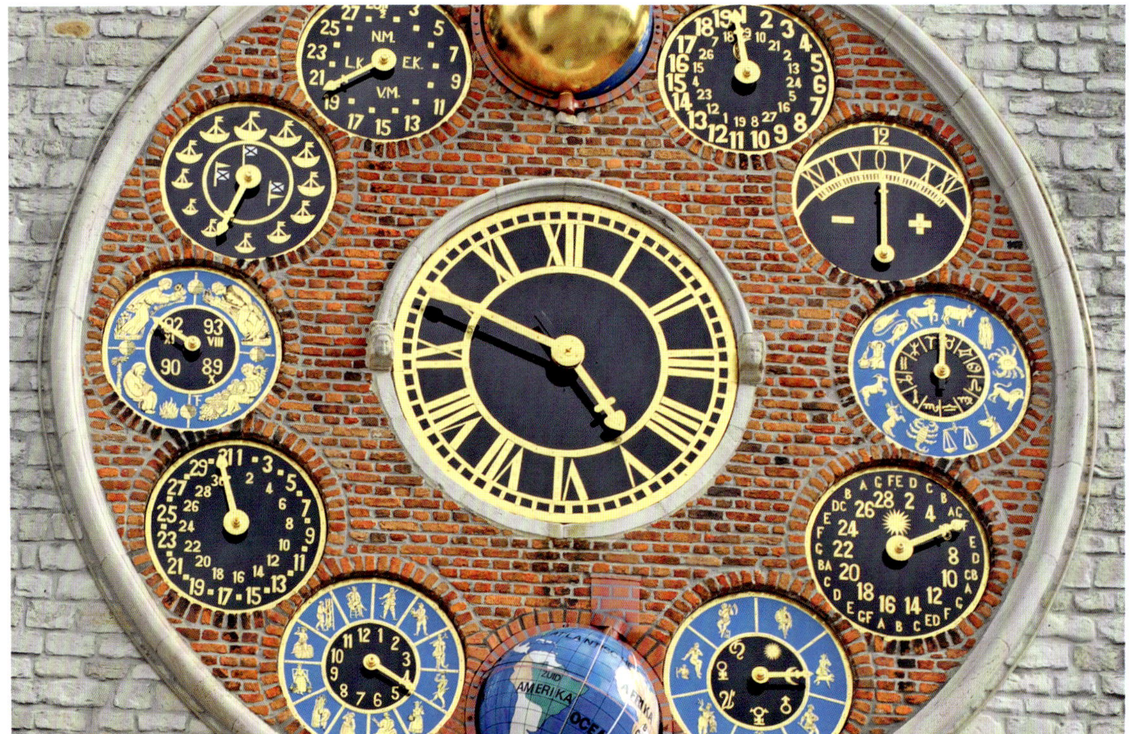

Zimmer Tower, Lier
Zimmertoren, Lier
La tour Zimmer, Lierre

Slowest hand in the world

The clockmaker and hobby astronomer, Louis Zimmer, built two monumental astronomical clocks. The mechanics convey the cosmic connections in a vivid way. One of the hands needs 25,800 years for one revolution, indicating the precession movement of the earth's axis. Zimmer was congratulated by, among others, Albert Einstein on this work.

La aguja más lenta del mundo

El relojero y aficionado a la astronomía Louis Zimmer construyó dos relojes astronómicos monumentales. El sistema mecánico transmite las conexiones cósmicas de una manera ilustrativa. Una aguja necesita 25 800 años para dar una vuelta e indica así el movimiento precesión del eje terrestre. Zimmer fue felicitado, entre otros, por Albert Einstein por este trabajo.

L'aiguille la plus lente du monde

Horloger et astronome amateur, Louis Zimmer construisit deux horloges astronomiques monumentales. Leur mécanique transmet clairement les informations astronomiques. Une aiguille a besoin de 25 800 ans pour faire le tour du cadran et indique ainsi le mouvement de précession de l'axe terrestre. Pour ce travail, Zimmer reçut les félicitations d'Albert Einstein, entre autres.

O ponteiro mais lento do mundo

O relojoeiro e astrônomo amador, Louis Zimmer, construiu dois relógios astronômicos monumentais. A mecânica transmite as conexões cósmicas de forma vívida. Um ponteiro precisa de 25 800 anos para completar um ciclo e assim indica o movimento de precessão do eixo da terra. Entre outros, Zimmer foi felicitado por Albert Einstein por este trabalho.

Langsamster Zeiger der Welt

Der Uhrmacher und Hobby-Astronom, Louis Zimmer, baute zwei monumentale astronomische Uhren. Die Mechanik vermittelt auf anschauliche Weise die kosmischen Zusammenhänge. Ein Zeiger braucht für einen Umlauf 25.800 Jahre und zeigt damit die Präzessionsbewegung der Erdachse an. Zimmer wurde unter anderem von Albert Einstein zu diesem Werk beglückwünscht.

Langzaamste wijzer ter wereld

De uurwerkmaker en amateur-astronoom Louis Zimmer bouwde twee monumentale, astronomische klokken. Het mechanisme brengt de kosmische verbindingen op een levendige manier in beeld. Een wijzer heeft 25 800 jaar nodig voor één omwenteling en geeft daarmee de precessiebeweging van de aardas aan. Zimmer werd o.a. door Albert Einstein gefeliciteerd met dit werk.

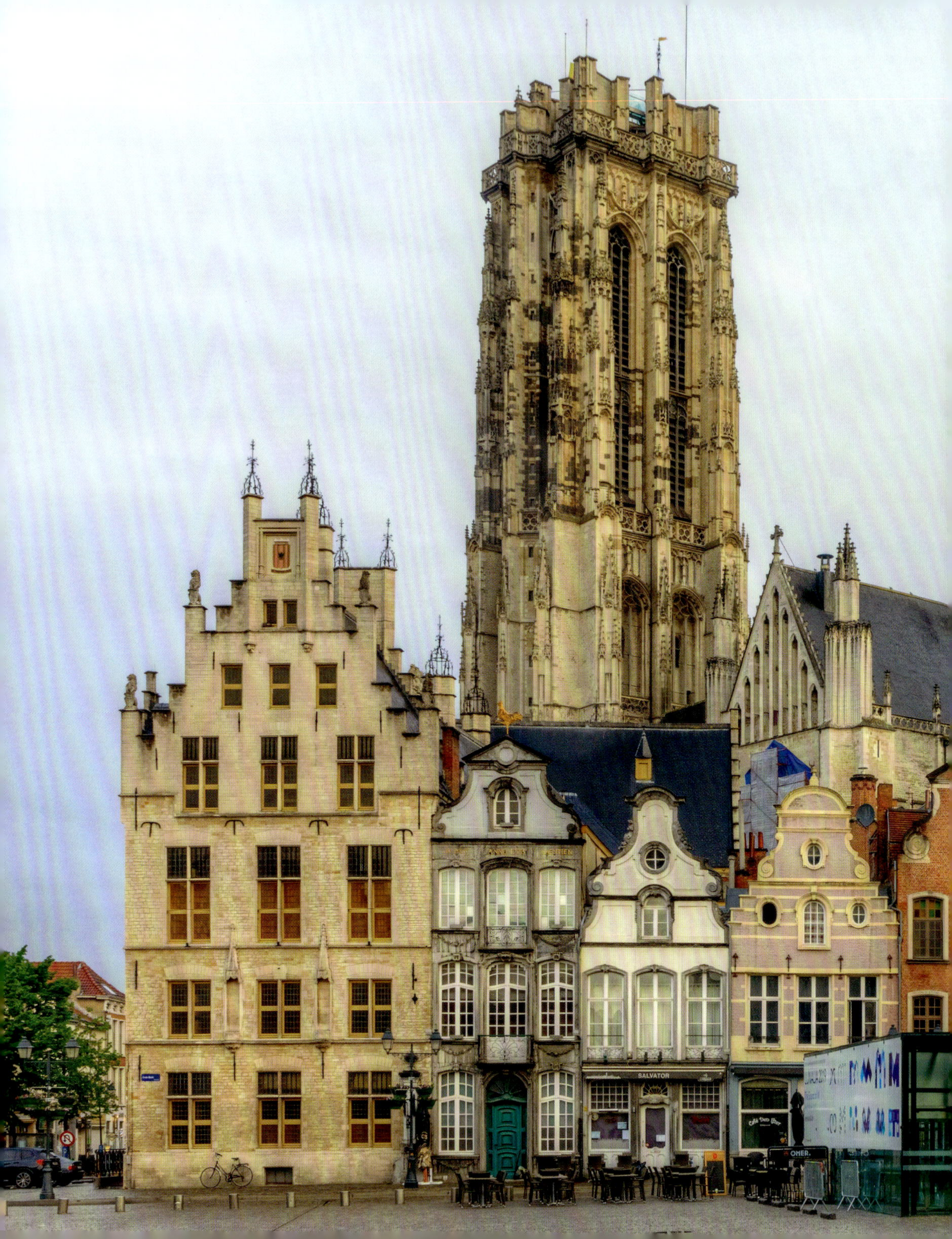

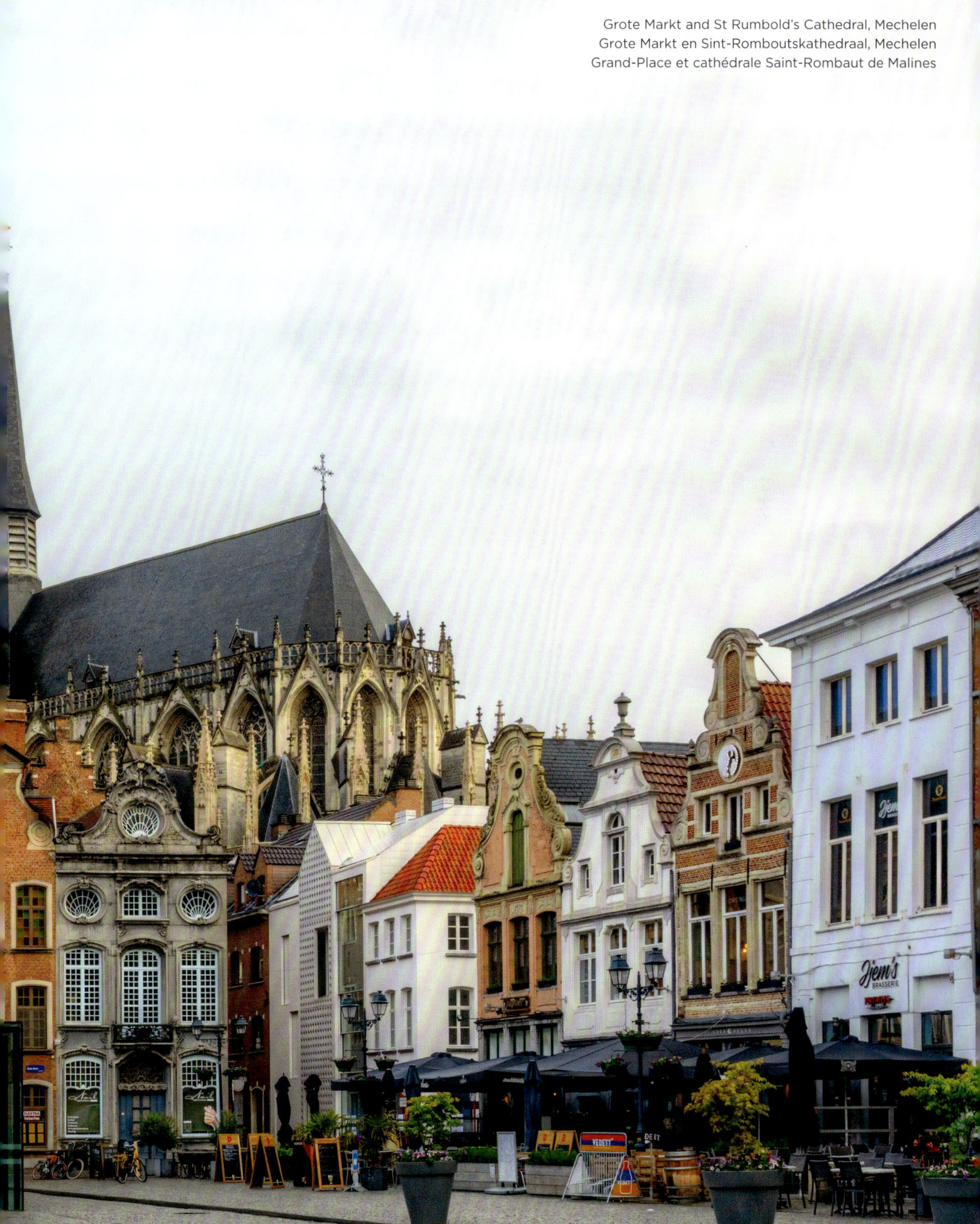

Grote Markt and St Rumbold's Cathedral, Mechelen
Grote Markt en Sint-Romboutskathedraal, Mechelen
Grand-Place et cathédrale Saint-Rombaut de Malines

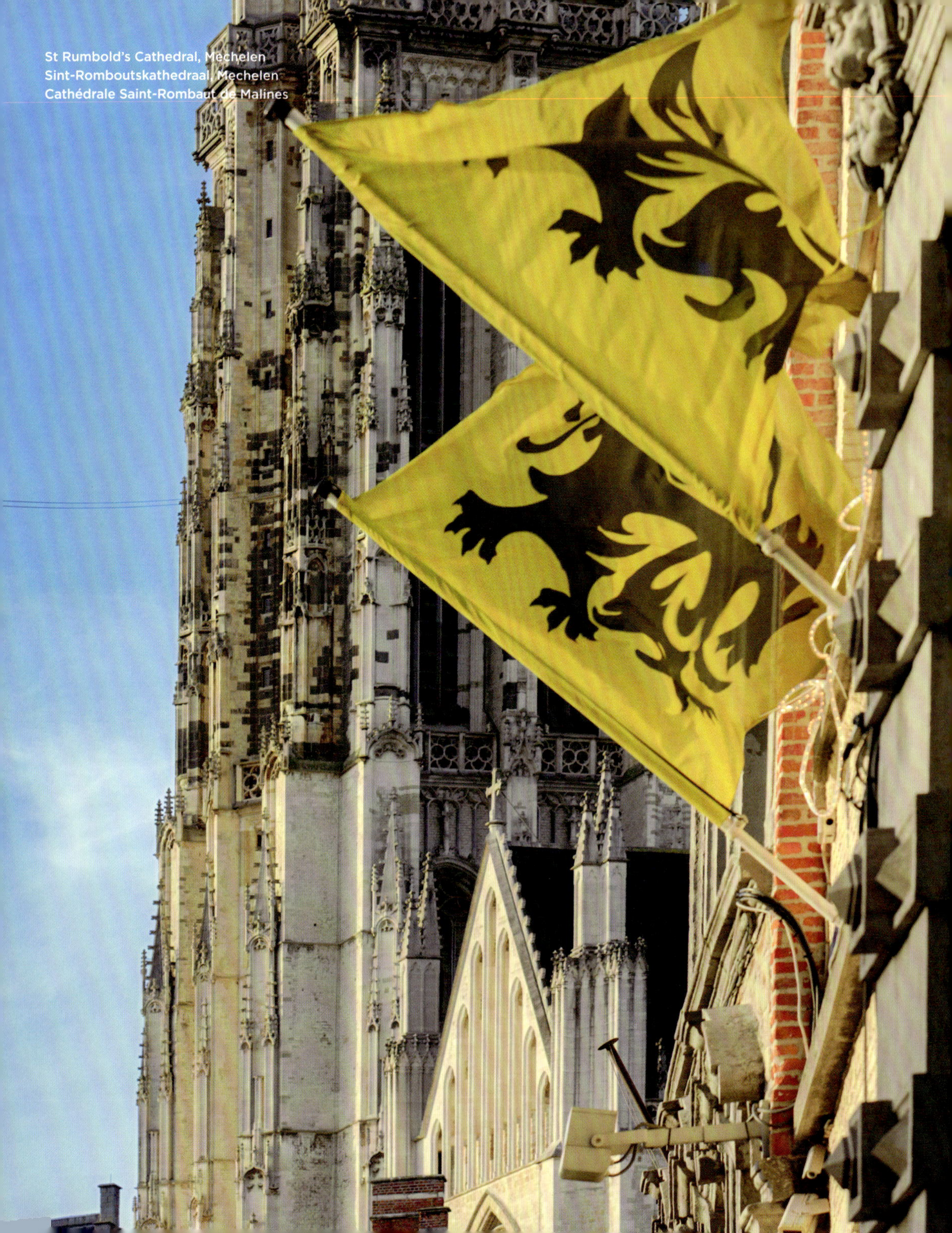

St Rumbold's Cathedral, Mechelen
Sint-Romboutskathedraal, Mechelen
Cathédrale Saint-Rombaut de Malines

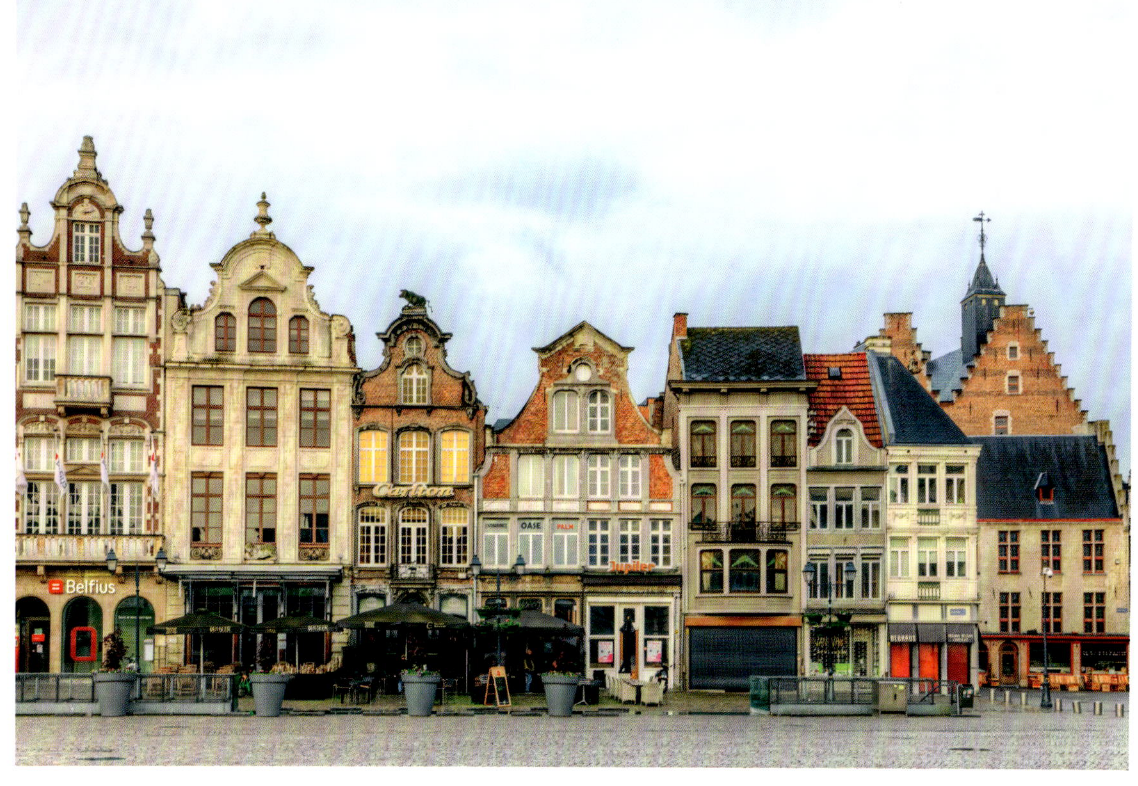

Grote Markt, Mechelen
Grand-Place de Malines

City of the Bell Ringers

The tranquil town of Mechelen, with its more than 300 listed buildings, is a real architectural treat. It even has two belfries—the town hall tower and the tower of St Rumbold's Cathedral, with its two carillons. The carillons may also be heard from the inner courtyard of the Palace of Margaret of Austria, who was once Governor of the Habsburg Netherlands.

Ciudad del carillón

La tranquila ciudad de Mechelen, con sus más de 300 edificios catalogados, es un verdadero paraíso arquitectónico. Incluso tiene dos campanarios: la torre del ayuntamiento y la torre de la Catedral de San Rombout, con dos carillones. El carillón también se puede escuchar en el patio interior del Palacio de Margarita de Austria, que una vez gobernó los Países Bajos de los Habsburgo.

La ville des carillonneurs

Avec plus de 300 bâtiments classés, la paisible ville de Malines est un véritable délice architectural. Elle possède même deux beffrois : la tour de la mairie et la tour de la cathédrale Saint-Rombaut, avec ses deux carillons. Le carillon retentit également dans la cour intérieure du palais de Marguerite d'Autriche, ancien siège du règne sur les Pays-Bas habsbourgeois.

Cidade dos tocadores de sinos

A tranquila cidade de Mechelen, com seus mais de 300 edifícios listados, é uma verdadeira iguaria arquitetônica. Tem ainda dois campanários: a torre da Câmara Municipal e a torre da Catedral de St. Rombout, com dois carrilhões. O carrilhão também pode ser ouvido no pátio interior do Palácio de Margarida da Áustria, que outrora governou a Holanda dos Habsburgos.

Stadt der Glockenspieler

Das beschauliche Mechelen ist, mit über 300 denkmalgeschützten Gebäuden, ein baugeschichtlicher Leckerbissen. Er hat sogar zwei Belfriede: den Rathausturm und den Turm der Kathedrale St. Rombout, mit zwei Glockenspielen. Auch im Innenhof des Palastes der Margarete von Österreich, von dem einst die habsburgischen Niederlande regiert wurden, erklingt das Glockenspiel.

Stad van de klokkenspellen

De ingetogen stad Mechelen is met meer dan 300 als monument beschermde gebouwen een bouwhistorische delicatesse en heeft 2 belforten: de toren van het stadhuis en de toren van de Sint-Romboutskathedraal met 2 beiaarden. Ook op de binnenplaats van het Hof van Savoye, van waaruit ooit de Habsburgse Nederlanden werden geregeerd, is het klokkenspel te beluisteren.

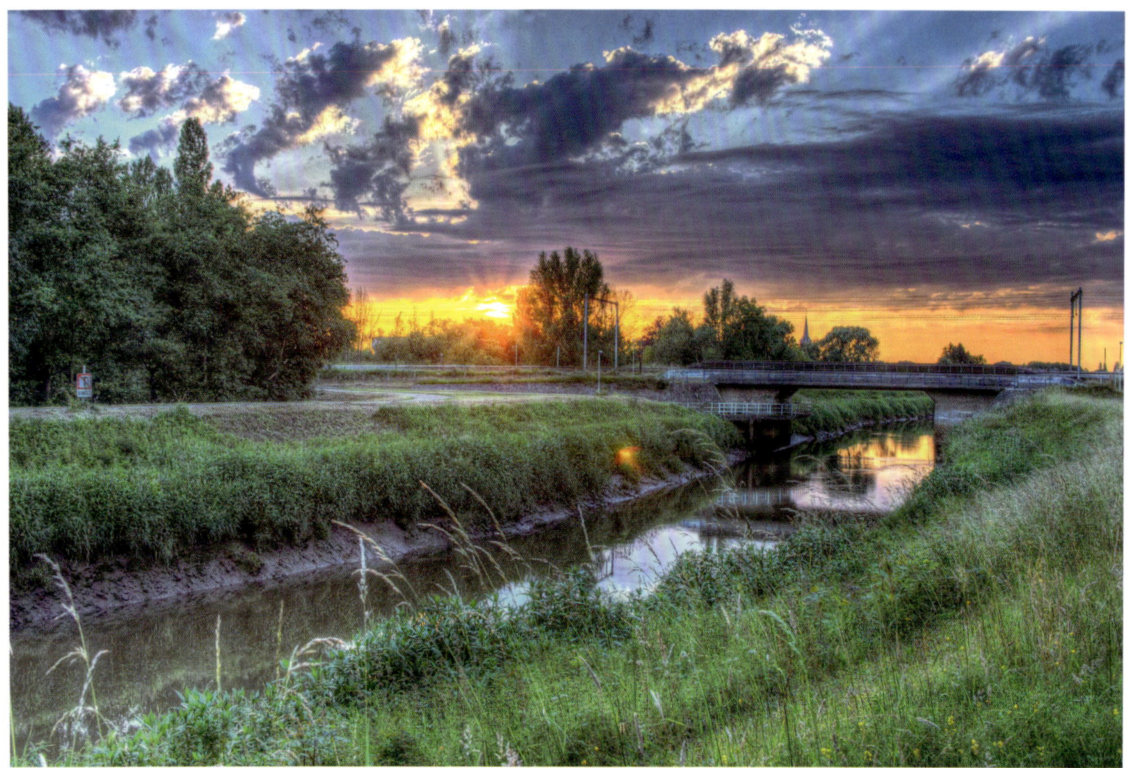

Landscape near Lier
Landschap bij Lier
Paysage près de Lierre

Port of Lier

The port city of Lier is connected to the sea by the river Nete and its canal, and formed a centre of the livestock trade in the Middle Ages. In the 15th century, the town had to decide on a princely privilege, hosting a market for livestock or a university. They decided to opt for the cattle market, and since then the people of Lier have been nicknamed "Schapenkoppen" (sheep heads).

Ciudad portuaria de Lier

La ciudad portuaria de Lier está conectada al mar por el río Nette y el canal y fue un centro de comercio de ganado en la Edad Media. En el siglo XV la ciudad tuvo que decidir sobre un privilegio principesco: derechos de almacenaje para el ganado o una universidad. Decidieron ir al mercado de ganado, y desde entonces los habitantes de Lier reciben el apodo de "cabezas de oveja".

Lierre, ville portuaire

La ville portuaire de Lierre est reliée à la mer par la Nèthe et le canal; au Moyen Âge, c'était l'un des centres du commerce de bétail. Au xve siècle, la ville dut choisir parmi deux privilèges princiers : soit le droit d'entreposer le bétail, soit une université. Elle trancha pour le marché au bétail : depuis lors, les Lierrois sont affublés du sobriquet «têtes de mouton».

Cidade portuária de Lier

A cidade portuária de Lier está ligada ao mar pelo rio Nette e pelo canal e foi um centro de comércio de gado na Idade Média. No século XV, a cidade teve de decidir sobre um privilégio principesco: direito básico para o gado ou uma universidade. Eles optaram pela parca agropecuária, desde então, os cidadãos de Lier foram apelidados de "cabeça de carneiro".

Hafenstadt Lier

Über den Fluss Nete und den Kanal ist die Hafenstadt Lier mit dem Meer verbunden und war im Mittelalter ein Zentrum des Viehhandels. Im 15. Jahrhundert musste sich die Stadt für ein fürstliches Privileg entscheiden: Stapelrecht für Vieh oder eine Universität. Sie entschieden sich für den Viehmarkt, seitdem tragen die Lierer den Spitznamen „Schafsköpfe".

Havenstad Lier

Via de rivier de Nete en het kanaal is de havenstad Lier met de zee verbonden en was in de Middeleeuwen het centrum van veehandel. In de 15e eeuw moest de stad kiezen uit twee vorstelijke beloningen: stapelrechten voor vee of een universiteit. Ze kozen voor de veemarkt en sindsdien hebben de inwoners van Lier de bijnaam schapenkoppen.

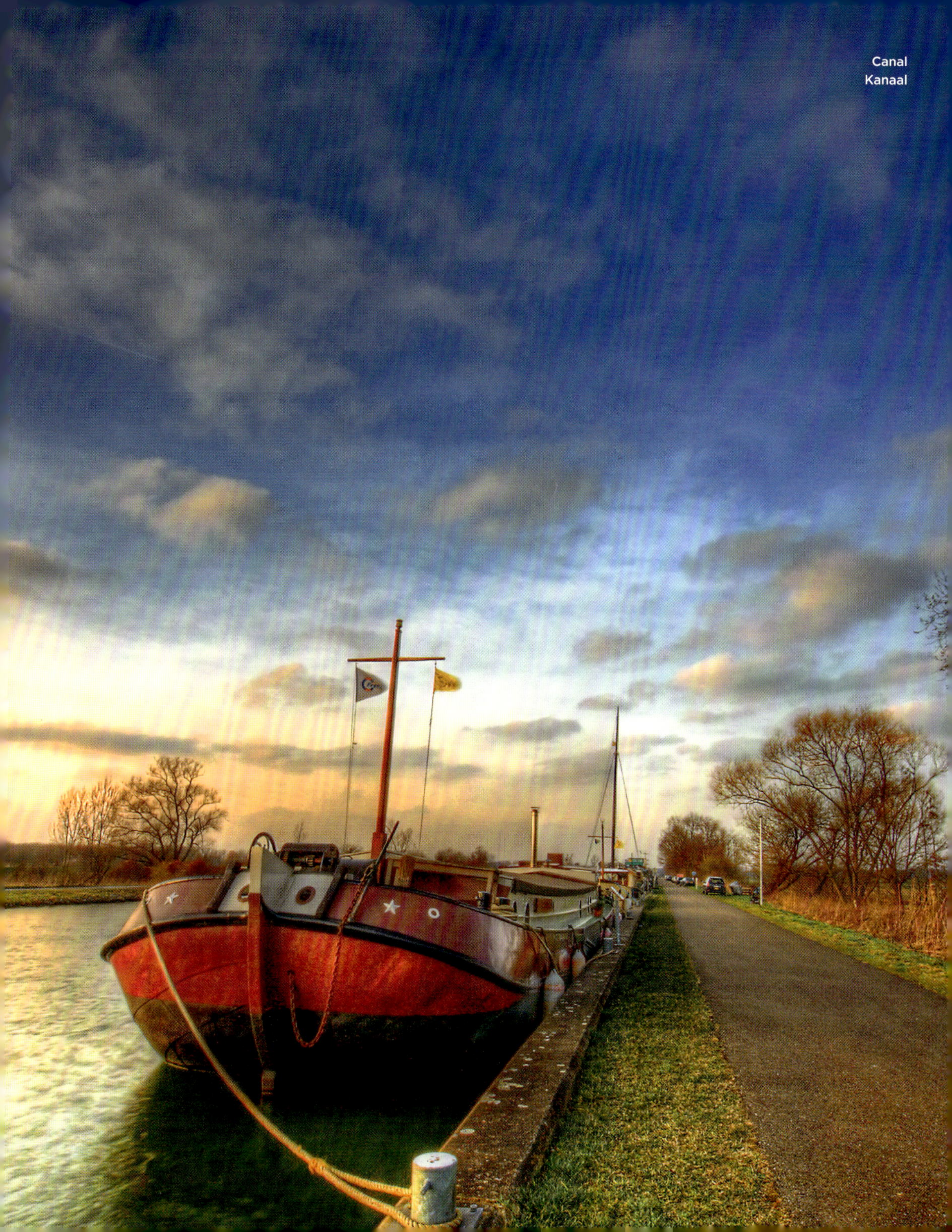

Canal
Kanaal

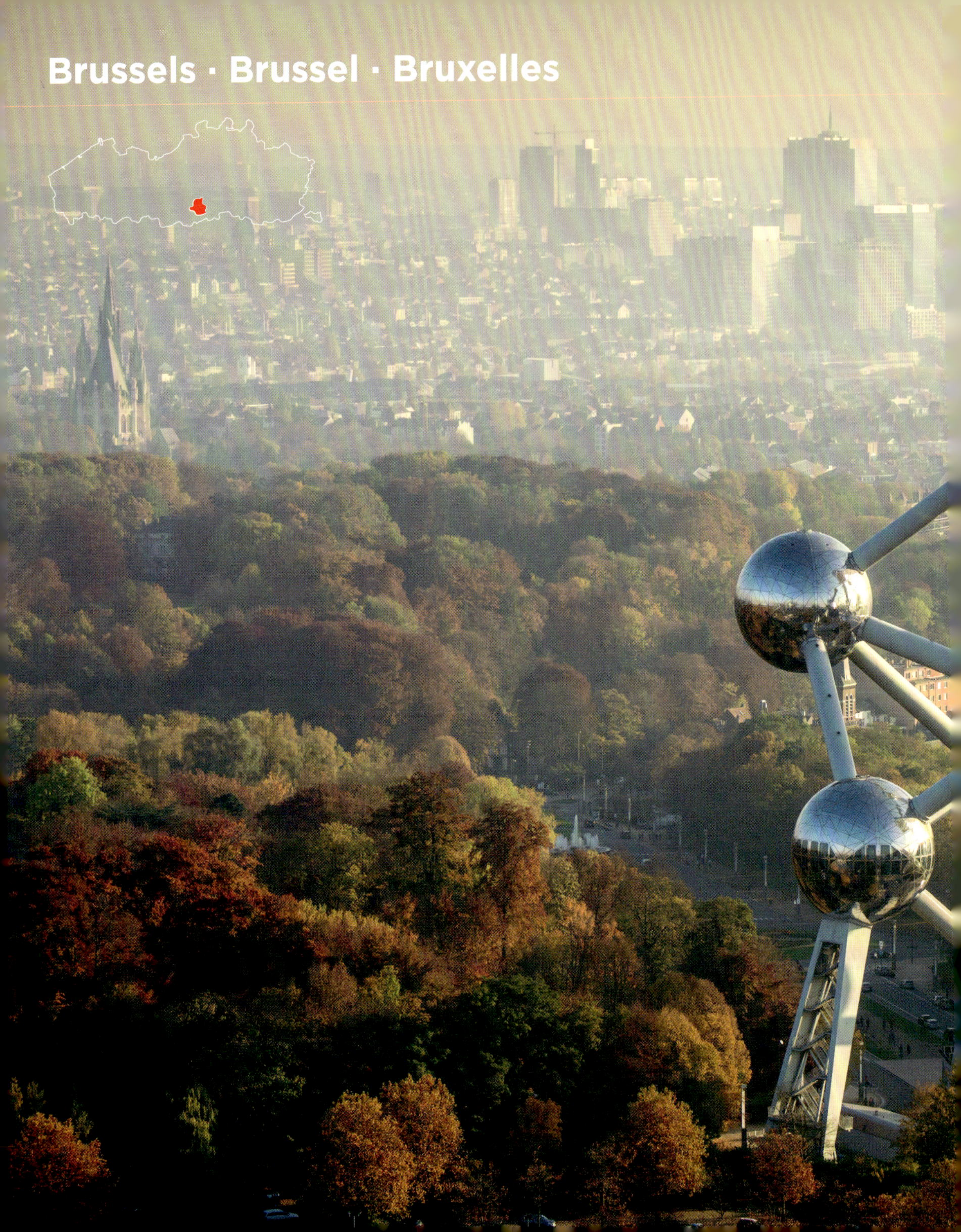

Brussels · Brussel · Bruxelles

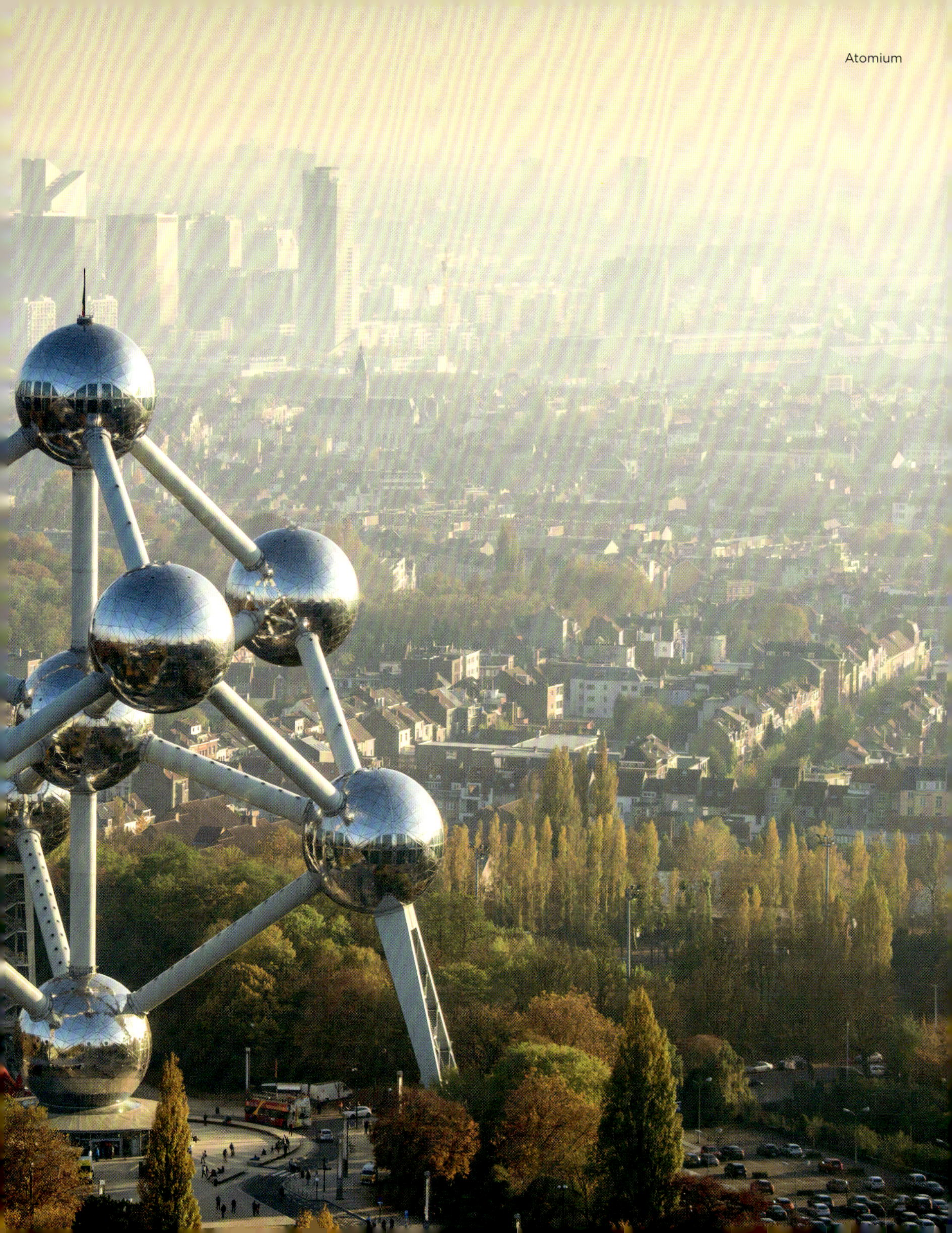

Atomium

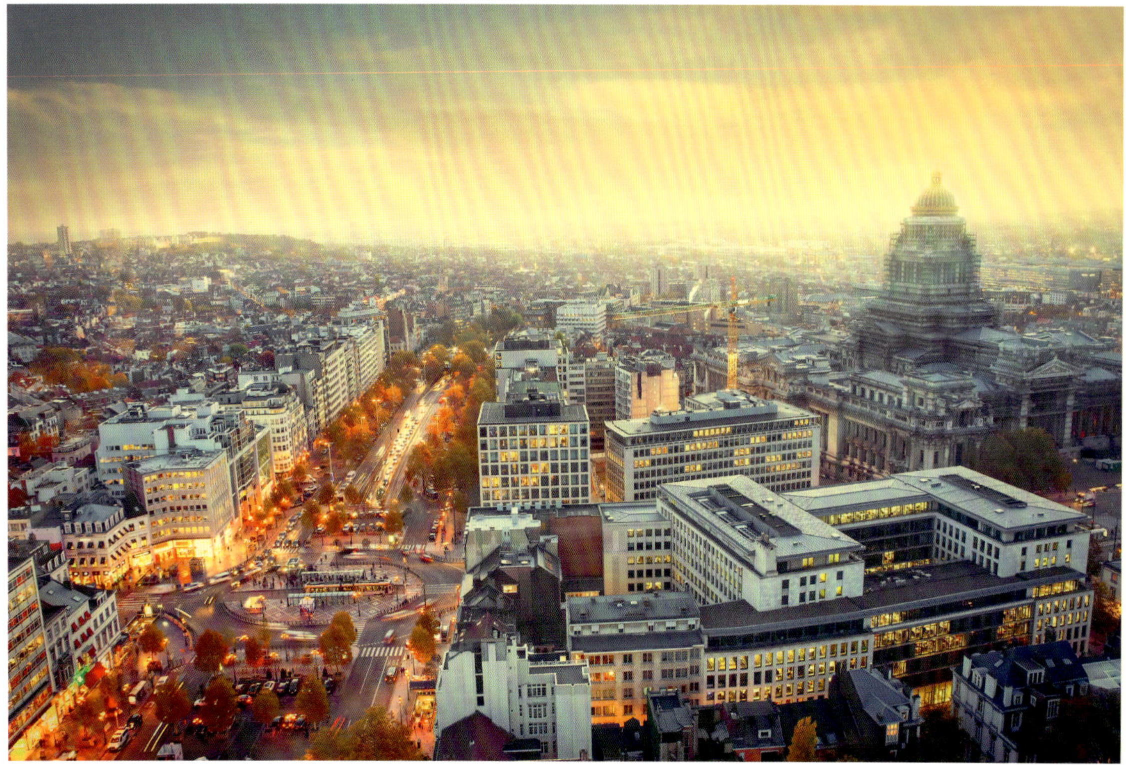

City of Brussels and Palace of Justice
De stad Brussel en Justitiepaleis van Brussel
Ville de Bruxelles et Palais de justice

Brussels

The Belgian capital is not only the headquarters of the European Union and NATO, but also a lively metropolis. It has perhaps the most beautiful marketplace in the world, and then so much more to offer, in its boulevards and magnificent buildings from the belle époque, Art Nouveau villas, museums exhibiting some of the world's greatest works of art and, as a symbol of the city, a little peeing boy.

Bruxelles

Siège de l'Union européenne et de l'OTAN, la capitale belge – métropole animée dont la grand-place est peut-être la plus belle au monde – offre bien plus encore : boulevards et somptueux bâtiments de la Belle Époque, villas Art nouveau, musées abritant certaines des plus grandes œuvres d'art, sans oublier l'emblème de la ville – un petit garçon qui pisse.

Brüssel

Die belgische Hauptstadt ist nicht nur Hauptsitz der Europäischen Union und der NATO, die quirlige Metropole mit dem vielleicht schönsten Marktplatz der Welt bietet mehr: Boulevards und Prachtbauten aus der Belle Époque, Jugendstil-Villen, Museen, die einige der größten Kunstwerke der Welt zeigen und als Wahrzeichen einen kleinen pinkelnden Jungen.

Bruselas

La capital belga no solo es la sede de la Unión Europea y de la OTAN, sino que la animada metrópoli, con el que puede que sea el mercado más bello del mundo, ofrece más: bulevares y magníficos edificios de la Belle Époque, villas modernistas, museos que muestran algunas de las más grandes obras de arte del mundo y como lugar emblemático, un niño haciendo pis.

Bruxelas

A capital belga não é apenas a sede da União Europeia e da OTAN, a animada metrópole com talvez o mais belo mercado do mundo oferece mais: avenidas e magníficos edifícios da Belle Époque, vilas em Art Nouveau, museus que mostram algumas das maiores obras de arte do mundo e como símbolo, o monumento de um pequeno menino a urinar para a bacia da fonte.

Brussel

De Belgische hoofdstad is niet alleen het hoofdkwartier van de Europese Unie en de NAVO, de levendige metropool met misschien wel het mooiste marktplein ter wereld biedt meer: boulevards en prachtige gebouwen uit de belle époque, art nouveau-villa's, musea die enkele van de grootste kunstwerken ter wereld tonen en als symbool een kleine plassende jongen.

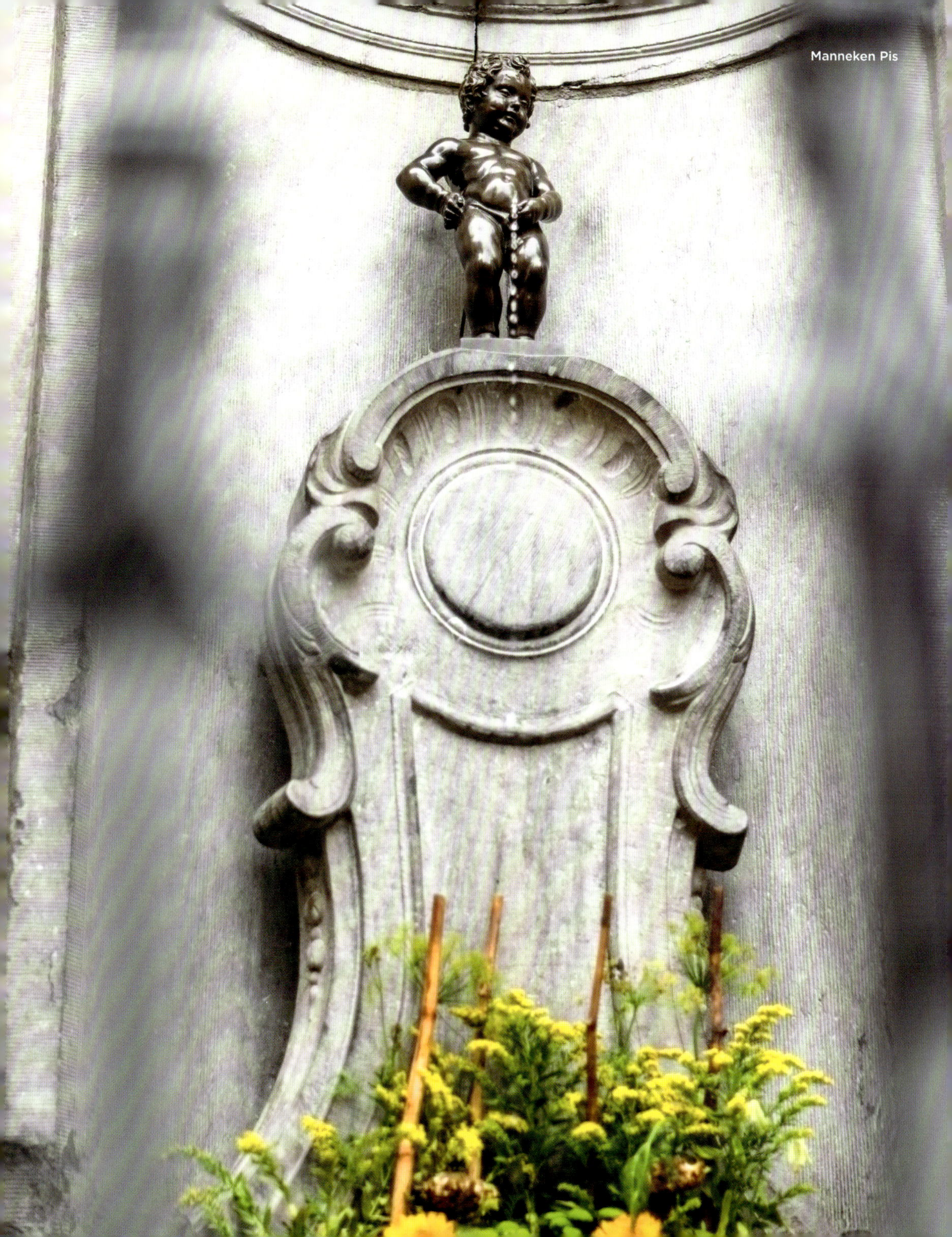
Manneken Pis

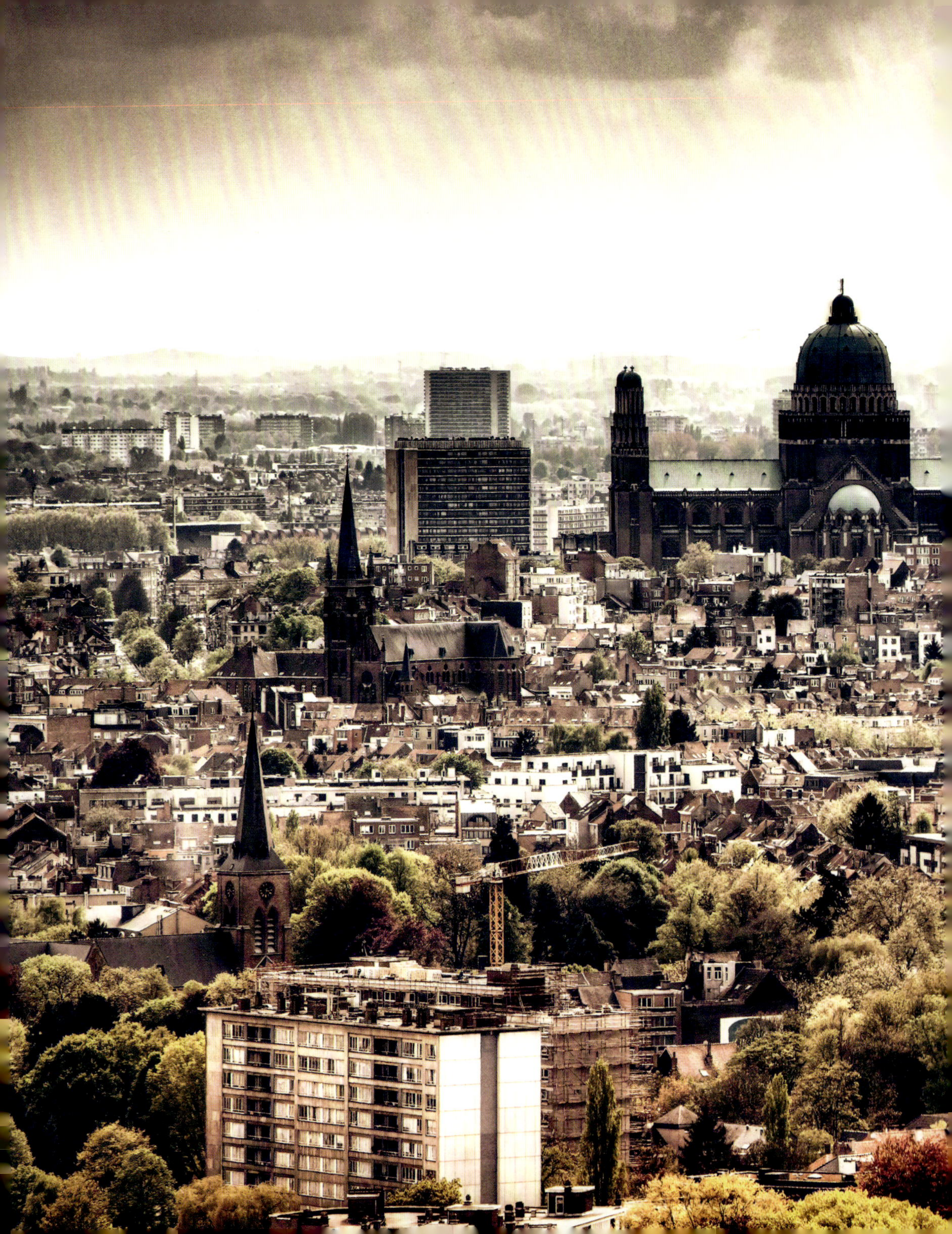

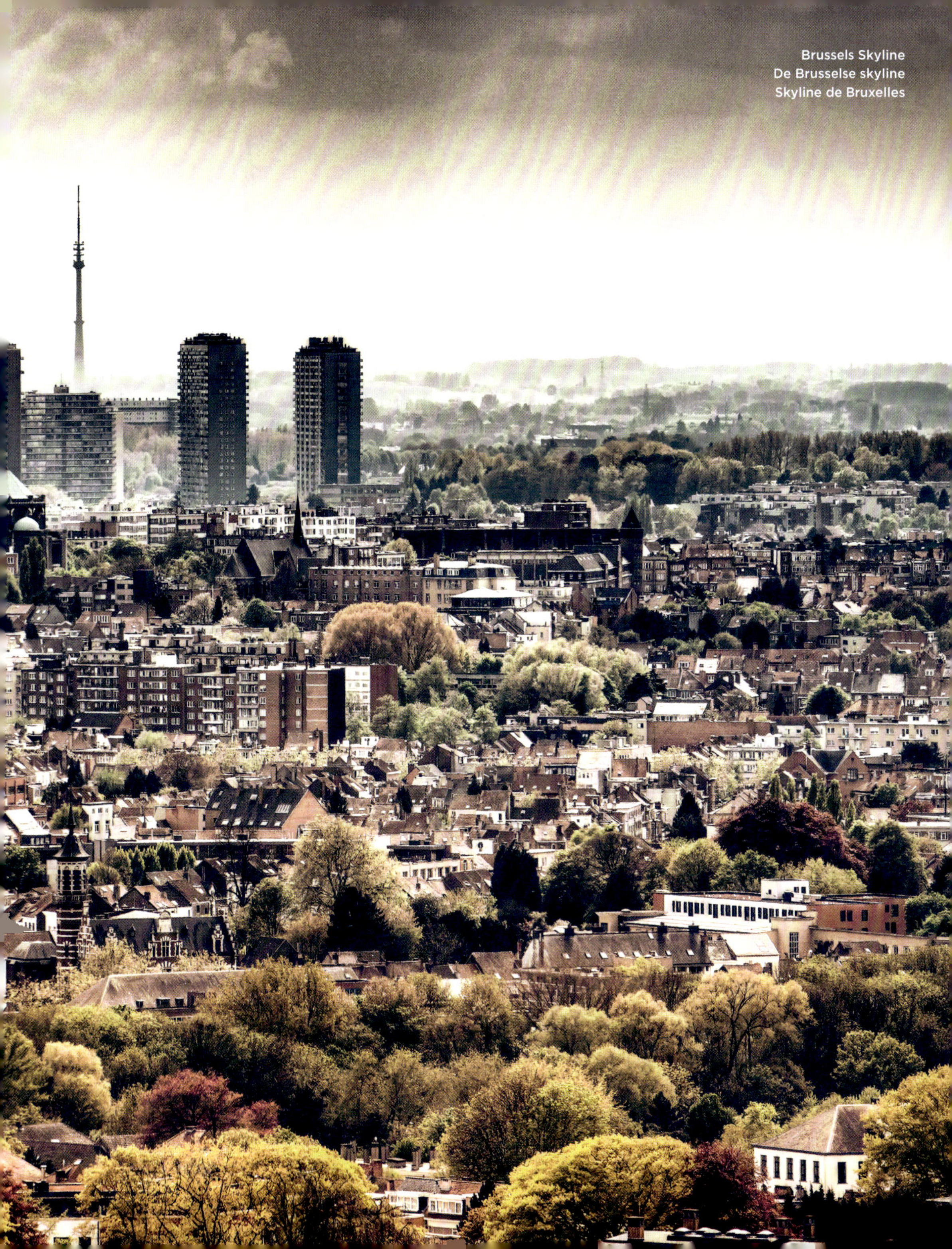
Brussels Skyline
De Brusselse skyline
Skyline de Bruxelles

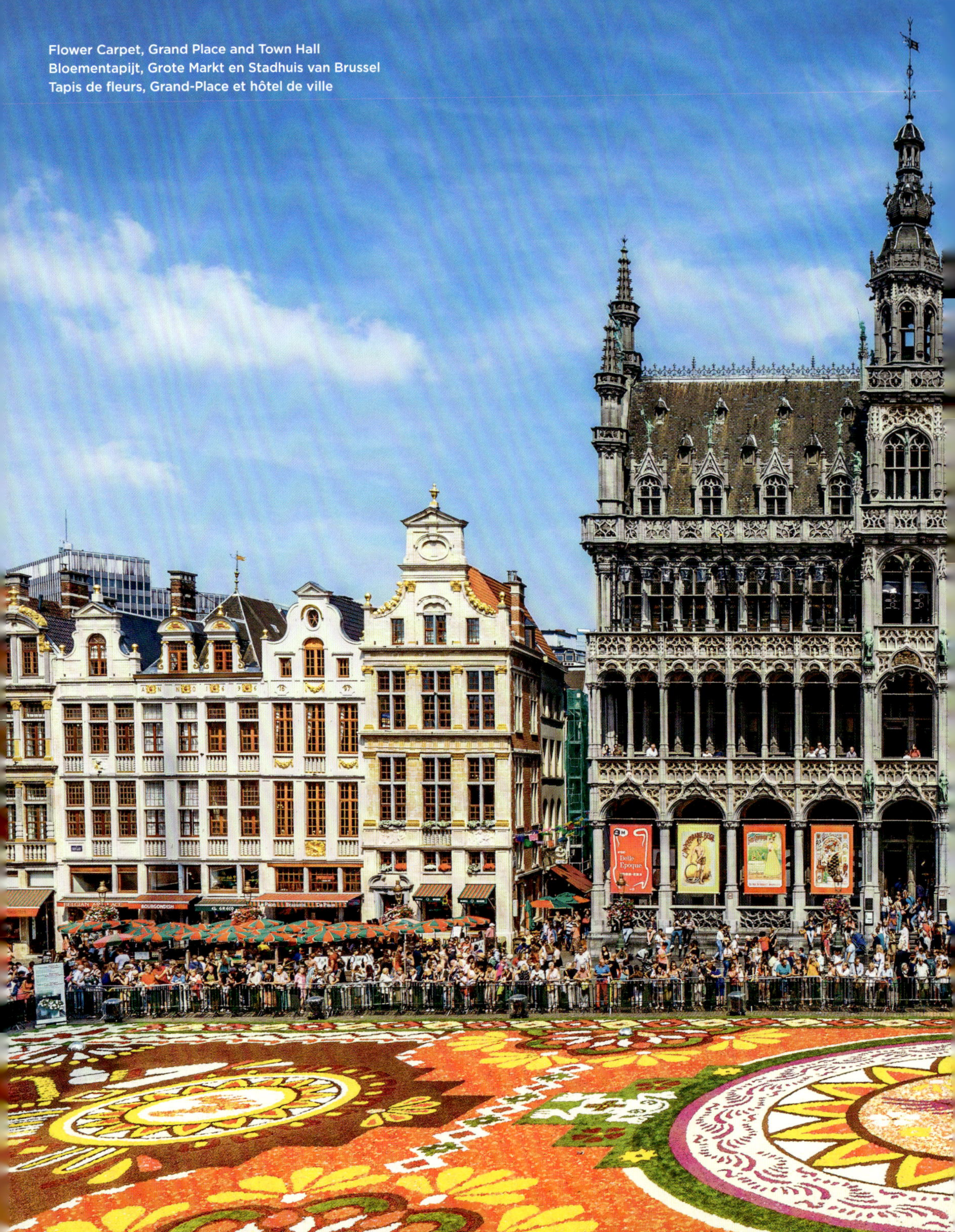

Flower Carpet, Grand Place and Town Hall
Bloementapijt, Grote Markt en Stadhuis van Brussel
Tapis de fleurs, Grand-Place et hôtel de ville

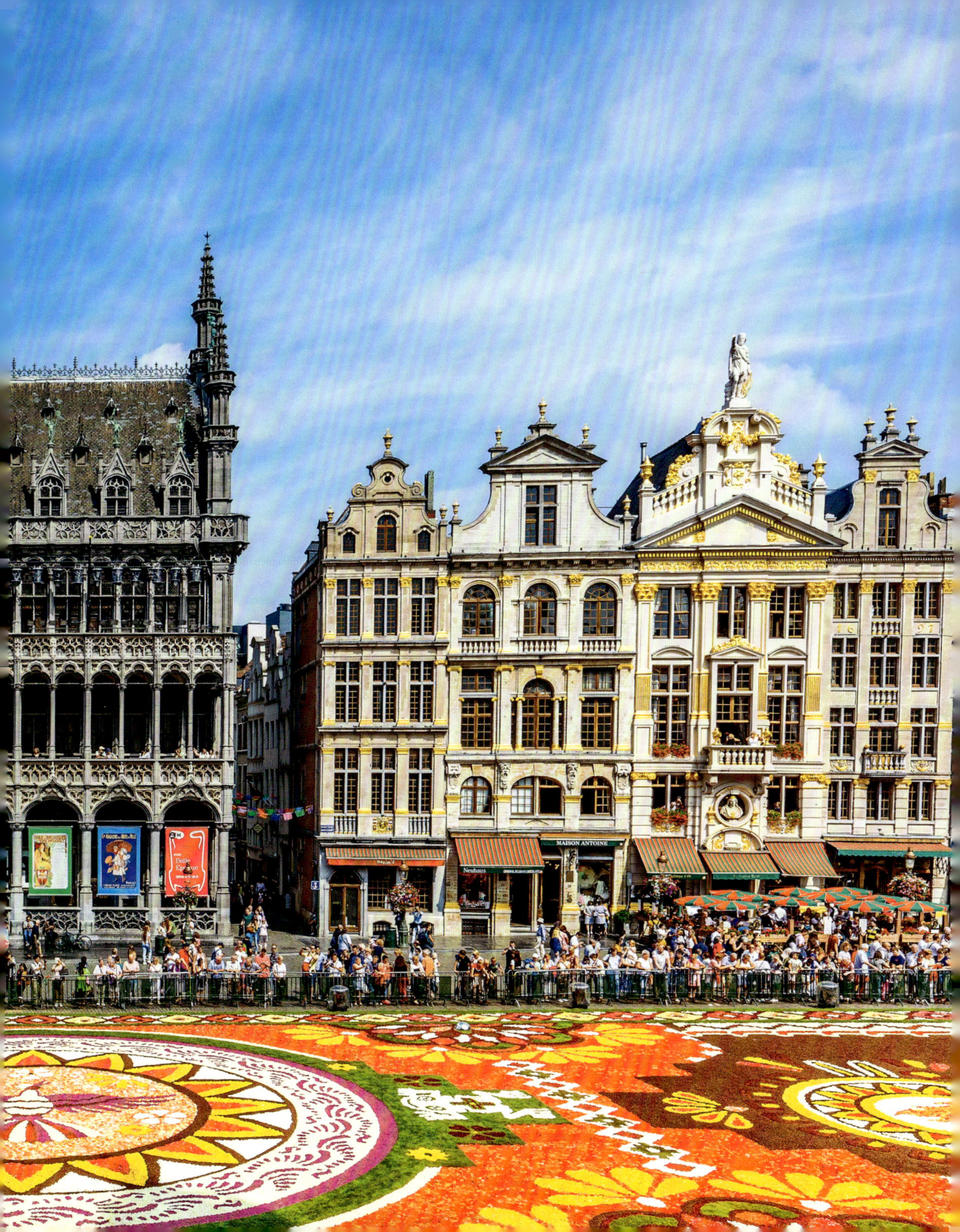

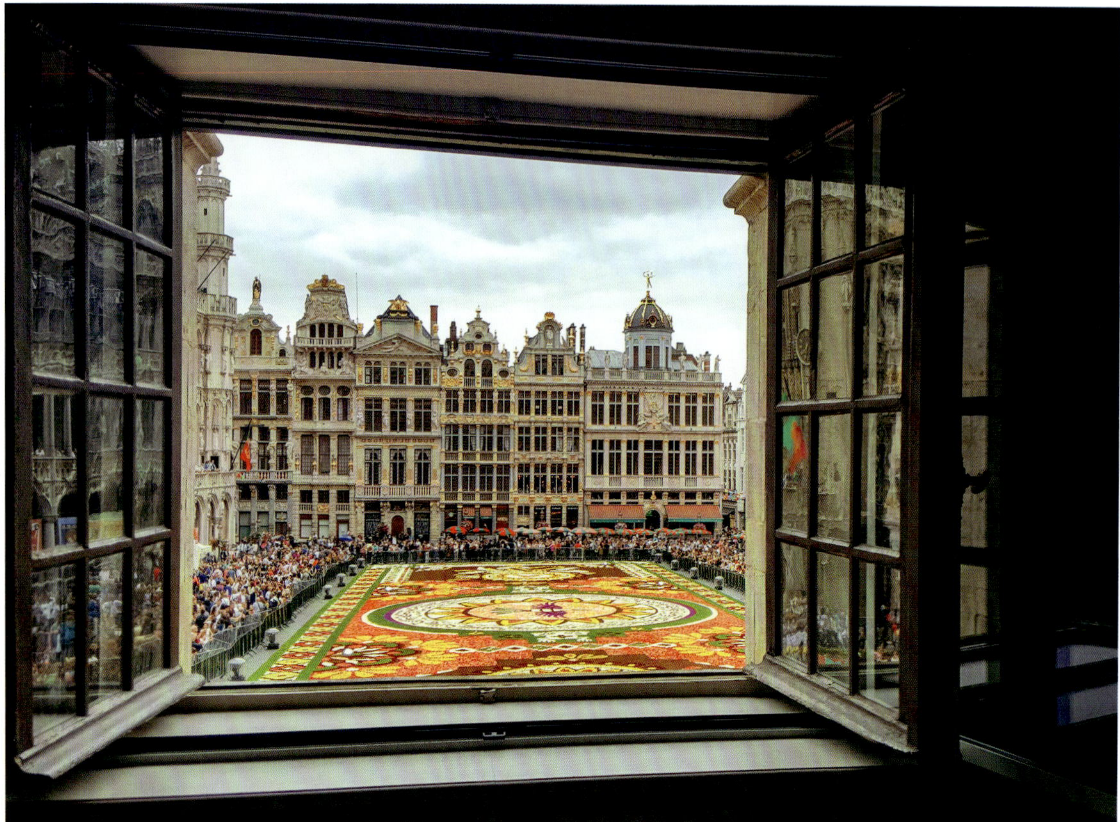

Flower Carpet
Bloementapijt
Tapis de fleurs

Carpet of flowers and the Grand Place

The market of the Flemish capital, with
its Gothic town hall and richly decorated
Baroque guild houses, is considered one
of the most beautiful squares in the world.
Every second year in summer, within a
few hours, hundreds of gardeners lay
out a colorful carpet of flowers at the
market. The 1800 m² (19,375 sq ft) floral
arrangement displays a total of 750,000
begonias, with around 400 flowers per
square metre. The very robust begonia
is the national flower of Flanders, with
around 80 percent of all begonias being
grown in the region of Ghent. Visitors have
the best view of the floral masterpiece
from the balcony of the town hall.

Tapis de fleurs et Grand-Place

Avec son hôtel de ville gothique et
ses maisons de corporation baroques
richement ornées, la Grand-Place de la
capitale flamande est considérée comme
l'une des plus belles places du marché
au monde. Tous les deux ans, en été, des
centaines de jardiniers y déroulent, en
quelques heures à peine, un tapis de fleurs
coloré. Cette peinture florale de 1800 m²
comprend 750 000 bégonias en tout – soit
environ 400 fleurs par m². Très résistant, le
bégonia est la fleur nationale des Flandres ;
environ 80 % des bégonias sont cultivés
dans la région de Gand. C'est le balcon de
l'hôtel de ville qui offre la meilleure vue sur
le chef-d'œuvre.

Blumenteppich und Grand Place

Der Markt der flämischen Hauptstadt gilt
mit seinem gotischen Rathaus und seinen
barocken reich verzierten Zunfthäusern
als einer der schönsten Plätze der Welt.
Jedes zweite Jahr im Sommer legen
innerhalb weniger Stunden Hunderte
Gärtner auf dem Markt einen farbenfrohen
Blumenteppich aus. Das 1800 m² große
Blumengemälde zählt, mit rund 400 Blüten
pro m², insgesamt 750 000 Begonien. Die
sehr robuste Begonie ist die Nationalblume
Flanderns, rund 80 Prozent aller Begonien
werden in der Region von Gent gezogen.
Den besten Blick auf das Meisterwerk
haben Besucher vom Balkon des
Rathauses aus.

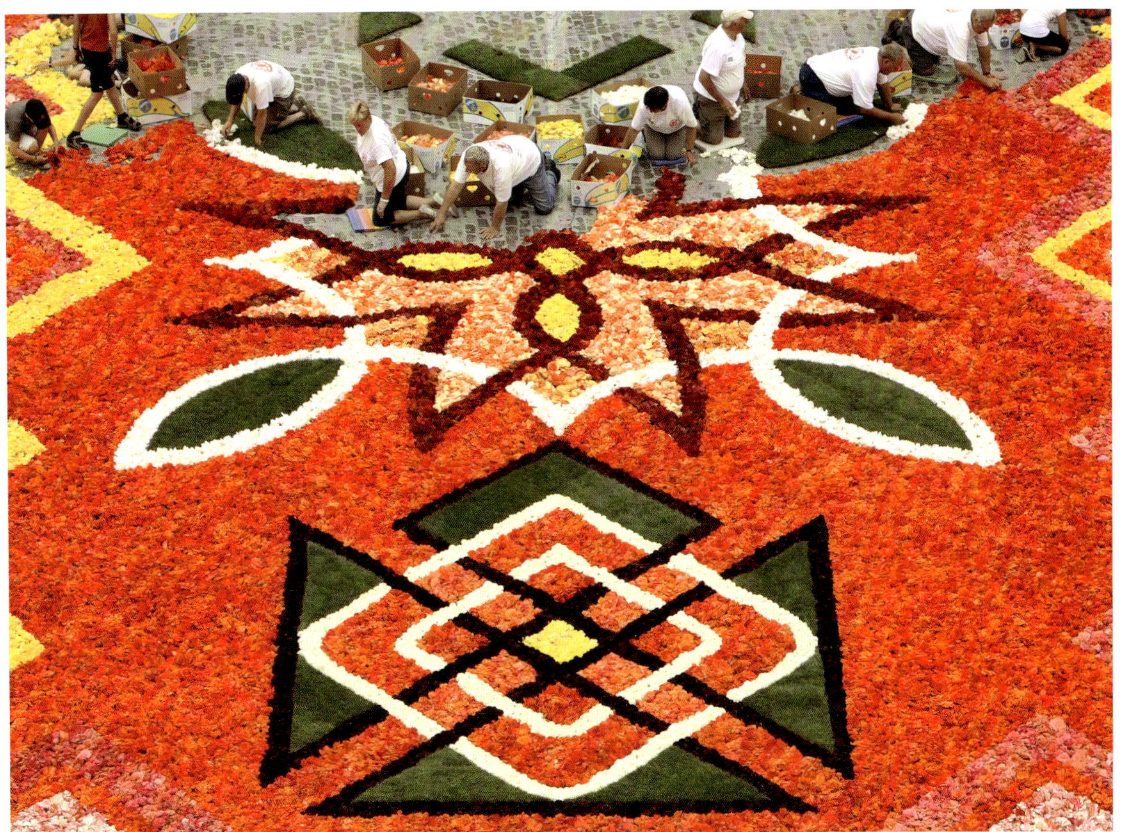

Flower Carpet
Bloementapijt
Tapis de fleurs

Alfombra floral y Grand Place

El mercado de la capital flamenca, con su ayuntamiento gótico y sus casas gremiales barrocas ricamente decoradas, se considera una de las plazas más bellas del mundo. Cada dos años en verano, en apenas unas pocas horas, cientos de jardineros colocan una colorida alfombra de flores en el mercado. La pintura floral de 1800 m² tiene un total de 750 000 begonias con alrededor de 400 flores por m². La robusta begonia es la flor nacional de Flandes; alrededor del 80 por ciento de todas las begonias se cultivan en la región de Gante. Los visitantes tienen la mejor vista de la obra maestra desde el balcón del ayuntamiento.

Tapete de flores e Grand Place

O mercado da capital flamenga, com sua câmara municipal gótica e casas das corporações barrocas ricamente decoradas, é considerada uma das mais belas praças do mundo. A cada dois anos no verão, em poucas horas, centenas de jardineiros colocam um tapete colorido de flores no mercado. A pintura floral de 1800 m² tem um total de 750 000 begónias com cerca de 400 flores por m². A begónia muito robusta é a flor nacional da Flandres, cerca de 80 por cento de todas as begónias são cultivadas na região de Gante. Os visitantes têm a melhor vista da obra-prima a partir da varanda da Câmara Municipal.

Bloementapijt en Grote Markt

De markt van de Vlaamse hoofdstad, met zijn gotische stadhuis en rijkelijk versierde barokke gildehuizen, wordt beschouwd als één van de mooiste pleinen ter wereld. Om de twee jaar rollen 's zomers honderden tuinders binnen een paar uur een kleurenrijk bloementapijt over de markt uit. Het 1800 m² grote bloemschilderij met ongeveer 400 bloemen per m² bevat in totaal 750 000 begonia's. De zeer robuuste begonia is de nationale bloem van Vlaanderen, ongeveer 80 procent van alle begonia's worden in de regio Gent geteeld. Vanaf het balkon van het stadhuis hebben de bezoekers het beste uitzicht op het meesterwerk.

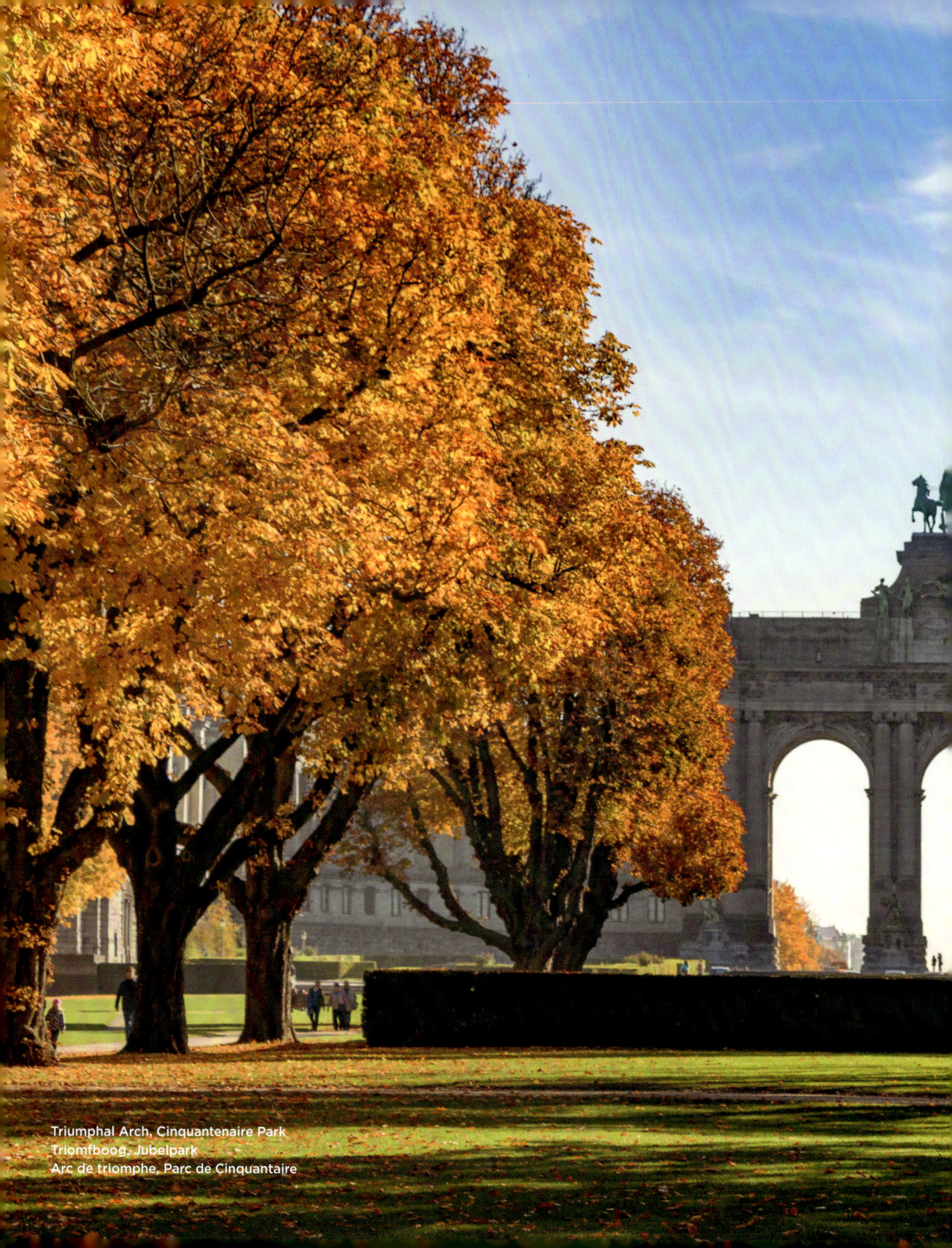

Triumphal Arch, Cinquantenaire Park
Triomfboog, Jubelpark
Arc de triomphe, Parc de Cinquantaire

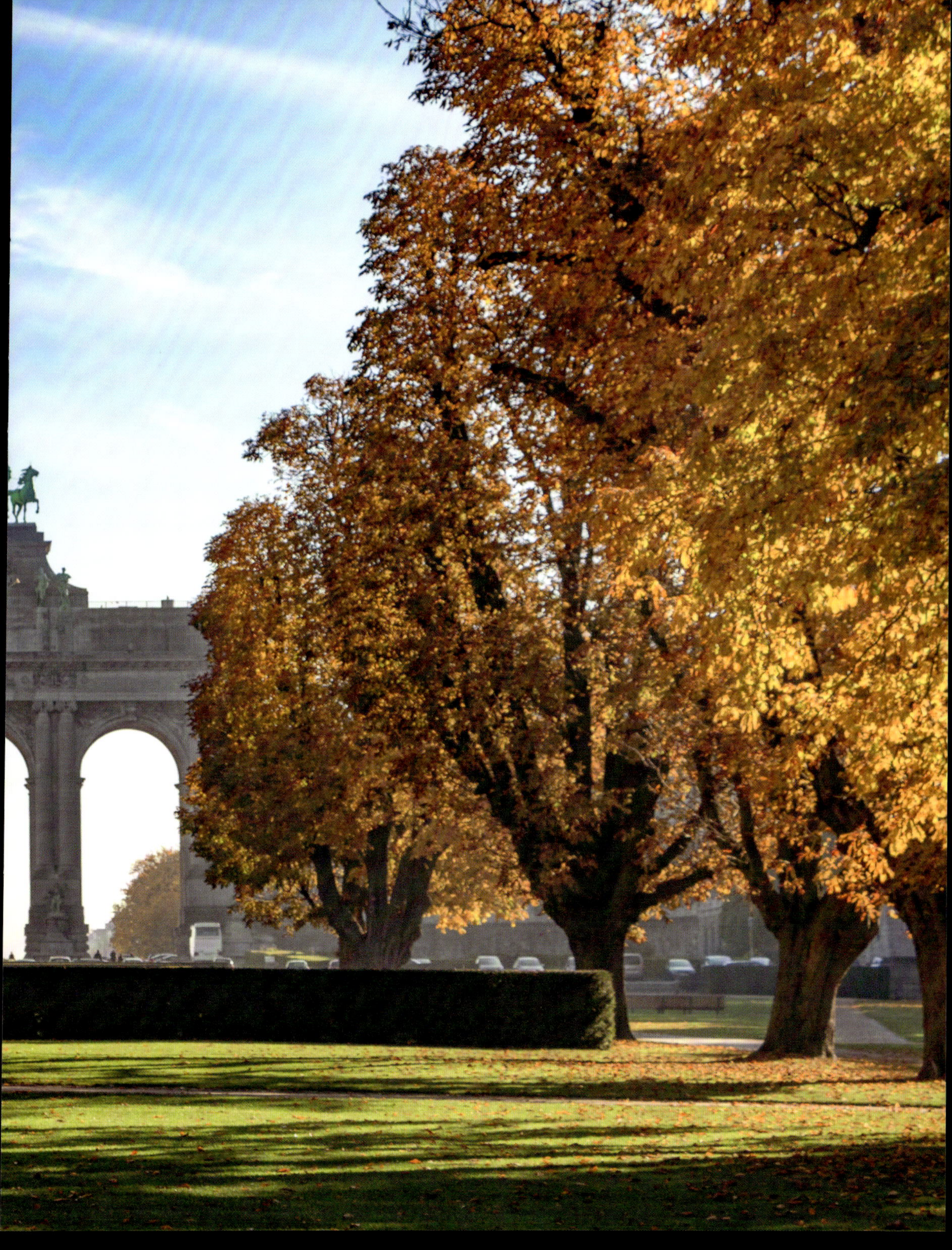

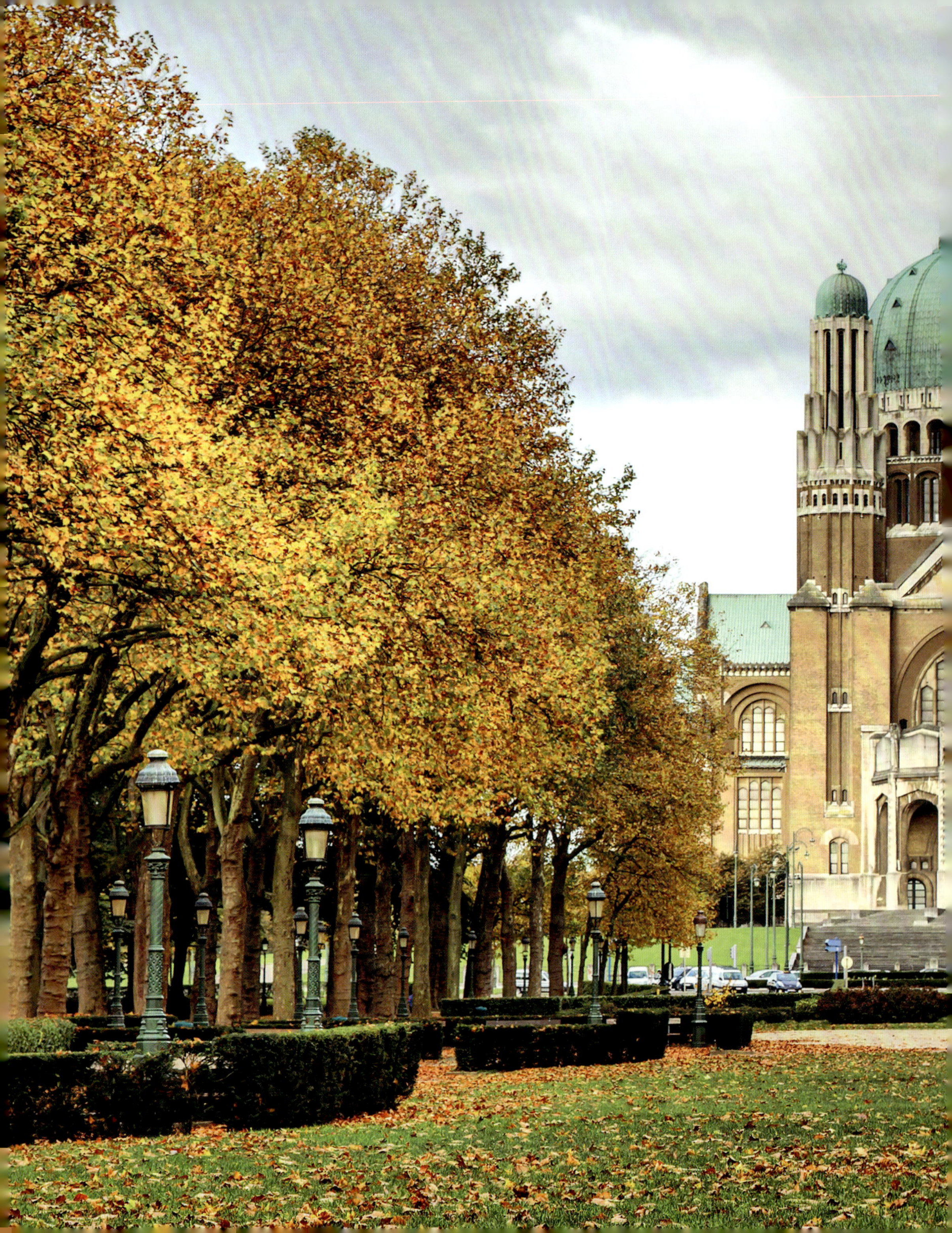

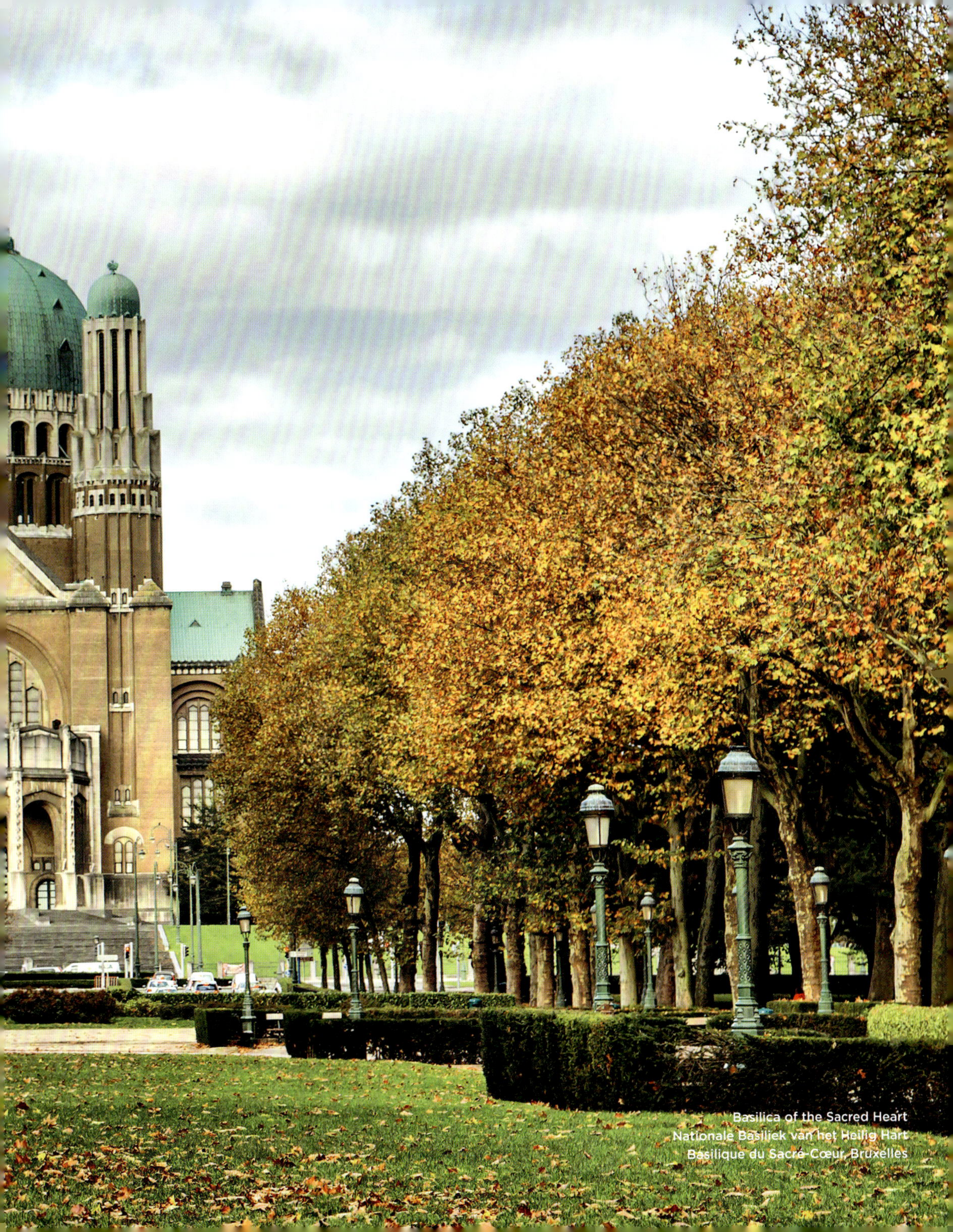

Basilica of the Sacred Heart
Nationale Basiliek van het Heilig Hart
Basilique du Sacré-Cœur, Bruxelles

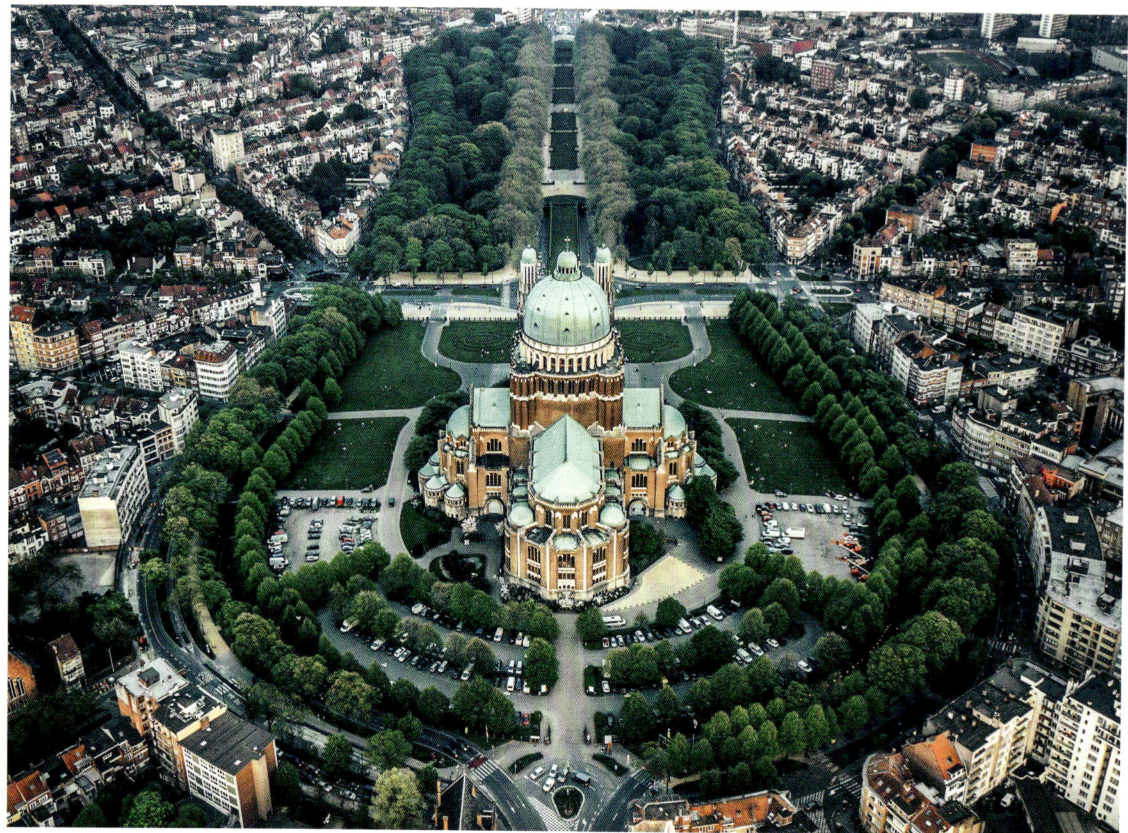

Basilica of the Sacred Heart
Nationale Basiliek van het Heilig Hart
Basilique du Sacré-Cœur, Bruxelles

Art Deco Basilica

The world's largest Art Deco building is the National Basilica of the Sacred Heart, can accommodate more than 2000 people. With its gigantic cathedral dome, the 89 m (292 ft) high basilica shapes the skyline of Brussels and has a viewing platform which offers a magnificent prospect of the capital. The interior of the church fits seamlessly into the architectural ensemble of splendour. Numerous round arches, columns and fantastic stained glass windows line the space. The basilica was commissioned under King Leopold II to celebrate the 75th anniversary of the independence of Belgium.

Basilique Art déco

La basilique nationale du Sacré-Cœur est le plus grand bâtiment Art déco du monde. Elle peut accueillir environ 2000 personnes. Avec son gigantesque dôme, la basilique de 89 m de haut fait partie intégrante de la skyline bruxelloise; une plate-forme panoramique offre une vue grandiose sur la capitale. L'intérieur de l'église s'intègre parfaitement à ce splendide ensemble architectural. D'innombrables arcs en plein cintre, colonnes et vitraux fantastiques ornent l'espace. La basilique a été commandée par le roi Léopold II à l'occasion du 75e anniversaire de l'indépendance de la Belgique.

Art déco-Basilika

Das weltweit größte Gebäude im Art déco-Stil ist die Nationalbasilika des Heiligen Herzens. Die Kirche bietet Platz für rund 2000 Menschen. Mit ihrer gigantischen Domkuppel prägt die 89 m hohe Basilika die Skyline von Brüssel und eine Aussichtsplattform bietet einen grandiosen Ausblick auf die Hauptstadt. Der Innenraum des Gotteshauses reiht sich nahtlos in das architektonische Prachtensemble ein. Zahlreiche Rundbögen, Säulen und fantastische Buntglasfenster säumen den Raum. Die Basilika wurde unter König Leopold II. zum 75. Jahrestag der Unabhängigkeit Belgiens in Auftrag gegeben.

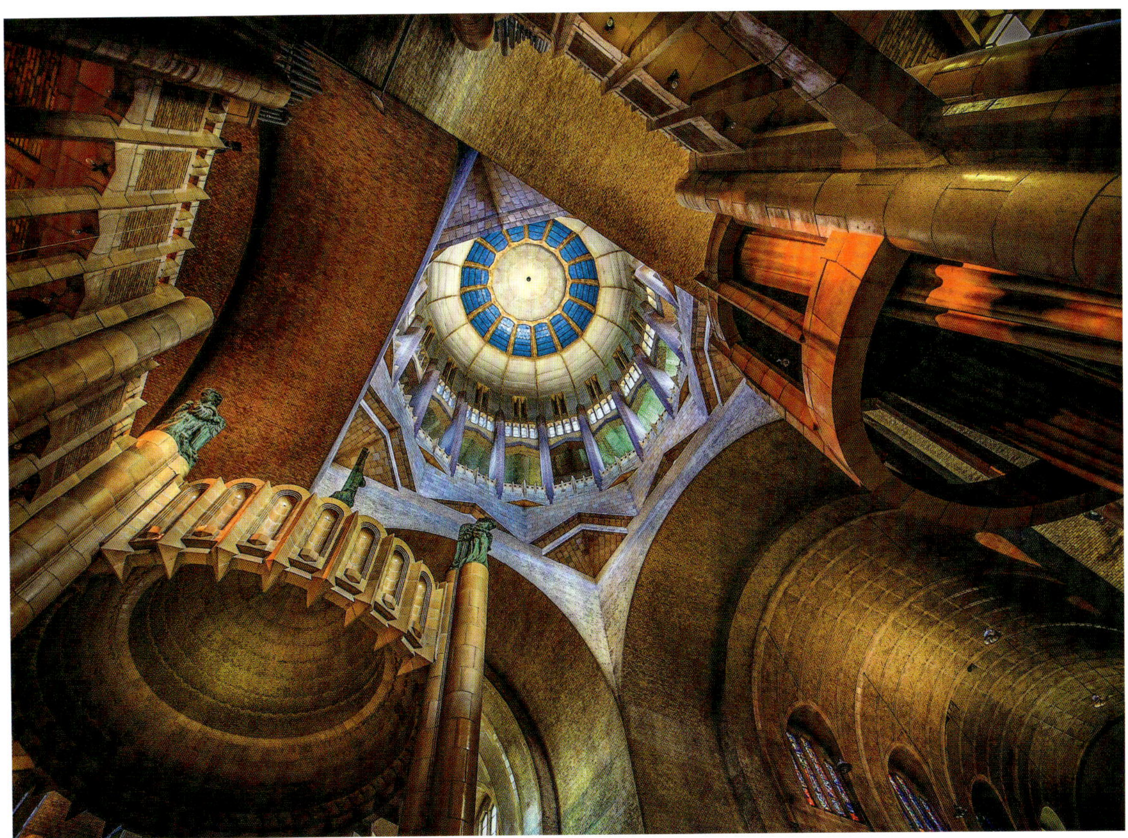

Basilica of the Sacred Heart
Nationale Basiliek van het Heilig Hart
Basilique du Sacré-Cœur, Bruxelles

Basílica Art Déco

El edificio Art Déco más grande del mundo es la Basílica Nacional del Sagrado Corazón. La iglesia tiene capacidad para unas 2000 personas. Con su gigantesca cúpula, la basílica de 89 m de altura conforma el horizonte de Bruselas y un mirador ofrece una magnífica vista de la capital. El interior de la iglesia encaja perfectamente en el conjunto arquitectónico de esplendor. Numerosos arcos de medio punto, columnas y fantásticos vitrales bordean la sala. La basílica fue encargada por el rey Leopoldo II con motivo del 75.º aniversario de la independencia de Bélgica.

Basílica Art Déco

O maior edifício em estilo Art Déco do mundo é a Basílica Nacional do Sagrado Coração. A igreja acomoda cerca de 2000 pessoas. Com a sua gigantesca cúpula de catedral, a basílica de 89 m de altura domina o horizonte de Bruxelas e uma plataforma de observação oferece uma vista magnífica da capital. O interior da igreja enquadra-se perfeitamente no esplendor arquitetónico. Numerosos arcos redondos, colunas e fantásticos vitrais revestem a sala. A basílica foi encomendada pelo rei Leopoldo II para o 75º aniversário da independência da Bélgica.

Art deco basiliek

Het grootste art-decogebouw ter wereld is de Nationale Basiliek van het Heilig Hart. De kerk biedt plaats aan ongeveer 2000 mensen. De 89 m hoge basiliek met zijn gigantische kathedraalkoepel vormt de skyline van Brussel. Een uitkijkplatform biedt een prachtig uitzicht op de hoofdstad. Het interieur van de kerk sluit naadloos aan bij het architectonisch ensemble van pracht en praal. Talrijke ronde bogen, zuilen en fantastische gebrandschilderde ramen omzomen de ruimte. De basiliek werd in opdracht van Koning Leopold II gebouwd ter gelegenheid van de 75ste verjaardag van de onafhankelijkheid van België.

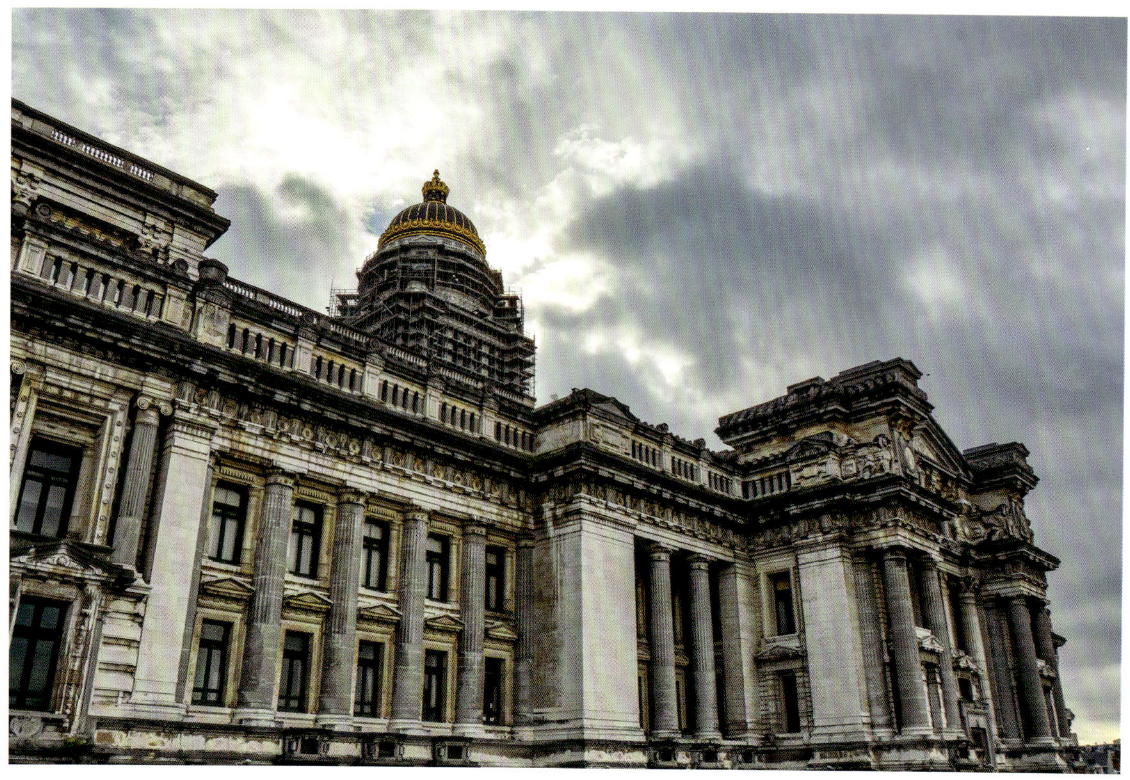

Palace of Justice of Brussels
Justitiepaleis van Brussel
Palais de justice de Bruxelles

Palace of Justice

The building is one of the largest stone buildings ever built by man. With a floor area of 26,000 m²(279,862 sq ft), it surpasses even St. Peter's Basilica in Rome. With this bombastic building, whose facade is teeming with columns, statues and superstructures, the Belgian king wanted to make an impression for the then still young Belgian state.

Palacio de Justicia

El edificio es una de las construcciones de piedra más grandes jamás construidas por el hombre. Con una superficie de 26 000 m², supera incluso a la Catedral de San Pedro de Roma. Con este edificio pomposo, cuya fachada está repleta de columnas, estatuas y superestructuras, los reyes belgas quisieron dar ejemplo para el entonces todavía joven estado belga.

Palais de justice

Voici l'un des plus grands bâtiments en pierre jamais construits par l'homme. D'une superficie de 26 000 m², il surpasse même la cathédrale Saint-Pierre de Rome. Avec ce bâtiment pompeux, dont la façade regorge de colonnes, de statues et de superstructures, les rois voulurent mettre en avant l'État belge, encore jeune à cette époque.

Palácio da Justiça

O edifício é um dos maiores edifícios de pedra já construídos pelo homem. Com uma área útil de 26 000 m², ultrapassa mesmo a Catedral de São Pedro em Roma. Com este edifício bombástico, cuja fachada está repleta de colunas, estátuas e superestruturas, os reis belgas quiseram dar um sinal para o então ainda jovem Estado belga.

Justizpalast

Das Gebäude zählt zu den größten Steinbauten, die je von Menschenhand errichtet wurden. Mit einer Grundfläche von 26 000 m² übertrifft es sogar den Petersdom in Rom. Mit dem bombastischen Gebäude, dessen Fassade von Säulen, Statuen und Aufbauten nur so wimmelt, wollten die belgischen Könige ein Zeichen für den damals noch jungen belgischen Staat setzen.

Justitiepaleis

Het gebouw is een van de grootste stenen gebouwen die ooit door de mens zijn gebouwd. Met een oppervlakte van 26 000 m² overtreft het zelfs de Sint-Pieterskathedraal in Rome. Met dit bombastische gebouw, waarvan de gevel wemelt van de zuilen, beelden en aangebouwde delen, wilden de Belgische koningen een signaal afgeven voor de toen nog jonge Belgische staat.

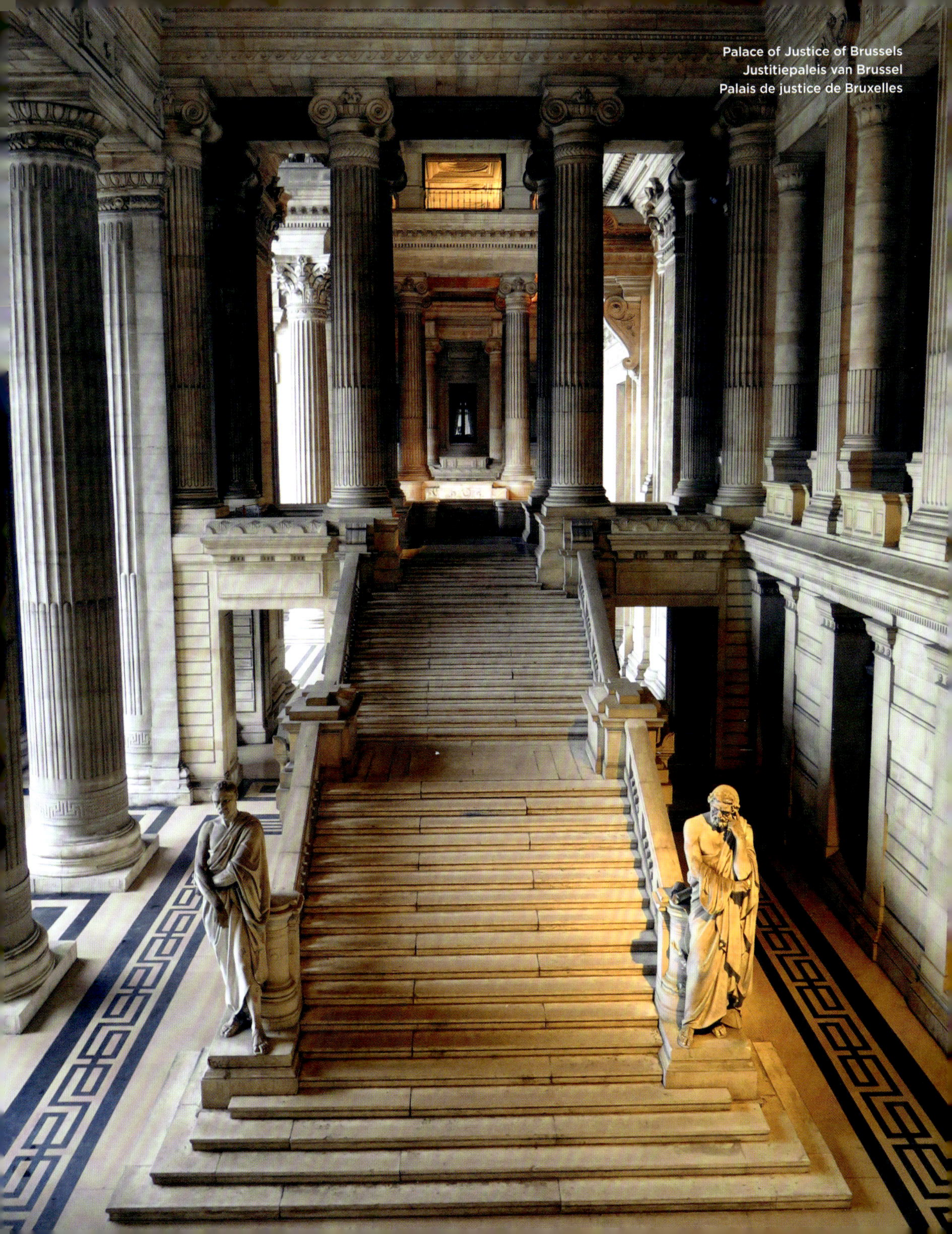
Palace of Justice of Brussels
Justitiepaleis van Brussel
Palais de justice de Bruxelles

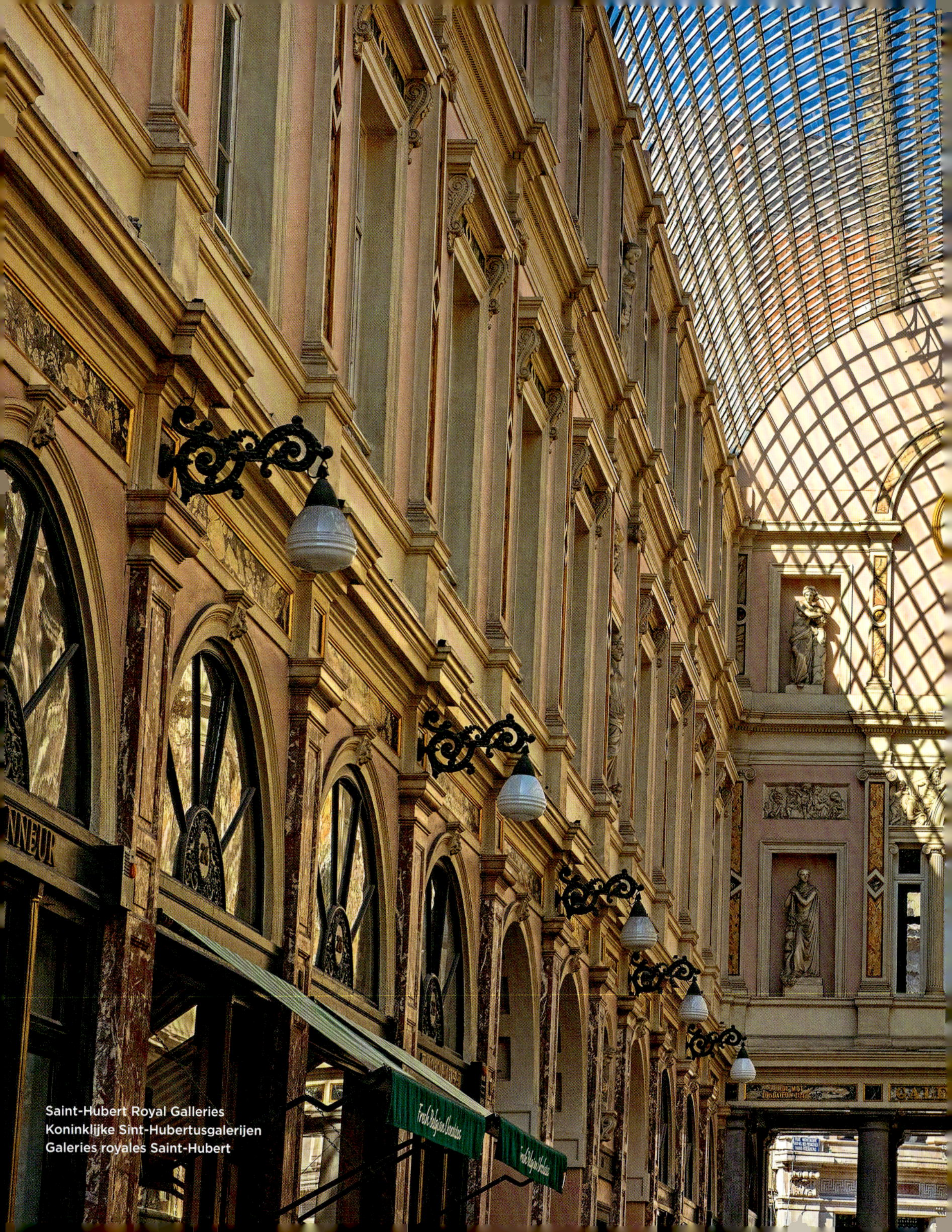

Saint-Hubert Royal Galleries
Koninklijke Sint-Hubertusgalerijen
Galeries royales Saint-Hubert

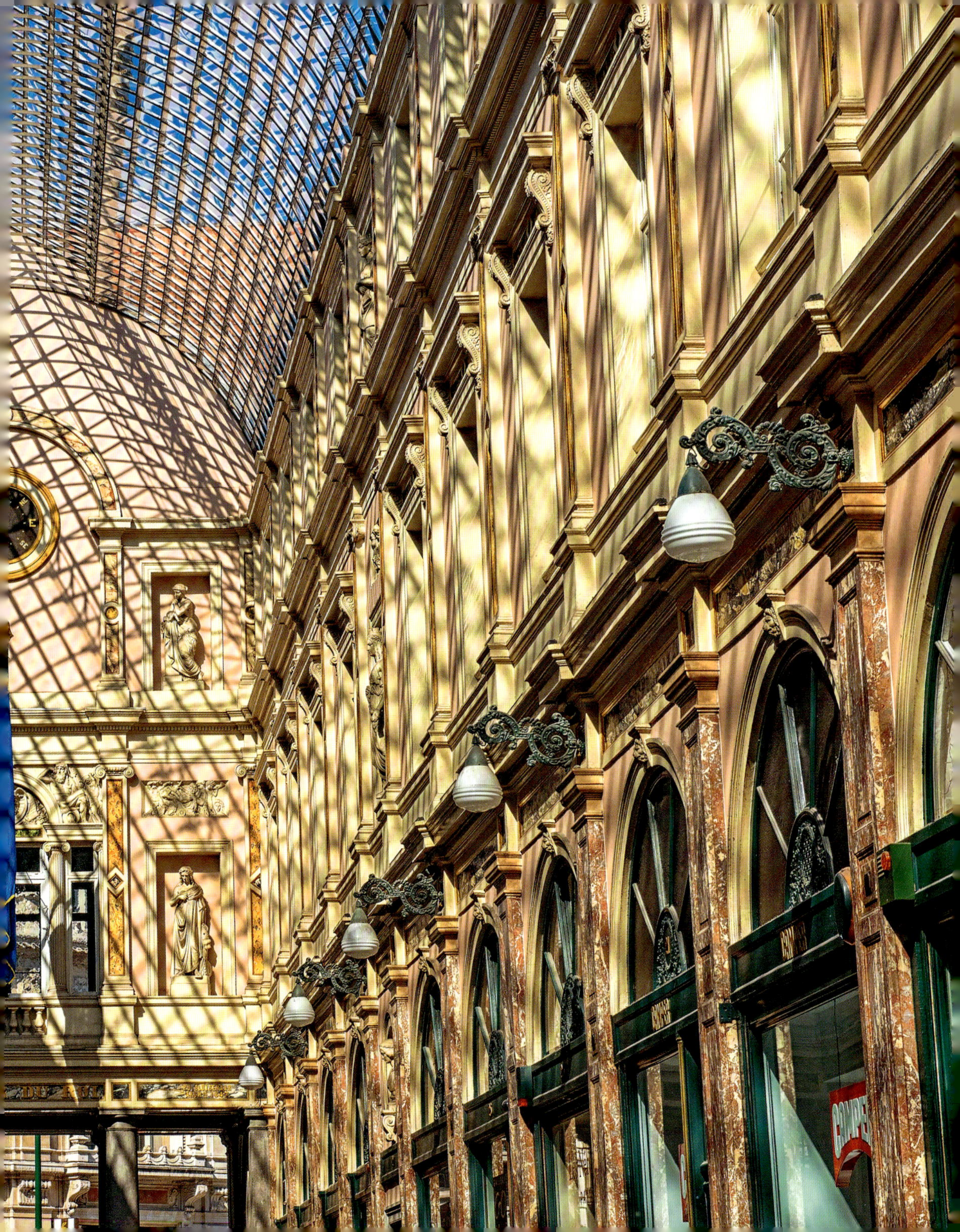

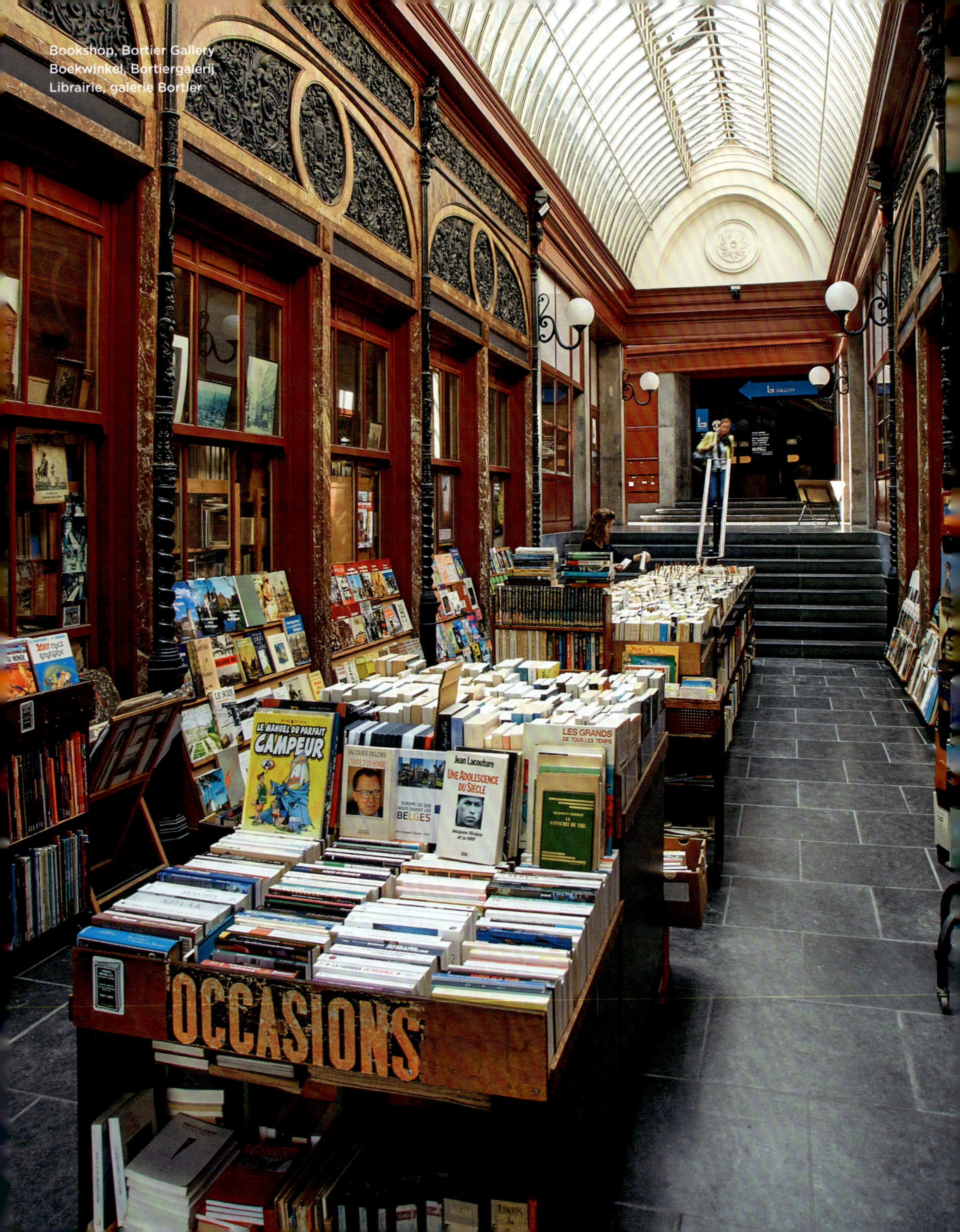

Bookshop, Bortier Gallery
Boekwinkel, Bortiergalerij
Librairie, galerie Bortier

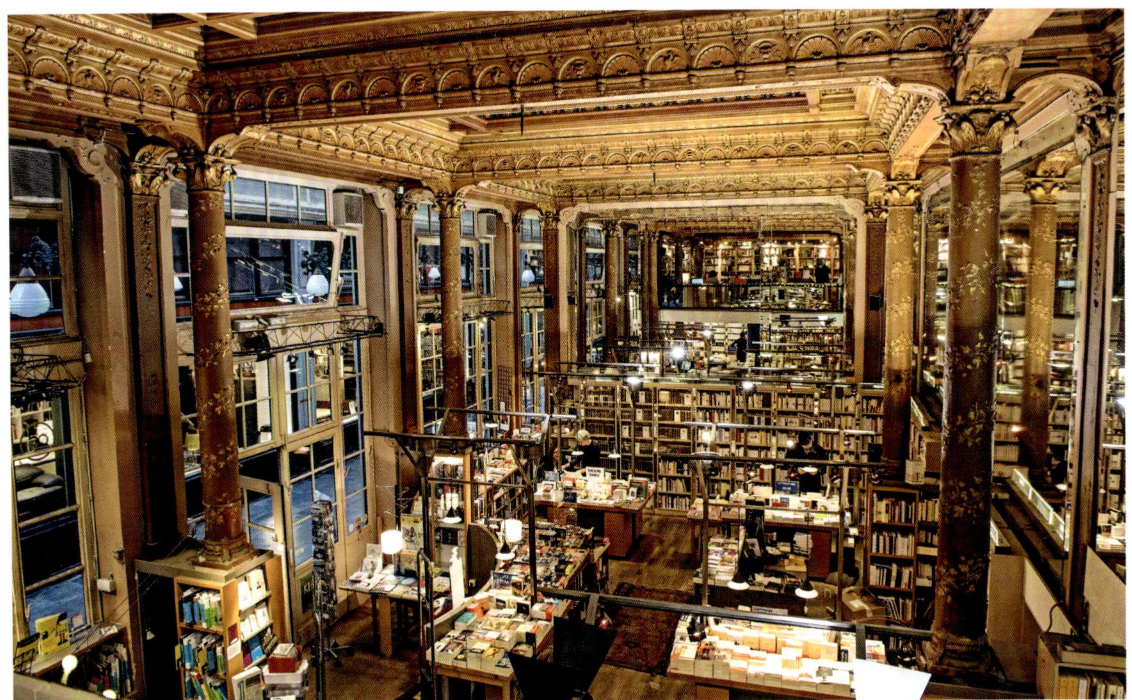

Bookshop, Saint-Hubert Royal Galleries
Boekwinkel, Koninklijke Sint-Hubertusgalerijen
Librairie, galeries royales Saint-Hubert

Galeries Royales Saint-Hubert

The Royal Galleries, opened in 1847, had a great influence on the later design of shopping arcades. From the beginning it attracted numerous luxury shops, which gave Brussels the flair of a European metropolis. In its well-lit interior, it was also possible to sit in "street cafés" despite Brussels' rainy maritime climate. On the 1st of March 1896 the Lumière brothers showed their first movies at the Galleries.

Galeries royales Saint-Hubert

Inaugurées en 1847, les galeries royales eurent une grande influence sur la conception ultérieure de galeries marchandes. Dès le début, elles attirèrent de nombreux magasins de luxe qui donnèrent à Bruxelles le charme d'une métropole européenne. L'intérieur bien éclairé des galeries permettait aux passants de s'installer dans des cafés malgré le climat maritime pluvieux de la ville. Le 1er mars 1896, les frères Lumière y présentèrent leurs premiers films.

Galeries Royales Saint-Hubert

Die 1847 eröffnete königliche Galerie hatte großen Einfluss auf die spätere Gestaltung von Ladenpassagen. Sie zog von Beginn zahlreiche Luxusgeschäfte an, die Brüssel das Flair einer europäischen Metropole gaben. In ihrem gut ausgeleuchteten Innern war es auch in Brüssels regnerischem Seeklima möglich, in Straßencafés zu sitzen. Am 1. März 1896 zeigten die Brüder Lumière hier ihre ersten Filme.

Galerías Reales Saint-Hubert

La galería real, inaugurada en 1847, tuvo una gran influencia en el diseño posterior de las galerías comerciales. Desde el principio atrajo a numerosas tiendas de lujo, lo que le dio a Bruselas el estilo de una metrópoli europea. En su interior bien iluminado, también era posible sentarse en las cafeterías de la calle a pesar del lluvioso clima marítimo de Bruselas. El 1 de marzo de 1896, los hermanos Lumière proyectaron aquí sus primeras películas.

Galerias Royales Saint-Hubert

A galeria real, inaugurada em 1847, teve grande influência na posterior concepção das arcadas comerciais. Desde o início, atraiu numerosas lojas de luxo, o que deu a Bruxelas o toque de uma metrópole europeia. No seu interior bem iluminado, também era possível sentar-se em cafés no clima marítimo chuvoso de Bruxelas. No dia 1º de março de 1896, os irmãos Lumière exibiram seus primeiros filmes aqui.

Koninklijke Sint-Hubertusgalerijen

De in 1847 geopende koninklijke galerij had een grote invloed op het latere ontwerp van de winkelgalerijen. Het trok van begin af aan luxewinkels aan die Brussel de flair van een Europese metropool gaven. In hun goed verlichte interieur was het ook mogelijk in het regenachtige Brusselse zeeklimaat in straatcafés te zitten Op 1 maart 1896 toonden de gebroeders Lumière hier hun eerste films.

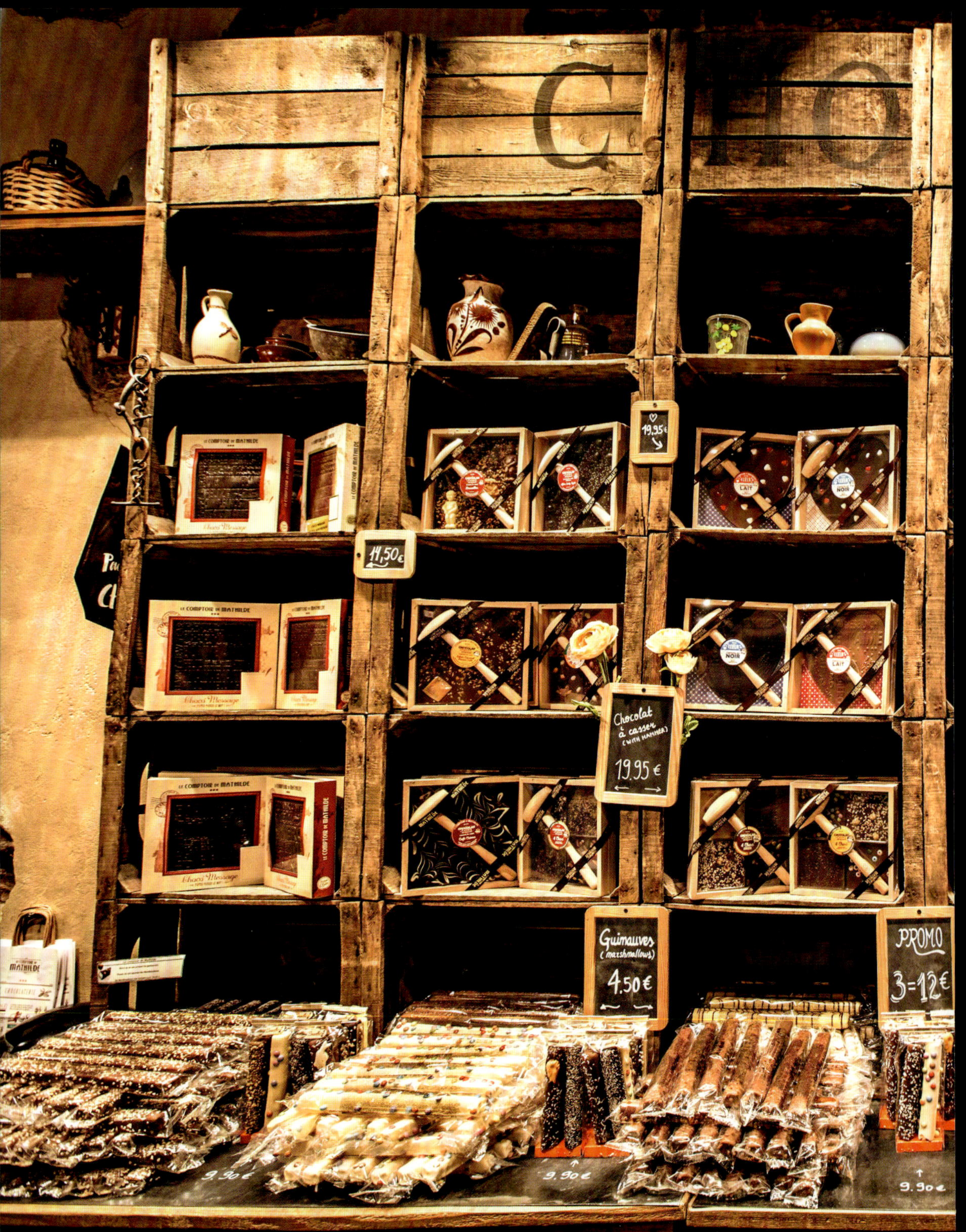
LE COMPTOIR de MATHILDE
19,95 €
14,50 €
Chocolat
à casser
(WITH HAMMER)
19.95 €
Guimauves
(marshmallows)
4.50 €
PROMO
3=12 €
9.90 €
9.90 €
9.90 €

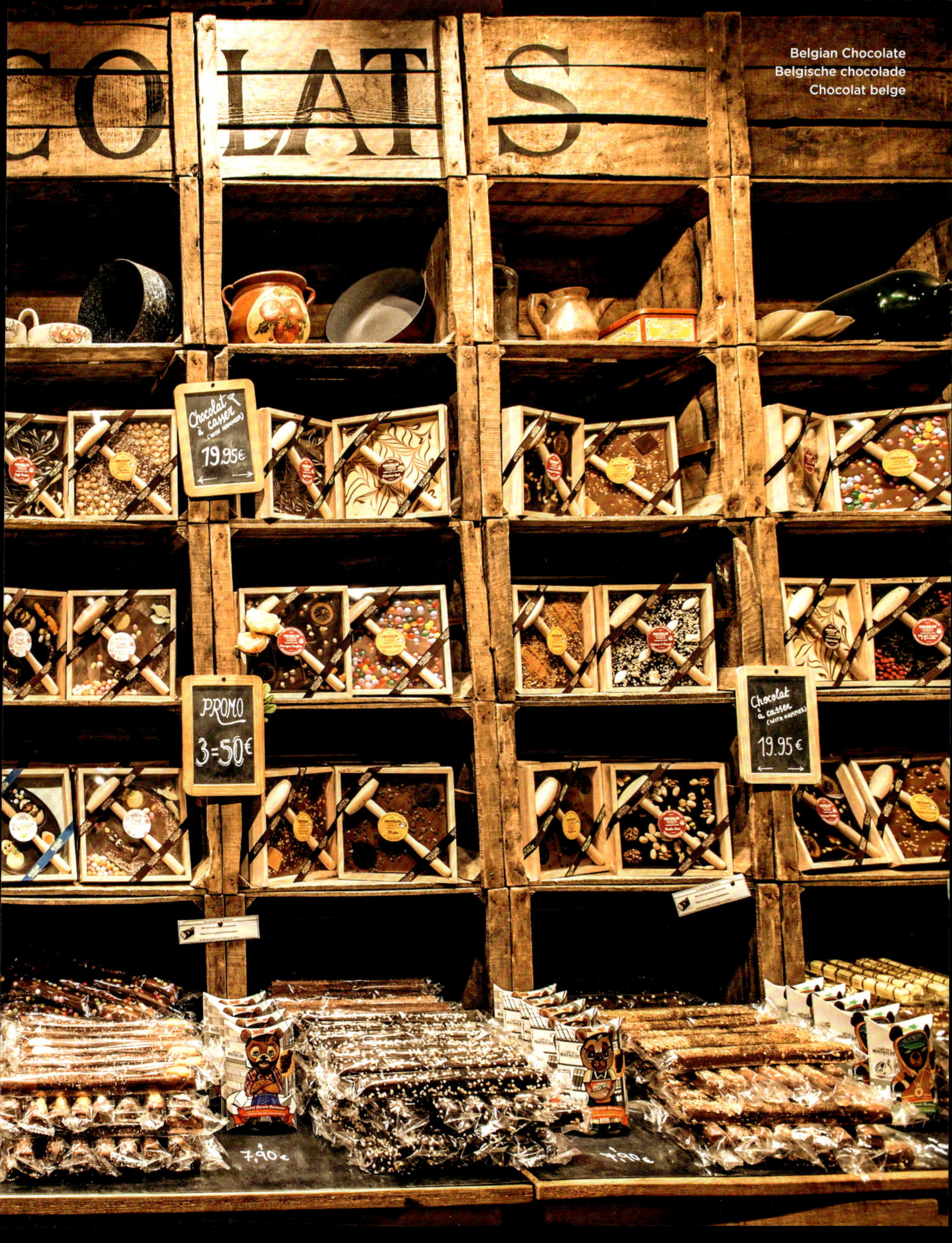
Belgian Chocolate
Belgische chocolade
Chocolat belge
Chocolat à casser (with hammer) 79.95€
PROMO 3=50€
Chocolat à casser (with hammer) 19.95€
7.90€
7.90€

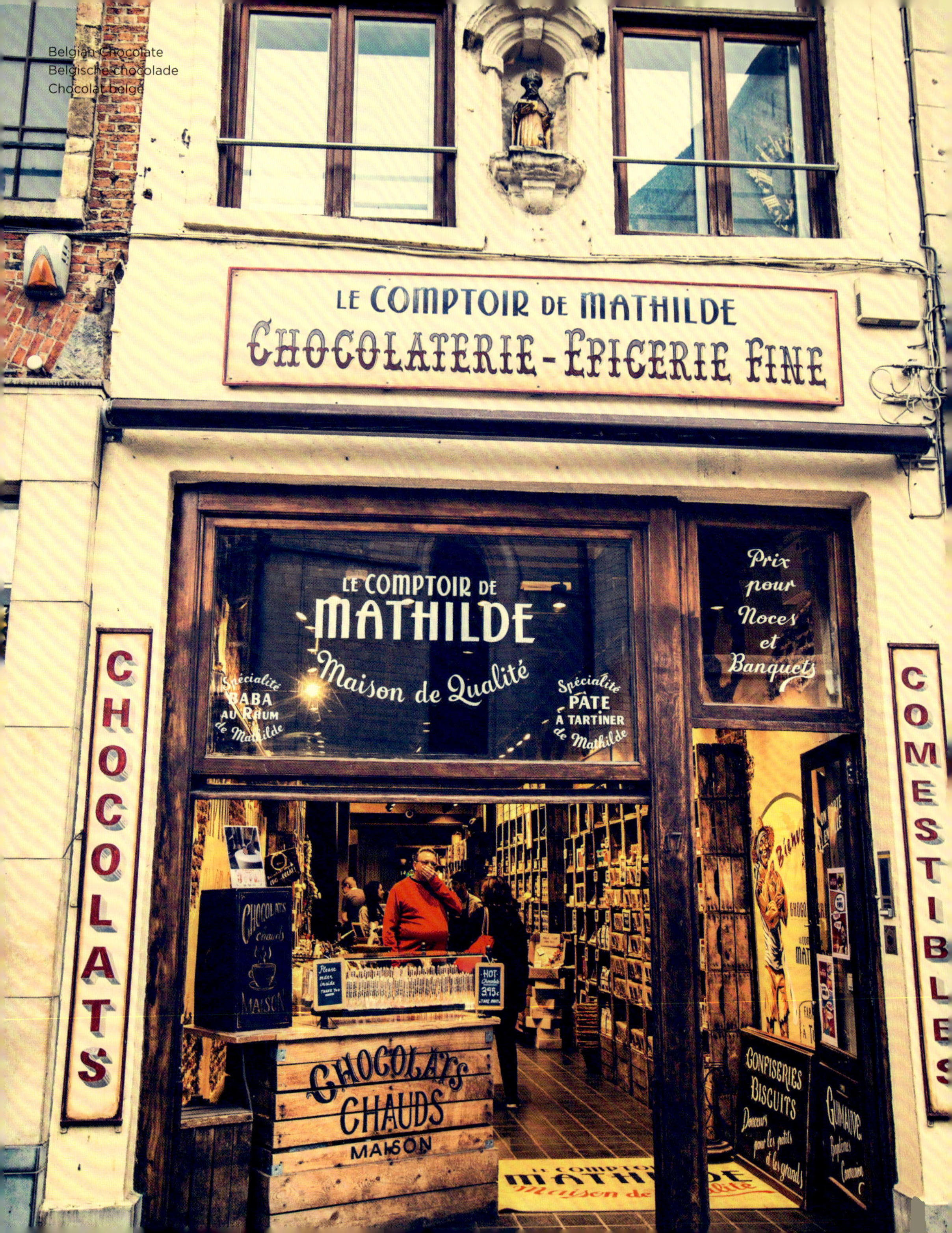
Belgian Chocolate
Belgische chocolade
Chocolat belge
LE COMPTOIR DE MATHILDE
CHOCOLATERIE - EPICERIE FINE
LE COMPTOIR DE
MATHILDE
Maison de Qualité
Spécialité
BABA
AU RHUM
de Mathilde
Spécialité
PATE
A TARTINER
de Mathilde
Prix
pour
Noces
et
Banquets
CHOCOLATS
CHOCOLATS
CHAUDS
MAISON
HOT
Chocolate
3.95€
TAKE AWAY
CHOCOLATS
CHAUDS
MAISON
COMESTIBLES
CONFISERIES
BISCUITS
Douceurs
pour les petits
et les grands
GUIMAUVE
LE COMPTOIR DE
MATHILDE
Maison de Qualité

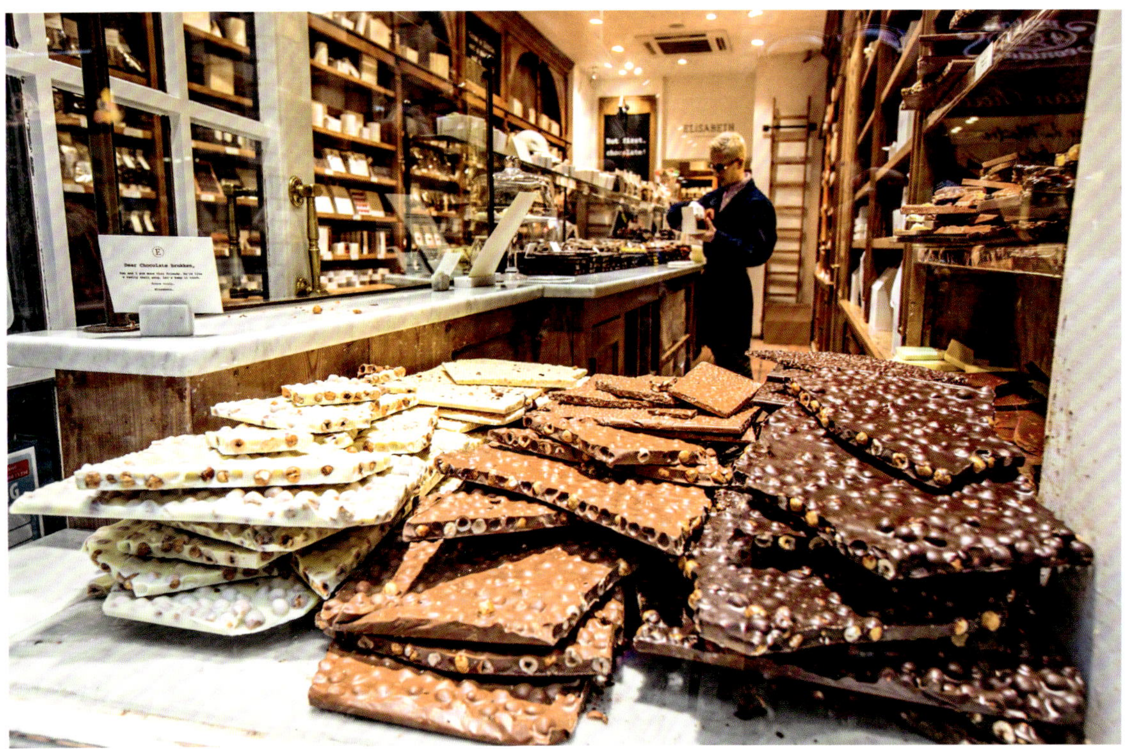

Belgian Chocolate
Belgische chocolade
Chocolats belges

Chocolate makers of Brussels

Brussels chocolate is famous all over the world, and as early as 1912 Jean Neuhaus created the first pralines in the city. Neuhaus, Godiva and Leonidas have marketed their ganache and truffles across the world, but they now face competition from the dozens of creative independent chocolatiers, whose idiosyncratic creations clearly stand out from the classic creamy-sweet pralines.

Chocolaterías de Bruselas

El chocolate de Bruselas es conocido en todo el mundo. Ya en 1912, Jean Neuhaus creó los primeros chocolates en Bruselas. Neuhaus, Godiva y Leonidas comercializaron sus ganache y trufas por todo el mundo, pero se enfrentaron a la competencia de docenas de creativos chocolateros cuyas creaciones idiosincrásicas destacaban claramente de los clásicos bombones cremosos y dulces.

Chocolatiers bruxellois

Le chocolat bruxellois est connu dans le monde entier. En 1912 déjà, Jean Neuhaus créa les premiers chocolats fourrés dans la capitale belge. Neuhaus, Godiva et Leonidas commercialisèrent leur ganache et leurs truffes aux quatre coins du globe, mais ils durent faire face à la concurrence de dizaines de chocolatiers imaginatifs, dont les créations originales se distinguent clairement des classiques chocolats fourrés, onctueux et sucrés.

Chocolataria de Bruxelas

O chocolate de Bruxelas é conhecido em todo o mundo. Já em 1912, Jean Neuhaus criou os primeiros chocolates em Bruxelas. Neuhaus, Godiva e Leonidas comercializaram seus ganache e trufas em todo o mundo, mas enfrentaram a concorrência de dezenas de chocolatiers criativos, cujas criações peculiares se destacaram claramente dos clássicos chocolates cremosos e doces.

Brüsseler Chocolatiers

Brüsseler Schokolade ist weltweit bekannt. Schon 1912 kreierte Jean Neuhaus in Brüssel die ersten Pralinen. Neuhaus, Godiva und Leonidas vermarkten ihre Ganache und Trüffel rund um den Globus, aber sie haben Konkurrenz bekommen von Dutzenden kreativen Chocolatiers, deren eigenwilligen Schöpfungen sich von den klassischen cremig-süßen Pralinen deutlich abheben.

Brusselse chocolatiers

Brusselse chocolade is wereldwijd bekend. Al in 1912 creëerde Jean Neuhaus in Brussel de eerste pralines. Neuhaus, Godiva en Leonidas brachten hun ganache en truffels over de hele wereld op de markt, maar kregen concurrentie van tientallen creatieve chocolatiers die zich met hun eigenzinnige creaties onderscheiden van de klassieke romige en zoete pralines.

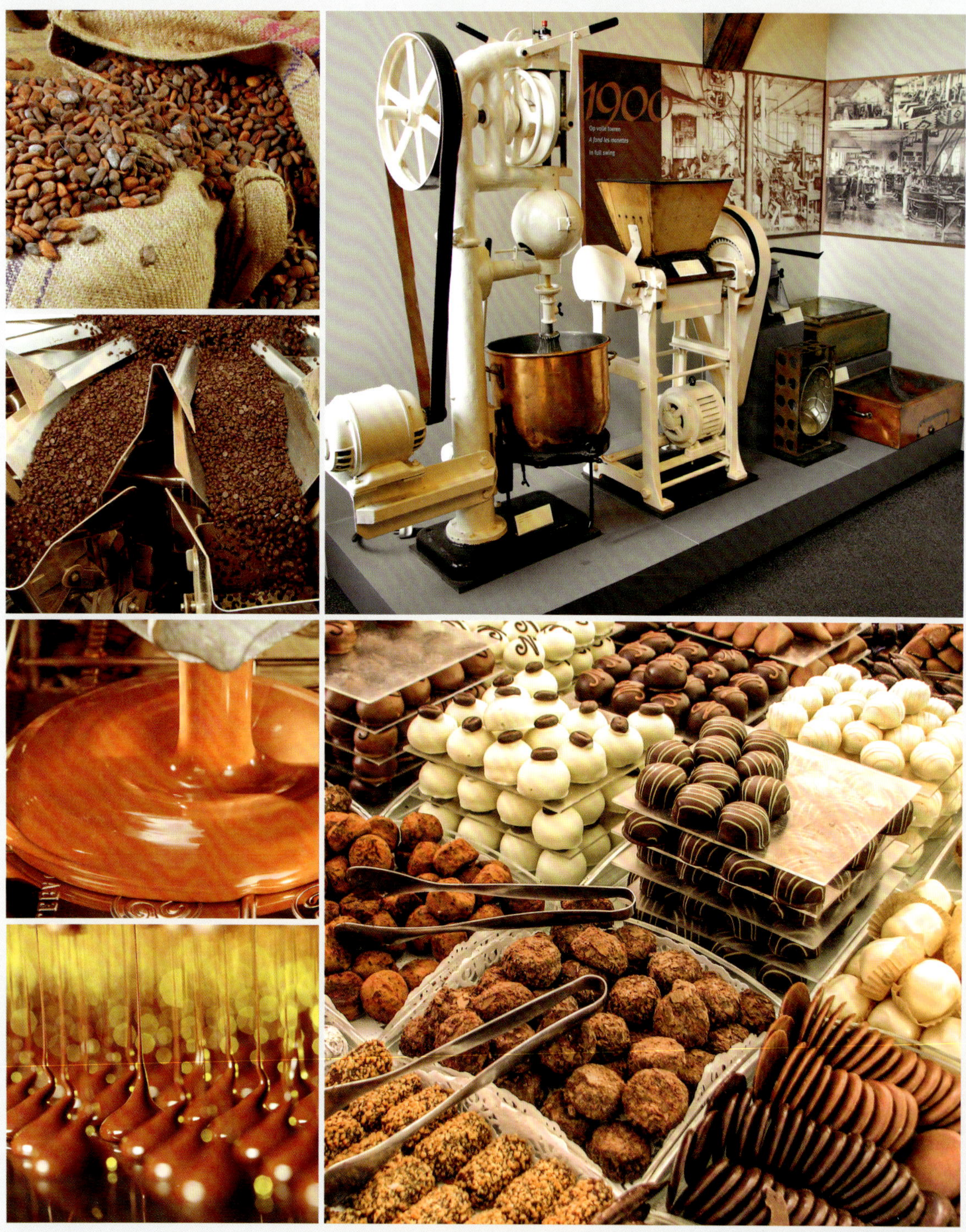

1900
Op volle toeren
À fond les manettes
in full swing

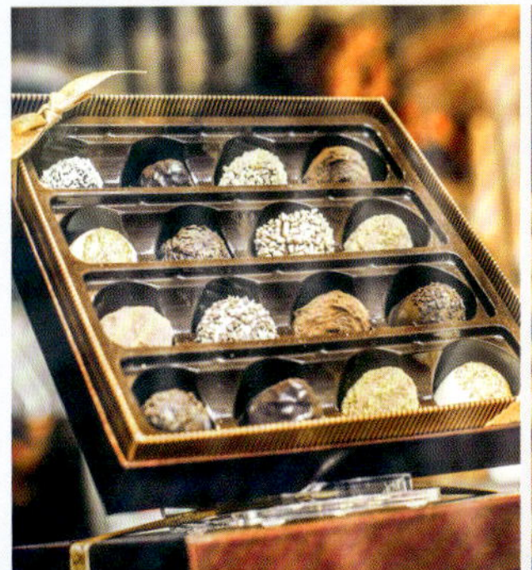

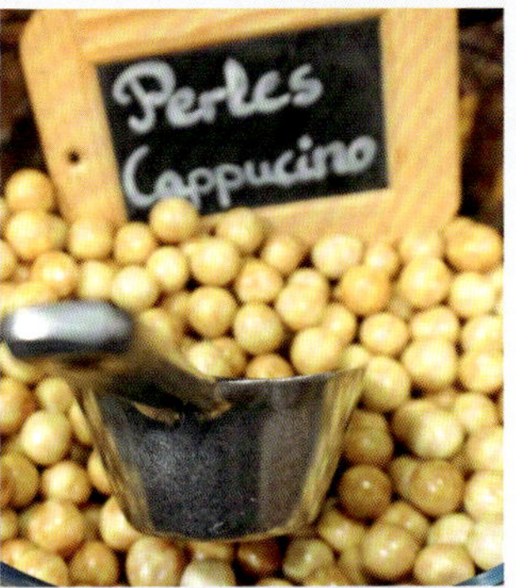

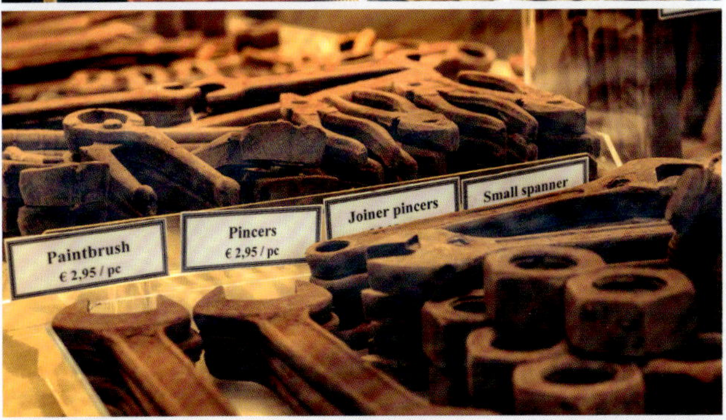

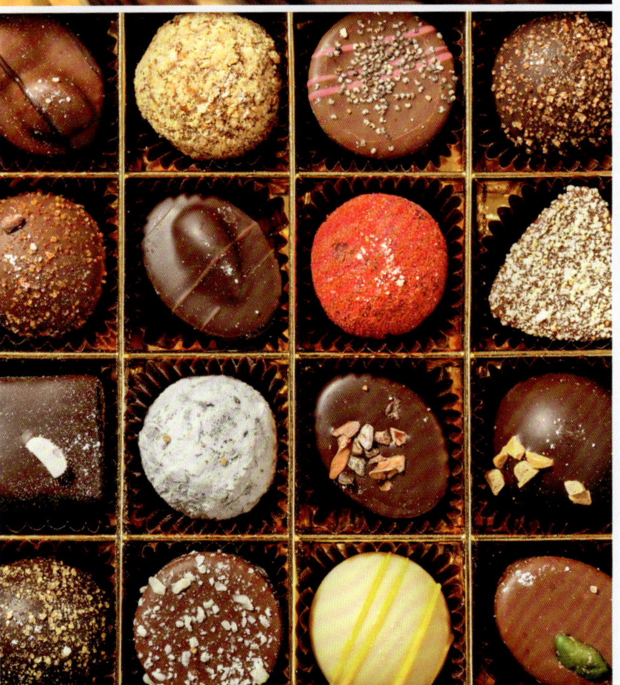

Chocolate and Crafts

Because of its elaborate production, the praline is regarded as the crowning glory of the art of chocolate making, although there may be considerable differences in quality. Most *chocolatiers* resort to industrially produced standard raw materials, whilst only a few of them roast, grind and conch themselves. The Belgian Chocolate Village museum, housed in a former chocolate factory, offers a good insight into the production of chocolate.

Chocolat et artisanat

Du fait de sa fabrication élaborée, le chocolat fourré est considéré comme le couronnement de l'art de la chocolaterie, qui présente d'importantes différences de qualité. La plupart des chocolatiers ont recours à des matières premières standards de production industrielle. Seuls quelques-uns d'entre eux s'occupent eux-mêmes de la torréfaction, du broyage et du conchage. Aménagé dans une ancienne chocolaterie, le Chocolate Village offre un aperçu de la production de chocolat.

Schokolade und Handwerk

Wegen ihrer aufwendigen Produktion gilt die Praline als die Krönung der Chocolatierskunst, bei der es beachtliche Qualitätsunterschiede gibt. Die meisten Chocolatiers greifen auf industriell gefertigte Standardrohmasse zurück. Nur wenige Chocolatiers rösten, mahlen und conchieren selbst. Einen Einblick in die Herstellung von Schokolade gewährt, in einer ehemaligen Schokoladenfabrik, das „Chocolate Village".

Chocolate y artesanía

Debido a su elaborada producción, el praliné es considerado como la coronación de la gloria del arte de la fabricación del chocolate, en el que existen considerables diferencias de calidad. La mayoría de los chocolateros recurren a materias primas estándar producidas industrialmente. Solo unos pocos chocolateros asan, muelen y trabajan con el conche ellos mismos. En una antigua fábrica de chocolate, la "Chocolate Village", se ofrece una visión de la producción de chocolate.

Chocolate e Artesanato

Devido à sua produção elaborada, o pralinê é considerado como a coroa da glória da arte de fazer chocolate, na qual há diferenças consideráveis na qualidade. A maioria dos chocolatiers recorre a matérias-primas padrão produzidas industrialmente. Apenas alguns chocolatiers assam, moem e fazem a conchagem eles mesmos. A "Vila do Chocolate" de uma antiga fábrica de chocolate, oferece uma visão na produção de chocolate.

Chocolade en ambachten

Vanwege zijn uitvoerige en gedetailleerde productie wordt de praline gezien als de bekroning van de kunst van het chocolade maken waarbij er aanzienlijke kwaliteitsverschillen zijn. De meeste chocolatiers grijpen terug op industrieel geproduceerde standaard grondstoffen. Slechts een paar chocolatiers roosteren, malen en concheren zelf. Een inzicht in de productie van chocolade biedt de "Belgian Chocolate Village".

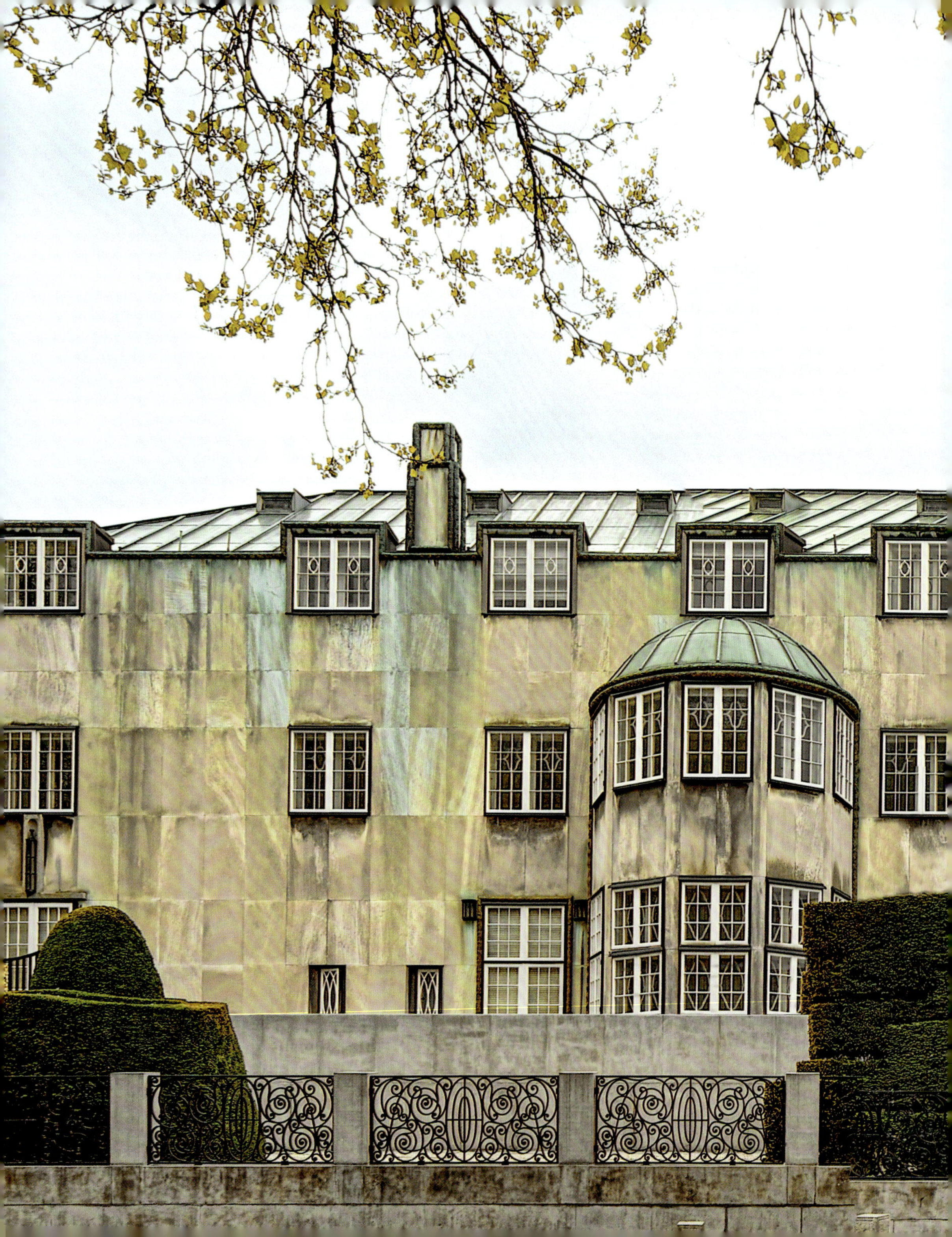

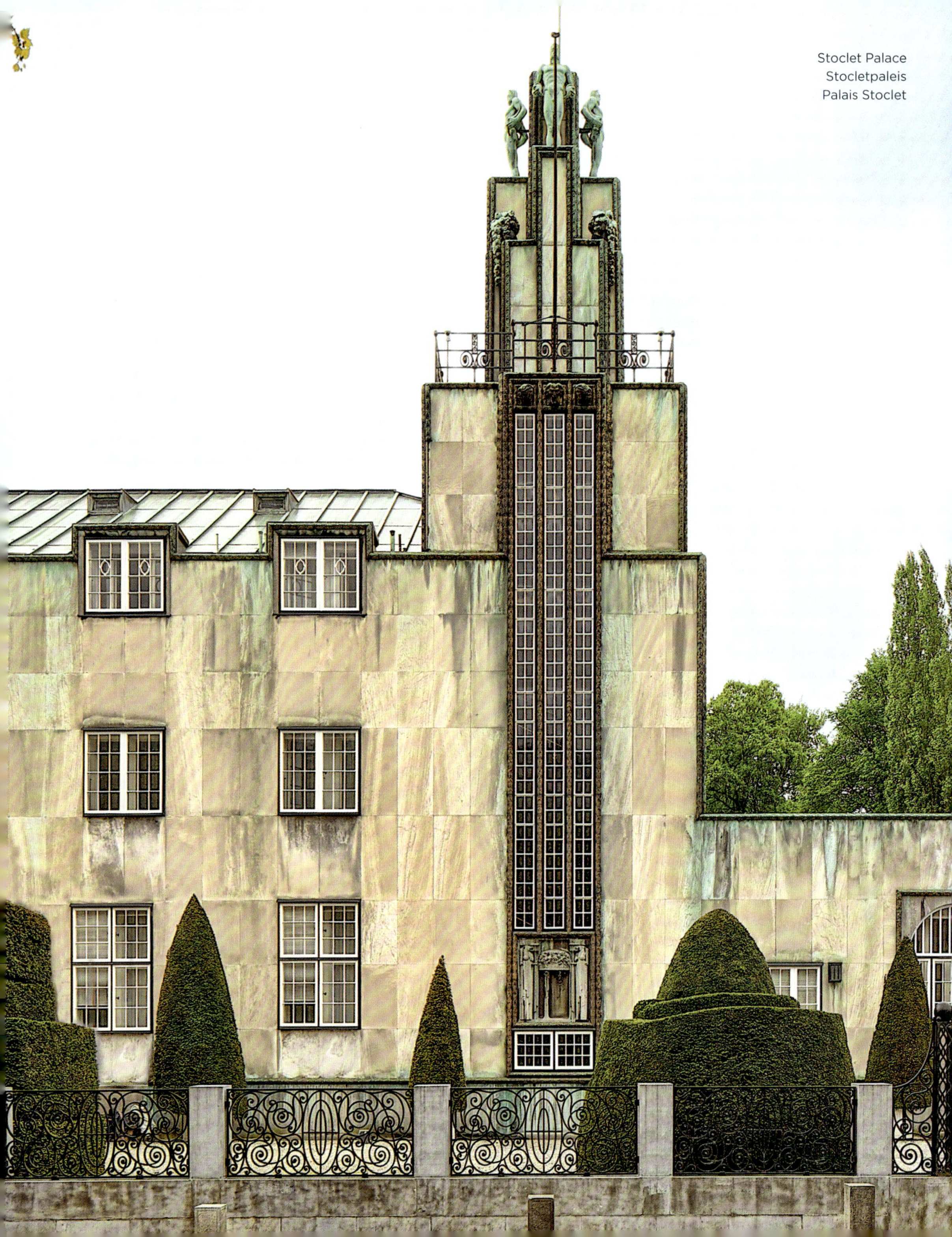

Stoclet Palace
Stocletpaleis
Palais Stoclet

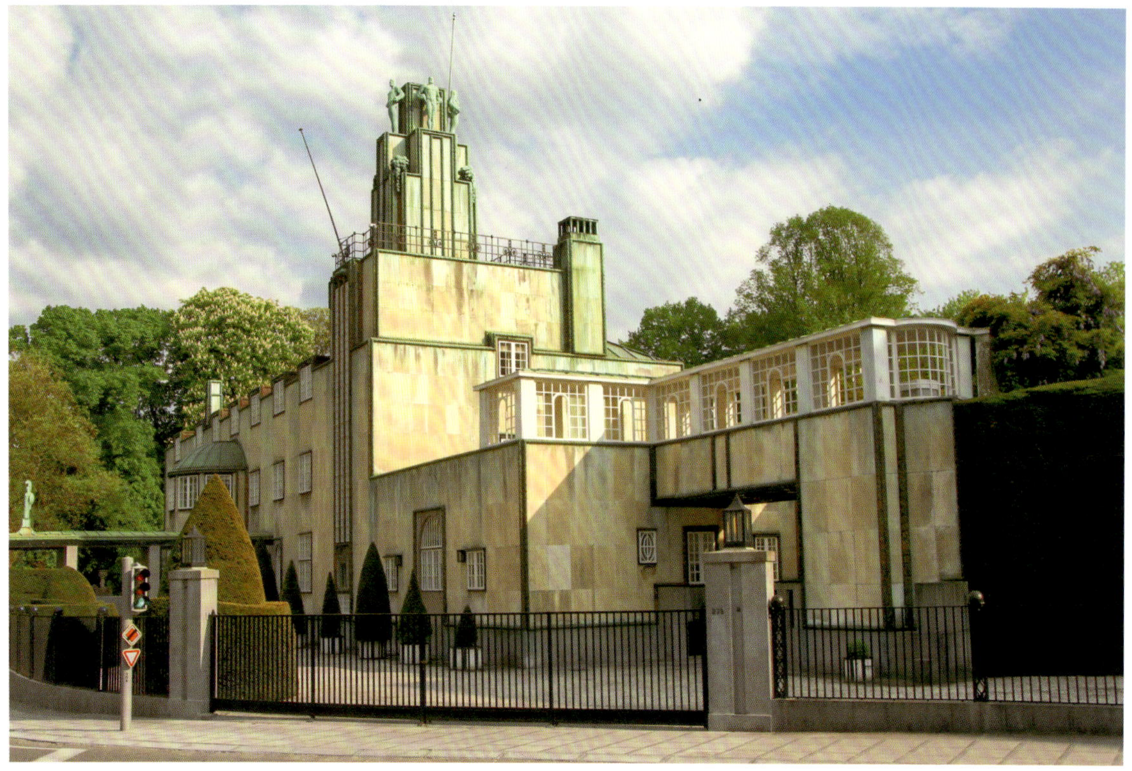

Stoclet Palace
Stocletpaleis
Palais Stoclet

Stoclet Palace

The Belgian banker's son, Adolphe Stoclet, financed what is probably the most impressive villa in Art Deco style. The strictly geometric and stepped construction made it clear, right from the start of construction in 1905, that the era of the playful Art Nouveau was over. The building, designed by Viennese architect Joseph Hoffmann, has been designated as a World Heritage Site by UNESCO.

Palacio Stoclet

El hijo del banquero belga, Stoclet, financió lo que probablemente sea la villa más impresionante en estilo Art Déco. El edificio estrictamente geométrico y escalonado dejó claro desde el inicio de la construcción en 1905 que la época del Art Nouveau juguetón había terminado. El edificio, diseñado por el arquitecto vienés Joseph Hoffmann, forma parte del Patrimonio Mundial de la UNESCO.

Palais Stoclet

Adolphe Stoclet, fils de banquiers belges, s'offrit la villa sans doute la plus impressionnante de style Art déco. Dès le début des travaux en 1905, sa structure étagée strictement géométrique montra clairement que l'époque de l'Art nouveau et de sa fantaisie était révolue. Conçu par l'architecte viennois Joseph Hoffmann, le bâtiment fait désormais partie du patrimoine mondial de l'Unesco.

Palácio Stoclet

O filho do banqueiro belga, Stoclet, financiou o que é provavelmente a vila mais impressionante no estilo Art Deco. A construção estritamente geométrica e em camadas deixou claro desde o início da construção, em 1905, que o tempo da lúdica Art Nouveau tinha acabado. O edifício, projetado pelo arquiteto vienense Joseph Hoffmann, agora faz parte do Patrimônio Mundial da UNESCO.

Palais Stoclet

Der belgische Bankierssohn, Stoclet, finanzierte sich die vermutlich imposanteste Villa im Art-déco-Stil. Der streng geometrische und stufige Aufbau brachte schon beim Baubeginn im Jahr 1905 deutlich zum Ausdruck, dass die Zeit der verspielten Art nouveau vorbei war. Das Gebäude, des Wiener Architekten Joseph Hoffmann, ist heute Teil des UNESCO Welterbes.

Stocletpaleis

De Belgische bankierszoon Stoclet financierde wat waarschijnlijk de indrukwekkendste villa in art-decostijl is. De strikt geometrische en trapvormige constructie maakte al bij het bouwen in 1905 duidelijk dat de tijd van de art nouveau voorbij was. Het gebouw, ontworpen door de Weense architect Joseph Hoffmann, staat op de werelderfgoedlijst van de UNESCO.

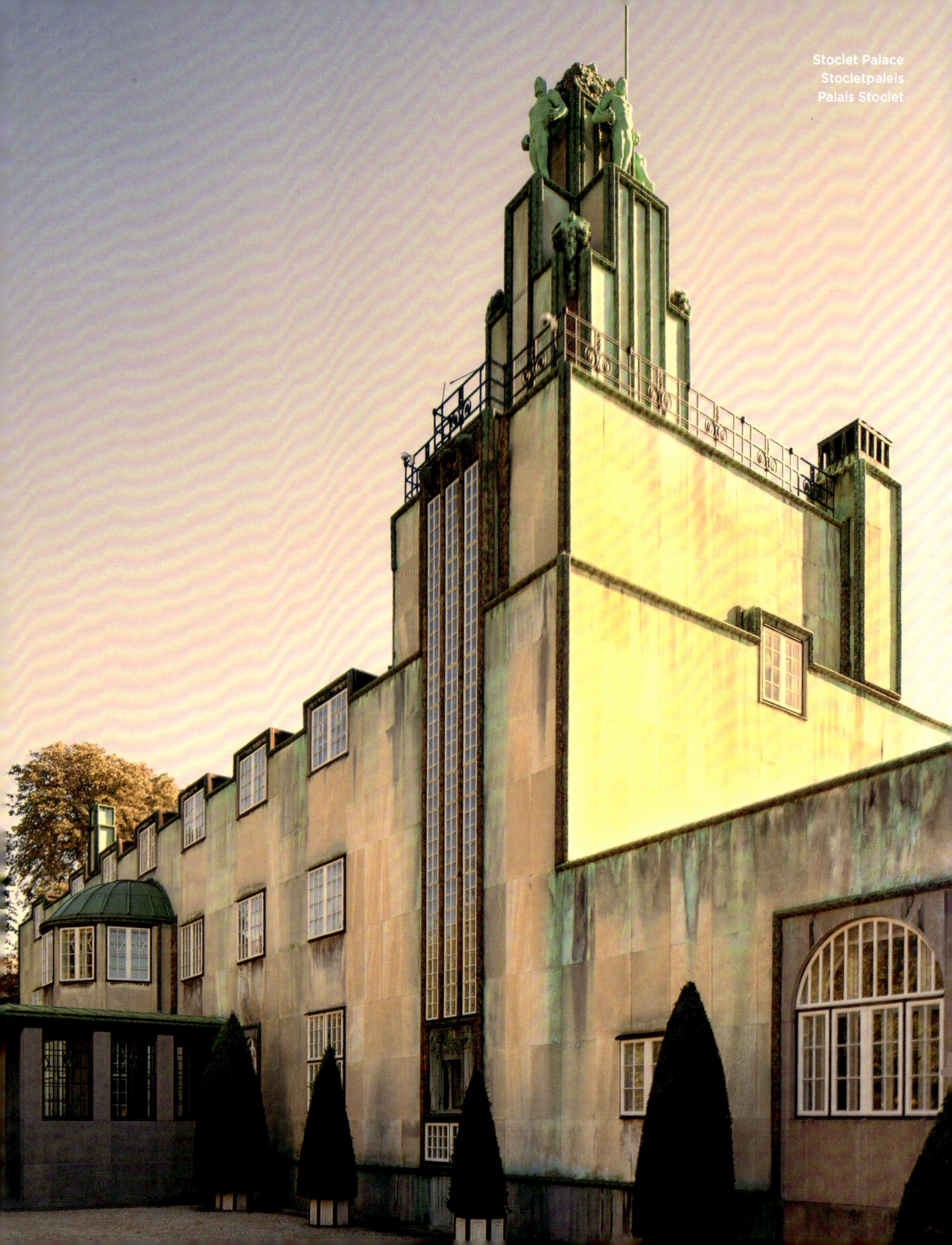

Stoclet Palace
Stocletpaleis
Palais Stoclet

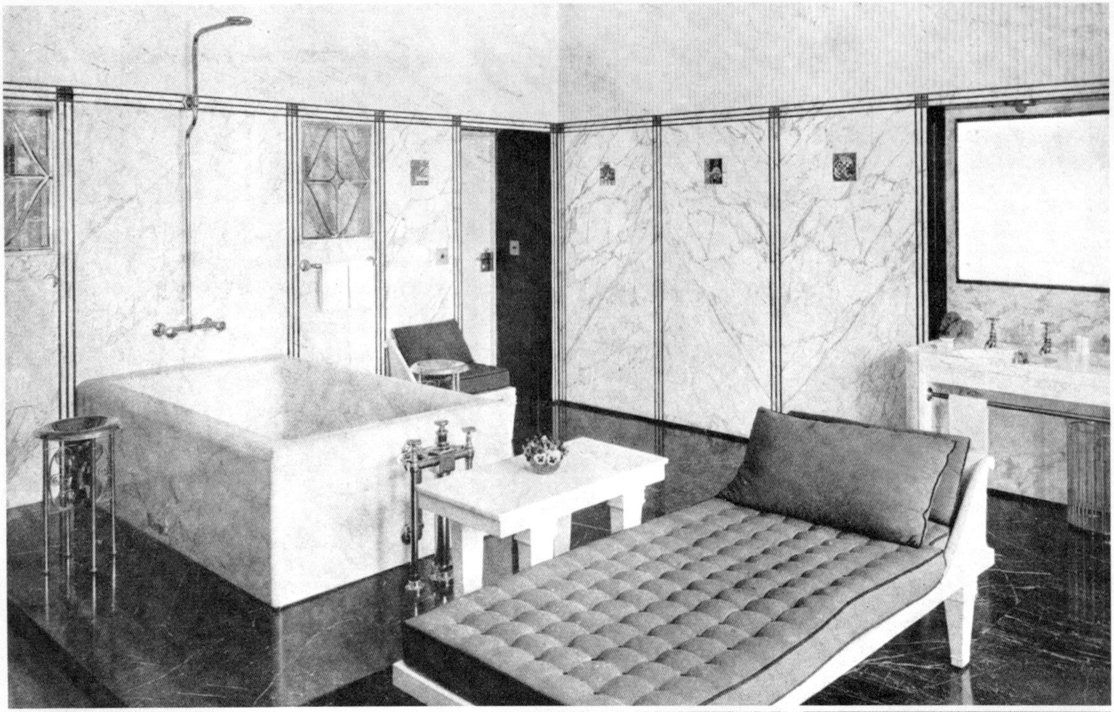

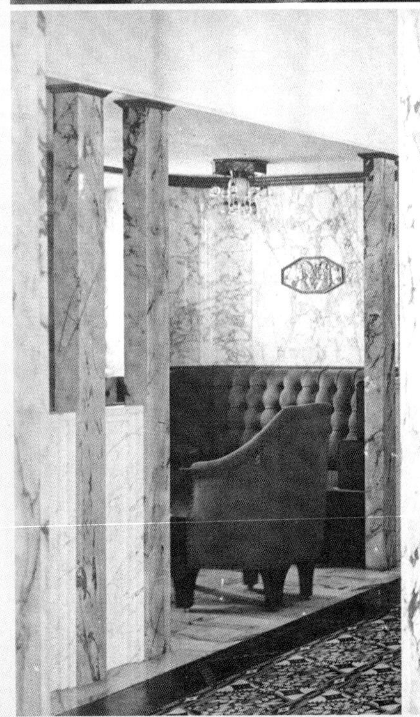
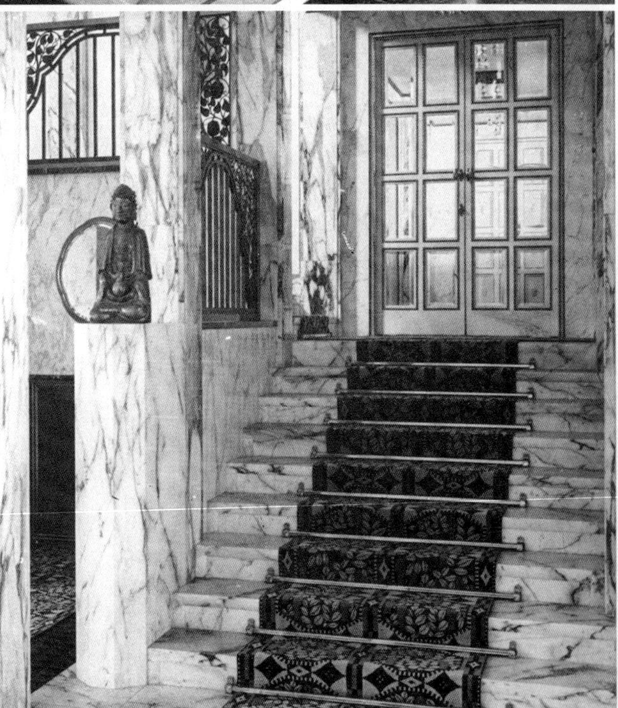

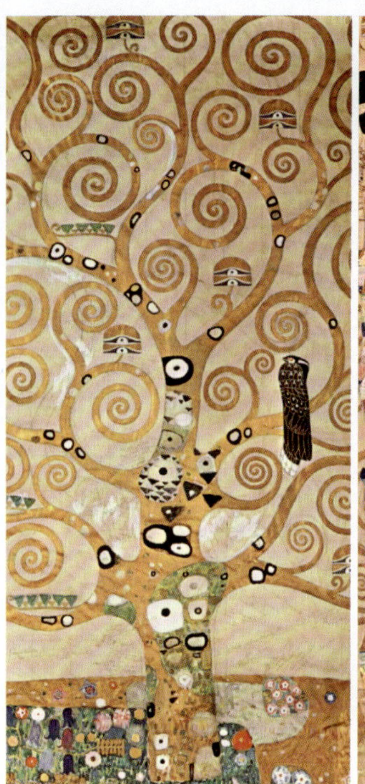 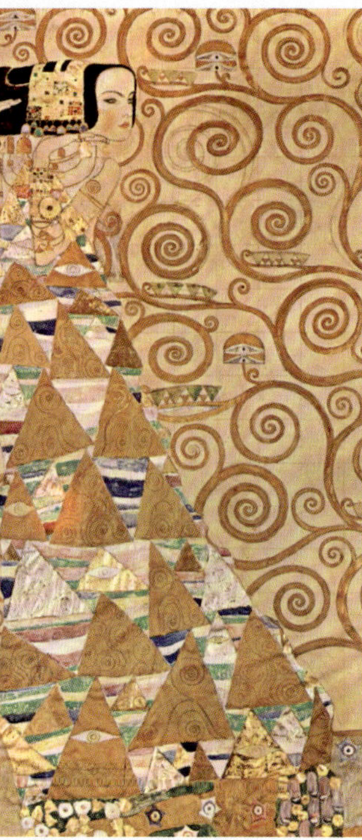

Klimt in Brussels

The Palace is a complete work of art. The exterior walls are entirely lined with white marble and framed by gilded stucco. The Vienna Workshop (Wiener Werkstätte) was responsible for the artistic design, whilst Gustav Klimt designed the legendary Stoclet Frieze for the dining hall. Numerous other Viennese artists were also involved in the overall concept. It is still privately owned and is not open to the public.

Klimt à Bruxelles

Avec ses murs extérieurs entièrement revêtus de marbre blanc et encadrés de stuc doré, le palais est une œuvre d'art à part entière. Sa conception artistique dépendait de la Wiener Werkstätte. Gustav Klimt conçut la légendaire frise Stoclet pour la salle à manger. De nombreux autres artistes viennois furent impliqués dans le concept global. Aujourd'hui encore, il s'agit d'une propriété privée, non accessible au public.

Klimt in Brüssel

Das Palais ist ein Gesamtkunstwerk. Die Außenwände sind komplett mit weißem Marmor ausgekleidet und von vergoldetem Stuck umrahmt. Die künstlerische Ausgestaltung übernahm die Wiener Werkstätte. Gustav Klimt gestaltete für den Speisesaal das legendäre Stoclet-Fries. Am Gesamtkonzept waren zahlreiche weitere Wiener Künstler beteiligt. Es ist nach wie vor in Privatbesitz und öffentlich nicht zugänglich.

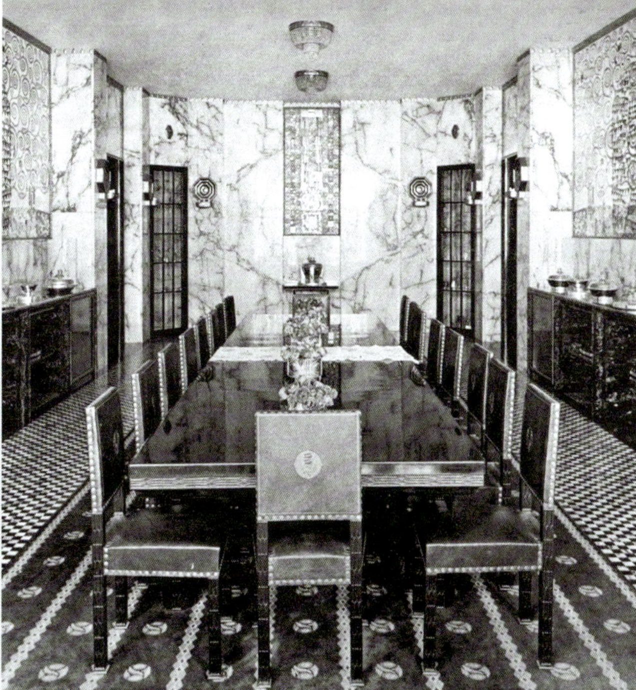

Klimt en Bruselas

El Palacio es una obra de arte total. Las paredes exteriores están completamente revestidas de mármol blanco y enmarcadas con estuco dorado. Los talleres vieneses se encargaron del diseño artístico. Gustav Klimt diseñó el legendario friso Stoclet para el comedor. Muchos otros artistas vieneses participaron en el concepto general. Sigue siendo de propiedad privada y no está abierto al público.

Klimt em Bruxelas

O palácio é uma obra de arte total. As paredes exteriores são totalmente revestidas a mármore branco e enquadradas por estuque dourado. A firma "Wiener Werkstätte" foi responsável pela concepção artística. Gustav Klimt projetou o lendário friso Stoclet para a sala de jantar. Muitos outros artistas vienenses estiveram envolvidos na concepção geral. O palácio continua a ser propriedade privada e não está aberto ao público.

Klimt in Brussel

Het Stocletpaleis is een totaalkunstwerk. De buitenmuren zijn volledig bedekt met wit marmer en omlijst door verguld stucwerk. De artistieke inrichting namen de Wiener Werkstätte op zich. Gustav Klimt ontwierp de legendarische Stoclet-fries voor de eetzaal. Talrijke andere Weense kunstenaars waren bij het totaalconcept betrokken. Het is nog steeds in particulier bezit en niet toegankelijk voor het publiek.

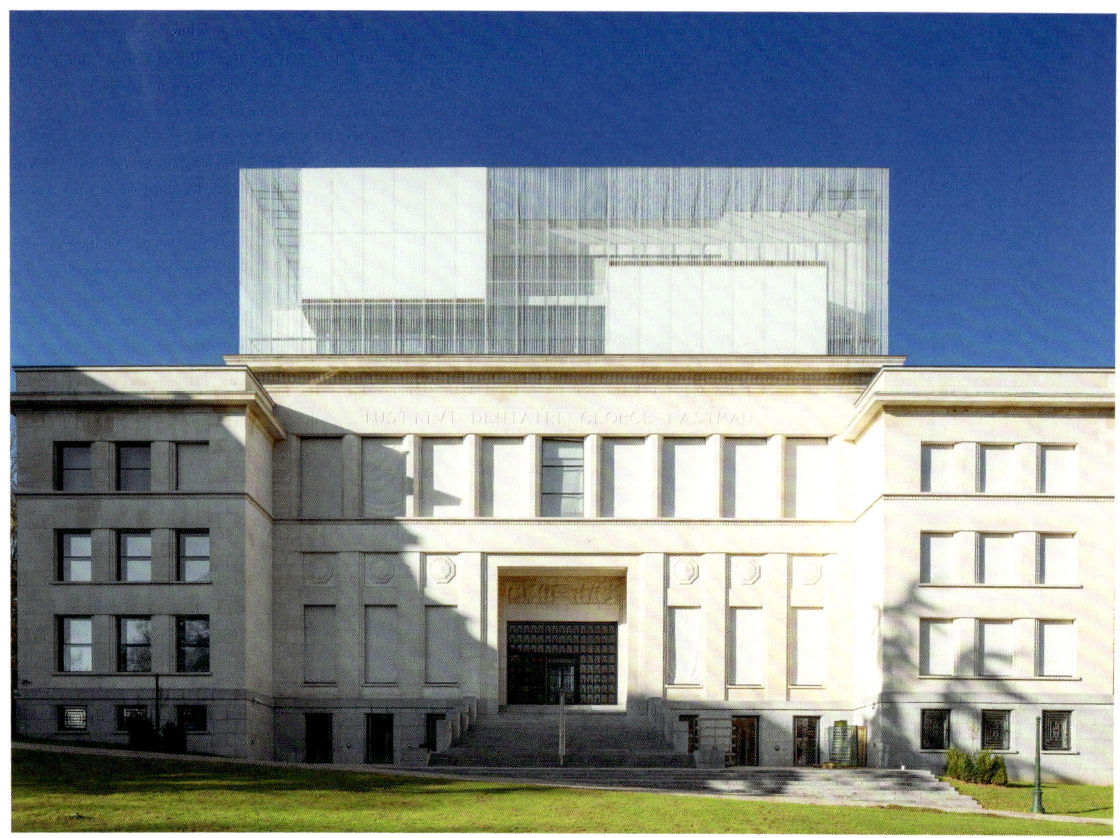

House of European History
Huis van de europese geschiedenis
Maison de l'histoire européenne

House of European History

The museum in the European or Leopold Quarter, near to the European Parliament, was conceived to help Europeans to better understand their common history. It is housed in the newly renovated Art Deco house of the American entrepreneur Georges Eastman. The permanent exhibition, with items from the Member States, reviews the great events of European history and presents the ideas and convictions of the 19th century. The exhibition also focuses on the destructive wars that shook Europe before the continent finally turned to unification.

Maison de l'histoire européenne

Situé dans le quartier européen, près du Parlement, ce musée a pour vocation d'aider les Européens à mieux comprendre leur histoire commune. Il se trouve dans la maison Art déco récemment rénovée de l'entrepreneur américain George Eastman. L'exposition permanente, qui comprend des pièces provenant des 28 États membres, passe en revue les événements marquants de l'histoire européenne et présente les idées et les convictions du XIXe siècle. L'exposition se concentre également sur les guerres destructrices qui secouèrent l'Europe, avant de se tourner vers l'unification européenne.

Haus der Europäischen Geschichte

Das Museum im Europaviertel, nahe dem Europa-Parlament, soll den Europäern helfen ihre gemeinsame Geschichte besser zu verstehen. Es wurde im frisch renovierten Art-déco-Haus des amerikanischen Unternehmers Georges Eastman untergebracht. Die Dauerausstellung mit Exponaten aus den Mitgliedstaaten lässt die großen Ereignisse der europäischen Geschichte Revue passieren und präsentiert die Ideen und Überzeugungen des 19. Jahrhunderts. Einen weiteren thematischen Schwerpunkt bilden die zerstörerischen Kriege, die Europa erschütterten, bevor die Ausstellung sich schließlich der europäischen Einigung zuwendet.

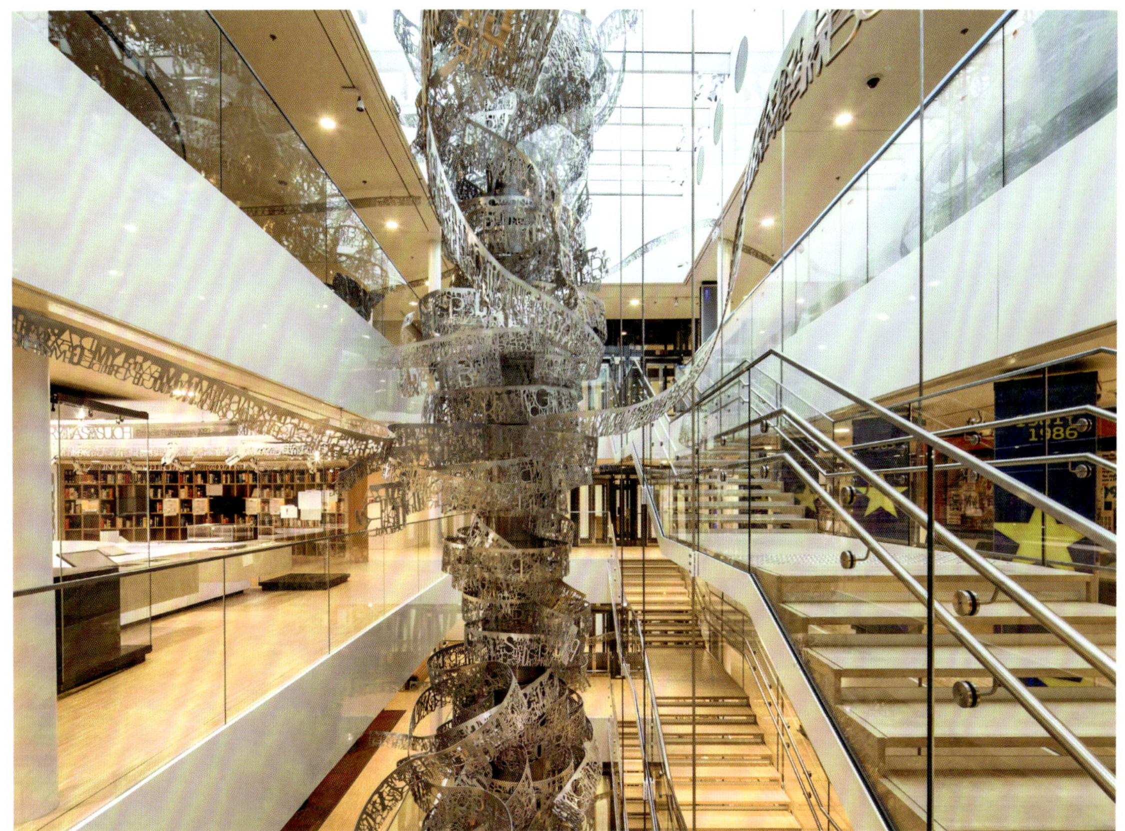

House of European History
Huis van de europese geschiedenis
Maison de l'histoire européenne

Casa de la Historia Europea

El museo del barrio europeo, cerca del Parlamento Europeo, ayuda a los europeos a comprender mejor su historia común. Se encuentra en la recién renovada casa Art Déco del empresario estadounidense Georges Eastman. La exposición permanente, con exposiciones de los estados miembros, repasa los grandes acontecimientos de la historia europea y presenta las ideas y convicciones del siglo XIX. La exposición también se centra en las destructivas guerras que sacudieron Europa antes de que tuviera lugar la unificación europea.

Casa da História Europeia

O museu no bairro europeu, próximo perto do Parlamento Europeu, dá aos europeus a oportunidade de compreender melhor a sua história comum. Ele está alojado na recém-renovada casa no estilo Art Déco do empresário americano Georges Eastman. A exposição permanente, com exposições dos Estados-Membros, expõe os grandes acontecimentos da história europeia e apresenta as ideias e convicções do século XIX. Outro foco temático são também nas guerras devastadoras, que abalaram a Europa, antes de chegar no tema final da exposição voltado finalmente para a unificação europeia.

Huis van de Europese geschiedenis

Het museum in de Europese wijk nabij het Europees Parlement dient ertoe de Europeanen te helpen om hun gemeenschappelijke geschiedenis beter te begrijpen. Het werd in het onlangs gerenoveerde art-decohuis van de Amerikaanse ondernemer Georges Eastman ondergebracht. De permanente tentoonstelling met exposities uit de lidstaten laat de grote gebeurtenissen in de Europese geschiedenis de revue passeren en presenteert de ideeën en overtuigingen van de 19e eeuw. Een ander thematisch accent vormen de destructieve oorlogen die Europa op zijn grondvesten deden schudden, voordat de tentoonstelling zich eindelijk met de Europese eenwording bezighoudt.

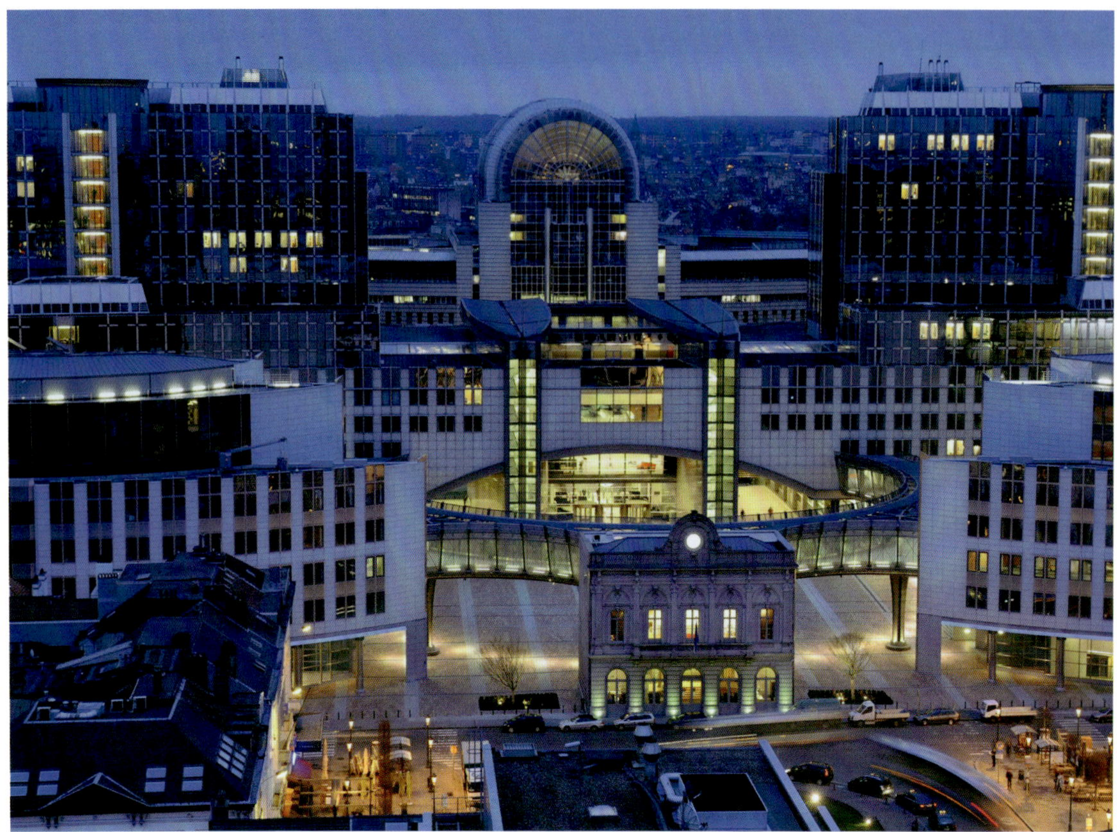

Bureau of the European Parliament, Luxemburg square
Bureau van het Europees Parlement, Luxemburgplein
Bureau du Parlement européen, place du Luxembourg

Heart of the European Union

The heart of the EU beats in the European Quarter. Around 100,000 people from all over the world work in the steel and glass castles of Europe. The political institutions are not isolated places—whether the EU Parliament, which is humorously called Caprice des Dieux due to its similarity to the shape of French soft cheese, the EU Council or the EU Commission—visitors are welcome to take a look around and learn how the institutions work. In the Parlamentarium you can experience Europe and the work of the Parliament in various multimedia installations.

Cœur de l'Union européenne

C'est dans le quartier européen que bat le cœur de l'UE. Environ 100 000 personnes du monde entier travaillent pour l'Europe dans les bureaux des monumentaux bâtiments de verre. Les institutions politiques ne sont pas des lieux fermés : les visiteurs sont les bienvenus, tant au Parlement européen – surnommé avec humour Caprice des Dieux en raison de sa ressemblance avec le fromage français à pâte molle –, qu'au Conseil de l'UE ou à la Commission européenne ; ils sont invités à explorer ces lieux et à se faire expliquer le fonctionnement des institutions. Le Parlamentarium permet de vivre de près l'Europe et le travail du Parlement au fil de différentes installations multimédias.

Herz der Europäischen Union

Im Europa-Viertel schlägt das Herz der EU. Rund 100 000 Menschen aus aller Herren Länder arbeiten in den gläsernen Büroburgen für Europa. Die politischen Institutionen sind keine abgeschirmten Orte: Ob EU-Parlament, das aufgrund seiner Ähnlichkeit mit der Form des französischen Weichkäses humorvoll auch Caprice des Dieux genannt wird, EU-Rat oder EU-Kommission – Besucher sind willkommen und können sich umsehen und sich erklären lassen, wie die Institutionen funktionieren. Im Parlamentarium kann man Europa und die Arbeit des Parlaments in verschiedenen Installationen multimedial erleben.

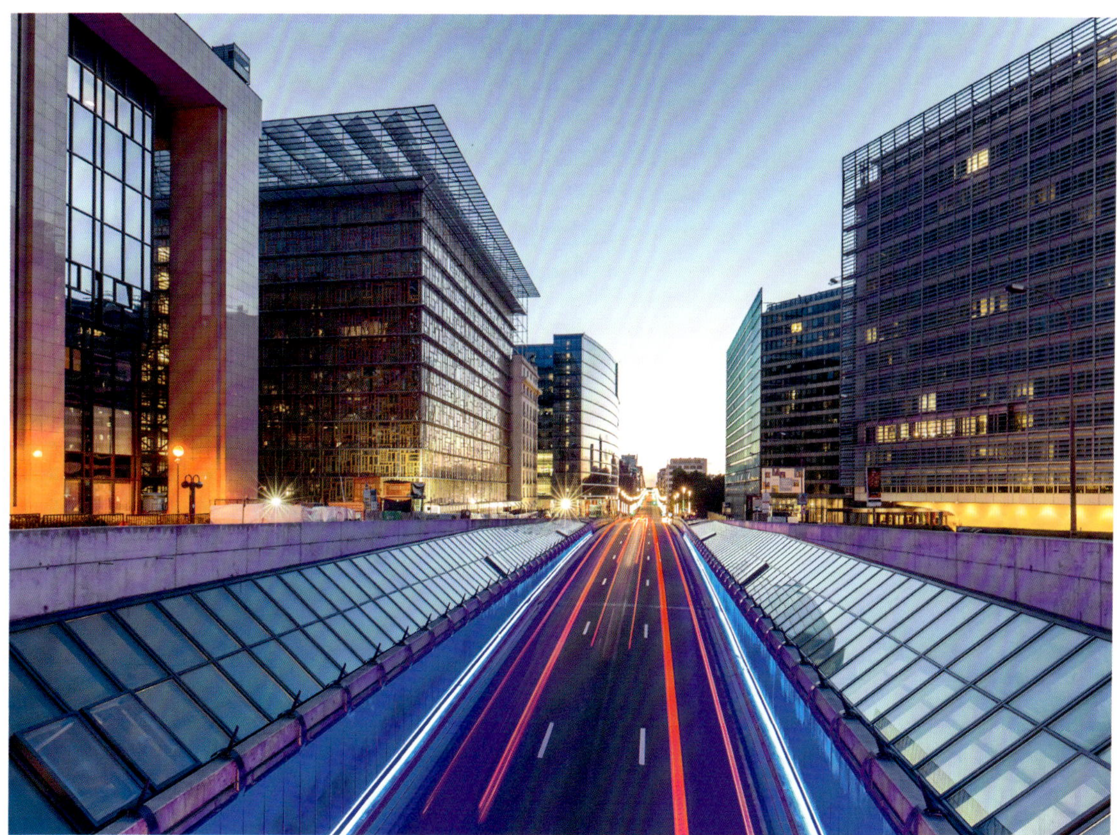

Rue de la Loi, European Quarter
Rue de la Loi, Europese wijk
Rue de la Loi, quatier européen

Corazón de la Unión Europea

El corazón de la UE late en el barrio europeo. Alrededor de 100 000 personas de todo el mundo trabajan en los castillos de oficinas de vidrio para Europa. Las instituciones políticas no son lugares aislados: tanto si se trata del Parlamento Europeo (llamado humorísticamente Caprice des Dieux por su similitud con la forma del queso blando francés) como del Consejo de la UE o de la Comisión de la UE, los visitantes son bienvenidos a echar un vistazo y conocer el funcionamiento de las instituciones. En el Parliamentarium se puede conocer mejor Europa y el trabajo del Parlamento en diversas instalaciones multimedia.

Coração da União Europeia

O coração da UE bate no bairro europeu. Cerca de 100 000 pessoas de todo o mundo trabalham para a Europa nas torres de escritórios de vidro. As instituições políticas não são lugares isolados: quer o Parlamento Europeu, que se chama humoristicamente "Caprice des Dieux" devido à sua semelhança com a forma do queijo fresco francês, o Conselho da UE ou a Comissão Europeia – os visitantes são bem-vindos e podem dar uma olhada no local e receber informações de como funcionam as instituições. No Parlamentarium pode-se viver a experiência da Europa e do trabalho do Parlamento através de várias instalações multimedia interativas.

Het hart van de Europese Unie

In de Europese wijk klopt het hart van de EU. Ongeveer 100 000 mensen uit de hele wereld werken in de glazen kantoorgebouwen voor Europa. De politieke instituten zijn geen afgeschermde plekken: Of het nu gaat om het Europees Parlement, dat op humoristische wijze Caprice des Dieux wordt genoemd vanwege de gelijkenis met de vorm van de Franse zachte kaas, de Europese Raad of de Europese Commissie – bezoekers zijn welkom een kijkje te nemen en zich te laten vertellen hoe de instituten werken. In het Parlementarium kan men in verschillende installaties Europa en het werk van het Parlement op multimediale wijze beleven.

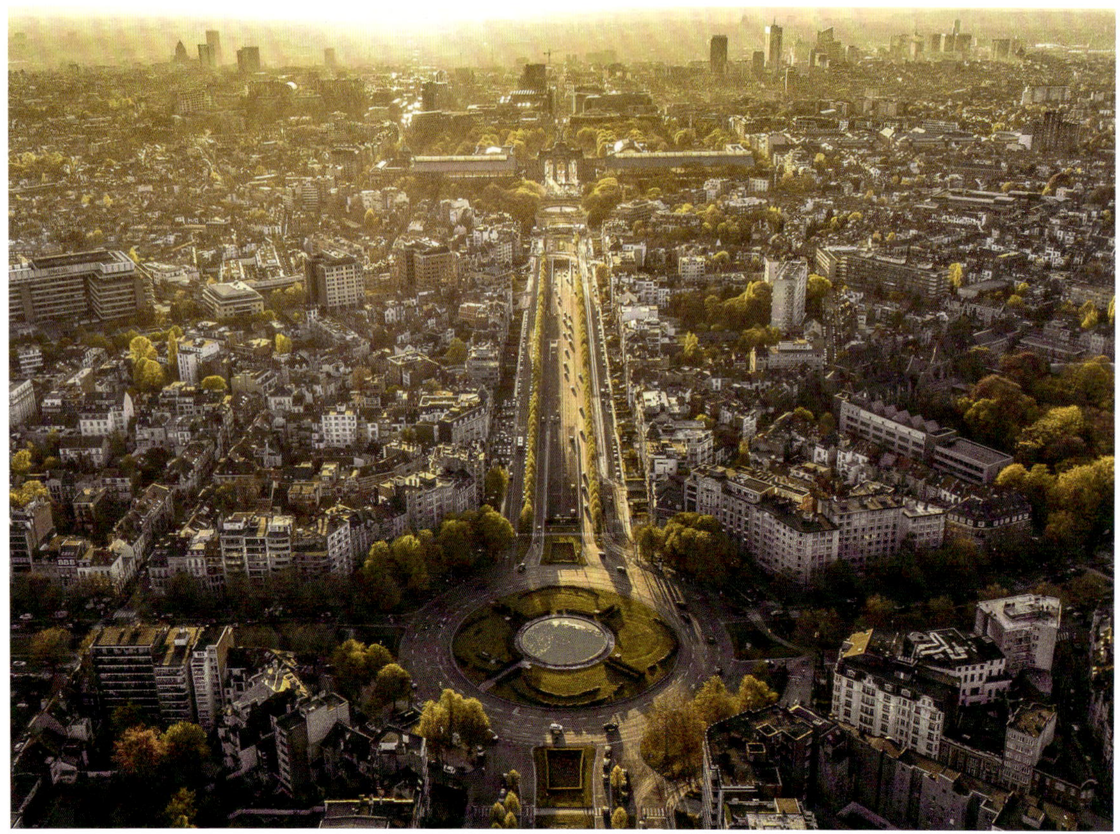

Montgomery Square, Avenue de Tervueren and Triumphal Arch, with Cinquantenaire Park
Montgomeryplein, Tervurenlaan en Triomfboog met Jubelpark
Square Maréchal Montgomery, avenue de Tervueren avec Arc de triomphe, parc du Cinquantenaire

Avenue de Tervueren

With this magnificent avenue, the Belgian king, Leopold II, wanted to surpass Paris in grandeur. Having a total length of more than 10 km (6,2 mi) and a width of 90 m (295 ft), it is 20 m (66 ft) wider than the Champs Elysées in Paris. For the Brussels World Exhibition in 1897, it connected the gigantic exhibition halls of the Jubelpark with the Palace of the Colonies (now the Royal Museum for Central Africa) in Tervuren. The avenue is lined with luxurious villas from the mid-19th century and provides access to the European quarter. The visual axis leads from the historic city centre, via the European Quarter, through the triumphal arch of the Jubelpark and on to Montgomery Square.

Avenue de Tervueren

En faisant construire cette somptueuse avenue de 10 kilomètres de long, le roi belge Léopold II voulut surpasser Paris. De fait, sa largeur de 90 mètres compte 20 mètres de plus que les Champs-Élysées. Lors de l'Exposition universelle de Bruxelles en 1897, l'avenue reliait les gigantesques salles d'exposition du parc du Cinquantenaire au palais des Colonies de Tervueren. L'avenue est bordée de luxueuses villas de style Gründerzeit et conduit au quartier européen. L'axe visuel part du centre-ville historique, passe par le quartier européen, traverse l'arc de triomphe du parc du Cinquantenaire pour aboutir à la place Montgomery.

Avenue Tervueren

Mit dieser Prachtallee wollte der belgische König, Leopold II. Paris überflügeln. Sie ist, mit einer Gesamtlänge von mehr als 10 km und einer Breite von 90 m, 20 m breiter als die Champs Elysées in Paris. Zur Brüsseler Weltausstellung 1897 verband sie die gigantischen Ausstellungshallen des Jubelparks mit dem Kolonialpalast in Tervueren (heute das Königliches Museum für Zentralafrika). Die Allee ist von luxuriösen Villen aus der Gründerzeit gesäumt und bildet den Zugang zum Europa-Viertel. Die Sichtachse führt vom historischen Stadtzentrum über das Europa-Viertel durch den Triumphbogen des Jubelparks zum Montgomery-Platz.

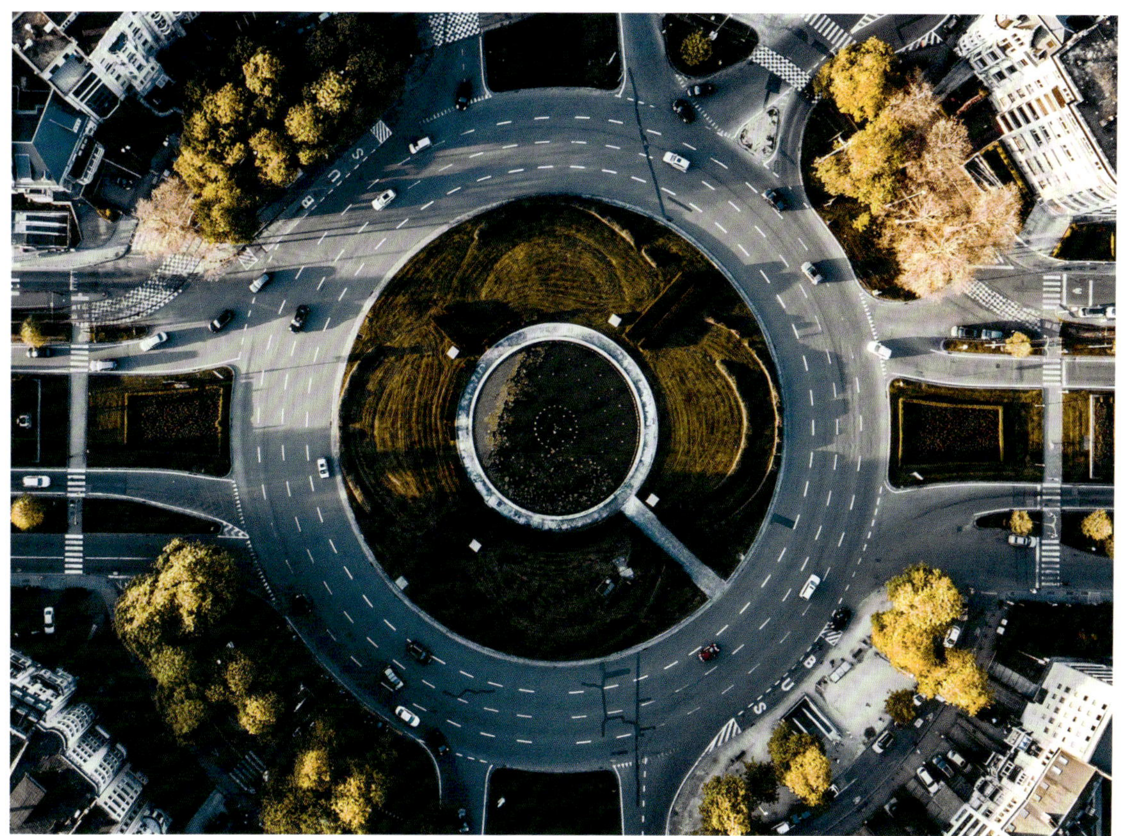

Montgomery Square
Montgomeryplein
Square Maréchal Montgomery

Avenida Tervueren

Con esta magnífica avenida, el rey
belga Leopoldo II quiso superar a París.
Con una longitud total de más de 10
km y una anchura de 90 m, es 20 m
más ancho que los Campos Elíseos de
París. Para la Exposición Universal de
Bruselas de 1897, conectó las gigantescas
salas de exposiciones del Parque del
Cincuentenario con el Palacio Colonial
de Tervueren (hoy el Museo real de
África central). La avenida está bordeada
de lujosas villas de los tiempos de la
fundación y da acceso al barrio europeo.
La línea de visión lleva desde el centro
histórico de la ciudad, pasando por el
barrio europeo, a través del arco de triunfo
del Parque del Cincuentenario, hasta la
plaza de Montgomery.

Avenida de Tervuren

Com esta magnífica avenida, o rei belga,
Leopoldo II, queria superar Paris. Com um
comprimento total de mais de 10 km e
uma largura de 90 m, é 20 m mais largo
que os Champs Elysées de Paris. Para a
Exposição Internacional de Bruxelas de
1897, ela se ligou às gigantescas salas de
exposição do Jubelpark com o Palácio
Colonial de Tervueren (hoje o Museu Real
da África Central). A avenida cercada por
vilas luxuosas do período dos fundadores
e oferece acesso ao bairro europeu. O eixo
de visão leva do centro histórico da cidade
através do bairro europeu ao arco triunfal
do Parque do Cinquentenário ou Jubelpark
até à Praça Montgomery.

Tervurenlaan

Met deze prachtige laan wilde de Belgische
koning, Leopold II, Parijs overtreffen.
Met een totale lengte van meer dan 10
km en een breedte van 90 m is het 20 m
breder dan de Champs Elysées in Parijs.
Voor de Brusselse Wereldtentoonstelling
van 1897 verbond het de gigantische
tentoonstellingszalen van het Jubelpark
met het Koloniënpaleis in Tervuren
(vandaag het Koninklijk Museum voor
Midden-Afrika). De laan is omzoomd met
luxe villa's uit de Gründerzeit en biedt
toegang tot de Europese Wijk. De zichtas
loopt van de historische binnenstad via de
Europese wijk door de triomfboog van het
Jubelpark naar het Montgomeryplein.

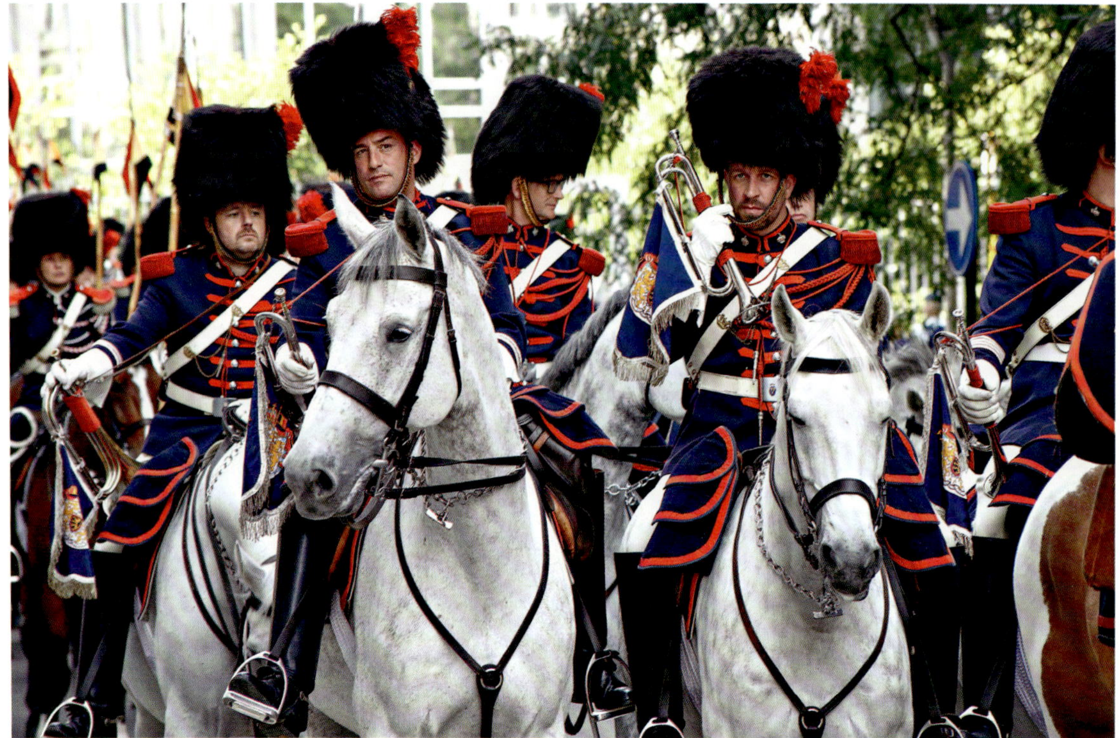

Royal Horse Guards during the Te Deum mass, Belgian National Day
Koninklijke Paardenwachters tijdens de Te Deum mis, de Nationale Feestdag van België
Garde royale à cheval pendant la messe du Te Deum, fête nationale belge

Parades and Processions

One of the most important medieval pageants in Flanders is the Ommegang, which celebrates a festival held in 1549 on the Grand Place in honour of Charles V. The pageant is one of the most important traditional parades in Flanders. The royal court, in its entire splendour, is present throughout the city, with more than 1000 extras in historical costumes, horses, chariots, flag wavers giants and stilt-walkers.

Défilés et processions

L'Ommegang est l'un des principaux cortèges folkloriques de Flandres. Il évoque une fête donnée en 1549 sur la Grand-Place en l'honneur de Charles Quint. La cour royale au complet sillonne la ville dans toute sa splendeur : plus de 1000 figurants en costumes historiques, des chevaux, des calèches, des lanceurs de drapeaux et des géants.

Umzüge und Prozessionen

Einer der wichtigsten traditionellen Umzüge in Flandern ist der Ommegang. Er zelebriert eine Feierlichkeit, die im Jahre 1549 auf dem Grand-Place zu Ehren von Karl V. veranstaltet wurde. Der vollzählige Königshof zieht in seiner ganzen Pracht durch die Stadt: mehr als 1000 Statisten in historischen Kostümen, Pferde, Wagen, Fahnenschwenker und Riesen.

Desfiles y Procesiones

Uno de los desfiles tradicionales más importantes de Flandes es el Ommegang. Celebra una celebración en 1549 en la Grand-Place en honor de Carlos V. El desfile es uno de los desfiles tradicionales más importantes de Flandes. La corte real en todo su esplendor está presente en toda la ciudad: más de 1000 extras en trajes históricos, caballos, carros, banderines y gigantes.

Desfiles e procissões

Um dos mais importantes desfiles tradicionais da Flandres é o Ommegang. Ele comemora uma solenidade realizada em 1549 na Praça Grande em homenagem a Carlos V. A corte real percorre toda a cidade em todo o seu esplendor: mais de 1000 figurantes em trajes históricos, cavalos, carruagens, lançadores de bandeiras e gigantes.

Optochten en Processies

Eén van de belangrijkste traditionele optochten in Vlaanderen is de Ommegang, de viering van een plechtigheid die in 1549 op de Grote Markt ter ere van Karel V werd gehouden. Het complete Koninklijk Huis trekt met al zijn pracht en praal door de stad: meer dan 1000 figuranten in historische kostuums, paarden, strijdwagens, wagens, vlaggetjes en reuzen.

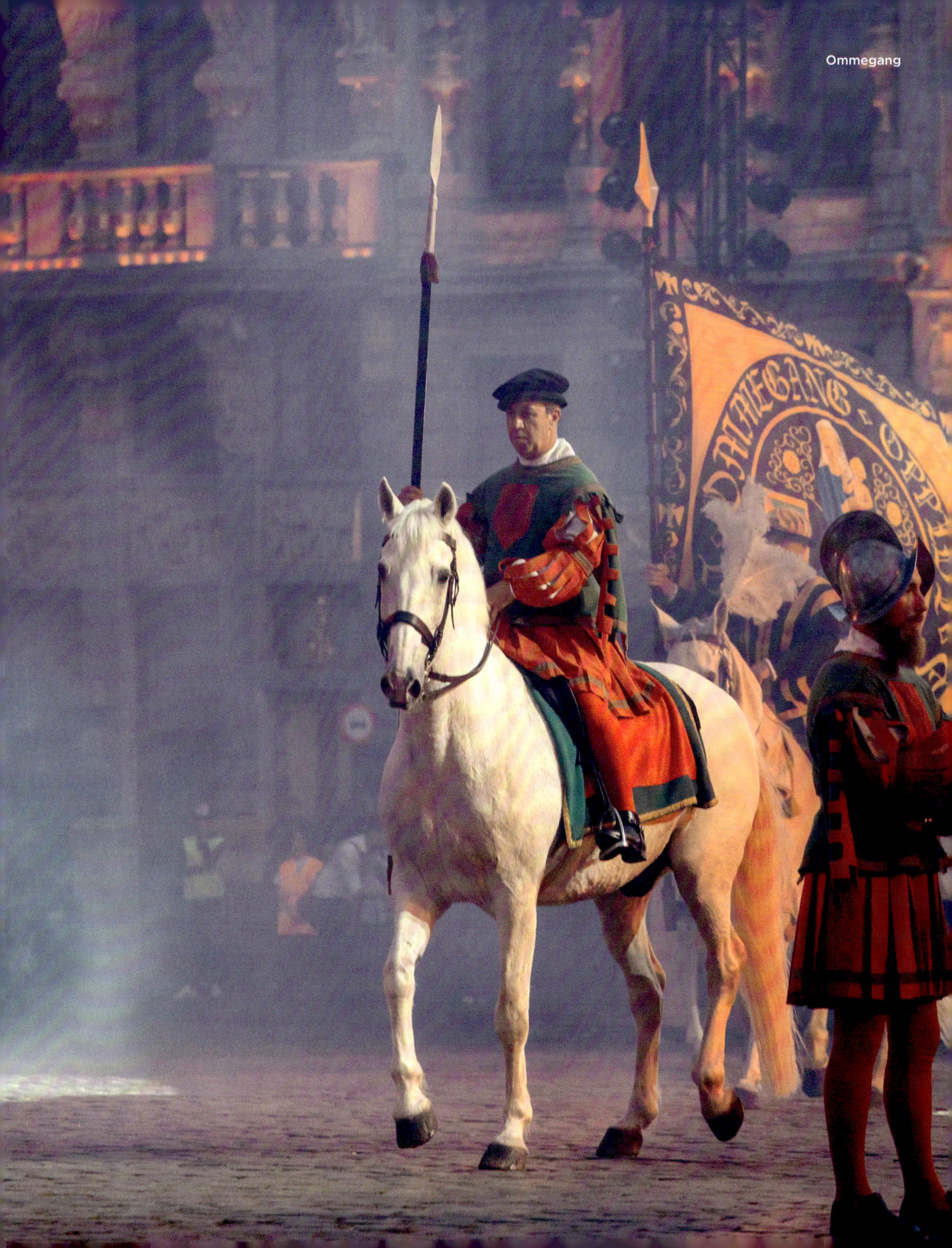
Ommegang

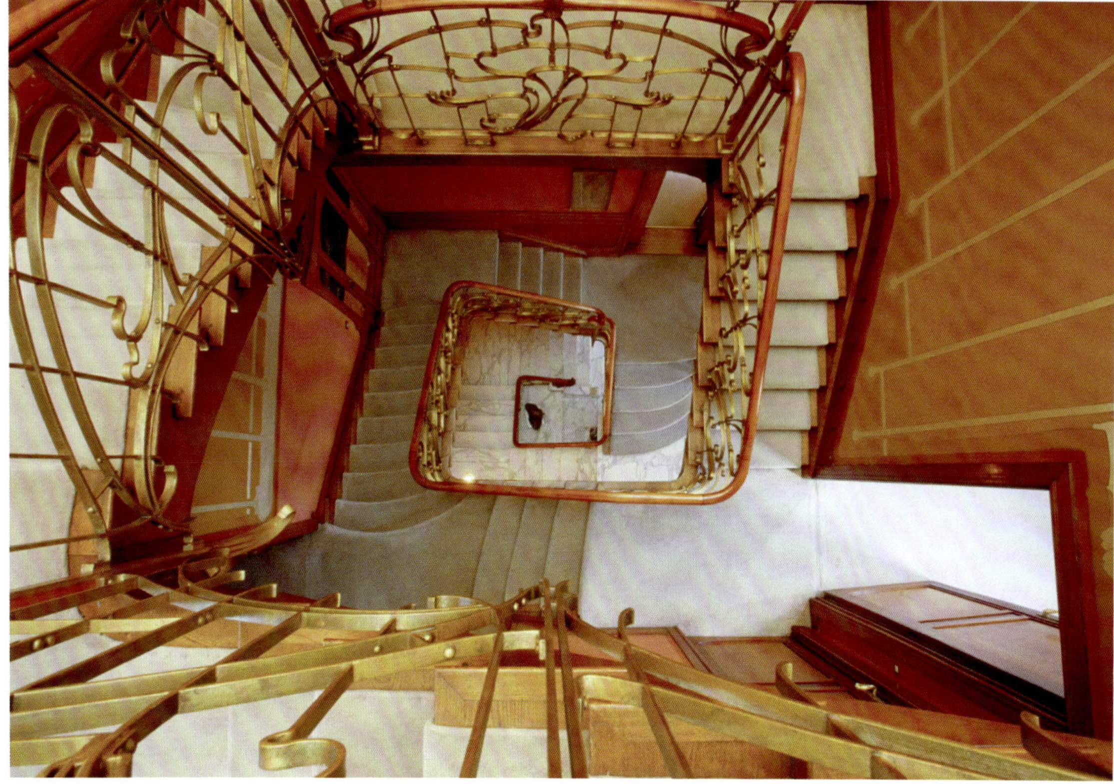

Hortamuseum
Musée Horta

Art Nouveau

Floral lines and flowing forms—the new building materials of steel and glass revolutionized architecture around 1900. The architect Victor Horta used steel, which at that time was a cheap building material for factory buildings, to construct prestigious buildings—an outrageous provocation! More than 1000 houses and shops were built in the new architectural style.

Art Nouveau

Las líneas florales y las formas fluidas; los nuevos materiales, el acero y el vidrio revolucionaron la arquitectura hacia 1900. El arquitecto Víctor Horta utilizó el acero, que en aquel entonces era un material de construcción barato para los edificios de las fábricas, para los edificios representativos. ¡Menuda provocación! Se construyeron más de 1000 casas y tiendas en el nuevo estilo arquitectónico.

Art nouveau

Lignes florales et formes fluides… Les nouveaux matériaux - le verre et l'acier - révolutionnèrent l'architecture vers 1900 : pour la construction de bâtiments représentatifs, l'architecte Victor Horta employa de l'acier, ce matériau bon marché réservé à l'époque aux bâtiments d'usine - quel scandale ! Plus de 1000 maisons et magasins furent édifiés dans ce nouveau style architectural.

Art Nouveau

Linhas florais e formas fluidas - os novos materiais, aço e vidro, revolucionaram a arquitetura por volta de 1900. O arquiteto Victor Horta usou aço na época material de construção barato para edifícios fabris, para edifícios representativos - uma provocação escandalosa! Mais de 1000 casas e lojas foram construídas no novo estilo arquitetônico.

Art nouveau

Florale Linien und fließende Formen – die neuen Materialien Stahl und Glas revolutionierten die Baukunst um 1900. Der Architekt Victor Horta nutzte Stahl, zu der Zeit billiges Baumaterial, für Fabrikhallen und für repräsentative Gebäude – eine ungeheuerliche Provokation! Mehr als 1000 Wohnhäuser und Geschäfte entstanden im neuen Architekturstil.

Art Nouveau

Florale lijnen en vloeiende vormen - de nieuwe materialen, staal en glas - zorgden rond 1900 voor een revolutie in de architectuur. De architect Victor Horta gebruikte staal, destijds goedkoop bouwmateriaal voor fabrieksgebouwen, voor representatieve gebouwen - een schandalige provocatie! Meer dan 1000 woonhuizen en winkels ontstonden in nieuwe architectuurstijl.

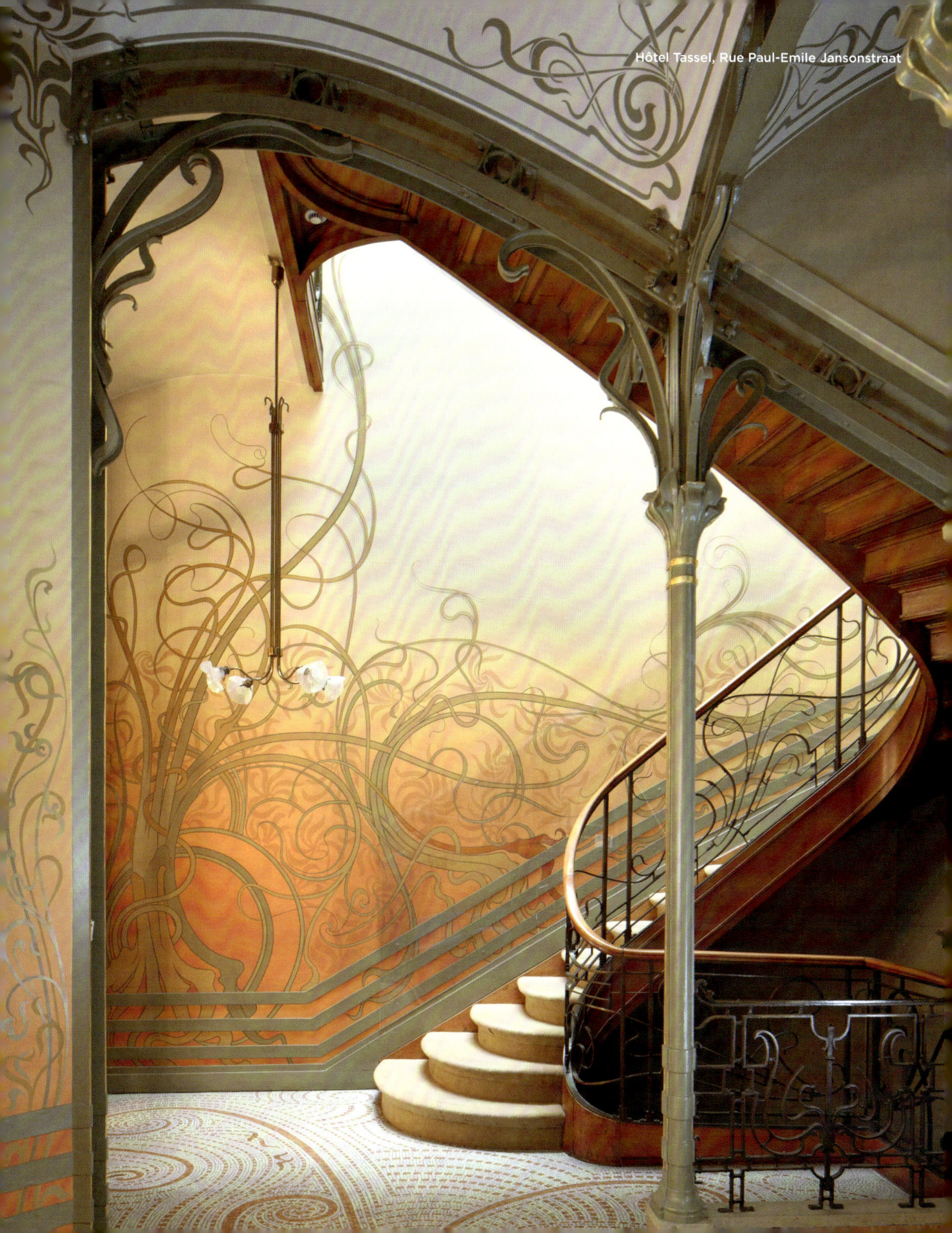

Hôtel Tassel, Rue Paul-Emile Jansonstraat

Victor Horta

Victor Horta always designed his buildings, from the floor plan to the door handle, as a complete work of art. The most important element of his architecture is light. The focus is on the spacious staircase, a glazed atrium that directs daylight to the various floors. Central filigreed atriums constructed from steel and glass elements, huge windows, organic shapes and soft lines define his style.

Victor Horta

Victor Horta conçut toujours ses bâtiments – des plans aux poignées de porte – comme des œuvres d'art. L'élément le plus important de son architecture est la lumière. L'accent est mis sur la spacieuse cage d'escalier, un atrium vitré qui oriente la lumière du jour vers les différents étages. Des cours intérieures centrales en filigrane, composées d'éléments en verre et en acier, d'immenses fenêtres, des formes organiques et des lignes douces définissent son style.

Victor Horta

Victor Horta entwarf seine Bauwerke vom Grundriss bis zur Türklinke stets als Gesamtkunstwerk. Das wichtigste Element seiner Architektur ist Licht. Im Mittelpunkt steht das großzügige Treppenhaus, ein verglastes Atrium, das das Tageslicht in die verschiedenen Etagen leitet. Zentrale filigrane Lichthöfe aus Stahl- und Glaselementen, riesige Fenster, organische Formen und weiche Linien bestimmen seinen Stil.

Víctor Horta

Victor Horta siempre diseñó sus edificios, desde la planta hasta la manilla de la puerta, como una obra de arte total. El elemento más importante de su arquitectura es la luz. La atención se centra en la espaciosa escalera, un atrio acristalado que dirige la luz del día a las distintas plantas. Atrios centrales de filigrana hechos de elementos de acero y vidrio, enormes ventanas, formas orgánicas y líneas suaves definen su estilo.

Victor Horta

Victor Horta sempre projetou os seus edifícios, desde a planta até ao puxador da porta, como uma obra de arte total. O elemento mais importante da sua arquitetura é a luz. O foco está na escadaria espaçosa, um átrio envidraçado que direciona a luz do dia para os vários andares. Pátios centrais de filigrana feitos de elementos de aço e vidro, grandes janelas, formas orgânicas e linhas suaves definem seu estilo.

Victor Horta

Victor Horta ontwierp zijn gebouwen, van de plattegrond tot de deurklink, altijd als een totaalkunstwerk. Het belangrijkste element van zijn architectuur is licht. De focus ligt op het ruime trappenhuis, een glazen atrium dat daglicht naar verschillende verdiepingen leidt. Centrale, filigreine overdekte binnenplaatsen van staal- en glaselementen, enorme ramen, organische vormen en zachte lijnen bepalen zijn stijl.

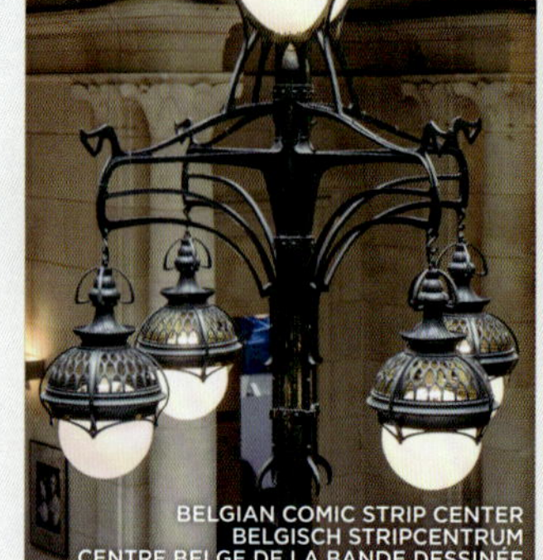

BELGIAN COMIC STRIP CENTER
BELGISCH STRIPCENTRUM
CENTRE BELGE DE LA BANDE DESSINÉE

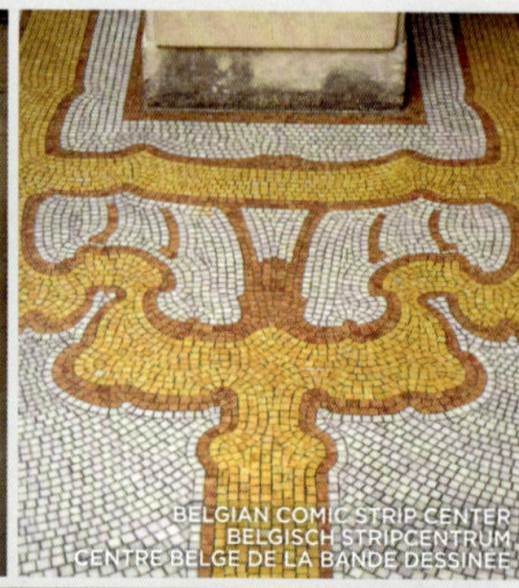

BELGIAN COMIC STRIP CENTER
BELGISCH STRIPCENTRUM
CENTRE BELGE DE LA BANDE DESSINÉE

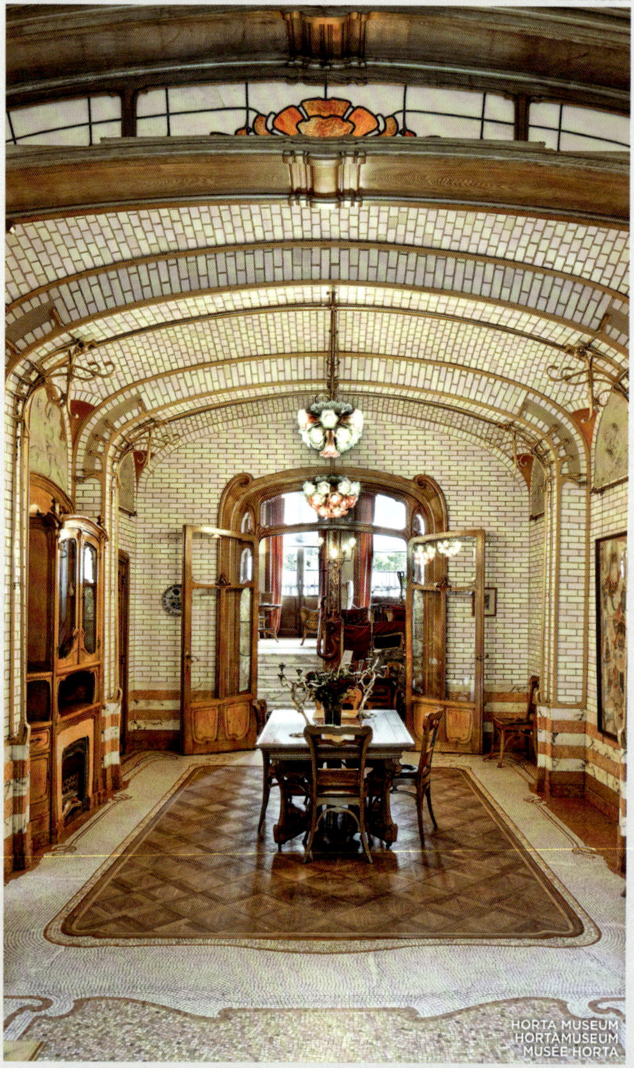

HORTA MUSEUM
HORTAMUSEUM
MUSÉE HORTA

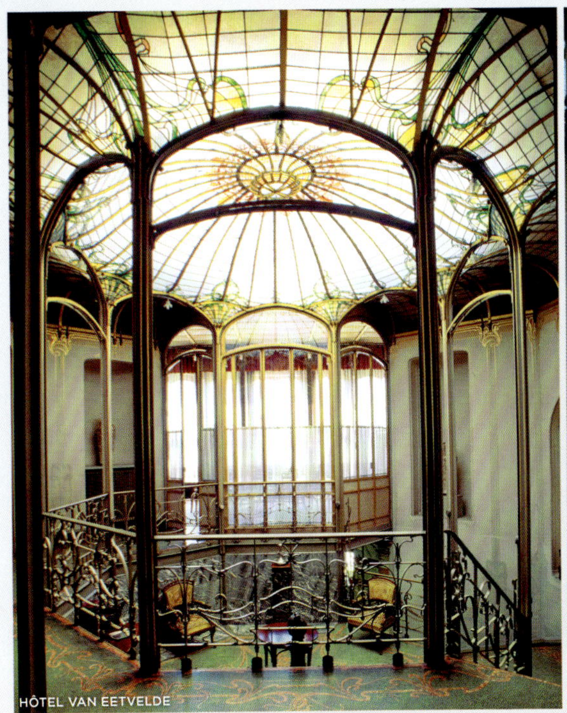

HÔTEL VAN EETVELDE

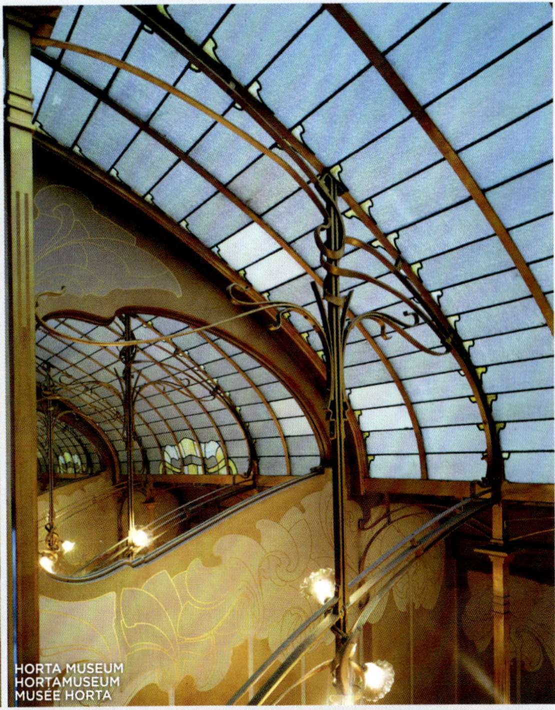

HORTA MUSEUM
HORTAMUSEUM
MUSÉE HORTA

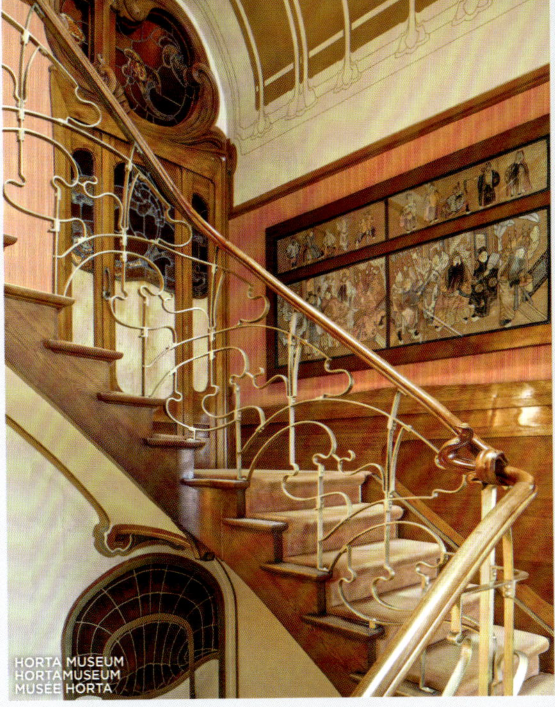

HORTA MUSEUM
HORTAMUSEUM
MUSÉE HORTA

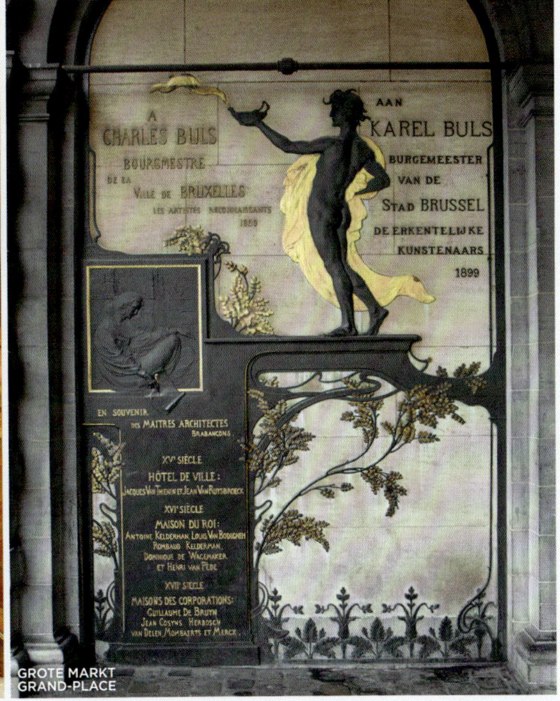

GROTE MARKT
GRAND-PLACE

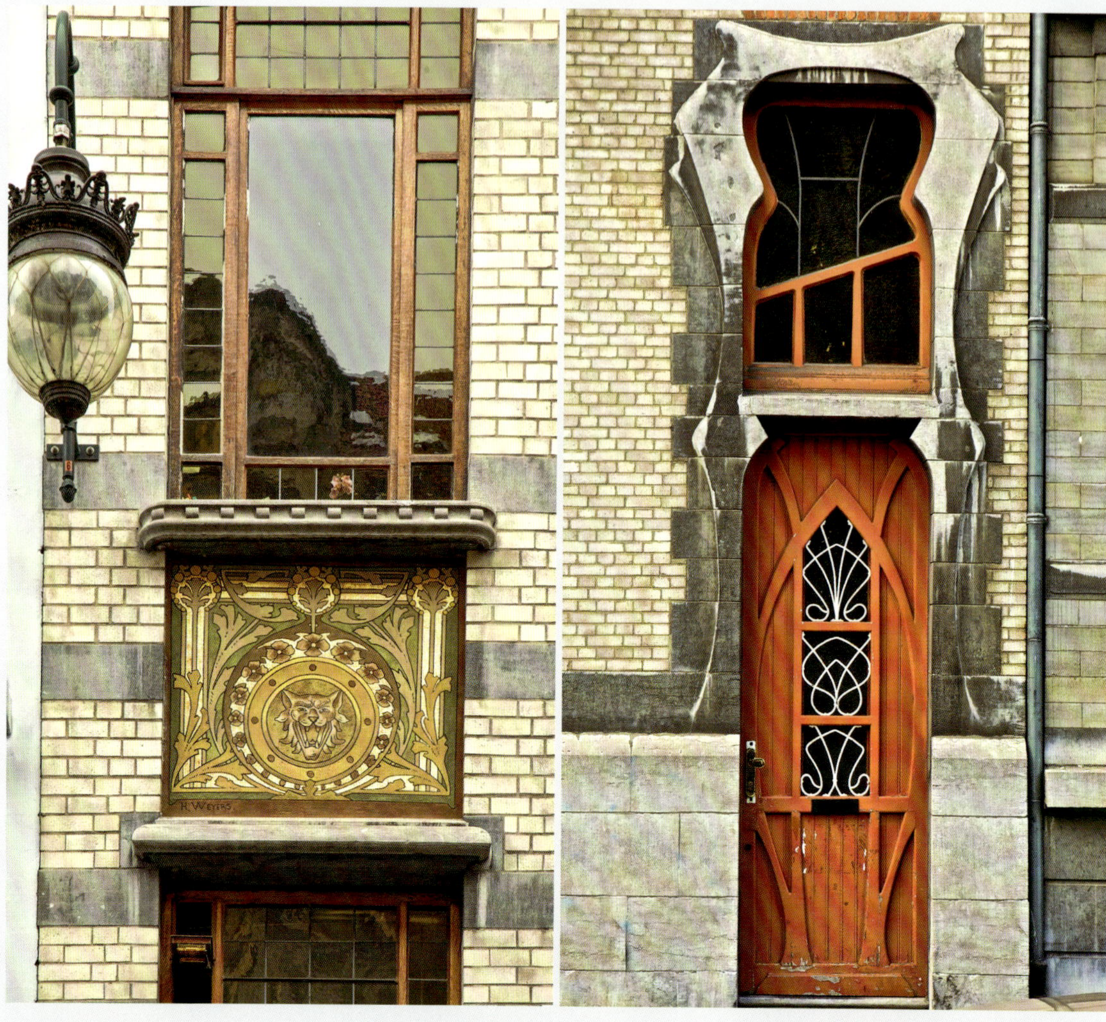

Art Nouveau facades

Art Nouveau shaped Brussels more than almost any other city in Europe. Around 500 residential buildings, shops and hotels have been preserved in Brussels. Anyone searching in the districts of St Gilles, Ixelles and Schaerbeek will discover the elegance of the facades, designed down to the smallest detail. Architects such as Victor Horta, Paul Hankar and Henry van de Velde created a style that had a lasting impact on all forms of artistic expression, encompassing furniture, decorative objects, crockery and haute couture. All became gently curved forms, featuring fauna and flora, color and light.

Façades Art nouveau

L'Art nouveau a façonné Bruxelles plus que toute autre ville européenne. Près de 500 immeubles d'habitation, commerces et hôtels y sont conservés. Dans les quartiers Saint-Gilles, Ixelles et Schaerbeek, vous découvrirez l'élégance des façades dessinées jusque dans les moindres détails. Des architectes tels que Victor Horta, Paul Hankar et Henry van de Velde créèrent un style qui a eu un impact durable sur toutes les formes d'expression artistique : mobilier, objets décoratifs, vaisselle et haute couture – tout adopta des formes aux courbes douces, incluant faune et flore, couleur et lumière.

Art-nouveau-Fassaden

Art nouveau prägte Brüssel wie kaum eine zweite Stadt in Europa. Rund 500 Wohnhäuser, Geschäfte und Hotels sind in Brüssel erhalten geblieben. Wer sich in den Stadtvierteln St. Gilles, Ixelles und Schaerbeek auf die Suche macht, entdeckt die Eleganz, der bis ins kleinste Detail gestalteten Fassaden. Architekten wie Victor Horta, Paul Hankar und Henry van de Velde schufen eine Stilrichtung, die sämtliche künstlerische Ausdrucksformen nachhaltig geprägt hat: Möbel, Ziergegenstände, Geschirr und Haute Couture – alles wurde zur sanft geschwungenen Form, Fauna und Flora, Farbe und Licht.

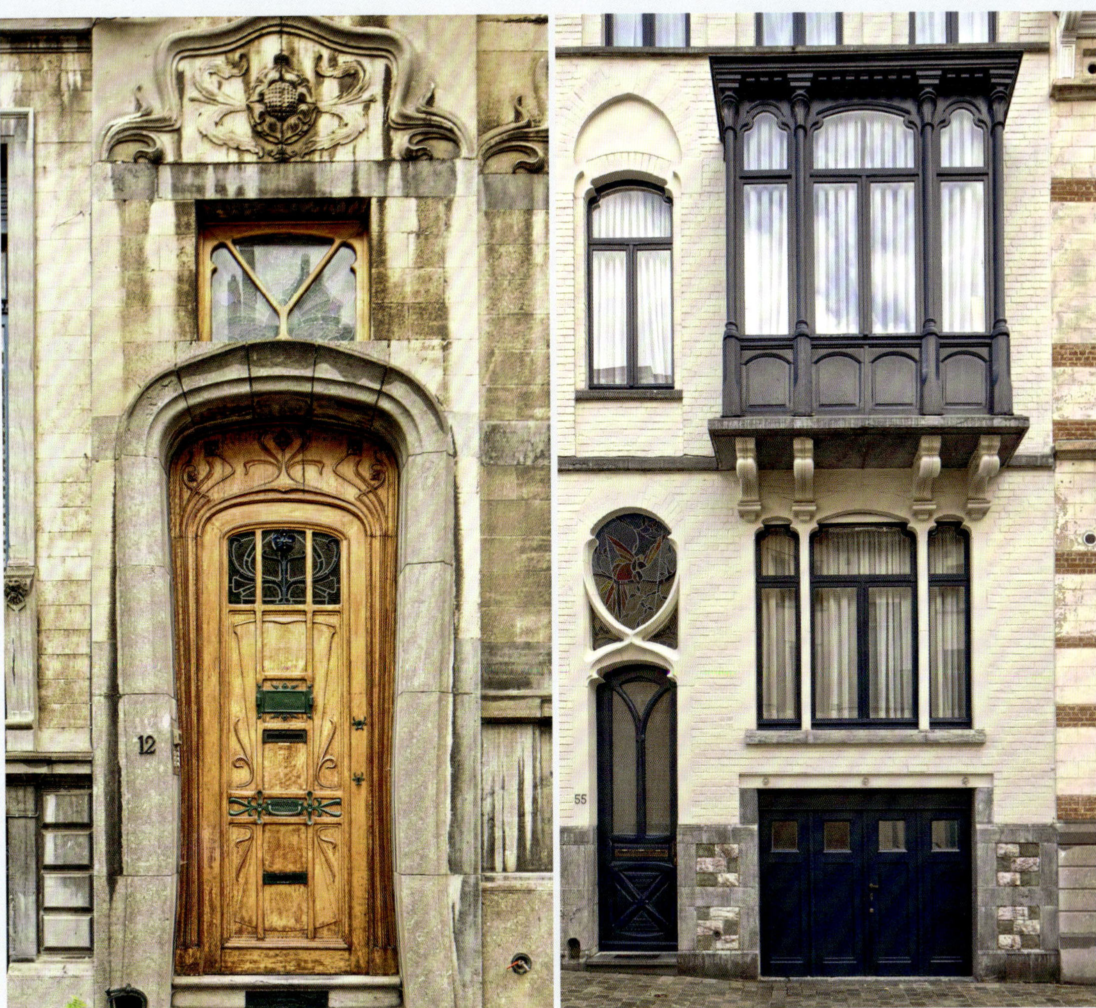

Fachadas Art Nouveau

El Art Nouveau dio forma a Bruselas más
que a cualquier otra ciudad de Europa.
En Bruselas se han conservado alrededor
de 500 edificios residenciales, tiendas y
hoteles. Quien busque en los barrios de
St. Gilles, Ixelles y Schaerbeek descubrirá
la elegancia de las fachadas, diseñadas
hasta el más mínimo detalle. Arquitectos
como Victor Horta, Paul Hankar y Henry
van de Velde crearon un estilo que tuvo
un impacto duradero en todas las formas
de expresión artística: muebles, objetos
decorativos, vajilla y alta costura. Todo se
convirtió en formas suavemente curvadas,
fauna y flora, color y luz.

Fachadas em Art Nouveau

O estilo Art Nouveau teve marcante
influência na cidade de Bruxelas, mais
do que qualquer outra cidade da Europa.
Cerca de 500 edifícios residenciais, lojas
e hotéis foram preservados em Bruxelas.
Quem procura nos bairros de St. Gilles,
Ixelles e Schaerbeek descobre a elegância
das fachadas, concebidas até no mínimo
detalhe. Arquitetos como Victor Horta,
Paul Hankar e Henry van de Velde criaram
um estilo que teve um impacto duradouro
em todas as formas de expressão artística:
mobiliário, objetos decorativos, louça e alta
costura – tudo se tornou em uma forma
suavemente curvada, fauna e flora, cor
e luz.

Art nouveau gevels

De art nouveau vormde Brussel zoals
nauwelijks een tweede stad in Europa.
Circa 500 woonhuizen, winkels en hotels
zijn in Brussel bewaard gebleven. Wie in de
wijken Sint-Gilles, Elsene en Schaarbeek
op zoek gaat, ontdekt de elegantie van de
tot in het kleinste detail ontworpen gevels.
Architecten zoals Victor Horta, Paul Hankar
en Henry van de Velde creëerden een
stijlrichting die voor altijd invloed had op
alle artistieke uitdrukkingsvormen: meubels,
decoratieve objecten, serviesgoed en haute
couture – het kreeg een zacht gebogen
vorm, fauna en flora, kleur en licht.

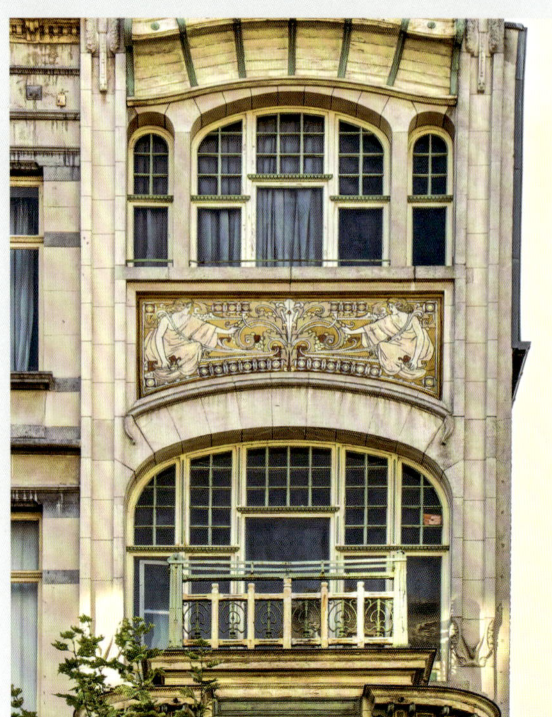
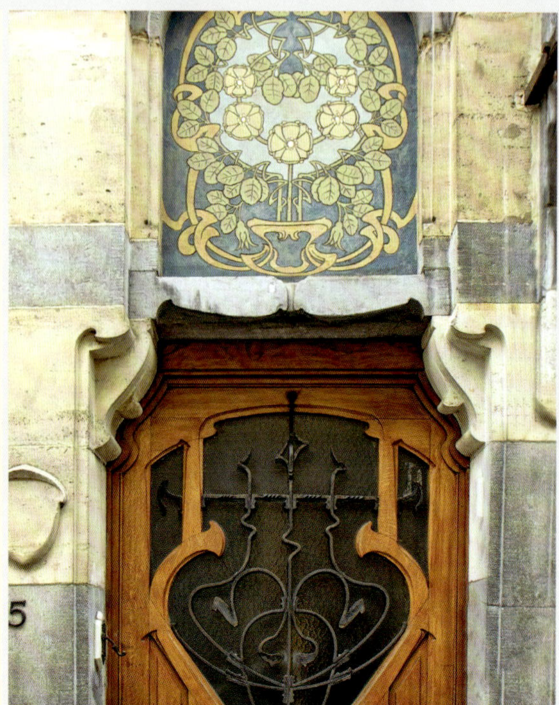
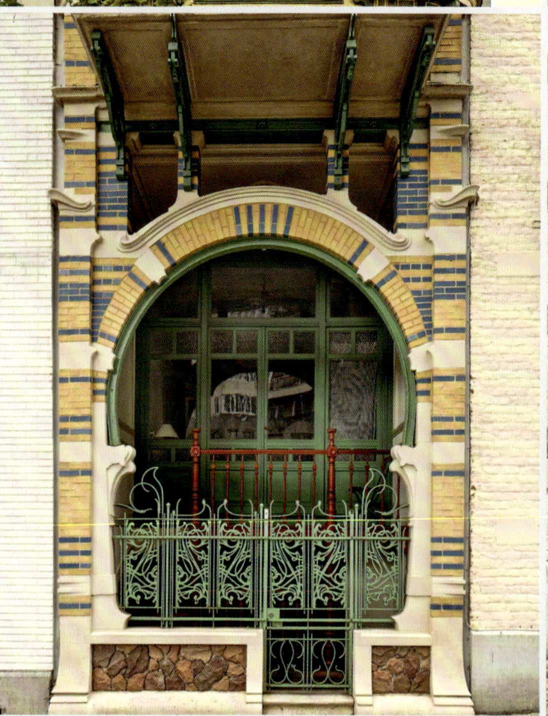
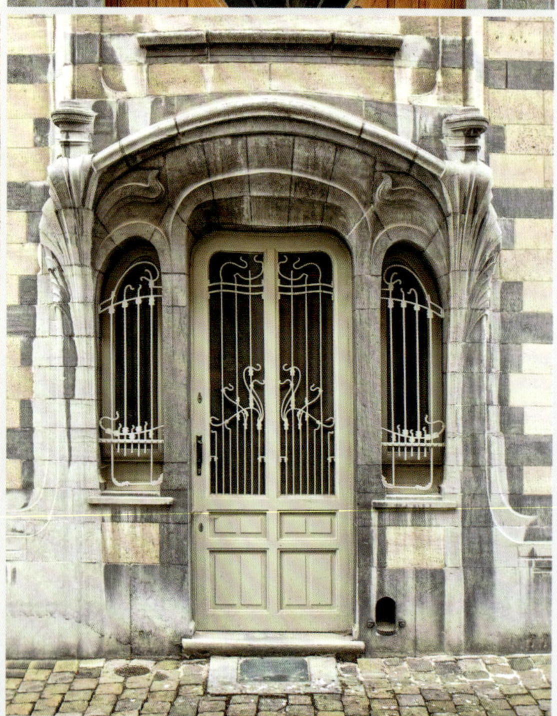

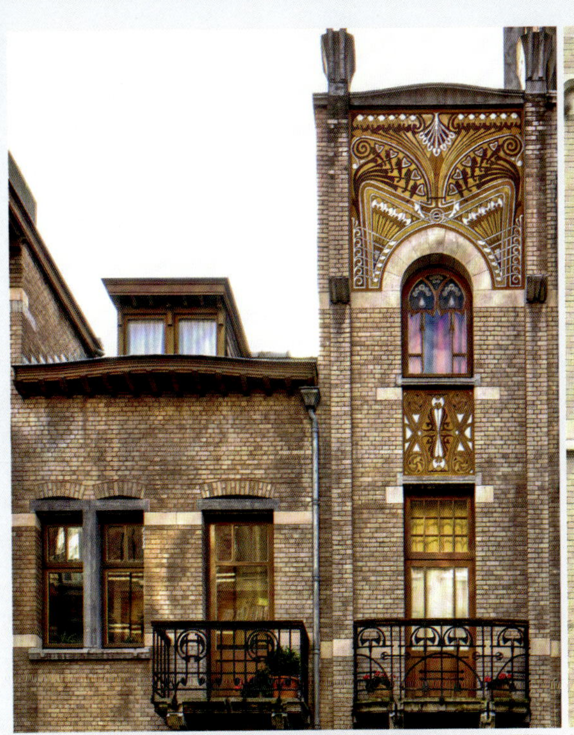
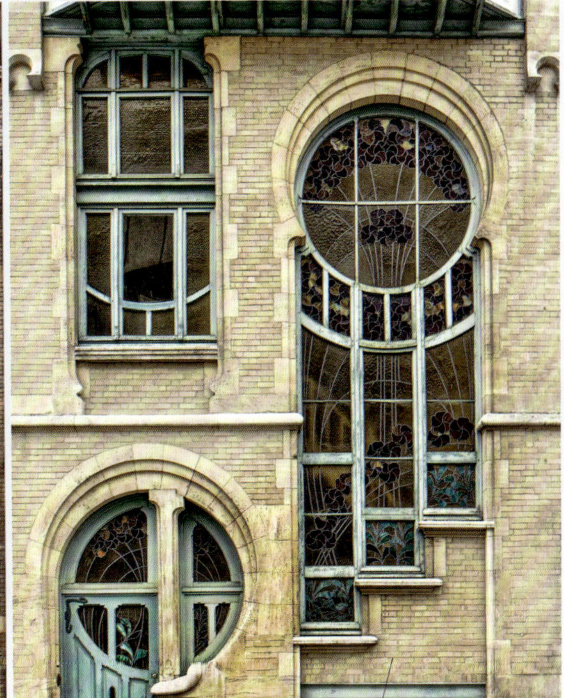
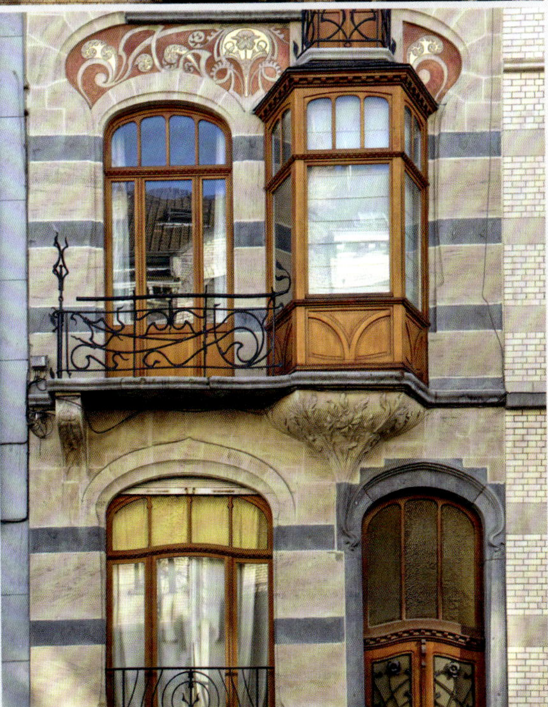
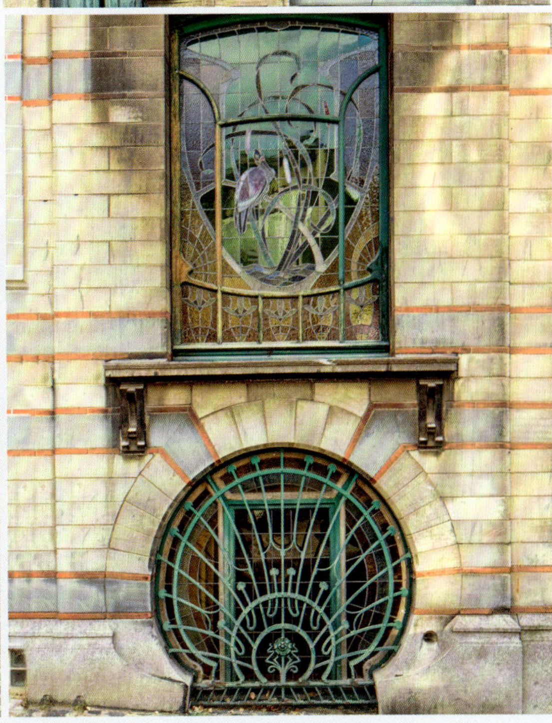

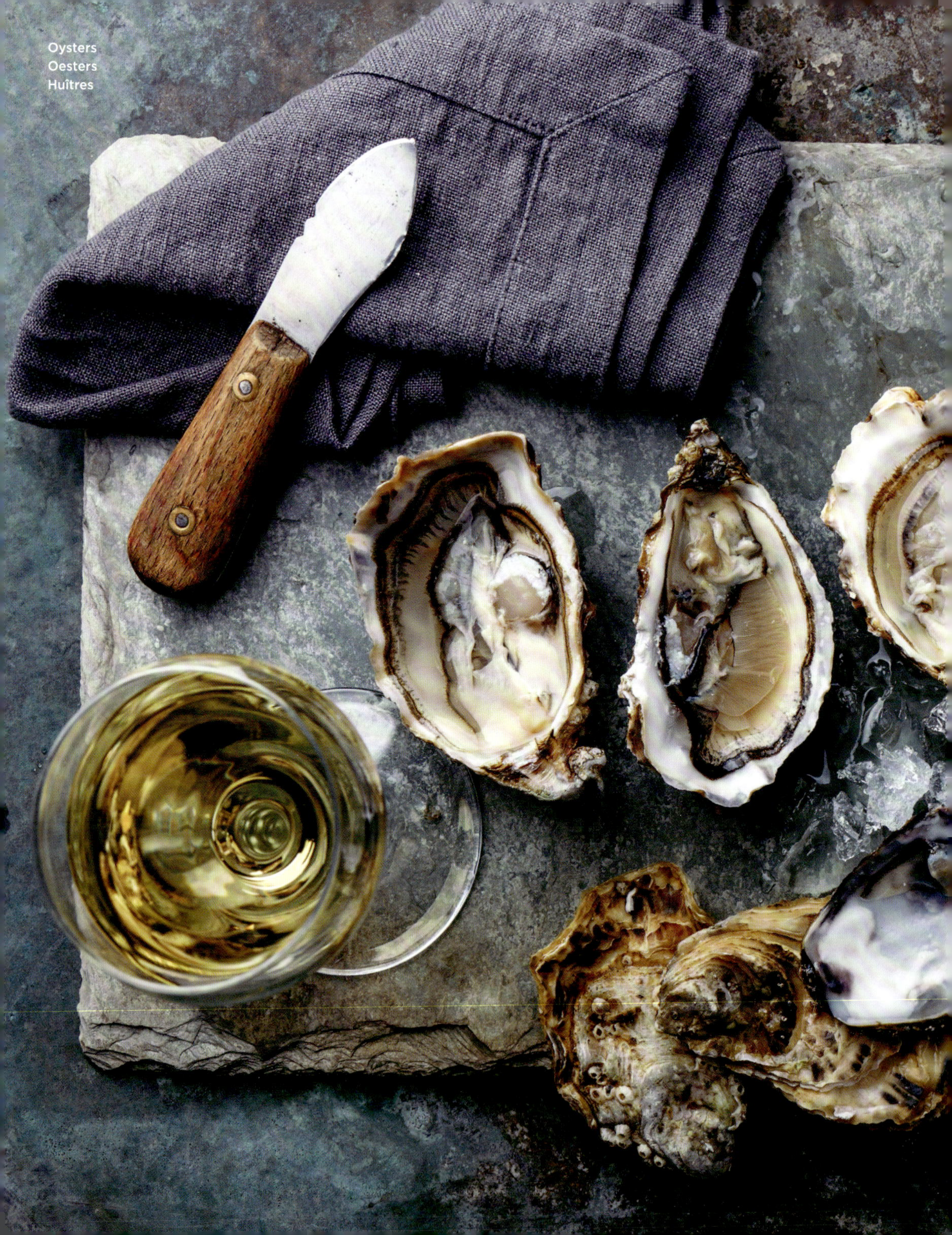
Oysters
Oesters
Huîtres

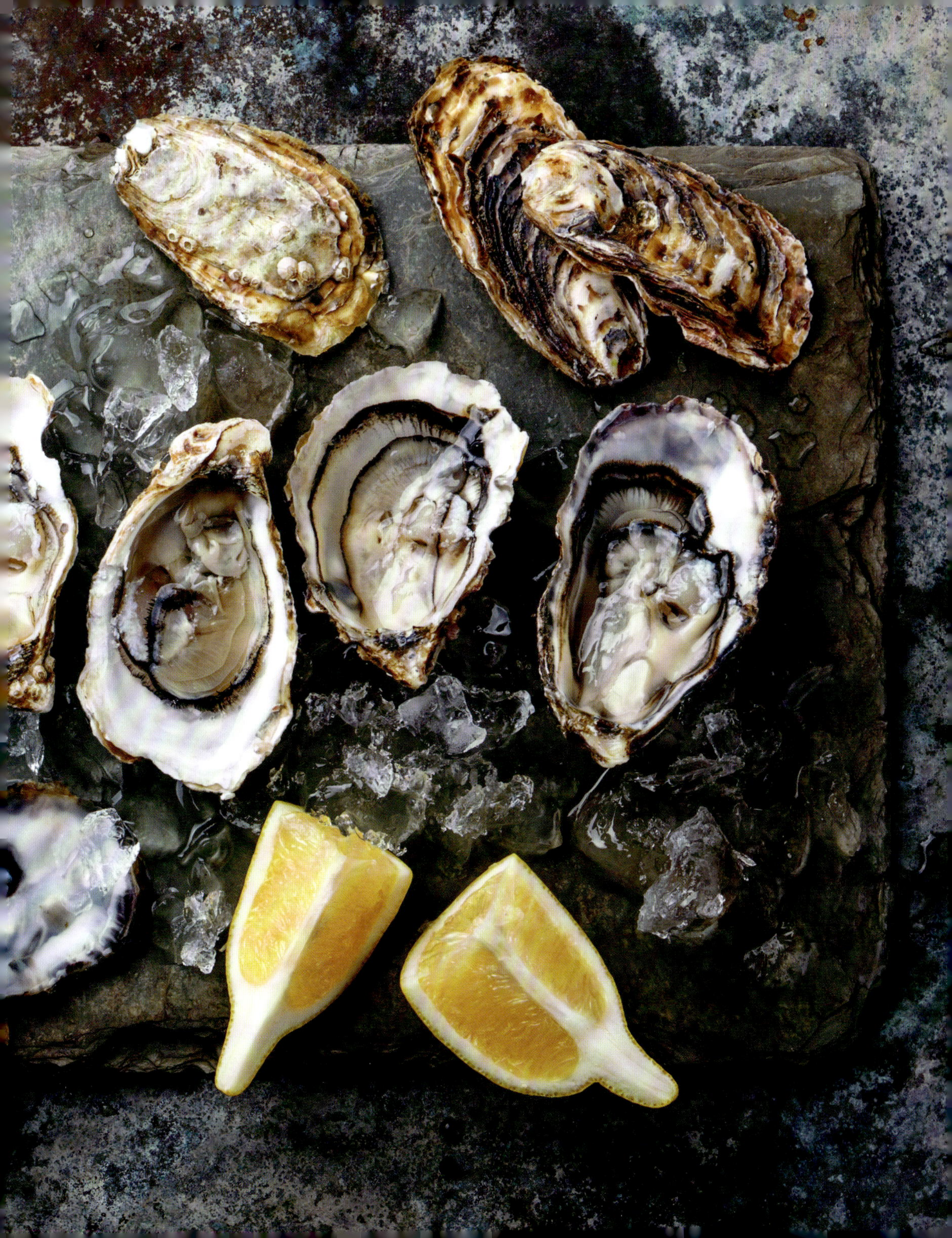

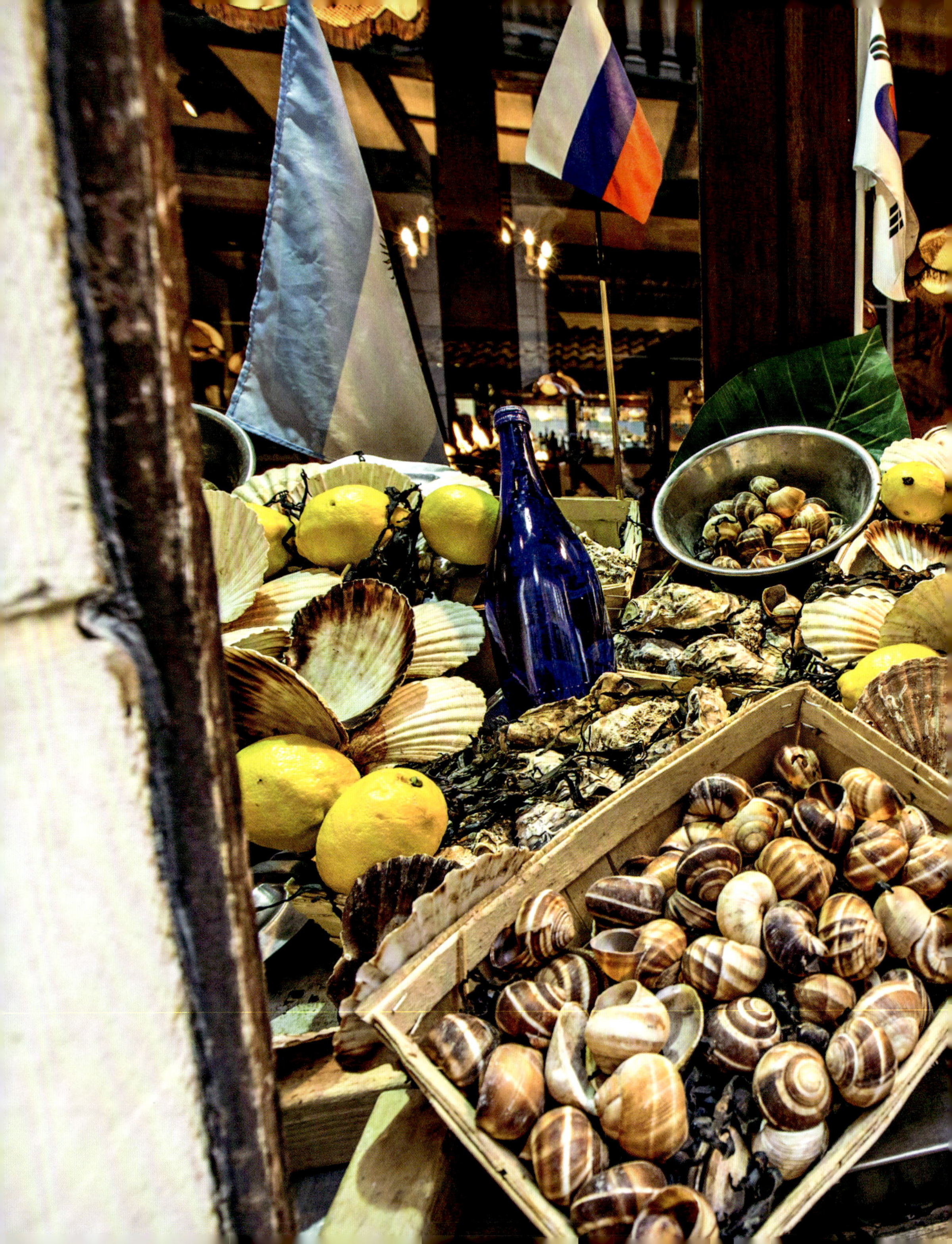

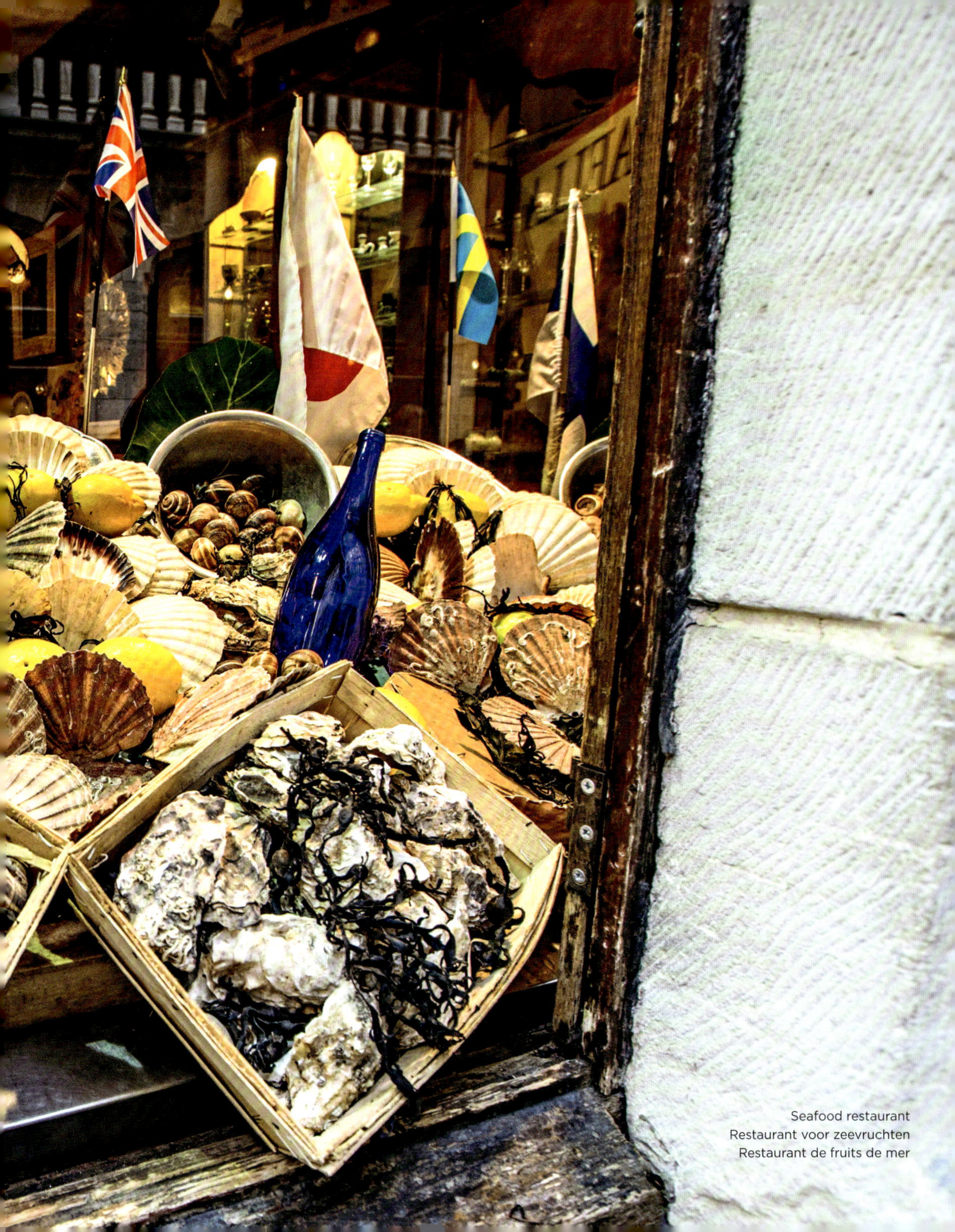

Seafood restaurant
Restaurant voor zeevruchten
Restaurant de fruits de mer

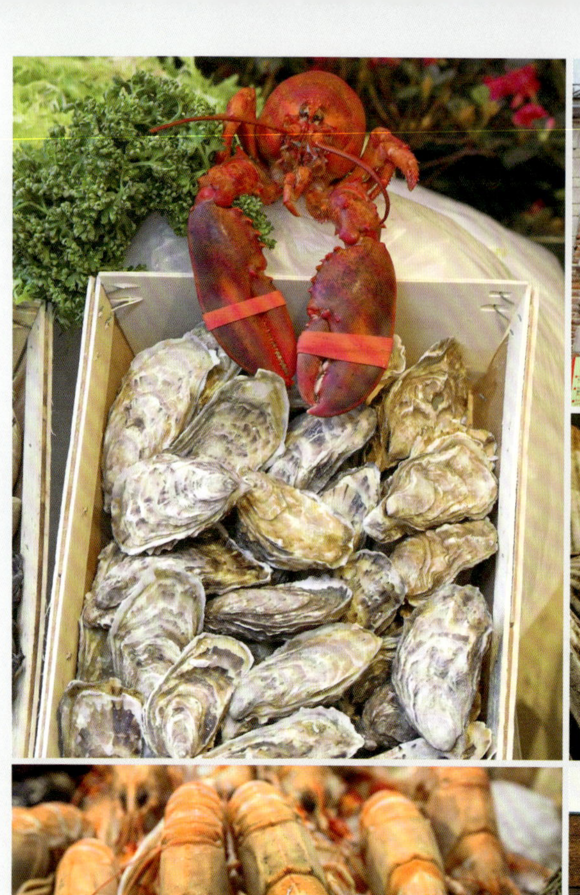
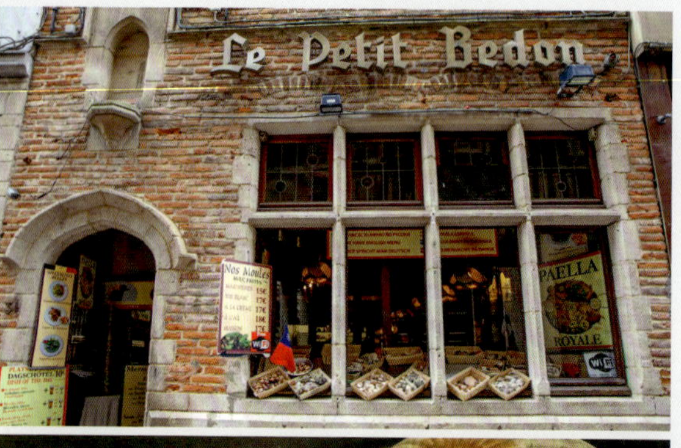
Le Petit Bedon
PAELLA
ROYALE
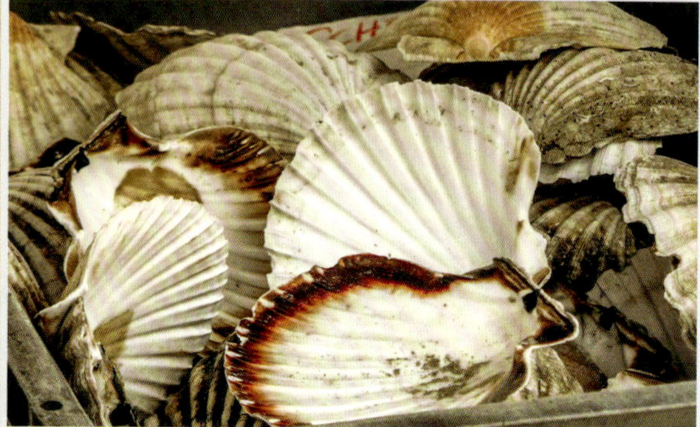
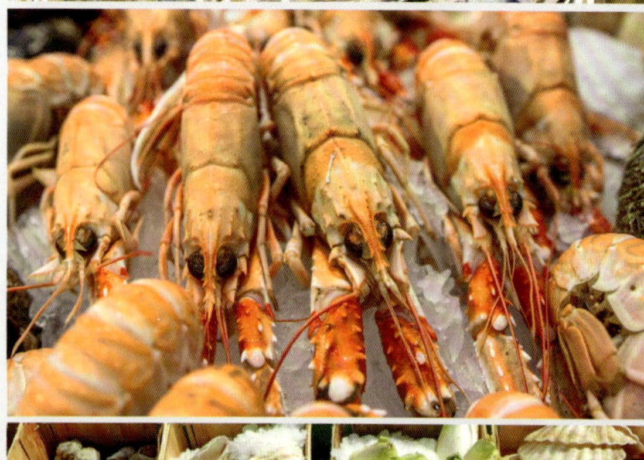
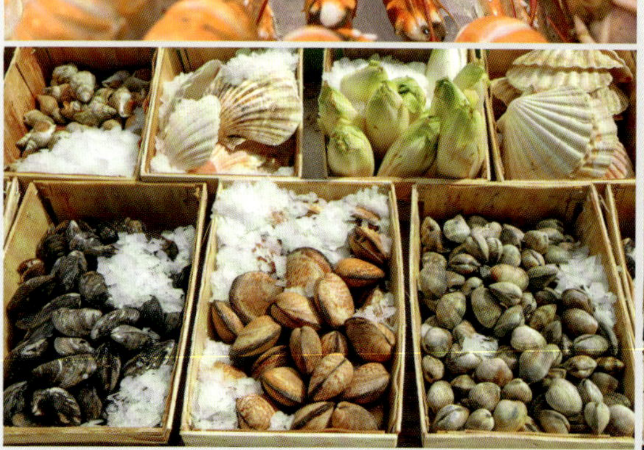
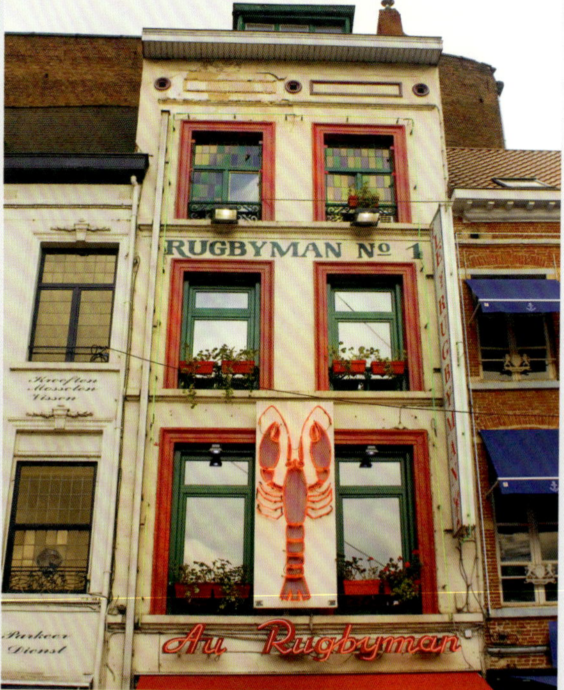
RUGBYMAN N° 1
Kreeften
Mosselen
Vissen
Au Rugbyman

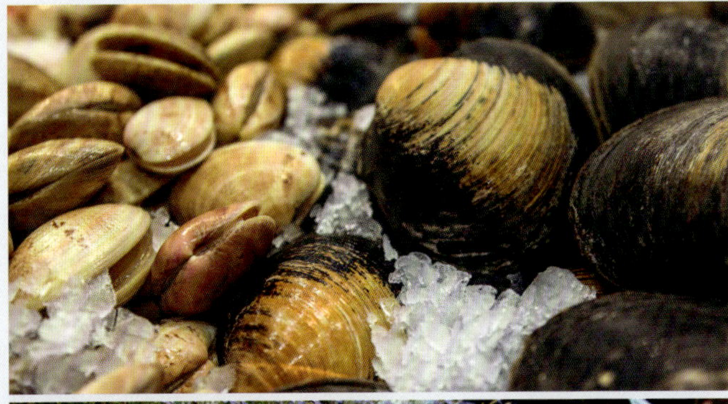

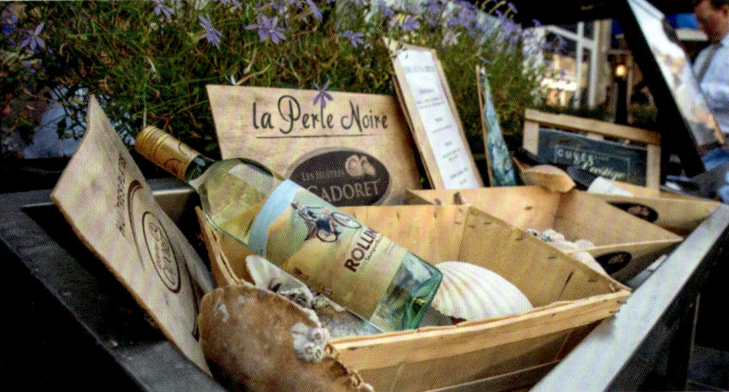

Young Chefs and Stars

With more than 30 Michelin stars, Flanders numbers considerably more top restaurants than France. It is above all the young chefs in Flanders, who are admired as much as pop stars, who give new impetus to the gastronomic scene. In doing so, they rely heavily on local ingredients. Due to their proximity to the North Sea, fish and seafood such as oysters and mussels are particularly popular.

Jeunes cuisiniers et étoiles

Avec plus de 30 étoiles au guide Michelin, les Flandres comptent bien plus de grands restaurants que la France par habitant. De jeunes chefs cuisiniers, que les Flamands vénèrent autant que des stars de la pop, donnent un nouvel élan à la scène gastronomique. Pour ce faire, ils misent sur des ingrédients locaux. Du fait de la proximité avec la mer du Nord, les poissons et fruits de mer, telles les huîtres et les moules, sont particulièrement appréciés.

Junge Köche und Sterne

Mit über 30 Michelin-Sterne zählt Flandern, auf den Einwohner umgerechnet, weit mehr Spitzenrestaurants als Frankreich. Es sind vor allem die jungen Küchenchefs, die in Flandern ähnlich verehrt werden wie Popstars, die der Gastro-Szene neuen Impulse geben. Dabei setzen sie auf heimische Zutaten. Aufgrund der Nähe zur Nordsee sind vor allem Fisch und Meeresfrüchte wie Austern und Muscheln beliebt.

Jóvenes cocineros y estrellas

Con más de 30 estrellas Michelin, Flandes cuenta con muchos más restaurantes que Francia. Son sobre todo los jóvenes cocineros de Flandes, admirados tanto como las estrellas del pop, los que dan un nuevo impulso a la escena gastronómica. Para ello, se basan en ingredientes locales. Debido a su proximidad al Mar del Norte, los pescados y mariscos como las ostras y los mejillones son particularmente populares.

Jovens Cozinheiros e Estrelas

Com mais de 30 estrelas Michelin, a Flandres conta por habitante muito mais restaurantes de alto nível do que a França. São sobretudo os jovens cozinheiros da Flandres, tão admirados como as estrelas pop, que dão novo ímpeto à cena gastronómica. Ao fazê-lo, confiam nos ingredientes locais. Devido à sua proximidade com o Mar do Norte, peixes e frutos do mar como ostras e mexilhões são particularmente populares.

Jonge koks en sterren

Omgerekend naar het aantal inwoners telt Vlaanderen met meer dan 30 Michelin-sterren veel meer toprestaurants dan Frankrijk. Het zijn vooral jonge chef-koks die in Vlaanderen net zo worden geadoreerd als popsteren en die de culinaire scene nieuwe impulsen geven. Daarbij vertrouwen ze op lokale ingrediënten. Door de nabijheid van de Noordzee zijn vooral vis en zeevruchten zoals oesters en mosselen populair.

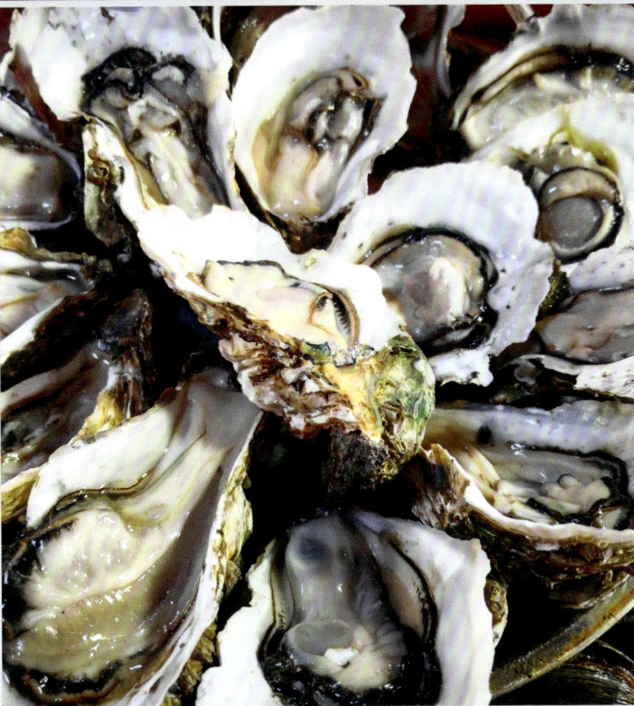

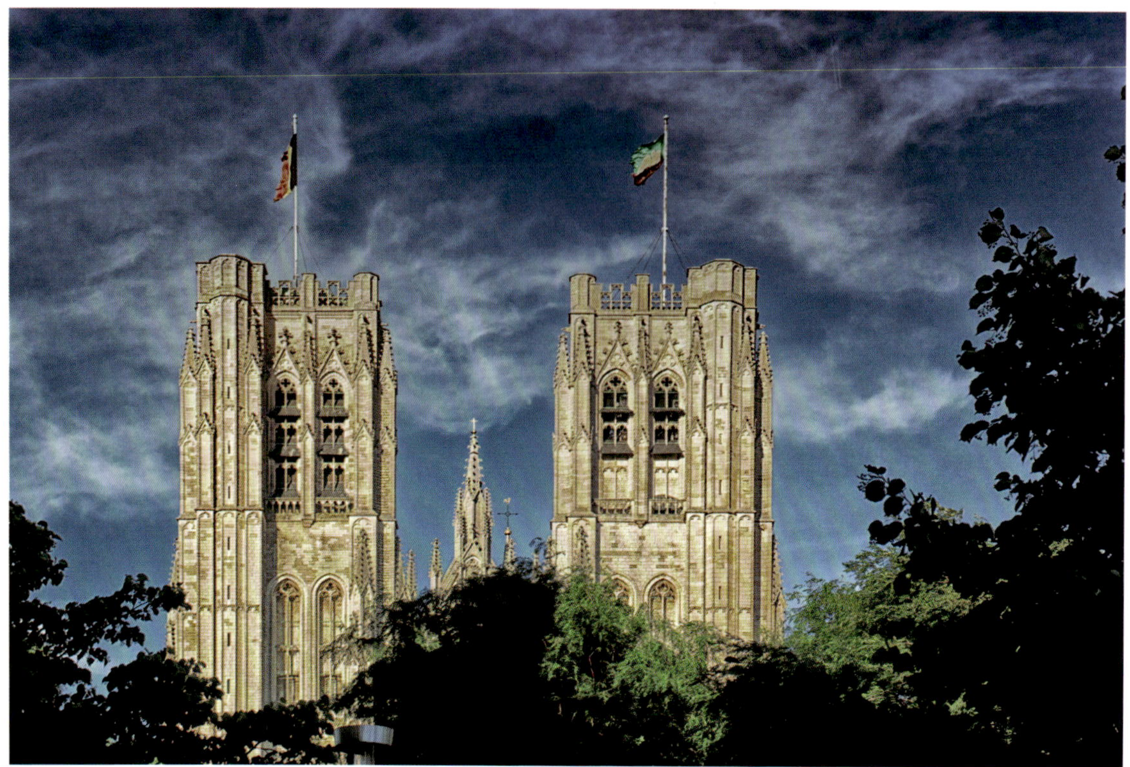

Cathedral of St Michael and St Gudula
Kathedraal van Sint-Michiel en Sint-Goedele
Cathédrale Saints-Michel-et-Gudule de Bruxelles

Cathedral of St Michael and St Gudula

The cathedral, built on a hill, plays an important role in the social life of both the city and the country, as the most important ceremonies of the royal family take place there. The 16 choir windows composed of hundreds of stained glass panels, the life-size statues of the 12 apostles and the baroque main altar, made of white and black marble, are all impressive.

Saints-Michel-et-Gudule

Construite en hauteur, la cathédrale joue un rôle important dans la vie sociale de la ville et du pays, car les principales cérémonies de la famille royale s'y déroulent. Les seize vitraux du chœur d'une richesse saisissante, les sculptures des apôtres grandeur nature et le maître-autel baroque en marbre blanc et noir valent le détour.

St. Michael und St. Gudula

Die auf einer Anhöhe erbaute Kathedrale spielt eine wichtige Rolle im gesellschaftlichen Leben der Stadt und des Landes, denn hier finden auch die wichtigsten Zeremonien der Königsfamilie statt. Eindrucksvoll sind die 16 Chorfenster mit Hunderten von Glasgemälden, die lebensgroße Apostelfiguren und der barocke Hauptaltar aus weißem und schwarzem Marmor.

San Miguel y San Gudula

La catedral, construida sobre una colina, juega un papel importante en la vida social de la ciudad y del campo, ya que en ella se celebran las ceremonias más importantes de la familia real. Son impresionantes las 16 ventanas del coro con cientos de vitrales, las figuras de apóstol a tamaño natural y el altar mayor barroco de mármol blanco y negro.

São Miguel e Santa Gúdula

A catedral, construída sobre uma colina, desempenha um papel importante na vida social da cidade e do país, já que as cerimônias mais importantes da família real acontecem aqui. São impressionantes as 16 janelas do coro com centenas de pinturas de vitrais, as figuras dos apóstolos em tamanho real e o altar-mor barroco em mármore branco e preto.

Sint-Michiel en Sint-Goedele

De kathedraal, gebouwd op een heuvel, speelt een belangrijke rol in het maatschappelijk leven van de stad en het land, omdat hier de belangrijkste ceremonies van de koninklijke familie plaatsvinden. Indrukwekkend zijn de 16 glasramen met honderden glas-in-lood schilderijen, de levensgrote apostelbeelden en het barokke hoofdaltaar van wit en zwart marmer.

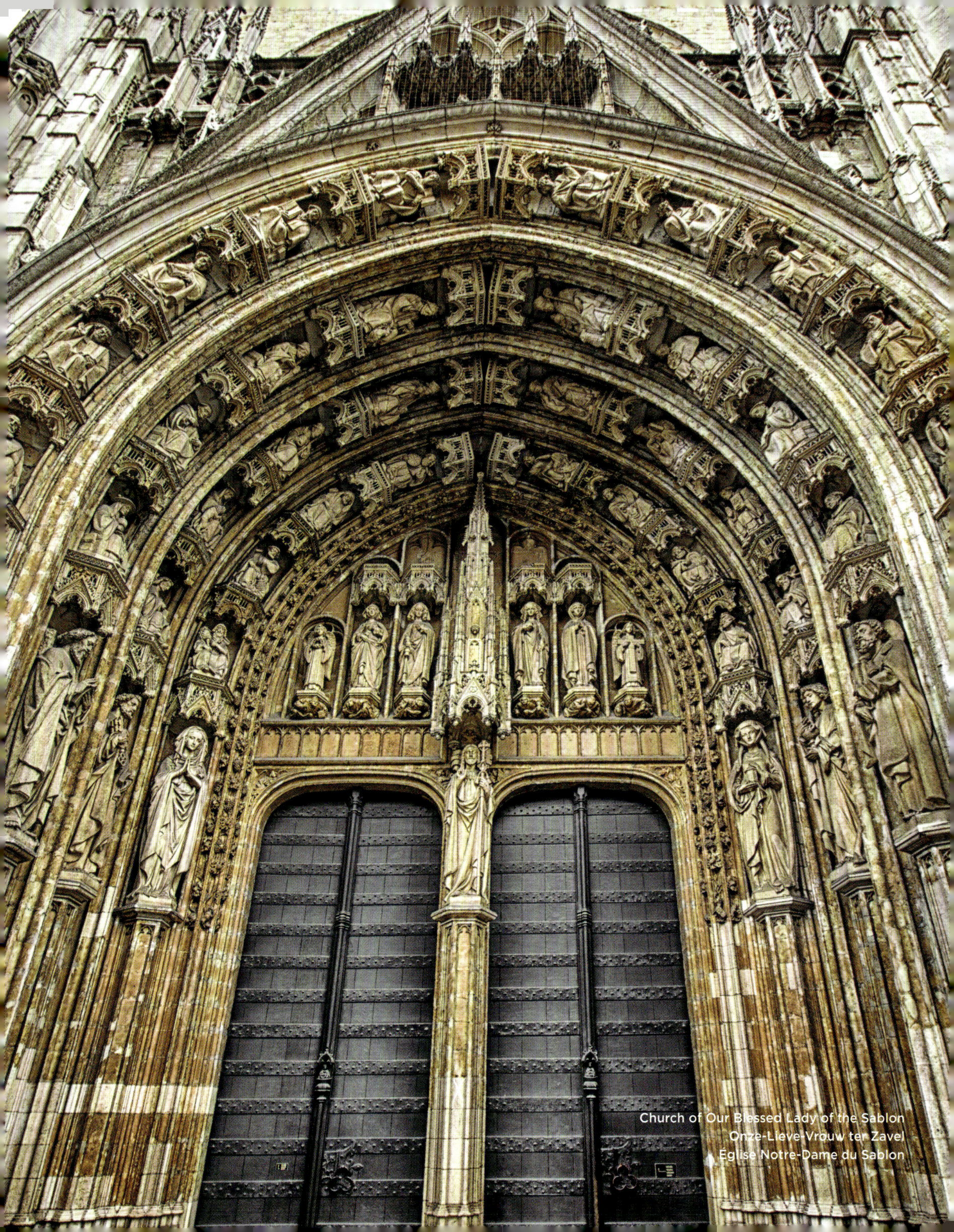

Church of Our Blessed Lady of the Sablon
Onze-Lieve-Vrouw ter Zavel
Église Notre-Dame du Sablon

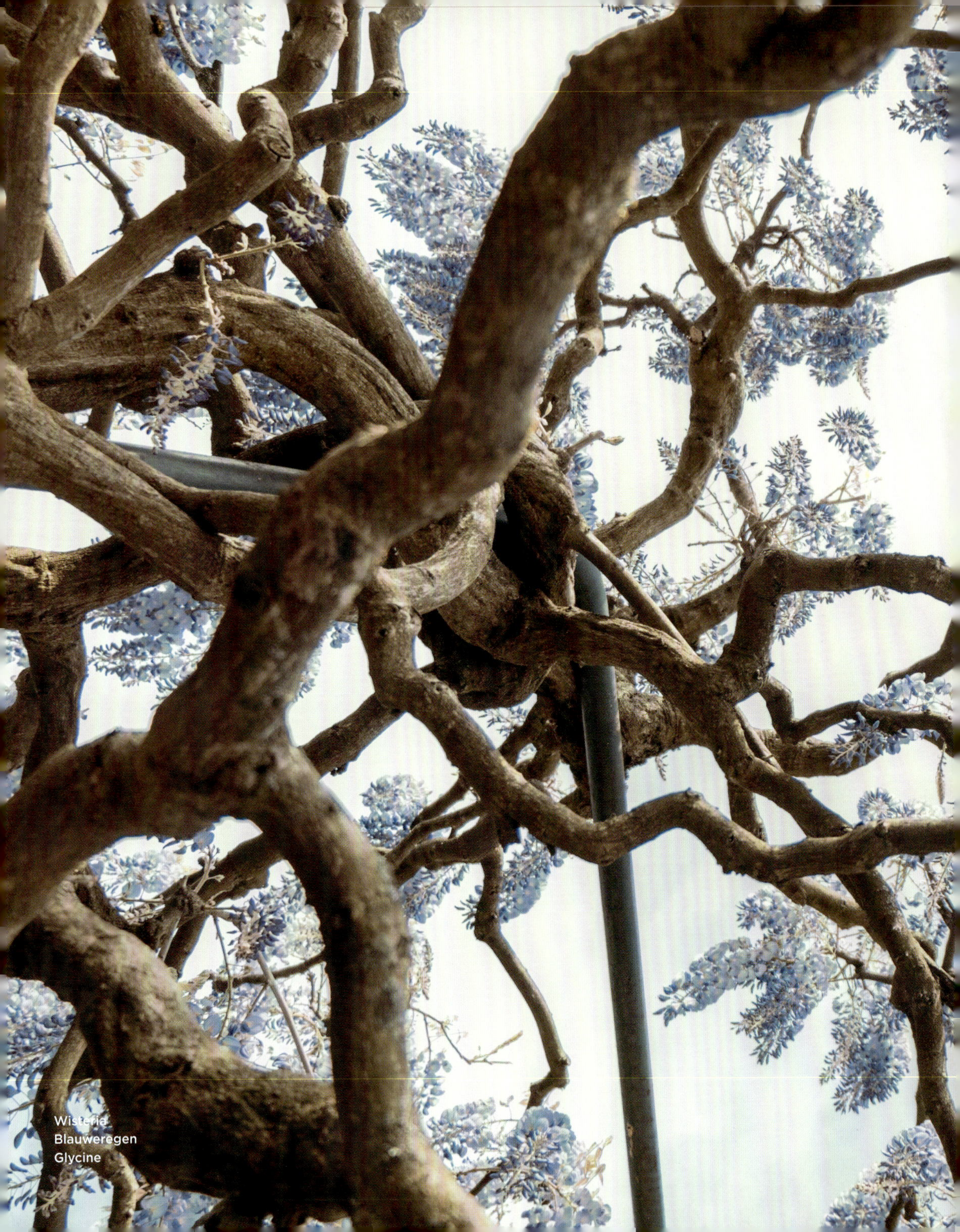
Wisteria
Blauweregen
Glycine

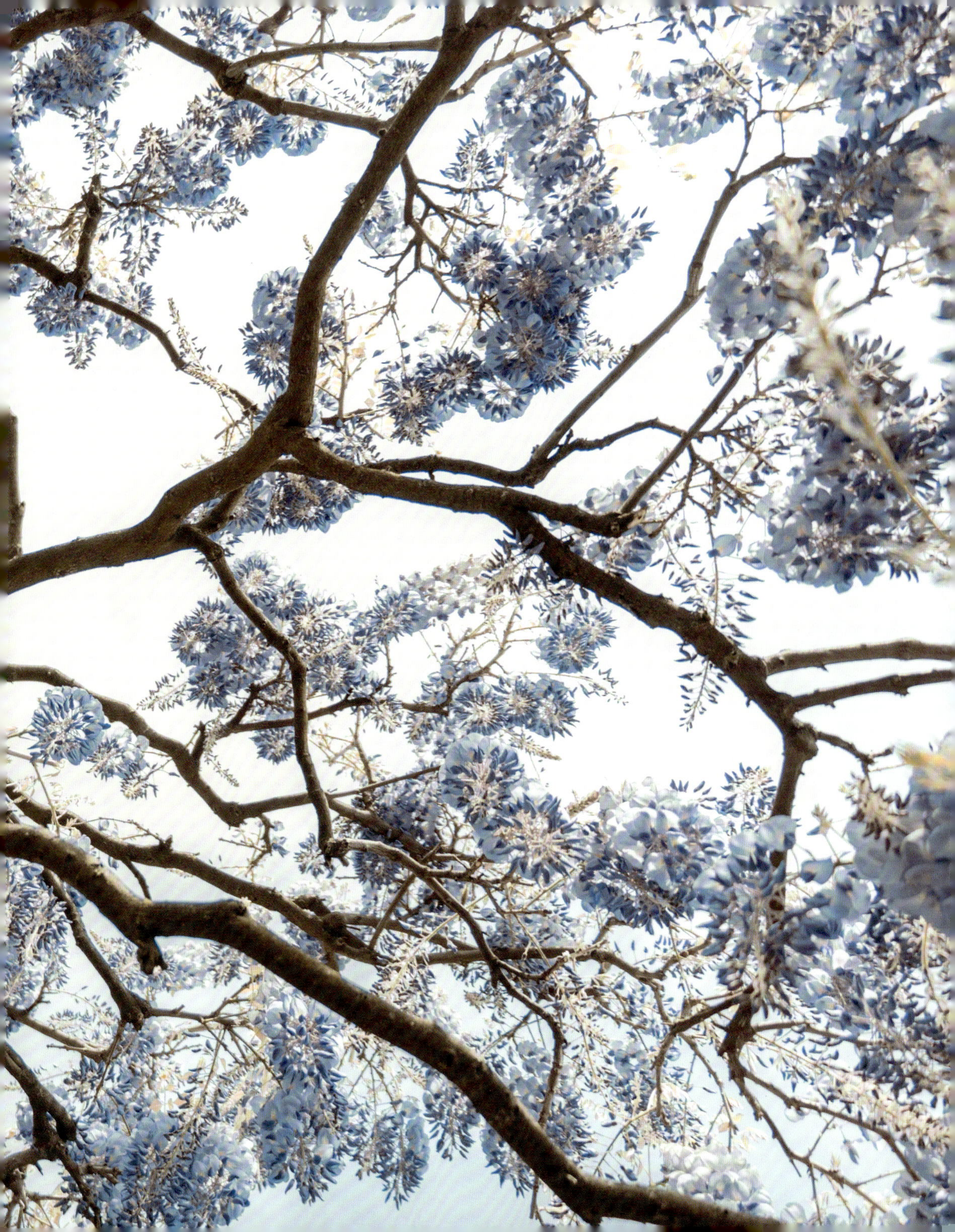

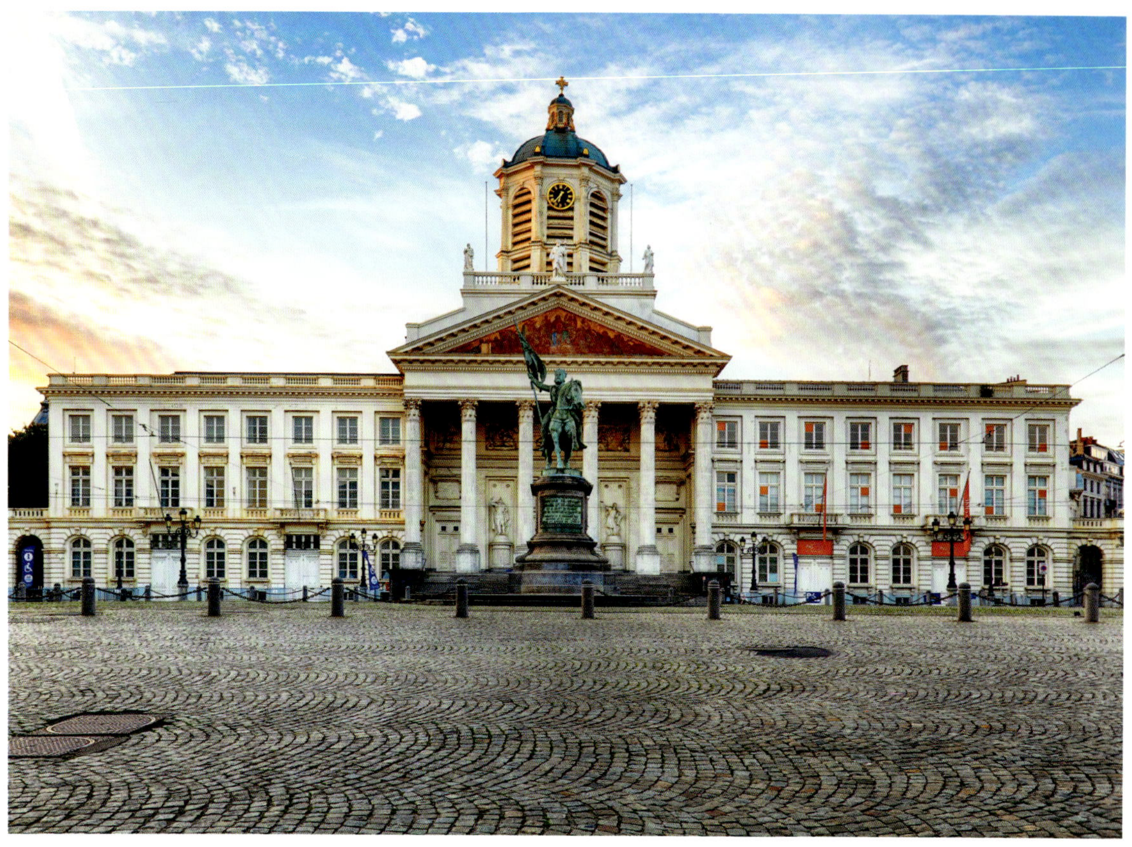

Church of Saint-Jacques on the Coudenberg and statue of Godfrey of Bouillon, Place Royale
Sint-Jacob-op-Koudenberg en standbeeld van Godfried van Bouillon, Koningsplein
L'église Saint-Jacques-sur-Coudenberg et la statue de Godefroid de Bouillon, place Royale

Centre for Fine Arts

Also known as BOZAR, it is perhaps the most important cultural and artistic centre in Belgium. Over more than 4000 sq m (43,056 sq ft), one may experience top-class international exhibitions, concerts, theatre, dance, literature and conferences all under one roof. Victor Horta's Art Deco Palace is also one of Brussels' great architectural treasures. The Place Royale, on a hill next to the Royal Palace, is flanked by large neoclassical white palaces. In one of these magnificent buildings, Brussels has dedicated a large museum to its famous son, the surrealist René Magritte.

Centre artistique

Le BOZAR est un centre culturel et artistique de premier ordre si ce n'est le plus important de Belgique. Sur plus de 4000 m² sont réunis des expositions internationales de premier ordre, des concerts, du théâtre, de la danse, de la littérature et des conférences. Le palais Art déco signé Victor Horta fait également partie des grands trésors architecturaux de Bruxelles. La Königsplatz, située en hauteur à côté du palais royal, est bordée de grands palais blancs néoclassiques. Dans l'un de ces somptueux bâtiments, Bruxelles a dédié un grand musée à son célèbre fils, le surréaliste René Magritte.

Zentrum der Kunst

Das BOZAR ist vielleicht das bedeutendste Kultur- und Kunstzentrum Belgiens. Auf mehr als 4000 m² gibt es hochkarätige internationale Ausstellungen, Konzerte, Theater, Tanz, Literatur und Konferenzen unter einem Dach. Der Art-déco-Palast aus der Feder Victor Hortas ist zudem einer der großen architektonischen Schätze Brüssels. Der Königsplatz, auf einer Anhöhe neben dem königlichen Palast, wird von großen neoklassizistischen weißen Palästen eingerahmt. In einem dieser Prachtbauten hat Brüssel ihrem berühmten Sohn, dem Surrealisten René Magritte, ein großes Museum gewidmet.

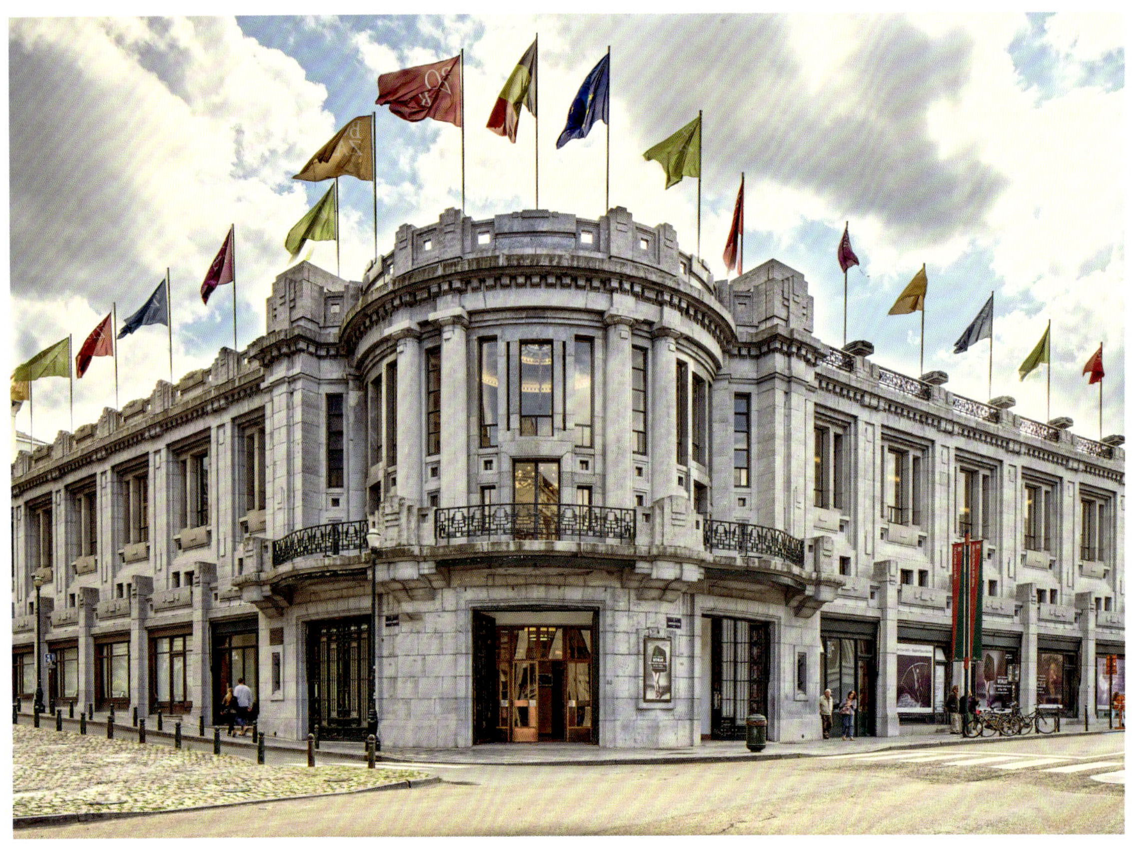

Centre for Fine Arts
BOZAR Paleis voor Schone Kunsten
Palais des Beaux-Arts de Bruxelles

Centro de arte

BOZAR es quizás el centro cultural y artístico más importante de Bélgica. En más de 4000 m² se celebran exposiciones internacionales de primera clase, conciertos, teatro, danza, literatura y conferencias bajo un mismo techo. El palacio Art Déco de Victor Horta es también uno de los grandes tesoros arquitectónicos de Bruselas. La Plaza Real, en una colina junto al Palacio Real, está enmarcada por grandes palacios blancos neoclásicos. En uno de estos magníficos edificios, Bruselas ha dedicado un gran museo a su famoso hijo, el surrealista René Magritte.

Centro de Arte

O BOZAR é talvez o mais importante centro cultural e artístico da Bélgica. Em mais de 4000 m² há exposições internacionais de primeira classe, concertos, teatro, dança, literatura e conferências sob o mesmo teto. O Palácio Art Deco de Victor Horta é também um dos grandes tesouros arquitetónicos de Bruxelas. A Praça Real, em uma colina ao lado do Palácio Real de Bruxelas, é emoldurada por grandes palácios brancos neoclássicos. Num destes magníficos edifícios, Bruxelas dedicou um grande museu ao seu famoso filho, o surrealista René Magritte.

Centrum van Kunst

BOZAR is misschien wel het belangrijkste cultuur- en kunstcentrum van België. Op meer dan 4000 m² zijn er internationale toptentoonstellingen, concerten, theater- en dansvoorstellingen, literaire evenementen en conferenties onder één dak. Het art-deco paleis van Victor Horta is bovendien één van de grote architectonische schatten van Brussel. Het Koningsplein, op dezelfde hoogte naast het Koninklijk Paleis, wordt omlijst door grote neoklassieke, witte paleizen. In n van deze prachtige gebouwen heeft Brussel een groot museum aan zijn beroemde zoon, de surrealist René Magritte, gewijd.

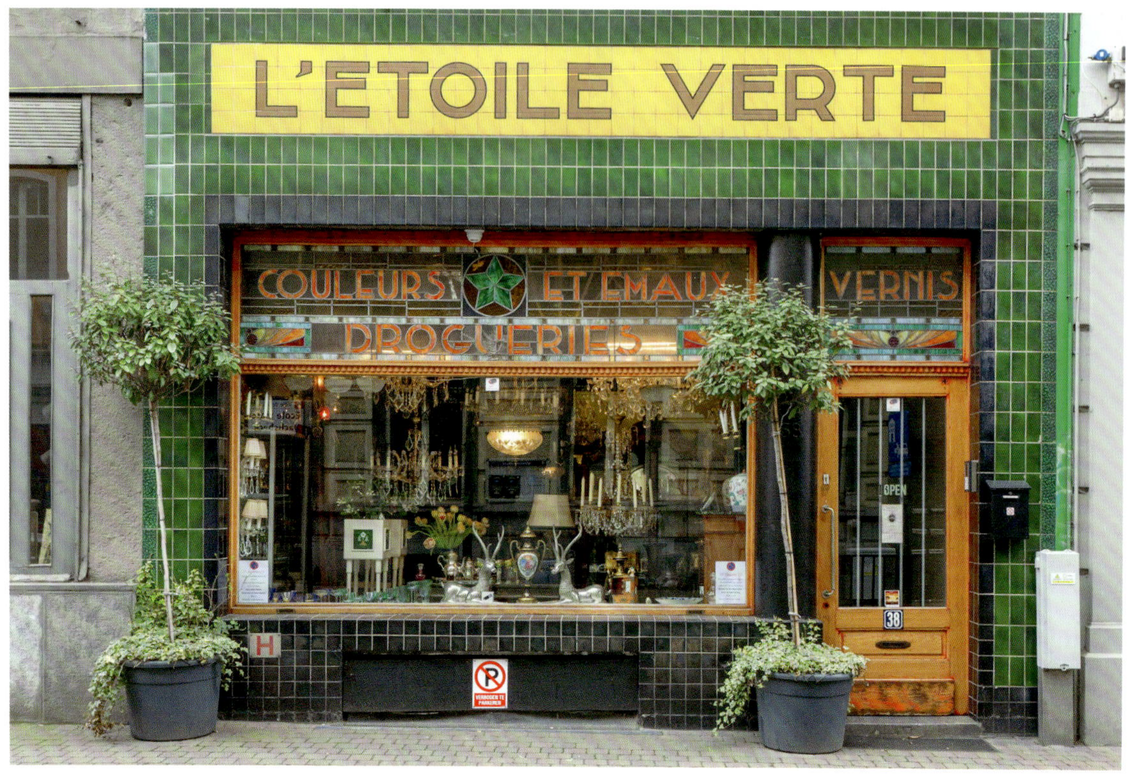

Antique store
Antiekwinkel
Magasin d'antiquités

Marolles Quarter

At the foot of the pompous Palace of Justice are the streets of the traders who work the daily flea market on the Place du Jeu de Balle. The ancient quarter, where the painter Breugel once lived, has evolved from a neglected working-class area into a colorful multicultural neighborhood with street art, numerous art galleries and furniture stores.

Barrio Marolles

Al pie del pomposo Palacio de Justicia se encuentran las calles de los comerciantes de baratijas y el mercadillo diario en la Place du Jeu de balle. El antiguo barrio donde vivió el pintor Breugel ha evolucionado, pasando de ser un barrio obrero descuidado a ser un colorido barrio multicultural con arte callejero, numerosas galerías de arte y tiendas de muebles.

Quartier des Marolles

Au pied du majestueux Palais de Justice s'étendent les rues des brocanteurs et le marché aux puces quotidien de la place du Jeu de Balle. Cet ancien quartier ouvrier délaissé, où vivait autrefois le peintre Brueghel, est désormais devenu un lieu multiculturel coloré où se côtoient le street art, d'innombrables galeries d'art et magasins de meubles.

Distrito de Marollen

Ao pé do pomposo Palácio da Justiça estão as ruas dos comerciantes de pulgas e o mercado diário de pulgas na Place du Jeu de Balle. O bairro antigo, onde já viveu o pintor Breugel, evoluiu de um bairro negligenciado da classe trabalhadora para um bairro multicultural colorido com arte de rua, inúmeras galerias de arte e lojas de design de interiores.

Marollen-Viertel

Zu Füßen des pompösen Justizpalastes erstrecken sich die Straßen der Trödelhändler und der tägliche Flohmarkt am Place du Jeu de Balle. Das uralte Viertel, in dem einst der Maler Breugel lebte, hat sich von einem vernachlässigten Arbeiterviertel zu einem bunten Multikulti-Stadtteil mit Street-Art, zahlreichen Kunstgalerien und Einrichtungsläden entwickelt.

De Marollen

Aan de voet van het pompeuze Justitiepaleis liggen de straten van de vlooienhandelaren en de dagelijkse rommelmarkt op het Vossenplein (Place du Jeu de Balle). De oeroude wijk waar ooit de schilder Breugel woonde, heeft zich van een verwaarloosde arbeiderswijk in een kleurrijke, multiculturele wijk met straatkunst, talrijke kunstgaleries en meubelzaken ontwikkeld.

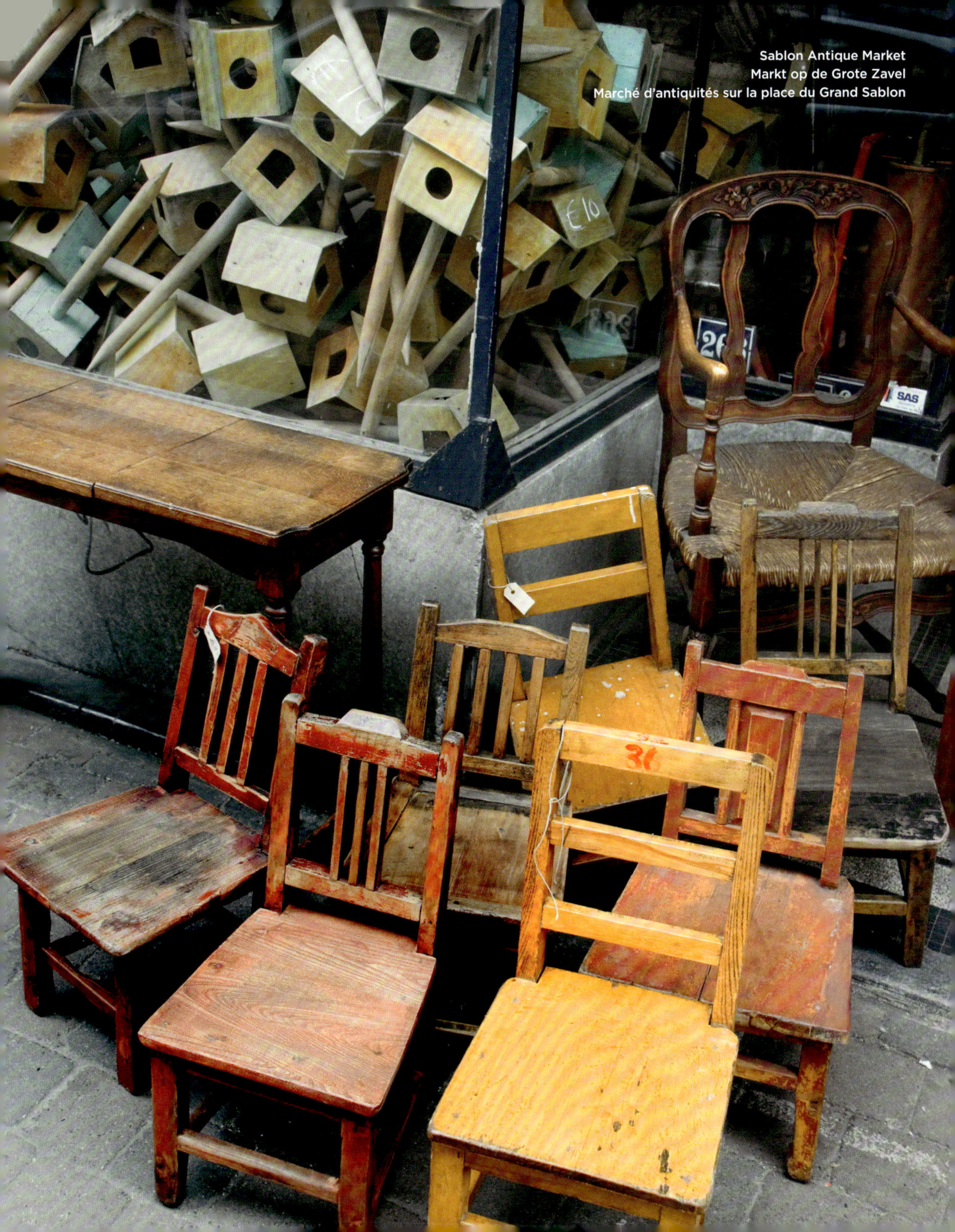

Sablon Antique Market
Markt op de Grote Zavel
Marché d'antiquités sur la place du Grand Sablon

Grand Sablon Square

Brussels is the perfect place for those who like to browse flea markets and search for antiques. In particular, the area around the Grand Sablon square is a Mecca for antique dealers and forms the backdrop for their market on weekends. The square is framed by superior antique shops, boutiques, restaurants and some of the finest Belgian chocolatiers.

Grand Sablon

Bruxelles comble tout amateur de brocantes et d'antiquités. La zone du Grand Sablon et de ses alentours, notamment, est la Mecque des antiquaires et elle accueille leur marché le week-end. La place est bordée d'élégants magasins d'antiquités, de boutiques, de restaurants et de quelques-uns des chocolatiers belges les plus éminents.

Grand Sablon

Wer gern auf Flohmärkten stöbert und nach Antiquitäten sucht, ist in Brüssel genau richtig. Insbesondere die Gegend rund um den Grand Sablon ist das Mekka der Antiquitätenhändler und bildet am Wochenende die Kulisse für ihren Markt. Eingerahmt wird der Platz von edlen Antiquitätengeschäften, Boutiquen, Restaurants und einigen der feinsten belgischen Chocolatiers.

Grand Sablon

Bruselas es el lugar perfecto para los amantes de los mercadillos y de la búsqueda de antigüedades. En particular, la zona alrededor del Grand Sablon es la meca de los anticuarios y constituye el telón de fondo de su mercado los fines de semana. La plaza está enmarcada por nobles tiendas de antigüedades, boutiques, restaurantes y algunas de los mejores chocolaterías belgas.

Grand Sablon

Bruxelas é o lugar perfeito para aqueles que gostam de passear pelos mercados de pulgas e procurar antiguidades. Em especial, a zona em torno Praça de Grand Sablon é a Meca dos antiquários e serve de cenário para o seu mercado nos fins-de-semana. A praça é emoldurada por nobres lojas de antiguidades, boutiques, restaurantes e alguns dos melhores chocolatiers belgas.

Grote Zavel

Wie graag over vlooienmarkten struint en naar antiquiteiten zoekt, is in Brussel op de juiste plek. Vooral het gebied rond de Grote Zavel is het Mekka van de antiekhandelaren en vormt in het weekend het decor voor hun markt. Het plein wordt omlijst door edele antiekwinkels, boetieks, restaurants en enkele van de beste Belgische chocolatiers.

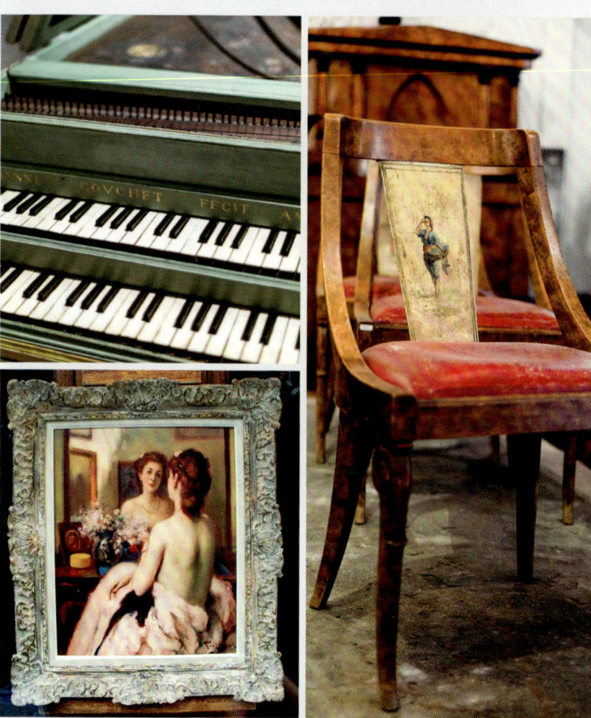

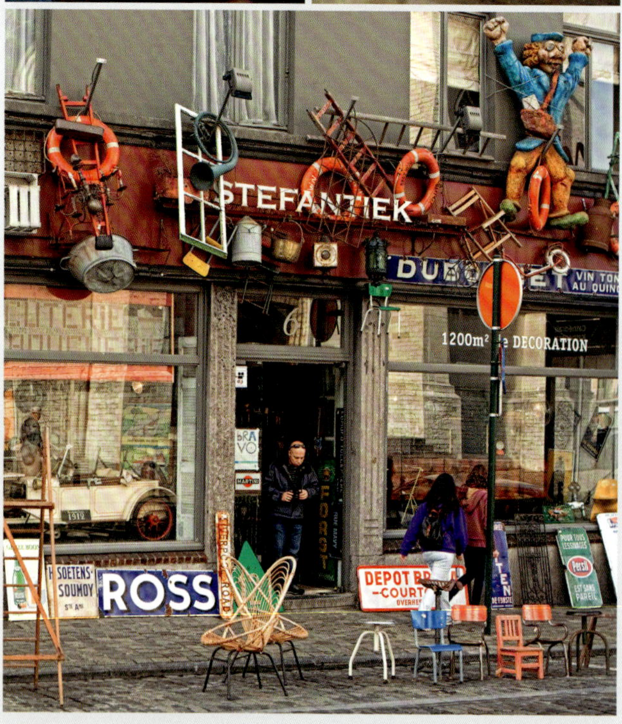

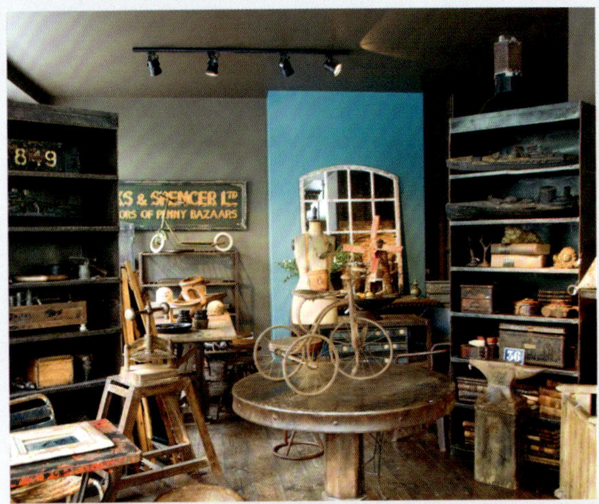
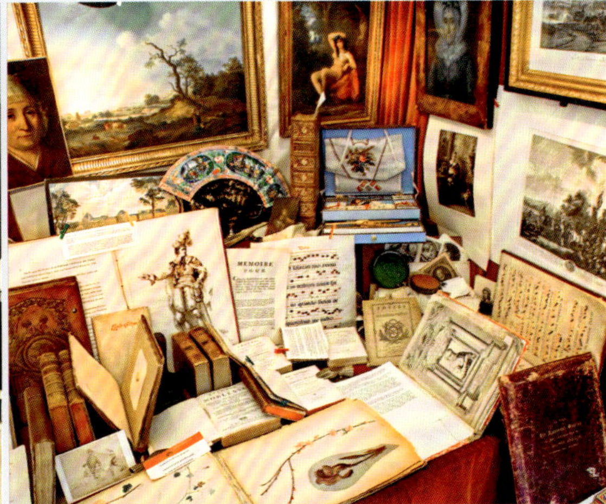
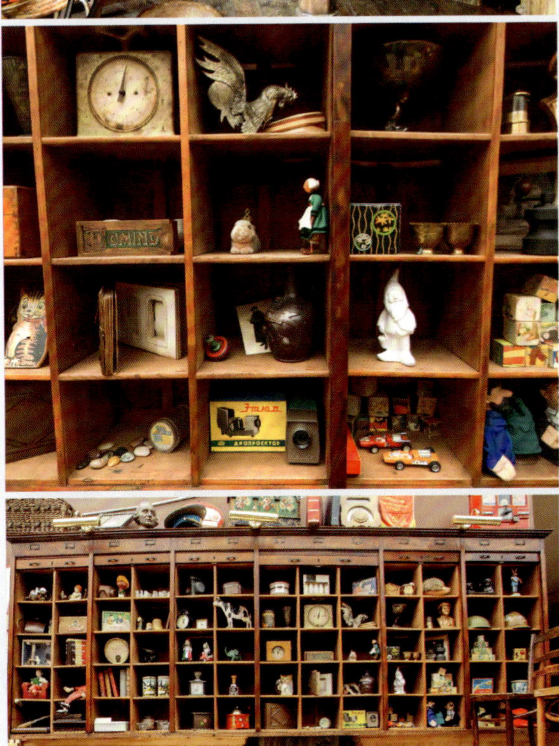
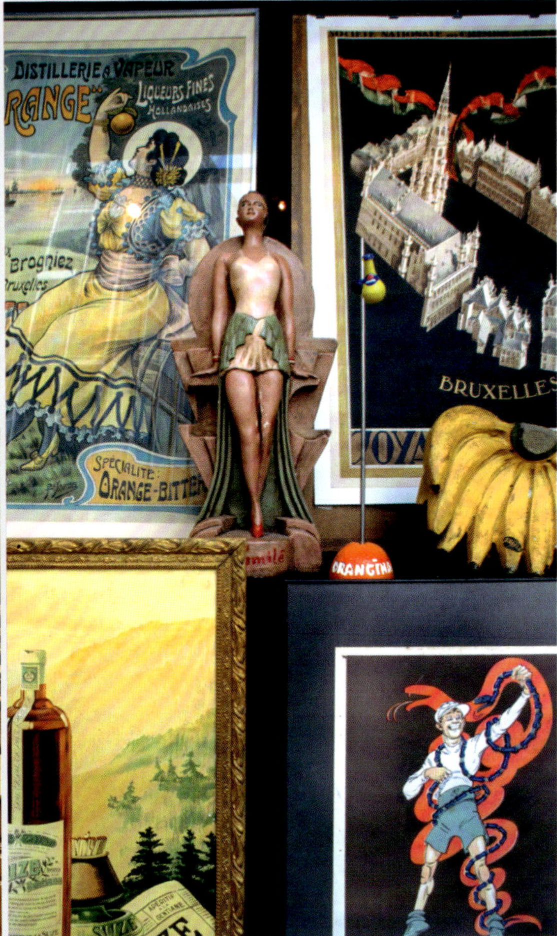

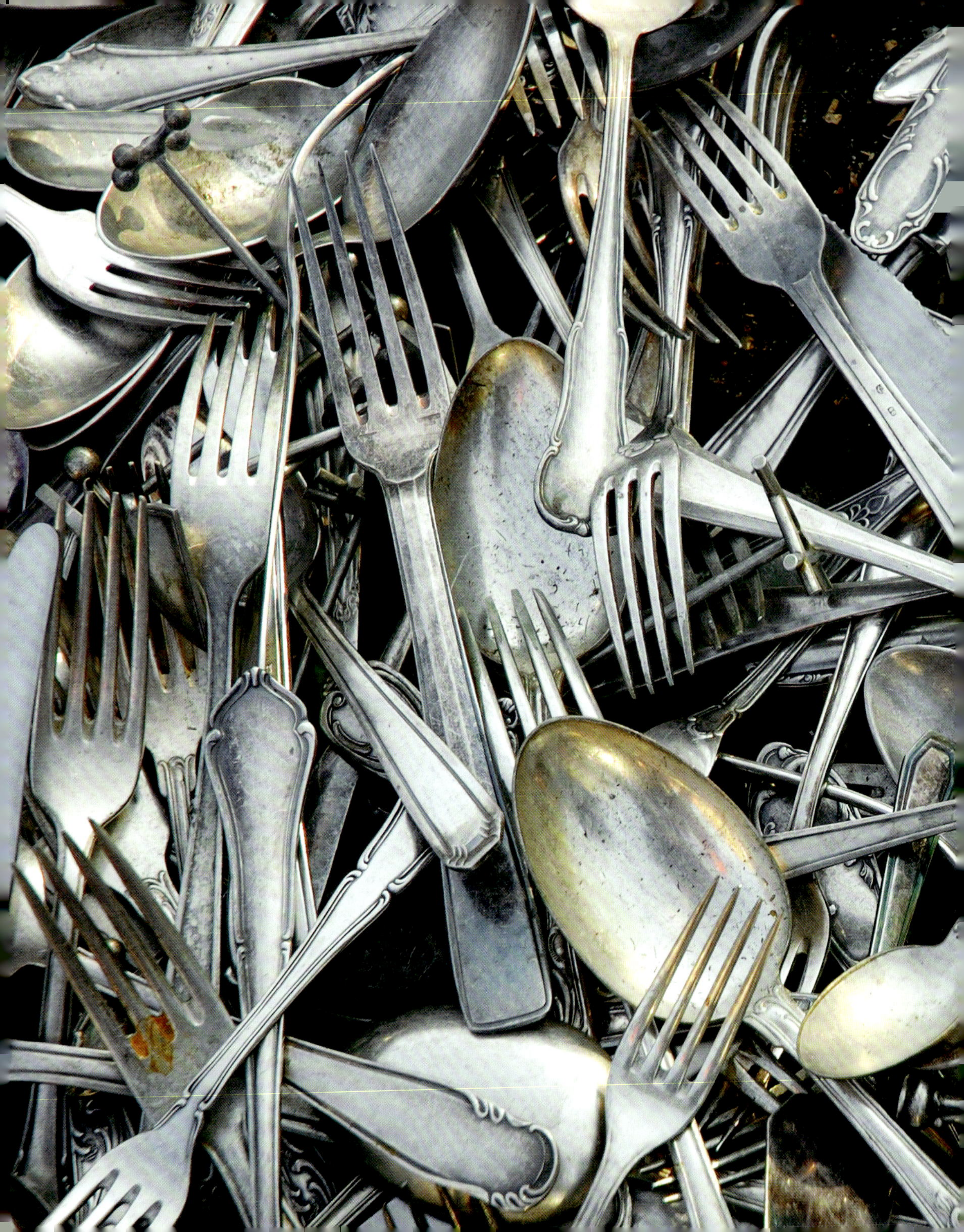

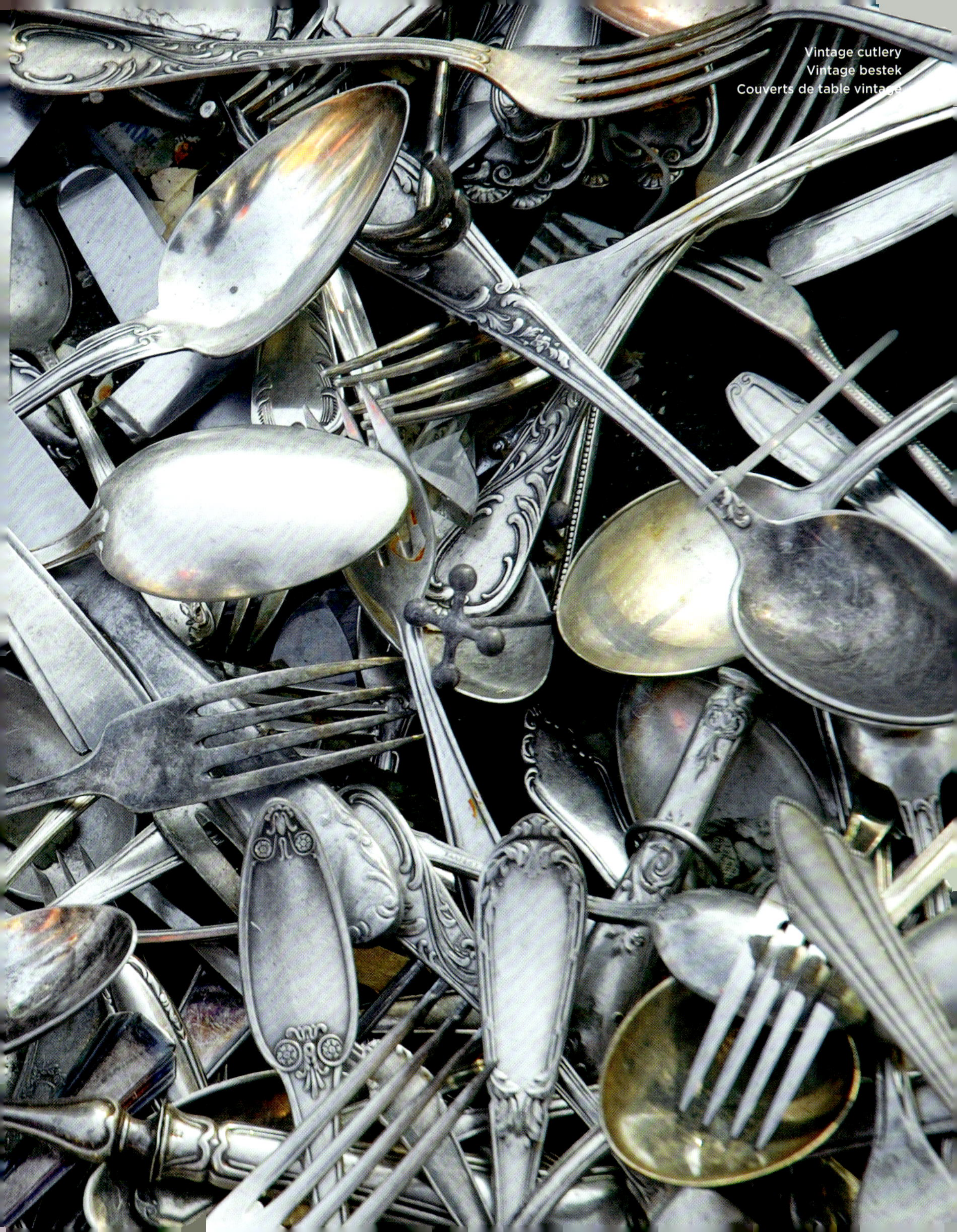
Vintage cutlery
Vintage bestek
Couverts de table vintage

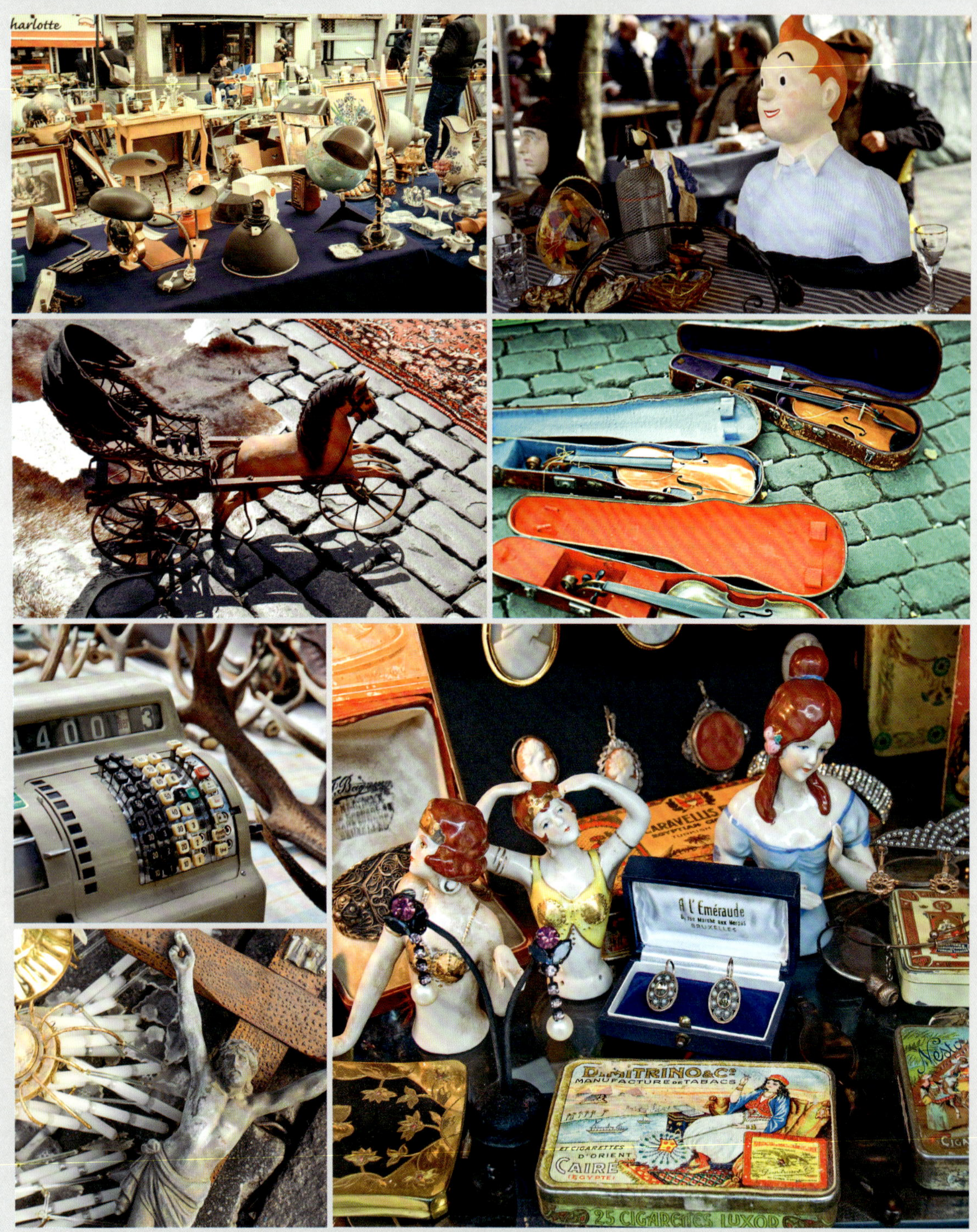

harlotte

Place du Jeu de Balle

On the Place du Jeu de Balle, a daily flea market has been held since 1873, which is an exception even in flea market-mad Flanders. From the extremely cheap to the highly expensive, around 200 stalls offer articles of all kinds, including paintings, furniture, household utensils and toys. Prices may range from a few cents to several thousand euros. On weekends the prices are often twice as high as during the week.

Place du Jeu de Balle

Auf der Place du Jeu de Balle, findet seit 1873 täglich ein Flohmarkt statt, was selbst im flohmarktverrückten Flandern eine Besonderheit ist. Von spottbillig bis edel, rund 200 Stände bieten Trödel aller Art an: Gemälde, Möbel, Haushaltsutensilien und Spielsachen. Die Preise reichen von wenigen Cent bis zu mehreren Tausend Euro. Am Wochenende sind die Preise oft doppelt so hoch wie unter der Woche.

Place du Jeu de Balle

La place du Jeu de Balle accueille un marché aux puces quotidien depuis 1873: même en Flandres, où les brocantes sont très populaires, il s'agit d'un état de fait exceptionnel. Environ 200 stands vendent un joyeux bric-à-brac, tant de la pacotille que des objets des plus raffinés: tableaux, meubles, ustensiles ménagers et jouets. Les prix varient de quelques centimes à plusieurs milliers d'euros. Le week-end, ils sont souvent deux fois plus élevés qu'en semaine.

Place du Jeu de Balle

En la Place du Jeu de Balle se celebra desde 1873 un rastro diario, que es una característica especial incluso en Flandes, la región de los mercadillos. Unos 200 puestos ofrecen artículos de todo tipo: pinturas, muebles, utensilios domésticos y juguetes, desde muy baratos hasta realmente costosos (los precios oscilan entre unos pocos céntimos y varios miles de euros). Los fines de semana los precios suelen ser dos veces más altos que entre semana.

Place du Jeu de Balle

Na Place du Jeu de Balle, um mercado de pulgas ocorre todos os dias desde 1873, o que constitui uma particularidade, mesmo na Flandres, onde são loucos por mercados de pulgas. Do barato ao nobre, cerca de 200 barracas oferecem objetos antigos de todos os tipos: pinturas, móveis, utensílios domésticos e brinquedos. Os preços variam entre alguns cêntimos e vários milhares de euros. Nos fins de semana os preços são frequentemente duas vezes mais altos do que durante a semana.

Vossenplein

Sinds 1873 vindt op het Vossenplein dagelijks een rommelmarkt plaats. Dat is zelfs in het door vlooienmarkten bezeten Vlaanderen bijzonder. Van spotgoedkoop tot edel, ca. 200 kraampjes bieden spullen in alle soorten en maten aan: schilderijen, meubels, huishoudelijke artikelen en speelgoed. Prijzen variëren van een paar cent tot duizenden euro's. In het weekend zijn de prijzen vaak dubbel zo hoog dan door de week.

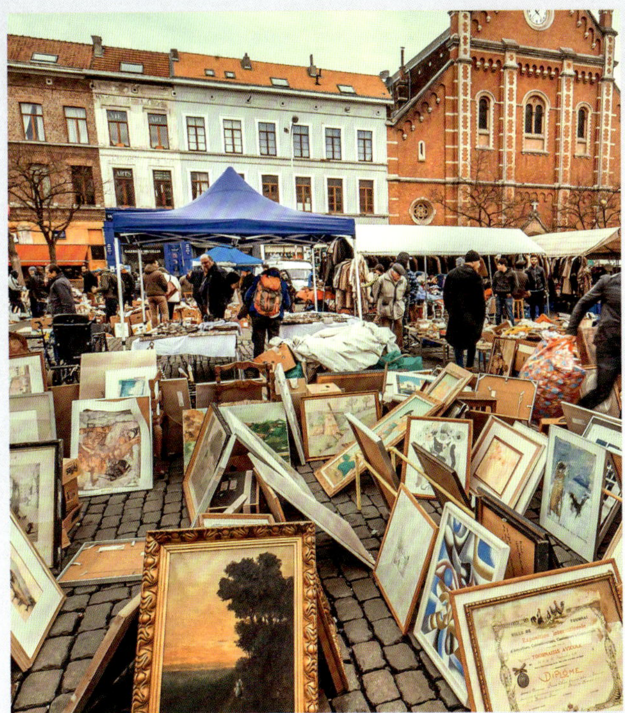

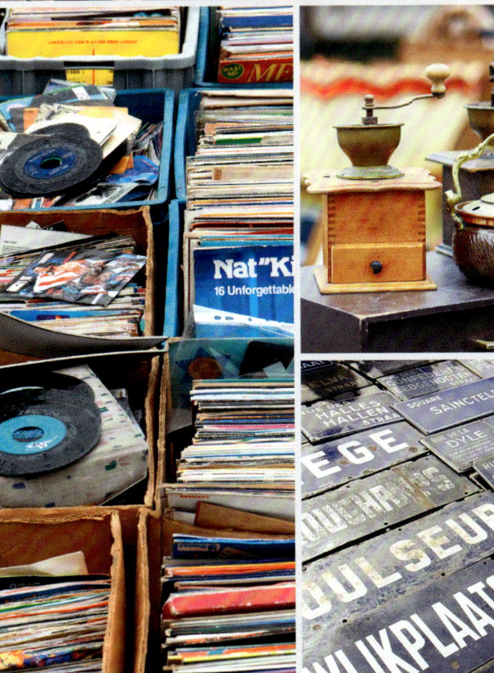

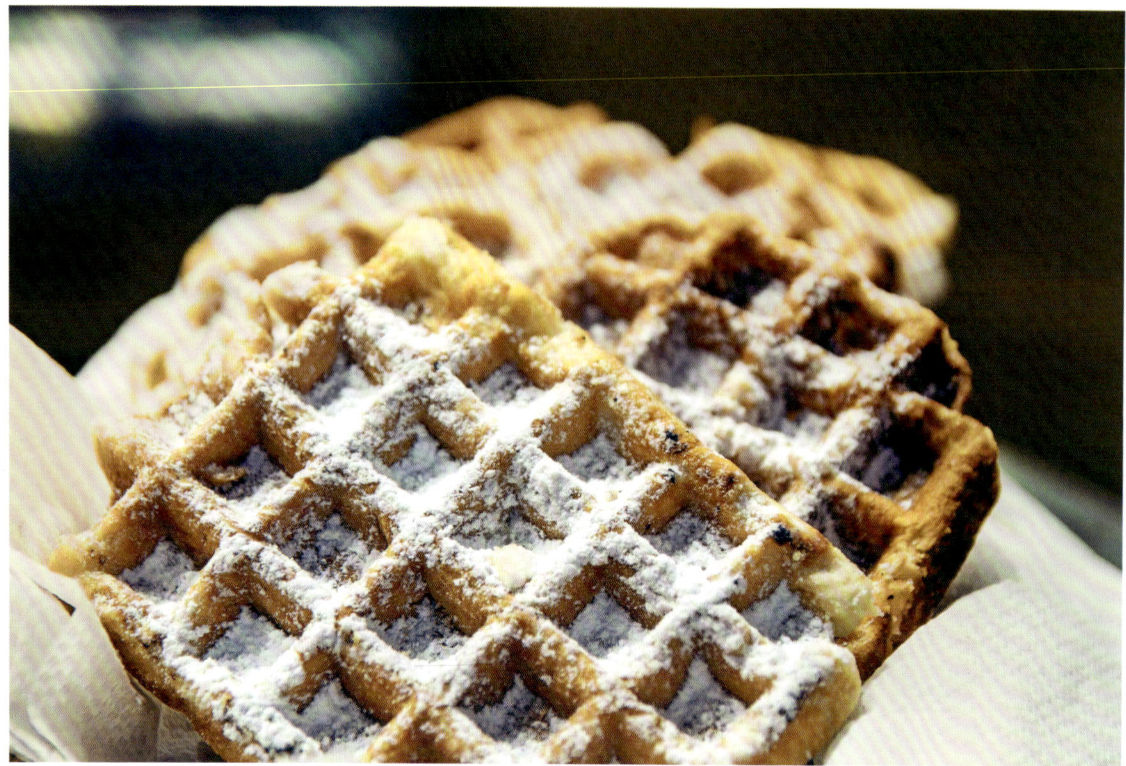

Belgian waffles
Wafels
Gaufres

Brussels waffles

For those who like it crispy on the outside and light and airy on the inside, Brussels waffles are the right choice. In Flanders, most waffles are served warm by street vendors. Despite their name, "Brussels waffles" were invented in Ghent, but Maurice Vermersch presented them at the 1964 World Fair in New York as Brussels waffles.

Gofre de Bruselas

Para aquellos a los que les gusta crujiente por fuera y ligero y blandito por dentro, los gofres de Bruselas son la elección correcta. En Flandes, la mayoría de los gofres son servidos calientes por vendedores ambulantes. A pesar de su nombre, "gofres de Bruselas", fueron inventados en Gante, pero Maurice Vermersch los presentó en la Feria Mundial de Nueva York de 1964 como gofres de Bruselas.

Gaufres de Bruxelles

Les gaufres de Bruxelles régaleront tout amateur de gourmandises croustillantes à l'extérieur, légères et moelleuses à l'intérieur. En Flandres, la plupart des gaufres sont servies chaudes par des vendeurs ambulants. Malgré leur nom, c'est à Gand qu'elles virent le jour, mais Maurice Vermersch les appela gaufres de Bruxelles lorsqu'il les présenta à l'Exposition universelle de New York en 1964.

Waffles de Bruxelas

Para aqueles que gostam de crocantes por fora e um pouco macios por dentro, os waffles de Bruxelas são a escolha certa. Na Flandres, a maioria dos waffles é servida quente por vendedores ambulantes. Apesar do seu nome, "waffles de Bruxelas", foram inventados em Gante, mas Maurice Vermersch apresentou-os na Feira Mundial de 1964 em Nova Iorque como "waffles de Bruxelas".

Brüsseler Waffeln

Wer es außen knusprig und innen locker-leicht mag, der ist bei den Waffeln aus Brüssel genau richtig. In Flandern werden die meisten Waffeln warm von Straßenhändlern serviert. Trotz ihres Namens „Brüsseler Waffeln" wurden sie in Gent erfunden, aber Maurice Vermersch präsentierte sie auf der Weltausstellung 1964 in New York als Brüsseler Waffeln.

Brusselse wafels

Wie knapperig van buiten en licht en luchtig binnenin prefereert, die komt met de Brusselse wafels aan zijn trekken. In Vlaanderen worden de meeste wafels warm door straatverkopers geserveerd. Ondanks hun naam "Brusselse wafels" werden ze in Gent uitgevonden, maar Maurice Vermersch presenteerde ze op de Wereldtentoonstelling van 1964 in New York als Brusselse wafels.

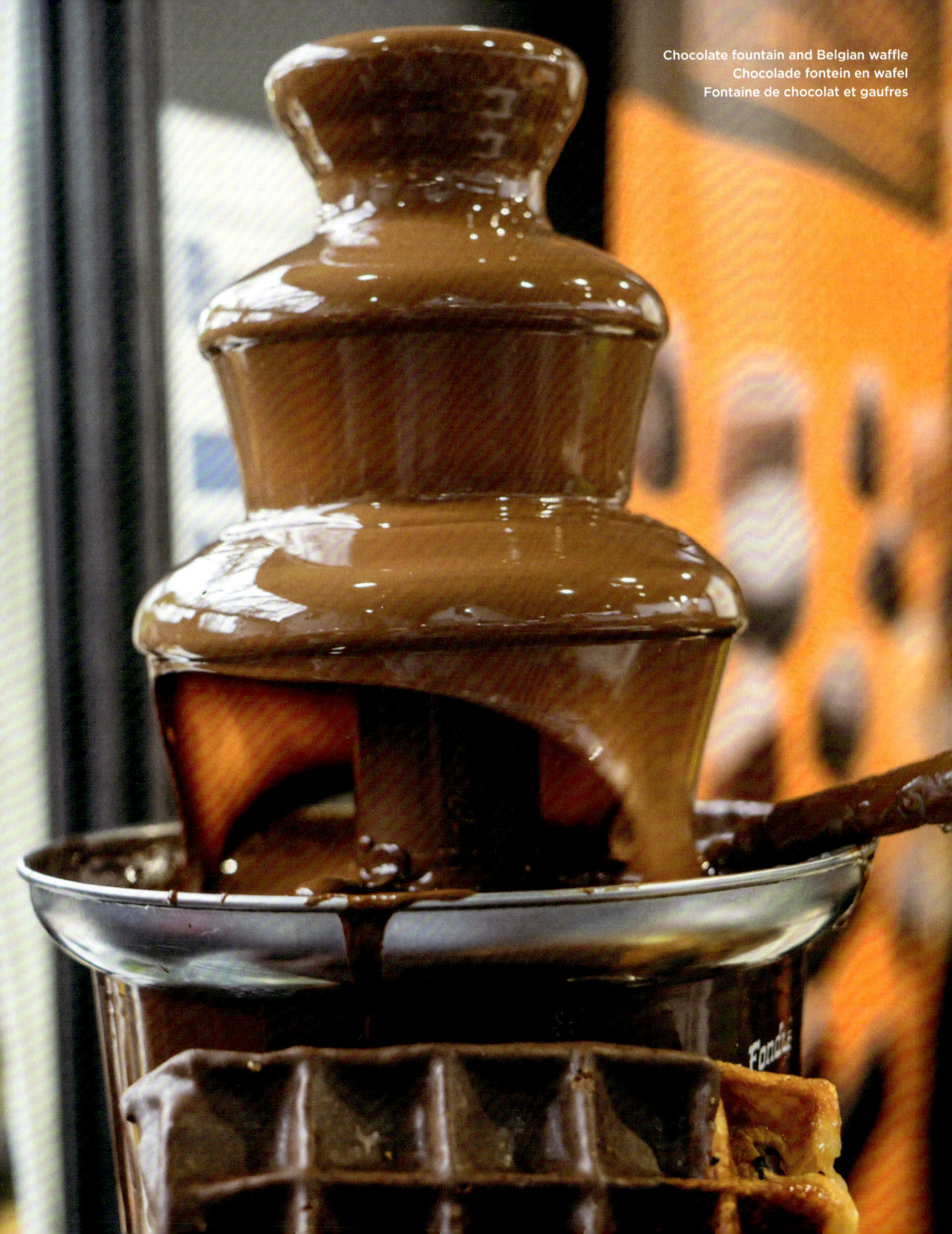
Chocolate fountain and Belgian waffle
Chocolade fontein en wafel
Fontaine de chocolat et gaufres

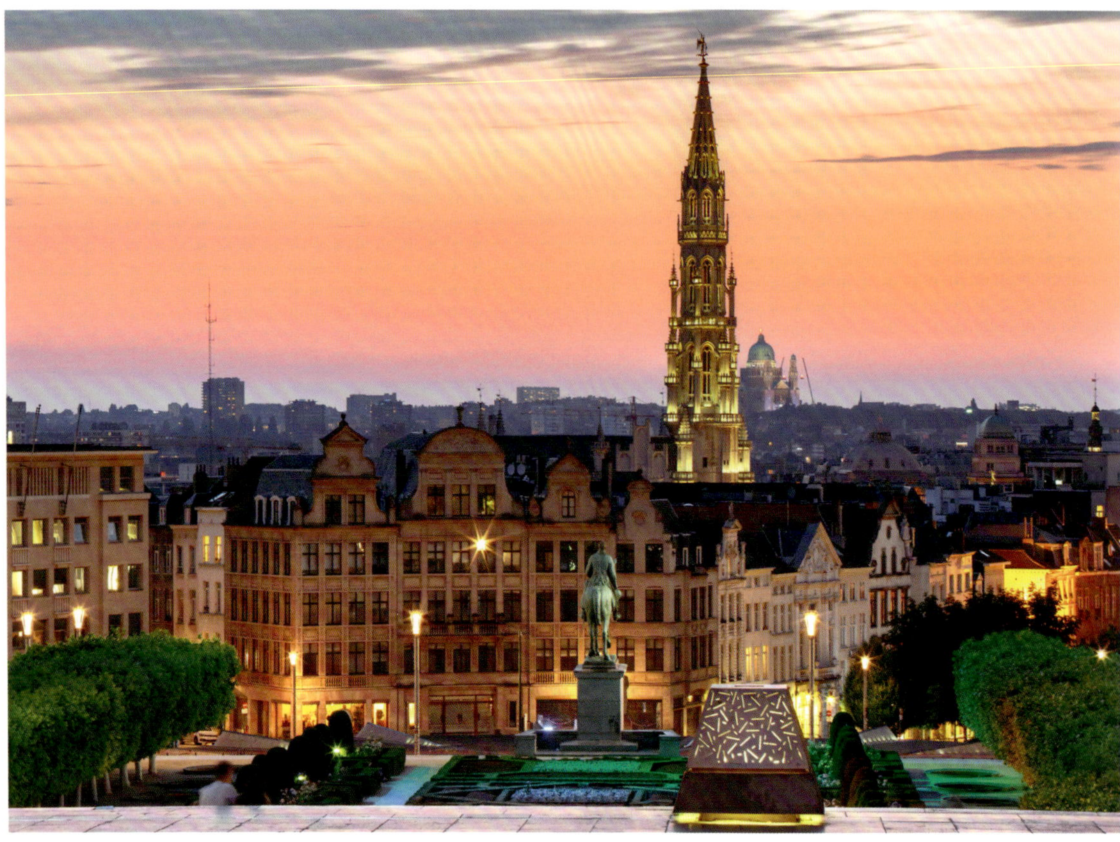

View from Kunstgerg (Hill of Arts), Brussels Town Hall
Ultzicht vanuit het kunstberg, stadhuis
Vue du monts des Arts, hôtel de ville

Mont des Art / Kunstberg

The Kunstberg (Hill of the Arts) offers one of the finest views of Brussels, including the Gothic Town Hall. If the weather is fine, the view extends as far as the National Basilica and the Atomium. Under Leopold II, the hill was converted into a Museum Mile. In the centre there is a park, which is surrounded by numerous museums. Particularly worth seeing are the Royal Museums of Fine Arts of Belgium, with their large collections of old art and fin-de-siècle, the Musical Instrument Museum (MIM) in an Art Nouveau building and the Magritte Museum. The equestrian statue depicts King Albert I, who promoted the democratisation of his country.

Musées du Mont des Arts

Le Mont des Arts offre une belle vue sur la ville basse de Bruxelles avec l'Hôtel de Ville. Lorsque le ciel est dégagé, cette vue s'étend jusqu'à la Basilique nationale et l'Atomium. Léopold II fit du Mont des Arts un quartier muséal. Au centre s'étend un parc entouré de nombreux musées. Les musées royaux des Beaux-Arts, qui abritent de vastes collections d'art ancien et fin de siècle, le musée des Instruments de musique dans le bâtiment Art nouveau et le musée Magritte méritent une visite particulière. La statue équestre représente le roi Albert Ier, qui fit avancer la démocratisation de son pays.

Museumsmeile Kunstberg

Der Kunstberg bietet einen schönen Ausblick auf die Unterstadt Brüssels mit dem Rathaus. Bei schönem Wetter reicht der Blick bis an die Nationalbasilika und das Atomium. Die Anhöhe wurde unter Leopold II. zur Museumsmeile umgebaut. Im Zentrum befindet sich ein Park, der von zahlreichen Museen umgeben wird. Besonders sehenswert sind die Königlichen Museen der Schönen Künste, mit großen Sammlungen zur alten Kunst und zum Fin-du-siècle, das Musikinstrumentenmuseum im Jugendstilgebäude und das Magritte-Museum. Das Reiterstandbild zeigt König Albert I., der die Demokratisierung seines Landes vorantrieb.

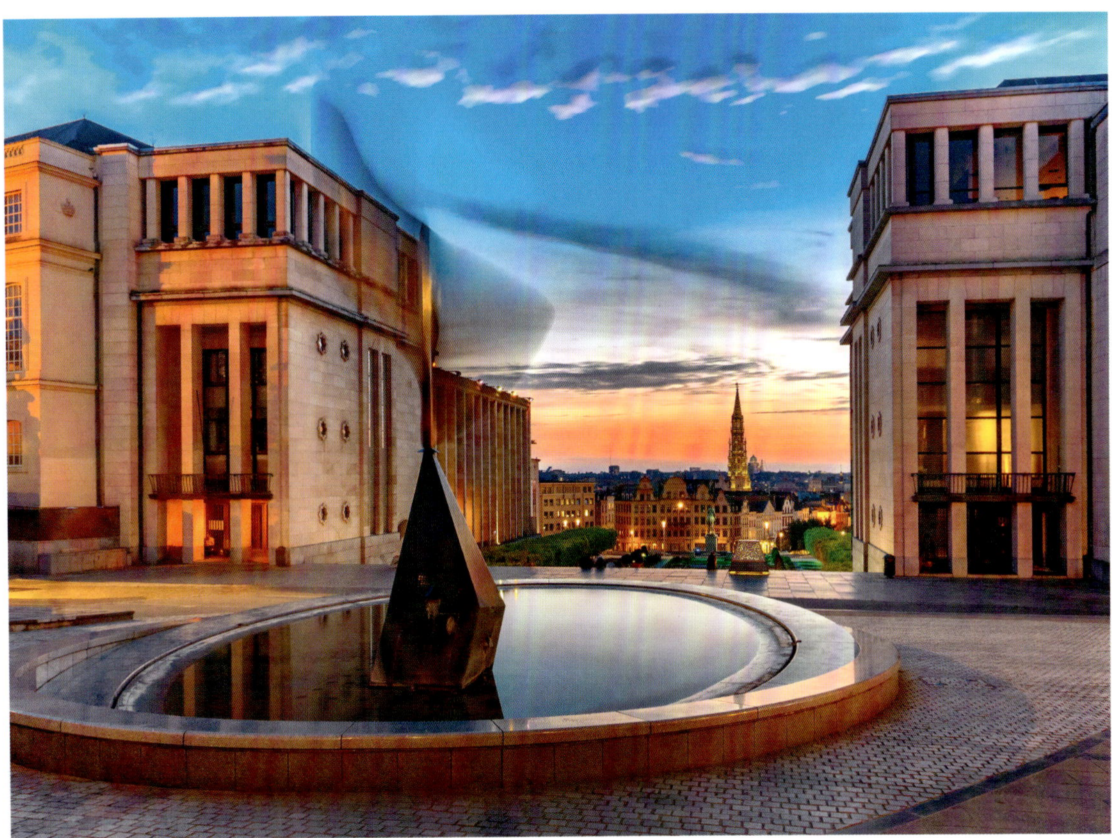

The Whirling Ear
Het Wervelend Oor
L'Oreille Tourbillonnante

Milla de museo Mont des Arts

El Mont des Arts ofrece una hermosa vista de la parte baja de la ciudad de Bruselas con el ayuntamiento. Cuando hace buen tiempo, la vista se extiende hasta la Basílica Nacional y el Atomium. Bajo el reinado de Leopoldo II, la colina se convirtió en una milla de museo. En el centro hay un parque que está rodeado de numerosos museos. Destacan los Reales Museos de Bellas Artes, con grandes colecciones de arte antiguo y Fin-du-siècle, el Museo de Instrumentos Musicales en el edificio Art Nouveau y el Museo Magritte. La estatua ecuestre muestra al Rey Alberto I, quien promovió la democratización de su país.

Milha dos Museus no Monte das Artes

O Monte das Artes oferece uma bela vista da cidade baixa de Bruxelas com a Câmara Municipal. Quando o tempo está bom, a vista estende-se até à Basílica Nacional e ao Atomium. Sob Leopoldo II, a colina foi transformada numa milha de museus. No centro há um parque, que está rodeado por numerosos museus. Particularmente dignos de nota são os Museus Reais de Belas Artes, com grandes coleções de arte antiga e Fin-du-siècle, o Museu de Instrumentos Musicais no edifício Art Nouveau e o Museu Magritte. A estátua equestre mostra o Rei Alberto I, que promoveu a democratização do seu país.

Museumwijk Kunstberg

De Kunstberg biedt een fraai uitzicht op de benedenstad van Brussel met het stadhuis. Bij mooi weer strekt het uitzicht zich uit tot de Nationale Basiliek en het Atomium. De heuvel werd onder Leopold II omgebouwd tot een museumwijk. In het centrum bevindt zich een park dat omgeven wordt door talrijke musea. Bijzonder bezienswaardig zijn de Koninklijke Musea voor Schone Kunsten van België met grote collecties oude kunst en fin de siècle, het Muziekinstrumentenmuseum in het art-nouveaugebouw en het Musée Magritte Museum. Het ruiterstandbeeld toont Koning Albert I die de democratisering van zijn land bespoedigde.

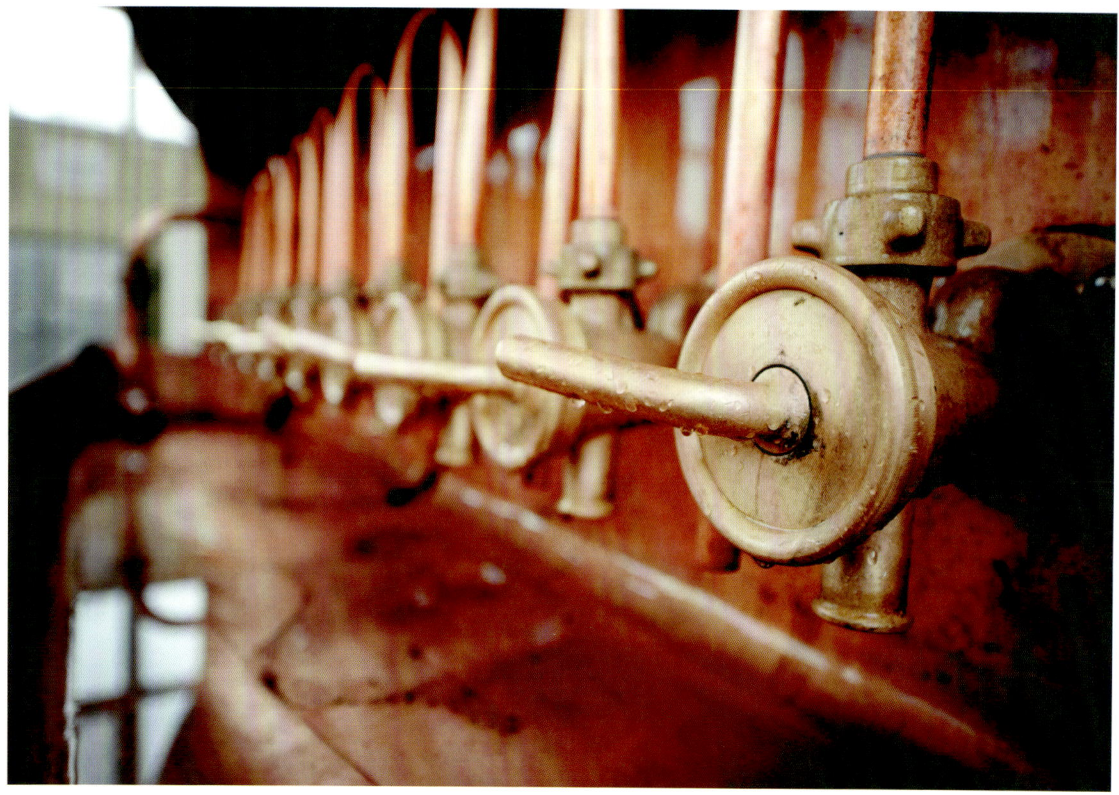

Mort Subite Brewery
Brouwerij Mort Subite
Brasserie Mort Subite

À la Mort Subite

This brasserie from the belle époque, with its high ceilings and large windows, has been featured in song by the chansonnier Jacques Brel. The brewery has this dramatic name due to the dice games which were played there, and where the loser died the "Mort Subite"(sudden death). In the restaurant you can enjoy the house beers, Geuze and Cherry beer.

À la mort subite

Esta brasserie de la Belle Époque, con techos altos y grandes ventanales, ya fue cantada por el chansonnier Jacques Brel. La cervecería tiene este nombre dramático porque solía ser un lugar de encuentro para los juegos de dados, donde el perdedor hacía de muerto por "mort subite" (muerte súbita). En el restaurante se puede disfrutar de las cervezas de la casa, Geuze y cerveza de cereza.

À la Mort Subite

Avec ses hauts plafonds et ses grandes fenêtres, cette brasserie de la Belle Époque était déjà chantée par Jacques Brel. Elle doit son nom dramatique aux jeux de dés auxquels on y jouait jadis : le perdant mourait de « mort subite ». Vous pourrez déguster ici les bières de la maison, la Gueuze et la Kriek.

À la mort subite

Esta brasserie da Belle Époque, com tetos altos e grandes janelas, já serviu de palco para o cantor belga francófono Jacques Brel. A cervejaria tem este nome dramático porque costumava ser um lugar de encontro para jogos de dados, onde o perdedor morria a "Mort Subite" (morte súbita). No restaurante você pode apreciar as cervejas da casa, Geuze e Kirschbier.

À la mort subite

Diese Brasserie aus der Belle Époque mit hohen Decken und großen Fenstern wurde schon von dem Chansonnier Jacques Brel besungen. Die Brauerei hat diesen dramatischen Namen, weil man sich hier einst zum Würfelspielen traf, bei dem der Verlierer den „Mort Subite" (Sekundentod) starb. Im Lokal kann man die Hausbiere Geuze und Kirschbier genießen.

À la Mort Subite

Deze brasserie uit de belle époque met hoge plafonds en grote ramen werd al bezongen door de chansonnier Jacques Brel. De brouwerij heeft deze dramatische naam, omdat het vroeger een ontmoetingsplaats was voor dobbelspelletjes waar de verliezer de "Mort Subite" (plotselinge dood) stierf. In het restaurant kunt u genieten van de lambiek-, geuze- en fruitbieren.

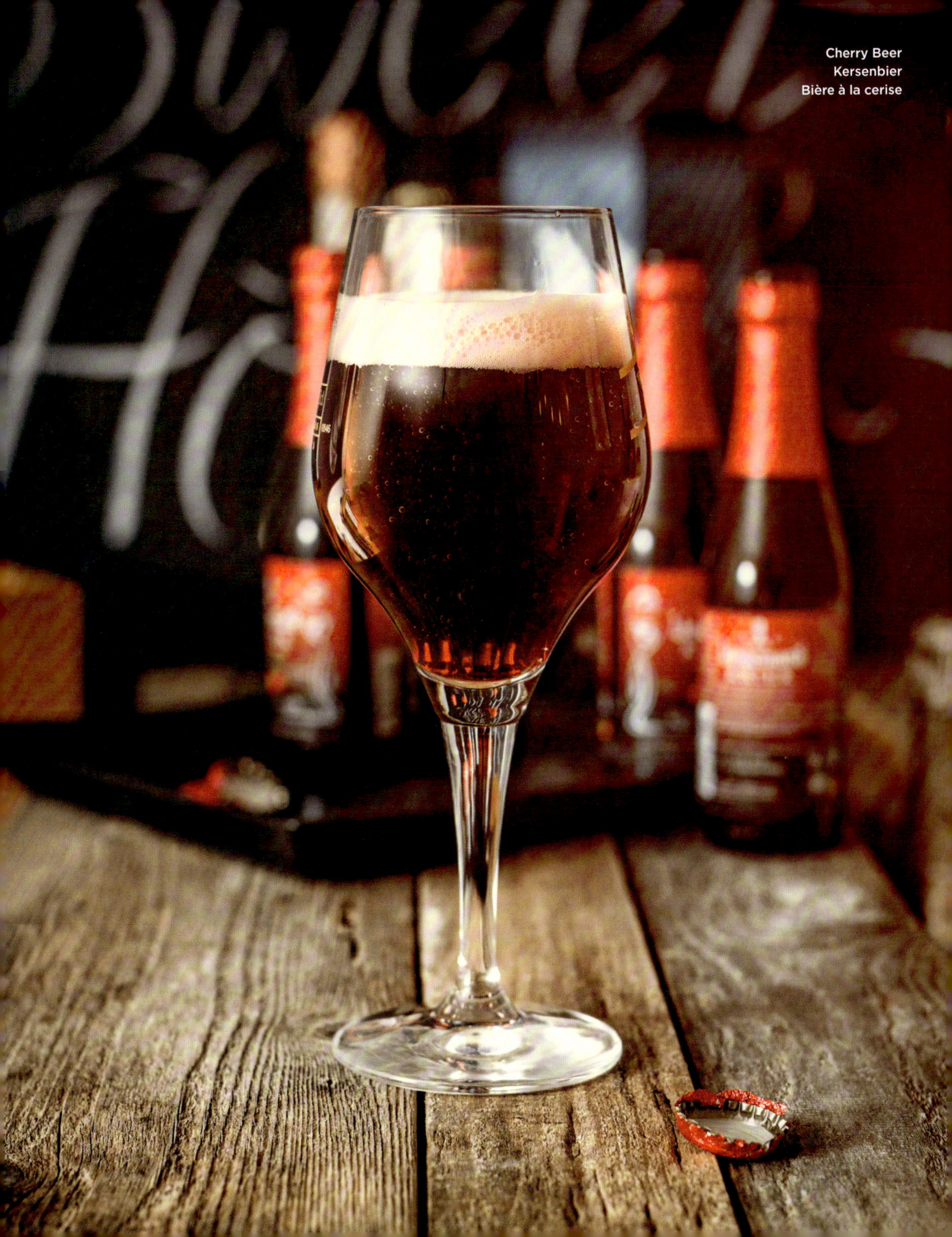
Cherry Beer
Kersenbier
Bière à la cerise

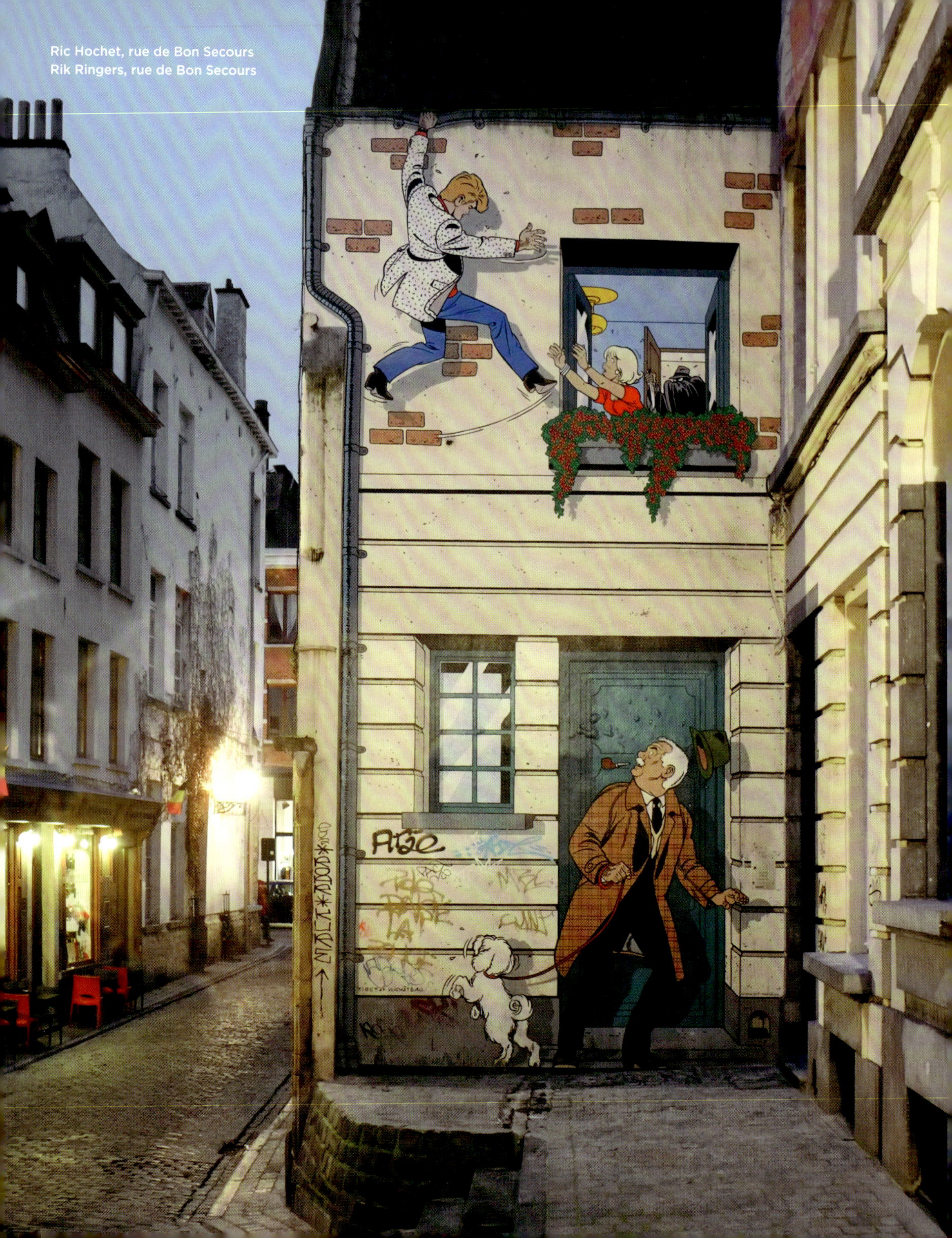

Ric Hochet, rue de Bon Secours
Rik Ringers, rue de Bon Secours

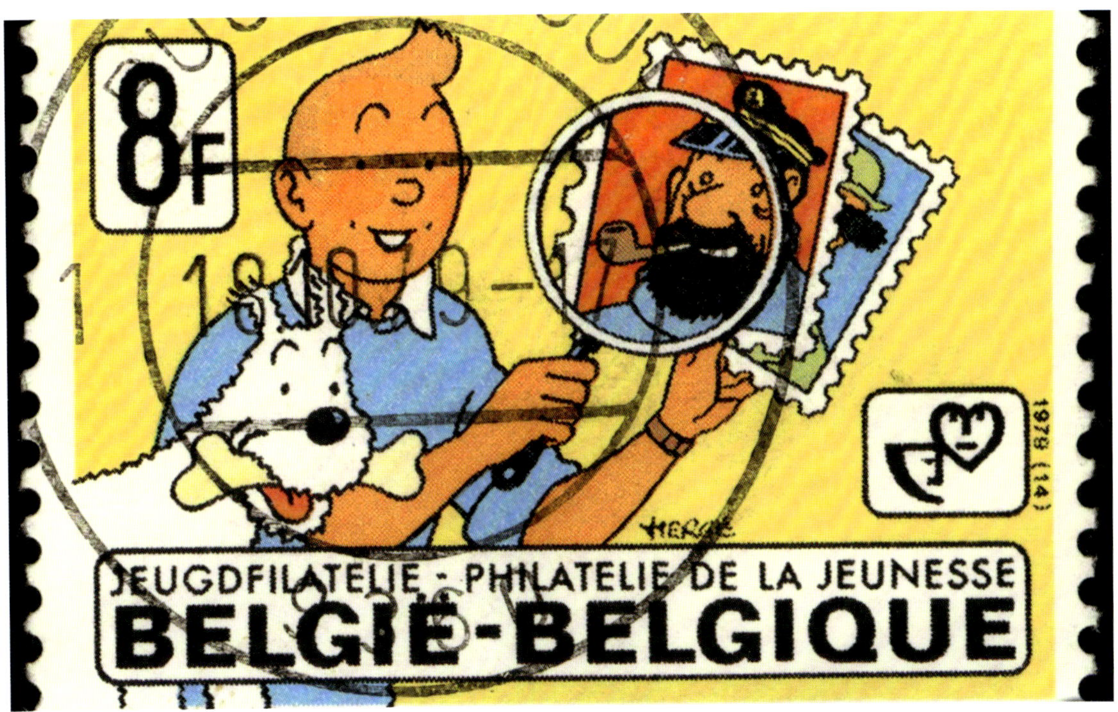

The Adventures of Tintin
De avonturen van Kuifje
Les Aventures de Tintin

Comic strips

Brussels is the capital of comic strips, with more comic strip artists living here than anywhere else and comic strip heroes depicted on walls across the city. It all started with Hergé, the cartoonist of Tintin and Snowy, followed by Lucky Luke, the Marsupilami and hundreds of other series. On Brussels' Comic Book Route one can discover the colorful world of Belgian comics on over 50 walls and buildings.

Paredes pintadas de cómic

Bruselas es la capital del cómic: en ningún otro lugar viven más artistas del mundo del cómic y en ningún otro lugar se encuentran tan a menudo como aquí héroes del cómic. Todo comenzó con Hergé, el dibujante de Tim y Struppi, seguido de Lucky Luke, el Marsupilami y cientos de otras series. En la Ruta del Cómic podemos descubrir el colorido mundo del cómic belga en más de 50 fachadas.

Murs de BD

Bruxelles est la capitale de la bande dessinée : aucun endroit ne renferme autant de dessinateurs de BD et nulle part ailleurs on ne tombe aussi souvent nez à nez avec leurs héros. Tout a commencé avec Tintin et Milou – de Hergé –, suivis de Lucky Luke, du Marsupilami et de centaines d'autres séries. Sur le parcours BD de Bruxelles, partez à la découverte de l'univers coloré de la bande dessinée belge au fil de plus de 50 peintures murales.

Paredes com bandas desenhadas

Bruxelas é a capital das bandas desenhadas: em nenhum lugar vive mais artistas de banda desenhada e em nenhum lugar se encontram heróis de banda desenhada com a mesma frequência que aqui. Tudo começou com Hergé, o cartunista de *As Aventuras de Tintim,* seguido por Lucky Luke, o Marsupilami e centenas de outras séries. Na Rota dos Quadrinhos (Comic-Strip Route) você pode descobrir o colorido mundo dos quadrinhos belgas em mais de 50 fachadas.

Comicwände

Brüssel ist die Hauptstadt der Comics: Nirgends leben mehr Comic-Zeichner und nirgends begegnet man so häufig den Comic-Helden wie hier. Mit Hergé, dem Zeichner von Tim und Struppi, fing alles an, es folgten Lucky Luke, das Marsupilami und hunderte weitere Serien. Auf der Comic-Route kann man auf über 50 Fassaden die bunte Welt der belgischen Comics entdecken.

Stripverhalen

Brussel is de hoofdstad van het stripverhaal: nergens anders wonen striptekenaars en ontmoet je zo vaak striphelden als hier. Het begon allemaal met Hergé, de tekenaar van Kuifje, gevolgd door Lucky Luke, de Marsupilami en honderden andere series. Op de striproute kan op meer dan 50 gevels de kleurrijke wereld van het Belgische stripverhaal worden ontdekt.

Belgian Comic Strip Center

In the land of Tintin, Snowy and the Smurfs, Brussels has dedicated a museum to comics as the "Ninth Art". In Victor Horta's impressive Art Nouveau building, everything revolves around comics, from their origins to avant-garde works. Visitors encounter life-size comic figures, colorful replicas from the world of comics and original drawings in the "treasure trove".

Centre belge de la bande dessinée

Au pays de Tintin et Milou et des Schtroumpfs, Bruxelles consacre un musée à la bande dessinée. Dans l'impressionnant bâtiment Art nouveau de Victor Horta, tout tourne autour du 9e art, de ses origines aux œuvres d'avant-garde. Le visiteur rencontre des personnages de BD grandeur nature, des répliques colorées de cet univers et – dans le « trésor » – les dessins originaux de leurs auteurs.

Belgisches Comic-Zentrum

Im Land von Tim und Struppi und den Schlümpfen widmet Brüssel dem Comic als 9. Kunst ein eigenes Museum. In dem eindrucksvollen Jugendstil-Bau von Victor Horta dreht sich, von den Ursprüngen bis hin zur avantgardistischen Werken, alles um Comics. Dem Besucher begegnen lebensgroße Comic-Figuren, farbenfrohe Nachbildungen aus der Comic-Welt und in der „Schatzkammer" die originalen Zeichnungen.

Centro Belga del Cómic

En la tierra de las aventuras de Tintín y los Pitufos, Bruselas dedica un museo al noveno arte: el cómic. En el impresionante edificio Art Nouveau de Victor Horta, todo gira en torno al cómic, desde sus orígenes hasta las obras más vanguardistas. Los visitantes se encuentran con figuras de cómic a escala real, réplicas a todo color del mundo del cómic y dibujos originales en la "cámara del tesoro".

Centro belga da banda desenhada

Na terra de Tintim e seu fiel cão Milu e dos Smurfs, Bruxelas dedica um museu próprio à banda desenhada como a 9ª arte. No impressionante edifício Art Nouveau de Victor Horta, tudo gira em torno de quadrinhos, desde suas origens até obras de vanguarda. Os visitantes encontram figuras cómicas em tamanho real, réplicas coloridas do mundo dos quadrinhos e desenhos originais na "sala do tesouro".

Belgisch Stripcentrum

In het land van Kuifje en de Smurfen wijdt Brussel een eigen museum aan strips als 9e kunst. In het indrukwekkende art-nouveau gebouw van Victor Horta draait alles om strips, van hun oorsprong tot avant-gardistische werken. De bezoekers ontmoeten levensgrote stripfiguren, kleurrijke replica's uit de stripwereld en de originele tekeningen in de "schatkamer".

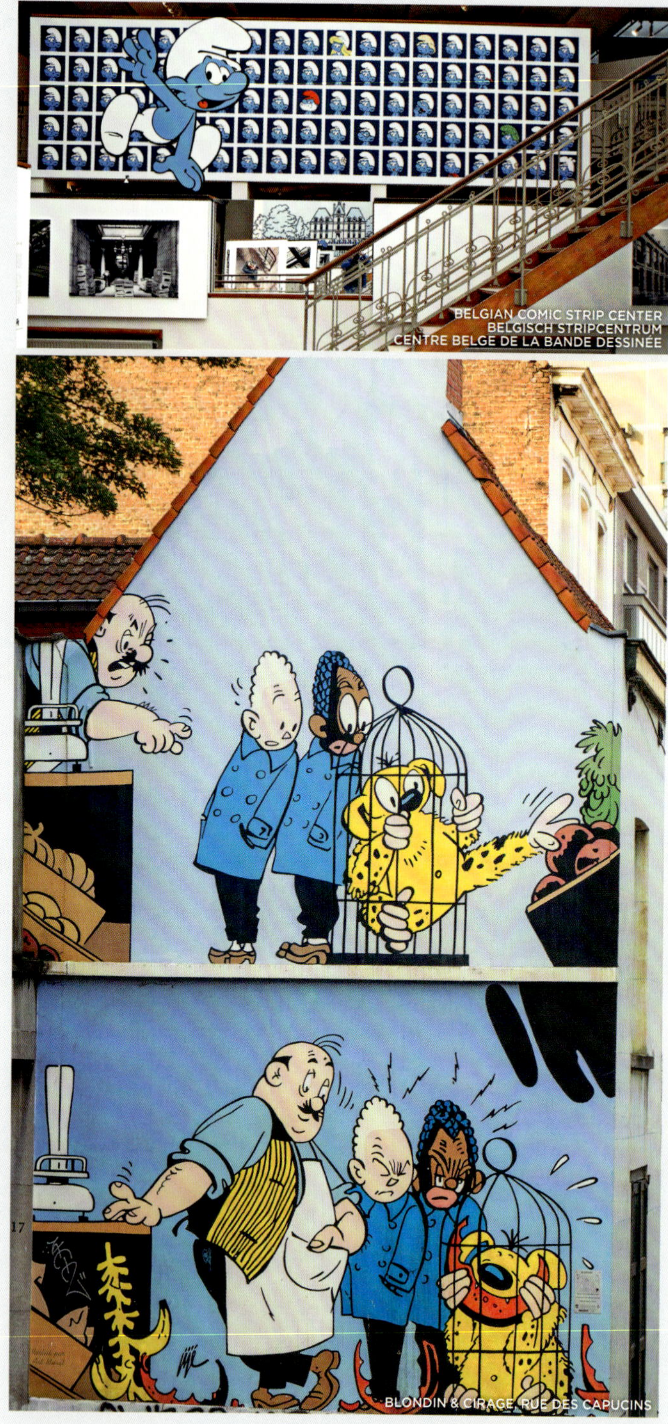
BELGIAN COMIC STRIP CENTER
BELGISCH STRIPCENTRUM
CENTRE BELGE DE LA BANDE DESSINÉE

BLONDIN & CIRAGE, RUE DES CAPUCINS

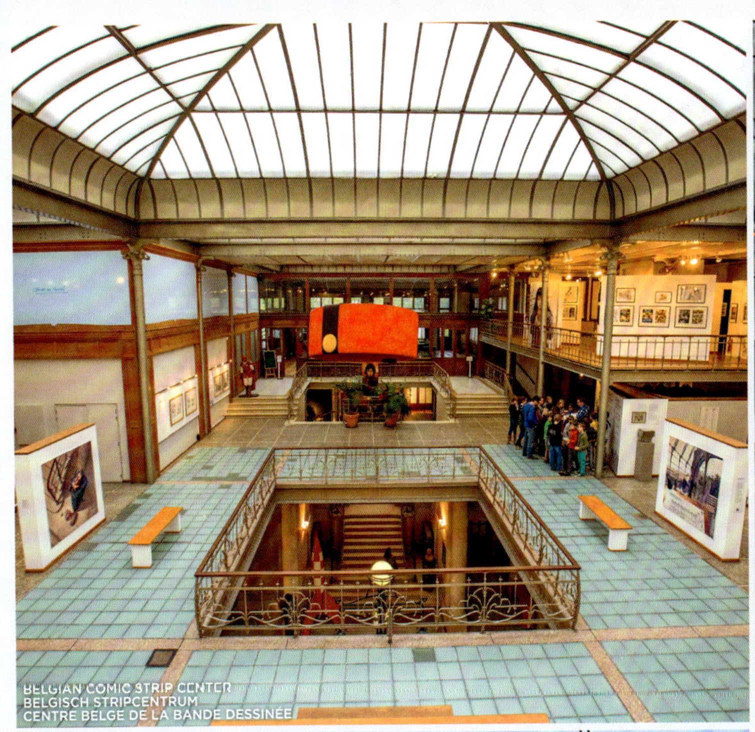

BELGIAN COMIC STRIP CENTER
BELGISCH STRIPCENTRUM
CENTRE BELGE DE LA BANDE DESSINÉE

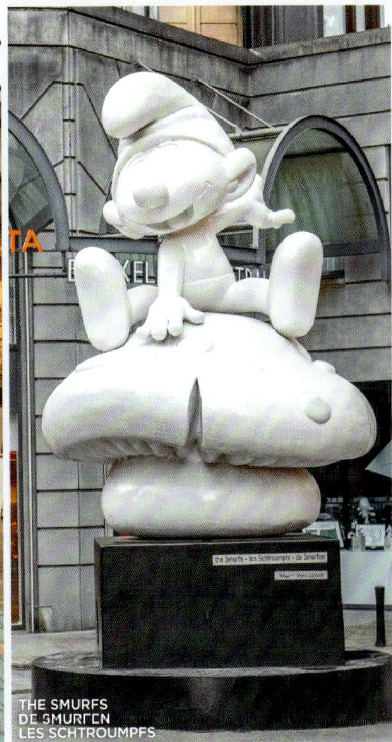

THE SMURFS
DE SMURFEN
LES SCHTROUMPFS

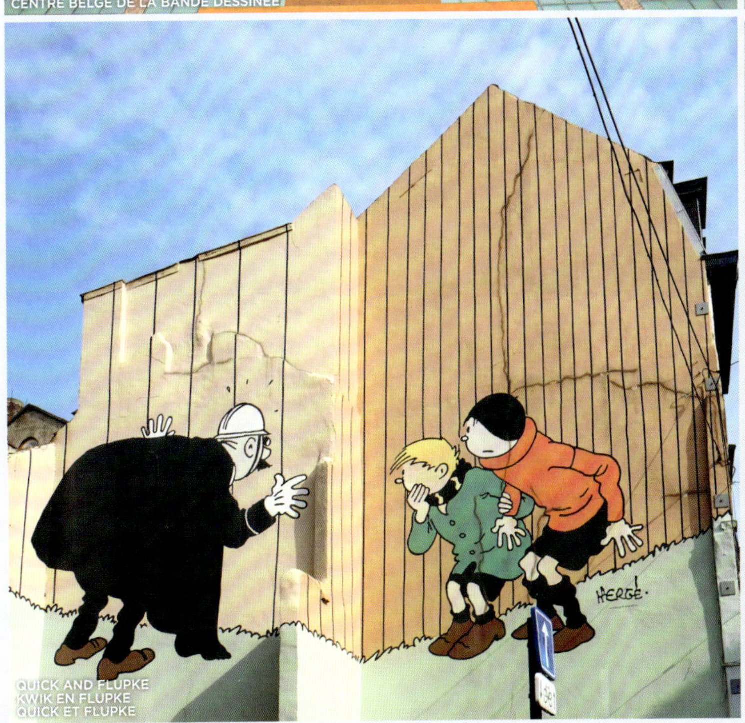

QUICK AND FLUPKE
KWIK EN FLUPKE
QUICK ET FLUPKE

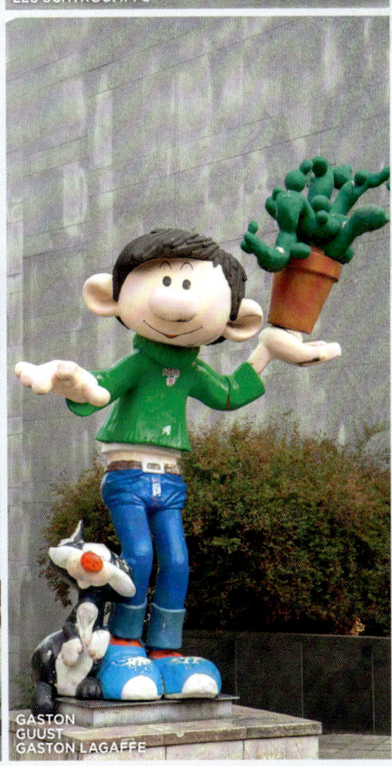

GASTON
GUUST
GASTON LAGAFFE

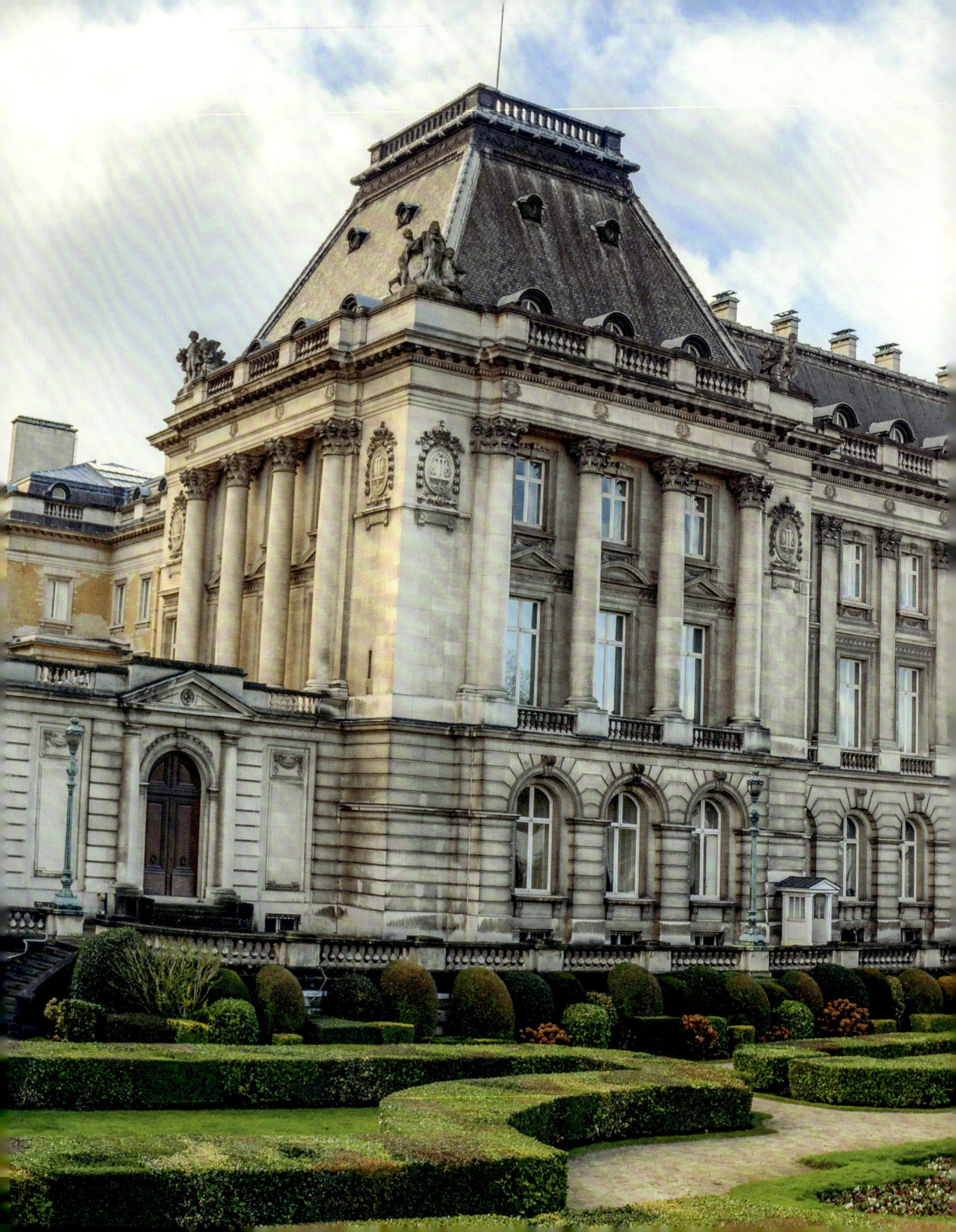

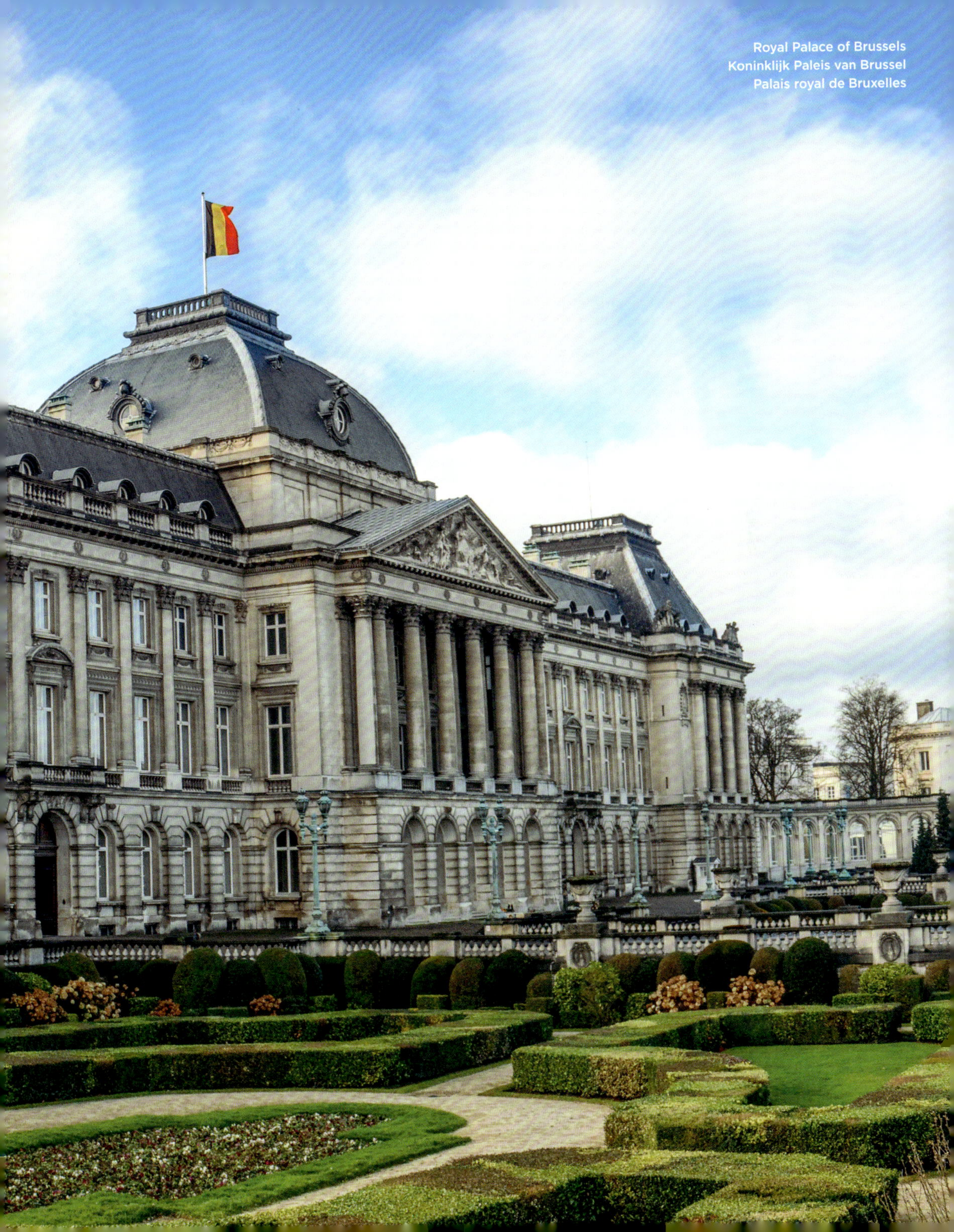

Royal Palace of Brussels
Koninklijk Paleis van Brussel
Palais royal de Bruxelles

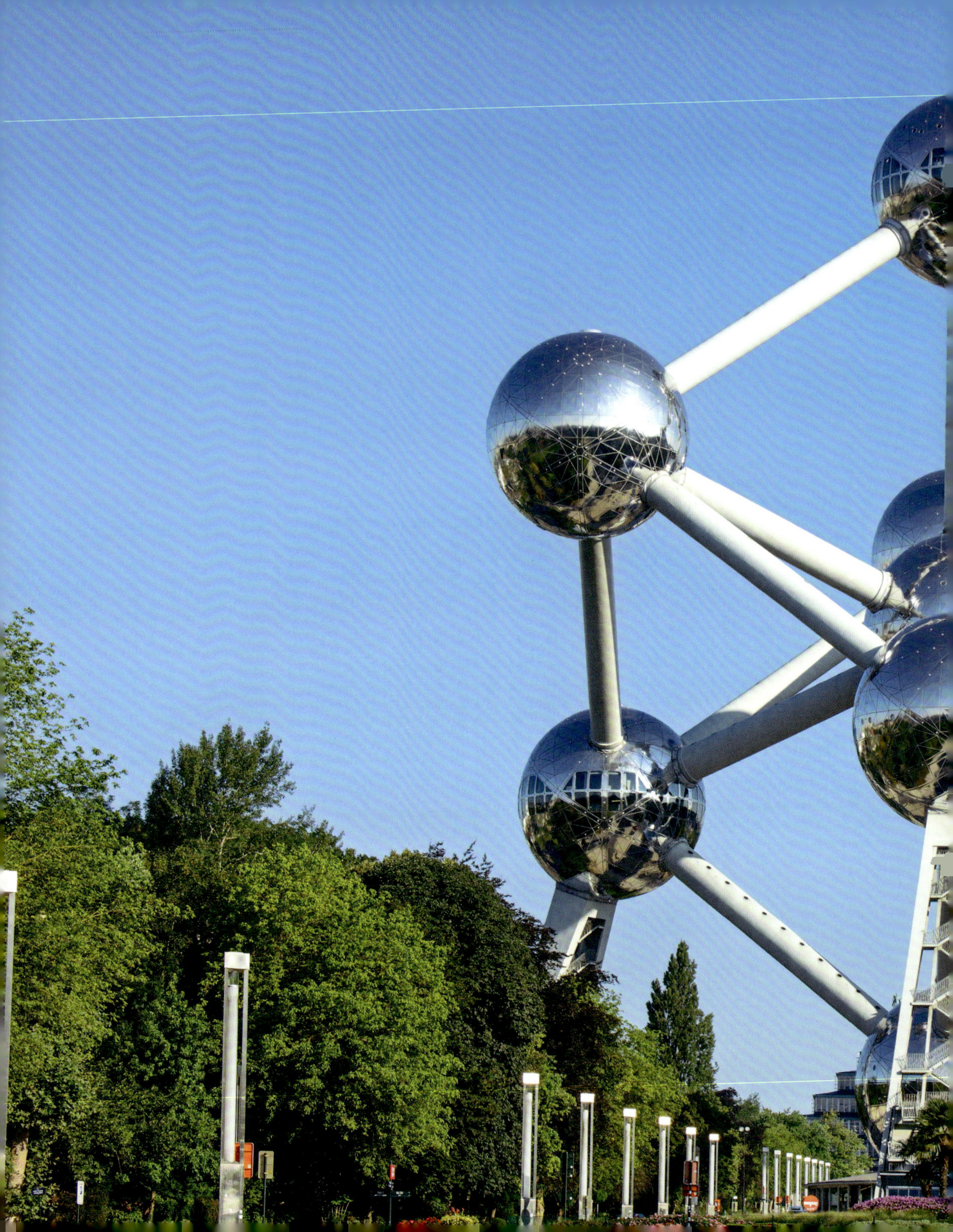

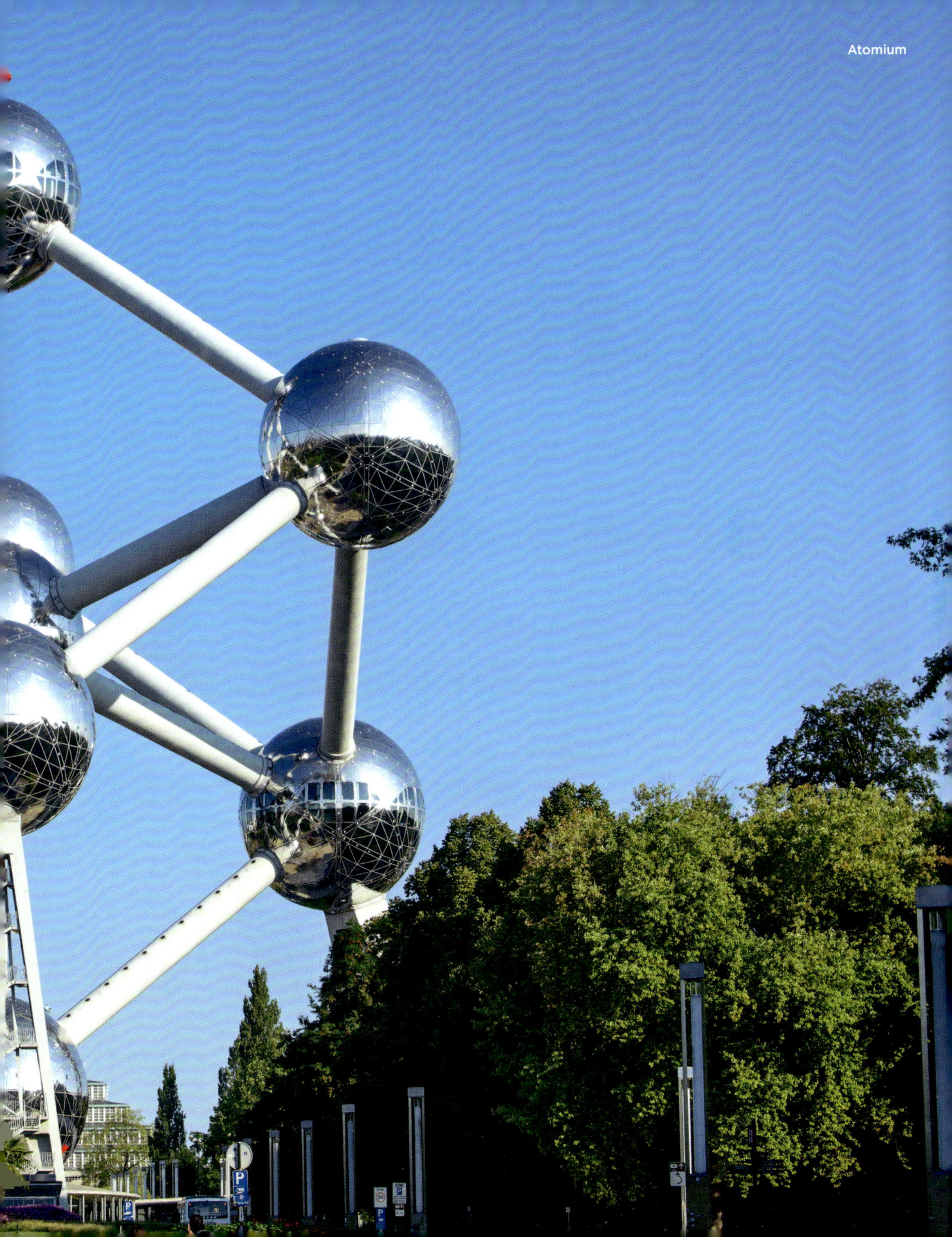
Atomium

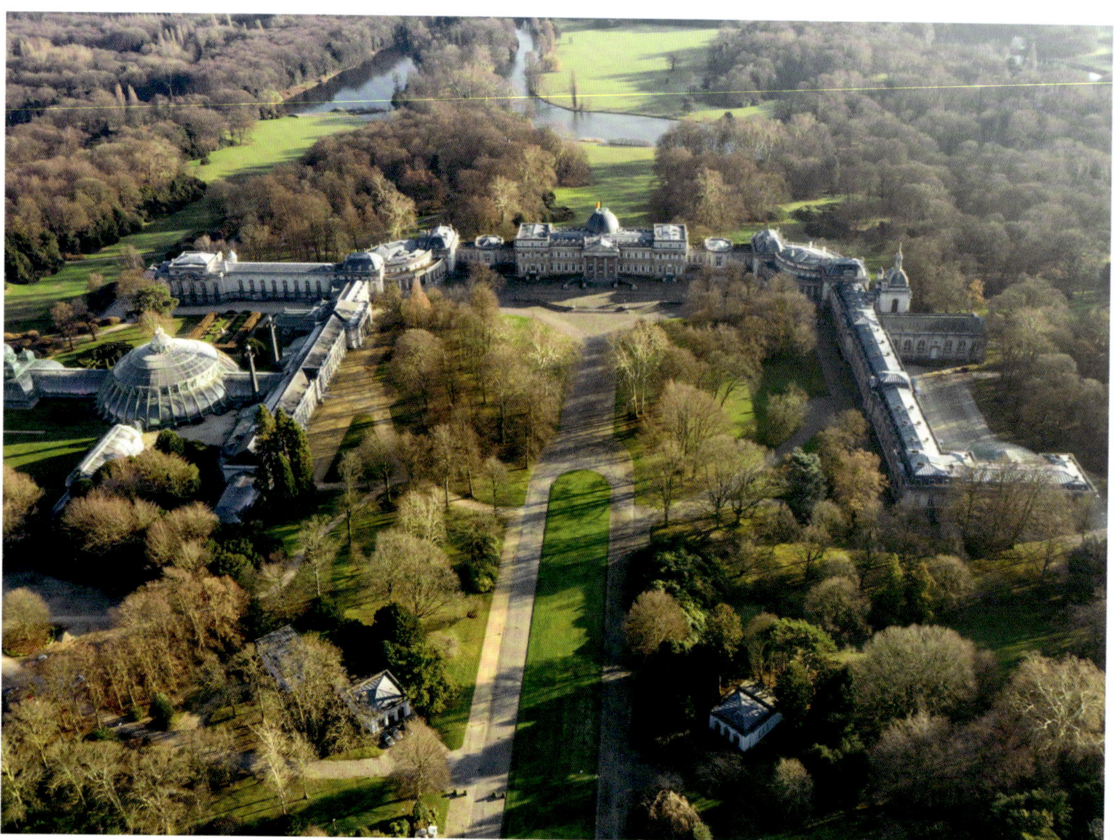

Castle of Laeken
Kasteel van Laken
Château de Laeken

Residence of the King

The Castle of Laeken is located in the north of Brussels and is the residence of the Belgian royal family. It was built in the 18th century in neoclassical style and served as the residence of the Dutch royal family. When Belgium split from the Netherlands in 1830, Laeken Castle became the residence of the Belgian King Leopold I.

Résidence du roi

Au nord de Bruxelles se dresse le château de Laeken, résidence de la famille royale belge. Construit au XVIIIᵉ siècle dans un style néoclassique, il servait alors de résidence à la famille royale néerlandaise. Lorsque la Belgique se sépara des Pays-Bas en 1830, le château de Laeken devient la résidence du roi belge Léopold Iᵉʳ.

Wohnsitz des Königs

Das Schloss Laken befindet sich im Norden von Brüssel und ist der Wohnsitz der belgischen Königsfamilie. Es wurde im 18. Jahrhundert im neoklassischen Stil errichtet und diente als Residenz für das niederländische Königshaus. Als sich Belgien 1830 von den Niederlanden abspaltete, wurde das Schloss Laeken der Wohnsitz des belgischen Königs Leopold I.

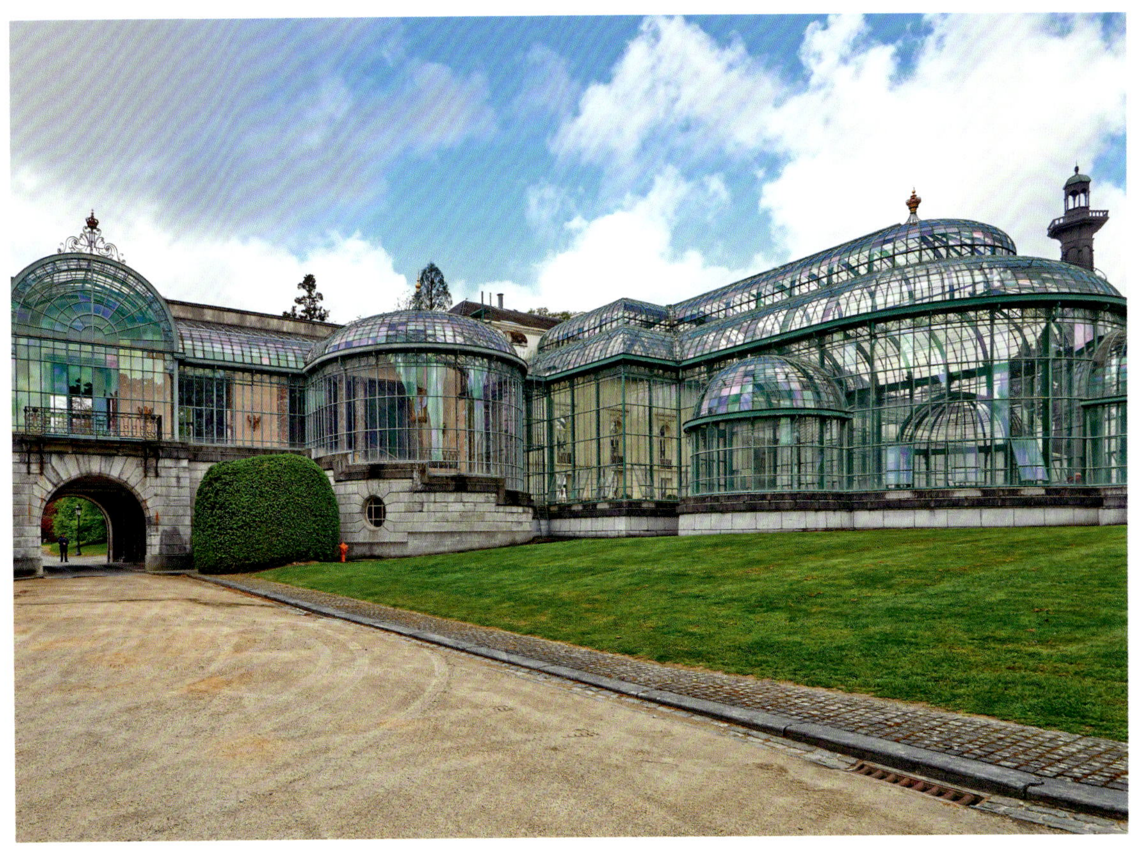

Royal Greenhouses of Laeken
Koninklijke Serres van Laken
Serres royales de Laeken

Residencia del rey

El castillo de Laeken está situado en el
norte de Bruselas y es la residencia de la
familia real belga. Se construyó en el siglo
XVIII en estilo neoclásico y sirvió como
residencia de la familia real holandesa.
Cuando Bélgica se separó de los Países
Bajos en 1830, el castillo de Laeken se
convirtió en la residencia del rey belga
Leopoldo I.

Residência do rei

O castelo de Laeken está localizado no
norte de Bruxelas e é a residência da
família real belga. Foi construído no século
XVIII em estilo neoclássico e serviu como
residência da família real holandesa.
Quando a Bélgica se separou dos Países
Baixos em 1830, o Castelo de Laeken
tornou-se a residência do rei dos belgas
Leopoldo I.

Residentie van de koning

Het Kasteel van Laken ligt in het noorden
van Brussel en is de residentie van de
Belgische koninklijke familie. Het werd
in de 18e eeuw in neoklassieke stijl
gebouwd en diende als residentie voor
het Nederlandse koningshuis. Toen België
zich in 1830 van de Nederlanden afsplitste,
werd het Kasteel van Laken de residentie
van de Belgische Koning Leopold I.

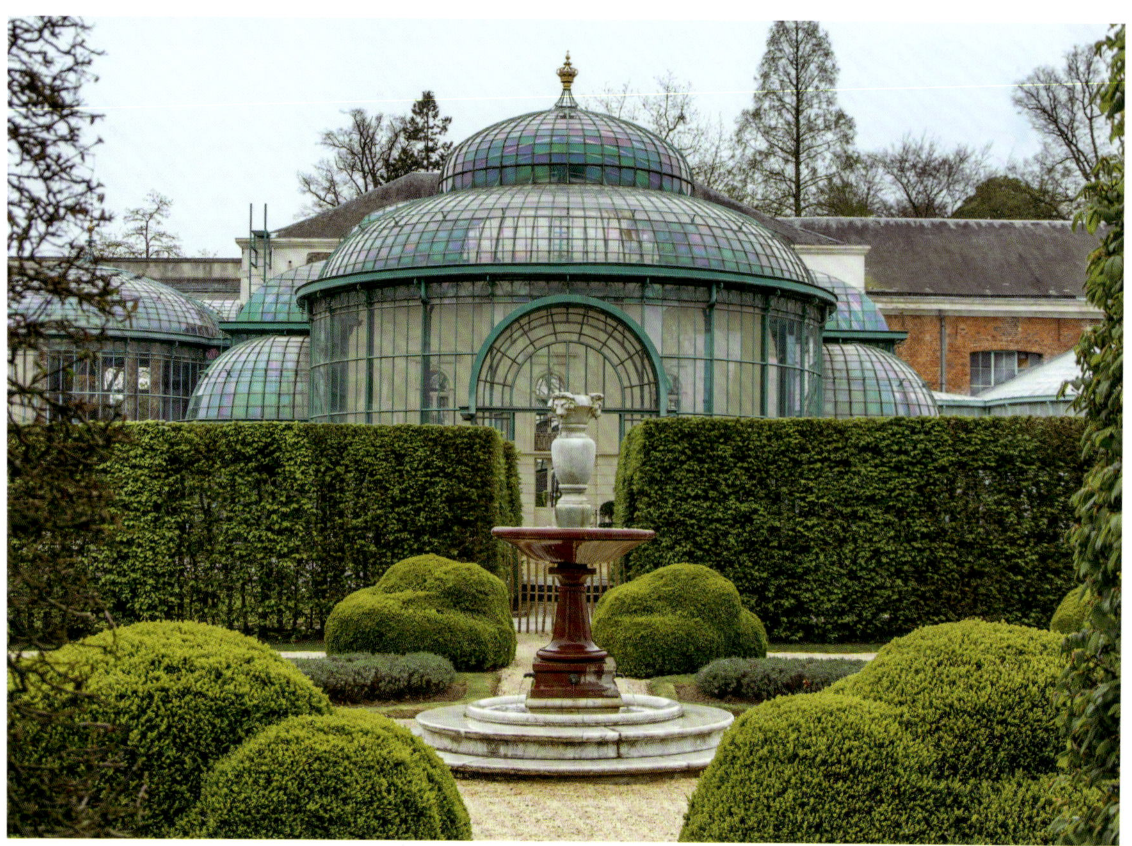

Royal Greenhouses of Laeken
Koninklijke Serres van Laken
Serres royales de Laeken

Royal Greenhouses of Laeken

Palm trees and other exotic plants thrive
in the huge greenhouses in the park of
the Royal Palace. The tour leads through
the Greenhouse of the Congo, the Palm
Garden, past orchids, orangeries and the
former studio of Queen Elisabeth. Inspired
by his passion for exotic plants, King
Leopold II commissioned the construction
of this architectural masterpiece of glass
and steel in 1873. It was here that he spent
the last years of his life, and even today his
wish to make these gardens accessible to
the public is still being fulfilled, for three
weeks each spring.

Serres royales

Palmiers et autres plantes exotiques
poussent dans les gigantesques serres du
parc du palais royal. La serre du Congo,
le pavillon des palmiers, les orchidées,
l'orangerie et l'ancien atelier de la reine
Élisabeth font partie de la visite. Inspiré
par sa passion pour les plantes exotiques,
le roi Léopold II fit construire ce chef-
d'œuvre architectural en verre et en acier
en 1873. Il y passa les dernières années de
sa vie. Aujourd'hui encore, on continue
à exaucer son souhait de rendre ces
jardins accessibles au public pendant trois
semaines au printemps.

Königliche Gewächshäuser

In den riesigen Gewächshäusern im Park
des Königsschlosses gedeihen Palmen
und andere exotische Pflanzen. Der
Rundgang führt durch das Kongohaus,
den Palmengarten, vorbei an Orchideen,
Orangerien und durch das ehemalige
Atelier der Königin Elisabeth. Von seiner
Leidenschaft für exotische Pflanzen
inspiriert, erteilte König Leopold II.
1873 den Auftrag für den Bau dieses
architektonischen Meisterwerks aus Glas
und Stahl. Hier verbrachte er seine letzten
Lebensjahre und noch heute wird seinem
Wunsch, diese Gärten für die Öffentlichkeit
zugänglich zu machen, für drei Wochen im
Frühling nachgegeben.

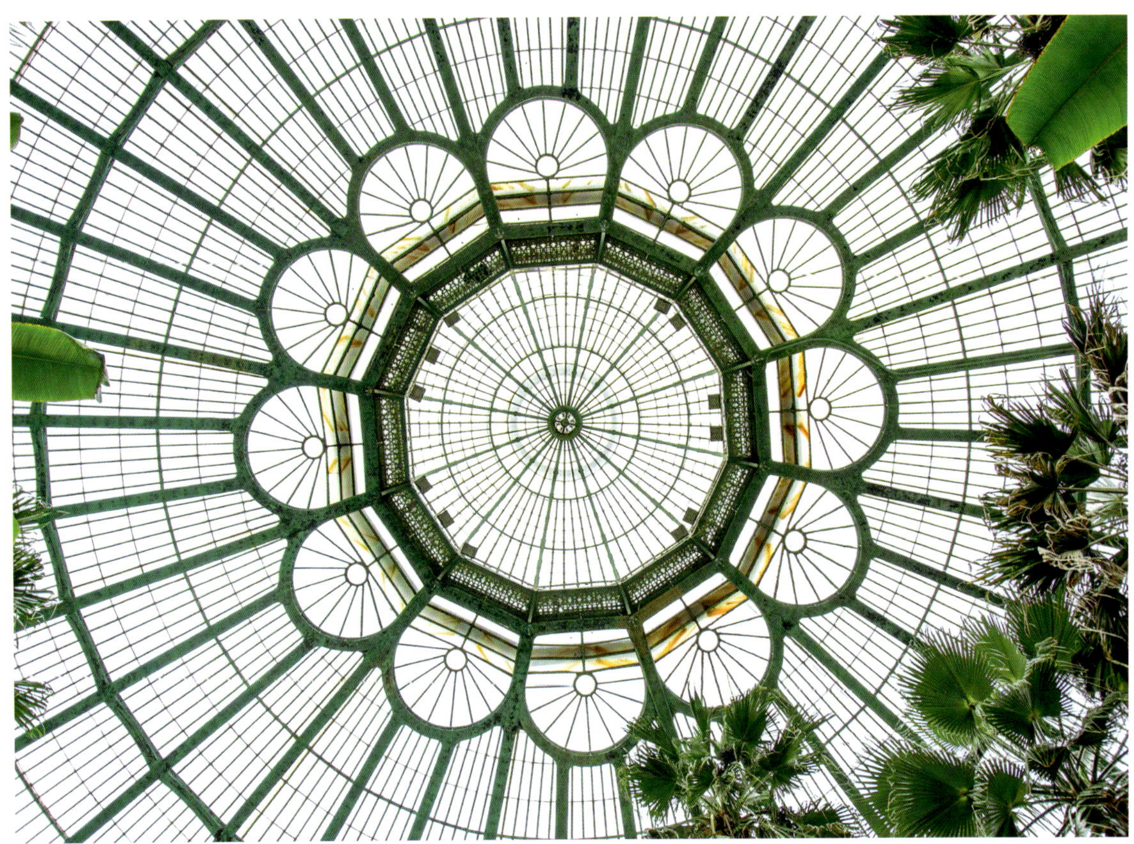

Royal Greenhouses of Laeken
Koninklijke Serres van Laken
Serres royales de Laeken

Invernaderos Reales

Las palmeras y otras plantas exóticas prosperan en los enormes invernaderos del parque del Palacio Real. Si damos una vuelta, pasaremos por la Casa del Congo, el Jardín de las Palmeras, las orquídeas, la Orangerie y el antiguo estudio de la Reina Elisabeth. Inspirado por su pasión por las plantas exóticas, el rey Leopoldo II encargó la construcción de esta obra maestra arquitectónica de vidrio y acero en 1873. Fue aquí donde pasó los últimos años de su vida, y aún hoy su deseo de hacer estos jardines accesibles al público se sigue cumpliendo durante tres semanas en primavera.

Estufas Reais

Palmeiras e outras plantas exóticas prosperam nas enormes estufas do parque do Palácio Real. A visita percorre a Casa do Congo, o Jardim das Palmeiras, passando pelas orquídeas, pelo hibernáculo e pelo antigo estúdio da Rainha Elisabeth. Inspirado por sua paixão por plantas exóticas, o Rei Leopoldo II encomendou a construção desta obra-prima arquitetónica de vidro e aço em 1873. Foi aqui que ele passou os últimos anos da sua vida, e ainda hoje o seu desejo de tornar estes jardins acessíveis ao público ainda está a ser realizado durante três semanas na primavera.

Koninklijke broeikassen

In de reusachtige broeikassen in het park van het Koninklijk Paleis gedijen palmen en andere exotische planten. De rondleiding gaat door de Congoserre, de tuin met palmen, langs orchideeën, oranjerieën en het voormalige atelier van koningin Elisabeth. Geïnspireerd door zijn passie voor exotische planten gaf koning Leopold II in 1873 opdracht tot de bouw van dit architectonische meesterwerk van glas en staal. Hier heeft hij de laatste jaren van zijn leven doorgebracht en zelfs vandaag de dag wordt zijn wens om deze tuinen toegankelijk te maken voor het publiek nog drie weken in het voorjaar vervuld.

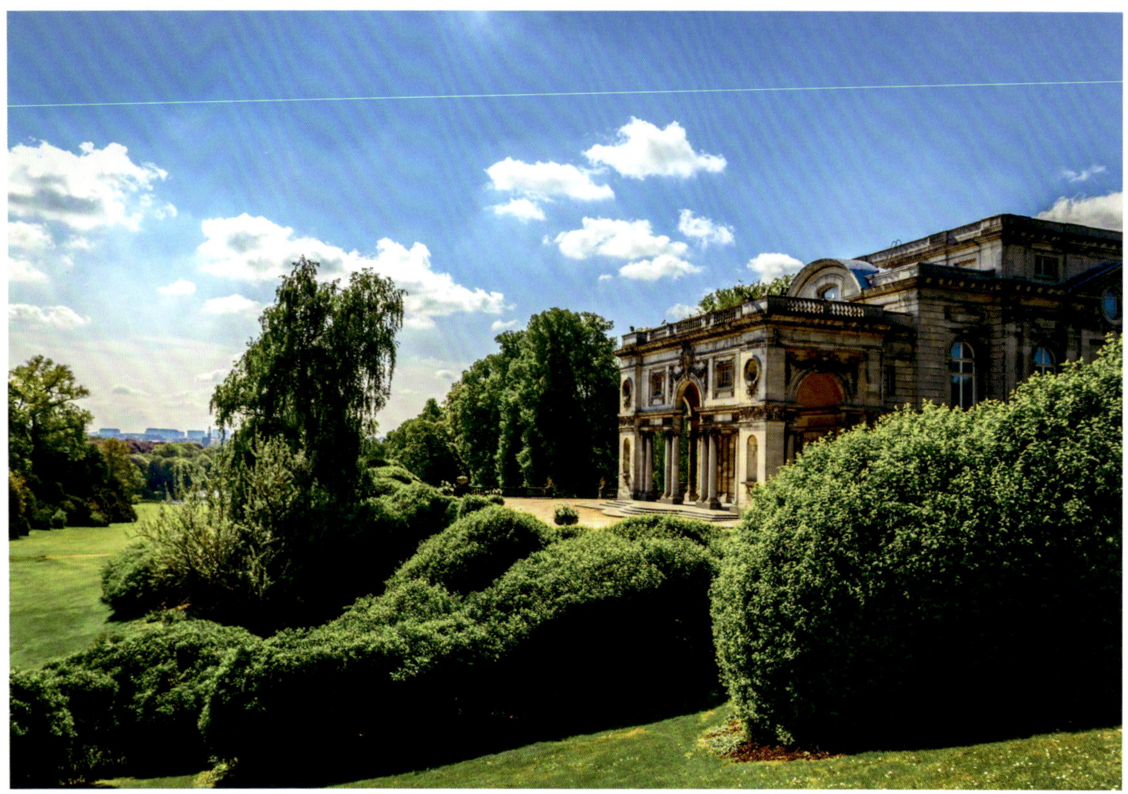

Castle of Laeken
Kasteel van Laken
Château de Laeken

Castle of Laeken

This Louis XVI style castle is built on the site of an old manor-house. Napoleon bought the estate and embellished it in order to give it to his wife Joséphine de Beauharnais. Later, it was King William I of the unified Netherlands who moved in there, then the Kings of the Belgians made it their residence.

Castillo Real de Laeken

Este castillo de estilo Luis XVI fue construido en el emplazamiento de una antigua mansión. Más tarde, Napoleón compró el dominio y lo embelleció para ofrecérselo a su esposa Joséphine de Beauharnais. El rey Guillermo I de los Países Bajos Unificados se instaló en el palacio, seguido por los reyes belgas, que lo convirtieron en su residencia.

Château de Laeken

Ce château de style Louis XVI est bâti sur l'emplacement d'un vieux manoir. Napoléon achèta le domaine et l'embellit pour l'offrir à son épouse Joséphine de Beauharnais. Ensuite le roi Guillaume Ier des Pays-Bas unifiés s'y installa, puis les rois des Belges en firent leur résidence.

Castelo Real de Laeken

Este castelo de estilo Louis XVI foi construído no local de uma antiga mansão. Mais tarde, Napoleão comprou o domínio e embelezou-o para o oferecer à sua esposa Joséphine de Beauharnais. O rei Guilherme I dos Países Baixos Unificados instalou-se no palácio, seguido dos reis belgas, que o fizeram a sua residência.

Schloss Laken

Das Schloss im Stil Ludwigs XVI. wurde an der Stelle eines alten Herrenhauses errichtet. Napoleon erwarb das Anwesen und verschönerte es, um es seiner Frau Joséphine de Beauharnais zu schenken. Dann ließ sich König Wilhelm I. der vereinigten Niederlande nieder, woraufhin die Könige der Belgier das Schloss zu ihrer Residenz wählten.

Kasteel van Laken

Het kasteel in Lodewijk XVI-stijl werd opgetrokken op de grondvesten van een oud landgoed. Napoleon koopt het domein en verfraait het om het te schenken aan zijn echtgenote Joséphine de Beauharnais. Na Napoleon neemt koning Willem I der Nederlanden zijn intrek in het kasteel. Tot slot zijn het de Belgische koningen die het kasteel als residentie nemen.

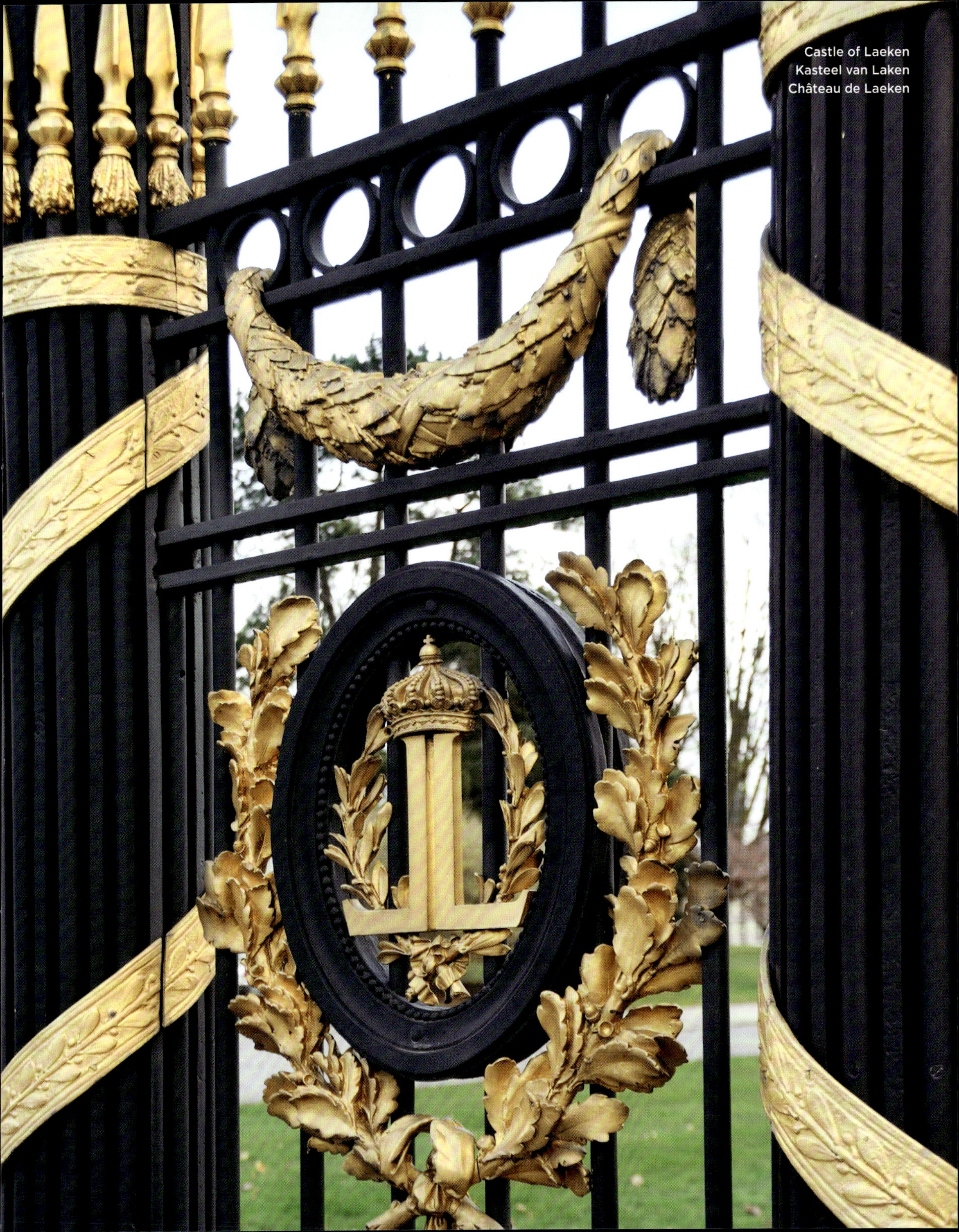

Castle of Laeken
Kasteel van Laken
Château de Laeken

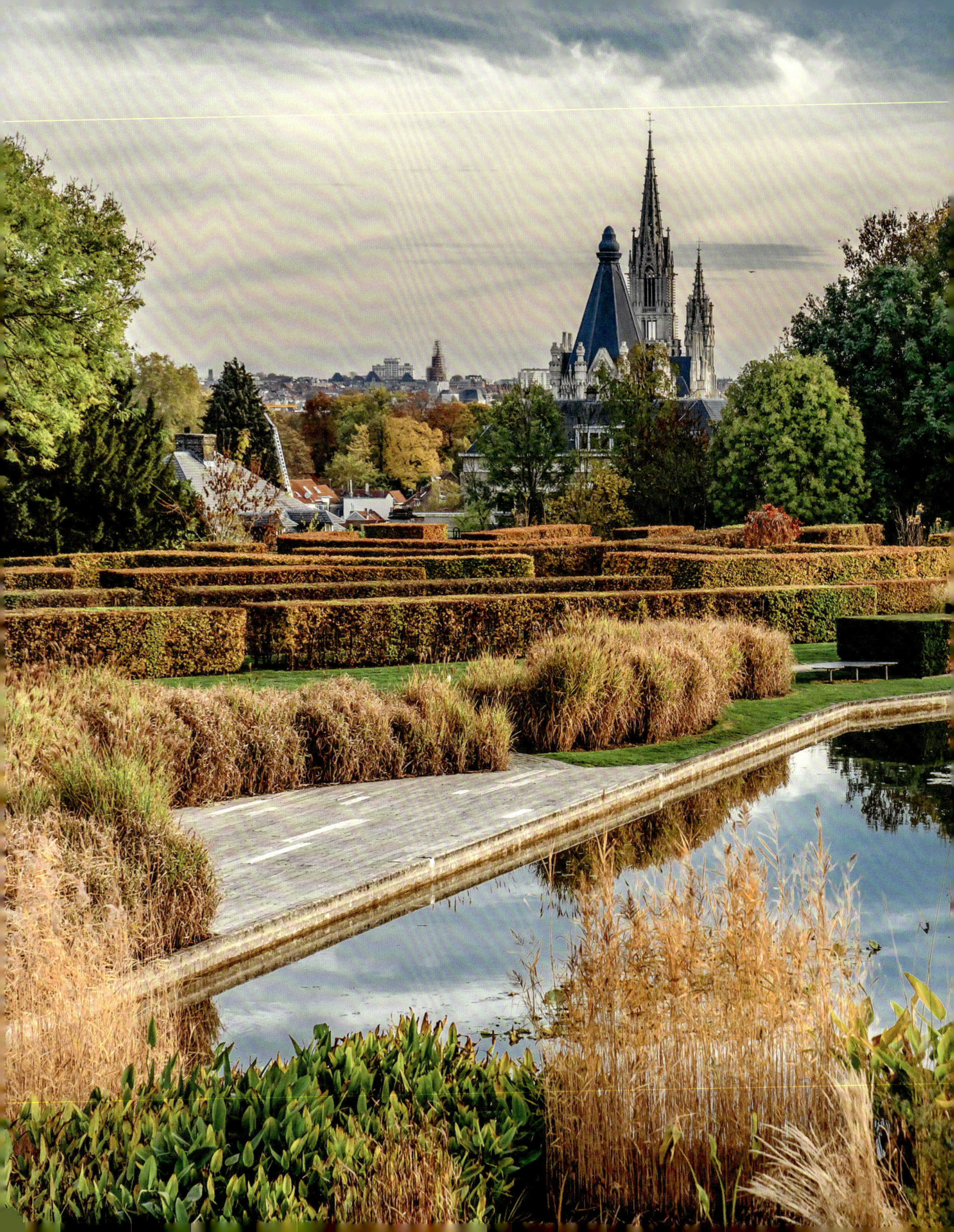

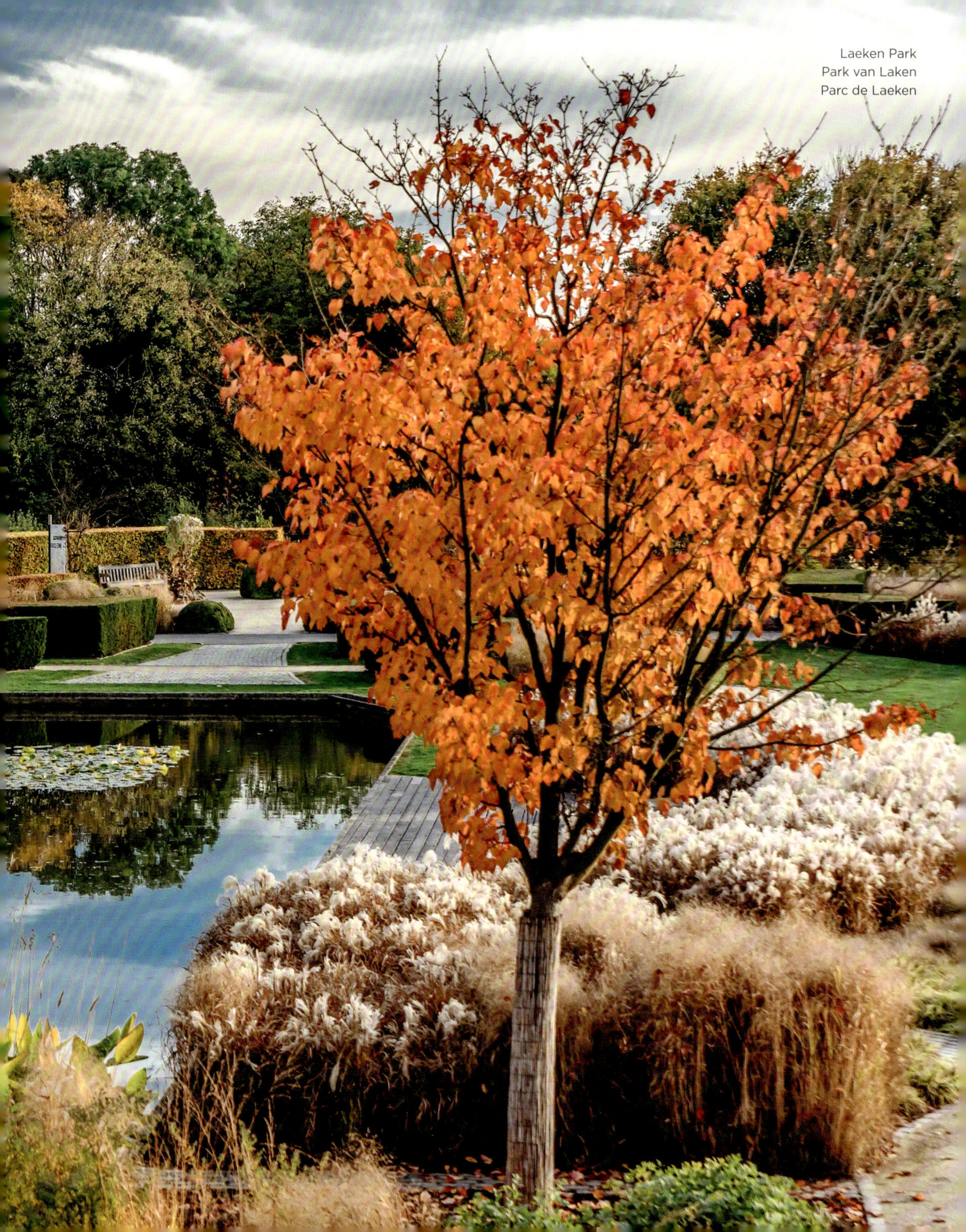

Laeken Park
Park van Laken
Parc de Laeken

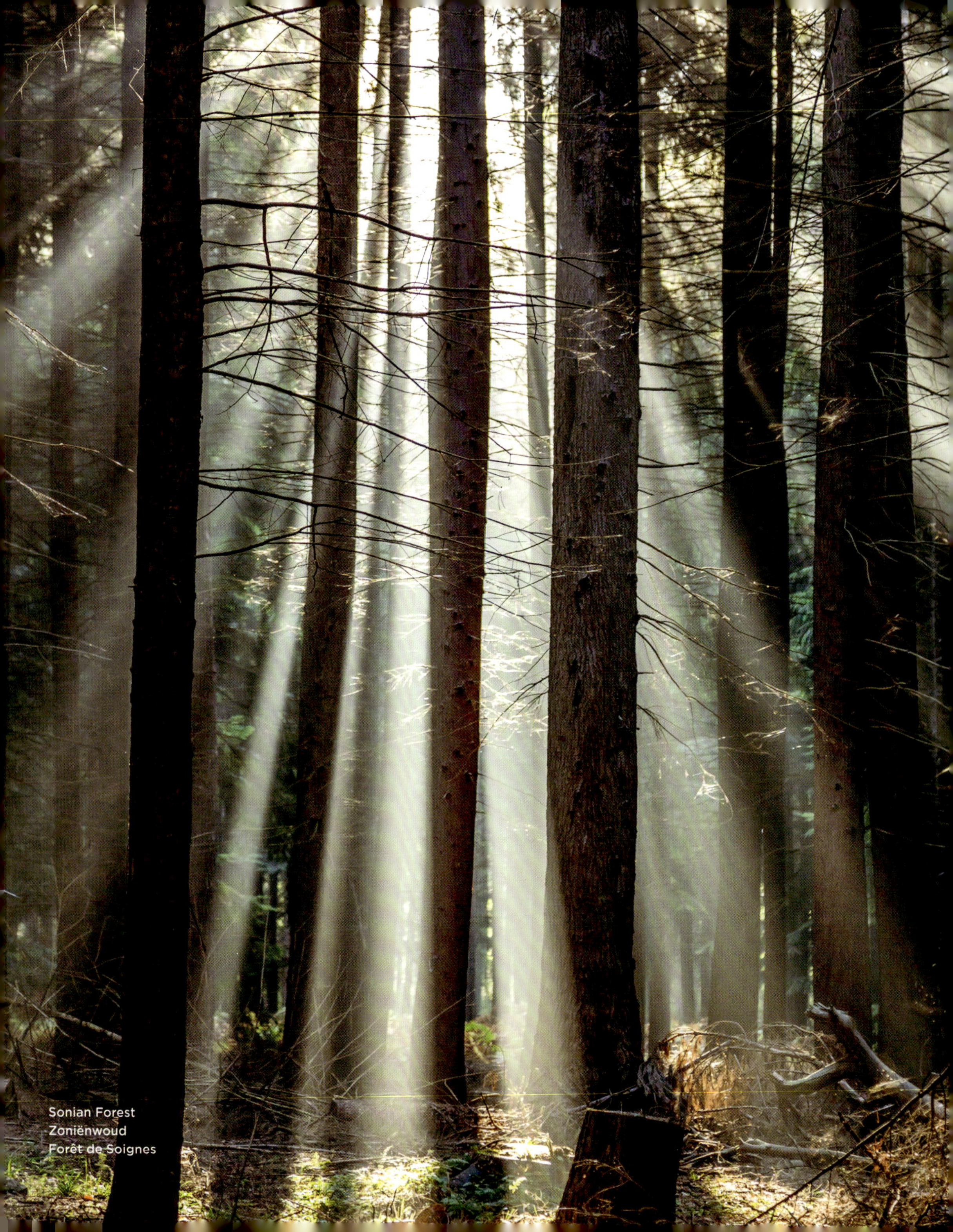
Sonian Forest
Zoniënwoud
Forêt de Soignes

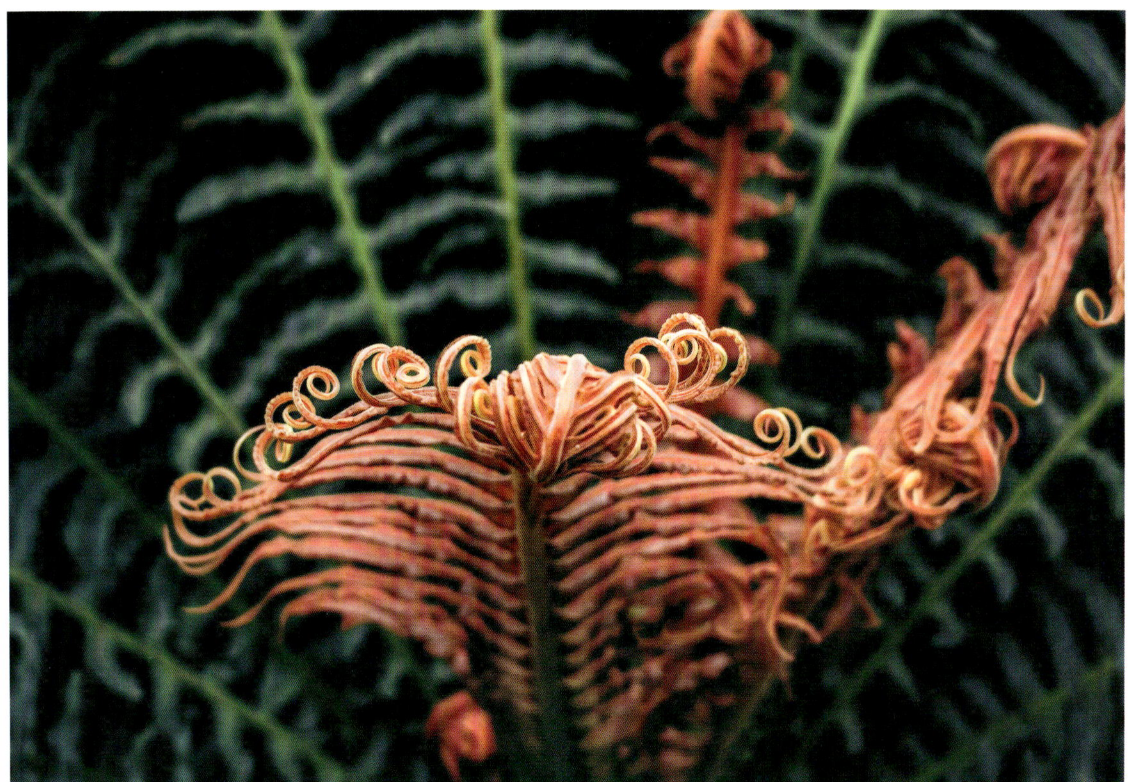

Fern
Varen
Fougère

A cathedral of beech trees

Covering almost 5000 ha (12,355 ac), the Sonian Forest is one of the largest urban forests in Europe and is only 4 km (2,5 mi) from Brussels city centre. In the 18th century, masses of beech trees were planted in the former charcoal forest, which today form the beech cathedral. In 2017, large parts of the forest were included in the UNESCO World Heritage List.

Hayedo catedral

Con casi 5000 ha, el bosque de Soignes es uno de los mayores bosques urbanos de Europa y se encuentra a solo 4 km del centro de la ciudad de Bruselas. En el siglo XVIII se plantaron múltiples hayas en el antiguo bosque carbonífero, que hoy forma el hayedo catedral. En 2017, gran parte del bosque se incluyó en la Lista del Patrimonio Mundial de la UNESCO.

Une cathédrale de hêtres

Avec ses près de 5 000 hectares, la forêt de Soignes est l'une des plus grandes forêts périurbaines d'Europe, à seulement 4 kilomètres du centre-ville de Bruxelles. Au XVIIIᵉ siècle, on planta des hêtres en grand nombre dans l'ancienne forêt Charbonnière, ce qui forme aujourd'hui la dénommée cathédrale de hêtres. Depuis 2017, une grande partie de la forêt fait partie du patrimoine mondial de l'Unesco.

Uma catedral feita de faias

Com quase 5000 ha, a Floresta de Soignes é uma das maiores florestas urbanas da Europa e fica a apenas 4 km do centro da cidade de Bruxelas. No século XVIII, foram plantadas faias em massa na antiga floresta de carvão, que hoje formam a catedral de faias. Em 2017, grande parte da floresta foi incluída na Lista do Património Mundial da UNESCO.

Eine Kathedrale aus Buchen

Der Sonienwald ist mit fast 5000 ha einer der größten stadtnahen Wälder Europas und ist nur 4 km vom Brüsseler Stadtzentrum entfernt. In dem ehemaligen Kohlenwald wurden im 18. Jahrhundert massenweise Buchen gepflanzt, die heute die Buchenkathedrale bilden. Im Jahr 2017 wurden große Teile des Waldes in die Liste des UNESCO-Welterbes aufgenommen.

Een kathedraal van beukenbomen

Het Zoniënwoud is met bijna 5000 ha één van de grootste stedelijke bossen van Europa en ligt op slechts 4 km van het centrum van Brussel. In het voormalige kolenwoud werden in de 18e eeuw massa's beuken geplant die nu de beukenkathedraal vormen. In 2017 werden grote delen van het bos opgenomen op de UNESCO Werelderfgoedlijst.

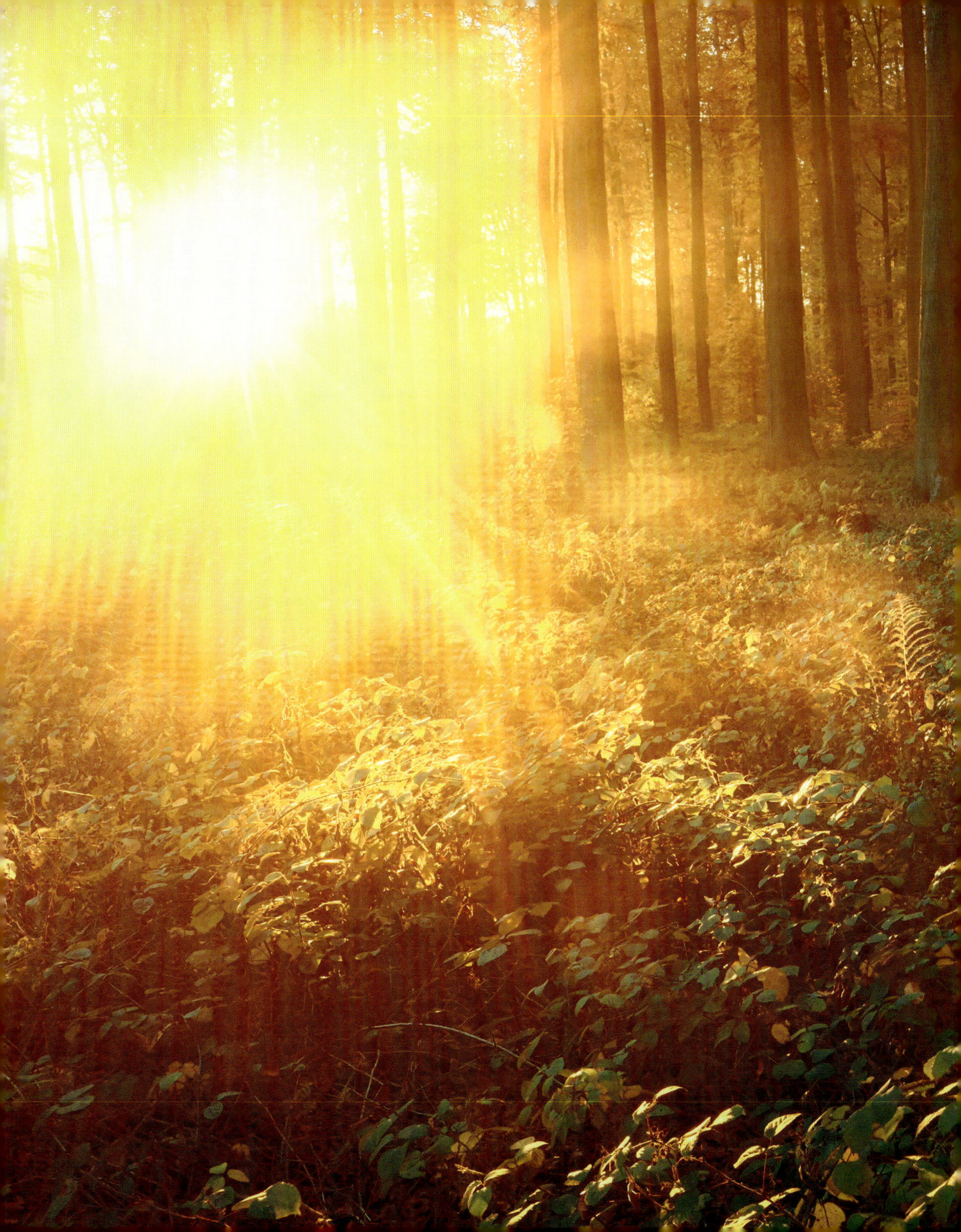

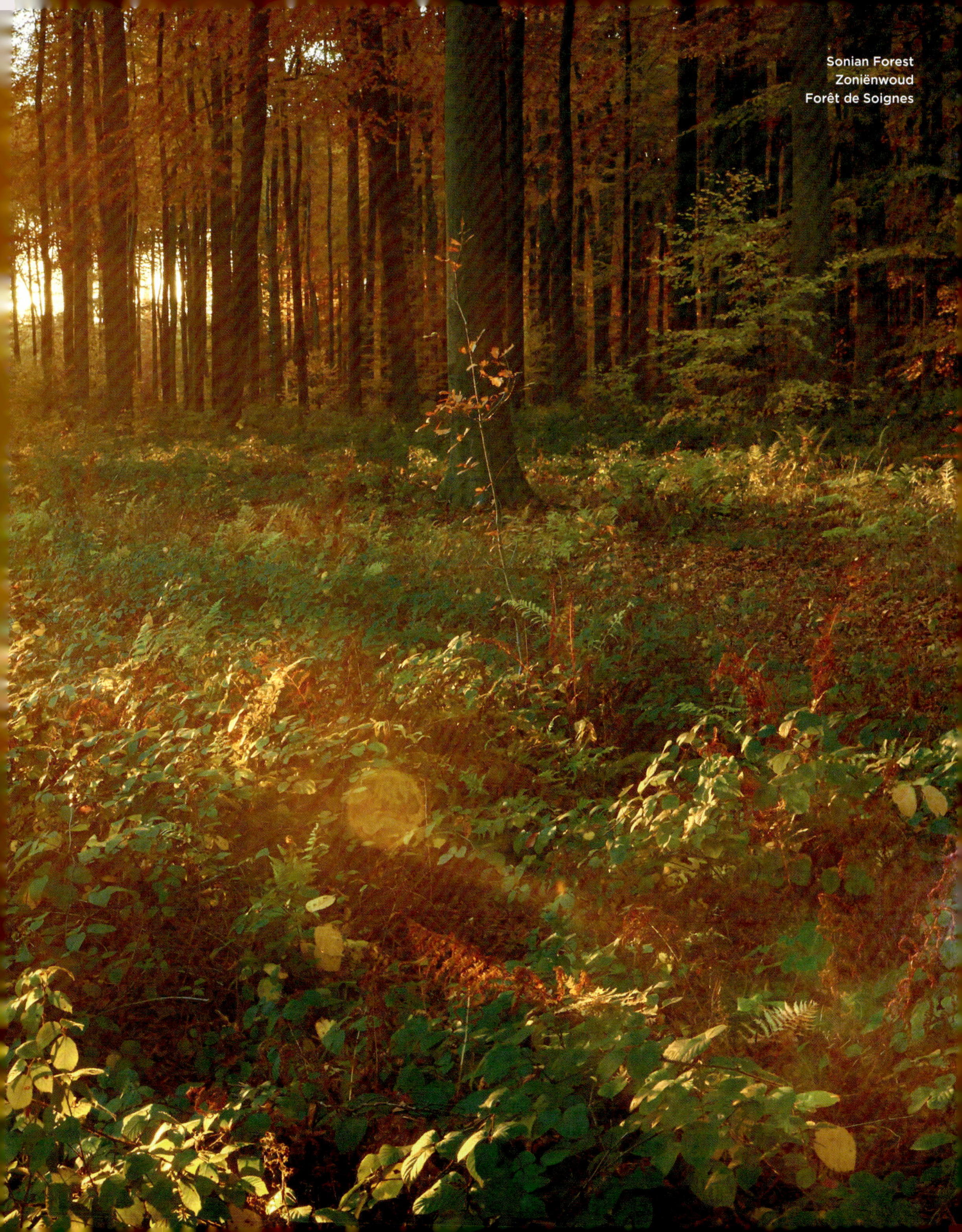

Sonian Forest
Zoniënwoud
Forêt de Soignes

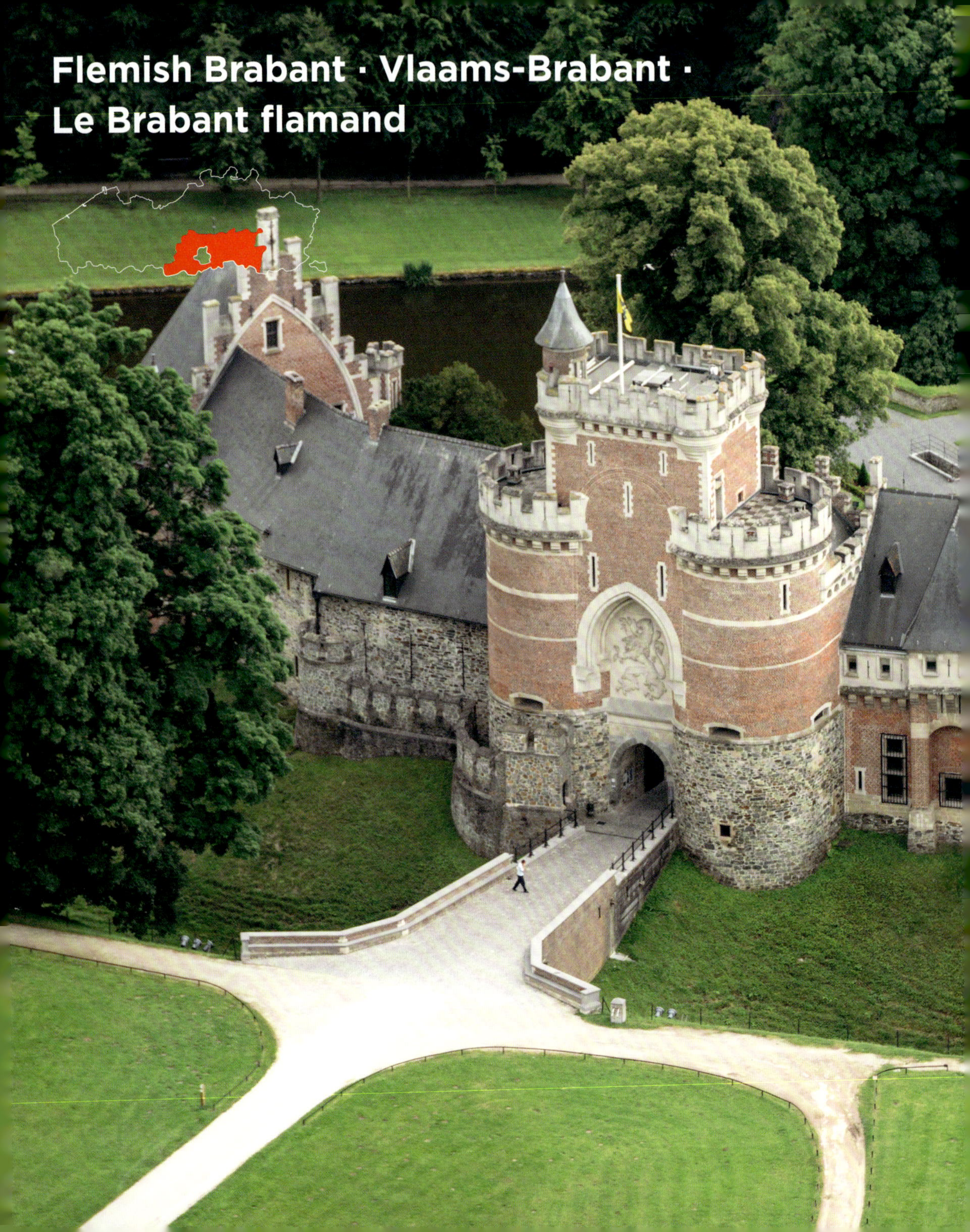

Flemish Brabant · Vlaams-Brabant ·
Le Brabant flamand

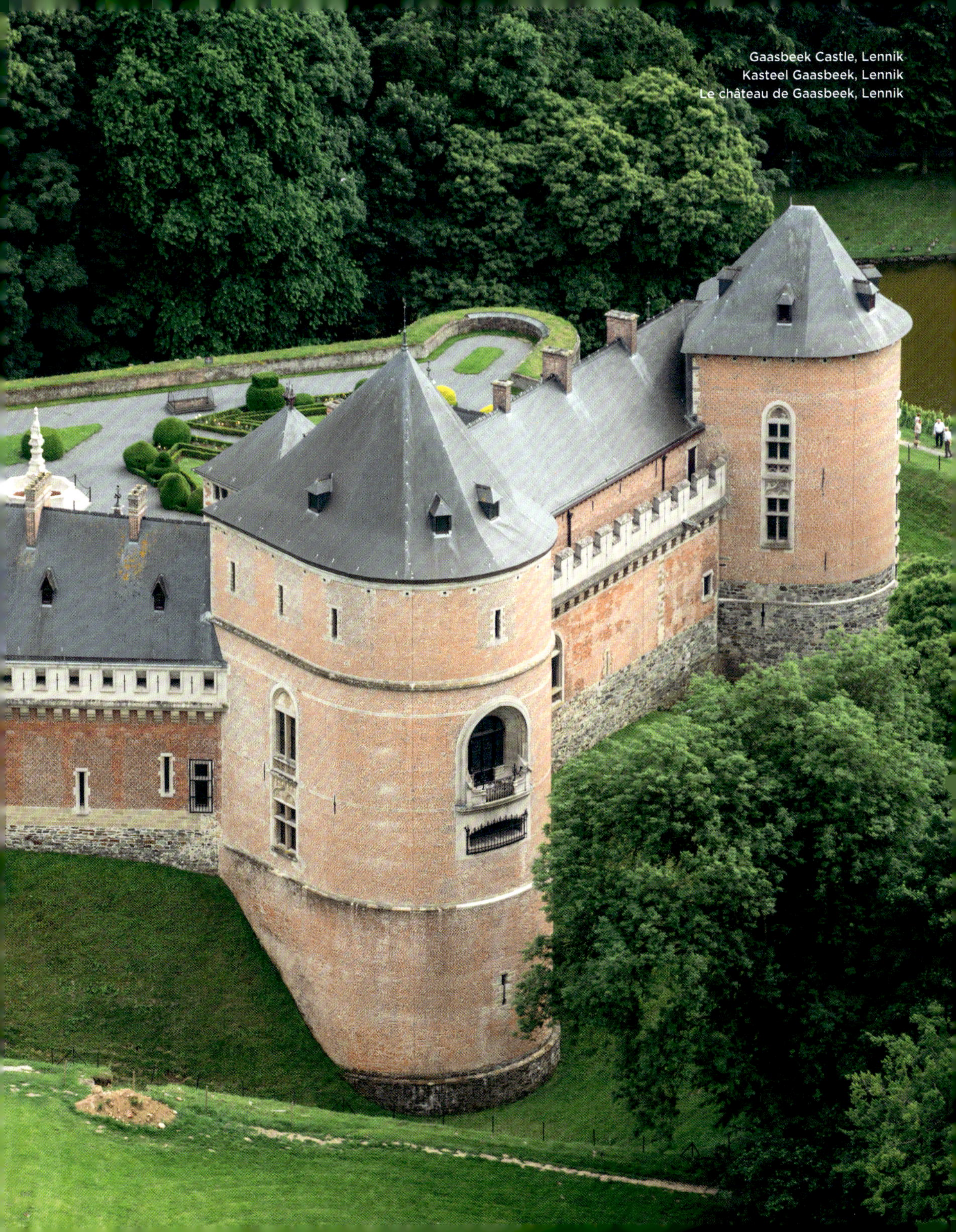
Gaasbeek Castle, Lennik
Kasteel Gaasbeek, Lennik
Le château de Gaasbeek, Lennik

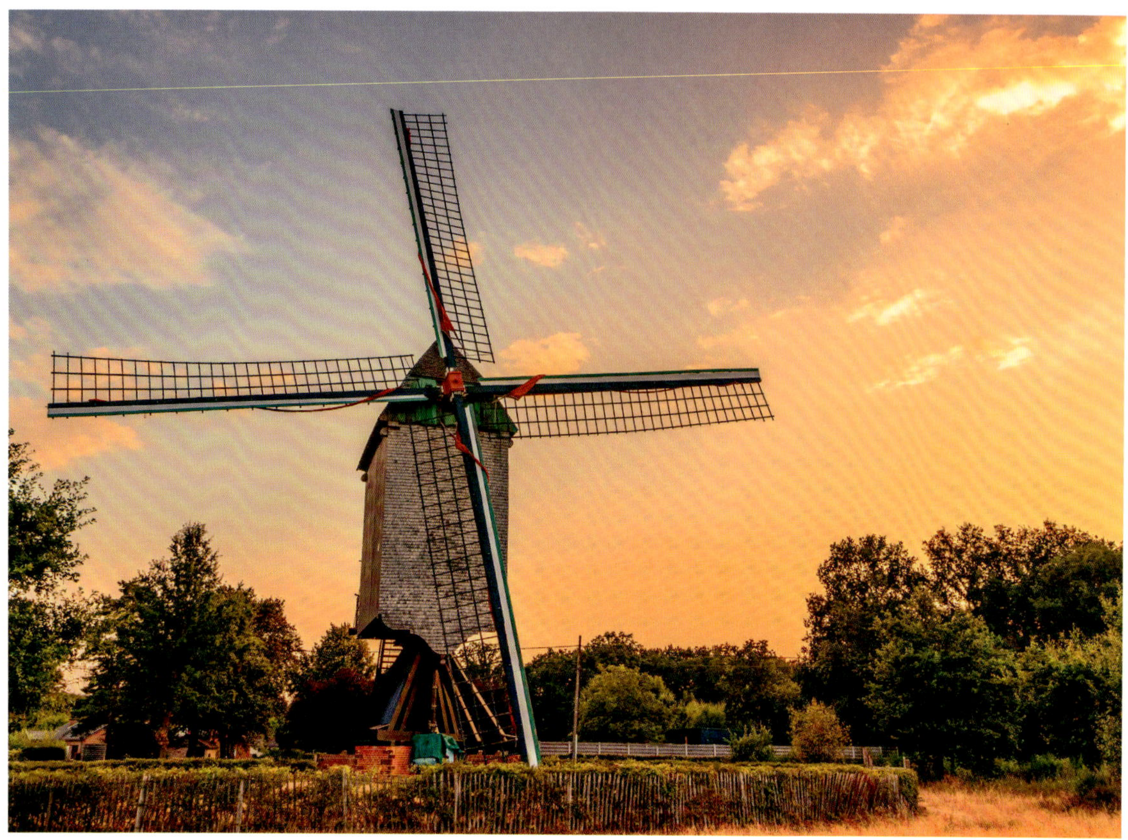

Windmill, Aarschot
Heimolen, Aarschot
Moulin à vent, Aarschot

Flemish Brabant

The Flemish painter Pieter Bruegel the Elder, known for his landscape painting and depictions of rural life, painted outside of the city of Brussels. His motifs of farmhouses, windmills and church towers can still be found today in the rural area around Brussels, a region where parades and processions take place in almost all towns and villages. The most visited place of pilgrimage in Flanders is Scherpenheuvel. What Lourdes is for the French, Scherpenheuvel is for the Belgians. The pretty city is grouped around the Basilica of Our Lady of Scherpenheuvel, in which a wooden statue of the Virgin Mary, which is said to have performed miracles, is revered.

Le Brabant flamand

Connu pour ses représentations de la vie rurale et sa peinture de paysage, l'artiste flamand Brueghel peignait aux portes de Bruxelles. Aujourd'hui encore, on retrouve ses motifs – fermes, moulins à vent, clochers – dans la région rurale autour de la capitale belge, une région dont presque toutes les villes et tous les villages ont leurs propres défilés et processions. Le lieu de pèlerinage le plus visité en Flandres est Montaigu. Ce que Lourdes est pour les Français, Montaigu l'est pour les Belges. La jolie ville s'organise autour d'une basilique où l'on vénère une statue en bois de la Vierge Marie, dont on dit qu'elle fait des miracles.

Flämisch-Brabant

Der flämische Maler Pieter Bruegel der Ältere, bekannt für seine Darstellungen des bäuerlichen Lebens und Landschaftsmalerei, malte vor den Toren Brüssels. Noch heute findet man seine Motive – Bauernhäuser, Windmühlen und Kirchentürme – in der ländlichen Region rund um Brüssel. Eine Region in der fast in allen Städten und Dörfern Umzüge und Prozessionen stattfinden. Der meistbesuchte Wallfahrtsort in Flandern ist Scherpenheuvel. Was den Franzosen ihr Lourdes, ist Scherpenheuvel für die Belgier. Die hübsche Stadt gruppiert sich rund um eine Basilika, in der eine Holzstatue der Jungfrau Maria angebetet wird, die Wunder vollbringen soll.

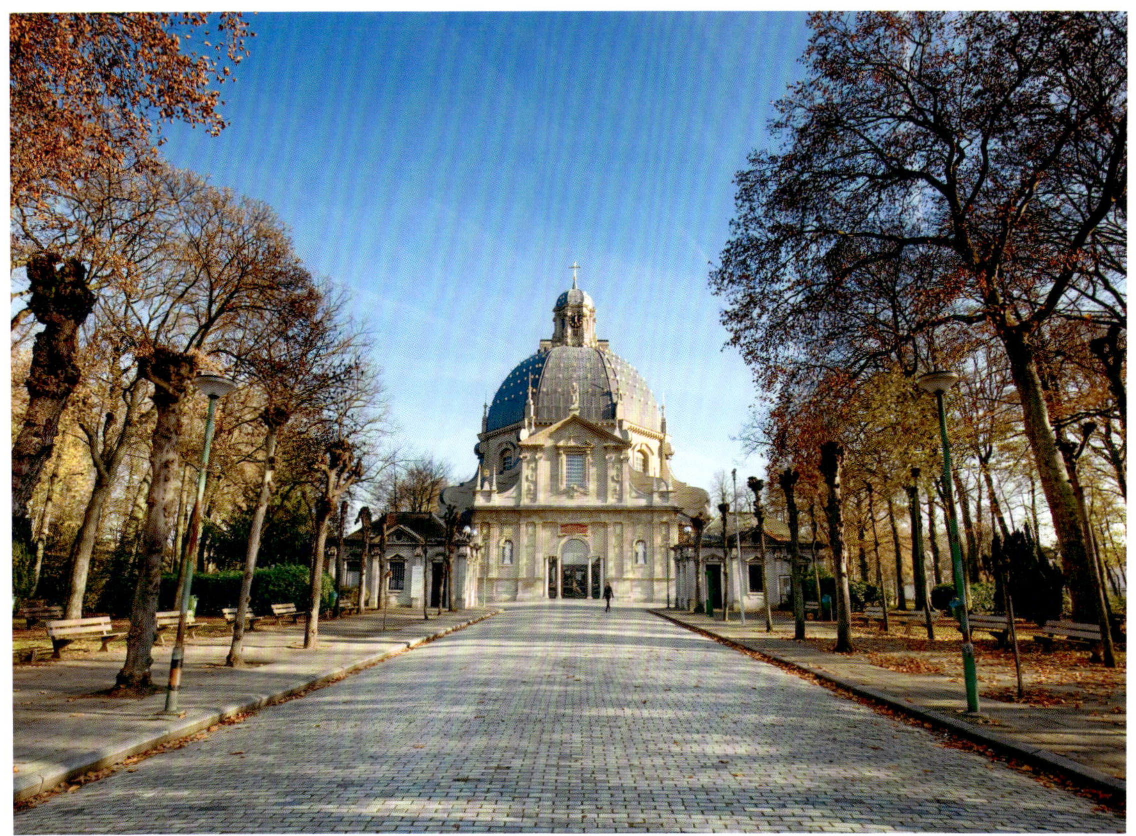

Basilica of Our Lady of Scherpenheuvel
Basiliek van Onze-Lieve-Vrouw van Scherpenheuvel
Basilique Notre-Dame de Montaigu

Brabante flamenco

El pintor flamenco Pieter Brueghel el Viejo, conocido por sus representaciones de la vida rural y la pintura paisajística, pintó a las puertas de Bruselas. Sus motivos, caseríos, molinos de viento y torres de iglesias todavía se pueden encontrar hoy en día en la región rural de los alrededores de Bruselas. Una región donde se realizan desfiles y procesiones en casi todas las ciudades y pueblos. El lugar de peregrinación más visitado de Flandes es Scherpenheuvel. Scherpenheuvel es para los belgas lo que Lourdes es para los franceses. La bonita ciudad está agrupada en torno a una basílica en la que se venera a una estatua de madera de la Virgen María, de la que se dice que hace milagros.

Brabante Flamengo

O pintor flamengo Pieter Brueghel o Velho, conhecido pelas suas representações da vida rural e pintura da paisagem, pintou nos arredores de Bruxelas. Os seus motivos, casas agrícolas, moinhos de vento e torres de igrejas ainda hoje podem ser encontrados na região rural de Bruxelas. Uma região na qual, em quase todas as cidades e vilas, desfiles e procissões acontecem. O lugar de peregrinação mais visitado da Flandres é Scherpenheuvel. O que Lourdes é para os franceses, Scherpenheuvel é para os belgas. A bela cidade é agrupada em torno de uma basílica em que uma estátua de madeira da Virgem Maria é adorada, para realização de milagres.

Vlaams-Brabant

De Vlaamse schilder Pieter Bruegel de Oude, bekend van zijn voorstellingen van het plattelandsleven en de landschapsschilderkunst, schilderde aan de poorten van Brussel. Zijn motieven, boerderijen, windmolens en kerktorens zijn nog steeds terug te vinden in de landelijke regio rond Brussel. Een regio waarin bijna in alle steden en dorpen parades en processies plaatsvinden. Het meest bezochte bedevaartsoord in Vlaanderen is Scherpenheuvel. Wat Lourdes is voor de Fransen, is Scherpenheuvel voor de Belgen. De fraaie stad groepeert zich rond een basiliek waarin een houten Mariabeeld wordt vereerd dat naar verluidt wonderen verricht.

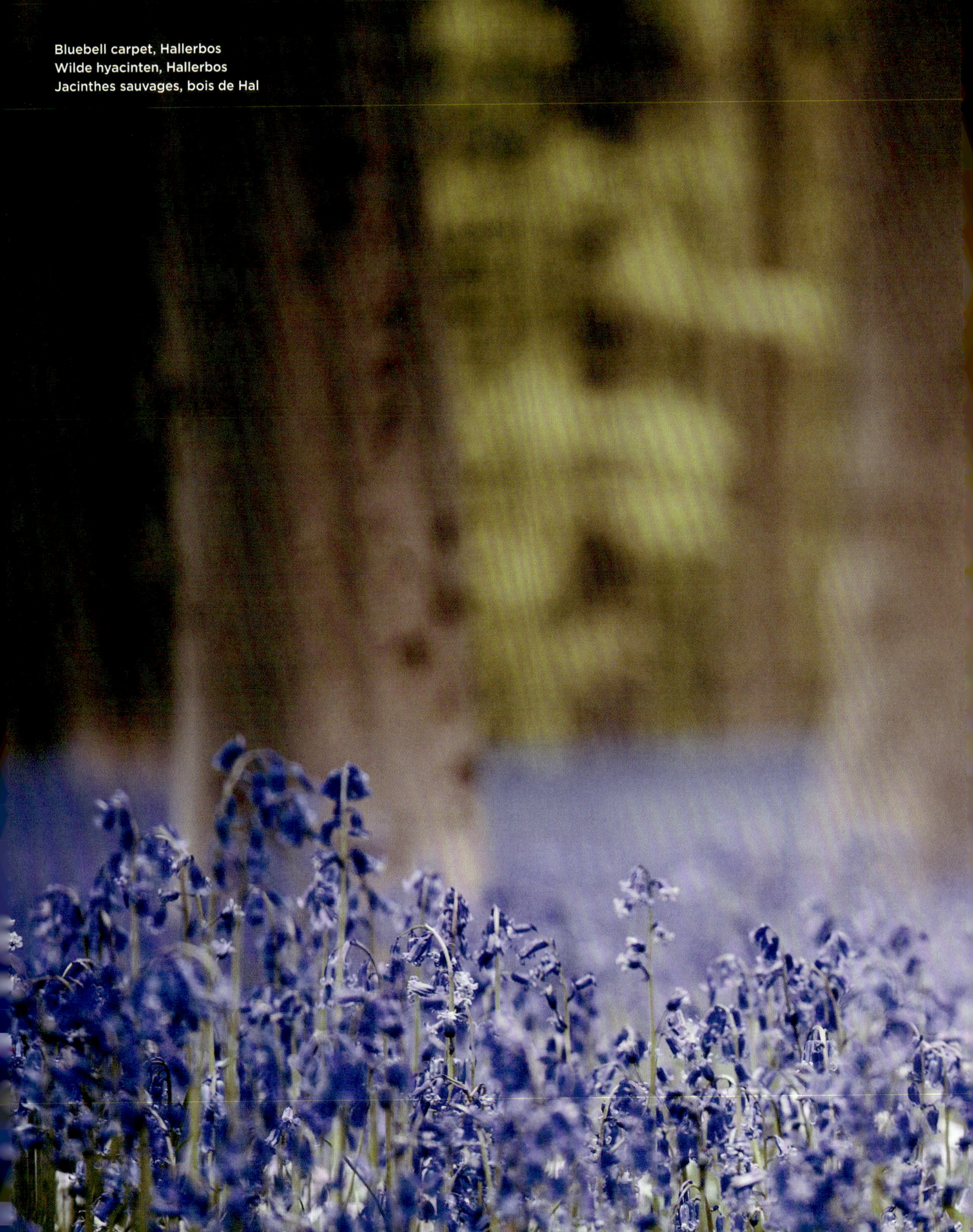

Bluebell carpet, Hallerbos
Wilde hyacinten, Hallerbos
Jacinthes sauvages, bois de Hal

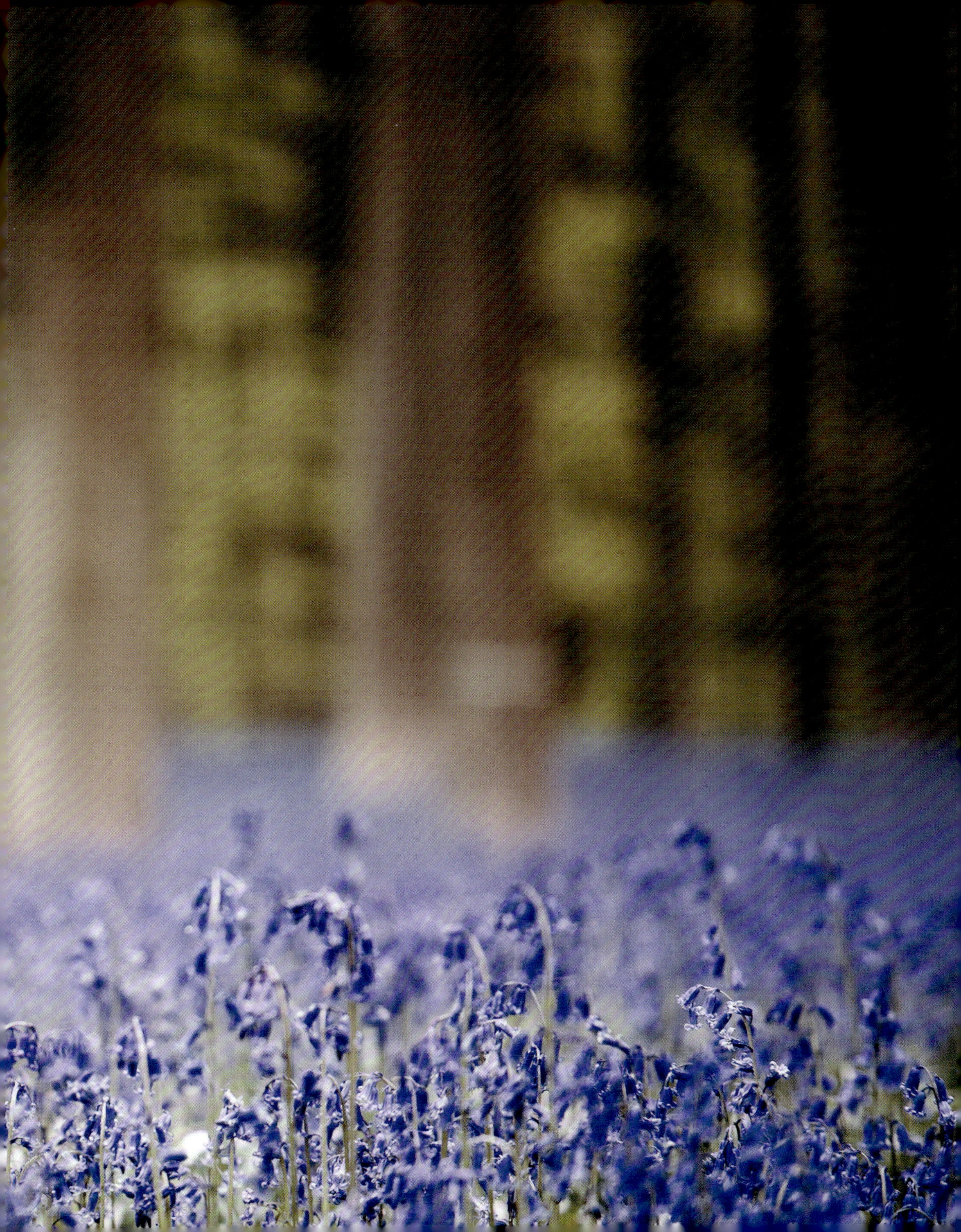

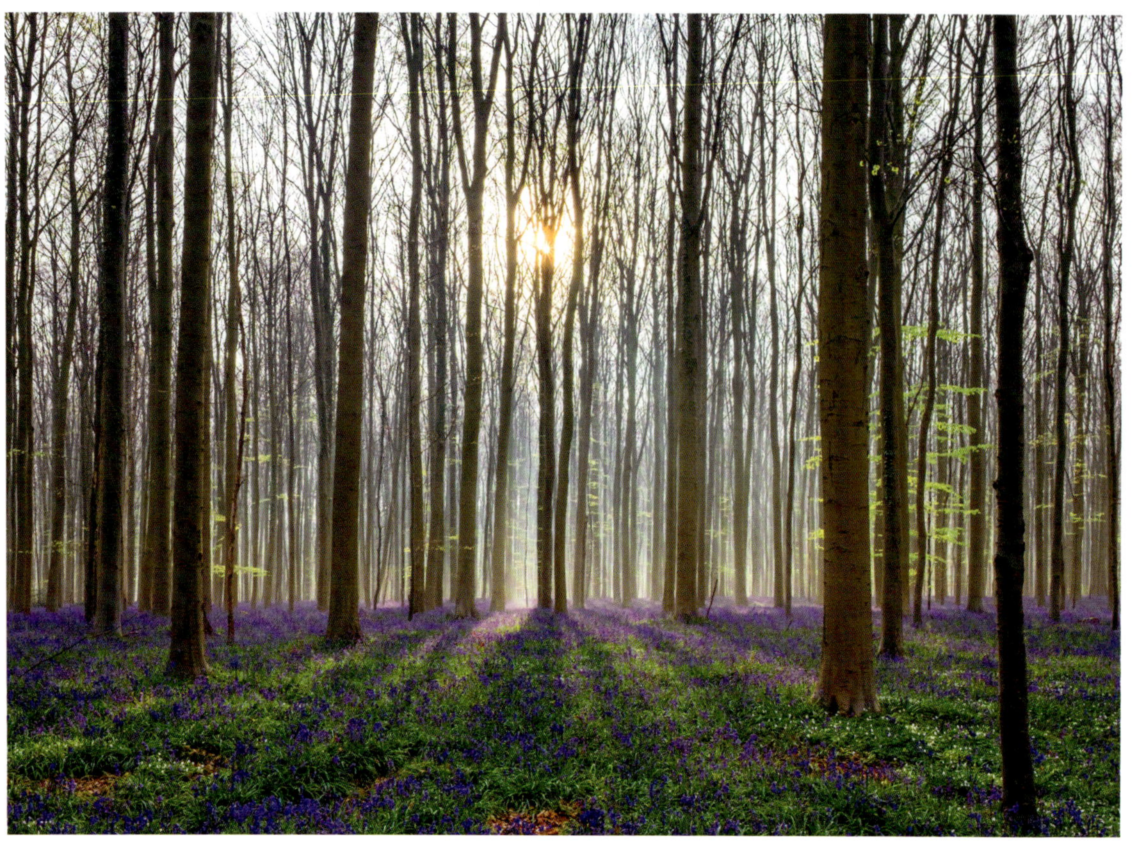

Hallerbos
Bois de Hal

The blue forest

The "blue forest" stretches about 20 km
(12,4 mi) southwest of Brussels. In spring,
a bright blue carpet of wild hyacinths,
or bluebells, covers the forest floor. The
beeches stand close together in a sea
of flowers. If the sun falls through the
treetops at the right angle, the atmosphere
created is magical. The mixed forest, near
the small town of Halle, is officially called
Hallerbos and is a remnant of the huge
charcoal forest of Silvia Carbona which in
ancient times stretched from the centre of
Flanders to the Meuse. The dense carpet of
hyacinths is estimated to have formed over
a period of 400 years.

La forêt bleue

La forêt bleue s'étend à environ 20 km
au sud-ouest de Bruxelles. Au printemps,
un tapis bleu vif de jacinthes des bois en
recouvre le sol. Les hêtres sont serrés
les uns près des autres dans un océan
de fleurs. Et lorsque les rayons du soleil
adoptent le bon angle pour traverser les
cimes des arbres, l'atmosphère devient
féerique. Vestige de la forêt Charbonnière
qui s'étendait autrefois du centre des
Flandres à la Meuse, cette forêt mixte
près de la petite ville de Hal s'appelle
officiellement Hallerbos (le bois de Hal).
On estime que la dense population de
jacinthes s'est formée en 400 ans.

Der blaue Wald

Rund 20 km südwestlich von Brüssel
erstreckt sich der blaue Wald. Im Frühling
legt sich ein leuchtend blauer Teppich aus
wilden Hyazinthen (Hasenglöckchen) über
den Waldboden. Dicht an dicht stehen
die Buchen in einem Meer aus Blüten.
Fällt dann noch die Sonne im richtigen
Winkel durch die Wipfel, herrscht eine
märchenhafte Atmosphäre. Der Mischwald
in der Nähe des Städtchens Halle, heißt
offiziell Hallerbos und ist ein Rest eines
Kohlenwalds, der sich in der Antike von der
Mitte Flanderns bis an die Maas erstreckte.
Das dichte Geflecht aus Hyazinthen soll
sich Schätzungen zufolge über 400 Jahre
gebildet haben.

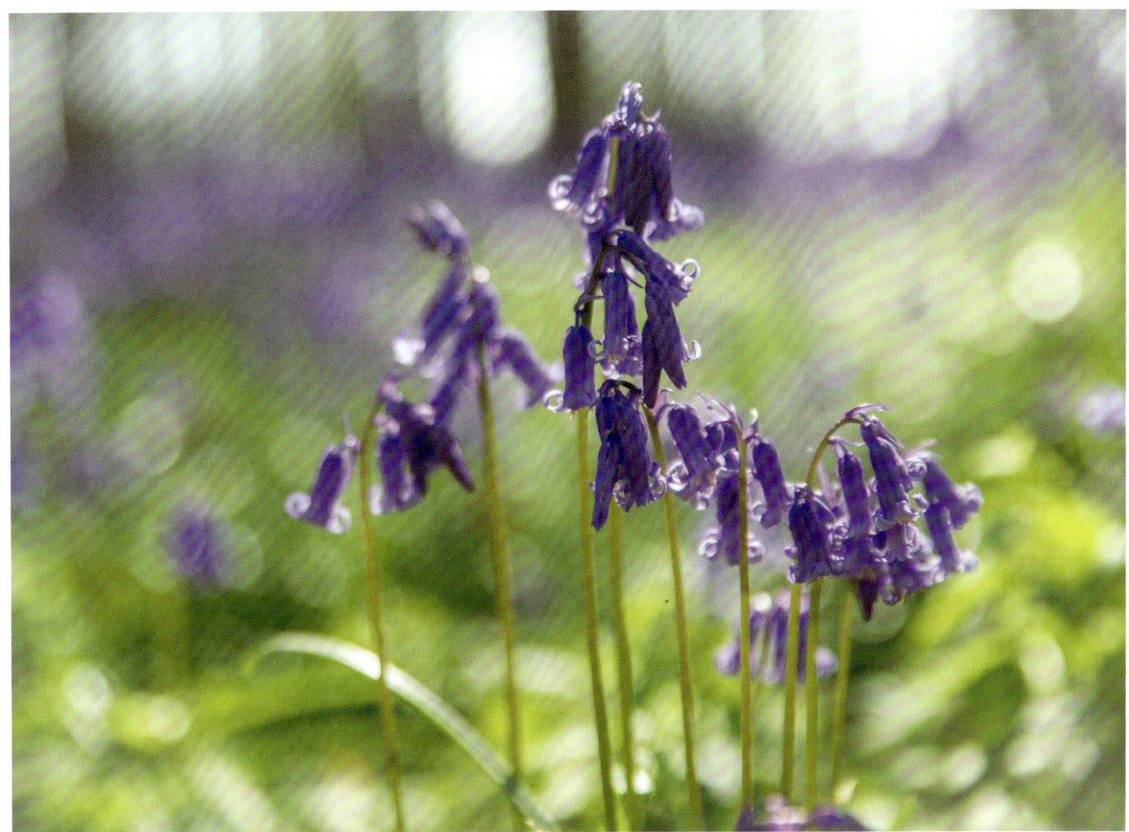

Bluebells
Wilde hycacinten
Jacinthes sauvages

El bosque azul

El bosque azul se extiende a unos 20 km al suroeste de Bruselas. En primavera, una alfombra azul brillante de jacintos salvajes *(Hyacinthoides)* cubre el suelo del bosque. Las hayas están juntas en un mar de flores. Si el sol cae a través de las copas de los árboles en el ángulo correcto, la atmósfera es mágica. El bosque mixto cerca de la pequeña ciudad de Halle se llama oficialmente Hallerbos y es un remanente de un bosque carbonífero que en la antigüedad se extendía desde el centro de Flandes hasta el Mosa. Se estima que la densa red de jacintos se ha formado durante 400 años.

A floresta azul

A floresta azul estende-se cerca de 20 km a sudoeste de Bruxelas. Na primavera, um tapete azul brilhante de jacintos da floresta (campainhas azuis) cobre o chão da floresta. Bem juntas uma com a outra, as faias encontram-se num mar de flores. Quando o sol cai no ângulo certo através das copas das árvores, prevalece uma atmosfera mágica. A floresta mista perto da pequena cidade de Halle é oficialmente chamada de Hallerbos e é um remanescente de uma floresta de carvão, que nos tempos antigos se estendia do centro da Flandres para o rio Mosa. Estima-se que a densa rede de jacintos se tenha formado ao longo de 400 anos.

Het blauwe bos

Het blauwe bos strekt zich ca. 20 km zuidwestelijk van Brussel uit. In het voorjaar bedekt een glanzend blauw tapijt van wilde hyacinten de bodem van het bos. In een zee van bloemen staan de beuken dicht bij elkaar. Als de zon dan in de juiste hoek door de boomtoppen valt, dan heerst er een sprookjesachtige sfeer. Het gemengde bos nabij het stadje Halle heet officieel Hallerbos en is een overblijfsel van een steenkoolbos dat zich in de klassieke oudheid uitstrekte van het centrum van Vlaanderen tot aan de Maas. Het dichte netwerk van hyacinten zou zich volgens schattingen in meer dan 400 jaar tijd hebben ontwikkeld.

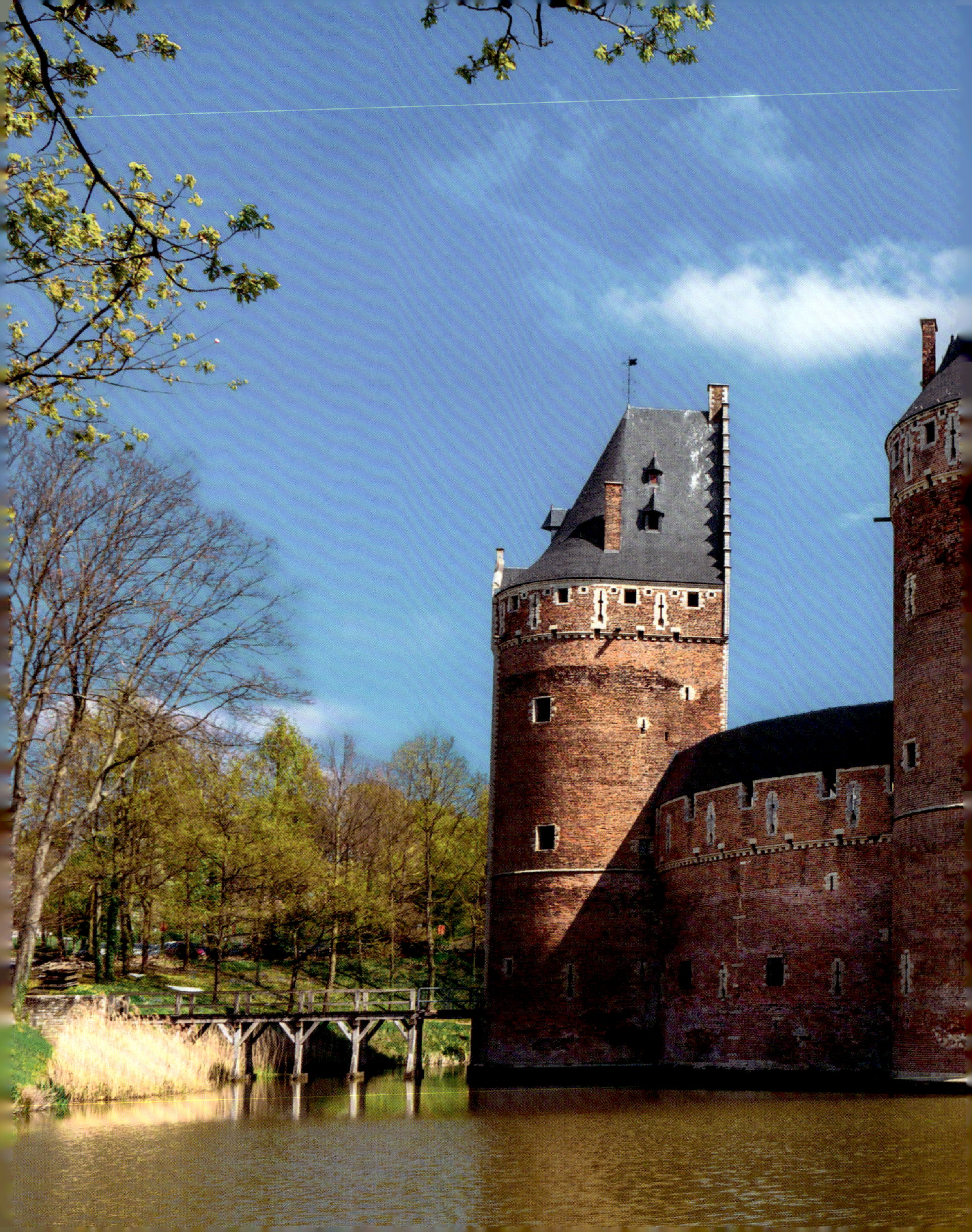

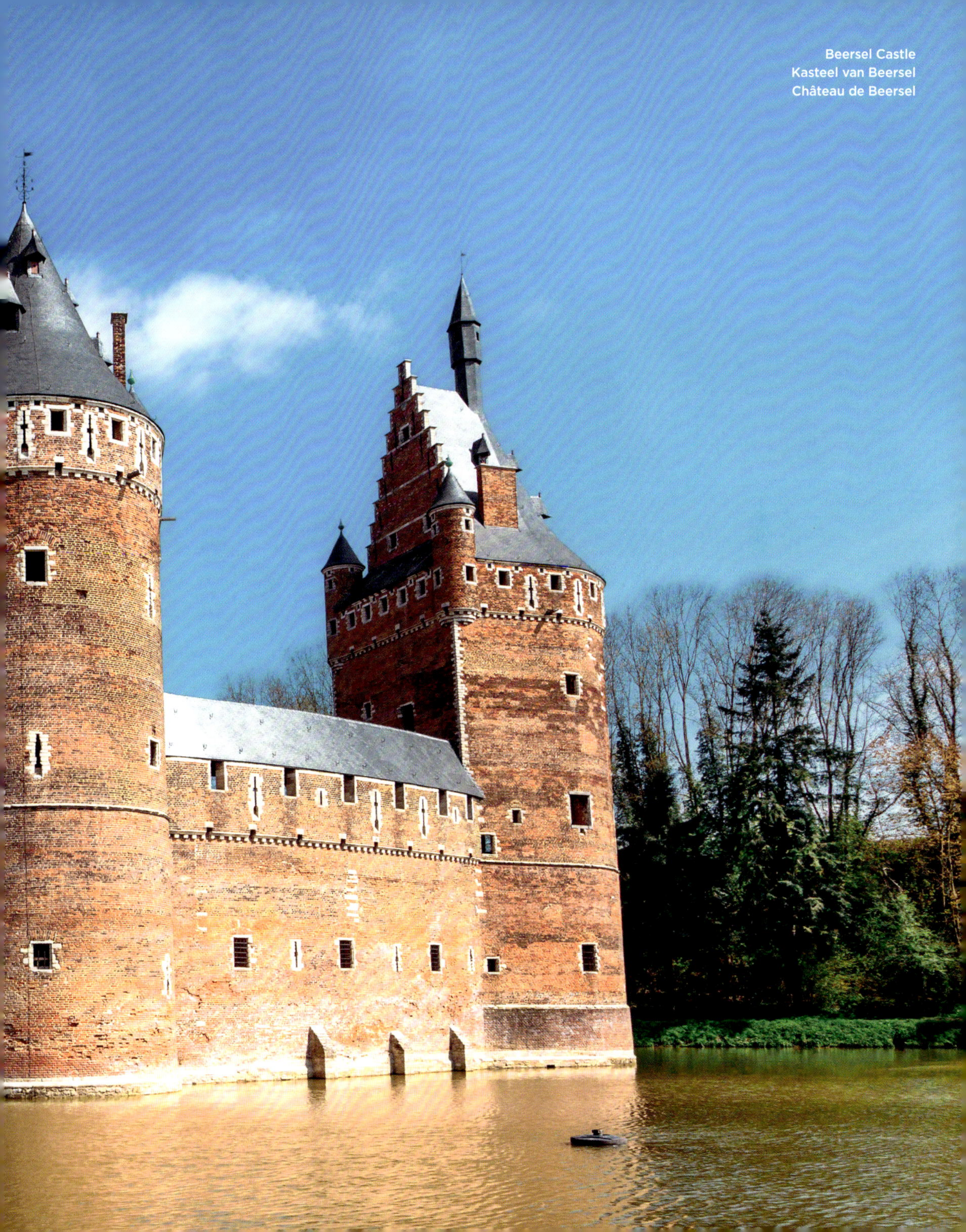

Beersel Castle
Kasteel van Beersel
Château de Beersel

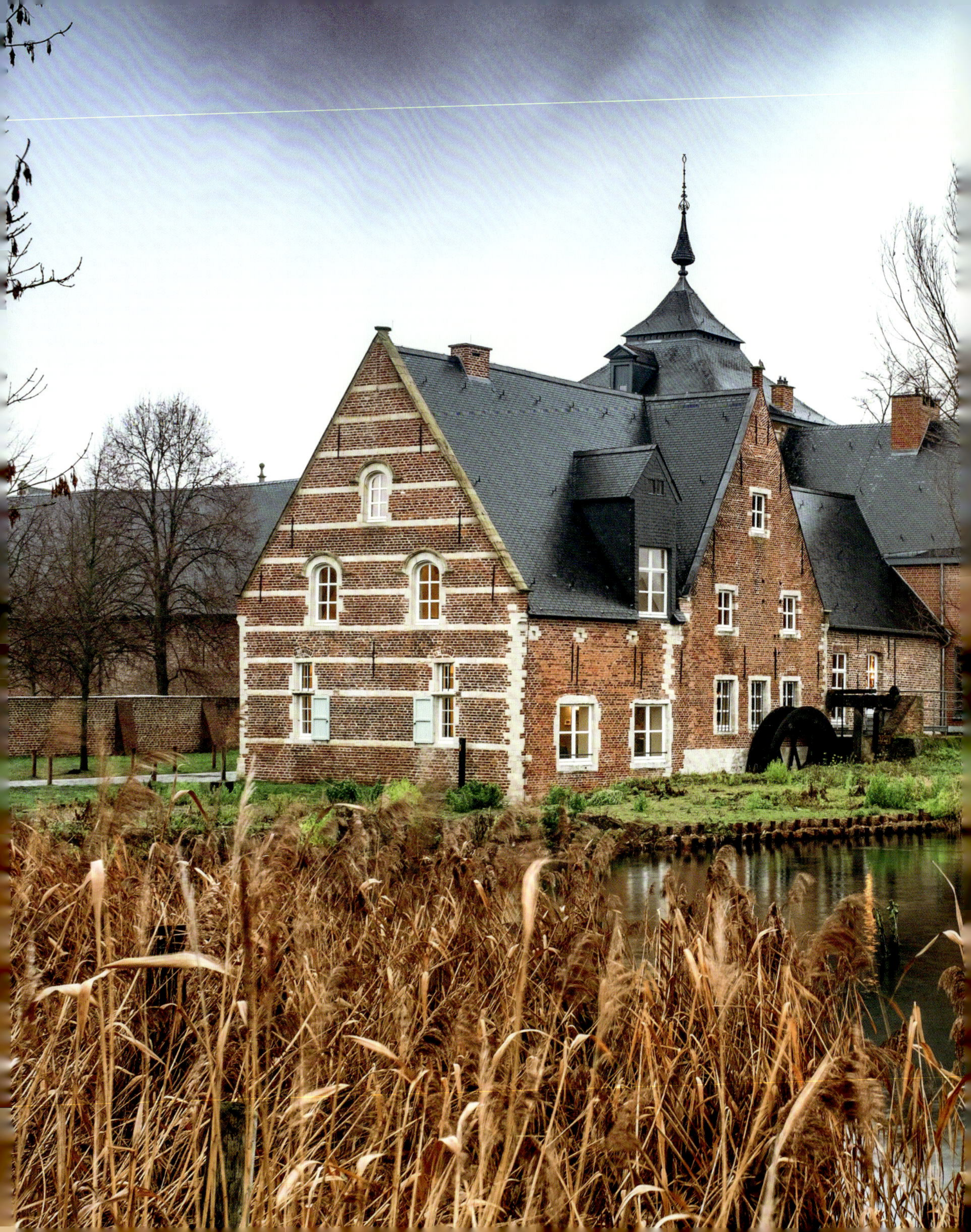

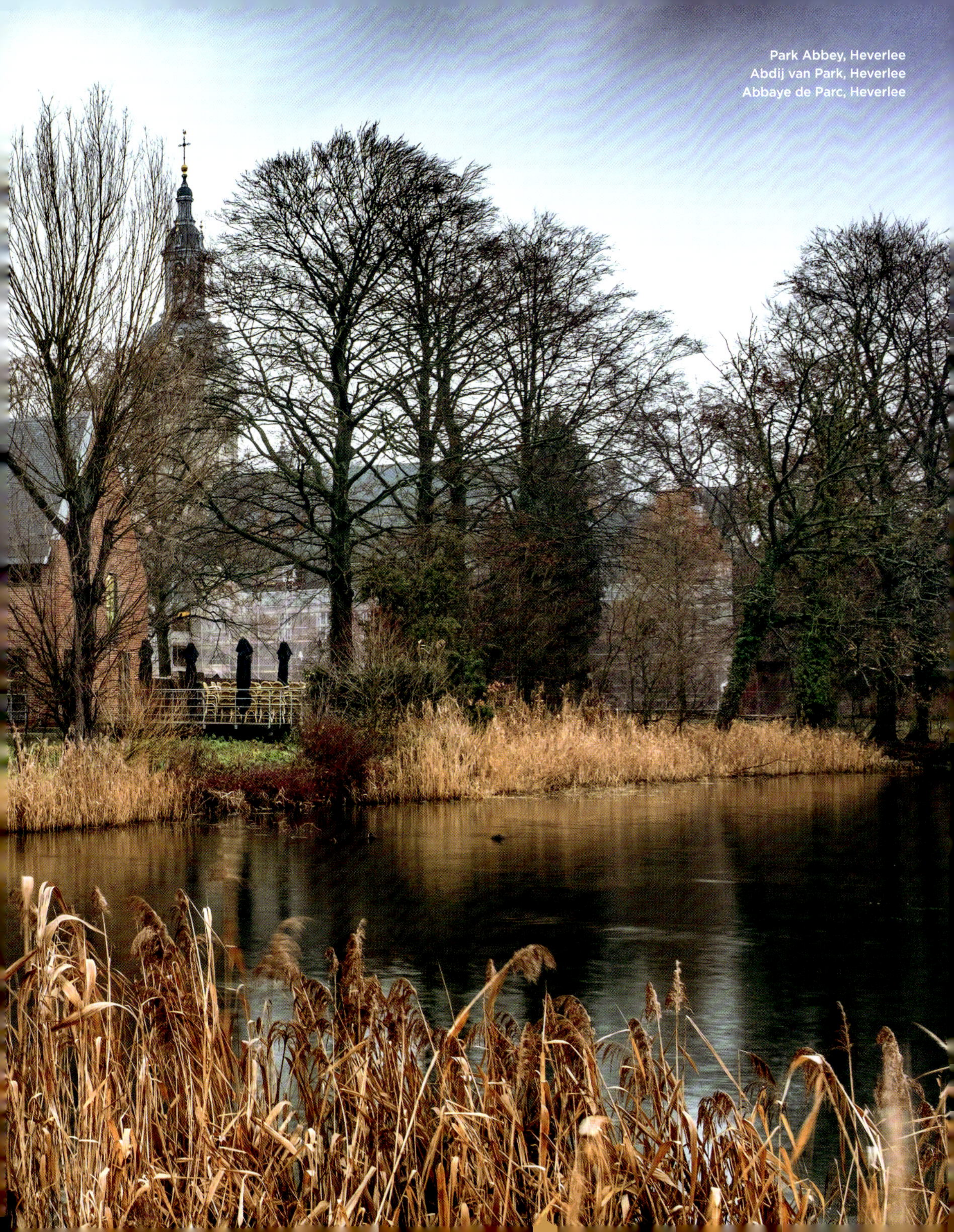

Park Abbey, Heverlee
Abdij van Park, Heverlee
Abbaye de Parc, Heverlee

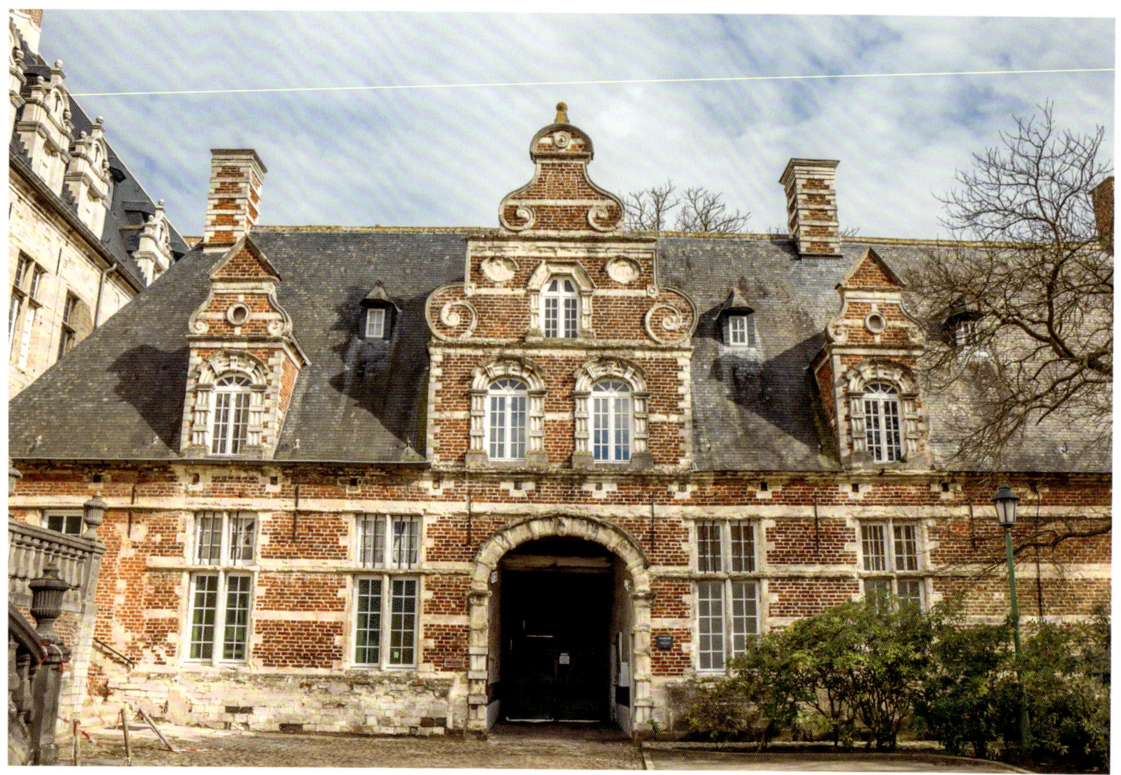

Park Abbey, Heverlee
Abdij van Park, Heverlee
Abbaye de Parc, Heverlee

Park Abbey near Löwen

The Park Abbey is one of the best preserved monasteries in Flanders. Since its foundation in 1129, the abbey has been inhabited by the Premonstratensian community. Worth seeing is the Romanesque monastery church and the monumental Norbertus Gate. The abbey is surrounded by walls, gates and a spacious park with avenues and fishponds.

Abadía del Parque de Lovaina

La abadía del Parque es una de las abadías mejor conservadas de Flandes. Desde su fundación en 1129, la abadía ha sido habitada por la comunidad premonstratense. Destacan la iglesia del monasterio románico y la monumental puerta de Norbertus. La abadía está rodeada de murallas, puertas y un amplio parque con avenidas y estanques.

L'abbaye de Parc près de Louvain

L'abbaye de Parc est l'une des abbayes les mieux conservées de Flandres. L'ordre des chanoines réguliers de Prémontré l'habite depuis sa fondation en 1129. Son église romane et le portail monumental Saint-Norbert valent le détour. L'abbaye est entourée de murs, de portes et d'un grand parc avec allées et étangs peuplés de poissons.

Abadia do parque perto de Lovaina

A abadia do parque é uma das abadias mais bem preservadas da Flandres. Desde a sua fundação em 1129, a abadia foi habitada pela ordem monástica premonstratense. Vale a pena ver a igreja românica do mosteiro e o monumental portão Norbertus. A abadia é cercada por muros, portões e um amplo parque com avenidas e tanques de peixes.

Parkabtei bei Löwen

Die Parkabtei ist eine der am besten erhaltenen Abteien Flanderns. Seit ihrer Gründung im Jahr 1129 wird die Abtei von der Ordensgemeinschaft der Prämonstratenser bewohnt. Sehenswert ist die romanische Klosterkirche und das monumentale Norbertustor. Rund um die Abtei erstrecken sich Mauern, Torbauten und ein großzügiger Park mit Alleen und Fischteichen.

Abdij van Park

De Abdij van Park is één van de best bewaarde abdijen van Vlaanderen. Sinds de oprichting in 1129 wordt de abdij bewoond door de kloosterorde van reguliere kanunniken van de Orde van Prém. Bezienswaardig is de romaanse kloosterkerk en de monumentale Norbertuspoort. De abdij is omgeven door muren, poorten en een ruim park met lanen en visvijvers.

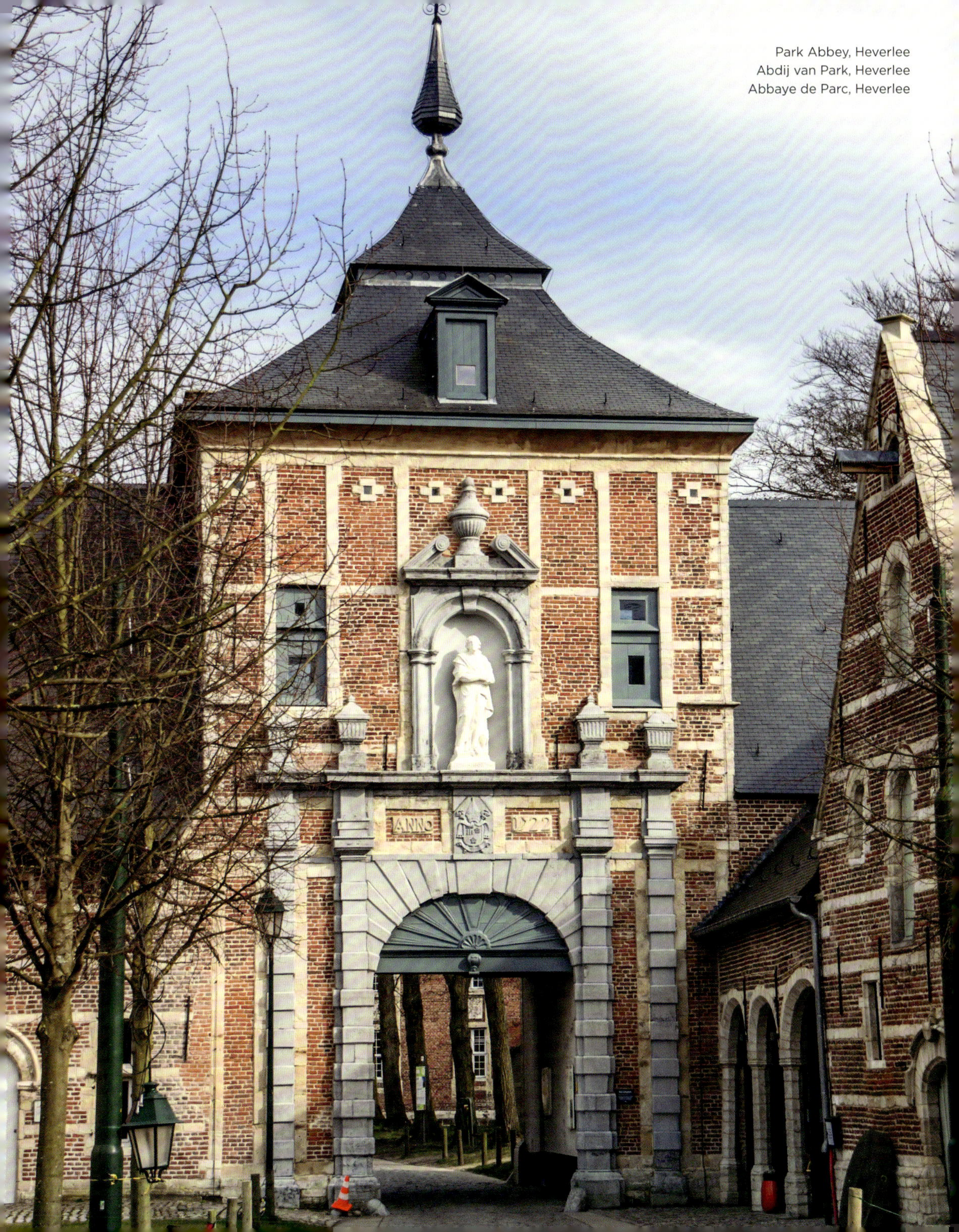

Park Abbey, Heverlee
Abdij van Park, Heverlee
Abbaye de Parc, Heverlee

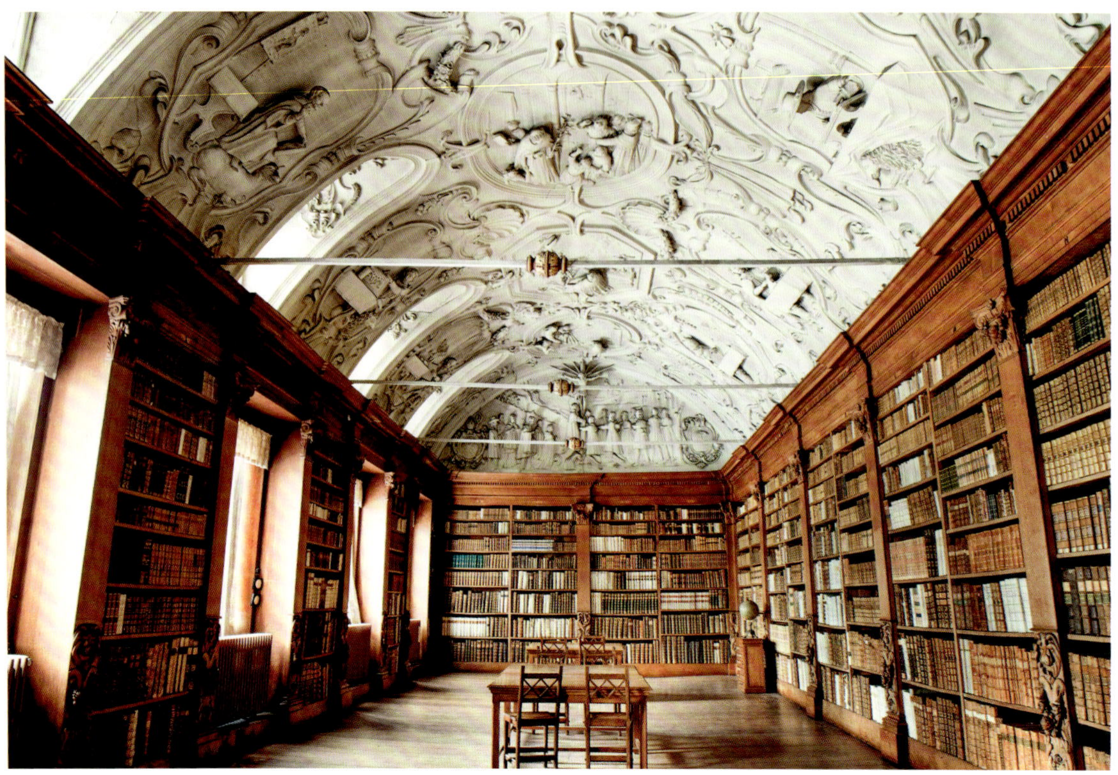

Library, Park Abbey, Heverlee
Libraberie, Abdij van Park, Heverlee
Bibliothèque, abbaye de Parc, Heverlee

Inside the abbey

Since the 17th century, the monastery buildings and their interiors have remained almost unchanged, housing the extraordinary stucco ceiling in the refectory, the library containing around 6000 old prints and the cloister with stained glass windows. In the newly created museum, temporary exhibitions provide in-depth insights into Flemish monastic and religious history.

À l'intérieur de l'abbaye

Depuis le XVIIᵉ siècle, les bâtiments de l'abbaye et leur aménagement intérieur n'ont guère changé : on y admire les extraordinaires plafonds en stuc du réfectoire, la bibliothèque abritant environ 6 000 anciens ouvrages et le cloître avec ses vitraux. Dans le musée tout juste ouvert, des expositions temporaires donnent un aperçu approfondi de l'histoire monastique et religieuse flamande.

Im Innern der Abtei

Seit dem 17. Jahrhundert sind die Klostergebäude und ihre Innenausstattung nahezu unverändert: außergewöhnliche Stuckdecken im Refektorium, die Bibliothek mit rund 6000 alten Drucken und der Kreuzgang mit Buntglasfenstern. Im neu geschaffenen Museum geben Wechselausstellungen vertiefte Einblicke in die flämische Kloster- und Ordensgeschichte.

Dentro de la abadía

Desde el siglo XVII, los edificios del monasterio y sus interiores han permanecido casi inalterados: extraordinarios techos de estuco en el refectorio, la biblioteca con unos 6000 grabados antiguos y el claustro con vidrieras. En el museo recientemente creado, las exposiciones temporales ofrecen una visión en profundidad de la historia monástica y religiosa flamenca.

Dentro da abadia

Desde o século XVII, os edifícios do mosteiro e seus interiores permaneceram quase inalterados: extraordinários tetos de estuque no refeitório, a biblioteca com cerca de 6000 gravuras antigas e o claustro com vitrais. No museu recém-criado, as exposições temporárias oferecem uma visão aprofundada da história monástica e religiosa flamenga.

In de abdij

Sinds de 17e eeuw zijn de kloostergebouwen en hun interieur vrijwel onveranderd gebleven: buitengewone stucplafonds in het refectorium, de bibliotheek met ongeveer 6000 oude drukken en de kloostergang met glas-in-loodramen. In het nieuw gecreëerde museum geven tijdelijke tentoonstellingen een diepgaand inzicht in de Vlaamse klooster- en godsdienstgeschiedenis.

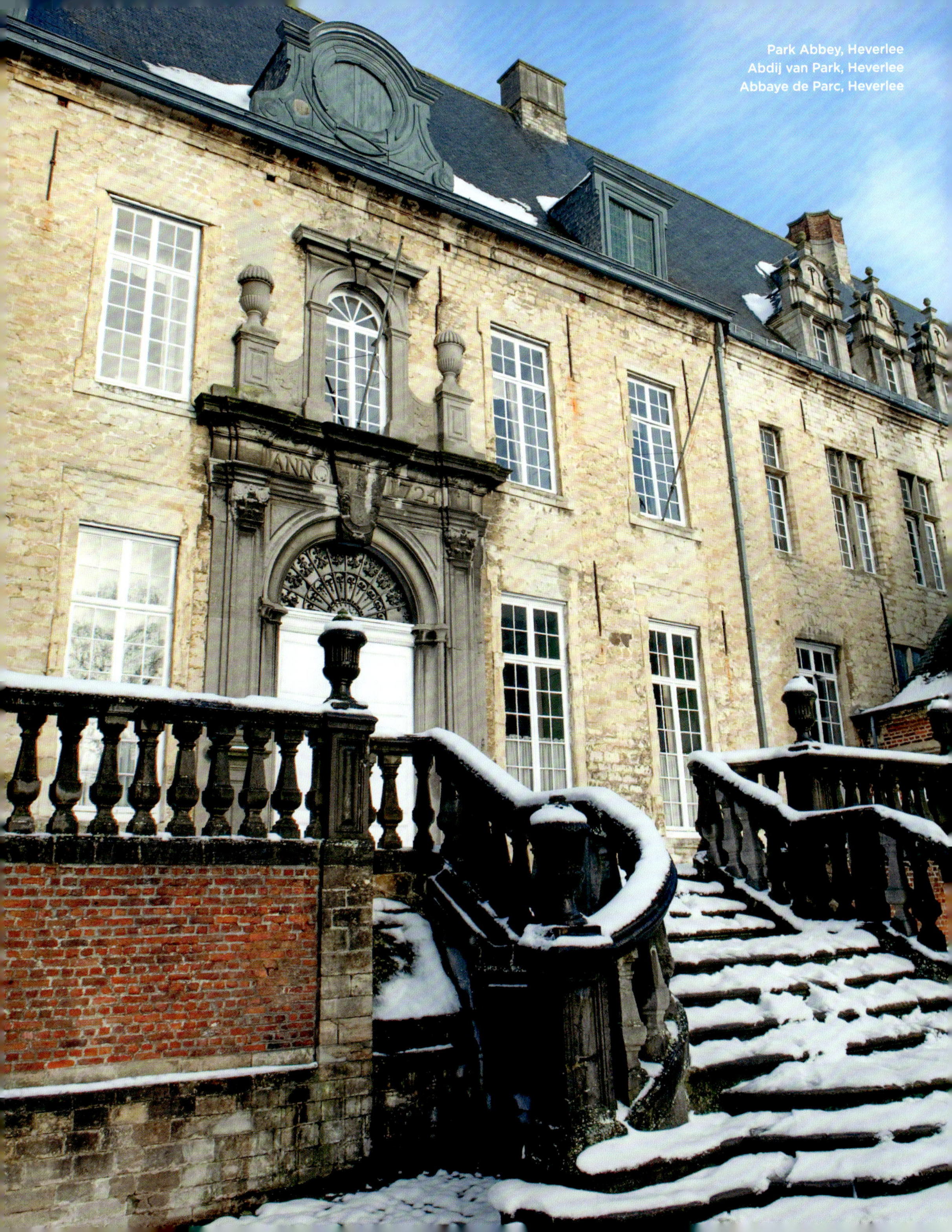

Park Abbey, Heverlee
Abdij van Park, Heverlee
Abbaye de Parc, Heverlee

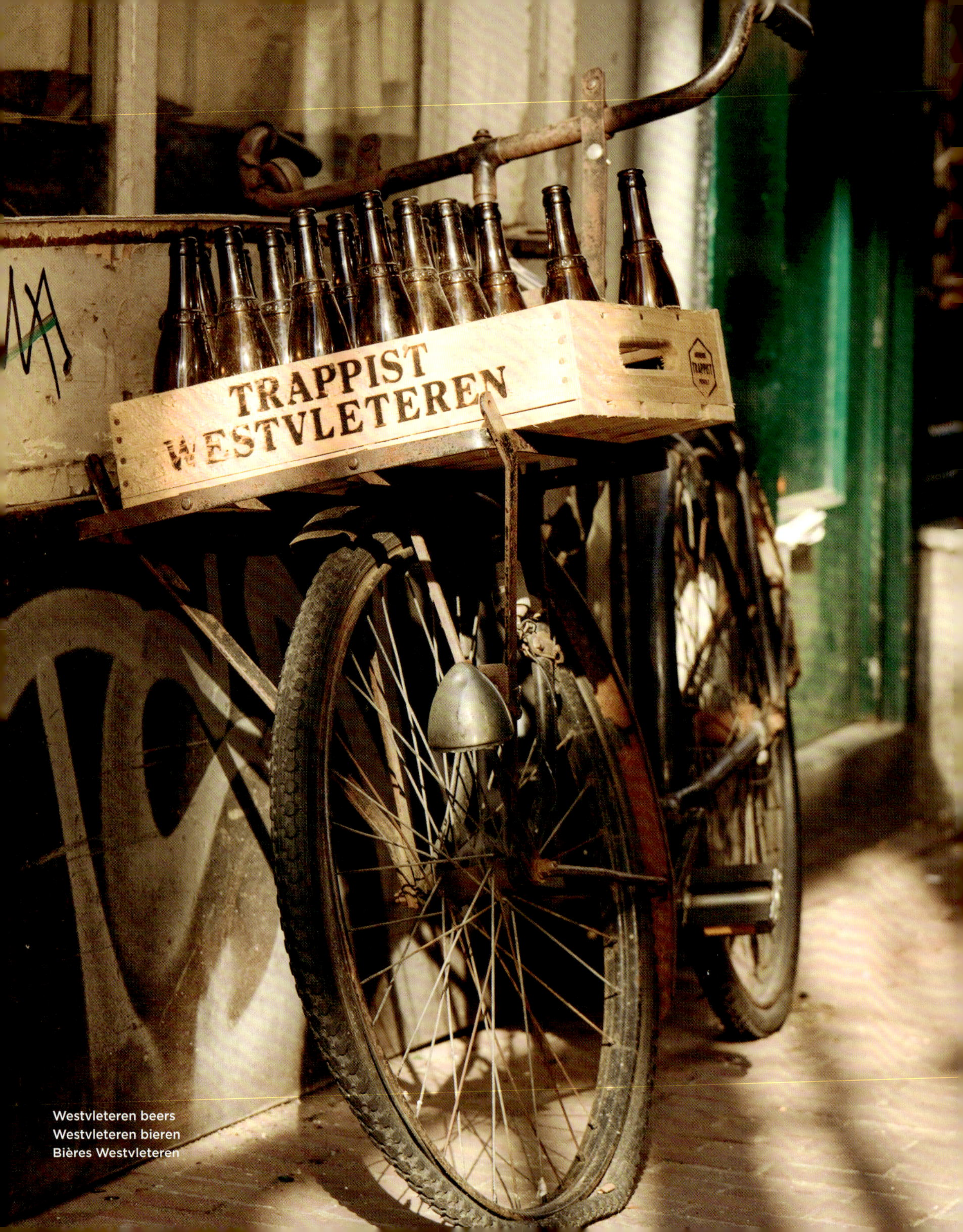

Westvleteren beers
Westvleteren bieren
Bières Westvleteren

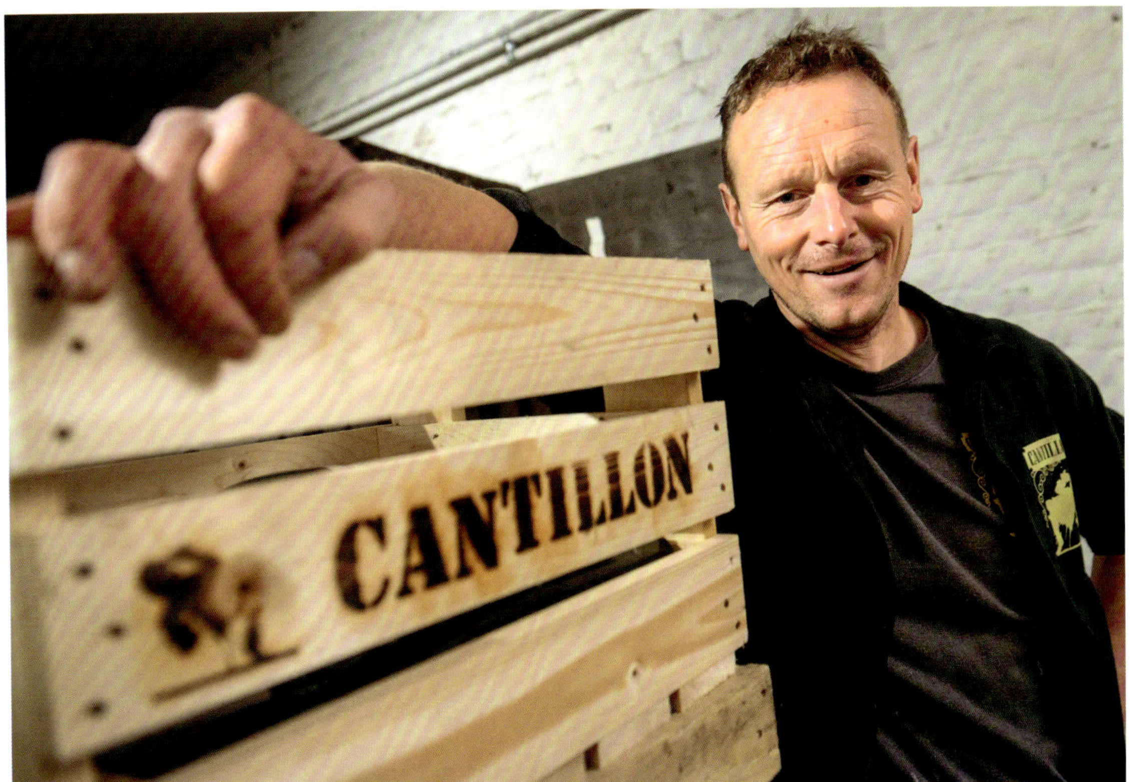

Cantillon Brewery
Cantillon Brouwerij
Brasserie Cantillon

Geuze and fruit beers

Geuze is a Flemish beer speciality that can only be produced in the area around Brussels. For the fermentation, the local airborne wild yeasts are necessary, with the yeast cultures not being artificially added. If sour cherries are included, the second fermentation after 3–18 months produces an intensely fruity cherry beer, Kriek.

Geuze y cervezas afrutadas

La Geuze es una especialidad de cerveza flamenca que solo puede producirse en la zona de Bruselas. Para la fermentación se necesitan las levaduras silvestres locales; los cultivos de levadura no se añaden artificialmente. Si se añaden cerezas frescas a la cerveza, la segunda fermentación después de 3–18 meses produce una cerveza de cerezas intensamente afrutada: la Kriek.

Gueuze et bières aux fruits

La Gueuze est une spécialité de bière flamande qui ne peut être produite qu'aux alentours de Bruxelles. Sa fermentation nécessite des levures sauvages locales; l'ajout artificiel de levure de culture est proscrit. Si l'on agrémente la bière de cerises fraîches, la deuxième fermentation produit, au bout de 3 à 18 mois, une bière à la cerise très fruitée, la Kriek.

Geuze e cervejas de fruta

O geuze é uma especialidade de cerveja flamenga que só pode ser produzida na região de Bruxelas. Para a fermentação é necessário o uso das leveduras silvestres locais, as leveduras de cultura não são adicionadas artificialmente. Se forem adicionadas cerejas frescas à cerveja, a segunda fermentação produz, após 3–18 meses, uma cerveja de cereja frutada intensa, Kriek.

Geuze und Fruchtbiere

Geuze ist eine flämische Bierspezialität, die nur in der Gegend rund um Brüssel hergestellt werden kann. Für die Gärung braucht man die lokalen wilden Hefen, die Hefekulturen werden nicht künstlich zugefügt. Wenn man dem Bier frische Kirschen hinzufügt, entsteht bei der zweiten Gärung nach 3–18 Monaten ein intensiv fruchtiges Kirschbier, Kriek.

Geuze en fruitbieren

Geuze is een Vlaamse bierspecialiteit die alleen in de omgeving van Brussel geproduceerd kan worden. Voor de gisting heb je de lokale, wilde gisten nodig, de gistculturen worden niet kunstmatig toegevoegd. Als verse kersen aan het bier worden toegevoegd, levert de tweede gisting na 3–18 maanden een intens fruitig kersenbier op; Kriek.

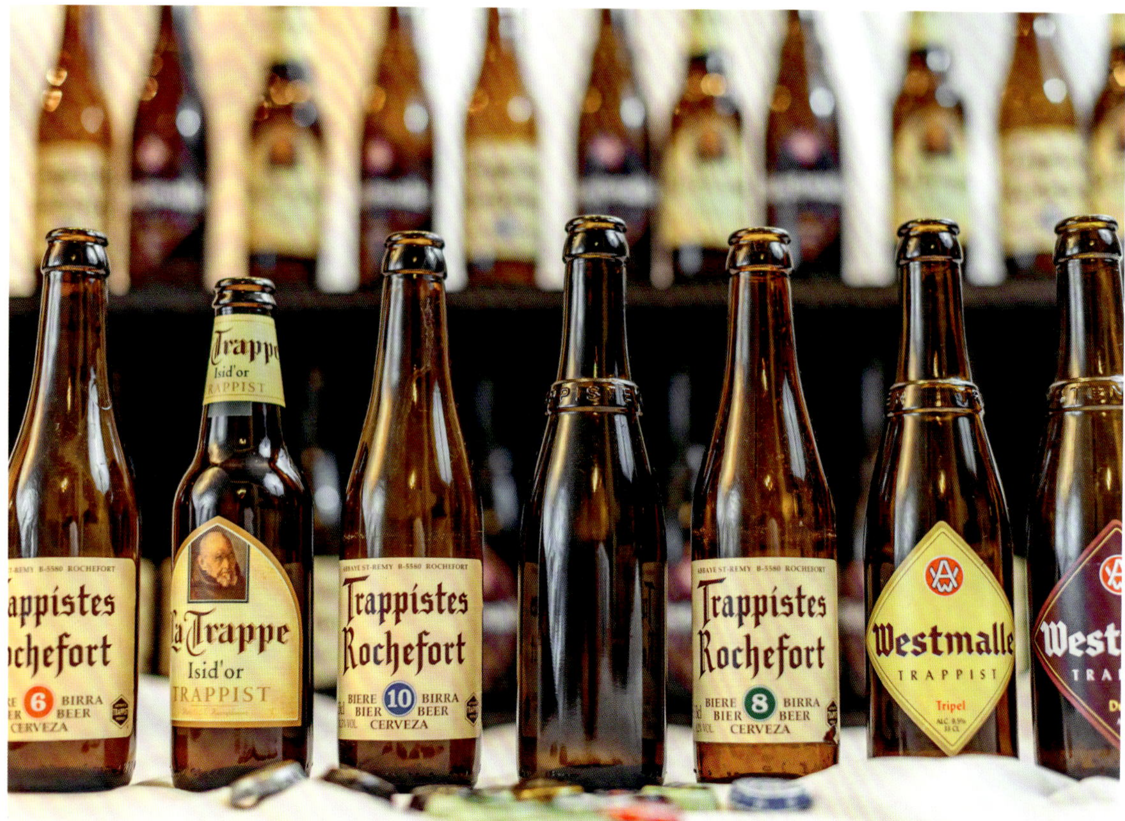

Selection of Trappist Beers
Selectie van trappistenbieren
Sélection de bières trappistes

Trappist beers

The beer culture originated in Flanders with the monastic breweries, and Trappist beers are still the most precious beers in the world. There are three monasteries in Flanders that brew Trappist beers: Westvleteren, Westmalle and Achel. Brewing beer is an important source of income, but part of the proceeds is used for social purposes. In contrast to the other abbey beers, Trappist beer is brewed by the monks themselves. There are about 43 different types of Trappist beer, the alcohol content of which varies between 6 and 12 percent. The designation "Bière Trappiste" is a designation of origin with strict criteria.

Bières trappistes

Dans les Flandres, la naissance de la culture de la bière est étroitement liée aux brasseries des monastères ; les bières trappistes sont toujours les bières les plus exquises au monde. En Flandres, trois monastères en brassent : Westvletern, Westmalle et Achel. Même si le brassage de la bière constitue une importante source de revenus, une partie des recettes est utilisée à des fins sociales. Contrairement aux autres bières d'abbaye, la bière trappiste est brassée par les moines eux-mêmes. Il en existe environ 43 variétés, dont la teneur en alcool se situe entre 6 et 12 %. Le nom de « bière trappiste » est une appellation d'origine répondant à des critères stricts.

Trappistenbiere

Die Bierkultur entstand in Flandern mit den Klosterbrauereien und noch immer sind die Trappistenbiere die kostbarsten Biere der Welt. In Flandern gibt es drei Klöster, die Trappistenbiere brauen: Westvletern, Westmalle und Achel. Das Bierbrauen ist eine wichtige Einnahmequelle, aber ein Teil des Erlöses wird für soziale Zwecke verwendet. Im Gegensatz zu den übrigen Abteibieren wird Trappistenbier von den Mönchen selbst gebraut. Es gibt etwa 43 verschiedene Sorten Trappistenbier, deren Alkoholgehalt zwischen 6 und 12 Prozent liegt. Die Bezeichnung „Bière Trappiste" ist eine Herkunftsbezeichnung mit strengen Kriterien.

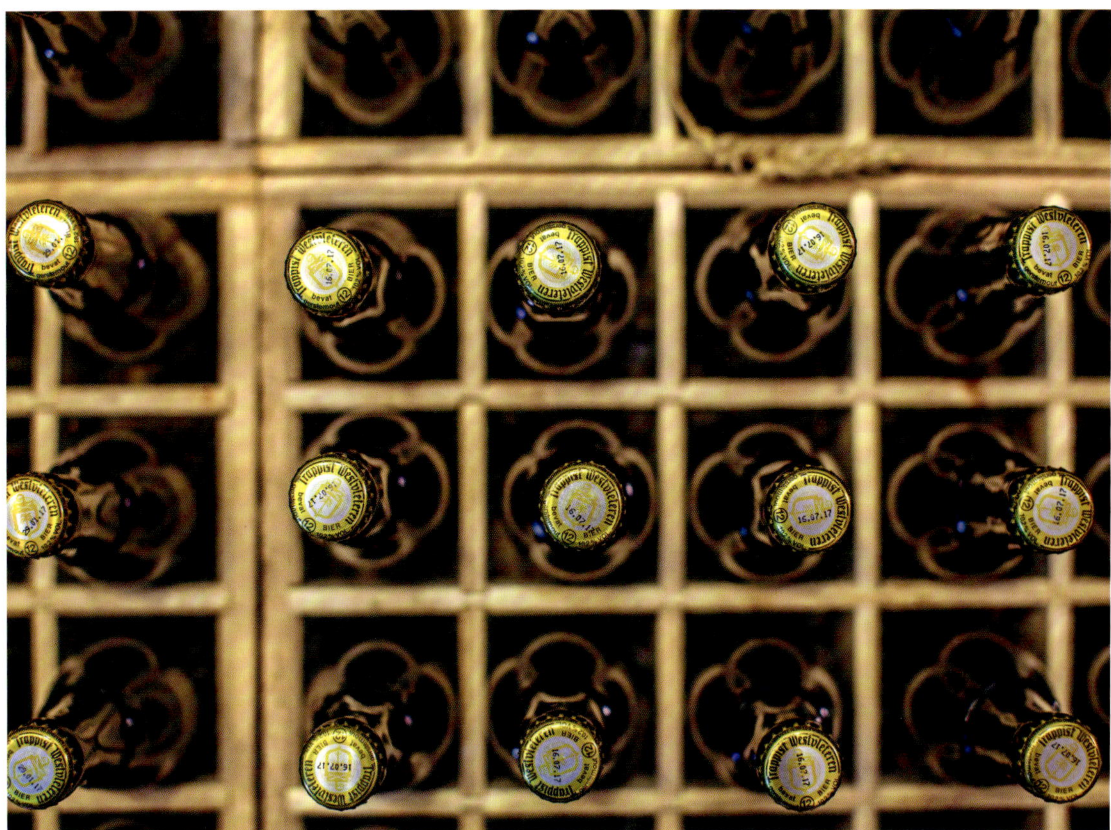

Westvleteren beers
Westvleteren bieren
Bières Westvleteren

Cervezas trapenses

La cultura cervecera se originó en Flandes
con las cervecerías del monasterio y las
cervezas trapenses siguen siendo las más
preciadas del mundo. Hay tres monasterios
en Flandes que elaboran cervezas
trapenses: Westvletern, Westmalle y
Achel. La elaboración de cerveza es una
importante fuente de ingresos, pero parte
de los ingresos se destina a fines sociales.
A diferencia del resto de cervezas de la
abadía, la cerveza trapense la elaboran
los propios monjes. Existen alrededor de
43 tipos diferentes de cerveza trapense,
cuya graduación alcohólica oscila entre el
6 y el 12 por ciento. La denominación Bière
Trappiste es una denominación de origen
con criterios estrictos.

Cervejas trapistas

A cultura da cerveja se originou em
Flandres com as cervejarias do mosteiro
e as cervejas trapistas ainda são as
cervejas mais preciosas do mundo. Na
Flandres existem três mosteiros que
fabricam cervejas Ttrapistas: Westvletern,
Westmalle e Achel. O fabrico de cerveja
é uma importante fonte de rendimento,
mas parte das receitas é utilizada para fins
sociais. Ao contrário das outras cervejas
de abadia, a cerveja trapista é fabricada
pelos próprios monges. Existem cerca de
43 tipos diferentes de cerveja trapista,
cujo teor alcoólico está entre 6 e 12 por
cento. A denominação Bière Trappiste
é uma denominação de origem com
critérios rigorosos.

Trappistenbieren

De biercultuur ontstond in Vlaanderen
met de kloosterbrouwerijen en nog altijd
zijn de trappistenbieren de kostbaarste
bieren ter wereld. In Vlaanderen zijn drie
kloosters die trappistenbieren brouwen:
Westvletern, Westmalle en Achel.
Bierbrouwen is een belangrijke bron
van inkomsten, maar een deel van de
opbrengst wordt gebruikt voor sociale
doeleinden. In tegenstelling tot andere
abdijbieren wordt trappistenbier door de
monniken zelf gebrouwen. Er zijn ongeveer
43 verschillende soorten trappistenbier,
waarvan het alcoholgehalte tussen de 6 en
12 procent ligt. De benaming trappist is een
oorsprongsbenaming met strikte criteria.

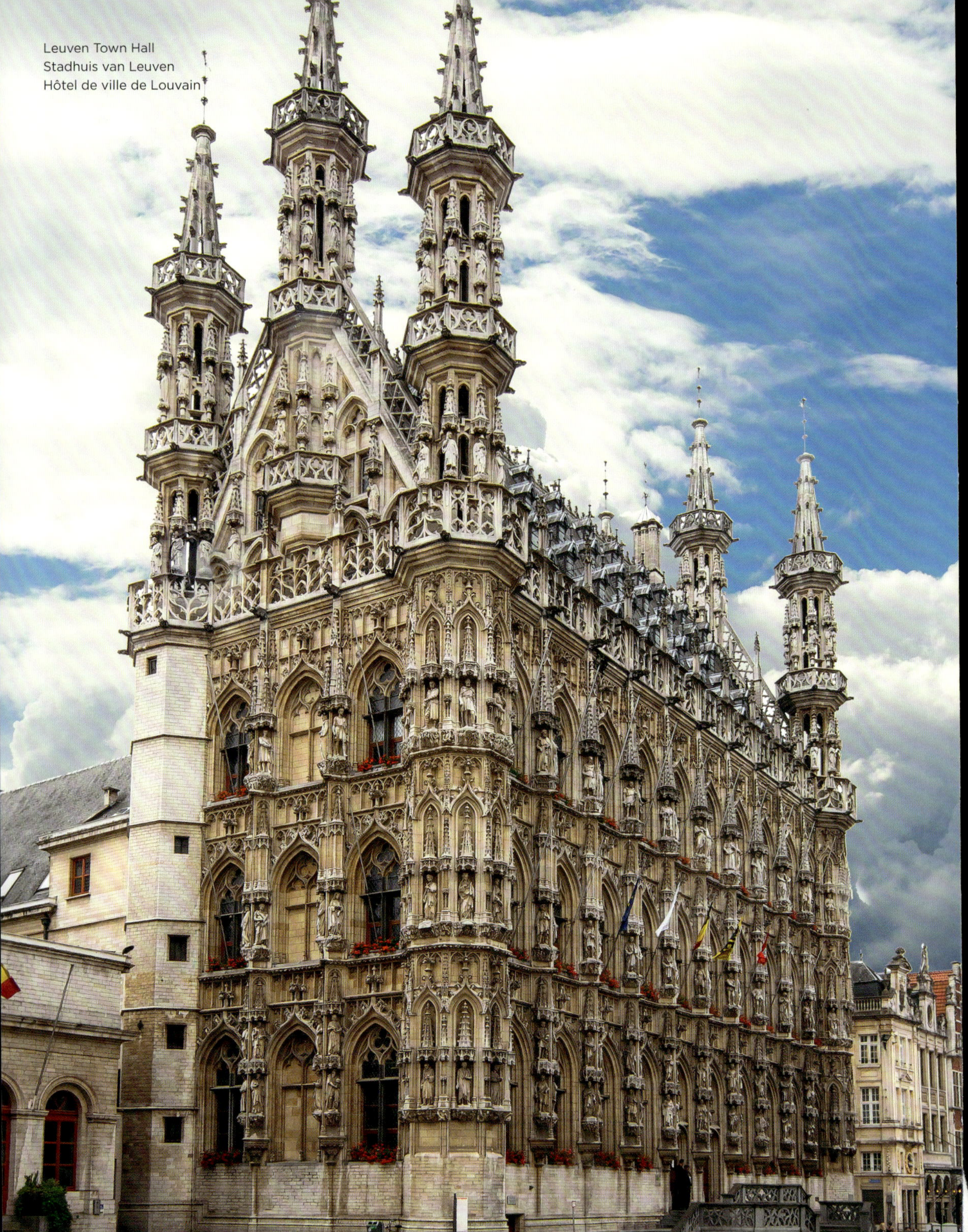

Leuven Town Hall
Stadhuis van Leuven
Hôtel de ville de Louvain

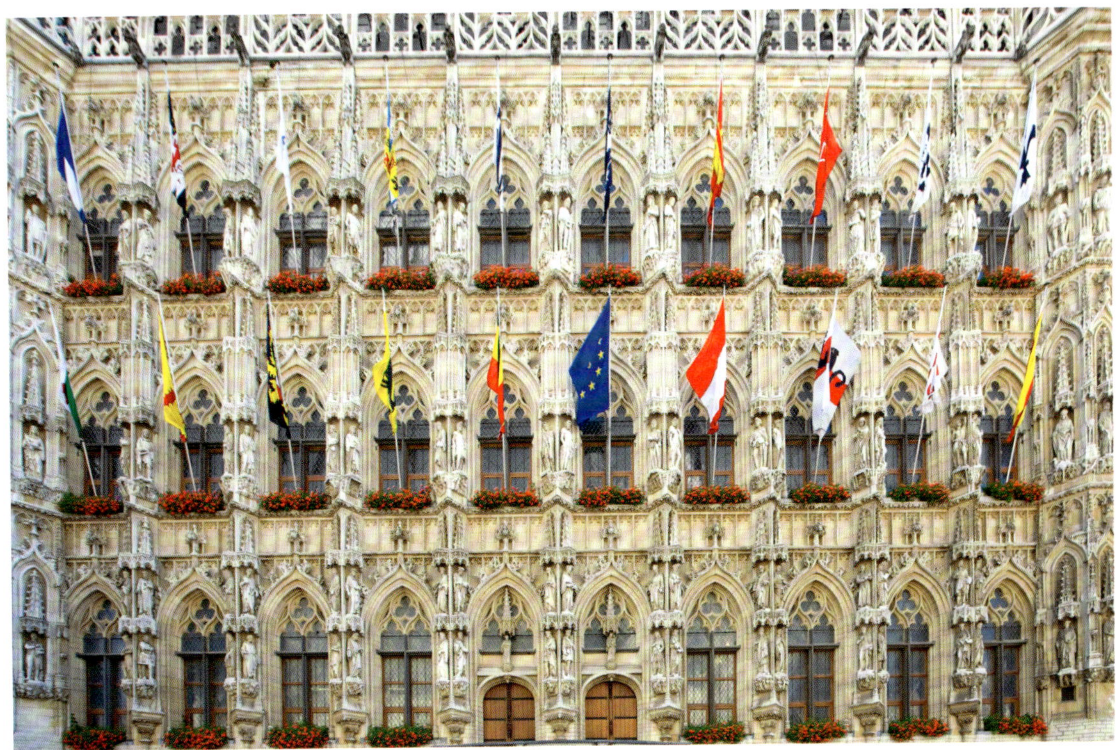

Facade detail, Leuven Town Hall
Detail van de gevel, Stadhuis van Leuven
Détail de façade, Hôtel de ville de Louvain

City Hall of Leuven

The filigreed town hall is one of the
highlights of Brabant's late Gothic period,
with six octagonal towers crowning the
building, and being decorated with over
200 statues of saints and important
local citizens. The present entrance hall
was originally a covered continuation of
the Great Market. The interior contains
numerous paintings and sculptures,
including those by Constantin Meunier.

Ayuntamiento de Lovaina

El ayuntamiento con estilo de filigrana es
uno de los puntos culminantes del gótico
tardío de Brabante. Seis torres octogonales
coronan el edificio, que está decorado
con más de 200 estatuas de importantes
personalidades de Lovaina. El actual
vestíbulo de entrada era originalmente una
continuación cubierta del Gran Mercado.
El interior contiene numerosas pinturas y
esculturas, entre las que se incluyen las de
Constantin Meunier.

Hôtel de ville de Louvain

L'hôtel de ville en filigrane est un bon
exemple du style gothique tardif du
Brabant. Six tours octogonales couronnent
le bâtiment, orné de plus de 200 statues
d'importantes personnalités louvanistes.
À l'origine, le hall d'entrée actuel était
un prolongement couvert de la Grand-
Place. L'intérieur abrite de nombreuses
peintures et sculptures, dont certaines de
Constantin Meunier.

Câmara Municipal de Lovaina

A câmara municipal de filigrana é um
dos destaques do período gótico tardio
de Brabantine. Seis torres octogonais
coroam o edifício, que é decorado com
mais de 200 estátuas de importantes
personalidades do povo de Lovaina. O
atual hall de entrada era originalmente
uma continuação coberta do mercado da
Grand Place. O interior contém numerosas
pinturas e esculturas, incluindo as de
Constantin Meunier.

Rathaus von Löwen

Das filigrane Rathaus gehört zu den
Höhepunkten Brabanter Spätgotik. Sechs
achteckige Türmchen krönen den mit
über 200 Statuen bedeutender Löwener
Persönlichkeiten verzierten Bau. Die
heutige Eingangshalle war ursprünglich
eine überdachte Fortsetzung des Großen
Markts. Das Innere birgt zahlreiche
Gemälde und Skulpturen, unter anderem
von Constantin Meunier.

Stadhuis van Leuven

Het sierlijke stadhuis van Leuven is een
van de hoogtepunten uit de laat Brabantse
gotiek. Zes achthoekige torens kronen het
met meer dan 200 beelden van belangrijke
Leuvens persoonlijkheden versierde
gebouw. De huidige entreehal was
oorspronkelijk een overdekte voortzetting
van de Grote Markt. Het interieur bevat
veel schilderijen en sculpturen, o.a. van
Constantin Meunier.

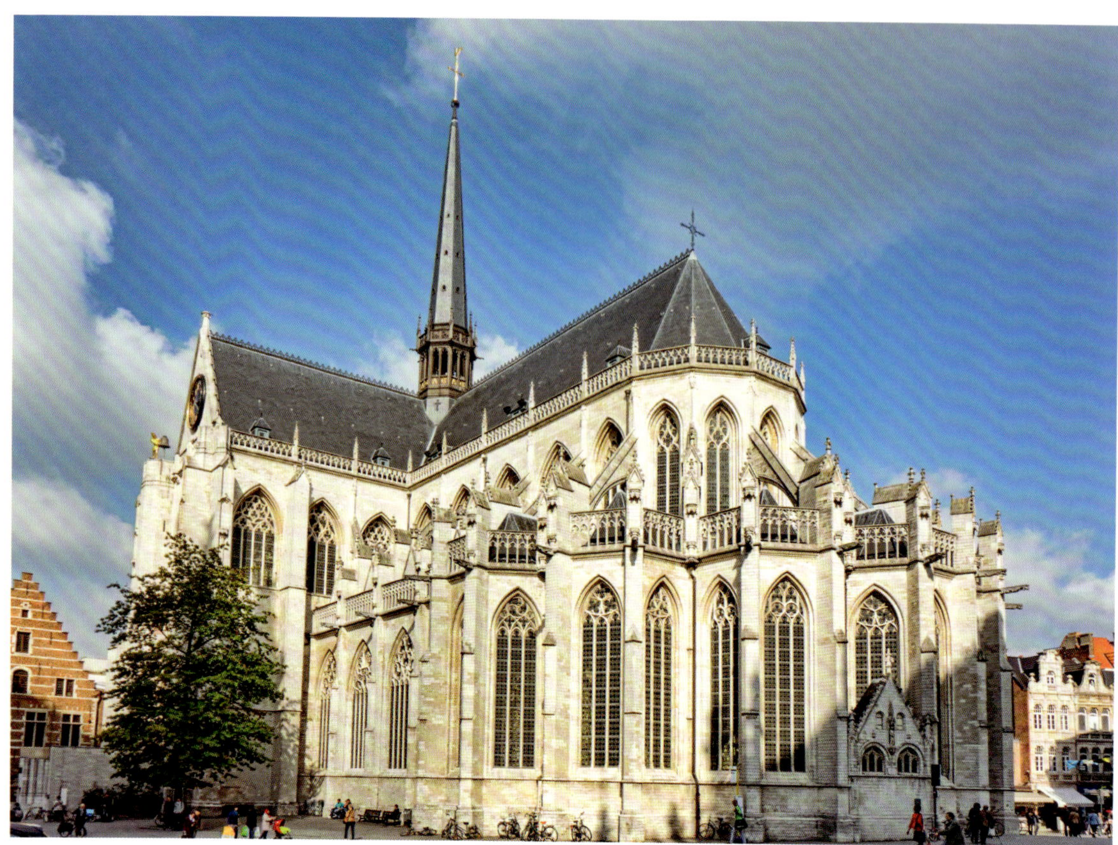

St Peter's Church, Leuven
Sint-Pieterskerk, Leuven
L'Église Saint Pierre, Louvain

Highest church in the world?

According to the building plans, the St Peter's Church in Leuven was to be the tallest church in the world, at 175 m (574 ft). One of the planned three towers was constructed, but collapsed in the 16th century. What we still see today are the bases for the towers. The imposing Gothic building houses one of the most important works of the Flemish Primitives, *The Last Supper* by Dirk Bouts. In the Saint Anthony's Chapel visitors can visit the tomb of Father Damian. The Flemish missionary was designated "Greatest Belgian of All Time" in December 2005 and canonised in Rome in 2009.

La plus haute église du monde ?

Selon les plans de construction, l'église Saint-Pierre de Louvain devait atteindre 175 mètres de hauteur, ce qui devait en faire la plus haute église du monde. L'une des trois tours prévues fut réalisée, mais s'effondra au xvie siècle. Seule la base des tours est encore visible aujourd'hui. L'imposant bâtiment gothique abrite l'une des principales œuvres des primitifs flamands, *La Cène* de Dirk Bouts. La chapelle Saint-Antoine abrite le tombeau du père Damien. Ce missionnaire flamand a été proclamé le «plus grand Belge de tous les temps» en décembre 2005 et canonisé à Rome en 2009.

Höchste Kirche der Welt?

Den Bauplänen nach sollte die Peters-Kirche in Löwen mit 175 m das höchste Gotteshaus der Welt werden. Einer der geplanten drei Türme wurde realisiert, stürzte aber im 16. Jahrhundert ein. Was wir heute noch sehen, ist die Basis für die Türme. In dem imposanten gotischen Bauwerk befindet sich eines der wichtigsten Werke der flämischen Primitiven, *Das letzte Abendmahl* von Dirk Bouts. In der Sint-Antoniuskapelle können die Besucher das Grab des Pater Damian besuchen. Der flämische Missionar wurde im Dezember 2005 zum „Größten Belgier aller Zeiten" ernannt und 2009 in Rom heiliggesprochen.

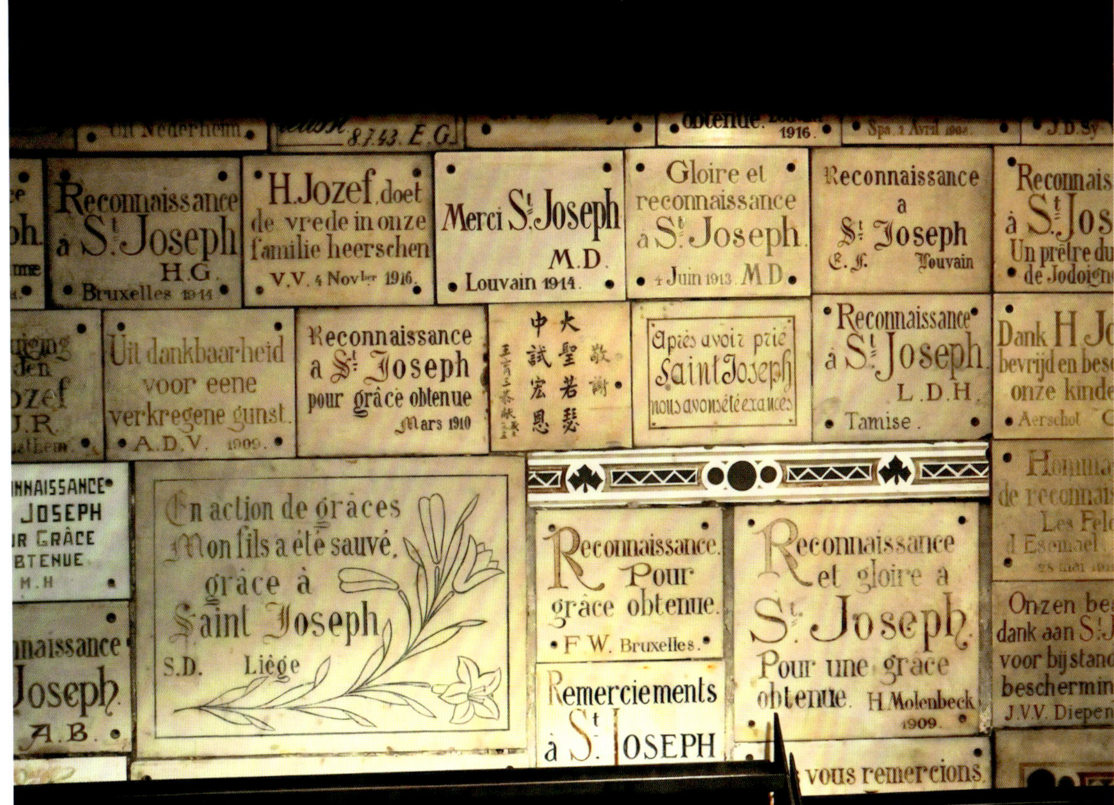

Saint Anthony's Chapel, Leuven
Sint-Antoniuskapel, Leuven
Chapelle Saint-Antoine, Louvain

¿La iglesia más alta del mundo?

Según los planos de construcción, la iglesia de San Pedro en Lovaina iba a ser la iglesia más alta del mundo, con 175 m. Una de las tres torres proyectadas se realizó, pero se derrumbó en el siglo XVI. Lo que todavía podemos ver es la base de las torres. La imponente construcción gótica alberga una de las obras más importantes de los primitivos flamencos, *La última cena* de Dirk Bouts. En la capilla de San Antonio se puede visitar la tumba del Padre Damián. El misionero flamenco fue nombrado "el mejor belga de todos los tiempos" en diciembre de 2005 y canonizado en Roma en 2009.

A igreja mais alta do mundo?

De acordo com os planos de construção, a Igreja de São Pedro em Lovaina deveria ser a igreja mais alta do mundo, com 175 m. Uma das três torres planeadas foi realizada, mas desabou no século XVI. O que ainda vemos hoje é a base para as torres. O imponente edifício gótico abriga uma das mais importantes obras dos primitivos flamengos, *A Última Ceia* de Dirk Bouts. Na capela de Santo Antônio, os visitantes podem visitar o túmulo do Padre Damião. O missionário flamengo foi nomeado "o maior belga de todos os tempos" em dezembro de 2005 e canonizado em Roma em 2009.

Hoogste kerk ter wereld?

Volgens de bouwplannen zou de Sint-Pieterskerk in Leuven met 175 m de hoogste kerk ter wereld worden. Eén van de drie geplande torens werd gebouwd, maar stortte in de 16e eeuw in. Wat we vandaag de dag nog zien is de basis voor de torens. In het imposante gotische bouwwerk bevindt zich *Het Laatste Avondmaal* van Dirk Bouts, één van de belangrijkste werken van de Vlaamse primitieven. In de Sint-Antoniuskapel kunnen bezoekers het graf van pater Damiaan bezoeken. De Vlaamse missionaris werd in december 2005 benoemd tot "Grootste Belg aller tijden' en in 2009 in Rome heiligverklaard.

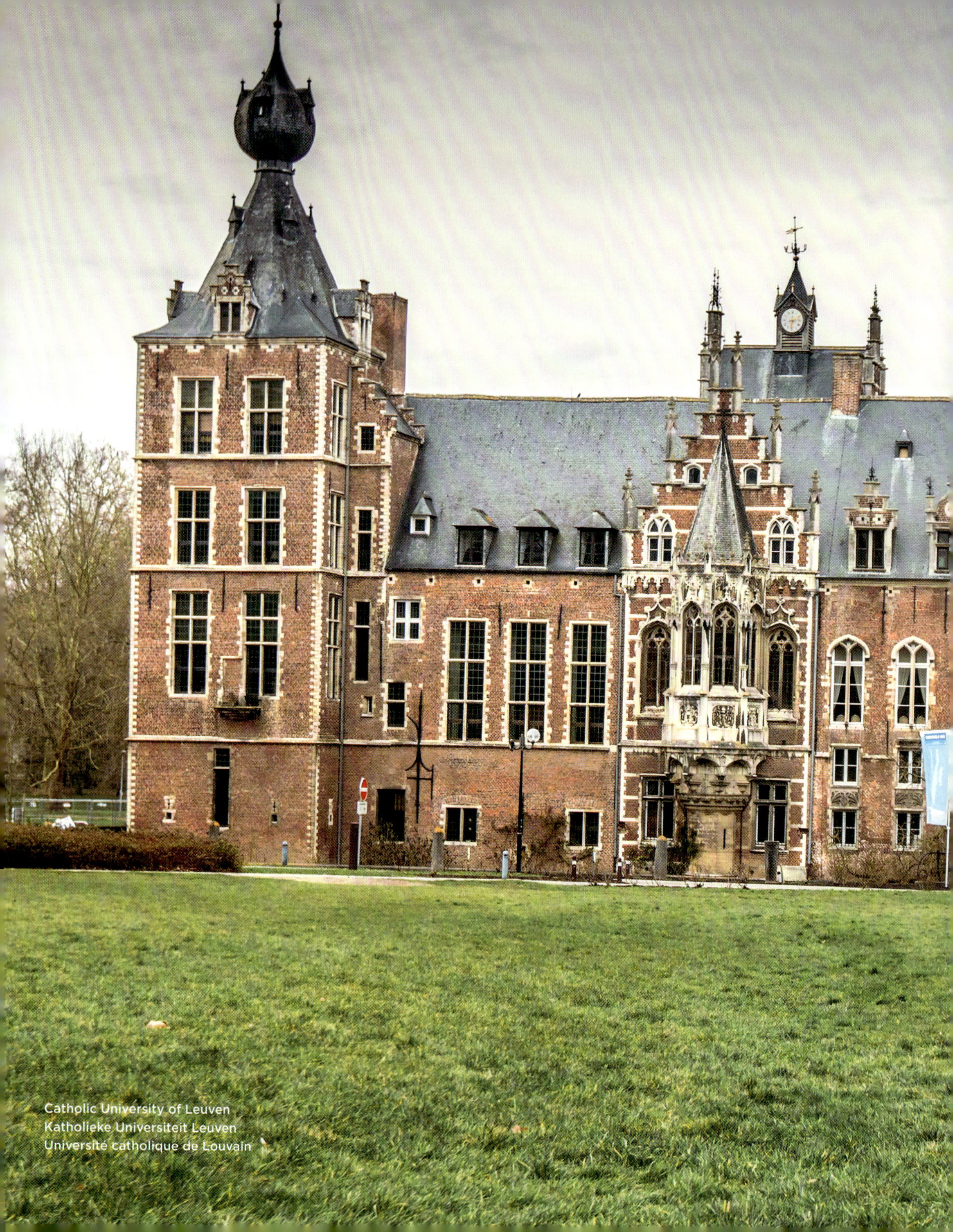

Catholic University of Leuven
Katholieke Universiteit Leuven
Université catholique de Louvain

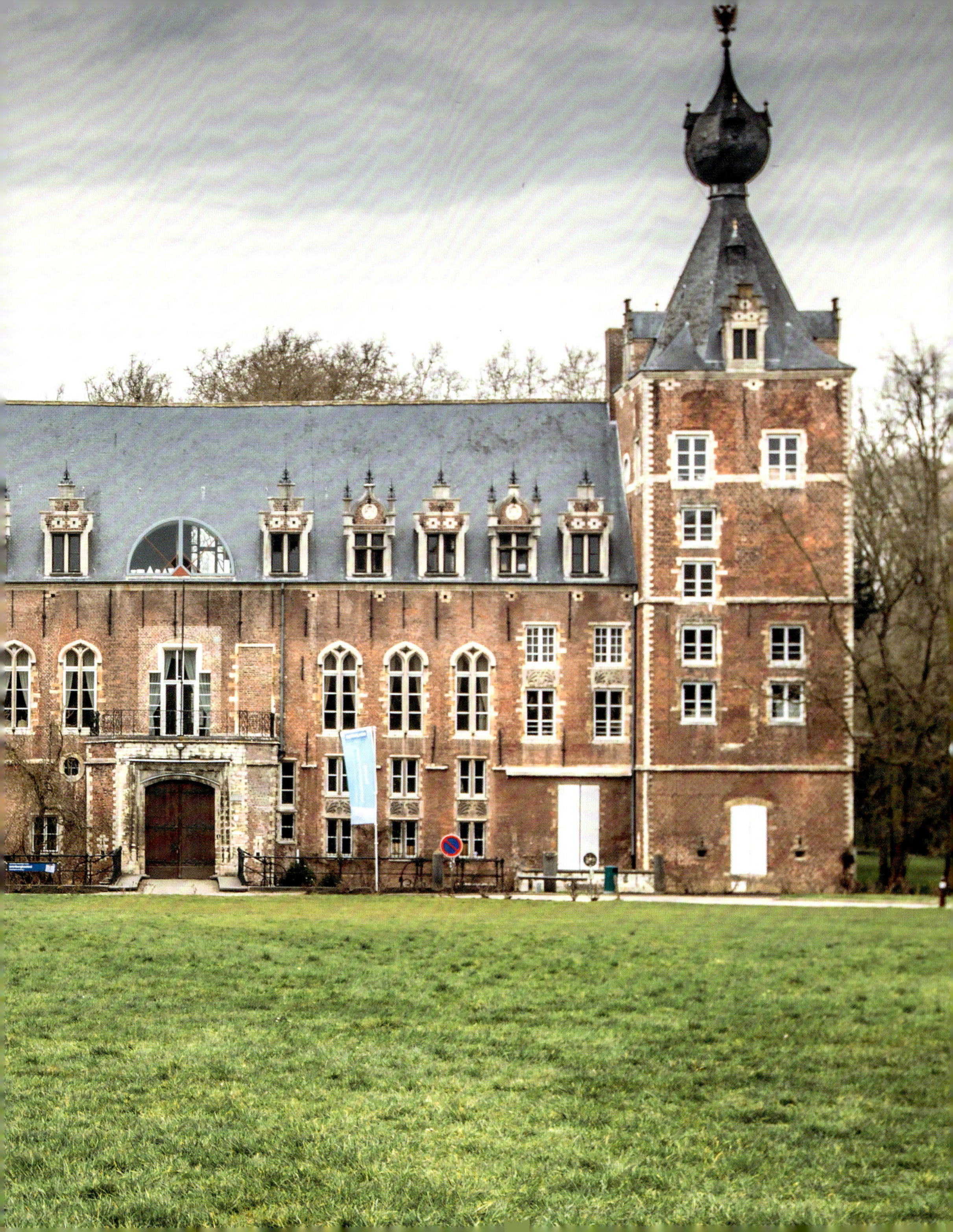

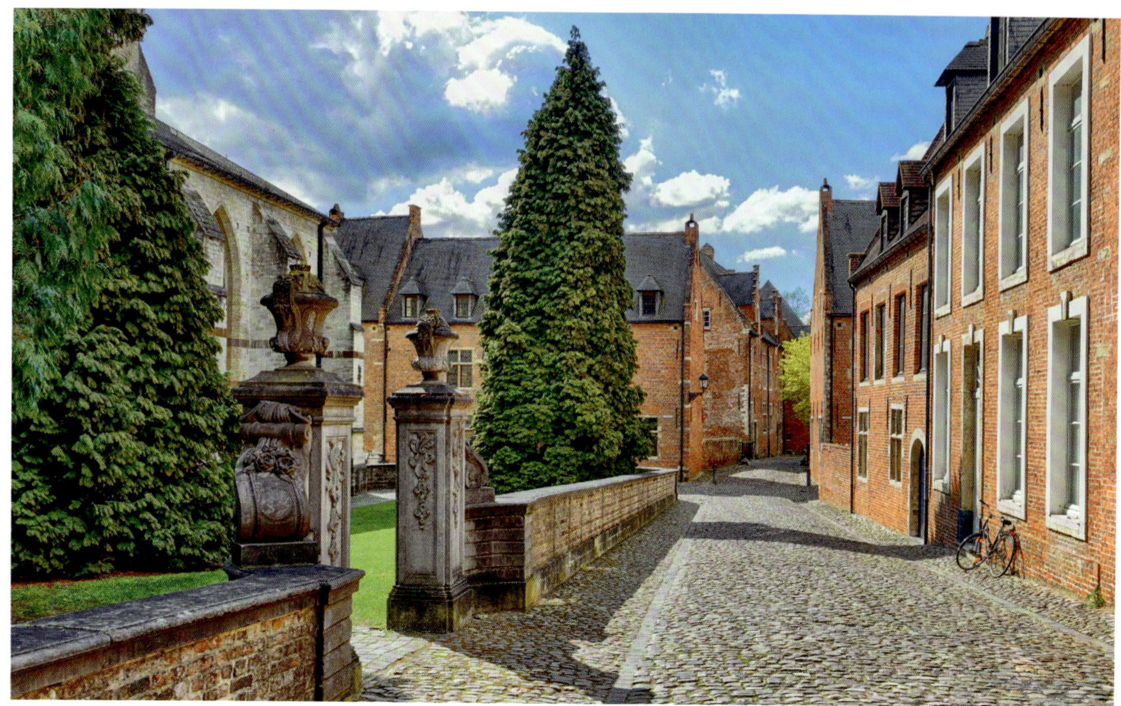

Great Beguinage of Leuven
Groot Begijnhof, Leuven
Grand béguinage de Louvain

The Great Beguinage

It is one of the largest existing beguinages in Flanders and a UNESCO World Heritage Site. The self-contained city quarter, with around 100 cottages, gardens, squares and three bridges is an oasis of peace. With no cars, only a few cyclists ride over the cobblestones. Students and visiting professors from the University of Leuven currently live in the approximately 300 apartments.

El Gran Beguinage

Es una de las mayores granjas de beguinage existentes en Flandes y forma parte del Patrimonio Mundial de la UNESCO. El barrio autónomo con alrededor de 100 casitas, jardines, plazas y tres puentes es un oasis de paz. No hay coches; tan solo unos pocos ciclistas conducen sobre los adoquines. Los estudiantes y profesores visitantes de la Universidad de Lovaina viven actualmente en los aproximadamente 300 apartamentos.

Grand Béguinage

Voici l'un des plus grands béguinages de Flandres ! Il fait partie du patrimoine mondial de l'Unesco. Ce quartier autonome composé d'une centaine de maisonnettes, de jardinets, de places et de trois ponts est une oasis de paix : pas de voitures, quelques cyclistes çà et là qui roulent sur les pavés. Actuellement, ces quelque 300 appartements accueillent étudiants et professeurs invités de l'université de Louvain.

Grande Beguinage

É um dos maiores agrupamento de pequenas construções usadas pelas beguinas existentes na Flandres e faz parte do Patrimônio Mundial da UNESCO. O bairro independente, com cerca de 100 pequenas casas, jardins, praças e três pontes é um oásis de paz. Sem carros, apenas alguns ciclistas circulam sobre os paralelepípedos. Estudantes e professores visitantes da Universidade de Lovaina vivem atualmente em aproximadamente 300 apartamentos.

Großer Beginenhof

Er ist einer der größten bestehenden Beginenhöfe Flanderns und Teil des UNESCO-Welterbes. Das in sich geschlossene Viertel mit rund 100 Häuschen, Gärtchen, Plätzen und drei Brücken ist eine Oase der Ruhe. Keine Autos, nur einzelne Radfahrer fahren über das Kopfsteinpflaster. Derzeit leben in den rund 300 Wohnungen Studenten und Gastprofessoren der Universität Löwen.

Groot Begijnhof

Het is één van de grootste bestaande begijnhoven in Vlaanderen en is onderdeel van het UNESCO-werelderfgoed. De op zichzelf staande wijk met ca. 100 huisjes, tuinen, pleinen en drie bruggen is een oase van rust. Geen auto's, alleen wat fietsers rijden over de kasseien. Nu wonen studenten en gastprofessoren van de KU Leuven in de ongeveer 300 woningen.

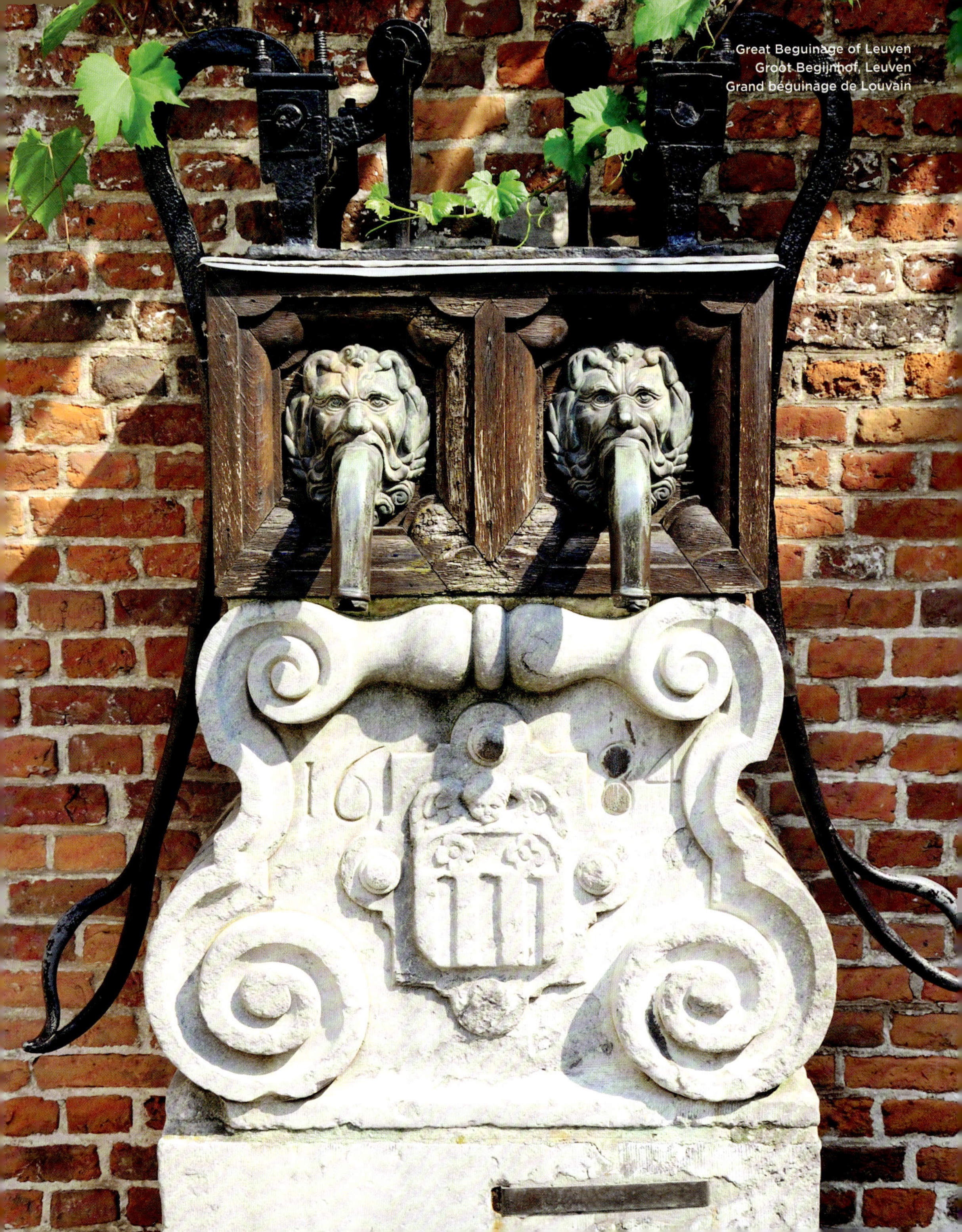

Great Beguinage of Leuven
Groot Begijnhof, Leuven
Grand béguinage de Louvain

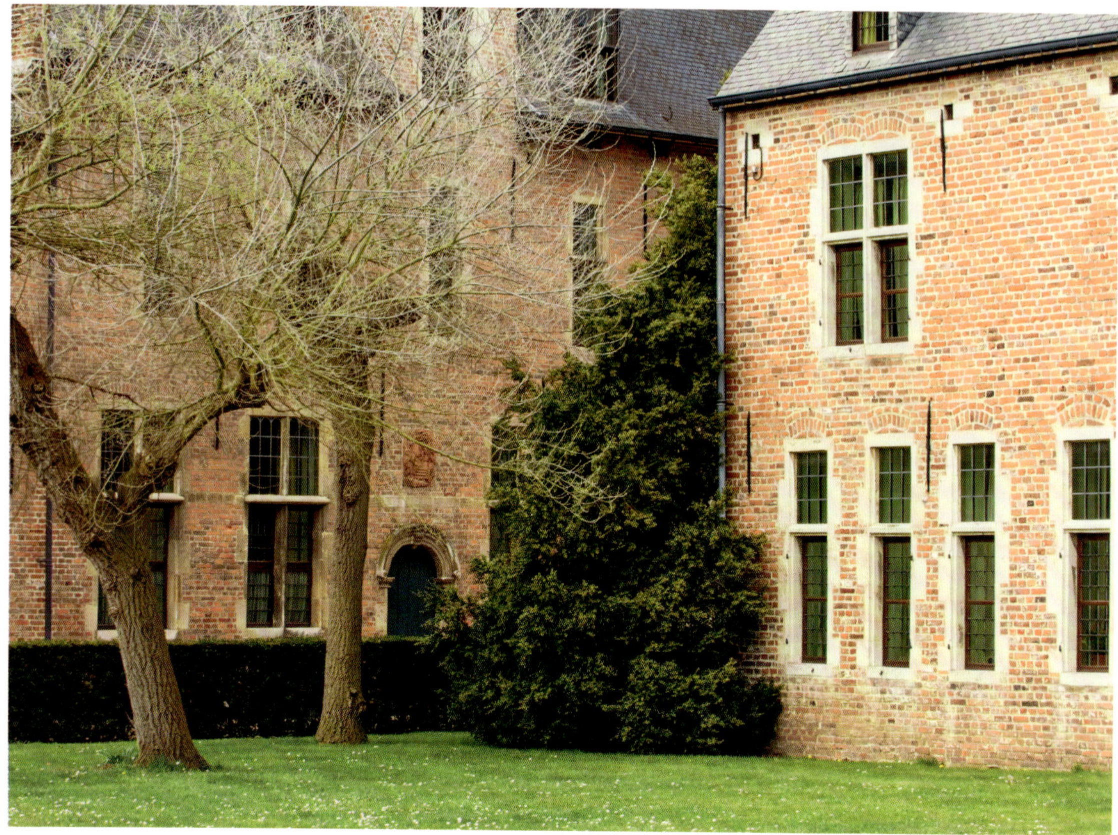

Great Beguinage of Leuven
Groot Begijnhof, Leuven
Grand béguinage de Louvain

The history of the Great Beguinage

This beguinage was founded in the early 13th century as a community for unmarried women. The community was led by a democratically elected "Grootjuffrouw". One of the pastors of the Beguinage was Adriaan Florensz Boeyens van Utrecht, who later became Pope Adrian VI. In the 17th century, about 360 Beguines lived in the court. During the French Revolution the Beguinage was not sold as state property, as were the monasteries and the Beguines were allowed to remain in their houses, but the empty rooms were rented to old women. Sister Julia, the last Beguine, died in 1988.

L'histoire du Grand Béguinage

Ce béguinage fut fondé au début du XIIIe siècle en tant que communauté de femmes non mariées. Celle-ci était dirigée par l'une d'entre elles, une «Grootjuffrouw» démocratiquement élue. L'un des pasteurs du béguinage fut, en 1490, Adriaan Florensz Boeyens van Utrecht, le futur pape Adrien VI. Au XVIIe siècle, environ 360 béguines vivaient en ces lieux. Pendant la Révolution française, le béguinage fut vendu comme propriété de l'État, contrairement aux monastères. Les béguines purent rester dans leurs maisons, mais on loua les espaces vides à des femmes âgées. Sœur Julia, la dernière béguine, est décédée en 1988.

Die Geschichte des Großen Beginenhofs

Dieser Beginenhof entstand im frühen 13. Jahrhundert als Gemeinschaft für unverheiratete Frauen. Die Gemeinschaft wurde von einer demokratisch gewählten „Grootjuffrouw" geleitet. Einer der Pastoren des Beginenhofs war 1490 Adriaan Floriszoon Boeyens van Utrecht, bekannt als späterer Papst Adrian VI. Im 17. Jahrhundert lebten rund 360 Beginen in dem Hof. Während der Französischen Revolution wurde der Beginenhof nicht wie die Klöster als Staatseigentum verkauft. Die Beginen durften in ihren Häusern wohnen, aber die leeren Räume wurden an alte Frauen vermietet. Schwester Julia, die letzte Begine starb 1988.

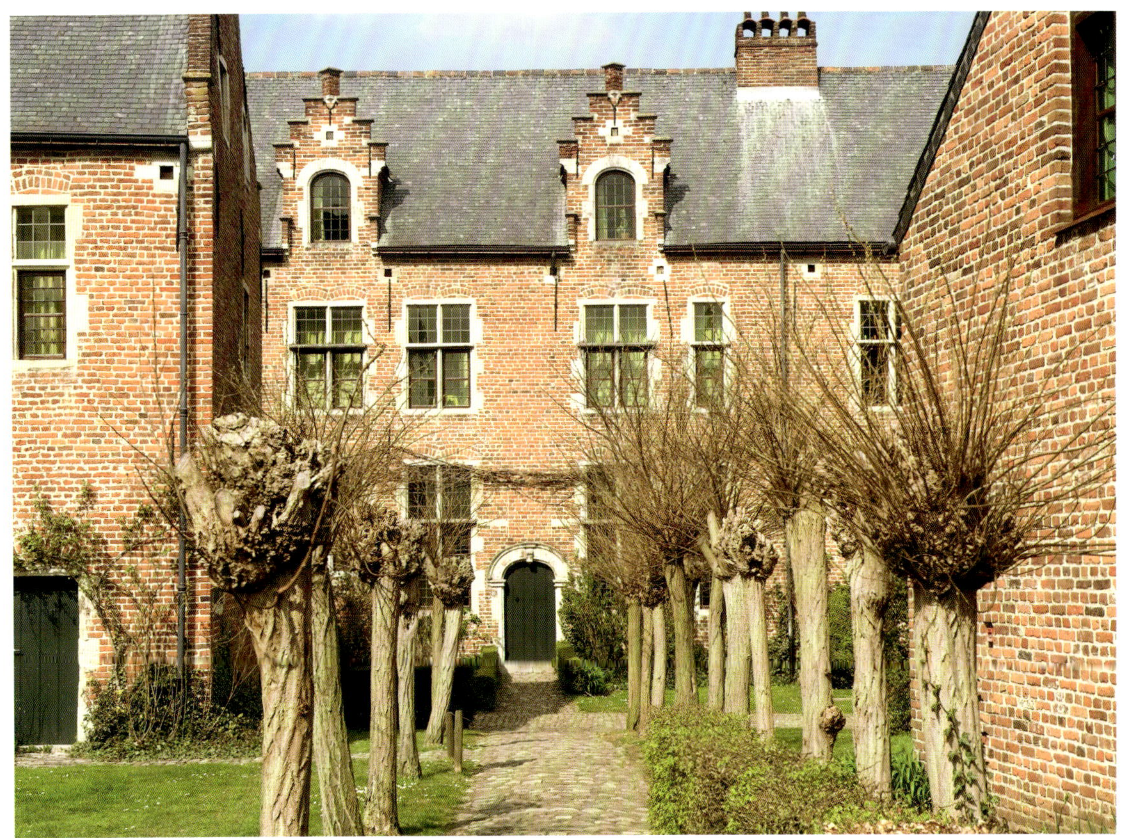

Great Beguinage of Leuven
Groot Begijnhof, Leuven
Grand béguinage de Louvain

La historia del Gran Beguinage

Este beguinage se creó a principios del siglo XIII como una comunidad para mujeres solteras. La comunidad fue dirigida por un "Grootjuffrouw" elegido democráticamente. Uno de los pastores del Beguinage fue Adriaan Floriszoon Boeyens en 1490, conocido más tarde como el Papa Adriano VI. En el siglo XVII vivían en la corte unas 360 beguinas. Durante la Revolución Francesa, la Beguinage no se vendió como propiedad estatal como los monasterios. A las beguinas se les permitía vivir en sus casas, pero las habitaciones vacías se alquilaban a ancianas. La hermana Julia, la última beguina, murió en 1988.

A história da Grande Beguinage

Esta beguinaria foi fundada no início do século XIII como uma comunidade para mulheres solteiras. A comunidade era liderada por uma madre superiora, ou "Grootjuffrouw", democraticamente eleita. Um dos pastores da Beguinage foi Adriaan Floriszoon Boeyens em 1490, conhecido como Papa Adrian VI. No século XVII, cerca de 360 beguinas viveram na comunidade. Durante a Revolução Francesa a Beguinage não foi vendida como propriedade do Estado como os mosteiros. As beguinas podiam viver nas suas casas, mas os quartos vazios eram alugados a mulheres idosas. Irmã Julia, a última begina, morreu em 1988.

De geschiedenis van het Groot Begijnhof

Dit begijnhof ontstond begin 13e eeuw als gemeenschap voor ongehuwde vrouwen. De gemeenschap werd geleid door een democratisch gekozen "Grootjuffrouw". Eén van de predikanten was Adriaan Florensz. Boeyens van Utrecht, later vooral bekend als paus Adrianus VI. In de 17e eeuw woonden er ca. 360 begijnen aan het hof. Tijdens de Franse Revolutie werd het begijnhof niet zoals de kloosters als staatseigendom verkocht. De begijnen mochten in hun huizen wonen, maar de lege kamers werden verhuurd aan oude vrouwen. Zuster Julia, de laatste begijn van het Groot Begijnhof, stierf in 1988.

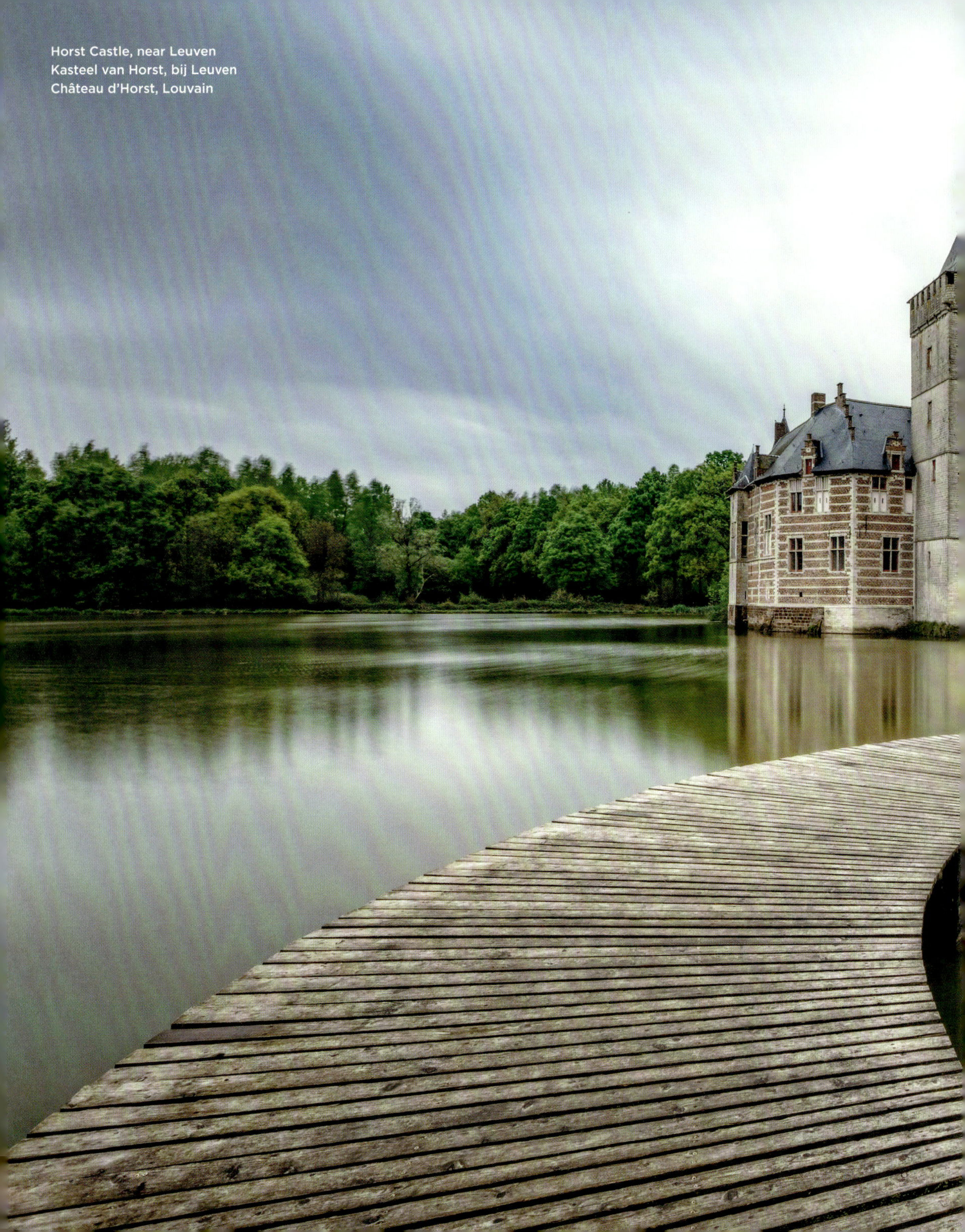
Horst Castle, near Leuven
Kasteel van Horst, bij Leuven
Château d'Horst, Louvain

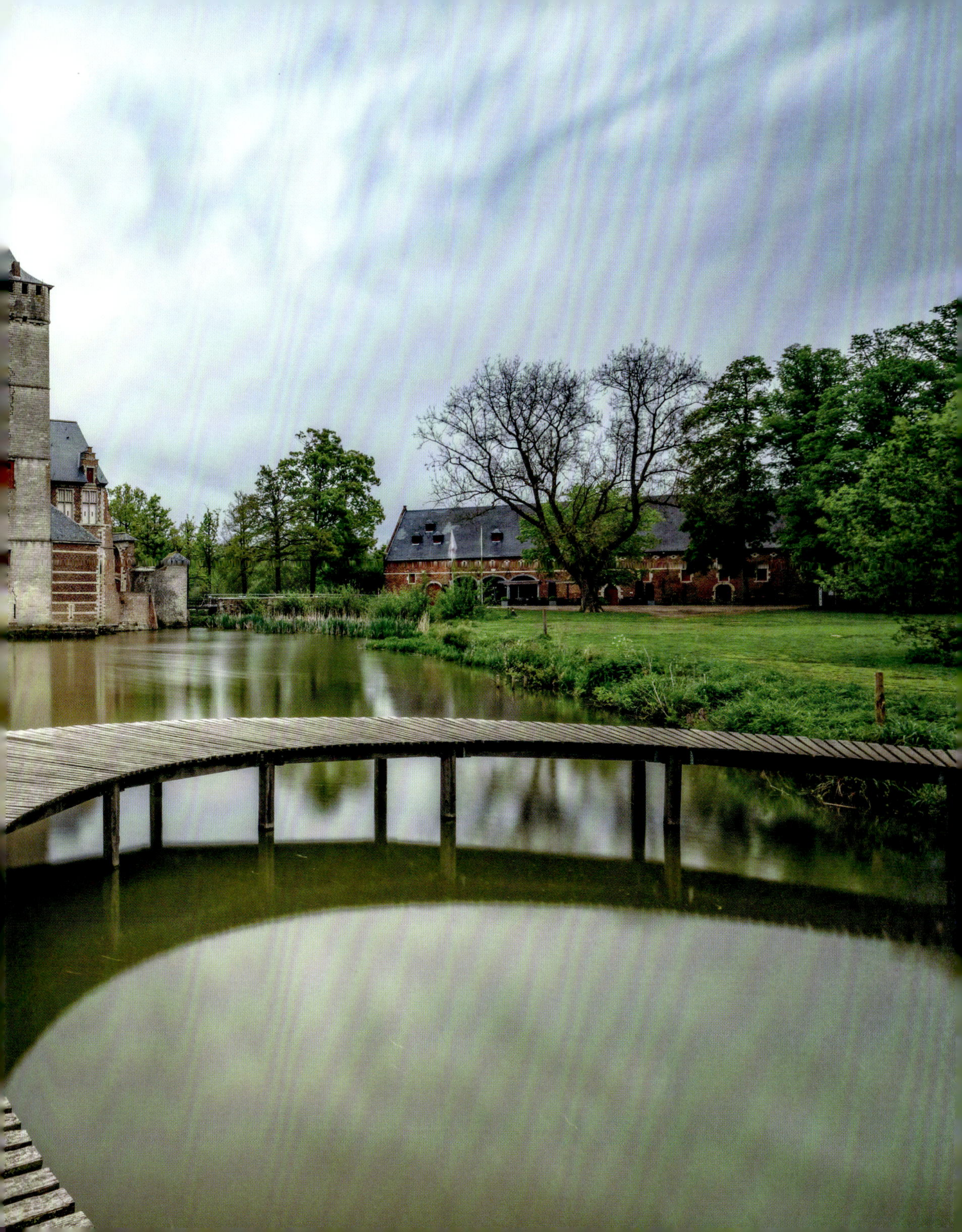

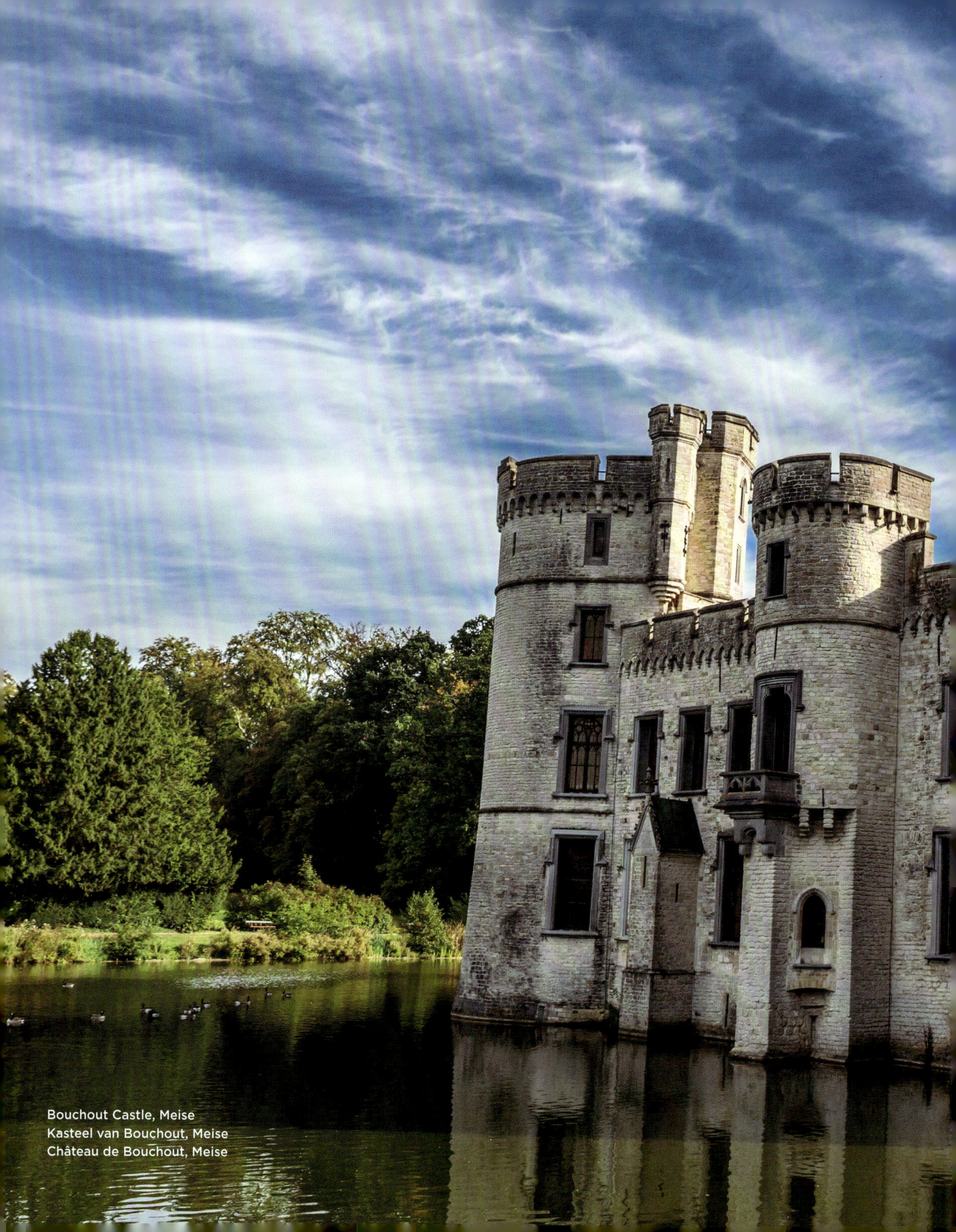

Bouchout Castle, Meise
Kasteel van Bouchout, Meise
Château de Bouchout, Meise

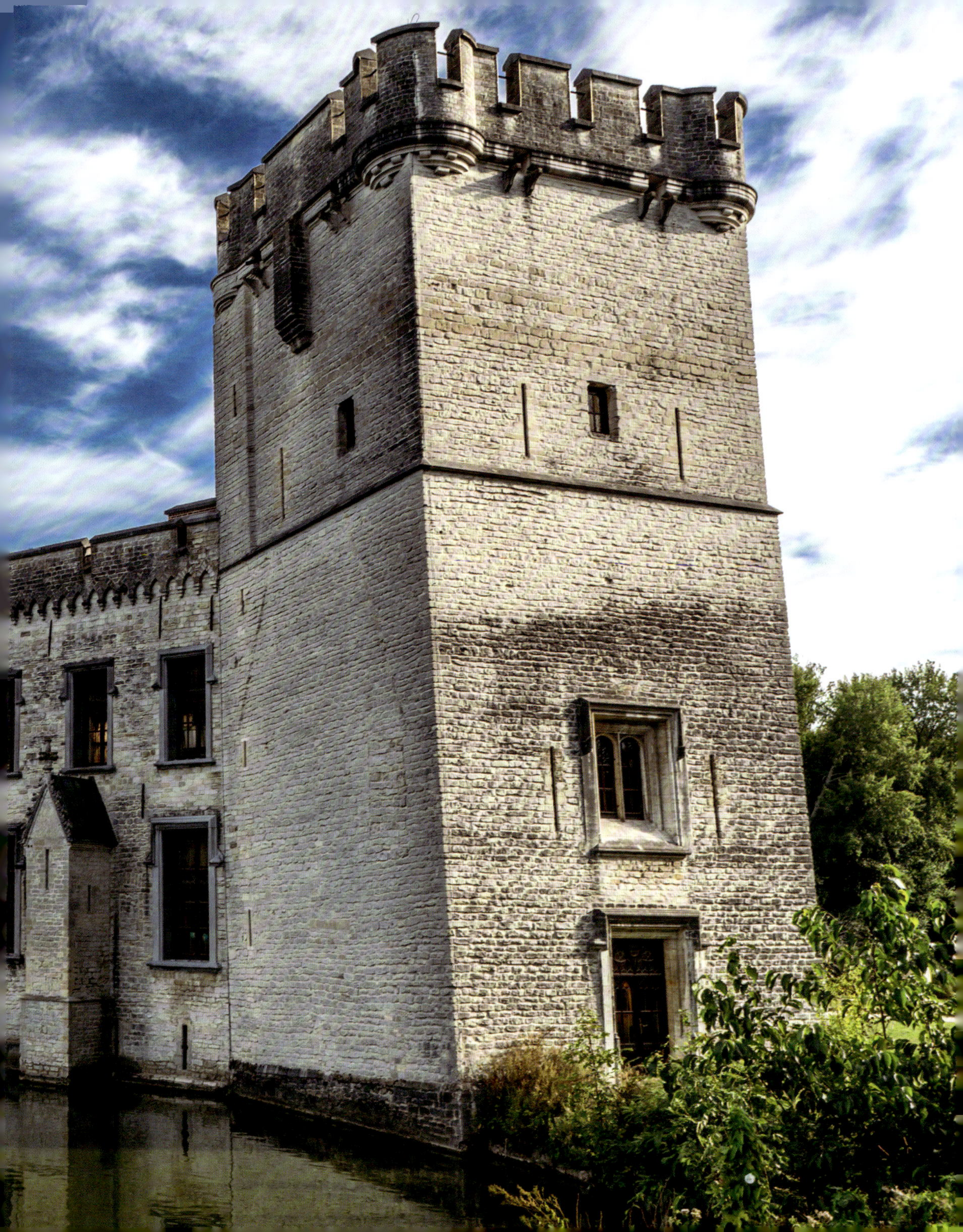

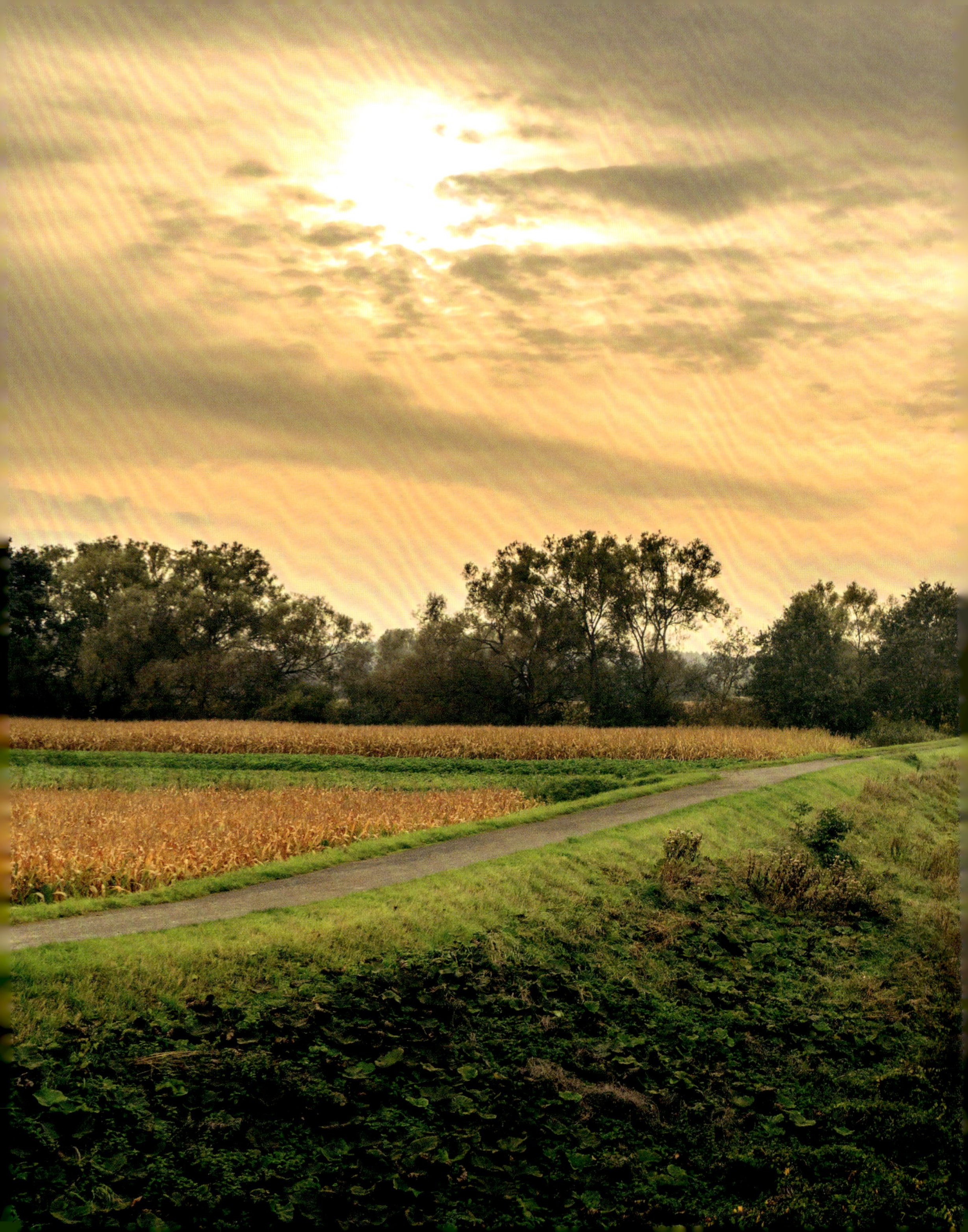

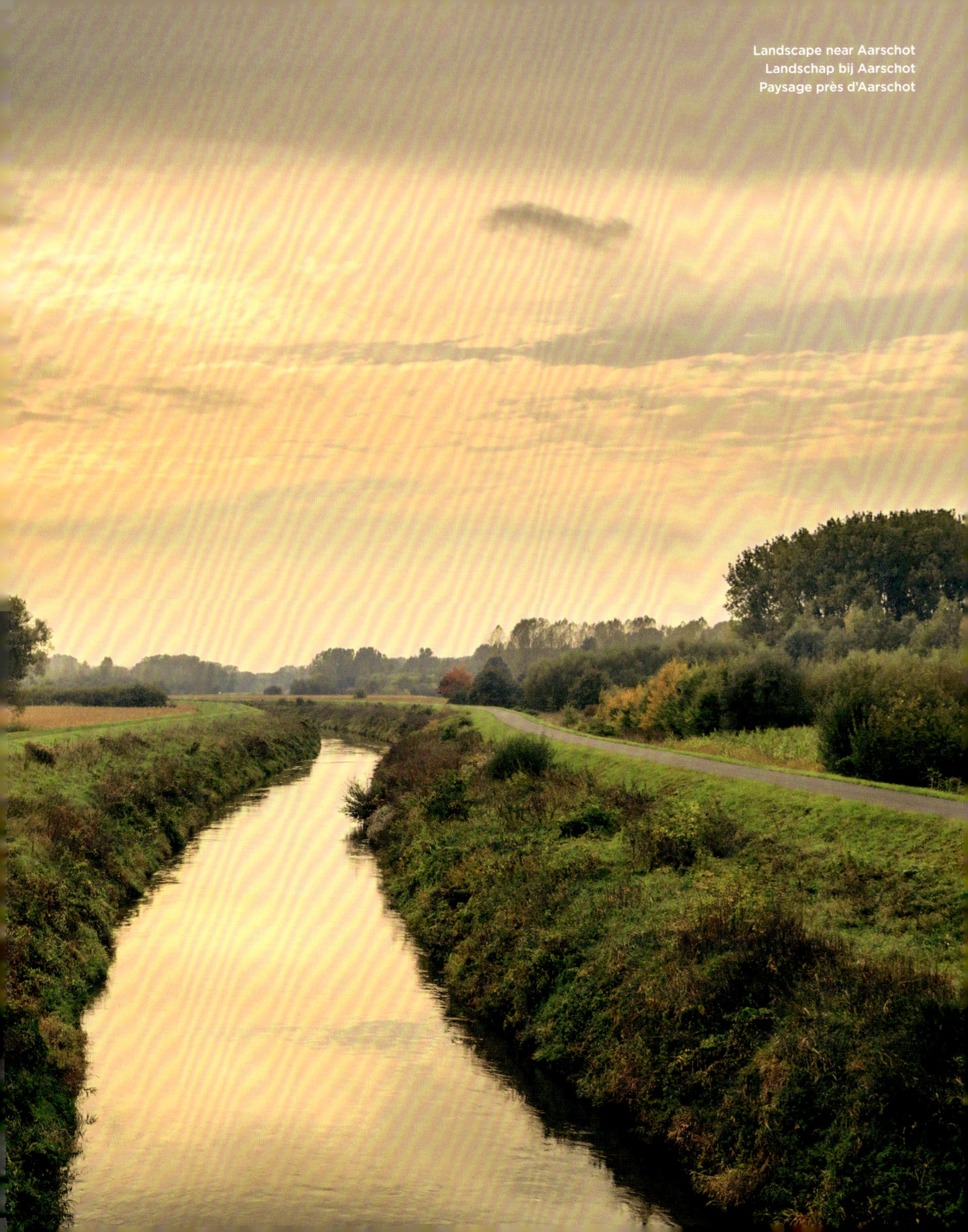
Landscape near Aarschot
Landschap bij Aarschot
Paysage près d'Aarschot

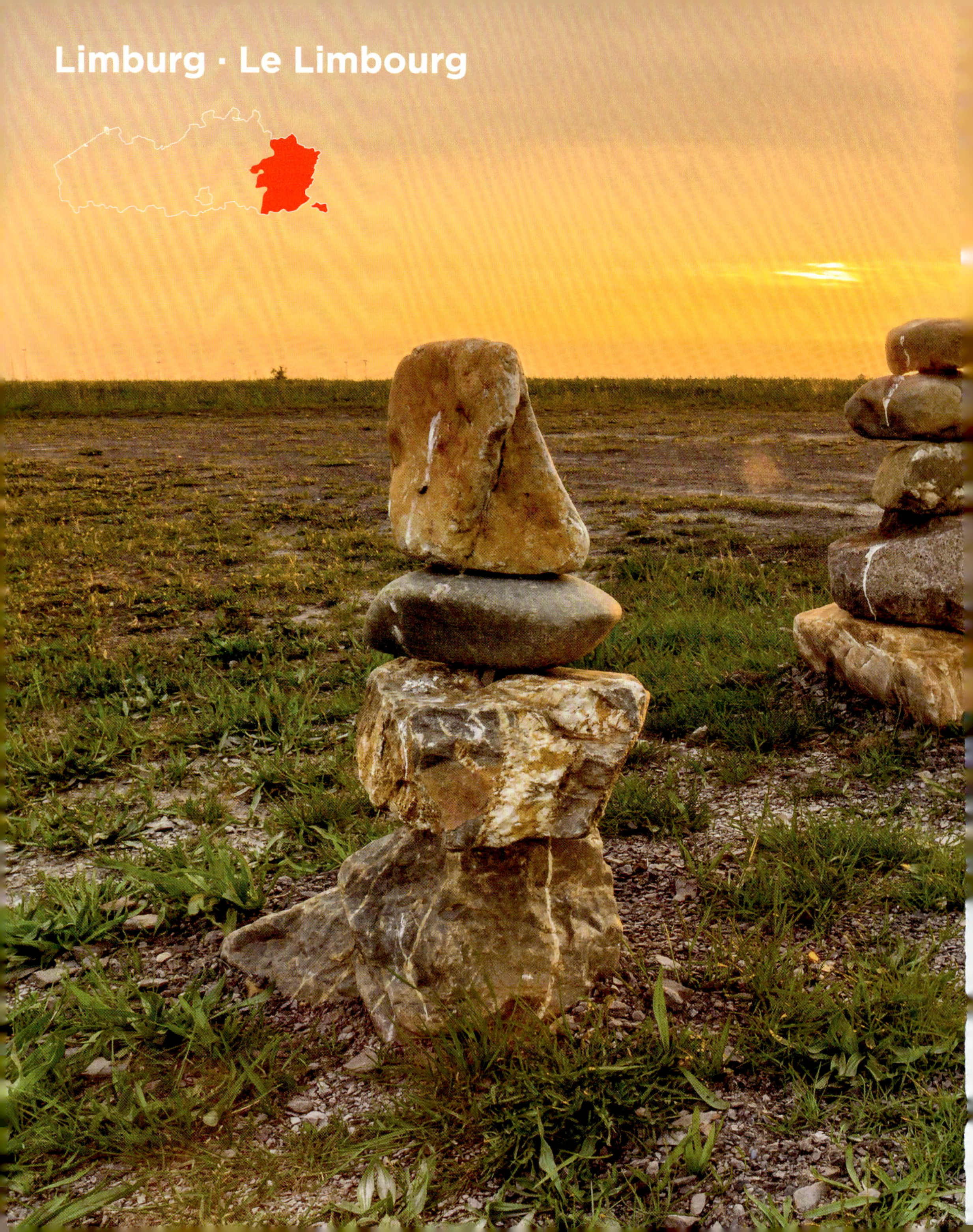

Limburg · Le Limbourg

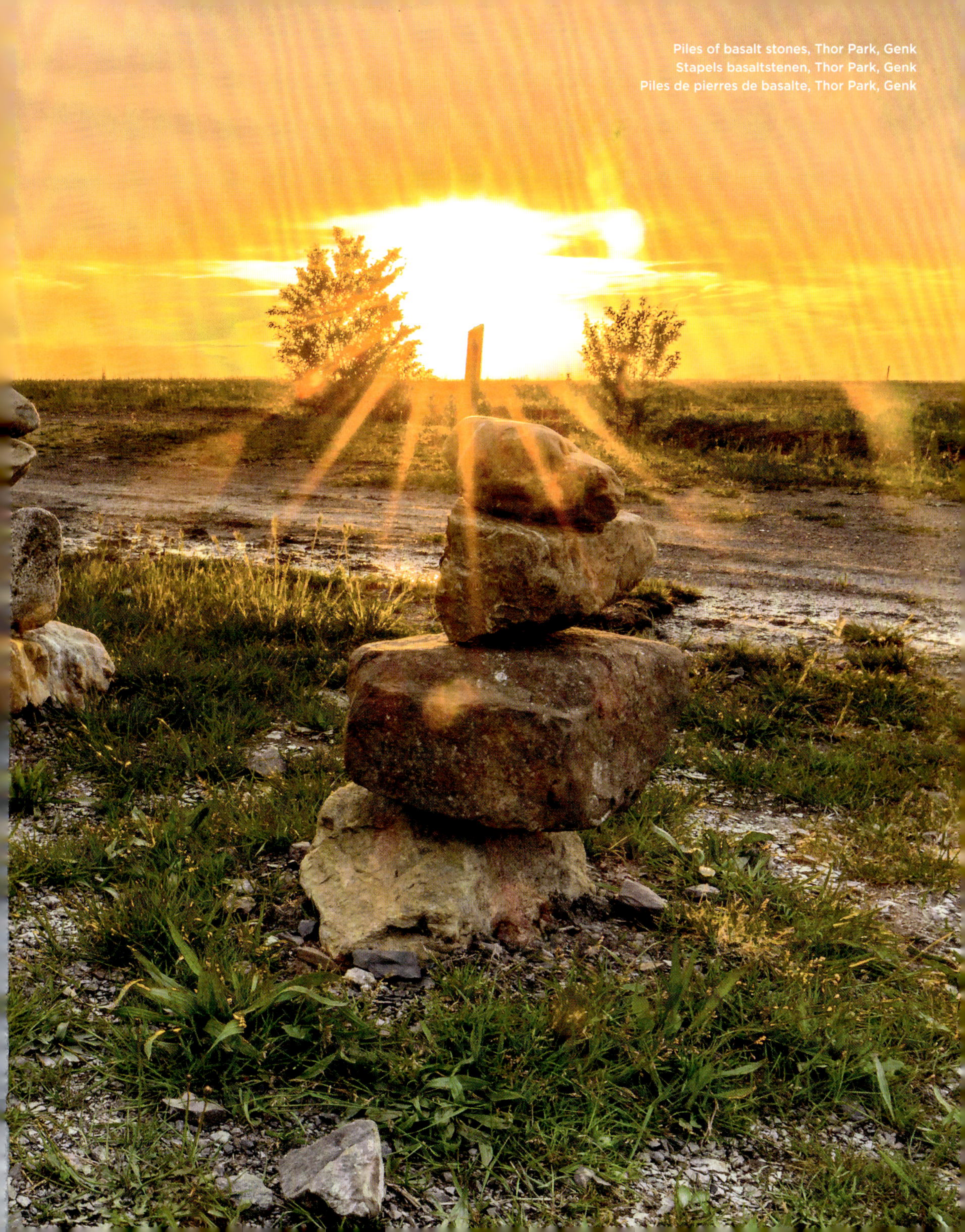

Piles of basalt stones, Thor Park, Genk
Stapels basaltstenen, Thor Park, Genk
Piles de pierres de basalte, Thor Park, Genk

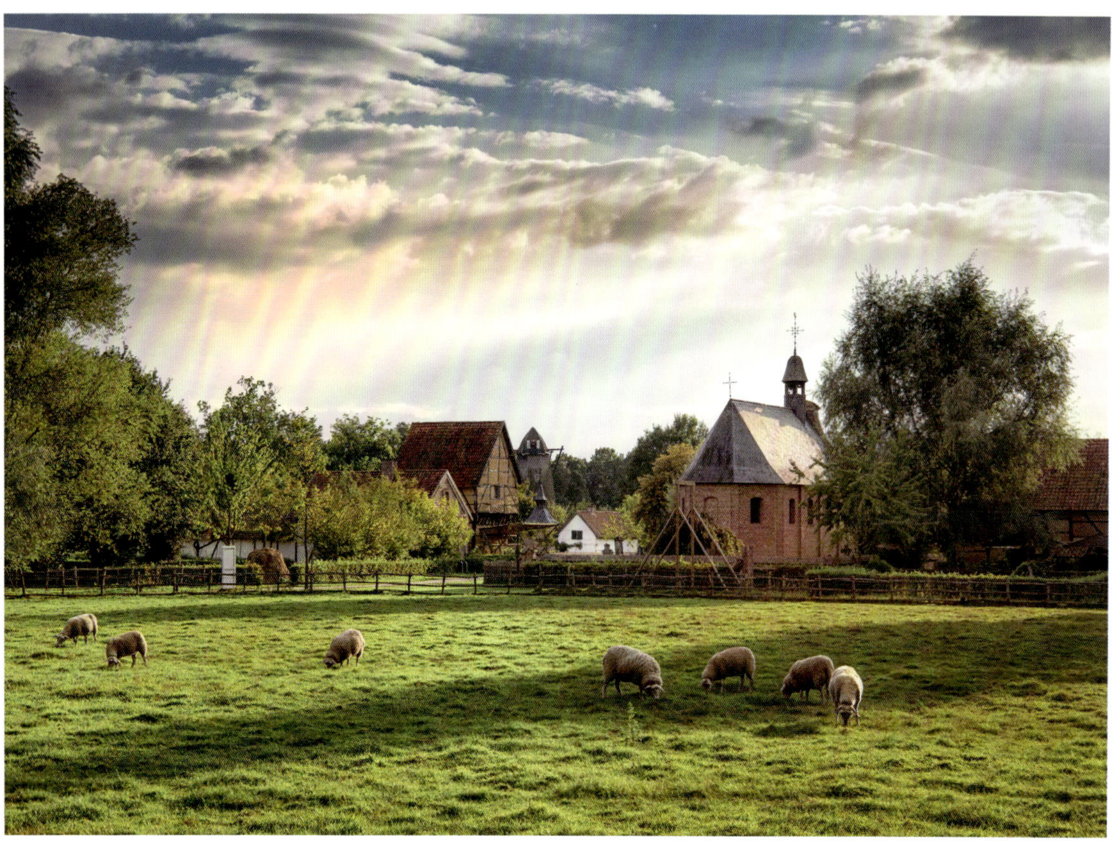

Bokrijk

Limburg

In the 18th century, Limburg was a region with many barely inhabited heaths and forest, which were ideal retreats for gangs of robbers, such as the so-called Buckriders, who attacked farms and monasteries and were then able to retreat to their hiding places in a flash. According to legend, the robbers rode on flying billy goats, and as they supposedly often shared their spoils with the poorest farmers, they were popular with large sections of the population, and are now seen as folk heroes. Today, Limburg with its heath landscapes and remote villages attracts cyclists and hikers, above all.

Le Limbourg

Au XVIIIe siècle, le Limbourg, guère peuplé alors, était une région de landes et de forêts – une retraite idéale pour les bandes de brigands, tels les dénommés « chevaliers du bouc », qui s'attaquaient aux riches domaines et monastères, se retirant dans leur cachette en un clin d'œil. Selon la légende, ces voleurs chevauchaient des boucs volants. Puisqu'ils partageaient souvent leur butin avec les paysans les plus démunis, une grande partie de la population les célébrait et on les considère aujourd'hui comme des héros populaires. De nos jours, les landes et villages isolés du Limbourg attirent avant tout cyclistes et randonneurs.

Limburg

Im 18. Jahrhundert war Limburg eine Region mit vielen kaum bewohnten Heiden und Wäldern. Ideale Rückzugsgebiete für Räuberbanden, wie den sogenannten Bockreitern, die reiche Güter und Klöster überfielen und sich blitzschnell in ihre Verstecke zurückziehen konnten. Der Legende nach ritten die Räuber auf fliegenden Ziegenböcken. Weil sie ihre Beute häufig mit den ärmsten Bauern teilten, waren sie bei weiten Teilen der Bevölkerung beliebt und werden heute als Volkshelden gesehen. Heute zieht Limburg mit seinen Heidelandschaften und abgelegenen Dörfern vor allem Radfahrer und Wanderer an.

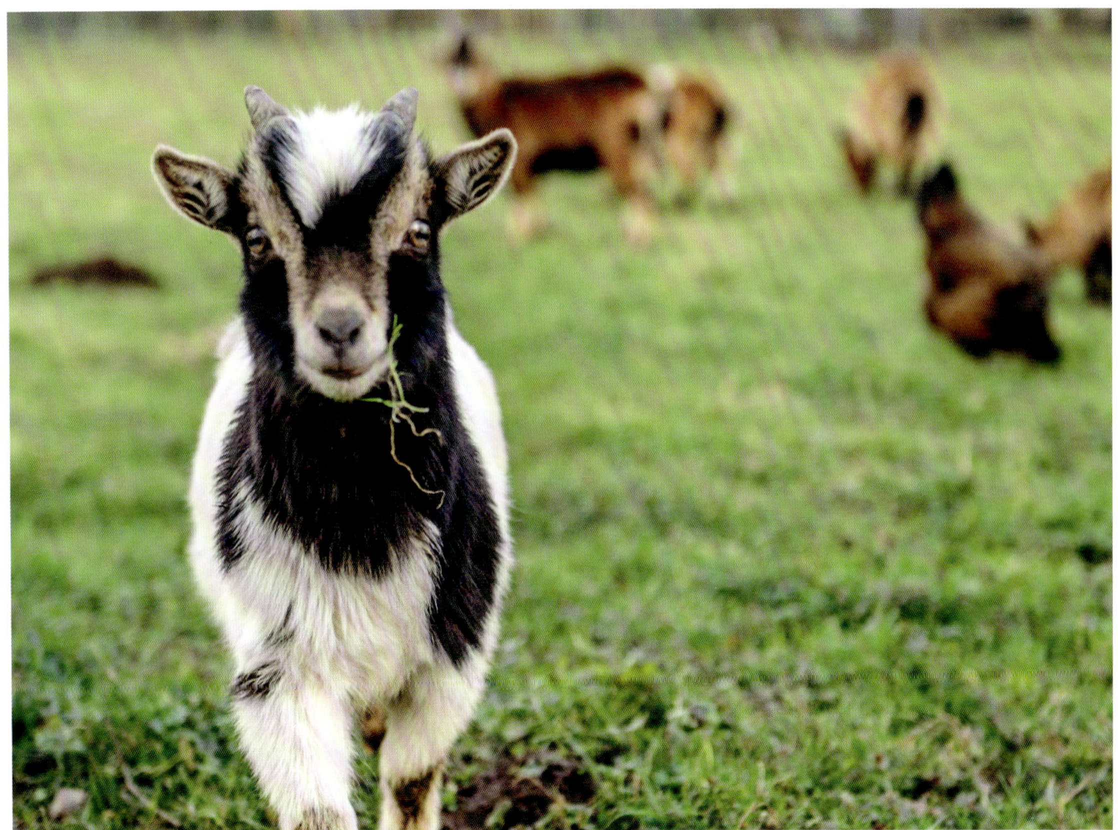

Young goat
Jonge geit
Jeune chèvre

Limburgo

En el siglo XVIII, Limburgo era una región con muchos brezales y bosques apenas habitados. Zonas ideales de retiro para bandas de ladrones, como los llamados Buckriders, que eran capaces de atracar fincas y monasterios ricos y retirarse a sus escondites en un abrir y cerrar de ojos. Según la leyenda, los ladrones montaban en cabras voladoras. Debido a que a menudo compartían sus presas con los agricultores más pobres, eran populares entre amplios sectores de la población y ahora se consideran héroes populares. Hoy en día, Limburgo, con sus paisajes de brezales y pueblos remotos, atrae sobre todo a ciclistas y excursionistas.

Limburgo

No século XVIII, Limburgo era uma região com muitas charnecas e florestas pouco habitadas. Refúgios ideais para gangues de ladrões, como os chamados cavaleiros do bode, ou "Bokkenrijders", que atacavam as propriedades ricas e os mosteiros, e eram capazes de recuar para seus esconderijos em um piscar de olhos. De acordo com a lenda, os ladrões cavalgavam em cabras voadoras. Porque muitas vezes partilhavam seus saques com os agricultores mais pobres, eles eram populares entre grandes grupos da população e agora são vistos como heróis populares.
Hoje em dia, o Limburgo, com as suas paisagens naturais e aldeias remotas, atria principalmenteciclistas e caminhantes.

Limburg

In de 18e eeuw was Limburg een regio met veel nauwelijks bewoonde heidevelden en bossen. Ideale toevluchtsoorden voor roversbendes, zoals de zogenaamde Bokkenrijders die rijke landgoederen en kloosters overvielen en zich bliksemsnel in hun schuilplaatsen konden terugtrekken. Volgens de legende reden de rovers op vliegende bokken. Omdat ze hun prooi vaak met de armste boeren deelden, waren ze populair bij grote delen van de bevolking en worden nu gezien als volkshelden. Vandaag de dag trekt Limburg met zijn heidelandschappen en afgelegen dorpen vooral fietsers en wandelaars aan.

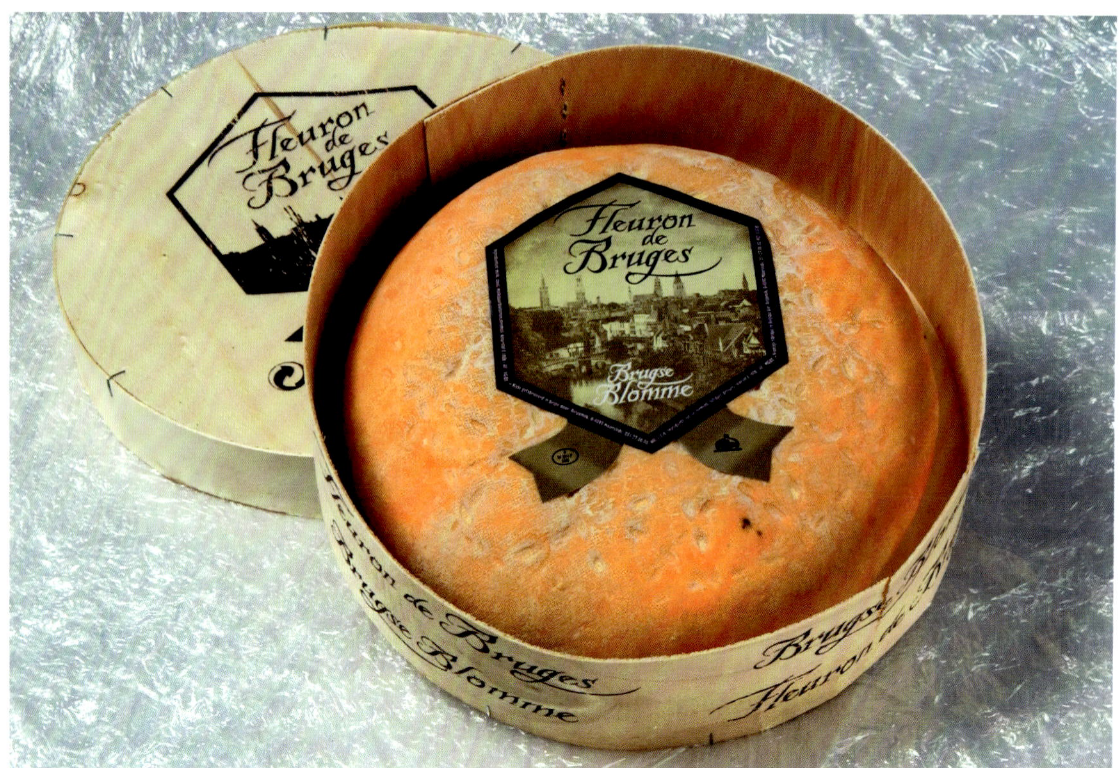

Brugge Blomme
Brugge Fleuron
Fleuron de Bruges

Cheese varieties

Flanders owes its diversity of cheeses to
the more than 30 abbeys there, almost all
of which produce their own cheese. These
cheeses, although produced in modern
cheese dairies, still bear the name of the
abbey. Only in the abbeys of Westmalle
and Postel is the cheese still made by
monks, where it is sold exclusively at the
monastery gate.

Variedad de queso

Flandes debe su diversidad de quesos a
las más de 30 abadías, casi todas ellas con
producción propia. Estos quesos, aunque
se producen en modernas queserías,
llevan el nombre de la abadía. Solo en
las abadías de Westmalle y Postel el
queso lo siguen fabricando los monjes
y se vende exclusivamente en la puerta
del monasterio.

Diversité de fromages en Flandres

Les Flandres doivent leurs nombreux
fromages à plus de 30 abbayes, dont la
quasi-totalité en avait une production
propre. Bien que fabriqués aujourd'hui
dans des fromageries modernes, ces
fromages portent le nom de l'abbaye
correspondante. Seuls les moines
des abbayes de Westmalle et de
Postel continuent à faire leur fromage
eux-mêmes ; ce dernier est vendu
exclusivement à la porte du monastère.

Variedade de queijo

A Flandres deve a sua diversidade de
queijos às mais de 30 abadias, quase
todas elas produtoras de queijos próprios.
Estes queijos, embora produzidos hoje em
laticínios de queijo modernos, ostentam
o nome de abadia. Somente nas abadias
de Westmalle e Postel é que o queijo
ainda é fabricado por monges e vendido
exclusivamente no portão do mosteiro.

Käsevielfalt

Die Vielfalt an Käsesorten verdankt
Flandern den über 30 Abteien, die fast
alle ihren eigenen Käse herstellten.
Diese Käsesorten tragen, auch wenn sie
heute in modernen Käsereien produziert
werden, den Namen der Abtei. Nur in
den Abteien von Westmalle und Postel
wird der Käse noch immer von Mönchen
hergestellt und ausschließlich an der
Klosterpforte verkauft.

Vele kaassoorten

Vlaanderen dankt zijn vele kaassoorten aan
de meer dan 30 abdijen die bijna allemaal
hun eigen kaas maakten. Deze kazen,
hoewel vandaag de dag geproduceerd
in moderne kaasmakerijen, dragen de
naam van de abdij. Alleen in de abdijen
van Westmalle en Postel wordt de kaas
nog steeds door monniken gemaakt en
uitsluitend aan de kloosterpoort verkocht.

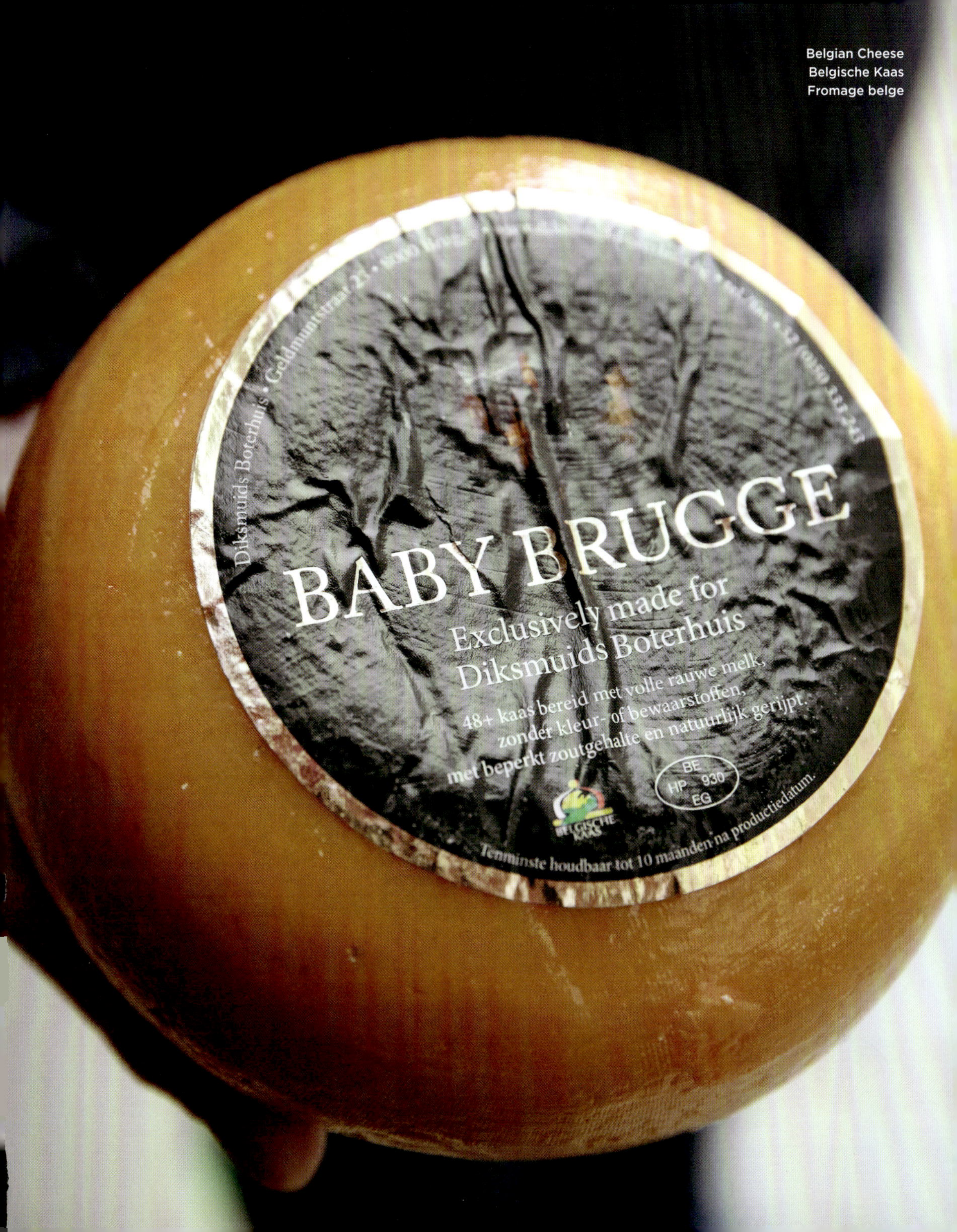

Belgian Cheese
Belgische Kaas
Fromage belge

Diksmuids Boterhuis · Geldmuntstraat 21 · 8000 Brugge

BABY BRUGGE
Exclusively made for
Diksmuids Boterhuis
48+ kaas bereid met volle rauwe melk,
zonder kleur- of bewaarstoffen,
met beperkt zoutgehalte en natuurlijk gerijpt.

BELGISCHE KAAS

BE
HP 930
EG

Tenminste houdbaar tot 10 maanden na productiedatum.

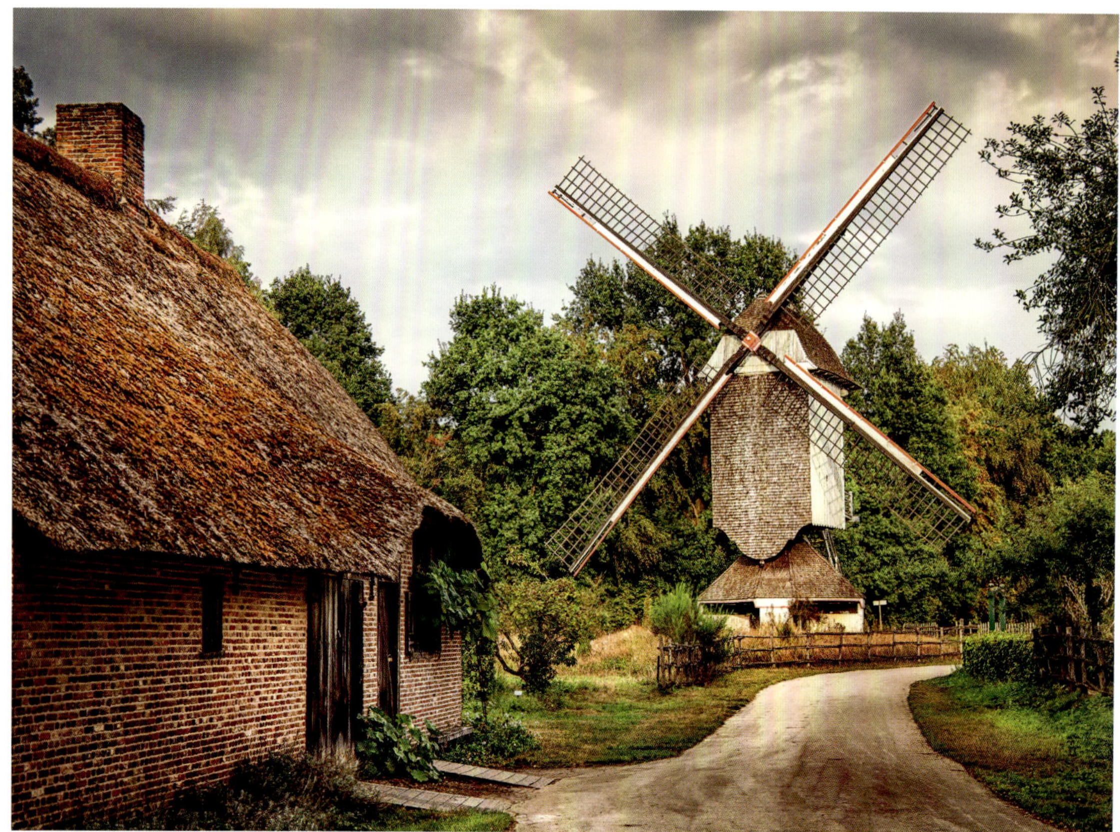

Open air museum, Bokrijk
Openluchtmuseum, Provinciaal Domein Bokrijk
Musée en plein air, domaine provincial de Bokrijk

Bokrijk, a journey back in time

The huge open-air museum of Bokrijk presents everyday Flemish life from circa 1900. Around 140 historical buildings, from farmhouses to windmills, are formed into a typical Flemish village. The village policeman, the pastor, the craftsmen and many other actors take the visitors back in time to 100 years ago. In the village you can go to school, walk into the houses, watch and ask people how they spin yarn, embroider or cook. The potter, the blacksmith and the tanner all provide insight into their craft and give workshops.

Bokrijk, un voyage dans le temps

Composé de trois villages, l'immense musée en plein air présente la vie quotidienne flamande vers 1900. De la ferme au moulin à vent, environ 140 bâtiments historiques ont été transformés en villages flamands typiques. Le policier du village, le pasteur, les artisans et bien d'autres acteurs emmènent les visiteurs un siècle en arrière. Ceux-ci peuvent retourner sur les bancs de l'école du village, entrer dans les maisons, regarder et demander comment filer, broder ou cuisiner. Le potier, le forgeron, le maroquinier donnent un aperçu de leur métier et animent des ateliers.

Bokrijk, eine Zeitreise

Das riesige, aus drei Dörfern bestehende, Freilichtmuseum präsentiert den flämischen Alltag um 1900. Rund 140 historische Bauwerke, vom Bauernhaus bis zur Windmühle, wurden zu typisch flämischen Dörfern geformt. Der Dorfpolizist, der Pastor, die Handwerker und viele andere Darsteller versetzen die Besucher in die Zeit von vor 100 Jahren zurück. Man kann in der Dorfschule die Schulbank drücken, in die Häuser gehen, zuschauen und fragen wie die Menschen Garn spinnen, sticken oder kochen. Der Töpfer, der Schmied, der Ledermacher geben Einblick in ihr Handwerk und geben Workshops.

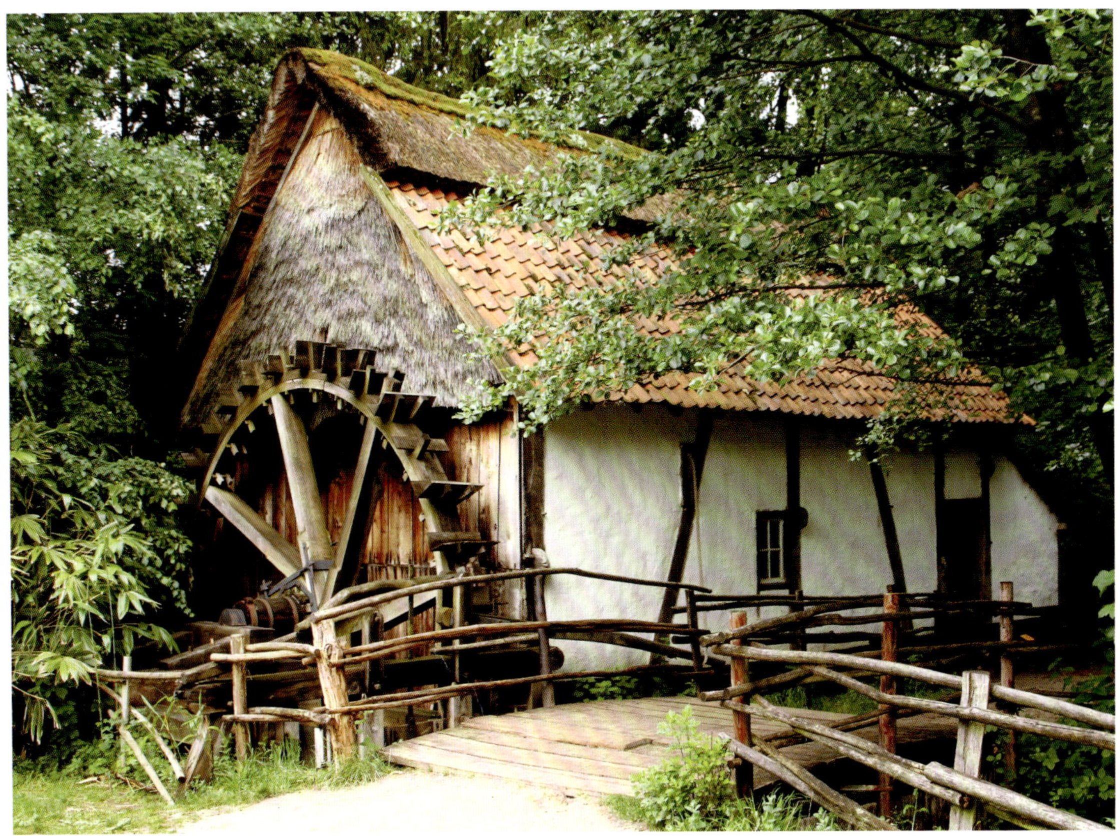

Open air museum, Bokrijk
Openluchtmuseum, Provinciaal Domein Bokrijk
Musée en plein air, domaine provincial de Bokrijk

Bokrijk, un viaje en el tiempo

El enorme museo al aire libre, formado por tres pueblos, nos muestra la vida cotidiana de los flamencos en torno a 1900. 140 construcciones históricas, desde granjas hasta molinos de viento, se convirtieron en pueblos flamencos típicos. El policía del pueblo, el párroco, los artesanos y muchos otros actores transportan a los visitantes en el tiempo hasta hace 100 años. En la escuela del pueblo se puede ir a la escuela, entrar en las casas, mirar y preguntar a la gente cómo hilan, bordan o cocinan el hilo. El alfarero, el herrero, el marroquinero, el marroquinero, dan una idea de su oficio y realizan talleres.

Bokrijk, uma viagem no tempo

O enorme museu ao ar livre, constituído por três aldeias, apresenta a vida quotidiana flamenga por volta de 1900. Cerca de 140 edifícios históricos, desde casas de quinta a moinhos de vento, foram transformados em típicas aldeias flamengas. O policial da aldeia, o pastor, os artesãos e muitos outros atores levam os visitantes de volta aos tempos de 100 anos atrás. Pode-se ir à escola na escola da aldeia, entrar nas casas, ver e perguntar às pessoas como é que elas tecem, bordam ou cozinham. O oleiro, o ferreiro, o cabeleireiro dão uma ideia do seu ofício e dão oficinas.

Bokrijk, een reis door de tijd

Het enorme openluchtmuseum, bestaande uit drie dorpen, toont het alledaagse Vlaamse leven van rond 1900. Ongeveer 140 historische gebouwen, van boerderij tot windmolen, werden tot typisch Vlaamse dorpen omgevormd. De dorpsagent, de pastoor, de ambachtslieden en vele andere acteurs nemen de bezoekers mee terug in de tijd van 100 jaar geleden. Je kunt in de dorpsschool in de schoolbank plaatsnemen, de huizen binnenlopen, kijken en vragen hoe mensen spinnen, borduren of garen spinnen. De pottenbakker, de smid en de leermaker geven een kijkje in hun ambacht en geven workshops.

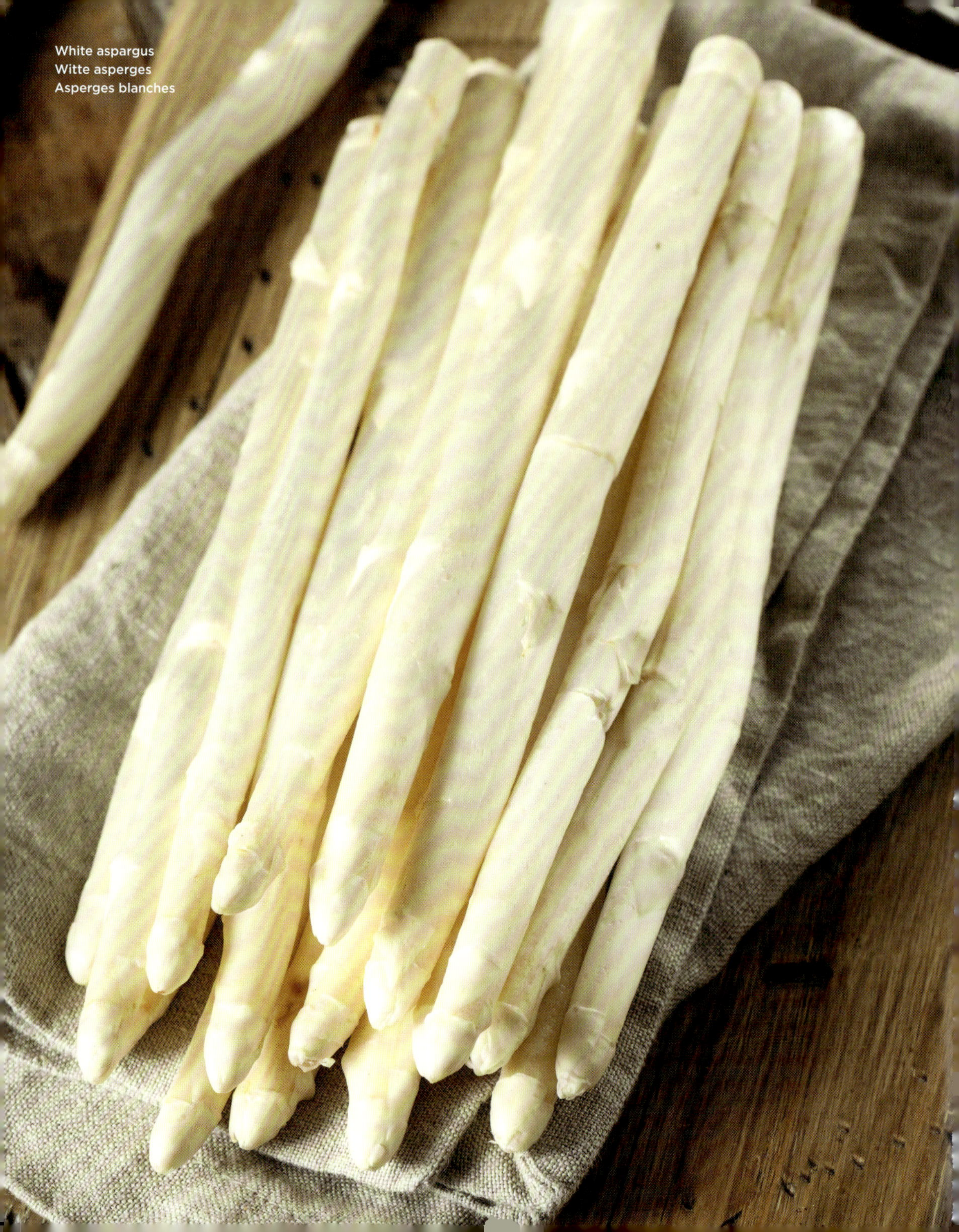
White aspargus
Witte asperges
Asperges blanches

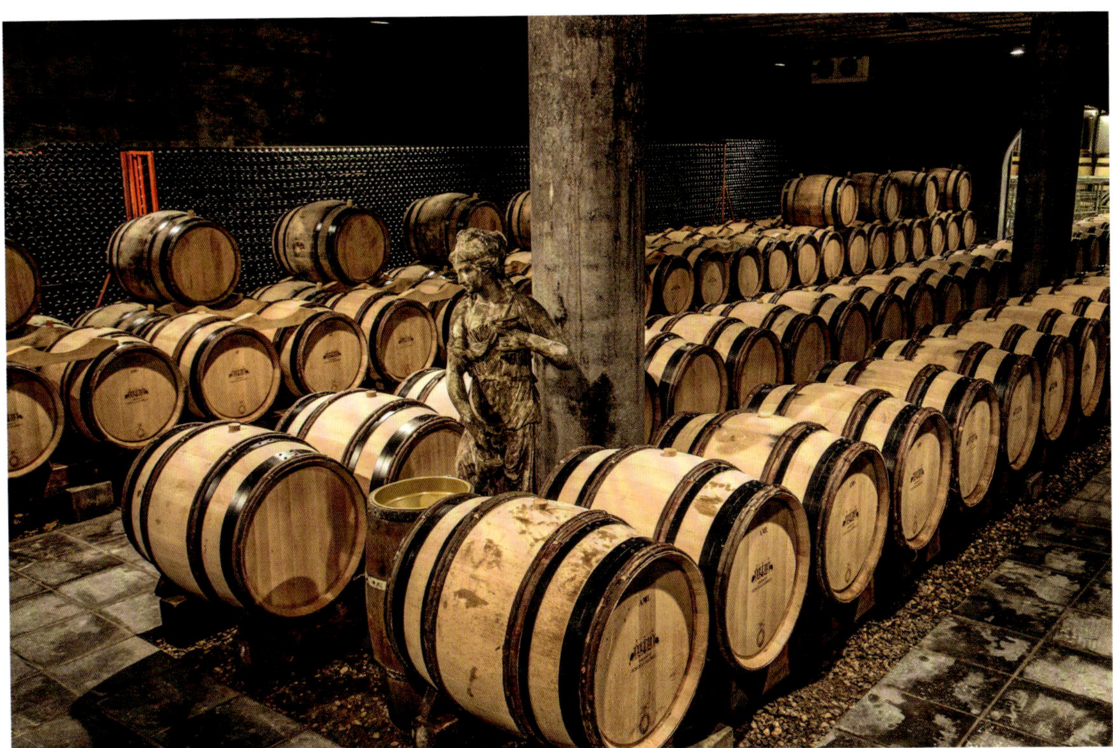

Wine Castle of Genoels-Elderen
Wijnkasteel Genoels-Elderen
Château viticole de Genoels-Elderen

Asparagus and Wine

White Flemish asparagus is the common type in Flanders, a gourmet vegetable which thrives very well in Limburg's sandy soils. A Pinot Blanc from Genoels-Elderen, the only wine castle in Flanders, accompanies this well. The vineyards, with more than 20 grape varieties, the wine cellar from the 13th century and the subsequent wine tasting are all worth a visit.

Vin et asperges

En Flandres, les asperges à la flamande sont la manière la plus courante de préparer ce légume de gourmet qui apprécie les sols sablonneux du Limbourg. Un Pinot blanc de Genoels-Elderen, le seul château viticole de Flandres, se conjugue à merveille avec ce mets. D'ailleurs, ce château vaut le détour pour ses vignobles comprenant plus de 20 cépages, sa cave du XIIIe siècle et la dégustation qui suit la visite.

Spargel und Wein

Spargel auf flämische Art ist die in Flandern gängige Art, das Feinschmeckergemüse, das auf Limburgs sandigen Böden sehr gut gedeiht zu genießen. Dazu passt ein Pinot blanc aus Genoels Elderen, dem einzigen Weinschloss in Flandern. Die Weingärten mit über 20 Traubensorten, der Weinkeller aus dem 13. Jahrhundert und die anschließende Weinverkostung lohnen einen Besuch.

Espárragos y vino

El espárrago a la flamenca es la forma común en Flandes. La verdura gourmet prospera muy bien en los suelos arenosos de Limburgo. Un Pinot blanc de Genoels Elderen (el único castillo de vinos de Flandes) acompaña muy bien el plato. Los viñedos con más de 20 variedades de uva, la bodega del siglo XIII y la posterior cata de vinos son dignos de una visita.

Espargos e Vinho

Os espargos flamengos são o tipo mais comum na Flandres, o vegetal gourmet que prospera muito bem nos solos arenosos do Limburgo. Para acompanhar nada melhor do que um Pinot blanc de Genoels Elderen, o único castelo de vinho da Flandres. Vale a pena visitar as vinhas com mais de 20 tipos de uvas, as adegas do século XIII e posteriormente a degustação de vinhos.

Asperges en wijn

Asperges op zijn Vlaams is in Vlaanderen de gebruikelijke bereidingswijze. De fijnproeversgroente gedijt goed op de Limburgse zandgronden. Een Pinot Blanc uit Genoelselderen, het enige wijnkasteel in Vlaanderen, past hier goed bij. De wijngaarden met meer dan 20 druivensoorten, de 13-eeuwse wijnkelder en de daaropvolgende wijnproeverijen zijn een bezoekje waard.

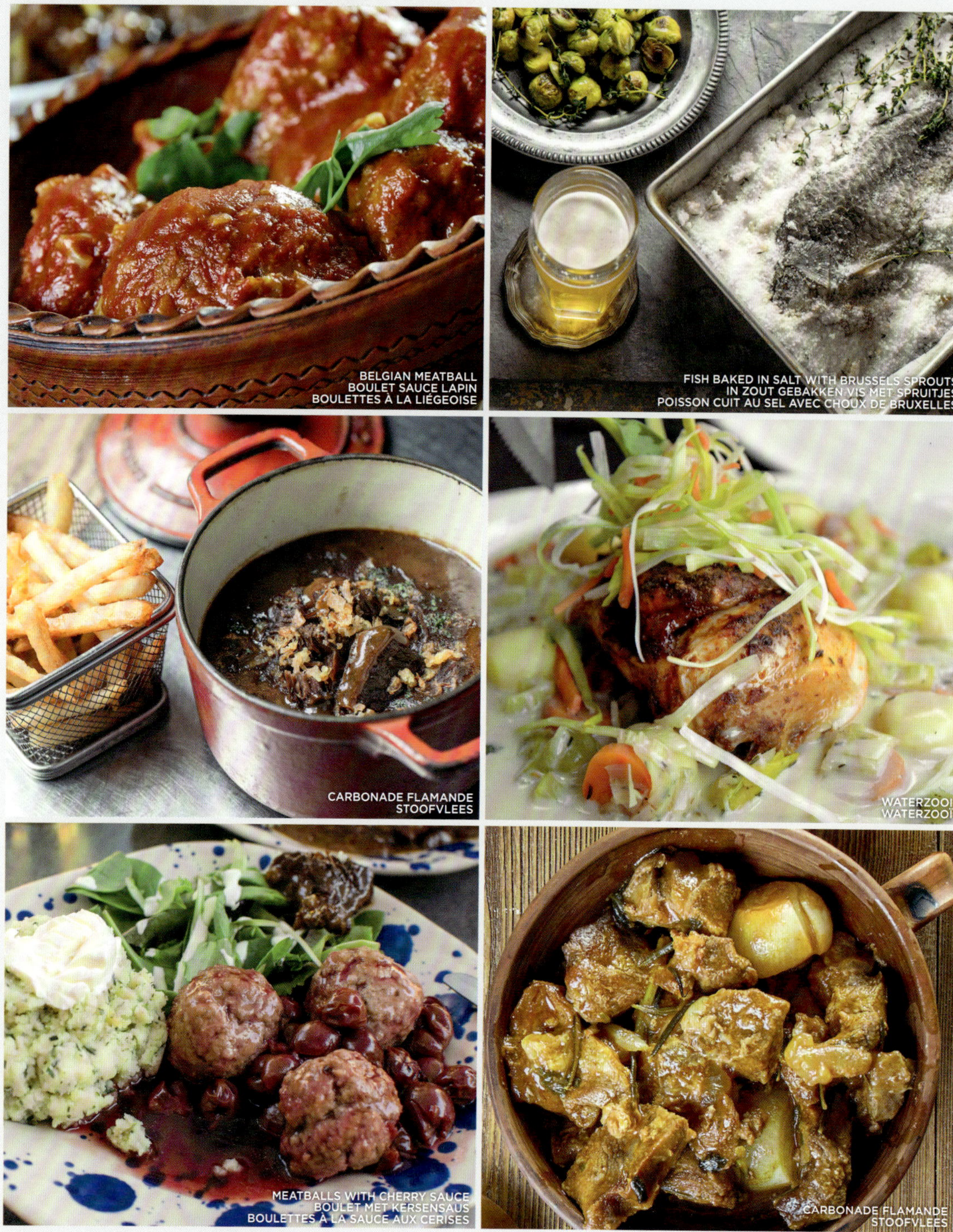

BELGIAN MEATBALL
BOULET SAUCE LAPIN
BOULETTES À LA LIÉGEOISE

FISH BAKED IN SALT WITH BRUSSELS SPROUTS
IN ZOUT GEBAKKEN VIS MET SPRUITJES
POISSON CUIT AU SEL AVEC CHOUX DE BRUXELLES

CARBONADE FLAMANDE
STOOFVLEES

WATERZOOI
WATERZOOÏ

MEATBALLS WITH CHERRY SAUCE
BOULET MET KERSENSAUS
BOULETTES À LA SAUCE AUX CERISES

CARBONADE FLAMANDE
STOOFVLEES

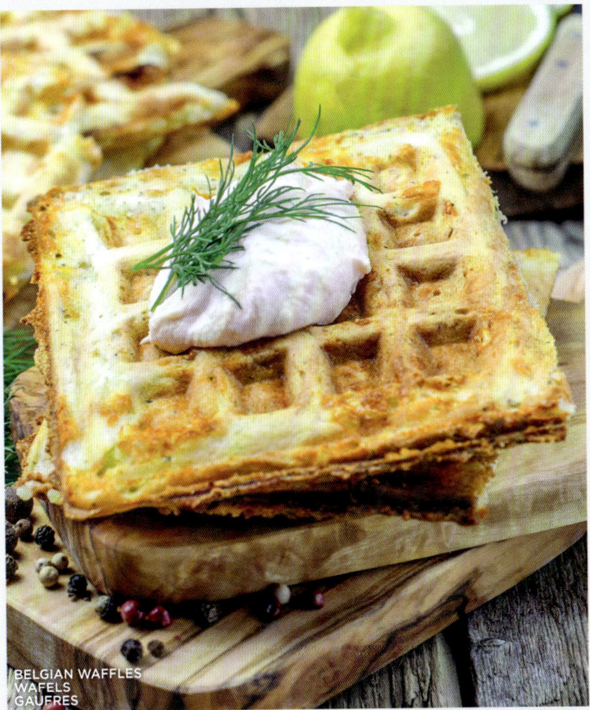

Flemish cuisine

The Flemish and Dutch often use the magic word "Burgundian" in connection with cuisine and lifestyle, which refers to the rich court culture of the Burgundians. Brussels sprouts and leeks, as well as fruit, characterise the typical Flemish dishes, such as meatballs in cherry sauce, *Stofvlees* (beef stewed for a long time with dark beer and onions), *Waterzooi* (a clear vegetable stew with fish or meat) and of course, waffles.

Cuisine flamande

En matière de cuisine et de style de vie, Flamands et Hollandais se plaisent à utiliser le mot magique «bourguignon», qui évoque la riche culture de la cour de Bourgogne. Les choux de Bruxelles et les poireaux ainsi que les fruits caractérisent les plats typiquement flamands, tels les boulettes aux cerises, la carbonade flamande (viande mijotée dans de la bière et des oignons), le waterzooï (un ragoût de légumes clair avec de la viande) et bien sûr les gaufres.

Flämische Küche

Flamen und Niederländer benutzen in Verbindung mit Küche und Lebensart oft das Zauberwort „burgundisch" was sich auf die reichhaltige Hofkultur der Burgunder bezieht. Rosenkohl und Lauch aber auch Obst prägen die typisch flämischen Gerichte, wie Bouletten in Kirschsoße, Stofvlees (in Bier und Zwiebeln ganz lange geschmortes Fleisch), Waterzooi (ein klarer Gemüseeintopf mit Fleisch) und natürlich Waffeln.

Cocina flamenca

Los flamencos y holandeses utilizan a menudo la palabra mágica "borgoñón" en relación con la cocina y el estilo de vida, que se refiere a la rica cultura de la corte de los borgoñones. Las coles de Bruselas y los puerros, así como las frutas, caracterizan los platos típicos flamencos, como los boulettes en salsa de cerezas, los Stofvlees (carne estofada durante mucho tiempo en cerveza y cebollas), el Waterzooi (un guiso de verduras claras con carne) y, por supuesto, los gofres.

Cozinha flamenga

Flamengos e holandeses muitas vezes usam a palavra mágica "borgonhesa" em conexão com a cozinha e o estilo de vida, que se refere à rica cultura da corte de Borgonha. As couves-de-bruxelas e os alhos-franceses, bem como as frutas, caracterizam os pratos típicos da Flandres, como as almôndegas em molho de cerejas, os Stofvlees (carne cozida durante muito tempo em cerveja e cebolas), os Waterzooi (um cozido de legumes claro com carne) e, claro, os waffles.

Vlaamse keuken

Bij keuken en levensstijl gebruiken de Vlamingen en Nederlanders vaak het toverwoord "Bourgondisch", wat betrekking heeft op de rijke hofcultuur van de Bourgondiërs. Spruitjes en prei, maar ook fruit kenmerken de typisch Vlaamse gerechten zoals gehaktballetjes in kersensaus, stoofvlees (vlees dat lange tijd in bier en uien is gestoofd), waterzooi (een heldere groentesoep met vlees) en natuurlijk wafels.

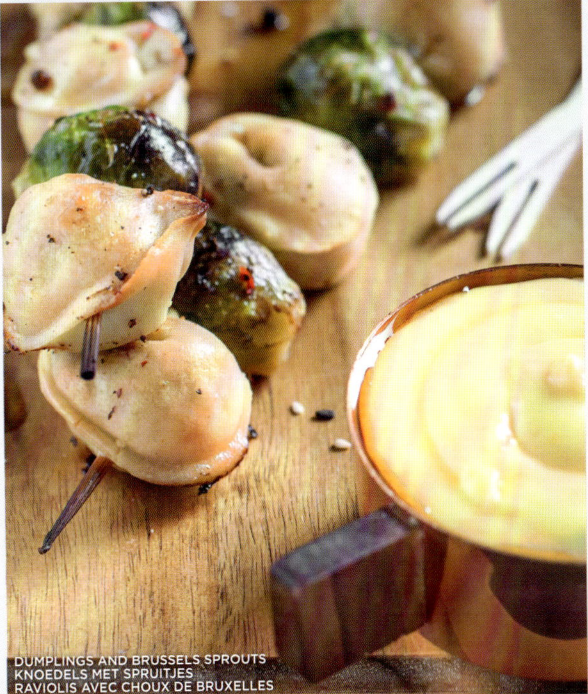

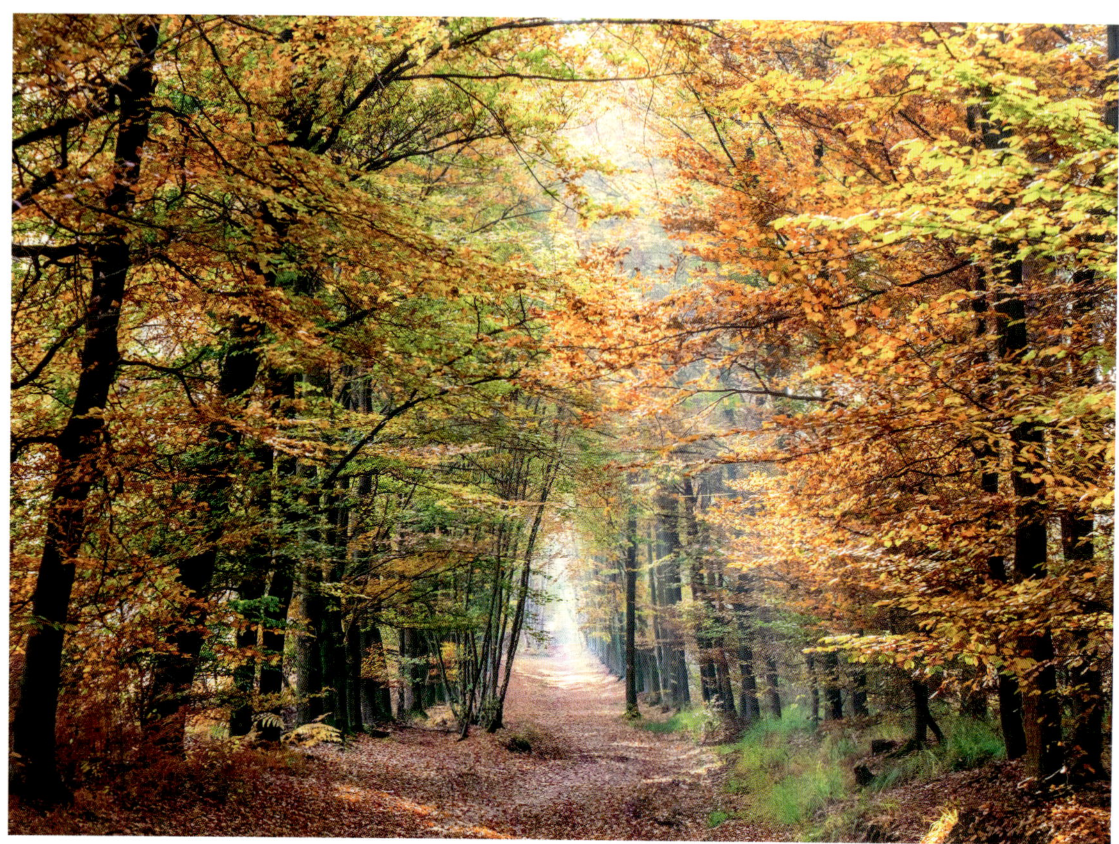

Hoge Kempen National Park
Nationaal Park Hoge Kempen
Parc national de la Haute Campine

Hoge Kempen National Park

The national park is the first, and so far only, national park in Belgium. The nature reserve covers 5750 ha (14,209 ac) of heath, pine forests and lakes. The main function of the national park is nature conservation, but the experience of the outdoors (hiking, cycling or forest games) is also promoted. In each municipality there is an entrance gate that explains an aspect of the national park. At each of these six gates is the start many circular hiking trails, forming a network of 200 km (124 mi). There are also many cycle paths through the National Park. Rangers offer nature tours, on foot or by bike, on various themes.

Parc national de la Haute Campine

Premier – et jusqu'à présent unique – parc national en Belgique, cette réserve naturelle couvre 5750 hectares de lande, de pinèdes et de lacs. Principalement voué à protéger la nature, le parc propose également des activités liées à cette dernière (randonnée, vélo ou jeux forestiers). Chaque commune possède un portail d'entrée, où un aspect du parc national est expliqué au visiteur. Chacune des six portes marque le début de nombreux sentiers de randonnée circulaires qui forment un réseau de 200 km en tout. Beaucoup de pistes cyclables sillonnent également le parc national. Les gardiens du parc proposent des visites guidées dans la nature portant sur différents thèmes, à pied ou à vélo.

Nationalpark Hoge Kempen

Der Nationalpark ist der erste und bislang einzige Nationalpark in Belgien. Das Naturreservat umfasst 5750 ha Heide, Kiefernwälder und Seen. Die Hauptfunktion des Nationalparks ist der Naturschutz, aber auch das Naturerlebnis (Wandern, Radfahren oder Waldspiele) wird gefördert. In jeder Gemeinde befindet sich ein Eingangstor, das einen Aspekt des Nationalparks erklärt. An jedem der sechs Tore starten viele Rundwanderwege und bilden ein Netz von 200 km. Auch zahlreiche Radwege führen durch den Nationalpark. Ranger bieten Naturführungen, zu Fuß oder mit dem Rad, zu unterschiedlichen Themen an.

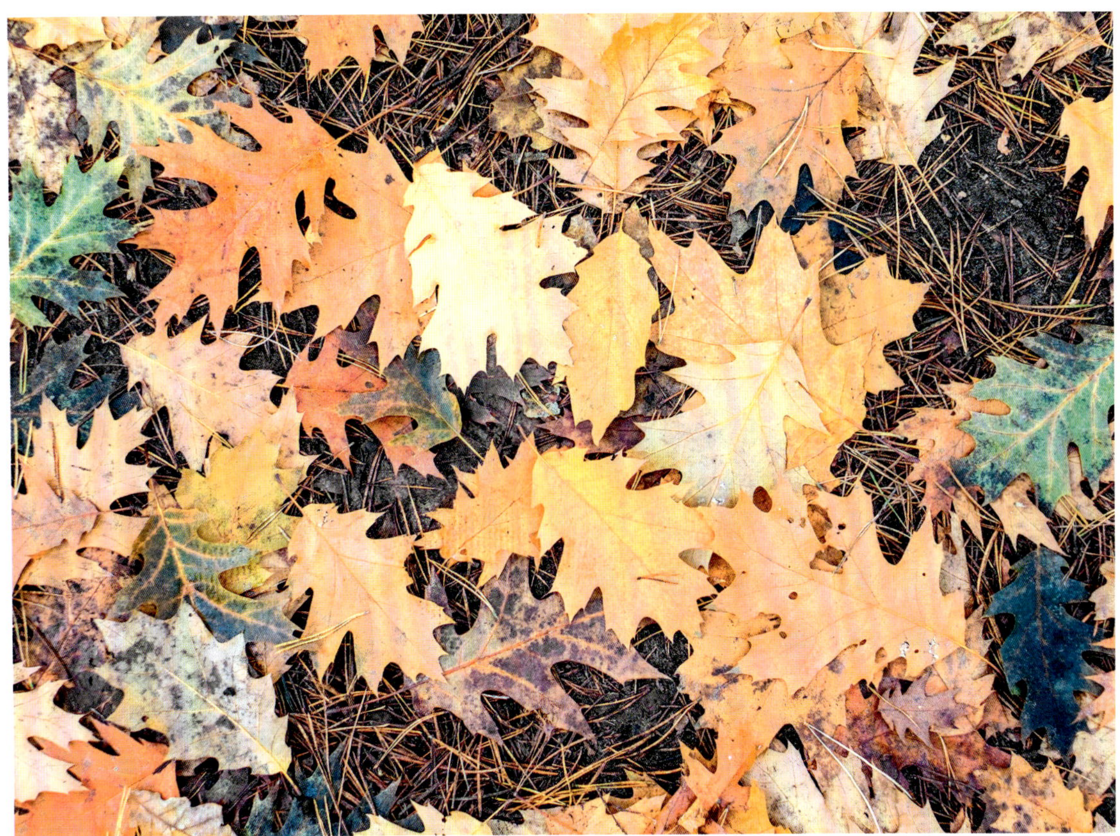

Hoge Kempen National Park
Nationaal Park Hoge Kempen
Parc national de la Haute Campine

Parque Nacional Hoge Kempen

El parque nacional es el primero y hasta ahora el único parque nacional de Bélgica. La reserva natural cubre 5750 ha de brezales, bosques de pinos y lagos. La función principal del parque nacional es la conservación de la naturaleza, pero también se promueve la experiencia de la naturaleza (senderismo, ciclismo o juegos en el bosque). En cada municipio hay una puerta de entrada que explica un aspecto del parque nacional. En cada una de las seis puertas hay muchos senderos circulares que comienzan y forman una red de 200 km. También hay múltiples carriles bici que atraviesan el parque nacional. Los guardabosques ofrecen excursiones a la naturaleza, a pie o en bicicleta, sobre diversos temas.

Parque Nacional Hoge Kempen

O parque nacional é o primeiro e até hoje o único parque nacional da Bélgica. A reserva natural abrange 5750 ha de charnecas, pinhais e lagos. A principal função do parque nacional é a conservação da natureza, mas a experiência da natureza (caminhadas, ciclismo ou jogos florestais) também é promovida. Em cada município existe um portão de entrada que explica um aspecto do parque nacional. Em cada um dos seis portões, começam muitas trilhas circulares e formam uma rede de 200 km. Há também muitas ciclovias pelo parque nacional. Os guardas-florestais oferecem passeios pela natureza, a pé ou de bicicleta, sobre vários temas.

Nationaal Park Hoge Kempen

Het nationaal park is het eerste en tot nu toe enige nationale park in België. Het natuurreservaat beslaat 5750 ha heide, dennenbossen en meren. De belangrijkste functie is natuurbehoud, maar ook de natuurbeleving (wandelen, fietsen of bosspelletjes) wordt gepromoot. In elke gemeente is er een toegangspoort die een aspect van het nationale park uitlegt. Bij elk van de zes poorten gaan vele rondwandelingen van start en vormen samen een netwerk van 200 km. Ook talrijke fietspaden leiden door het nationaal park. Rangers bieden natuurwandelingen rond verschillende thema's aan, te voet of met de fiets.

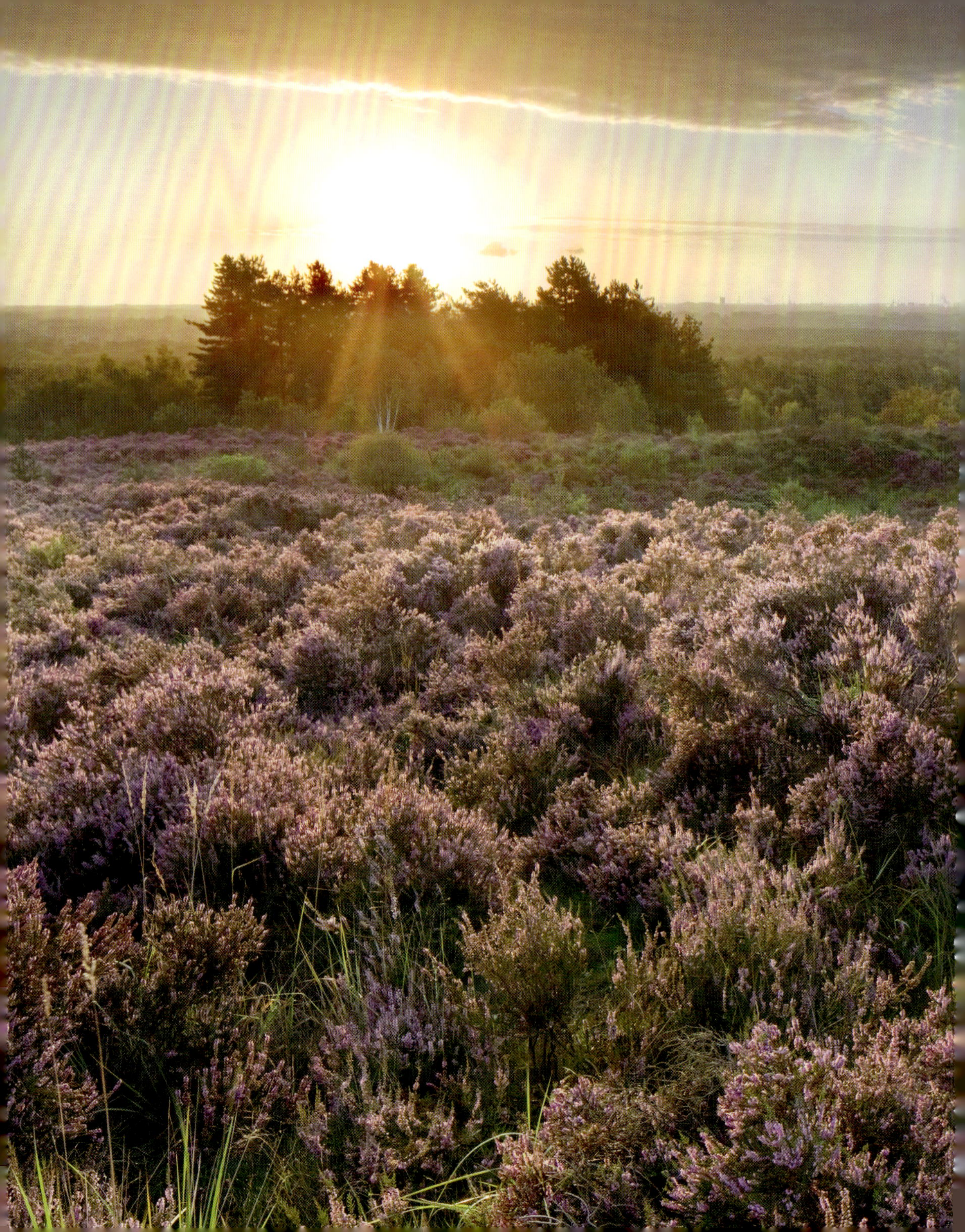

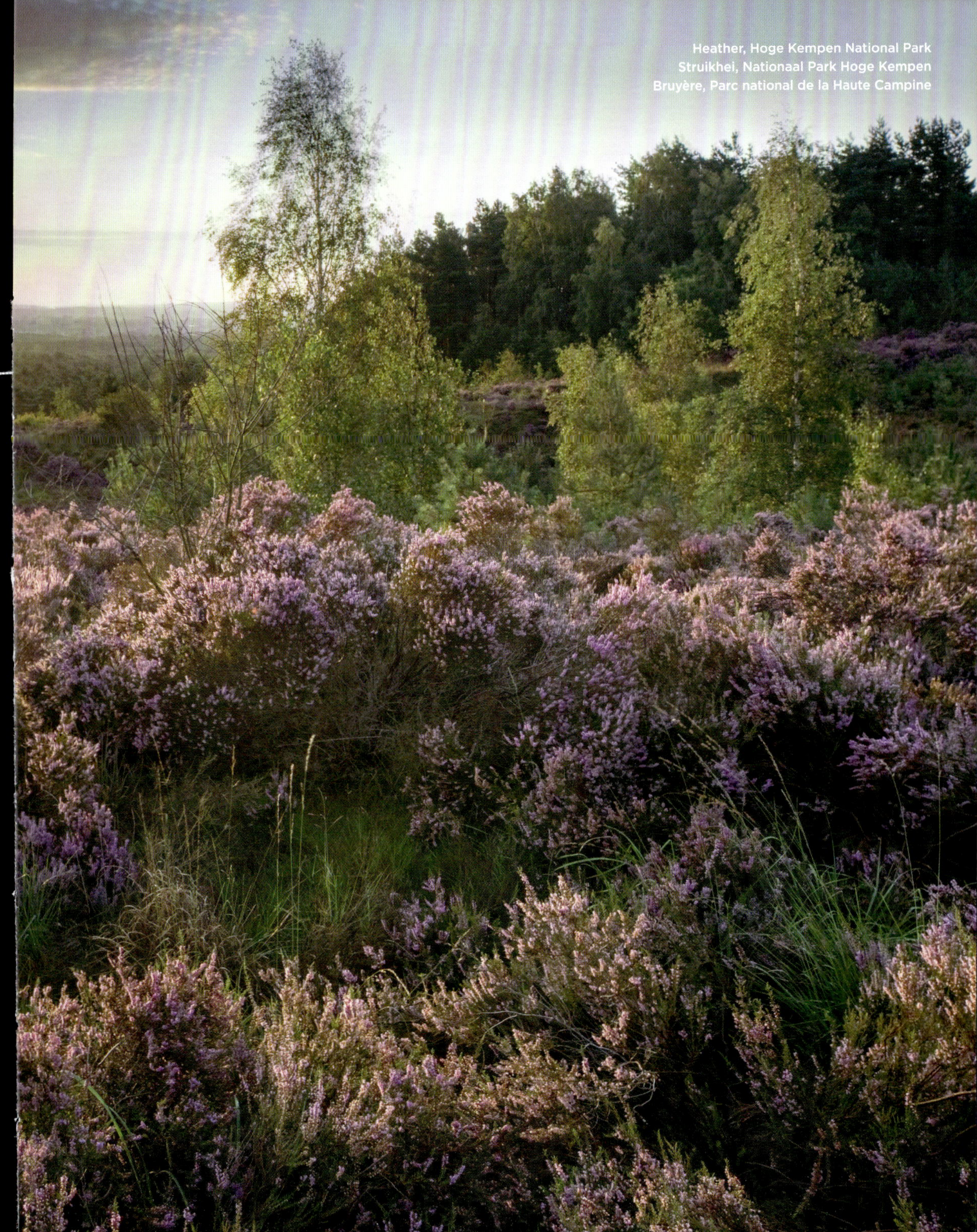
Heather, Hoge Kempen National Park
Struikhei, Nationaal Park Hoge Kempen
Bruyère, Parc national de la Haute Campine

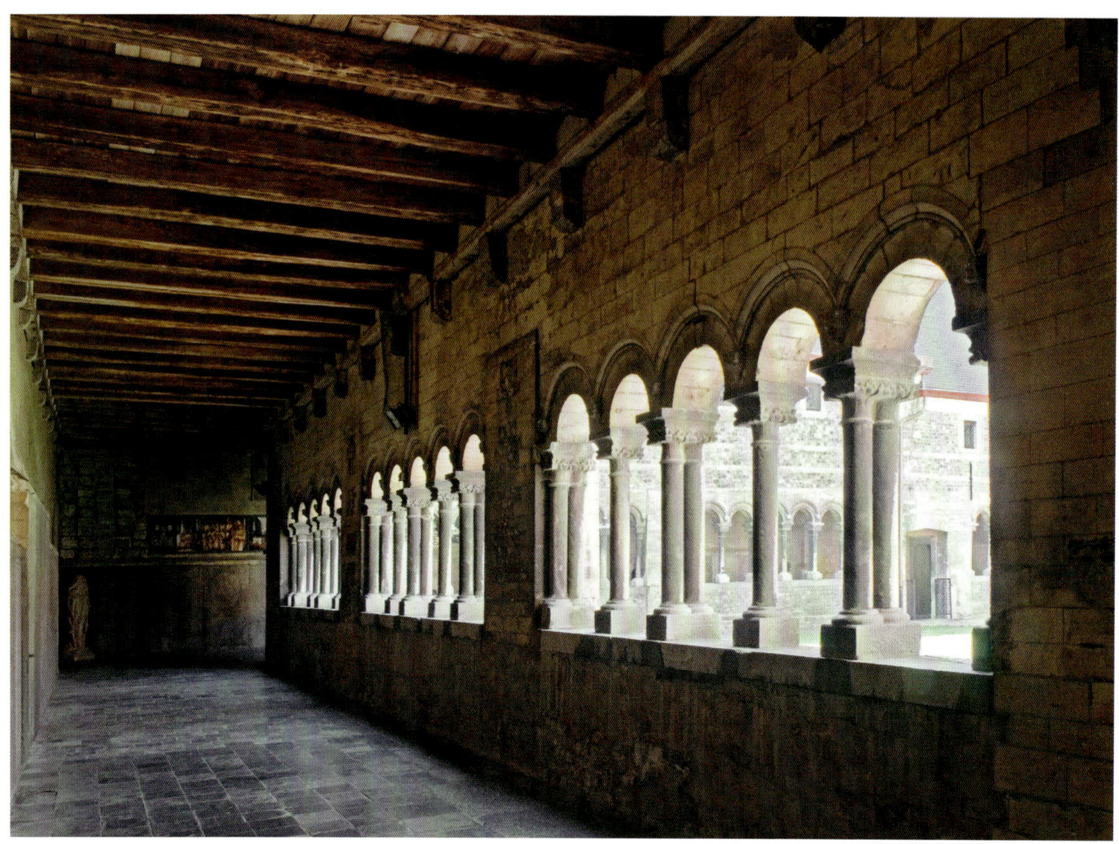

Basilica of Our Lady, Tongeren
Onze-Lieve-Vrouwe Basilica, Cloister, Tongeren
Basilique Notre-Dame de Tongres

Tongeren, oldest city in Flanders

Approaching Tongeren, the UNESCO World Heritage Site of the Gothic tower of the Basilica of Our Lady, can be seen from the distance. Also worth visiting is the Romanesque cloister with its monastery garden, the religious art treasures in the "Teseum" and the archaeological site below the basilica, in which 2000 years of the city's history are displayed, including wooden houses from the 1st century, a Roman stone house, a Roman basilica from the 4th century, and seven more churches. The Roman city is well known, particularly, for hosting Belgium's largest flea market, by the old city walls.

Tongres, la plus ancienne ville de Flandres

Sur la route vers Tongres, la tour gothique de la basilique Notre-Dame, inscrite au patrimoine mondial de l'Unesco, se dessine déjà au loin. Découvrez-y le cloître roman et le jardin du monastère, les trésors de l'art religieux du Teseum et le site archéologique sous la basilique, qui retrace 2000 ans d'histoire de la ville : des maisons en bois du Ier siècle, une maison romaine en pierre, une basilique romaine du IVe siècle, suivies de sept autres églises. La ville romaine de Tongres doit son renom, notamment, au plus grand marché aux puces de Belgique, qui se tient devant les remparts de la vieille ville.

Tongern, älteste Stadt Flanderns

Auf dem Weg nach Tongern sieht man bereits aus weiter Ferne den gotischen Turm der Liebfrauenbasilika, der zum Weltkulturerbe der UNESCO gehört. Sehenswert ist der romanische Kreuzgang mit Klostergarten, die religiösen Kunstschätze im „Teseum" und die archäologische Stätte unterhalb der Basilika, in der 2000 Jahre Stadtgeschichte gezeigt werden: Holzwohnhäuser aus dem 1. Jahrhundert, ein römisches Steinhaus, eine römische Basilika aus dem 4. Jahrhundert, darauf folgen weitere sieben Kirchen. Bekannt ist die Römerstadt vor allem auch für den größten Flohmarkt Belgiens vor den alten Stadtmauern.

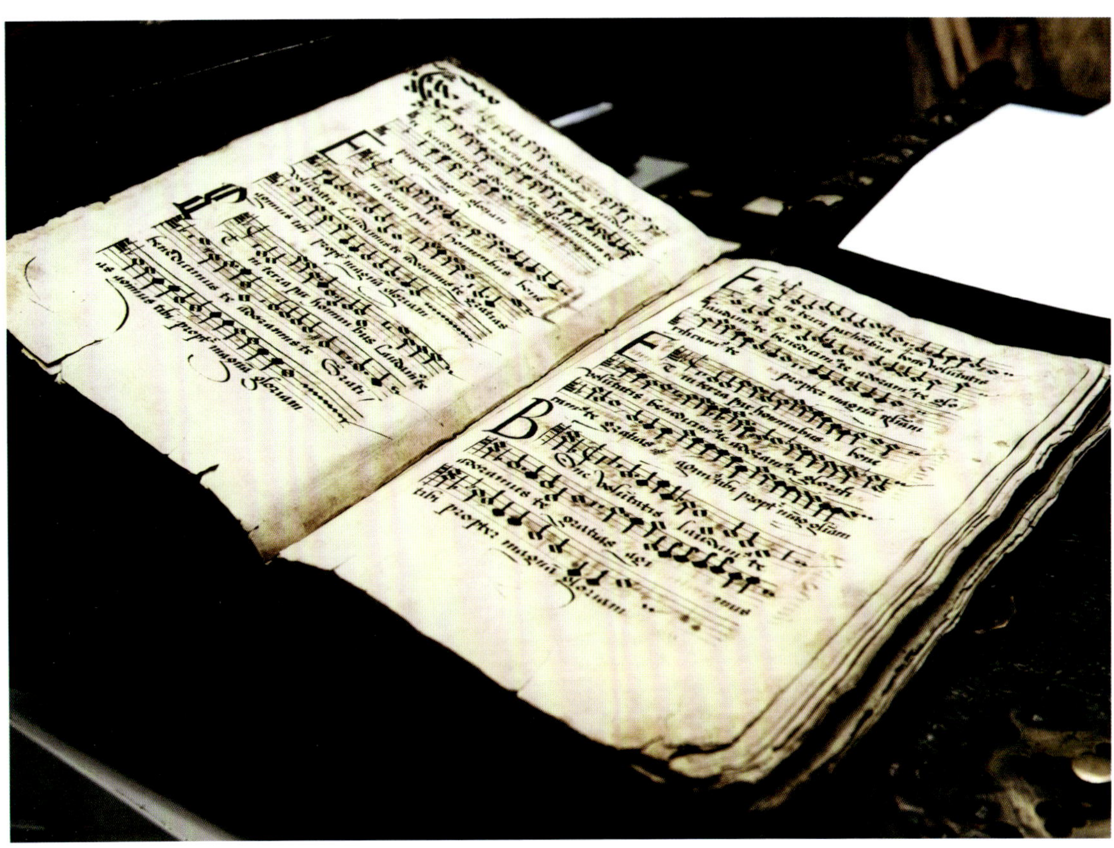

Gregorian musical notation, Basilica of Our Lady, Tongeren
Gregoriaanse muzikale handschriften, Onze-Lieve-Vrouwe Basilica, Cloister, Tongeren
Écritures musicales grégoriennes, basilique Notre-Dame de Tongres

Tongeren, la ciudad más antigua de Flandes

En el camino a Tongeren, se puede ver desde lejos la torre gótica de la Basílica de Nuestra Señora, que es Patrimonio de la Humanidad de la UNESCO. Destacan el claustro románico con jardín del monasterio, los tesoros de arte religioso del "Teseum" y el yacimiento arqueológico situado bajo la basílica, en el que se muestran 2000 años de historia de la ciudad: casas de madera del siglo I, una casa romana de piedra, una basílica romana del siglo IV, seguida de siete iglesias más. La ciudad romana es bien conocida, especialmente por el mercadillo más grande de Bélgica situado frente a las antiguas murallas de la ciudad.

Tongeren, a cidade mais antiga da Flandres

No caminho para Tongeren, a torre gótica da Basílica de Nossa Senhora, que é um Patrimônio Mundial da UNESCO, pode ser vista de longe. Vale a pena ver o claustro românico com jardim do mosteiro, os tesouros da arte religiosa no sítio arqueológico "Teseum" e os sítios arqueológicos abaixo da basílica, no qual são mostrados 2000 anos de história da cidade: casas de madeira do século I, uma casa de pedra romana, uma basílica romana do século IV, seguida de mais sete igrejas. A cidade romana é bem conhecida, especialmente pelo maior mercado de pulgas da Bélgica, em frente às muralhas da cidade velha.

Tongeren, oudste stad van Vlaanderen

Op weg naar Tongeren is de gotische toren van de Onze-Lieve-Vrouwebasiliek, die op de Werelderfgoedlijst van UNESCO staat, al van veraf te zien. Bezienswaardig is de romaanse kloostergang met kloostertuin, de religieuze kunstschatten in het "Teseum" en de archeologische opgravingen onder de basiliek, waar 2000 jaar stadsgeschiedenis wordt getoond: houten huizen uit de 1e eeuw, een Romeins stenen huis, een Romeinse basiliek uit de 4e eeuw, gevolgd door zeven andere kerken. De Romeinse stad is vooral bekend vanwege de grootste rommelmarkt van België voor de oude stadsmuren.

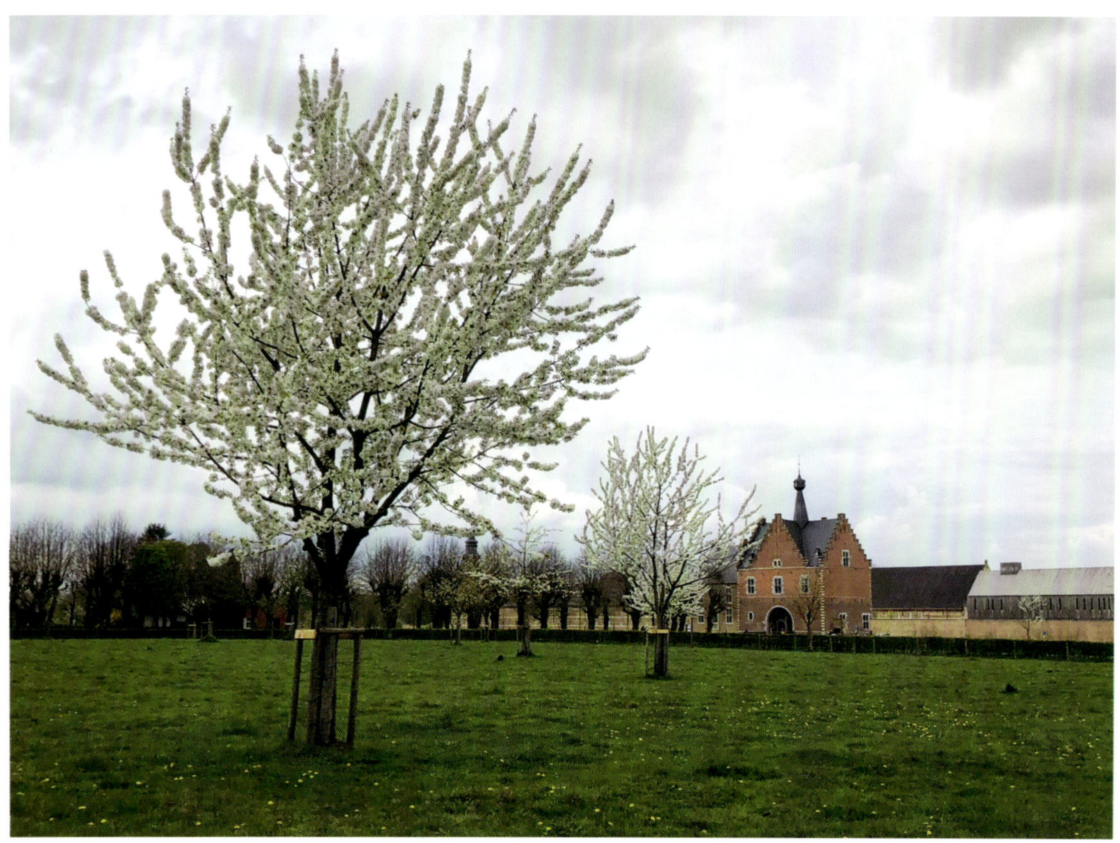

Herkenrode Abbey, Hasselt
Abdij van Herkenrode, Hasselt
Abbaye de Herkenrode, Hasselt

Herkenrode Abbey and Japanese Garden

The Cistercian monastery is one of the oldest and richest abbeys in Flanders. The large monastery complex also encompasses a 2 ha (5 ac) herb park. Also to be found near Hasselt is the Japanese Garden, which was created with the help of the Japanese twin town of Itami. At 2.5 ha (6 ac), it is the largest of its kind in Europe. It stands as an authentic symbol for inner peace and natural beauty, reflecting the landscape of the 17th century tea garden model—including waterfalls, a tea house and more than 250 Japanese cherry trees.

Abbaye de Herkenrode et Jardin japonais

Ce monastère cistercien fait partie des abbayes les plus anciennes et les plus riches de Flandres. Son grand complexe comprend aussi un parc d'herbes aromatiques de 2 hectares. Près de Hasselt se trouve également le Jardin japonais, créé avec l'aide de la ville jumelle japonaise Itami. Avec ses 2,5 hectares, c'est le plus grand d'Europe. Symbole authentique de paix intérieure et de beauté naturelle, il reflète le modèle des jardins japonais du XVIIe siècle, incluant chutes d'eau, salon de thé et plus de 250 cerisiers japonais.

Abtei Herkenrode und Japanischer Garten

Das Kloster der Zisterzienserinnen zählt zu den ältesten und auch reichsten Abteien Flanderns. Zur großen Klosteranlage zählt auch ein 2 ha großer Kräuterpark. Ebenfalls in der Nähe von Hasselt liegt der Japanische Garten, der mithilfe der japanischen Partnerstadt Itami angelegt wurde. Er ist mit 2,5 ha der größte seiner Art in Europa. Er steht als authentisches Symbol für innere Ruhe sowie natürliche Schönheit und spiegelt die Landschaft nach dem Teegartenmodell des 17. Jahrhunderts wider - inklusive Wasserfällen, Teehaus und mit mehr als 250 japanischen Kirschbäumen.

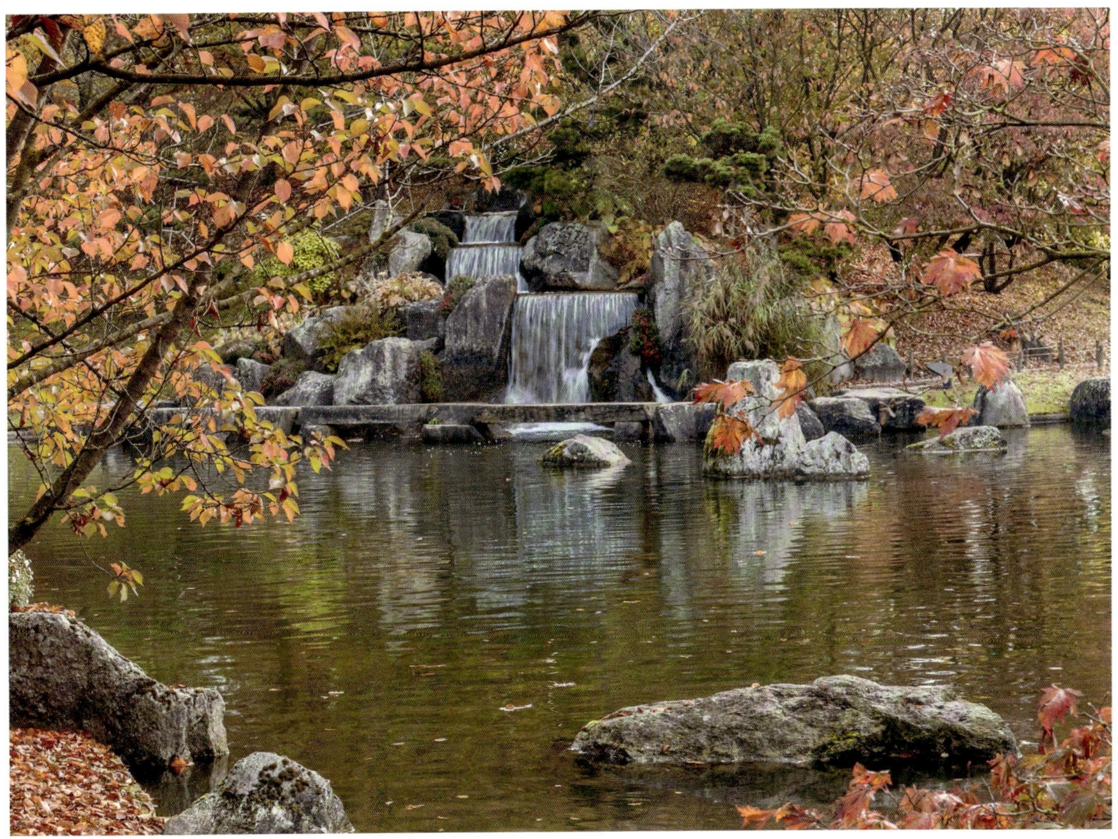

Japanese Garden, Hasselt
Japanse Tuin, Hasselt
Jardin japonais, Hasselt

Abadía de Herkenrode y jardín japonés

El monasterio cisterciense es una de las abadías más antiguas y ricas de Flandes. El gran complejo del monasterio también incluye un parque de hierbas de 2 hectáreas. Cerca de Hasselt se encuentra también el jardín japonés, que se creó con la ayuda de la ciudad gemela japonesa Itami. Con 2,5 ha, es el más grande de Europa en su género. Es un auténtico símbolo de paz interior y belleza natural, y refleja el paisaje del modelo de jardín de té del siglo XVII, que incluye cascadas, casas de té y más de 250 cerezos japoneses.

Abadia de Herkenrode e Jardim Japonês

O mosteiro das freiras cistercienses é uma das mais antigas e ricas abadias da Flandres. O grande complexo do mosteiro também inclui um parque de ervas de 2 ha. Também perto de Hasselt está o Jardim Japonês, que foi criado com a ajuda da cidade germinada japonesa Itami. Com 2,5 ha, é o maior do seu género na Europa. É um símbolo autêntico da paz interior e da beleza natural e reflete a paisagem do modelo do jardim do chá do século XVII – incluindo cascatas, casas de chá e mais de 250 cerejeiras japonesas.

Abdij Herkenrode en Japanse Tuin

Het cisterciënzerklooster behoort tot één van de oudste en rijkste abdijen van Vlaanderen. Ook een kruidenpark van 2 ha maakt deel uit van het grote kloostercomplex. Eveneens in de buurt van Hasselt ligt de Japanse Tuin die met de hulp van de Japanse zusterstad Itami is aangelegd. In Europa is hij met 2,5 ha de grootste in zijn soort. De Japanse Tuin is een authentiek symbool voor innerlijke rust en natuurlijke schoonheid en weerspiegelt het landschap van de theetuinen uit de 17e eeuw, inclusief watervallen, theehuis en meer dan 250 Japanse kersenbomen.

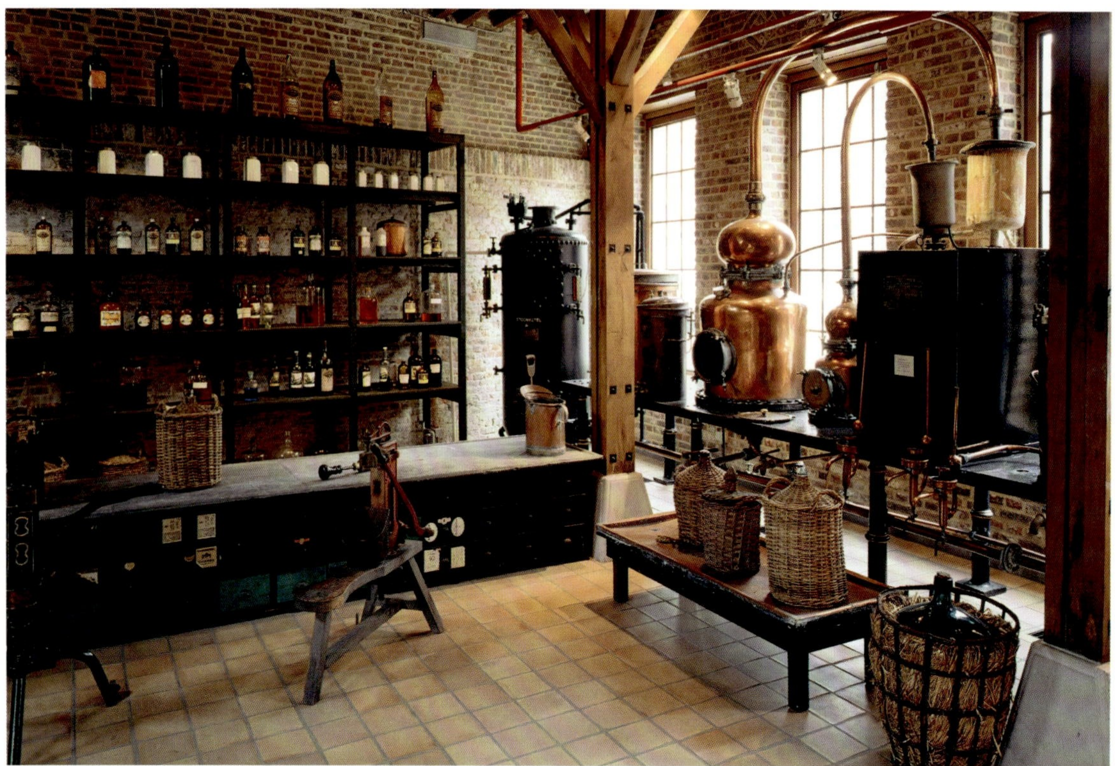

Genever Museum, Hasselt
Jenevermuseum, Hasselt
Musée du Genièvre, Hasselt

Genever Museum

The museum at Hasselt is located in the former Stellingwerff-Theunissen distillery, in the old town. Here, everything revolves around the more than 500-year-old national drink, Genever, and a schnapps is included in a visit. In the old distillery, with its restored and newly commissioned steam engine and grain mill, the history of the beverage can be experienced.

Musée national du Genièvre

Le musée est aménagé dans l'ancienne distillerie Stellingwerff-Theunissen, située dans la vieille ville. Ici, tout tourne autour de cette boisson nationale de plus de 500 ans qu'est le genièvre – d'ailleurs, la visite en inclut la dégustation. Avec sa machine à vapeur restaurée et récemment mise en service ainsi que son moulin à grains, l'ancienne distillerie permet de découvrir l'histoire de la boisson.

National Genevermuseum

Das Museum befindet sich in der früheren Brennerei Stellingwerff/Theunissen in der Altstadt. Hier dreht sich alles um das mehr als 500 Jahre alte Nationalgetränk Genever – ein Schnäpschen ist bei einem Besuch inklusive. In der alten Brennerei mit restaurierter und neu in Betrieb genommener Dampfmaschine sowie Getreidemühle wird die Geschichte des Getränks erlebbar.

Museo Nacional del Jenever

El museo se encuentra en la antigua destilería Stellingwerff/Theunissen en el casco antiguo. Aquí, todo gira en torno a la bebida nacional Jenever, de más de 500 años de antigüedad, y en la visita se incluye un chupito. En la antigua destilería, con su máquina de vapor restaurada y recién puesta en marcha y su molino de grano, se puede conocer la historia de la bebida.

Museu Nacional de Genebra

O museu está localizado na antiga destilaria Stellingwerff/Theunissen na cidade velha. Aqui, tudo gira em torno da bebida nacional Genebra, de mais de 500 anos de idade – um licorzinho está incluído em uma visita. Na antiga destilaria, com a sua máquina a vapor e moinho de grãos restaurados e recentemente colocado em funcionamento, a história da bebida pode ser vivida.

Nationaal Jenevermuseum

Het museum is gevestigd in de voormalige stokerij Stellingwerff/Theunissen in de oude binnenstad. Hier draait alles om de meer dan 500 jaar oude nationale drank jenever – een borrel is bij het bezoek inbegrepen. In de oude stokerij met zijn gerestaureerde en nieuw in gebruik genomen stoommachine en graanmolen wordt de geschiedenis van de drank weer levendig.

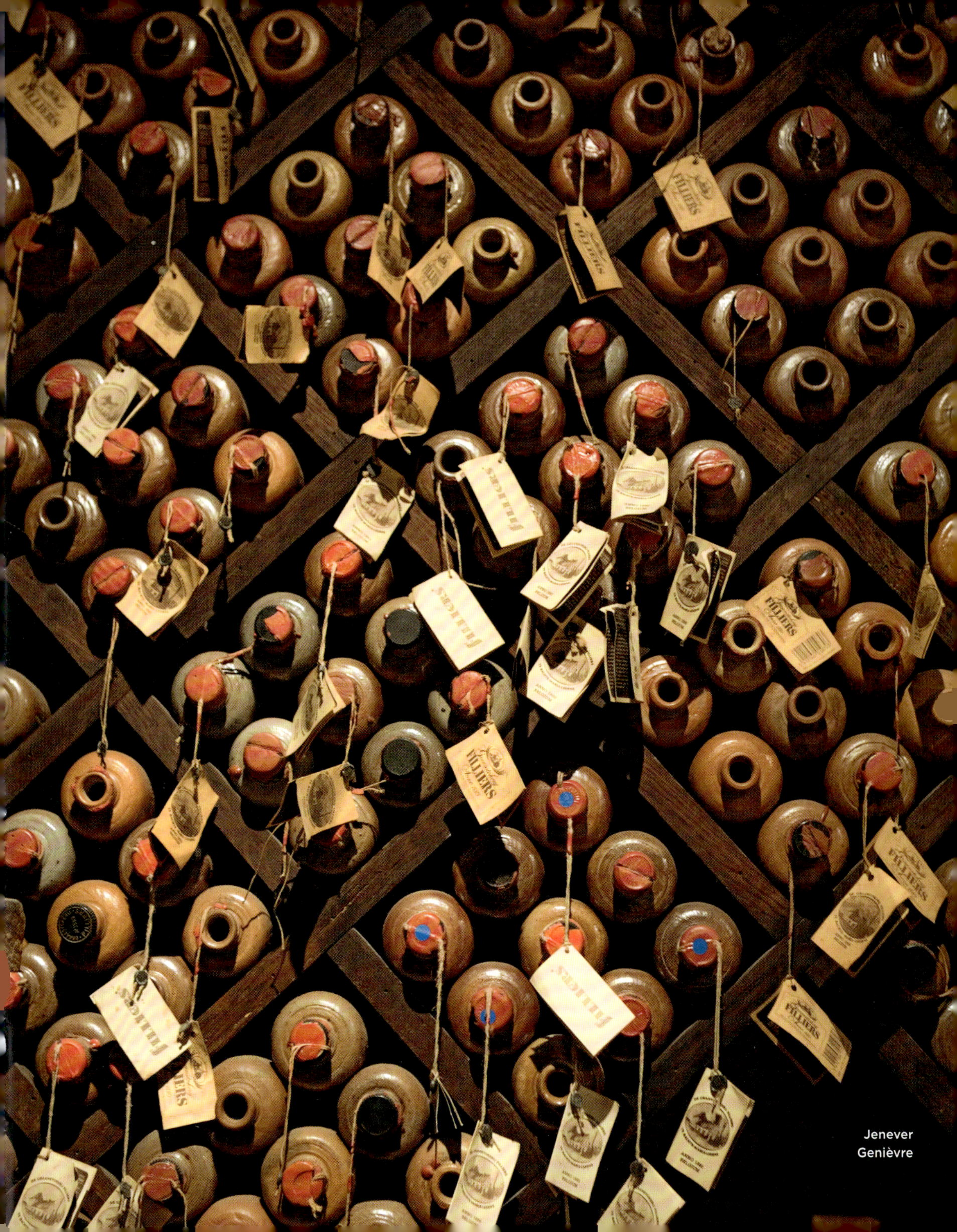

Jenever
Genièvre

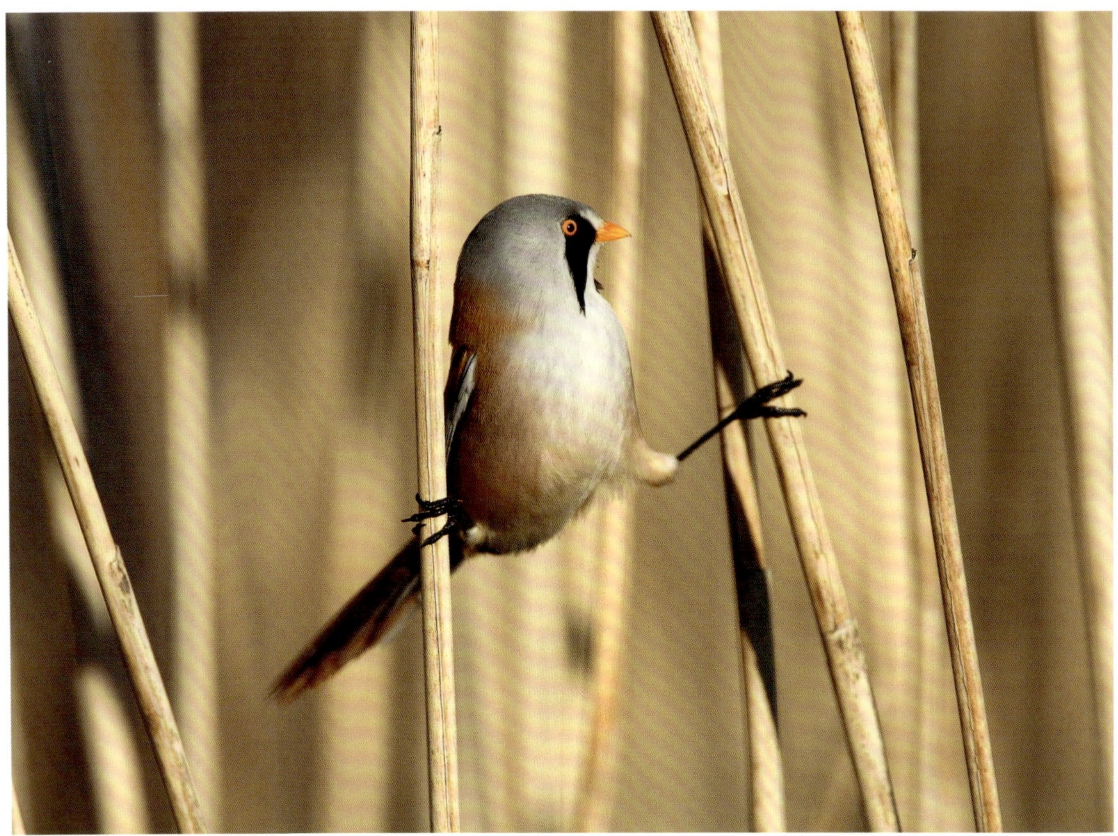

Bearded reedling
Baardman
Panure à moustaches

Meuse

In the very east of Flanders, where the Meuse has created a unique landscape over the centuries, lies the Maasland. The capricious Meuse has long since created silted river arms and man has created numerous gravel pits, which are now surrounded by natural reed beds. Many water birds, such as the bearded tit, live in the extensive old reed beds. On the banks of the Meuse lies the picturesque hamlet of Oud-Rekem, which was voted the most beautiful village in Flanders. One may easily cycle from village to village and cross to the Netherlands on a free ferry across the Meuse.

Le Maasland

À l'extrême est des Flandres, là où la Meuse a créé un paysage unique au fil des siècles, s'étend le Maasland. Il y a fort longtemps, la Meuse capricieuse façonna des bras de rivière aujourd'hui ensablés et l'homme créa d'innombrables lacs artificiels, désormais entourés d'une ceinture naturelle de roseaux qui forme l'habitat de nombreux d'oiseaux aquatiques, comme la panure à moustaches. Sur les rives de la Meuse, le pittoresque village d'Oud-Rekem a été élu plus beau village de Flandres. Les environs s'explorent à merveille par le biais d'une balade à vélo de village en village ; on peut même emprunter un ferry gratuit pour traverser la Meuse et se rendre aux Pays-Bas.

Maasland

Ganz im Osten Flanderns, wo die Maas im Laufe der Jahrhunderte eine einzigartige Landschaft geschaffen hat, liegt das Maasland. Die launische Maas schuf längst versandete Flussarme und der Mensch zahlreiche Baggerseen, die inzwischen mit einem natürlichen Schilfgürtel umgeben sind. Viele Wasservögel, wie die Bartmeise, leben in den ausgedehnten Altschilffeldern. An den Ufern der Maas liegt der malerische Weiler, Oud-Rekem, der zum schönsten Dorf von Flandern gewählt wurde. Ganz entspannt kann man von Dorf zu Dorf radeln und mit einer kostenlosen Fähre über die Maas in die Niederlande gelangen.

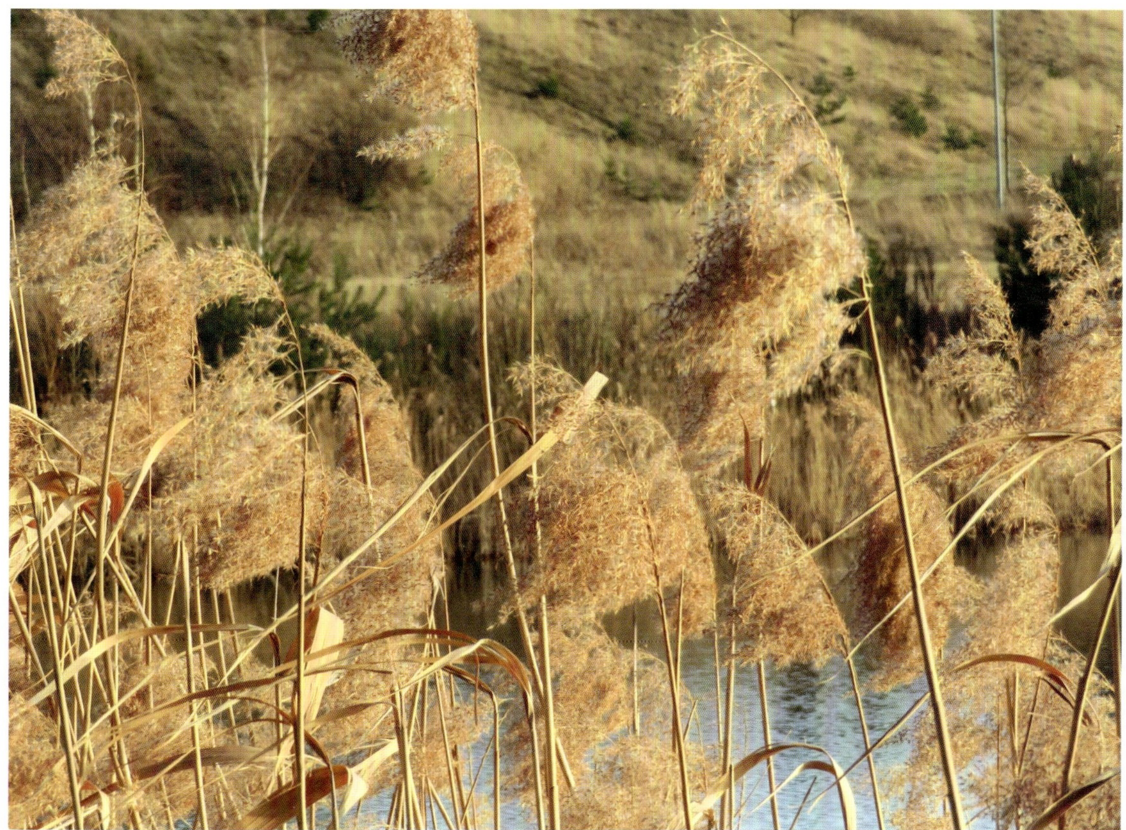

Landscape near Genk
Landschap beij Genk
Paysage près de Genk

Maasland

En el extremo oriental de Flandes, donde el río Mosa ha creado un paisaje único a lo largo de los siglos, se encuentra Maasland. El caprichoso Mosa ha creado desde hace mucho tiempo brazos de río entarquinados y el hombre ha creado numerosos lagos de dragado, que ahora están rodeados por un cinturón de caña natural. Muchas aves acuáticas, como el bigotudo, viven en los extensos y antiguos cañaverales. En la ribera del Mosa se encuentra la pintoresca aldea de Oud-Rekem, que fue elegida el pueblo más bello de Flandes. Se puede ir de pueblo en pueblo y llegar a los Países Bajos en un ferry gratuito a través del Mosa.

Mosa

No extremo leste da Flandres, onde o rio Mosa criou uma paisagem única ao longo dos séculos, encontram-se as regiões perto do rio Mosa, o "Maasland". O inconstante Mosa há muito tempo criou braços de rio assoreados e o homem criou numerosos lagos de dragagem, que estão agora rodeados por uma vegetação costeira natural. Muitas aves aquáticas, como o bico-grossudo, vivem nos extensos e velhos canaviais. Nas margens do rio Mosa encontra-se a pitoresca aldeia de Oud-Rekem, que foi eleita a aldeia mais bonita da Flandres. Você pode andar de bicicleta de aldeia em aldeia em um ambiente descontraído e chegar à Holanda em uma balsa gratuita através do Mosa.

Maasland

In het uiterste oosten van Vlaanderen, waar de Maas door de eeuwen heen een uniek landschap heeft gecreëerd, ligt het Maasland. De grillige Maas bracht allang verzandde rivierarmen voort en de mens talrijke met water gevulde grindgaten, die nu door een natuurlijke rietkraag worden omgeven. Veel watervogels, zoals de baardmees, leven in de uitgestrekte oude rietvelden. Aan de oevers van de Maas ligt het pittoreske gehucht Oud-Rekem dat uitgeroepen werd tot het mooiste dorp van Vlaanderen. Men kan zeer ontspannen van dorp naar dorp fietsen en met een gratis pontje over de Maas naar Nederland gaan.

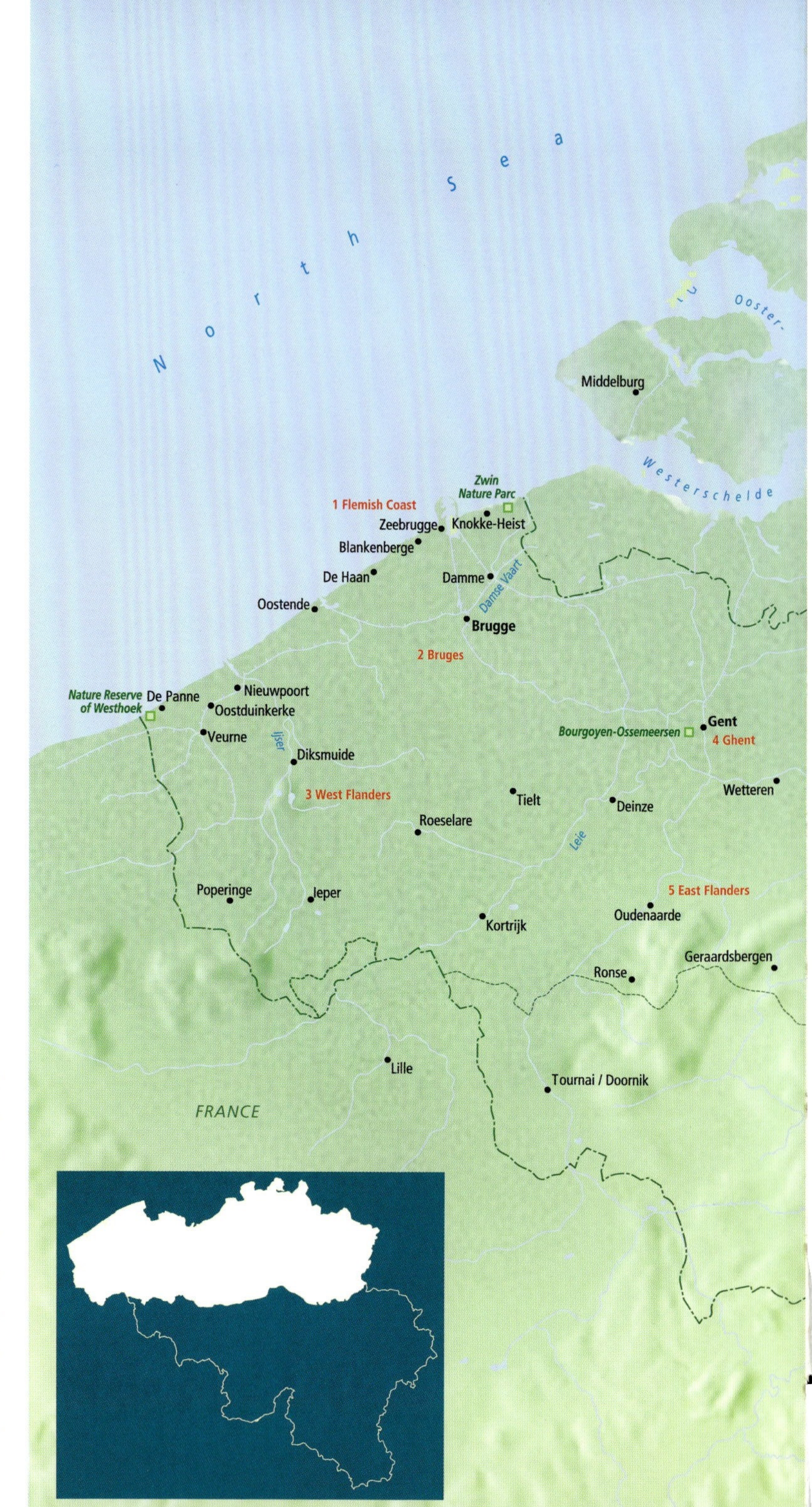

North Sea
Ooster-
Westerschelde
Middelburg
Zwin Nature Parc
1 Flemish Coast
Zeebrugge
Knokke-Heist
Blankenberge
De Haan
Damme
Damse Vaart
Oostende
Brugge
2 Bruges
Nieuwpoort
Nature Reserve of Westhoek
De Panne
Oostduinkerke
Bourgoyen-Ossemeersen
Gent
4 Ghent
Veurne
IJzer
Diksmuide
Wetteren
3 West Flanders
Tielt
Deinze
Roeselare
Leie
5 East Flanders
Poperinge
Ieper
Oudenaarde
Kortrijk
Geraardsbergen
Ronse
Lille
Tournai / Doornik
FRANCE

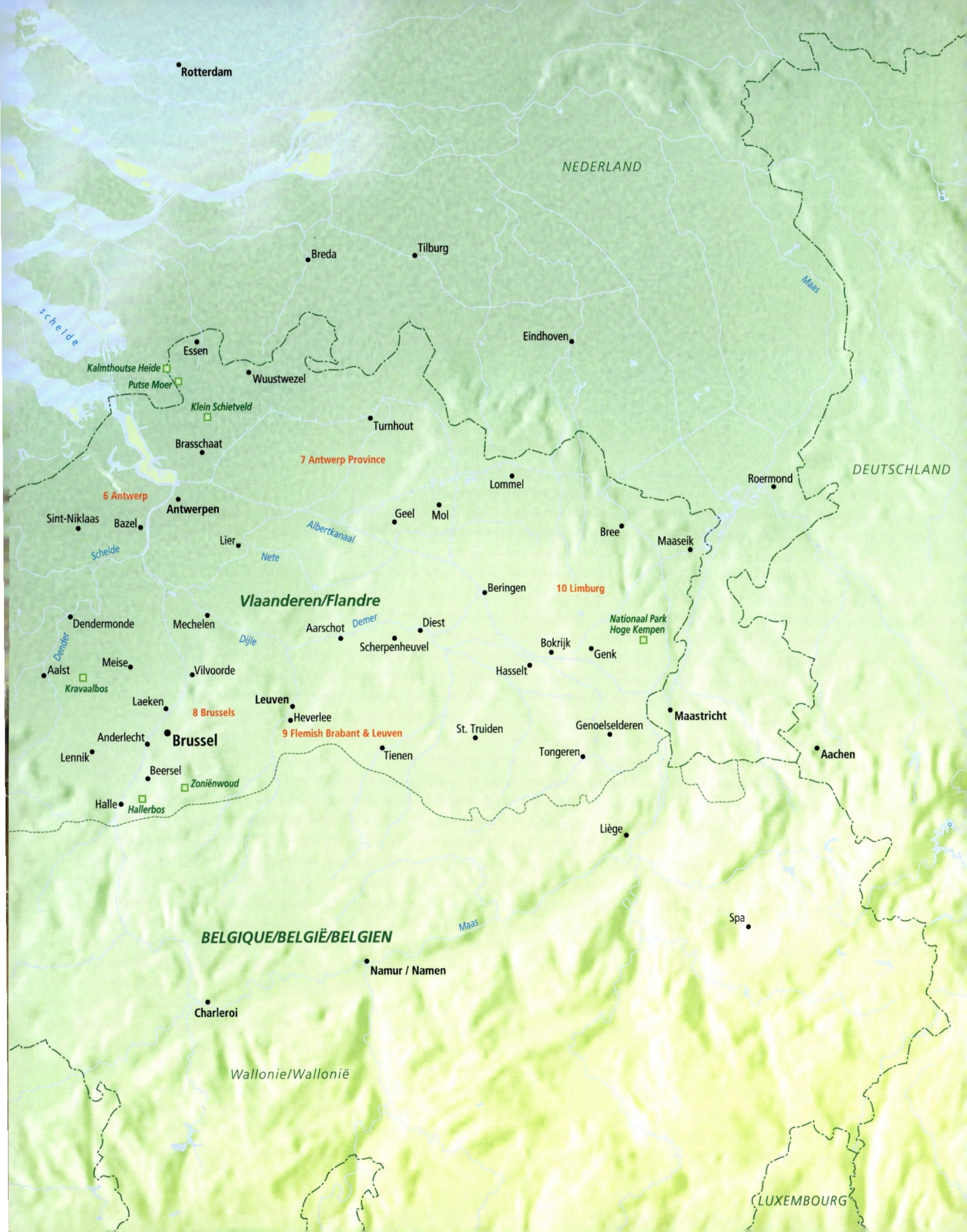

Rotterdam
NEDERLAND
Breda
Tilburg
Eindhoven
Maas
Schelde
Essen
Kalmthoutse Heide
Putse Moer
Wuustwezel
Klein Schietveld
Turnhout
Brasschaat
7 Antwerp Province
Lommel
Roermond
DEUTSCHLAND
6 Antwerp
Antwerpen
Sint-Niklaas
Bazel
Geel
Mol
Bree
Maaseik
Lier
Schelde
Albertkanaal
Nete
Beringen
10 Limburg
Vlaanderen/Flandre
Dendermonde
Mechelen
Aarschot
Demer
Diest
Nationaal Park
Hoge Kempen
Dender
Dijle
Scherpenheuvel
Bokrijk
Genk
Meise
Vilvoorde
Hasselt
Aalst
Kravaalbos
Laeken
8 Brussels
Leuven
Heverlee
9 Flemish Brabant & Leuven
St. Truiden
Genoelselderen
Maastricht
Anderlecht
Brussel
Lennik
Tienen
Tongeren
Aachen
Beersel
Zoniënwoud
Halle
Hallerbos
Liège
BELGIQUE/BELGIË/BELGIEN
Maas
Spa
Namur / Namen
Charleroi
Wallonie/Wallonië
LUXEMBOURG

Photo credits

KÖNEMANN

© 2020 koenemann.com GmbH
www.koenemann.com

© Éditions Place des Victoires
6, rue du Mail – 75002 Paris
www.victoires.com
Dépôt légal : 1ᵉʳ trimestre 2020
ISBN 978-2-8099-1781-9

Series Concept: koenemann.com GmbH

Responsible Editor: Jenny Tiesler
Picture Editing: Katja Sassmannshausen, Nicole Wustrack
Layout: Regine Ermert
Colour Separation: Prepress, Cologne
Text: Joel Etzold
Translation into French: Catherine Livet
Translation into English, Spanish, Portuguese and Dutch: koenemann.com GmbH
Maps: Angelika Solibieda
Front Cover: Getty Images/Rudy Balasko

Printed in China by Shyft Publishing / Hunan Tianwen Xinhua Printing Co., Ltd

ISBN 978-3-7419-2519-1